P9-ARU-893

WITHDRAWN

Gramley Library
Salem Academy and College
Winston-Salem, N.C. 27108

Madres del Verbo/
Mothers of the Word

Madres del Verbo/ Mothers of the Word

Early Spanish–American Women Writers
A Bilingual Anthology

Edited, Translated, and with an Introduction by
NINA M. SCOTT

Gramley Library
Salem Academy and College
Winston-Salem, N.C. 27108

University of New Mexico Press
Albuquerque

© 1999 by the University of New Mexico Press

All rights reserved.

First edition

Library of Congress Cataloging-in-Publication Data

Madres del verbo - Mothers of the word : early Spanish-American
   women writers : a bilingual anthology / edited, translated, and
   with an introduction by Nina M. Scott.

 p. cm.

 Includes bibliographical references and index.

 ISBN 0-8263-2145-3 (cloth : alk. paper).—ISBN 0-8263-2144-5
(pbk. : alk. paper)

 1. Spanish American literature—Women authors—Translations
into English. 2. Spanish American literature—Women authors.
I. Scott, Nina M. II. Title: Mothers of the word.

PQ7087.E5M23 1999

860.8'09282—dc21   99-37410

                CIP

To Jim

Contents

Acknowledgments

During the many years I worked on this anthology, I often affectionately called it my "old girls" project, with no disrespect meant to the authors whose works I have included. On the contrary—the older I get, the more I respect the wit and wisdom of older women, and here I want to pay tribute to four very special "old girls" in my life: my mother, Hildegard Koppermann Budde, my mother-in-law, Elizabeth Tompkins Scott, and two aunts, Hertha Hamdorff Koppermann and Barbara Tompkins Stowell.

Many people have helped me directly and have inspired me with their scholarship. I owe a great deal to the generosity of Cristina González, Mary Berg, Kathryn McKnight, Montserrat Ordóñez, Asunción Lavrin, Kathleen Myers, and Frederick Luciani. My former graduate students Raúl Marrero-Fente and Carolina Alzate-Cadavid were also most generous in sharing their research. I continue to be enriched by the work of Stephanie Merrim, Doris Sommer, Jean Franco, Georgina Sabàt-Rivers, Mabel Moraña, Emilie Bergmann, Walter Mignolo, Rolena Adorno, Margarita Zamora, Rosa Perelmuter, Electa Arenal, Stacey Schlau, Susan Kirkpatrick, and Marie-Cécile Bénassy-Berling. Amanda Powell, Frances López-Morillas, Luis Harss, Margaret Peden, and Alan Trueblood are my model translators. I have major debts to scholars in Mexico: Elías Trabulse, Margo Glantz, Josefina Muriel, Clara Bargellini, Aureliano Tapia-Méndez, Sara Poot-Herrera, and Antonio Alatorre and the special friendship of Elena Poniatowska and Elena Urrutia. My list would not be complete without Márgara Russotto and Luisa Campuzano. To my many wonderful graduate students at the University of Massachusetts: *gracias por todo.*

My translation of Sor Juana's letter to her confessor was previously published in 1988. It is reprinted with permission from *Women's Studies International Forum,* vol. 11, Nina M. Scott, "'If You Are Not

Pleased to Favor Me, Put Me Out of Your Mind . . . ': Gender and Authority in Sor Juana Inés de la Cruz" and "Translation of Her Letter to the Reverend Father Maestro Antonio Núñez of the Society of Jesus," Copyright 1988, Pergamon Press Ltd, Headington Hill Hall, Oxford, OX3 OBW, United Kingdom.

I am especially grateful to Barbara Guth of the University of New Mexico Press, who was unfailingly kind, patient, and helpful. My greatest thanks go to my husband, Jim, whose constant help, encouragement, and computer skills really brought this book to fruition.

Nina M. Scott
Amherst, Massachusetts, 1999

Introduction

This anthology has been many years in the making—far more than I had anticipated when the idea for it first occurred to me. A number of years ago I developed an advanced seminar dealing with the literature of Spanish-American women writers from colonial times to the end of the nineteenth century and found it difficult to obtain the texts I wanted my students to read. Many of them were rare and practically unavailable, so I put together my own anthology of photocopied materials, garnered through Inter-Library Loan or the generosity of friends and colleagues. I had so many requests for these materials that I felt I should try to publish an anthology in order to provide a useful text for classroom use in Spanish-American Literature. The editors at the University of New Mexico Press suggested that a bilingual anthology would be an even better idea, as many of these authors and their texts are unknown to non-Spanish speakers. This almost quadrupled my work in producing this book, but I hope that the final result will prove useful for courses in Women's Studies, Cultural Studies, Hemispheric American Studies, to name a few, as well as enjoyable for the general reader.

At the turn of the twenty-first century, it is difficult to remember how few women's voices and texts were recorded in the colonial era of Spanish America, and even those that have managed to reach our times were for years ignored or denigrated by literary historians and critics as peripheral, unworthy, uninteresting, second-rate literature. Feminist, cultural, and interdisciplinary studies have taught us new ways to approach traditional canons, to read and appreciate texts by women, slaves, indigenous peoples—all those heretofore relegated to the margins of the margins. As Kathleen Myers points out,

> The recuperation, translation, and publication of texts that had been lost or devalued as nonliterary characterize the current sta-

tus of the field as much as the new theoretical and interdisciplinary readings. Often for the first time, scholars are studying works by previously marginalized indigenous, mestizo, and women writers. The definition of what is considered a literary text has radically changed. . . . As a result, the canon continues to be drastically altered and expanded. (260)

The selections I have chosen range from Isabel de Guevara (first half of the sixteenth century) to Soledad Acosta de Samper (1833–1913). I have taught all of the texts included in this anthology on a number of occasions, and with great success. I have included four writers from the colonial period and five from the nineteenth century; the majority of the texts are autobiographical, and many are epistolary. All of the authors belonged to the middle or upper class and all are white, for in the past these were the only women who were literate or had access to publication. For the colonial era there is material from one married woman, one transvestite, and two nuns who were very famous in their time. For the nineteenth century I have given particular emphasis to networks of friendship and support among women writers, as well as to their roles in nation building (*el proyecto nacional*). In all cases I have tried to show that in spite of the limited roles society allowed women to play in their respective times, many of these writers still managed to assert their individuality and their talent.

Isabel de Guevara participated in the exploration and settlement of what is now Buenos Aires, Argentina, and Asunción, Paraguay. She arrived with Pedro de Mendoza's expedition in 1535. Hundreds of people died from hunger and disease on that ill-fated venture, and when the survivors, among whom were a number of women, realized that they would also die unless they went to a healthier location with better sources of food, the group made its way up the Paraná River to what is now Asunción. Twenty-one years later Doña Isabel wrote a letter to Princess Juana of Castile describing this trek and especially the role of the women in saving the lives of the remaining men; just as innumerable male explorers had, she asked for a land grant in return. This letter is one of the only published documents to record the experiences of a woman in the earliest years of Spanish America.

Catalina de Erauso, known as "la Monja Alférez" (the Ensign Nun), was born in Spain of Basque origin in 1592(?); her family placed her in a convent at the age of four, from which she escaped eleven years later, before taking her final vows. She shed her habit in favor of men's cloth-

ing, changed her name, and embarked for the New World, where she held a number of professions, including trader and mercenary soldier. Catalina gambled, brawled, dueled (she allegedly killed her own brother), and seduced other women until she confessed her identity to a clergyman. She was sent back to Spain, and her case became no- torious. After she appeared before the king of Spain and the pope, she was granted permission to continue cross-dressing and returned to the New World; when last heard of she was a muleteer in Mexico. Erauso's autobiographical account may have been tampered with by subsequent authors, for much of it sounds fantastic, but then so was her life.

The largest body of writing in the initial years of the Spanish-American colonies was by nuns, as most convents accepted only women from the white elite, and many of these were literate. I have chosen two of the best-known nuns: Sor Juana Inés de la Cruz (1648/51?–95) from Mexico and La Madre Castillo (1671–1742) from Colombia. I have chosen to pair them because they are such diametrically opposite women: the brilliant intellectual and the devout mystic, each tormented by her own set of demons.

Sor Juana is such a gigantic figure that it is hard to choose just a few selections from her vast oeuvre. I have included some of her better-known poems, as well as others that are less familiar, especially the re-ligious poems, often ignored by our more secular age. I have also in-cluded an autobiographical letter to her confessor that was discovered only in 1981; in it she exercised a nun's right to dismiss her confessor and spiritual father but did it in such a rebellious and insolent fashion that it shocks even today. The letter is a measure of the rage she felt at the unequal treatment of women by the male Church hierarchy, and, given the circumstances under which this letter was written, for once she was able to vent her anger openly.

The selections from Madre Castillo's *Vida* (Life) illustrate not only her religious vocation and mystical experiences but also some of the infighting among the nuns of her convent, the harsh treatment by her confessors, and the very ambivalent attitude she had about writing her autobiography. Whereas Sor Juana lived to write and used her pen to carve out as much intellectual freedom as was possible in her day, Madre Castillo was tormented by her confessors' order to write about herself. As was the case with many spiritual autobiographies by nuns, this text followed certain set parameters of hagiographic writing: early religious vocation and desire for the monastic life; an experience that makes the nun reject marriage; descriptions of an ascetic life filled with doubts, joys, self-accusations of sinfulness, and the striving toward union with her mystical bridegroom, Christ. Madre Castillo's autobiographical writing has neither the brilliance nor the assurance of Sor Juana's authorial voice, but it gives us a good record of life within a colonial convent and of the psychological processes of a woman bound to perpetual enclosure and self-sacrifice.

The jump to Gertrudis Gómez de Avellaneda and nineteenth-century writers is a quantum one, but the neoclassical poetry and essays of the eighteenth–century writers offer neither the stylistic interest nor the thematic concerns of the rest of this anthology. Enormous changes had taken place, not only politically, in that most Spanish-American countries achieved independence in the early part of the nineteenth century, but also with respect to women's place in literature. Many more women were now literate, meaning that there was a female reading public and women writers who wrote for this market. Although women were now writing and publishing, they still experienced anxiety of authorship, only for different reasons. In her analysis of women writers during the Romantic era, Susan Kirkpatrick has shown that the male ideal of womanhood was that of a modest, self-effacing, and self-sacrificing person (the "angel in the house," as Virginia Woolf called her), yet male Romantics simultaneously extolled the importance of human sentiments and emotions, long identified by Western society as the particular preserve of women. Women writers were thus caught in a paradoxical situation: how could they express powerful emotional selves and still remain modest and angelic?

Gertrudis Gómez de Avellaneda (1814–72) was one of the most successful writers of her day, one who lived by her pen and was famous both in Spain and in her native Cuba. (Cuba was an anomaly in the nineteenth-century Americas in that it was still a Spanish colony.) For this anthology I have chosen excerpts from her private correspondence, which show to perfection how she was trying to bridge the chasm between the conflictive roles of woman and writer. Avellaneda's love letters to Ignacio de Cepeda and Antonio Romero Ortiz oscillate between promising the men of her heart love and abject obedience and then fighting tooth and claw for her creative freedom. In her correspondence Avellaneda also made some incisive observations on nineteenth-century gender roles.

Juana Manuela Gorriti (1816–92) came from an upper-class Argentinian family. Because her father fought against the dictator Juan Manuel de Rosas in the civil wars of the early nineteenth century, the family had to go into exile in Bolivia, where their headstrong daughter insisted on marrying a Bolivian army officer when she was only fourteen. Manuel Isidoro Belzú eventually became president of Bolivia, but the marriage was a disaster and Gorriti ultimately moved to Lima, where she supported herself by teaching and writing. Gorriti's literary talents and her prolific writings on many subjects, from short stories to personal memoirs, make her Argentina's leading woman writer of the nineteenth century. The melodramatic novella included here records the horrors of Rosas's death squads and is eerily reminiscent of the literature that has recently come out of Argentina, especially by women authors who graphically recorded the torture and violence of the so-called Dirty War (1976–82).

Gorriti had a circle of women friends who made their living in much the same way that she did, such as the Peruvian novelist and essayist Mercedes Cabello de Carbonera (1845–1909) and Teresa González de Fanning (1835–?) who also wrote novels and was headmistress of a school. Gorriti did not have much money, but she hosted a literary salon at her house that attracted the leading intellectuals of Lima, both male and female, and provided a place for the exchange of ideas, musical performances, and the reading of new pieces of literature. I have selected two short essays written for these gatherings by Cabello de Carbonera and González de Fanning which illustrate topics of great interest to them and to other women of the nineteenth century: the merits of beauty versus intelligence and the need to give women sufficient professional training so that they could achieve economic independence. Although these topics might appear banal today, and the essays are not literary masterpieces, the topics presented were of vital interest to women like themselves—widows coping with straitened financial circumstances once their husbands had passed away. Male essayists of the nineteenth century produced ringing prose that spoke to heroic futures and national identity, yet "in their search for an Americanist equation of cultural authenticity, male essayists—even self-declared liberals—were virtually oblivious to the one-sided nature of their discourse" (Meyer 3). For example, it never seemed to have occurred to any of them what their wives and families would do if they died first. Women, too, wrote essays—most completely ignored until recently—that addressed problems that were to them more immediate and vital than national identity.

Soledad Acosta de Samper was, like Gorriti, the daughter of a general and a highly prolific author; in Colombia she is considered the leading nineteenth-century woman writer, yet she is little known in the United States. I have chosen her novella "Dolores" (1867) for two reasons: it is stylistically interesting in the alternation between male and female narrative voices; and her descriptions of the psychological processes for facing terminal illness, in this case leprosy, are strikingly modern. As opposed to many novels of the time written by males, in which terminally ill women expire beautifully and uncomplainingly, Dolores exhibits both rage at her fate and callousness toward those around her. This story is another example of the way early women writers resisted the roles and values that a male-dominated society imposed on them.

A word of explanation about the title of this anthology. It comes from Sor Juana's reference to the Virgin Mary as "Madre del Verbo" (Mother of the Word), an attribute based on the Gospel according to Saint John: "In the beginning was the Word, and the Word was with God, and the Word was God" (John 1.1). In Saint John's context, "Word" referred to the Greek *logos*: "in Greek thought the divine principle of reason that gives order to the universe and links the human mind to the mind of God" (*HarperCollins Study Bible* 2013). This reference to Mary is not original with Sor Juana; it existed not only in literature but also in the visual arts, as for example in the portraits of Mary as Mother of the Word by the Renaissance painter Giovanni Bellini (Kimbell Museum, Ft. Worth) and by Sandro Botticelli (Museo Poldi Pezzoli, Milan). However, given the nun/poet's reverence for language, Mary as Mother of the Word takes on a radical meaning. We must not forget that for a long time women had been considered a source of evil and corruption, to be kept both silent and enclosed. Just a century before, in 1583, the Spanish cleric Fray Luis de León wrote a highly popular manual entitled *La perfecta casada* (The Perfect Wife), in which he laid out the rules: "it is right that all women should strive to be silent, those for whom it is best to hide the little knowledge they have, as well as those who might without shame proclaim what they know, for in all women to be silent and to say little is not only an agreeable condition but proper virtue" (123). Sor Juana used Mary as her ally in countering this code of ignorance and silence for women. Besides seeing Mary as Mother of the Word, Sor Juana often extolled the Virgin's intellectual properties, hailing Mary as poet and even as Doctor of Divine Studies. As the critic Jean Franco so aptly observed,

> Sor Juana's celebration of the Virgin allows her to envisage female power and intellect. She describes Mary as Mother of the Word. When this is taken literally, it means that the female body is the matrix that gives birth to the logos. The womb is not only the sullied and impure repository of original sin but the source of redemption without which there would be neither life nor meaning. (52–53)

It is this prioritizing of women's voices I want to underscore in this anthology. Until very recently the curricula of courses dealing with Spanish America's early literary production might include Sor Juana and Avellaneda but usually ignored the many other significant women writers who also form part of this heritage. With this book their voices will now be available to both a Spanish- and an English-speaking public, so that their remarkable stories will not be forgotten.

A Note on Translation: As all of the introductory biographies to these writers are in English, I have translated all Spanish citations into English. All translations in this book, unless otherwise noted, are mine. Given the long, often-convoluted syntax that characterized the Spanish of earlier centuries, I have sometimes altered the punctuation, or made two sentences out of what was originally one, hoping to make the translations more readable without altering the original meaning.

Isabel de Guevara

*T*he letter that Isabel de Guevara wrote to Princess Juana, asking to be rewarded for services rendered, is one of the only published documents to record the participation of Spanish women in the settlement of the Americas.[1] As we have no information on Doña Isabel apart from her letter, I thought this introduction would be very brief, but the more I thought about her, the more I wanted to know the answers to some very basic questions. When did Spanish women begin to come to the Americas? What was the context in which Isabel de Guevara made these initial voyages? Was she unusual in asking for a *repartimiento,* or share, for herself; that is, were these privileges ever given to women? And finally, why did she wait twenty years after her arrival in Asunción before asking for this reward?[2]

Consuelo Varela, in her edition of Columbus's four voyages, notes that women sailed for the New World as early as his second voyage (20, esp. n. 5). The colonial historian Samuel Eliot Morison has only two references to women in his famous biography of Columbus, *Admiral of the Ocean Sea,* but even these are contradictory. He states that he could find no record of women on the island of Hispaniola before 1498 (397) yet maintains that women and children had come in 1494 with Antonio de Torres, who was bringing provisions to Columbus and his Spanish settlers on the north coast of that island (490). According to Morison, in 1498 Columbus was given permission to recruit one woman for every ten male emigrants (397), and as of that date Spanish women appeared to have come in greater numbers. In 1509 the first woman's name appeared on the passenger lists, which at that time were compiled by the Casa de Contratación, the administrative center in Seville that kept all records having to do with the American colonies (Schurz 286). As James Lockhart and Enrique Otte note, the wives and female relatives of the conquerors "begin to appear in the new country almost before the fighting was over" (14).

At the beginning of the sixteenth century women were expressly barred from expeditionary voyages (as opposed to establishing settlements), and there was a real effort made to control female emigration. As it was felt that the presence of single women aboard the ships to the colonies would prove troublesome on the voyages, at first only married women were legally allowed to embark, but there is little doubt that from the beginning such rules were bent with fair regularity. In her delightful book, *Algunas mujeres de la conquista* (Some Women of the Conquest), the Paraguayan writer Josefina Plà maintains that there must have been many single women, some quite respectable and others not very, who successfully smuggled their way across the Atlantic, because the captain looked the other way, or they hid as stowaways, or they dressed as men. Historians agree that cross-dressing was not as implausible as it may sound, and we have an example of it in Catalina de Erauso. Many of the soldiers of the time were teenagers, so that a woman's beardless face and slender build would not necessarily have attracted attention (Lopreto 45). Supposing women were discovered during a voyage? Tongue in cheek, Plà suggests that a captain would have three options: marry them off, return to port, or throw them overboard. Since none of these made real sense, most likely the women continued with the ship (13–14).

What about Isabel de Guevara's own journey to the Americas? In 1534 Pedro de Mendoza, a Spanish nobleman of great wealth, was granted permission to organize one of the largest and most ambitious expeditions to explore the Americas. A fleet of eleven ships transported some twelve hundred men, a few of them with their wives, and a hundred horses to the estuary of the River Plate, the site of present-day Buenos Aires. Settlement began in 1536, in a location that proved to be just as bad as Jamestown was for John Smith and his English compatriots some seventy years later. Disease, hunger, and hostile Indians decimated the group in short order, leaving a starving group of settlers who were reduced to eating "rats, mice, snakes, lizards, even their shoes, and all available hides. Some gorged on the bodies of those who had died" (Crow 131).

As Pedro de Mendoza was incapacitated during these events by a virulent case of syphilis, one of his lieutenants, Capt. Juan de Ayolas, took a group of the starving settlers up the Paraná River in 1537; in the following year they established Asunción, Paraguay. When Ayolas was killed by a group of Indians, Domingo Martínez de Irala was elected governor of the colony, Mendoza having died on his way back to Spain. Irala is considered the founder of present-day Paraguay. In 1580 a group of Spaniards from Asunción retraced the journey down the Paraná, and their leader, Blas de Garay, established the second, successful settlement of Buenos Aires.

Isabel de Guevara was one of the women who joined Mendoza's expedition. Even though it was apparently illegal, this being clearly an exploratory voyage, eight women are mentioned in the documents of this venture. The Argentine historian Gladys Lopreto, who has studied the history of this expedition, found no Isabel de Guevara among the eight listed but did notice a certain "Carlos de Guevara and Isabel de Laserna," though the relationship between the two was unclear (46). Guevara died in the same skirmish with the Indians in which Ayolas perished.

Isabel de Guevara participated in the trek upriver from Buenos Aires, as she records in the letter that was written some twenty years after this group arrived in Asunción. She waited until 1556 to write because in 1555 Governor Irala was granted permission by the Crown to distribute sizable *encomiendas* to the Spaniards residing in Asunción, and Isabel de Guevara had not received one (Lopreto 48; Marrero 4–5). It was not unusual for a woman to ask for a repartimiento for herself. Luis Marín has shown that women were indeed the beneficiaries of such privileges: "One of the first Spanish women to obtain an encomienda in America was Doña María de Toledo, the daughter-in-law of the discoverer, who with her husband, Diego Colón, arrived in Hispaniola in 1509. This precedent was followed later in Panamá and Mexico, where women encomenderas date back to the early days of the conquest" (46). Another example of this is María de Estrada, a Spanish woman who participated in Hernán Cortés's campaign, and perhaps foreshadows the exploits of Catalina de Erauso:

[She] was already noted for her readiness to take up arms with the men. After the fall of Tenochtitlán [the Aztec capital] she participated in an attack on a mountain town in the foothills of Popocatepetl. Charging on horseback with lance in hand and shouting the war cry of Santiago, enemy of the heathen, she frightened the defenders out of their wits. In recognition of her valor, certified by Cortés, she and her husband were awarded a grant of Indian service there. (Karttunen 17)

At some point in her life Isabel de Guevara married Pedro de Esquivel, a Sevillian who had come to Paraguay with Alvar Núñez Cabeza de Vaca (Tieffemberg 287), and thus had not been with her on the trek from Buenos Aires to Asunción. Isabel de Guevara and her husband may have been left out because Esquivel was not a supporter of Irala's; he was later jailed and beheaded, leaving Isabel a widow (Plà 26). In any event, Isabel de Guevara felt slighted by Irala, took pen in hand, and wrote to Juana of Austria, the emperor Charles V's youngest daughter, who was governor of Castile and of Spain's overseas possessions from 1554 to 1559 (Tieffemberg 288).[3] Did it make a difference to her that the recipient of her letter was a woman? Most likely, as Guevara bypassed all intermediary functionaries to write directly to Princess Juana (Lopreto 44).

As the letter is in fact a petition for a specific reward, it was necessary for Isabel de Guevara to tell her story to justify the grant by Princess Juana.[4] Letters from male explorers and colonizers to the Crown requesting a reward for their actions in subjugating the Americas were not unusual, but the insertion of a female protagonist's voice certainly was. In her narration she consistently foregrounds the heroic actions of the women and obscures the ratio of women to men to such a degree that the activities of the latter become completely secondary. A number of critics (Lopreto, Tieffemberg, Alzate-Cadavid) have remarked on the fact that Guevara almost always uses the third-person plural, "las mugeres," "ellas" (the women, they), when she refers to their participation in the upriver journey, switching to the first person only in the last paragraph, in which she asks for her personal reward. Silvia Tieffemberg also points out an alternation between an objective narrative and a more intimate, "woman-to-woman" tone that Guevara adopted in addressing the princess (289–90). It is important to note that she requests that the repartimiento be granted to her, not to her husband, and that it be given in perpetuity, as her actions had warranted it. In so doing Isabel de Guevara gives us a glimpse of a stalwart woman, one with a strong sense of self and worth. As was the case with many other documents of this kind, the letter she wrote articulated not only her personal frustration but also a common complaint among Spain's immigrants to the Americas: the resentment of the established colonists toward the newcomers, who were enriching themselves without having suffered the dangers and hardships of the original settlers.

Notes

1. Mary G. Berg has done research in the Archives of the Indies in Seville and has found other letters by women asking for redress of wrongs, but none of them tell as complete a story as Isabel de Guevara's. Berg is planning to publish some of her finds, which will add greatly to what we know about European women in the early colonial years.

2. The repartimiento she requested was given by the Spanish Crown under a system called *encomienda* (the entrusting of one person to another). A repartimiento was not a land grant per se—although in practice it turned out to be tantamount to one—but the right to the tribute and labor of a determined number of Indians on a specific parcel of land, given either for a limited time or in perpetuity. In return for this tribute or labor the Indians were entrusted to the Spanish *patrón* for instruction in the Christian faith. The two terms, *repartimiento* and *encomienda,* are often used interchangeably.

3. Juana governed in the absence of her brother Philip II, who was away in England for several years, having married Mary Tudor in 1555.

4. Raúl Marrero-Fente points out that her letter followed legal models for establishing a claim: she first narrates the facts, then denounces the injustice done her, and subsequently asks that her grievance be addressed.

Carta a la princesa doña Juana

Carta de doña ISABEL DE GUEVARA á la princesa gobernadora doña JUANA, exponiendo los trabajos hechos en el descubrimiento y conquista del Rio de la Plata por las mugeres para ayudar á los hombres, y pidiendo repartimiento para su marido.[1]

Muy alta y muy poderosa señora:

A esta probinçia del Rio de la Plata, con el primer gouernador della, don Pedro de Mendoça, avemos venido çiertas mugeres, entre las quales a querido mi ventura que fuese yo la vna; y como la armada llegase al puerto de Buenos Ayres, con mill é quinientos hombres, y les faltase el bastimento, fué tamaña la hambre, que, á cabo de tres meses, murieran los mill; esta hambre fué tamaña, que ni la de Xerusalen se le puede ygualar, ni con otra nenguna se puede conparar. Vinieron los hombres en tanta flaqueza, que todos los travajos cargavan de las pobres mugeres, ansi en lavarles las ropas, como en curarles, hazerles de comer lo poco que tenian, alimpiarlos, hazer sentinela, rondar los fuegos, armar las vallestas, quando algunas vezes los yndios les venien á dar guerra, hasta cometer á poner fuego en los versos, y á levantar los soldados, los questavan para hello, dar arma por el canpo á bozes, sargenteando y poniendo en orden los soldados; porque en este tienpo, como las mugeres nos sustentamos con poca comida, no aviamos caydo en tanta flaqueza como los hombres. Bien creerá V. A. que fué tanta la soliçitud que tuvieron, que, si no fuera por ellas, todos fueran acabados; y si no fuera por la honrra de los hombres, muchas más cosas escriviera con verdad y los diera á hellos por testigos. Esta relaçion bien creo que la escrivirán á V. A. más largamente, y por eso sesaré.

Pasada esta tan peligrosa turbunada, determinaron subir el rio arriba, asi, flacos como estavan y en entrada de ynvierno, en dos ver-

gantines, los pocos que quedaron viuos, y las fatigadas mugeres los
curavan y los miravan y les guisauan la comida, trayendo la leña á
cuestas de fuera del navio, y animandolos con palabras varoniles, que
no se dexasen morir, que presto darian en tierra de comida, metien-
dolos á cuestas en los vergantines, con tanto amor como si fueran sus
propios hijos. Y como llegamos á vna generaçion de yndios que se
llaman tinbues, señores de mucho pescado, de nuevo los serviamos
en buscarles diversos modos de guisados, porque no les diese en rostro el pescado, á cabsa que lo comian sin pan y estavan muy flacos.

Despues, determinaron subir el Parana arriba, en demanda de
bastimento, en el qual viaje, pasaron tanto trabajo las desdichadas
mugeres, que milagrosamente quiso Dios que biviesen por ver que
hen ellas estava la vida dellos; porque todos los serviçios del navio
los tomavan hellas tan á pechos, que se tenia por afrentada la que
menos hazia que otra, serviendo de marear la vela y gouernar el
navio y sondar de proa y tomar el remo al soldado que no podia
bogar y esgotar el navio, y poniendo por delante á los soldados que
no desanimasen, que para los hombres heran los trabajos: verdad es,
que á estas cosas hellas no heran apremiadas, ni las hazian de obli-
gaçion ni las obligaua, si solamente la caridad. Ansi llegaron á esta
çiudad de la Asunçion, que avnque agora está muy fertil de basti-
mentos, entonçes estaua dellos muy neçesitada, que fué nesesario
que las mugeres boluiesen de nuevo á sus trabajos, haziendo rosas
con sus propias manos, rosando y carpiendo y senbrando y reco-
gendo el bastimento, sin ayuda de nadie, hasta tanto que los soldados
guareçieron de sus flaquezas y començaron á señorear la tierra y al-
querir yndios y yndias de su serviçio, hasta ponerse en el estado en
que agora está la tierra.

E querido escrevir esto y traer á la memoria de V. A., para hazerle
saber la yngratitud que comigo se a vsado en esta tierra, porque al
presente se repartió por la mayor parte de los que ay en ella, ansi de
los antiguos como de los modernos, sin que de mí y de mis trabajos
se tuviese nenguna memoria, y me dexaron de fuera, sin me dar
yndio ni nengun genero de serviçio. Mucho me quisiera hallar libre,
para me yr á presentar delante de V. A., con los serviçios que á S. M.
e hecho y los agravios que agora se me hazen; mas no está en mi

mano, por questoy casada con vn cauallero de Sevilla, que se llama
Pedro d'Esquiuel, que, por servir á S. M., a sido cabsa que mis trabajos quedasen tan oluidados y se me renovasen de nuevo, porque tres
vezes le saqué el cuchillo de la garganta, como allá V. A. sabrá. A
que suplico mande me sea dado mi repartimiento perpétuo, y en
gratificaçion de mis serviçios mande que sea proveydo mi marido
de algun cargo, conforme á la calidad de su persona; pues él, de su
parte, por sus serviçios lo merese. Nuestro Señor acreçiente su Real
vida y estado por mui largos años. Desta çibdad de la Asunçion y de
jullio 2, 1556 años.

Serbidora de V. A. que sus Reales manos besa
Doña Ysabel de Guevara.

[Sello] Sobre. — *A la muy alta y muy poderosa señora la Princesa doña
Joana, Gouernadora de los reynos d'España, etc.— En su Consejo de Yndias.*

Notas

1. Es interesante ver cómo los que clasificaron este documento leyeron
mal su mensaje central: Doña Isabel pide recompensa principalmente
para sí misma, y no tanto para el marido.

Gramley Library
Salem Academy and College
Winston-Salem, N.C. 27108

Letter to the Princess Doña Juana

Letter from Doña ISABEL DE GUEVARA to the Governing Princess Doña JUANA, explaining the hardships endured in the discovery and conquest of the River Plate by the women in order to help the men, and asking for a land grant for her husband.[1]

Very High and Very Powerful Lady:

To this province of the River Plate, with Don Pedro de Mendoza being the first governor thereof, there came certain women, of whom my destiny willed it that I should be one, and as the fleet arrived at the port of Buenos Aires with fifteen hundred men and they were in need of food, the starvation was so great that after three months a thousand of them died. So great was the famine that not even in Jerusalem could it have been worse, nor can it be compared to any other. The men became so weak that all the work fell on the poor women: from washing their clothes to caring for the sick, making them eat the little they had, cleaning them, standing guard, tending the watch-fires, arming the crossbows when sometimes there were Indian attacks and even firing the culverins; we would sound the alarm to the soldiers with loud voices, we drilled them and put them in order, for at that time we women could get by with less food and had not fallen into such a state of weakness as the men. Your Highness will understand that had it not been for the care and concern we had for them, all of them would have been finished, and were it not for the honor of the men, I might truly write a great deal more and offer the [men] as witnesses. I am sure they will write this report to Your Highness in greater detail, and for that reason I will desist.

When this terrible time was over the few who remained alive determined to go upriver in two brigantines, as weak as they were and with winter about to begin. And the exhausted women cared for them and watched over them and cooked their food, lugging firewood onto the ships on their backs, and encouraging them with manly words not to let themselves die, that soon they would get to lands where there would be food, and carrying them aboard the brigantines on their backs with as much love as if they had been their own children. And when we came to a tribe of Indians called Timbues, lords of good places to fish, again we served the men by thinking up different ways of preparing the fish so that it would not disgust them, for they had to eat it without bread and were very feeble.

After that they decided to go up the Paraná River in search of food, on which journey the unfortunate women underwent such hardships that God determined that they should survive miraculously because He saw that the men's lives were in their hands, for the women took all the labors on board so to heart that one would feel affronted if she did less than another, so they all worked at handling the sails and steering the ship, taking soundings at the bow and taking over the oar from a soldier unable to row, and bailing the ship and encouraging the soldiers not to lose heart; this was men's work, and in truth the women were not rewarded for it, nor did it out of obligation, but only out of love. So they got to this city of Asunción which, although now it produces a great deal of food, was then very much in need of it, and thus it was necessary for the women to set to work again, clearing the land with their own hands, digging, weeding, sowing, and harvesting the food with no help from anyone until the soldiers had recovered from their weakness and began to govern the land and acquire Indian men and women as their servants, until the land came to be in the state it is now.

I have wanted to write and bring this to Your Highness's attention, to let you know the ingratitude that has been shown me in this country, because by now the greater part of it has been granted to those who reside here, the old colonists as well as the new, without any acknowledgment whatsoever of me and of my work, and I was left out, not having been given an Indian or any other kind of reward. I would dearly love to be free to go and appear before Your Highness, and tell you about the many services I have rendered His Majesty and the injuries now being done to me, but this is not in my power because I am married to a gentleman of Seville named Pedro d'Esquivel, whose services to His Majesty have caused mine to be quite forgotten, and they should be told again, because thrice I have saved his life when he had a knife at his throat, as Your Highness over there must know. And so I beg you to order that my repartimiento be given me in perpetuity and that in appreciation of my services my husband be assigned a position worthy of his person, as he for his services also merits this. May Our Lord God increase your royal life and state for many years. From this city of Asunción and on July 2, 1556.

> Your Highness's servant who kisses your royal hands
> Doña Ysabel de Guevara.

[Seal]   Envelope— *To the very high and very powerful lady the Princess Doña Juana, Governor of the kingdoms of Spain, etc.—At her Council of the Indies*

Notes

1. It is interesting to see how the person who classified this document misread her central message: Doña Isabel's request is principally for herself, not so much for her husband.

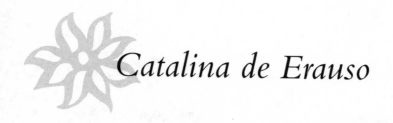

Catalina de Erauso

Catalina de Erauso from The Nun Ensign. *James Fitzmaurice-Kelly
(London: T Fisher Unwin, 1907).*

*T*he scandalous story of Catalina de Erauso, a transvestite with marked homoerotic tendencies, known in her day as the "Ensign Nun," has shock value even today. She was born in 1592 into a prominent family in the city of San Sebastián, in the Basque country in northern Spain. As a child Catalina was placed in a convent where her aunt was abbess, and was fully expected to take the veil; instead, she fled her convent when a teenager (she was a novice at the time), dressed as a boy, and lived a wandering life in Spain for about three years. She then embarked for the New World and joined the throngs of Spaniards looking for a way to make their fortunes. She lived as a man for more than twenty years, as merchant's apprentice, soldier, muleteer, constantly switching employers, clothes, jobs, names, and countries. She seduced women, brawled, cheated, stole, gambled, fought in major battles against the fierce Araucanian Indians in Chile, and killed her own brother in a duel. In Peru Catalina finally met a saintly bishop who showed her great kindness, and to him she confessed her true gender and identity, thus becoming instantly notorious. The bishop insisted that she return to the religious life until it could be proven that she indeed had not taken her final vows; while she waited for this information she lived in convents in Peru for about three years, once again wearing the habit she had discarded so many years earlier. When she returned to Spain, she appeared before King Philip IV, who was extremely curious to meet her. The king not only did not punish her, but gave her money, a land grant, and permission to continue dressing as a man. As the pope wanted to see her as well, Catalina subsequently went to Rome, where His Holiness, too, granted her permission to retain her male attire. In 1630 she returned to America and lived out her life as Antonio de Erauso, a teamster who, like many of his fellow Basques, transported the New World's goods by mule train. She died in Mexico in about 1650.

Catalina was a legend in her own time, and her story took many forms. She was so notorious on her return to Spain that at least one play, *La monja alférez* (The Ensign Nun), was written about her and performed on the Madrid stage—not after her death, but in 1626, the very year she was on her way to see the pope. If anything more of note happened to her, the playwright, Juan Pérez de Montalbán, promised a sequel. Catalina's portrait was painted twice, once by Francisco Pacheco, the father-in-law of Diego Velázquez. Her story—albeit somewhat sanitized—was incorporated into the colonial history of Chile (Merrim 190) and circulated in three versions on broadsheets in Mexico. Catalina purportedly wrote her own autobiography—or dictated it to someone—when she was in Seville, waiting to return to the New World, but the original manuscript has been lost.[1]

Although Catalina continued to exist in the legends of Mexico and Chile, not to mention her own Basque country, her autobiography had never been published. A fellow Basque, Joaquín María Ferrer, obtained a version of the manuscript in the early nineteenth century and, after some careful archival research, published it in Paris in 1829. It was an immediate sensation and was translated into German and French the following year. The first English translation was done by James Fitzmaurice-Kelly in 1908, but has long been out of print; another translation was published in 1996. Two films have been made about the life of the Ensign Nun: a Mexican one in 1940, starring María Félix in the title role, and a Basque one, made in Spain.[2] There is no doubt that Catalina de Erauso's story has continued to exert a powerful appeal.

Social and literary historians, especially those working on matters of sexuality and gender roles in early modern Europe, have long been aware of the story of Catalina de Erauso; especially good studies on this topic are those by Stephanie Merrim (1993) and Mary Elizabeth Perry (1990). In Catalina's day, and indeed in her own family, "the men served the king; the women entered religion" (Fitzmaurice-Kelly xvii). Four of the Erauso brothers went to the New World; three sisters became nuns, and only one married (Stepto xxvii). Catalina straddled these gender roles in a way that was both peculiar and successful. Perry underscores her primary desire to live a man's free and adventurous existence: "Catalina, in fact, refused feminization and embraced only masculine qualities. . . . Aware of the restrictions that gender imposed on her life, she did not try to change the inequity between the sexes. Instead, she chose to change herself, to deny her body, to repudiate the convent, habit, and submission expected of her as a woman, and to construct for herself a male persona who would completely obliterate her identity as a woman" (134). She was not punished for these transgressions—indeed she was rewarded—because she knew how to present her case: on the one hand, once her identity as a woman was revealed to the bishop, she proved that she was still a virgin: on the other, she presented herself before king and pope as exemplary for having renounced her femininity and aspired to become something superior, a man (Perry 134–35; Merrim 180, 188).

Catalina's autobiography is a problematic document for many reasons. There are many discrepancies with respect to the dates mentioned within it, including the date of her birth, which she gives as 1585 while her baptismal certificate is dated 1592, and we know that Catholic children are routinely baptized as soon after birth as possible. Then there is the question of authorship. Most trained readers immediately notice a familiar "literary" quality in her text. As Fitzmaurice-Kelly noted, "The dividing line between the personal narrative and certain specimens of picaresque romance is faint and shifting" (xxxix). Merrim feels that there are essentially three positions one can take on this issue: (a) Catalina actually wrote the entire document herself; (b) she dictated it to a trained author, who may have given it literary form; or (c) a later author changed the original version or inserted material of his own (196). This puzzle has not been resolved.

While the autobiography is certainly full of adventure and stirring action, a modern reader may long for some sort of introspection or psychological explanation in the narration. This is conspicuously absent, yet Catalina's tale keeps us in suspense because of "the constant risk that her 'secret' will be discovered" (Garber xii). In terms of gender, the narrative voice in Spanish is particularly distinctive, given the shifting masculine and feminine adjectives Erauso uses with respect to herself.[3] Social historians such as Rudolf Dekker and Lotte van de Pol, Diane Dugaw, and Perry have all called attention to the importance of

Erauso's story as it pertains to gender roles prevalent in her time. Although the Bible specifically forbade cross-dressing (Deut. 22.5), in sixteenth- and seventeenth-century Europe women who dressed as men were not infrequent, both in literature and in real life. What makes Erauso's case unique, however, is the bravado and skill with which she presents her story, how, in modern terms, she "markets" herself before the world. As Merrim so perceptively observed, she has "a keen awareness of the worth of a singular and prodigious tale" (192) in an age—much like ours today—in which the bizarre and the peculiar were appreciated and applauded.

Notes

1. This would have been sometime between 1626, when she left Rome, and 1630, when Erauso reembarked for the Americas.

The whole convoluted story of the manuscript is too complex and long to be told in its entirety here. Merrim (179–80) gives a concise summary of its vicissitudes; a complete account is in Rima de Vallbona's edition of *Vida i sucesos de la Monja Alférez escrita por ella misma.*

2. Adrienne Martin, "Catalina de Erauso: The Undressing of a Golden Age Transvestite," lecture at Mt. Holyoke College, South Hadley, MA, April 9, 1996.

To cast the sensuously beautiful María Félix in the title role was taking considerable visual license with the protagonist: contemporaries who knew her described Catalina as tall, of strong build, neither handsome nor ugly, a little stooped, with some facial hair, and the general appearance of a eunuch (Fitzmaurice-Kelly xxii–xxiii).

3. Critics have called attention to the fact that Basque, Catalina's native language, has no grammatical gender (Merrim 183), and thus she may have been unsure when using gender-inflected adjectives in Spanish. Ferrer's version (which I have used in this anthology) differs from Vallbona's transcription of the manuscript with respect to the gendered adjectives (Merrim 203 n. 7).

Vida i sucesos de la monja alférez

CAPÍTULO I

Su patria, padres, nacimiento, educación, fuga y correrías por varias partes de España.

Nací yo, doña Catalina de Erauso, en la villa de San Sebastián, de Guipúzcoa, en el año de 1585, hija del capitán don Miguel de Erauso y de doña María Pérez de Galarraga y Arce, naturales y vecinos de aquella villa. Criáronme mis padres en su casa, con otros mis hermanos, hasta tener cuatro años. En 1589 me entraron en el convento de San Sebastián el Antiguo, de dicha villa, que es de monjas dominicas, con mi tía doña Ursula de Unzá y Sarasti, prima hermana de mi madre y priora de aquel convento, en donde me crié hasta tener quince años, en que se trató de mi profesión.

Estando en el año de noviciado, ya cerca del fin, me ocurrió una reyerta con una monja profesa llamada doña Catalina de Aliri, que, siendo viuda, entró y profesó. Era ella robusta y yo muchacha; me maltrató de mano y yo lo sentí. A la noche del 18 de marzo de 1600, víspera de San José, levantóse el convento a media noche a maitines. Entré en el coro y hallé allí arrodillada a mi tía, la cual me llamó, y dándome la llave de su celda, me mandó traerle el breviario. Yo fuí por él. Abrí y lo tomé, y viendo en un clavo colgadas las llaves del convento, dejéme la celda abierta y volvíle a mi tía su llave y breviario. Estando ya las monjas en el coro y comenzados los maitines con solemnidad, a la primera lección llegué a mi tía y le pedí licencia, porque estaba mala. Mi tía, tocándome con la mano en la cabeza, me dijo: "Anda, acuéstate." Salí del coro, tomé una luz y fuíme a la celda de mi tía; tomé allí unas tijeras, hilo y una aguja; tomé unos reales de a ocho que allí estaban, y tomé las llaves del convento y me salí. Fuí abriendo puertas y emparejándolas, y en la última dejé mi escapulario y me salí a la calle, que nunca había visto, sin saber por dónde echar ni adónde ir. Tiré no sé por dónde, y fuí a dar en un castañar que está fuera y cerca de la espalda del convento. Allí acogíme y estuve tres días trazando, acomodando y cortando de vestir. Híceme, de una basquiña de paño azul con que me hallaba, unos calzones, y de un faldellín verde de perpetuán que traía debajo, una ropilla y polainas: el hábito me lo dejé por allí, por no saber qué hacer con él. Cortéme el pelo, que tiré, y a la tercera noche, deseando alejarme, partí no sé por dónde, calando caminos y pasando lugares, hasta venir a dar en Vitoria, que dista de San Sebastián cerca de veinte leguas, a pie, cansada y sin haber comido más que hierbas que topaba por el camino.

Entré en Vitoria sin saber adónde acogerme. A los pocos días encontré al doctor don Francisco de Cerralta, catedrático de allí, el cual me recibió fácilmente, sin conocerme, y me vistió. Era casado con una prima hermana de mi madre, según luego entendí; pero no me dí a conocer. Estuve con él cosa de tres meses, en los cuales, viéndome él leer bien el latín, se me inclinó más y me quiso dar estudio; pero como yo rehusara, me porfió y me instaba hasta ponerme las manos. Yo, con esto, determiné dejarle, e hícelo así. Cogíle unos cuartos, y concertándome en doce reales con un arriero que partía para Valladolid, que dista cuarenta y cinco leguas, partí con él.

Entrado en Valladolid, donde estaba entonces la Corte, me acomodé en breve por paje de don Juan de Idiáquez, secretario del rey, el cual me vistió luego bien. Allí me llamé Francisco Loyola y estuve bienhallado siete meses. Al cabo de ellos, estando una noche a la puerta con otro paje compañero, llegó mi padre, preguntándonos si estaba en casa el señor don Juan.

Respondió mi compañero que sí. Dijo mi padre que le avisase que estaba él allí, y subió el paje, quedándome yo con mi padre, sin hablarnos palabra ni él conocerme. Volvió el paje, diciendo que subiese, y subió, yendo yo tras de él. Salió don Juan a la escalera, y, abrazándole, dijo: "¡Señor capitán, que buena venida es ésta!" Mi padre habló de modo que él conoció que traía disgusto, y despidiendo una visita con que estaba, volvió y sentáronse, preguntándole qué había de nuevo. Mi padre dijo cómo se le había ido del convento aquella muchacha, y esto le traía por los contornos en su busca. . . .

Yo, que oí la conversación y sentimiento de mi padre, salíme atrás y fuíme a mi aposento. Cogí mi ropa y salí, llevándome cosa de ocho doblones con que me hallaba, y fuíme a un mesón, donde dormí aquella noche y donde entendí a un arriero que partía por la mañana a Bilbao. Ajustéme con él, y partimos a otro día, sin saberme yo qué hacer ni adónde ir, sino dejarme llevar del viento como una pluma. . . .

De allí, luego que salí, me pasé a Estella, de Navarra, que distará veinte leguas a lo que me parece. Entré en Estella, donde me acomodé por paje de don Carlos de Arellano, del hábito de Santiago,[1] en cuya casa y servicio estuve dos años, bien tratado y bien vestido. Pasado este tiempo, sin más causa que mi gusto, dejé aquella comodidad y me pasé a San Sebastián, mi patria, diez leguas distante de allí, y donde me estuve, sin ser de nadie conocido, bien vestido y galán. Y un día oí misa en mi convento, la cual misa oyó también mi madre, y vide que me miraba y no me conoció, y acabada la misa, unas monjas me llamaron al coro, y yo, no dándome por entendido, les hice muchas cortesías y me fuí. Era esto entrado ya el año de 1603.

Paséme de allí . . . a Sanlúcar. Hallé allí al capitán Miguel de Echarreta, natural de mi tierra, que lo era de un patache de galeones, de que era general don Luis Fernández de Córdoba, y de la armada, don Luis Fajardo, año 1603, que partía para la Punta de Araya. Senté plaza de grumete en un galeón del capitán Esteban Eguiño, tío mío, primo hermano de mi madre, que vive hoy en San Sebastián, y embarqué y partimos de Sanlúcar, Lunes Santo, año de 1603.

CAPÍTULO II

Parte de Sanlúcar para Punta Araya, Cartagena, Nombre de Dios y Panamá.

Pasé algunos trabajos en el camino por ser nuevo en el oficio. Inclinóseme mi tío sin conocerme, y haciéndome agasajos, oído de dónde era y el nombre supuesto de mis padres, que yo di, tuve en él gran arrimo. Llegamos a Punta de Araya y hallamos allí una armadilla enemiga fortificada en tierra, y nuestra armada la echó. Arribamos finalmente a Cartagena de las Indias, y estuvimos allí ocho días.

Híceme borrar de la plaza de grumete y pasé a servir al dicho capitán Eguiño, mi tío. De allí pasamos a Nombre de Dios, donde estuvimos nueve días, muriéndosenos en ellos mucha gente, lo cual hizo dar mucha prisa a salir.

Estando ya embarcada la plata y aprestado todo para partir de vuelta a España, yo le hice un tiro cuantioso a mi tío, cogiéndole quinientos pesos. A las diez de la noche, cuando él estaba durmiendo, salí y dije a los guardas que me enviaba a tierra el capitán a un negocio. Como me conocían, dejáronme llanamente pasar, y salté a tierra; pero nunca más me vieron. De allí a una hora dispararon pieza de leva y zarparon hechos a la vela.

Levada ya la flota, me acomodé allí con el capitán Juan de Ibarra, factor de las cajas de Panamá, que hoy vive. De allí a cuatro o seis días nos partimos para Panamá, donde él residía y donde estuve con él cosa de tres meses. Hacíame poca comodidad, que era escaso, y hube allí de gastar cuanto de mi tío había traído, hasta no quedarme ni un cuarto, con lo cual me despedí para buscar por otra parte mi remedio.

Haciéndome mi diligencia descubrí allí a Juan de Urquiza, mercader de Trujillo, y acomodéme con él, y con él me fué muy bien, y estuvimos en Panamá tres meses.

CAPÍTULO III

De Panamá pasa con su amo Urquiza, mercader de Trujillo, al puerto de Paita y a la villa de Saña.

De Panamá partí con mi amo Juan de Urquiza, en una fragata, para el puerto de Paita, donde él tenía un gran cargamento. Llegando al puerto de Manta, nos cargó un tiempo tan fuerte que dimos al través, y los que supimos nadar, como yo, mi amo y otros, salimos a tierra: los demás perecieron. En el dicho puerto de Manta nos volvimos a embarcar en un galeón del rey que allí hallamos y costó dinero, y en él partimos y llegamos al puerto de Paita, donde halló mi amo toda su hacienda, como esperaba, cargada en una nao del capitán Alonso Cerrato, y dándome a mí orden de que toda, por sus números, la fuese remitiendo allá, partió.

Yo puse luego por obra lo que me mandó, y fuí descargando la hacienda por sus números, y por ellos fuíla remitiendo. Mi amo, en Saña, que dista de Paita unas sesenta leguas, fué recibiéndola, y a lo último, con las últimas cargas, yo partí de Paita y llegué a Saña.

Llegado a Saña, me recibió mi amo con gran cariño, mostrándose contento de lo bien que lo había hecho, y con todo buen trato, hízome luego al punto dos vestidos muy buenos, uno negro y otro de color. Púsome en una tienda suya, entregándome por géneros y por cuenta mucha hacienda, que importó más de ciento treinta mil pesos, poniéndome por escrito en un libro los precios a cómo había de vender cada cosa. Dejóme dos esclavos que me sirviesen y una negra que me guisase, señalándome tres pesos para el gasto de cada día, y hecho esto, cargó él con la demás hacienda y se fué con ella a Trujillo, distante de allí treinta y dos leguas.

También me dejó escrito y advertido en el dicho libro las personas a quienes podía fiar la hacienda que pidiesen y quisiesen llevar, por ser de su satisfacción y seguras, pero con cuenta y razón y asentando cada partida en el libro. Y especialmente me advirtió esto, para en cuanto a mi señora doña Beatriz de Cárdenas, persona de toda su satisfacción y obligación. Fuése él a Trujillo y yo me quedé en Saña con mi tienda, vendiendo conforme a la pauta que él me dejó, y cobrando y asentando en mi libro, con día, mes, y año, género, varas, nombre de compradores y precios: de la misma suerte con lo fiado.

Comenzó mi señora doña Beatriz de Cárdenas a sacar ropas, prosiguió y fué sacando tan largamente, que yo llegué a dudar, y sin dárselo a ella a entender, se lo escribí todo por extenso al amo a Trujillo. Respondióme que estaba muy bien todo, y que en este particular de la señora, si toda la tienda entera me la pedía, se la podía entregar; con lo cual, y guardando yo esta carta, proseguí . . .

[Catalina de Erauso tiene más problemas con la justicia y tiene que dejar a este amo.]

CAPÍTULO V

Parte de Trujillo a Lima.

Partido de Trujillo a Lima, y andadas más de ochenta leguas, entré en la ciudad de Lima, cabeza del opulento reino del Perú . . .

Di mi carta a Diego de Solarte, mercader muy rico, que es ahora cónsul mayor de Lima, y a quien me remitió Juan de Urquiza, el cual me recibió luego en su casa con mucho agrado y afabilidad, y a pocos días me entregó su tienda, señalándome seiscientos pesos al año, y allí lo fuí haciendo muy a su agrado y contento.

Al cabo de nueve meses me dijo que buscase mi vida en otra parte, y fué la causa que tenía en casa dos doncellas, hermanas de su mujer, con las cuales, y sobre todo con una que más se me inclinó, solía yo jugar y triscar. Y un día, estando en el estrado peinándome acostado en sus faldas y andándole en las piernas, llegó acaso a una reja, por donde nos vió y oyó a ella que me decía que fuese al Potosí² y buscase dineros y nos casaríamos. Retiróse, y de allí a poco me llamó, me pidió y tomó cuentas, y despidióme y me fuí.

Hallábame desacomodado y muy remoto de favor. Estábanse allí entonces levantando seis compañías para Chile; yo me llegué a una y senté plaza de soldado, y recibí luego doscientos ochenta pesos, que me dieron de sueldo. Mi amo, Diego de Lasarte, que lo supo, lo sintió mucho, que parece que no lo decía por tanto. Ofrecióme hacer diligencias con los oficiales para que me borrasen de la plaza y volver el dinero que recibí; pero no vine en ello, diciendo que era mi inclinación andar y ver mundo. En fin, asentada la plaza en la compañía del capitán Gonzalo Rodríguez, partí de Lima en tropa de mil seiscientos hombres, de que iba por maestro de campo Diego Bravo de Sarabia, para la ciudad de la Concepción, que dista de Lima quinientas cuarenta leguas.

CAPÍTULO VI

Llega a la Concepción de Chile y halla allí a su hermano. Pasa a Paicabí, y hallándose en la batalla de Valdivia, gana una bandera. Vuelve a la Concepción, mata a dos y a su propio hermano.

Llegamos al puerto de la Concepción en veinte días que se tardó en el camino. Es ciudad razonable, con título de *noble y leal*, y tiene obispo. Fuimos bien recibidos por la falta de gente que había en Chile. Llegó luego orden del gobernador, Alonso de Ribera, para desembarcarnos, y trájola su secretario, el capitán Miguel de Erauso. Luego que oí su nombre me alegré y vi que era mi hermano, porque aunque no le conocía ni había visto porque partió de San Sebastián para estas partes siendo yo de dos años, tenía noticias de él, si no de su residencia. Tomó la lista de la gente, fué pasando y preguntando a cada uno su nombre y patria, y llegando a mí y oyendo mi nombre y patria, soltó la pluma y me abrazó y fué haciendo preguntas por su padre, y su madre, y hermanos, y por su querida Catalina, la monja. Yo fuí a todo respondiendo como podía, sin descubrirme ni caer él en ello. Fué prosiguiendo la lista, y en acabando me llevó a comer a su casa y me senté a comer. Díjome que aquel presidio que yo llevaba de Paicabí era de mala pasadía de soldados; que él hablaría al gobernador para que me mudase de plaza. En comiendo subió a ver al gobernador, llevándome consigo. Dióle cuenta de la gente que venía y pidió de merced que mudase a su compañía a un mancebito que venía allí de su tierra, que no había visto otro de allá desde que salió. Mandóme entrar el gobernador, y en viéndome, no sé por qué, dijo que no me podía mudar. Mi hermano lo sintió y salióse; pero de allí a un rato llamó a mi hermano el gobernador, y díjole que fuese como pedía.

Así, yéndose las compañías, quedé yo con mi hermano por su soldado, comiendo a su mesa casi tres años sin haber dado en ello. Fuí con él algunas veces a casa de una dama que allí tenía, y de ahí, algunas otras veces, me fuí sin él, y alcanzó a saberlo y concibió mal y díjome que allí no entrase. Acechóme y me cogió otra vez, y esperándome, al salir me embistió a cintarazos y me hirió en una mano. Fué forzoso defenderme, y al ruido acudió el capitán Francisco de Aillón, y metió paz; pero yo me hube de entrar en San Francisco por temor al gobernador, que era fuerte y lo estuvo en esto, aunque mi hermano intercedió, hasta que vino a desterrarme a Paicabí, y sin remedio hube de irme, y estuve allí tres años.

Hube de salir a Paicabí y pasar allí algunos trabajos por tres años, habiendo antes vivido alegremente. Estábamos siempre con las armas en la mano, por la gran invasión de los indios que allí hay, hasta que vino finalmente el gobernador Alonso de Sarabia con todas las compañías de Chile. Juntámonos otros cuantos con él y alojámonos en los llanos de Valdivia, en campaña rasa, cinco mil hombres, con harta incomodidad. Tomaron y asaltaron los indios la dicha Valdivia. Salimos a ellos, y batallamos tres o cuatro veces, maltratándolos siempre y destrozándolos; pero llegándoles la vez última socorro, nos fué mal y nos mataron mucha gente, y capitanes, y a mi alférez, y se llevaron la bandera. Viéndola llevar, partimos tras ella yo y dos soldados de a caballo, por medio de gran multitud, atropellando y matando y recibiendo daño. En breve cayó muerto uno de los tres. Proseguimos los dos y llegamos hasta la bandera; pero cayó de un bote de lanza mi compañero. Yo, con un mal golpe en una pierna, maté al cacique[3] que la llevaba, se la quité y apreté con mi caballo, atropellando, matando e hiriendo a infinidad; pero malherido y pasado de tres flechas y de una lanza en el hombro izquierdo, que sentía mucho; en fin, llegué a mucha gente y caí luego del caballo. Acudiéronme algunos, y entre ellos mi hermano, a quien no había visto y me fué de consuelo. Curáronme y quedamos allí alojados nueve meses. Al cabo de ellos, mi hermano me sacó del gobernador la bandera que yo gané, y quedé alférez de la compañía de Alonso Moreno, la cual poco después se dió al capitán Gonzalo Rodríguez, el primer capitán que yo conocí y holgué mucho. . . .

A este tiempo, y entre otros, vino un día don Juan de Silva, mi amigo, alférez vivo, y me dijo que había tenido unas palabras con don Francisco de Rojas, del hábito de Santiago, y lo había desafiado para aquella noche, a las once, llevando cada uno a un amigo, y que él no tenía otro para eso sino a mí. Yo quedé un poco suspenso, recelando si habría allí forjada alguna treta para prenderme. El, que lo advirtió, me dijo: "Si no os parece, no sea; yo me iré solo, que a otro no he de fiar mi lado." Yo me dije que en qué reparaba, y acepté.

En dando la oración, salí del convento y me fuí a su casa. Cenamos y parlamos hasta las diez, y en oyéndolas tomamos las espadas y capas, y salimos al puesto señalado. Era la obscuridad tan suma que no nos veíamos las manos; y advirtiéndolo yo, hice con mi amigo, para no desconocernos en lo que se pudiera ofrecer, que nos pusiéramos cada uno en el brazo atado su lenzuelo.

Llegaron los dos, y dijo el uno, conocido en la voz por don Francisco de Rojas: "¿Don Juan de Silva?" Don Juan respondió: "¡Aquí estoy!" Metieron ambos mano a las espadas y se embistieron, mientras estábamos parados el otro y yo. Fueron bregando, y a poco rato sentí que se sintió mi amigo la punta que le había entrado. Púseme luego a su lado, y el otro al lado de don Francisco. Tiramos dos a dos, y a breve rato cayeron don Francisco y don Juan; yo y mi contrario proseguimos batallando, y entréle yo una punta, según después pareció, por bajo de la tetilla izquierda, pasándole, según sentí, coleto de dos antes, y cayó. "¡Ah, traidor—dijo—, que me has muerto!" Yo quise reconocer el habla de quien yo no conocía; preguntéle quién era, y dijo: "El capitán Miguel de Erauso." Yo quedé atónito. Pedía a voces confesión, y pedíanla los otros. Fuí corriendo a San Francisco, y envié dos religiosos, que los confesaron. Dos expiraron luego; a mi hermano lo llevaron a casa del gobernador, de quien era secretario de guerra. Acudieron con médico y cirujano a la curación, e hicieron cuanto alcanzaron; luego hízose lo judicial, preguntándole el nombre del homicida; y como él clamaba por un poco de vino y el doctor Robledo se lo negaba, diciendo que no convenía, él porfió, el doctor negó y él dijo: "Más cruel anda usted conmigo que el alférez Díaz"; y de ahí a un rato expiró. . . . Muerto el capitán Miguel de Erauso, lo enterraron en el dicho convento de San Francisco, viéndolo yo desde el coro, ¡sabe Dios con qué dolor! . . .

CAPÍTULO XX

Entra en Guamanga, y lo que allí le sucedió hasta descubrirse al señor obispo.

Entré en Guamanga y fuíme a una posada. . . . Salí a ver la ciudad, que parecíame bien, de buenos edificios: los mejores que vide en el Perú. Vi tres conventos, de franciscanos, mercedarios y dominicos; uno de monjas y un hospital; muchísimos vecinos indios y muchos españoles; bello temple de tierra, fundada en un llano, sin frío ni calor; de grandes cosechas de trigo, vino, frutas y semillas, buena iglesia, con tres dignidades y dos canónigos y un santo obispo, fraile agustino, don fray Agustín de Carvajal, que fué mi remedio; aunque faltó, muriendo de repente el año veinte, y decían que lo había sido allí desde el año doce.

Estuve allí unos días, y quiso mi desgracia que me entrara unas veces en una casa de juego, donde estando un día entró el corregidor, don Baltasar de Quiñones, y mirándome y desconociéndome, me preguntó de dónde era. Dije que vizcaíno. Dijo: "¿De dónde viene ahora?" Dije: "Del Cuzco." Suspendióse un poco mirándome, y dijo: "Sea preso." Dije: "De buena gana"; y saqué la espada, retirándome a la puerta. El dió voces pidiendo favor al rey, y hallé en la puerta tal resistencia que no pude salir. Saqué una pistola de tres bocas, y salí y desaparecíme, entrando en casa de un amigo que me había hallado. Partió el corregidor y embargóme la mula y no sé qué cosillas que tenía en la posada. Estúveme allí unos días, habiendo descubierto que aquel amigo era vizcaíno. Entretanto no sonaba ruido del caso ni sentía que la justicia tratase de ello; pero todavía nos pareció ser forzoso mudar tierra, pues tenía allí lo mismo que en otra parte. Resuelto a ello, salí un día a boca de noche, y a breve rato quiere mi desgracia que tope con dos alguaciles. Pregúntanme: "¿Qué gente?" Respondo: "Amigos." Pídenme el nombre, y digo, que no debí decir: "El diablo." Vanme a echar mano, y saco la espada, armándose gran ruido. Ellos dan voces diciendo: "¡Favor a la justicia!," y acude gente. Sale el corregidor, que estaba en casa del obispo; avánzanme más ministros, hállome afligido, disparo una pistola y derribo a uno. Crece más el empeño, y hállome al lado aquel vizcaíno mi amigo y otros paisanos con él. Daba voces el corregidor que me matasen; sonaron muchos traquidos de ambas partes, hasta que salió el obispo con cuatro hachas y entróse por medio, encaminándolo hacia mí su secretario, Juan Bautista de Arteaga. Llegó y me dijo: "Señor alférez, déme las armas." Dije: Señor, hay aquí muchos contrarios." Dijo: "Démelas, que seguro está conmigo, y le doy palabra de sacarle a salvo, anuque me cueste cuanto soy." Dije: "Señor ilustrísimo, en estando en la iglesia[4] besaré los pies a V. S. [Vuestra Señoría] ilustrísima." En esto me acometen cuatro esclavos del corregidor, y me aprietan, tirándome ferozmente, sin respeto a la presencia de su ilustrísima; de modo que, defendiéndome, hube de entrar la mano y derribar a uno. Acudióme el secretario del señor obispo con espada y broquel, con otros de la familia, dando muchas voces, ponderando el desacato delante de su ilustrísima, y cesó algo la puja. Asióme su ilustrísima por el brazo, quitóme las armas, y poniéndome a su lado, me llevó consigo y entróme en su casa. Hízome luego curar una pequeña herida que llevaba, y mandóme dar de cenar y recoger, cerrándome con llave, que se llevó. Vino luego el corregidor, y tuvo su ilustrísima larga conversación y alteraciones con él sobre esto, lo cual después entendí.

A la mañana, como a las diez, su ilustrísima me hizo llevar a su presencia, y me preguntó quién era y de dónde, hijo de quién, y todo el curso de mi vida y causas y caminos por donde vine á parar allí. Y fuí en esto desmenuzando tanto, mezclando buenos consejos y los riesgos de la vida y espantos de la muerte y contingencias de ella, y el asombro de la otra si no me cogía bien apercibido, procurándome sosegar, y reducir, y arrodillarme a Dios, que yo me puse tamañito. Y viéndolo tan santo varón, pareciéndome estar ya en la presencia de Dios, descúbrome y dígole: "Señor, todo esto que he referido a V. S. ilustrísima no es así. La verdad es ésta: Que soy mujer, que nací en tal parte, hija de Fulano y Zutana; que me entraron de tal edad en tal convento, con Fulana mi Tía; que allí me crié; que tomé el hábito y tuve noviciado; que estando para profesar, por tal ocasión me salí; que me fuí a tal parte, me desnudé, me vestí, me corté el cabello, partí allí y acullá; me embarqué, aporté, trajiné, maté, herí, maleé, correteé, hasta venir a parar en lo presente, y a los pies de su señoría ilustrísima."

El santo señor, entretanto que esta relación duró, que fué hasta la una, se estuvo suspenso, sin hablar, ni pestañear, escuchándome, y después que acabé se quedó también sin hablar, llorando a lágrima viva. Después me envió a descansar y a comer. Tocó una campanilla, hizo venir a un capellán anciano, y envióme a su oratorio, donde me pusieron la mesa y un trasportín, y me encerraron; yo me acosté y me dormí. A la tarde, como a las cuatro, me volvió a llamar el señor obispo, y me habló con gran bondad de espíritu, conduciéndome a dar gracias a Dios por la merced usada conmigo, dándome a ver el camino perdido que llevaba derecho a las penas eternas. Exhortóme a recorrer mi vida y hacer una buena confesión, pues ya por lo más la tenía hecha y me sería fácil; después, Dios ayudaría para que viésemos lo que se debía hacer. Y en esto y en cosas ocurrentes se acabó la tarde. Retiréme, diéronme bien de comer, y me acosté.

A la mañana siguiente dijo misa el señor obispo, que yo oí, y después dió gracias. Retiróse a un desayuno, y me llevó consigo. Fué moviendo y siguiendo su discurso, y vino a decirme que tenía éste por el caso más notable, en este género, que había oído en su vida, y re-mató diciendo: "En fin, ¿esto es así?" Dije: "Sí, señor." Replicó: "No se espante que su rareza inquiete a la credulidad." "Señor" —dije—, "es así, y si quiere salir de dudas V. S. ilustrísima por experiencia de matronas, yo me allano." Dijo: "Conténtame oírlo, y vengo en ello." Y retiréme por ser la hora del despacho. A medio día comí, después reposé un rato, y a la tarde, como a las cuatro, entraron dos matronas y me miraron y se satisficieron, y declararon después ante el obispo, con juramento, haberme visto y reconocido cuanto fué menester para certificarse, y haberme hallado virgen intacta, como el día en que nací. Su ilustrísima se enterneció, despidió a las comadres y me hizo comparecer, y delante del capellán, que vino conmigo, me abrazó enternecido, en pie, y me dijo: "Hija, ahora creo sin duda lo que me dijisteis, y creeré en adelante cuanto me dijereis; os venero como una de las personas notables de este mundo, y os prometo asistiros en cuanto pueda y cuidar de vuestra conveniencia y del servicio de Dios."

Mandóme poner cuarto decente, y estuve en él con comodidad y ajustando mi confesión, la cual hice en cuanto pude, y después, su ilustrísima me dió la comunión. Parece que el caso se divulgó, y era inmenso el concurso que allí acudió, sin poder excusar la entrada a personajes, por más que yo lo sentía y su ilustrísima también.

En fin, pasados seis días, acordó su ilustrísima entrarme en el convento de monjas de Santa Clara de Guamanga, que allí de religiosas no hay otro, [y] púsome el hábito. Salió su ilustrísima de casa, llevándome a su lado, con un concurso tan grande, que no hubo de quedar persona alguna en la ciudad que no viniese; de suerte que se tardó mucho en llegar allá. Llegamos finalmente a la portería, porque a la iglesia, donde pensaba su ilustrísima entrar antes, no fué posible; entendido así, se había llenado. Estaba allí todo el convento, con velas encendidas, y otorgóse allí, por la abadesa y ancianas, una escritura en que prometía el convento volverme a entregar a su ilustríssima o prelado sucesor cada vez que me pidiesen. Abrazóme su ilustrísima, echóme su bendición, y entré. Lleváronme al coro en procesión e hice oración allí. Besé la mano a la señora abadesa, fuí abrazando y fuéronme abrazando las monjas, y lleváronme a un locutorio, donde su ilustrísima me estaba esperando. Allí me dió buenos consejos y exhortó a ser buena cristiana y dar gracias a Dios Nuestro Señor y frecuentar los sacramentos, ofreciéndose su ilustrísima a venir a ello, como vino muchas veces, y ofrecióme largamente todo cuanto hubiese menester. Corrió la noticia de este suceso por todas partes, y los que antes me vieron y los que antes y después supieron mis cosas en todas las Indias, se maravillaron. Dentro de cinco meses, año 1620, repentinamente, se quedó muerto mi santo obispo, que me hizo gran falta.

[Catalina de Erauso se va a Lima y pasa los dos años siguientes en un convento allí hasta que llegan las noticias de España que nunca había sido monja profesa; por eso puede salir del convento y dejar su hábito monjil. Se va a España y se presenta ante el Rey Felipe IV, que le otorga una pensión de 800 escudos de por vida; le vuelve a ver en Barcelona, después de que la hayan robado en el camino, y el rey le vuelve a regalar dinero. Luego viaja a Italia para ver al papa.]

CAPÍTULO XXV

Parte de Barcelona a Génova, y de allí, a Roma.

. . . Partí de Génova a Roma. Besé el pie a la Santidad de Urbano VIII, y referíle en breve y lo mejor que supe mi vida y correrías, mi sexo y virginidad. Mostró Su Santidad extrañar tal cosa, y con afabilidad me concedió licencia para proseguir mi vida en hábito de hombre, encargándome la prosecución honesta en adelante y la abstinencia de ofender al prójimo, teniendo la *ulción* [venganza] de Dios sobre su mandamiento *non occides* [no mates]. Hízose el caso allí notorio, y fué notable el concurso de que me vi cercado: personajes, príncipes, obispos, cardenales. Dondequiera me hallé lugar abierto, de suerte que en mes y medio que estuve en Roma fué raro el día en que no fuese convidado y regalado de príncipes; y especialmente un viernes fuí convidado y regalado por unos caballeros, por orden particular y encargo del Senado romano, y me asentaron en un libro por ciudadano romano. El día de San Pedro, 29 de junio de 1626, me entraron en la capilla de San Pedro, donde vi los cardenales y las ceremonias que se acostumbran aquel día. Todos, o los más, me mostraron notable agrado y caricia y me hablaron muchos. A la tarde, hallándome en rueda con tres cardenales, me dijo uno de ellos, que fué el cardenal Magalón, que [yo] no tenía más falta que ser español, a lo cual le dije: "A mí me parece, señor, debajo de la corrección que se debe a vuestra señoría ilustrísima, que no tengo otra cosa buena."

CAPÍTULO XXVI

De Roma viene a Nápoles.

Pasado mes y medio que estuve en Roma, me partí de allí para Nápoles, el día 5 de julio de 1626. Embarcamos en Ripa.

En Nápoles, un día, paseándome en el muelle, reparé en las risotadas de dos damiselas que parlaban con dos mozos. Me miraban, y mirándolas, me dijo una: "Señora Catalina, ¿adónde se camina?" Respondí: "Señoras p . . . , a darles a ustedes cien pescozones y cien cuchilladas a quien las quiera defender." Callaron y se fueron de allí.

FIN

Notas

1. La orden de Santiago era una de las órdenes militares de más prestigio en España.

2. Potosí era una ciudad riquísima en el virreinato del Perú (hoy Bolivia) donde se descubrió una fabulosa mina de plata en 1545, la cual enriqueció a muchos hombres.

3. "Cacique" era la palabra indígena para "jefe" o "capitán."

4. Erauso aquí se refiere al derecho de santuario, bajo el cual las autoridades seculares no podían llevarse a los criminales y fugitivos de la justicia que se refugiaban en una iglesia.

Life and Adventures of the Ensign Nun

Her homeland, parents, birth, education, flight, and journeys throughout various parts of Spain.

I, Doña Catalina de Erauso, was born in the town of San Sebastián, in Guipúzcoa, in the year 1585, the daughter of Captain Don Miguel de Erauso and of Doña María Pérez de Galarraga y Arce, natives and residents of that town. My parents brought me up at home with my other siblings until I was four years old. In 1589 they put me in the convent of San Sebastián el Antiguo, in said town, which belongs to Dominican nuns, with my aunt Doña Ursula de Unzá y Sarasti, my mother's cousin and the abbess of that convent; there I was raised until I was fifteen, when the matter of my profession came up.

When I was almost at the end of my year of the novitiate, I had a quarrel with a professed nun named Doña Catalina de Aliri, who, being a widow, had professed and entered the convent. She was strong and I but a girl; she slapped me, and I resented it. On the night of March 18, 1600, the eve of St. Joseph, the convent arose at midnight for Matins. I went into the choir and found my aunt kneeling there; she called me over, gave me the key to her cell, and told me to bring her her prayer book. I went to get it. I unlocked [the cell] and took it, and, seeing all the keys to the convent hanging from a nail, I left the cell open and gave my aunt her key and the prayer book. The nuns were already in the choir and had solemnly begun Matins; at the first lesson I went up to my aunt and asked her permission to withdraw, as I was feeling ill. My aunt put her hand to my forehead and said, "Go lie down." I left the choir, took a lamp, and went to my aunt's cell; there I took a pair of scissors, thread, and a needle; I took some coins (*reales de a ocho*) that were lying there and took the convent keys and left. I went along opening doors and shutting them behind me, and at the final one left my scapulary and went out into the street, which I had never seen, with no idea which way to turn or where to go. I don't remember where I went, but I came on a stand of chestnut trees that was outside [of town] but close behind the convent. There I hid, and spent three days designing, fitting, and cutting out clothes. I made myself a pair of breeches from a blue cloth petticoat I was wearing, and from an underskirt of coarse green wool, a sleeved doublet and leggings; I left the habit there because I didn't know what to do with it. I cut off my hair, which I threw away, and on the third night, since I wanted to get away from there, I left for parts unknown, slogging over roads and skirting villages until I came to Vitoria, which is about twenty leagues from San Sebastián, on foot, weary and without having eaten anything but plants I found along the way.

I entered Vitoria with no idea where to stay. A few days later I met Dr. Don Francisco de Cerralta, a professor there, who, without knowing me, took me in with no difficulty and gave me some clothes. He was married to a cousin of my mother's, as I found out later, but I did not reveal who I was. I was with him for about three months, during which time, as he saw that I read Latin well, he liked me more and wanted to educate me, but when I refused he insisted and even laid hands on me. When that happened I made up my mind to leave him, and did so. I took some of his money, agreed to pay twelve *reales* to a muleteer who was leaving for Valladolid, forty-five leagues away, and departed with the latter.

When I got to Valladolid, where the Court was at that time, I soon got a position as a page to Don Juan de Idiáquez, the king's secretary, who clothed me well. There I called myself Francisco Loyola, and was very comfortable for seven months. At the end of that time, while I was standing in the doorway one evening with a fellow page, my father arrived and asked us if Señor Don Juan was at home.

My comrade said he was. My father said to let him know that he was there, and the page went upstairs while I stayed with my father; we said nothing to each other and he did not recognize me. The page came back and said that he should go upstairs, so up he went and I behind him. Don Juan came out on the staircase and, embracing him, said, "Señor Captain, what a welcome visit!" My father spoke in such a way that the Señor knew he was annoyed, so Don Juan sent away another visitor, then came back and they sat down. He asked what was the matter. My father told how that girl of his had left the convent, and the search for her had brought him to that region. . . .

I, when I heard my father's conversation and feelings, withdrew and went to my room. I took my clothes and left, taking with me some eight doubloons which I happened to have, and went to a tavern; I slept there that night, and heard a muleteer say that he was leaving for Bilbao in the morning. I came to terms with him and we left the next day; with no idea as to what to do or where to go, I simply let myself be borne by the wind like a feather. . . .

After I got out I went to Estella, in Navarre, which I think is about twenty leagues away. I reached Estella, where I became the page of Don Carlos de Arellano, who belonged to the order of Santiago,[1] in whose house and service I remained for two years, well treated and well attired. Afterward, for no other reason than my fancy, I left that comfortable position and went to my native San Sebastián, where I, a well-dressed dandy, spent some time without anyone recognizing me. One day I went to mass at my convent, the same service my mother attended, and saw that she looked at me without recognizing me; when mass was over, some nuns called me over to the choir, but I pretended not to understand, paid them many compliments and left. This was well into the year 1603.

From there I went to . . . Sanlúcar. There I found Captain Miguel de Echarreta, another Basque, who commanded a tender to the galleons under General Don Luis Fernández de Córdoba, part of Don Luis Fajardo's armada, which was sailing for Punta de Araya. I signed on as a cabin boy in Captain Esteban Eguiño's galleon—he was my uncle, my mother's cousin, and today lives in San Sebastián. I went aboard and we left Sanlúcar on Holy Monday in the year 1603.

CHAPTER II

She leaves Sanlúcar for Punta Araya, Cartagena, Nombre de Dios, and Panama.

As I was new to the job, I had some difficulties on the voyage. Without knowing who I was my uncle was kind to me, and thought very highly of me; when he heard where I was from, and my parents' fictitious name, I had in him a great protector. When we got to Punta Araya we came upon a small enemy force entrenched on the shore and our fleet drove it away. We finally reached Cartagena de las Indias, and were there eight days.

I had my name taken off the list as cabin boy, and went into the service of the said Captain Eguiño, my uncle. From there we went to Nombre de Dios, where we stayed for nine days; many of our men died, which made us leave there very quickly.

When the silver was already aboard and everything was ready for our return voyage to Spain, I played a major trick on my uncle, making off with five hundred of his pesos. At ten at night, when he was asleep, I went on deck and told the sentries that the captain was sending me ashore on an errand. As they knew me, they let me pass with no trouble and I jumped ashore, but they never saw me again. An hour later they fired the departure gun and weighed anchor, ready to sail.

When the fleet had left, I took employment with Captain Juan de Ibarra, the agent for the Panama treasury, who is still alive today. Four to six days later we left for Panama, where he lived and where I stayed with him for about three months. He did not treat me well, for he was miserly, and I had to spend all the money I had lifted from my uncle until I had not a penny left; thereupon I departed in order to look for better employment elsewhere.

When I looked around I found Juan de Urquiza there, a merchant from Trujillo, and reached an agreement with him; things went well for me with him, and we were in Panama three months.

CHAPTER III

From Panama she goes with her master Urquiza, a merchant from Trujillo, to the port of Paita and the town of Saña.

I sailed from Panama in a frigate with my master Juan de Urquiza, bound for the port of Paita, where he had a large cargo. When we got to the port of Manta the ship was hit broadside by a tremendous storm, and those who knew how to swim, like me, my master, and some others, made it ashore; the rest perished. In the said port of Manta we reembarked in one of the king's galleons we found there, for a handsome price; we sailed on this ship and got to the port of Paita, where, just as he expected, my master found all of his property loaded onto Captain Alonso Cerrato's vessel. Giving me instructions to dispatch all of it in numbered order, he left.

I immediately did as he had ordered, unloading the merchandise by number, and sending it along to him. My master, who was in Saña, some sixty leagues away, received it and at the end, along with the last shipments, I left Paita for Saña.

When I got to Saña, my master greeted me very affectionately, for he was very pleased with the good job I had done; right away he ordered two suits to be made for me, one black and one colored, and treated me very well. He employed me in one of his shops, entrusting me with a considerable amount of both goods and cash, which amounted to more than one hundred thirty thousand pesos in value, and in a ledger annotated the prices at which I was to sell each item. He gave me two slaves to serve me and a negress to cook for me, setting aside three pesos for each day's expenses, and when he had done that, he took the rest of the merchandise and departed with it for Trujillo, about thirty-two leagues away.

He also left written instructions in the said ledger as to the people who could buy merchandise they wanted on credit and take it away, because they were people he trusted and whose credit was good, but I was to annotate and justify each transaction in the ledger. And he particularly stressed this with respect to Doña Beatriz de Cárdenas, a person he held in the highest regard. He left for Trujillo and I stayed in Saña with my shop, selling things according to the instructions he had left with me, collecting the money and noting it down in my book with the day, month, year, type and yards of cloth sold, names of the buyers, prices charged, etc., and the same procedure with merchandise bought on credit.

Then my lady doña Beatriz de Cárdenas began to buy material, and kept on doing so, and charged so much that I began to have my doubts; without informing her I wrote at length to my master in Trujillo. He replied that everything was just fine, and that with respect to this particular lady, should she ask for the entire shop I should let her have it; with those instructions, and holding on to the letter, I went on with my work.

[Catalina de Erauso has another brush with the law and has to leave this employer.]

CHAPTER V

She leaves Trujillo for Lima.

Having left Trujillo for Lima and having gone more than eighty leagues, I entered the city of Lima, capital of the prosperous realm of Peru. . . .

I gave my letter to Diego de Solarte, a very wealthy merchant who is now chief consul of Lima, and to whom Juan de Urquiza had recommended me; he immediately took me into his home with great courtesy and kindness, and a few days later entrusted his shop to me, assigning me a salary of six hundred pesos a year, and there I did my job much to his satisfaction and pleasure.

At the end of nine months he told me that it was time to make my living elsewhere, and the reason for this was that there were two young girls in his house, his wife's sisters, with whom I used to play and romp about, especially with one who showed a decided liking for me. And one day, while I was in the drawing room with my head in her lap and caressing her legs, while she was combing my hair, he happened to look in through the grille and see us, and heard her say to me that I should go to Potosí[2] to get some money and we would be married. He withdrew, soon after that summoned me, asked me to explain myself, discharged me, and I left.

I found myself unemployed and very out of favor. At that time six companies of men were being assembled to go to Chile; I went to one of them and enlisted as a soldier, for which I immediately received eighty pesos in wages. My employer Diego de Lasarte, who found out about it, was very sorry, for it seemed that he had not wanted it to come to this. He offered to intercede with the officers so that they would take me off the muster roll and return the money I had been given, but I refused, telling him that I had a taste for roving and seeing the world. Finally, having been assigned to the company of Captain Gonzalo Rodríguez, whose camp-master was Diego Bravo de Sarabia, I left Lima in a detachment of sixteen hundred men for the city of Concepción, which is five hundred forty leagues from Lima.

CHAPTER VI

She arrives in Concepción, Chile, and finds her brother. She goes to Paicabí and, while participating in the battle of Valdivia, captures a standard. She returns to Concepción and kills two men and her own brother.

It took us twenty days traveling time to get to the port of Concepción. It's a fair-sized city, with the title of *noble and loyal*, and has a bishop. Because of the scarcity of people in Chile we were well received. Soon an order came from the governor, Alonso de Ribera, that we should disembark, and it was brought by his secretary, Captain Miguel de Erauso. As soon as I heard his name I was delighted, and saw that he was my brother; even though I didn't know him, nor had seen him—because he left San Sebastián for these parts when I was two years old—I had had news of him, but not of his whereabouts. He took the list of soldiers, read it off, and asked each one his name and place of origin; when he got to me and heard my name and place of birth, he threw down the pen, embraced me, and asked many questions about his father and mother and siblings, and about his beloved Catalina, the nun. I answered everything as best I could, without betraying my identity, nor he guessing it. He went through the list, and when he finished he took me to his home for dinner and I sat down to eat. He told me that the garrison at Paicabí to which I was assigned was a terrible place for soldiers and that he would speak to the governor to have me transferred. During the meal he went over to see the governor, taking me along. He reported on the recent arrivals, and asked as a favor that a young lad from his part of the country be transferred to his company, for since his departure he had come across no others from there. The governor had me come in, and when he saw me, I don't know for what reason, he said that he could not transfer me. My brother was upset and left, but a short while later the governor called my brother back again and told him that things could be the way he wanted them.

And so, when the troops left, I stayed with my brother as his soldier, eating at his table for almost three years without having him guess a thing. A few times I accompanied him to his mistress's house; afterward I went a few other times without him, and he found out and took offense and told me not to go back. He spied on me, and caught me at it again; he waited for me when I came out, and whipped me with a belt, injuring my hand. I was forced to defend myself. When he heard the altercation Captain Francisco de Aillón showed up and made peace, but I had to slip into [the church of] San Francisco because I feared the governor, [known to be] a severe man, as he proved to be in this instance, although my brother interceded. Ultimately he banished me to Paicabí; there was no recourse but to go, and I stayed there for three years.

I was obliged to go to Paicabí and suffer hard times for three years, after having lived such a carefree life earlier. Because of the great Indian invasion there, we always lived with our weapons at the ready, until finally Governor Alonso de Sarabia and all the Chilean troops arrived. We all joined forces with him, and five thousand men camped on the open plains of Valdivia with a great deal of discomfort. The Indians captured and attacked said Valdivia. We went out to meet them and fought them three or four times, always besting and destroying them, but in the last battle their reinforcements came, things went badly for us, and they killed many of our men, our captains, and my ensign; they also took our standard. Seeing them make off with it, I and two other mounted soldiers went after them through a great multitude, charging and killing and being wounded in turn. Soon one of the three fell dead. The two of us kept on, and we got to the standard, but a lance thrust felled my companion. I, with a bad wound in one leg, killed the cacique[3] who had it in his possession, took the standard away and spurred my horse, charging, killing and wounding indiscriminately; badly injured, pierced by three arrows and with a very painful lance wound in the left shoulder, I finally reached our men and then fell from my horse. Several rushed to my help, among them my brother, whom I had not seen, and this was a great consolation to me. They dressed my wounds, and we stayed in camp there for nine months. At the end of that time my brother got the standard I had captured away from the governor and I became the ensign of Alonso Moreno's company, which was subsequently assigned to Captain Gonzalo Rodríguez, the first captain I had known, and I was very pleased. . . .

At this time, and among others, one day there appeared my friend Don Juan de Silva, a lively ensign, and he told me he had had an altercation with Don Francisco de Rojas, of the order of Santiago, and had challenged him to a duel that night at eleven. Each man was to bring a friend, and he had no one else but me. I was a little reluctant, wondering if this was some ruse to trap me. He noticed this and said, "If you do not wish to, don't do it; I will go alone, for I trust no one else at my side." I asked myself what was he thinking of, and accepted.

I left the convent when the bells rang for devotions, and went to his house. We dined and talked until ten, and when we heard it strike the hour, took our swords and cloaks and went to the designated spot. The darkness was so intense that we could not see our hands in front of our eyes, and when I noticed this I made a pact with my friend that each of us would tie a pocket handkerchief around his arm, so that we would know each other no matter what happened.

The other two arrived and one, whose voice we knew to be that of Don Francisco de Rojas, said, "Don Juan de Silva?" Don Juan answered, "Here I am!" They both drew their swords and began to fight, while the other man and I stood on the side. They fought on, and a little while later I sensed that my friend had been injured by a thrust he had received. Then I took my place at his side, and the other man joined Don Francisco. We fought two by two, and soon thereafter both Don Francisco and Don Juan fell; my opponent and I continued, and I wounded him with a thrust, which, as it subsequently turned out, pierced his chest underneath the left nipple. I felt my sword go through a double jerkin and he went down. "Oh, traitor," he said, "you have killed me!" I wanted to identify the voice of the unknown man; I asked him who he was, and he said, "Captain Miguel de E-rauso." I was astounded. He loudly called for confession, and the others did as well. I ran to San Francisco and sent two priests, who confessed them. Two men subsequently died; my brother was taken to the house of the governor, whose secretary of war he was. A doctor and a surgeon were brought to aid him, and they did what they could. Later on legal matters were attended to, and my brother was asked for the name of his assailant. He begged for a little wine, but Dr. Robledo refused to give it to him, saying it would do him harm; when he insisted the doctor refused again, and he said, "You're worse to me than Ensign Díaz," and shortly afterward he died. . . . After Captain Miguel de Erauso had expired, he was buried in the said monastery of San Francisco, I witnessing it from the choir with God alone knows what sorrow! . . .

CHAPTER XX

She goes to Guamanga, and what happened to her there, until she reveals her identity to the Bishop.

I got to Guamanga and went to an inn. . . . I went to look at the city, and liked it, as it had handsome buildings, the best I had seen in Peru. I found three monasteries (Franciscan, Mercedarian, and Dominican), a convent and a hospital, many Indian and Spanish residents, [and] a wonderful climate for settling this plain, neither hot nor cold. There are great harvests of wheat, wine, fruits, and grain, a fine church with three prebendaries, two canons and a saintly bishop, an Augustinian friar [named] Don Agustín de Carvajal, who people said had been there since 1612, and who was my salvation, though he was taken from me by his sudden death in 1620.

I was there for a few days, and my ill luck would have it that I sometimes visited a gaming house. One day when I was there, the magistrate, Don Baltasar de Quiñones, entered; he looked at me, and as he did not recognize me, asked me where I was from. I said I was Basque. He said, "Where have you come from just now?" I answered, "Cuzco." He hesitated a moment while observing me, and said,

"You're under arrest." I said, "Fine with me," drew my sword and re-treated toward the door. He shouted for help in the king's name, and I found the door so blocked that I was unable to leave. I drew a three-barreled pistol, got away and disappeared, finding refuge in the house of a friend I had made there. The magistrate thereupon seized my mule, and some other trifles I had left in the inn. I spent a few days in hiding, having discovered that my friend was a Basque. Meanwhile there was no word of the matter, nor did I feel that the authorities were doing anything about it, but it still seemed a good idea to us for me to move to another place, for I had the same problem there as I did everywhere. Determined to do this, I left one day at nightfall, and, as my misfortune would have it, immediately ran into two constables. They ask me, "Who goes there?" I reply, "A friend." They demand my name, and I answer, "The devil," which I shouldn't have said. They begin to lay hands on me, and I take out my sword, causing a great commotion. They cry out, "Help us in the name of the Law!" and people gather. The magistrate comes out of the Bishop's house, where he had been, more constables come, I find myself in a desper-ate situation, fire my pistol, and one goes down. The brawl gets big-ger, and I find my Basque friend and some of his compatriots at my side. The magistrate shouted that I should be killed, and shots were exchanged on both sides, until the Bishop came out with four torch-bearers, and stepped into the middle of the fray, directing his secretary Juan Bautista de Arteaga my way. This man stepped up to me and said, "Ensign, give me your weapons." I said, "Sir, there are many enemies here." He said, "Hand them over, for you are safe with me, and I give you my word that I will get you out of this, cost me what it may." I said, "Exalted Sir, when I get into the church⁴ I will kiss your illus-trious feet." As I was saying this, four of the magistrate's slaves fell upon me and put me into a tight spot, pulling at me ferociously with no regard for His Lordship's presence, so that I had to defend myself and knock one of them down. The Bishop's secretary, with sword and shield, along with others of his retinue, came to my aid, shouting loudly and denouncing the disrespect shown the Bishop, after which the brawling abated somewhat. His Lordship seized my arm, took away my weapons, and, placing me at his side, took me with him into his house. He had a slight wound of mine dressed, and ordered some dinner brought to me; thereupon he told me to go to bed, locked me in, and took the key with him. The magistrate subsequently arrived, and, as I later heard, had a long conversation and high words with His Lordship concerning this matter.

In the morning about ten, His Lordship summoned me into his presence, and asked me who I was and from where, who my parents were, and the whole course of my life: the hows and the whys of how I came to be there. I embellished my tale considerably, mixing in good advice, the perils of life, my fear of death and the consequences thereof, and how I terrified I was lest the afterlife catch me unawares; I tried to calm and humble myself and to kneel before God, which made me feel very small. And when I saw what a saintly man he was, it seemed that I was already in the presence of God, so I took off my hat and said to him: "Sir, all I have just told Your Lordship is false. The truth is this: I am a woman, I was born in such-and-such a place, the daughter of so-and-so, and at a certain age was placed in a certain convent with my aunt so-and-so. There I grew up, put on the habit and was a novice. When I was about to profess, for such-and-such a reason I left. I went to such-and-such a place, took off my habit, put on other clothes, cut my hair, went hither and thither; went aboard ship, put into port, went to and fro, killed, wounded, cheated, ran around, and finally landed here, at the feet of Your Most Illustrious Lordship."

During the time it took to tell this story, which took until one o'clock, the saintly man was all ears: he listened to me without speaking or batting an eyelash, and when I finished he said not a word, but wept bitterly. Afterward he sent me off to rest, and to eat something. He rang a bell, bid an old chaplain come, and sent me to his oratory where they put a table and a mattress for me, and locked me in. I lay down and slept. In the afternoon about four, the Bishop called me to him again, and spoke to me with great kindness of spirit, beseeching me to give thanks to God for the great favor He had shown me by making me see the path of perdition, which leads one straight to everlasting torment. He exhorted me to go back over my past and to make a proper confession, for I had already come a long way, and it would be easy for me. After this God would lend His help so that we could figure out what to do next. In these and other matters the afternoon drew to a close. I withdrew, was given a good meal, and went to bed.

The next morning the Lord Bishop said Mass, which I attended, and afterward he gave thanks. He withdrew to have breakfast, and took me with him. He expounded on his sermon, and told me that mine was the most curious case of this sort he had heard in his life, and finally said, "But is it really true?" I said, "Yes, Sir." He replied, "Don't be affronted if its peculiar nature strains the imagination." "Sir," I said, "it really is true and if Your Lordship wants to make sure by having me examined by some women, I am willing to do it." He said, "I'm glad to hear you say that, and I agree." I withdrew because it was his reception time. At noon I ate, then rested a bit, and in the afternoon about four, two matrons came in, examined me, and were convinced; later they swore before the Bishop that they had examined me to a sufficient degree to be sure, and had found me as intact a virgin as the day I was born. His Lordship was touched, dismissed the women and had me sent for; in the presence of the chaplain, who had come with me, he stood up and tenderly embraced me, saying, "My daughter, now I believe what you told with no doubts whatsoever, and will henceforth believe anything you tell me. I respect you as one of the amazing people of this world, and promise to help you in any way I can, to take care of your needs, and to do that to serve God."

He ordered me put in a suitable room, where I was comfortable and prepared my confession, which I made as soon as possible, and afterward His Lordship gave me communion. Apparently my story got around, and the number of people that came was huge; we were unable to keep them out, as much as I minded it, and His Lordship as well.

Finally, six days later, His Illustrious Lordship ordered me to go into the convent of the Poor Clares of Guamanga, as there was no other, and to put on the habit. His Lordship left his house with me at his side, surrounded by such a mob of people that I don't think there was anyone in the city who didn't come, and for that reason it took a long time to get there. We finally got to the porter's lodge, because going into the church, as His Lordship had initially intended, was out of the question, for it was completely full. The whole convent was there, bearing lit candles, and the abbess and senior nuns signed a document in which the convent promised to hand me over to the Bishop or a prelate who might succeed him, any time they gave the word. His Lordship embraced and blessed me, and I went in[to the convent]. I was escorted in procession to the choir, and prayed there. I kissed the lady abbess's hand, was embraced by and in turn embraced the other nuns; they then took me to a locutory where His Lordship awaited me. There he gave me good advice, and exhorted me to be a good Christian woman, to give thanks to Our Lord God and to make frequent use of the sacraments; His Lordship offered to come and administer them personally, as he indeed did many times, and generously offered me anything at all I might need. News of this event spread everywhere very quickly, and people who had seen me before, and people, both before and after, who heard my story all over the Indies, were amazed. In 1620, within five months, my saintly bishop suddenly died, and I felt his loss keenly. . . .

[Catalina de Erauso goes to Lima and spends the next two years in a convent there, until word arrives from Spain that she was never a professed nun, and can therefore leave the convent and take off her nun's habit. She goes to Spain and presents herself before King Philip IV, who grants her a life pension of 800 escudos; she sees him again in Barcelona, having been robbed along the way, and he gives her another gift of money. She subsequently travels to Italy to see the pope.]

CHAPTER XXV

She goes from Barcelona to Genoa and thence to Rome.
 . . . I left Genoa for Rome. I kissed the foot of His Holiness Urban VIII and told him succinctly, and as best I could all about my life, adventures, gender, and virginity. His Holiness appeared to be astonished thereby, and graciously gave me permission to continue to lead my life dressed as a man, urging me to lead an honest life from now on, and to refrain from offending my fellow man, reminding me of God's jus-

tice with reference to His commandment "Thou shalt not kill." My case became well known there and I was constantly surrounded by a throng of illustrious persons: princes, bishops, and cardinals. Every door was open to me, so that in the month and a half that I was in Rome, rarely a day went by that I was not invited and made much of by princes. One Friday in particular, on specific request by the Roman Senate, I was invited and entertained by some gentlemen who entered my name in a book as a Roman citizen. On St. Peter's Day, June 29, 1636, I was taken to St. Peter's chapel, where I saw the cardinals and the usual ceremonies they hold on that day. All—or most—of them were extremely courteous and kind, and many spoke to me. In the afternoon, while three cardinals stood around me, one of them, Cardinal Magalón, told me that I had no other flaw than being a Spaniard, to which I replied, "It seems to me, Sir, keeping in mind the deference one owes your illustrious person, that it is the only good thing I have."

CHAPTER XXXVI

From Rome she goes to Naples.

When I had been in Rome for a month and a half, I left to go to Naples on June 5, 1626. We went aboard in Ripa.

One day in Naples, as I was strolling on the wharf, I heard the guffaws of two wenches who were talking to two lads. They stared at me, and when I stared back, one of the women said, "Lady Catalina, where are you going?" I replied, "My lady whores, to give you a hundred whacks on the head, and a hundred knife thrusts to any who would defend you." They fell silent and went off.

THE END

Notes

1. The order of Santiago (Saint James) was one of the most prestigious military orders in Spain.
2. Potosí was the colonial boomtown in the viceroyalty of Peru

(today this region is in Bolivia) where a fabulously rich hill of silver ore was discovered in 1545 and made many men very wealthy.

3. *Cacique* was the indigenous word for a chieftain.

4. Erauso here refers to the right of sanctuary, whereby criminals and fugitives from justice who took refuge in a church could not be removed by secular authorities.

Sor Juana Inés de la Cruz

Sor Juana Inés de la Cruz, by Juan de Miranda. Courtesy of Patrimonio Universitario of the National Autonomous University of Mexico.

"*I* became a nun, even though I knew that that state entailed many things . . . that were repugnant to my nature, but with all that, given the total antipathy I felt toward marriage, it was the least unsuitable and most seemly [state] I could choose in light of the assurance I desired with respect to my salvation. . . . [When I became a nun] I thought I was fleeing from my self, but oh, misery! I brought my self along, and brought my greatest foe in this inclination [to study], for I cannot determine if Heaven bestowed it on me as a gift or as a punishment."

So spoke Sor Juana Inés de la Cruz in an autobiographical letter ("La Respuesta a Sor Filotea") she wrote in 1691, four years before her death. The greatest poet of colonial Spanish America was born in either 1648 or 1651 (most scholars prefer the latter date) in the hamlet of Nepantla, in the valley of Mexico, the illegitimate daughter of Isabel Ramírez and a Spanish officer, Pedro Manuel de Asbaje. Isabel was a *criolla,* a term that denoted someone of Spanish blood who was born in the New World. Sor Juana was thus of pure Spanish extraction and belonged to the white elite of New Spain, though her family was not wealthy and her social status was somewhat impaired for having been born out of wedlock. As Asunción Lavrin has shown, illegitimacy was a fairly common occurrence in colonial America, even among the upper classes (154 ff.). Isabel Ramírez bore six "natural" children, three to Asbaje and three to another Spaniard, Diego Ruiz de Lozano. Asbaje seems to have disappeared from his daughter's life when she was about eight, and soon afterward she was sent to Mexico City to live with a maternal aunt, who was both rich and socially prominent. Mexico City at the time was a city of some four hundred thousand inhabitants and the capital of the Viceroyalty of New Spain. Its cultural center was the glittering viceregal court, with which Juana was soon to have contact.

Juana had had a minimal education in a girl's school in Nepantla but had devoured the books in her grandfather's library and begun writing poetry at the age of eight. In her autobiographical letter she states that when she was six or seven and heard of the existence of a university in Mexico City, she begged her mother to let her dress as a boy in order to attend but that this request was denied. Many people in the capital knew of her prodigious intelligence and her poetic genius, and soon the viceroy, the Marquis of Mancera, and his wife, Leonor Carreto, asked to meet her. The vicereine was so taken with the pretty, bright girl that Juana was appointed one of her ladies-in-waiting, something that placed her in the center of court life. She continued her poetic activities, and her fame grew apace.

When Juana turned eighteen she had to make a decision as to her future, and for girls of her class there were only two options: marriage or the convent. According to Octavio Paz, at that time there were twenty-two convents in Mexico City (165), reserved for the legitimate daughters of the white elite, who paid a considerable dowry to become members of a prestigious group of women. What attracted the worldly court lady to choose the veil over marriage? Juana's consuming passion was her intellectual life, and she knew very well that once she married she would most likely face yearly pregnancies, as well as a husband who would have total control over her person and could easily forbid her studies and her writing. The convent offered her far more control over her personal life; many nuns were literate, and the Church encouraged study and writing, as long as it was in the service of God. The convent also offered her social prestige and economic security, no small matters for a woman in her position.

Another factor in the decision to profess was her confessor, the powerful Jesuit Antonio Núñez de Miranda, who was also the confessor of the viceroys. Given her fame at court, coupled with her considerable physical attraction, Father Núñez feared for Juana's future and desired nothing more fervently than to remove her from the public eye and have her safely enclosed by the walls of a convent; he also felt that she should devote her God-given intellect solely to her Creator. Her own inclinations, Núñez's influence, and a wealthy relative's willingness to pay her dowry decided her. Juana initially chose the order of the Barefoot Carmelites, the reformed order founded by Saint Teresa of Avila, but the severity of their lifestyle was too much for her. After falling ill, she withdrew and opted for the far more worldly and relaxed order of the Hieronymites. In 1669 Juana took the veil, taking vows of chastity, obedience, poverty, and perpetual enclosure. The vow of obedience would give her the most trouble; the vow of poverty was quite relative.

The convent of Saint Paula was one of the most prestigious in Mexico. It still stands in the historic center of the city, and has now been converted into a small private university. The dimensions of its two-story cloister, the spacious, flower-filled patio, and attendant church all attest to its wealth and prominence. The nuns who lived there in Sor Juana's time had luxurious quarters, with far more private space than any married woman of the time. They wore elegant habits of fine cloth and, as portraits of the time show, even wore jewelry; servants and slaves tended to their needs, and they could—and did—receive many visitors in the convent locutory. Given Sor Juana's fame before she became a nun, succeeding viceroys sought her out and requested that she continue to write verses for them. This explains why fully a third of her prolific output is secular poetry, much of it written for the court. As a reward for composing these poems, Sor Juana received gifts of money, books, musical or scientific instruments, and the like. Her private library in her convent cell was one of the finest in New Spain. In spite of her continuing connection to the viceregal court, however, the main body of her work is religious: prayers and devotions in honor of the Virgin or the saints, religious drama, carols to be sung at popular religious festivals. These carols, known as *villancicos,* are receiving a good bit of critical attention at the moment, as they are excellent examples of the popular culture of seventeenth-century Mexico. Sor Juana, in spite of living in perpetual enclosure, remembered the polyglot accents of the streets of the capital: the speech of the black street vendors, the soft sounds of indigenous Nahuatl, voices of Portuguese immigrants, even the fractured Latin of poorly educated clerics and students.

Núñez's two wishes, to remove Juana from the public eye and to have her devote herself completely to God, were not being realized, and relations between them became strained. Sor Juana had chosen the convent to be able to continue her intellectual life, but she was ambitious in her goals and definitely transgressing the parameters the Church permitted her. The other religious superior who frowned on her was the archbishop of Mexico, Francisco de Aguiar y Seijas, a Jesuit like Núñez. Aguiar y Seijas had arrived in Mexico in the early 1680s, about the same time as a new viceregal couple, the Marquis of la Laguna and his wife, María Luisa, the Countess of Paredes, both of the highest Spanish nobility. Sor Juana and the countess soon became intimate, if not passionate friends, and during the eight years these viceroys were in Mexico (1680–88), the nun skillfully played off the power of the State against that of the Church to assure herself maximum creative freedom. This was her happiest and most productive time.

From her earliest years Sor Juana was a consummate poet. The baroque was an age splendidly suited to her talents: she loved the play of dialectical opposites, puns and double entendres, labyrinthine syntax and imagery, much of it derived from classical mythology. She was skilled at all the poetic forms in use at the time and enjoyed showing her mastery in them. Not that all her poetry is uniformly great: she wrote a number of occasional verses that are quite forgettable or simply do not interest the modern reader. She excelled at the sonnet, and the best of these are among the masterworks of the Spanish language.

Although Sor Juana was always dutiful about her responsibilities as a nun, there is no doubt that in her writing she gave her superiors much to criticize. That a nun should write love poetry, satiric verses aimed at the double standard men imposed on women, some bawdy burlesque sonnets, and dramas of romantic intrigue, in one of which a male servant cross-dresses as a woman, certainly exceeded permissible boundaries and brought her relentless criticism. As long as María Luisa and her husband were there to protect her, Sor Juana was fairly safe, and she made the most of this. So safe did she feel that in 1681 she wrote a letter of dismissal to her confessor Núñez, a step not many nuns dared to take, but his public criticism of her had long rankled. The nun composed many affectionate, even impassioned verses to her benefactress (whom she addressed as "Lysi" in her poetry), leading

some *sorjuanistas* to wonder if there was ever a sexual attraction between the two women. In Alan Trueblood's opinion, what Sor Juana
felt was "a mixture of love and friendship in which affection, devotion, gratitude, respect, and a Neoplatonically accented idealization all
have a part" (13). Had it been more than that, it would have been a
very serious transgression, for "until the end of the eighteenth century
the existence of sexual feelings of women for other women was
nearly inconceivable."[1] Whatever the nature of their personal relationship, the vicereine played a decisive role in the nun's life in another
way: she assured the publication of Sor Juana's verses in Spain. We
must remember that her poems circulated among court and religious
circles in manuscript form and were essentially dispersed all over the
capital. Before her departure for Spain in 1688 the countess commanded Sor Juana to give her copies of as much material as she could
gather together and, once back in Europe, used her wealth and influence to have these verses published. *Inundación castálida* (Castalian
Flood) came out in 1689 and was so successful that by 1725 it had been
republished nine times. As I discussed in a previous study ("Ser mujer
. . . "), without the intervention of the countess, and especially in light
of subsequent Church persecution of Sor Juana, it is possible that much
of her poetry might have been lost forever.

After the departure of the viceroys in 1688, storm clouds began to
gather on Sor Juana's horizon. Pressure from the archbishop escalated,
and general criticism of her worldliness increased while there were few
powerful allies to fight for her. And, given the religious sentiment of
the times, Sor Juana could indeed be censored for vanity, the undue attention to the ephemeral attractions of the world. In 1691 the bishop
of Puebla, who admired the nun very much, made what appears to be
a very contradictory gesture: on the one hand, he published a critique
she had written of a sermon by the Portuguese Jesuit Antonio de
Vieyra, entitling it "A Letter Worthy of Athena" (the Greek goddess
of wisdom); on the other, he sent Sor Juana a more or less open letter
of censure, in which he reminded her that her amazing intelligence
was God's gift, a talent she should thus devote exclusively to His service, risking eternal damnation if she did not do so. To make this letter appear less harsh, he signed it "Sister Philotea," making it appear

as if it came from a sister nun instead of from a male superior, though everyone knew the real identity of the signatory.

Sor Juana's famous "Reply to Sister Philotea" is one of the unique documents of the seventeenth century, for it is one of the only ones to record so eloquently a woman's cry for intellectual freedom. Sor Juana used every argument at her disposal to make her case, beginning with the bishop's main premise. If God Himself had given her the gift of intelligence, then how could it logically follow that to use it was a sin? Sor Juana knew perfectly well that the crucial issue for the Church was her gender. Why was she being accused of censoring Vieyra, when he had written against several of the Fathers of the Church? "Is not my reason, such as it is, as free as his, seeing that both emanate from the same source?" she asked. The answer was, of course, no.

Events both inside and outside Sor Juana's convent walls conspired to make the atmosphere around her apocalyptic. There was famine in the land, and hungry bands of the poor rioted in the streets of the capital. The archbishop stepped up his campaign to bring her to heel. The nun at this point stood totally alone, and could hold out no longer against the power of the institutionalized Church. About two years before her death she underwent a radical change: she recalled Núñez as her confessor, appeared to stop all intellectual activity, and engaged in long hours of prayer and mortification of the flesh. Under pressure from the archbishop, she sold her library and other treasures and gave the money to the poor. She renewed her vows of profession several times, calling herself "the worst in the world" and signing them in her own blood. Other nuns did this as well, so it was not a unique gesture, but all of this was so uncharacteristic for Sor Juana that critics have long debated what brought on this radical change in her. Some believed that she had had a true religious conversion, had recognized the folly of her worldliness, and had thrown herself into acts of penitence to atone for her past. Others were just as convinced that she cracked under the pressure, perhaps had a nervous breakdown, and saw no alternative but to obey her superiors. Octavio Paz, for his part, conjectured that perhaps she was pretending remorse while waiting for better times (598, 601). Up until 1995, the tercentenary of Sor Juana's death, no one had resolved this mystery, but then the historian Elías Trabulse of the Colegio de México made some startling new finds. One is a poem, ostensibly written by one "Sor Serafina de Cristo," which attacked Núñez and supported Sor Juana—and which Trabulse believes Sor Juana herself composed.[2] His other find, no less startling, came when he reviewed the account books of the convent. Sor Juana had been elected treasurer of her convent twice, and oversaw the myriad economic transactions involved in the administration of her large community. Her account books, which had to be checked yearly by a Church official, showed that in the midst of her persecution by the archbishop she was clandestinely investing some of her own funds with a wealthy banker, probably to replace what she had been forced to give Aguiar y Seijas. A third find, by the historian Teresa Castello, was an item scholars had wanted to unearth for years: the inventory of Sor Juana's cell when she died. Although Aguiar y Seijas had made her divest herself of all her books and manuscripts, the inventory shows that at the time of the nun's death there were some 170 books and 180 bundles of manuscripts in her cell.[3] All of the above has given us final proof of what many Sor Juana scholars had hoped all along: she did, in fact, never surrender to the Church authorities.

In 1695 an epidemic of some highly contagious disease appeared in Mexico City and did not spare the Hieronymite convent. Sor Juana nursed her sisters until she herself succumbed to the disease. She died on April 17, 1695, and is buried in the chapel of her convent.

Notes

1. Rudolf M. Dekker and Lotte C. van der Pol, *The Tradition of Female Transvestism in Early Modern Europe* (New York: St. Martin's Press, 1989) 69. The intimate relationship between Sor Juana and the countess is the subject of María Luisa Bemberg's film *Yo, la peor de todas* (I, the Worst of All).

2. See his *El enigma de Serafina de Cristo: Acerca de un manuscrito inédito de Sor Juana Inés de la Cruz* (1691) (Toluca: Instituto Mexiquense de Cultura, 1995); and "La guerra de las finezas," *Memoria del Coloquio Internacional Sor Juana Inés de la Cruz y el pensamiento novohispano 1995* (Toluca: Instituto Mexiquense de Cultura, 1995): 483–93. Noted scholars who do not agree with Trabulse are Antonio Alatorre and Martha Lilia Tenorio. See their

Serafina y Sor Juana (con tres apéndices) (México: El Colegio de México, 1998).

3. Trabulse's and Castello's discoveries were presented at the November 1995 conference, "Sor Juana y su mundo," which was held at the Universidad Claustro de Sor Juana in her convent in Mexico City. Publication of the papers presented at this conference is forthcoming.

Carta al R. P. M. Antonio Núñez

Carta de la Madre Juana Inés de la Cruz escrita al R. P. M. Antonio Núñez, de la Compañía de Jesús.

Pax Xpti. [Christi]

Aunque ha muchos tiempos que varias personas me han informado de que soy la única represible en las conversaciones de V. R. [Vuestra Reverencia], fiscalizando mis acciones con tan agria ponderación como llegarlas a *escándalo público*, y otros epítetos no menos horrorosos, y aunque pudiera la propia conciencia moverme a la defensa, pues no soy tan absoluto dueño de mi crédito, que no esté coligado con el de un linaje que tengo, y una comunidad en que vivo, con todo esto, he querido sacrificar el sufrimiento a la suma veneración y filial cariño con que siempre he respetado a V. R. queriendo más aína que cayesen sobre mí todas las objeciones, que no que pareciera pasaba yo la línea de mi justo, y debido respeto en redargüir a V. R. en lo cual confieso ingenuamente que no pude merecer nada para con Dios, pues fue más humano respeto a su persona, que cristiana paciencia; y esto no ignorando yo la veneración y crédito grande que V. R. (con mucha razón) tiene con todos, y que le oyen como a un oráculo divino y aprecian sus palabras como dictadas del Espíritu Santo, y que cuanto mayor es su autoridad tánto más queda perjudicado mi crédito; con todo esto nunca he querido asentir a las instancias que a que responda me ha hecho, no sé si la razón o si el amor propio (que éste tal vez con capa de razón nos arrastra) juzgando que mi silencio sería el medio más suave para que V. R. se desapasionase; hasta que con el tiempo he reconocido que antes parece que le irrita mi paciencia, y así determiné responder a V. R. salvando y suponiendo mi amor, mi obligación y mi respeto.

La materia, pues, de este enojo de V. R. (muy amado Padre y

Señor mío) no ha sido otra que la de estos negros versos de que el cielo tan contra la voluntad de V. R. me dotó.[1] Estos he rehusado sumamente el hacerlos y me he excusado todo lo posible no porque en ellos hallase yo razón de bien ni de mal, que siempre los he tenido (como lo son) por cosa indiferente, y aunque pudiera decir cuántos los han usado santos y doctos, no quiero entrometerme a su defensa, que no son mi padre ni mi madre: sólo digo que no los haría por dar gusto a V. R. sin buscar, ni averiguar la razón de su aborrecimiento, que es muy propio del amor obedecer a ciegas; demás que con esto también me conformaba con la natural repugnancia que siempre he tenido a hacerlos, como consta a cuantas personas me conocen; pero esto no fue posible observarlo con tánto rigor que no tuviese algunas excepciones, tales como dos villancicos a la Santísima Virgen que después de repetidas instancias y pausa de ocho años, hice con venia y licencia de V. R., la cual tuve entonces por más necesaria que la del Sr. Arzobispo Virrey mi Prelado,[2] y en ellos procedí con tal modestia, que no consentí en los primeros poner mi nombre, y en los segundos se puso sin consentimiento ni noticia mía, y unos y otros corrigió antes V. R.

A esto se siguió el Arco de la Iglesia.[3] Esta es la irremisible culpa mía a la cual precedió habérmel[o] pedido tres o cuatro veces y tántas despedídome yo, hasta que vinieron los dos señores jueces hacedores que antes de llamarme a mí, llamaron a la Madre Priora y después a mí, y mandaron en nombre del Excmo. Señor Arzobispo lo hiciese porque así lo había votado el Cabildo pleno y aprobado Su Excelencia.

Ahora quisiera yo que V. R. con su clarísimo juicio, se pusiera en mi lugar y consultara ¿qué respondiera en este lance? ¿Respondería que no podía? Era mentira. ¿Que no quería? Era inobediencia. ¿Que no sabía? Ellos no pedían más que hasta donde supiese. ¿Que estaba mal votado? Era, sobre descarado atrevimiento, villano y grosero desagradecimiento a quien me honraba con el concepto de pensar que sabía hacer una mujer ignorante, lo que tan lucidos ingenios solicitaban: luego no pude hacer otra cosa que obedecer.

Estas son las obras públicas que tan escandalizado tienen al mundo, y tan [d]edificados a los buenos y así vamos a l[a]s no públic[a]s: apenas se hallará tal o cual coplilla hecha a los años, al obsequio de tal o tal persona de mi estimación, y a quienes he debido socorro en mis necesidades (que no han sido pocas, por ser tan pobre y no tener renta alguna). Una loa a los años del Rey Nuestro Señor hecha por mandato del mismo Excmo. Señor Don Fray Payo, otra por orden de la Excma. Sra. Condesa de Paredes.[4]

Pues a[h]ora Padre mío y mi señor, le suplico a V. R. deponga por un rato el cariño del propio dictamen (que aun a los muy santos arrastra) y dígame V. R. (ya que en su opinión es pecado hacer versos) ¿en cuál de estas ocasiones ha sido tan grave el delito de hacerlos? Pues cuando fuera culpa (que yo no sé por qué razón se le pueda llamar así) la disculparan las mismas circunstancias y ocasiones que para ello he tenido, tan contra mi voluntad, y esto bien claro se prueba, pues en la facilidad que todos saben que tengo, si a ésa se juntara motivo de vanidad (quizá lo es de mortificación) ¿qué más castigo me quiere V. R. que el que entre los mismos aplausos que tanto [l]e duelen, tengo? ¿De qué envidia no soy blanco? ¿De qué mala intención no soy objeto? ¿Qué acción hago sin temor? ¿Qué palabra digo sin recelo?

Las mujeres sienten que las exceda, los hombres, que parezca que los igualo;[5] unos no quisieran que supiera tánto, otros dicen que había de saber más, para tánto aplauso; las viejas no quisieran que otras supieran más, las mozas que otras parezcan bien, y unos y otros que viese conforme a las reglas de su dictamen, y de todos juntos resulta un tan extraño género de martirio cual no sé yo que otra persona haya experimentado.

¿Qué más podré decir ni ponderar? que hasta el hacer esta forma de letra algo razonable me costó una prolija y pesada persecución, no por más de porque dicen que parecía letra de hombre, y que no era decente, con que me obligaron a malearla adrede, y de esto toda esta comunidad es testigo; en fin, ésta no será materia para una carta, sino para muchos volúmenes muy copiosos. Pues ¿qué dichos son estos tan culpables? ¿los aplauses y celebraciones vulgares los solicité? y los particulares favores y honras de los Excelentísimos Señores Marqueses que por sola su dignación y sin igual humanidad me hacen ¿los procuré yo?

Tan a la contra sucedió que la Madre Juana de San Antonio, Priora de este Convento y persona que por ningún caso podrá mentir, es testigo de que la primera vez que Sus Excelencias honraron esta casa, le pedí licencia para retirarme a la celda y no verlos, ni ser vista (como si Sus Excelencias me hubiesen hecho algún daño) sin más motivo que huir el aplauso, que así se convierte en tan pungentes espinas de persecución, y lo hubiera conseguido a no mandarme la Madre Priora lo contrario.

¿Pues qué culpa mía fue el que Sus Excelencias se agradasen de mí? Aunque no había por qué ¿podré yo negarme a tan soberanas personas? ¿podré sentir el que me honren con sus visitas?

V. R. sabe muy bien que no; como lo experimentó en tiempo de los Excmos. Sres. Marqueses de Mancera, pues oí yo a V. R. en muchas ocasiones quejarse de las ocupaciones a que le hacía faltar la asistencia de Sus Excelencias sin poderlas no obstante dejar; y si el Excmo. Sr. Marqués de Mancera entraba cuantas veces quería en unos conventos tan santos como Capuchinas y Teresas, y sin que nadie lo tuviese por malo ¿cómo podré yo resistir que el Excmo. Sr. Marqués de la Laguna entre en éste? De más que yo no soy prelada, ni corre por mi cuenta su gobierno.

Sus Excelencias me honran porque son servidos, no porque yo lo merezca, ni tampoco porque al principio lo solicité.

Yo no puedo, ni quisiera aunque pudiera, ser tan bárbaramente ingrata a los favores y cariños (tan no merecidos, ni servidos) de Sus Excelencias.

Mis estudios no han sido en daño ni perjuicio de nadie, mayormente habiendo sido tan sumamente privados que no me he valido ni aun de la dirección de un maestro, sino que a secas me lo he habido conmigo y mi trabajo, que no ignoro que el cursar públicamente las escuelas, no fuera decente a la honestidad de una mujer, por la ocasionada familiaridad con los hombres, y que ésta sería la razón de prohibir los estudios públicos;[6] y el no diputarles lugar señalado para ellos, será porque como no las ha menester la República para el gobierno de los magistrados (de que por la misma razón de honestidad están excluídas) no cuida de lo que no le ha de servir; pero los privados y particulares estudios ¿quién los ha prohibido a las mujeres? ¿No tienen alma racional como los hombres? Pues ¿por qué no gozará el privilegio de la ilustración de las letras como ell[o]s?[7] ¿No es capaz de tanta gracia y gloria de Dios como la suya? Pues ¿por qué no será capaz de tántas noticias y ciencias, que es menos? ¿Qué revelación divina, qué determinación de la Iglesia, qué dictamen de la razón hizo para nosotras tan severa ley?

¿Las letras estorban, sino que antes ayudan a la salvación? ¿No se salvó San Agustín, San Ambrosio, y todos los demás Santos Doctores? Y V. R., cargado de tántas letras ¿no piensa salvarse?

Y si me responde que en los hombres milita otra razón, digo: ¿No estudió Santa Catalina, Santa Gertrudis, mi Madre Santa Paula[8] sin estorbarle a su alta contemplación, ni a la fatiga de sus fundaciones, el saber hasta griego? ¿El aprender hebreo? ¿Enseñada de mi Padre San Jerónimo, el resolver y el entender las Santas Escrituras, como el mismo santo lo dice? Ponderando también en una epístola suya en todo género de estudios doctísima a Blesilla, hija de la misma santa, y en tan tiernos años que murió de veinte?

Pues ¿por qué en mí es malo lo que en todas fue bueno? ¿Sólo a mí me estorban los libros para salvarme?

Si he leído los profetas y oradores profanos (descuido en que incurrió el mismo Santo [Jerónimo]) también leo los Doctores Sagrados y Santas Escrituras, demás que a los primeros no puedo negar que les debo innumerables bienes, y reglas de bien vivir.

Porque ¿qué cristiano no se corre de ser iracundo a vista de la paciencia de un Sócrates gentil? ¿Quién podrá ser ambicioso a vista de la modestia de Diógenes Cínico? ¿Quién no alaba a Dios en la inteligencia de Aristóteles? Y en fin ¿qué católico no se confunde si contempla la suma de virtudes morales en todos los filósofos gentiles?

¿Por qué ha de ser malo que el rato que yo había de estar en una reja hablando disparates, o en una celda murmurando cuanto pasa fuera y dentro de casa, o pelea[ndo] con otra, o riñendo a la triste sirviente, o vagando por todo el mundo con el pensamiento, lo gastara en estudiar? Y más cuando Dios me inclinó a eso y no me pareció que era contra su ley santísima, ni contra la obligación de mi estado. Yo tengo este genio, si es malo, yo [no] me hice,[9] nací con él y con él he de morir.

V. R. quiere que por fuerza me salve ignorando. Pues amado

Padre mío, ¿no puede esto hacerse sabiendo? Que al fin es camino para mí más suave. Pues, ¿por qué para salvarse ha de ir por el camino de la ignorancia, si es repugnante a su natural?

¿No es Dios como suma bondad, suma sabiduría? Pues, ¿por qué le ha de ser más acepta la ignorancia que la ciencia?

Sálvese San Antonio con su ignorancia santa, norabuena, que San Agustín va por otro camino, y ninguno va errado.

Pues ¿por qué es esta pesadumbre de V. R. y el decir "que a saber que yo había de hacer versos no me hubiera entrado religiosa, sino casádome?"

Pues, Padre amantísimo (a quien forzada y con vergüenza insto lo que no quisiera tomar en boca), ¿cuál era el dominio directo que tenía V. R. para disponer de mi persona y del albedrío (sacando el que mi amor le daba y le dará siempre) que Dios me dio?

Pues cuando ello sucedió había muy poco que yo tenía la dicha de conocer a V. R., y aunque le debí sumos deseos y solicitudes de mi estado, que estimaré siempre como debo, lo tocante a la dote,[10] mucho antes de conocer yo a V. R. lo tenía ajustado mi padrino el Capitán D. Pedro Velázquez de la Cadena, y agenciádomelo estas mismas prendas, en las cuales, y no en otra cosa, me libró Dios el remedio. Luego no hay sobre qué caiga tal proposición, aunque no niego deberle a V. R. otros cariños y agasajos muchos que reconoceré eternamente, tal como el de pagarme maestro, y otros; pero no es razón que éstos no se continúen, sino que se hayan convertido en vituperios, y en que no haya conversación en que no salgan mis culpas, y sea el tema espiritual el celo de V. R. [por] mi conver[sión].[11]

¿Soy por ventura hereje? Y si lo fuera ¿había de ser santa a pura fuerza? Ojalá y la santidad fuera cosa que se pudiera mandar, que con eso la tuviera yo segura; pero yo juzgo que se persuade, no se manda, y si se manda, prelados he tenido que lo hicieran; pero los preceptos, y fuerzas exteriores, si son moderados y prudentes, hacen recatados y modestos, si son demasiados, hacen desesperados; pero santos, sólo la gracia y auxilios de Dios saben hacerlos.

¿En qué se funda, pues, este enojo? ¿En qué este desacreditarme? ¿En qué este ponerme en concepto de escandalosa con todos? ¿Canso yo a V. R. con algo? ¿Héle pedido alguna cosa para el socorro de mis necesidades? ¿O le he molestado con otra espiritual ni temporal?

¿Tócale a V. R. mi corrección por alguna razón de obligación, de parentesco, crianza, prelacía, o tal que cosa?

Si es mera caridad, parezca mera caridad, y proceda como tal, suavemente, que el exasperarme, no es buen modo de reducirme, ni yo tengo tan servil naturaleza que haga por amenazas lo que no me persuade la razón, ni por respetos humanos, lo que no haga por Dios, que el privarme yo de todo aquello que me puede dar gusto, aunque sea muy lícito, es bueno que yo lo haga por mortificarme, cuando yo quiera hacer penitencia; pero no para que V. R. lo quiera conseguir a fuerza de represiones, y éstas no a mí en secreto como ordena la paternal corrección (ya que V. R. ha dado en ser mi padre, cosa en que me tengo ser muy dichosa) sino públicamente con todos, donde cada uno siente como entiende y habla como siente.

Pues esto, Padre mío ¿no es preciso yo lo sienta de una persona que con tánta veneración amo y con tánto amor reverencio y estimo?

Si estas represiones cayeran sobre alguna comunicación escandalosa mía, soy tan dócil, que (no obstante que ni en lo espiritual, ni temporal he corrido nunca por cuenta de V. R.), me apartara de ella y procurara enmendarme y satisfacerle, aunque fuera contra mi gusto.

Pero, si no es sino por la contradicción de un dictamen que en sustancia tánto monta hacer versos como no hacerlos, y que éstos los aborrezco de forma que no habrá para mí penitencia como tenerme siempre haciéndolos ¿por qué es tánta pesadumbre?

Porque si por contradicción de dictamen hubiera yo de hablar apasionada[mente] contra V. R. como lo hace V. R. contra mí, infinitas ocasiones suyas, me repugnan sumamente (porque al fin, el sentir en las materias indiferentes es aquel *alius sic, et alius sic*) pero no por eso las condeno, sino que antes las venero como suyas y las defiendo como mías; y aun quizá las mismas que son contra mí, llamándolas buen celo, sumo cariño, y otros títulos que sabe inventar mi amor y reverencia cuando hablo con los otros.

Pero a V. R. no puedo dejar de decirle que rebosan ya en el pecho las quejas que en espacio de los años pudiera haber dado; y que pues tomo la pluma para darlas redarguyendo a quien tánto venero, es porque ya no puedo más, que como no soy tan mortificada como otras hijas en quien se empleara mejor su doctrina, lo siento demasiado.

Y así le suplico a V. R. que si no gusta ni es ya servido favorecerme (que eso es voluntario) no se acuerde de mí, que aunque sentiré tánta pérdida mucho, nunca podré quejarme, que Dios que me crió y redimió, y que usa conmigo tántas misericordias, proveerá con remedio para mi alma, que esper[o] en su bondad no se perderá, aunque le falte la dirección de V. R., que [al] cielo hacen muchas llaves, y no se estrechó a un solo dictamen, sino que hay en él infinidad de mansiones para diversos genios, y en el mundo hay muchos teólogos, y cuando faltaran, en querer más que en saber consiste el salvarse, y esto más estará en mí que en el confesor.

¿Qué precisión hay en que esta salvación mía sea por medio de V. R.? ¿No podrá ser otro? ¿Retringióse y limitóse la misericordia de Dios a un hombre, aunque sea tan discreto, tan docto, y tan santo como V. R.?

No por cierto, ni hasta ahora he tenido yo luz particular ni inspiración del Señor que así me lo ordene; conque podré gobernarme con las reglas generales de la Santa Madre Iglesia, mientras el Señor no me da luz de que haga otra cosa, y elegir libremente Padre espiritual el que yo quisiere: que si como Nuestro Señor inclinó a V. R. con tánto amor y fuerza mi voluntad, conformara también mi dictamen, no fuera otro que V. R. a quien suplico no tenga esta ingenuidad a atrevimiento, ni a menos respeto, sino a sencillez de mi corazón con que no sé decir las cosas sino como las siento, y antes he procurado hablar de manera que no pueda dejar a V. R. rastro de sentimiento o quejas.

Y no obstante, si en este manifiesto de mis culpas hubiere alguna palabra que haya escrito mala, [será] inadvertencia que la voluntad no sólo digo de ofensa, pero de menos decoro a la persona de V. R., desde luego la retracto, y doy por mal dicha y peor escrita, y borrara desde luego si advirtiera cuál era.

Vuelvo a repetir que mi intención es sólo suplicar a V. R. que si

no gusta de favorecerme, no se acuerde de mí, si no fuere para en-
comendarme al Señor, que bien creo de su mucha caridad lo hará
con todas veras.

> Yo pido a Su Majestad me guarde a V. R. como deseo.
> De este convento de mi Padre San Jerónimo de México.
> Vuestra
> Juana Inés de la Cruz[12]

Notas

1. Hay varios errores en el texto de la carta, debidos o al descuido de
parte de Sor Juana, o a los errores de transcripción del amanuensis en
cuestión. Como nota Paz con mucha razón, la intención de Sor Juana aquí
no es sugerir que son los *versos* los que son desafortunados, sino el talento
que Dios le dio para componerlos (634). Para una versión anotada y co-
rregida del texto de la carta, véase Antonio Alatorre, "La *Carta* de Sor
Juana al P. Núñez," *Nueva Revista de Filología Hispánica* 15 (1987): 591–673.

2. Esto se refiere a Fray Payo Enríquez de Rivera, que fue primero Arzobispo de México, y luego virrey de 1674 a 1680.

3. Lo que ella llama "el Arco de la Iglesia" era una alegoría poética
a Neptuno, compuesta para acompañar un provisional arco triunfal
eregido para celebrar la llegada en 1680 de los nuevos virreyes, el Marqués
de la Laguna y su esposa. Sor Juana escogió la referencia mitológica a Neptuno para aludir al apellido acuático del virrey. Este arco, que consistía de
un *collage* de pintura y poesía, lo comisionaron por orden directa el Capítulo de la Catedral y el Arzobispo Fray Payo, mencionado arriba.

4. María Luisa Manrique de Lara y Gonzaga, Condesa de Paredes y
Virreina de México, fue la amiga más íntima de Sor Juana y la que hizo
publicar la poesía de la monja en Sevilla en 1689.

5. El texto original es algo diferente: "Las mujeres sienten que las excedan los hombres, que parezca que los igualo," una frase muy confusa de
sintaxis por el subjuntivo de "parecer"; estoy de acuerdo con la opinión
de Marie-Cécile Bénassy-Berling, que cree que debe decir "Las mujeres
sienten que las exceda, los hombres que parezca que los igualo," y así lo
he traducido (Carta personal, 28 de febrero de 1987).

6. En el original el verbo es "publicar los estudios públicos," que no
tiene sentido alguno y probablemente es un error; lo he cambiado a "prohibir." El segundo error ocurre con "disputarles lugar," cuando debe ser

"diputarles lugar señalado," o sea "designar lugar especial" para estudiar esta materia. Le agradezco a Antonio Alatorre señalarme este punto.

7. Otra vez el original tiene poco sentido: "¿Pues por qué no gozará el privilegio de la ilustración de las letras con ellas?" Bénassy-Berling sugiere que debe ser "como ellos" que me parece más razonable.

8. Aquí Sor Juana se refiere a la legendaria Santa Catarina de Alejandría (s. III), famosa por su belleza y su erudición, martirizada por el Emperador Maximino II cuando ella rehusó casarse con él. Gertrudis "la Magna" (s. XIII) era monja benedictina que redactó trozos del "Legatus Divinae Pietatis," una de las obras más destacadas del misticismo alemán, y también es santa patrona de las Indias; Santa Paula (s. V), adinerada matrona romana, era una de las discípulas más devotas de San Jerónimo; él la nombró superiora de una de las comunidades monásticas gemelas que él fundó en Belén. Era la santa patrona del convento de Sor Juana.

9. El original dice "yo me hice," que parece contradecir todo el mensaje de este pasaje; Tapia Méndez ya lo cambió en su texto (*Carta* 25) y yo le seguí en mi traducción, pero Alatorre (623) y Paz (643) mantienen "yo me hice," que también tiene sentido. Que decidan los lectores.

10. Aparentemente la gente pensaba que Núñez le había procurado la dote a Sor Juana, y que por eso ella le debía algo. Este punto—antes desconocido—es uno de los más importantes descubrimientos biográficos que el hallazgo de esta carta ha aportado a los estudios sorjuaninos.

11. El original dice "conversación," en vez de "conversión," que sería mucho más verosímil; parece ser otro error de transcripción. Tapia Méndez está de acuerdo que el término correcto debe ser "conversión" (*Carta* 25).

12. El texto aquí reproducido se basa en tres versiones anteriores de la carta descubierta por Aureliano Tapia Méndez: en la *Carta*, publicada por este último; en la versión incluida en el apéndice de la 3ª edición de *Sor Juana Inés de la Cruz o Las trampas de la fe* de Octavio Paz, y en la versión de Antonio Alatorre en "*La Carta* de Sor Juana al P. Núñez (1682)." Para facilitar la lectura de este texto para los lectores modernos he alterado algo la puntuación y los párrafos.

Letter to the R. F. M. Antonio Núñez

Letter of Mother Juana Inés de la Cruz written to the Reverend Father Maestro Antonio Núñez of the Society of Jesus.

The Peace of Christ.

Although for a long time now various persons have informed me that I am the only one to blame in Your Reverence's conversations, as you criticize my actions with such bitter criteria so as to classify them as a *public scandal* and other epithets no less dreadful, though it would be only natural for me to defend myself, as I am not the absolute mistress of my reputation, linked as it is to the state in which I exist and the community in which I live, in spite of all that I have wanted to sacrifice my suffering to the highest veneration of filial affection with which I have always respected Your Reverence, desiring sooner that all these objections fall on me rather than that it seem that I were deviating from just and proper respect by engaging in a counterargument with Your Reverence; in this matter I confess openly that my actions do not merit divine reward because it was more a matter of human respect for your person than of Christian patience; [I say] this not ignoring the veneration and great esteem which Your Reverence (with good reason) receives from everyone, for they listen to you as to a divine oracle and value your words as though dictated by the Holy Spirit, so that the greater your authority, the more my reputation suffers; yet even so, in view of all of this, I have never wished to yield to the desire to answer that has impelled me, I know not whether it was a matter of reason or of self-esteem (for perhaps the latter in the guise of reason sways us), judging that my silence would be the gentlest means whereby Your Reverence might be restored to calm, until in time I came to realize that it appears that my patience irritates you, and so I resolved to reply to Your Reverence, all the while certifying and implying my love, my duty, and my respect.

The focus, then, of Your Reverence's anger (most beloved Father and Sir) has been none other than those unfortunate verses which Heaven—most contrary to Your Reverence's wishes—has bestowed on me.[1] I have always tried mightily to refrain from writing them and I have excused myself from doing so as much as possible, not because I found in them either good or evil, as I have always held them (as indeed they are) as something quite indifferent, and though I could tell you how many holy and learned persons have made use of them, I do not want to get involved in defending them for they are not that important (they are neither my father nor my mother); I only say that in order to please Your Reverence I would refrain from composing them without even searching for or attempting to ascertain the reason for your displeasure, for one of the characteristics of love is to obey blindly; furthermore, by doing this I would also be able to give in to the natural aversion which I have always felt while writing them, as is well known to all who know me; however, it was not possible to do this so rigorously as not to admit some exceptions, as for example two pieces to the Most Holy Virgin which, after repeated requests and an interval of eight years, I composed with the permission and leave of Your Reverence, which at the time I thought more important even than those of my Prelate, the Lord Archbishop and Viceroy,[2] and proceeded with them with such modesty that I refused to sign my name to the first, and as to the second, my name appeared on it with neither my consent nor prior notice to me, and both the former as well as the latter were first submitted to Your Reverence for correction.

These [pieces] were followed by the Church's Arch.[3] This is my unforgivable fault, which was preceded by my having been asked to write it three or four times and I having refused as many until two lay magistrates went to the Mother Superior before coming to me and summoned me to do it in the name of His Excellency the Lord Archbishop, because the entire municipal council had voted in favor and His Excellency had approved it.

Now I ask that Your Reverence, with your great clarity of judgment, put yourself in my position and ask yourself what you would have done under similar circumstances? Would you have answered that you were unable to comply? That would be a lie. That you did not want to? That would be disobedience. That you did not know how? They did not ask me to go beyond the extent of my knowledge. That they had voted badly? That would be bold-faced impudence, base and rude ingratitude toward those brilliant minds who honored an ignorant woman with their request. Therefore I could do no less than to obey.

These are the public works which have so scandalized the world and contributed to the detriment of good souls, so let us go on to those works which are private: one will find perhaps a couplet here or there written to honor the birthday of some person whom I esteemed and who has helped me with things I needed (which were not a few, given the fact that I am very poor and have no income whatever). A panegyric on the occasion of the birthday of Our Lord the King, written by order of His Excellency Don Fray Payo, another by order of Her Excellency the Countess of Paredes.[4]

Well, then, my Father and good Sir, I beg Your Reverence to suspend for a while the affection you feel for your own advice (even the most holy are swayed by this tendency) and tell me, Your Reverence (since in your opinion it is a sin to write poetry), in which of these occasions was it a grave sin to compose verses? And even supposing it was a sin (though I cannot conceive for which reason it would be deemed such), the same circumstances and occasions which forced me do it so much against my will would excuse it, and this can be clearly proved, for should the gift which all know I possess be joined to vanity (perhaps it is actually chagrin), what greater punishment could Your Reverence envision for me than the pain which this very applause occasions me? Of what envy am I not the target? Of which evil intention am I not the object? What action do I take without quailing? What word do I utter without misgiving?

Women take offense that I surpass them, men that I seem to equal them;[5] some wish that I did not know quite so much, others say I should know more to merit such praise; old women do not want others to know more than they do, young women resent those who attract more attention and one and all want me to comply with the rules of their judgment; all these sources together produce such a strange kind of martyrdom that I know of no one else who has undergone the like.

What more can I say or think? Why, even writing a more or less reasonable hand has cost me lengthy and difficult persecution only because they say my writing looked like a man's and that was unseemly, so I was purposely made to alter it and to this the whole community can bear witness; in short, this is a matter not just for a letter but for a number of very lengthy volumes. For what have I said that is so sinful? Did I ask for praise and common approval? And the special favors and honors which Their Excellencies the Lords Marquesses bestow on me only by their favor and unequaled kindness, did I strive to obtain these?

So differently did it happen that Mother Juana de San Antonio, Prioress of this convent and a person incapable of lying under any circumstances, is witness to the fact that the first time that Their Excellencies honored this house with their visit, I asked her permission to withdraw to my cell and neither see them nor be seen (as though Their Excellencies had done me some harm), with no other motive than to flee from the praise that subsequently is turned into most painful barbs of persecution, and I would have been able to do it had the Mother Superior not commanded me otherwise.

What fault is it of mine that Their Excellencies find my company pleasant? Even if there were no reason for this, can I refuse to see such highborn persons? Should I regret the honor they do me with their visits?

Your Reverence knows very well I should not, as you yourself experienced in the times of Their Excellencies the Lords Marquesses of Mancera, for many was the time that I heard Your Reverence complain of the occupations you had to put aside in order to attend Their Excellencies without being able to do otherwise, and if His Excellency the Lord Marquis of Mancera entered convents as saintly as those of the Capuchins and the Barefoot Carmelites any time he wished without anyone thinking ill of it, how can I prevent His Excellency the Marquis of Laguna from visiting this one? Besides, I am not the one in charge here, nor is the governance of this convent my responsibility.

Their Excellencies do me honor because they wish to, not because I deserve it nor because I originally courted it.

I cannot, and would not wish to even if I could, be so barbarously ungrateful for the favors and affection of Their Excellencies (favors so undeserved and so unmerited).

My studies have not been undertaken to hurt or harm anyone and have principally been so private that I have not even made use of the guidance of a teacher but have relied solely upon myself and my work, for I know that studying publicly in schools is unseemly to a woman's modesty because of the hazardous familiarity with men and this would be the reason for keeping women[6] from public studies; not delegating a special place for their study is probably because as the Republic has no need of women for the government of magistrates (from which area, for the same reasons of propriety, the former are also excluded), [the state] is not concerned with that of which it has no need, but who has forbidden women to engage in private and individual studies? Have they not a rational soul as men do? Well, then, why cannot a woman profit by the privilege of enlightenment as they do?[7] Is her soul not as able to receive the grace and glory of God as that of a man? Well, then, why should she not be just as capable in matters of information and knowledge which are of less import? What divine revelation, what rule of the Church, what reasonable judgment formulated such a severe law for us women?

Does learning now prevent, when in other times it furthered salvation? Were not Saint Augustine, Saint Ambrosius and all the other Doctors of the Church saved? And Your Reverence, bowed down under the weight of so much learning, do you not plan to be saved?

And if you answer that men are governed by other rules I say: did not Saint Catherine, Saint Gertrude and my mother Saint Paula[8] study without harming their lofty contemplations, and was the latter's travail in the founding of convents impeded by her knowledge even of Greek? By having learned Hebrew? By having been instructed by my Father Saint Jerome to understand and interpret

Holy Writ, as the Saint himself tells us? Who also, in one of his epistles dealing with all manner of knowledge, praised Saint Paula's daughter Blesilla as being extremely learned, [and this] when the latter was very young indeed, dying as she did when she was twenty?

Then why is that, which in all others was considered good, judged to be evil in my case? Is it only I whose salvation is hindered by books?

If I have read the prophets and secular orators (a lapse of which Saint Jerome himself was guilty), I also read the Holy Doctors and Scripture and cannot deny that to the former I owe countless gifts and rules of good conduct.

For which Christian will not avoid wrath when confronted by the patience of a pagan Socrates? Who can be ambitious in view of the modesty of the Cynic Diogenes? Who does not praise God in Aristotle's intelligence? And finally, what Catholic can fail to be astonished when contemplating the sum of moral virtues in all of the pagan philosophers?

Why should it be judged evil that the time which I might spend in foolish chatter at the grille, or in a cell sniping at everything that goes on in and out of this house, or fighting with someone or shouting at a poor servant or wandering idly through the world with my thoughts, be invested in studying?

And all the more so since God disposed me to be this way and it does not appear to me to be against His most holy law nor contrary to the obligations of my profession; I have this inclination and if it is evil I am not the one who formed me thus[9]—I was born with it and with it I shall die.

Your Reverence wishes that of necessity I should be saved in a state of ignorance, but my beloved Father, can one not accomplish this end and be learned? In the final analysis, for me it is the easier path. Because why should one be led to salvation by the way of ignorance if this is repugnant to one's nature?

Is not God as ultimate goodness also ultimate wisdom? Well, then, why should ignorance be more pleasing to Him than learning?

Let Saint Anthony achieve salvation with his holy ignorance and well and good, while Saint Augustine goes by a different path and neither one of the two is wrong.

Then from whence comes Your Reverence's displeasure and your saying that "had you known I was going to write poetry you would not have made me a nun but would have arranged for me to marry"?

Well, dearly beloved Father (to whom, obliged and with all modesty, I say that which I would prefer not to utter), what direct authority (leaving aside that which my love gave and always will give you) did you have to dispose of my person and my God-given free will?

Because when all that happened I had only very recently had the pleasure of knowing Your Reverence, and although I was indebted to you for your very great concern and interest in my condition, for which I will always be very grateful as indeed I ought to be, as to the matter of my dowry,[10] long before I got to know Your Reverence my sponsor Captain Pedro Velázquez de la Cadena had already set it aside and in making the arrangements for this same sum, and in no other way, God gave me the means [to enter the convent], for which reason I do not know on what your assumption is based, though I do not deny that I owe Your Reverence other kindnesses and favors for which I will be eternally grateful, such as having paid for a teacher of mine, and others; there is no reason that these might not continue except that they have been converted into insults and there seems to be no conversation in which my faults are not mentioned and in which my conversion[11] is not the topic of Your Reverence's zeal.

Am I perchance a heretic? And even if I were, could sheer force make me a saint? Would that saintliness were something to be commanded, for then I would be sure to possess it, but I feel that one must be persuaded of it, not ordered, and if it were a matter to be commanded I have had prelates who have done it; if external precepts and pressures are tempered and prudent they make a person circumspect and modest, but if they are excessive, result in despair. Only the grace and assistance of God are capable of producing saints.

On what, then, is this anger based? Why this descrediting of my person? Why this attitude of making me out to be scandalous in front of everyone? Do I annoy Your Reverence in some way? Have I asked you to help me in remedying any of my needs? Or have I importuned you with any other spiritual or temporal request?

Has Your Reverence any stake in my betterment by reason of obligation, blood relation, upbringing, Church authority, or anything else?

If it is pure charity, let it seem pure charity and have it proceed as such, gently, because exasperating me is not a good way to bring me around, for I do not possess such a servile nature that I will do something when threatened which reason would not persuade me to do; neither would I do for human respect that which I would not do for God, for to give up everything that might give me pleasure —even though it might be very just—is good if I do it to humble myself when I might want to do penance, but it is not when Your Reverence wishes to obtain it by dint of reprimands, and these not in secret as befits paternal correction (given that Your Reverence has decided to be my Father, something for which I consider myself to be very fortunate) but publicly, in front of everyone, where each one reacts to a situation to the extent of his understanding and speaks as he may feel.

Then in all this matter, my Father, is it not natural that I should be hurt by a person whom I love with such veneration and whom with such love I esteem and revere?

If these admonishments were to fall upon some scandalous statement of mine, I am so obedient that (in spite of the fact that neither in matters secular nor spiritual have I been answerable to Your Reverence) I would desist from it and would try to reform and please you, even though it went against my will.

But this not being the case, as our dispute centers on the fact that it amounts to the same thing whether I write verses or not and, considering that I dislike them intensely, so that for my penance there could be no greater punishment than constantly to oblige me to write them, why then do you feel such troublesome affliction?

Because if, to contradict this opinion, I were to speak as passionately against Your Reverence as Your Reverence does against me, countless actions of yours have displeased me (because, after all, in different matters feeling is a question of one doing it this way, the other that), but I do not condemn them for that but instead revere them for being yours and defend them as though they were my own, and perhaps even those same ones which are directed against me, calling them laudable zeal, supreme affection and other merits which my love and reverence are able to invent when I converse with others.

But I cannot refrain from telling Your Reverence that my heart is bursting with the recriminations which for years I might have uttered, and if now I take up the pen to vent them and reply to one I venerate so highly, it is because I can bear no more, for as I am not as submissive as others of your daughters in whom you might better employ your doctrine, [I do it] because I am too deeply affected by this.

And so I beg Your Reverence that if you no longer wish or are disinclined to favor me (for this is voluntary), put me out of your mind, for though I will regret so great a loss, I will have no grounds for complaint, for the God who created and redeemed and bestows so many mercies on me will provide a means whereby my soul, which trusts in His goodness, will not go astray even if it be without Your Reverence's guidance, for Heaven has many keys and is not restricted to one judgment only, but there are many mansions for diverse temperaments and in the world there are many theologians and even if these were lacking, salvation consists more in the desiring than in the knowing and the former depends more on me than on a confessor.

What rule dictates that this salvation of mine must be by means of Your Reverence? Cannot it be someone else? Is God's mercy restricted and limited to one man, even if he be as prudent, as learned and as saintly as Your Reverence?

Surely not, nor have I had up to now particular enlightenment or inspiration of the Lord that He has so ordained and so I will be able to govern myself by the general rules of the Holy Mother Church—as long as the Lord does not enlighten me otherwise—and thus freely choose the spiritual Father I wish, for just as our Lord has disposed Your Reverence to feel such love for me, were He to influence my heart and help me arrive at a firm judgment, I would choose none other than Your Reverence. I beg you not to judge this candor as boldness or lack of respect but as simplicity of heart, as I do not know how to say things other than how I feel them, for which reason I have attempted to speak so that Your Reverence would not have a shred of regret or complaint. Notwithstanding, if in this declaration of my faults there be any word which I have written by inadvertent oversight rather than intentionally and which might be not only offensive but discourteous to Your Reverence's person, consider it retracted and judge it to be ill said and worse written and if I could discern which phrase might cause offense, I would immediately expunge it.

I repeat once again that my intention is solely to beg Your Reverence that if you are not pleased to favor me that you put me out of your mind, unless it be to entrust me to the Lord, as I truly believe that in your great charity you will do this most fervently.

I entreat God's Majesty to keep you.

From this my Father St. Jerome's convent in Mexico.

Your

Juana Inés de la Cruz[12]

Notes

1. There are a number of errors in the text of the letter, caused either by carelessness on Sor Juana's part or through errors of transcription of the original letter by the amanuensis involved. As Paz rightly notes, Sor Juana's intention here is not to suggest that it is her *verses* that are unfortunate but her God-given talent for composing them (634). For a corrected and extensively annotated version of the letter's text, see Antonio Alatorre, "La *Carta* de Sor Juana al P. Núñez," *Nueva Revista de Filología Hispánica* 15 (1987): 591–673.

2. This is a reference to Fray Payo Enríquez de Rivera, who was first archbishop of Mexico and subsequently viceroy from 1674 to 1680.

3. What she calls "the Church's Arch" was a poetic allegory on Neptune, composed to accompany a temporary triumphal arch erected to celebrate the arrival in 1680 of the new viceroys, the Marquis de la Laguna and his wife. Sor Juana chose the mythological reference to Neptune to allude to the water-related last name of the viceroy (Laguna = lake). This

arch, which consisted of a collage of painting and poetry, was commissioned by direct order of the Cathedral's Chapter and of Archbishop Payo, mentioned above.

4. María Luisa Manrique de Lara y Gonzaga, Countess of Paredes and Vicereine of Mexico, was Sor Juana's most intimate woman friend and the one who arranged for the publication of the nun's poetry in Seville in 1689.

5. The original text here reads somewhat differently: "Las mujeres sienten que las excedan los hombres, que parezca que los igualo," a syntactically confusing sentence because of the subjunctive form of "parecer"; I agree with the opinion of Marie-Cécile Bénassy-Berling, who believes it should read "Las mujeres sienten que las exceda, los hombres que parezca que los igualo," which is how I have translated it (Personal letter, February 28, 1987).

6. In the original the verb used is "publicar los estudios públicos," which in context makes no sense and is in all likelihood an error; I have translated it as "prohibir. " The second error is in the phrase "disputarles lugar," when it should read "diputarles lugar señalado," that is, "designate a special place" for women to study these matters. I am grateful to Antonio Alatorre for pointing this out.

7. Again the original makes very little sense: "¿Pues por qué no gozará el privilegio de la ilustración de las letras con ellas?" Bénassy-Berling suggests it should read "como ellos," which also seems more plausible to me.

8. Sor Juana here refers to the legendary Saint Catherine of Alexandria (third century), famous for her beauty and learning, who was martyred by the Emperor Maximin II when she refused to become his bride; Saint Gertrude "the Great" (thirteenth century) was a Benedictine nun who wrote parts of the "Legatus Divinae Pietatis," one of the most important works of German mysticism, and is also the patron saint of the West Indies; Saint Paula (fifth century) was the wealthy Roman matron who was one of Saint Jerome's most devoted disciples; he named her head of one of the twin monastic communities he founded in Bethlehem. She was the patron saint of Sor Juana's convent.

9. The original text reads "yo me hice" (I made myself), which appears to contradict the whole thrust of this passage; Tapia Méndez changed it in his text (*Carta* 25), and I followed him in my translation, but Alatorre (623) and Paz (643) keep "yo me hice," which is also plausible. Let the readers decide.

10. People were apparently under the impression that Núñez had procured Sor Juana's dowry for her and that she was therefore beholden to him. This is one of the most important points of heretofore unknown biographical information that the discovery of this letter has contributed to Sor Juana studies.

11. The original text says "conversación" instead of the more plausible "conversión," which again appears to be an error of transcription. Tapia Méndez is also persuaded that the correct term should be "conversión" (*Carta* 25).

12. I wish to express my sincere thanks to David Lagmanovich and to Antonio Alatorre for their help in this translation.

POESÍA
Poesía religiosa

361
Dos letras sueltas para cantar en la solemnidad del nacimiento [de Cristo].

LETRA I
Estribillo
¿Cómo será esto, mi Dios,
que yo creo en Vos,
y aunque creo lo que veo
no veo todo lo que creo?

Coplas
Si la Fe y la vista son
tan encontradas, ¿por qué
aquí ha de hacer fe la vista
y no hacer vista la Fe?

Niño os miro, y que lo sois
es necesario creer;
mas también sé que sois Grande,
y mis ojos no lo ven.

Cuando allá en la Eucaristía
estáis, más fácil me es,
porque ya sé que al contrario
de la vista he de creer.

Pero aquí, ¿qué me mandáis?
Que crea mi sencillez
lo que veo y que no veo,
lo que es y que no es.

Hombre parecéis, y sois,
Señor, lo que parecéis;
pero lo Dios no se os mira,
y sé que sois Dios también.

En fin, el sentido aquí
no se engaña, pero es
Infinito más lo que hay
que lo que se alcanza a ver.

219

Compuesto para la fiesta de la Asunción de la Virgen 1676.

VILLANCICO III

La soberana Doctora
de las Escuelas divinas,
de que los Angeles todos
deprenden sabiduría,

por ser quien inteligencia
mejor de Dios participa,
a leer la suprema sube
Cátedra de Teología.

Por Primaria de las ciencias
es justo que esté aplaudida,
quien de todas las criaturas
se llevó la primacía.

Ninguno *de Charitate*
estudió con más fatiga,
y la materia *de Gratia*
supo aun antes de nacida.

Después la *de Incarnatione*
pudo estudiar en sí misma,

con que en la *de Trinitate*
alcanzó mayor noticia.

Los soberanos Cursantes
que las letras ejercitan
y de la Sagrada Ciencia
los secretos investigan,

con los Espíritus puros
que el eterno Solio habitan
(e Inteligencias sutiles,
Ciencia de Dios se apellidan),

todos la votan iguales,
y con amantes caricias,
le celebran la victoria
y el triunfo le solemnizan.

Estribillo
Y con alegres voces de aclamación festiva,
hinchen las raridades del aire de alegrías,
y sólo se percibe en la confusa grita:
—¡Vítor, vítor, vítor, vítor María,
a pesar del Infierno y de su envidia!
¡Vítor, vítor, vítor, vítor María![1]

Poesía cortesana

Soneto 167

Continúa [del soneto 166]² el mismo asunto y aun le expresa con más viva elegancia.³

Feliciano me adora y le aborrezco;
Lisardo me aborrece y yo le adoro;
por quien no me apetece ingrato, lloro,
y al que me llora tierno, no apetezco.

A quien más me desdora, el alma ofrezco;
a quien me ofrece víctimas, desdoro;
desprecio al que enriquece mi decoro,
y al que le hace desprecios, enriquezco.

Si con mi ofensa al uno reconvengo,
me reconviene el otro a mí, ofendido;
y a padecer de todos modos vengo,

pues ambos atormentan mi sentido:
aquéste, con pedir lo que no tengo;
y aquél, con no tener lo que le pido.

Soneto 168

Prosigue el mismo asunto, y determina que prevalezca la razón contra el gusto.

Al que ingrato me deja, busco amante;
al que amante me sigue, dejo ingrata;
constante adoro a quien mi amor maltrata;
maltrato a quien mi amor busca constante.

Al que trato de amor, hallo diamante,
y soy diamante al que de amor me trata;
triunfante quiero ver al que me mata,
y mato al que me quiere ver triunfante.

Si a éste pago, padece mi deseo;
si ruego a aquél, mi pundonor enojo:
de entrambos modos infeliz me veo.

Pero yo, por mejor partido, escojo
de quien no quiero, ser violento empleo,
que, de quien no me quiere, vil despojo.

Sor Juana Inés
de la Cruz
87

Poesía satírica

Epigrama 95 [4]
Que dan el Colirio merecido a un soberbio.

El no ser de Padre honrado,
fuera defecto, a mi ver,
si como recibí el ser
de él, se lo hubiera yo dado.

Más piadosa fue tu Madre,
que hizo que a muchos sucedas:
para que, entre tantos, puedas
tomar el que más te cuadre.

Poemas a la Virreina (la Condesa de Paredes)

82

ENDECHAS REALES

Expresa su respeto amoroso: dice el sentido en que llama suya a la Señora Virreina Marquesa de la Laguna.

Divina Lysi mía:
perdona si me atrevo
a llarmarte así, cuando
aun de ser tuya el nombre no merezco.

Y creo, no osadía
es llamarte así, puesto
que a ti te sobran rayos,
si en mí pudiera haber atrevimientos.

Error es de la lengua,
que lo que dice imperio
del dueño, en el dominio,
parezcan posesiones en el siervo.

Mi rey, dice el vasallo;
mi cárcel, dice el preso;
y el más humilde esclavo,[5]
sin agraviarlo, llama suyo al dueño.

Así, cuando yo mía
te llamo, no pretendo
que juzguen que eres mía,
sino sólo que yo ser tuya quiero.

Yo te vi; pero basta:
que a publicar incendios
basta apuntar la causa,
sin añadir la culpa del efecto.

Que mirarte tan alta,
no impide a mi denuedo;
que no hay Deidad segura
al altivo volar del pensamiento.

Y aunque otras más merezcan,
en distancia del Cielo
lo mismo dista el valle
más humilde, que el monte más soberbio.

En fin, yo de adorarte
el delito confieso;
si quieres castigarme,
este mismo castigo será premio.

Soneto 195[6]

A la excma. Sra. Condesa de Paredes, Marquesa de la Laguna, enviándole estos papeles que su excia. Le pidió y que pudo recoger Soror Juana de muchas manos, en que estaban no menos divididos que escondidos, como tesoro, con otros que no cupo en el tiempo buscarlos ni copiarlos.

El hijo que la esclava ha concebido,
dice el Derecho que le pertenece
al legítimo dueño que obedece
la esclava madre, de quien es nacido.

El que retorna el campo agradecido,
opimo fruto, que obediente ofrece,
es del señor, pues si fecundo crece,
se lo debe al cultivo recibido.

Así, Lysi divina, estos borrones
que hijos del alma son, partos del pecho,
será razón que a ti te restituya;

y no lo impidan sus imperfecciones,
pues vienen a ser tuyos de derecho
los conceptos de una alma que es tan tuya.

Ama y Señora mía, besa los pies de V. Excia., su criada
Juana Inés de la Cruz.

Poesía filosófica

Soneto 149

Encarece de animosidad la elección de estado durable hasta la muerte.

Si los riesgos del mar considerara,
ninguno se embarcara; si antes viera
bien su peligro, nadie se atreviera
ni al bravo toro osado provocara.

Si del fogoso bruto ponderara
la furia desbocada en la carrera
el jinete prudente, nunca hubiera
quien con discreta mano lo enfrenara.

Pero si hubiera alguno tan osado
que, no obstante el peligro, al mismo Apolo[7]
quisiese gobernar con atrevida

mano el rápido carro en luz bañado,
todo lo hiciera, y no tomara sólo
estado que ha de ser toda la vida.

Soneto 145

Procura desmentir los elogios que a un retrato de la poetisa[8] inscribió la verdad, que llama pasión.

Este que ves, engaño colorido,
que del arte ostentando los primores,
con falsos silogismos de colores
es cauteloso engaño del sentido;

éste, en quien la lisonja ha pretendido
excusar de los años los horrores,
y venciendo del tiempo los rigores
triunfar de la vejez y del olvido,

es un vano artificio del cuidado,
es una flor al viento delicada,
es un resguardo inútil para el hado:

es una necia diligencia errada,
es un afán caduco, y, bien mirado,
es cadáver, es polvo, es sombra, es nada.

Soneto 146

Quéjase de la suerte: insinúa su aversión a los vicios, y justifica su diverti-
miento a las Musas.

En perseguirme, Mundo, ¿qué interesas?
En qué te ofendo, cuando sólo intento
poner bellezas en mi entendimiento
y no mi entendimiento en las bellezas?

Yo no estimo tesoros ni riquezas;
y así, siempre me causa más contento
poner riquezas en mi pensamiento
que no mi pensamiento en las riquezas.

Y no estimo hermosura que, vencida,
es despojo civil de las edades,
ni riqueza me agrada fementida,

teniendo por mejor, en mis verdades,
consumir vanidades de la vida
que consumir la vida en vanidades.

Notas

1. El tradicional grito triunfal de "Vítor" que Sor Juana emplea aquí se usaba cuando un estudiante aprobaba sus exámenes doctorales, o cuando un profesor ganaba una serie de exámenes muy rigurosos y competitivos, *las oposiciones*, para ocupar una cátedra.

2. En un ciclo de tres sonetos, de los cuales he escogido el segundo y el tercero, Sor Juana trabaja con el tema de las "encontradas correspondencias," o sea las antítesis triangulares amorosas. Esta era una convención popular en la poesía cortesana de la época.

3. Sor Juana no redactó estos breves resúmenes al principio de sus versos; los puso algún editor.

4. Alguién debe de haber aludido al nacimiento ilegítimo de Sor Juana, para que ella respondiera con tal poema. En su época se les echaba la culpa de la bastardía a los hijos, lo cual a ella le parece ilógico e injusto. ¿Cómo se puede culpar a la criatura de la forma en que fue concebida? Son los padres los responsables de sus hijos. Por eso, razona Sor Juana, la única manera por la cual le pueden echar la culpa a ella por su estado social es ser ella la progenitora de su propio padre (que sea él el hijo de ella).

5. Sor Juana se considera "esclava" de amor y de gratitud de la Virreina.

6. Este soneto funcionaba como prefacio a la *Inundación castálida*, el primer libro impreso de Sor Juana, gracias a los esfuerzos y la influencia de la condesa.

7. Sor Juana aquí hace referencia al destino de Faetón, hijo de Apolo. El rey sol le había prometido a su hijo cumplir cualquier deseo suyo, y Faetón eligió conducir el carro de su padre, que llevaba el ardiente disco solar a través del cielo. Apolo le advirtió a su hijo que el joven carecía de fuerza para controlar a los caballos que tiraban del carro, pero Faetón no le hizo caso. Efectivamente, poco después de comenzar a regir el carro, perdió el control, y el sol empezó a girar tan violentamente por el cielo que amenazaba destruir la tierra y el Monte Olimpo, hogar de los dioses. Para evitar el desastre, Júpiter mató al conductor con un rayo, y el joven se precipitó al mar y a la muerte. Sor Juana aludía a Faetonte con mucha frecuencia en sus escritos, destacando su atrevimiento y su voluntad de arriesgarlo todo; es obvio que ella se identificaba con este mismo deseo.

8. Los críticos, basándose en la sinopsis del editor, siempre han interpretado este poema como si Sor Juana estuviera hablando de un retrato de sí misma, pero una cuidadosa lectura del soneto no nos indica tal cosa.

Religious Poems

361

Two separate lyrics to sing on the solemn occasion of the birth of Christ.

SONG I

Refrain
How can this be, my God,
That I believe in You,
And though I believe what I see
see not all I believe?

Verses
If Faith and sight are
so opposite, why must sight
be taken on faith, and not
Faith on sight?

I see You as Child,
and must believe that You are such,
yet I also know You are Great,[1]
though this my eyes cannot see.

Things are easier for me
When You are present in the Eucharist,
for then I know I must believe
the opposite of what I see.

But here, what do You wish me to do?
That my simplicity may believe
what I see and do not see,
that which is and yet is not.

You seem a Man, and You are,
My Lord, that which You seem.
But that You are God is not obvious,
Yet I know You are God as well.

In any case, sense here
cannot be fooled, for what there is
is Infinitely more
than that which is possible to see.

219

Composed for the feast of the Assumption of the Virgin 1676.

VILLANCICO III

The unsurpassed Doctor
of divine Doctrine,
from whom all the Angels
learn wisdom,

for as she is the one who best
shares in God's intelligence,
she rises to lecture
from the highest Chair[2] of Theology.

It is right to praise her
as First [in her class] in knowledge,
she who has won
first place among all creatures.

No one studied *Charity*
with greater effort than she,
while she mastered the course on *Grace*
even before her birth.

The assignment on the *Incarnation*
she could study in her own person,

in the matter of the *Trinity*
even greater acclaim was hers.

The sovereign Students [3]
whose business is literature
research the secrets
of Divine Knowledge,

along with the pure Spirits
who dwell in the eternal Throne of Heaven
(and the subtle Minds
who call themselves God's Knowledge),

all these together cast their vote for her,
and with loving affection
celebrate her victory
and solemnize her triumph.

Refrain
And with happy voices of festive acclaim
the highest spheres with joy do swell,
in the confused uproar one hears but this:
"Vítor, vítor, vítor, vítor, Mary,
in spite of Hell and its envy!
Vítor, vítor, vítor, vítor, Mary!"[4]

Courtly Poems

Sonnet 167

She continues the same topic [from Sonnet 166]⁵ and expresses it with even
livelier elegance.⁶

> Feliciano adores me, and I loathe him;
> Lisardo loathes me, and I adore him;
> I weep for him who ungratefully shuns me,
> and shun him who tenderly weeps for me.
>
> To him who most debases me, I offer my soul;
> he who offers me [sacrificial] victims, I debase;
> I scorn him who enriches my good name,
> and enrich him who shows me scorn.
>
> If, by my offense, I rebuke the one,
> the other, offended, rebukes me;
> and either way I come to suffer,
>
> for both torment my judgment:
> the one, by pleading for what I do not have;
> and the other, by not having that for which I plead.

Sonnet 168

She continues the same theme and determines that reason must prevail over
desire.

> He who ungratefully leaves me, I lovingly long for;
> he who lovingly pursues me, I ungratefully leave;
> steadfastly I adore him who abuses my love;
> abusing him who steadfastly seeks my love.

He, to whom I would speak of love, I find diamond-obdurate,
obdurate as diamond am I with him who speaks of love;
he who slays me, I would see triumphant,
yet would I kill the one who longs to see me triumph.

If I please the latter, my desire suffers;
if I beg the former, I vex my honor:
both ways lead to my unhappiness.

But I, as the better option, choose
to be the constrained object of him I do not love,
than for him who does not love me, degraded plunder.

*Sor Juana Inés
de la Cruz*

99

Satiric Poems

Epigram 95[7]

Where eyewash is administered to an arrogant man who needs it.

As I see it, not to be born of an honorable father,
Might indeed be judged a flaw,
If, instead of receiving my life from him,
[My father] had received his life from me.

Far more charitable was your mother
with you, the successor of many:
So that among infinite fathers
You might choose the sire you liked.

Poems to the Vicereine (the Countess of Paredes)

ENDECHAS REALES

She expresses her loving respect: she explains the sense in which she calls the Vicereine Marchioness of la Laguna her own.

My divine Lysi:
forgive me if I dare
to call you thus, when as yet
I do not deserve to be called yours.

It is not too bold, I think,
to call you thus
for you have thunderbolts to spare,
with which to blast any boldness of mine.

It is an error of the tongue,
when what it calls the lord's realm
appears instead to be
the property of the servant.

My King, says the vassal;
my prison, says the prisoner,
and the humblest of slaves,[8] with no insult intended,
calls the master his as well.

And so, when I call you
my own, I do not claim
that others should judge you mine;
For I only wish to be yours.

I saw you—but enough:
when one shouts "Fire,"
it is enough to point out the cause,
without adding blame to the effect.

Seeing you there so high,
does not affect my daring;
there is no Deity who is safe
from thought's proud flight.

Though others may be more worthy,
when one measures distance from Heaven,
the humblest valley is just as far
as the proudest mountain of all.

And so, I confess
to the crime of adoring you;
should you desire to punish me
that same punishment would be glory.

Sonnet 195[9]

To Her Excellency the Countess of Paredes, Marchioness of la Laguna, on sending her these papers which Her Excellency requested of her and which Sor Juana was able to collect from many hands, where they were no less scattered than hidden, like treasure, along with others which for lack of time she could neither find nor copy over.

The child the slave woman has conceived,
the Law says belongs
to the rightful master [whom] the slave mother
—from whom the child is born—obeys.

The lush harvest the grateful earth
obediently returns to its master,
should by rights be his, for if the earth bears fruit,
[the earth] owes it to the care it has received.

So then, divine Lysi, these scribbles,
which are my soul's children, births of my heart,
are rightfully restored to you;

no matter their imperfections,
by right they belong only to you,
the concepts of a soul which is utterly yours.

Sor Juana Inés
de la Cruz

103

My Mistress and My Lady, your servant kisses
Your Excellency's feet.
Juana Inés de la Cruz.

Philosophical Poems

Sonnet 149

She ponders the choice of a state that lasts until death.

> If one considered the dangers of the sea,
> no one would embark; if first one clearly saw
> one's peril, no one would dare
> to bravely provoke the raging bull.
>
> If the prudent rider
> would ponder the wild steed's fury
> no guiding hand would ever be found
> to check his headlong frenzy in the race.
>
> But were there one of such daring
> that, mindless of the danger, he would
> with fearless hand aspire
>
> to steer the sun-bathed chariot of Apollo himself:[10]
> he would risk all, and would not deign
> to accept a state that bound him all his days.

Sonnet 145

She attempts to prove false the praise which truth inscribed on a portrait of the poetess,[11] which she terms enthusiasm.

> This, which you see, a colored deception,
> displaying art's exquisite beauties
> with false syllogisms of color,
> is a guileful deception of sense;

this, in which flattery has attempted
to exonerate the years' ravaged traces,
and, overcoming time's harsh sentence,
to triumph over old age and oblivion,

is a vain artifice of care,
is a delicate flower exposed to the wind,
is a useless defense against fate:

is a foolish, misguided effort,
is a fruitless desire, and, truly seen,
is corpse, dust, shadow, naught.

Sonnet 146

*She bemoans her fate; she suggests her aversion to vices and justifies her
diversion with the Muses.*

In persecuting me, World, what is your intention?
How do I offend you, when all I desire
is to place beauty in my mind
instead of focusing my mind on worldly beauty?

I esteem neither treasures nor riches,
and thus, am always more content
to put riches into my thoughts
than to waste my thoughts on riches.

I esteem not that beauty which, vanquished,
is the ravaged prey of passing years,
nor do false riches please me;

for I prize more to consume
the vanities of life with my truths
than to have my life consumed by vanity.

Notes

1. Sor Juana here is playing with the double meaning of *grande* in Spanish, where it can mean both "great" and "adult."

2. In the Middle Ages professors read from a high chair and podium (*cátedra*) on a level above the student body. "Chair" and "professorship" later became synonymous terms.

3. The Students, Spirits, and Minds to which Sor Juana refers all dwell in Heaven.

4. The Spanish cheer "Vítor" that Sor Juana uses here was, and is today, the traditional shout of triumph when a student passed his doctoral examinations, or a professor attained a coveted professorship after winning a series of *oposiciones* (highly competitive academic examinations).

5. In a cycle of three sonnets, of which I have selected the second and third, Sor Juana addresses the subject of "encontradas correspondencias" or triangular antitheses on the subject of love. This was a popular convention in the courtly love poetry of the time.

6. Sor Juana did not write these brief synopses that precede her poems; they were added by an editor.

7. Someone must have alluded to Sor Juana's illegitimate birth in order for her to write such a response. In her time children were blamed for the stain of illegitimacy, which to her seems illogical and unjust. How can the child help the way he or she is conceived? It is the parents who are responsible for their children. Therefore, Sor Juana reasons, the only way she could be blamed for her social status is for her to have given birth to her own father.

8. Sor Juana considers herself the Vicereine's "slave," chained by feelings of love and gratitude.

9. This sonnet functioned as a preface to the *Inundación castálida* [Castalian Flood], Sor Juana's first published work, thanks to the effort and influence of the countess.

10. Sor Juana here refers to the fate of Apollo's son Phaeton; the Sun God had promised to fulfill any wish of his, and Phaeton chose to drive his father's chariot, which pulled the sun's burning disk across the sky. Apollo warned his son that he lacked the strength to control the horses that drew the chariot, but Phaeton would not listen. Soon after he began to drive the chariot he indeed lost control, and the sun careened wildly across the sky, threatening to burn the earth and Mount Olympus, the

home of the gods. Jupiter killed Phaeton with a thunderbolt to prevent this from happening, and the young man fell headlong into the sea to his death. In her writing Sor Juana frequently alluded to Phaeton's daring and willingness to risk all; it is obvious that she identified with this desire.

11. Although critics have always read this poem as though Sor Juana were speaking to a portrait of herself, basing themselves on the editor's synopsis, a careful reading of the sonnet itself shows no such reference.

Madre Francisca Josefa de Castillo

*Madre Francisca Josefa de Castillo, courtesy
of Biblioteca Luis Angel Arango, Bogotá.*

*F*rancisca Josefa de la Concepción de Castillo y Guevara was born in Tunja, Colombia—known as New Granada during the colonial era—in 1671, to a family that wielded a great deal of influence in the small, provincial city. Her father was from Spain, from the province of Toledo, and her mother was a criolla. Francisca learned to read from her mother, and although she never had any formal education, the fact that she was literate at all made her different from many of her peers. Religious life attracted her from a very early age; she shared with Sor Juana a distinct aversion to marriage, but her family was totally opposed to her desire to enter a convent. They offered her space in their house to use for her devotions and agreed to let her wear a religious habit (*Obras* 1: 15–17), but it was not enough: Francisca ran away from home to join the Real Convento Franciscano de Santa Clara. This was the first religious community for women established in New Granada (1572), and the founders were directly related to Francisca.

In spite of her deep commitment to the religious life, Francisca was never happy in her community. Her autobiography chronicles many conflicts with her sister nuns, some of whom were verbally and others even physically abusive. There were several reasons for this. As upper-class women had only two life choices, marriage or the veil, convents housed many women who had little or no religious vocation (McKnight, "Voz" 86; Mújica 7), who spent their time gossiping about each other, and who may well have resented someone as devout, socially powerful, and literate as Francisca. Her own personality may also have put them off, so that when she claimed to have experienced mystical unions with God, many of the nuns reacted not with joy but with disbelief and envy.[1] The community also resented the many members of her family who joined the order, including her widowed mother and sister. In Madre Castillo's writings the Tunja convent often comes across more as a snake pit than a house of God. In spite of these frictions, however, she was elected abbess on three different occasions, though rumor had it that she had been somewhat heavy-handed in wielding her influence to get elected. During her terms she appears to have run the convent very efficiently, once even saving it from bankruptcy.

Madre Castillo is known for two very different works: the *Afectos espirituales,* devotional meditations on a variety of themes, and *Su Vida,* the spiritual autobiography that covers her life from about 1713 to 1723. Her confessors were aware of her piety and encouraged her to write down her thoughts and mystical experiences. She began to write the *Afectos* very soon after entering the convent in 1689 (she professed in 1694) and continued to work on them for most of her life. These meditations are considered of better literary quality than her autobiography: lyrical, positive, the product of an assured authorial voice that derived deep spiritual satisfaction from this activity. For the modern reader, however, it is her autobiography that is of greater interest.

Although she wrote some of the *Afectos* and the *Vida* more or less at the same time, the *Vida* is so different that, as Elisa Mújica says, "it seems that they could not have come from the same pen" (30). One explanation may be that the time covered by the *Vida* was a particularly difficult one for the nun (McKnight, "Sister Acts" 91). Another is that whereas she *wanted* to write the *Afectos,* she composed her autobiography under duress. As happened with many nuns who were renowned for their piety, Madre Castillo's confessors compelled her to relate her life story, and her trepidation at doing this is palpable in the text. It is no wonder that it should be so (many other nuns made to write their autobiographies expressed similar feelings): having been trained to subject, even annihilate all personal will and volition in the service of God, a nun who was ordered to write her life, the most self-affirming form of writing there is, would often react with confusion, resistance, and fear. While Madre Castillo composed the *Afectos* for the greater glory of God, recounting the particulars of her own life must have seemed out of place and even sinful to her. Thus there is a marked difference in authorial voice: in the *Afectos* she is serving as a conduit for *God's* voice, not as principal author of the text, as was the case in her autobiography. Hence she is surer of herself, and less nervous about narrative responsibility.

The *Vida* is not particularly pleasant reading, but it offers fascinating insights into the life of an exceptionally devout nun and into the nature of her mystical experiences as a Bride of Christ. It records a life of ascetic discipline, morbid mortification of her own body, celestial visions and erotic nightmares, recurrent ill health, and the ongoing enmity of her community. Although Madre Castillo casts herself into the role of perpetual sinner and victim, she also insists that all her suffering is for the sake of her beloved Bridegroom. What is so interesting in the *Vida* is the author's strategy of subjectivity, which is less obvious than it seems. Madre Castillo presents herself in a dual role: she may be a vile sinner, yet she is also the chosen Bride of Christ (McKnight, "Voz" 80). Her narrative strategy is elusive and paradoxical: her very humility is simultaneously self-affirming.

The *Afectos* should also be read with care. After the ecclesiastical reforms of the sixteenth-century Council of Trent, nuns were forbidden to read the Bible in the vernacular or to teach religious matters. They had always been forbidden to preach. Madre Castillo had somehow learned Latin, and was familiar with the Bible in this language. Though the *Afectos* appear to fall squarely within the mainstream of what a nun was permitted to write, McKnight shows that in many of these meditations Madre Castillo was actively paraphrasing and interpreting Scripture, as well as adopting an instructional tone while purportedly only preaching to her own soul ("Nexos" 249). Her humility thus was not quite what it appeared to be. Stacey Schlau noted a similar strategy in the nun's writing: while insisting on her total obedience to Catholic tradition and dogma, the Madre is nevertheless affirming her own uniqueness (166). Madre Castillo's strategies in the formation of her subjective voice are thus much more complex and transgressive than first meets the eye.

The other aspect of her narrative self we must not forget is that in spite of her affinity for spiritual withdrawal, Madre Castillo as abbess had to deal with the outside world on a daily and direct basis. This was especially true in the administration of the convent's finances and property, which led to frequent lawsuits (McKnight, "Voz" 75–76).

She herself came under fire from her community when she inherited her late sister's extremely valuable jewelry. Just like Sor Juana with her "nest egg," Madre Castillo did not donate these assets directly to her convent: she gave most of the inheritance to fashion a beautiful and costly *custodia* (monstrance), a ceremonial piece of altar plate used to exhibit the consecrated Host. This monstrance, known as "La Custodia de los Andes," is made of eight pounds of gold, emeralds, amethysts, topazes, diamonds, and the like; considered a major national treasure, it now reposes in the vaults of Colombia's Banco de la República (Mújica 18).[2] Just as in her writing, Madre Castillo has engaged in a double-edged act: she neatly bypassed her sister nuns while exalting her own name as pious donor.

The manuscripts of both the *Afectos* and *Su Vida* are in the Luis Angel Arango Library in Bogotá. There is also a third manuscript known as "El cuaderno de Enciso" (The Enciso Notebook), an accounting ledger given to Madre Castillo by her brother-in-law, José Enciso; as paper was always very scarce, she used the blank pages to rework some of the "Afectos," or to copy works of other authors she admired. Among these was Sor Juana, several of whose verses Madre Castillo copied without recording her source; for a while these poems were attributed to the Colombian nun until the mistake was rectified. It is fortunate that this mix-up occurred, as it established a direct link between the two most famous nuns of Spanish America.

After the Madre died in 1742, the Clarissan nuns gave her writings to the Castillo family. *Su Vida,* curiously enough, was first published in Philadelphia in 1817 by one of her descendants because Colombia was undergoing a period of political instability that made publishing there difficult (Mújica 21–22). The *Afectos* were published in 1843.

There is no doubt that in temperament and in religious vocation the Madre Castillo is very different from Sor Juana, but both left their mark on the colonial literature of their respective countries. They are but the tip of the iceberg: many more life stories of religious women lie in the archives of libraries and convents, waiting for the critical attention that has been denied them for so many centuries.[3]

Notes

1. As Electa Arenal and Stacey Schlau show, hers was not the only text to record such reactions by other nuns, many of whom were openly hostile to claims of mystic experiences.

2. Sor María del Niño Jesús relates that other nuns contributed what they could to the monstrance, but Madre Castillo gave the lion's share (389).

3. Arenal and Schlau's *Untold Sisters* is an invaluable resource in this area. Kathleen Myers has also recently published the writings of a Mexican nun who was Sor Juana's contemporary: *Word from New Spain: The Spiritual Autobiography of Madre María de San José (1656–1719)* (Liverpool: Liverpool University Press, 1993). See also Kathryn McKnight, *The Mystic of Tunja: The Writings of Madre Castillo, 1671–1742* (Amherst, MA: U of Massachusetts Press, 1997).

Su Vida

Padre mío: Hoy día de la Natividad de Nuestra Señora, empiezo en su nombre a hacer lo que vuestra paternidad me manda y a pensar y considerar delante del Señor todos los años de mi vida en amargura de mi alma, pues todos los hallo gastados mal, y así me alegro de hacer memoria de ellos, para confundirme en la divina presencia y pedir a Dios gracia para llorarlos, y acordarme de sus misericordias y beneficios, y uno de ellos he entendido fue el darme padres cristianos y temerosos de Dios, compasivos y recatados; tánto, que a mi padre jamás se le oyó una palabra menos compuesta, ni se le vió acción que no fuera; siempre nos hablaba de Dios, y eran sus palabras tales, que en el largo tiempo de mi vida aún no se me han olvidado; antes, en muchas ocasiones, me han servido de consuelo y aliento, y también de freno. En hablando de Nuestra Señora (de quien era devotísimo) o de la pasión de Nuestro Señor, siempre era con los ojos llenos de lágrimas, y lo mismo cuando daba limosna a los pobres, que se juntaban todos los de la ciudad en casa los viernes, y yo lo vía, porque lo acompañaba a repartir la limosna, y vía la ternura, humildad y devoción con que la repartía, besando primero la que daba a cada pobre; y aun con los animales enfermos tenía mucha piedad, de que pudiera decir cosas muy particulares. Asimismo, mi madre era tan temerosa de Dios, cuanto amiga de los pobres, y enemiga de vanidades, de aliños ni entretenimientos, y de tánta humildad, que habiendo enviudado y estando casi ciega, le dio una criada muchos golpes en una iglesia por que se quitara del lugar donde estaba, lo cual llevó con mucha mansedumbre, y se quitó medio arrastrando; y me lo refería alabando a Dios y bendiciéndolo, porque la había traído de tánta estimación a tiempo en que padeciera algo; de esto pudiera decir mucho, y de los buenos ejemplos que vía en mi niñez; sino que yo como las arañas volvía veneno aun las cosas más saludables.

Padeció mucho mi madre cuando yo hube de nacer al mundo, hasta que llamando a su confesor, que era el padre Diego Solano, de la Compañía de Jesús, para confesarse y morir, que ya no esperaba otra cosa, confesándose y teniéndose del bordón del padre, nací yo—y lo que al decir esto siente mi corazón, sólo lo pudieran decir mis ojos hechos fuentes de lágrimas. Nací, Dios mío, Vos sabéis para qué, y cuánto se ha dilatado mi destierro, cuán amargo lo han hecho mis pasiones y culpas, Nací, ¡ay Dios mío!, y luego aquel santo padre me bautizó y dio una grande cruz, que debía de traer consigo, poniéndome los nombres de mi padre san Francisco y san José; dándome Nuestro Señor desde luégo estos socorros y amparos, y el de los padres de la Compañía de Jesús, que tánto han trabajado para reducirme al camino de la verdad. Quiera Nuestro Señor que éntre por él, antes de salir de la vida mortal.

Nací día del bienaventurado san Bruno, parece quiso Nuestro Señor darme a entender cuánto me convendría el retiro, abstracción y silencio en la vida mortal, y cuán peligroso sería para mí el trato y conversación humana, como lo he experimentado desde los primeros pasos de mi vida, y lo lloro, aunque no como debiera. A los quince o veinte días, decían que estuve tan muerta, que compraron la tela y recados para enterrarme, hasta que un tío mío, sacerdote, que despúes me aconsejó (sólo él, que en los demás hallé mucha contradicción) que entrara monja; éste me mandó, como a quien ya no se esperaba que viviera, aplicar un remedio con que luégo volví y estuve buena. En esto sólo la voluntad de Dios me consuela, pues, ¿a quién no pareciera mejor que hubiera muerto luégo quien había de ser como yo he sido?

Siendo aún tan pequeña, que apenas me acuerdo, me sucedió que uno de los niños que iban con sus madres a visita (como suele acaecer, según después he visto), me dijo había de casarse conmigo, y yo sin saber qué era aquello, a lo que ahora me puedo acordar, le respondí que sí; y luégo me entró en el corazón un tormento tal, que no me dejaba tener gusto ni consuelo; parecíame que había hecho un gran mal; y como con nadie comunicaba el tormento de mi corazón, me duró hasta que ya tendría siete años; y en una ocasión hallándome sola en un cuarto donde habían pesado trigo, y quedado el lazo pendiente, me apretó tánto aquella pena, y debía de ayudar el enemigo, porque luégo me propuso fuertemente que me ahorcara, pues sólo este era remedio; mas el santo ángel de mi guarda debió de favorecerme, porque a lo que me puedo acordar, llamando a Nuestra Señora, a quien yo tenía por madre y llamaba en mis aprietos y necesidades, me salí de la pieza, asustada y temerosa; y así me libró Nuestro Señor de aquel peligro, cuando no me parece que tendría siete años. Hasta esta edad, y algún tiempo adelante, todo mi recreo y consuelo era hacer altares y buscar retiros; tenía muchas imágenes de Nuestro Señor y de Nuestra Señora, y en componerlas me pasaba sola y retirada. . . .

Pues el temor que digo despertaba Nuestro Señor en mí, algunas noches en sueños vía cosas espantosas. En una ocasión me pareció andar sobre un entresuelo hecho de ladrillos, puestos punta con punta, como en el aire, y con gran peligro, y mirando abajo vía un río de fuego, negro y horrible, y que entre él andaban tántas serpientes, sapos y culebras, como caras y brazos de hombres que se vían sumidos en aquel pozo o río; yo desperté con gran llanto, y por la mañana vi que en las extremidades de los dedos y las uñas tenía señales de fuego: aunque yo esto no pude saber cómo sería. Otras veces, me hallaba en un valle tan dilatado, tan profundo, de una oscuridad tan penosa, cual no se sabe decir, ni ponderar, y al cabo de él estaba un pozo horrible de fuego negro y espeso; a la orilla andaban los espíritus malos haciendo y dando varios modos de tormentos a diferentes hombres, conforme a sus vicios. Con estas cosas y otras me avisaba Dios misericordioso, para que no le ofendiera, del castigo y pena de los malos; mas nada de esto bastó para que yo no cometiera muchas culpas, aun en aquella edad.

Criábame muy enferma, y esto, y el grande amor que mis padres me tenían, hacía que me miraran con mucho regalo y compasión, y aunque me habían puesto el hábito de santa Rosa de Lima,[1] que se lo prometieron a la santa porque me diera salud Nuestro Señor, mi madre se esmeraba en ponerme joyas y aderezos, y yo era querida de toda la casa, y gente que asistía a mis padres. Con todo eso, jamás tuve contento, ni me consolaba cosa ninguna de la vida, ni los entretenimientos de muñecas y juegos que usan en aquella edad; antes me parecía cosa tan sin gusto, que no quería entender en ello. Algunas veces hacía procesiones de imágenes o remedaba las profesiones y hábitos de las monjas, no porque tuviera inclinación a tomar ese estado; pues sólo me inclinaba a vivir como los ermitaños en los desiertos y cuevas del campo.

[Los trozos que siguen se refieren a su vida después de ser monja.]

En este tiempo vino a confesarme el padre Francisco de Herrera, a quien vuestra paternidad lo dejó encomendado, y yo procuré darme del todo al trato interior con Nuestro Señor, de quien recibía tánta luz; y me parece tenía tan embebida en sí mi alma, como si no viviera en esta vida. El padre me trataba con severidad, y hacía que trabajara de manos lo más del día, y si alguna vez le pedía licencia para gastar el medio día en oración, me la daba, con condición que a la tarde doblara el trabajo. Mandóme muchas veces que escribiera y le mostrara los sentimientos que Nuestro Señor me daba; fue grande mi pena y vergüenza en eso; mas al fin lo hice. . . .

Pocas noches podía irme a acostar, detenida de aquella fuerza de mi alma; parecíame que tenía en lo íntimo de mi corazón una brasa viva, que me enseñaba sin palabras, y encendía en un fuego más dulce que la vida. . . .

Así pasé casi dos años, pareciéndome todas las cosas de esta vida un sueño, y cosa de risa. Un día, estando recogida con Nuestro Señor, me parecía ver a mí misma con una vestidura encarnada que cogía del cuello a los pies, y que los cabellos tenía tan dilatados que llegaban hasta el suelo; dos espíritus malos andaban por allí en forma humana, echando y queriendo trabar con las puntas de aquellos cabellos, para enredarlos; yo me quedé confusa, sin saber qué sería aquello. De ahí a unos días le dijeron al padre algunas cosas de mí, que le causaron un grande enojo: decíame cosas muy sensibles, y me dejaba en el confesionario y se iba sin oírme, hasta que paró en dejarme de confesar, y yo, como quien no tiene fundamento en cosa buena, no hacía sino llorar y desconsolarme de muerte, y darme por engañada, pues mi confesor así me echaba de sí, y me daba por errada; bien veo ahora que el camino hubiera sido rogarle con humildad me enseñara y ayudara a la enmienda de aquellas faltas, y entrar por el camino que me mostrara. . . .

[La Madre Castillo luego obedece al P. de Herrera y redacta algunos de sus pensamientos sobre la verdadera devoción a Dios.]

Este papel como va aquí, vio mi confesor, el padre Francisco, cuando había pasado su enojo; y me respondió: que, aunque más lo miraba, no hallaba en él las señales que suele dejar la serpiente en las cosas por donde anda; que antes, a todo su entender, era Dios; que sólo lo que me aconsejaba era que, aunque más el confesor me azotara e hiriera, no huyera de él, etc.; y así, con la gracia de Dios, lo he procurado hacer en lo que después he vivido, pasando por esto grandes trabajos. . . .

Y así, un día, como yo rehusara mucho escribir lo que el padre Francisco me mandaba, me parecía que vía escribirse en el corazón de Nuestro Señor con su misma sangre, aquellos sentimientos que El mismo daba a mi alma, y los afectos que contenían aquellos papeles; aunque por entonces yo no entendí lo que esto significaba. . . .

Muchas veces, en pasando, aunque fuera de prisa, por donde está el Santísimo Sacramento, sentía, en lo más escondido de mi alma, estas su[a]vísimas palabras, como que salían de Su Divina Majestad: *¿Quis nos separabit?* (Rom. 8.35). Eran estas palabras, como si dijera: *"ninguno será poderoso a apartarnos."* Eran tan dulces, tan tiernas y tan suaves, que no sé yo quién, si no es mi corazón de tierra, ingrato y vil, pudiera volver a tener gusto en cosa que no fuera Dios; ni sé por qué gasto el tiempo corto de la vida en otra cosa que en llorar mis culpas e ingratitudes. Asimismo, me advirtió que El solo debía ser mi consuelo; porque un día, como hubiera venido mi confesor, y se fuera sin consolarme, yo quedé con pena y tristeza por esto, y luégo entendí estas palabras: *Cur fles? et quare non comedis? et quam ob rem affligitur cor tuum? Numquid non ego melior tibi sum quam decem filii?* (I Sam. 1.8). Fueron estas palabras tan sentidas en mi alma, que me hicieron casi salir de mí con la alegría y amor que habían infundido en ella. No entendí, yo, que dejara de buscar el asilo y la enseñanza en el confesor, sino que el consuelo lo buscara en Dios.

[La Madre Castillo sueña con conversaciones iniciadas por el diablo.]

También había tomado Nuestro Señor otro medio para sacarme de aquellas conversaciones, y éste fue, en medio de ellas ver yo a vuestra paternidad junto a mí, no sé si dormida o despierta, reprendiéndome con severidad y caridad, y acordándome de lo que debía a Dios; con esto tomé más horror a aquellas cosas, aunque yo se lo tenía grande, y tánto, que para escribirle a vuestra paternidad (que ya había vuelto a Santa Fe) el desconsuelo en que me hallaba; me acuerdo que me puse a llorar sobre el tintero, para mojarlo con las lágrimas que lloraba, porque estaba seco, y temía yo tánto el abrir la celda, ni pedir nada, para no dar lugar a que entraran, que más quise mojarlo con mis lágrimas y escribir con ellas; cosa que podía hacer con facilidad, por lo mucho que lloraba.

Después que estuvo acá [mi confesor Juan Martínez], estaba yo un día en mi retiro, considerando en el paso de los azotes que dieron a Nuestro Señor, y pareciéndome caía al desatarlo de la columna, sentía lo mismo que la vez pasada, aquella ansia y deseo de ayudarlo a levantar, pero ahora, al contrario de lo que me sucedió la otra vez, sentía, al llegar mi alma a El, que se desaparecía su cuerpo, porque se hacía como espiritualizado, o yo no sé cómo me dé a entender: parece que se desaparecía de los ojos o conocimiento del alma, y la hacía quedar con gran pena. Esto me parece fue prevenirme para el trabajo, y trabajos que me vinieran. También me sucedió que habiendo entrado en ejercicios con la novicia, a quien yo deseaba encaminar lo mejor que pudiera, estando una tarde en oración, vi pasar el enemigo en hábito de religioso por la puerta de la celda, y que mirando, con unos ojos que daban horror, hacia donde estábamos, se entró en la celda de otra religiosa que estaba junto a la mía; yo no entendí qué sería aquello, mas quedé llena de pavor y tristeza.

Pues por aquel tiempo yo vía mi alma tan mudada, y tan renovados en ella los buenos deseos que en otro tiempo Nuestro Señor me había dado, que yo misma no me conocía, ni sabía con qué así me había encendido Nuestro Señor el alma. Estaba lo más del día retirada, previniendo mi confesión general de aquel año, cuando una noche, a las oraciones, que no se habían hecho maitines,[2] viene a la celda aquella religiosa en cuya celda vi entrar al enemigo, tan llena de furor, y dando gritos contra mí, que yo me quedé pasmada; hízome muchas amenazas, diciendo que no era la novicia mi criada, que ahora vería lo que hacía la madre abadesa. Dio tántas voces, y se levantó tal murmullo de criadas y gritos, que yo me hallé cortada, y no tuve más alivio que meterme en una tribuna, mas desde allí oía tales voces en el coro, tal algazara y cosas que se decían de mí, que estaba medio muerta de oírlas, y no saber en qué pararía aquel furor y gritos; cuando fueron a buscarme la madre vicaria, la religiosa que he dicho, y un tropel de criadas, con linternas y luces. Las cosas que allí me dijeron fueron sin modo, y la cólera con que iban. . . . Las cosas que me levantaron no son para dichas, yo no hallaba dónde acogerme, porque la celda había quedado llena sólo de pavor, y con el susto no me podía tener ya en pie. Mis criadas habían levantádose también contra mí, con que hube de acogerme a las puertas de una religiosa a quien le habían dicho cosas que la pudieran enojar mucho contra mí; mas viéndome en tan miserable estado, se movió a compasión, y fue la única que en toda la casa la tuvo de mí en mis trabajos. Luégo caí enferma de una enfermedad tal, que el sudor que sudaba me dejaba las manos como cocidas en agua hirviendo. La boca se me volvía a un lado, y me daban unos desmayos tan profundos que duraban tres y cuatro horas largas. En estos desmayos tiraba a ahogarme una criada que había allí, amiga de aquellas religiosas que digo, porque me tapaba la boca y las narices con toda fuerza; y si su ama, que era en cuya celda yo estaba no la advirtiera, según me decía después, no sé qué hubiera sido. Yo pienso que no tiraría a ahogarme, sino sólo a mortificarme. . . .

. . . y cuando se lo avisaban a la madre abadesa, que había tántas horas que [yo] estaba sin sentido, respondía: "darle unos cordeles bien fuertes, que la hagan reventar." Otras veces decía: "ya he estado amolando muy bien un cuchillo para enviárselo que se lo meta, y le enviaré soga para que se ahorque." Yo, en volviendo en mí de los desmayos, lloraba amargamente, y les preguntaba: "Señoras mías, madres mías, ¿qué motivo, qué causa les he dado?". . .

Las veces que yo salía al confesonario, o a esconderme en una parte

muy sola y retirada de la casa, las criadas que me topaban, o me atro-
pellaban, y otras me ponían nombres muy afrentosos y ridículos, di-
ciéndomelos con gritos y repetidas veces a mí misma. La madre
abadesa prometía cada día en comunidad, que me había de poner en
un cepo, y brearme a azotes, que era una loca y que ella me haría
cuerda . . . mas no dejaba por esto de valerme mucho de la Virgen Santísima, . . . y poniéndome en su presencia como la más enferma en lo
espiritual, como la más pobre de virtudes, como la más ciega, baldada
y llagada, llena de enfermedades incurables, sentía una grande consolación, esperando por mano de la Madre de las misericordias el remedio de mi alma, como por ella lo han recibido tántos. Aunque en esta
ocasión, que voy contando a vuestra paternidad, estaba yo tan llena
de turbación, confusión y congoja, que no me entendía.

[Después de esta temporada difícil, la Madre Castillo siente mayor
comprensión.]

Otras muchas cosas entendí por entonces, que algunas escribí, por
mandármelo mi confesor.

Andaba mi alma como una ligera pluma, que es llevada del viento
suave; así me parecía que yo no tenía parte en mí, para nada, sino que
andaba como sin alma, que mi alma se había entrado en su Dios, y
que era gobernada por otro impulso, suave, dulce, amoroso y eficaz.
Todo lo que vía y oía, era Dios, era sumo bien; y era un bien sobre
todo sentido y conocimiento. No me estorbaba nada exterior; antes
todo era como soplos que hacían arder aquella llama, y más ardía, con
todo lo que era desprecio y humillación mía.

Mi confesor me mortificaba, cuanto alcanzaba su industria, y en
esto se la daba Nuestro Señor muy grande, y tal, que a veces me decía:
que había estado vacilando sobre qué modo hallaría de mortificarme;
y que ya no se le ofrecía ninguno. Tratábame mal, cuanto se podía, de
palabra, y me respondía ásperamente. A veces, y lo más ordinario, se
enojaba tánto, y tan de veras, reprendiéndome sobre cosas que a mí
me parecían buenas, que me quedaba temblando y temiendo, y después me decía que las prosiguiera, que bien iba. Algunas veces me
echaba del confesionario, con tal enojo y desprecio, que parecía le

había dado alguna grave causa; en particular en algunas ocasiones me escribió: "Que ya había echado de ver que yo y todas mis cosas, sólo para quemadas eran buenas y que estaba determinado a huir de mí, porque mi camino era perdición"; y otras cosas muy duras, a que parece concurría Nuestro Señor, porque me dejaba en una escuridad y confusión, que me parecía era así verdad que el padre lo decía de veras, y lloraba amargamente, sin más consuelo que la determinación que en mí hallaba, de hacer todo aquello que me dijera, era voluntad de Dios, fuera lo que fuera; mas, para hallar quién me guiara en esto, se me cerraba el camino, porque el padre me decía: no volvería más y que mis culpas lo desterraban. Pero luégo venía y me volvía a reñir y reprender, porque no había sabido llevar bien aquella mortificación y cruz. Con todo esto y otras muchas cosas, yo vía y conocía el cuidado que tenía de mi alma y el gran deseo de mi aprovechamiento; y así, aquel rigor era lo que más me animaba, porque me había puesto en sus manos con deseo de quitar de mí todo lo que fuera desagradable a los ojos de Dios. Dióme licencia muy larga para todo cuanto pudiera de mortificación y penitencia, y mientras más hacía, con más salud me hallaba; porque así lo debía de querer Dios, por entonces. . . .

Y así he llegado a los cuarenta y cuatro años de vivir en este mundo; y así le pido, padre mío, que pues con el favor de Nuestro Señor yo he vencido tánto y pasado tántas tribulaciones en escribir esto, y darle cuenta de toda mi vida, la mire bien, y los pasos que lleva mi alma, para que no se pierda; pues de nuevo la vuelvo a poner en sus manos, que miro en ellas las de Dios, para que, libre de mí misma, pueda llegar a conseguir el fin para que Nuestro Señor nos crió, y lo veamos allá, y lo alabemos; donde espero, por la misericordia de Dios y la intercesión de la Virgen Santísima, ver a vuestra paternidad.

Padecí en este tiempo enfermedades, trabajos y desconsuelos grandes, en lo exterior e interior, y como se fuera llegando la cuaresma, me parecía ver con los ojos del alma, un mar de aguas tan turbias y oscuras, que causaba el verlas una gran congoja, amargura, y aprieto interior. Parecíame que Nuestro Señor Jesucristo andaba en medio de aquel mar, y entendí significar algún grande padecer, que quería enviarme, y quedé con grande temor a esta cuaresma. . . . Junto con esto llevaba muchas pesadumbres y contradicciones, en las cosas más sensibles; padeciendo también la persecución del enemigo malo, no sólo con las tentaciones graves y continuas, sino también con espantos malos y aborrecibles. En llegando la noche, llegándose y cargándose sobre mí, etc., con figuras abominables, y sobre toda ponderación aborrecibles, etc. Teníame yo ya por perdida, y que toda mi vida había sido engañada, y sólo andaba a que me dejaran quemar aquellos papeles, que por obediencia había escrito. Y ahora conozco la astucia del enemigo, pues sólo aquello me acordaba por culpa. . . .

Con estas cosas y otras, que escribí en aquellos papeles, consoló y animó la infinita piedad de Dios, entonces, mis desconsuelos, y me detuvo a que no quemara lo que había escrito, según yo lo había muchas veces propuesto y pedido a vuestra reverencia. Especialmente, un día de Pascua de Espíritu Santo, habiendo comulgado, entendí con mucha claridad y razones que para ello me ofreció Nuestro Señor, que ninguna cosa de las que había escrito era mía, ni del demonio. . . .

Proseguiré, padre mío, obedeciendo por la voluntad de Dios, que es el único fin que yo en esto pueda tener para atropellar mi repugnancia y vergüenza, y las muchas cosas con que se aflige mi corazón en esta obediencia. Y si quisiera decir cuántas se me ofrecen para no proseguir, llenara mucho papel, y lo gastara en balde. . . .

También escribiré aquí algunas razones de consuelo que recibía el alma, no porque yo piense que me hablaba Nuestro Señor como a las almas justas, mas para explicarme, es como si dijera: "Pobrecilla, combatida por la tempestad, sin ninguna consolación, no temas, no morirás. Yo soy el Señor Dios tuyo, mira que yo te adornaré con piedras preciosas. Yo te daré aquella corona y diadema de diamantes, que es mi fiel, piadosa y amorosa Madre. Yo pondré en tu pecho aquella cruz de rubíes, que soy yo, tu esposo, humanado, amantísimo, y ensangrentado. Yo te daré aquella piedra que, siendo blanca, toda es fuego, que te adorne y abrase en el sacramento, y sea para ti un rico tesoro de esperanza y amor. . . .

"Sufre la vida, suspira por la muerte, sujeta siempre a mi voluntad, y encerrada en el fiel y fuerte muro de mi eterno querer. . . .

"¡Ea! alienta tu corazón, pobrecilla, mujer, anégate en el mar de las misericordias mías. Mira que vendrá la aurora, y se acabará la lucha y batalla, y se dará fin a las tinieblas, en entrando la aurora María, fuerte, suave, apacible y misericordiosa; terrible para los espíritus malos como un ejército bien ordenado. ¿No es tu Madre, y Madre de su esposo? ¿Pues, qué temes? ¿No es escogida, como el sol, para alegrar, beneficiar y vivificar, desde el águila real hasta la más pequeña avecilla, desde el león coronado hasta el animalito más pequeño, desde el cedro del Líbano hasta el hisopo y hierba más humilde? Pues, ¡oh gusanito pobre! también gozarás de las beneficencias de esta aurora y sol clarísimo, hermosísimo, y purísimo. Arrójate a sus pies, escóndete en este mar de piedades, bebe de esta fuente purísima, cuando recibas a su Hijo Sacramentado, etc." Con estas razones se alienta y respira mi corazón en la fuerza de los desconsuelos y angustias. . . .

Padre mío: hasta aquí he cumplido mi obediencia, y por el amor a Nuestro Señor le pido me avise si es esto lo que vuestra paternidad me mandó, o he excedido en algo, y si será este camino de mi perdición, como me afligen algunas veces terribles temores, que me parece me atan de pies y manos. Puede ser lo haga el enemigo para que no corresponda con el agradecimiento que debiera, a los beneficios de mi Señor y Dios. Me propone que todo son engaños e ilusiones mías; y estas noches que estaba escribiendo, me ha afligido el enemigo, poniéndose tres noches arreo: una, atajándome el oratorio, y riéndose mucho; otra, diciéndome hartos oprobios, y entre ellos, que era una habladora, que no callaba nada; otra, haciendo unas acciones de extraordinario desprecio y asco, y aunque de esto no hago caso, por ser en sueños, pero los modos que él tiene de afligirme y atormentarme, sólo Nuestro Señor lo sabe; y sólo El, por intercesión de su Santísima Madre, me puede librar y dar aliento y paciencia para no haber desfallecido. Bendito sea Dios, y alabado.

Notas

1. Santa Rosa de Lima (1586–1617), joven peruana muy devota, canonizada en 1668; es la primera santa americana.

2. Hora de oración al principio del día.

Her Life

My Father: Today, the day of the birth of Our Lady, I shall in her name begin to do what Your Reverence orders and to think and ponder all the years of my life before the Lord with grief in my soul, for I consider them ill spent. Therefore I rejoice to write them down, so that I may be shamed in the divine presence and to ask God's grace to lament them and to remember His mercies and benefits. One of these I understand was to give me Christian and God-fearing parents, compassionate and modest, to such a degree that my father never uttered a word nor took an action which was not circumspect. He always spoke to us of God, and his words were such that in my whole long life I have never forgotten them; more than that, on many occasions they have given me consolation and strength, and restraint as well. In speaking of Our Lady (to whom he was extraordinarily devoted) or of Our Lord's Passion, his eyes always filled with tears, just as they did when he gave alms to the city's poor, who would gather at our house on Fridays. I would watch him, for I used to accompany him to distribute the alms, and saw the tenderness, humility and devotion with which he distributed them, first kissing [the coin] before he gave it to each one of the poor; he was also very kind to sick animals, of which I could give some very specific examples. In the same way my mother was as respectful of God as she was a friend to the poor, and an enemy of [worldly] vanities, of fancy clothing and entertainments. She was so humble that when she was widowed and nearly blind, [one day] in church a servant woman hit her many times so that she would give up her place, all of which she bore with great meekness and left the church half limping. She told me about this while praising and blessing God Who had seen fit to think so highly of her that He had given her something to suffer. I could tell much more about this and about the good examples I observed in my childhood, but I, just as spiders do, was able to convert even the most wholesome things into poison.

My mother suffered terribly when I was about to be born, and even called her confessor, Father Diego Solano of the Jesuit Order, in order to make her last confession and to die, for she was convinced she would; while she was making her confession and holding on to the father's staff, I was born—and to describe what my heart feels when I say this, only my overflowing eyes could express. I was born, oh God, [and] You must know why, as You know how long my exile has been, and how bitter my passions and faults have made it. I was born, oh Lord! and afterward my saintly father baptized me and donated a large cross which he must have brought with him, giving me the names of my Father Saint Francis and of Saint Joseph, Our Lord bestowing on me henceforth this help and aid, as well as that of the fathers of the Company of Jesus who have worked so hard to compel me to the way of truth. May it be Our Lord's will that I find it before I depart this mortal life.

I was born on the day of the blessed Saint Bruno; it seems that Our Lord wished me to understand how much I would benefit from seclusion, introspection and silence in this mortal life, and how perilous dealings and conversations with people would be for me, just as I have experienced from the first stages of my life, and I regret this, though not as much as I should. People said that fifteen to twenty days [after my birth] I was so near death that the cloth and other trappings for my burial had been bought, until an uncle of mine, a priest, who later on advised me to become a nun (only he, for in the others I encountered much opposition), ordered that a certain remedy be given me, as to someone who was not expected to live, to which I responded and later got well. In this matter only the will of God consoles me, for who would not agree that it would have been better for me to die than to have become the person I am?

When I was still so young that I can hardly remember it, I had this experience: one of the little boys who used to come and visit with his mother (these things often happen, as I later realized) told me that he was going to marry me. I, as far as I can remember now, had no idea what that meant and agreed. Then such a torment afflicted my heart that it allowed me neither pleasure nor consolation and it seemed to me that I had committed a terrible evil, but as I told no one of this pain in my heart, it stayed with me until I must have been seven. On one occasion when I was alone in the room where grain was weighed and the rope had been left hanging, I felt so tormented and the Devil must have had a hand in it as well, because he strongly urged me to hang myself as the only solution. My guardian angel must have been looking out for me, because as far as I can recall I cried out to Our Lady, whom I regarded as a mother and on whom I called in my distress and affliction, [and] ran out of the room, startled and afraid. This is how Our Lord helped me out of that peril, when I don't think I was even seven years old. Until that age, and even a little beyond, all my amusement and consolation came from building altars and seeking seclusion; I had many images of Our Lord and Lady, and alone and secluded spent many hours arranging them. . . .

Because of the fear which I said Our Lord awoke in me, some nights I saw terrible things in my dreams. One time I thought I was walking on a raised floor made of bricks that were stood on end, as though up in the air and in great danger. Looking down I saw a fiery river, black and horrible, and within it a great number of serpents, frogs and snakes, as well as the faces and arms of men who were floating in that well or river. I awoke racked by sobs, and in the morning saw that the ends of my fingers and my nails bore marks of fire, although I had no idea how that could happen. Other times I was in a valley so wide, so deep and so wretchedly dark I cannot describe nor imagine it, and at the end was a horrible well of thick, black fire. On the bank evil spirits wandered about inflicting various torments on other people, in accordance with their sins. So that I would not offend Him, by means of these and other things God the Merciful warned me as to the punishment and the pain of evildoers, but none of this sufficed to keep me from committing many sins, even at that age.

I grew up a very sickly child, and this and the great love my parents had for me, caused them to look upon me with great affection and understanding. Although they dressed me in the habit of Saint Rose of Lima,[1] a promise they had made the saint so that Our Lord would give me good health, my mother took great pains in adorning me with jewels and finery, and I was the darling of the house and of all the people who served my parents. But in spite of this, I never derived pleasure or consolation from any of life's objects, neither playing with dolls nor games children engage in at that age; on the contrary, they held so little attraction for me that I wanted nothing to do with them. Sometimes I would organize processions of religious images, or imitate nuns' professions or customs, but not because I had any inclination to take the veil; all I wanted was to live the way hermits did in the desert and in caves out in the country.

[The following passages refer to events after Madre Castillo had become a nun.]

About this time Father Francisco de Herrera came to confess me, whom Your Reverence had recommended; I attempted to surrender myself completely to inner discourse with Our Lord, from Whom I received so much light, and it seemed to me that my soul was so innerly absorbed with this that it was as though I were not living in this life. The Father treated me harshly and made me do manual labor the greater part of the day; if at some time I asked his permission to spend half a day in prayer he would grant it, on the condition that I would do twice as much work in the afternoon. Many times he ordered me to write and to explain to him the feelings Our Lord produced in me. This caused me much suffering and shame, but I finally did it. . . . There were few nights I could sleep, being kept therefrom by that power in my soul; it seemed that I had live coals in the innermost part of my heart which showed me [things] without words, which ignited into a fire sweeter than life itself. . . .

I spent two years like this, in which all the things of this life seemed dreamlike and laughable to me. One day, while withdrawn with Our

Lord, I thought I saw myself dressed in a scarlet garment which went from my neck to my feet, and my hair was so long it reached the ground. Two evil spirits in human form were there, giving off sparks and wanting to play with the ends of my hair in order to snarl them. I was perturbed, not knowing what to make of it. Some days later some things were said to the Father about me which made him exceedingly angry. He said some very hurtful words to me; he would leave me in the confessional and go away without listening to me, until finally he stopped hearing my confession. I, as one who had no sure foundation, could only weep and become disconsolate unto death; I believed myself deceived and mistaken because my confessor rejected me in this way, but I see clearly now that what I should have done was to ask him humbly to instruct me, to help me to correct those faults and to take the path he would show me. . . .

[Madre Castillo subsequently obeys Father de Herrera and writes down some of her thoughts on true devotion to God.]

My confessor, Father Francisco, looked over this paper when his anger had abated and gave me his response: that the closer he examined it, the less he could find any of the marks the serpent [i.e., the Devil] leaves in matters in which he is involved; that, on the contrary, as far as he was concerned, it was God's work, and the only thing he advised me to do was not to flee from my confessor, no matter how much he chastised and hurt me, etc. In my later life, with God's grace, I have attempted to do this, suffering great travail because of it. . . .

And so one day, as I was strongly resisting writing what Father Francisco ordered, it seemed to me that I saw those same emotions which Our Lord instilled in my soul and the feelings which those pages expressed were being written on His heart with His very own blood, though at that time I did not understand what all this meant. . . .

Many times, as I hurried by the place where the Holy Sacrament was, I would feel in the innermost part of my soul these exceedingly gentle words as though emanating from His Divine Majesty: "Who shall separate us [from the love of Christ]?" (Rom. 8.35). Those were the words, as though He were saying, "No one will be strong enough to separate us." The words were so sweet, so tender and so gentle that I know not what, unless it be my stony, vile and ungrateful heart, would ever again take delight in anything that were not God, nor do I know why I waste the short span of my life in anything but lamenting my faults and ingratitude. In the same way He indicated that He alone should be my comfort, because one day, when my confessor had come and gone without consoling me, I was left with sorrow and sadness because of it and then I heard these words: "Why do you weep? And why do you not eat? And why is your heart sad? Am I not more to you than ten sons?" (1 Sam. 1.8). My soul felt these words so deeply that I was nearly beside myself with the joy and love they had instilled therein. I understood that I should not stop looking to a confessor for refuge and instruction but should look to God for consolation.

[Madre Castillo dreams about conversations instigated by the Devil.]

Our Lord also devised another way to get me away from those conversations, and this was when in the midst of them I saw Your Reverence at my side (I know not if I was asleep or awake), reprimanding me with severity and kindness, and reminding me of what I owed God. Therewith those matters filled me with even greater horror, although it was already very bad, so much so that I began to write Your Reverence (who had already returned to Santa Fe) about the distress in which I found myself. I remember that I began to weep into the inkwell in order to moisten it with the tears I was shedding, for it was dry, and I was so afraid to open my cell or to ask for anything so that [the demons] couldn't enter, that I wished to fill up the inkwell with my tears and to write with them, something I could easily do because of the copious tears I shed.

After [my confessor Juan Martínez] was here, one day I was in my retreat thinking about the lashes Our Lord was given and it seemed to me that He fell when they untied Him from the column; I felt the same thing as the time before, that anxiety and desire to help Him rise, but now, as opposed to what happened to me the other time, I felt that when my soul reached Him that His body disappeared because it became somehow spiritualized—I don't know how to explain it: it seemed that He disappeared from view or from the soul's knowledge, leaving it feeling great sorrow. I think this was to warn me for what lay ahead, and for the trials that were destined for me. It also happened that when I had begun spiritual exercises with the novice, whom I wished to direct the best I could, we being at prayer one afternoon I saw the Devil go by the door of the cell dressed in a religious habit; he watched us where we were with eyes that horrified, then went into the cell of another nun which was next to my own; I did not understand what all that might be, but was filled with fear and sadness.

About then I saw that my soul was so changed, and so renewed with the good impulses that on another occasion Our Lord had bestowed on me, that I hardly knew myself, nor understood by what means Our Lord had kindled my soul. I had been in seclusion the better part of the day, anticipating my general confession for that year, when one night at prayers, because there had been no Matins,[2] the nun into whose quarters I had seen the Devil disappear entered my cell. She was so filled with rage and screamed at me that I was dumbfounded. She uttered numerous threats against me, saying that the novice was not my servant and that now we would see what the Mother Abbess would do. She shouted so loudly and there was such an outcry by the maids and general commotion that I was cut off and could find no refuge but that of slipping into a gallery, but from there heard such cries in the choir, such a tumult and things that were said about me that I was half dead with shame from hearing them. I had no idea where all this anger and shouting would end when the assistant mother superior, the nun I described earlier, and a throng of servant women with lanterns and lights came to find me. Their anger and what they said to me there were beyond description. . . . The things that they accused me of were unspeakable, and I didn't know where to hide, for anger had filled my cell and I could not stand up I was so afraid. My servant women had also rebelled against me so I was forced to knock at the door of a nun who had been told things that might make her feel angry toward me, but when she saw me in such an afflicted state she was moved to compassion, and she was the only one in the whole house who was on my side during my travails. Afterward

I fell ill with a sickness so grievous that the sweat which poured from my body left my hands as though scalded in boiling water. My mouth twisted to one side, and I had such terrible fainting spells that they would last three and four long hours. During those spells one of the servant women there, a friend of the nuns I described, tried to suffocate me because she covered my nose and mouth with all her might, and if her mistress, in whose cell I was, had not noticed it, who knows what might have happened to me, as she later told me. I think perhaps she wasn't trying to suffocate but only to torment me. . . .

When they told the Mother Abbess that I had been unconscious for so many hours she responded, "Give her some stout lashes, and let her drop dead." Other times she said, "I've been putting a good edge on a knife so that I can send it to her and she can stab herself, and I'll send her a rope so that she can go hang." And I, when I would regain consciousness, wept bitterly and asked them, "Good ladies, my mothers, what cause, what motive have I given you?" . . .

The times I would leave my room to go to the confessional or to withdraw to a solitary and out-of-the-way part of the house, the servant women I would meet would either knock me down or call me insulting and ridiculous names, screaming them at me repeatedly. The Mother Abbess would promise every day when we were in community that she was planning to put me in the stocks and mortify me with a whip, that I was a madwoman and that she would bring me to my senses. . . . But in spite of this I did not cease appealing to the Most Holy Virgin. . . . And when I presented myself before her as the sickest in spirit, the poorest in virtue, the blindest, most incapacitated and wounded being, stricken with incurable illnesses, then I would feel a great consolation, hoping for the healing of my soul at the hand of the Mother of mercies, from whom so many others have received help. However, on this occasion, which I am describing to Your Reverence, I was so filled with anxiety, confusion and distress that I did not understand myself.

[After this difficult time Madre Castillo experiences greater understanding.]

I understood many other things then, some of which I wrote down because my confessor bade me. My soul floated like a light feather which is carried on a gentle wind; in that way it seemed to me that I no longer belonged to myself for anything, but that I went about without a soul, for my soul had entered into its God and was ruled by another impulse that was gentle, sweet, loving and effective. All that I saw and heard was God; it was supreme good, a good beyond all feeling and knowledge. Nothing outward affected me; rather, everything was like little puffs which made that flame burn, and it burned higher, fed by all that was my scorn and my humiliation.

My confessor tormented me to the best of his ability, which Our Lord increased greatly in him, so much so that at times I speculated that he must have been having difficulty figuring out what new way he could devise to torment me, and that perhaps there weren't any left. He spoke to me as badly as he could, and answered me harshly. Usually he would get so profoundly angry, reproving me for things that to me seemed good, that I would end up trembling and afraid; then afterward I would think that perhaps he should go on doing them, that he was doing well. Sometimes he would throw me out of the confessional with such anger and scorn that it seemed I had given him some serious reason for doing so; at times he wrote to me specifically, "That he had seen that I and all my affairs were good only for burning, and that he had resolved to leave me because my path was that of perdition," and other very harsh things. And Our Lord must have agreed because He left me in such a state of darkness and confusion that I was convinced that things really were the way the Father had said and I would cry bitterly. I had no comfort but my own inner determination to do all that he bade me, for it was God's will, be what may. However, to find someone to guide me through this was almost impossible, because the Father told me that he was not coming back, that my sins drove him away. But then he would come back to scold and reprove me because I had not known how to bear that burden and mortification well. In spite of this and many other things, I saw and knew the care he felt for my soul and his great desire for my improvement, and thus his severity was what most spurred me on because I had put myself in his hands with the desire that all be taken from me that might be offensive in the sight of God. He gave me extended permission to do all I was able in the way of penitence and mortification, and the more I did, the better I felt, because that was what God must have wanted then. . . .

And thus I have reached the age of forty-four years of living in this world, and thus I beg you, my Father, that as with the help of Our Lord I have overcome so much and have endured so many trials in writing this and in telling you about my life, that you look on it with favor. [This also goes for] the steps my soul has taken in order not to lose its way, and again I place it in your hands, for to me they are the hands of God, so that, freed from myself, I may come to attain the end for which God has created us, where we shall see Him and praise Him. And there, through God's mercy and the intercession of the Most Holy Virgin, I hope to see Your Reverence.

About that time I was very ill and suffered from troubles and great distress, both interior and exterior, and as we were approaching Lent, I seemed to see in my soul's eye a sea with such muddy, dark waters that looking at it caused me great affliction, bitterness and inner pangs. I seemed to see Our Lord Jesus Christ walking in the midst of that sea and I understood that that meant that He wanted to send me a great trial and during that Lent I was very afraid. . . .

Along with this I bore many cares and contradictions in the most sensitive matters, suffering as well the persecution of the Devil, not only with grave and continuous temptations, but also with evil and loathsome fears. When night came they would come and throw themselves on me, etc., with abominable shapes and disgusting beyond all belief. I gave myself up for lost and felt that all my life I had been deceived, and only wanted permission so I could burn those papers which I had written for the sake of obedience. And now I know the enemy's astuteness, because only that occurred to me as a sin. . . .

By means of these and other things I wrote on those pages, the infinite mercy of God consoled and encouraged [me in] my disconsolateness, and kept me from burning what I had written, which is what I have so often proposed and asked Your Reverence to let me do. One Pentecost in particular, when I had just taken Communion, I understood very clearly and for many reasons which Our Lord showed me, that not one thing which I had written belonged either to me or to the Devil. . . .

I will go on [writing], Father, obeying by the will of God, which is the only goal which in all this I can have in order to overcome my loathing and my shame, and the many other things which afflict my heart in this obedience [to you]. And if I wanted to count up the reasons I can think of not to continue, I would fill up a great deal of paper and waste it. . . .

I will also write down some reasons for consolation which I received in my soul, not because I think that Our Lord spoke to me as to one of the just, but to explain that it is as though He said: "Poor thing, tossed about by the storm without any consolation, fear not, you will not die. I am the Lord your God and see, I will adorn you with jewels. I will give you the crown and diadem of diamonds that is my faithful, pious and loving Mother. I will place on your breast a cross of rubies which is I, your husband, made flesh, most loving and stained with blood. I will give you that stone, which, though white, is fire itself, that it may adorn you and sear you in the sacrament, and be for you a rich treasure of hope and love.

"Endure life, long for death, be subject always to my will and enclosed in the faithful and strong wall of my eternal love. . . .

"There! Cheer your heart, poor little one, woman, and drown in the sea of my mercies. Look, for the dawn will come, the strife and battle will be over and there will be an end to darkness when the dawn which is Mary, strong, gentle, mild and merciful, breaks, and she will be as terrible for evil spirits as a well-ordered army. Is she not your Mother, and the Mother of your Husband? Then what do you fear? Is she not chosen like the sun to cheer, to benefit and to bestow life, from the royal eagle to the smallest bird, from the crowned lion to the least little creature, from the cedar of Lebanon to the hyssop and the lowliest plant? And you poor little worm, you too will enjoy the rewards of this dawn and of the brightest, loveliest and purest sun. Throw yourself at her feet, hide in this sea of mercies, and drink of this purest of springs when your receive her Transsubtantiated Son, etc." When in the grip of discouragement and anguish, thoughts such as these restore my heart and it breathes anew. . . .

Father: up to this point I have met my obligations, and for love of Our Lord I beg you to tell me if this is what Your Reverence ordered me to do, or if I have done too much, and if this will be the path to my perdition, as sometimes I am afflicted with terrible fears which seem to bind me hand and foot. It may be that this is caused by the Devil so that I do not repay the benefits of my Lord and God with the gratitude I should. He suggests that all is deception and illusion on my part, and these past evenings as I have been writing the Enemy has tormented me, appearing on three successive nights. On one he headed me off on the way to chapel and laughed heartily; on another he said extremely disgraceful things, among them that I was a chatterbox, and could keep nothing to myself; and on yet another he made extraordinarily scornful and disgusting gestures (though I don't pay attention to this because it was in a dream). Only Our Lord knows the ways [the Devil] has of distressing and tormenting me, and only He, by the intercession of his Most Holy Mother, can free me from this and give me strength and patience so as not to weaken. Blessed and praised be God.

Notes

1. Saint Rose of Lima (1586–1617), a very devout young Peruvian woman, was canonized in 1668 and became the first American saint.

2. An early-morning hour of prayer.

Gertrudis Gómez de Avellaneda

Gertrudis Gómez de Avellaneda from La Avellaneda y sus obras,
Emilio Cotarelo y Mori (Madrid: Tipografía de archivos, 1930).

*J*ust like Sor Juana and Madre Castillo, Gertrudis Gómez de Avellaneda was the daughter of a Spanish father and a criolla mother. She was born in the central Cuban city of Camagüey in 1814 and was raised in comfortable circumstances. She was very proud of her father's aristocratic lineage, and her mother, too, came from Cuba's landed gentry—which meant, of course, that they were slaveholders.

Cuba's white population in the early nineteenth century was an uneasy society, primarily because the successful slave uprising in nearby Haiti (1791) was seen as a direction Cuban blacks and mulattoes might take as well. Domingo del Monte, a wealthy Venezuelan planter who opposed the further importation of slaves to Cuba, organized a group of intellectuals to compose antislavery (but not abolitionist) literature; as the critics Ivan Schulman and Antonio Benítez Rojo have shown, these writings marked the beginning of a national Cuban literature. Avellaneda would play her part in this, albeit indirectly, as she lived in Spain most of her life.

She was eight when her father died, and within the year her mother married another Spaniard, Isidoro de Escalada, a handsome military officer who was part of Spain's colonial garrison on the island. Gertrudis (or Tula, as she was called) could not bear her stepfather—nor he her—but, true to the patriarchal nature of nineteenth-century families, she had no alternative but to obey him, especially because of her financial dependence on him. Tula's grandfather had disinherited her when she refused to marry a man he had chosen but whom she did not love, and all her life she remained sensitive to women's powerlessness due to a lack of money. This, as we shall see, is an issue that was also very important to other nineteenth-century writers in this anthology: Gorriti, Cabello de Carbonera, and González de Fanning.

Escalada was worried about the possibility of a Cuban slave uprising and in 1836 took the family back to Spain: Tula, her brother Manuel, and three new siblings. They went first to Galicia, Escalada's home. The strong-willed Tula detested both his conservative family and the gloomy, wet climate. With her mercurial temperament she must have made everyone's life so miserable that she and Manuel were subsequently allowed to go to Seville, her father's birthplace. Andalusia suited her a great deal better. She lost no time in joining Seville's literary circles and published both poetry and her first play. Tula was also writing *Sab,* her first and today most famous novel, which she published in Madrid in 1841. It was a radical story, especially for a Cuban woman author. Set on the island, it concerned the doomed love of a mulatto slave for his white owner's daughter. It was immediately banned in Cuba.

Tula was a talented writer, and she also knew how to present herself to her best advantage. As a Cuban in Spain, she was considered exotic, and she knew it; she was also very attractive and knew that as well. She was ambitious in her goal to become a recognized writer and knew that Seville was too small a pond for her. She moved to Madrid and parlayed her many contacts with writers and intellectuals into acceptance into their circles. Tula was now writing and publishing poetry, novels, and plays and was successfully supporting herself by her pen.

While she was still in Seville, Tula had fallen passionately in love with Ignacio de Cepeda, a local aristocrat about two years younger (she actively lied about her age all her life). The tempestuous emotions he aroused in her were definitely *not* reciprocated: Cepeda was socially and intellectually conservative, cool of temperament, dictatorial, and apparently often embarrassed by Tula's passion. They had an on-again, off-again relationship until 1854, when Cepeda married another woman. He fortunately kept all of Tula's letters to him, with instructions to have his wife publish them after his death, which she did.[1]

Today, with telephones, voice mail, e-mail, and the like, it is hard to appreciate what letters meant in the nineteenth century, and how much time people spent writing them—even if they saw each other almost daily, as was the case with Tula and Cepeda. The letters she wrote to her reluctant lover are not only compelling insights into her psyche, they are helpful in providing a background against which her literature developed. They are also, as Emil Volek noted, more appealing to modern readers than much of her other literature.

In the early stage of their relationship Cepeda had asked her to write him about her past, and she provided him with her epistolary autobiography.[2] At this juncture Avellaneda was twenty-five years old. Epistolary writing was one genre women had always been able to practice freely, and, in Susan Kirkpatrick's opinion, Tula's private writing was good training for her later career: "It was in letters and in diaries that the very young Gómez de Avellaneda, before she had the confidence to enter the man's world of publication, had cultural permission and precedent to construct and represent herself as a woman in writing" (135). Even as she attempted to construct a submissive, dutiful self who would appeal to someone like Cepeda, Tula also realized that that was not where she wanted to be: "The autobiography is of particular interest because it shows her working out in a very personal mode of writing an image of the self that draws on Romantic literary models while registering acute awareness that these models were antithetical to the cultural pattern of feminine existence" (Kirkpatrick 135). The same could be said of many of her other letters, not only to Cepeda but also later on to another suitor, Antonio Romero Ortiz. I have included examples of her correspondence with both of these men in this anthology.

After *Sab* Avellaneda wrote *Dos mugeres* (Two Women; 1842), another radical novel that took a sympathetic and tolerant view of adultery; it was also banned in Cuba. Tula also established herself as one of Madrid's most successful playwrights, in spite of some harsh criticism because of her gender. She took her writing very seriously, as can be seen in her correspondence with both Cepeda and Romero Ortiz, in which she would often alternate between phrases of endearment and very businesslike assessments of the reception her writing was receiving. After a blowup with Cepeda in 1840, for instance, she sent him a letter enumerating her numerous successes with *Sab* and a play and concluded by saying, "You see that I ought to be very satisfied with the brilliant success of my literary endeavors. God willing that when people get to know the novel and the play it will not affect their enthusiasm [for my poetry], and just because I want to be a playwright and a novelist, [I hope] they will not forget the reputation I have acquired as a lyric poet" (*Diario íntimo* 99).

We can see the same tendency in her letters to Romero Ortiz. Eight years her junior, he was a reporter for *La Nación,* and Tula thought nothing of writing him a steamy love letter ("I love you, Antonio; you are my lover; I know nothing else," etc.) and then, in a postscript, giving him precise instructions on how he was to write a review of one of her plays (*Cartas inéditas* 67–68).

In 1844 Tula had an affair with Gabriel García Tassara, a poet and diplomat, which resulted in a pregnancy and the birth of their daughter, Brenhilde. Tassara left her and would not acknowledge the child, who died before she was a year old. Two years later Tula married Pedro Sabater, who was already terminally ill with throat cancer and died within four months of their wedding. In 1853 came one of her cruelest disappointments: her failure to be elected a member of the Royal Spanish Academy. Her literary accomplishments certainly qualified her, and she had many *académicos* who supported her, but a majority of the all-male members of the Academy voted her down. When the poet Carmen Conde was elected an *académica* in 1977, it was reported that she was the first women to receive this honor, but this is not true. While doing research on Avellaneda's only essay, "La mujer," I noticed her reference to a "Doctora de Alcalá" and wondered about her identity. She was Doña María Isidra Quintina de Guzmán y de la Cerda (1768–1803), a very intelligent young noblewoman who had the favor of King Charles III and of his prime minister, Floridablanca. The king wanted her admitted to the Royal Academy and arranged for her to get a doctorate from the University of Alcalá to qualify her for admission. There was a great deal of resistance from the *académicos,* but the king was not to be denied, and in 1784, at the age of eighteen, she was admitted to their ranks. The most amazing part of her story, however, is that she was the granddaughter of María Luisa Manrique de Lara, Countess of Paredes—Sor Juana's friend and benefactress (Serrano y Sanz 493–95).

Avellaneda was deeply disappointed and embittered by this defeat. In the same year she began her relationship with Antonio Romero

Ortiz; just as had been the case with Cepeda, the lovers used romantic aliases to hide their affair and their correspondence.[3] This relationship also had its ups and downs. In her amorous correspondence Tula would use the familiar "tú" or the formal "Ud." in addressing her lovers, depending on the state of her feelings for them at the moment of writing. Just as she had done with Cepeda, in her letters Tula actively courted Romero Ortiz, which resulted in frightening both of them off. At one point Tula toyed with the idea of marrying Romero Ortiz but ultimately broke off their relationship.

She dallied briefly with Tassara again but in 1855 married Domingo Verdugo, who was close to Queen Isabel II of Spain and to her consort, King Francisco. The ceremony took place in the Royal Palace, with the monarchs as witnesses. Tula was now at the pinnacle of society and continued her successful career as a playwright. Unfortunately Verdugo had an altercation with a spectator who had attempted to disrupt one of his wife's plays; the man stabbed him in the chest, and although Verdugo survived, his health was permanently impaired.

Late in 1859 the couple went to Cuba with the new Spanish governor, and the famous Tula was celebrated in high style by her native country, though there were some Cuban patriots who criticized her alliance with the Spanish colonial administration. She was crowned with a diadem of gold laurel leaves in Havana's Teatro Tacón and lionized wherever she went—surely a source of great satisfaction after her exclusion from the Royal Academy. While in Cuba she founded the island's first journal for women, the *Album Cubano de lo Bueno y lo Bello* (The Cuban Album of the Good and the Beautiful). Though it lasted only a year, the issues are excellent examples of popular women's literature in the nineteenth century. Aside from a number of her poems, Tula contributed the essay "La mujer," some sketches of famous women of the past, and gave the *Album* the prestige of her name.

Verdugo died in 1863, after which Avellaneda returned to Spain via the United States. She lived first in Seville and then went back to Madrid, continuing her writing and preparing an edition of her complete works. The five volumes, published between 1869 and 1871, do not, however, contain either *Sab* or *Dos mugeres,* partly because she herself was now much more conservative than in her youth and also because these novels were banned in Cuba and she did not want to endanger sales in that country. Her real *Obras completas* were published in Havana in 1914.

Tula died of diabetes in February 1873. After Cepeda's death, her love letters to him were published (*Diario íntimo*), and the passion of her voice was heard again.

Cepeda! You have not understood me; you have not understood my love. I want your heart, your heart without any kind of ties. I am free and so are you; both of us should always be free; the man who acquires a right to humiliate a woman, the man who abuses his power, tears that woman's precious freedom away, because she who acknowledges a master is no longer free. (81)

I don't know if I am always prudent; sometimes I fear I will never be, but I dare anyone to prove that I am false or meanspirited. My defects are of the same measure as my good qualities, and I have presented myself to you just the way I am. Did you love me the way I am? Do you think me worthy? . . . I don't know, but I do know that you will not find other women on this earth like me. They may be better or worse, but they will not be like

TULA. (119)

She was very right.

Notes

1. The letters to Cepeda were compiled and published by Lorenzo Cruz de Fuentes, who edited out certain parts. As the originals have disappeared, we have no idea what the editor suppressed. He also put the letters in the order in which they appear here, which may or may not be correct, as many of the letters were undated.

2. I translated this autobiography earlier, in *Sab* and *Autobiography*, for which reason I am not including it in this anthology.

3. Cepeda was from the small town of Almonte, and when writing to him, Avellaneda called herself "Doña Amadora de Almonte"; Romero Ortiz signed his first letters to her "Armand Carrel," and it took her a while to find out his real identity.

Cartas a Ignacio de Cepeda

CARTA I

Una hora de desvelo y melancolía en la noche del 13 de julio [1839].
Dedicada a mi "compañero de desilusión." Para él solo.

[Avellaneda empieza su carta con un largo poema que habla de su desilusión personal con la vida, y cómo estos sentimientos la vinculan a Cepeda; ella cree que él siente lo mismo.]

Me hace mal, mucho mal, oír a usted expresar sus ideas, dolores y esperanzas. Ya ve usted por esta composición qué pensamientos me inspira. Atienda usted a los versos y no a las ideas.

Efectivamente, a veces me abruma esta *plenitud de vida* y quisiera descargarme de su peso. He trabajado mucho tiempo en minorar mi existencia moral para ponerla al nivel de mi existencia física. Juzgada por la sociedad, que no me comprende, y cansada de un género de vida que acaso me ridiculiza; superior e inferior a mi sexo, me encuentro extranjera en el mundo y aislada en la naturaleza. Siento la necesidad de morir, y, sin embargo, vivo y pareceré dichosa a los ojos de la multitud. . . .

Usted me habla de amistad, y no ha mucho que sintió usted amor. Yo no creo ni en una ni en otro. Busco en emociones pasajeras, en afectos ligeros, un objeto en que distraer mis devoradores pensamientos y me siento así menos atormentada, porque inconstante en mis gustos, cánsome fácilmente de todo, y los afectos ligeros, que apenas me ligan, no me privan del derecho de seguir el instinto de mi alma que codicia libertad. Alguna vez deseo hallar sobre esta tierra un corazón melancólico, ardiente, altivo y ambicioso como el mío; compartir con él mis goces y dolores y darle este exceso de vida, que yo sola no puedo soportar. Pero más a menudo temo en mí esta inmensa facultad de padecer, y presiento que un amor vehemente suscitaría en mi pecho tempestades, que trastornaría acaso mi razón y mi vida. Además, ¿llenaría aún el amor el abismo de mi alma? Todo lo he probado y todo lo desecho: amor y amistad. ¿Qué puedo, pues, ofrecer a usted, querido mío? ¡La compasión de un corazón atormentado! . . . y mis versos para distraerle un momento de ocupaciones graves.

CARTA 2

[1° de agosto de 1839]

Estoy avergonzada, ¡Dios mío! ¿Qué habrá usted pensado de mí, Cepeda, después de la extraña y ridícula conducta que tuve anoche? Si fuese usted un fatuo presumido, uno de estos hombres vanidosos de que abundan en la ciudad, ya sé lo que pensaría.

Aun no siéndolo usted, aun creyéndole a usted modesto y no ligero en sus juicios, tiemblo al reflexionar en mis locuras el concepto que usted se formará y lo que usted supondrá. ¿Qué hombre habrá bastante modesto que viendo en una mujer el arrebato indominable que usted vió anoche en mí, no creyera que sólo los celos . . . ? ¡Dios mío!, mi mano tiembla y mi frente se cubre de vergüenza al pensarlo. He dado motivo para que usted no crea nada de cuanto le he dicho hasta el presente acerca de la naturaleza de mis sentimientos para con usted; he dado motivo para que usted me crea *enamorada y celosa*; he dado motivo para que usted me coloque en la lista de esas cuatro o cinco a quienes inspiró, sin pretenderlo, una pasión desgraciada. ¡Maldición! Yo sufro una humillación que no creía estuviese en la lista de mis padecimientos. ¡Qué papel he querido representar, o, mejor dicho, he representado involuntariamente! ¡El de enamorada celosa! ¡Yo, yo, Dios mío! No sé como no muero sofocada de rabia. Es cierto que no hay en mí ni amor ni celos; es bien cierto que ni le he mirado a usted como amante, ni le deseo como tal, ni lo admitiría . . . ¡lo juro a Dios y por mi dignidad de mujer! Juro que no lo admitiría a usted por mi amante, así como hasta ahora no le he considerado a usted como a tal.

Es bien cierto todo esto y que el afecto mutuo que nos ha ligado hasta el alma, ha sido tan puro como desinteresado; y, sin embargo de esto, ¡qué papel hago desde anoche! ¡Cómo me he degradado por un capricho inconcebible, por una violencia pueril y extravagante! ¡A qué suposiciones humillantes he dado lugar! Ya lo ve usted probado; ya ve usted probado lo que yo le he dicho muchas veces: que hay en mi carácter algo de tan ligero, tan caprichoso y tan inconsecuente, que me ha de causar en mi vida muchas pesadumbres.

Las gentes me creen mujer de algún talento y mundo, y yo misma lo he pensado así; pero nos engañábamos: ya lo sé por experiencia. A los veinticuatro años[1] soy más niña que una de cinco. Yo no tengo talento ninguno, ni tengo mundo, ni tengo prudencia: no tengo más que una desgraciada cualidad, que yo maldigo: una ingenuidad que raya en necedad y en locura. Usted debe haberse reído de mí; ya lo creo. No puedo quejarme. Pero tenga usted la bondad de escucharme un momento, que aunque no pueda ni pretenda justificar la ligereza y extravagancia de mi conducta anoche, acaso haré comprender a usted sus verdaderos motivos y evitaré, ya que no sea el concepto de arrebatada y de indiscreta en que usted debe justamente tenerme, al menos el de *celosa*, que me humilla lo que no es decible y que ciertamente no merezco. . . .

. . . Mi dolor, mi sorpresa, mi exaltación eran efectos de una misma causa. No vi en usted en aquel momento el amigo de mi corazón, que asegurándome una *amistad grande, tierna y santa*, me había dicho: "*puedes aceptarla sin temor ni reserva, porque te la ofrece el más puro y ardiente de los corazones.*"[2] En vez de este corazón *puro y ardiente*, yo no vi en aquel momento rápido de sorpresa y de dolor sino un corazón usado al extremo, un corazón dividido entre muchos objetos. . . .

Lo que dije, lo que hice, yo no lo sé exactamente. Sé que me volví loca nada más; loca de dolor, al ver destruída mi última y más querida ilusión: la ilusión divina que me hizo creer había hallado al fin un corazón sensible, puro, ardiente, capaz de grandes pasiones y acaso de grandes faltas, pero no capaz de tibios y multiplicados afectos. . . .

Todo esto, agolpándose súbitamente en mi cabeza, la trastornó en términos que ya no supe más lo que hice. Parecíame que me habían transportado a otro mundo, a un infierno, y aquella carta de usted, que tenía en mi seno, me quemaba como una ascua de fuego. Hice mil locuras, locuras que pudieron ser bien siniestramente interpretadas; y lo que más siento, lo que más me humilla, es el pensar que usted mismo, Cepeda, usted mismo, habrá creído ver un arrebato de celos en lo que no era más que un exabrupto de dolor. ¡Cuán avergonzada estoy, Dios mío! ¡Hubiera querido morir antes de salir anoche de mi casa! . . .

Por lo demás, nada me resta que decir. Retíreme usted su confianza; no la merezco; soy demasiado violenta y ligera. Soy también muy joven todavía para ser confidente de un hombre de la edad de usted y de sus méritos, y diré, aun más, de un hombre que se halla en posición tan delicada. No tengo ni la madurez, ni el talento necesario para aconsejar con acierto, y sólo podré afligirme o hacer locuras como anoche. Seré siempre su amiga de usted. . . .

¡Adiós, mi amable amigo, feliz viaje! Déjeme usted cuatro letras en el correo, acusándome recibo de ésta, pues no estaría tranquila si no supiese con certeza que usted la había recibido. Diviértase usted en Elmonte o Almonte, y consérvese bueno y estudioso para que le veamos pronto. Repito y ruego encarecidamente, de rodillas si es preciso, que olvide usted mis miserias de anoche. Si no puede usted impedirse el creer que sólo el amor, y un amor exaltado y celoso, pudo arrastrar a tales loca ni tonta, créalo usted; pero crea usted también en que, si existió, ya no existe, y que si existió, era sin conocerlo yo misma. En fin, lo que deseo, sobre todo, es que se olvide de todo lo pasado.

CARTA 6

Señor don Ignacio Cepeda:

He recibido la amable de usted, mi caro amigo, con tanta mayor satisfacción cuanto que informada por Concha[3] de que no estaba usted en Almonte, sino en otra parte que designó su hermano y de cuyo nombre no me acuerdo, temía hubiese padecido extravío mi carta. Varias veces mandé una criada al correo, y siempre me dijo que no había carta, hasta que ayer, siéndome imposible salir yo, me valí de Concha, la cual fué ella misma al correo y me trajo al momento la suspirada de usted.

Celebro que esté usted bueno, como en ella me dice, y menos melancólico que en ésta. Yo, por mi parte, quisiera poder decir otro tanto, pero, por desgracia, no es así, Mis dolores de estómago me han dado mucho que hacer, y mi melancolía se aumenta cada día. ¡Usted me pide que la venza! . . . Ciertamente, es grande el influjo que una súplica de usted ejerce en mi corazón; pero en este punto acaso no esté en mi poder el complacer la solicitud de su tierna amistad. Aparte de la ausencia de mi mejor, de mi único amigo, que es suficiente causa para melancolizarme, ¡tengo tantos otros motivos de tristeza! ¡La expectativa de una separación acaso próxima y larga de una madre que amo con ternura! ¡La indecisión en que batallo sin saber qué partido tomar ni qué suerte me espera! ¡La necesidad de independencia y el temor de la opinión, que me impide proporcionármelo! . . . En fin, tantas y tantas cosas me agitan al presente (en que según las apariencias se aproxima el día de la crisis), que la amistad misma, la dulce y lisonjera amistad de Cepeda no será poderosa a darme tranquilidad. Pero, ¡basta! Hablemos de otra cosa. ¡Yo quisiera que mis cartas fuesen tan risueñas! ¡Ah, ya lo veo, imposible! La amargura de mi corazón se mezcla en todas ellas. ¡Perdón!

Mandaré mi traducción por el conducto que me indica; pero será luego que tenga tiempo para escribirla, pues el borrador está ininteligible y la única copia leíble que tenía la he mandado a Cádiz por compromiso. Los señores redactores del nuevo periódico de literatura, que sale en dicha ciudad con el nombre de *La Aureola*, me han escrito una lisonjera carta rogándome cediese a su periódico algunas de mis composiciones, y aunque quise negarme, me he visto forzada a complacerles por haber intervenido en el asunto un paisano mío, a quien estimo, y que se ha empeñado de un modo que no podía yo, sin desairarle, mantener mi negativa. Así, pues, he cedido a *La Aureola* mi traducción, poniendo la condición de que no se imprimiera firmada con mi nombre sino enteramente anónima.

Ya enviaré a usted, tan pronto pueda, una copia, y de antemano reclamo su indulgencia. Preciso fuera que usted conociese el original, para que se formase un juicio exacto de la grandísima dificultad de la traducción. Lamartine, uno de los más grandes poetas de la moderna escuela, y acaso el más dulce y fácil, tiene, sin embargo, algo de vago y metafísico en su poesía y una manera de decir que es, ciertamente, intraducible. Sus ideas en muchas composiciones son tan delicadas, que se marchitan, por decirlo así, bajo la pluma del traductor, y sus giros son a veces tan atrevidos, que intimidan. He procurado en *La Fuente* traducir con la exactitud posible, penetrándome de los pensamientos e ideas del autor; pero estoy muy lejos de la satisfacción de creer que he logrado imitar con mediano acierto su versificación flúida y armoniosa y aquel colorido místico y melancólico que distingue sus composiciones.

Respecto a mi novela [*Sab*], he sometido sus diez primeros capítulos a la censura de mi compatriota, ya mencionado, hombre instruido y de gusto que, felizmente, se halla ahora en esta ciudad, y he tenido el gusto de que mereciese su aprobación. Él ha animado mi tímida pluma, asegurándome que la parte descriptiva está trazada con exactitud y variedad y que los caracteres están bien delineados y desenvueltos con vigor. Su bondad le ha hecho propasarse hasta dar al estilo elogios inmerecidos y juzgar de altamente interesante el plan de la novela. A pesar de mi amor propio, he conocido el favor de este juicio; pero me ha animado, sin embargo, a continuar haciendo esfuerzos para merecer lo mejor.

Ya ve usted, mi buen amigo, que le hablo de cosas que no son más que cosas; ya ve usted que evito un lenguaje que usted llama de la imaginación y que yo diría del corazón: usted lo juzga peligroso y lo destierra de nuestras cartas. Yo suscribo a su formidable sentencia; pero, ¿qué temes tú, amigo mío? ¿qué peligro quieres evitar? Acaso oyendo y empleando el idioma del corazón, ¿temerás no poder impedirle adelantarse demasiado? ¿Temerás sentir o inspirar un sentimiento más vivo que el de la amistad . . . ? Si es cierto, tranquilízate, yo te aseguro que no me amarás nunca sino como a tu hermana, y que en mi alma no hallarás jamás otros afectos que los que hoy día me envanezco de expresarte. Yo he meditado mucho en estos días sobre la naturaleza de nuestros sentimientos, y, te lo juro, este examen me ha tranquilizado. Yo perdería mucho si tú dejases de ser mi amigo para ser mi amante. ¡Amantes! . . . ¡Cercan tantos a una mujer joven y de tal cual mérito! Pero, ¿dónde hallar un amigo como tú? ¡Amantes! . . . Mira, me empalagan ya; esa cáfila de aduladores que asedian nuestro sexo, me parecen poca cosa aún para divertirse una un rato con sus necios galanteos. ¡Ni puedo yo creer que me amen! Uno me obsequia porque soy una forastera que no conoce, cuya clase acaso juzga dudosa, cuyas costumbres ignora y acaso puedan ser fáciles; cuya conquista no le parecerá dudosa, y me obsequia creyendo que puedo ser su capricho, su juguete, su pasatiempo, su placer de algunos días. Otro me obsequia porque hace profesión de obsequiante de cuantas mujeres bien parecidas se le presentan: sin ideas, sin cálculos, sin esperanzas, y sólo por el prurito de galantear y hacer de elegante. Otro me obsequia porque anda a la cuarta pregunta, como suele decirse, y oliendo donde guisan. Soy americana, y por ser americana supone que soy rica, lo cual basta para que forme sus cálculos de matrimonio. En fin, otro me hace el amor sólo por vanidad: porque se lisonjearía de ser mi novio, no porque yo le guste, sino porque cree darse importancia en la sociedad con la preferencia de una mujer que es celebrada, que dicen tiene algún talento. He aquí, querido Cepeda, los motivos que impulsan a la mayor parte de aquellos que me hacen la corte. Y estando yo en esta persuasión, ¿podré oírlos con otro objeto que el de burlarme de ellos?

¿Y usted qué hallará en más mujeres que digan amarle? Una dice que le ama, y no ama más que su colocación. Desea un marido, un estado, que es la ambición de las mujeres vulgares y lo busca en usted. Otra dice amarle, y sólo ama en usted a su pasatiempo, al que le regaló el oído y la lisonjea en la sociedad, al que satisface su vanidad y al que dejaría sin pesar por otro más galán, de más representación social, de más nombradía, etcétera, etcétera. Otra dice amarle, y sólo ama en usted sus propios placeres, y . . . ¡oh! —rubor causa decirlo—, pero lo vemos cada día para vergüenza nuestra. Vemos esta clase de mujeres que degradan la dignidad de su sexo, y son a mis ojos más despreciables que la escoria más vil de la tierra.

¡Y tal es el amor en nuestra triste y corrompida sociedad! ¿Cómo podía él existir entre nosotros? ¡Oh, no, jamás! Esos profanados nombres de amante y querida déjalos a otros y a otras. Tú serás mi amigo, yo tu amiga de toda la vida, y no debes temer que sea degradado nunca el santo carácter de nuestros vínculos. ¿Temerás tú cuando yo no temo? Todo lo dicho te prueba que nada arriesgas en dejar hablar tu corazón. No interpretará la vanidad tus palabras, ni puede tu amiga confundir la expresión de tus sentimientos con la jerga insípida del galanteo que llaman amor. En cuanto a mí, haré lo que quieras; no te expresaré si esto te hace mal, pero ¡me cuesta tanto este esfuerzo!

Cepeda: ya lo ve usted: mi pluma corre a pesar mío y dice más de lo que quiero decir. Yo debiera ofenderme en vez de halagarle a usted; pero mi orgullo, tan susceptible en otras, no lo es en esta ocasión. No tema usted, *vanidoso*, no tema usted, que yo le crea *enamorado* si usa conmigo un lenguaje tierno. ¿Me cree usted una niña o una vieja? No tema usted, repito, y para tranquilizarse enteramente, sepa usted que el día en que le creyese a usted *enamorado* de mí, ese día cesaría de amarle y no le vería a usted más. Con que con esta seguridad su libertad no corre ningún riesgo conmigo, ni tiene usted necesidad de alarmarse de mi ternura, como si viese en ella un lazo de hierro pronto a aprisionarlo. ¡Amable melancólico! ¡Qué poco mundo tiene usted! Perdóname, amigo, esta frase, pero me hace gracia, tanta gracia ver tu temor y adivinar tu corazón al través de ese velo con que piensas cubrirlo! Me temes, Cepeda, no lo niegues; temes que me posesione yo de tu corazón; temes los lazos de hierro que pudieran ser consecuencia de tu amor por mí, y crees evitar algo acogiéndote a la sagrada sombra de la amistad. ¡Oh!, eres un niño si tal crees. Cuánto te engañas, querido, cuánto, si crees que la amistad señalaría límites que el corazón respetara! ¿Qué importa el nombre a los sentimientos? ¿Dejan de ser los mismos? Lo que debe tranquilizarte no es eso, sino el saber que no hallas en mí *un enemigo de tu libertad* y que, por mi propio interés, cuidaré de no dar a tu corazón más vehementes afectos que los que hoy abrigue.

Raro, original es el papel que hago contigo. Yo, mujer, ¡tranquilizándote a ti del miedo de amarme! ¡Es cosa peregrina! Pero contigo no soy mujer, no: soy toda espíritu, y ninguna regla es aplicable a este cariño excepcional que me inspiras.

Muy larga es esta carta; pero no imitaré yo a los que acaban las suyas jurando (nada menos que jurando) ser más corto en lo sucesivo. Esta es larga; pero aún lo será más la que escriba cuando no se me ordene *no usar expresiones que conmuevan demasiado y hagan mucho daño*. . . .

¡Adiós, mi amado amigo! Cuídese usted, diviértase y vuelva pronto donde le llaman los votos más sinceros de una amistad tiernísima.

Expresiones de Concha, y mil afectos de su invariable TULA.

Sevilla, agosto 28 de 1839

P.D.: Ruego a usted disimule la incoherencia de ésta [carta] y su poca unidad y defecto de estilo. Veo que está rara; pero va según mi cabeza. ¡Tengo tanta confusión en ella! Y luego, mi humor hoy es malísimo.

CARTA 9

[Sin fecha—sobre noviembre de 1839]

Anteanoche te dije que había enviado a tu casa un libro, y no pude añadir, por los testigos que había, que dicho libro era, como lo es el que hoy te mando, un pretexto para escribirte sin que el portador se haga cargo. La fatalidad hizo que no te encontrase en tu casa el mensajero, y rasgué la carta en un momento de impaciencia contra la mala suerte, que la hizo volver por dos veces a mis manos cuando la suponía en las tuyas.

Nada, empero, contenía dicha carta de importancia; era solamente la expresión de mi tristeza en varios días, que no te veía, y una proposición que ahora voy a repetir en pocas palabras. Veremos si te agrada.

Pronto vas a graduarte, y creo que saliendo de eso podrás verme con más frecuencia: aún antes de graduarte nos hemos de ver algunas veces, porque, ¿cómo vivir así, querido amigo? ¿Quién tiene resistencia? La mía comienza a faltarme, no obstante todos mis propósitos. He pensado, pues, que debemos convenir en una cosa, y es que siempre que tú vengas y esté yo sola aprovechemos tales momentos para realizar un deseo, que tengo desde hace mucho tiempo, y que es el de leer contigo alguna obra interesante. Aun estando mamá podemos, si nos agrada, entretener un rato en la lectura, pues ningún inconveniente veo en ello si a ti no te desagrada mi proyecto. Con este objeto he hecho una lista de algunas obras de mi gusto, que voy a nombrarte para que tú escojas la que te parezca y me lo digas. Yo la tendré en casa inmediatamente, y la comenzaremos en la primera oportunidad. ¡Qué placer presiento, mi dulce amigo, en leer contigo una obra interesante!

En primer lugar, porque quiero que conozcas al primer prosista de Europa, el novelista más distinguido de la época. Tengo en lista: *El pirata*; *Los privados rivales*; *El Waverley* y *El anticuario*, obras del célebre Walter Scott.

Seguidamente, *Corina o Italia*, por Madame Staël. Novela descriptiva del más hermoso y poético país del mundo, y hecha esta descripción por la pluma de una escritora cuyo mérito conoces. Además, han dado algunos amigos en decirme que hay semejanzas entre mí y la protagonista de esta novela, y deseo por eso volver a leerla contigo y buscar la semejanza, que se me atribuye con este bello ideal de un genio como el de la Staël.[4]

Sigue la *Atala* del inmortal Chateaubriand, porque te agradan todas las escenas de la naturaleza, todos los *corazones primitivos*, en fin, el hombre en su estado normal; y esta linda obra te satisfará. Luego, las poesías de Lista, Quintana y Heredia, porque, como dice uno de estos poetas:

> *. . . Verás la poesía*
> *del corazón y mente descendiendo*
> *al corazón y mente arrebatarse.*

Esta es mi lista: escoge tú la obra que mejor te parezca y avísamelo. ¡Verás qué placer gozamos en los momentos que pasemos juntos! A tu elección dejo también tus visitas a casa, pero no quiero que dejemos de vernos por un motivo. . . . Leeremos juntos. ¿No es éste un placer? Adiós, mi bien.

CARTA 10

Señor don Ignacio Cepeda:

Hasta hoy sábado, que vino el correo general, no se ha traído la carta de usted, querido Cepeda, y para que ésta no duerma hasta el miércoles en la estafeta, determino enviarla directamente a su casa de usted.

Cuando anteanoche me dijo usted que mandase al correo, porque me había usted escrito, se olvidó advertirme que la carta venía a mi nombre y no al adoptado en nuestra correspondencia. Así, aunque ayer mandé, no me la trajeron, porque la persona encargada buscó a Doña Amadora de Almonte[5] y no a mi nombre. En fin, ya está en mis manos esta querida carta.

¡Una vez por semana . . . ! ¡Solamente te veré una vez por semana . . . ! Bien: Yo suscribo, pues así lo deseas y lo exigen tus actuales ocupaciones. Una vez por semana te veré únicamente: pues señálame, por Dios, ese día feliz entre siete para separarle de los otros días de la larga y enojosa semana. Si no determinases ese día, ¿no comprendes tú la agitación que darías a todos los otros? En cada uno de ellos creería ver al amanecer *un día feliz*, y después de muchas horas de agitación y expectativa pasaría el día, pasaría la noche, llevándose una esperanza a cada momento renovada y desvanecida, y sólo me dejaría el disgusto del desengaño. Dime, pues, para evitarme tan repetidos tormentos, qué día es ese que debo desear: ¿será el viernes? En ese caso comenzaremos por hoy; si no, será el sábado. ¿Qué te parece? Elige tú: si hoy, lo conoceré viéndote venir; si mañana, avísamelo para que yo no padezca esta noche esperándote, que tendrá para mí luz y alegría.

¡Ya lo ve usted, me arrastra mi corazón, no sé usar con usted el *lenguaje moderado*, que usted desea y emplea; pero en todo lo demás soy dócil a su voz de usted, como lo es un niño a la de su madre! Ya ve usted que suscribo a no verle sino semanalmente. Pero, ¿no irá usted al Liceo? ¿no al baile? Para decidirle a usted ¿no será bastante que yo le asegure no habrá placer para mí en estas diversiones si usted no asiste? . . .

¡Cepeda! ¡Cepeda! Debes gozar y estar orgulloso, porque este poder absoluto que ejerces en mi voluntad debe envanecerte. ¿Quién eres? ¿qué poder es ése? ¿quién te lo ha dado? . . . Tú no eres un hombre, no, a mis ojos. Eres el Angel de mi destino, y pienso muchas veces al verte que te ha dado el mismo Dios el poder supremo de dispensarme los bienes y los males que debo gozar y sufrir en este suelo. Te lo juro por ese Dios que adoro, y por tu honor y el mío; te lo juro que mortal ninguno ha tenido la influencia que tú sobre mi corazón. Tú eres mi amigo, mi hermano, mi confidente, y, como si tan dulces nombres aún no bastasen a mi corazón, él te da el de su Dios sobre la tierra. ¿No está ya en tu mano dispensarme un día de ventura entre siete? ¡Así pudieras también señalarme uno de tormento y desesperación, y yo lo recibiría, sin que estuviese en mi mano evitarlo! Ese día, querido hermano mío, ese día sería aquel en que dejases de quererme; pero yo lo aceptaría de ti sin quejarme, como aceptamos de Dios infortunios inevitables con que nos agobia.

No me haga usted caso; tuve jaqueca a medianoche y creo que me ha dejado algo de calentura: ¿no es verdad? Mi cabeza no está en su ser natural.

Adiós. Lo que es esta noche, si usted me ve, será en casa, porque C. ha quedado en venir, y no puedo ir a su casa sabiendo [que] viene ella a la mía.

Deseo leer a usted un himno patriótico, que acabo de componer, y otros versos a un jilguero.

Adiós otra vez, mi dulce amigo; no conserves ésta, rásgala, te lo ruego. Es una carta de dislates, que sólo la desconfianza de que todas las que escriba hoy salgan lo mismo me hace mandar ésta. Hay días en que está uno no sé cómo: días en que el corazón se rompería si no se desahogase. Yo tenía necesidad de decirte todo lo que te he dicho; ahora ya estoy más tranquila. No me censures, por Dios.

CARTA 12

Caro amigo: Aprovecho la visita, que ha venido a hacerme una de mis antiguas criadas, menos torpe que las que tengo actualmente, para ponerte estas líneas, encargándola de llevártelas.

No irás al baile, ya lo sé, y no quiero infringir mis propósitos importunándote con objeto de verte en él. Pero como deseo contarte qué tal estuvo y lo que hice, y lo que vi, y lo que hablé . . . ¡todo!: como deseo referirte las personas que estaban, los trajes de las señoras, en fin, todo, todo como ya dije, espero que tú tengas también alguna curiosidad de saberlo, y te invito (sin comprometerte) a que vengas mañana por la noche.

El baile, según parece, no estará demasiado concurrido, pues anoche mismo vimos despachando en el teatro billetes sueltos, y se nos dijo que había sido preciso hacerlo, porque no había más que 44 suscritores. Pero si usted estuviera, ¿no estaría harto concurrido para mí . . . ? ¡No será! ¡paciencia! Voy adquiriendo con usted una resignación admirable, de la que no me creía capaz: porque a la verdad, vida mía, puedo muy bien decirle a usted aquel verso de una comedia de Moreto:[6]

¡Qué tibio galán hacéis!

Y, sin embargo, yo lo sufro con un estoicismo heroico. ¿Sabes que a veces me pregunto a mí misma por qué he de querer a un hombre tan poco complaciente, tan poco asiduo, tan poco apasionado como tú? Me lo pregunto y no alcanzo respuesta de mi pícaro corazón, tan caprichoso. Pero, no, Ignacio mío, ¡no es verdad! El me responde siempre satisfactoriamente y me dice que te ama porque eres bueno, noble, sincero, porque eres el mejor hombre del mundo, y es justicia amarte cuando se ha tenido la dicha de conocerte.

Ya lo ves: aunque mis cartas comiencen algunas veces amargas o festivas, siempre las concluyo más tiernas que debieran ser, y tú abusas, ingrato, de esta ternura mía para hacer cuanto se te antoja y nunca lo que yo deseo. Ya me las pagará usted, señor mío, el día en que esté yo de humor de hacer desesperar a usted; digo, si acaso usted se desespera por alguna cosa. . . . Vaya esta heridita entre tantas flores como le prodigo, porque, a fe mía, no merece usted tanta bondad.

Adiós.—Mañana, ¿eh? . . . esto es, *si puede usted*, si se lo permiten sus estudios, visitas, etc.; y ahora acuérdate un momento de que te ama a pesar de tus *indocilidades* tu demasiada buena

G.

CARTA 13

Voy a probarte que no soy tan dócil, como anoche me reprochaste, a tu antigua orden. Voy a saludarte con la pluma, ya que verbalmente no puedo hacerlo hoy. ¡Vida mía! ¡qué mala noche he pasado, qué mala estoy, qué triste . . . ! No tengo vida sino para amarte; para todo lo que no es tu amor estoy insensible. Ni me agrada escribir, ni leer, ni bordar, ni la calle, ni mi casa. Si algún talento he tenido, creo positivamente que lo he perdido ya, porque me encuentro lo más necia y fastidiada. He leído no sé donde:

> *Un momento ha vencido*
> *mi audacia imprudente,*
> *este alma tan soberbia . . . ,*
> *¡vedla ya dependiente!*

Yo he mandado siempre en mi corazón y en mis acciones con mi entendimiento, y ahora mi entendimiento está subyugado por mi corazón, y mi corazón por un sentimiento todo nuevo, todo extraordinario.

¡Posible es, Dios mío, que cuando yo me creía libre ya del dominio de amor, cuando me persuadía de haberlo conocido, cuando me lisonjeaba de experta y desilusionada, haya caído como una víctima débil e indefensa en las garras de hierro de una pasión desconocida, inmensa y cruel! . . . !Posible es, Cepeda, que yo ame ahora con el corazón de una niña de trece años! . . . ¿Qué es esto que por mí pasa? ¿Qué es esto que yo siento? . . . Dímelo, dímelo, porque yo no lo sé. Es harto nuevo para mí, te lo juro. Y yo he amado antes que a ti, he amado, o lo he creído así, y, sin embargo, nunca, nunca he sentido lo que ahora siento. ¿Es amor esto? No, hay algo de más, a mi corazón. ¡Qué feliz era! ¡Cuán tiernamente te amaba! ¡Los ángeles me envidiarían! Y ahora, ahora, ¡cuán desgraciada! ¡Cuánto sufro! ¡Cuánto, querido mío! ¿Y por qué? ¿Qué ha sucedido? ¿Qué cosa me atormenta? Nada, yo no lo sé. ¿Es acaso que Dios castiga el exceso de amor, haciéndole un martirio? ¿Es que el corazón humano es estrecho y se rompe cuando está demasiado lleno? . . . ¿Es un presentimiento de desgracia? ¿Es una plenitud de felicidad? ¿Es un defecto de mi organización, o una inconsecuencia de mi espíritu? . . . Yo no lo sé, pero estoy abatida, padezco, soy desgraciada.

No te pido que vengas a menudo, no, ni aun el lunes, como has ofrecido. Mejor será más tarde: el martes, el miércoles, el jueves . . . en fin, cuando yo esté menos triste que ahora, porque tu presencia, tan cara, tan deseada antes, ahora aumentaría mi tristeza. ¡Cuidado,

Cepeda, cuidado! . . . Ten cuidado de mi corazón, tenlo . . . , mira que puedo morir. Tú no sabes, no puedes saber, que puedes matarme, no lo sabes. Pues bien, acaso te es muy fácil. Si quieres mi vida, si quieres conservar tu amiga, cuídala; dale tranquilidad, dale sosiego. Yo conozco que eres más prudente que yo, y me acuerdo de que alguna vez me has pedido *paz y olvido*. Olvido, no, pero paz, yo quiero dártela y quiero tenerla. Tú tenías razón, la tenías. ¡Paz, sí, paz! Yo la necesito como tú y como tú la demando. De hoy en adelante, de común acuerdo, nos daremos paz, bien mío. ¡Desgraciados los que quieren apretar el corazón hasta romperlo, los que dan impulso a una máquina sin saber si tienen fuerza para detenerla cuando quieren! Es santa, es sagrada la vida del corazón, y nos empeñamos en gastarla. ¡Porque todo se gasta, todo! ¡Hoy no puedo resistir, mi corazón me ahoga! Mañana acaso estará parado y frío. ¡Nada es inexhausto! Se deben respetar los sentimientos y se debe temerlos. Ellos pueden dar la dicha o la desgracia. Tú no querrás darme sino felicidad. Si para dármela al presente es preciso más. Es preciso que me compadezcas, y acaso . . . acaso que dejes de verme. ¡Cuánto me cuesta decírtelo! Rompe ésta, y adiós.

CARTA 32

Madrid, 25 de julio de 1845

Querido Cepeda: Perdona el innoble papel en que te escribo; se va el correo, estoy demudada y no encuentro otro papel a mano. Te ofrezco, antes de todo, mi nueva habitación, calle del Horno de la Mata, número 9, cuarto principal, y luego voy a contestar brevemente tu grata última. . . .

¡Conque piensas casarte? . . . No te lo censuro, ni lo apruebo. Para mí la verdadera felicidad no consiste en el estado que se tiene; así como no creo que la bondad de los gobiernos consista en su forma. El matrimonio es mucho o poco, según se considere; es absurdo o racional, según se motive.

Yo no me he casado, ni me casaré nunca; pero no es por un fanatismo de libertad, como algunos suponen. Creo que no temblaría por ligarme para toda la vida, si hallase un hombre capaz de inspirarme una estimación tal que garantizase la duración de mi afecto. Más; tengo la convicción de que no hay dicha en lo que es pasajero, y digo, como Chateaubriand, que si tuviese la locura de creer en la felicidad la buscaría en la costumbre. El matrimonio es un mal necesario del cual pueden sacarse muchos bienes. Yo lo considero a mi modo, y a mi modo lo abrazaría. Lo abrazaría con la bendición del cura o sin ella; poco me importaría; para mí el matrimonio garantizado por los hombres o garantizado por la recíproca de los contrayentes únicamente, no tiene más diferencia sino que el uno es más público y el otro más solemne: el uno puede ser útil a la impunidad de los abusos y el otro los dificulta; el uno es más *social* y el otro más *individual*. Para mí es santo todo vínculo contraído con recíproca confianza y buena fe, y sólo veo deshonra donde hay mentira y codicia. Yo no tengo ni tendré un vínculo, porque lo respeto demasiado; porque el hombre a quien me uniese debía ser no solamente amable, sino digno de *veneración*; porque no he hallado, ni puedo hallar un corazón bastante grande para recibir el mío sin oprimirlo, y un carácter bastante elevado para considerar *las cosas y los hombres* como yo los considero.

Tú no estás en ese caso; eres el hombre y puedes buscar felicidad en una mujer aun cuando ella no esté a tu altura. Créeme, sin embargo: no te cases con una tonta; la mayor virtud no compensa el defecto de talento, y aun me atrevo a decir que no hay virtud en la estupidez. Las ligerezas, las faltas mismas de una mujer son males más remediables que la incapacidad de comprender aun las mismas virtudes que acaso se practican. El talento se extravía, pero la tontería no sabe siquiera que sigue el buen camino, y si lo deja no lo recobra jamás. Cásate, si lo crees conveniente; pero acuérdate siempre de que una amiga te aconseja no juzgar nunca virtud la frialdad de las almas ineptas, ni pensar, como algunos, que la ignorancia garantiza el corazón.

Ésta es ya muy larga, y aun no te he dicho que pienso establecerme en París. Sí, amigo mío; parece que en aquella capital puedo prometerme mayores ventajas de mi pluma, y como no soy rica y quiero asegurarme una vejez sin privaciones, pienso irme *adonde mejor paguen*. Esto, sin embargo, aun no es cosa decidida. Veremos.[7]

Estoy cansada del mundo, de los obsequios, de las calumnias, de la adulación, de la gloria y hasta de la vida. Necesito otro espacio mayor o menor que éste, otra vida de más calma o de más agitación. El amor no existe ya para mí; la gloria no me basta; quiero *dinero*, pues quiero la vida de los viajes o la vida del *retiro muelle y lleno de goces del lujo.* Tampoco me sería ingrato irme a una pobre aldea a criar pichones; pero aun no puedo, porque necesito de mi pluma.

En fin, si tú te casas con una buena chica que tenga talento, que sea bonita para que no sea celosa, que te quiera mucho y merezca ser correspondida, suspenderé mi curso vagabundo para ir dondequiera que estéis a cantaros un lindo epitalamio y a pasar ocho días con vosotros. ¿Aceptas?

Adiós; acabo de publicar una oda, que ha alborotado a Madrid, y que me ha valido un gran regalo del Infante D. Francisco de Paula. Te la mandaré un día de éstos, y hoy me repito tu amiguísima,

TULA

P.D. . . . Yo he dicho en una novela: "No acuséis al corazón de perder sus ilusiones; así como no se acusa al árbol por ceder sus hojas al inclemente soplo de viento." ¿Pero el árbol desnudo y el corazón desengañado no pueden llorar la pérdida de sus flores? Sin acusar a nadie se puede decir: han hecho a mi corazón un daño con voluntad o sin ella.

Carta a Antonio Romero Ortiz[8]

Día 5 de Mayo (1853)

Querido Antonio, parece que no tienes ni chispa de impaciencia por repetir tu visita à Eloisa. Nada me dices de eso; nada de vernos. Acaso haces bien: creo que el comunicarnos por cartas tiene grandes ventajas bien examinado. Por mi parte, aunque se me hacen muy largos los dias privada de tu presencia, con todo, conozco que mas bien nos conviene qᵉ. nos daña este [*sic*] lejania, que no me impide saber tus pensamientos y comunicarte los mios. El amor, ese tirano insaciable que con nada sé da por satisfecho, sabe ser tambien un niño dócil y hasta pueril, qᵉ. se entretiene con cualquier cosa, y se alegra y se reputa dichoso. He deseado algunas veces que Armand[9] hubiese continuado siendo por largo tiempo mi *invisible caballero*; que solo su pensamiento hubiese llegado à mi, siempre envuelto en esas nubes de rosa del misterio, como la eterna promesa de una felicidad nunca poseida pº. incesantemᵗᵉ. esperada. Al adquirir una forma, y un caracter determinado, mi fantástico caballero se ha hecho amar mucho, si ciertamᵗᵉ . . . mucho! pero es indudable qᵉ. lo qᵉ. ahora me inspira es un sentimiento agitador y doloroso; mientras que todo era dulce, tranquilo, ideal en lo que esperimentaba por mi Armand.

Sin pensarlo, amigo mio, he contestado à la pregunta que me haces en tu carta de ayer. Si, Antonio, yo te amo, eso es una verdad: pero quieres tambien que te esplique *como te amo* y eso lo espresare mejor cuando no quiera qᵉ. cuando de intento me ponga à definirlo. Te amo, à lo que entiendo, de varios modos, y eso es lo que me disgusta: si te amase de uno solo ambos seriamos mas felices y nos entenderiamos mejor. Te amo cuando no te veo, cuando no te escucho, cuando solo llegan à mi tus cartas y no te veo mas qᵉ. en mi corazon, te amo entonces con un afecto en qᵉ. gozo; con un afecto q^e. me engrandece à mis propios ojos: Siento en tales instantes q^e. aunq^e. fueras viejo, de fea figura, despreciable p^a. todas las mujeres, serias bello p^a. mi por tu alma; joven por tu amor. Siento q^e. mi corazon noble y puro se lanza al tuyo por un movimiento de santa confianza y de casta simpatia, y que nos unimos con un vínculo sin nombre, pero augusto, indisoluble, eterno: por aquel consorcio de las inteligencias que he deseado tanto conocer y q^e. no he visto jamas. Entonces, Antonio, no dudo de ti, ni de mi: entonces no te llamo esposo, porq^e. no encuentro nombre que darte en el lenguaje humano: entonces eres p^a. mi *la esperanza*, q^e. es lo unico grande que puede gozar el hombre: entonces respiro contigo en una atmósfera tan pura, tan embalsamada, tan suave, que me parece imposible la puedan surcar jamas las pasiones terrenales. He aqui como te amo algunas veces; como quisiera amarte para siempre; como debo amarte si aspiro à ser feliz por el amor. Pero desgraciadam^{te}. en mi organizacion desventurada todos los estremos se tocan: cuando te veo, cuando te oigo, cuando respiro tu aliento, cuando me haces una caricia, me arrancas subitam^{te}. de mi region encantada, me haces desear delicias terrenales, me das fiebre, Antonio, una fiebre tal que quedo enferma por muchas horas; me transformas en una mujer vulgarisima; me haces avergonzar de mi misma y de la flaca naturaleza humana . . . en fin, te amo entonces con un amor tan violento como receloso, tan ambicioso como impotente: con un amor que logrando cuanto anhela no seria feliz; que dandolo todo no daria nada. Si, te amo entonces con pasion pero con cólera contra ti y contra mi, y contra la naturaleza: te amo dudando de tu corazon y del mio, porq^e. en tales momentos me parece muy dudoso que sea algo ese q^e. llamamos corazon: en esos momentos, querido mio, me pregunto con pavura si es cierto q^e. el hombre está llamado à mas alto destino que el q^e. vé en el bruto; si no ha nacido, lo mismo que este, para multiplicarse y morir . . . me parece entonces que lo q^e. llamamos alma, sentimiento, idea, acaso no son en suma sino seducciones que emplea la pícara naturaleza material p^a. llevarnos ciegos à cumplir sus leyes: esas leyes q^e. el bruto obedece por instinto, y q^e. el *animal pensador* cumple mas fatalm^{te}. todavia, arrastrado por la esperanza de un bien mentiroso, irrealizable.

Oh! no sabré nunca esplicarte lo que yo veo y siento y juzgo en estas cosas: no podré por mas que diga hacerte comprender la lucha q^e. hay entre mi orgullo de inteligencia y mi naturaleza de mujer apasionada: no se definen estas contrariedades, Antonio: se sienten, no se pintan. ¿Quieres saber como te amo? . . . Como tu quieras: esta es la verdad. Con un afecto que no puede darte ninguna otra mujer; con una ternura y un idealismo infinito; con una felicidad íntima y duradera . . . y tambien puedo amarte como Safo à Faon:[10] tambien puedo decir como ella,

> Ante mis ojos desparece el mundo
> y por mis venas circular ligero
> el fuego siento de placer profundo . . .
> Trémula, en vano resistirte quiero,
> de ardiente llanto mi méjilla inundo,
> deliro, gozo, te bendigo, y muero!

Oh! si! desgraciadam^{te}. hay en mí estas dos naturalezas poderosas del poeta y de la mujer: hay en mí idealismo bastante p^a. vivir toda la vida de un suspiro de tu amor, y bastante sangre p^a. agotar en un momento todo tu amor y el mio. Desgraciadam^{te}. tambien, has tenido el poder de despertar à la vez ambas naturalezas, y se empeñan en una lucha cuyo exito ignoro. En los momentos en q^e. la victoria se inclina por la *naturaleza ideal*, entonces es cuando te amo con fé, en ti y en mi; cuando creo q^e. seré feliz y me hallo digna de serlo. En los momentos en q^e. gana terreno la *naturaleza terrestre*, entonces es cuando te amo dudando, cuando temo q^e. no podamos querernos ni estimarnos largo tiempo; cuando me desprecio à mi misma al mismo tiempo q^e. se revela mi insensato orgullo contra el fallo de mi propia conciencia: entonces sufro, y te hago sufrir, y soy caprichosa, y desigual, y llena de inconsecuencias. Entonces me parece q^e. ha sido ridículo todo mi idealismo de poeta, puesto q^e. había de parar por donde comienza el instinto de la bestia. Y sin embargo, en medio de aquellas tempestades de alma, q^e. se venga tan cruelm^{te}.[*sic*], en mí, de los momentáneos triunfos de mi otra naturaleza terrestre, sucede q^e. te amo locam^{te}. y te llamo *mon homme* [mi hombre], y me parece en aquel instante q^e. no hay dicha mayor q^e. ser tuya de todos modos; tuya por todos los vínculos posibles. Una hora despues, por cuanto existe en el orbe no querria que se me cumpliese semejante deseo: por cuanto hay no querria que me uniesen à ti lazos vulgares, fuese cualquiera su nombre: no querria dar un destino vulgar à este hermoso sueño que encanta à mi alma: à esta página de mi vida en q^e. has escrito con rasgos originales y nuevos el nombre de Armand; de Antonio. Pero otra hora despues vuelvo à verte y entonces . . . entonces digo q^e. solo à Dios se puede amar en *su esencia incomprensible*; q^e. tu eres mi amante, mi esposo, que mi idealismo es una locura, una profanacion . . . q^e. la felicidad del amor está en tus brazos y no en mis sueños: entonces, Antonio, quisiera inventar lazos todavia mas estrechos que los q^e. conocemos, y mas corpóreos, y mas sensibles, p^a. ligarme à ti con todos ellos. De todos estos modos te amo: yo no sé de mi corazón mas de lo q^e. te digo: te lo juro, Antonio. ¿Me haras feliz? no lo sé. ¿Lo soy ahora? No; estoy muy disgustada conmigo misma, y de rechazo contigo tambien. ¿Está en tu mano terminar mis disgustos? Creo q^e. no, por ahora al menos: ¿estará despues? Es muy probable. ¿De que modo? . . . Casi no lo alcanzo. Lo único q^e. veo claro es q^e. te quiero, que si sabes no escitar en mi estas luchas, mi amor puede hacerme mucho bien: que si te gozas en matar mi idealismo, acaso luego querras en balde hacerlo renacer. Si; tengo un poder terrible sobre mi corazón; es mi orgullo: respétalo siempre, Antonio: no me digas jamas una sola palabra que me haga sospechar q^e. me crees flaca y esclava de mis pasiones: con solo eso me harias fuerte, me harias invencible; pero ¡ah! ¿viviria mi amor despues de haber sido una vez violentam^{te}. ahogado?—Basta de esto p^a. siempre, amigo mio: te suplico que volvamos à ser por algunos dias Armand y Gertrudis: escríbeme como entonces: véme ò no me veas, segun te parezca conveniente: te dejo dueño absoluto de tu conducta en este punto. Recibiré tus cartas con placer intimo: te veré con felicidad siempre q^e. quieras; pero ni te exijo que dediques algun rato cada dia à hablar con tu amiga, ni me quejaré si dejas de verme mas ó menos tiempo. Sé libre, Antonio mio, sé siempre libre en tus relaciones conmigo, y cree q^e. aunq^e. tan celosa, tan exijente, tan inconstante en mi caracter, soy bastante firme en mis sentimientos, y no decaerá mi amor mientras tu seas noble, bueno, sincero, leal, aunq^e. seas menos apasionado si asi lo crees conveniente. ¿Que mas puedo decirte?

¿Dudaras aun? no me entenderas todavia? ¿Seguiras creyendo que no te amo lo q^c. tu deseas? Oh! serias bien injusto. Antonio, antes q^c.

serlo pideme pruebas à tu placer. No es la primera vez q^c. te he dicho q^c. *serás arbitro de mi suerte:* te repito ahora q^c. *te amaré como tu quieras*; q^c. seré p^a. ti, hoy mismo si te place, *la q^c. tu quieras q^c. sea*; pero dejame creer, amigo mio, Armando mio, mi leal caballero, déjame creer q^c. tu no quieres sino mi felicidad, y q^c. comprendes que mi felicidad será grande si me haces sentir que tu la posees, y q^c. ambos la merecemos. Si soy una pobre sensitiva q^c. sufre con los cámbios atmosféricos, eso, ya lo ves, no es culpa mia. Si deseo verte y me enojo alguna vez porque no lo adivinas . . . tampoco es culpa mia. Se indulgente: sufre mis desigualdades y ámame siempre, como esposo, como hermano, como quieras, Antonio, pero estimandome siempre. La idea de q^c. tu amor era meram^{te}. fisico me haria mucho, muchisimo daño. Tuya.

T.

Notas

1. En realidad tenía un año más.

2. Estas son palabras de Cepeda, citadas de una carta que él le había mandado el 15 de julio de 1839.

3. Concepción Noriega, amiga de la Avellaneda.

4. Esta novela describe las frustraciones de la mujer como artista creadora a causa de los límites que la sociedad se la impone.

5. Cepeda era del pueblo de Almonte. "Amadora" era el nombre ficticio bajo el cual la Avellaneda se carteaba con Cepeda.

6. Agustín de Moreto y Cabaña (1618–69), Famoso dramaturgo.

7. Nunca lo hizo.

8. Para estas cartas, sí hay acceso a las que Tula escribió de su puño y letra. He conservado la ortografía original.

9. El nombre ficticio con el cual Romero Ortiz firmaba sus cartas iniciales a la Avellaneda.

10. Safo: poeta griega (600 *a.C.*). Hay una leyenda, probablemente ficticia, que dice que se enamoró de un hombre, Faón, y cuando él no le correspondió su amor, Safo se tiró de un precipicio. Se sabe muy poco de su vida.

Letters to Ignacio de Cepeda

LETTER I

During an hour of sleeplessness and melancholy on the night of July 13 [1839]. Dedicated to my "companion in disillusionment." For him alone.

[Avellaneda begins her letter with a lengthy poem that speaks to her personal disappointment with life and to how these feelings link her to Cepeda, who she thinks feels similarly.]

It disturbs me very, very much to hear you express your ideas, sufferings and hopes. You see by the above creation what thoughts this produces in me. Listen to the verses and not to the ideas.

In actual fact, sometimes this *fullness of life* oppresses me and I would like to be rid of its weight. I have worked for a long time to diminish my moral existence so as to bring it to the same level as my physical one. Judged by a society which fails to understand me, and weary of a lifestyle that perhaps makes me look foolish, superior and inferior to my sex, I feel like a stranger in the world and isolated in nature. I feel the need to die, yet nevertheless live and in the eyes of many must seem happy. . . .

You speak to me of friendship, and not long ago you felt love. I believe in neither one nor the other. In fleeting emotions, in superficial affections I look for something to distract my consuming thoughts, and in this way I feel less tormented, for [as I am] inconstant in my tastes I easily tire of everything, and superficial feelings which hardly bind me do not take away the right to follow the instinct of my soul, which longs for freedom. Sometime I hope to find on this earth a melancholy, ardent, proud and ambitious heart like my own, to share with him my pleasures and sorrows, and to give him this excess of life which alone I am unable to bear. But more often I fear this enormous capacity of mine for suffering, and have a foreboding that an impassioned love would arouse [such] storms in my breast that they might perturb my reason and my life. Besides, would even love fill my soul's abyss? I have tried everything and discarded it all: love and friendship. What, then, can I offer you, my dear? The compassion of a tormented heart! . . . and my verses to distract you for a bit from momentous cares.

LETTER 2

[August 1, 1839]

I am ashamed. My Lord! What must you have thought of me, Cepeda, after the strange and ridiculous conduct I displayed last night? If you were one of those conceited fools, one of those vain men who abound in this city, then I'd know what you were thinking.

Even though you are not one of those, even knowing that you are a modest man and not hasty in your judgments, I tremble when I reflect on what you must think of my foolishness, and the opinion you must have of me. What moderately modest man could there be, who, seeing the immoderate outburst you observed in me last evening, would not believe that only jealousy . . . ? My Lord! My hand trembles and I blush to think of it. I have given you cause not to believe anything I have told you up to now about the nature of my feelings toward you; I have given you cause to think that I am *in love and jealous*. I have given you cause to put me on the list of the four or five women in whom, without desiring it, you inspired an unfortunate passion. Damnation! I am feeling a humiliation which I did not think was on my list of afflictions. What kind of a role did I want to play, or, better yet, have I unwillingly played? That of the jealous woman! I, I, good Lord! I can't understand why I do not die choked with rage! I certainly feel neither love nor jealousy; it is absolutely certain that I have not regarded you as a lover nor want you as such, nor would I permit it . . . I swear this by God and my dignity as a woman! I swear that I would not have you as my lover, just as until now I have not thought of you as such.

All of this is absolutely true, as is the fact that the mutual affection which has linked us even unto our souls is as pure as it is self-
less, yet in spite of this, what a role have I played since last night!
How I have degraded myself for an inconceivable whim, for a child-
ish and bizarre outburst! To what humiliating conjectures have I laid
myself open! There you have the proof, the proof of what I have
often told you: there is something in my character that is so frivolous, so capricious and unstable that it will cause me much sorrow in
my life.

People think me a woman of some talent and sophistication, and
I myself have felt this way, but we were wrong: I know this from
experience. At the age of twenty-four[1] I have no talent, no sophistication, no prudence; I only have an unfortunate trait which I curse:
an ingenuity which borders on stupidity and madness. You must
have laughed at me; I do believe you must have. I cannot complain.
But please be so good as to hear me out for a moment, for although
I do not pretend to justify the frivolous and unrestrained nature of
my conduct last evening, perhaps I can make you understand the
true motivation thereof and will avoid, if not the impression you
must justifiably have of me as rash and indiscreet, having you think
of me as a *jealous woman*, which humiliates me beyond words and
which I most certainly do not deserve.

. . . My pain, my surprise and my agitation were the result of
the same cause. At that moment I could not see in you my heart's
friend, who assured me of a *great, tender and holy friendship* and had
told me: "you can accept it without fear or reservation, because the
purest and most fervent of hearts offers it to you."[2] Instead of this
"pure and fervent heart" at that instant of surprise and hurt I saw
only a heart which had reached its limit, a heart torn between many
alternatives. . . .

I don't recall exactly what I did or said. I know that I went mad,
nothing more, mad with pain when I saw my last and dearest illusion shattered: the divine illusion which let me think that at last I
had found a sensitive heart, pure [and] ardent, capable of great passions and perhaps of great mistakes, but not of lukewarm and multiple affections. . . .

All this, rushing suddenly to my head, upset it to such a degree that I no longer knew what I did. It seemed that I had been transported to another world, a hell, and that letter of yours which I had in my breast burned me like a glowing ember. I committed a thousand improprieties, improprieties which could be disastrously interpreted, and what I feel worst about, what most humiliates me, is to think that you, Cepeda, you thought you were seeing an outburst of jealousy when it was only a pained rebuff. My God, how ashamed I am! Would that I had died before going out last evening! . . .

Other than that I have nothing left to say. Withdraw your trust from me; I do not deserve it, for I am too violent and frivolous. I am also still very young in order to be the confidante of a man of your age and worth, and, I would even say of a man in such a delicate position. I have neither the necessary maturity nor the talent in order to give sound advice, and can only get upset or engage in foolishness like last night. I will always be your friend. . . .

Good-bye, my dear friend, bon voyage! Leave me a few lines at the post office, acknowledging receipt of this letter, for I would have no peace if I did not know for sure that you had received it. Have a good time in Elmonte or Almonte, take care of your health and be studious so that we will see you again soon. I repeat and fervently beg you, on my knees if necessary, that you forget my wretched behavior last night. If nothing can stop you from believing that only love, a jealous and exalted love at that, could drive a woman who normally is neither mad nor stupid to commit such foolishness, then believe it. But you must also believe that if such a love existed, it does so no longer, and if it existed, it was without my knowledge. In any case, what I most desire is that all that is past be forgotten.

LETTER 6

Mr. Ignacio Cepeda:

I have received your kind letter, my dear friend, with even greater satisfaction ever since Concha[3] informed me that since you were not in Almonte, but somewhere else your brother had men-

tioned and whose name I could not remember, I was afraid my letter might have gotten lost. I sent a maid to the post office several
times and she always told me that there was no letter, until yesterday, when it was impossible for me to go out and I availed myself of
Concha, who went to the post office herself and immediately
brought me the longed-for letter from you.

I am so glad that you are well, as you write me, and less melancholy than in your former [letter]. For my part I would like to be
able to say the same but, unfortunately, this is not the case. My
stomach pains have given me a great deal of trouble and my melancholy is worse every day. You tell me to get over it! . . . A wish of
yours certainly exercises strong influence on my heart, but in this
matter it is perhaps not within my power to accommodate the request made by your tender friendship. Besides the absence of my
best, indeed of my only friend, which is reason enough to make me
melancholy, I have so many other reasons to be sad! The prospect of
soon having to face a protracted separation from a mother I love
very dearly! The indecision with which I struggle without knowing
which side to take nor what life has in store for me! The need for
independence and the fear of public opinion which impedes my taking it! . . . In any event, so many, many things are upsetting me at
the present moment (during which time, if appearances are any indication, the day of crisis is approaching), that even Cepeda's friendship, that sweet and flattering friendship, will not be enough to give
me peace. But enough! Let's speak of other matters. I do wish my
letters were more cheerful! But oh, I see that that is impossible! The
bitterness of my heart becomes entangled in all of them. Do forgive
me!

I will send on my translation by the channels you indicated, but
it will have to be later on, when I have the time to do it, for the
rough draft is unintelligible and the only readable copy I had, I had
promised to send on to Cádiz. The editors of the new literary journal, which is published there under the name of *The Aureole*, sent me
a flattering letter asking me to let the journal publish some of my
works, and even though I wished to say no, I was obliged to do
them the favor because a relative of mine, of whom I think highly,

was so insistent in this matter that I could not refuse without insulting him. Therefore I have let *The Aureole* have my translation, under the condition that it not be published under my name, but entirely anonymously.

As soon as I can I will send you a copy, and from the outset beg your indulgence. You would really need to know the original to fully appreciate just how difficult the translation was. Lamartine, one of the greatest poets of the modern school, and perhaps the sweetest and easiest, nevertheless has something undefined and metaphysical in his poetry and a way of speaking that is really quite untranslatable. In many of his works his ideas are so delicate that they can wither, so to speak, under the translator's pen, and his expressions on occasion are so daring as to be intimidating. In *The Fountain* I have tried to translate with the greatest possible precision, letting the author's thoughts and ideas penetrate me, but I am still very far from the satisfaction of thinking that I have been able to imitate with even middling success his fluid and harmonious versification or that mystical, melancholy coloring which is characteristic of his works.

As far as my novel [*Sab*] is concerned, I have submitted the first ten chapters to the scrutiny of the compatriot whom I already mentioned, a cultivated man who fortunately is now here in this city, and have had the pleasure of gaining his approval. He has encouraged my timid pen, assuring me that the descriptive parts are rendered with precision and variety, and that the characters are well drawn and forcefully developed. His kindness has made him go so far as to bestow undeserved praise on my style and to judge the novel's organization extremely interesting. For all my self-esteem, I know that he has done me a good turn with his opinion, but in spite of that he has encouraged me to keep on trying in order to deserve the best.

So you see, my good friend, that I speak to you of things that are only things; you see that I am avoiding what you call the language of the imagination and I call the language of the heart: you judge it to be dangerous and banish it from our letters. I obey your formidable verdict, but what are you afraid of, my friend? What danger do you wish to avoid? Perhaps if you heard and used the language of the heart, are you afraid that you would be unable to prevent it getting away from you? Would you be afraid to feel or inspire a feeling stronger than that of friendship . . . ? If that is the case, calm yourself, for I assure you that you will never love me as anything but a sister, and that you will never find other affections in my soul other than those which today I am vain enough to express to you. These past few days I have thought a great deal about the nature of our feelings, and, I swear to you, this examination has given me peace. I would lose a great deal if you stopped being my friend in order to become my lover. Lovers! . . . So many of them besiege a young woman and what good are they? But where to find a friend such as you? Lovers! . . . Look, I'm fed up with them; that gaggle of flatterers that pesters our sex seems to me hardly worth bothering with, even to amuse oneself for a while with their idiotic compliments. I don't for a minute believe that they are in love with me! One man courts me because I'm an foreigner he hasn't met, whose class he perhaps judges as doubtful, whose customs he doesn't know and thinks are probably lax, of whose conquest he has no doubt and woos me with the idea that I could be his little whim, his toy, his amusement, his short-term pleasure. Another man courts me because he is a professional flatterer of any pretty women he meets: devoid of ideas, of sense, of prospects, just for the sake of courting and cutting an elegant figure. Yet another courts me because he hasn't got a plugged nickel, as the saying goes, and is sniffing around the fleshpots. I'm American, and because I am American he supposes I have money, which is reason enough for him to begin to make his matrimonial calculations. And last, there is the man who makes love to me only for the sake of vanity: it would flatter him to be my fiancé, not because I appeal to him, but because he could give himself airs in society that a woman with a modicum of fame and who people say has some talent has chosen him. Here, my dear Cepeda, you have the motives of the great majority of the men who come to pay me court. And given my frame of mind, can I even listen to them with any other motive but to make fun of them?

And what will you find in the majority of women who say they are in love with you? One declares she loves you and all she cares about is your profession. She wants a husband, a social position, which is the goal of common women, and they look for it in you. Another says she loves you and all she sees in you is her own amusement, a man who gives her his ear, who flatters her in public and who satisfies her vanity, and whom she would jilt without a second thought for another who is a more consummate flatterer, of higher social position, more distinguished name, etc., etc. Another says she loves you and all she loves in you is her own pleasure, and . . . Oh!— I blush to mention it—but we women see it every day, to our shame. We see that class of women which degrades the dignity of their sex, and which to my eyes are more despicable than the vilest scum of the earth.

Such is love in our unhappy and corrupt society! How could it even exist between us? Oh no, never! Let us leave the tainted words of lover and beloved for other men and women. You will be my friend and I yours all our lives, and you must never fear that the holy nature of our bonds will be degraded. Will you be afraid when I am not? All I have said proves to you that you risk nothing when you let your heart speak. Vanity will not interpret your words, nor can your friend confuse the expression of your sentiments with the insipid gibberish of courtship which is termed love. As far as I am concerned I will do whatever you wish; I won't express my feelings if this bothers you, but it's such an effort for me!

You see, Cepeda: my pen runs on in spite of me and says more than I want to say. I should be offended instead of showing my affection for you, but my pride, normally so sensitive in other matters, on this occasion is not affected. Don't be afraid, *you conceited person*, don't be afraid that I shall think you are *in love* when you use tender words with me. Do you take me for a little girl or an old woman? I repeat: do not be afraid, and so that you may have complete peace of mind, know that the day I believe you are *in love* with me is the day I stop caring for you and would never see you again. With this assurance your freedom runs absolutely no risk with me, nor have you any reason to be alarmed at my affection, nor need to envision it as an iron shackle ready to make you a prisoner. Dear melancholy man! How little sophistication you have! Forgive my using this sentence, my friend, but it tickles me, it really does, to see your fear and to try to find your heart under the veil with which you try to shroud it! You are afraid of me, Cepeda, don't deny it; you're afraid I will take possession of your heart, you fear the iron shackles that might be the consequences of your love for me and you think you can avoid things by clinging to the sacred protection of friendship. Oh, if you think that, you are a child. How much you deceive yourself, dear one, how very much, if you think friendship will delineate the limits the heart should respect! What difference does it make what you call feelings? Do they stop being what they are? It is not this that should calm you, but rather the knowledge that in me you do not have *a threat to your freedom*, and that, for the sake of my own interests, I will take care not to bestow on your heart more impassioned affection than that which I feel right now.

Strange and novel is the role I play with you. I, a woman, calming your fears of loving me! That's an odd thing! But with you I am not a woman; no: I am all spirit and there are no applicable rules for the exceptional affection you arouse in me.

This letter is very long, but I refuse to imitate those people who end their letters swearing (nothing less than swearing) to be briefer in subsequent ones. This letter is long, but longer still will be the one I write when I am not told to *avoid using expressions which are too moving and do a lot of harm.* . . .

Good-bye, my dear friend! Take care of yourself, have a good time and come back soon to where the sincerest desires of a most tender friendship call you.

Concha sends her best, and from me a thousand greetings from your unchanging

Tula

Seville, August 28, 1839

P.S. I beg you to disregard the incoherence, lack of organization and defective style of this letter. I realize that it's odd, but it follows my head. It's so confused! And besides, I'm in an awful mood today.

[Undated—about November 1839]

Night before last I told you that I had sent a book to your house, but because there were other people who were around, I couldn't add that the book in question (just like the one I am sending you today) was just a pretext so that I could write you without having the messenger be any wiser. Luck had it that the man didn't find you at home, so in a fit of pique I tore up the letter to protest the bad luck that sent it back to me twice when I supposed it was already in your hands.

Anyway, the letter contained nothing of importance; it was only an expression of my sadness at not having seen you for several days, and a proposition which I shall repeat in a few brief words. Let's see if you like it.

Soon you will be graduating, and I think that when you are out from under that you can see me more often. We have to see each other sometimes even before you graduate, because who can live like this, dear friend? Who can stand it? My own resistance is beginning to fail me, in spite of all my intentions. Anyway, I thought we should agree on one thing, and that is that whenever you come and I am alone, we should take advantage of such moments to satisfy one desire, and that is for me to read some interesting book with you. Even when Mother is around we could, if we feel like it, amuse ourselves a while by reading, as I see no problem with this if the idea appeals to you. With this in mind I've drawn up a list of some works I enjoy, which I will identify so that you can choose the one you like best and then tell me. I will have it here at home right away, and we can start the first chance we have. What pleasure I envision, my sweet friend, on reading an interesting book with you!

In the first place, I want you to get to know the most eminent European prose writer, the most distinguished novelist of our time. On the list I have *The Pirate, The Rival Favorites,*[4] *Waverley* and *The Antiquary*, works by the famous Walter Scott.

Right afterward, *Corinne or Italie*, by Madame Staël. A descriptive novel of the most beautiful and poetic country in the world, the descriptions written by the pen of a woman writer of whose worth you are aware. Besides, some friends have begun to say that there are similarities between me and the heroine of this novel, for which reason I would like to reread it with you and look for the similarity which people say I have with this lovely ideal created by the genius of Mme. Staël.[5]

Then there is *Atala*, by the immortal Chateaubriand, because you like all those nature scenes, all those *primitive hearts*, anyway, man in his natural state, and this lovely work will please you. Then poetry by Lista, Quintana and Heredia, because, as one of these poets says:

> . . . You will see that poetry
> which comes from the heart and the mind
> will carry the heart and the mind away.

That's my list: you choose the work that appeals to you the most and let me know. You'll see what pleasure we derive from the moments we spend together! I'll let you choose your visits to my house as well, but I don't want us to stop seeing each other for a reason. . . . We'll read together. Isn't that a pleasure? Good-bye, my love.

LETTER 10

Mr. Ignacio Cepeda:

There was no letter from you, my dear Cepeda, until today, Saturday, when the regular mail came, and so that this letter will not slumber in the post office until Wednesday, I have decided to send it directly to your house.

When night before last you told me to inquire at the post office because you had written me, you forgot to mention that the letter was addressed to my name and not to the one we adopted for our correspondence. So, even though I sent someone to inquire yesterday, they couldn't bring it to me because the messenger looked under Doña Amadora de Almonte and not under my name.[6] In any event, now the cherished letter is in my hands.

Once a week . . . ! I will see you only once a week! All right, I agree, because that's how you want it and your present occupations demand. I will see you only once a week. For God's sake indicate to me which one will be the happy day to separate it from the other seven of the long and tedious week. If you don't select a day, don't you understand the agitation you would cause on the other days? On every one of them I would expect the dawn to bring me *a happy day*, and after many hours of fretting and waiting the day would go by, and the night would go by, taking away with it a hope continually renewed and fading, which would only leave me with the disappointment of disillusion. For that reason, and to spare me such repeated torments, tell me, then, which day is it to which I should look forward? Shall it be Friday? In that case let's start with today; if not, let it be Saturday. What do you think? You choose: if it's today, I'll know it when I see you coming; if it's tomorrow, let me know so that I don't suffer through the night waiting for you to come; it will hold light and happiness for me.

 · You see, my heart sweeps me away; with you I don't know how to use the *moderated language* you ask for and yourself employ, but in all else I am docile to your voice, just as a child to the voice of his mother! You see that I do agree not to see you more than once a week. But won't you be going to the Lyceum? To the ball? So that you can make up your mind, isn't it enough for me to assure you that I will find pleasure in none of these activities if you aren't there? . . .

Cepeda! Cepeda! You must be satisfied and very proud, because this absolute power you have over my will must make you arrogant. Who are you? What power is this? Who gave it to you? . . . In my eyes you are not a man; no, you aren't. You are the Angel of my fate, and many times when I see you I think that God Himself gave you the supreme power to bestow on me the good and the evil I am fated to enjoy and to suffer on this earth. I swear this to you by the God I worship, by your honor and by mine; I swear that no mortal has ever had the influence over my heart that you do. You are my friend, my brother, my confidant, and if such sweet terms were not enough for my heart, it gives you the title of its God on earth. Isn't it in your hands to assure me one day of happiness among seven? That way you could also designate one day of torment and desperation, and I would accept it, for it is not in my hands to do otherwise. That day, my dear brother, that day would be the one on which you stopped loving me, but from you I would accept this without complaint, as we accept from God the inevitable misfortunes by which He weighs us down.

Don't mind me; I had a splitting headache at midnight and I think it's left me with a little fever, don't you think so? My head is not in its normal state.

Good-bye. With respect to tonight, if you see me it will be at home, because C. has arranged to come by, and I can't go to her house knowing that she is coming to mine.

I'd like to read you a patriotic hymn I've just composed, and some verses to a goldfinch.

Good-bye again, my sweet friend; don't keep this [letter], tear it up, I implore you. It's a letter filled with nonsense, and only the suspicion that any others I might write today would come out the same impels me to send you this one. There are days when one is in I don't know [what kind of state], days in which one's heart would break were it not able to vent its feelings. I needed to tell you everything I have said; now I feel more composed. For God's sake, don't censure me.

LETTER 12

Dear Friend: I am taking advantage of a visit by one of my former maids, less dim-witted than the ones I have now, in order to write you these lines, requesting her to deliver them to you.

I know you're not going to the ball, and I don't want to infringe on my plans by pestering you with the purpose of seeing you there. But since I want to tell you how it was and what I did, what I saw and what I said . . . everything! Because I want to give you an account of the people who were there, the ladies' dresses, well, everything, just as I said, I hope that you are just a little curious to know these things, and so I am inviting you (with no commitment on your part) to come by tomorrow evening.

The way it looks not too many people will be going to the ball, because last night they were selling single tickets in the theatre, and we were told it was necessary to do so because there had been only 44 subscribers. But if you were there, wouldn't it be filled to over-flowing for me? But it won't be! Patience! With you I am acquiring an admirable resignation, one of which I did not think myself capable, because in truth, my love, I really can quote you this line from a play by Moreto:[7]

What a lukewarm lover you are!

But nevertheless, I bear this with heroic stoicism. Do you know that sometimes I ask myself why I had to fall in love with a man who is as little agreeable, as little devoted, as little passionate as you? I pose this question and get no answer from my mischievous and fickle heart. But no, my Ignacio, it's not true! My heart always an-swers me very satisfactorily and tells me that it loves you because you are good, noble, sincere, because you are the best man in the world, and it is right to love you when one has had the pleasure of knowing you.

You see: even though my letters sometimes begin in a bitter or a joyful vein, I always end them more tenderly than they ought to be, and you, ingrate, take advantage of this tenderness to do whatever pleases you and never what I'd like. You'll pay for that someday, Mister, the day I'm in the mood to drive you to despair, that is, in the event that you ever despair of anything. . . . Let this little insult be sent along with all the compliments with which I shower you, because, on my oath, you don't deserve that much kindness.

Good-bye. — Tomorrow, right? . . . that is *if you can*, if your stud-ies, company, etc. permit, and now recall for one moment that in spite of your *intractableness* you are loved by your too good

G.

LETTER 13

I am going to prove to you that I am not as docile as you re-proached me for being last night, according to your old system. I shall use my pen to say hello to you, as I cannot do so verbally today. My dearest! What a ghastly night I had, how awful I feel, how sad. . . . I have no life but loving you; I am insensitive to anything that is not your love. I don't even care about writing, or reading, or embroidering or going out, or staying home. If ever I had any talent at all, I am positive that by now I have lost it, as I feel so foolish and irritated. Somewhere or another I read:

> [In] one instant
> this supremely proud soul
> has vanquished my reckless audacity . . .
> Look how dependent it has become!

I have always controlled my heart and my actions by means of my mind, yet now my mind is in thrall to my heart, and my heart to a feeling that is completely new and completely extraordinary.

It is possible, my God, that when I thought myself free at last from love's power, when I convinced myself that I knew what it was all about, when I flattered myself I was an expert and undeceived [thereby], I have fallen like a weak and defenseless victim into the iron claws of an unknown, immense and cruel passion! . . . It is possible, Cepeda, that I now love with the heart of a thirteen-year-old girl! . . . What is happening to me? What is this I feel? . . . Tell me, tell me, for I don't know. It is totally new to me, I swear to you. I have been in love before loving you, I have loved, or at least I thought I did, and nonetheless I have never, ever felt what I do now. Is this love? No, there's something more, it isn't just love. It is hell that has come to lodge in my heart. How happy I was! How tenderly I loved you! Angels would envy me! And now, now—how unhappy I am! How I suffer! How very much, my love! And why? What has happened? What is torturing me? I just don't know. Could it be that God punishes an excess of love, making it martyrdom? Is it that the human heart has a restricted capacity and bursts when it is too full? . . . Is it a foreboding of disaster? A deluge of happiness? Is it a defect in my makeup or an inconsistency in my spirit? . . . I have no idea, but I am dispirited, I suffer, I am unhappy.

I'm not asking you to come by often, no, not even on Monday, as you offered to do. It would be better a little later: Tuesday, Wednesday, Thursday . . . eventually, when I am less unhappy than now, because your presence, which was so dear and desired ere this, at present would heighten my sadness. Careful, Cepeda, careful! . . . Be careful of my heart, be . . . you know I might die. You don't know, you can't know, that you could kill me; you really don't know. Really, it might be quite easy for you. If you value my life, if you want to keep your friend, take care of her; give her peace, give her calm. I know that you are more prudent than I am, and I remember that once you asked me for *peace and forgetfulness*. Forgetfulness, no, but I want to give you peace and want it for myself as well. You were right, you were right. Peace, yes, peace! I need it and demand it just the way you do. From today on, by mutual agreement, my dearest, we will give each other peace. Woe to those who want to squeeze the heart until it breaks, and those who set a machine in motion without knowing if they are strong enough to stop it when they so desire! The life of the heart is holy and sacrosanct, and we insist on squandering it. Because everything gets squandered, everything! Today I can't bear it, my heart is choking me! Tomorrow perhaps it will have stopped and be cold. Nothing is inexhaustible! Feelings should be respected and feared. They can bring joy or misfortune. I know you only want to give me happiness. But it takes more to give this to me now. You must have pity on me and perhaps . . . perhaps you have to stop seeing me. How hard it is for me to tell you this! Tear this up and good-bye.

LETTER 32

Madrid, June 25 [1845]

Dear Cepeda: Forgive the poor quality of the paper on which I am writing you; the mail is about to go out, I am upset and can't find any other. First of all I want to give you my new address: Horno de la Mata Street, Number 9, fourth floor, and then I will briefly answer your last letter, which was greatly appreciated. . . .

. . . So you're going to get married? I neither approve, nor disapprove. For me true happiness does not depend on one's status, just as I don't believe that a government's goodness depends on its type. Matrimony is a lot or a little, depending on how you look at it; it is absurd or rational, depending on how it works.

I have not married, nor do I ever plan to, but this is not because of some kind of fanatic desire for freedom, the way some people suppose. I don't think I would hesitate to bind myself for a lifetime if I were able to find a man capable of inspiring in me such esteem as to guarantee the duration of my affection. Furthermore: I am convinced that there is no joy in what is temporary, and I say with Chateaubriand that were I mad enough to believe in happiness, I would look for it in what is habitual. Marriage is a necessary evil from which one can extract a number of benefits. I look at it my way, and in my way would embrace it. I would embrace it with or without benefit of clergy; [their blessing] matters very little to me because in my opinion there is no difference between a marriage that is vouched for by men and one that is vouched for solely by the reciprocal word of the parties involved. The only difference is that one is more public and the other more serious, one can facilitate the impunity of abuses and the other makes it more difficult, one is more *social* and the other more *individual*. In my opinion any bond is holy which is entered into with reciprocal trust and good faith, and I see dishonor only where there are lies and greed. I have not and will not enter into such a bond because I respect it too much; because the man to whom I bind myself must be not only kind but worthy of *veneration*; because I have not found and cannot find a heart great enough to accept mine without oppressing it, nor a character lofty enough to look at *things and men* as I do.

You are not in this position: you are the man and can look for happiness with a woman even when she is not on the same level as you. Nevertheless, believe me: don't marry a stupid woman; the greatest virtue does not make up for a lack of talent, and I would go so far as to say that there is no virtue in stupidity. A woman's indiscretions and even her mistakes are faults which are more easily remedied than the incapacity to understand the very virtues which might be put into practice. Talent may err, but stupidity doesn't even know that it is on the right path, and once off the path, will never find it again. Marry, if you think it's worthwhile, but always remember that a friend advises you never to judge as a virtue the coldness of inept souls, nor to think, as some do, that ignorance guarantees [the affections of] the heart.

This letter is already very long, and I haven't even told you that I am planning to take up residence in Paris. Yes, my friend, in that capital city it appears likely that I will be able to garner greater advantages from my pen, and as I am not wealthy and want to assure myself of an old age without privation, I plan to go *where they pay the best*. Nevertheless, this is not yet totally decided. We shall see.[8]

I am tired of the world, of its flattery, its slander, its adulation, its glory, and of life itself. I need another space either larger or smaller than this one, another life, either calmer or more exciting. Love no longer exists for me; glory isn't enough; I want *money* because I want to be able to travel or have *a comfortable retreat filled with luxurious pleasures*. I wouldn't even mind going to a poor village to raise pigeons, but I can't do that yet because I am dependent on my pen.

Anyway, if you are marrying a nice girl who has some talent, who is pretty so that she need not be jealous, who loves you a lot and deserves to be loved in turn, I will end my vagabond ways and go wherever you all may be to sing you a pretty wedding song and spend a week with you. Do you accept?

Good-bye. I have just published an ode which has put Madrid on its ear and earned me a substantial gift from Prince Francisco de Paula. I'll send you [the ode] one of these days, and today sign myself your very good friend,

Tula

P.S. . . . In one of my novels I said, "Don't blame the heart for losing its illusions, just as you can't blame the tree for surrendering its leaves to the inclement wind." But can't the bare tree and the disillusioned heart mourn the loss of their blossoms? Without accusing anyone it could be said that voluntarily or involuntarily my heart has been dealt a wound.

Letter to Antonio Romero Ortiz[9]

LETTER 15

May 5 [1853]

Dear Antonio, it seems you don't feel the slightest bit of impatience to repeat your visit to Eloisa. You say nothing to me about it, nothing about seeing each other. Perhaps you do well: I think that for us to communicate by letter has, on close scrutiny, many advantages. For myself, although the days on which I am deprived of your presence are very long, nevertheless I understand that this distance is better for us, rather than doing us harm, as it does not stop me from knowing your thoughts or communicating mine to you. Love, that insatiable tyrant who is never satisfied with anything, also knows how to be a docile and even an immature child who can amuse himself with trifles, is content and considers himself happy. Sometimes I have wished that Armand[10] could have kept on being my *invisible gentleman*, that only his thoughts had reached me, always shrouded in those pink clouds of mystery, like the eternal promise of a happiness that is never possessed but incessantly hoped for. When he acquired a shape and a particular character, my fantastic gentleman became extremely cherished . . . that most certainly! But there is no doubt that what he produces in me now is an agitated and painful feeling, whereas what I felt for my Armand was completely sweet, tranquil and ideal.

Without intending to, my friend, I have answered the question you asked me in your letter of yesterday. Yes, Antonio, I love you, that is the truth, but you also want me to explain to you *how I love you*, and that I can express better when I'm not thinking about it than when I try to define it. As I understand it, I love you in different ways and that annoys me: if I only loved you one way both of us would be happier and we'd understand each other better. I love you when I don't see you, when I don't hear you, when only your letters reach me and I see you only in my heart. Then I love you with an emotion that exalts me in my own eyes. At such moments I feel that even though you were old, ugly in body, worthless to all other women, to me you would be beautiful because of your soul, and young because of your love. I feel that my noble heart hurls itself toward yours in a gesture of sacred trust and chaste affection, and that we are united by a bond that is nameless, but august, indissoluble, eternal, by an intellectual partnership I have wanted so much to know and which I have never seen. Then, Antonio, I have no doubt either of you or of me; then I do not call you "husband," because in human speech I can find no name to give you. Then you are *hope* for me, which is the only great thing man can enjoy; then I breathe with you an atmosphere so pure, so sweetly scented, so soft, that it seems impossible to me that earthly passions could ever destroy it. This is how I sometimes love you, how I'd like to love you forever, how I ought to love you if I aspired to happiness through love. But unfortunately in my hapless makeup all extremes come together: when I see you, when I hear you, when I feel your breath, when you caress me, you suddenly tear me out of my enchanted region, you make me desire earthly delights, you inflame me, Antonio, with such a fever that I become ill for many hours. You transform me into a totally common woman, you make me ashamed of myself and of weak human nature . . . in short, then I love you with a love that is as violent as it is suspicious, as ambitious as it is powerless, with a love that were it to attain what it wishes, would not be happy, and giving all would give nothing. Yes, at those times I love you with passion, but also with rage at you, at me and at nature; I love you while doubting your heart and mine because in those moments it seems very doubtful to me that something we call a heart even exists. At those times, my darling, I ask myself with dread if it is true that man is called to a higher destiny than the one he sees in animals, if he has not been born, just like the latter, to multiply and die . . . then it seems to me that those things we call soul, feeling, idea, are all only seductions which mischievous material nature uses to get us blindly to fulfill her laws, those laws an animal obeys instinctively and which the *thinking animal* fulfills even more fatefully, dragged along by the hope of a deceptive, unattainable good.

Oh! I will never be able to explain to you what I see and feel and judge in these matters; no matter how much I say I will never be able to make you understand the battle that goes on between my pride in being intelligent and my nature as a passionate woman—these contradictions cannot be defined, Antonio, they are felt, not described. You want to know how I love you? . . . Any way you want, that's the truth. With an affection no other woman can give you, with infinite tenderness and idealism, with an intimate and lasting happiness . . . and I can also love you the way Sappho loved Phaon[11] and say as she did:

> The world disappears from before my eyes
> and lightly through my veins I feel
> the fire of a deep pleasure circulate . . .
> Trembling, I want vainly to resist you,
> my cheek is washed by ardent tears,
> I feel delirium, pleasure, I bless you, and die!

Ah, yes! Unhappily, there are within me these two powerful temperaments: that of the poet and that of the woman. I have enough idealism in me to live all my life on the breath of your love, enough blood to exhaust in one moment all of your love and mine. Unhappily, too, you have had the power to awaken both of these temperaments simultaneously, and they are locked in a struggle whose outcome I do not know. In those moments where victory seems to be on the side of *ideal nature*, that's when I love you with faith in you and in me, when I believe I will be happy and feel I deserve it. In those moments when *earthly nature* gains ground is when I love you uncertainly, when I am afraid we will be incapable of loving and respecting each other for long, when I hate myself while my foolish pride is rebelling against the errors of my own conscience. Then I suffer, and make you suffer, am capricious and difficult and full of inconsistencies. Then all of my idealism as a poet seems ridiculous, as it must end up where animal instinct begins. But nevertheless, in

Gertrudis Gómez de Avellaneda

191

the midst of those tempests in my soul—which exacts such cruel revenge of me—[in the midst] of the short-lived triumphs of my other, earthly nature, it happens that I love you madly, and call you *my man*; at that instant it seems to me that there could be no greater joy than to be yours in every way, yours by any bonds whatsoever. An hour later, nothing in the world would induce me to wish for any such destiny; nothing on earth would want me to be bound to you by common bonds, whatever their name. I would not want a common destiny for this beautiful dream that bewitches my soul, for this my life's page on which you have written with a new and original script the name of Armand, of Antonio. Another hour later I see you again and then . . . then I say that one can only love God in his *incomprehensible essence*, that you are my lover, my husband, that my idealism is madness, desecration . . . that love's happiness is in your arms and not in my dreams and then, Antonio, I would like to think up even closer bonds than any we know of, more physical, more sensitive, to bind myself to you with them all. I love you in all these ways; I do not know more of my heart than what I say to you: I swear it, Antonio. Will you make me happy? I have no idea. Am I now? No: I am very annoyed with myself, and indirectly with you as well. Is it in your power to end my vexation? I don't think so, at least not now. Later perhaps? Quite probably. How? . . . I can hardly explain it. The only thing I see clearly is that I love you, that if you know how not to provoke these inner battles, my love can do me a great deal of good; if you enjoy destroying my idealism, perhaps later on you will try in vain to bring it back. Yes, I have a terrible power over my heart: my pride. Always respect it, Antonio: don't ever say a single word that would make me suspect that you think me weak and a slave to my passions. With that alone you would make me strong, you would make me invincible, but ah! Would my love survive once it had been violently extinguished?

Let us leave this matter forever, my friend; I beg you to let us be Armand and Gertrudis again for a few days. Write to me as you did then, see me or not, according to what even seems convenient for you; in this matter I leave you totally in charge of your conduct. I will receive your letters with intimate pleasure, I will happily see you whenever you wish, but I don't insist that you devote some part of every day to chat with your friend, nor will I complain if you see me a little more or a little less time. Be free, my Antonio, always be free in your relationship with me, and believe that although I am so jealous, so demanding, so inconstant in character, I am quite stead-fast in my feelings, and my love will not fail as long as you are noble, good, sincere, loyal, though perhaps less passionate if you think it's best that way. What else can I tell you? Do you still doubt? Do you still not understand me? Will you keep on thinking that I don't love you as much as you wish? Oh! You would be very unjust, Antonio, and before you are, ask me for any proof you want. This is not the first time I have told you that *you will be the judge of my destiny*. I now repeat to you that *I will love you any way you want me to*, that I will be for you—today if that's what you want—*the woman you wish me to be*, but allow me to believe, my friend, my Armand, my loyal gentleman, allow me to believe that you only want my happiness, and that you understand that my happiness will be great if you make me feel that you have it in your hands, and that we both deserve it. If I am a poor woman who is sensitive to atmospheric changes, that, you see, is not my fault. If I want to see you and I sometimes get angry because you don't sense this . . . that isn't my fault, either. Be indulgent: bear with my inconsistencies and always love me, as a husband, a brother, any way you wish, Antonio, but always with respect for me. The idea that your love was only physical would hurt me very, very much. Yours,

T.

Notes

1. She was making herself out to be a year younger than she was.
2. These are Cepeda's own words, quoted from a letter he had sent her on July 15, 1839.
3. Avellaneda's friend, Concepción Noriega.
4. I have been unable to track down the correct title of this work in English.
5. This novel describes the frustrations of the woman as creative artist, because of the constraints that society places on her.

6. Almonte was the town from which Cepeda came; "Amadora" roughly means "the loving woman," the fictitious name under which Avellaneda wrote to Cepeda.

7. Agustín de Moreto y Cabaña (1618–69), a famous playwright.

8. She never did go to Paris.

9. For these letters, the originals in Tula's handwriting do exist.

10. A fictional name with which Romero Ortiz signed his initial letters to Avellaneda.

11. Sappho was a Greek woman poet who lived about 600 B.C.; the story of her unrequited love for Phaon, which caused her to throw herself off a cliff, is probably fictitious. Very little is known of her life.

Juana Manuela Gorriti

Juana Manuela Gorriti

*J*ust like Gertrudis Gómez de Avellaneda, Juana Manuela Gorriti could truly be said to have lived a "Romantic" life, this one marked by the dramatic constants of war, exile, violence, and almost perpetual movement.

Juana Manuela was born in 1818 in the northern Argentinian province of Salta, the daughter of a prominent landholding family. Her father, José Ignacio Gorriti, was a distinguished military officer who fought first in the wars of independence from Spain and later in the interminable, bloody civil wars that marked the early years of the Argentine Republic. General Gorriti opposed the rising power of Juan Manuel de Rosas, the tyrant who began to be a force in Argentine politics about 1829 and, when he became dictator, would impose a bloody reign of terror that lasted from 1835 to 1852. On the losing side in this struggle, the Gorriti family had to flee the country for Bolivia in 1831, leaving behind them their lands, their home, and their past. The critic Cristina Iglesia has pointed out very adroitly how the ruins of the paternal house are a leitmotiv in Gorriti's writing, both in the content and in the fragmented style (19).

The adolescent Juana Manuela—again like Avellaneda—was attractive, intelligent, and headstrong. She had had a minimal formal education but from the beginning had been an avid reader, and literature was her passion. She felt passion of a different kind for a dashing Bolivian officer, Juan Manuel Isidoro Belzú, and insisted on marrying him when she was fourteen. Belzú rose to power quickly and became president of his country on two different occasions, but the marriage was a rocky one and, in spite of the birth of two daughters, Edelmira and Mercedes, ended in separation and divorce. Gorriti chose to settle in Lima, Peru, and, as she had no personal funds, supported herself and her daughters by establishing the first coeducational primary school in Lima as well as a high school for girls. Besides teaching and administration, she founded several women's magazines and wrote prolifically. She also organized the leading literary salon in the city, where men and women of letters and the arts met, read their writings to each other, listened to music, and exchanged ideas. Mercedes Cabello de Carbonera and Teresa González de Fanning, the two writers who appear next in this anthology, were close friends and active participants in these literary and social activities.

Gorriti's personal life continued to be unconventional: she had a number of affairs and two children out of wedlock, but this did not appear to dissuade the parents of Lima's leading families from sending their daughters to her schools (Berg, "Rereading Fiction" 129). Belzú —who had demanded his girls' return to Bolivia—was assassinated in 1865, just when his wife happened to be in La Paz to visit her daughters; in spite of their past marital differences, Gorriti organized a formal wake and burial for her late husband and pronounced a stirring funerary oration before returning to Peru.

The following year was also a politically turbulent one: Callao, Lima's port city, was besieged by the Spanish fleet, and many people were killed or injured in the bombardments. Gorriti aided the victims so heroically that she was awarded a medal by the Peruvian government.

From then on Gorriti alternated living in Lima and Buenos Aires and became a famous literary figure in both countries. During her life she wrote essays, stories, personal reminiscences, novels, historical biographies, and much travel literature, publishing in newspapers, women's magazines, and books. She was an indefatigable traveler between Bolivia, Argentina, and Peru, crossing the Andes many times by horse or mule; she also rounded the Horn several times by ship. A glance at a topographic map of South America shows that these journeys were tremendously arduous and dangerous, but this never kept her at home. Not only did Gorriti often document her own journeys in her writing, she cast many of her literary protagonists as travelers or exiles in search of physical or spiritual homes (Berg, "Viajeras" 69–70).

As Gorriti was so closely tied to major political figures and events in all three of the countries in which she lived, it is no wonder that her writing should reflect this. In the nineteenth century many writers from the newly independent Spanish-American nations were preoccupied with nation building and the identification of a national self ("el proyecto nacional"), but, given women's domestic roles that precluded their involvement in the public sphere, this writing was almost exclusively from a male perspective. Gorriti, however, actively participated in her country's historical discourse, partially for economic reasons. On repeated occasions she made it a point to remind her Argentine readers of her father's role as soldier and patriot and of the fact that he (and hence she) had lost their sizable fortune as a result of his opposition to Rosas (Mizraje 48, 52, 58). She thus consciously kept her illustrious name before her reading public, and, near the end of her life, the Argentine government indeed awarded her a pension in recognition of her father's service to his country. Besides her personal reminiscences, she also wrote biographies of some of the heroic generals of her father's circle (Puch, Güemes), another way of inserting herself into the discourse of nation building. "Without a doubt," says Iglesia, "her greatest audacity consists in presenting herself as a *patriotic writer*, and from there to narrate the national legend" (8).

Gorriti was also unique in telling of the horrors of war and terrorism from a woman's perspective, as she does in this highly melodramatic tale, "La hija del mashorquero," and in several other stories as well. Many leading Argentine politicians and intellectuals (Sarmiento, Mitre, Echeverría, Mármol) used their pens to oppose Rosas, for which they suffered prison or exile. A whole school of anti-Rosas literature came into being during the long years of his tyranny; one of the most famous examples is Esteban Echeverría's harrowing short story, "El matadero," in which Rosas's government is equated to a bloody slaughterhouse. When one compares these two stories the gendered viewpoints are strikingly different. Whereas Echeverría deals with issues of class, race, and society, Gorriti describes what terrorism does to the family.[1] If one recalls that in the literature of the nineteenth century stories of love, matrimony, and the family were often used as allegories for reconciling national interests,[2] the metaphorical charge of her story becomes even greater. Seen through a woman's eyes, and from inside the home, institutionalized terrorism takes on new meanings: children rebel against parents; parents kill their children; children from rival bands may fall in love, but their relationships are aborted or truncated by violence.[3] According to Isabel Quintana, Gorriti's heroine, Clemencia, is not only a kind of ghost but also a voluntary celibate because in this kind of world it is madness to procreate (77); Quintana also points out the stylistic counterpoint between the brutality of the father's dialogue and the ameliorating, suffering female voices (87).

The original title of the story, "La hija del mashorquero" (1865), which I have translated as "The Executioner's Daughter," needs some explanation. It refers to the Mashorca, the secret police who had networks of spies among the population, and would engage in undercover acts of torture and terrorism. The term "mashorca" is a play on words: "horca" is the gallows, so "más horca" is "more gallows"; a "mazorca" (pronounced the same way in Spanish America) is also a corncob, and, in a brutal play on the similarity of these words, the goons who tortured their victims would leave some of them hanging in public places, with corncobs sticking from bodily orifices. With this story and several others of the same sort, as well as her historical biographies and personal recollections of her family's involvement in opposing the dictator, Gorriti has surely earned a place both in the discourse of nation building and in the anti-Rosas school of Argentine literature, though this has not been acknowledged until fairly recently.

Gorriti went to Buenos Aires to live out her final years, still writing and publishing prolifically, founding more women's journals, and remaining involved in the education of young women. Two years before she died she published an unusual cookbook, *Cocina ecléctica* (The Eclectic Kitchen), which is a more interesting text than one might suppose, as many of her contributors were celebrities, and most embedded their recipes in entertaining anecdotes that reveal much about these women's cultural history and about Gorriti's network of friends.[4] Before her death in 1892 she wrote—among other things—some short biographies and her memoirs, *Lo íntimo*. Today she is celebrated as nineteenth-century Argentina's foremost woman writer.

I would like to add one additional note on Gorriti as a precursor to the contemporary literature of women's opposition to terrorism. The Rosas era became a popular topic during and after the recent Dirty War (1976–82), another period of institutionalized terrorism in Argentina, as it was not hard to see the grisly parallels. Like Gorriti, many women artists who protested the activities of the military junta also focused on issues of terrorism and its impact on the family. A famous true story of the Rosas era is that of Camila O'Gorman, who defied society and parental authority by fleeing with her priest/lover; Rosas made it a point to pursue the lovers, who were ultimately caught and executed, in spite of the fact that Camila was pregnant at the time. This event was made into the famous film *Camila* (1984) by María Luisa Bemberg.[6] In a similar vein, the playwright Griselda Gambaro wrote "La malasangre" in 1982,[5] a play that alludes to the brutal relationship between a Rosas-like father and his rebellious daughter. One could cite numerous other examples. There is no doubt that Juana Manuela Gorriti was a groundbreaking precursor in this type of literature.

Notes

1. Harriet Beecher Stowe took much the same approach in *Uncle Tom's Cabin,* in which she foregrounds how destructive slavery is to family life, both black and white.

2. See Doris Sommer, *Foundational Fictions: The National Romances of Latin America* (Berkeley: University of California Press, 1991), esp. ch. 3.

3. On this topic, see the excellent article by Liliana Zuccotti, "Legados de guerra" (The Legacy of War), *El ajuar de la patria: Ensayos críticos sobre Juana Manuela Gorriti,* ed. Cristina Iglesia (Buenos Aires: Feminaria Editora, 1993), 80–93.

4. See my article, "Juana Manuela Gorriti's *Cocina ecléctica*: Recipes as Feminine Discourse."

5. This play has been translated into English twice: "Bitter Blood," by Evelyn Picón Garfield in her volume on *Women's Fiction from Latin America* (Detroit: Wayne State University Press, 1988), 111–57; and *Bad Blood (La malasangre)* by Marguerite Feitlowitz (Woodstock, IL: Dramatic Publishing Company, 1994).

6. It is interesting that Bemberg should also turn to Sor Juana in her

1990 film, *Yo, la peor de todas* (I, the Worst of All), to illustrate the silencing and victimization of women by a despotic male hierarchy. See my "Sor Juana and Her World," *Latin American Research Review* 29 (1994): 143–54.

La hija del mashorquero

Roque Alma-negra era el terror de Buenos Aires. Verdugo por excelencia entre una asociación de verdugos llamada Mas-horca y consagrado en cuerpo y alma al tremendo fundador [Rosas] de aquella terrible hermandad, contaba las horas por el número de sus crímenes, y su brazo, perpetuamente armado de puñal, jamás se bajaba sino para herir. Su huella era un reguero de sangre, y había huído de él hacía tanto tiempo la piedad, que su corazón no conservaba de ésta ningún recuerdo, y los gemidos del huérfano, de la esposa y de la madre, lo encontraban tan insensible, como la fría hoja de acero que hundía en el pecho de sus víctimas. Cada semejanza con la humanidad había desaparecido de la fisonomía de aquel hombre, y su lenguaje, expresión fiel del nombre que sus delitos le habían dado, era una mezcla de ferocidad y de blasfemia que hacía palidecer de espanto a todos aquellos que tenían la desgracia de acercársele.

Sin embargo, entre aquel horrible vocabulario de crueldades y de impiedad, como una flor nacida en el cieno, había una palabra de bendición que Roque pronunciaba siempre.

—Clemencia—decía aquel hombre de sangre, cuando fatigado con los crímenes de la noche entraba a su casa al amanecer. Y a este nombre, que sonaba como un sarcasmo en los labios de asesino, una voz tan dulce y melodiosa que parecía venir de los celestes coros, respondía con ternura:—¡Padre!—y una figura de ángel, una joven de dieciséis años, con grandes ojos azules y ceñida de una aureola de rizos blondos salía al encuentro del mashorquero y lo abrazaba con dolorosa efusión. Era su hija.

Roque la amaba como el tigre ama a sus cachorros, con un amor feroz. Por ella hubiera llevado el hierro y el fuego a los extremos del mundo; por ella hubiera vertido su propia sangre; pero no le habría sacrificado ni una sola gota de su venganza, ni uno solo de sus instintos homicidas.

Clemencia vivía sola en el maldecido hogar del mashorquero. Su madre había muerto hacía mucho tiempo víctima de una dolencia desconocida.

Clemencia la vio languidecer y extinguirse lentamente en una larga agonía, sin que sus tiernos cuidados pudieran volverla a la vida, ni sus ruegos y lágrimas arrancar de su corazón el fatal secreto que la llevaba a la tumba. Pero cuando su madre murió, cuando la vio desaparecer bajo la negra cubierta del ataúd y que espantada del inmenso vacío que se había hecho en torno suyo, fue a arrojarse en los brazos de su padre, los vio manchados en sangre y la luz de una horrible revelación alumbró de repente el espíritu de Clemencia. Tendió una mirada al pasado, y trajo a la memoria escenas misteriosas entonces para ella, y que ahora se le presentaban claras, distintas, horribles. Recordó las maldiciones dirigidas a Roque el Mashorquero, que tantas veces habían herido sus oídos y que ella en su amor, en su veneración por su padre, estaba tan distante de pensar que caían sobre él. Ella, que hasta entonces había vivido en un mundo de amor y de piedad, hallóse un día de repente en otro de crímenes y de horror. La verdad toda entera se mostró a sus ojos, y comparando con su propio dolor el dolor que su madre había devorado en silencio, comprendió por qué había preferido a la vida la eternidad y al lecho conyugal la fría almohada del sepulcro. Pero en el dolor de Clemencia no se mezcló ningún sentimiento de amargura. El alma de aquella hermosa niña se parecía a su nombre: era toda dulzura y misericordia. Su fatal descubrimiento en nada disminuyó la ternura que profesaba a su padre. Al contrario, Clemencia lo amó más, porque lo amó con una compasión profunda; y viéndolo marcharse solo con sus crímenes en un sendero regado con sangre, llevando el odio bajo sus pies y la venganza sobre su cabeza, lejos de envidiar el reposo eterno de su madre, Clemencia deseó vivir para acompañar al desdichado como un ángel guardián en aquella vía de iniquidad, y si no le era posible apartarlo de ella, ofrecer al menos por él a Dios una vida de dolor y de expiación.

Clemencia rechazó con horror el lujo que la rodeaba, porque en él vio el precio del crimen, y olvidando que era joven, olvidando que era bella, y que en el mundo hay goces celestes para la juventud y la belleza, ocultó su esbelto talle, y sus deliciosas formas bajo una larga túnica blanca, cubrió los sedosos rizos de su espléndida cabellera con un tupido velo, acalló los latidos con que su corazón la pedía amor, y se consagró toda entera al alivio de los desgraciados. Sobreponiéndose al profundo horror de su alma, hojeó esas sangrientas listas en que su padre consignaba el nombre de sus víctimas, y guiada por estos fúnebres datos, corría a buscar para adoptarlos a los huérfanos y viudas que el puñal de aquél había dejado sin amparo en el mundo. Empleó para socorrerlos los talentos adquiridos en la esmerada educación que había recibido de su madre: dio lecciones de música y de pintura, y consagró sus horas a un constante trabajo. La pobre niña, llena la mente de lúgubres pensamientos y con el corazón destrozado de dolor, tocaba alegres polkas que sus discípulos danzaban alegres y felices; y en la pavorosa soledad de sus noches, ella, que había dicho un eterno adiós a todas las dichas de la vida, se ocupaba en bordar vaporosos ramilletes en el velo de una desposada o en la transparente y coqueta falda de un vestido de baile, sin que le desanimaran las ideas dolorosas que esos accesorios de una felicidad a que ella no podía ya aspirar, despertaban en su alma; y con el precio de esos trabajos tan llenos de tristes emociones, corría a derramar el consuelo y la paz en el hogar de aquéllas a quienes había sacrificado el hacha de su padre. Como una tierna madre acariciaba e instruía a los niños, velaba a los enfermos con la ardiente solicitud de una hermana de caridad y auxiliaba a los moribundos con una elocuencia llena de unción y piedad.

Enteramente olvidada de sí misma, Clemencia parecía vivir sólo en la vida de los otros. Y sin embargo el mundo la sonreía a lo lejos, le abría los brazos, y le mostraba sus goces. Frecuentemente en sus piadosas correrías, Clemencia oía tras de sí voces apasionadas que exclamaban:

—¡Cuán bella es! ¡Dichoso, mil veces dichoso, aquel que merezca una mirada de esos ojos!

Pero aquellas palabras de galantería y amor en medio del sepulcral silencio de la ciudad desolada, escandalizaban los oídos de Clemencia como cantos profanos entre las tumbas de un cementerio, y ocultando el rostro entre los pliegues de su velo, se apartaba con el corazón oprimido de tristeza y disgusto.

II

Un día al anochecer, Clemencia vio entrar en su casa y dirigirse al cuarto de su padre algunos hombres de fisonomía patibularia, envueltos en largos ponchos bajo cuyos pliegues se veían brillar los mangos de sus puñales. Clemencia previó algo funesto en la presencia de aquellos hombres, y después de haber vacilado algunos instantes corrió a aplicar el oído a la cerradura de una puerta que se abría sobre la habitación de su padre.

Roque, de pie cerca de una mesa, tenía en la mano algunos papeles, y hablaba en voz alta a su auditorio.

—Sí, amigos míos—decía,—¡guerra a muerte a los unitarios![1] ¡guerra a muerte a esos malvados! ¿Vosotros cr[e]éis hacer mucho? Pues sabed que os engañáis. Leed sino la lista de nuestras ejecuciones de este mes y cotejadla con las delaciones que hemos recibido hoy solamente. Leed y veréis que aún queda una inmensa obra al cuchillo de la Mashorca, cuando comparéis el número de los que han caído con el de aquellos que caerán . . . ¡que caerán sí, aunque se escondan bajo el manto de María!

—¡Reina del cielo!—murmuró Clemencia juntando las manos con angustia y volviéndose hacia la imagen de la Virgen, su única compañera en aquella morada solitaria.—Si esa blasfemia ha llegado al pie de vuestro divino trono, no la escuchéis ¡madre buena! desechadla con indulgencia y alumbrad con una sonrisa de compasión al desdichado que camina en las tinieblas.

Al pronunciar estas últimas palabras, Clemencia volvió a oir la voz de su padre que leía:

"A las nueve de esta noche, un hombre embozado se detendrá al pie del obelisco de la plaza de la Victoria, y dará tres silbidos. Ese hombre es Manuel de Puirredón, el incorregible conspirador unitario, amigo de Lavalle [2] y emigrado en Montevideo. La señal es dirigida a la hija de un federal que unida a él secretamente y convertida en su auxiliar más poderoso, le entrega los secretos de su padre e instruído por esa señal del regreso del conspirador, irá a reunírsele para segundar sin duda el infame plan que le trae a Buenos Aires."

—¿Lo oís, camaradas? ¡Y aun están nuestros puñales en el cinto!— exclamó Roque con ira feroz.

—¡Muera Manuel de Puirredón!—gritaron los asesinos desenvainando sus largos puñales.

Clemencia dirigió una mirada por la cerradura a la péndula que estaba enfrente de su padre, y se estremeció.

La aguja marcaba las ocho y cincuenta y cinco.

—¡Cinco minutos para salvar la vida a un hombre! ¡Cinco minutos para preservar a mi padre de un crimen más! ¡Oh! Dios mío, alarga este corto espacio, y presta alas a mis pies.

Y envolviéndose en su largo velo blanco, salió de su casa corriendo, no sin volver muchas veces la cabeza por temor de que los asesinos se le adelantaran, inutilizando el deseo de salvar al desgraciado que sin saberlo se encaminaba a la muerte.

Al llegar al ángulo que forma la calle de la Victoria con la del Colegio, Clemencia divisó un bulto negro que cortando diagonalmente la plaza se dirigía al obelisco.

—¡Es él!—murmuró con voz temblorosa, y corriendo en pos suya alcanzóle en el momento que tocaba ya la verja de hierro.

Muchos paseantes vagaban en aquel sitio halagados por la brisa de la noche, e impedían a Clemencia hablar con el desconocido.

Entonces ella se volvió hacia atrás; pasó cerca de él y tocóle ligeramente la espalda haciéndole una imperceptible seña de seguirle.

El embozado se volvió con impetuosidad y acercándose a Clemencia—¡Emilia! ¡Emilia mía!—exclamó ciñendo apaciblemente el cuerpo de la joven con uno de sus brazos, sin que ella pudiera impedirlo por temor de llamar sobre ellos la atención.

Obligada así a callar, Clemencia, al través de su velo contempló al desconocido, cuyo rostro estaba iluminado en aquel momento por los rayos de la luna. Era un hombre joven y bello como jamás Clemencia había visto otro ni aún en sus poéticos ensueños de dieciséis años. Era alto y esbelto. En todos sus movimientos revelábase esa elegancia fácil, casi descuidada, que sólo dan el uso del mundo y un nacimiento distinguido. La mirada a la vez profunda y lánguida de sus hermosos ojos, tenía un poder irresistible de atracción que aliándose a la mágica armonía de su voz, hacía de aquel hombre uno de esos seres que una vez vistos no pueden olvidarse jamás, y que dejan en nuestra vida una huella imborrable de felicidad o de dolor.

Y el desconocido, bajo el poder de su engaño, repetía al oído de Clemencia:

—Emilia, héme aquí, amada mía, no como un conspirador, a envolverte de nuevo en la ruína de mis quiméricas esperanzas, sino como esposo apasionado a arrebatarte de los brazos de tu padre, y llevarte en los míos, lejos, muy lejos, al fondo de los desiertos, a algún paraje desconocido que tu amor convertirá para mi en un delicioso Edén. Ven, Emilia mía, abandonemos esta patria fatal. Dios la ha maldecido y nuestros esfuerzos y sacrificios para salvarla son vanos. . . .

—¡Oh—continuó el proscrito con voz ahogada y estrechando aún más a Clemencia contra su pecho,—lo ves, Emilia: esta idea despedaza mi corazón . . . pero aquí estás tú para calmar sus dolores y llenarlo de alegría . . .

¿Y nuestro hijo? Qué bello será! Cuánto habrás sufrido al separarte de él en la cruel necesidad de ocultar su existencia! . . .

En aquel momento llegaban a un paraje solitario de la plaza. Clemencia tendió una mirada en torno suyo y separándose precipitadamente de los brazos del desconocido, alzó el velo para hacerle conocer su error.

—¡Cielos!—exclamó él,—¡no es Emilia!

—No, señor; pero si vos os llamáis Manuel de Puirredón, huid de este sitio funesto donde cada segundo es para vos un paso hacia la muerte . . . ¿No lo veis?—continuó ella con terror, señalando un grupo negro al otro extremo de la plaza.—Son ellos, son los puñales sangrientos de la Mas-horca que os acechan. . . . Huid en nombre del cielo, por vuestra esposa, por vuestro hijo. . . . Id con ellos lejos de este antro de fieras a realizar ese hermoso sueño de dicha que halaga vuestra mente. . . . Huid, huid—repitió,—señalando al proscrito una calle sombría y alejándose ella por otra.

Al entrar en su casa Clemencia, fue a postrarse a los pies de la Virgen, y ocultando su rostro bajó el velo de la sagrada imagen, lloró largo tiempo, murmurando entre sollozos palabras misteriosas: quizás algún dulce y doloroso secreto que ella había querido ocultarse a si misma, y que sólo osaba confiar a aquella que guarda la llave del corazón de las vírgenes.

Desde ese día el hechicero y melancólico rostro de Clemencia, palideció más todavía, revistiéndose de una tristeza profunda. ¡Quién sabe que halagüeña visión cruzó por su mente con las palabras apasionadas de ese hombre! ¡Quién sabe que sentimiento hizo nacer su vista en aquel corazón joven y solitario!

Algunas veces con la mirada perdida en el vacío, sonreía dulcemente; pero luego, como asaltada por un amargo recuerdo, movía la cabeza en ademán de dolorosa resignación murmurando en voz baja:

—Hija de la desgracia, heredera del castigo celeste, víctima expiatoria, piensa en tu voto; acuérdate que tu reino no es de este mundo.

Y sumida de nuevo en su mortal tristeza, consagrábase con mayor ardor a la misión de piedad que se había impuesto.

—Clemencia—dijo a su hija un día el mashorquero,—¿por qué te hallo cada vez más triste y meditabunda? ¿quién se atreve a causarte pesadumbre? Nómbralo, por vida mía, y muy luego podrás añadir: ¡Desdichado de él!

—¡Nadie! ¡padre . . . nadie!—respondió ésta estremeciéndose, y levantó instintivamente la mano al corazón, como si hubiese temido que su padre leyera allí algún secreto.

—No . . . tú me engañas. . . . Hace tiempo que advierto lágrimas hasta en tu voz cuando vienes a abrazarme.

—Padre . . . —replicó la joven interrumpiéndolo y fijando en los sangrientos ojos del asesino los suyos azules y piadosos,—¿no lo adivina? Cuando después de una noche de vigilia y ansiedad te veo llegar en fin y salgo a abrazarte, pienso con profundo dolor que los hijos de esos desdichados que diariamente siega el hacha de tu bando, no podrían gozar ya de esa felicidad que Dios me concede a mi todavía. ¡Oh padre! ¿no es este un gran motivo de tristeza y de lágrimas? ¿En medio de esas sangrientas escenas no has llevado alguna vez la mano al corazón, y te has preguntado qué harías tú mismo si vieras una mano armada del puñal bajarse sobre tu hija y degollarla?

—¡Calla . . . ! ¡calla, Clemencia . . . !—gritó el bandido,—¿qué haría? El infierno mismo no tiene una rabia semejante a la que entonces movería el brazo de Roque para vengarte . . . ¡Pero tú estas loca, niña! ¿No sabes que los salvajes unitarios no tienen corazón como nosotros, que amamos y aborrecemos con igual violencia . . . ?

—¡Padre, tú sabes que eso no es cierto! ¿qué dicen pues los gritos desgarradores de esas madres, los gemidos de esas esposas y el triste llanto de esos huérfanos que a todas horas oigo elevarse al cielo contra nosotros? ¿No te dicen que las fibras rotas por tu puñal en el fondo de sus almas son tan sensibles como las nuestras?

—¡Calla—repitió,—calla,—Clemencia! Tienes una voz tan insinuante y persuasiva que me lo harías creer; y entonces ¿qué pensaría el general Rosas de su servidor? ¡Cómo se burlaría Salomón y Cuitiño de su compañero! No . . . ¡Vete! no quiero escucharte, hoy sobre todo que Manuel Puirredón, ese bandido unitario a quien he jurado degollar, vaga entre nosotros invisiblemente y como protegido por un poder sobrenatural . . . ¡Oh! pero en vano me inquieto . . . ¡qué locura! Este corazón está lleno de odio, y ya no cabría en él la piedad . . . Escucha sino esta historia . . .

Hace algunos meses entré a oir misa en la iglesia del Socorro.

—¡Padre! ¡Osasteis entrar en el templo de Dios con las manos manchadas!

—¿De sangre? Sí, por cierto ¿por qué no, si es sangre de unitarios, esos enemigos de Dios?

Entré, como decía, en la iglesia del Socorro. Apenas había comenzado la misa un hombre a cuyo lado me había arrodillado volvióse de repente y habiéndome contemplado un segundo como para reconocerme paseó sobre mí una mirada de desprecio y apartándose con insolente repugnancia, fue a colocarse muy lejos de aquel sitio. Aquella acción me denunció un unitario. El miserable había reconocido a Roque, pero ignoraba lo que era la venganza de Roque.

Mis ojos no se apartaron de él durante la misa y al salir de la iglesia vile entrar al frente de una casa pequeña, casi arruinada.

En la noche de ese día, mientras aquel hombre olvidado del agravio que me había hecho y con dos niños en los brazos estaba tranquilamente al lado de su mujer, ocupada en bordar el ajuar para el tercero que iba a nacer, yo guié a su casa, la Mashorca; y entre los brazos de su esposa y de sus hijos hundí mil veces mi puñal en su corazón salpicando los pañales del que aun no había visto la luz.

—¡Clemencia! ¡Clemencia! ¿qué tienes?

El asesino alargó el brazo para sostener a su hija, que vacilante y trémula lo rechazó con mal disimulado horror.

—Por algún tiempo—continuó él,—creí que sería "eso" que llaman remordimiento el recuerdo imborrable que aquella escena de sangre, de gritos y de lágrimas dejó en mi imaginación; pero ¡ah! era sólo el contento de una venganza satisfecha. El día en que Roque conociera la compasión o el remordimiento, la hoja de esta arma se empañaría y . . . mira como resplandece . . . —dijo el bandido, haciendo brillar su ancho puñal a los ojos de su hija.

Y ocultándolo en seguida entre la faja de su chiripá ³ se alejó, sin duda para volver a su horrible tarea.

Clemencia se sintió anonadada bajo el peso de las espantosas palabras que había escuchado. Débil, quebrantada, exánime fue a caer a los pies de su divina protectora elevando hacia ella las manos en angustiosa plegaria.

A medida que oraba, la esperanza y la fe descendían a su corazón; y cuando se levantó, su frente volvió a iluminarse con la serenidad de la resignación.

—Nunca es tarde para tu infinita misericordia, Dios mío—dijo ella alzando al cielo su mirada.—La hora del arrepentimiento no ha llegado todavía; pero ella sonará.

En seguida visitó el tesoro que guardaba para los desgraciados; tomó consigo una cesta de provisiones y un bolsillo de oro; y a favor de las sombras de la noche, fue a buscar aquella casa de que había hablado su padre.

Reconocióla en la huella del hacha de los bandidos que rompiendo el postigo la habían dejado abierta; Clemencia iba a pasar el umbral de una habitación desnuda y miserable, cuando oyendo una voz que hablaba dentro se detuvo y contempló el cuadro que se ofrecía a su vista.

En un rincón del cuarto, sobre un lecho pobre y desabrigado, yacía una mujer joven, pero pálida y enflaquecida, con un recién nacido entre sus brazos. Más lejos un niño de seis años y otro de cuatro estaban sentados bajo las mantas de una camita suspendida en forma de cuna por cuatro cuerdas reunidas y pendientes de una viga del techo.

La luz opaca de una vela que ardía en el suelo daba a aquella morada un aspecto lúgubre que, unido al recuerdo de la espantosa escena ocurrida allí despedazó de dolor el alma de Clemencia.

—Mamá—decía con voz lamentable el menor de los dos niños,—tengo hambre. ¿Qué has hecho del pan que comimos ayer?

La madre exhaló un profundo gemido al mismo tiempo que el otro niño respondió con acento grave y resignado:

—Lo comimos, Enrique, lo comimos y mamá no tiene dinero para comprar otro, porque está enferma y no puede trabajar. No la atormentes; y durmamos como el pobre angelito que ayer cayó del cielo entre nosotros.

—¡Ay! ¡él tiene el pecho de mi mamá y yo tengo hambre . . . tengo hambre!—replicaba Enrique llorando.

—¡Dios mío!—exclamó la madre entre sollozos,—si en la sabiduría de tus designios quisiste que el hacha homicida abatierra [sic] el árbol más robusto, yo adoro tu voluntad y me resigno; pero ten piedad de estas tiernas flores que comienzan a abrirse a los rayos de tu sol. ¡Señor! tú que alimentas las avecillas del aire, los gusanos de la tierra y que oyes llorar de hambre a mis hijos ¿no enviarás en su socorro uno de los millares de ángeles que habitan tu cielo . . . ?

—¡Ah! helo ahí—murmuró viendo a Clemencia que arrodillada ante la cama de los niños les presentaba las provisiones que había traido.

La madre juntó las manos y contempló con religiosa admiración a aquella bellísima joven, cuyo blanco velo plegado como una aureola en torno de su frente parecía iluminar las tinieblas que la rodeaban, y que inclinada sobre sus hijos como el genio de la misericordia los cubría con una mirada de ternura y de dolor. La pobre mujer creíala un ángel descendido a su ruego; e inmóvil, temía que un ademán, que un soplo, desvanecieran la divina visión, restituyéndola a la horrible realidad. Y cuando Clemencia se acercó a su lecho, la sencilla hija del pueblo alargó ansiosamente la mano para tocar las suyas y convencerse de que no era una aparición sobre-humana.

—¡Oh! tú, que has venido a derramar el consuelo en esta morada de dolor—exclamó abrazando las rodillas de la joven,—¿quien eres, criatura angelical?

—Soy un ser desventurado como vosotros y vengo a buscar a mis compañeros de dolor. Vengo a deciros: Madre cristiana, confiad en aquél que enjuga toda lágrima y acalla todo gemido. El vela sobre todo de lo alto de su cielo y puede hacer de la más débil criatura un instrumento de su misericordia. ¿Habéis quedado sola y desamparada? Yo estaré cerca de vos y seréis mi hermana querida. ¿Vuestros hijos necesitan de un protector? Yo lo seré. ¿Os halláis falta de todo? He aquí oro para que lo procuréis.

—¡Ah! ¡sois una santa! . . . —dijo la viuda, inclinándose devotamente,—bendecid a mi hijo y dadle un nombre; porque todavía no está bautizado.

Y puso al recién nacido en los brazos de Clemencia.

—Llamadle "Manuel"—dijo ella en voz baja, y al pronunciar este nombre la pálida frente de la virgen se ruborizó, y sus ojos brillaron con extraño fulgor.

—Manuel—continuó, besando al niño con timidez,—yo seré para tí una nodriza solícita y apasionada. Tu madre no tendrá celos, pues para ella serán todas tus caricias; para mí sólo la dicha de poder decir cada día.—Manuel ¡yo te amo!

—¡Ay de mí!—exclamó la pobre madre, cubriendo sus ojos con la mano de Clemencia, y sollozando profundamente,—bien pronto lo seréis todo para él. Mi esposo me llama desde la eternidad. El puñal del asesino no ha podido romper el lazo que unía nuestras almas, y la mía se va, aunque a pesar suyo, y gimiendo amargamente por estas otras almas que se quedan penando en la tierra. Y la infeliz señalaba a los niños con ademán desesperado.

Clemencia la escuchaba con terror. La hija del asesino pensó estremecida de espanto en los crímenes de su padre, cuya imagen nunca se le había presentado tan horrible. Pero sobreponiéndose a las lúgubres ideas que la abrumaban, llamó a la madre al cumplimiento de su deber en la tierra, y a la cristiana a la resignación en la voluntad del cielo.

—Madre mía—dijo el mayor de los niños cuando quedaron solos, —¿cuál de los ángeles del señor es éste que ha venido a visitarnos?

¡Qué hermosos son sus largos cabellos rizados como los de Nuestra Señora del Socorro!

—Y sus ojos, mamá—replicó el más pequeño,—sus ojos azules como el cielo y sus pestañas ¿no es cierto que se parecen a los rayos de esa estrella que nos está mirando por la ventana?

—Sí, hijos míos—dijo la viuda sonriendo tristemente a sus niños, —es un bello ángel que Dios tiene en la tierra para consolar a los infelices.

—¡Ah! es un ángel de la tierra; por eso está tan triste. Yo la he visto llorar mientras arreglaba nuestra cama.

—¿Cuál es el nombre de ese ángel, madre mía?

—Cualquiera que sea, bendigámoslo, hijos míos, y pidamos a Dios que enjugue sus lágrimas como ha enjugado las nuestras—dijo la viuda, haciendo arrodillar a los niños para la oración de la noche.

IV

Clemencia entre tanto se alejaba con lentos y vacilantes pasos. La expresión de su semblante revelaba un profundo desconsuelo. Pensaba en la omnipotencia del mal y en la omnipotencia del bien. Un solo golpe de puñal había bastado a su padre para abrir el insondable abismo de infortunio que acababa de contemplar y ella con toda una vida de sacrificios y abnegación, ¿qué había alcanzado? Aliviar el hambre y la desnudez; curar dolores materiales: para los del alma nada había hallado sino lágrimas. Y a esta idea Clemencia se sintió abrumada por un inmenso desaliento. Pero como siempre cuando temía que su fe vacilara, la virgen elevó su pensamiento a Dios, pidiéndole algún grande sacrificio que la revelase el secreto de hacer descender la felicidad donde reinaba el dolor.

Un nombre pronunciado muchas veces con acento feroz, despertó bruscamente a Clemencia de su triste meditación. Miró en torno suyo, y se encontró entre un grupo de hombres cuyo aspecto siniestro llamó su atención. Embozábanse en largos "ponchos"; y armados todos de puñales guardaban cuidadosamente una puerta. La hija del mashorquero los reconoció. Aquellos hombres eran los compañeros de su padre; aquella casa era la "Intendencia," el sitio consagrado a las ejecuciones secretas, el "in pace" donde los unitarios entraban para no salir jamás, y en cuyas bóvedas el dedo del terror había grabado para ellos la lúgubre inscripción del Dante.[4]

Mientras Clemencia trémula y palpitante de ansiedad procuraba oculta detrás de una columna escuchar lo que hablaban aquellos hombres, un jinete montado en un caballo negro, y cuya espada de largos tiros chocaba ruidosamente contra el encuentro de la lanza que empuñaba, detuvo con una sofrenada y una maldición la fogosa carrera de su corcel; y acercándose al grupo que custodiaba la puerta:

—Teniente Corbalán—gritó con voz ronca y breve—toma veinte hombres y ronda el Bajo, mientras yo hago una batida en Barracas. ¡Por las garras del diablo! Consiento en dejar de ser quien soy si el sol de mañana no encuentra la cabeza de Manuel Puirredón clavada en esta lanza.

Y hundiendo las espuelas en los flancos de su caballo, se alejó como un sombrío torbellino.

Clemencia pálida y helada de espanto cayó sobre sus rodillas. El hombre que acababa de hacer ese horrible juramento era su padre.

—Corbalán—dijo uno de aquellos bandidos,—llévame contigo . . . Quiero matar hombres y no guardar mujeres.

—Si Alma-negra te hubiera entregado la que está en el calabozo de las Tres Cruces, no te habría pesado guardarla para tí—dijo riendo atrozmente otro de ellos.

—¡Ah, viejo tigre! sorprender a la hermosa que esperaba a su galán, atarla como un cordero al arzón de la silla, traerla bajo el poncho a la Intendencia, encerrarla en el calabozo de las Tres Cruces donde hay más de cincuenta sepulturas . . . ¿qué pensará hacer de ella?

—¡Poca cosa! Matarla en lugar de su marido, y matarla con él si logra atraparlo.

Clemencia no escuchó más. Alzóse fuerte y resuelta; acercóse con entereza al jefe de los bandidos, y dando a sus ojos la negra mirada de su padre, levantó el velo y le dijo con voz imperiosa.

—Teniente Corbalán ¿me conocéis?

—¡La hija del comandante!—exclamó el mashorquero descubriéndose.

Los bandidos se apartaron respetuosamente, y la joven sin dignarse añadir una palabra, pasó el umbral y se internó en las sombras del fatídico edificio.

En la obscuridad del lóbrego portal que daba entrada al patio de los calabozos, Clemencia divisó un hombre de pie, inmóvil y apoyado en una alabarda. Vestía el uniforme de gendarme y ella le creyó un centinela; pero al acercarse a él se estremeció.

La joven no tuvo para reconocerlo necesidad de ver su rostro que cubría la ancha manga de una gorra de cuartel.

—¡Desventurado!—murmuró Clemencia al oído de aquel hombre y estrechando su brazo con terror. ¿Qué hacéis aquí? ¿No habéis oído?

—Sí—respondió él cerrándola el paso.—Soy aquel que los asesinos buscan con tan feroz afán. Sus puñales están sobre mi cabeza, pero yo he venido a salvar a mi amada o perecer con ella. Mirad—continuó hiriendo con el pie un objeto sin forma que yacía en tierra,—he matado un centinela, y armado con sus despojos velo aquí para tender a mis pies al primero que atraviese el dintel de esa puerta.

—¡Manuel Puirredón!—dijo Clemencia descubriendo su bello rostro y posando en los ojos del proscrito una mirada inefable, ¿os acordáis?

¡Ella!...exclamó el unitario,—¡el ángel que me salvó!...

—¿Tenéis confianza en mí? Me abandonaréis el cuidado de salvar a aquélla que buscáis?

—¡Ah!—respondió él con un transporte que Clemencia reprimió asustada,—por esas solas palabras, hermosa criatura, heme aquí a vuestros pies. Pedid mi sangre...mi alma...todo os lo daré.

—Alejaos, pues, de esto funesto lugar; trasponed esa puerta fatal, y esperad a vuestra amada donde ella os esperaba poco há.

—¡No! Todo...menos alejarme un paso de aquí.

—¡Oh! ¡Dios mío! ¡quiere perderse!...Pues bien...juradme al menos permanecer inmóvil bajo vuestro disfraz, y no atacar a nadie cualquiera que sea que pase por este sitio.

—¡Duro es hacer esa promesa!...pero, pues lo queréis, ¡sea!

—¡Gracias! ¡gracias!...—exclamó ella estrechando la mano del proscrito, en la que éste sintió caer una lágrima.—Sed feliz, Manuel Puirredón...¡Adiós!

Y la joven bajando el velo se perdió entre las sombras.

El unitario oyó a lo lejos un ruido áspero de cerrojos y dijo:

—Es la puerta de su calabozo. ¡Emilia! ¡Emilia mía!

Y con la mirada y el oído atento, interrogaba angustiosamente a la noche y al silencio. Y así pasaron con la lentitud de los siglos dos, cinco, diez minutos; y Puirredón, en su mortal inquietud, estaba ya próximo a quebrantar el juramento y a correr tras aquélla que se lo había impuesto.

Al fin allá a lo lejos el blanco velo de Clemencia apareció de repente entre las tinieblas de un lóbrego pasadizo. Puirredón lo vio venir sola y olvidando su promesa, olvidando su peligro, olvidándolo todo, arrojó una exclamación de dolor y corrió a su encuentro. Pero al llegar a ella dos brazos cariñosos rodearon su cuello, y unos labios de fuego ahogaron en los suyos un grito de gozo.

—¡Silencio, amado mío!—dijo una voz querida al oído del proscrito.—Un milagro me ha salvado. La virgen del Socorro ha descendido a mi calabozo para librarme. Sí. Yo la he reconocido en su celeste belleza y en la melancólica sonrisa de su labio divino. Este es su sagrado velo . . . él nos protegerá . . . Huyamos.

Y la mujer encubierta arrastró tras de sí al proscrito.

Cuando los fugitivos llegaban a la puerta vieron avanzar un jinete que haciendo dar botes a su caballo entró en el portal, y arrojándose en tierra desenvainó su puñal y en un silencio feroz se encaminó al patio de los calabozos.

A su vista Puirredón sintió estremecerse entre las suyas la mano de su compañera, y la oyó murmurar bajo su velo con acento de terror!

—¡Alma-negra!

Mas luego traspusieron ambos el umbral maldito, y respiraron el aura embalsamada de la libertad.

Entre tanto Alma-negra atravesó el patio y llegando al calabozo de las Tres-Cruces descorrió los pesados cerrojos y buscó a tientas entre las tinieblas.

Un rayo perdido de la luna menguante deslizándose por la estrecha claraboya de la bóveda, formaba una mancha lívida en el húmedo pavimento, haciendo más densas las tinieblas de aquella espantosa mazmorra. Sin embargo, el ojo ávido del bandido descubrió una forma blanca.

Fuése hacia ella, extendió su mano sangrienta, y palpando el cuello de una mujer, hundió en él su puñal, gritando con rabia:

—Delatora de nuestros secretos, cómplice de los infames unitarios, muere en lugar del conspirador que amas, pero sabe antes que ni tus huesos se juntarán con los suyos porque tu sepulcro será el fondo de este calabozo.

Y hablando así, arrojó una espantosa carcajada.

Al sentirse herida de muerte la desventurada llevó las manos a su cuello dividido, y conteniendo la sangre que se escapaba a torrentes de la herida.

—¡Dios mío!—murmuró,—¡mi sacrificio está consumado! cumplida está la misión que me impuse en este mundo: haced ahora, Señor, que mi sangre lave esa otra sangre que clama a vos desde la tierra.

Al acento de aquella voz Alma-negra sintió romperse su corazón, y los cabellos se erizaron sobre su cabeza. Alzóse rápido y levantando a su víctima corrió a la claraboya y miró al rayo de la luna su rostro ensangrentado.

—¡Clemencia!—gritó el asesino con un horrible alarido.

—¡Padre! . . . ¡pobre padre! . . . eleva al cielo tus miradas, y búscala allí—balbuceó la dulce voz de la joven al exhalar el último aliento.

El bandido cayó desplomado en tierra, arrastrando entre sus brazos el cadáver de su hija degollada . . .

Pero la sangre de la virgen halló gracia delante de Dios, y como un bautismo de redención, hizo descender sobre aquel hombre un rayo de luz divina que lo regeneró.

Notas

1. Los unitarios eran los enemigos políticos de Rosas. Rosas encabezaba el partido federal.

2. El general Lavalle había tratado de apoderarse del gobierno argentino en 1829, pero Rosas le venció en una batalla; después de esta derrota, Lavalle se fue al exilio en el Uruguay.

3. El chiripá es el ancho pantalón de los gauchos.

4. "Abandonad toda esperanza, los que entráis aquí." Del *Inferno* de Dante Alighieri, Canto III.

The Executioner's Daughter

Roque Blacksoul was the terror of Buenos Aires. Executioner par excellence in an association of executioners called "Mas-horca" and devoted heart and soul to the dreadful founder [Rosas] of that terrible fraternity, he measured the hours by the number of his crimes, and his hand, always armed with a dagger, never moved except to wound. His tracks were a pool of blood, and pity had left him so long ago that there was no trace of it left in his heart; the cries of the orphan, the wife, and the mother left him as unfeeling as the cold steel blade he plunged into the breast of his victims. All resemblance to humanity had disappeared from the man's countenance, and his language, faithful expression of the name with which his crimes had endowed him, was a mixture of ferocity and blasphemy that made all those who had the ill fortune to cross his path blanch with fear.

Nevertheless, within that awful storehouse of expressions of cruelty and blasphemy, like a flower which blooms in a swamp, there was one word of goodness which Roque always uttered.

"Clemencia," the bloody executioner would say when he came home at dawn, worn out from the crimes he had committed that night. And at this name, which sounded sarcastic coming from the assassin's lips, a voice so sweet and melodious that it seemed to come from celestial choirs responded tenderly, "Father!" and the angelic figure of a young girl of sixteen, with great blue eyes and a halo of blonde curls, came to meet the executioner and embraced him with painful effusiveness. She was his daughter.

Roque loved her with fierce affection, as a tiger loves his cubs. For her sake he would have taken fire and destruction to the ends of the earth, for her he would have given his own blood; yet he would not have sacrificed one drop of his vengeance nor one of his murderous instincts for her.

Clemencia lived alone in the accursed house of the executioner. Her mother had died long ago, the victim of some unknown ailment. Clemencia had seen her languish and wither away in a slow death, but in spite of her tender care she could not restore her mother to health, nor could Clemencia's pleas and tears wrest from her mother's heart the fatal secret that was taking her to the grave. But when her mother died, and she saw her disappear under the coffin's black lid, and when, terrified at the enormous void in which this left her, she had flung herself into her father's arms, she saw that they were stained with blood, and an awful revelation suddenly flashed in Clemencia's soul. She looked back on the past and remembered scenes that had been mysterious for her at the time, but that now appeared clear, sharp and awful. She recalled the curses hurled at Roque the Executioner that had hurt her ears so many times, and which she, in the love and veneration she felt for her father, could not have conceived were meant for him. She, who until then had lived in a world of love and piety, one day suddenly found herself in another, marked by crimes and horror. The whole truth was revealed to her eyes, and when she compared her own pain to that which her mother had suffered in silence, she understood why the latter had preferred eternity to life and the cold pillow of the grave to the conjugal bed. But no feeling of bitterness mingled with Clemencia's suffering. The beautiful girl's soul was like her name: she was all sweetness and mercy. The awful discovery she had made in no way diminished the tenderness she felt for her father. On the contrary, Clemencia loved him all the more because she loved him with deep compassion, and when she saw him go forth alone to his crimes on a blood-drenched path, with hatred under his feet and vengeance over his head, far from envying her mother's eternal rest, Clemencia wanted to live in order to stand by the wretched man on his road to iniquity like a guardian angel, and, if she could not persuade him to leave this path, she could at least offer God a life of suffering and atonement on her father's behalf.

Clemencia rejected with horror the luxury which surrounded her, for in it she saw the price of crime, and, forgetting that she was young and beautiful, and that in the world there are heavenly pleasures for youth and beauty, she hid her slender figure and delicious curves under a long, white tunic, covered the silken curls of her magnificent hair with a thick veil, quieted the beating of a heart that longed for love, and devoted herself entirely to helping the unfortunate. Controlling her soul's profound horror, she leafed through the bloody lists to which her father consigned the names of his victims, and, guided by these hideous facts, hurried to aid the widows and orphans her father's dagger had left unprotected in the world. In order to help them she used the skills she had acquired from the scrupulous education her mother had given her: she gave lessons in painting and music and dedicated her hours to constant work. The poor girl, whose mind was full of dreadful thoughts and whose heart was rent with pain, played happy polkas which her pupils danced with joy and abandon, and in the terrifying silence of her nights, she, who had bid eternal farewell to all of life's joys, busied herself by embroidering airy bouquets on a bridal veil or the transparent and flirtatious skirt of a ballgown, without having her soul become dispirited by the painful thoughts that these were accessories of a happiness to which she could no longer aspire. With the money she earned by these labors, so full of sad emotions, she hastened to spread consolation and peace in the homes of the victims of her father's axe. Like a tender mother she cuddled and taught the children, watched over the sick with the fervent solicitude of a sister of Charity, and helped the dying with an eloquence full of devotion and piety.

Totally forgetting her own self, Clemencia seemed to exist solely in the lives of others. Yet nevertheless the world smiled on her from afar, opened its arms to her and showed her its pleasures. On her charitable errands Clemencia would often overhear fervent voices exclaim:

"How lovely she is! Fortunate the man who deserves one glance from those eyes!"

But those remarks of gallantry and love uttered in the depths of the aggrieved city's tomblike silence affronted Clemencia's ears like bawdy songs sung among graves in a cemetery, and, shielding her face within the folds of her veil, she drew away, her heart weighed down by sorrow and distaste.

One day at nightfall, Clemencia saw several men of dreadful appearance enter her house and make their way to her father's room. The men were wrapped in long ponchos, under whose folds one could see the handles of their daggers gleam. Clemencia perceived something threatening in the presence of those men, and after vacillating for a few moments, ran to put her ear to the keyhole of a door that opened onto her father's room.

Roque, who stood next to a table, had some papers in his hands, and spoke in a loud voice to his listeners.

"Yes, my friends," he said, "a fight to the death to the Unitarians![1] A fight to the death for those cursed people! You think you're accomplishing a lot? Well, know that you're wrong. Just read the list of our executions for this month and compare it to the denunciations we have received today alone. Read it and you will see that there is still a huge job to be done by the knives of the association of the Mas-horca, especially when you compare the number of the fallen with those who will fall . . . yes, who will fall, even though they hide under the Virgin Mary's cloak!"

"Queen of Heaven," whispered Clemencia, wringing her hands in anguish, and turning toward the image of the Virgin, her only companion in that lonely dwelling. "If this blasphemy has reached the foot of your divine throne, don't listen to it! Good Mother: cast it aside indulgently, and with a smile of compassion enlighten the unfortunate man who walks in darkness."

As she uttered these last words Clemencia again heard her father's voice read:

"Tonight at nine a muffled man will stop at the foot of the obelisk in Victoria Square and whistle three times. This man is Manuel de Puirredón, the incorrigible Unitarian conspirator, Lavalle's[2] friend and exiled in Montevideo. The signal is intended for a Federalist's daughter who has secretly joined him and, converted into his most powerful ally, is handing over her father's secrets. As this signal will tell her of the conspirator's return, she will then join him, doubtlessly to help in the vile plan which brings him to Buenos Aires.

"Do you hear, friends? And our daggers are still in our belts!" exclaimed Roque with ferocious rage.

"Death to Manuel de Puirredón!" shouted the assassins, unsheathing their long knives.

Clemencia shot a look through the keyhole at the pendulum clock in front of her father, and shuddered.

The hand showed eight fifty-five.

"Five minutes to save a man's life! Five minutes to keep my father from committing one more crime! Oh God, make this short time last, and put wings on my feet."

Wrapping herself in her long, white veil, she ran out of the house, not without turning her head many times, in fear that the murderers would get there ahead of her, thus ruining her desire to save the unfortunate man who, without knowing it, was going to his death.

When she got to the corner formed by Victoria and Colegio streets, Clemencia spied a black shape walking diagonally across the square and heading for the obelisk.

"It is he!" she murmured with trembling voice, and running after him, caught up with him just as he reached the iron fence.

Many pedestrians strolled about this place, enjoying the evening breeze, and prevented Clemencia from speaking with the stranger.

Then she turned back; she passed close by him and touched him lightly on the shoulder, making an imperceptible sign to follow her.

The muffled man turned impetuously and, drawing near to Clemencia, exclaimed, "Emilia, my Emilia!" gently embracing the young woman's body with one arm, she being unable to stop this without calling attention to them both.

In this way obliged to silence, Clemencia regarded the unknown man through her veil, whose countenance was at that moment lit by the rays of the moon. He was a young man, and more handsome than any Clemencia had ever envisioned, even in the poetic dreams of a sixteen-year-old girl. He was tall and slender. In all of his movements he showed an easy, almost careless grace, that only experience in the world and distinguished birth can bestow. The deep and yet languid glance of his beautiful eyes had an irresistible force of attraction which, combined with the magic harmony of his voice, made this man one of those beings that once seen, is never forgotten, and who leaves an indelible mark of happiness or pain on our lives.

The stranger, in the throes of deception, repeated into Clemencia's ears:

"Emilia, here I am, my love, not as a conspirator who will once again involve you in the ruin of my fantastic hopes, but as the ardent husband who will tear you from your father's arms and carry you off in mine, far, far away, to the ends of the earth, to some unknown spot which your love will change into a delectable Eden for me. Come, my Emilia, let us leave this fatal homeland. God has cursed it and our attempts and sacrifices to save it are in vain . . .

"Oh," the fugitive went on with a choking voice, and drawing Clemencia even closer to his chest, "you see, Emilia: this idea wreaks havoc on my heart, but you are here to calm its pain and fill it with happiness . . .

"And our son? How handsome he will be! How you must have suffered when you separated from him in the cruel necessity of hiding his existence! . . . "

At that moment they reached a deserted part of the square. Clemencia cast a look around and, drawing back suddenly from out of the stranger's arms, lifted her veil to let him see his mistake.

"Good Heavens!" he said, "It isn't Emilia!"

"No, Sir, but if your name is Manuel de Puirredón, flee from this fateful place as every second you stay here means a step closer to death . . . Don't you see?" she continued, pointing to a dark group at the other end of the square. "It is they, the bloody henchmen of the Mashorca who are going to ambush you . . . Flee, in God's Name, for the sake of your wife and son . . . Take them far away from this savage lair to realize the beautiful dream of happiness your mind envisions . . . Flee, flee," she repeated, pointing out a dark street to the fugitive and disappearing down another.

III

When Clemencia got home she fell at the feet of the Virgin, and, hiding her face under the sacred image's own veil, wept for a long time, while murmuring strange words among her sobs: perhaps some sweet and painful secret she had wanted to hide from herself, and which she only dared to confess to the one who keeps the key to all maidens' hearts.

From this day on Clemencia's enchanting and melancholy face became still paler, and took on a profound sadness. Who knows what pleasant vision crossed her mind, brought on by that man's passionate words? Who knows what feeling the sight of him had awakened in that lonely young heart?

Sometimes, with distracted gaze, she smiled sweetly, but then, as though beset by a bitter memory, shook her head with a movement of painful resignation, murmuring in a low voice:

"Daughter of misfortune, inheritor of heavenly punishment, sacrificial victim, think of your vow and remember that your kingdom is not of this world."

Sunk anew in her definitive sadness, she rededicated herself with even greater fervor to the mission of mercy she had imposed on herself.

"Clemencia," the executioner said to his daughter one day, "why are you continually more pensive and sad? Who dares to cause you grief? Tell me his name, and you can instantly add, 'Poor devil!'"

"No one, Father, no one!" his daughter exclaimed, instinctively lifting her hand to her heart as though fearing that her father could read some secret there.

"No, you are deceiving me . . . For some time now I have even noticed tears in your voice when you come to greet me."

"Father," replied the young woman, interrupting him and looking into his bloodstained eyes with her blue and pious gaze, "can't you guess? When at last you come home after a night of anxiously waiting up for you, and I go to embrace you, I think with great sadness of the children of the unfortunate men cut down by your group, and that those poor beings will never enjoy the happiness that God has still granted me. Oh Father, is this not a good reason for tears and sadness? In the midst of those bloody events, have you never lifted your hand to your heart and asked yourself what you would do if you saw a hand with a dagger descend upon your daughter and cut her throat?"

"Be still, Clemencia, be still!" shouted the outlaw. "What would I do? Hell itself would not equal the rage with which Roque's arm would move to avenge you . . . But you are mad, child! Don't you know that the barbarous Unitarians lack a heart such as ours, we who love and hate with equal intensity?"

"Father, you know that isn't true! What, then, do the mothers' heartrending cries mean, or the sobs of the wives and the sad weeping of the orphaned children which I constantly hear raised to Heaven against us? Don't they tell you that the heartstrings severed by your dagger are as sensitive as our own?"

"Be quiet, Clemencia, be quiet!" he repeated. "You have such a suggestive and persuasive voice that you will have me believing this, and then what would General Rosas think of his servant? How Solomon and Cuitiño would make fun of their compatriot! No! Get out! I don't want to listen to you, above all not today, when Manuel Puirredón, that Unitarian outlaw whose throat I have sworn to cut, walks among us as though invisible and protected by a supernatural force . . . Oh, I am getting upset over nothing. What madness! My heart is full of hatred, and there would be no room for mercy in it. Just listen to this story . . .

"A few months ago I went to hear mass at the Perpetual Help Church."

"Father! You dared to enter God's temple with your hands stained with blood?"

"With blood? Yes, of course, and why not, if it is Unitarian blood, and they are God's enemies?

"Anyway, as I was saying, I went into the Perpetual Help church. Mass had barely begun when the man at whose side I had knelt down, suddenly turned around, and, regarding me for a second as though to place me, threw me a scornful look, and, drawing away with insolent disgust, moved to a spot very far from me. That act betrayed him as a Unitarian. The wretch had recogized Roque, but he had no idea what Roque's vengeance would be.

"I kept my eyes on him during mass, and when he left the church I saw him go into a small, almost ruined house, that was across the street.

"That night, while the man had forgotten his insulting behavior toward me, he sat quietly by his wife's side, holding his two children in his arms. His wife was busy embroidering baby clothes for the third child that was soon expected, while I guided the Mas-horca to his house. While the arms of his wife and children embraced him I buried my dagger countless times in his breast, spattering blood on the clothing of the yet unborn baby.

"Clemencia, Clemencia, what's the matter?"

The murderer reached out his arm to support his daughter, who, trembling and shaking, refused it with ill-concealed horror.

"For a while," he continued, "I thought that the indelible memory that bloody scene, with all its screams and tears, had left in my imagination what is referred to as remorse, but no—it was only the pleasure of satisfied revenge. The day Roque knows compassion or remorse is the day the blade of this knife would be dulled and . . . just look how it shines," the outlaw said, making the wide blade glitter before his daughter's eyes.

And thrusting it quickly into the belt of his wide trousers he left, doubtless to go back to his gruesome task.

Clemencia felt crushed under the weight of the frightful words she had just heard. Feeling weak, broken, and faint she fell at the feet of her divine patroness, raising her hands to her in anguished prayer.

While she prayed hope and faith came into her heart, and when she arose, her face once again shone with serene resignation.

"It is never too late for Your divine mercy, oh Lord," she said, raising her eyes to Heaven. "The hour of repentance has not yet come, but it will toll."

Quickly she went to the fund she kept for the victims. She took a basket of food and a purse of gold with her, and, under cover of night, went to look for the house her father had mentioned.

She recognized it from the marks of the axes the criminals had used to break down the side gate, and had left open. Clemencia was about to cross the threshold of a poor, bare room, when she heard a voice speak inside and held back, contemplating the scene before her eyes.

In one corner, stretched out on a bed so poor it had nearly no covers, lay a pale, thin young woman who held a newborn in her arms.

At a distance a boy of about six and another of four sat under the blankets of a bed that was suspended like a cradle from four ropes attached to a roofbeam.

The faint light of a candle which burned on the floor gave this dwelling a gloomy atmosphere, which, when joined to the memory of the hideous scene which had taken place there, tore Clemencia's soul apart with grief.

"Mother," said the younger of the two children with a sad voice, "I'm hungry. Where is the bread we had yesterday?" The mother let out a deep sigh while the other boy answered with a grave and resigned tone:

"We ate it, Enrique, we ate it and Mother has no more money to buy more because she is ill and can't work. Don't bother her, and let's go to sleep like the little angel that fell down from Heaven here yesterday."

"Oh, he has my mother's breast and I'm hungry, I'm hungry!" wailed Enrique.

"Oh Lord," cried the mother between sobs, "if in the wisdom of Your designs you wished the executioner's axe to fell the strongest tree, I worship Your will and resign myself to it, but have mercy on these tender flowers that are only beginning to open to the sun's rays. Lord! You who feed the birds of the air and the worms of the earth, and hear my children weep with hunger, can't You send one of the countless angels who dwell in Heaven to help them?"

"Ah, here is one," she murmured when she saw Clemencia kneeling by the children's bed and handing them some of the food she had brought.

The mother clasped her hands and with pious adoration looked at the beautiful young girl, whose white veil fell like a halo around her face and seemed to light up the gloom which surrounded them. Bent over the children like a spirit of mercy she gazed at them with a look of tenderness and sorrow. The poor woman held her to be an angel who had come in answer to her prayers and tried to keep as still as possible, fearing that a gesture, a breath would destroy that heavenly vision, bringing her back to her painful reality. And when Clemencia drew near her bed, the simple woman of the people anxiously stretched out her hands to touch Clemencia's, as though to convince herself that she was not a supernatural illusion.

"Oh, you who have come to bring consolation to this unhappy home," she exclaimed, embracing the young woman's knees, "who are you, angelic creature?"

"I am an unfortunate being just like you, and I have come to seek my companions in grief. I have come to tell you this: Christian Mother, trust in the One Who wipes away all tears and quiets all weeping. He watches over everything from on high and can make the weakest creature the instrument of His mercy. Have you been left alone and abandoned? I will be near you and you will be my dear sister. Do your children need someone to protect them? I shall be the one. Do you have need of things? Here is gold so that you can buy them."

"Oh, you are a saint!" said the widow, bending down reverently, "Bless my son and give him a name, for he has not yet been baptized."

And she placed the newborn in Clemencia's arms.

"Call him Manuel," she said in a low voice, and when she said this, the maiden's pale face blushed and her eyes shone with a peculiar brilliance.

"Manuel," she continued, kissing the child shyly, "I will be a solicitous and devoted wetnurse for you. Your mother will not be jealous, for all your caresses will be for her. I only want the joy of being able to say to you every day, 'Manuel, I love you!'"

"Oh, Lord!" exclaimed the poor mother, covering her eyes with Clemencia's hands and sobbing hard. "Soon you will be everything to him. My husband calls to me from Eternity. The assassin's knife could not sever the bonds that unite our souls, and mine is about to depart, even though it does not wish to and cries bitterly for these other beings who must remain and suffer on earth." And the unhappy woman pointed to the children with a desperate gesture.

Clemencia listened to her, terrified. With profound horror the assassin's daughter thought about her father's crimes, which had never seemed more awful to her. But, rising above the gloomy thoughts which depressed her, she reminded the mother of her responsibilities on earth, and as a Christian of the need to resign herself to God's will.

"Mother," said the oldest of the children when they were alone again, "which of God's angels is it who has come to see us? How beautiful she is with her long curls, just like Our Lady of Help!"

"And her eyes," replied the youngest, "her eyes are blue like the sky and her eyelashes—isn't it true that they look like the rays of that star that shines in our window?"

"Yes, children," said the widow, smiling sadly at her little ones, "she is a lovely angel whom God has put on earth to console the unfortunate."

"What's the angel's name, Mother?"

"Whatever it is, let us bless it, children, and ask God to dry her tears as He has dried ours," said the widow, making the children kneel for bedtime prayer.

I V

Meanwhile Clemencia walked away with slow, hesitant steps. The expression on her face bore witness to her profound distress. She thought about the omnipotence of good and evil. One blow of her father's dagger had sufficed to create the bottomless abyss of misery she had just witnessed, and she, what had she gained by an entire life of sacrifice and self-abnegation? Alleviate hunger and nakedness, cure some material hurt, perhaps, but for the soul's afflictions the only remedy she had found was weeping. At this thought Clemencia felt overcome by profound dejection. But as she always did when she feared her faith might waver, the maiden lifted up her thoughts to God, asking Him for some great sacrifice that would uncover for her the secret of replacing suffering with happiness.

Clemencia was roused out of her sad reverie by the sound of a name which was uttered often and menacingly. Looking around her, she saw that she was surrounded by a group of men whose sinister aspect aroused her attention. Wrapped in long ponchos and armed with daggers, they were carefully guarding a door. The executioner's daughter recognized them. They were her father's henchmen, the building was "Headquarters," the place devoted to carrying out secret executions, the "R.I.P." where Unitarians entered never to come out again, and on whose vaults the finger of terror had written for them Dante's funereal warning.[3]

While Clemencia, trembling and shaking with anxiety, hid behind a column and attempted to hear what the men were talking about, a rider on a black horse, whose long sword clanked noisily against the handle of the lance he was holding, checked the headlong rush of his mount with a curse, and approached the group on guard at the door.

"Lieutenant Corbalán," he shouted with hoarse, curt voice, "take twenty men and patrol el Bajo, while I raid Barracas. The Devil! I shall renounce who I am if by tomorrow at sunrise Manuel Puirredón's head isn't stuck on this lance!"

Plunging his spurs into his horse's flanks, he departed like a black whirlwind.

White and cold with fear, Clemencia fell to her knees. The man who had just pronounced this terrible oath was her father.

"Corbalán," said one of the bandits, "take me with you. I want to kill men and not keep watch over women."

"If Blacksoul had given you the one who was in the Tres Cruces jail, you wouldn't have minded keeping her for yourself," said another man with savage laughter.

"The old dog! Surprising the lovely lady who was awaiting her gallant gentleman, tying her up like a sheep to his saddle, bringing her to Headquarters under his poncho, and locking her up in the Tres Cruces jail where there are more than fifty graves—what do you suppose he plans to do with her?"

"Not much! Kill her instead of her husband, or kill her with him if he catches him."

Clemencia listened no further. She drew herself up, strong and resolute. She firmly approached the bandits' leader, giving her eyes the same black look as her father's, and spoke in an imperious voice.

"Lieutenant Corbalán, do you know me?"

"The commandant's daughter!" exclaimed the assassin, taking off his hat.

The men drew aside respectfully, and the young woman, without bothering to add another word, crossed the threshold and disappeared into the shadows of the fateful building.

In the darkness of the gloomy portico which gave out onto the patio where the cells were, Clemencia made out a man, standing immobile and leaning on a halberd. He was dressed in a guard's uniform and she took him for a sentinel, but on approaching him she trembled.

The young woman did not need to see his face in order to recognize him, a face which was covered by the wide band of an army cap.

"Poor man!" Clemencia murmured in his ear and clutched his arm in fright. "What are you doing here? Didn't you hear?"

"Yes," he answered, blocking her path. "I'm the one those killers are looking for so desperately. Their daggers are aimed at my head, but I have come to save my beloved or die with her. Look," he went on, kicking at a formless shape that lay on the ground, "I have killed a sentinel, and armed with his things am awaiting the first man to cross this threshold in order to bring him down."

"Manuel de Puirredón!" said Clemencia, uncovering her face and casting an indescribable glance at the fugitive's eyes. "Do you remember?"

"It is she!" exclaimed the Unitarian. "The angel who saved me!"

"Do you trust me? Will you let me take over saving the one you seek?"

"Ah!" he replied with such ecstasy that Clemencia stifled it in fear. "For those words alone, beautiful creature, I fall at your feet. Ask me for my blood, my soul . . . I will give you everything."

"Then get away from this dreadful place; cross that fatal threshold, and wait for your beloved where she was waiting for you a little while ago."

"No! I'll do anything but take even one step away from here."

"Oh, my God! Do you want your doom! Well then, swear to me to keep still in your disguise, and not to attack anyone who walks by here."

"That's a hard promise, but since you wish it, so be it!"

"Thank you, thank you," she said, clasping the fugitive's hand. He felt a tear fall on it. "Be happy, Manuel de Puirredón. Farewell!"

Lowering her veil, the young woman disappeared into the shadows.

The Unitarian heard from afar the harsh sound of the lock, and said, "That's the door to her cell . . . Emilia, my Emilia!"

With eyes and ears alert, he anxiously probed the night and the silence. Two, five, ten minutes crept by at a snail's pace, and in his mortal anxiety Puirredón came close to breaking his oath and running after the one who had exacted it from him.

Finally, there in the distance Clemencia's white veil suddenly appeared among the shadows of the dismal corridor. Puirredón saw her coming alone and, forgetting his promise, forgetting everything, let out an exclamation of pain and ran to meet her. But when he reached her two loving arms encircled his neck and fiery lips sealed the cry of ecstasy that was about to burst from his own.

"Silence, my darling," a beloved voice whispered into the fugitive's ear. "A miracle has saved me. The Virgin of Help came down to my cell to free me. Yes,—I recognized her by her celestial beauty and by the sad smile of her divine lips. This is her holy veil which will protect us. Let us flee!"

Covering her face, the woman dragged the man behind her.

When the fugitives reached the door they saw a rider come up; making his horse prance he entered the gateway, dismounted and unsheathed his dagger, then headed for the cell area in menacing silence.

When they saw him Puirredón felt his companion's hand tremble in his, and under her veil heard her say in a terrified voice, "Blacksoul!"

Then they crossed the accursed threshold together and breathed in the sweet scent of freedom.

Meanwhile Blacksoul crossed the patio, and when he reached the dungeon of Tres Cruces, opened the massive locks and groped about in the dark.

A solitary ray of the waning moon which shone through the narrow skylight of the vault made a livid splash on the damp floor, heightening the dense shadows of the fearful dungeon. Nevertheless, the criminal's sharp eye discerned a white shape.

He went over to it, extended his bloodstained hand, and, feeling a woman's throat, plunged his dagger into it, shouting furiously, "Informer of our secrets, accomplice of the filthy Unitarians, die in place of the conspirator you love, but know ere you do that not even your bones will lie by his because your grave will be the bottom of this cell!"

As he said this he broke into a chilling laugh.

Feeling herself wounded unto death, the unhappy woman brought her hands up to her cleft throat, holding back the blood that gushed in streams from the wound.

"My God!" she whispered, "My sacrifice has been accomplished! The mission I assigned myself here on earth has been completed. Lord, let my blood cleanse this other blood that cries to You from below."

At the sound of her voice Blacksoul felt his heart break and the hair rise on his head. Quickly he stood up, carried his victim over to the skylight, and examined her bloodstained face by the light of the moon.

"Clemencia!" the assassin shouted with a horrible scream.

"Father, poor Father! Raise your eyes to Heaven and look there for mercy," faltered the young woman's gentle voice as she breathed her last.

The criminal fell heavily to the floor, the body of his murdered daughter in his arms.

But the maiden's blood found favor before God, and He, in an act of redemptive baptism, sent down a ray of divine light which re-formed her father.

Notes

1. The Unitarians were Rosas's political enemies. Rosas headed the Federalist party.

2. General Lavalle had attempted to take over the Argentine government in 1829, but Rosas defeated him in a battle; after this defeat, Lavalle went into exile in Uruguay.

3. "All hope abandon, ye who enter here." From Dante Alighieri's *Inferno*, Canto III.

Mercedes Cabello
de Carbonera

Mercedes Cabello de Carbonera from Elvira García y García, La mujer peruana a través de los siglos. Serie Historiada de estudios y observaciones. *(Lima: Imprenta Americana, 1924–25).*

*B*orn in 1845 to an upper-class family in the Peruvian provinces, Mercedes Cabello moved to Lima when she was twenty and married a distinguished medical doctor, Urbano Carbonera. Hers was an active and probing intelligence. As university studies were not permitted to women in her time, she read voraciously on her own and began to write at an early age, at first under the pseudonym Enriqueta Pradel (Mazquiarán 98–99). She was widowed after only a few years of marriage (there were no children) and became an active participant in Lima's circle of intellectuals and literary salons. Juana Manuela Gorriti, her close friend, said of her, "She is one of the most remarkable and eminent women of Peru, distinguished for her beauty, intelligence, and erudition" ("Chincha" 65).

Cabello de Carbonera wrote many articles for newspapers and journals, both in Spanish America and in Europe. She is one of the most important essayists in nineteenth-century Latin America, one who, like many other women, spoke out against women's inequality in society and before the law. The importance of women's ever-increasing publications in newspapers and journals cannot be underestimated. As Mary Louise Pratt observed, "Fortunately, their access to literacy, print culture, and the public sphere was established *before* the republican era. They could not be silenced completely" (15). Because she felt her own lack of formal education keenly, Cabello de Carbonera became a fervent advocate for the education of women. She looked at this issue not only in practical terms but in ideal terms as well: as did many women of her time, she felt that educated women contributed to the moral progress of nations. Here, then, is another example of a female perspective in the nation-building process.

Cabello de Carbonera was an outspoken social critic, to which her journalistic articles and also her novels attest. She loathed the materialism and social pretentiousness of the Peruvian upper classes, in which many women unfortunately were the most active participants. Outward show, stylish fashions, and material possessions counted for everything in these social circles. Cabello de Carbonera also spoke out against their sham religiosity, often abetted by the Catholic clergy of Peru.

Among her five novels, *Blanca Sol* (1888), a novel of social realism, is probably the most widely read, and presents a portrait of just such a shallow and hypocritical woman. Blessed with considerable beauty and native intelligence (but almost no education), Blanca had been raised by her mother to covet wealth and social position, and to do anything to get it. She marries a stupid and ugly man she does not love, has six children whom she neglects, and for a while becomes a leader of fashionable Lima society. When her husband goes insane she loses everything, and the book ends with her poised to become the proprietress of a house of prostitution. Cabello de Carbonera has insinuated all along that upper-class women routinely sell themselves into marriage, so that Blanca Sol's ultimate profession is not very different from what she has been doing all her life. Blanca herself realizes this in a moment of reflection: "Her state as a married woman, and wed to a man whom . . . she could not love, presented itself to her with all the frightening reality of her life. Marriage without love, she thought, was nothing more than prostitution sanctioned by society" (118). In spite of the author's stated intentions to condemn her protagonist's sinful end, the final pages of the novel leave little doubt that Blanca will become an eminently successful madam: "She got ready to make many men lose their wits and their money. . . . [I]t was the shamelessness, the insolence of a woman who wished to express by means of her actions what cannot be said by spoken language" (189). Lucía Guerra Cunningham sees in Blanca's end an inversion of the traditional bildungsroman, in which the protagonist finally realizes—and exploits—her true status (41).

Cabello de Carbonera not only wrote novels, she theorized on them. One of her most important essays was "La novela moderna" (1892), in which she lays out the directions she believes this genre should take in Latin America and shows herself very much in touch with French theorists such as Balzac, Zola, and the positivism of Comte. She saw the novel as linked to the experimental sciences and endorsed social realism as the best approach for novels to speak to the emerging young nations of Latin America: "The novel is called upon to collaborate in the solution of the great problems with which science presents it" (iv). With this essay Cabello de Carbonera won major prizes in Buenos Aires and in the 1892 Chicago Exposition.

Gorriti says of her friend that she was a fine cook, and Elvira García y García tells us a number of other personal details about this energetic and efficient woman. She apparently was an avid gardener and sewed beautifully, often making items for the trousseaus of the daughters of impoverished friends. When her husband died her personal fortune disappeared, but she learned how to manage the money she earned by her writing, and even acquired several ranches (García 21). At the end of her life she unfortunately had a nervous breakdown and slipped into permanent mental illness. She died alone, after ten years in what can only be called horrific conditions in Lima's insane asylum.

The brief essay presented in this anthology examines a topic that was very important to many nineteenth-century women: the relative importance of beauty versus intelligence in a woman. It spoke to a woman's destiny as wife and mother and, by implication, to the role of the family as national allegory. Women's literature of this century is full of attacks on the institution of marriage and foregrounds many women's ignorance and powerlessness in the choice of a marital partner, often with disastrous results. Because men and women often barely knew each other before marrying, men could hardly be blamed for preferring an attractive woman to a plain one, but Cabello de Carbonera is quick to point out that to create lasting and happy relationships between marital partners there has to be more than physical attraction. She also shows that the concept of female beauty is both relative and a social construct. Implicit in her opposition of beauty and intelligence in a woman is the idea that the estimation of a woman's beauty depends on the male gaze in general, while appreciation of a woman's mind belonged only to equally intelligent and talented men, thus fitting partners for a lasting relationship. Cabello de Carbonera focused on a woman's domestic role, but at the same time she and her contemporaries "sought to assert themselves as citizens, as social subjects, as agents of history, and as *pensadoras* [thinkers]" (Pratt 15).

This essay was first read in one of Juana Manuela Gorriti's literary gatherings, the so-called *veladas,* and Cabello dedicated it to her hostess and friend, whose drive and intelligence matched her own.

Estudio comparativo de la inteligencia y la belleza en la muger

TRABAJO DE LA SEÑORA MERCEDES CABELLO
DE CARBONERA LEÍDO POR SU AUTORA

A mi querida amiga Juana Manuela Gorriti.

La eminente é ilustre escritora, á quien tengo el honor de dedicar el presente trabajo, fué la que me sujirió este hermoso á la par que difícil tema, comprometiéndome á tratarlo en esta velada. Ella bien sabe que sus deseos, aun los mas pequeños, son para mi órdenes, que en cumplirlas complázcome, y que su inspirada palabra, será siempre un poderoso móvil para mi pluma.

Así, despues de esta breve esplicacion que doy en salvedad de cualquiera interpretacion que sobre el tema pudiera hacerse, procuraré satisfacer á la amiga, llenando al mismo tiempo mi compromiso.

Por fuerza habré de tratarlo lijera y superficialmente, de otro modo, necesario sería al hablar de la belleza, escribir un tratado de estética, para manifestar hasta qué punto la idea de la belleza es relativa, estando sujeta á mil cambios, que ora se relacionan con las modas y las costumbres de un país, ora dependen de otras muchas circunstancias que dificultan y hacen casi imposible poder establecer un principio general, aplicable á todas las épocas y á todos los pueblos. Con mucha razon ha dicho un escritor, que de la belleza se puede decir lo mismo que dijo Pascal de la justicia: "Lo que es á esta parte de los Pirineos belleza, es á la otra fealdad." Prozer-Collard dice: "Lo bello se siente y no se define."

Asi por ejemplo, en los pueblos meridionales, donde parece que el sol tropical hubiera teñido de subidos tintes los ojos y los cabellos y tostado con su calor la tez de los habitantes, allí se toma como el tipo de la belleza, á las mugeres cuyos rúbios cabellos, nos parece que simuláran las hebras del oro, y cuyos ojos celestes, miramos como el reflejo de nuestro azulado y límpido cielo. Al contrario de los pueblos que se alejan del Ecuador, en los que las brumas de un cielo siempre opaco y nebuloso, hace que el sol se muestre avaro de su luz y de su calor, allí se tiene por bella á la muger de ojos negros y pelo de azabache. Así veremos que los Griegos, esos maestros del arte, pintaban á sus Venus con cabellos rubios, y Byron, el inmortal cantor de la belleza, celebraba á las españolas con su color moreno y con sus cabellos de ébano, encontrándolas muy superiores á las inglesas con sus tintes descoloridos.

No hablaré de los pueblos donde los beneficios de la civilizacion no se han dejado sentir, educando el gusto hasta poder formular el tipo de la belleza; entre estos se ve las mayores aberraciones. Hay algunas tribus salvajes, entre las que se usa teñir de negro los dientes con una yerba, y miran como una cosa feísima y propia, segun dicen ellos, de los perros ó de otros animales, el tener los dientes blancos.

Aun mas lijera y superficialmente, será necesario tratar este tema, considerando, que para establecer una comparacion entre la belleza y la inteligencia, preciso es mirar á la muger bajo la seductora y risueña faz que presenta en los salones, considerándola solamente, como un adorno, como un dije, ó si se me permite el calificativo, como una hada que arrebata con su belleza y encanta con su talento.

Forzoso será olvidar la grandiosa mision que la ha sido encomendada por la naturaleza; mision augusta y sublime, de esposa y de madre, en la que la belleza entra por tan poco, y la inteligencia tiene que entrar por tanto. Si hubiera de considerarla bajo de esta última faz, absurdo seria y muy grande, establecer una comparacion entre la importancia de la belleza y la de la inteligencia.

Al tomar á la belleza para ponerla en parangon con la inteligencia, hablaré de ella segun nuestro tipo, es decir, de aquella con ojos de cielo, cabellos de oro, cútis alabastrino, y cuerpo de esbeltas y delicadas formas.

¿Preciso será acaso, que os presente tambien un tipo de la muger inteligente? No, el talento no tiene mas que un solo tipo, y no puede jamás confundirse, ni ocultarse, y si bien es cierto, que entre el vulgo de las inteligencias hay muchas formas y gradaciones, el verdadero talento no tiene mas que una sola forma, una forma única y eterna, puesto que su modelo es Dios.

Para juzgar del poder de la una y de la otra, imaginémonos dos tipos, opuestos el uno del otro; la una dotada de una belleza perfecta y deslumbradora y sin ninguna inteligencia; la otra de una inteligencia poderosa y clara y sin ninguna belleza.

¡Una muger bella! estas palabras nos parece que simbolizan estas otras—Una muger perfecta.

La belleza es la manifestacion mas elocuente que tiene la naturaleza, para despertar en nuestra alma la idea de un Ser infinito, grande y perfecto: he allí por qué en todo corazon noble, existe un culto ferviente para todo lo que es bello; he allí por qué una muger bella nos inspira admiracion y simpatia.

La belleza tiene un lenguaje, una elocuencia que le es propia, peculiar de ella sola. Una muger bella, habla con su mirada, habla con su sonrisa, habla hasta con su frente inmóvil y tersa. Lenguaje admirable que se presta á que cada cual lo traduzca á su deseo; así el hombre soñador y espiritual, lo traduce con su alma, como el hombre material y vulgar, lo interpreta tambien á su modo. Esas son las razones por las que la belleza tiene el privilegio de seducir y fascinar á todos los hombres.

No así la inteligencia, que solo seduce al hombre de talento. El gran Voltaire ha dicho: Solo al genio le es dado comprender al genio.

Sucede con el mérito de una muger inteligente, lo mismo que con el de un hermoso cuadro: mostradle á un hombre torpe y vulgar, un cuadro de gran mérito, en el que, en medio de los tintes vagos y oscuros, se ve sin embargo brillar la idea del autor, es decir, el alma del cuadro; despues de mirarle mucho tiempo, quedará convencido que el cuadro no dice nada, y sin embargo, allí hay una idea, una idea grandiosa, que solo puede comprender el hombre inteligente.

Muchas veces héme preguntado, ¿por qué la belleza no va siempre unida á la inteligencia? ¿Por qué la muger que nos fascina con su hermosura, nos decepciona con su inteligencia, y por qué la que es un encanto para los ojos, suele ser un desencanto para el alma?

Cuántas mugeres conozco, cuya belleza ganaria mucho si enmudecieran; así tendrian solo el lenguaje simbólico de la belleza; ese lenguaje que, como dije ya, tiene el privilegio de que cada cual pueda interpretarlo á su modo; así, sus lábios no serian sus eternos enemigos, que van divulgando á cada momento, que en su cerebro hay tanta incorreccion de forma, como hay en su fisonomia correccion de lineas.

Una belleza sin inteligencia es una ilusion que está muy próxima al desengaño. Es una hada que nos fascina, mientras la miramos á traves del prisma encantador de su belleza; pero que desaparece tan luego que la luz de la razon penetra mas allá de donde miran los ojos.

Una inteligencia sin belleza, es como un rico tesoro oculto entre las escabrosidades de un terreno árido y montañoso, que se esconde para enriquecer al hombre feliz que llega á encontrarlo. Se puede decir que es un magnífico libro encuadernado á la rústica, que los nécios desprecian, solo porque le juzgan mirándole por fuera.

La violeta de los campos por mas que se oculta, la denuncia su perfume; así es la muger inteligente, solo no la encuentra el que es incapaz de comprenderla.

A un hombre de talento, una muger bella puede hacerle concebir la felicidad, solo á una muger inteligente le es dado el realizársela. La primera le hará soñar, la segunda le hará sentir y pensar.

En el turbulento y borrascoso mar de las pasiones, soñar es navegar sin brújula ni timon, á merced de las tempestades; por eso, todo sueño tiene su triste y amargo despertar. Sentir y pensar, es viajar asegurado contra todos los escollos y peligros, atravesando el encantado y risueño paraiso de las dulces emociones, á do mora la verdadera felicidad.

Hé aquí, al fin, llegado el momento de resolver el problema de la importancia de la belleza y de la inteligencia, concediendo la supremacía á una de las dos.

Mi opinion ya la habreis adivinado. Hubiera querido no dejarla comprender, sinó que promoviendo una discusion, someter la solucion de este problema á la ilustrada decision de ustedes, pero ¿cómo establecer un paralelo entre dos cosas tan esencialmente distintas?

¿Cómo comparar lo que constituye la belleza del alma, con lo que solo puede constituir la perfeccion de las formas?

¿Cómo igualar la inteligencia que brilla y perfuma la existencia entera, con la belleza, esa flor primaveral que nace, se colora y resplandece, tan solo en una época de la vida[?]

¿Cómo comparar lo que es efímero y fugaz, como una centella que pasa sin dejar en pos de sí, ni los vestigios de su claridad, con un foco de luz purísima que se irradia sobre nuestra propia existencia y la de todos los seres que nos rodean?

Admiradora entusiasta de todo lo bello, ríndole ferviente culto; pero no he podido encontrar un término siquiera, para establecer una comparacion, entre el mérito de la belleza y el de la inteligencia: así, no creo equivocarme reconociendo la superioridad que tiene la inteligencia sobre la belleza de la muger.

A Comparative Study on Intelligence and Beauty in Women

A PAPER BY SEÑORA MERCEDES CABELLO DE
CARBONERA, READ BY THE AUTHOR

To my dear friend Juana Manuela Gorriti.

The eminent and famous author, to whom I have the honor of dedicating the present paper, was the one who suggested this lovely and yet also difficult topic, making me promise to discuss it during this meeting. She is well aware that her wishes, even the least of them, for me are commands that I enjoy fulfilling, and that her inspired word will always be a powerful impulse for my pen.

So, after this brief explanation which I offer to clarify any interpretation which might be made on this subject, I will attempt to satisfy my friend and at the same time meet my obligation.

Of need I will have to treat it briefly and superficially; to do otherwise when speaking of beauty would necessitate my writing a treatise on aesthetics in order to show to what degree the idea of beauty is relative, being as it is subject to a thousand modifications, at times related to the fashion and customs of a country, at times dependent on many other circumstances which impede and indeed make it almost impossible to establish a general principle which would be applicable to all times and all people. With good reason an author remarked that the same thing could be said of beauty that Pascal said of justice: "What is beauty on this side of the Pyrenees is ugliness on the other." Prozer-Collard says: "What is beautiful is felt and not defined."

For example, it appears that in southern countries, where the tropical sun tints eyes and hair with stronger tones, and by its heat browns people's skin, those women are considered beautiful whose blonde hair resembles strands of gold and whose blue eyes seem to reflect our clear blue sky. On the other hand, in those countries which are far from the equator, in which the mists of a perennially opaque and cloudy sky force the sun to be miserly with its light and heat, there the woman with black eyes and jet hair is considered beautiful. Thus we see that the Greeks, those masters of art, painted their Venuses with blonde hair, while Byron, the immortal bard of beauty, praised Spanish women with their dark skin and ebony hair, considering them far superior to Englishwomen with their faded coloring.

I don't plan to speak of the nations where the benefits of civilization have not yet been felt, [benefits] which educate taste so as to be able to formulate a type of beauty; among these nations one can see the greatest aberrations. There are some savage tribes who use a plant to dye their teeth black, and, according to their own testimony, hold the white teeth of dogs or other animals to be genuinely ugly.

I will have to discuss this topic even more quickly and superficially when I consider that in order to set up a comparison between beauty and intelligence, one must look at a woman with the seductive and smiling countenance she puts on in the salons, regarding her only as a decoration, a trinket, or, if I may be permitted the qualifying noun, as a spirit who enthralls with her beauty and enchants with her talent.

One must of needs forget the great mission that has been entrusted to women by nature, the majestic and sublime mission of wife and mother, in which beauty matters so little and intelligence counts for so much. If a woman is to be considered in this role, it would be absurd in the extreme to establish a comparison between the importance of beauty and of intelligence.

When I take beauty to establish a comparison with intelligence, I will speak of it with our type in mind, that is, the woman with sky-blue eyes, golden hair, alabaster skin, and a body of slender and delicate contours.

Will I also have to establish a type for the intelligent woman? No, for talent has only one type, and can never be mistaken for another, nor hidden, and while it is true that among the masses there are many kinds and gradations of intelligence, true talent has only one form, a unique and eternal form, because its model is God.

To judge the power of one and the other [beauty and intelligence], let us imagine two completely opposite types: one blessed with stunning, perfect beauty and no intelligence at all, and the other with clear, powerful intelligence and no beauty.

"A beautiful woman!"—To us these words seem to symbolize these others: "A perfect woman."

Beauty is the most eloquent manifestation Nature has to awaken in our soul the concept of an infinite, great and perfect Being; this is why there exists in every noble heart a passionate cult to all that is beautiful; this is why a lovely woman inspires admiration and affection in us.

Beauty has a language, an eloquence of its own that is unique to it alone. A beautiful woman speaks with her glance, her smile, even with her firm, smooth brow. An admirable language which lends itself to allow each person to translate it according to his fancy: the dreamy, spiritual man translates it with his soul, just as the coarse materialist interprets it in his way. These are the reasons why beauty has the gift of seducing and bewitching all men.

This is not the case with intelligence, which only seduces the man of talent. The great Voltaire said: "Only genius is able to understand genius."

The merit of an intelligent woman is measured in the same way as that of a beautiful painting: show a great painting to a coarse and vulgar man, one in which among vague, dark hues one can nevertheless see the painter's idea or the painting's soul shine forth; after looking at it at length [this man] will be convinced that the picture says nothing, and yet there is an idea there, a splendid idea that only an intelligent man can understand.

I have often asked myself why beauty and intelligence are not always linked? Why is it that the woman who enchants us with her beauty disappoints us with her intelligence, and why does the one who delights the eye frequently disillusion the soul?

I know many women whose beauty would gain considerably if they kept their mouths shut; in that way they would speak only the symbolic language of beauty, the language which, as I said before, has the advantage that each person can interpret it as he wishes. In that way their mouths would not be their perennial enemies which continually show the world that the flaws within their heads stand in direct contrast to the perfection of their physical features.

Beauty without intelligence is an illusion that is very close to disillusion. It is a spirit that enchants us while we perceive it through the bewitching prism of its beauty, but which disappears as soon as the light of reason penetrates deeper than what the eye can see.

Intelligence without beauty is like a rich treasure concealed in the harshness of an arid, mountainous landscape, a treasure which has been hidden in order to enrich the happy man who finds it. One might compare it to a magnificent book bound in paper, which fools scorn because they look no farther than the cover.

The violet of the field, no matter how it tries to hide, is given away by its scent; it is the same with an intelligent woman: the one who is unable to understand her will never find her.

A beautiful woman can make a gifted man envision happiness, but only an intelligent woman has the power to give it to him. The former will make him dream, the latter feel and think.

In the turbulent and stormy sea of passionate feelings, to dream is to navigate with neither compass nor tiller, at the mercy of the tempest; because of this all dreams have their sad and bitter awakening. To feel and to think is to travel protected against all dangers and pitfalls, and to cross over to the enchanted and smiling paradise of sweet emotions, where true happiness dwells.

I have finally reached the moment to resolve the problem of the importance of beauty versus intelligence, and to assign supremacy to one of the two.

You will have already guessed my opinion. I would have preferred not to have it be understood, but instead have engaged in a discussion, submitting the solution of this problem to your educated decision, but how are we to establish a parallel between two things which are so essentially different?

How is one to compare what constitutes beauty of soul with what makes up perfection of form?

How can one equate intelligence, which illuminates and perfumes an entire lifetime, with beauty, that springtime flower that is born, assumes its color and brilliance, but only in one moment of its life?

How is one to compare that which is ephemeral and fleeting, like a spark which is gone without leaving behind even a trace of its brightness, with a beacon of exceedingly pure light which radiates over our own life and the lives of all those around us?

An impassioned admirer of all things beautiful, I worship them fervently, but I haven't even been able to find the words to set up a comparison between the merits of beauty and intelligence, and thus, I do not believe I am mistaken in recognizing the superiority which intelligence has over beauty in women.

*Teresa González
de Fanning*

Teresa González de Fanning from Elvira García y García, La mujer peruana a través de los siglos. Serie Historiada de estudios y observaciones. *(Lima: Imprenta Americana, 1924–25).*

*T*hat we do not know Teresa González de Fanning's date of death is an indication of how little is known about her, but she was an important member of Lima's circle of women writers and intellectuals in the nineteenth century.

One of the best sources of information about her is the two-volume *La mujer peruana a través de los siglos* (Peruvian Women Across the Centuries), published in 1925 and edited by Elvira García y García, who, it says on the title page, was the director of the Liceo Fanning in Lima. It is obvious from her article that she knew her subject well. García points out that Teresa González de Fanning was known primarily as an educator and writer. She made her first timid forays into the world of literature when she was very young, says García, "with all the scruples and reservations which a woman in our social milieu always has when she launches herself on this exceedingly harsh path" (30).

Even after her marriage to naval Capt. Juan Fanning Teresa continued to write, though, just like Soledad Acosta de Samper after her, often under cover of a pseudonym. In 1880 Fanning was killed in the battle of Miraflores against the Chileans, an encounter that was part of the War of the Pacific (1879–83), after which his widow's formerly comfortable economic position became very precarious. As was the case with so many nineteenth-century women who were forced to make a living, González de Fanning turned to writing and to education to support herself.

She was socially well connected in Lima, and the girls' school she founded soon became one of the best in the city, not so much because it was socially elite, but because it was based on sound pedagogy. García relates that as director of the school González de Fanning always put "education over instruction" (30). In later years, when she had retired from the directorship of the school, she wrote numerous articles about women's education, which were published in Lima in 1905. In so doing González de Fanning was joining in a wider struggle to allow women access to higher education. The basic questions asked in the nineteenth century were the following:

> Were women physically or emotionally capable of meeting the rigorous demands of higher education? Even if they were, was it moral for women to abandon their "natural" sphere of home and hearth to pursue higher education? Must women choose between roles as mothers and wives and activity in the public sphere? (Kimmel 50)

Prose fiction was another outlet for her writing talents, and she published a series of novels, generally under another pseudonym, María de la Luz. Some of these are *Regina* (1886), which was awarded the silver medal in an international competition by Lima's Atheneum, *Lucecitas* (Little Lights) (1893), and *Indómita* (Indomitable) and *Roque Moreno,* both published in 1904.

García points out that because Peruvian society did not heed González de Fanning's advice on the education of women, she became somewhat embittered in old age, especially since she had little patience with "the social farce" and was "truthful to the point of recklessness" (32). Having suffered economic hardship on the death of her husband, González de Fanning was passionate in her pleas to educate women—both intellectually and practically—so that no matter what happened to their men, they would be in a position to support themselves and their families financially. The essay that follows makes this point eloquently, and González de Fanning makes it completely clear how her topic is related to the well-being of the family, society, and the nation. Few of the male essayists of the time who spoke of a woman's domestic destiny as wife and mother thought about the consequences of the husband's death for his family, yet it was a painful reality to many women who suddenly found themselves bereft of spouse and breadwinner and without the skills either to manage the assets they might still have or to earn an independent living. Inserting the feminine point of view into this socioeconomic discourse—as González de

Fanning, Cabello de Carbonera, and Gorriti did—results in a contestatory work that Mary Louise Pratt terms the *gender essay*, "whose topic is the status and reality of women in modern society" (15), and one of whose salient discursive practices is "the analytical commentary on the spiritual and social condition of women" (18). This essay certainly falls into that category. The gender essay, as opposed to the canonical male essays on national identity, has received much less critical attention thus far, but here again it is time the women's voices are also heard.

Trabajo para la muger

DE LA SEÑORA TERESA GONZALEZ DE FANNING
(MARÍA DE LA LUZ) LEÍDO POR RICARDO PALMA[1]

Una nación está tanto mas adelantada en el camino del progreso, cuanto mayor es la suma de moralidad, libertad y cultura de que disponen los miembros que la componen para alcanzar todo el desarrollo y perfectibilidad de que son susceptibles.

Apoyándonos en esta verdad generalmente reconocida, vamos á examinar, si bien muy á la ligera, una de las faces [sic] de la situación moral de la muger en nuestra sociedad, y como resultado de este exámen, á pedir para ella, no la emancipación, no el éjercicio de los derechos políticos, sino pura y simplemente el éjercicio del santo derecho del trabajo. Abrigamos la esperanza de que todos los corazones generosos se pondrán de parte nuestra y en favor de esa pobre esclava de su propia ignorancia y de antiguas y arraigadas preocupaciones.

Para principiar penetremos siquiera sea con la imaginación á la morada donde un recién nacido acaba de ver la primera luz; y observemos como, siendo varon, el padre lo acoge con orgullosa satisfacción y la familia toda lo recibe como una bendición del cielo. Mas, si es muger, qué decepción! se la considera como una nueva carga para los suyos y hasta la tierna madre que tanto ama el fruto de sus entrañas, se conduele al considerar que es una desgraciada mas que viene á soportar las penalidades de la vida y cuya suerte es doblemente incierta y azarosa á causa del sexo á que pertenece.

El niño desde bien temprano ofrece á sus padres mayores dificultades que vencer; en lo general se muestra mas terco, mas indómito, mas dificil de conducir: su educación es incomparablemente mas dispendiosa, pero su sexo lo hace acreedor á que aun á costa de sacrificios, se procure darle no solamente una instrucción tan completa como sea posible, sino además y de preferencia, una profesión que poniéndolo á cubierto de las vicisitudes de la fortuna, lo haga al mismo tiempo un miembro útil de la sociedad y de la familia.

La educación de la muger es mucho mas fácil y limitada. Para ella, el porvenir solo presenta dos caminos practicables: el claustro que hoy dia está ya casi abolido y el matrimonio. Para este esclusivamente se la educa ó por lo menos hácia ese norte se dirigen sus aspiraciones.

Es indudable que la maternidad en el matrimonio es acaso la misión mas santa que ella puede ejercer sobre la tierra y uno de los fines principales para que ha sido creada; pero tambien es cierto que para llenar ese fin, su voluntad entra en parte, solo de una manera secundaria y no es, no puede ser justo que se haga depender esclusivamente su felicidad y su porvenir, de causas hasta cierto punto, independientes de su voluntad, como vamos á demostrarlo.

Nadie nos negará que es el hombre el que tiene la prerogativa de elegir á su compañera y que solo cuando está ya decidido á ligar su suerte, es cuando solicita el consentimiento de la que ha elegido y como la indulgencia social lo absuelve tan fácilmente de las faltas que comete contra la moral, raro es que se apresure á cambiar la independencia y los goces fáciles de su estado de célibe, por los graves deberes é indisolubilidad del matrimonio.

La muger, aunque por naturaleza mas sensible que el hombre, se vé precisada á reprimir los mas vehementes impulsos de su corazón.

En vano será que el amor, ese dulce y espontáneo sentimiento que poetiza la vida y que está en la esencia de nuestro sér, le haga sentir su influjo poderoso; debe esconderlo cuidadosamente so pena de esponerse á la burla, tal vez hasta del mismo que se lo inspiró y que dificilmente se dejará arrebatar el derecho de iniciativa que la costumbre le ha otorgado.

No es necesario recurrir á la estadística, basta la simple observación para adquirir el convencimiento de que en esta capital especialmente, los matrimonios no guardan proporcion con el número de habitantes. Si á esto se agrega la mayor mortalidad de los hombres por la guerra, el abuso de los licores y tantas otras causas, se comprenderá cómo forzosamente tiene que quedar un gran número de mugeres en estado de viudez ó de perpétua soltería.

Estas tristes víctimas del destino, aguardando ver satisfechas sus justas aspiraciones con la venida de ese Mesias que se les habia prometido, ven agostarse su juventud y llegar los treinta años, que si para el hombre es como ha dicho un poeta español: "Funesta edad de amargos desengaños," para la muger soltera es la tumba de sus ilusiones y esperanzas.

Aun cuando sienta la vida en toda su plenitud, el porvenir es para ella un desierto árido sin un solo oasis en que reposar. Como el imprudente jugador que aventuró toda su fortuna en una carta y al verla perdida se encuentra sumido en un abismo sin fondo, así la que cifrara toda su ventura en la idea del matrimonio, al ver que esta se desvanece, se siente herida de muerte y desorientada sin saber el rumbo que le conviene seguir.

El mundo, que antes la acogiera con halagos y distinciones cuando se hallaba adornada con las gracias seductoras de la primera juventud, la recibe friamente cuando no la persigue con sus burlas y sarcasmos, porque ha ingresado en el número de las solteronas y todos se creen con derecho para escarnecerla.

Al perder á sus padres que son su natural apoyo, se encuentra de huéspeda en hogar ageno y sin que le sea dado gozar de independencia, porque la educacion y las costumbres se unen para arrebatárselas. Y desgraciada de la que pretendiera arrostrar las preocupaciones sociales! á mas de los inconvenientes que le resultarian del aislamiento, espondria su honra á los ataques venenosos de la calumnia, siempre dispuesta á cebarse en el honor de la muger.

Si agriada por las decepciones y sintiendo hastío de la vida, se acoge como último recurso á la religión, si bien logra calmar en parte sus angustias y llenar el vacío de su existencia, se conquista el despreciativo apodo de beata, que unido al de solterona, acaban de transformarla en un sér antipático y repulsivo, especialmente para los miopes de espíritu que no alcanzan á penetrar los sufrimientos del alma.

Este es á grandes rasgos el porvenir que se les prepara á muchísimas mugeres que no carecen de méritos y virtudes, y de una despejada inteligencia, que si se cultivara, podria aprovecharse en beneficio de la sociedad á que pertenecen y de la cual vienen á ser miembros paralizados, porque se les condena á una absoluta esterilidad y á perpétua dependencia: la dependencia de la debilidad centuplicada por la ignorancia.

Mucho se ha escrito ya y reconocemos que con algun fruto, sobre la necesidad y conveniencia de acrecentar la ilustracion de la muger. Abundando en las mismas ideas nos limitamos, por hoy, á pedir para ella que lo mismo que al hombre, se la enseñe algun arte, profesion ú oficio proporcionados á su sexo y posicion social, que, á la vez que ocupen y desarrollen su inteligencia, le proporcionen cierto grado de independencia á que tiene derecho á aspirar, sobre todo cuando carece del apoyo del ser fuerte que debiera acompañarla en la penosa peregrinación de la vida.

Como nos dirigimos especialmente á las personas de buena intencion y recto juicio, no nos ocuparemos de combatir la vana preocupacion de que la muger solo ha nacido para el desempeño de las tareas domésticas y que redunda en perjuicio de estas, el darle ocupacion y cultura á su inteligencia. Admitir esto, seria colocarla en un nivel muy poco mas elevado que el de las bestias de carga y animales de servicio.

Tampoco seria su debilidad escusa para negarle el derecho de trabajar. No todas las profesiones exigen fuerza física y en cuanto á la moral, está bien probado que la posee.

La fuerza y extensión de su inteligencia bien puede decirse que aun no se conoce, desde que nadie casi ha cuidado desarrollarla sino en muy estrechos límites. Sin embargo, en todos los siglos ha dado, aunque aisladas, brillantes pruebas de que existe. Omitimos citar ejemplos, porque seria á mas de difuso, repetir lo que todos saben.

Seria una insensatez el pretender clasificar por sexos las inteligencias y darle la preferencia ciegamente á la del hombre, que, si bien tiene ciertas cualidades que le hacen superior, en cambio la de la muger la supera en muchas otras. Si se compara la de un hombre inculto con la de una muger medianamente educada, no estará la ventaja de parte del primero, por mas de que pertenezca al sexo privilegiado.

Solicitando inmigracion como un elemento de bienestar y prosperidad para el país, ciertamente que no solo se busca el concurso de las fuerzas materiales, pues las intelectuales son de tanto ó mas valor, que ellas, para hacer floreciente y respetada á una nación. Y esto supuesto ¿es razonable que se dejen en la inercia y el abandono tantas inteligencias que pudieran utilizarse en servicio del bien público y del particular del individuo? ¿Es justo acaso que á seres dotados de una alma inmortal, que aspira á perfeccionarse, se les sujete á una perpétua infancia sin llegar á adquirir nunca su legitimo y natural desarrollo?

Ciertamente que la cultura y el trabajo ya sea manual ó intelectual, solo pueden ser considerados como elementos que deben contribuir á formar la felicidad de la muger; pero que nunca pueden completarla ni menos aun destruir esa irresistible inclinacion que impele á ambos sexos á reunirse, porque ambos son parte de un todo que el matrimonio completa, formando el perfecto ser humano en conformidad con la idea de su divino Hacedor.

Siempre quedará un inmenso vacío que solo Dios podrá llenar en el corazon de las que su fatal destino condene á no conocer jamás los puros goces, las santas fruiciones de esposa y madre, pero para los males del alma, lo mismo que para los del cuerpo, si no se encuentra el remedio que pueda curarlos radicalmente, debe á lo menos buscarse el que, aliviándolos, los haga mas soportables.

Para esos pobres seres condenados á un perpétuo aislamiento, es justamente para los que el trabajo seria un bien mayor y un recurso salvador, y para ellos lo pedimos con mayor instancia.

Dése interés á esas vidas que languidecen en una forzada inercia. Utilícese esa actividad, que bien dirigida puede rendir ópimos frutos. Ábranse nuevos horizontes á las que la injusticia irreflexiva, vilipendia y casi escluye de la comunion social.

Que al perder la esperanza de unir su destino al de un hombre que pudiera labrar su felicidad, no se marque á la inocente víctima de la suerte con el estigma de la burla y el desprecio.

Que no se la condene á una muerte moral tan inmerecida y tanto mas terrible, cuanto que es indefinida.

Que no se la reduzca á la triste condicion de pária de la humanidad.

Si la sociedad fuera justa en sus fallos, el desden y el sarcasmo que emplea con la muger forzadamente célibe, deberia hacerlos recaer y con mayor acritud sobre el hombre que se conserva indefinidamente en tal estado, porque á éste solo el desórden de sus pasiones y un frio egoismo y pésimo cálculo, han podido impedirle que formando una familia llene la misión que el mismo Dios le ha impuesto.

Ojalá que estas consideraciones, que tan desaliñadamente y tan á la ligera apuntamos, pero cuya exactitud nadie podrá negar, lográran fijar la atencion de los padres celosos de la felicidad de sus hijos y los indujeran á tentar una reforma en la educación de la muger.

Ojalá que meditaran sobre el inmenso beneficio que para ella seria en cualquier estado que el porvenir le reserve, si siendo opulenta tuviera una fructuosa ocupacion para distraer sus ocios, si poseyendo una escasa fortuna pudiera acrecentarla para sí ó unir sus esfuerzos á los de su esposo, si lo tiene, para aumentar el bienestar comun, y por último si perteneciendo á la clase pobre ó desheredada pudiera, con ayuda de un inteligente trabajo, hacer mas llevadera la pesada carga de la miseria.

Cuántos bienes se la procurarian si tal sucediera, y de cuántos males se la libertaria!

Teniendo una honrosa ocupacion que la libertara de los azares de la miseria ó del hastío de una vida estéril por falta de un objeto digno que la llene, esperaria tranquila que se presentara el hombre, que, reuniendo las cualidades que ella pudiera apetecer, fuera acreedor á que le entregara sin reserva su corazón y le confiara la felicidad de su vida entera.

Entonces no se apresuraria á aceptar el primer partido que se le presentara, si al dar su mano, su alma hubiera de permanecer insensible ó indiferente á las tiernas afecciones conyugales.

Tal vez entonces no serian tan frecuentes esos matrimonios llamados de razon ó mas bien de conveniencia, que se arreglan por medio de operaciones aritméticas y en los cuales el corazón, como que es ignorante en cálculo, para nada es consultado.

Y acaso desaparecerían esos repugnantes enlaces que no titubeamos en llamar inmorales, de viejos, que casi tocan en la decrepitud, con jóvenes lozanas, que encontrándose en la primavera de la vida, se sacrifican por huir de la miseria porque carecen á la vez de fortuna y de medios honrados y dignos de adquirir la subsistencia.

De ese modo la que tuviera la desgracia de perder con su esposo su sosten y el de sus tiernos hijos, no se veria precisada, tal vez, á mendigar el pan para su alimento ó á prostituirse por huir de la miseria y el desamparo. Apelaría á sus propios recursos y podria ganar su sustento y el de sus hijos, siendo pobre, ó conservaría y adelantaría su fortuna sin tener que recurrir á extraño é inseguro apoyo.

Si al hombre fuerte se cree necesario darle armas para combatir en la penosa campaña de la vida, con cuanta mayor razon la débil muger ha de necesitarlas para que no sucumba y desfallesca [*sic*]? Se nos dirá que no las ha menester porque en el hombre encuentra el natural apoyo de su debilidad. Pero no nos cansaremos de repetirlo, ese apoyo es incierto y eventual y de ello dan testimonio tantas y tan innumerables huérfanas, viudas y solteras que gimen en el mas completo desamparo ó comen el duro pan de una forzada caridad.

Muchos padres amantes y previsores buscan en las compañias de seguros el medio de afianzar el porvenir de sus hijos. Cuánto mas garantido quedaria éste si se les proveyera de los medios para asegurarlo por sí mismos y hacer frente á las eventualidades de la fortuna ó del destino!

Cuánto ganarian la moral y el progreso sociales, si á la muger se le educara, no solo para esposa, sino tambien para miembro útil de la sociedad á que pertenece!

Cuánto no ganaria la sociedad si se tratára de obtener algun fruto de esas inteligencias que con harta frecuencia, por desgracia, se esterilizan, rindiendo culto á los estravagantes caprichos de la moda ó entregándose por completo á las vanas fórmulas de un exagerado misticismo.

En nombre de tan sagrados intereses, levantamos nuestra humilde voz pidiendo: Trabajo para la muger.

Notas

1. Ricardo Palma (1833–1919). Político y escritor, creador de las llamadas *tradiciones peruanas*, cuentos históricos que se basaban en la época colonial del Perú. Alcanzó gran fama con este género. Era muy amigo de Juana Manuela Gorriti y de su círculo femenino, y participaba activamente en sus *veladas literarias*.

Work for Women

BY SEÑORA TERESA GONZÁLEZ DE FANNING
(MARÍA DE LA LUZ) READ BY RICARDO PALMA[1]

A nation is that much farther down the road to progress the greater the sum of morality, liberty and culture at the disposal of the people who compose it, in order to attain all the development and perfectibility of which these people are capable.

Using this generally accepted truth as our bastion, let us examine, even though very briefly, one of the aspects of the moral situation of women in our society, and, to claim for her, not emancipation, not the exercise of political rights, but pure and simply the exercise of the sacred right to work. We hold to the hope that all generous hearts will rally to our point of view, and in favor of the poor slave of her own ignorance and of old, entrenched prejudices.

To begin, let us enter, albeit only by means of our imagination, the home where a newborn has just seen the light of day, and we will observe that if it is a boy, the father welcomes him with proud satisfaction, and the entire family receives him like a gift from Heaven. But if it is a girl, what a disappointment! She is considered a new burden for the family, and even the tender mother who loves the fruit of her womb is saddened at the thought that there is one more unfortunate soul who has come to bear life's sufferings, and whose fate is doubly uncertain and chancy because of the sex to which she belongs.

From an early age the boy presents his parents with greater difficulties to overcome: in general he tends to be more stubborn, more difficult to lead; his education is incomparably more expensive, but his sex makes him deserving, so that even at the cost of sacrifices an attempt is made to give him not only the best education possible, but, above and beyond, a profession which, by protecting him against the vicissitudes of fate, will simultaneously make him a useful member of society and of the family.

Women's education is much easier and restricted. For her the future holds only two possible paths: the convent, which today is already almost done away with, and marriage. She is educated exclusively toward this end, or at least that is the guiding principle toward which she orients her aspirations.

Undoubtedly motherhood within matrimony is the most sacred mission a woman can perform on earth, and one of the principal reasons for her creation, but it is also true that in order to fulfill this goal her [own] will comes in only partially, in a secondary way, and it is not right—nor can it be—that her happiness and her future should come to depend exclusively on causes that up to a certain point are, as we plan to demonstrate, independent of her will.

No one will deny to us that it is the man who has the prerogative of choosing his mate, and only when he has decided he wants to bind his fate does he solicit the consent of the woman he has chosen; as social indulgence absolves him so easily of the sins he commits against morality, it is rare for a man to rush to exchange the independence and easy pleasures of his celibate state for the serious responsibilities and the indissolubility of marriage.

The woman, although by nature more sensitive than the man, sees herself forced to restrain her heart's most passionate impulses.

Love, that sweet, spontaneous feeling which makes life poetic and is there in the essence of our being, has her feel its powerful influence in vain: she must carefully hide it, or risk exposing herself to mockery, perhaps even from the very man who inspires [this feeling] in her, and who would hardly allow his right to take the initiative (which custom has granted him) to be taken from him.

It is not necessary to consult statistics: simple observation is enough to show that especially in this capital city, there is a discrepancy between the number of marriages and the number of inhabitants. If to this you add the higher mortality rate of men because of war, alcohol abuse and many other causes, one can see why perforce there are a large number of women in states of widowhood or perpetual spinsterhood.

These unfortunate victims of fate, while awaiting the satisfaction of their just aspirations by the arrival of the Messiah who had been promised them, see their youth fade and reach the age of thirty, which, if for a man (in the words of a Spanish poet), is the "doomed age of bitter disillusion," for the single woman it marks the grave of her dreams and aspirations.

Even if she still feels the fullness of life, the future for her is an arid desert without a single oasis which offers repose. Like the reckless gambler who has staked his entire fortune on one card, and who, when he sees that all is lost, feels himself in a bottomless pit, so she, who has invested all her luck in the concept of marriage and sees this fade, feels mortally wounded and disoriented, with no idea which path best to take.

The world, which earlier might have embraced her with compliments and rewards when she was still endowed with the seductive graces of early youth, now greets her coldly, when it is not pursuing her with mockery and sarcasm because she has joined the ranks of the old maids, and all feel entitled to ridicule her.

When a woman loses the parents who are her natural support, she becomes a guest in a strange household without being afforded the pleasure of independence because education and custom unite to take it from her. And woe to her who tries to defy social custom! Besides the problems she would have because of isolation, she exposes her honor to the poisonous attacks of slander, always eager to feed on a woman's honor.

If, soured by disappointment and weary of living, a woman seeks ultimate recourse in religion, if she is partially successful in alleviating her anxieties and filling the emptiness of her existence, she garners for herself the scornful epithet of being overly pious, and this, on top of being an old maid, is enough to make of her a disagreeable and repulsive human being, especially for those who are myopic of spirit and have no way of understanding the agonies of the soul.

This, in broad strokes, is the future which awaits many women who are in no way deficient in merit or virtue or clear intelligence, which, were it cultivated, could be utilized to benefit the society to which they belong, and of which they come to be paralyzed members because they are condemned to absolute sterility and perpetual dependence: the dependence of weakness multiplied a hundredfold by ignorance.

A great deal has already been written, and we grant to some effect, about the need and usefulness of expanding a woman's education. While agreeing with those same ideas, we will for now limit ourselves to asking that she, just like a man, be taught some skill, profession or occupation suitable to her sex and social position, which, while it engages and develops her intellect, simultaneously gives her a certain degree of independence to which she has the right to aspire, above all when she lacks the support of the stronger being who should be at her side on the painful pilgrimage of life.

As we are directing our remarks especially to people of good intentions and sound judgment, we will not waste time combating the foolish notion that a woman is born solely to take care of domestic chores, and that giving her an education and cultivating her intelligence will lead to their neglect. To admit this would relegate her to a level not far above that of beasts of burden and domestic animals.

Nor is a woman's weakness an excuse to deny her the right to work. Not all professions demand physical strength, and with respect to moral fortitude, it has been adequately proven that she possesses it.

It could well be said that the power and range of a woman's intellect is as yet unknown, as practically no one has bothered furthering it outside of very narrow limits. Nevertheless, in all ages there have been examples, albeit isolated ones, of brilliant proof that this intellect exists. We will forgo citing examples because, besides becoming wordy, we would repeat what everyone already knows.

It would be foolhardy to attempt to classify intelligence by gender and blindly give preference to that of the man; although he has some qualities which make him superior, a woman's intellect, on the other hand, surpasses his in many other ways. If one compared the intellect of an uncultured man with that of a moderately educated woman, the former would not have advantage on his side, however much he belonged to the privileged sex.

When looking to immigration as a means to the prosperity and well-being of a nation, one certainly would not look solely for physical strength, as intellectual power is worth as much or more in order to make a nation flourish and earn respect. And this being so, does it make sense to leave so many minds in a state of inertia and abandonment when these might be put to use in the service of both the public and the private good of the individual? Can it be right that human beings endowed with an immortal soul which aspires to perfect itself, should be subjected to perennial infancy without ever attaining their legitimate and natural development?

Certainly culture and work, be it manual or intellectual, can only be considered elements which should contribute to forming a woman's happiness, but they can never completely fulfill her, much less destroy the irresistible inclination that impels the sexes to unite, for both are part of a whole that is completed by marriage, forming the perfect human being in conformity with the idea of his divine Maker.

A huge void only God can fill will always remain in the hearts of those women whose fatal destiny has condemned them never to know the pure pleasures, the sacred fulfillment of wife and mother, but if no remedy can be found to radically cure these ills of the soul as well as of the body, one should at least seek out the balm which, by alleviating them, makes life more bearable.

It is precisely for those poor beings condemned to perpetual isolation that work would be a great good and a saving resource, and we plead for this on their behalf with mounting insistence.

Give interest to lives that languish in forced inertia. Make use of this activity, which, if well directed, will yield abundant fruit. Open new horizons to those women whom unthinking injustice insults, and practically excludes from social association.

When a woman loses hope of uniting her fate to that of a man who could make her happy, don't let the innocent victim of chance be branded with the stigma of mockery and scorn.

Don't let her be condemned to such an undeserved moral death which is that much worse for being indefinite.

Let her not be reduced to the sad condition of a pariah of humankind.

If society were just in its verdicts, the disdain and sarcasm directed against the woman who is forced to be unmarried, should come down even more harshly on the man who remains indefinitely in this state, because only the disorder of his passions, a cold egotism and extremely bad sense have prevented him from founding a family, and thereby fulfilling the mission that God Himself imposed on him.

Hopefully these remarks, which we are penning in so superficial and disorganized a fashion, but whose truth no one can deny, will succeed in attracting the attention of those parents who are concerned about their children's happiness, and will induce them to attempt a reform in women's education.

Let us hope that they will think about the enormous benefit this would mean to [their daughter], in whatever position the future might hold for her—should she be rich, she would have a useful occupation to fill her leisure hours, and if she has a meager fortune she can make it grow for herself or join her efforts to those of her husband, should she have one, in order to augment their common welfare, and last, should she belong to the poor or disinherited class she could, with the aid of intelligent work, make the heavy burden of poverty more bearable.

How much good could be accomplished if this were to happen, and from how much evil it would rescue her!

Were she to have an honest occupation that would free her from the vicissitiudes of poverty or the boredom of a life that has become sterile for lack of the right person to fulfill it, she could wait calmly for the right man to come along, one who possessed the qualities that appealed to her, and who would be the deserving recipient to whom she would unreservedly surrender her heart and entrust the happiness of an entire life.

Then she would not rush to accept the first man who came along, to whom, if she gave her hand, her soul would remain insensitive or indifferent to tender conjugal affections.

Perhaps then we would not have so many so-called arranged marriages, or, better still, "marriages of convenience," which are agreed upon on the basis of mathematical computations and in which the heart, as it is ignorant of calculation, is in no way consulted.

And then perhaps those ghastly marriages would disappear which we do not hesitate to call immoral, between old men, who are practically decrepit, with lovely young women in the springtime of life, who sacrifice themselves to flee from poverty because they have neither money nor any means of earning a living which are either honorable or suitable.

In this way, a woman who might have the misfortune of losing her husband, and with him the support of herself and her children, would perhaps not see herself forced to beg for her daily bread or to prostitute herself in order to escape poverty and homelessness. She could call upon her own resources and, if she were poor, could earn a living for herself and her children, or maintain and increment her fortune without having to rely on outside or uncertain support.

If people think it necessary to give the strong man arms to fight in the hard campaign of life, with what greater reason does a weak woman have need of them so that she will not succumb and perish! We will be told that she doesn't need them because in a man she will find the natural support for her weakness. But we do not tire of repeating that this support is uncertain and chancy, and the proof thereof are the innumerable orphans, widows and spinsters who weep in the most desperate circumstances, or eat the bitter crust of forced charity.

Many loving and farsighted parents look to insurance companies for the means to secure their children's future. How much more secure the latter would be if the children were given the means to secure it for themselves and face the vicissitudes of fortune or destiny!

How much social morality and progress would gain if a woman were educated, not only to be a wife, but also a useful member of the society to which she belongs!

How much society would profit if it attempted to gain some benefit from those minds which unfortunately so often become sterile, either worshiping extravagant whims of fashion or surrendering completely to empty formulas of exaggerated mysticism.

In the name of such sacred interests we lift our humble voice to plead: Give women work.

Notes

1. Ricardo Palma (1833–1919) was a politician and writer who invented the genre known as *Peruvian traditions*, short stories based on Peru's colonial past. He became very famous because of these stories. He was a good friend of Juana Manuela Gorriti's and of her circle of women friends, and participated actively in her literary salon.

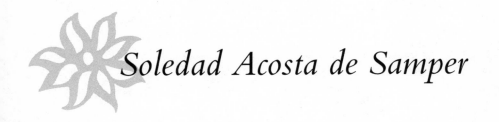

Soledad Acosta de Samper

Soledad Acosta de Samper, courtesy of Biblioteca Luis Angel Arango, Bogotá.

Soledad Acosta de Samper is an author waiting to be discovered. One of the most prolific women writers of the nineteenth century, few readers outside of her native Colombia know her name, but it is hoped that this will change in the future.

Her background is both international and distinguished. Born in Bogotá in 1833, she was the only child of Joaquín Acosta, a general and Colombian patriot of the wars of independence, and of Caroline Kemble, of Scottish ancestry. She spent her youth not only in Colombia but also in Ecuador, Washington, D.C., Halifax, Nova Scotia (where her grandmother lived), and Paris, where she was educated and lived for five years. Acosta de Samper was thus at least trilingual, and much better educated than most Colombian women of her time. In 1855 she married José María Samper, a politician, journalist, and prolific writer, and became the mother of four daughters. The family spent more time in Europe and also in Lima, Peru, where Acosta de Samper founded a journal, then returned to Colombia. Two of the daughters later died in an epidemic, and her husband died in 1888, but her active writing career was never interrupted. At one time, when her husband was away on national business, the government confiscated his printing press and the family home. Acosta de Samper kept herself and her children solvent by writing (Otero Muñoz 373). She died in 1913.

Her literary production is astounding, and there is doubtless more that has not been officially cataloged, as she often wrote under pseudonyms and published mainly in newspapers and journals, many of which have likely been lost. According to Flor María Rodríguez-Arenas, her salvaged works form a corpus of 192 texts: 37 novels, 49 short stories, 59 studies, essays, and articles, 21 historical works, 4 plays, 12 travel narratives, 5 journals founded and directed by her, plus

10 translations of essays and novels from English, French, and German (137 n. 2). Paulina Encinales de Sanjinés has shown that in spite of a conservative, moralistic, and religious frame of mind, Acosta de Samper nevertheless did her share to highlight women's participation in Colombia's nation building, sharing González de Fanning's feelings about the need to train women to work and to strive for personal independence:

> Only those who try to degrade the feminine sex in order to debase it, have been able to advance the absurd idea that a woman's only function is to adorn her husband's home. The working-class woman (and even she who belongs to the upper classes) should always learn a lucrative and useful occupation by means of which she might at any time earn a living, so that she knows that she is free and in no way dependent on a man's work. (232 n. 13)

Although Soledad Acosta de Samper belonged to the social and intellectual elite of Colombia (and lived into the twentieth century), during her lifetime it was still extremely difficult for a woman to publish a book in her country. Her husband, José María, obviously very proud of his wife, urged her to collect some of her prose fiction and had it published in Belgium. This collection, *Novelas y cuadros de la vida sur-americana,* came out in Ghent in 1869 and contained the story "Dolores." Apparently the latter was translated into English as *Dolores: The Story of a Leper,* but we do not know when, and to date no one has located this text. For this reason I have done a new translation and have included it in this anthology.

In an effort to get Acosta de Samper better known, some of her works were republished in Colombia in 1988 by the Fondo Cultural Cafetero in a volume entitled *Soledad Acosta de Samper: Una nueva lectura.* It contains an excellent introduction by Montserrat Ordóñez, some critical studies, and a bibliography of Doña Soledad's works, which give the reader an overview of the astounding scope of her interests. Rodríguez-Arenas published an extensive study of Acosta de Samper in 1991, but there is little available on her in English.

"Dolores" is an amazing story, one well worth knowing and appreciating. The content itself is riveting: a beautiful, upper-class young woman—the ideal romantic heroine—contracts leprosy and, after a number of years in which the disease ravages her body and mind, dies. Leprosy was a disease that in Samper's time had a symbolic/moral charge very like AIDS does today, and it is still prevalent in South America. (Gabriel García Márquez and Mario Vargas Llosa mention lepers in their fiction.) Both the Old and the New Testament speak of leprosy and lepers. It was a common disease in Europe but began to disappear on that continent in the sixteenth century. In the Middle Ages it was considered the outward manifestation of an inner corruption of the soul, and lepers were cast out of society to wait for death alone. As Susan Sontag observed, "Nothing is more punitive than to give a disease a meaning—that meaning being invariably a moralistic one" (58). The bacillus that causes leprosy was discovered by the Norwegian Armauer Hansen in 1873–74, shortly before "Dolores" was published, but Acosta de Samper appears to be unaware of this medical breakthrough, for in her story leprosy, although known to be contagious, is primarily considered hereditary.

What we encounter in this text is the radical deconstruction by illness of a beautiful female body, a woman's ultimate marginalization from society, and a surprisingly modern description of the way the human mind copes with terminal illness. Acosta de Samper is skilled in evoking the psychological journey this entails and shows us how this process can, to some degree, even become a liberating one for the doomed heroine (Rodríguez-Arenas 144–47). Not only the plot, but the style in which the story was written, is unusual. Ordóñez points out the stylistic modernity of Acosta de Samper's fragmented narrative, using alternating male and female narrators and interweaving letters and diaries written by the protagonist (*Una nueva lectura* 22).

"Dolores" first appeared in a journal in 1867, the same year that Jorge Isaacs published *María,* Colombia's most important historical romance, and to date one of the most popular novels in all of Latin America (Sommer 172). It is interesting that both novels deal with a woman's terminal illness, a topic of much interest in nineteenth-century Western fiction. Sontag notes that this literature "is stocked with descriptions of almost symptomless, unfrightened, beatific deaths" (15) where "the actual agony is simply suppressed" (29) and "the ultra-virtuous . . . boost[ed] themselves to new moral heights" (41). In a related vein, the critic Lucía Guerra Cunningham observed that "illness should be considered an attribute which beautifies the submissive, weak body to the law of the father and of the husband" (355). The gendered treatment of the terminally ill heroine differs markedly in the works of Isaacs and Acosta de Samper. María, who suffers from epilepsy, expires wordlessly and beautifully within the bosom of her adopted family, whereas Dolores, a social outcast and thus completely alone, records in her diary wild mood swings brought on by the hideous deformation of her body, rage at the Almighty and at her fate, and personal liberation via the writing of her story. In retrospect, it is Acosta de Samper's text that is the more complex and the more compelling for the modern reader, in terms of both content and narrative style.

Dolores
Cuadros de la vida de una mujer

PARTE PRIMERA

La nature est un drame avec des personnages.[1]

Victor Hugo

—¡Qué linda muchacha! exclamó Antonio al ver pasar por la mitad de la plaza de la aldea de N★★★ algunas personas a caballo, que llegaban de una hacienda con el objeto de asistir a las fiestas del lugar, señaladas para el día siguiente.

Antonio González era mi condiscípulo y el amigo predilecto de mi juventud. Al despedirnos en la Universidad, graduados ambos de doctores, me ofreció visitarme en mi pueblo en la época de las fiestas parroquiales, y con tal fin había llegado el día anterior a N★★★. Deseosos ambos de divertirnos, dirigíamos, con el entusiasmo de la primera juventud, que en todo halla interés, la construcción de las barreras en la plaza para las corridas de toros del siguiente día. A ese tiempo pasó, como antes dije, un grupo de gente a caballo, enmedio del cual lucía, como un precioso lirio enmedio de un campo, la flor más bella de aquellas comarcas, mi prima Dolores.

—Lo que más me admira, añadió Antonio, es la cutis tan blanca y el color tan suave, como no se ven en estos climas ardientes.

Efectivamente, los negros ojos de Dolores y su cabellera de azabache hacían contraste con lo sonrosado de su tez y el carmín de sus labios.

—Es cierto lo que dice usted, exclamó mi padre que se hallaba a mi lado; la cutis de Dolores no es natural en este clima . . . ¡Dios mío! dijo con acento conmovido un momento después, yo no había pensado en eso antes.

Antonio y yo no comprendimos la exclamación del anciano. Años después recordábamos la impresión que nos causó aquel temor vago, que nos pareció tan extraño . . .

Mi padre era el médico de N★★★ y en cualquier centro más civilizado se hubiera hecho notar por su ciencia práctica y su caridad. Al contrario de lo que generalmente sucede, él siempre había querido que yo siguiese su misma profesión, con la esperanza, decía, de que fuese un médico más ilustrado que él.

Hijo único, satisfecho con mi suerte, mimado por mi padre y muy querido por una numerosa parentela, siempre me había considerado muy feliz. Me hallaba entonces en N★★★ tan sólo de paso, arreglando algunos negocios para poder verificar pronto mi unión con una señorita a quien había conocido y amado en Bogotá.

Entre todos mis parientes la tía Juana, señora muy respetable y acaudalada, siempre me había preferido, cuidando y protegiendo mi niñez desde que perdí a mi madre. Dolores, hija de una hermana suya, vivía a su lado hacía algunos años, pues era huérfana de padre y madre. La tía Juana dividía su cariño entre sus dos sobrinos predilectos.

Apenas llegamos a una edad en que se piensa en esas cosas, Dolores y yo comprendimos que el deseo de la buena señora era determinar un enlace entre los dos; pero la naturaleza humana prefiere las dificultades al camino trillado, y ambos procurábamos manifestar tácitamente que nuestro mutuo cariño era solamente fraternal. Creo que el deseo de imposibilitar enteramente ese proyecto contribuyó a que sin vacilar me comprometiese a casarme en Bogotá, y cuando todavía era un estudiante sin porvenir. Considerando a Dolores como una hermana, desde que fui al colegio le escribía frecuentemente y le refería las penas y percances de mi vida de colegial, y después mis esperanzas de joven y de novio.

Esta corta reseña era indispensable para la inteligencia de mi sencilla relación.

Después de permanecer en la plaza algunos momentos más, volvimos a casa. La vivienda de mi padre estaba a alguna distancia del pueblo; pero como se anunciaban fuegos artificiales para la noche, Antonio y yo resolvimos volver al poblado poco antes de que se empezara esta diversión popular.

La luna iluminaba el paisaje. Un céfiro tibio y delicioso hacía balancear los árboles y arrancaba a las flores su perfume. Los pajarillos se despertaban con la luz de la luna y dejaban oír un tierno murmullo, mientras que el filósofo buho, siempre taciturno y disgustado, se quejaba con su grito de mal agüero.

Antonio y yo teníamos que atravesar un potrero y cruzar el camino real antes de llegar a la plaza de N★★★. Conversábamos alegremente de nuestras esperanzas y nuestra futura suerte, porque lo futuro para la juventud es siempre sinónimo de dichas y esperanzas colmadas! Antonio había elegido la carrera más ardua, pero también la más brillante, de abogado, y su claro talento y fácil elocuencia le prometían un bello porvenir. Yo pensaba, después de hacer algunos estudios prácticos con uno de los facultativos de más fama, casarme y volver a mi pueblo a gozar de la vida tranquila del campo. Forzoso es confesar que N★★★ no era sino una aldea grande, no obstante el enojo que a sus vecinos causaba el oirla llamar así, pues tenía sus aires de ciudad y poseía en ese tiempo jefe político, jueces, cabildo y demás tren de gobierno local. Desgraciadamente ese tren y ese tono le producían infinitas molestias, como le sucedería a una pobre campesina que, enseñada a andar descalza y usar enaguas cortas, se pusiese de repente botines de tacón, corsé y crinolina. . . .

Antonio y yo nos acercamos a la casa de la tía Juana que, situada en la plaza, era la mejor del pueblo. En la puerta y sentadas sobre silletas recostadas contra la pared, reían y conversaban muchas de las señoritas del lugar, mientras que las madres y señoras respetables estaban adentro discutiendo cuestiones más graves, es decir, enfermedades, víveres y criadas. Los *cachacos*[2] del lugar y los de otras partes que habían ido a las fiestas, pasaban y repasaban por frente a la puerta sin atreverse a acercarse a las muchachas, que gozaban de su imperio y atractivo sin mostrar el interés con que los miraban.

Me acerqué a la falange femenina con todo el ánimo que me inspiraba el haber llegado de Bogotá, grande recomendación en las provincias, y la persuasión de ser bien recibido como pariente. Presenté mi amigo a las personas reunidas dentro y fuera de las casa, y tomando asientos salimos a conversar con las muchachas. . . .

Propuse entonces que fuéramos todos los que estábamos reunidos en casa de la tía Juana a dar una vuelta por la plaza.

La tropa femenina se formó en columna y los del sexo feo, desplegándonos en guerrilla, dábamos vuelta a su rededor. La simpatía es inexplicable siempre: en breve Antonio y Dolores se acercaron el uno al otro y trabaron al momento una alegre conversación.

La plaza estaba cubierta de mesas de diferentes juegos de lotería, *bisbis, pasa-diez, cachimona*, etc., en los que con la módica suma de un cuartillo se apuntaban todos aquellos que querían probar la suerte. En otras mesas y bajo de toldos algunos tomaban licores de toda especie: *chicha* de coco, *guarapo*, anisado, mistela, y hasta brandi y vino no muy puros; mientras que otros encontraban el *ideal* de sus aspiraciones en suculentos guisos, *ajiacos*, pavos asados y *lechonas* rellenas con ajos y cominos. Más lejos se veían orchatas, aguas de lulos, de moras, de piña, *guarruz* de maíz ye de arroz, que se presentaban en sus botellas tapadas con manojitos de claveles o rosas. Los bizcochuelos cubiertos con batido blanco o canela, los huevos *chimbos*, las frutas acarameladas, las cocadas, los panderos, las arepitas de diversas formas, y todo el conjunto de golosinas que lleva compendiosamente el nombre de colación, yacían en bandejas de varios tamaños y colores, en hileras sobre manteles toscos pero limpios. . . .

Después de haber inspeccionado las mesas de la plaza, en las cuales campeaba la alegría popular, nos dirigimos hacia un baile de *ñapangas*[3] o *cintureras*. Era tal la compostura de estas gentes, que las señoras gustaban ir a verlas bailar, sin temor de que sus modales pudiesen ser tachados. Se había anunciado este baile como muy ruidoso y en extremo concurrido; así fue que hallamos una multitud de curiosos que rodeaban la puerta o prendidos de las ventanas se asomaban a la sala. Sin embargo, al vernos llegar se hicieron a un lado, y las señoritas se situaron al pie de las ventanas y nosotros detrás de ellas. . . .

Las *ñapangas* vestían enaguas de fula azul con su arandela abajo, camisa bordada de rojo y negro, pañolón rojo o azul y sombrerito de paja fina con lazos de cinta ancha. Algunas se quitaban los sombreros para bailar y descubrían sus profusas cabelleras negras partidas en dos trenzas que caían por las espaldas terminando en lazos de cinta.

Los hombres, casi todos con pretensiones a ser los cachacos de la sociedad, fumaban y tomaban copitas de aguardiente, fraternizando con los músicos, quienes situados en la puerta interior de la sala templaban sus instrumentos.

—¡Arriba, don Basilio! exclamaron varias voces desde la puerta, al momento que empezaban a tocar un alegre *bambuco*: ¡la pareja lo aguarda!

Y todas las miradas se dirigieron a un hombre de unos cuarenta años, grueso, lampiño, de cara ancha, frente angosta y escurrida hacia atrás: su mirada torva y la costumbre de cerrar un ojo al hablar le daban un aire singularmente desagradable.

—Nos vamos a divertir esta noche si baila don Basilio, dijo Antonio.

—Cállate, le contesté, que si te oye no te perdonará jamás; ese hombre es presuntuoso y vengativo.

—Bailo, exclamó don Basilio con aire importante, si Julián me acompaña.

—¡Adelante, Julián! gritaron los cachacos; y sacando a Julián de enmedio de ellos los obligaron a que diera la mano a una alegre y desenvuelta *ñapanga*, cuyos negros ojuelos hacían contraste con un ramo de azahares que llevaba en la cabeza. Entre tanto don Basilio tiraba a otra de la mano diciéndole al oído palabras que la hicieron sonrojarse, y adelantándose con aire complacido se situó frente a ella y empezó a bailar el bambuco. La muchacha, joven y ligera, daba vueltas en torno de su pareja poniendo en ridículo el grueso talle y toscos ademanes de su galán, el cual parecía un enorme oso jugando con una gatita. Aunque afeminado y lleno de afectación, Julián formaba con la otra muchacha un cuadro más agradable.

Pero mientras acaban de bailar, digamos quiénes eran estos personajes, uno de los cuales figura en esta relación.

Basilio Flores era hijo de una pobre campesina de los alrededores de Bogotá. Su genio vivo y natural talento llamaron la atención a un rico hacendado en cuyo terreno su madre cultivaba su semterilla de papas y maíz. El hacendado lo llevó a su casa y le enseñó a leer en sus ratos de ocio; y encantado con la facilidad que el muchacho tenía para aprender, se propuso sacar de él un buen dependiente, sobre quien pudiese, con el tiempo, descargar una parte de sus complicados negocios. Lo envió, pues, a un colegio en donde pronto hizo grandes adelantos. Tenía Basilio 18 años cuando estalló la guerra de la independencia, y el español que lo protegía creyó necesario emigrar. Antes de partir llamó al muchacho con mucho sigilo y le exigió bajo juramento que cuando se calmasen las revueltas públicas sacase una suma que había enterrado en un sitio de la casa de su habitación y que con ella lo fuese a buscar a España.

La situación del país impedía que se tuviese comunicación alguna con la madre patria, y enmedio de las emociones políticas que lo rodeaban el protegido del español seguramente olvidó la recomendación de su patrón. . . .

Cuando volvió a reinar alguna paz en el país se supo que, entre los españoles que habían salido prófugos, el patrón de Basilio, después de haber vagado por las costas de Colombia y enfermádose en las Antillas, apenas había tenido tiempo de llegar a España y morir sin dar sus últimas disposiciones. . . .

Basilio volvió a la capital diciendo haber heredado a [un] incógnito pariente, y haciendo alarde de su riqueza trató de introducirse en la sociedad distinguida, pero fue rechazado con desdén.

Disgustado, pero decidido a poner todos los medios que tenía a su alcance para hacer olvidar su origen, partió para Europa y permaneció algunos años en París. Sin relaciones ni disposición, se entregó a los vicios y acabó de corromper el escaso corazón con que la naturaleza lo había dotado. . . .

Resuelto a crearse una carrera brillante en su país, volvió con mil proyectos ambiciosos, y muy pronto se hicieron notar sus artículos en los periódicos de uno y otro partido. Poseía una memoria muy feliz, una instrucción regular y cierta elocuencia irónica, aunque superficial, con que se engaña fácilmente. Se firmaba B. de Miraflores, y decían que en París había pasado por *barón*. Hablaba francés e inglés con bastante corrección y siempre adornaba su conversación con frases y citas de autores extranjeros. Se vestía con un lujo extravagante y de mal gusto, y daba almuerzos en que desplegaba un boato charro con que alucinaba al vulgo.

Pero, desgraciadamente, si tenía memoria para algunas cosas la había perdido completamente para otras, y durante su viaje olvidó a la pobre madre, única persona que lloraba su ausencia. A su regreso de Europa no quiso verla ni dejarse visitar por ella (¡eso lo podría desacreditar!) pero fingiendo la generosidad que distingue a los nobles corazones, enviaba, por medio de un joven que le servía de *factotum*, una pensión mensual a "la pobre estanciera que le había servido de nodriza," según decía arqueando las cejas.

Deseando, al cabo de algunos años, *faire une fin*,[4] como él decía, propuso casamiento sucesivamente a las señoritas más ricas, bellas y virtuosas de Bogotá: naturalmente todas lo desdeñaron hiriendo su amor propio, lo que hizo recordar la famosa máxima de que: "de la calumnia siempre queda algo." Y tarde o temprano se vengó de ellas.

Desalentado en sus proyectos matrimoniales entró de lleno en la política; pero aquí también lo aguardaban desengaños. Sus antecedentes poco claros, su lenguaje acerbo y mordaz y sus malas costumbres lo hicieron despreciable entre los hombres de algún valer en todos los partidos. No pudiendo hacerse apreciar y admirar se hizo temible, y juró burlarse de la sociedad y vengarse de todos los que lo habían humillado. Se alió con los hombres más corrompidos de uno y otro partido y logró por medio de intrigas formarse cierta reputación entre los escritores públicos del país. . . .

La carrera política de nuestro héroe no podía ser completa si no agregaba un lauro más a su gloria: quería ser diputado. En las provincias del centro y del Magdalena era demasiado conocido para ser popular, y le aconsejaron que fuese a las provincias del Sur, donde podría ganarse a los lectores con algunos discursos *bien* sentidos. Este era el motivo que había llevado a *don* Basilio de Miraflores a mi pueblo, en el que se detuvo de paso al saber que se preparaban fiestas.

Julián era el tipo de cierta clase de cachacos que desgraciadamente se han hecho muy comunes en los últimos años; aumentando sus malas cualidades en cada generación y perdiendo las pocas buenas que los distinguían.

Hijo de un rico propietario de las provincias del Sur y educado en Bogotá, en cuyos colegios había permanecido siete años, no había sufrido nunca aquella heroica pobreza que forma el carácter del estudiante. Su tez blanca y rosada, su talle flexible y su mirada lánguida le habían granjeado la admiración de las señoritas de Bogotá, mientras que la riqueza conocida y la posición que ocupaba su familia le habían ganado el corazón de las madres de familia. Durante los siete años de colegio y los dos más en que permaneció *repasando* lo que había estudiado, como escribía a sus padres, aprendió a hablar algo en francés y tal cual frase en latín; de historia, sabía la de las novelas de Dumas; muy poco de filosofía y menos de geografía. . . . [B]ailaba todas las danzas conocidas y hablaba con gravedad del tedio de su existencia, de la pérdida de sus ilusiones y de su adolorido corazón; pero al ver la frescura de su fisonomía y la alegría de su aspecto, se comprendía que su salud no había sufrido con tamañas desgracias y tantas pérdidas irreparables. . . .

Inspirado por el baile y la ruidosa música, don Basilio recordó los tiempos de su mocedad y adornó los últimos compases del bambuco con varios saltos en tosca imitación del *cancán* de los famosos bailes de "Mabille" y "Valentino."

—¡Bravo! le gritaron los cachacos, y al concluir se acercaron para ofrecerle una copa de licor por vía de refrescante. . . .

En ese momento los instrumentos tocaron un valse del país y todos los jóvenes se apresuraron a sacar parejas entre las *ñapangas* más agraciadas. Algunos usaban ruana y todos bailaban con el sombrero puesto y el cigarro en la boca.

Las señoritas que acompañábamos miraban en silencio aquella escena, y se sentían naturalmente vejadas y chocadas al ver que los jóvenes que las visitaban eran tratados de igual a igual por aquellas mujeres.

—Vámonos, dijeron, y se quitaron de las ventanas.

Antonio y yo acompañamos a las señoras hasta sus respectivas casas y volvimos a tomar el camino de nuestra habitación.

El corazón tiene a veces presentimientos que no podemos explicarnos. No sé por qué la suerte de Dolores me preocupaba aquella noche: recordaba mil causas que debían hacerla feliz, y con todo no podía desechar una aprehensión sin motivo que me molestaba sin comprenderla. Antonio, por su parte, sentía los primeros síntomas de una gran pasión: las tempestades que se desarrollan en el corazón siempre se anuncian por un sentimiento de melancolía dolorosa. La dulzura del sentimiento no inspira sino cuando uno ha perdido ya el poder de voluntad y ama sin reflexionar.

Antonio sufría; yo me sentía triste, y ambos volvimos a casa en silencio.

En los días siguientes concurrimos a los encierros y corridas de toros y los bailes por la noche. Antonio se mostraba completamente subyugado por los encantos de Dolores, y cada vez que nos hallábamos juntos no se cansaba de elogiarme sus gracias y hermosura. Recuerdo que una vez casi se enfadó conmigo porque le cité riendo aquel proverbio latino: "No es la naturaleza la que hace bella a la mujer, sino nuestro amor."

Dolores recibía los homenajes de Antonio con su buen humor e inagotable alegría. Ella no podía estar nunca triste y perseguía con alegres chanzas a los que se mostraban melancólicos. Mi amigo correspondía a su genio vivo contestándole con mil chistes y agudezas propias del cachaco bogotano. El amor entre estos dos jóvenes era bello, puro y risueño como un día de primavera. En donde quiera que se reunían comunicaban su innata alegría a cuantos los rodeaban. No he visto nunca dos personas más adecuadas para amarse y saber apreciar sus mutuas cualidades. No hay duda que es un grave error el que encierra aquel axioma de que los contrastes simpatizan. Eso puede dar cierto brillo, animación y variedad a un sentimiento fugaz, a una inclinación pasajera; pero entre personas que aman verdaderamente es preciso una completa armonía, armonía en sentimientos, en educación, en posición social y en el fondo de las ideas. La tranquilidad moral es el resultado de la armonía, y ése debe ser el principal objeto del matrimonio, en lo que debe consistir su bello ideal.

Don Basilio pronto descubrió que Dolores, además de ser bella y virtuosa, poseía una dote regular, e inmediatamente puso sitio ante aquella nueva fortaleza; creyó que no sería mal *negocio* encontrar en su viaje una diputación y una novia. El caudal de su difunto *tío* empezaba a desaparecer muy de veras y no quería ver llegar la vejez unida a la pobreza. Le confió a Julián su propósito diciendo: —Una sencilla *villageoise* es una conquista fácil de obtener . . . Además es bella, y la podré presentar en Bogotá sin bochorno; y añadía con su acostumbrada fatuidad, citando a un autor francés: "Elle a d'assez beaux yeux . . . pour des yeux de province."[5]

—Pero, observaba Julián, ¿no ve usted que ya tiene un rival en Antonio?

—Mejor, mejor, joven inexperto ¿no sabe usted que el gran Corneille dijo:"A vaincre sans péril on triomphe sans gloire?"[6]

Un día le presentó a Dolores una composición rimada que le dedicaba, en la cual declaraba su ardiente amor en versos glaciales: tenía tantas citas que casi no se encontraba una palabra original; mezclaba la mitología con la historia antigua invocando a Venus y a Lucrecia, a Minerva y a Virginia, y acababa diciendo: "que, guiado por el destino, había montado en el Pegaso para caer a sus pies."[7] A instancias de la tía Juana, Dolores nos mostró a Antonio y mí la sonora composición, y naturalmente no escaseamos nuestras burlas.

Después de haber permanecido algunos días en N*** don Basilio siguió su marcha en busca de popularidad, bien persuadido de que allí no podría conseguir nada, y comprendiendo que Dolores le preparaba, si los provocaba, unos *nones* como los que él estaba enseñado a recibir. Fácil nos era ver que partía furioso con Antonio y yo, pues, no habíamos ocultado nuestras burlas, y que se prometía hacérnoslas pagar algún día.

Las fiestas se habían concluido. Cada cual de los que habían ido a ellas fueron dejando el lugar de uno en uno.

El día antes del de la partida de Antonio promoví un paseo en que debían reunirse las principales personas que se hallaban todavía en el pueblo. A algunas horas de N*** corre un caudaloso río sombreado por altísimos árboles, y muy cerca de él se halla la casa de un trapiche que ofrece recursos y lugar en que dejar las cabalgaduras. Este es el sitio predilecto de los que organizan los paseos de todas las inmediaciones.

A las siete de mañana, como veinte personas aguardábamos a la puerta de la casa de tía Juana a que saliera Dolores. Pronto se presentó ésta montada en un brioso caballo, con su traje largo, sombrerito redondo, velillo al viento, la mirada brillante y ademán gracioso. Después de atravesar bulliciosamente las calles tomamos un angosto camino orillando potreros, y allí se fueron formando grupos según las simpatías de cada uno. Yo dejé que Antonio buscase el lado de Dolores, acordándome de que no sé qué autor ha dicho que el tiempo más a propósito para una declaración es cuando uno anda a caballo. Y efectivamente, la animación del paseo, el aire libre que sopla en torno, la facultad de apurar o detener el caballo, de atrasarse, o adelantarse sin aparente motivo, de hablar o callar de repente, volver la cabeza o buscar la mirada de su compañera, todo esto da ánimo y presenta fácilmente ocasiones de aislarse aún enmedio de una numerosa concurrencia. Sin embargo, Antonio callaba ese día, y la fisonomía de ambos se velaba por momentos con una dulce melancolía; acaso porque pensaban que debían separarse aquella tarde.

Acompañamos a las señoras hasta la orilla del río, y mientras que ellas se bañaban, nos reunimos en el trapiche conversando y riendo alegremente. Antonio no recobró, sin embargo, animación hasta que nos volvimos a reunir todos con la parte femenina de la concurrencia en el punto en que se había preparado el almuerzo. El campo estaba bellísimo: la fragancia de las flores, el susurro de los insectos, el murmurante río que bajaba entre lucientes piedras a nuestro lado, el rumor del viento entre las hojas de los árboles que se balanceaban sobre nuestras cabezas, y toda aquella vida y movimiento de la naturaleza tropical, nos hacían gozar y convidaban al reposo y a la dicha perezosa del vivir . . . Antonio y Dolores se habían alejado insensiblemente de los demás y se sentaron al pie de una gran piedra cubierta de amarillento musgo. Dolores tiraba al río con distracción los pétalos de un ramo de flores que llevaba en la mano; y mientras que el agua salpicaba la dorada arena a su pies, ambos miraban con interés la suerte de aquellas florecillas en la espumosa corriente. Algunas bajaban lentamente y se detenían muy pronto sobre la blanda orilla: otras, arrastradas con ímpetu por el agua, se engolfaban de improviso en un remolino y desaparecían al punto: otras salían al principio con rapidez y alegremente, pero al llegar a una concavidad formada por las piedras, tropezaban allí y no pudiendo salir, se impregnaban de agua y se consumían poco a poco; por último, las más afortunadas se unían en grupos y salían a la mitad del río, descendiendo por medio de la corriente sin encontrar tropiezo alguno.

—¿Ven ustedes la filosofía de ese espectáculo? dije acercándome de improviso a los dos.

Antonio y Dolores se estremecieron como si se los hubiera interrumpido; y en efecto, ellos se comunicaban sus pensamientos con una mirada y se hablaban en su mismo silencio.

—¿Qué filosofía? preguntaron.

—La que encierra esa flor que Dolores tira a la corriente. Ella es la imagen de la Providencia y cada uno de esos pétalos lo es de una vida humana. ¿Cuál suerte preferirías tú, Dolores? La de las que pronto se retiran a la playa sin haber tenido emociones; la de las que se precipitan a la corriente y se pierden en un remolino . . .

—¿Yo? . . . no sé. Pero las que me causan pena son aquellas que se encuentran encerradaas en un sitio aislado y sin esperanza de salir . . . Mira, añadió, cómo se van hundiendo poco a poco y como a pesar suyo.

—Yo, decididamente, señor filósofo, dijo Antonio fijando la mirada en la de Dolores, prefiero la suerte de las que bajan de dos en dos por la corriente de la vida.

Las mejillas de mi prima se cubrieron de carmín y levantándose turbada se unió a los demás grupos de amigas.

Las risas y conversaciones, los cantos y armonía de los tiples y bandolas, el baile en el patio del trapiche y el buen humor general, nada de esto pudo animar a Dolores. Estaba contenta, dichosa tal vez por momentos, pero se veía en su frente una sombra y cierta modulación dolorosa suavizaba el timbre de su voz. Antonio estaba en aquella situación en que los enamorados se vuelven taciturnos y atolondrados, sin poder hacer otra cosa que contemplar el objeto amado, sin poder atender sino a lo que *ella* dice, ni admirar a otra persona u objeto; estado de ánimo sumamente fastidioso para todos, menos para la que inspira y comprende tal situación.

Volvimos al pueblo por la noche; estaba muy oscura no obstante que las estrellas lucían en el despejado cielo. Al atravesar un riachuelo en un punto peligroso se creyó necesario que cada hombre fuese al lado de una señora. El caballo de Dolores se asustó al resbalar en las piedras, y si Antonio no la hubiese sostenido con un brazo y afirmándola nuevamente en el galápago, al brincar el caballo la habría hecho caer al agua. Cuando Antonio se encontró nuevamente en tierra, seguramente se le conoció el susto y la emoción que había sentido en aquel lance, y su voz temblaba al contestar a mi pregunta. Entonces comprendí cuán verdadera y tiernamente amaba a Dolores. El amor sincero no es egoísta; y nunca es más cobarde el corazón que cuando la persona amada está en peligro, aunque éste parezca insignificante para los demás.

¡Media hora después se separaron, tal vez para simpre, aquellos dos seres que habían nacido para amarse tan profundamente!

Luego a solas me confió Antonio que no había podido hablar a Dolores de su amor, que siendo tan vehemente y elevado, no había hallado palabras con que expresarlo. Me rogó que le dijera a mi prima en nombre suyo que no había pedido su mano formalmente porque su posición no se lo permitía aún; pero teniendo esperanzas de ser correspondido me pedía la suplicara que no lo olvidase.

El mismo día que partió Antonio para Bogotá, la tía Juana volvió a su hacienda con Dolores. Yo había visto la despedida de Dolores y Antonio, y aunque ella tenía la sonrisa en los labios comprendí que necesitaría algún consuelo. Así, al domingo siguiente me dirigí muy temprano a la hacienda, llamada Primavera, situada en una llanura al pie de altos cerros cubiertos de bosques y vestida principalmente de ganados y extensos cacaotales.

Cuando llegué, mi tía estaba ausente y la casa completamente silenciosa. Me desmonté y entregando mi caballo a un sirviente, atravesé el patio que antecedía a la casa y me dirigí al retrete de Dolores en el cual me dijeron se encontraba.

El sitio favorito de mi prima era un ancho corredor hacia la parte de atrás de la casa y con vista sobre una semi-huerta, semi-jardín. . . . La pajarera de Dolores era afamada en los alrededores: en una gran jaula que ocupaba todo el ángulo del corredor había reunido muchos pájaros de diversos climas, que se habían enseñado a vivir unidos y en paz. . . . Enmedio de sus flores y pájaros Dolores pasaba el día cosiendo, leyendo, y cantando con ellos. Desde lejos se oía el rumor de la pajarera y la dulce voz de su ama.

Ese día todo estaba en silencio. El calor era sofocante, y la naturaleza parecía agobiada y abochornada por los rayos de un sol de fuego que reinaba solo en un cielo despejado. Los pájaros callaban y sólo se oía el ruido del chorro de la alberca que corría sin cesar bajo su enramada de flores. Desde lejos vi a Dolores vestida de blanco y llevando por único adorno su hermoso pelo de matiz oscuro. Recostada sobre un cojín al pie del asiento en que había estado sentada, apoyaba la cabeza sobre el brazo doblado, mientras que la otra manecita blanca y rosada caía inerte a su lado. Detúveme a contemplarla creyéndola dormida, pero había oído el ruido de mis espuelas al acercarme, y se levantó de repente, tratando de ocultar las lágrimas que se le escapaban y cogiendo al mismo tiempo un papel que tenía sobre su mesita de costura.

—¿Qué es esto, prima? le pregunté señalándole el papel, después de haberla saludado.

—Estaba escribiendo y . . .

—¿A quién?

—A nadie.

—Cómo, ¿Antonio ya logró . . . ?

—No, Pedro, me contestó con dignidad; él no me pidió tal cosa, ni yo lo haría.

—Dolores, le dije tomando entre mis manos la suya fría y temblorosa ¿no te juró Antonio que te amaba locamente, como me lo dijo mil veces? ¡Confiésame que te suplicó que le guardaras tu fe!

—No; me hizo comprender que me prefería tal vez, pero nunca me dijo más.

—¿Y esa carta?

—¡No es carta!

—Misiva, pues, dije riéndome, epístola, billete, como quieras llamarla.

—¿No quieres creerme? Toma el papel; haces que te muestre lo que sólo escribía para mí.

Y me presentó un papel en que acababa de escribir unos preciosos versos, que mostraban un profundo sentimiento poético y cierto espíritu de melancolía vaga que no le conocía. Era un tierno adiós a su tranquila y feliz niñez y una invocación a su juventud que se le aparecía de repente como una revelación. Su corazón se había conmovido por primera vez, y ese estremecimiento la hacía comprender que la vida del sufrimiento había empezado.

Avergonzada y conmovida bajaba los ojos a medida que yo leía. Su tez blanca y rosada resaltaba aun con mayor frescura en contraste con su albo vestido y cabello destrenzado. Un temor vago me asaltó a mí también, como a mi padre, al notar el particular colorido de su tez; pero esa impresión fue olvidada nuevamente para recordarla después.

Pasé el día en casa de mi tía, cumplí la recomendación de Antonio y me persuadí de que ella lo amaba también. Debía volver a Bogotá en esos días: estaba impaciente y deseaba tener la dicha de ver otra vez a mi novia después de mes y medio de ausencia.

Al tiempo de despedirme quisieron acompañarme hasta cierto punto del camino para que Dolores me mostrara un lindo sitio al pie de la serranía, que ella había *descubierto* algunos días antes en uno de sus paseos.

Dolores se manifestaba muy risueña y festiva. El amor que la animaba formaba como una aureola en torno suyo. ¿Qué importa la ausencia si hay seguridad de amar y ser amado? Al llegar a una angosta vereda que había hecho abrir por enmedio del monte, tomó la delantera. Yo la seguía, admirando su esbelto talle y su gracia y serenidad para manejar un brioso potro que sólo con ella se había mostrado obediente y dócil.

Pocos momentos después llegamos a un sitio más abierto: un riachuelo cristalino bajaba saltando por escalones de piedras y reposaba en aquel lugar entre un bello lecho de musgos y de temblantes y variados helechos. Altísimos árboles se alzaban a un lado del riachuelo, impidiendo con su tupida sombra que otros arbustos creciesen a su lado. Varios troncos viejos y piedras envueltas en verde lama cubrían el suelo, alfombrado por una suave arena dorada. Empezaba a caer el sol y la sombra de aquel sitio producía un delicioso fresco. Bandadas de pájaros vistosos, entre los que charlaban numerosos loros y pericos, llegaban a posarse en las altas copas de los árboles, dorados por los últimos rayos del sol.

Nos desmontamos, y sacando mi tía algunos dulces y un coco curiosamente engastado en bruñida plata, nos invitó a que tomásemos un refrigerio campestre.

—Qué bello sería pasar su vida aquí, ¿no es cierto? exclamó Dolores.

—¿Sola? contesté sonriéndome.

No replicó sino con sólo una mirada tierna que se dirigía a mi amigo ausente, y continuó conversando alegremente. ¡Pobre niña! . . . pero feliz todavía en su ignorancia de lo porvenir.

PARTE SEGUNDA

La douleur est une lumière qui nous éclaire la vie.[8]

Balzac

Dos meses después de haber llegado a Bogotá recibí de Dolores su primera carta, la que he conservado con otras muchas como recuerdos de mi prima, cuyo claro talento fue ignorado de todos menos de mí.

"Querido primo," me decía: aguardaba recibir noticia de tu lle-

gada para escribirte, y después, cuando quise hacerlo, los acontecimientos que han tenido lugar en casa y en mi vida, me lo habían
impe-dido . . . No sabía si debería confiarte el horrible secreto que
he descubierto; pero el corazón necesita desahogarse, y sé bien que
eres no solamente mi hermano sino un amigo muy querido que
simpatiza con mis penas. No hace mucho que leía que lo que hace
las amistades indisolubles y duplica su encanto, es aquel sentimiento
que falta al amor: la seguridad. ¡Oh! la amistad es lo único que
puede ahora consolarme, ya que otro sentimiento me será prohibido
. . . No hace mucho, ¿te acuerdas? veía el mundo bello, alegre, encantador; todo me sonreía . . . pero ahora, ¡gran Dios! . . . ¡un terre-
moto ha cubierto de ruinas el sitio en que se levantaba el templo de
mis esperanzas!

Perdóname, Pedro, esta palabrería con que procuro retardar la
confesión de mis penas: esto sólo te demuestra el terror que me
causa ver escrito lo que casi no me atrevo a pensar.

Pero, ¡valor! empezaré.

Algunos días después de tu partida me dirigía una tarde a la pieza
de mi tía, cuando al pasar por el corredor del patio de entrada, oí
que un viejo arrendatario que vivió en los confines de la hacienda
preguntaba por ella. Llevaba una carta en la mano, y al saber que era
para mi tía la tomé y me preparaba a entregársela, cuando al notar
que el viejo Simón la había llevado dio un grito diciendo:—Tira esa
carta, Dolores, ¡tírala!

Yo hice instintivamente lo que mandaba y la dejé caer. Mi tía
hizo entonces que me lavara las manos, y mandando llevar un
brasero, no tomó la carta en sus manos sino después de haberla
hecho fumigar.

Yo estaba tan admirada al ver aquella escena, que casi no acertaba
a preguntar la causa de los súbitos temores de mi tía; al fin la cosa
me pareció hasta chistosa y exclamé riéndome:—¿Está envenenado
ese papel, tía? El viejo Simón tendrá sus rasgos a lo Borgia,[9] como en
la historia que leíamos el otro día?

—No te burles, hija mía, me contestó con seriedad: el veneno que
puede contener ese papel es más horrible que todos los que han in-
ventado los hombres.

Al decir estas palabras, acabó de leer la carta y tirándola al brasero, la vio consumirse lentamente.

—Es preciso que me explique usted este misterio . . .

—En esto no creas que hay misterio romántico, me dijo con acento triste, interrumpiéndome. ¿No sabes que en las inmediaciones de N★★★ hay lazarinos? Uno de esos desgraciados me ha enviado esa carta.

—¿Y quién es?

—¡Quién! un infeliz a quien he mandado algunos socorros y vive en una choza arruinada no lejos de la de Simón.

—¡Pobrecito! Y vive solo como todos ellos! Solo, enmedio del monte, sin que nadie le hable ni se le acerque jamás. Vivirá y morirá aislado sin sentir una mano amiga . . . ¡Dios mío! qué horrible suerte, ¡qué crueldad!

Y se me apretaba el corazón con indecible angustia.

—La sociedad es muy bárbara, tía, añadí; rechaza de su seno al desgraciado . . .

—Así es, me contestó, ¿pero qué remedio? Se dice que esa espantosa enfermedad se comunica con la mayor facilidad. ¿No es mejor en tal caso que sufra uno solo en vez de muchos? Por mi parte, Dolores, te confieso que el aspecto de un lazarino me espanta y querría más bien morir que acercármele.

—¿Y cómo conoció usted a ese infeliz? ¿Por qué lo protege, tía? Mucho me ha interesado: el sobrescrito de la carta estaba muy bien puesto . . . y aún me parece que la letra no me es enteramente desconocida.

—¿Por qué lo protejo, me preguntas? ¿No se ha de procurar siempre aliviar a los que sufren?

Mi tía cortó la conversación bruscamente. Aunque en los subsiguientes días no hablamos del episodio de la carta; esto me había impresionado mucho. El invierno entró con toda la fuerza con que tú sabes se desencadenan las lluvias en estos climas. Estábamos completamente solas en la hacienda: nadie se atrevía a atravesar los ríos crecidos y los caminos inundados para venirnos a visitar. A veces me despertaba en medio de la noche al ruido de una fuerte tempestad, y al oír caer la lluvia, el trueno rasgar el aire y mugir el viento contra las ventanas bien cerradas, y sintiéndome abrigada en mi pieza y rodeada de tantas comodidades, mi espíritu se trasportaba a las chozas solitarias de esos parias de nuestra sociedad: los lazarinos. Veía con la imaginación a esos infelices, presas de terribles sufrimientos, enmedio de las montañas y de la intemperie, y solos, siempre solos . . .

Una noche había leído hasta muy tarde, estudiando francés en los libros que me dejaste: procuraba aprender y adelantar en mis estudios, educar mi espíritu e instruirme para ser menos ignorante: el roce con *algunas* personas de la capital me había hecho comprender últimamente cuán indispensable es saber. Me acosté pues tarde, y empezaba a dormitar cuando creí oír pasos en el patio exterior y como el cuchicheo de dos voces que hablaban bajo. Mi perro favorito, que pasa la noche en mi cuarto, se levantó de repente y se salió por ventana abierta al corredor, y un momento después oí que se abalanzaba sobre alguien en el patio. La voz de mi tía lo hizo retirarse. ¡Cosa extraña! ¡mi tía que se recogía a las ocho, andaba por los corredores de la casa a media noche! Me levanté resuelta a indagar esto y entreabrí la puerta que daba al corredor extremo. Entonces oí una voz de hombre que decía por lo bajo: '¡Adiós, Juana!' Esta voz me causó grande estremecimiento: creí soñar . . .

—Aguárdese un momento, contestó mi tía, voy a traerle el retrato que mandé hacer para usted por un pintor quiteño que por casualidad estuvo aquí ahora días.

Al decir esto sentí que la tía Juana entró a su cuarto y aprovechándome de la oscuridad, salí al corredor prontamente y me situé en un ángulo desde donde, agazapada, pude ver un bulto que aguardaba inmóvil enmedio del patio.

El temor y la vaga aprehensión que había sentido al oír la voz del desconocido desaparecieron al ver que no era una fantasma, un sueño de mi imaginación. Sin embargo, no podía comprender que la tía Juana tuviera *citas* a media noche y regalara su retrato! . . . Era cierto que poco antes le rogué que se hiciese retratar por un pintor de paso que hizo el mío también. Un momento después volvió, y apoyándose sobre la baranda del corredor dijo, atando a una cuerda un paquete envuelto:—No está tan parecida como yo quisiera; y cuando el bulto se acercó, añadió: va también [el libro] la 'Imitación de Cristo,' de Dolores, que se la cambié por una nueva.

No sabe usted cuánto provecho me hará esto, exclamó con voz conmovida el desconocido . . . ¡Oh! ¡pobre hija mía! . . . ¡su retrato!

Esa voz, ese acento me heló la sangre, y por un momento no sé lo que pasó por mí. Una idea increíble, un terror horrible me dejó como anonadada. Me puse en pie, fría, temblando.

Váyase pronto, Jerónimo, contestó mi tía, he oído un ruido del lado del cuarto de Dolores y . . .

Nada más oí. Había conocido la voz de mi padre y mi tía lo nombró. ¡Mi padre, que yo creía muerto hacía seis años! No reflexioné en el misterio de aquella aparición, y bajando las gradas del corredor que caían al patio corrí hacia el bulto, y acercándome le eché los brazos al cuello. Al ver mi acción, tanto mi tía como mi padre, pues él era, dieron un grito de horror: éste último se separó de mí con desesperación, se cubrió la cara con la *ruana* en que estaba envuelto y quiso huir; yo pugnaba por seguirlo, y mi tía que había bajado detrás de mí me detuvo.

—Dolores, gritaba ésta, Dolores, no te acerques, ¡por Dios! . . . ¡está lazarino!

¿Lazarino? ¡qué me importa! Mi padre no ha muerto y quiero abrazarlo.

No te puedes figurar la escena que hubo entonces . . . al fin mi tía logró que mi padre se fuera, y llamando a las sirvientas me llevó por fuerza a mi cuarto; y allí quitándome los vestidos que tenía los hizo tirar al patio para ser quemados al día siguiente.

No consentí que mi tía me dejase hasta que no me refiriera la causa de este acontecimiento y me hiciera saber inmediatamente porqué se hallaba mi padre oculto y en aquel estado . . . Conversamos largo tiempo y no me quedé sola sino cuando empezaban a entrar los primeros rayos de la aurora por la ventana abierta. Me levanté entonces y recostándome contra la ventana contemplé el bello paisaje que se extendía a mis ojos. . . . ¡El día, el paisaje, los rumores campestres eran bellos y admirables! . . . pero yo veía todo triste y sin animación. La faz de mi vida ha cambiado; ya nada puede ser risueño para mí. ¡Mi padre vive, pero vive sufriendo!

¿No es cierto, Pedro, que el lázaro es una enfermedad horrorosa? Al saber cuál es la herencia que me aguarda, todos tratarían de retirarse de mi lado y procurarían descubrir en mí los síntomas precursores; ¡estaría condenada a vivir aislada! Mi padre que me amaba con ternura no quiso que esa mancha empañase mi frente, y por eso resolvió desaparecer. Ha vivido escondido en los más recónditos rincones de la provincia y hace apenas un año que mi tía y tu padre saben dónde se halla . . . ¿Pero, yo podré vivir contenta lejos de mi desgraciado padre? ¿Sería justo que engañase a los demás ocultando la enfermedad a que la suerte puede condenarme? Mi padre me ha hecho saber que de ningún modo permitirá que se sepa que él existe . . . En tu última carta me dices que Antonio tiene esperanzas de alcanzar más pronto de lo que creía una posición que le permita pedir mi mano. Ya es tarde, primo mío: es preciso que renuncie a esa idea . . . ¡que me olvide! Mi desdicha no debe encadenarlo. No le digas nunca la causa, pero hazle perder la esperanza. Me creerá variable, ingrata . . . pero ¿qué puedo hacer? Este sacrificio es grande, muy grande, pero no tiene remedio.

Adiós. Escríbele palabras de consuelo a la que sufre tanto.

—Dolores

Al cabo de algunos días recibí esta otra carta:

Me escribes, querido primo, y tus palabras han sido para mí un verdadero consuelo: ¡gracias, oh, mil gracias! Me preguntas con interés los pormenores de la desaparición de mi padre y cómo vivió tanto tiempo oculto, sin que nadie adivinase ni pudiese sospechar que vivía.

He reunido todo lo que acerca de este particular he podido descubrir, y procuraré explicarte las cosas como pasaron.

Tú sabes que desde que murió mi madre, mi padre había concentrado en mí todo su afecto y me cuidaba con la ternura de una mujer. Tenía yo doce años, cuando sintiendo mi padre algunas novedades en su salud que lo alarmaron partió para Bogotá. Allí consultó varios médicos que le dijeron que los síntomas que sentía eran los de una enfermedad incurable y horrorosa: el lázaro. Desesperado, volvió para N*** sin determinar la conducta que debía seguir. Pero al llegar a las márgenes del Magdalena, su espíritu exaltado le presentó la imagen del suicidio como la única salida menos mala y el solo remedio que tenía su situación. Se desmontó y en un momento de demencia se precipitó al río con la intención de dejarse ahogar. Pero tú recordarás que mi padre era muy buen nadador. El instinto natural y el apego que se tiene a la vida lo obligaron a no dejarse consumir, y aunque exánime arribó al otro lado. Allí lo amparó un infeliz que vivía en una triste choza en la orilla de río. ¡Qué casualidad! su protector estaba también lazarino, y vivía en aquellas soledades manteniéndose con algunos socorros que le enviaban del vecino pueblo y el producto de un platanal y otras semerterillas que cultivaba y mandaba a vender a las inmediaciones con sus dos hijos que lo acompañaban. Mi padre permaneció con él algunos días y concibió la idea de huir del mundo para siempre, y ocultando sus padecimientos no dejarle esa misteriosa herencia a su hija.

Con el producto de una cantidad de oro y algunas joyas que llevaba entre el bolsillo vivió algún tiempo en aquellos desiertos. Pronto se separó del lazarino. ¿Vivir bajo el pie de igualdad con un ser vulgar no es la peor de las desgracias? Compró pues una choza en el monte y allí vegetó solo, aislado y profundamente desgraciado más de cinco años. Algunas veces bajaba a las márgenes del Magdalena, visitaba al lazarino y estudiaba en él los progresos y estragos que hacía el mal que ambos padecían. Otras ocasiones, vestido como campesino, penetraba de noche a los pueblos más cercanos y preguntaba por la suerte de su familia. ¡Cuántas veces no podía tener noticia alguna y se volvía desconsolado a su montaña!

Un día bajó a la choza de su compañero en infortunio, y encontró a los dos muchachos llorando en el quicio de la puerta.

El lazarino había muerto. Ese espectáculo conmovió a mi padre y les propuso que lo siguieran a su desierto. Ellos, una niña de doce años y un muchacho de catorce, aceptaron su oferta con gratitud. Hacía muchos meses que mi padre no había sabido nada con certeza de su familia, y estaba sumamente inquieto; por otra parte, la muerte del lazarino le hizo comprender que la suya podía estar cercana, y no pudo menos que desear verme por la última vez.

Emprendió, pues, viaje hacia N★★★, viaje penosísimo al través de aquellas desiertas llanuras de pajonales interminables, acompañado por los dos muchachos.

En los confines de la hacienda de mi tía había una choza abandonada, y allí eligió su domicilio. Sus compañeros no sabían quién era él y así pudo mandar sin cuidado una carta dirigida a tu padre, revelándole su existencia y pidiéndole noticias de su familia. Ya te puedes figurar la admiración que semejante revelación le causaría a tu padre. Nunca se había tenido la menor duda de que el mío no se hubiese ahogado al atravesar imprudentemente el Magdalena. Cuando aquel se persuadió de la verdad consultó con la tía Juana lo que debía hacer: su primer impulso había sido buscar a mi infeliz padre y llevarlo nuevamente a su casa, aunque él rehusase seguirlo. Pero tú sabes el horror que mi tía le tiene a esa enfermedad, y de ningún modo accedió a la propuesta. Decía (me aseguran que en esto tenía razón) que teniendo yo por herencia predisposición a ese mal, era preciso precaverme en lo posible de todo contagio. Convinieron en que de la hacienda se le enviaría todo lo que necesitaba, pero que viviría lejos de todos sus parientes y su existencia continuaría ignorada por todos. Mi padre, ¡oh infeliz! nunca había tenido otra pretensión que la de verme ocultamente y de lejos . . . ¿Te acuerdas de la tarde en que te despediste de nosotros? él se hallaba oculto entre las breñas a orillas del riachuelo; nos contemplaba alegres y el eco de nuestra risa llegaba hasta sus oídos.

Me dicen que su enfermedad está el último período . . . que sufre horriblemente; pero no me es permitido verlo ni aliviarlo. Vivo ahora siempre triste, retraída: mi carácter ha cambiado totalmente. Dime ¿qué ha dicho Antonio? ¿Me olvida con facilidad? . . . Preguntas necias, ¿no es cierto? Hablemos de ti: me dices que tu matrimonio no podrá ser tan presto como pensabas, pero tú al menos vives en una atmósfera de esperanza. Hemos sido hermanos: a ti te toca la dicha, a mí . . . No, Dios sabe lo que hace: habrá medido mis fuerzas y resignación. Adiós . . .

Estas noticias de N★★★ me entristecieron mucho. El estado de dolor mórbido a veces, exaltado otras que revelaban las cartas de Dolores me alarmó. Escribí a mi padre aconsejándole que procurasen distraerla, pues ese pensamiento continuo en una cosa tan dolorosa podía presdisponerla más que todo a que estallase en ella la enfermedad de su padre. Una reflexión me consolaba: rara vez se han visto casos de que los hijos de los lazarinos sufran la enfermedad: casi siempre salta una generación para aparecer en los nietos. Sin embargo, comprendía y aprobaba su noble conducta al desear romper con Antonio. Yo no me atrevía a quitar repentinamente las esperanzas a mi amigo; lo veía tan feliz que me parecía una crueldad inútil apagar aquel fuego y vida, aquel vigor y energía que animaban sus trabajos y lo hacían triunfar de todas las dificultades.

Así se pasaron varios meses. Al fin recibí la noticia de la muerte del padre de Dolores: escribió ella algunas líneas en que me manifestaba su angustia. No podía llorar públicamente la pérdida que había hecho, ni vestirse de luto, pues él le había hecho saber en sus últimos momentos que quería que su sacrificio sirviera al menos para preservar a su hija de las miradas recelosas de una sociedad que sabría lo que ella debía esperar al conocer la causa de su muerte.

Viéndola tan abatida, mi tía quiso distraerla y la llevó hasta el Espinal.[10] Ambas me escribieron entonces rogándome que fuese a verlas por algunos días, ya que estaban más cerca de Bogotá.

Accedí a ese deseo y fuí a pasar una semana con ellas. ¡Cómo podía prever las consecuencias que esa visita tendría para mí!

Nada podía consolar a Dolores; estaba pálida y en todos sus movimientos se veía la profunda pena que la agobiaba. Entonces me volvió a pedir encarecidamente que desengañase a Antonio, pero me hizo prometer que jamás le diría la causa del rompimiento que ella deseaba.

A mi vuelta procuré hacer comprender a Antonio la repugnancia que Dolores manifestaba por el matrimonio, y lo imposible que sería que se realizasen sus esperanzas. Esta era una obra ardua, y frecuentemente no tenía valor para desconsolarlo enteramente.

Por otra parte mis proyectos matrimoniales habían tomado un aspecto que me causaba mucha desconfianza en lo porvenir. Don Basilio se había hecho presentar en casa de mi novia como aspirante a la mano de Mercedes, quien le mostraba siempre un ceño esquivo; pero los padres lo acogían con cierta atención que me disgustaba. Poco a poco descubrí que a medida que se acataba a don Basilio se me trataba con mayor indiferencia. Una vez me dijo Mercedes que estaba muy triste porque sus padres habían tenido malos informes de mí; que ella me había defendido, pero no podía impedir un viaje que se preparaba con dirección a Chiquinquirá.[11] Hacía muchos años que su madre había hecho una promesa a la Virgen, pero hasta entonces no le ocurrió cumplirla, sin duda con la intención, me decía Mercedes, de separarnos. Quise tener una explicación acerca de los informes que de mí habían tenido, pero Mercedes no me lo permitió, asegurándome que no sabía cuáles eran los cargos que se hacía, y que, cuando ella averiguase de qué se me acusaba yo podría defenderme mejor.

Comprendí que ésta debía ser obra de don Basilio y prometí esperar. A los pocos días la familia de Mercedes partía para Chiquinquirá. Durante las primeras semanas de su ausencia estuve profundamente abatido y mi mayor gusto era conversar largamente con Antonio de nuestras mutuas penas. Mercedes me escribía con frecuencia, pero al fin me dijo que no volverían a Bogotá tan pronto como habían pensado; que su madre había deseado quedarse algunos meses en San Gil con la familia que tenía allá. Cada vez que recibía una carta de Mercedes era motivo de fiesta para mí, pero al fin empezaron a escasear, bajo pretexto de que su madre le había prohibido que me escribiese. Entonces todavía amaba y me creía amado, y aunque sufría mucho en aquel tiempo lo recuerdo con ternura: "todos los demás placeres no equivalen a nuestras penas," decía un autor francés. Pero poco a poco me fui enseñando a su silencio y ya no deseaba sus cartas con tanta impaciencia. No sé por qué motivo dieron en esos días en Bogotá muchos bailes y tertulias: asistí a ellos y confieso que no estuve triste. Sin embargo, llevaba siempre en el alma un malestar, una pena oculta que revestía la memoria de Mercedes.

Se habían pasado cuatro meses sin recibir noticia alguna de ella cuando un día llegó a mis mano una carta suya, y comprendí con profunda tristeza que mi corazón ya no sentía la dicha de antes. Mercedes me decía que habiéndole dicho a su padre que debían volver a Bogotá porque ya se cumplía el plazo en que se debía verificar nuestro matrimonio, éste le había notificado que con su consentimiento nunca sería mi esposa. No le quiso explicar la causa de su resolución, pero añadió que tenía seguridad de que bastaría una ausencia prolongada para que mutuamente nos olvidásemos. La carta de Mercedes era sumamente afectuosa, tal vez más que ninguna otra; pero con aquel magnetismo, aquella intuición que hay entre dos personas que se aman y que queda aún después de haberse amado; con esa revelación del alma, digo, que se comprende sin poderse explicar, sentí hasta en sus expresiones más cariñosas cierto despego y frialdad. La cadena de sentimientos y simpatías estaba a punto de romperse entre los dos. Desde ese día empecé a resignarme a su ausencia y a familiarizarme con la posibilidad de que nuestra suerte podía ser desunida.

Un negocio importante del padre de Mercedes trajo a toda la familia a Bogotá por fin. Apenas supe su llegada imprevista mi corazón se galvanizó por un momento y me dirijí inmediatamente a su casa. ¡Triste desengaño! aquella impresión fue pasajera y pronto me sentí otra vez tranquilo. Sin embargo, hacía un esfuerzo para pensar que al verla sería otra vez dichoso, y al entrar a la casa repasaba con la imaginación todas las soñadas escenas con que antes había revestido la esperanza que ahora iba a ser colmada. Llegué, la vi bella como siempre, pero en sus ojos se había apagado la luz que faltaba en los míos. Nos hablamos: yo procuré ocultar mi indiferencia; ella estaba distraída . . . Al despedirme se apoderó de mí un pesar inmenso. ¡Es tan desalentador sentir el corazón vacío, sin emociones ni entusiasmo!

No quería tener ninguna explicación con ella y temía que hubiera entre nosotros una reconciliación que ya no se deseaba. Así me fui retirando de su casa, y aunque ella no podía menos que notar la frialdad que había en nuestras relaciones nada me dijo. La vi más hermosa que nunca, cubierta de galas, en el teatro y en tertulias: oí hablar de las conquistas que había hecho y de los pretendientes que tenía, entre los cuales se hallaban en primer lugar don Basilio y Julián que había vuelto a Bogotá; pero en lugar de los celos y la pena que antes hubiera sentido al verla tan obsequiada, mi corazón permaneció tranquilo. Había perdido la facultad de sentir aquellos nobles celos que son el síntoma del amor. No hay duda que hay celos, o más bien cierta envidia, en un corazón que no ama, pero no puede haber amor vehemente sin ellos.

¡Pobre Mercedes! A veces procuraba llamarme a su lado y encubría su indiferencia cuando le era posible, como yo la mía. Yo estaba muy triste entonces: el corazón humano, sin exceptuar el mío, me parecía tan pequeño, variable e indigno, bien que en lo íntimo de él guardase el recuerdo de la mujer que amé como un ángel, ¡pero que se había convertido para mí en un ser débil, fútil, y fácilmente llevado por la voluntad ajena! A veces la conciencia me acusaba de haber cambiado yo también. Era cierto, pero no había empezado a sentirme indiferente sino cuando advertí en ella despego. Su silencio y sus vacilaciones durante nuestra separación me la habían mostrado bajo otra luz, y el antiguo ideal había desaparecido para mí.

Fluctuaban mis sentimientos en este vaivén anárquico, en que nada espera uno ni desea, cuando recibí otra carta de Dolores, carta que me llenó de aprehensión penosísima. Luego que la leí, tomé la resolución de partir al día siguiente para N★★★. La misma noche fuí a despedirme de Mercedes.

Estaba muy abatido, y en esa situación el ánimo está dispuesto a aceptar con agradecimiento cualquiera simpatía. Creo que si Mercedes me hubiera acogido aquella noche como en otro tiempo, tal vez habría recuperado su imperio sobre mi corazón. Cuánta gratitud hubiera tenido hacia ella al ser inspirado por el sentimiento que creía ser el mayor bien dado a los mortales: ¡el amor!

Subí muy conmovido las escaleras de su casa; mi voz tembló al saludarla.

La tertulia estaba completa como la de casi todas las noches. En un lado de la sala y alrededor del piano había un grupo compuesto de Mercedes y algunas amigas: una de ellas tocaba una pieza, mientras que don Basilio disertaba sobre la ópera de donde había sido tomada: Julián volvía las hojas del papel de música y miraba lánguidamente a Mercedes. Al lado opuesto, el padre de ella jugaba tresillo con dos o tres amigos de don Basilio, sencillos congresistas de provincias lejanas, que vestían casacas muy apretadas, cuellos muy tiesos, trabillas muy tirantes, por último *usaban* unas manos tan negras y toscas, que se conocía cuáles habían sido sus antecedentes.

Noté que mi llegada produjo impresión. Todos los ojos se fijaron en mí con curiosidad y se interrumpieron las conversaciones empezadas. Mercedes me recibió desdeñosamente, volteándome la espalda después de haberme saludado ligeramente y sin mirarme. El dueño de casa apenas me contestó y toda la concurrencia me recibió con frialdad. Enmedio del silencio general causado por mi llegada don Basilio se dirigió a mí y dijo con voz sonora y su acostumbrada pedantería: —"Hablando del rey de Roma," etc., o más bien como dicen los ingleses: "*Talk of the devil. . . .*" Se hablaba de usted, joven, hace un momento. Y añadió mirando a todos con aire significativo ¿ha tenido usted últimamente noticias de sus interesantes parientas a quienes conocí el año pasado en N★★★?

No sé qué le contesté. Un momento después, acercándome a Mercedes le dije que venía a despedirme porque tenía que ausentarme algunos días.

—Naturalmente, me contestó sonrojándose con suma contrariedad.

—¿Por qué naturalmente? Usted no sabe a dónde voy . . .

—¿Cómo no he de adivinar? . . . El engañado puede a veces abrir los ojos.

—¿El engañado?

—O la engañada, si usted gusta.

—Explíquese, Mercedes.

—Lo haré. Sepa usted que hoy ya comprendo la falsedad de la conducta de usted, y tenga por seguro que entre nosotros acabó todo compromiso.

—¿Y de qué soy culpable, por Dios?

—Ahora no tengo tiempo para explicarme. Bástele saber que lo sé todo . . . y añadió con ironía: ¡comprendo que usted quiera ir a visitar a la persona que prefiere!

—No entiendo.

—¿No? Pues, entonces hágame el favor de saludar a su prima Dolores de mi parte.

—Mercedes, usted es muy injusta, y no sé quién ha podido inventar semejante . . .

Ella no pudo menos que volver lo ojos hacia don Basilio al interrumpirme diciendo:—No sé por qué se ha tomado usted la pena de venir a despedirse. Entre usted y yo no hay ni puede haber simpatía: yo no me intereso en sus asuntos particulares.

Inmediatamente comprendí que todo esto era obra de don Basilio. Mi orgullo se exaltó, y no quise humillarme pidiendo explicaciones.

—Ya veo, le contesté mirando a mi rival, ya veo que mi dignidad me impide defenderme; la fortaleza está en manos del enemigo y sería inútil procurar rechazar las calumnias que ciertas personas saben inventar.

Y saludando con aire altivo a Mercedes y a toda la concurrencia salí de la sala seguido por la mirada maligna y la perversa sonrisa de don Basilio. En la puerta me alcanzó Julián, y ofreciéndome la mano me dijo:—No crea usted, Pedro, que yo he tenido parte en la conspiración que comprendo se había preparado contra usted, pues yo soy enemigo de estas cosas y tengo verdadero aprecio por usted.

Le agradecí este acto de espontaneidad y nos separamos.

Atravesé las calles que me separaban de casa, y odio, deseo de vengarme, profunda humillación al verme vencido por ese aventurero de pluma, desprecio por Mercedes que servía de instrumento, todo esto bullía en mi mente y hacía latir mi corazón. Enmedio de todo recordaba que al salir había visto que la mirada de Mercedes me siguió, humedecida y melancólica . . . No volví a verla sino años después y ¡en qué circunstancias!

Al llegar a casa me dijeron que alguien me aguardaba: era Antonio. Al acercarme para saludarlo dio un paso atrás y rechazando mi mano dijo con destemplanza:—Deseo primero saber si le doy la mano a un amigo o a un traidor a la amistad!

—¡A un traidor! . . . ¿yo Antonio?

—¡Usted!

—Explícate . . . ¡Esto me faltaba! exclamé con desaliento. Esto me faltaba para volverme loco . . . Vengo de casa de Mercedes que rompió conmigo definitivamente.

—¿Y no dijo la causa?

—Me dio a entender que creía en una calumnia . . .

—¡Calumnia! tal vez ella tenía razón . . . ¡Pedro, Pedro! todavía me queda una esperanza: ¡tu lealtad de tantos años! Dime la verdad, añadió tuteándome otra vez; es tan triste perderlo todo en un día . . . contéstame ¿amabas acaso a Dolores antes de conocerla yo? O en tu viaje al Espinal, ahora cuatro meses . . . ¡Oh! ¡dime la verdad!

—Te juro en nombre de nuestra vieja amistad y por todo lo que hay más sagrado, que Dolores ha sido siempre solamente una hermana para mí.

—No sé qué creer . . . He estado pensando mucho en tu conducta últimamente y es inexplicable. Desde que estuviste en el Espinal has procurado siempre disuadirme de mis proyectos con respecto a Dolores, y no me permites que hable de ella; todo esto con cierto aire misterioso que no puedes ocultar y sin decirme la causa de tan extraño cambio. El amigo Durán me dijo también en días pasados que ya nadie veía a Dolores, que vivía siempre retirada en su hacienda . . . En estos días han circulado aquí rumores acerca de ella y de ti que no acierto a repetirlos . . . ¡Dime si esto es verdad!

—¿Qué verdad? pregunté angustiado y sin saber qué contestar.

—Dime si . . . ¡tú debes casarte con ella?

—Esa es una infame mentira forjada por don Basilio; ¡y que tú, Antonio, hayas podido dar oídos a esto!

—¡Por don Basilio! . . .

Y un momento después añadió:

—Tienes razón, Pedro, debe ser mentira entonces. Me admiro cómo no lo había pensado antes. Me dijeron aquí que pensabas irte mañana para N★★★: no espero más tiempo: no quiero creer en la repugnancia de Dolores por el matrimonio: ¿no me has dicho que me ama? Pues bien, tú mismo llevarás una carta pidiendo la mano de tu prima, y de cualquier modo haremos el matrimonio. Este es el mejor modo de contestar a semejante calumnia.

—Eso no puede ser! exclamé sin pensar en las consecuencias de mis palabras.

—¿Por qué?

—Ella dice que jamás se casará.

Antonio me miró sin contestarme y yo añadí:—Hay en su vida un misterio que no puedo revelar.

—¿Un misterio?

—Sí.

—Un misterio en la vida de una mujer no puede ser bueno. Exijo que se me diga en qué consiste. Yo no soy héroe de novela, y si se me engaña que sea con algo verosímil.

—No tengo libertad para revelártelo: Dolores me ha exigido el secreto.

—¡El secreto! ¡Y yo que empezaba a creerle! . . .

Y levantándose, se caló el sombrero con aire decidido, y con voz temblorosa de rabia me impuso silencio diciendo:—Basta ya. Nadie se burla de mí impunemente. No me replique usted; no quiero cometer una falta aquí; yo mandaré amigos que arreglen el asunto entre los dos.

—¡Un desafío!

—Así lo entiendo ¿acaso la cobardía es otra de las cualidades que lo distinguen a usted?

—La cólera te ciega, Antonio, contesté procurando guardar mi razón. Entre los dos no puede haber desafío. ¡Esto es hasta ridículo! Escúchame: te he dado mi palabra de que en esto hay una horrible equivocación.

—¿Qué pruebas me puede usted dar para creer que sus palabras son verídicas, puesto que asegura que Dolores no puede casarse?

—El tiempo . . .

—¡El tiempo! . . . ¡Usted es un cobarde!

—¡No permito que nadie me diga semejante cosa!

—Entonces acepta mi reto, o contesta a mi pregunta.

—Antonio, exclamé, haciendo el último esfuerza para no perder mi serenidad, Antonio, esto es absurdo. Si las circunstancias lo exigen, se-parémonos, ¡pero no como enemigos!

Antonio fuera de sí ya, se acercó con el brazo levantado.

—¡Cobarde e hipócrita! gritó.

Entonces olvidé toda consideración, y mostrándole la puerta dije:—Salga usted. Arregle las cosas como quiera y para cuando quiera.

Al día siguiente a las seis de la tarde me llevaban desmayado para la casa en que vivía. Cuando volví a recuperar mis sentidos me encontré tendido en la cama. Era de noche, y sentada a los pies de la cama vi dormida a la casera: traté de hablar y moverme, pero un dolor agu-dísimo en el pecho me obligó a estarme quieto. Estaba solo, sin pa-riente ni amigo que se condoliera de mí; la caridad de los dueños de casa era mi único amparo. Recordé entonces lo que me había sucedido: me ví nuevamente al frente de Antonio detrás de las colinas de San

Diego: cada uno de nosotros tenía una pistola en la mano: Julián me servía de testigo. La expresión de la fisonomía de Antonio era temible: me miraba con todo el odio nacido de su anterior cariño. En ese momento olvidé todo sentimiento religioso, todo recuerdo de mi padre . . . un profundo desaliento de la vida me dominaba; deseaba verdaderamente morir en aquel momento. Le apunté a Antonio, pero la memoria de Dolores y de su pena al saber que yo habría causado su muerte me hizo volver a mejores sentimientos y disparé al aire; pero al mismo tiempo sentí una fuerte conmoción y sin saber cómo, me encontré en el suelo . . . No recordaba más.

Volví a perder el juicio y por muchos días estuve entre la vida y la muerte. Cuando mis ojos se abrieron nuevamente a la luz y a la razón encontré a mi lado a mi padre, que acababa de llegar de N★★★ sin haber tenido noticia del estado en que me hallaba.

La siguiente carta de Dolores hará comprender mejor que otras explicaciones la causa del viaje imprevisto de mi padre.

No sé si recibiste una carta que te escribí hace algunos días. Es posible que se haya extraviado o que no hubieras entendido lo que en ella te decía. Ahora pienso explicarte con más claridad la causa del desorden de mi espíritu: estoy en completa calma y me creo capaz de abarcar con ánimo mi situación . . . ¡Con ánimo! ¡gran dios! En calma . . . ¡qué ironía! . . . no, Pedro estoy loca, desesperada.

He tenido momentos de verdadera demencia . . .

Sin embargo, quiero vencer la repugnancia, el horror que siento. Es preciso referírtelo todo.

Desde que estuve en el Espinal empecé a sentir mucho malestar, una agitación de nervios constante y una completa postración de ánimo. Sentía por turnos y en algunas horas, frío, calor, fuerza, debilidad, valor, desaliento, temor, audacia, en fin los sentimientos más contradictorios y las sensaciones más diversas. Al volver a N★★★ consulté a tu padre: me hizo varias preguntas y leí en su semblante la mayor emoción y desconsuelo a medida que le refería los síntomas del extraño mal que padecía. El pobre tío procuró infundirme valor asegurándome que esas novedades provenían de mis recientes penas.

Mi tía se empeñó en que consultase con otros médicos, pero yo no quería que me viese nadie. Al fin viendo que mi salud no mejoraba, llamaron sin consultarme a varias personas de los alrededores que pasan aquí por médicos, y su experiencia, si no el diploma, los hace dignos del título de doctores que les dan.

Se reunieron, pues, un día en la hacienda. Yo me presenté temblando, pero me acogieron con tanta bondad y me trataron con tan alegres chanzas, que fui perdiendo en presencia de ellos el horrible temor que me asaltaba. Antes de separarme comprendí que esos señores debían reunirse en la sala para dar su opinión. Quise saber la verdad y resolví oír ocultamente la consulta. Me retiré a mi cuarto, pero saliendo inmediatamente entré a una alcoba vecina de la sala y separada de ésta sólo por un cancel.

Me había tardado algunos momentos y cuando llegué a mi observatorio ya estaba empezada la conversación.

—¡Pobre niña! decía uno de ellos; me parece que no hay esperanza . . .

—El lázaro está en su segundo período apenas, repuso otro, y creo que se podría hacer algún esfuerzo.

—Eso apenas retardaría por algunos días más . . .

—Es cierto, dijeron todos, no hay ya remedio . . .

No supe qué más dijeron, ni lo que pasó por mí. Había procurado hacerme fuerte y ver con serenidad el mal que podía, que debía esperar. Pero al tener la seguridad de que era cierto lo que sólo temía, al encontrarme cara a cara con el espectro que había presentido, al contemplar de repente el horror de mi situación, no pude resistir a semejante dolor, y aunque no perdí el sentido, me tiré al suelo dominada por una completa postración de espíritu. No lloraba, ni me quejaba: mi desesperación no admitía desahogo. Un sollozo prolongado en el corredor me hizo volver en mí. Conocí la voz de mi tía, salí . . . al menos, pensé, ¡podremos llorar juntas! Guiada por el mismo interés que me animaba, también había querido conocer el fallo de los médicos, y al oír sus palabras no había podido resistir a su emoción.

Me le acerqué, pero al levantar los ojos y verme a su lado no pudo reprimir cierto movimiento de repugnancia que corrigió inmediatamente con una tierna mirada.

—Hija mía, me dijo alargándome la manos, ven, abrázame.

Pero su primer movimiento había sido como una puñalada para mí: no lo pude olvidar, y huyendo entré a mi cuarto sin querer oírla, y me encerré. ¡Me sentía sola, completamente abandonada en el mundo! Después de esto no recuerdo más. Parece que mi tía, cansándose de llamarme y no teniendo contestación alguna se había alarmado, y auxiliada por tu padre forzaron la puerta y ¡me encontraron loca!

Sí, Pedro: fue tal mi desesperación que perdí el juicio por algunos días. Cuando volví a la razón y contemplé la horrible existencia que me aguardaba, en lo primero que pensé fue en escribirte. Tú has sido siempre un amigo en cuya simpatía creo; un hermano, cuyo apoyo ha sido mi consuelo siempre. A ti apelé: no recuerdo qué te decía; todavía había en mi mente una nube de demencia. Tu padre me dice que no ha perdido completamente la esperanza, y parte para Bogotá a consultar él mismo los mejores médicos del país. Si hubiera esperanza, ¡Dios mío! . . . ¡si hubiera esperanza!

La carta a que se refería Dolores era la que había determinado mi partida para N★★★, partida que se había interrumpido trágicamente.

Apenas pude levantarme quise acompañar a mi padre a casa de los mejores médicos de Bogotá, quienes nos dieron algunos medicamentos con los cuales decían haberse mejorado notablemente varios lazarinos. Mi padre regresó a N★★★. Yo me quedé solo, triste, enfermo todavía, desalentado y sin proyectos ya para lo porvenir.

En eso supe que un rico capitalista partía enfermo para Europa y deseaba llevar un médico que lo asistiera durante su viaje. Me le ofrecí y me aceptó con gusto: pero antes de partir no pude resistir al deseo de ir a abrazar a mi padre y ver a mis parientes. Por otra parte deseaba arreglar las pocas propiedades de que podía disponer para tener algunos recursos con que subsistir algunos años en Europa.

Llegué inesperadamente a N★★★, y después de haber pasado algunas horas con mi padre fui a casa de la tía Juana. Estaba sola y muy triste: la enfermedad de Dolores no tenía ningún alivio. Me decía que no quería vivir sino en la hacienda; y prorrumpiendo en llanto la pobre tía añadió que no se dejaba ver de nadie, y no permitía que se le acercasen. Yo traté de consolarla diciendo que iría a verla y procuraría dulcificar sus pensamientos y mejorar su género de vida.

Al principio mi prima rehusó verme, pero cuando le hice saber que partía pronto para un viaje tan lejano accedió a mi deseo.

Estaba sentada en un sillón y el cuarto muy oscuro: así con su vestido blanco se veía como un espectro entre las sombras. No quería que yo me acercase a ella; pero usando de mis prerrogativas de primo y hermano le tomé las manos por fuerza y abriendo de improviso una ventana quise contemplar los estragos que aquel mal había hecho en ella.

Estaba ya empezando el tercer período de la enfermedad. La linda color de rosa que había asustado a mi padre, y que es el primer síntoma del mal, se cambió en desencajamiento y en la palidez amarillenta que había notado en ella en el Espinal: ahora se mostraba abotagada y su cutis áspera tenía un color morado. Su belleza había desaparecido completamente y sólo sus ojos conservaban un brillo demasiado vivo. Comprendí que ya no tenía esperanzas de mejoría, pero procuré ocultar mi sorpresa: ciertamente no esperaba encontrar en ella semejante cambio. Al principio permaneció callada, pero cuando le expliqué las penas de la tía Juana, me confió que su aparente despego y el deseo de aislarse provenían de un plan que había ideado y que tenía la determinación de llevar a cabo.

—Quiero que mi tía se enseñe a nuestra separación, pues no pienso vivir más tiempo a su lado.

—¿Y dónde te irás?

—Viviré sola. Mi tía tiene un horror, una repugnancia singular al mal que sufro, y sé que vivirá martirizada. Por otra parte, es tal el temor que me causa una voz extraña . . . veo a la humanidad entera como un enemigo que me persigue, que me acosa, y he resuelto separarme de todo el que me tema.

—¿Pero cómo?

—¿No recuerdas aquel sitio tan lindo donde nos despedimos la última vez que estuviste aquí?

—¿La quebradita?

—Allí quiero mandar hacer una casita y acompañada por los muchachos que sirvieron a mi padre hasta sus últimos momentos (ellos no me tienen repugnancia) viviré aislada, pero en mi soledad estaré tranquila.

—Esa es una locura, Dolores ¿cómo sería tu vida enmedio del monte? no, eso no puede ser.

—En lugar de disuadirme, Pedro, ténme lástima y ayúdame a llevar a cabo mi propósito, Si no, añadió apretándose las manos con ademán desesperado, si no, huiré, me iré sola al monte y moriré como una fiera de los bosques. Mira: he sentido mayor desesperación al comprender que inspiro horror. ¡Dios mío! si no me permiten vivir sola, ocultarme a todos los ojos, no sé qué haré . . . no es difícil quitarse uno la vida.

El estado de exasperación en que se hallaba la pobre joven no admitía razonamientos y tuve que ofrecerla mi cooperación a su plan.

—¿Y Antonio? preguntó al cabo de un momento de silencio y haciendo un esfuerzo para serenarse.

—No lo he visto, ¿acaso no has sabido? . . .

—Sí, tu padre me lo refirió todo. ¡Yo he sido la causa de tus penas y peligros, y sin embargo ni un consuelo, ni una señal de gratitud has recibido de mí! Perdóname: las penas nos hacen egoístas. Te confesaré mi debilidad: me llena de espanto la idea de que Antonio me recuerde con repugnancia.

—¿Pero no es peor que te tenga en mal concepto?

—Sí, es cierto; no lo había pensado. ¡Que lo sepa todo!

Y al decir esto prorrumpió en amargo llanto.

—Dile también a Mercedes lo que quieras, añadió.

—Ya Mercedes no es nada para mí. No quiero darle explicaciones: ella debió haber tenido fe en mi lealtad.

Dolores me miró un momento.

—Tú no la amaste nunca, pues cuando uno ama no tiene orgullo: no puede haber resentimiento duradero, ni pique, ni mala voluntad respecto del ser amado.

—No hablemos más de ella. Mercedes tiene otros pretendientes y yo ni la recuerdo.

Me despedí prometiéndole hablar con mi tía, lo que efectivamente hice, procurando hacerle comprender que la vida de Dolores dependía de que hiciese su voluntad.

Algunos días después me reuní con mi compañero en Honda y bajamos el Magdalena sin novedad, embarcándonos en Santamarta a principios del siguiente mes.

PARTE TERCERA

Sólo busco en la selva más lejana
Tétrico albergue, asilo tenebroso
No pisado jamás de huella humana.

Vicenta Maturana

Je meurs, et sur ma tombe, ou lentement j'arrive,
Nul ne viendra verser des pleurs.[12]

Gilbert

Durante los primeros meses de mi permanencia en Europa recibí varias cartas de mi padre en que me daba cuenta de la salud de Dolores. Empeoraba cada día, y al cabo de algunos meses ya todos habían perdido completamente las esperanzas. A pesar de los esfuerzos que hacían, consultando a los médicos más afamados del país, la horrible y misteriosa enfermedad continuaba con su mano desoladora destruyendo la belleza y aún la figura humana de mi infeliz prima. Ella vivía oculta, sin aire y sin luz, rogando que le permitiesen huir lejos de aquella atmósfera que la sofocaba.

Al fin entre otras cartas recibí la siguiente, de Dolores:

¡Ya no hay remedio, mi querido Pedro! Hace dos meses que he muerto para el mundo y me hallo en esta soledad. Tú escucharás con paciencia mis quejas, ¡oh! ¡ténme piedad!

Pero no, ¿por qué quejarme? la Providencia es ciega, y hay momentos . . . No me atrevo a leer lo que hay en el fondo de mi alma. Voy a referirte cómo fue mi despedida de mi tía y la llegada aquí. Si mi carta es incoherente, perdónamela: ¡mi espíritu cede a veces a tantos sufrimientos!

No sé si tú lo sabías, pero fueron tantas mis instancias, que al fin logré que se empezara a construir una casita, una pequeña choza, aunque aseada y cómoda, en el sitio que indiqué. Yo misma quise ir a mostrar el lugar exacto en que debía quedar. Sin embargo se pasaron meses antes de que la acabasen, y aunque yo rogaba que la concluyeran pronto, conocí que mi tía no podía resolverse a esta separación. Pero fatigada ya de rogar, amenacé seriamente que me huiría de la casa y conseguí mi deseo.

Yo permanecía oculta siempre y hablaba con mi tía y tu padre al través de la reja de la ventana de mi cuarto, y por entre las rendijas de mi puerta.

Un día me vinieron a decir que la casa estaba concluida y habían llevado los muebles necesarios, mis pájaros y algunas flores. Mi pobre tía se había esmerado en que tuviese cuantas comodidades podía apetecer. Tu padre me vino a decir, después de hacerme algunas recomendaciones higiénicas, que entre lo que habían llevado a mi futura casa se hallaba un pequeño botiquín y una relación sobre el modo de usarlo. 'Ahí encontrarás todo, me dijo, según la marcha de la enfermedad hasta, hasta. . . . ' Al pronunciar estas palabras el buen anciano que tanto me había mimado prorrumpió en sollozos. Yo había entreabierto la puerta para hablar con él más cómodamente, y al oír aquella señal de vivísimo dolor, sentí en mi corazón una desesperación indomable, y abriendo la puerta enteramente me hinqué en el suelo exclamando con angustia:—¡Oh! tío, tío . . . usted tiene en su poder el hacerme penar menos; ¡oh! por Dios, deme un remedio . . . un remedio que acorte mi vida!

Tu padre se cubrió la cara con las manos y no me contestó. Pero en eso oí que mi tía venía por el corredor e inmediatamente me volvió el juicio, y haciendo un esfuerzo de voluntad violento me levanté y entrando a mi pieza cerré la puerta. Pero ella me había visto y me gritó golpeando en la puerta:—¡Dolores, Dolores! este sacrificio es demasiado grande, tú no puedes dejarme así.

Tuve una debilidad de un instante; pero eso ya pasó, le contesté con voz segura:—mañana me quiero ir a la madrugada, pero ruego por última vez que a mi salida nadie se me acerque.

Esa noche dormí tranquila. Ya había pasado la agitación y me sentía fuerte ante mi resolución. Antes de aclarar el día me vinieron a decir que mi caballo estaba preparado. Me levanté, y saliendo de mi cuarto atravesé el corredor en que estaba mi pajarera y ví por última vez el jardín, la alberca, los árboles . . . todo, todo lo que me recordaba mi feliz niñez y los sueños de mi corta juventud. No quise pensar, ni detenerme: la luz fría y triste del amanecer empezaba a iluminar los objetos que tomaban un aspecto fantástico. Mi perro favorito me siguió dando saltos de alegría.

El mayordomo, que debía acompañarme hasta mi choza y dos o tres sirvientes más me esperaban en el patio. Yo no quise aceptar el apoyo de nadie y de un salto monté a caballo.

—¡Adios! dije con voz ahogada dirigiéndome a los criados, díganle a mi tía . . .

No pude añadir otra cosa, y azotando con las riendas al caballo, que es muy brioso, salí como un relámpago del patio seguida por el mayordomo. No sé qué sentí entonces. Mi vida entera en sus más íntimos pormenores pasó ante mi imaginación, como dicen sucede a los que se están ahogando. Creo que iba a perder el sentido y dejarme caer del caballo, cuando un grito ahogado por la distancia me hizo detener mi cabalgadura, y mirando hacia atrás vi venir a mi tía que había montado y me seguía.

—¡Hija mía, Dolores! me dijo al acercarse. ¿Creías que yo permitiría que salieras de mi casa como una criminal sin que te acompañara siquiera hasta tu destierro?

—Perdón, tía; sí lo creí, y me desgarraba el corazón esta idea; pero como usted me había ofrecido no volverme a ver . . .

—Sí, sí lo dije. ¿Pero cómo dejar de verte, de hablarte por la última vez?

Dejé volar mi pañuelo al viento para ver de dónde venía y poniéndome del lado opuesto le contesté:—Una sola vez y al aire libre no podrá serle funesto. Prométame, sin embargo, que no se me acercará; si no me lo ofrece, juro, tía, que pondré en acción mi amenaza y me iré lejos de aquí: me ocultaré y moriré en el fondo del monte.

—Tía, añadí después, ésta es nuestra última conversación. Hablemos con toda la cordura y resignación que puede tener un cristiano en su lecho de muerte. No permitamos que nos interrumpan lágrimas, y no seamos débiles. El sacrificio indispensable está hecho;

aceptémoslo como una prueba enviada por la Providencia. Cuando lleguemos a orillas del monte me adelantaré sin decir nada. No pronunciemos la palabra adiós; ambas necesitamos de un valor que nos abandonaría si nos despidiésemos.

Así se hizo. Conversamos tranquilamente, en apariencia, del modo como arreglaría mi vida, pero teníamos el corazón despedazado. Cuando llegamos al estrecho camino que recordarás, me adelanté en silencio y al cruzar por la vereda que conduce a mi choza volví involuntariamente la cara: al través de los árboles vi a mi tía que se había detenido y me miraba partir con profunda pena. ¡Probablemente no la volveré a ver jamás! . . .

Por mucho tiempo no volví a recibir noticias de Dolores: mi padre me decía apenas que continuaba en su soledad y había prohibido que nadie se le acercase. Una vez me escribió lleno de tribulación. Parece que un día le vinieron a decir que Dolores estaba sumamente indispuesta: él se hallaba en la hacienda de mi tía y no pudo evitar que supiese lo que decían de Dolores. La tía Juana se alarmó y quiso a todo trance, y sin acordarse de su promesa, acompañar a mi padre a la choza de mi prima.

Llegaron hasta la casa, sin ser vistos, compuesta de una salita y una alcoba; separábala de la cocina y despensa un patiecito lleno de flores, y entre los bejucos que enredaban en el diminuto corredor colgaban jaulas llenas de pájaros. Penetraron a la salita, adornada con varios muebles y muchos libros sobre las mesas. Al ruido que hicieron al entrar, Dolores salió de la alcoba sin precaución alguna. Estaba tan desfigurada que mi tía dio un grito de espanto y se cubrió la cara con las manos. Dolores se detuvo un momento, y al ver la expresión de la fisonomía de sus tíos pasó cerca de ellos sin decir nada y tomó la puerta. Mi padre la siguió llamándola y la vio internarse en el monte. Viendo que no contestaba corrió hacia el sitio en que había desaparecido: caminó por la orilla de la quebrada, llamándola a cada paso, hasta que llegó a un sitio más abierto; pero el monte espeso se cerraba completamente más arriba, y la quebrada encajonándose entre dos rocas, no podía atravesarse sino llevando el agua hasta las rodillas. Dolores no parecía ni contestaba: mi padre creyó que había tomado otra senda y volvió a la casa para consultar con los sirvientes de mi prima. Ellos no la habían visto nunca salir así, pero inmediatamente corrieron a buscarla. Mi tía estaba tan conmovida e inmutada, que mi padre le aconsejó que volviera a la hacienda mientras que él se quedaría buscando a Dolores.

Se pasaron horas y no era posible encontrarla. Los sirvientes y todos los peones de la hacienda se pusieron en movimiento, pero llegó la noche, la que pasó también sin noticia alguna. Los primeros rayos del sol encontraron todavía a mi padre lleno de angustia, pues además de la desaparición de Dolores, mi tía se había enfermado gravemente.

Mejor será trascribir ahora una parte de la carte que recibí de Dolores, dándome noticia de lo sucedido.

. . . Creí, Pedro, que nunca volverías a saber de mí . . . quise morir, amigo mío, y no pude lograrlo. En días pasados me sentía muy enferma, tanto material como espiritualmente: mi postración era horrible y pasé días sin hablar ni tomar casi alimento alguno. Isidora y su hermano probablemente se alarmaron al verme en ese estado, y dieron aviso a la familia: no he querido preguntarles cómo llegaron repentinamente a mi choza tu padre y mi tía Juana. Al verme, fue tal el horror que se pintó en sus semblantes, que comprendí en un segundo que yo no debía hacer parte de la humanidad, y sin saber lo que hacía salí de la casa. Creo que perdí el juicio: me parecía oír tras de mí la carrera de cien caballos desbocados que me perseguían, y oía el ladrar de innumerables perros . . . Subí desalada por la orilla de la quebrada, y al llegar a un sitio más inculto atravesé sus aguas sin sentir que me mojaba ni pensar que me hería en los espinos del monte. Al fin se me acabaron las fuerzas y me detuve. Ya no oía los gritos ni las carreras de los que creí me perseguían y me encontré sola en medio de la montaña: no había más ruido que el zumbido de los insectos, el trinar de los pájaros y el chasquido de las hojas secas al romperlas con los pies. Estaba completamente exánime: no sé si me dormí o me desmayé, pero caí al suelo como un cuerpo inerte. Cuando volví en mí la oscuridad era casi completa en el fondo del bosque. ¿Qué hacer? La muerte se me presentó como un descanso. Me levanté para buscar un precipicio, pero la montaña en aquel sitio está en un declive suave del cerro y no hallé lugar alguno que fuera a propósito.

No sentía dolor ninguno (tú sabes que a consecuencia de la enfermedad se pierde la sensibilidad cutánea) y sin embargo me había desgarrado y estaba inundada de sangre y los vestidos hechos pedazos.

Después de haber vagado largo tiempo llegué a un sitio más abierto en donde al pie de algunos árboles altísimos se veían anchas piedras cubiertas de musgo. Se sentía allí un fresco delicioso: me recosté sobre una piedra y levanté los ojos al cielo. La noche había llegado, y a medida que el suelo se cubría de sombras el cielo se poblaba de estrellas. Las lámparas celestes se encendían una a una como cirios en un altar. ¡Cuántas constelaciones, qué maravillosa titilación en esos lejanos soles, qué inmensidad de mundos y de universos sin fin . . . ! Poco a poco la misteriosa magnificencia de aquel espectáculo fue calmando mi desesperación. ¿Qué cosa era yo para rebelarme contra la suerte? Esos rayos de la luz morían antes de llegar a mi rincón, y sin embargo parecían mirarme con compasión . . . ¡Compasión! ¿todos no me tienen horror? No, hay tal vez algún ser que me recuerde todavía con ternura: te diré la verdad; la memoria de Antonio me salvó, y creí comprender como por intuición que no me había olvidado. ¿No bastaría la seguridad de su lejana simpatía para vivir resignada? No me creas ingrata: también te recordé; tú al menos no te mostraste espantado al verme.

La noche estaba estrellada pero muy oscura. Me sentía sin valor para pasarla entera en medio de aquella selva. Al desaparecer la agitación nerviosa que me animaba, sentí una gran postración y deseaba encontrar un sitio seguro en que pudiera recostarme sin temor. Recordé que había subido por la quebrada, y por la vista de las estrellas que tanto había contemplado en mi soledad me orienté. Busqué un lucero que brilla siempre en el confín del cielo al caer el sol, y me dirigí hacia un lado en que debía hallarse la choza de una pobre tullida que vivía en el monte con un hijo tonto. A poco comprendí que había encontrado un angosto sendero y procuré seguirlo. No sé cómo no me picaron mil animales venenosos que se arrastraban por el suelo, colgaban de las ramas y volaban chillando en torno mío. Desapareció la estrella tras de los árboles y la noche se hacía cada vez más oscura: había perdido los zapatos, y los pies rehusaban llevarme más lejos, cuando oí el ladrido de un perro: ¡qué música tan deliciosa fue aquella para mí! Algunos pasos más lejos encontré la choza y defendiéndome del perro con un palo que había tomado en el monte y me servía de bastón, empujé el junco que servía de puerta y despertando a la tullida pedí licencia para acostarme en un rincón.

Pasé la noche como una miserable, despertándome sobresalta[da] a cada momento, pero el cansancio me hacía dormir otra vez. Cuando amaneció, el tonto se levantó y encendiendo fuego enmedio del rancho, puso una olla sobre tres piedras que había allí e hizo un caldo con yucas, plátanos y carne salada. Yo permanecía en mi rincón sin moverme, hasta que habiéndome brindado un plato con hirviente caldo comprendí que mi mayor debilidad provenía de la falta de alimentos. Acepté y tomé con gusto lo que me ofrecían y al acabar rompí el plato como por descuido y tiré la cuchara.

A medida que subía el sol el calor aumentaba en el rancho y al fin salí a la puerta a respirar el aire. Mi vestido enlodado y hecho pedazos, los cabellos desgreñados y mi aspecto indudablemente terrible causaron impresión a los dueños de casa. Imposible que me reconocieran, aunque en otro tiempo había visitado algunas veces a la enferma. Pero aunque no sabían quien era, la tullida adivinó la enfermedad de que padecía y me dijo con dulzura que sería mejor que me fuera a sentar en el alar . . . Comprendí la repugnancia que inspiraba aún a aquellos desgraciados y me salí profundamente humillada. Deseaba mandar decir a mis parientes que no volvería otra vez a mi choza hasta que no me ofreciesen solemnemente que jamás irían a ella. El tonto no podía hablar claro ¿cómo mandar a decir lo que deseaba? Busqué un lápiz que llevaba en el bolsillo y que por casualidad no se había perdido en mi huida, y la tullida me dio un pedacito de papel que el tonto había llevado con unos remedios enviados por la tía Juana. Sobre un tronco de árbol caído que había cerca de la casa, puse el papelito y con mano trémula escribí algunas líneas y se las di al tonto para que las llevase a la hacienda, prometiendo pagarle bien.

Esa tarde llegaron mis dos sirvientes. Isidora me trajo ropa y Juan un caballo ensillado y una carta de tu padre en la que me decía que mi tía estaba gravemente enferma a causa de las penas que yo les había dado: por último me ofrecía no intentar verme sin mi consentimiento.

Volví a mi choza a cuidarme . . . sí, ¡me cuidé! ¡Oh triste humanidad! ¿No era mejor dejarme morir? Siempre encontramos en nuestro corazón este amor a la vida, y por lo mismo que es miserable como que nos complacemos en conservarla . . . Sí, Pedro: mientras yo cuidaba mi horrible existencia, mientras recuperaba fuerzas para seguir viviendo, mi pobre tía moría de resultas del terror, de la aprehensión y de la angustia que yo le había causado. Parece que se le declaró una fiebre violenta y al cabo de dos días sucumbió sin conocer a nadie, pero asediada por mi recuerdo y llamándome sin cesar. Acaso me creerás insensible, desnaturalizada, al ver que puedo hablar tranquilamente de la muerte de la que me quiso tanto. No sé qué decir: no me comprendo a mí misma y creo que hasta he perdido la facultad de sentir. Nunca lloro: la fuente de las lágrimas se ha secado; no me quejo, ni me conmuevo. Deseo la muerte con ansia, pero no me atrevo a buscarla y aun procuro evitarla.

Mi espíritu es un caos: mi existencia una horrible pesadilla. Mándame, te lo suplico, algunos libros. Quiero alimentar mi espíritu con bellas ideas: deseo vivir con los muertos y comunicar con ellos.

La carta de Dolores me impresionó vivamente. Comprendí que su carácter tan dulce había cambiado con el sufrimiento, y esto me dio la medida de sus penas. Busqué algunos libros buenos y se los envié. Durante los siguientes años recibí apenas algunas breves cartas de Dolores: el fondo de ellas era de una tristeza desgarradora a veces, con cierta incredulidad religiosa y odio al género humano en sus pensamientos, que me llenaban de pena. Mi padre me escribía que nunca la había vuelto a ver, pero que mandaba una persona todas las semanas a llevarle lo que podía necesitar y recoger noticias de ella.

Antonio se había arrepentido de su conducta ligera conmigo, y continuábamos una correspondencia muy activa. El primer golpe de dolor al comprender la horrible suerte de Dolores y la imposibilidad de que jamás fuera suya; ese rudo golpe no fue para él causa de desaliento: su carácter enérgico no permitía eso, y al contrario procuró vencer su pena dedicándose a un trabajo arduo y a un estudio constante. Pronto se hizo conocer como un hombre de talento, laborioso y elocuente, y alcanzó a ocupar un lugar honroso entre los estadistas del país.

Había pasado varios años estudiando en Europa y me preparaba a volver a la patria, cuando llegó la noticia de la muerte de mi padre. No diré lo que sentí entonces . . . Dolores me escribió también manifestándome la desolación en que había quedado.

Aunque al principio me repugnaba la idea de visitar mi hogar vacío, no pude resistir al deseo de volver al lado de Dolores y me embarqué.

Llegué a Bogotá de paso, pero allí me detuvo António para que asistiese a su matrimonio. Se casaba con una señorita de las mejores familias de la capital, rica y digna de mucha estimación. Inmediatamente le escribí a Dolores la causa de mi detención, participándole la noticia del brillante matrimonio que hacía Antonio.

El matrimonio fue rumboso si no alegre. La novia no era bella; pero sus modales cultos, educación esmerada y bondad natural, hacían olvidar sus pocos atractivos. Cuando, después de la ceremonia me despedí de Antonio en la puerta de su casa, me entregó una carta para Dolores; carta que había escrito ese día, y en sus ojos vi brillar una lágrima, último tributo a sus ensueños juveniles.

Ocho días después llegaba a las cercanías de N★★★ y en vez de entrar al pueblo me dirigí inmediatamente por un camino extraviado al rincón del valle en que vivía Dolores. Al llegar a la vereda que años antes había pasado con mi prima, mi imaginación me trajo otra vez el recuerdo del esbelto talle de Dolores, su brillante mirada y alegres palabras: oía de nuevo el eco de su argentina risa que me parecía vibraba todavía en aquellas soledades. ¡Cómo había cambiado mi vida desde entonces! Mi tía había muerto, mi pobre padre también, mi novia era la esposa de otro (no sé si he dicho, que casó con don Basilio) y en fin, mi prima, la alegre niña de otro tiempo, era un ser profundamente desgraciado. No había querido entrar al pueblo que tenía para mí tan tristes recuerdos, y nada sabía de Dolores.

Cuando me acerqué al sitio en que debía hallarse la choza de mi prima, sentí cierto rumor que me admiró. Bajo un árbol estaban varios caballos ensillados: piqué el mío y llegué a la puerta de la casita a tiempo que salían de ella el cura y varios vecinos de N★★★.

—¡Qué encuentro tan casual! dijo el cura al reconocerme y deteniéndome en la puerta.

Era un respetable anciano que había sido cura de mi pueblo desde mi infancia.

—¿Dolores está adentro? pregunté después de haberle saludado.

—¡Dolores! No sabía usted acaso . . . ?

—¿Qué? Deseo hablarla.

—No, no entre, me contestó tomándome la mano.

—¿Qué ha sucedido?

—¡Pobre niña! me dijo con voz conmovida: ¡esta mañana dejó de padecer!

—¡Dios mío! exclamé sintiendo que hasta el último eslabón que me ligaba a los recuerdos de mi provincia había desaparecido; y entonces comprendí cuán necesario había sido para mí ese afecto.

Sentándome en silencio en el quicio de la puerta de la casa de Dolores, escondí la cara entre las manos. Los que rodeaban al cura se alejaron por un sentimiento de delicadeza; el cura se sentó a mi lado.

—Su muerte fue la de una cristiana, dijo el buen sacerdote. Hace algunos días me mandó rogar que viniera a verla; que no había necesidad de que me acercase, pues hablaría conmigo al través de la puerta de su alcoba. Vine varias veces y ayer se confesó y recibió lo auxilios de la religión. Esta mañana me fueron a decir que se estaba muriendo, y hasta entonces no pude verla: ¡no le diré a usted cuán cambiada estaba!

—Ahora, añadió al cabo de un momento, habiéndola visto expirar volvía a la parroquia para disponer el entierro.

Yo cumplí con mi deber. Asistí al entierro. Había dispuesto que la enterrasen en el patio de la casita y mandó que todo aquello quedase inhabitado.

Entre sus papeles hallé un testamento a mi favor y varias composiciones en prosa y verso. He aquí algunos fragmentos de un diario que llevaba y que hacen comprender mejor su carácter y los horribles padecimientos morales que sufría, sus vacilaciones y su desesperación.

23 de junio 1843.

Hace un año que sufro sola, aislada, abandonada por el mundo entero en este desierto. ¡Oh! si hubiera alguien que se acordara de mí ¿cómo no me hubieran de llegar ráfagas de consuelo que inspiraran resignación a este corazón desgarrado? A lo lejos en la llanura corren y se divierten. Mañana es día de San Juan, aniversario de las fiestas de N★★★. ¡Las fiestas! ¡qué de recuerdos me traen a la memoria! Hoy encontré por casualidad un ramo de jazmines secos ¿podrá creerse que este ser monstruoso que aparece ante mí al acercarme al espejo es la bella niña a quien fueron regaladas estas flores? Antonio, Antonio, tú a quien amo en el secreto de mi alma, cuya memoria es mi único consuelo, Antonio, ¿te acordarás acaso todavía de la infeliz a quien amaste? ¡Si supieras cómo me persigue tu imagen! Resuena tu nombre en el susurrante ramaje de los árboles, en el murmullo de la corriente, en el perfume de mis flores favoritas, en el viento que silba, entre las páginas del libro en que me fijo, en la punta de la pluma con que escribo; veo tus iniciales en el ancho campo estrellado, entre las nubes al caer el sol, entre la arena del riachuelo en que me baño . . . ¡Dios Santo! que este amor sea tan grande, tan profundo, tan inagotable, y sin embargo mi corazón ardiente yace mudo para siempre!"

Diciembre 8 de 1843.

La vida es un negro ataúd en el cual nos hallamos encerrados. ¿La muerte es acaso principio de otra vida? ¡Qué ironía! En el fondo de mi pensamiento sólo hallo el sentimiento de la nada. Si hubiera un Dios justo y misericordioso como lo quieren pintar ¿dejaría penar una alma desgraciada como yo? ¡Oh! muerte, ven, ¡ven a socorrer al ser más infeliz de la tierra! Soledad en todas partes, silencio, quietud, desesperante calma en la naturaleza . . . El cielo me inspira horror con su espantosa hermosura: la luna no me conmueve con su tan elogiada belleza: el campo me causa tedio: las flores me traen recuerdos de mi pasada vida. Flores, campos, puros aromas, armonías de la naturaleza que son emblemas de vida ¿por qué venir a causar tan hondos sentimientos a la que ya no existe? . . .

Mayo de 1844.

. . . Espantoso martirio . . . la enfermedad no sigue su curso ordinario. ¿Viviré aun muchos años? Hay noches en que despierto llena de agitación: soñé que al fin pude conseguir una pistola; pero al quererme matar no dio fuego y en mi pugna por dispararla desperté . . . Otras veces imagino que estoy nadando en un caudaloso

río, y me dejo llevar dulcemente por las olas que van consumién-
dome; pero al sentir que me ahogo, me despierta un intenso
movimiento de alegría.

Febrero de 18[45.][13]

Recibí hoy una carta de Pedro que me ha consolado. Hay todavía
alguien, además de mi buen tío, que se acuerda de mí . . . Había
dicho que esta carta me había consolado . . . ¡mentira! La he vuelto
a leer y me ha causado un sufrimiento nuevo. Me habla de su vida
tranquila, de sus estudios y proyectos para lo porvenir. Los hombres
son los seres más crueles de la creación: se complacen en hacernos
comprender nuestro infortunio. En los siglos de la edad media,
cuando se le declaraba lázaro a alguno, era inmediatamente considerado como un cadáver: lo llevaban a la iglesia, le cantaban la misa de
difuntos y lo recluían por el resto de sus días como ser inmundo . . .
Pero al menos ellos no volvían a tener comunicación con la sociedad; morían moralmente y jamás llegaban a sus oídos los ecos
de la vida de los seres que amaron. Y yo, yo que me he retirado al
fondo de un bosque americano, hasta aquí me persigue el recuerdo
. . . ¿Amar qué es? Amar es sentir gratas emociones: los médicos
dicen que el lazarino ha perdido el sistema nervioso ¿para qué siento
yo, por qué recuerdo con ternura los seres que amé? . . .

Abril de 1845.

. . . ¡Dios, la religión, la vida futura! ¡Cuestiones insondables!
¡Terribles vacilaciones de mi alma! ¡Si mi mal fuera solamente físico,
si tuviera solamente enfermo el cuerpo! Pero cambia la naturaleza
del carácter y cada día siento que me vuelvo cruel como una fiera
de estos montes, fría y dura ante la humanidad como las piedras de
la quebrada. Hay momentos en que en un acceso de locura vuelo a
mis flores, que parecen insultarme con su hermosura, y las despe-
dazo, las tiro al viento: un momento después me vuelve la razón, las
busco enternecida y lloro al encontrarlas marchitas. Otras veces mi
alma se rebela, no puede creer en que un Dios bueno me haga
sufrir tanto, y en mi rebeldía niego su existencia: después . . . me
humillo, me prosterno y caigo en una adoración sin fin ante el Ser
Supremo. . . .

Septiembre de 1845.

Siempre el silencio, la soledad, la ausencia de una voz amiga que me acaricie con un tono de simpatía. ¡La eterna separación! ¿Podrá haber idea más aterradora para un ser nacido para amar?

1 de enero de 1846.

Atravieso una época de desaliento y de letargo completo. He vivido últimamente como en sueños . . . No estoy triste ni desesperada. Siento que en mi corazón no hay nada: todo me es indiferente: la vida es el sufrimiento, la muerte . . . todo pasa y se mezcla en las tinieblas de mi alma, y nada me llega a conmover. ¡Una emoción! una emoción aunque fuera de pena, de miedo, de espanto (lo único a que puedo aspirar) sería bendecida por mí como un alivio: ¡tal es el estado en que me encuentro! Es peor esto que mi loca desesperación de los tiempos pasados. Vegeto como un árbol carcomido: vivo como una roca en un lugar desierto. . . .

Marzo de 1846.

A veces me propongo estudiar, leer, aprender para hacer algo, dedicarme al trabajo intelectual y olvidar así mi situación: procuro huir de mí misma, pero siempre, siempre el pensamiento me persigue, y como dice un autor francés: *"Le chagr[i]n monte en croupe et galope avec moi."*[14]

La mujer es esencialmente amante, y en todos los acontecimientos de la vida quiere brillar solamente ante los seres que ama. La vanidad en ella es por amor, como en el hombre es por ambición. ¿Para quién aprendo yo? Mis estudios, mi instrucción, mi talento, si acaso fuera cierto que lo tuviera, todo esto es inútil, pues jamás podré inspirar un sentimiento de admiración: estoy sola, sola para siempre. . . .

6 Septiembre de 1846.

Ya todo acabó para mí. Pronto moriré: mi mano apenas puede trazar estas líneas con dificultad. ¡Cuánto había deseado este día! pero ¿por qué no he tenido la dicha de morir antes, cuando tenía una ilusión? Acaso soy injusta; pero este golpe aflojó, por decirlo así, la última cadena que me ligaba a la existencia. Recibí una carta de Pedro fechada en Bogotá: ¡pobre primo mío! pensé al abrirla; pronto podré oír tu voz; y también por él tendré alguna noticia directa de Antonio . . . Mi corazón latía con una dulce emoción y me sentía desfallecer. Me senté a orillas del riachuelo que corre murmurando cerca de mi habitación. ¡Con cuánto gusto había visto llegar al sirviente que trajo la carta! La imagen de Antonio vagaba en torno mío. . . .

Después de leer las primeras líneas una nube pasó ante mis ojos. Pedro me daba parte del matrimonio de Antonio ¡el matrimonio de Antonio! ¿Por qué rehusaba creerlo al principio? ¿No es él libre para amar a otra? Sin embargo, la desolación más completa, más agobiadora se apoderó de mí: me hinqué sobre la playa y me dejé llevar por toda la tempestad de mi dolor. Me veía sola, ¡oh! cuán sola, sin la única simpatía que anhelaba. Todo en torno mío me hablaba de Antonio, y sólo su recuerdo poblaba mi triste habitación. No había rincón de mi choza, no había árbol o flor en mi jardín, ni estrella en el azul del cielo, ni pajarillo que trinara, que no me dijera algo en nombre de él. Mi vida hacía parte de su recuerdo; ¿y ahora? El ama a otra ¡qué absurda idea! ¡a cuántas no habrá amado desde que nos separamos! ¡Cosa rara! esto no me había preocupado antes, y ahora esta idea no me abandona un momento. Como que mi alma esperaba este último desengaño para desprenderse de este cuerpo miserable. Comprendo que todos los síntomas son de una pronta muerte. ¡Gracias, Dios mío! Dejo ya todo sufrimiento; pero *él* es mi pensamiento en estos momentos supremos: ¡oh! ¡*él* me olvidará y será dichoso!

FIN

Notas

1. "La naturaleza es un drama con personajes."
2. Un *cachaco* es un joven elegante, de Bogotá o del centro del país.
3. Una *ñapanga* es una mujer mestiza.
4. Hacer un buen partido; casarse bien.

5. "Ella tiene bastante bonitos ojos . . . para ojos de provincia."

6. "El que vence sin peligro, triunfa sin gloria."

7. Venus es la diosa del amor; Lucrecia, matrona romana, es el modelo de la fidelidad conyugal; Minerva es la diosa de la sabiduría; Virginia es la heroina de la novela popular *Paul et Virginie* (1787) de Bernardin de St. Pierre; Pegaso es el caballo alado de la mitología griega.

8. "El dolor es una luz que nos aclara la vida."

9. Los Borgia (o Borja), era una famosa familia de origen español en los siglos XV y XVI, uno de cuyos miembros llegó a ser santo (San Francisco Borja), pero otros, como el Papa Alejandro VI, y su hijo, Cesare, tenían pocos escrúpulos y fama de eliminar a sus enemigos por medio del veneno.

10. El Espinal es un pueblo pequeño al suroeste de Bogotá, en la provincia de Tolima.

11. Chiquinquirá, unos 140 km al norte de Bogotá, tiene un culto importante a una Virgen milagrosa.

12. "Me muero, y sobre mi tumba, a la cual lentamente me acerco,/ Nadie vendrá a verter sus lágrimas."

13. El original dice "1864," lo cual tiene que ser un error.

14. "La tristeza monta a la grupa y corre al galope conmigo."

Dolores
Scenes from a Woman's Life

FIRST PART

La nature est un drame avec des personnages.[1]
Victor Hugo

"What a lovely girl!" exclaimed Antonio when he saw a group of people on horseback cross the center of the plaza of the village of N★★★, people who had come from a ranch for the purpose of attending the village festival, slated for the following day.

Antonio González was my classmate and favorite childhood friend. When we said good-bye at the university, both having graduated with our doctorates, he offered to come and visit me in my hometown at the time of the religious festival, and with that end in mind had arrived in N★★★ the previous day. As we were both anxious to have a good time, we oversaw with all the enthusiasm of early youth (which can muster interest in everything) the construction of the barriers in the plaza for the following day's bullfights. Just then, as I said before, a group on horseback went by, in whose midst there shone like a lovely lily in a field the area's most beautiful flower: my cousin Dolores.

"What strikes me the most," added Antonio, "is such a white complexion, and a soft tint you don't see in this hot climate."

In effect, Dolores's black eyes and long, jet black hair stood out against her rosy skin and the crimson of her lips.

"What you say is true," exclaimed my father, who happened to be at my side. "Dolores's skin is not normal for this climate . . . Good Heavens!" he said with a troubled voice a moment later. "I hadn't thought of that before."

Antonio and I didn't understand the old man's comment. Years later we would remember the impression that his vague fear caused in us, a fear that seemed so strange. . . .

My father was the doctor in N★★★ and in any other more civilized place he would have been famous for his practical knowledge and his charity. Contrary to the norm, he had always wanted me to follow in his same profession, with the hope, he said, that I would be a better-educated doctor than he.

An only child, satisfied with my lot, spoiled by my father and dearly cherished by numerous relatives, I had always considered myself very fortunate. At that time I was in N★★★ only temporarily, taking care of some business so that soon I could formalize my engagement to a young lady I had met, and with whom I had fallen in love in Bogotá.

Among all my relatives I had always been Aunt Juana's favorite; she was a most respectable and wealthy lady who had taken care of me and overseen my childhood from the time I lost my mother. Dolores, one of her sister's children, had been living with her for several years, as the girl had lost both of her parents. Aunt Juana shared her affection between her favorite niece and nephew.

Hardly had we reached the age when one begins to think of these matters, when Dolores and I realized that the good lady's dearest wish was to arrange our engagement, but human nature prefers the difficult to the smooth path, and both of us tacitly attempted to make it clear to her that our mutual affection was only fraternal. I think that the desire to thwart this project once and for all contributed to my urgent desire to get married in Bogotá at a time when I was still a student without a clear future. As I regarded Dolores as a sister, from the time I went off to high school I wrote to her often, describing the ups and downs of my student life, and later my plans as a young man and a fiancé.

This short summary is indispensable for understanding my simple tale.

After staying in the plaza a little while longer we returned home. My father's house was a little distance from the village, but as there were to be fireworks that night, Antonio and I decided to return to town a little before this popular spectacle was to begin.

The moon lit up the landscape. A warm, delicious breeze ruffled the trees and brought out the flowers' scent. Birds awakened with the moonlight and twittered gently, while the philosophical owl, ever silent and gloomy, complained with his unlucky call.

Antonio and I had to cut through a horse pasture and cross the main road before reaching N***'s plaza. We talked happily of our hopes and future plans, because for youth the future is always synonymous with happiness and fulfilled expectations! Antonio had chosen the more difficult but also more brilliant career of law, and his evident ability and easy eloquence promised him a fine future. As for myself, after doing some practical training with one of the best-known professors, I planned to get married and return home to enjoy quiet country life. I have to confess that N*** was really no more than a large village, no matter how much its inhabitants minded having it called that, for it gave itself the airs of a city and back then had a governor, judges, a city council and the other trappings of local government. Unfortunately these trappings and pretensions were the source of countless problems, much like those of a simple country girl, who, used to going barefoot and wearing short skirts, suddenly puts on high-heeled boots, a corset, and crinolines. . . .

Antonio and I went to Aunt Juana's house, which was located on the plaza and was the finest in town. Many of the local young ladies sat on low chairs in the doorway and against the walls, laughing and chatting, while their mothers and respectable ladies sat inside discussing more serious matters, such as ailments, food, and maids. Dandies from the village and from other places who had come for the festival strolled up and down in front of the doorway without daring to approach the girls, while the latter reveled in their glory and fine appearance without revealing the interest with which they regarded the young men.

I approached the female phalanx with all the high spirits that came from having arrived from Bogotá, something that carried considerable weight in the provinces, and the knowledge that as a relative I would be well received. I introduced my friend to everyone inside and outside the house, and, taking chairs, we went outside to talk to the girls.
. . .

I then suggested that all of us who were from Aunt Juana's house should take a stroll around the plaza.

The female contingent formed a line, and we of the unfair sex took up guerrilla positions, patrolling the outskirts of the group. Attraction is always inexplicable: very soon Antonio and Dolores were drawn to each other and immediately began an animated conversation.

The plaza was full of tables offering different games of chance, at which for the modest sum of a penny everyone who wished to could try his luck. Around other tables and under tents people were drinking a variety of alcoholic beverages: fermented coconut juice, cane liquor, anise and fruit-flavored spirits, and even rather bad wine and brandy. Others satisfied their heart's desire with succulent food: soups, roast turkey, and suckling pigs stuffed with garlic and cumin. There were also tropical fruit drinks, some of blackberry and pineapple, and beverages made with corn or rice, proffered in bottles stoppered with bunches of carnations or roses. Cookies with white or cinnamon icing, almond and egg desserts, candied fruit, coconut macaroons, dry biscuits and little griddle cakes in a variety of shapes; the whole assortment of delicacies commonly known as "snacks" was spread out on trays of various colors and sizes, arranged in rows on coarse but clean tablecloths. . . .

After having inspected the tables in the plaza, where rustic enjoyment reigned, we went to the mestizas' dance. So colorful were these women that ladies liked to go and see them dance, without fearing that their reputations might be compromised. As this dance was supposed to be very noisy and extremely crowded, we found a great number of curious onlookers around the door or glued to the windows that gave onto the dance floor. Nonetheless, when they saw us coming they stepped aside so that the girls could stand by the windows, and we men behind them. . . .

The mestizas wore blue silk skirts with a frill on the bottom, a red and black embroidered blouse, a red or blue shawl, and a small hat of fine straw with wide ribbon ties. Some of the women took off their hats to dance, exposing their thick black hair to view, hair that was parted into two braids, the ends tied up with ribbons, and which hung down their backs.

The men, practically all of whom had pretensions of being social dandies, smoked and drank small glasses of aguardiente,[2] chatting with the musicians who sat by the inner door of the room while they tuned their instruments.

"Hey, Don Basilio!" several voices shouted from the doorway, just as the band began to play a sprightly *bambuco.* "Your partner's waiting for you!"

All eyes focused on a man of some forty years of age, heavyset, beardless, broad of face, with a narrow brow which slanted backward, an irritable look, and the habit of closing one eye when he spoke, all of which combined to give him a singularly disagreeable appearance.

"If Don Basilio dances tonight we're going to have some fun," said Antonio.

"Quiet," I answered. "If he hears you he'll never forgive you. That man is conceited and vengeful."

"I'll dance," exclaimed Don Basilio with self-importance, "if Julian will dance, too."

"Go on, Julian," the dandies shouted, and, hauling Julian out of their midst they made him give his hand to a cheerful and spirited mestiza, whose little black eyes contrasted with a sprig of orange blossoms she wore in her hair. Meanwhile Don Basilio pulled another woman by the hand, whispering things in her ear that made her blush, and, stepping out with a complacent air, stood in front of her and began to dance the *bambuco.* The girl, who was young and light, circled around him, mocking the thick waist and awkward gestures of her swain, so that he looked like a huge bear playing with a kitten. Although he was effeminate and very affected, Julian and the other girl made a much better pair.

But while they finish dancing, let us tell you who these people are, one of whom is important to this story.

Basilio Flores was the son of a poor country woman from the outskirts of Bogotá. His cleverness and natural aptitude came to the attention of a rich landowner, on whose property Basilio's mother cultivated her plot of potatoes and corn. The landowner took him home, and in his free time taught Basilio to read; pleased at the facility with which the boy learned, he determined to make a good employee out of him, onto whose shoulders he could in time shift some of the burden of his complicated business dealings. He sent him to a school where the boy quickly made great strides. Basilio was eighteen when the War of Independence broke out, and his Spanish protector felt obliged to emigrate. Before leaving he secretly summoned the boy, and made him promise under oath that when things calmed down, Basilio should dig up a sum of money that had been buried somewhere in the house where he lived, and use it to travel to Spain to fetch his master.

Circumstances in the country made any kind of communication with the motherland impossible, and, in the midst of the political turmoil which engulfed him, the Spaniard's protégé doubtless forgot his patron's request. . . .

When some sort of peace finally returned to the nation, it came to light that, among the Spaniards who had fled the country, Basilio's master, who had wandered about the Colombian coast, and had fallen ill in the Antilles, had barely had time to reach Spain before he died, leaving no will. . . .

Basilio went back to the capital claiming to have been an unknown relative's inheritor, and, making a great show of his wealth, attempted to enter good society but was rejected with disdain.

Angry, yet determined to use all the means at his disposal to gloss over his origin, he left for Europe and lived in Paris for several years. Lacking connections and ability, he surrendered to vice, and managed to corrupt the meager heart with which nature had endowed him. . . .

Resolved to forge a brilliant career for himself in his own country, he returned with a thousand ambitious projects, and very soon the articles he wrote for the newspapers of this or that political party began to attract attention. He had a very good memory, an average education, and some ironic, though superficial eloquence, the kind that deceives people easily. He signed himself B. de Miraflores, and there were people who said that in Paris he made himself out to be a baron. He spoke French and English fairly correctly, and always embellished his conversation with phrases or quotations by foreign authors. He dressed with extravagant luxury and bad taste, and gave luncheons where he flaunted the gaudy ostentation with which he dazzled the masses.

But unfortunately, if he had a good memory for some things, it failed him completely in others, and during his trip abroad he forgot about his poor mother, the only person to weep for his absence. On his return from Europe he refused to see her, nor did he permit her to come to his house (this might discredit him!), but pretending a generosity that distinguishes noble hearts, by means of a young man who served as his factotum he sent a monthly pension to "the poor country woman who had been his wet nurse," as he said, arching his eyebrows.

When, after a few years he wanted to *faire une fin*,[3] in his words, he successively proposed marriage to the richest, prettiest, and most virtuous young ladies of Bogotá society; naturally all scorned him and wounded his self-esteem, which brings to mind the famous maxim: "When it comes to insults, there is always a legacy." And sooner or later he got even with them.

Discouraged in his marital plans, he turned wholeheartedly to politics, but here, too, disappointments awaited him. His more than humble origin, his coarse, biting tongue, and his bad habits made him undesirable among men of any worth in all the political parties. Unable to make himself esteemed and admired, he made men fear him, and swore to mock society and take revenge on all those who had humiliated him. He allied himself with the most corrupt men of any party, and by means of intrigue succeeded in forging some sort of reputation among the well-known public writers of the nation. . . .

Our hero's political career would not be complete if he were unable to add yet one more laurel to his crown: he wanted to be elected to the national government. In the central and the Magdalena provinces he was too well known to be popular, and was advised to go to the southern provinces, where he might be able to win over his readers by some impassioned articles. This was the reason why *Don Basilio de Miraflores* had come to my town, in which he stayed on when he found out about the coming festival.

Julian belonged to a certain type of dandy that unfortunately has become very common of late, their bad traits worsening with each generation while losing the few good ones they had.

The son of a rich landowner of the southern provinces and educated in Bogotá, in whose preparatory schools he had spent seven years, he had never experienced the heroic poverty that molds a student's character. His pink and white complexion, willowy build, and languid gaze had captured the admiration of the young ladies of Bogotá, while word of his wealth and of the social position of his family won the hearts of their mothers. In the course of his seven years of preparatory school, and a further two in which, according to what he wrote his parents, he was *reviewing* what he had studied, he learned to speak a smattering of French and one or two sentences in Latin; in history he knew Dumas's novels, very little philosophy and even less geography. . . . [He] could dance all the latest dances, and spoke with great seriousness about the tedium of his life, the loss of his illusions, and his wounded heart, but when one saw his fresh face and cheerful demeanor, it was clear that his health had not been impaired by great misfortune or numbers of irreparable losses. . . .

Spurred on by the dance and the loud music, Don Basilio recalled his own youth, and embellished the last strains of the *bambuco* with various leaps which were clumsy imitations of the cancan, performed at the famous Mabille and Valentino balls.

"Bravo!" the dandies shouted to him, and when he finished came over to offer him a glass of liquor as refreshment. . . .

At that instant the musicians struck up a popular waltz and the young men hurried to find partners from among the prettiest mestizas. Some men wore *ruanas*,[4] and all danced with hats on and cigarettes in their mouths.

The young ladies whom we had escorted looked on in silence, naturally feeling affronted and shocked to see that the young men who called upon them were treated very familiarly by those women.

"Let's go," they said and left the windows.

Antonio and I saw the ladies to their respective homes and ourselves resumed the road to our lodging.

At times the heart has premonitions that we cannot explain. I don't know why Dolores's fate worried me so that night: I thought of many things that should make her happy, but in spite of that I could not shed an apprehension that had no motive but that bothered me without my understanding why. For his part Antonio was feeling the first symptoms of a great love: the storms that develop in a heart always begin with a sense of painful melancholy. The sweetness of love is not felt until one has already lost one's willpower and loves unthinkingly.

Antonio suffered, I felt sad, and both of us returned home in silence.

The following days we went to the penning of the bulls and to the bullfights, and in the evenings to dances. Antonio was completely enthralled by Dolores's charms, and any time we were together never wearied of praising her grace and beauty to me. I remember that once he nearly got angry with me because I laughingly quoted the Latin proverb that says, "It is not Nature which makes a woman beautiful, but our love."

Dolores received Antonio's attentions with her good humor and irrepressible happiness. She was unable to be sad, and went after those who appeared melancholy with good-natured barbs. My friend matched her lively character by countering with many jokes and witticisms characteristic of the Bogotá dandy. The love between those two young people was as beautiful, clear, and smiling as a spring day. Wherever they were, they communicated their innate happiness to all around. I have never seen two people more suited to fall in love, and to appreciate each other's mutual qualities. There is no doubt that the axiom which says that opposites attract is a serious error. It may lend a certain glitter, liveliness, and variety to a fleeting sentiment, but between people who love deeply there has to be complete harmony: harmony of feelings, upbringing, social position, and the background of one's ideas. The result of this harmony is moral peace, and this should be the principal goal and beautiful ideal of matrimony.

Don Basilio soon discovered that Dolores, besides being pretty and virtuous, had a fair-sized dowry, and immediately began to lay siege to this new fortress; he thought it would not be bad *business* to garner both a political post and a bride on his trip. The late *uncle's* fortune was beginning to disappear at an alarming rate and he had no desire to grow old in a state of poverty. He confided his plan to Julian, saying: "A simple *villageoise* is an easy conquest . . . Besides, she's pretty, and I could show her in Bogotá without embarrassment," adding with his usual fatuousness by quoting a French writer: "Elle a d'assez beaux yeux . . . pour des yeux de province."[5]

"But," observed Julian, "don't you see that you have a rival in Antonio?"

"Better yet, my young novice. Don't you know that the great Corneille said, 'A vaincre sans péril on triomphe sans gloire?'"[6]

One day he gave Dolores a poem dedicated to her, in which he declared his torrid love in glacial verses: it had so many quotes there was hardly an original word in it, he jumbled mythology with ancient history when he invoked Venus and Lucrece, Minerva and Virginia, and ended by saying, "that led by fate, I mounted Pegasus to fall at your feet."[7] On Aunt Juana's urging Dolores showed the ringing verses to Antonio and me, and naturally we did not spare our jokes.

After having stayed in N✦✦✦ for several days, Don Basilio continued his journey in search of popularity, totally convinced that there was nothing to be gained in our town, and realizing that if he asked for it, Dolores was set to give him the kind of *no* he was accustomed to receiving. It was not hard for Antonio and me to see that he was furious with us when he left, for we had openly made fun of him, something he promised himself he would make us pay for some day.

The festival was over. One by one the people who had come for it began to leave.

The day before Antonio's departure I organized an outing to which the most important people who were still in town were to come. A few hours from N✦✦✦ flows a good-sized river shaded by very tall trees, and nearby is the house of a sugar mill that offers refreshments and a place to leave the horses. This is the favorite destination for anyone hereabouts who organizes excursions.

At seven in the morning some twenty of us were waiting at the entrance of Aunt Juana's house for Dolores to come out. She soon appeared, mounted on a spirited horse, with her long habit, round little hat with flying veil, bright look, and charming air. After noisily clattering through the streets we took a narrow path along some horse pastures, and there groups formed according to each person's preference. I let Antonio ride alongside Dolores, recalling that some writer once said that the best time for a declaration of love is when one is on horseback. And indeed, the liveliness of the outing, the fresh air blowing, the ability to spur on or rein in your horse, to ride ahead or stay back for no apparent reason, of speaking or falling silent, to turn your head or catch your companion's eye—all this enlivens things and easily presents opportunities for being alone, even in the midst of a large group. Nonetheless, that day Antonio was silent, and both their faces were at times shadowed by a sweet melancholy, perhaps because they were thinking of having to separate that very afternoon.

We accompanied the ladies to the riverbank, and while they were bathing we gathered in the sugar mill, talking and laughing happily. But Antonio never recovered his spirits until we rejoined our group's female contingent when lunch was ready. The landscape was extraordinarily beautiful: the scent of the flowers, the buzzing of the insects, the murmuring river that on our side flowed downstream among glistening rocks, the sound of the wind in the leaves of the trees that fluttered over our heads—all the life and motion of tropical nature made us revel in it, enticing one to leisure and the lazy joy of living . . . Antonio and Dolores had imperceptibly drawn apart from the others and were seated at the base of a huge rock covered with yellow moss. Dolores was distractedly tossing the petals of a bunch of flowers she held in her hand into the river, and while the water splashed the golden sand at her feet, both of them regarded with interest the fate of those little blossoms in the foaming current. Some floated slowly downstream, and soon came to rest on the soft bank; others, swept away forcefully by the river, were suddenly caught in a whirlpool and immediately disappeared; others initially sailed off quickly and joyfully, but when they came to a cavity the rocks had formed, ran into each other, and, unable to escape, became waterlogged and sank little by little; in the end, the most fortunate ones clung together, and made their way into the middle of the river, floating downstream without encountering any obstacles whatever.

"Do you see the philosophy behind this event?" I asked, suddenly coming upon the two of them.

Antonio and Dolores started as though they had been interrupted, and in fact communicated their thoughts to each other with a glance, speaking through their very silence.

"What philosophy?" they asked.

"The one in the flower Dolores is casting into the stream. It is the symbol of Providence, and each one of the petals is a human life. What fate would you like, Dolores? That of the blossoms which quickly come to rest on the sand without ever having felt any emotions? That of those that are swept away by the current and are swallowed up in a whirlpool?"

"I? I don't know. But those I feel sorry for are the ones that are trapped in a lonely place, and have no hope of getting out . . . Look," she added, "how they sink little by little, and seemingly against their will."

"I, most assuredly, Sir Philosopher," said Antonio, catching Dolores's eye, "prefer the fate of those who float down the river of life two by two."

My cousin's cheeks flushed crimson, and getting up in a fluster, she went to rejoin the other groups of her girlfriends.

Laughter and conversation, songs and the harmony of guitars and mandolins, a dance in the patio of the sugar mill and general good spirits, none of this could cheer Dolores. She was content, momentarily even happy, but there was a shadow in her face and a kind of sad tone modulated the timbre of her voice. Antonio was in that state in which people in love fall silent and are bewildered, unable to do anything but gaze at their beloved, hear what *she* has to say, not see anything or anyone else — a state of mind which is extremely annoying to everyone except the woman who inspires these feelings and understands the situation.

We returned to town at night; it was very dark, in spite of the stars which sparkled in the cloudless sky. While crossing a stream at a dangerous point, we thought it a good idea for each man to cross beside one of the ladies. Dolores's horse shied when it slipped on the rocks, and if Antonio had not caught her with one arm and sat her back in her saddle, her horse's lunge would have thrown her into the water. When Antonio finally regained the bank, one could plainly see the fright and emotion he had felt in that endeavor, and his voice shook when he answered my question. It was then I realized how tenderly and truly he loved Dolores. True love is not selfish, and the heart is never more fearful than when the beloved person is in danger, even though it might not seem all that serious to others.

Half an hour later they parted, perhaps forever, those two people who had been born to love each other so deeply!

Later, when we were alone, Antonio confided to me that he had not been able to speak to Dolores of his love, for as it was so strong and noble, he had found no words to express it. He asked me to tell my cousin for him that he had not formally asked for her hand because his present position did not yet allow him to do so, but as he had hopes that she felt the same way, asked me to beg her not to forget him.

The same day Antonio left for Bogotá, Aunt Juana returned to her ranch with Dolores. I had witnessed Antonio and Dolores's parting, and although she had a smile on her lips I understood that she might need some comforting. And so, very early the following Sunday, I rode off to the ranch, which was called Springtime, and was located on a plain at the foot of some high, forested hills, a plain where livestock and extensive cacao plantings flourished.

When I got there my aunt was out, and the house absolutely quiet. I dismounted and, giving my horse to a servant, crossed the patio in front of the house and headed for the room in which I was told Dolores could be found.

My cousin's favorite place was a wide passageway toward the rear of the house, with a view over a combined garden and orchard. . . . Dolores's aviary was famous round about: in a great cage which took up the entire corner of the passageway she had collected from all over many birds who had been taught to live together peacefully. . . . Among her flowers and birds Dolores spent the days sewing, reading, and singing along with them. From afar one heard the sound of the aviary, and the gentle voice of its mistress.

On that day everything was still. The heat was asphyxiating, and Nature seemed oppressed and scorched by the rays of a fiery sun which ruled by itself in a cloudless sky. The birds were silent, and the only sound that one heard was that of a stream of water from the pond, which flowed unceasingly under the arbor of flowers. From afar I could see Dolores, dressed in white, her lovely dark hair her only adornment. Resting on a pillow at the foot of the chair on which she had been seated, she leaned her head on her folded arm, while her other small hand, rosy and white, lay inert at her side. I stopped when I spied her, thinking her asleep, but she had heard the jingle of my spurs when I approached, and suddenly stood up, attempting to hide the tears that sprang to her eyes, and simultaneously picking up a paper she had put on her little sewing table.

"What's this, cousin?" I asked her, pointing to the paper after having greeted her.

"I was writing, and . . . "

"To whom?"

"To no one."

"What? Has Antonio already managed . . . ?"

"No, Pedro," she answered with dignity, "he hasn't asked me any such thing, nor would he."

"Dolores," I said, taking her cold, trembling hand between my own, "didn't Antonio swear to you that he loved you madly, just like he's told me thousands of times? Confess that he asked you to be true to him!"

"No; he indicated that perhaps he liked me somewhat, but never told me any more than that."

"And this letter?"

"It isn't a letter!"

"Message, then," I said laughing, "epistle, note, whatever you want to call it."

"You won't believe me? Take it; you're making me show you what I wrote only for myself."

And she gave me the page whereupon she had just written some beautiful verses which showed deep poetic sensitivity, and a kind of vague melancholy spirit I did not know she possessed. It was a tender farewell to her peaceful, happy childhood, and a prayer to her youth, which suddenly seemed like a revelation to her. Her heart had been touched for the first time, and that trembling had made her understand that a life of suffering had begun.

Embarrassed and moved, she dropped her eyes as I read. Her rosy white skin stood out with greater freshness against her white dress and loose hair. A vague fear gripped me, as it had my father, when I noted the particular coloration of her skin, but this impression was again forgotten, only to be recalled later.

I spent the day at my aunt's house, attended to Antonio's request, and was convinced that she loved him, too. About that time I had to return to Bogotá: I was restless, and longed for the joy of seeing my fiancée again after an absence of a month and a half.

When I was leaving the two ladies wanted to accompany me up to a certain point in the road, so that Dolores could show me a pretty spot at the base of the hills, which she had *discovered* a few days before on one of her outings.

Dolores was most happy and joyful. The love that vitalized her formed a kind of halo around her. What does absence matter if we are sure we love and are loved in return? When she reached a narrow trail she had had broken through the wilderness, she rode on ahead. I followed her, admiring her slender figure and the grace and sureness with which she controlled a spirited colt that had shown itself obedient and docile only with her.

A few moments later we reached a more open place: a crystalline stream leaped down stony steps and came to rest in a lovely bed of moss and of quivering, variegated ferns. Extremely tall trees rose on one side of the stream, their dense shade preventing other shrubs from growing beside them. A number of old trunks and stones encased in green moss covered the earth, carpeted by a soft, golden sand. The sun was beginning to set and the shade in that spot produced a delicious coolness. Groups of colorful birds, among which chattered many parrots and parakeets, flew up to land in the high crowns of the trees, gilded by the sun's last rays.

We dismounted, and my aunt, who brought out some sweets and a coconut curiously set in polished silver, invited us to share in a rustic repast.

"How lovely it would be to spend one's life here, wouldn't it?" exclaimed Dolores.

"Alone?" I answered, smiling.

Her only reply was a tender glance that was meant for my absent friend, then she continued talking gaily. The poor girl! . . . But still happy in the ignorance of what was to come.

La douleur est une lumière qui nous éclaire la vie.[8]

Balzac

Two months after I had gotten back to Bogotá I received Dolores's first letter, which I have kept along with many others as mementos of my cousin, whose truly gifted nature no one knew but I.

"Dear Cousin," she wrote me,

I was awaiting news of your arrival before I wrote you, and later, when I wanted to write, the events which have taken place at home and in my life prevented me from doing so . . . I didn't know if I should confide the terrible secret I have discovered to you, but the heart needs to let go, and I well know that you are not only my brother but a very beloved friend who will feel compassion at my troubles. Recently I read that what makes friendships last and doubles their joy is a feeling that love does not have: security. Oh! Friendship is the only thing that can comfort me now, as other feelings will be forbidden me. Not long ago, remember? I saw the world as beautiful, happy, enchanting; everything smiled on me . . . but now, great God, an earthquake has strewn with ruins the place where the temple of my hopes once stood!

Forgive me, Pedro, for this chatter with which I am trying to put off confessing my troubles; this itself will indicate to you the terror I feel when I see in writing that which I hardly dare even to think.

But courage! I shall begin.

A few days after your departure I was going to my aunt's room one afternoon, when I went by the passageway of the entrance patio, and heard that an old tenant who lived within the borders of the ranch was asking for her. He had a letter in his hand, and when I found out it was for my aunt I took it, and was about to hand it to her, but when she found out that it was old Simon who had brought it, she screamed, "Throw that letter away, Dolores, throw it away!"

Instinctively I did as she asked and dropped it. My aunt then had me wash my hands, and, ordering a brazier brought to her, did not pick up the letter in her own hands until she had had it fumigated.

I was so surprised at seeing this that I could barely ask the reason for my aunt's sudden fear; in the end the whole thing even seemed funny, and I exclaimed, laughing,

"Is the paper poisoned, Aunt? Is old Simon like the Borgias,[9] as in the story we read the other day?"

"Don't joke, my dear," she answered me seriously, "for the poison this letter might contain is far more dreadful than any men have invented."

As she said these words she finished reading the letter, and, tossing it on the brazier, watched it slowly go up in flames.

"You have to explain this mystery to me . . ."

"Don't think there's any romantic mystery here," she interrupted me with a sad tone. "Don't you know that there are lepers on the outskirts of N***? One of those unfortunate beings sent me this letter."

"And who is it?"

"Who indeed? A poor wretch whom I have sent some help and who lives in a tumbledown cabin not far from old Simon's."

"The poor man! And he lives alone the way they all do? Alone, right in the wilderness, with no one to speak to him nor ever approach him. He will live and die in isolation, without the touch of a helping hand . . . My God, how cruel, what an awful fate!"

And my heart ached with unspeakable anguish.

"Society is very cruel, Aunt," I added. "It casts out the unfortunate man from its bosom . . ."

"That's the way it is," she answered me, "but what is there to do? Apparently this ghastly disease is terribly contagious. Given that, isn't it better for one to suffer than many? As for me, Dolores, I confess that the very sight of a leper horrifies me, and I would rather die than get close to one."

"And how did you get to know this poor man? Why do you help him, Aunt? This really interests me, for the address was beautifully written . . . and the handwriting even looks familiar to me."

"Why do I help him, you ask? Shouldn't one always help those who suffer?"

My aunt abruptly ended the conversation. Although during the

following days we did not talk about the business of the letter, it
had impressed me greatly. Winter came with all the fury with
which you know the rains fall here in this climate. We were completely alone on the ranch; no one dared cross the swollen rivers and
flooded roads to come and see us. Sometimes I awoke in the middle
of the night at the noise of a tremendous storm, and when I heard
the rain fall, thunder rip the air, and the wind moan against the
tightly shut windows, and when I felt secure in my room, surrounded by so much comfort, my spirit flew to the lonely huts of
those pariahs of our society: the lepers. In my imagination I saw the
poor wretches, beset by terrible suffering, in the midst of the
wilderness and the storm, and alone, always alone . . .

One night I had read until very late, studying French in the
books you left me; I tried to learn and progress in my studies, to
educate my spirit and teach myself so as to be less ignorant: contact
with *certain* people from the capital city had lately made me realize
how indispensable it is to be educated. I thus went to bed late, and
was just falling asleep when I thought I heard steps in the outside
patio, and something like the whispering of two voices speaking
in low tones. My favorite dog, who spends the night in my room,
suddenly jumped up and went out the open window to the passageway; a moment later I heard him leap up on someone in the
patio. My aunt's voice made him stop. How strange! My aunt, who
usually went to bed at eight, was wandering about corridors of the
house at midnight! I got up, determined to find out what was
going on, and slightly opened the door which went out into the
farthest passage. Then I heard a man who said in a low voice,
"Good-bye, Juana!" This voice caused me to tremble greatly; I
thought I was dreaming . . .

"Wait a moment," answered my aunt, "and I will bring the portrait I had done for you by a painter from Quito who happened by
here a few days ago."

After saying this I heard Aunt Juana go into her room, and, under
cover of darkness, I quickly slipped into the corridor and hid in a
corner from which, by crouching down, I could see a shape that
stood motionless in the center of the patio.

Fear and a vague apprehension I had felt when I heard the

stranger's voice vanished when I saw he was no ghost, no figment of my imagination. Nevertheless, I could not understand how Aunt Juana could have *appointments* at midnight and give away her portrait! It was true that a short time previously I had asked her to have her portrait done by an itinerant painter who did mine as well. A moment later she returned, and, leaning on the railing of the corridor, tied a string around a wrapped package while saying, "It's not as good a likeness as I would have wished," and when the shape drew nearer, she added, "I'm also giving you Dolores's [book] *Imitation of Christ*, which I replaced with a new one."

"You don't know how much good this will do me," the stranger said with feeling. "Oh, my poor daughter! Her portrait!"

The voice, the tone froze my blood, and for a moment I don't know what happened to me. An incredible idea, a horrible terror left me feeling as though I had been struck down. I stood up, cold and trembling.

"You must go soon, Jerome," my aunt replied, "I heard a noise from Dolores's room and . . ."

I heard no more. I had recognized my father's voice and my aunt called him by name. My father, whom I had thought dead for six years! I thought no further about the mystery of that apparition. Racing down the corridor steps which led to the patio, I ran toward the figure, and when I reached him, threw my arms around his neck. When they saw what I had done, both my aunt and my father let out cries of horror: the latter pushed me away in desperation, covered his face with the *ruana* in which he was wrapped, and attempted to flee. I fought to run after him, but my aunt, who had followed me down, stopped me.

"Dolores," she shouted, "Dolores, don't go near him! Good God, he's a leper!"

"A leper? What do I care? My father isn't dead, and I want to put my arms around him."

You can't imagine the scene that followed. My aunt finally got my father to leave, and, calling the servants, forcibly took me to my room. There she took off my clothes and had them thrown out onto the patio to be burned the next day.

I did not allow my aunt to leave me until she had told me the cause of this incident, and explained to me on the spot why my father was hiding and in that state . . . We spoke for a long time, and I was finally alone only when the first rays of dawn appeared through the open window. Then I got up, and, leaning against the window, regarded the beautiful landscape that lay before my eyes. . . . The day, the landscape, the farmyard sounds were so lovely and so good! . . . But to me everything looked sad and lifeless. My whole life has changed; nothing can be happy for me again. My father is alive, but he lives a life of suffering!

Isn't it true, Pedro, that leprosy is a hideous disease? When people find out what a legacy awaits me, everyone will try to avoid me, and attempt to discern my first symptoms. I will be condemned to live in isolation! My father, who loved me tenderly, did not want this stain to mar my life, and so he decided to disappear. He has lived hidden away in the farthest reaches of the region, and it has only been for a year or so that my aunt and your father have known where he was . . . But I, can I live happily far from my unhappy father? Is it right to deceive everyone else by hiding the disease to which fate may condemn me? My father has made it clear that under no circumstances will he allow it to be known that he exists . . . In your last letter you tell me that somewhat sooner than he had anticipated Antonio hopes to get a position that would allow him to ask for my hand. It's too late, cousin: he has to give up this idea . . . Let him forget me! My misfortune should not tie him down. Do not ever tell him the reason, but make him forget his hopes. He will think I am inconstant and ungrateful . . . but what can I do? This is a very, very great sacrifice, but there's no other way.

Farewell. Write some comforting words to one who suffers greatly.

Dolores

A few days later I received this other letter:

You have written me, dear cousin, and your words have been a real comfort to me—many, many thanks! You have asked with concern for details as to the disappearance of my father, and how he lived hidden away for so long without anyone suspecting nor guessing that he was alive.

I have collected everything I have been able to find out about this matter, and will try to explain to you how things happened.

You know that ever since my mother died, my father bestowed all his affection on me, and cared for me with a woman's tenderness. I was twelve years old when my father discovered some changes in his health that disturbed him, and went to Bogotá. There he consulted various doctors who told him that the symptoms he had were those of a ghastly and incurable disease: leprosy. Desperate, he started for N*** without knowing what he was going to do. But when he reached the banks of the Magdalena, his distraught spirit presented him with the idea of suicide as the best way out, and the only solution to his plight. He dismounted, and in a moment of madness threw himself into the river with the intention of letting himself drown. But you will recall that my father was a very good swimmer. Natural instinct and the will to live made him not succumb, and, although exhausted, he reached the other side. There he was taken in by an unfortunate soul who lived in a poor hut on the riverbank. What a coincidence! His savior was also a leper, and lived in that desolate spot; he managed to exist thanks to some help with which a neighboring town provided him, as well as the harvest from a banana tree and other crops which he grew and sold in the surrounding area by means of his two children who lived with him. My father stayed with him for a few days; he thought of fleeing from the world for ever, and, by hiding his affliction, avoid passing on this secret legacy to his daughter.

With the assets of some gold and jewels he had in his possession, he lived for a while in that desolate area. He soon took leave of the leper. To live as an equal with a common person, is that not the worst tragedy of all? So he bought a cabin in the mountains and there vegetated alone, isolated and deeply afflicted for over five years. Sometimes he went down to the banks of the Magdalena to visit the leper, and observed in him the progress and ravages of the disease from which they both suffered. On other occasions, dressed as a peasant he would roam about the neighboring towns at night, asking how his family was. How often he failed to find out anything at all, and returned disconsolate to his wilderness!

One day he went down to his fellow sufferer's cabin, and found the two children weeping in the doorway.

The leper had died. This event moved my father deeply, and he asked the children to follow him into his exile. They, a girl of twelve and a boy of fourteen, gratefully accepted his offer. For many months my father had not heard anything definite about his family, and was extremely uneasy; besides, the leper's death made him realize that his own might not be far off, and he could not resist wanting to see me for the last time.

So, accompanied by the two children, he began the trek to N***, a terribly difficult journey through desolate plains of interminable grassy fields.

There was an abandoned cabin within the boundaries of my aunt's ranch, and there he chose to live. His companions had no idea who he was, and thus he could send a letter to your father with no difficulty, revealing his existence to him, and asking him for word of his family. You can well imagine the surprise which such a revelation would cause your father. There had never been the slightest doubt but that my father had died while rashly crossing the Magdalena. When he was convinced of the truth he went to talk to Aunt Juana as to what he should do; his first impulse had been to look for my unfortunate father and take him home again, even though the latter might refuse to go with him. But you know the extreme aversion my aunt has to this disease, and would in no way agree to the plan. She said (and I have been assured that in this she was right), that as I had a hereditary propensity for contracting this disease, it was essential to protect me as much as possible from any contagion. They agreed that they would send him anything he needed from the ranch, but that he would live far from all of his family and his existence would continue to be concealed from everyone. My father, poor man, never had had any other wish than to see me secretly and from afar . . . Do you remember the afternoon you came to say good-bye to us? He was hidden in the bramble thicket at the bank of the stream; he saw us so happy and the echo of our laughter reached his ears.

I am told that his illness is in the last stages . . . that he is suffering terribly, but I am not permitted to see nor to help him. I am living in a state of perennial sadness and withdrawal; my character has changed completely. Tell me, what has Antonio said? Has he forgotten me easily? . . . Silly questions, aren't they? Let's talk about you: you tell me that your wedding will not be as soon as you thought, but you at least live in a state of hope. We have been like brother and sister: you will attain happiness, and I . . . No, God knows what He is doing: He will have taken measure of my strength and my obedience. Farewell . . .

This news from N*** made me very unhappy. The at times morbid, at times overwrought state of suffering revealed by Dolores's letters alarmed me. I wrote to my father, advising him to try to get her mind off this, because constant fixation on such a painful matter could predispose her more than anything else to having her father's disease break out in her. One thought consoled me: rarely had there been cases in which the children of lepers caught the disease; it almost always skips a generation, and appears in the grandchildren. Nevertheless, I understood and approved of her noble conduct at wishing to break with Antonio. I did not dare dash my friend's hopes suddenly; I saw him so happy that it seemed a useless act of cruelty to quench the fire and life, the vigor and energy which vitalized his work and made him overcome all obstacles.

Several months went by like this. At last I received word of the death of Dolores's father: she wrote a few lines in which she gave vent to her grief. She could not openly weep for the loss she had sustained, nor put on mourning, for in his last moments he had let her know that he wanted his sacrifice to be of at least some use in protecting his daughter from the suspicious glances of a society that would know what awaited her when it learned the cause of his death.

Seeing her so depressed, my aunt wanted to cheer her up and took her to El Espinal.[10] The two of them thereupon wrote me, asking me to come and see them for a few days, now that they were a little closer to Bogotá.

I consented to this request, and went to spend a week with them. How was I to foresee the consequences this visit would have for me!

Nothing could console Dolores: she was pale, and in all of her gestures one could see the deep sorrow that distressed her. She then begged me insistently to tell Antonio that things were over, but made me promise that I would never tell him the reason for the break she desired.

On my return I tried to make clear to Antonio the aversion Dolores felt toward the prospect of matrimony, and the impossibility of realizing his hopes. This was a difficult task, and I often lacked the courage to distress him too much.

On the other hand, my own marital plans had taken a turn that caused me to feel a great deal of doubt about the future. Don Basilio had had himself introduced in my fiancée's house as a suitor for Mercedes's hand; she had always regarded him with a disdainful frown, but her parents treated him with the sort of attention I did not like at all. Little by little I began to realize that while Don Basilio was treated with growing respect, I was shown increasing indifference. One time Mercedes told me that she was very sad because her parents had heard some bad things about me; she had come to my defense, but could not prevent an upcoming trip to Chiquinquirá[11] that was being organized. Her mother had made a vow to the Virgin many years ago, but up until then had not considered fulfilling it; as Mercedes told me, it was doubtless with the intention of separating us. I wanted an explanation as to what had been said about me to them, but Mercedes would not allow it, assuring me that she did not know of what I was being accused, and that when she found out the charges I would be able to defend myself better.

I realized that this must be Don Basilio's doing, and promised to wait. A few days later Mercedes's family left for Chiquinquirá. During the first weeks of her absence I was deeply dejected, and my greatest pleasure was to have long talks with Antonio about our respective heartaches. Mercedes wrote me often, but finally told me that they would not be returning to Bogotá as soon as they had thought, as her mother wanted to stay a few months in San Gil with relatives she had there. Whenever I received a letter from Mercedes it was cause for celebration for me, but gradually they became fewer and fewer, under the pretext that her mother had forbidden her to write me. Back then

I was still in love and believed myself loved in return, and though I was very unhappy at the time, remember it fondly; as a French writer said, "None of our other pleasures can compare with our sorrows." But gradually I became used to her silence, and did not wait for her letters with my previous impatience. I don't know the reason why there were so many balls and functions given in Bogotá during that time, but I attended them, and confess that I was not unhappy. Nevertheless, deep down I was always uneasy, with a hidden pain that clung to the memory of Mercedes.

Four months had passed with no word at all from her, when one day a letter from her arrived and I realized with deep sorrow that my heart no longer felt the joy of previous times. Mercedes told me that when she told her father they ought to be returning to Bogotá because the time had come when our engagement was to be formalized, he had informed her that she would never become my wife with his consent. He refused to give her an explanation for his decision, but added that he was sure a prolonged separation would suffice to have us forget about each other. Mercedes's letter was extremely affectionate, perhaps more than any other one of hers, but with the attraction, the intuition that exists between people who love each other and which remains even after they have stopped being in love, I mean with that revelation of the soul that is understood without the possibility of explanation, I felt a certain disdain and coldness even in her most loving phrases. The bond of feeling and intimacy between us was about to snap. From that day on I became resigned to her absence, and used to the idea that our paths might diverge.

At last some important business of her father's brought the whole family back to Bogotá. Hardly had I learned of her unexpected arrival than my heart beat high for an instant, and I immediately went to her house. What a sad disappointment! The excitement was fleeting, and I calmed down again very quickly. Nevertheless, I made an effort to think that when I saw her my old joy would return again, and when I entered her house I recalled all the imagined scenes with which I had embellished the hopes that now were to be fulfilled. I arrived, found her as lovely as ever, but in her eyes as in mine the old spark had died. We spoke, I attempted to hide my indifference, and she was distracted. When I said good-bye a deep sorrow took hold of me. How depressing it is to feel your heart empty, with neither emotions nor enthusiasm!

I wanted no explanation from her, fearing there might be a reconciliation between us that was no longer desirable. So I withdrew from her house, and though she could not fail to notice the chill in our relationship, she said nothing to me. I saw her at the theatre and at functions, lovelier than ever and beautifully dressed; I heard of the conquests she had made and the suitors she attracted, among whom Don Basilio and Julian, who had returned to Bogotá, figured most prominently, but instead of the jealousy and hurt I would have felt earlier at seeing her thus courted, my heart remained calm. I had lost the ability to feel the noble jealousy that is symptomatic of love. Though doubtless a heart which does not love can feel jealousy, or perhaps a certain envy, there can be no passionate love without jealousy.

Poor Mercedes! At times she tried to coax me to her side and hid her indifference when she could, as I did mine. During that time I felt very sad: the human heart, my own not excepted, seemed to me so small, fickle, and despicable, though in its inner reaches it still retained the memory of the woman I had loved like an angel, but who in my opinion had changed into a weak, trivial person, easily swayed by the will of others! At times my conscience accused me of having changed as well. This was true, but I had not begun to feel indifferent until I sensed the coolness in her. Her silence and her vacillations during our separation had revealed her to me in another light, and for me the old ideal had disappeared.

My feelings were fluctuating in those uncontrolled mood swings, in which one neither wants nor hopes for anything, when I received another letter from Dolores, a letter which filled me with the most painful apprehension. As soon as I had read it I resolved to leave for N★★★ the following day. That same evening I went to say good-bye to Mercedes.

I was very distressed, and in that frame of mind would gratefully have accepted any sign of friendship. I think if Mercedes had received me that evening the way she did in former times, she might have recovered her hold over my heart. How grateful I would have been to her had she been inspired by the emotion I held to be the greatest good given to humankind: love!

I was very troubled when I went up the steps to her home; my voice shook as I greeted her.

The function was well attended, as it was almost every evening. In one part of the living room around the piano stood a group made up of Mercedes and some of her girlfriends; one of them was playing a piece, while Don Basilio pontificated about the opera from which it came. Julian turned the pages of the music and gazed languidly at Mercedes. Across the room her father was playing cards with two or three of Don Basilio's friends, country bumpkin politicians from distant provinces who sported very tight jackets, very stiff collars, very taut gaiters, and to top it off had such coarse, black hands that it was quite obvious who their forebears had been.

I saw that my entrance had caused a stir. All eyes turned on me curiously, and conversations in progress broke off. Mercedes received me disdainfully, turning her back once she had extended a cursory greeting without looking at me. The master of the house barely acknowledged me, and the entire crowd treated me coldly. In the midst of the silence produced by my arrival Don Basilio turned to me, saying with resonant voice and his usual pedantry:

"Well, well, the man of the hour, etc., or better yet, 'Talk of the devil,' as the English say. You were being spoken of just a moment ago, young man." And, looking at everyone meaningfully, he added, "Have you had any news lately of your interesting relatives whom I met in N★★★ last year?"

I don't know what I answered. A moment later I went up to Mercedes and told her that I had come to say good-bye because I had to be away for a few days.

"Naturally," she answered, flushing with marked annoyance.

"Why naturally? You don't even know where I'm going . . ."

"How could I fail to guess? The man being deceived can sometimes open his eyes."

"The man deceived?"

"Or the woman, as you wish."

"Explain yourself, Mercedes."

"I will. I want you to know that I now understand how false your conduct has been, and you can be sure that any relationship between us is over."

"And of what in Heaven am I guilty?"

"I haven't time to explain now. It suffices for you to know that I'm aware of everything." And she added ironically, "I understand your wanting to visit the person you prefer!"

"I don't understand."

"No? Well then, do me the favor of saying hello to your cousin Dolores for me."

"Mercedes, you're quite unfair, and I have no idea who could have made up such a . . . "

She could not help looking at Don Basilio as she interrupted me and said, "I don't know why you even bothered to come to say goodbye. There is nothing between us, nor can there ever be; I'm not interested in your private affairs."

I immediately realized that this was all Don Basilio's doing. My pride flared, and I had no desire to be humiliated by asking for an explanation.

"Well, I see," I answered her while looking at my rival, "I see that my dignity prevents my defending myself; the fortress is in enemy hands and it would be pointless to try to rebut the falsehoods that certain people know how to fabricate."

Paying my respects disdainfully to Mercedes and to the other guests, I left the room, followed by the malignant look and perverse smile of Don Basilio. In the doorway Julian caught up with me, and, offering me his hand, said, "Pedro, please don't think I had a hand in this conspiracy which I gather has been set up against you, because I am against this sort of thing, and hold you in genuine esteem."

I thanked him for this spontaneous gesture and we parted.

I crossed the streets between me and my home, and hatred, a longing to get even, profound humiliation at seeing myself bested by this windbag, disdain for Mercedes who was his instrument—all of this seethed in my head and made my heart pound. In the midst of it all, I remembered that when I had left Mercedes had looked after me with a misty, saddened glance . . . I did not see her again for many years and then, under what circumstances!

When I got home I was told that someone was waiting for me: it was Antonio. When I went up to greet him he stepped back and pushed my hand away, saying harshly, "The first thing I want to know is if I am shaking hands with a friend or a traitor to friendship!"

"A traitor! . . . I, Antonio?"

"You!"

"Explain yourself . . . This is the last straw!" I said with dismay. "This is just what I needed to go absolutely mad . . . I've just come from Mercedes's house, who has definitively broken off our relationship."

"And she didn't say why?"

"She gave me to understand that she believed a lie . . . "

"A lie! But maybe she's right . . . Pedro, Pedro! I still have one hope left: your loyalty of so many years' standing! Tell me the truth," he added, speaking to me more familiarly, "for it is so heartbreaking to lose everything in one day . . . Answer me: were you perhaps in love with Dolores before I met her? Or when you went to El Espinal, four months ago now? Oh, tell me the truth!"

"I swear to you by our old friendship and by all I hold sacred that Dolores has always been only a sister to me."

"I don't know what to believe . . . Lately I've been thinking a great deal about your behavior and it's inexplicable. From the time you went to El Espinal you have constantly tried to dissuade me from my plans with respect to Dolores, and you won't let me speak of her at all. And all this with a kind of mysteriousness you can't hide, and without telling me the reason for such a startling change. My friend Durán also told me that of late no one has seen Dolores anymore, that she was living in constant seclusion at her ranch. Lately rumors have begun to circulate here about her and you that I can't bring myself to repeat . . . Tell me if this is true!"

"What's true?" I asked him, disconcerted and not knowing what to answer.

"Tell me if . . . are you going to marry her?"

"That's an outrageous lie fabricated by Don Basilio. I'm amazed that you, Antonio, would have even listened to it!"

"By Don Basilio?"

A moment later he added, "You're right, Pedro, then it must be a lie. I'm amazed I hadn't thought of it before. They told me here that you were planning to leave for N★★★ tomorrow; I won't wait any longer. I refuse to believe in Dolores's aversion to marriage; didn't you tell me she loved me? Well then, you yourself will take along a letter asking for your cousin's hand, and we'll get married any way we can. That's the best way to answer a lie like that."

"That cannot happen!" I exclaimed, without thinking about the consequences of my words.

"Why?"

"She says she will never marry."

Antonio looked at me without answering and I added, "There is a secret in her life I cannot reveal."

"A secret?"

"Yes."

"A secret in a woman's life cannot be good. I demand that you tell me what it's about. I'm not a hero in a novel, and if people are going to deceive me it had better be with something plausible."

"I am not at liberty to reveal it to you; Dolores has made me keep the secret."

"The secret! And I was beginning to believe you!"

Getting up, he firmly put on his hat, and, in a voice that shook with anger, silenced me by saying, "That's enough. No one makes a fool of me and gets away with it. Don't answer me because I don't want to do anything rash here. I will send friends to arrange the matter between us."

"A challenge!"

"That's the way I see it. Is cowardice perhaps another one of your distinguishing characteristics?"

"Anger is blinding you, Antonio," I answered, trying to keep my reason. "There can't be a challenge between the two of us. This is totally ridiculous! Listen to me: I have given you my word that this is a terrible misunderstanding."

"What proof can you give me to make me believe what you say is true, given that you say Dolores can't get married?"

"Time . . ."

"Time! . . . You're a coward!"

"I will not have anyone call me that!"

"Then accept my challenge or answer my question."

"Antonio," I cried, making a last effort not to lose my temper. "Antonio, this is absurd. If circumstances demand it, then let us part, but not as enemies!"

Antonio was already beside himself and approached with raised arm.

"Coward and hypocrite!" he shouted.

Then I forgot all restraint, and, showing him the door, said, "Get out. Set things up for when and where you want."

The following day at six in the evening I was carried unconscious to the house where I lived. When I came to I was lying in bed. It was nighttime, and I saw my landlady asleep at the foot of the bed; I tried to speak and to move, but an extremely sharp pain in my chest forced me to lie still. I was alone, with neither a relative nor a friend to feel sorry for me; my only comfort was the kindness of my landlords. Then I remembered what had happened to me: I saw myself once again facing Antonio behind the San Diego hills. Each of us had a pistol in his hand, and Julian was serving as my second. The expression on Antonio's face was fearsome: he regarded me with all the hatred born of his earlier affection. At that moment I forgot all religious feeling, all memory of my father . . . profound despair with regard to life held sway over me; at that instant I truly wanted to die. I aimed at Antonio, but the thought of Dolores and of her sorrow when she found out I had caused his death appealed to my better nature, and I fired into the air. But simultaneously I felt a strong jolt, and without knowing how, found myself on the ground: I remembered nothing more.

I lost consciousness again, and for many days hovered between life and death. When I opened my eyes again to light and consciousness I found my father at my side, who had just arrived from N*** without having received word of the state I was in.

The following letter from Dolores will explain better than anything else the reason for my father's unexpected journey.

I don't know if you received a letter I wrote you a few days ago. It may have gotten lost, or you might not have understood what I was telling you in it. Now I plan to explain to you more clearly the reason for the turmoil within my soul; I am completely calm and able, I think, to face my situation with courage. "With courage"— great God! "Calm" . . . what irony! No, Pedro, I'm crazy, desperate. I have had moments of true madness.

Nevertheless, I want to overcome the revulsion, the horror I feel. I must tell you everything.

From the time I was at El Espinal I began to feel very ill, a constant nervous agitation and total depression. In the space of a few hours I would feel alternating heat, cold, strength, weakness, courage, despair, fear, bravery—in short, the most contradictory emotions and disparate feelings. When I returned to N★★★ I went to see your father: he asked me some questions, and in his face I could read the greatest agitation and sorrow as I described the symptoms of the strange disease afflicting me. Poor Uncle tried to give me courage, assuring me that these changes were a result of my recent trials.

My aunt insisted that I consult other doctors, but I didn't want anyone to examine me. Finally, seeing that my condition was not improving, without consulting me they called in some local persons who hereabouts pass for doctors, for their experience, rather than a diploma, makes them worthy of the title of doctor that people give them.

They all met then, one day at the ranch. I appeared before them trembling, but they received me with such kindness and treated me with such good humor, that in their presence I began to forget about the awful terror that haunted me. Before I left them, I gathered that these gentlemen were to convene in the living room to give their opinions. I wanted to know the truth, and decided to eavesdrop on their session. I withdrew to my room, but, leaving immediately, slipped into a bedroom which adjoins the living room and is separated from it only by a screen.

This took me a few minutes, and when I reached my vantage point their conversation had already begun.

"The poor girl!" one said. "It seems to me there's no hope . . . "

"The leprosy is scarcely in its second phase," another replied, "and I think some effort should be made."

"That would only slow it down for a few more days . . ."

"That's true," they all agreed. "There's no cure any longer."

I didn't find out what else they said, nor knew what came over me. I had made an effort to be strong, and to face with serenity the illness that I could—should—expect. But when I was certain something was true that [up to then] I only feared, when I was face-to-face with the specter that had filled me with foreboding, when I suddenly grasped the horror of my situation, I could not fight the excruciating pain, and, though I did not faint, I threw myself on the floor in the throes of complete spiritual anguish. I neither wept nor lamented: my desperation tolerated no release. A deep sob in the hallway made me come to. I recognized my aunt's voice and left the room . . . at least, I thought, we can cry together! Guided by the same desire that impelled me, she, too, had wished to know the opinion of the doctors, and when she heard their words had not been able to control her feelings.

Soledad Acosta de Samper

361

I approached her, but when she raised her eyes and saw me at her side she could not repress a kind of revulsive shudder, which she immediately mediated with a tender look.

"My dear," she said, holding out her hands, "come, give me a hug."

But her first reaction had been like a knife thrust for me: I could not forget it, and fleeing to my room without wanting to hear her, locked myself in. I felt alone, completely abandoned in the world! After that I don't remember anything. Apparently my aunt, exhausted from calling me and not getting a response, became frightened. With your father's she help broke open the door, and found me deranged!

Yes, Pedro, my despair was such that I lost my mind for several days. When I recovered my reason, and thought about the horrible existence that awaited me, the first thing I thought about was writing to you. You have always been a friend in whose kindness I have believed, a brother whose support has ever been my consolation. I cried out to you: I can't recall what I told you because my mind was still clouded by madness. Your father tells me that he has not given up hope completely, and is leaving for Bogotá to consult in person with the finest doctors in the nation. If only there were hope, dear God! . . . if only there were hope!

The letter to which Dolores referred was the one that had impelled me to go to N★★★, a departure which had been tragically interrupted.

No sooner was I up again than I insisted on accompanying my father to the practices of Bogotá's best doctors, who gave us some remedies by means of which, they said, a number of lepers had significantly improved. My father went back to N★★★. I was left alone, sad, still ill, discouraged, and now with no set plans for the future.

At this point I heard of a wealthy businessman who was ill, and en route to Europe; he wanted to take along a doctor to attend him during his trip. I offered him my services, and he gladly accepted me, but before my departure I could not resist the desire to go and embrace my father and see my relatives. Furthermore I wanted to put the little property I had in order, so that I would have some funds on which to live in Europe for several years.

I arrived unexpectedly in N★★★, and, after spending a few hours with my father, went to Aunt Juana's house. She was alone and very sad: there was no help for Dolores's affliction. She told me that Dolores only wanted to live on the ranch, and, bursting into tears, the poor aunt added that she let no one see her or come near her. I tried to comfort her, saying that I would go and see Dolores, to try to cheer her thoughts and improve her way of life.

At first my cousin refused to see me, but when I told her that soon I was leaving on a trip very far away, she gave in to my wish.

She was seated in an armchair, and the room was very dark, so that in her white dress she looked like a ghost among the shadows. She did not want me to come near her, but, taking advantage of my privileged status as cousin and brother, I forcibly took her hands, and, suddenly opening a window, insisted on seeing the damage the malady had done to her.

The third phase of the disease was already beginning. The lovely rosy color that had alarmed my father, and is the first symptom of the illness, had now blanched and changed into the yellowish pallor I had noted in her in El Espinal; [her face] was swollen and the rough skin had a purple color. Her beauty had completely disappeared, and only her eyes still retained an unnatural brightness. I realized that she no longer had any hope of getting better, but attempted to hide my surprise: I surely had not counted on seeing such a change in her. At first she remained silent, but when I described Aunt Juana's grief to her, she confided in me that her apparent indifference and the desire to isolate herself were part of a plan she had devised, and was determined to put into action.

"I want my aunt to get used to our separation, for I do not plan to live with her any longer."

"And where will you go?"

"I shall live alone. My aunt is horrified and singularly repulsed by the illness I have, and I know that she would live like a martyr. Besides, a stranger's voice causes me such terror . . . I look on all of humanity as an enemy that pursues me, that lies in wait for me, and have resolved to part company from all who fear me."

"But how?"

"Don't you remember the lovely spot where we said good-bye the last time you were here?"

"The little stream?"

"I want to have a small house built there, and, accompanied by the young people who served my father until his last moments (they are not repulsed by me), I will live alone, but I will be content in my solitude."

"This is madness, Dolores. What would your life be out in the wilderness? No, you can't do that."

"Instead of dissuading me, Pedro, have pity on me and help me carry out my plan. If you don't," she added, wringing her hands with a desperate gesture, "I'll run away, I'll go into the wilderness alone, and die like a wild forest animal. Look: my greatest despair comes from knowing I produce horror in people. My God! If I am not allowed to live alone, to hide from all eyes, I don't know what I'll do . . . it isn't hard to end one's life."

The poor young woman's state of despair was such that there was no room for reason, and I had to offer her my help with her plan.

"And Antonio?" she asked after a moment of silence, making an effort to regain her composure.

"I haven't seen him. Perhaps you didn't know?"

"Yes, your father told me everything. I have been the cause of grief and danger to you, and you have never received any comfort nor sign of gratitude from me! Forgive me: suffering makes one an egotist. I'll confess my most vulnerable point to you: I am terrified at the thought that Antonio should remember me with loathing."

"But isn't it worse that he should think ill of you?"

"That's true; I hadn't thought about that. Let him know everything!"

On saying that she burst into bitter tears.

"Tell Mercedes anything you want as well," she added.

"Mercedes doesn't mean anything to me anymore. I don't want to give her any explanation: she should have had faith in my constancy."

Dolores looked at me for a moment.

"You never loved her at all, because when one loves one is not proud: it's impossible to harbor lasting resentment, or pique, or ill will toward one you love."

"Let's not discuss her further. Mercedes has other suitors and I don't even think about her."

I said good-bye, promising to speak with my aunt, which indeed I did, attempting to make her understand that Dolores's life depended on doing what she wanted.

A few days later I joined my companion in Honda, and we sailed down the Magdalena without incident, boarding our ship in Santa Marta the beginning of the following month.

THIRD PART

> In the remotest of forests I seek
> But a gloomy shelter, a shadowy refuge
> Where man's footstep has never trod.
>
> *Vicenta Maturana*

> Je meurs, et sur ma tombe, ou lentement j'arrive
> Nul ne viendra verser des pleurs.[12]
>
> *Gilbert*

During the first months of my stay in Europe I received various letters from my father, in which he gave me an account of Dolores's health. She was getting worse every day, and at the end of several months' time everyone had totally given up hope. In spite of their efforts and consultations with the nation's most renowned doctors, the destructive hand of this horrible and mysterious disease continued to ravage the beauty and even the human body of my unhappy cousin. She lived hidden away, without air or light, begging for permission to flee from the atmosphere which was stifling her.

Finally, among other letters I received the following one from Dolores:

There's no help anymore, my dear Pedro! For two months now I have been dead to the outside world, and find myself in this solitude. You will listen patiently to my troubles; oh, have pity on me!

But no—why complain? Providence is blind, and there are times . . . I don't dare read what is at the bottom of my soul. I'll tell you how my parting from my aunt was, and the arrival here. If my letter is incoherent, forgive me: at times my spirit gives way under so much suffering!

I don't know if you knew this, but I insisted so long that finally I got them to begin to construct a small house, a little cabin, but clean and comfortable, on the site I had picked. I wanted to go myself and show them the exact spot where it should be built. Nevertheless, months went by before it was finished, and even though I begged that it be completed quickly, I realized that my aunt could not bring herself to this separation. Tired of pleading, however, I seriously threatened to run away from home, and got what I wanted.

I always stayed hidden away, and spoke with my aunt and your father through the grille over the window of my room, or though the crack in the door.

One day they came to tell me that the house was finished, and that the necessary furniture, my birds, and some flowers had been taken over there. My poor aunt had gone to great pains to see that I had all the comforts I might want. After making some suggestions as to personal hygiene, your father came to tell me that among other things that had been taken to my future home, there was a small medical kit and instructions as to its use. "There you will find everything," he told me, "that should see you through the different stages of the disease, until, until . . . " When he said these words, the dear old man who had cared for me so much burst into tears. I had opened the door a bit to speak with him more easily, and when I heard the sound of that intense pain, I felt an overwhelming despair in my heart; opening the door completely, I knelt down on the floor and cried out in anguish, "Oh, Uncle, Uncle . . . you have it in your power to ease my suffering; oh, for God's sake, give me something . . . something to shorten my life!"

Your father covered his face with his hands, and did not answer me. But then I heard my aunt coming down the hall, and I immediately came to my senses; by an enormous effort of will I stood up, went into my room, and closed the door. But she had seen me, and, while pounding on the door, shouted, "Dolores, Dolores, that's too great a sacrifice; you can't leave me like this!"

I felt a momentary weakness, but it passed and I answered her with a firm voice: "I want to leave tomorrow at dawn, and I am asking for the last time that no one come near me when I go."

That night I slept well. My agitation had gone, and I felt strong in the face of my decision. Before dawn broke people came to tell me that my horse was ready. I got up, and, leaving my room, crossed the hall where I had my aviary, took a last look at the garden, the pond, the trees . . . everything that reminded me of my happy childhood and the dreams of my brief youth. I refused to think, or linger: the cold, sad light of dawn began to illuminate things, which took on a fantastic appearance. My favorite dog followed me, leaping joyfully.

The foreman, who was to accompany me to my cabin, and two or three other servants were waiting for me in the patio. I wanted no one's help and with one bound leapt into the saddle.

"Good-bye," I said with a choked voice, as I spoke to the servants, "tell my aunt . . . "

Unable to say another thing, I lashed the horse with the reins, and, as he is very spirited, I shot out of the patio like lightning, followed by the foreman. I don't know what I felt then. My whole life, in its most intimate details, went through my mind, the way they say happens to people who are drowning. I thought I was going to faint and fall off the horse, when a faraway cry, muffled by distance, made me rein in my mount, and, looking behind me, I saw my aunt, who had gotten on a horse and was following me.

"Dolores, my darling!" she said when she reached me. "Do you think I would let you leave my house like a criminal without accompanying you to your place of exile?"

"I'm sorry, Aunt; I did think so, and my heart broke at the thought, but as you had promised not to see me again . . . "

"Yes, yes, I did say that. But how could I not see you or speak to you for the last time?"

I let my handkerchief flutter in the wind to see from whence it blew, and, placing myself in the opposite direction, answered her: "Only once, and out in the open air can't hurt you. Promise me, though, that you won't come near me; if you don't, I swear, Aunt, I'll carry out my threat and go far, far away; I'll hide, and die in the depths of the wilderness."

"Aunt," I added, "this is our last conversation. Let us speak with all the judiciousness and resignation a Christian can muster on his deathbed. Let no tears interrupt us, and don't let's break down. The essential sacrifice has been made; let us accept it as a test sent us by Providence. When we reach the edge of the mountain I will go on ahead without saying anything. We will not utter the word 'good-bye'; we both need a strength we would lose were we to say farewell."

And that's what we did. We spoke with apparent calm of how I would organize my life, but our hearts were broken. When we reached the narrow trail you will recall, I rode ahead in silence, and, when I crossed the path that leads to my cabin I involuntarily turned my head; through the trees I saw that my aunt had stopped, and was looking after me with deep sorrow. I will probably never see her again!

For a long time I received no other word from Dolores; my father told me only that she continued in her isolation, and had forbidden anyone to come near her. On one occasion he wrote me in a very troubled state. It seems that one day he was told that Dolores was extremely ill; he was at my aunt's ranch and could not keep her from finding out what was being said about Dolores. Aunt Juana became alarmed, and, forgetting about her promise, insisted on accompanying my father to my cousin's cabin at all cost.

Without being seen they reached the house, which consisted of a small living room and a bedroom; a tiny, flower-filled patio separated the latter from the kitchen and the pantry, and among the vines which trailed in a diminutive corridor hung cages filled with birds. They went into the living room, which held several pieces of furniture and many books on the tables. When she heard them come in, Dolores came out of the bedroom without taking any precautions. She was so disfigured that my aunt let out a horrified shriek, and covered her face with her hands. Dolores paused a moment; when she saw the expression on the faces of her aunt and uncle, she passed them by without a word, and went out the door. My father followed her, calling her name, and saw her vanish into the forest. As she did not answer, he ran to the place where she had disappeared; he walked along the edge of the stream, continually calling her name, until he got to a clearing. The dense forest closed in completely farther up the hill, and the stream, compressed between two boulders, could not be crossed without getting wet up to one's knees. Dolores neither appeared nor answered; my father thought she had taken another path and went back to the house to consult with my cousin's servants. They had never seen her leave like this, and immediately ran to look for her. My aunt was so upset and worried that my father urged her to return to the ranch while he stayed behind to look for Dolores.

Hours passed, and it was impossible to find her. The servants and all the ranch hands joined in, but night came and went without any news of her. The first light of dawn found my father still filled with anguish, for besides Dolores's disappearance, my aunt had fallen gravely ill.

At this point it would be better to transcribe part of the letter I received from Dolores, in which she told me what had happened.

. . . I thought, Pedro, that you would never hear from me again . . . I wanted to die, dear friend, and I couldn't make it happen.

Lately I had felt very ill, in body and in spirit: I was horribly weak, and spent days without speaking or eating much of anything. Isidora and her brother were probably alarmed at seeing me in this state, and notified the family; I have not wanted to ask them how it was that your father and Aunt Juana suddenly appeared at the cabin. When they saw me the expression of horror on their faces was such that in a second I understood that I was no longer a member of the human race, and without knowing what I was doing, I left the house. I think I went mad: I seemed to hear the hoofbeats of a hundred runaway horses that were after me, and heard the baying of countless dogs . . . Hurriedly I climbed up the bank of the stream, and, when I reached a particularly wild spot, waded through the water without feeling myself getting wet, or realizing that I was getting scratched by the hawthorns in the forest. At last my strength gave out and I stopped. I no longer heard the shouts or the running of those I thought were after me, and found myself alone in the midst of the wilderness: the only sound was the buzzing of the insects, the trill of the birds, and the crunching of the dry leaves when I walked on them. I was completely exhausted; I don't know if I went to sleep or fainted, but I fell to the ground as one dead. When I came to it was almost totally dark there in the heart of the forest. What to do? Death seemed to me a release. I got up to look for a cliff, but up there the mountain is a gentle, hilly slope, and I found no appropriate place.

I felt no pain at all (you know that one of the consequences of the disease is that your skin loses feeling), but nevertheless I was badly scratched, covered with blood, and my clothes were in tatters. After having wandered about for a long time, I came to a clearing where broad, moss-covered rocks lay at the feet of some very tall trees. It was deliciously cool there; I lay down on one of the rocks and looked up at the sky. Night had fallen, and as darkness fell on the earth the sky became covered with stars. The heavenly lanterns lit up one by one, like candles on an altar. So many constellations, such wonderful sparkling in those faraway suns, such an immensity of worlds and endless universes . . . ! Little by little the mysterious magnificence of that spectacle assuaged my despair. Who was I to rebel against fate? Those rays of light were dying before they ever reached my remote spot, yet still seemed to look on me with compassion . . . Compassion! Isn't everyone horrified by me? No, perhaps there is some person who still remembers me tenderly. I'll tell you the truth: Antonio's memory saved me, as I think I knew by intuition that he had not forgotten me. Wouldn't the certainty of his distant affection be enough for me to live on with resignation? Don't think me ungrateful: I remembered you, too; you, at least, did not appear to be horrified when you saw me.

The night was starry, but very dark. I did not feel I had the courage to spend the whole night in the heart of that wilderness. When the nervous excitement which stirred me up had abated, I felt tremendous exhaustion, and wanted to find a safe spot where I could lie down without being afraid. I recalled that I had gone upstream, and oriented myself by the stars at which I had gazed so long in my solitude. I looked for a bright star that always shines on the horizon when the sun goes down, and went in a direction in which I would find the hut of a poor paralyzed woman who lives there in the wilderness with a retarded son. I soon realized I had come across a narrow path, and attempted to follow it. I don't know why I wasn't bitten by the thousands of poisonous animals that crawled on the ground, hung from branches or flew shrieking round about me. The star vanished behind the trees, and the night became progressively darker; I had lost my shoes, and my feet refused to carry me any further when I heard a dog bark: what a delightful sound for me! A few steps farther on I found the hut; warding off the dog with a stick I had found in the forest and was using as a cane, I pushed aside the rushes that served as a door and, waking the invalid woman, I asked permission to curl up in a corner.

I spent the night in misery, constantly waking up in a fright, but my weariness made me fall asleep again. When dawn came, the retarded boy got up, lit a fire in the center of the hut, placed a pot on three stones lying there, and made a soup from yucca, bananas, and salted meat. I remained motionless in my corner until he offered me a plate of hot soup, and realized that the major part of my weakness stemmed from a lack of food. I accepted and ate heartily what they put before me; when I finished I broke the bowl as though by accident and threw away the spoon.

As the sun rose it got hotter in the hut and at last I went to the door to get some air. My muddy, ragged dress, disheveled hair, and undoubtedly dreadful appearance had an effect on the owners of the house. There was no way for them to recognize me, although in previous times I had visited the sick woman on several occasions. But although they did not know who I was, the paralyzed woman guessed the nature of the illness which afflicted me, and gently told me that it would be better if I sat outside the hut on the ground . . . I was aware of the revulsion I caused even in those unfortunate beings and went out, completely humiliated. I wanted to let my relatives know that I would not return to my cabin again until they solemnly promised me they would never return there. The retarded boy could not speak intelligibly, so how could I get my message across? In my pocket I found a pencil which by chance had not been lost during my flight, and the paralyzed woman gave me a scrap of paper the retarded boy had brought along with some medicines sent by Aunt Juana. I placed the paper on the trunk of a fallen tree which lay near the house, and with a shaking hand wrote a few lines, then gave them to the boy to take to the ranch, promising to pay him well.

That afternoon my two servants arrived. Isidora brought me clothes, and Juan a saddled horse and a letter from your father, in which he told me that my aunt was gravely ill, on account of the grief I had caused them; in the end he promised not to try to see me without my consent.

I returned to my cabin to take care of myself . . . yes, I took care of myself! Oh unhappy humanity! Wasn't it better to let myself die? In our hearts there is always this love of life, and as miserable as it is, we take pleasure in prolonging it . . . Yes, Pedro: while I took care of my horrible existence, while I regained strength to keep on living, my poor aunt was dying as a result of the fright, the worry, and the anguish I had caused her. Apparently she developed a violent fever and died two days later without recognizing anyone, but haunted by my memory and continually calling my name. Perhaps you think me insensitive, unnatural when you see that I can speak calmly of the death of someone who loved me so dearly. I don't know what to say: I don't understand myself, and think that I may have lost the ability to feel. I never cry; I think the source of my tears has dried up. I never complain, nor am I moved. I long anxiously for death, but don't dare seek it out, and even attempt to avoid it.

My spirit is chaos, my existence a ghastly nightmare. I beg you to send me some books. I want to nourish my spirit with beautiful thoughts; I want to live with the dead, and communicate with them.

Dolores's letter made a deep impression on me. I saw that her particularly sweet character had changed because of her suffering, and that helped me assess the extent of her troubles. I got together some good books and sent them to her. During the years that followed I received only a few short letters from Dolores: their essence was at times one of wrenching sadness, and there was a certain lack of religious faith and a hatred of humankind in her thoughts that filled me with sorrow. My father wrote me that he had never seen her again, but that every week he sent a person with things she might need and to bring word of her.

Antonio had repented of his thoughtless conduct toward me, and we continued a very active correspondence. The first painful shock when he grasped Dolores's awful fate and the impossibility of her ever being his were not enough to discourage him: his vigorous character would not allow that. On the contrary, he attempted to get over his sorrow by throwing himself into his demanding work and constant study. He was soon known as a man of talent, hardworking and eloquent, and succeeded in attaining an honorable place among the nation's statesmen.

I had spent several years studying in Europe and was preparing to return home when I received word of my father's death. I cannot express what I felt at that point . . . Dolores wrote me as well, describing the bereavement in which she had been left.

Although at first I loathed the idea of visiting my empty home, I could not resist the desire to return to Dolores's side, and took passage home.

I was just passing through Bogotá, but Antonio detained me there in order to attend his wedding. He was marrying a young woman of one of the city's best families, wealthy, and very respected. I wrote Dolores immediately, explaining the reason for my delay, and telling her the news of Antonio's brilliant match.

The wedding was sumptuous, though not joyful. The bride was not beautiful, but her cultured manners, polished education, and natural goodness made one forget her lack of physical charms. After the ceremony, when I was saying good-bye to Antonio at the door of his house, he gave me a letter for Dolores, a letter he had written that day, and in his eyes I saw a single tear glisten, the last tribute to his youthful dreams.

Eight days later I reached the outskirts of N***, and instead of going into town, immediately took the little-traveled road to that corner of the valley where Dolores lived. When I reached the path I had taken years ago with my cousin, my imagination brought back to me once again Dolores's slender figure, her brilliant eyes and lighthearted words; once more I heard the echo of her silvery laugh which to me still hovered in that desolate spot. How my life had changed since then! My aunt had died, my poor father as well, my fiancée was someone else's wife (I don't know if I've told that she married Don Basilio), and finally my cousin, that happy girl of former times, was a profoundly unfortunate human being. I had not wanted to go to the town which held such sad memories for me, and I knew nothing of Dolores.

When I approached the place where my cousin's cabin should have been, I heard a certain sound which astonished me. Several saddled horses stood under a tree; I spurred my own, and reached the door of the little house just as the priest and several people from N*** were leaving.

"What an amazing coincidence!" said the priest when he recognized me and detained me in the doorway.

He was a respected old man who had been the village priest ever since I was a child.

"Dolores is inside?" I asked, after I had greeted him.

"Dolores? But didn't you know . . . ?"

"What? I want to speak with her."

"No, don't go in," he answered, taking my hand.

"What's happened?"

"Poor girl!" he said with a shaken voice. "This morning her suffering came to an end."

"My God!" I exclaimed, feeling that the last link that bound me to the memories of this place had disappeared, and then I realized just how essential this attachment had been for me.

Sitting down in silence on the threshold of Dolores's house, I hid my face in my hands. The people surrounding the priest moved away out of respect for my feelings; the priest sat down beside me.

"Her death was a Christian one," said the good clergyman. "A few days ago she asked me to come to see her, saying that there was no need to come near her because she would speak to me through her bedroom door. I came several times, and yesterday she made her final confession and received the last rites. This morning I was told that she was dying; up to that point I had not been able to see her, and I won't tell you how greatly she had changed!

"Now," he said a moment later, "having been present when she died, I was just going back to the parish to make arrangements for the burial."

I did my duty. I went to the funeral. She had asked to be buried in the patio of her little house, and ordered that all was to be left uninhabited.

Among her papers I found a will leaving everything to me, and some works in prose and verse. Here are a few fragments of a diary she kept, which help one to understand her character better, as well as the terrible moral suffering she underwent, her misgivings and her despair.

June 23, 1843

For a year now I have been suffering alone, isolated, abandoned by the whole world in this wilderness. Oh! If there were only someone to remember me, how could I not feel bursts of consolation that would inspire this tormented heart to resignation? Far away, down on the plain, people run about and enjoy themselves. Tomorrow is Saint John's day, the anniversary of the festival in N★★★. The festival! What memories come to mind! Today by chance I found a bouquet of dried jasmine—is it possible that this monstrous being that appears before me when I draw near the mirror is the pretty girl to whom these flowers were given? Antonio, Antonio, you whom I love in the secret recesses of my soul, whose memory is my only consolation, Antonio, do you perchance still remember the unhappy girl you loved? If you knew how your image haunts me! Your name resounds in the whispering branches of the trees, in the murmuring of the stream, in the scent of my favorite flowers, in the wind that whistles, among the pages of the book I am reading, in the tip of the pen with which I write; I see your initials in the wide, starry sky, among the clouds at sunset, in the sand of the brook in which I bathe . . . Holy God! That this love should be so great, so deep, so boundless, and yet my burning heart lies mute forever!

December 8, 1843

Life is a black coffin into which we find ourselves locked. Is death perhaps the beginning of another life? What irony! In the depths of my thoughts I only find a sensation of nothingness. If there were a God Who was as just and merciful as people are wont to describe Him, would He let an unfortunate soul like me suffer? Oh, Death, come, come to the aid of the unhappiest being on earth! Solitude everywhere, silence, stillness, Nature's maddening calm! . . . The sky with its ghastly beauty fills me with horror, I am not moved by the moon and its highly exalted loveliness, the countryside bores me, flowers remind me of my past life. Flowers, earth, pure scents, harmonies of Nature which are emblems of life: why come and arouse deep feelings in one who no longer exists? . . .

May 1844

. . . Awful martyrdom . . . the illness is not following its normal course. Will I live many more years? There are nights I wake up totally agitated: I dreamt I finally got hold of a pistol, but when I tried to kill myself it wouldn't go off, and in my struggle to get it to fire I woke up . . . Other times I dream I am swimming in an abundantly flowing river, and I let myself be carried gently by the waves which are engulfing me, but when I feel I am drowning, an intense rush of joy awakens me.

February 18[45][13]

Today I received a letter from Pedro which consoled me. There still is someone, aside from my good uncle, who remembers me . . . I said that the letter consoled me: that's a lie! I reread it and it caused me new pain. He tells me of his quiet life, his studies, and his plans for the future. Men are creation's cruelest beings: they take pleasure in making us aware of our misfortune. In the Middle Ages, when a person was declared a leper, he was immediately considered a corpse: he was taken to the church, the funeral mass was sung, and he was shut away the rest of his days like a filthy being . . . But at least they never again had any contact with society; morally they were dead, and never heard echoes of the lives of the persons they held dear. Yet I, I who have withdrawn to the depths of an American wilderness: even here memory follows me . . . What does it mean to love? To love is to have pleasant feelings. Doctors say lepers have lost their nervous system. Then for what purpose do I feel? Why do I tenderly recall the people I loved?

April 1845

. . . God, religion, future life! Unfathomable questions! Terrible vacillations of my soul! If my disease were only physical, if it were only my body that was sick! But the nature of one's character changes, and every day I feel I have become cruel, like the animals in this wilderness, cold and hard toward humanity like the rocks in the stream. There are times when in a fit of madness I rush to my flowers which seem to insult me with their loveliness, and I shred them, I throw them to the winds; a moment later my reason returns, I tenderly look for them and weep when I find they are withered. Other times my soul rebels: it cannot believe that a good God would make me suffer so much, and in my rebellion I deny His existence; afterward . . . I humble myself, I throw myself on my knees, and fall into endless adoration of the Supreme Being . . .

September 1845

Ever the silence, the loneliness, the absence of a friendly voice which might caress me with an affectionate tone. Eternal separation! Can there be a more terrifying concept for one who was born to love?

January 1, 1846

I am going through a time of discouragement and total lethargy. Lately I have lived as though in dreams . . . I am neither sad nor desperate. I feel that in my heart there is nothing: I am indifferent to everything; life is suffering, death . . . everything passes, and mingles in my soul's shadows; nothing can move me. One feeling! One feeling, even if it were of sorrow, fear, horror (the only thing to which I can aspire) would be blessed by me as a consolation: such is the state I am in! This is worse than my maddened desperation in the past. I vegetate like a worm-eaten tree; I live like a stone in some deserted spot . . .

March 1846

At times I intend to study, read, learn, in order to do something, devote myself to intellectual tasks, and thus forget my condition; I try to flee from myself, but always, always, thought pursues me, and, as a French writer said, "Le chagrin monte en croupe et galope avec moi."[14]

Woman is essentially a loving being, and in all of life's events wants only to shine before those whom she loves. In her, vanity is for the sake of love, as in man it is for ambition. For whom do I learn? My studies, my education, my gifts, even if it is true that I have them, all of this is useless, for I can never inspire a feeling of admiration: I am alone, forever alone . . .

September 6, 1846

Everything is over for me now. I am going to die soon: even with an effort my hand is scarcely able to write these lines. How I had longed for this day! But why was I not fortunate enough to die sooner, when I [still] had a dream? Perhaps I am unjust, but this blow, so to speak, undid the last link that chained me to life. I received a letter from Pedro, dated in Bogotá. My poor cousin, I thought on opening it, soon I will hear your voice, and through him, too, I will have some direct news of Antonio . . . My heart beat with sweet emotion and I felt faint. I sat down by the banks of the stream which runs burbling near my room. How happy I had been to see the servant who brought the letter! Antonio's image hovered around me . . .

After reading the first lines a cloud passed before my eyes. Pedro told me of Antonio's wedding. Antonio's wedding! Why did I initially refuse to believe it? Is he not free to love another? Nevertheless, the most awful, overwhelming grief came over me: I knelt down on the beach and let myself be swept away by the gale force of my pain. I envisioned myself alone, oh, so alone, bereft of the only affection for which I longed. Everything around me spoke of Antonio, and his memory alone dwelt in my sad abode. No corner of my hut, no tree or flower in my garden, no star in the blue heaven, no singing bird failed to tell me things in his name. My life was part of his memory, and now? He loves another woman. What an absurd idea! How many others will he most likely have loved since we parted! How strange! Earlier this did not bother me, and now I can't relinquish this idea for one moment. It was as though my soul were waiting for this last disillusionment in order to depart this miserable body. I understand that all of these symptoms portend a speedy death. Thank you, dear God! I am about to end all my suffering, but *he* is all I think about in these final moments. Oh! *He* will forget me and be happy!

THE END

Notes

1. "Nature is a play with characters."
2. Liquor; literally "burning water."
3. Make a good match.
4. A type of poncho.

5. "Her eyes are quite pretty . . . for provincial eyes."

6. "He who wins without danger, triumphs without glory."

7. Venus is the goddess of love; Lucrece, a Roman matron, is the symbol of conjugal fidelity; Minerva is the goddess of wisdom; Virginia is the heroine of the popular novel *Paul et Virginie* (1787), written by Bernardin de St. Pierre; Pegasus is the winged horse of mythology.

8. "Pain is a light which illuminates our life."

9. The Borgias (or Borjas) were a famous Spanish family of the fifteenth and sixteenth centuries, one of whose members became a saint (Saint Francis Borgia); others, such as Pope Alexander VI and his illegitimate son, Cesare, had few scruples, and were known to do away with their enemies by poison.

10. El Espinal is a small town southwest of Bogotá, in the province of Tolima.

11. Chiquinquirá, due north of Bogotá, is a town where there is a cult to a miraculous Virgin.

12. "I am dying, and over my grave, to which I am slowly borne / No one will come to shed tears."

13. The date in the original is 1864, which is an error.

14. "Suffering leaps up behind my saddle and gallops along with me."

Works Cited

Acosta de Samper, Soledad. *Novelas y cuadros de la vida sur-americana.*
Gante: Imprenta de Eug. Vanderhaegen, 1869.

———. *Una nueva lectura.* Introd. Montserrat Ordóñez. Bogotá: Fondo
Cultural Cafetero, 1988.

Alzate-Cadavid, Carolina. "Cristóbal Colón e Isabel de Guevara: Voz
narrativa y autoridad." Unpublished paper. October 1993.

Antoni, Claudio G. "A Comparative Examination of Style in the Works
of Madre Castillo." Diss. City University of New York, 1979.

Arenal, Electa, and Stacey Schlau. *Untold Sisters: Hispanic Nuns in Their
Own Works.* Trans. Amanda Powell. Albuquerque: University of New
Mexico Press, 1989.

Auerbach, Emily. *Sor Juana Inés de la Cruz.* The Courage to Write Series.
With Electa Arenal, Nina M. Scott, and Margarita Zamora. Audio-
cassette. University of Wisconsin–Madison, 1997.

Bénassy-Berling, Marie-Cécile. *Humanismo y religión en Sor Juana Inés de
la Cruz.* Trans. Laura López de Belair. México: Universidad Nacional
Autónoma de México, 1983.

Benítez-Rojo, Antonio. "Power/Sugar/Literature: Toward a Reinterpre-
tation of Cubanness." Trans. Jorge Hernández Martín. *Cuban Studies*
16 (1986): 9–31.

Berg, Mary. "Viajeras y exiliadas en la narrativa de Juana Manuela Gorriti." *Mujeres y cultura en la Argentina del siglo XIX.* Ed. Lea Fletcher.
Buenos Aires: Feminaria Editora, 1994. 69–79.

———. "Rereading Fiction by 19th-Century Latin American Women
Writers: Interpretation and Translation of the Past into the Present."
Translating Latin America: Culture as Text. Ed. William Luis and Julio
Rodríguez Luis. Binghamton, NY: Center for Research in Transla-
tion, 1991. 127–33.

Bergmann, Emilie L. "Sor Juana Inés de la Cruz: Dreaming in a Double
Voice." *Women, Culture, and Politics in Latin America.* Ed. Emilie
Bergmann et al. Berkeley: University of California Press, 1990.
151–72.

Bravo-Villasante, Carmen. *25 mujeres a través de sus cartas*. Madrid: Editorial Almena, 1975. 27–31.

―――. *Una vida romántica: La Avellaneda*. Madrid: Instituto de Cooperación Iberoamericana, 1986.

Cabello de Carbonera, Mercedes. *Blanca Sol*. Lima: Torres Aguirre, 1888.

―――. "Estudio comparativo de la inteligencia y la belleza en la mujer." Juana Manuela Gorriti. *Veladas literarias de Lima, 1876–1877*. Tomo 1. Veladas 1–10. Buenos Aires: Imprenta Europea, 1892. 207–12.

―――. "La novela moderna: Estudio filosófico." 1892. 2d ed. Lima: Ediciones Hora del Hombre, 1948.

Castillo, Francisca Josefa de. "Madre Castillo's *Afectos espirituales*. Trans. and comm. Kathleen Jeanette Jarvis. Master's thesis. University of Texas at Austin, 1985.

―――. *Obras completas de la Madre Francisca Josefa de la Concepción del Castillo,* según fiel transcripción de los manuscritos originales que se conservan en la Biblioteca Luis-Angel Arango. 2 vols. Introducción, notas e índices elaborados por Darío Achury Valenzuela. Bogotá: Talleres Gráficos del Banco de la República, 1968.

Cotarelo y Mori, Emilio. *La Avellaneda y sus obras: Ensayo biográfico y crítico*. Madrid: Tipografía de Archivos, 1930.

Crow, John A. *The Epic of Latin America*. 1946. 3d ed. Berkeley: University of California Press, 1980.

Cruz, Sor Juana Inés de la. *Inundación castálida*. Ed. Georgina Sabàt de Rivers. Madrid: Editorial Castalia, 1982.

―――. *Obras completas*. 4 vols. Vols. 1–3, ed. Alfonso Méndez Plancarte. Vol. 4, ed. Alberto G. Salceda. México: Fondo de Cultura Económica, 1951–57.

Dekker, Rudolf, and Lotte van der Pol. *The Tradition of Female Transvestism in Early Modern Europe*. New York: St. Martin's Press, 1989.

De la Maza, Francisco. *Sor Juana Inés de la Cruz ante la historia*. Rev. Elías Trabulse. México: Universidad Nacional Autónoma de México, 1980.

Dugaw, Diane. *Warrior Woman and Popular Balladry, 1650–1850*. Cambridge: Cambridge University Press, 1989.

Encinales de Sanjinés, Paulina. "La obra de Soledad Acosta de Samper ¿Un proyecto cultural?" *Mujeres latinoamericanas: Historia y cultura. Siglos XVI al XIX*. 2 vols. Ed. Luisa Campuzano. Tomo II. La Habana: Fondo Editorial Casa de las Américas, 1997. 227–32.

Epple, Juan Armando. "Mercedes Cabello de Carbonera y el problema de la novela moderna en el Perú." *Doctores y proscritos*. Ed. S. Muñoz. Minneapolis: Institute for the Study of Ideologies and Literature, 1987. 233–53.

Erauso, Catalina de. *Historia de la monja alférez Doña Catalina de Erauso, escrita por ella misma*. 1829. Ed. Joaquín María Ferrer. Madrid: Tipografía Renovación, 1918.

———. *Lieutenant Nun: Memoir of a Basque Transvestite in the New World*. Trans. Michele Stepto and Gabriel Stepto. Boston: Beacon Press, 1996.

———. *The Nun Ensign*. Trans. James Fitzmaurice-Kelly. Also *La monja alférez*, a Play in the Original Spanish, by Juan Pérez de Montalbán. London: T. Fisher Unwin, 1908.

———. *Vida i sucesos de la Monja Alférez: Autobiografía atribuida a Doña Catalina de Erauso*. Ed. Rima de Vallbona. Tempe, AZ: ASU Center for Latin American Studies, 1992.

Figarola Caneda, Domingo, y Doña Emilia Boxhorn. *Gertrudis Gómez de Avellaneda: Biografía, bibliografía e iconografía, incluyendo muchas cartas, inéditas y publicadas, escritas por la gran poetisa o dirigidas a ella, y sus memorias*. Madrid: Sociedad General Española de Librería, 1929.

Fitzmaurice-Kelly, James. Introduction. *The Nun Ensign*. Trans. James Fitzmaurice-Kelly. Also *La monja alférez*, a Play in the Original Spanish, by Juan Pérez de Montalbán. London: T. Fisher Unwin, 1908. xv–xl.

Fletcher, Lea, ed. *Mujeres y cultura en la Argentina del siglo XIX*. Buenos Aires: Feminaria Editora, 1994.

———. "Patriarchy, Medicine, and Women Writers in Nineteenth-Century Argentina." *The Body and the Text: Comparative Essays in Literature and Medicine*. Ed. Bruce Clark and Wendell Aycock. Lubbock: Texas Tech University Press, 1990. 91–110.

Franco, Jean. *Plotting Women: Gender and Representation in Mexico*. New York: Columbia University Press, 1989.

———. "Writers in Spite of Themselves: The Mystical Nuns of Seventeenth-Century Mexico." *Plotting Women: Gender and Representation in Mexico*. New York: Columbia University Press, 1989. 3–22.

Garber, Marjorie. "Foreword: The Marvel of Peru." *Lieutenant Nun: Memoir of a Basque Transvestite in the New World*. Trans. Michele Stepto and Gabriel Stepto. Boston: Beacon Press, 1996. vii–xxiv.

García y García, Elvira, ed. "Mercedes Cabello de Carbonera." *La mujer peruana a través de los siglos: Serie historiada de estudios y observaciones.* 2 vols. Lima: Imprenta Americana, 1924–25. II: 18–22.

———. "Teresa González de Fanning." *La mujer peruana a través de los siglos: Serie historiada de estudios y observaciones.* 2 vols. Lima: Imprenta Americana, 1924–25. 2: 29–32.

Glantz, Margo. *Sor Juana Inés de la Cruz: ¿Hagiografía o autobiografía?* México: Editorial Grijalbo, 1995.

Gómez de Avellaneda, Gertrudis. *Cartas inéditas existentes en el Museo del Ejército.* Ed. José Priego Fernández del Campo. Madrid: Fundación Universitaria Española, 1975.

———. *Diario íntimo.* Ed. Lorenzo Cruz de Fuentes. Buenos Aires: Ediciones Universal, 1945.

———. *Obras de doña Gertrudis Gómez de Avellaneda.* 6 vols. Habana: Imprenta A. Miranda,1914.

———. *Sab* and *Autobiography.* Trans. and ed. Nina M. Scott. Austin: University of Texas Press, 1993.

———. "Women." ["La mujer."] Trans. Nina M. Scott. *Rereading the Spanish American Essay: Translations of 19th- and 20th-Century Women's Essays.* Ed. Doris Meyer. Austin: University of Texas Press, 1995. 25–39.

González de Fanning, Teresa. *Educación femenina: Colección de artículos pedagógicos, morales y sociológicos.* Lima: "El Lucero," 1905.

———. "Trabajo para la muger." Juana Manuela Gorriti. *Veladas literarias de Lima: 1876–1877.* Buenos Aires: Imprenta Europea, 1892. 286–93.

Gorriti, Juana Manuela. "Chincha." Trans. Mary G. Berg. *Rereading the Spanish American Essay: Translations of 19th- and 20th-Century Women's Essays.* Ed. Doris Meyer. Austin: University of Texas Press, 1995. 61–66.

Guerra, Lucía. "Estrategias femeninas en la elaboración del sujeto romántico en la obra de Gertrudis Gómez de Avellaneda." *Revista Iberoamericana* 51 (July-Dec. 1985): 707–22.

Guerra Cunningham, Lucía. "La modalidad hermética de la subjetividad romántica en la narrativa de Soledad Acosta de Samper." Acosta de Samper, *Una nueva lectura,* 353–67.

———. "Mercedes Cabello de Carbonera: Estética de la moral y los desvíos no-disyuntivos de la virtud." *Revista de Crítica Literaria Latinoamericana* 26 (1987): 25–41.

————. "Visión marginal de la historia en la narrativa de Juana Manuela Gorriti." *Ideologies and Literature* 11 (Fall 1987): 59–76.

Guevara, Isabel de. "Carta de Doña Isabel de Guevara a la princesa gobernadora Doña JUANA . . . " *Cartas de Indias.* Madrid: Imprenta de Manuel G. Hernández, 1877. 619–21.

HarperCollins Study Bible. New Revised Standard Version. Gen. ed. Wayne A. Meeks. New York: HarperCollins, 1989.

Harter, Hugh A. *Gertrudis Gómez de Avellaneda.* Boston: Twayne, 1981.

Hinds, Harold E., Jr. "Life and Early Literary Career of the Nineteenth-Century Colombian Writer Soledad Acosta de Samper." *Latin American Women Writers: Yesterday and Today.* Ed. Yvette E. Miller and Charles M. Tatum. Pittsburgh: Latin American Literary Review, 1977. 32–41.

Iglesia, Cristina. "Prólogo." *El ajuar de la patria: Ensayos críticos sobre Juana Manuela Gorriti.* Ed. Cristina Iglesia. Buenos Aires: Feminaria Editora, 1993. 5–10.

Johnson, Julie Greer. *Women in Colonial Spanish American Literature: Literary Images.* Westport, CT: Greenwood Press, 1983. 169–83.

Karttunen, Frances. *Between Worlds: Interpreters, Guides, and Survivors.* New Brunswick: Rutgers University Press, 1994.

Kimmel, Michael S. "The Struggle for Gender Equality: How Men Respond." *Thought and Action* 8 (Winter 1993): 49–76.

Kirkpatrick, Susan. *Las Románticas: Women Writers and Subjectivity in Spain, 1835–1850.* Berkeley: University of California Press, 1989.

Lavrin, Asunción. "Female Religious." *Cities and Society in Colonial Latin America.* Ed. Louisa Schell Hoberman and Susan Migden Socolow. Albuquerque: University of New Mexico Press, 1986. 165–95.

————. "*Lo femenino:* Women in Colonia Historical Sources." *Coded Encounters: Writing, Gender and Ethnicity in Colonial Latin America.* Ed. Francisco Javier Cevallos-Candau, Jeffrey A. Cole, Nina M. Scott, and Nicomedes Suárez-Araúz. Amherst: University of Massachusetts Press, 1994.

León, Fray Luis de. *La perfecta casada.* Duodécima edición. Madrid: Espasa Calpe, 1983.

Leonard, Irving A. *Baroque Times in Old Mexico.* Ann Arbor: University of Michigan Press, 1959.

Lewis, Bart L. "Art, Society and Criticism: The Literary Theories of Mercedes Cabello de Carbonera and Clorinda Matto de Turner." *Letras Femeninas* 10 (1984): 66–73.

Lockhart, James, and Enrique Otte, eds. *Letters and People of the Spanish Indies: The Sixteenth Century*. London: Cambridge University Press, 1976. 15–17.

Lopreto, Gladys. "Isabel de Guevara: La primera feminista." *Todo es Historia* 34 (March 1991): 43–49.

Luciani, Frederick. "The Burlesque Sonnets of Sor Juana Inés de la Cruz." *Hispanic Journal* 8 (1986): 85–95.

Ludmer, Josefina. "Tretas del débil." *La sartén por el mango: Encuentro de escritoras latinoamericanas*. Ed. Patricia Elena González and Eliana Ortega. Río Piedras, Puerto Rico: Ediciones Huracán, 1984. 47–54. This essay has also been published in English as "Tricks of the Weak" in Stephanie Merrim's *Feminist Perspectives on Sor Juana Inés de la Cruz*, 86–93.

McKnight, Kathryn Joy. *The Mystic of Tunja: The Writings of Madre Castillo, 1671–1742*. Amherst: University of Massachusetts Press, 1997.

———. "Nexos del discurso femenino y la vida conventual de Sor Juana Inés de la Cruz y Sor Francisca Josefa de la Concepción de Castillo." *Memoria del Coloquio Internacional Sor Juana Inés de la Cruz y el pensamiento novohispano. 1995*. Toluca: Instituto Mexiquense de Cultura, 1995. 241–52.

———. "Sister Acts: Subject, Voice and Intertextuality in the Works of Madre Castillo (1671–1742)." Diss. Stanford University, 1992.

———. "Voz, subjetividad y mística en la Madre Castillo: Tres elementos de una escritura femenina conventual." *Texto y Contexto* 17 (Sept.-Dec. 1991): 66–96.

Marín, Luis. *Daughters of the Conquistadores: Women of the Viceroyalty of Peru*. Dallas: Southern Methodist University Press, 1983.

Marrero-Fente, Raúl. "De retórica y derechos: Estrategias de la reclamación en la carta de Isabel de Guevara." *Hispania* 79 (Mar. 1996): 1–7.

Martin, Leona. "Las veladas literarias de Juana Manuela Gorriti: Un momento dorado del feminismo hispanoamericano." *Mujeres latinoamericanas: Historia y cultura. Siglos XVI al XIX*. Ed. Luisa Campuzano. Tomo II. La Habana: Fondo Editorial Casa de las Américas, 1997. 219–26.

Martínez-San Miguel, Yolanda. "Sujetos femeninos en *Amistad funesta* y *Blanca Sol*: El lugar de la mujer en dos novelas latinoamericanas de fin de siglo XIX. *Revista Iberoamericana* 52 (Jan.-Mar. 1996): 27–45.

Mazquiarán de Rodríguez, Mercedes. "Mercedes Cabello de Carbonera." Trans. Alicia Valero Covarrubias. *Escritoras de Hispanoamérica: Una guia bio-bibliográfica.* Ed. Diane Marting. (Ed. de la edición en español, Montserrat Ordóñez.) Bogotá: Siglo XXI Editores, 1991. 98–108.

Masiello, Francine. "Between Civilization and Barbarism: Women, Family and Literary Culture in Mid-Nineteenth-Century Argentina." *Cultural and Historical Grounding for Hispanic and Luso-Brazilian Feminist Literary Criticism.* Ed. Hernán Vidal. Minneapolis: Institute for the Study of Ideologies and Literature, 1989. 517–66.

———. "Disfraz y delincuencia en la obra de Juana Manuela Gorriti." *El ajuar de la patria: Ensayos críticos sobre Juana Manuela Gorriti.* Ed. Cristina Iglesia. Buenos Aires: Feminaria Editora, 1993. 62–71.

Meehan, Thomas C. "Una olvidada precursora de la literatura fantástica argentina: Juana Manuela Gorriti." *Chasqui* 10 (Feb.-May 1981): 3–19.

Merrim, Stephanie. "Catalina de Erauso: From Anomaly to Icon." *Coded Encounters: Writing, Gender and Ethnicity in Colonial Latin America.* Ed. Francisco Javier Cevallos-Candau, Jeffrey A. Cole, Nina M. Scott, and Nicomedes Suárez Araúz. Amherst: University of Masssachusetts Press, 1993. 177–205.

Merrim, Stephanie, ed. *Feminist Perspectives on Sor Juana Inés de la Cruz.* Detroit: Wayne State University Press, 1991.

Meyer, Doris, ed. *Reinterpreting the Spanish American Essay: Women Writers of the 19th and 20th Centuries.* Austin: University of Texas Press, 1995.

Mignolo, Walter. "Cartas, crónicas y relaciones del descubrimiento y la conquista." *Historia de la literatura hispanoamericana.* Tomo I: *Epoca colonial.* Ed. Iñigo Madrigal. Madrid: Cátedra, 1982. 57–75.

Miller, Beth. "Gertrude the Great: Avellaneda, Nineteenth-Century Feminist." *Icons and Fallen Idols: Women in Spanish American Literature.* Ed. Beth Miller. Berkeley: University of California Press, 1983. 201–14.

Miller, Martin C. "Clorinda Matto de Turner and Mercedes Cabello de Carbonera: Societal Criticism and Morality." *Latin American Women Writers: Yesterday and Today.* Ed. Yvette E. Miller and Charles M. Tatum. Pittsburgh: Latin American Literary Review Press, 1975. 25–32.

Mizraje, María Gabriela. "Juana Manuela Gorriti: Cuentas pendientes." *Mujeres y cultura en la Argentina del siglo XIX.* Ed. Lea Fletcher. Buenos Aires: Feminaria Editora, 1994. 47–60.

Moraña, Mabel. "Orden dogmático y marginalidad en la *Carta de Monterrey* de Sor Juana Inés de la Cruz." *Hispanic Review* 58 (1990): 205–25.

Morison, Samuel Eliot. *Christopher Columbus: Admiral of the Ocean Sea.* Boston: Little, Brown, 1942.

Mújica, Elisa. *Sor Francisca Josefa del Castillo.* Bogotá: Procultura, 1991.

Myers, Kathleen A. 1998. "Broader Canon, Interdisciplinary Approaches: Recent Works in Colonial Latin American Literary Studies." *Latin American Research Review* 33.2 (1998): 258–70.

Netchinsky, Jill Ann. "Engendering a Cuban Literature: Nineteenth-Century Antislavery Narrative (Manzano, Suárez y Romero, Gómez de Avellaneda, A. Zambrana)." Diss. Yale University, 1986.

Niño Dios, Sor María Antonia del. *Flor de santidad: La Madre Castillo.* Tunja: Academia Boyacense de Historia, 1993.

Otero Muñoz, Gustavo. "Doña Soledad Acosta de Samper." Acosta de Samper, *Una nueva lectura,* 369–76.

Ordóñez, Montserrat. "One Hundred Years of Unread Writing: Soledad Acosta, Elisa Mújica and Marvel Moreno." *Knives and Angels: Women Writers in Latin America.* Ed. Susan Bassnett. London: Zed Books, 1990. 132–44.

———. "Soledad Acosta de Samper: Una nueva lectura." Acosta de Samper, *Una nueva lectura,* 11–24.

Pagés-Rangel, Roxana. *Del dominio público: Itinerarios de la carta privada.* Amsterdam: Teoría Literaria: Texto y Teoría 20, 1996.

Paz, Octavio. *Sor Juana Inés de la Cruz o Las trampas de la fe.* Barcelona: Seix Barral, 1982. English translation by Margaret Sayers Peden, *Sor Juana or The Traps of Faith.* Cambridge, MA: Harvard University Press, 1988.

Perry, Mary Elizabeth. *Gender and Disorder in Early Modern Seville.* Princeton: Princeton University Press, 1990.

Picon Garfield, Evelyn. *Poder y sexualidad: El discurso de Gertrudis Gómez de Avellaneda.* Amsterdam: Teoría Literaria: Texto y Teoría 12, 1993.

Plà, Josefina. *Algunas mujeres de la conquista.* Asunción, Paraguay: Newprint, 1985.

Poot Herrera, Sara, ed. *Sor Juana y su mundo: Una mirada actual.* México: Universidad del Claustro de Sor Juana, 1995.

Poot Herrera, Sara, and Elena Urrutia, eds. "*Y diversa de mí misma/entre vuestras plumas ando*": *Homenaje internacional a Sor Juana Inés de la Cruz.* México: El Colegio de México, 1993.

Pratt, Mary Louise. "'Don't Interrupt Me': The Gender Essay as Conversation and Countercanon." *Reinterpreting the Spanish American Essay: Women Writers of the 19th and 20th Centuries.* Ed. Doris Meyer. Austin, TX: University of Texas Press, 1995. 10–26.

Quintana, Isabel A. "Juana Manuela Gorriti y sus mundos." *El ajuar de la patria: Ensayos críticos sobre Juana Manuela Gorriti.* Ed. Cristina Iglesia. Buenos Aires: Feminaria Editora, 1993. 72–79.

Robledo, Angela. "La pluralidad discursiva como mecanismo de afirmación personal en *Su vida* de Francisca Josefa de Castillo y Guevara." *¿Y las mujeres? Ensayos sobre literatura colombiana.* Ed. María Mercedes Jaramillo, Angela Inés Robledo, and Flor María Rodríguez-Arenas. Antioquia: Universidad de Antioquia, 1991. 65–73.

Rodríguez-Arenas, Flor María. "Soledad Acosta de Samper, pionera de la profesionalización de la escritura femenina colombiana en el siglo XIX: *Dolores, Teresa la limeña, y El corazón de la mujer.*" *¿Y las mujeres? Ensayos sobre literatura colombiana.* Ed. María Mercedes Jaramillo, Angela Inés Robledo, and Flor María Rodríguez-Arenas. Antioquia: Otraparte, Editorial Universidad de Antioquia, 1991. 133–75. Bibliografía de Soledad Acosta de Samper: 289–307.

Sabàt de Rivers, Georgina. "Sor Juana Inés de la Cruz." *Historia de la literatura hispanoamericana.* Tomo I: *Epoca colonial.* Ed. Luis Iñigo Madrigal. Madrid: Ediciones Cátedra, 1982. 275–93.

Schlau, Stacey. "Madre Castillo." *Spanish American Women Writers: A Bio-Bibliographical Source Book.* Ed. Diane Marting. New York: Greenwood Press, 1990. 156–64.

————. "Madre Francisca Josefa de Castillo (1671–1742)." *Escritoras de Hispanoamérica: Una guía bio-bibliográfica.* Ed. Diane Marting. (Ed. de la edición en español, Montserrat Ordóñez.) Bogotá: Siglo Veintiuno Editores de Colombia, 1991. 161–69.

Schulman, Ivan A. "The Portrait of the Slave: Ideology and Aesthetics in the Cuban Antislavery Novel." *Annals of the New York Academy of Sciences* 292 (1977): 356–67.

Schurz, William Lytle. "The Woman." *This New World.* New York: Dutton, 1954. 276–338.

Scott, Nina M. "Juana Manuela Gorriti's *Cocina ecléctica*: Recipes as Feminine Discourse." *Recipes for Reading: Community Cookbooks, Stories, Histories.* Ed. Anne L. Bower. Amherst: University of Massachusetts Press, 1997. 189–99, 260–63.

————. "'La gran turba de las que merecieron nombres': Sor Juana's

Foremothers in 'La Respuesta a Sor Filotea.'" *Coded Encounters: Writing, Gender and Ethnicity in Colonial Latin America.* Ed. Francisco Javier Cevallos-Candau, Jeffrey A. Cole, Nina M. Scott, and Nicomedes Suárez-Araúz. Amherst: University of Massachusetts Press, 1994. 206–23.

———. "Ser mujer, ni estar ausente,/No es de amarte impedimento": Los poemas de Sor Juana a la Condesa de Paredes." *"Y diversa de mí misma/entre vuestras plumas ando": Homenaje internacional a Sor Juana Inés de la Cruz.* Ed. Sara Poot Herrera and Elena Urrutia. México: El Colegio de México, 1993.

———. "Shoring up the 'Weaker Sex': Avellaneda and Nineteenth-Century Gender Ideology." *Reinterpreting the Spanish American Essay: Women Writers of the 19th and 20th Centuries.* Ed. Doris Meyer. Austin: University of Texas Press, 1995. 57–67.

Serrano y Sanz, Manuel. *Apuntes para una biblioteca de escritoras españolas desde el año 1401 al 1833.* Tomo I, Segunda Parte. Madrid: Establecimiento Tipolitográfico "Sucesores de Rivadeneyra," 1903.

Sommer, Doris. *Foundational Fictions: The National Romances of Latin America.* Berkeley: University of California Press, 1991.

———. "Sab c'est moi." *Foundational Fictions: The National Romances of Latin America.* Berkeley: University of California Press, 1991. 114–37.

Sontag, Susan. *Illness as Metaphor.* New York: Farrar, Straus and Giroux, 1977.

Stepto, Michele. Introduction and Translators' Note. *Lieutenant Nun: Memoir of a Basque Transvestite in the New World.* Trans. Michele Stepto and Gabriel Stepto. Boston: Beacon Press, 1996. xxv–xlviii.

Tieffemberg, Silvia. "Isabel de Guevara o la construcción del yo femenino." *Filología* 24 (1989): 287–300.

Trabulse, Elías. *La memoria transfigurada: Tres imágenes históricas de Sor Juana.* México: Universidad Claustro de Sor Juana, 1996.

Trueblood, Alan. *A Sor Juana Anthology.* Cambridge, MA: Harvard University Press, 1988.

Vallbona, Rima de. "Realidad histórica y ficción en *Vida y sucesos de la monja alférez.*" Diss. Middlebury College, 1981.

Varela, Consuelo, ed. *Los cuatro viajes: Testamento.* By Cristóbal Colón. Madrid: Alianza Editorial, 1986.

Volek, Emil. "Cartas de amor de la Avellaneda." *Cuadernos Hispanoamericanos* (Madrid) 511 (Jan. 1993): 103–13.

Yeager, Gertrude. "Juana Manuela Gorriti: Writer in Exile." *The Human Factor in Latin America: The Nineteenth Century.* Ed. William H. Beezley and Judith Ewell. Wilmington, DE: Scholarly Resources, 1989. 114–27.

Yo, la peor de todas. Dir. María Luisa Bemberg. GEA Cinematográfica, 1990. Available with English subtitles.

Zaldívar, Gladys, y Rosa Martínez de Cabrera, eds. *Homenaje a Gertrudis Gómez de Avellaneda: Memorias del simposio en el centenario de su muerte.* Miami: Ediciones Universal, 1981.

Index

Gramley Library
Salem Academy and College
Winston-Salem, N.C. 27108

Herbert H. Lamson Library

Plymouth State College

PLYMOUTH, N. H.

PRESENTED BY

Scott Meyer

1871

The Challenge of Democracy

Government in America

FOURTH EDITION

COMPLIMENTARY COPY NOT FOR SALE

COMPLIMENTARY COPY — NOT FOR SALE

The Challenge of Democracy

Government in America

FOURTH EDITION

■

Kenneth Janda
Northwestern University

Jeffrey M. Berry
Tufts University

Jerry Goldman
Northwestern University

LIBRARY
COLBY-SAWYER COLLEGE
NEW LONDON, NH 03257

Houghton Mifflin Company   Boston   Toronto
Geneva, Illinois   Palo Alto   Princeton, New Jersey

JK 274 .J36 1995
OCLC 31906763
The challenge of democracy

1995

Senior Sponsoring Editor: Jean L. Woy
Senior Associate Editor: Frances Gay
Senior Project Editor: Susan Westendorf
Production/Design Coordinator: Carol Merrigan
Senior Manufacturing Coordinator: Marie Barnes

Copyright © 1995 by Houghton Mifflin Company. All rights reserved.

No part of this work may be reproduced or transmitted in any form or by any means, electronic or mechanical, including photocopying and recording, or by any information storage or retrieval system without the prior written permission of Houghton Mifflin Company unless such copying is expressly permitted by federal copyright law. Address inquiries to College Permissions, Houghton Mifflin Company, 222 Berkeley Street, Boston, MA 02116-3764.

Printed in the U.S.A.

Library of Congress Catalog Card Number: 94-76514

Student text ISBN: 0-395-70882-6
Examination text ISBN: 0-395-71715-9
123456789-VH-98 97 96 95

Illustration Credits
Cover Designer: Harold Burch Design, *NYC*
Cover photographer: Burton Pritzker Photography
Frontispiece: Bob Llewellyn
Preface photo: Alexander Stephens
  Digital Services: David Andrew

Chapter 1: **2:** **(Opener):** Bob Llewellyn; **4:** Alan Hanes/Sygma; **6:** Bettmann; **8:** Wide World; **12-13:** Photo courtesy of The Norman Rockwell Museum at Stockbridge; **14:** © Chicago Tribune Company, All Rights reserved; **18:** Flip Horvat/SABA; **25:** © Chicago Tribune Company, All Rights reserved.
Chapter 2: **29:** **(Opener):** Joe Sohm/The Image Works; **31:** Chris Brown/SABA; **32:** Peter DeJong/ Wide World; **33:** Baldev/Sygma; **35:** Spratt/The Image Works; **38:** © Mel Rosenthal/Impact Visuals; **43:** Terry Ashe/Time Magazine; **44:** Paul Conklin; **51:** Rick Reinhard/Impact Visuals.
Chapter 3: **58:** **(Opener):** N.R. Rowan/The Image Works; **60:** Gjon Mili/Life Magazine © Time Warner; **64:** Library of Congress; **65:** Courtesy of the John Carter Brown Library at Brown University; **69:** Copyright Yale

Copyright page continues on A99.

To our wives
  Ann Janda
  Lori Berry
  Susan Kennedy

COMPLIMENTARY COPY NOT FOR SALE

COMPLIMENTARY COPY

COMPLIMENTARY COPY

COMPLIMENTARY COPY

COMPLIMENTARY COPY NOT FOR SALE

COMPLIMENTARY COPY

COMPLIMENTARY COPY

Brief Contents

Boxed Features

Compared with What?

Politics in a Changing America

Features

COMPLIMENTARY COPY NOT FOR SALE

COMPLIMENTARY COPY

Contents

xi

Preface

More than a decade has passed since we contracted to write an American government textbook. Because we wanted to write a book that students would actually read, we sought to discuss politics, a complex subject, in a captivating and understandable way. American politics isn't dull, and its textbooks needn't be either. But equally important, we wanted to produce a book that students would credit for stimulating their thinking about politics. While offering all the essential information about American government and politics, our book was built around a framework for analyzing politics that students could use long after their studies ended.

In brief, our conceptual framework is built upon two enduring foundations of American politics: the clash among the values of freedom, order, and equality, and the tensions between pluralist and majoritarian visions of democracy. As discussed more extensively below, knowledge of these conflicts enables citizens to recognize and analyze the difficult choices they face in politics.

Based on the reactions to our first three editions, we believe we succeeded in developing a lively book based on a framework that fulfills our goal of helping students analyze and interpret the political process in the United States. Moreover, our framework travels well over time. Our first and second editions (1987 and 1989) were written when Republican president Ronald Reagan was in the White House. Our third edition (1992) analyzed politics under George Bush's administration. In this, our fourth edition, we are able to apply our framework for the first time to a government headed by a Democrat in the White House. Bill Clinton's presidency has charted quite a different course among the values of freedom, order, and equality from that taken by his Republican predecessors. Although we extensively revised each chapter to deal with changes under the Clinton administration, we easily accommodated the developments within our analytical framework.

Our framework also seems to travel well over space—to other countries with a very different political heritage. At the time we devised our analytical themes, the Soviet Union (in Ronald Reagan's words) stood as the "evil empire." Now the USSR stands no more, and the former communist countries in central and eastern Europe engage in the transition to democratic government and deal with alternative models of democracy. Little did we know that our book would become so widely used in teaching students in these countries about democratic politics. Houghton Mifflin Company has donated copies of earlier editions of our book to English-speaking faculty and students in Bulgaria, Croatia, the Czech Republic, Georgia, Hungary, Poland, Romania, Slovakia, and of course, Russia itself. Moreover, the brief edition of our book is under contract for translation

xix

into Hungarian and Georgian, and plans are underway for translation into several other central and eastern European languages. We are pleased that *The Challenge of Democracy* will soon be available to many more students in these countries, students who are confronting the challenge of democracy in a time of political transition.

THEMATIC FRAMEWORK	Two themes run through our book. One deals with the conflict among values and the other with alternative models of democracy. In Chapter 1, we suggest that American politics often reflects conflicts between the values of freedom and order and between the values of freedom and equality. These value conflicts are prominent in contemporary American society, and they help to explain political controversy and consensus in earlier eras.

For instance, in Chapter 3 we argue that the Constitution was designed to promote order, and it virtually ignored issues of political and social equality. Equality was later served, however, by several amendments to the Constitution. In Chapter 15, "Order and Civil Liberties," and Chapter 16, "Equality and Civil Rights," we demonstrate how many of this nation's most controversial issues represent conflicts among individuals or groups who hold differing views on the values of freedom, order, and equality. Views on issues such as abortion are not just isolated opinions; they also reflect choices about the philosophy citizens want government to follow. Yet choosing among these values is difficult, sometimes excruciatingly so.

The second theme, introduced in Chapter 2, asks students to consider two competing models of democratic government. One way that government can make decisions is by means of majoritarian principles—that is, by taking the actions desired by a majority of citizens. For instance, in Chapter 20, "Global Policy," we discuss the impact of public opinion in making foreign policy. A contrasting model of government, pluralism, is built around the interaction of decision makers in government with groups concerned about issues that affect them. Pluralism is a focus of Chapter 17, "Policymaking," which discusses issue networks in the nation's capital.

These models are not mere abstractions; we use them to illustrate the dynamics of the American political system. In Chapter 9, "Nominations, Elections, and Campaigns," and Chapter 12, "The Presidency," we discuss the problem of divided government. In most presidential elections from 1968 to 1988, Americans elected Republican presidents and at the same time returned Democrats to Congress in large numbers; in fact, Democrats have typically controlled both the House and the Senate. When the two branches of government are divided between the two parties, majoritarian government is difficult. As Bill Clinton is finding out, even when the same party controls both branches, the majoritarian model is not always realized.

Throughout the book we stress that students must make their own choices among the competing values and models of government. Although the three of us hold diverse and strong opinions about which choices are best, we do not believe it is our role to tell students our answers to the broad questions we pose. Instead, we want our readers to learn first-hand that a democracy requires thoughtful choices. That is why we titled our book *The Challenge of Democracy*.

FEATURES OF THE FOURTH EDITION

The fourth edition maintains the basic structure of the previous edition while capturing important developments in American politics—for example, the election of a Democratic president and the two years of his administration.

To accommodate the major changes and new issues in politics that have occurred since the last edition, every chapter in the text has been updated and revised. For instance, Chapter 3 on "Federalism" discusses the problems that states face when Congress mandates programs without providing the funds to carry them out. Chapter 5, "Public Opinion and Socialization," replaces the issue of communism with that of abortion in the analysis of ideological types. Of course, Chapter 8 on "Political Parties" and Chapter 9 on "Nominations, Elections, and Campaigns" evaluate the impact of Ross Perot, the independent presidential candidate in 1992. Ironically, Chapters 11 ("Congress") and 12 ("The Presidency") describe politics in Washington which have become even more partisan, with a new, seemingly unified Republican majority in both houses facing a Democrat in the White House. Chapter 18, "Economic Policy," deals with Clinton's deficit reduction program, which involves new taxes on the wealthy in a stark departure from Reaganomics.

Finally, Chapter 20, "Global Policy," has been significantly revised to reflect the declining importance of military might and the growing influence of economic policy in international relations. This chapter details Clinton's efforts to forge a new foreign policy in the "messy and ambiguous" world, to quote the Air Force Chief of Staff, that has followed the fall of the Soviet Union.

As in previous editions, each chapter begins with a vignette that draws students into the substance of the material that chapter examines and suggests one of the themes of the book. For example, we begin Chapter 15, "Order and Civil Liberties," by discussing the debate over the exhibition of Robert Mapplethorpe's photographs at Cincinnati's Contemporary Arts Center. Were the efforts of city officials to ban these photographs, which they considered obscene, an appropriate attempt to maintain order or an infringement on freedom of expression?

In every chapter in this edition, we introduce a new feature, "Politics in a Changing America," designed to illustrate changes over time in the political opportunity, participation, and status of groups such as women, African Americans, youth, Hispanics, and religious fundamentalists. For example, the feature in Chapter 1 describes how women's sports programs at American colleges and universities have grown as a consequence of Title IX of the 1972 Civil Rights law that outlawed gender discrimination in institutions receiving federal funds.

We believe that students can better evaluate how our political system works when they compare it with politics in other countries. Once again, each chapter has at least one boxed feature called "Compared with What?" which treats its topic in a comparative perspective. How much importance do citizens in other parts of the world place on freedom, order, and equality? Do American television reporters color the news with their commentary more than reporters in other countries? Are Americans more or less supportive of redistributing wealth than are citizens of other countries?

We also make frequent use of other boxed features throughout the text. They allow us to explore some topics in more detail or discuss matters that don't fit easily into the regular flow of text. Examples include an inside look at how CBS news reporter Lesley Stahl tried to expose the Reagan administration's manipulation of the media, a historical account of Martin Luther King, Jr.'s "I Have a Dream" speech, and a description of how a Washington interest group designed a mail campaign to increase its membership.

Each chapter concludes with a brief summary, a list of key terms, and a short list of recommended readings. At the end of the book, we have included the Articles of Confederation, the Declaration of Independence, an annotated copy of the Constitution, *Federalist* Nos. 10 and 51, a glossary of key terms, and some other valuable appendices.

THE TEACHING/LEARNING PACKAGE	When we began writing *The Challenge of Democracy,* we viewed the book as part of a tightly integrated set of instructional materials. We have worked closely with some very talented political scientists and with educational specialists at Houghton Mifflin to produce what we think is a superior set of ancillary materials to help both students and instructors.

The primary purpose of the *Instructor's Resource Manual,* written by the authors (and ably updated by Mona Field at Glendale College) is to provide teachers with material that relates directly to the thematic framework and organization of the book. It includes learning objectives, chapter synopses, detailed full-length lectures, including a new type of lecture format that encourages class participation, bonus features, and suggested classroom and individual activities.

The Test Item Bank, prepared by Nicholas Strinkowski of Siena College, provides over 1,500 test items—identification, multiple-choice, and essay. The Study Guide, written by Melissa Butler of Wabash College, contains an overview of each chapter, exercises on reading tables and graphs, topics for student research, and multiple-choice questions for practice. The transparency package, containing forty full-color overhead transparencies, is available to adopters of the book. Adopters may also receive the six videotapes from Houghton Mifflin's *Videotape Program in American Government,* written and produced by Ralph Baker and Joseph Losco of Ball State University. A corresponding Video Guide contains summaries and scripts of each tape, definitions of key terms, multiple-choice questions, and ideas for class activities.

Perhaps the most promising new research tool for students is the Internet. Therefore a free guide to political science resources on the Internet is available with each new copy of *The Challenge of Democracy.* This 32-page booklet explains to students how to access the Internet and how to find such resources as Supreme Court cases and White House briefings.

Software ancillaries available to instructors include *LectureBank,* an inventory of complete lectures, and a computerized test generation program containing all the items in the printed Test Item Bank. Other software ancillaries are designed to enhance students' understanding. They include a computerized study guide and IDEAlog, an award-winning interactive exercise we designed that illuminates for students the value-conflicts theme in the book. For instructors who want to introduce students to data analysis, a disk and workbook called Crosstabs allows students to do research using survey data on the 1992 presidential election and data on voting in Congress, updated after the 1992 election.

The fourth edition will also be accompanied by a 60-minute videodisc composed of archival footage on four topics: Campaigns and Elections, The Presidency, Civil Rights, and Watergate. The video segments range from half a minute to about three minutes. A video guide with shot descriptions and barcodes is packaged with the disc. Instructors will find this most useful in designing illustrated lectures.

We invite your questions, suggestions, and criticisms. You may contact us at our respective institutions, or, if you have access to an electronic mail service, you may contact us through our collective e-mail address—cod©nwu.edu—and we will try to respond to you.

Acknowledgments

All authors are indebted to others for inspiration and assistance in various forms. Textbook authors are notoriously in hock to others for help. In producing this edition, we especially want to thank Gloria Hamilton and Sally Roberts of Northwestern University Library; Phyllis Siegel, Northwestern's Program in American Culture; Ronald Inglehart, the University of Michigan; Peter S. Ginsberg, Esq.; Adam Kalai; Alexander Stephens; Tom Smith, National Opinion Research Center; and Ken Thomson, Lincoln Filene Center for Citizenship and Public Affairs at Tufts.

Our colleagues at Northwestern and Tufts are a constant source of citations, advice, and constructive criticism. Special thanks to T. H. Breen, Dennis Chong, William Crotty, Herbert Jacob, Jane Mansbridge, Jock McLane, and Carl Smith (Northwestern); and Lisa Brandes, Richard Eichenberg, Don Klein, Tony Messina, Kent Portney, and Pearl Robinson (Tufts). Our research assistants were indispensable: at Northwestern, David Andrew, Scott Barclay, Jason Castillo, Mark Farris, Kathryn Ibata, and David Wrobel; and at Tufts, Debra Candreva and Tracy Turner.

Kenneth Janda revised some of his chapters while serving as the John Marshall Chair at the Budapest University of Economics, where he taught American government under the Fulbright Program in 1993–94. Thanks to Attila Agh and his colleagues in the Department of Political Science for their support in Budapest and to Donna Culpepper and Philip Reeker of the United States Information Agency, who arranged to translate the brief edition of our text into Hungarian.

We all owe special thanks to Ted and Cora Ginsberg, whose research endowment helped launch several small investigations by our students that eventually found their way into this edition.

Once again in this edition we were lucky enough to have Melissa Butler

The authors (left to right):
Kenneth Janda, Jeffrey Berry,
Jerry Goldman

contribute Chapter 20, "Global Policy." She is also the author of the excellent Study Guide that accompanies the text.

We have been fortunate to obtain the help of many outstanding political scientists across the country who provided us with critical reviews of our work as it has progressed through three separate editions. We found their comments enormously helpful, and we thank them for taking valuable time away from their own teaching and research to write their detailed reports. More specifically, our thanks go to

David Ahern, University of Dayton
James Anderson, Texas A & M University
Theodore Arrington, University of North Carolina, Charlotte
Denise Baer, Northeastern University
Linda L. M. Bennett, Wittenberg University
Stephen Earl Bennett, University of Cincinnati
Thad Beyle, University of North Carolina, Chapel Hill
Michael Binford, Georgia State University
Bonnie Browne, Texas A & M University
J. Vincent Buck, California State University, Fullerton
Gregory A. Caldeira, University of Iowa
Robert Casier, Santa Barbara City College
James Chalmers, Wayne State University
John Chubb, Stanford University
Allan Cigler, University of Kansas
Stanley Clark, California State University, Bakersfield
Ronald Claunch, Stephen F. Austin State University
Gary Copeland, University of Oklahoma

Cornelius P. Cotter, University of Wisconsin, Milwaukee
Christine L. Day, University of New Orleans
Victor D'Lugin, University of Florida
Art English, University of Arkansas
Henry Fearnley, College of Marin
Elizabeth Flores, Del Mar College
Patricia S. Florestano, University of Maryland
Steve Frank, St. Cloud State University
Mitchel Gerber, Hofstra University
Dorith Grant-Wisdom, Howard University
Sara A. Grove, Shippensburg University
Kenneth Hayes, University of Maine
Ronald Hedlund, University of Wisconsin, Milwaukee
Marjorie Randon Hershey, Indiana University
Roberta Herzberg, Indiana University
Peter Howse, American River College
Scott Keeter, Virginia Commonwealth University
Sarah W. Keidan, Oakland Community College (Mich.)
Beat Kernen, Southwest Missouri State University
Vance Krites, Indiana University of Pennsylvania
Clyde Kuhn, California State University, Sacramento
Jack Lampe, Southwest Texas Junior College
Joseph Losco, Ball State University
Wayne McIntosh, University of Maryland
Michael Maggiotto, University of South Carolina
Edward S. Malecki, California State University, Los Angeles
Steve J. Mazurana, University of Northern Colorado
Jim Morrow, Tulsa Junior College
William Mugleston, Mountain View College
David A. Nordquest, Pennsylvania State University, Erie
Bruce Odom, Trinity Valley Community College
Laura Katz Olson, Lehigh University
Bruce Oppenheimer, University of Houston
Richard Pacelle, Indiana University
Robert Pecorella, St. John's University
James Perkins, San Antonio College
Denny E. Pilant, Southwest Missouri State University
Curtis Reithel, University of Wisconsin, La Crosse
Ronald I. Rubin, Borough of Manhattan Community College–CUNY
Gilbert K. St. Clair, University of New Mexico
Barbara Salmore, Drew University
William A. Schultze, San Diego State University
Thomas Sevener, Santa Rosa Junior College
Kenneth S. Sherrill, Hunter College
Sanford R. Silverburg, Catawba College
Mark Silverstein, Boston University
Robert J. Spitzer, SUNY Cortland
Candy Stevens Smith, Texarkana College
Charles Sohner, El Camino College
Dale Story, University of Texas, Arlington
Nicholas Strinkowski, Eastern Oregon State College

Neal Tate, University of North Texas
James A. Thurber, The American University
Gary D. Wekkin, University of Central Arkansas
Jonathan West, University of Miami
John Winkle, University of Mississippi
Clifford Wirth, University of New Hampshire
Ann Wynia, North Hennepin Community College
Jerry L. Yeric, University of North Texas

Finally, we want to thank the many people at Houghton Mifflin who helped make this edition a reality. Jean Woy, Senior Sponsoring Editor, signed us to do the book. Jean suffered through the traumas of the First Edition, and she took charge of this edition too. Ann Goodsell and Beth Welch, our development editors; Susan Westendorf, our Senior Project Editor; and June Smith, Director of the College Division, all made us do things that we didn't plan to do but which ultimately improved the quality of the book.

Our experience proves that authors, even experienced authors working on their fourth edition, can benefit from the suggestions and criticisms of a gifted staff of publishing experts. No publisher has a more capable group of dedicated professionals than Houghton Mifflin, and we have been fortunate to have their guidance over the past decade and the four editions of our text.

K.J., J.B., J.G.

COMPLIMENTARY COPY NOT FOR SALE

PART I

Dilemmas of Democracy

CHAPTER 1

Freedom, Order, or Equality?

THEY BRANDED HIM "DR. DEATH" for helping gravely ill people commit suicide. From 1990 through 1993, Dr. Jack Kevorkian, a retired Michigan pathologist, assisted in twenty suicides. Facing prosecution for his actions, he said, "I have never cared about anything but the welfare of the patient in front of me. I don't care about the law."[1]

Dr. Kevorkian eluded prosecution for murder because he was careful to let his patients trigger the lethal action. Moreover, until he came along, Michigan had no law against assisting a suicide. That changed in December, 1992, when the state made it a felony. Dr. Kevorkian soon defied that law by helping others die, and this time was jailed. In late 1993, however, he was released after pledging that he would stop the practice, saying "I can't help humans who are suffering any more, because I have given my word."[2]

Dr. Kevorkian turned to working to legalize the practice of *euthanasia*, the term for ending the life of an individual suffering from a terminal or incurable condition. His case raises the issue of the government's right to prevent a person from committing suicide to avoid protracted suffering. In fact, a state judge later struck down the Michigan law under which Dr. Kevorkian was jailed, citing a constitutionally protected right to commit suicide.[3] Test your own feelings about this controversial issue. On what basis would you decide whether the government's interest in protecting life outweighs an individual's freedom to end his life?

Which is better: to live under a government that allows individuals complete freedom to do whatever they please or under one that enforces strict law and order? Which is better: to allow businesses and private clubs to choose their customers and members or to pass laws that require them to admit and serve everyone, regardless of race or sex?

For many people, none of these alternatives is satisfactory. All pose difficult dilemmas. The dilemmas are tied to opposing philosophies that place different values on freedom, order, and equality.

This book explains American government and politics in light of these dilemmas. It does more than explain the workings of our government; it encourages you to think about what government should—and should not—do. And it judges the American government against democratic ideals, encouraging you to think about how government should make its decisions. As its title implies, *The Challenge of Democracy* argues that good government often involves difficult choices.

3

Things Will Never Be the Same

The Citadel military college in South Carolina had been an all-male institution for 151 years. Some women had tried to enroll, but their applications were rejected. Then Shannon Faulkner applied, avoiding any mention of her sex. When the school learned that Shannon was a she, it withdrew her acceptance. In turn, Shannon sued for admission, contending that The Citadel, as a state institution, could not bar her because of her sex. Shannon won and began classes in 1994—to considerable opposition from many male cadets who favored the all-male education historically associated with The Citadel.

College students frequently say that American government and politics are hard to understand. In fact, many people voice the same complaint. Two-thirds of a national sample interviewed after the 1992 presidential election agreed with the statement "Politics and government seem so complicated that a person like me can't understand what's going on."[4] With this book, we hope to improve your understanding of "what's going on" by analyzing the norms, or values, that people use to judge political events. Our purpose is not to preach what people ought to favor in making policy decisions; it is to teach what values are at stake.

Teaching without preaching is not easy; no one can completely exclude personal values from political analysis. But our approach minimizes the problem by concentrating on the dilemmas that confront governments when they are forced to choose between important policies that threaten equally cherished values—as between the freedom of speech and personal security.

Every government policy reflects a choice between conflicting values. We want you to understand this idea, to understand that all government policies reinforce certain values (norms) at the expense of others. We want you to interpret policy issues (for example, should assisted suicide go unpunished?) with an understanding of the fundamental values in question (freedom of action versus order and protection of life) and the broader political overtones (liberal or conservative politics).

By looking beyond specifics to underlying normative principles, you should be able to make more sense out of politics. Our framework for analysis does not encompass all the complexities of American government, but it should help your knowledge grow by improving your comprehension of political information. We begin by considering the basic purposes of government. In short, why do we need it?

THE PURPOSES OF GOVERNMENT

Most people do not like being told what to do. Fewer still like being coerced into acting a certain way. Yet every day, millions of American motorists dutifully drive on the right-hand side of the street and obediently stop at red lights. Every year, millions of U.S. citizens struggle to complete their income tax forms before midnight on April 15. In both examples, the coercive power of government is at work. If people do not like being controlled, why do they submit to it? In other words, why do we have government?

Government may be defined as the legitimate use of force—including imprisonment and execution—within territorial boundaries to control human behavior. All governments require citizens to surrender some freedom in the process of being governed. Although some governments minimize their infringement on personal freedom, no government has as a goal to maximization of personal freedom. Governments exist to control; *to govern* means 'to control.' Why do people surrender their freedom to this control? To obtain the benefits of government. Throughout history, government seems to have served two major purposes: maintaining order (preserving life and protecting property) and providing public goods. More recently, some governments have pursued a third purpose: promoting equality.

Maintaining Order

Maintaining order is the oldest objective of government. *Order* in this context is rich with meaning. Let's start with "law and order." Maintaining **order** in this sense means establishing the rule of law to preserve life and to protect property. To the seventeenth-century English philosopher Thomas Hobbes (1588–1679), preserving life was the most important function of government. In his classic philosophical treatise, *Leviathan* (1651), Hobbes described life without government as life in a "state of nature." Without rules, people would live as predators do, stealing and killing for personal benefit. In Hobbes's classic phrase, life in a state of nature would be "solitary, poor, nasty, brutish, and short." He believed that a single ruler, or sovereign, must possess unquestioned authority to guarantee the safety of the weak from the attacks of the strong. Hobbes characterized his all-powerful government as Leviathan, a biblical sea monster. He believed that complete obedience to Leviathan's strict laws was a small price to pay for the security of living in a civil society.

Most of us can only imagine what a state of nature would be like. We might think of the "Wild West" in the days before a good guy in a white hat rode into town and established law and order. But in some parts of the world today, people actually do live in a state of lawlessness. This occurred in Somalia in 1992 after the central government collapsed. Many thousands died from starvation as warring factions destroyed the economy and then disrupted the flow of relief supplies from international agencies. President George Bush sent U.S. troops into Somalia to restore a semblance of order and prevent further starvation. (That done, President Bill Clinton learned how difficult it was to maintain order in Somalia.) Throughout history, authoritarian rulers have used people's fears of civil disorder to justify their governments. Ironically, the ruling group itself—whether monarchy, aristocracy, or political party—became known as the *established order.*

Leviathan, Hobbes's All-Powerful Sovereign

This engraving is from the 1651 edition of Leviathan, *by Thomas Hobbes. It shows Hobbes's sovereign brandishing a sword in one hand and the scepter of justice in the other. He watches over an orderly town, made peaceful by his absolute authority. But note that the sovereign's body is composed of tiny images of his subjects. He exists only through them. Hobbes explains that such government power can be created only if people "confer all their power and strength upon one man, or upon one assembly of men, that may reduce all their wills, by plurality of voices, unto one will."*

Hobbes's focus on life in the cruel state of nature led him to view government primarily as a means for survival. Other theorists, taking survival for granted, believed that government protected order by preserving private property (goods and land owned by individuals). Foremost among them was John Locke (1632–1704), an English philosopher. In Two Treatises on Government (1690), he wrote that the protection of life, liberty, and property was the basic objective of government. His thinking strongly influenced the Declaration of Independence. It is reflected in the Declaration's famous phrase that identifies "Life, Liberty, and the Pursuit of Happiness" as "unalienable Rights" of citizens under government.

Not everyone believes that the protection of private property is a valid objective of government. The German philosopher Karl Marx (1818–1883) rejected the private ownership of property that is used in the production of goods or services. Marx's ideas form the basis of **communism,** a complex theory that gives ownership of all land and productive facilities to the people—in effect, to the government. In line with communist theory, the 1977 constitution of the former Soviet Union set forth the following principles of government ownership:

> State property, i.e., the common property of the Soviet people, is the principal form of socialist property.
>
> The land, its minerals, waters, and forests are the exclusive property of the state. The state owns the basic means of production in industry, construction, and agriculture; means of transport and communication; the banks; the property of state-run trade organizations and public utilities, and other state-run undertakings; most urban housing; and other property necessary for state purposes.[5]

Even after the Soviet Union collapsed and the Russians elected Boris Yeltsin as president, the public was deeply split over changing the old communist-era constitution to permit the private ownership of land. Even outside the formerly communist societies, the extent to which government protects private property is a political issue that forms the basis of much ideological debate around the world.

Providing Public Goods

After governments have established basic order, they can pursue other ends. Using their coercive powers, they can tax citizens to raise money to spend on **public goods,** which are benefits and services that are available to everyone—such as education, sanitation, and parks. Public goods benefit all citizens but are not likely to be produced by the voluntary acts of individuals. The government of ancient Rome, for example, built aqueducts to carry fresh water from the mountains to the city. Road building was another public good provided by the Roman government—which also used the roads to move its legions and to protect the established order.

Government action to provide public goods can be controversial. During President James Monroe's administration (1817–1825), many people thought that building the Cumberland Road (between Cumberland, Maryland, and Wheeling, West Virginia) was not a proper function of the national government, the Romans notwithstanding. Over time, the scope of government functions in the United States has expanded. During President Dwight Eisenhower's administration in the 1950s, the federal government outdid the Romans' noble road building. Despite his basic conservatism, Eisenhower launched the massive Interstate Highway System at a cost of $27 billion (in 1950s dollars). Yet some government enterprises that have been common in other countries—running railroads, operating coal mines, generating electric power—are politically controversial or even unacceptable in the United States. People disagree about how far the government ought to go in using its power to tax to provide public goods and services and how much of that realm should be handled by private business for profit.

Promoting Equality

The promotion of equality has not always been a major objective of government. It has gained prominence only in this century, in the aftermath of industrialization and urbanization. Confronted by the paradox of poverty amid plenty, some political leaders in European nations pioneered extensive government programs to improve life for the poor. Under the emerging concept of the **welfare state,** government's role expanded to provide individuals with medical care, education, and a guaranteed income, "from cradle to grave." Sweden, Britain, and other nations adopted welfare programs aimed at reducing social inequalities. This relatively new purpose of government has been by far the most controversial. People often oppose taxation for public goods (building roads and schools, for example) because of its cost alone. On principle, they oppose more strongly taxation for government programs to promote economic and social equality.

The key issue here is government's role in redistributing income—taking from the wealthy to give to the poor. Charity (voluntary giving to the poor) has a strong basis in Western religious traditions; using the power of the state to support the poor does not. (In his nineteenth-century novels,

Rosa Parks: She Sat for Equality

Rosa Parks had just finished a day's work as a seamstress and was sitting in the front of a bus in Montgomery, Alabama, going home. A white man claimed her seat, which he could do according to the law in December 1955. When she refused to move and was arrested, angry blacks, led by Dr. Martin Luther King, Jr., began a boycott of the Montgomery bus company.

Charles Dickens dramatized how government power was used to imprison the poor, not to support them.) Using the state to redistribute income was originally a radical idea, set forth by Marx as the ultimate principle of developed communism: "from each according to his ability, to each according to his needs."[6] This extreme has never operated in any government, not even in communist states. But over time, taking from the rich to help the needy has become a legitimate function of most governments.

That legitimacy is not without controversy, however. Especially since the Great Depression of the 1930s, the government's role in redistributing income to promote economic equality has been a major source of policy debate in the United States. Food stamps and Aid to Families with Dependent Children (AFDC) are typical examples of government welfare programs that tend to redistribute income—and generate controversy.

Government can also promote social equality through policies that do not redistribute income. For example, it can regulate social behavior to enforce equality—as it did when the Supreme Court of Texas in 1993 cleared the way for homosexuals to serve in the Dallas police department. Policies that regulate social behavior, like those that redistribute income, inevitably clash with the value of personal freedom.

A CONCEPTUAL FRAMEWORK FOR ANALYZING GOVERNMENT

Citizens have very different views of how vigorously they want government to maintain order, provide public goods, and promote equality. Of the three objectives, providing for public goods usually is less controversial than maintaining order or promoting equality. After all, government spending for highways, schools, and parks carries benefits for nearly every citizen. Moreover, services merely cost money. The cost of maintaining order and promoting equality is greater than money; it usually means a tradeoff in basic values.

To understand government and the political process, you must be able to recognize these tradeoffs and identify the basic values they entail. Just as people sit back from a wide-screen motion picture to gain perspective, to understand American government you need to take a broad view, a view much broader than that offered by examining specific political events. You need to use political concepts.

A concept is a generalized idea of a set of items or thoughts. It groups various events, objects, or qualities under a common classification or label. The framework that guides this book consists of five concepts that figure prominently in political analysis. We regard the five concepts as especially important to a broad understanding of American politics, and we use them repeatedly throughout the book. This framework will help you evaluate political events long after you have read this text.

The five concepts that we emphasize deal with the fundamental issues of what government tries to do and how it decides to do it. The concepts that relate to what government tries to do are order, freedom, and equality. All governments by definition value order; maintaining order is part of the meaning of government. Most governments at least claim to preserve individual freedom while they maintain order, although they vary widely in the extent to which they succeed. Few governments even profess to guarantee equality, and governments differ greatly in policies that pit equality against freedom. Our conceptual framework should help you evaluate the extent to which the United States pursues all three values through its government.

How government chooses the proper mix of order, freedom, and equality in its policymaking has to do with the process of choice rather than the outcome. We evaluate the American governmental process using two models of democratic government: the majoritarian and the pluralist. Many governments profess to be democracies. Whether they are or are not depends on their (and our) meaning of the term. Even countries that Americans agree are democracies—for example, the United States and Britain—differ substantially in the type of democracy they practice. We use our conceptual models of democratic government both to classify the type of democracy practiced in the United States and to evaluate the government's success in fulfilling that model.

The five concepts can be organized into two groups.

- Concepts that identify the values pursued by government:
  Freedom
  Order
  Equality

- Concepts that describe models of democratic government:
  Majoritarian democracy
  Pluralist democracy

The rest of this chapter examines freedom, order, and equality as conflicting values pursued by government. Chapter 2 discusses majoritarian democracy and pluralist democracy as alternative institutional models for implementing democratic government.

THE CONCEPTS OF FREEDOM, ORDER, AND EQUALITY

These three terms—*freedom, order,* and *equality*—have different connotations in American politics. Both freedom and equality are positive terms that politicians have learned to use to their own advantage. Consequently, freedom and equality mean different things to different people at different times—depending on the political context in which they are used. Order, on the other hand, has negative connotations for many people, for it symbolizes government intrusion in private lives. Except during periods of social strife, few politicians in Western democracies call openly for more order. Because all governments infringe on freedom, we examine that concept first.

Freedom

Freedom can be used in two major senses: freedom to and freedom from. President Franklin Delano Roosevelt used the word in both senses in a speech he made shortly after the United States entered World War II. He described four freedoms—freedom of religion, freedom of speech, freedom from fear, and freedom from want. The noted illustrator Norman Rockwell gave Americans a vision of these freedoms in a classic set of paintings published in the *Saturday Evening Post* (see Feature 1.1).

Freedom to is the absence of constraints on behavior. In this sense, freedom is synonymous with *liberty*. Two of Rockwell's paintings—*Freedom of Worship* and *Freedom of Speech*—exemplify this type of freedom.

Freedom from underlies the message of the other paintings, *Freedom from Fear* and *Freedom from Want*. Here freedom suggests immunity from fear and want. In the modern political context, **freedom from** often symbolizes the fight against exploitation and oppression. The cry of the civil rights movement in the 1960s—"Freedom Now!"—conveyed this meaning. If you recognize that freedom in this sense means immunity from discrimination, you can see that it comes close to the concept of equality.[7] We avoid using freedom to mean freedom from; for this sense of the word, we simply use *equality*. When we use freedom, we mean freedom to.

Order

When order is viewed in the narrow sense of preserving life and protecting property, most citizens would concede the importance of maintaining order and thereby grant the need for government. For example, "domestic Tranquility" (order) is cited in the preamble to the Constitution. However, when order is viewed in the broader sense of preserving the social order, people are more likely to argue that maintaining order is not a legitimate function of government (see Compared with What? 1.1). Social order refers to established patterns of authority in society and to traditional modes of behavior. It is the accepted way of doing things. The prevailing social order prescribes behavior in many different areas: how students should dress in school (neatly, no purple hair) and behave toward their teachers (respectfully); under what conditions people should have sexual relations (married, different sexes); what the press should not publish (sexually explicit photographs); and what the proper attitude toward religion and country should be (reverential). It is important to remember that social order can change. Today, perfectly respectable men and women wear bathing suits that would have caused a scandal at the turn of the century.

COMPARED WITH WHAT? 1.1

The Importance of Order as a Political Value

Compared with citizens in other nations, Americans do not value maintaining order as much as others do. Surveys in the United States and in fifteen other countries asked respondents to select which of the following four national goals was the "most important in the long run":

- Maintaining order in the nation
- Giving the people more say in important government decisions
- Fighting rising prices

- Protecting freedom of speech

Just 28 percent of those surveyed in the United States chose "maintaining order." Only respondents in Belgium and Canada attached appreciably less importance to maintaining order. Compared with citizens in most other Western countries and Russia, Americans seem to want less government control of social behavior.

Source: World Values Survey, *1990–1991. The tabulation was provided by Professor Ronald F. Inglehart, University of Michigan.*

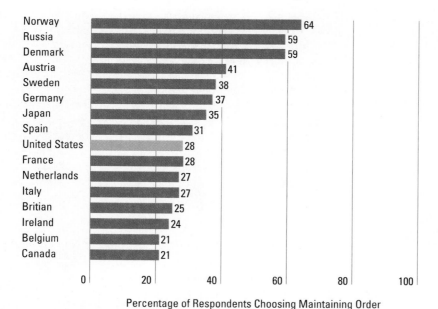

Percentage of Respondents Choosing Maintaining Order

A government can protect the established order under its **police power**—its authority to safeguard residents' safety, health, welfare, and morals. The extent to which government should use this authority is a topic of ongoing debate in the United States and is constantly being redefined by the courts. In the 1980s, many states used their police powers to pass legislation that banned smoking in public places. In 1990, a Fort Lauderdale jury convicted a record store owner of obscenity for selling a 2 Live Crew album that made explicit references to sexual violence (the conviction

■ The Four Freedoms

Norman Rockwell became famous in the 1940s for the humorous, home-spun covers he painted for the *Saturday Evening Post*, a weekly magazine. Inspired by an address to Congress in which President Roosevelt outlined his goals for world civilization, Rockwell painted *The Four Freedoms*, which were reproduced in the *Post*. Their immense popularity led the government to print posters of the illustrations for the Treasury Department's war bond drive. The Office of War Information also reproduced *The Four Freedoms* and circulated the posters in schools, clubhouses, railroad stations, post offices, and other public buildings. Officials even had copies dropped into the European front to remind soldiers of the liberties for which they were fighting. It is said that no other paintings in the world have ever been reproduced or circulated in such vast numbers as *The Four Freedoms*.

Freedom of Speech

Freedom of Worship

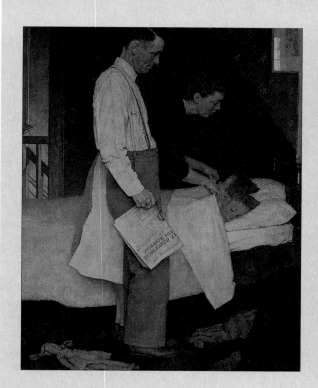

Freedom from Fear

Freedom from Want

was later overturned). There are those who fear the evolution of a police state—government that uses its power to regulate nearly all aspects of behavior. For example, South Africa had laws governing intermarriage between blacks and whites and prescribing where an interracial married couple could live. It is no accident that the chief law enforcement officer in South Africa was the minister of law and order.

Most governments are inherently conservative; they tend to resist social change. But some governments have as a primary objective the restructuring of the social order. Social change is most dramatic when a government is overthrown through force and replaced by a revolutionary government. Governments can work at changing social patterns more gradually through the legal process. Our use of the term *order* in this book includes all three aspects: preserving life, protecting property, and maintaining traditional patterns of social relationships.

Welcome Home, Soldier
During World War II, the men went away to fight while the women stayed home. Today, as a result of the drive for sexual equality, many women are soldiers, too. And many men found themselves in interesting role reversals when their loved ones were called to duty during the Persian Gulf crisis.

Equality

As with freedom and order, *equality* is used in different senses, to support different causes.

Political equality in elections is easy to define: Each citizen has one and only one vote. This basic concept is central to democratic theory—a subject explored at length in Chapter 2. But when some people advocate political equality, they mean more than one person, one vote. These people contend that an urban ghetto dweller and the chairman of the board of General Motors are not politically equal despite the fact that each has one vote. Through occupation or wealth, some citizens are more able than others to influence political decisions. For example, wealthy citizens can exert influence by advertising in the mass media or by contacting friends in high places. Lacking great wealth and political connections, most citizens do not have such influence. Thus, some analysts argue that equality in wealth, education, and status—that is, **social equality**—is necessary for true political equality.

There are two routes to achieving social equality: providing equal opportunities and ensuring equal outcomes. **Equality of opportunity** means that each person has the same chance to succeed in life. This idea is deeply ingrained in American culture. The Constitution prohibits titles of nobility and does not make owning property a requirement for holding public office: public schools and libraries are free to all. To many people, the concept of social equality is satisfied just by offering opportunities for people to advance themselves. It is not essential that people end up being equal after using those opportunities. For others, true social equality means nothing less than **equality of outcome.**[8] They believe that society must see to it that people are equal. It is not enough for governments to provide people with equal opportunities; they must also design policies that redistribute wealth and status so that economic and social equality are actually achieved. In education, equality of outcome has led to federal laws that require comparable funding for men's and women's college sports (see Politics in a Changing America 1.1). In business, equality of outcome has led to certain affirmative action programs to increase minority hiring and to the active recruitment of women, blacks, and Hispanics to fill jobs. Equality of outcome here also has produced federal laws that require employers to pay men and women equally for equal work.

Some link equality of outcome with the concept of governmental **rights**—the idea that every citizen is entitled to certain benefits of government, that government should guarantee its citizens adequate (if not equal) housing, employment, medical care, and income as a matter of right. If citizens are entitled to government benefits as a matter of right, government efforts to promote equality of outcome become legitimized.

Clearly, the concept of equality of outcome is quite different from that of equality of opportunity, and it requires a much greater degree of government activity. It is also the concept of equality that clashes most directly with the concept of freedom. By taking from one to give to another—which is necessary for the redistribution of income and status—the government clearly creates winners and losers. The winners may believe that justice has been served by the redistribution. The losers often feel strongly that their freedom to enjoy their income and status has suffered.

TWO DILEMMAS OF GOVERNMENT

The two major dilemmas facing American government in the 1990s stem from the oldest and the newest objectives of government—maintaining order and promoting equality. Both order and equality are important social values, but government cannot pursue either without sacrificing a third important value: individual freedom. The clash between freedom and order forms the original dilemma of government; the clash between freedom and equality forms the modern dilemma of government. Although the dilemmas are different, each involves trading some amount of freedom for another value.

The Original Dilemma: Freedom Versus Order

The conflict between freedom and order originates in the very meaning of government as the legitimate use of force to control human behavior. How much freedom must a citizen surrender to government? The dilemma has occupied philosophers for hundreds of years. In the eighteenth century, French philosopher Jean Jacques Rousseau (1712–1778) wrote that the problem of devising a proper government "is to find a form of association which will defend and protect with the whole common force the person and goods of each associate, and in which each, while uniting himself with all, may still obey himself alone, and remain free as before."[9]

The original purpose of government was to protect life and property, to make citizens safe from violence. How well is the American government doing today in providing law and order to its citizens? More than 40 percent of the respondents in a 1993 national survey said that they were afraid to walk alone at night within a mile of their homes.[10] In the cities, their fears seem justified. Almost three in ten people in urban areas reported in 1990 that they, or a member of their family, had been touched by a crime within the past year.[11] Visitors to New York are well advised to keep out of Central Park after dark. Simply put, Americans do not trust their urban governments to protect them from crime when they go out alone at night.

POLITICS IN A CHANGING AMERICA

1.1 The Attempt to Achieve Gender Equity in College Sports

 Since the 1970s, the number of women's sports programs at American colleges and universities has risen steadily. This graph shows the growth in the number of men's programs in basketball and tennis and women's programs in basketball and volleyball (the sports with the largest numbers of programs for each sex) as a percentage of all member institutions of the National Collegiate Athletic Association (NCAA) since the mid-1950s. (Comparable data for women's sports begin in the mid-1960s.) The men's programs have held fairly steady over time but have declined slightly in recent years. The women's programs, however, jumped markedly after 1972 and increased somewhat thereafter. While some growth in women's programs may owe to voluntary acts by the institutions, a good deal of it can be attributed to the federal government's demand for equal treatment of the sexes under the 1972 Civil Rights law. Title IX of that law outlawed gender discrimination in any institution that receives federal funding.

As applied to sports, Title IX requires that men and women have (1) equal opportunities for participation, (2) equitable shares of athletic scholarships, and (3) equitable conditions for athletes in coaching, scheduling, equipment, recruiting, and facilities. Many institutions responded by increasing the number of sports programs for women, as shown here for basketball and volleyball. Nevertheless, inequities in sports programs for men and women have remained at virtually every participating institution, with men's sports getting most of the athletic scholarship funds and other spending. In large part, this is because of men's football programs, which cost so much to run.

With more attention being focused on gender equity in college sports and with increasing numbers of investigations under Title IX by the Office of Civil Rights, institutions are responding by cutting men's sports (e.g., gymnastics) and adding more women's sports (e.g., soccer). Jack Weidenbach, the athletic director of the University of Michigan, said that the effect will inevitably be felt by cut-

When the old communist governments still ruled in Eastern Europe, the climate of fear in urban America stood in stark contrast to the pervasive sense of personal safety in such cities as Moscow, Warsaw, and Prague. Then it was common to see old and young strolling late at night along the streets and in the parks of these communist cities. The formerly communist regimes gave their police great powers to control guns, monitor citizens' movements, and arrest and imprison suspicious people—which enabled them to do a better job of maintaining order. Communist governments deliberately chose order over freedom. It is perhaps not surprising that some Russians who emigrated to the United States found life here too threatening and returned to the security of the Soviet Union. After living for eight years in New York City, Rebecca Katsap (age sixty-seven) returned to Odessa in 1987, saying, "I was afraid to go out in the street after four in the afternoon."[12] But with the collapse of order under communism, things have changed in the former Soviet Union. In early 1993, more than

ting men's sports: "If you're going to have gender equity, you're going to have to take the money from some place, and the men are the only place left." In a changing America, enforcing social equality does have its costs.

Sources: National Collegiate Athletic Association, The Sports and Recreational Programs of the Nation's Universities and Colleges, Report Number 7, 1956–87 (Mission, Kansas: NCAA, 1990); data for 1991–1992 were kindly provided by Todd Petr of the NCAA; and Ed Sherman, "Men vs. Women: It's a Brand New Ball Game," Chicago Tribune *(April 28, 1993), p. 1.*

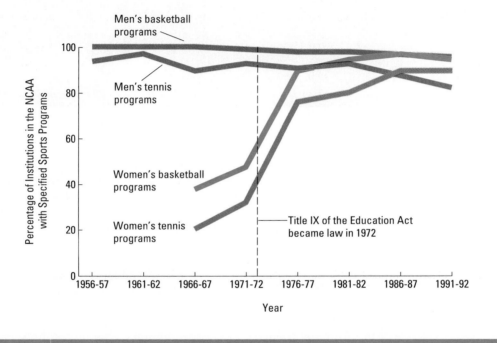

two thousand residents of Russia's capital were asked, "Do you feel protected from criminal action in Moscow?" Only 7 percent said yes and 86 percent said no.[13] So most Muscovites had no complaint when President Yeltsin took advantage of the emergency immediately after the 1993 rebellion to establish a curfew and deport immigrants.[14]

The crisis over acquired immune deficiency syndrome (AIDS) adds a new twist to the dilemma of freedom versus order. Some health officials believe that AIDS, for which there is no known cure, is the greatest threat in the medical history of the United States. The U.S. Public Health Service estimated that more than 1 million Americans were infected with the AIDS virus by late 1992, when 233,907 cases of the disease had been reported to the Centers for Disease Control, and 158,243 people had died.[15] There were 103,500 cases of AIDS in 1993 alone.[16]

To combat the spread of the disease in the military, the Department of Defense began testing all applicants for the AIDS virus. Other government

Freedom as a Weapon in the Velvet Revolution

Armed with banners proclaiming "Svobodu"— 'freedom,' in Czech—students in Prague confront police in November 1989. The confrontation was no contest. Within weeks, the nonviolent "Velvet Revolution" in Czechoslovakia forced the communist government out of power, ending more than four decades of authoritarian rule. Free elections were held the next year and again in 1992.

agencies have begun testing current employees. And some officials are calling for widespread mandatory testing within the private sector as well. The programs are strongly opposed by those who believe they violate individual freedom. Those who are more afraid of the spread of AIDS than of an infringement on individual rights support aggressive government action to combat the disease.

The value conflict between freedom and order represents the original dilemma of government. In the abstract, people value both freedom and order; in real life, the two values inherently conflict. By definition, any policy that works toward one value takes away from the other. The balance of freedom and order is an issue of enduring matters (whether to allow capital punishment) and of contemporary challenges (how to deal with urban gang members who spray-paint walls; whether to allow art galleries to display sexually explicit photographs). And in a democracy, policy choices hinge on how much citizens value freedom and how much they value order.

The Modern Dilemma: Freedom Versus Equality

Popular opinion has it that freedom and equality go hand in hand. In reality, the two values usually clash when governments enact policies to promote social equality. Because social equality is a relatively recent government objective, deciding between policies that promote equality at the expense of freedom, and vice versa, is the modern dilemma of politics. Consider these examples:

• During the 1960s, Congress (through the Equal Pay Act) required employers to pay women and men the same rate for equal work. This means that some employers are forced to pay women more than they would if hiring were based on their free choice.

• During the 1970s, the courts ordered the busing of schoolchildren to achieve a fair distribution of blacks and whites in public schools. This action was motivated by concern for educational equality, but it also impaired freedom of choice.

• During the 1980s, some states passed legislation that went beyond the idea of equal pay for equal work to the more radical notion of pay equity—equal pay for comparable work. Women had to be paid at a rate equal to men's—even if they had different jobs—providing the women's jobs were of "comparable worth." For example, if the skills and responsibilities of a female nurse were found to be comparable to those of a male sanitation engineer in the same hospital, the woman's salary and the man's salary would have to be the same.

• In the 1990s, Congress prohibited discrimination in employment, public services, and public accommodations on the basis of a person's physical or mental disability. Under the 1990 Americans with Disabilities Act, businesses with twenty-five or more employees cannot pass over an otherwise qualified disabled person in employment or promotion, and new buses and trains have to be made accessible to them.

These examples illustrate the problem of using government power to promote equality. The clash between freedom and order is obvious, but that between freedom and equality is more subtle. Americans, who think of freedom and equality as complementary rather than conflicting values, often do not notice the clash. When forced to choose between the two, however, Americans are far more likely to choose freedom over equality than are people in other countries (see Compared with What? 1.2). The emphasis on equality over freedom was especially strong in the former Soviet Union, which traditionally guaranteed its citizens medical care, inexpensive housing, and other social services under communism. Although the quality of the benefits was not much by Western standards, Soviet citizens experienced a sense of equality in sharing their deprivations. Indeed, there was such aversion to economic inequality that citizens' attitudes hindered economic development in a free market. In 1990, one Russian politician said, "The ideal of social justice here is that everybody should have nothing, not that entrepreneurs should prosper and spread the wealth."[17]

The conflicts among freedom, order, and equality explain a great deal of the political conflict in the United States. The conflicts also underlie the ideologies that people use to structure their understanding of politics.

IDEOLOGY AND THE SCOPE OF GOVERNMENT

People hold different opinions about the merits of government policies. Sometimes their views are based on self-interest. For example, most senior citizens vociferously oppose increasing their contributions to Medicare, the government program that defrays medical costs for the elderly, preferring to have all citizens pay for their coverage. Policies also are judged according to individual values and beliefs. Some people hold an assortment of values and beliefs that produce contradictory opinions on government policies. Others organize their opinions into a **political ideology**—a consistent set of values and beliefs about the proper purpose and scope of government.

COMPARED
WITH WHAT? 1.2

The Importance of Freedom and Equality as Political Values

Compared with citizens' views of freedom and equality in fifteen other nations, Americans value freedom more than others do. Respondents in each country were asked which of the following statements came closer to their own opinion:

- "I find that both freedom and equality are important. But if I were to make up my mind for one or the other, I would consider personal freedom more important, that is, everyone can live in freedom and develop without hindrance."
- "Certainly both freedom and equality are important. But if I were to make up my mind for one of the two, I would consider

equality more important, that is, that nobody is underprivileged and that social class differences are not so strong."

Americans chose freedom by a ratio of nearly 3 to 1. No other nation showed such a strong preference for freedom, and citizens in four countries favored equality instead. When we look at this finding together with Americans' disdain for order (see Compared with What? 1.1), the importance of freedom as a political concept in the United States is clear.

Source: World Values Survey, *1990–1991. The tabulation was provided by Professor Ronald F. Inglehart, University of Michigan.*

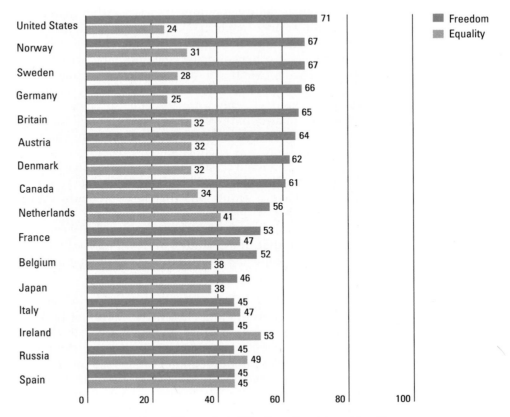

Percentage of Respondents Who Chose Freedom and Equality

How far should government go to maintain order, provide public goods, and promote equality? In the United States (as in every other nation), citizens, scholars, and politicians have different answers. We can analyze their positions by referring to philosophies about the proper scope of government—the range of its permissible activities. Imagine a continuum. At one end is the belief that government should do everything; at the other is the belief that government should not exist. These extreme ideologies—from most government to least government—and those that fall in between are shown in Figure 1.1.

Totalitarianism

Totalitarianism is a belief that government should have unlimited power. A totalitarian government controls all sectors of society: business, labor, education, religion, sports, the arts. A true totalitarian favors a network of laws, rules, and regulations that guides every aspect of individual behavior. The object is to produce a perfect society serving some master plan for "the common good." Totalitarianism has reached its terrifying potential only in literature and films (for example, George Orwell's *1984*), but several real societies have come perilously close to "perfection." One thinks of Germany under Hitler and the Soviet Union under Stalin. Not many people openly profess totalitarianism today, but the concept is useful because it anchors one side of our continuum.

Socialism

Whereas totalitarianism refers to government in general, **socialism** pertains to government's role in the economy. Like communism, socialism is an economic system based on Marxist theory. Under socialism (and communism), the scope of government extends to ownership or control of the basic industries that produce goods and services. These include communications, mining, heavy industry, transportation, and power. Although socialism favors a strong role for government in regulating private industry and directing the economy, it allows more room than communism does for private ownership of productive capacity.

Many Americans equate socialism with the communism practiced in the old closed societies of the Soviet Union and Eastern Europe. But there is a difference. Although communism in theory was supposed to result in a "withering away" of the state, communist governments in practice tended toward totalitarianism, controlling both political and social life through a dominant party organization. Some socialist governments, however, practice **democratic socialism.** They guarantee civil liberties (such as freedom of speech and freedom of religion) and allow their citizens to determine the extent of government activity through free elections and competitive political parties. Outside the United States, socialism is not universally viewed as inherently bad. In fact, the governments of Britain, Sweden, Germany, and France—among other democracies—have at times since World War II been avowedly socialist. More recently, the formerly communist regimes of Eastern Europe have abandoned the controlling role of government in their economies in favor of elements of capitalism.

FIGURE 1.1   ■ Ideology and the Scope of Government

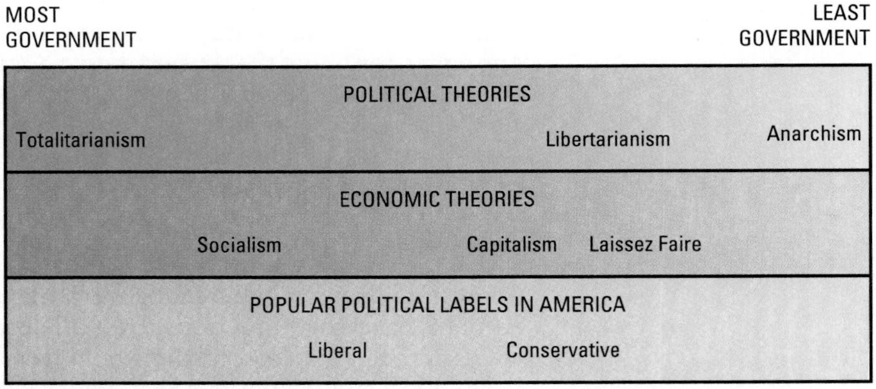

*We can classify political ide-
ologies according to the scope
of action that people are willing to give government in
dealing with social and economic problems. In this chart,
the three lines map out various philosophical positions
along an underlying continuum ranging from "most" to
"least" government. Notice
that conventional politics in
the United States spans only a
narrow portion of the theoretical possibilities for government action.*

*In popular usage, liberals
favor a greater scope of government; conservatives want
a narrower scope. But over
time, the traditional distinction has eroded and now
oversimplifies the differences
between liberals and conservatives. See Figure 1.2 for a
more discriminating classification of liberals and conservatives.*

MOST
GOVERNMENT

LEAST
GOVERNMENT

POLITICAL THEORIES		
Totalitarianism	Libertarianism	Anarchism

ECONOMIC THEORIES		
Socialism	Capitalism	Laissez Faire

POPULAR POLITICAL LABELS IN AMERICA	
Liberal	Conservative

Capitalism

Capitalism also relates to the government's role in the economy. In contrast to both socialism and communism, **capitalism** supports free enterprise—private businesses operating without government regulation.
Some theorists, most notably economist Milton Friedman, argue that free
enterprise is necessary for free politics.[18] This argument, that the economic system of capitalism is essential to democracy, contradicts the
tenets of democratic socialism. Whether it is valid depends in part on our
understanding of democracy, a subject discussed in Chapter 2.

The United States is decidedly a capitalist country, more so than Britain
or most other Western nations. Despite the U.S. government's enormous
budget, it owns or operates relatively few public enterprises. For example,
railroads, airlines, and television stations are privately owned in the
United States; these businesses are frequently owned by the government
in other countries. But our government does extend its authority into the
economic sphere, regulating private businesses and directing the overall
economy. American liberals and conservatives both embrace capitalism,
but they differ on the nature and amount of government intervention in
the economy.

Libertarianism

Libertarianism opposes all government action except that which is necessary to protect life and property. **Libertarians** grudgingly recognize the necessity of government but believe that it should be as limited as possible.
For example, libertarians grant the need for traffic laws to ensure safe and
efficient automobile travel. But they oppose as a restriction on individual
actions laws that set a minimum drinking age—and even oppose laws outlawing marijuana and other drugs. Libertarians believe that social programs that provide food, clothing, and shelter are outside the proper scope
of government. Helping the needy, they insist, should be a matter of individual choice. Libertarians also oppose government ownership of basic industries; in fact, they oppose any government intervention in the

economy. This kind of economic policy is called **laissez faire**—a French phrase that means 'let (people) do (as they please).' Such an extreme policy extends beyond the free enterprise advocated by most capitalists.

Libertarians are vocal advocates of hands-off government—in both social and economic spheres. Whereas those who favor a broad scope of government action shun the description *socialist,* libertarians make no secret of their identity. The Libertarian party ran candidates in every presidential election from 1972 through 1992. However, not one of these candidates won more than 1 million votes.

Do not confuse libertarians with liberals. The words are similar, but their meanings are quite different. Libertarianism draws on *liberty* as its root and means 'absence of governmental constraint.' In American political usage, liberalism evolved from the root word *liberal.* **Liberals** see a positive role for government in helping the disadvantaged. Over time, liberal has come to mean something closer to *generous,* in the sense that liberals (but not libertarians) support government spending on social programs. Libertarians find little benefit in any government social program.

Anarchism

Anarchism stands opposite totalitarianism on the political continuum. Anarchists oppose all government, in any form. As a political philosophy, **anarchism** values freedom above all else. Because all government involves some restriction on personal freedom (for example, forcing people to drive on one side of the road), a pure anarchist would object even to traffic laws. Like totalitarianism, anarchism is not a popular philosophy, but it does have adherents on the political fringes.

In July 1989, more than 1,500 anarchists from around the world convened in San Francisco. The conference featured more than one hundred workshops on history, philosophy, culture, sexuality, and the environment. But the older organizers who wanted to discuss history and debate philosophy were countered by "punk anarchists" with shaved heads marked by fluorescent streaks who knew more about Sid Vicious and Johnny Rotten than about the philosophy of anarchism. As at their previous convention in Chicago in 1986, this one erupted in rioting that broke store windows in nearby Berkeley—underscoring the anarchists' rejection of order.[19] For our purposes, anarchism serves to anchor the right side of the government continuum and to indicate that libertarians are not as extreme in opposing government as is theoretically possible.

Liberals and Conservatives—The Narrow Middle

As shown in Figure 1.1, practical politics in the United States ranges over only the central portion of the continuum. The extreme positions—totalitarianism and anarchism—are rarely argued in public debate. And in this era of distrust of "big government," few American politicians would openly advocate socialism—although one did in 1990 and won election to Congress as an independent candidate. On the other hand, about 150 people ran for Congress in 1992 as candidates of the Libertarian party. Although none won, American libertarians are sufficiently vocal to be heard in the debate over the role of government.

Still, most of that debate is limited to a narrow range of political thought. On one side are people commonly called *liberals*; on the other are *conservatives.* In popular usage, liberals favor more government, conservatives less. This distinction is clear when the issue is government spending to provide public goods. Liberals favor generous government support for education, wildlife protection, public transportation, and a whole range of social programs. **Conservatives** want smaller government budgets and fewer government programs. They support free enterprise and argue against government job programs, regulation of business, and legislation of working conditions and wage rates.

But in other areas, liberal and conservative ideologies are less consistent. In theory, liberals favor government activism, yet they oppose government regulation of abortion. In theory, conservatives oppose government activism, yet they support government control of the publication of sexually explicit material. What's going on? Are American political attitudes hopelessly contradictory, or is something missing in our analysis of these ideologies today? Actually, something is missing. To understand the liberal and conservative stances on political issues, we have to look not only at the scope of government action but also at the purpose of government action. That is, to understand a political ideology, it is necessary to understand how it incorporates the values of freedom, order, and equality.

AMERICAN POLITICAL IDEOLOGIES AND THE PURPOSE OF GOVERNMENT

Much of American politics revolves around the two dilemmas just described: freedom versus order and freedom versus equality. The two dilemmas do not account for all political conflict, but they help us gain insight into the workings of politics and organize the seemingly chaotic world of political events, actors, and issues.

Liberals Versus Conservatives: The New Differences

Liberals and conservatives are different, but their differences no longer hinge on the narrow question of the government's role in providing public goods. Liberals still favor more government and conservatives less, but this is no longer the critical difference between them. Today, that difference stems from their attitudes toward the purpose of government. Conservatives support the original purpose of government, maintaining social order. They are willing to use the coercive power of the state to force citizens to be orderly. They favor firm police action, swift and severe punishment for criminals, and more laws regulating behavior. Conservatives do not stop with defining, preventing, and punishing crime, however. They tend to want to preserve traditional patterns of social relations—the domestic role of women and the importance of religion in school and family life, for example.

Liberals are less likely than conservatives to use government power to maintain order. In general, liberals are more tolerant of alternative lifestyles—for example, homosexual behavior. Liberals do not shy away from using government coercion, but they use it for a different purpose—to promote equality. They support laws that ensure equal treatment of homosexuals in employment, housing, and education; that require busing

A Kiss Is but a Kiss

A city worker stares at a controversial poster on an elevated train station in Chicago. Part of a national AIDS awareness campaign, this advertisement was intended to show that AIDS is not transmitted through kissing. Public officials and clergy who tried to ban the ad found that they could not, because it was neither untruthful nor obscene; it simply conveyed unconventional images of a conventional act.

schoolchildren to achieve racial equality; that force private businesses to hire and promote women and members of minority groups; that require public carriers to provide equal access to the disabled; that order cities and states to reapportion election districts so that minority voters can elect minority candidates to public office.

Conservatives do not oppose equality, but they do not value it to the extent of using the government's power to enforce equality. For liberals, the use of that power to guarantee equality is both valid and necessary.

A Two-Dimensional Classification of Ideologies

To classify liberal and conservative ideologies more accurately, we have to incorporate freedom, order, and equality in the classification. We do this using the model in Figure 1.2. It depicts the conflicting values along two separate dimensions, each anchored in maximum freedom at the lower left. One dimension extends horizontally from maximum freedom on the left to maximum order on the right. The other extends vertically from maximum freedom at the bottom to maximum equality at the top. Each box represents a different ideological type: libertarians, liberals, conservatives, and populists.*

Libertarians value freedom more than order or equality. (We will use this term for people who have libertarian tendencies but who may not accept

---

* *The ideological groupings we describe here conform to the classification in William S. Maddox and Stuart A. Lilie,* Beyond Liberal and Conservative: Reassessing the Political Spectrum *(Washington, D.C.: Cato Institute, 1984), p. 5. However, our formulation—in terms of the values of freedom, order, and equality—is quite different.*

FIGURE 1.2 ■ Ideologies: A Two-Dimensional Framework

The four ideological types below are defined by the values they favor in resolving the two major dilemmas of government: How much freedom should be sacrificed in pursuit of order and equality? Test yourself by thinking about the values that are most important to you. Which box in the figure best represents your combination of values?

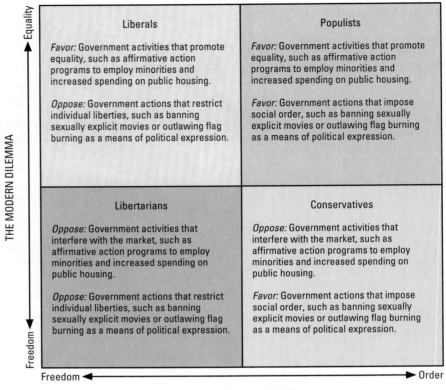

THE MODERN DILEMMA — Equality / Freedom

THE ORIGINAL DILEMMA — Freedom ◄ ► Order

Liberals

Favor: Government activities that promote equality, such as affirmative action programs to employ minorities and increased spending on public housing.

Oppose: Government actions that restrict individual liberties, such as banning sexually explicit movies or outlawing flag burning as a means of political expression.

Populists

Favor: Government activities that promote equality, such as affirmative action programs to employ minorities and increased spending on public housing.

Favor: Government actions that impose social order, such as banning sexually explicit movies or outlawing flag burning as a means of political expression.

Libertarians

Oppose: Government activities that interfere with the market, such as affirmative action programs to employ minorities and increased spending on public housing.

Oppose: Government actions that restrict individual liberties, such as banning sexually explicit movies or outlawing flag burning as a means of political expression.

Conservatives

Oppose: Government activities that interfere with the market, such as affirmative action programs to employ minorities and increased spending on public housing.

Favor: Government actions that impose social order, such as banning sexually explicit movies or outlawing flag burning as a means of political expression.

the whole philosophy.) In practical terms, libertarians want minimal government intervention in both the economic and the social spheres. For example, they oppose food stamp programs and laws that restrict abortion.

Liberals value freedom more than order but not more than equality. Liberals oppose laws that restrict abortion but support food stamp programs. Conservatives value freedom more than equality but would restrict freedom to preserve social order. Conservatives oppose food stamp programs but favor laws that restrict abortion.

Finally, we arrive at the ideological type positioned at the upper right in Figure 1.2. This group values both equality and order more than freedom. Its members support both food stamp programs and laws that restrict abortion. We will call this new group *populists*. The term **populist** derives from a rural reform movement that was active in the United States in the late 1800s. Populists thought of government as an instrument to promote the advancement of common people against moneyed or vested interests. They used their voting power both to regulate business and to enforce their moral judgments on minorities whose political and social values differed from the majority's.[20] Today, the term aptly describes those who favor government action both to reduce inequalities and to ensure social order.

By analyzing political ideologies on two dimensions rather than one, we can explain why people seem to be liberal on one issue (favoring a broader scope of government action) and conservative on another (favoring less government action). The answer hinges on the action's purpose: Which value does it promote, order or equality? According to our typology, only libertarians and populists are consistent in their attitudes toward the scope of government activity, whatever its purpose. Libertarians value freedom so highly that they oppose most government efforts to enforce either order or equality. Populists are inclined to trade freedom for both order and equality. Liberals and conservatives, on the other hand, favor or oppose government activity depending on its purpose. As you will learn in Chapter 5, large groups of Americans fall into each of the four ideological categories. Because Americans choose four different resolutions to the original and modern dilemmas of government, the simple labels of *liberal* and *conservative* no longer describe contemporary political ideologies as well as they did in the 1930s, 1940s, and 1950s.

SUMMARY

The challenge of democracy is making difficult choices—choices that inevitably bring important values into conflict. The *Challenge of Democracy* outlines a normative framework for analyzing the policy choices that arise in the pursuit of the purposes of government.

The three major purposes of government are maintaining order, providing public goods, and promoting equality. In pursuing these objectives, every government infringes on individual freedom. But the degree of that infringement depends on the government's (and, by extension, its citizens') commitment to order and equality. What we have, then, are two dilemmas. The first—the original dilemma—centers on the conflict between freedom and order. The second—the modern dilemma—focuses on the conflict between freedom and equality.

Some people have political ideologies that help them resolve the conflicts that arise in political decision making. These ideologies outline the scope and purpose of government. At opposite extremes of the continuum are totalitarianism, which supports government intervention in every aspect of society, and anarchism, which rejects government entirely. An important step back from totalitarianism is socialism. Democratic socialism favors government ownership of basic industries but preserves civil liberties. Capitalism, another economic system, promotes free enterprise. A significant step short of anarchism is libertarianism, which allows government to protect life and property but little else.

In the United States, the terms *liberal* and *conservative* are used to describe a narrow range toward the center of the political continuum. The usage is probably accurate when the scope of government action is being discussed. That is, liberals support a broader role for government than do conservatives. But when both the scope and the purpose of government are considered, a different, sharper distinction emerges. Conservatives may want less government but not at the price of maintaining order. In other words, they are willing to use the coercive power of government to impose social order. Liberals, too, are willing to use the coercive powers of government but for a different purpose—promoting equality.

It is easier to understand the differences between liberals and conservatives and their views on the scope of government if the values of freedom,

order, and equality are incorporated in the description of political ideologies. Libertarians choose freedom over both order and equality. Populists
are willing to sacrifice freedom for both order and equality. Liberals value
freedom more than order and equality more than freedom. Conservatives
value freedom more than order and order more than freedom.

The concepts of government objectives, values, and political ideologies
appear repeatedly as we determine who favors what government action
and why. So far, we have said little about how government should make its
decisions. In Chapter 2, we complete our normative framework for evaluating American politics by examining the nature of democratic theory.
There, we introduce two key concepts for analyzing how democratic governments make decisions.

Key Terms

government	political ideology
order	totalitarianism
communism	socialism
public goods	democratic socialism
welfare state	capitalism
freedom to	libertarianism
freedom from	libertarians
police power	laissez faire
political equality	liberals
social equality	anarchism
equality of opportunity	conservatives
equality of outcome	populists
rights	

Selected Readings

Bock, Gisela, and Susan James (eds.). *Beyond Equality and Difference: Citizenship, Feminist Politics, and Female Subjectivity.* New York: Routledge, 1992. A collection of essays by women on the meaning of equality and its relationship to the differences between the sexes, with special reference to sexual politics.

Bowie, Norman E. (ed.). *Equal Opportunity.* Boulder, Col.: Westview, 1988. A series of essays on the theory of equal opportunity and its practice and social influence on education, employment, and political participation.

Ebenstein, William, and Edwin Fogelman. *Today's Isms: Communism, Fascism, Capitalism, Socialism.* 10th ed. Englewood Cliffs, N.J.: Prentice-Hall, 1994. This standard source describes the history of each of the four major "isms" and relates each to developments in contemporary politics. It is concise, informative, and readable.

Foley, Michael. *American Political Ideas: Traditions and Usages.* New York: St. Martin's Press, 1991. A foreigner's perspective on the major concepts in American political thought. It has chapters on freedom, equality, capitalism, liberalism, and conservatism, among other topics.

Gans, Chaim. *Philosophical Anarchism and Political Disobedience.* New York: Cambridge University Press, 1992. Inquires into the meaning of duty to obey laws, makes a case for limits to strict obedience to laws, and analyzes intolerance for legal disobedience.

Institute for Cultural Conservatism. *Cultural Conservatism: Toward a New National Agenda.* Washington, D.C.: Free Congress Research and Education Foundation, 1987. This book assumes that traditional values are necessary for individual fulfillment and that society and government must play an active role in upholding traditional culture.

Skogan, Wesley G. *Disorder and Decline: Crime and the Spiral of Decay in American Neighborhoods.* New York: The Free Press, 1990. This study of neighborhood crime and disorder in six cities explores the nature of disorder and the limits to the state's police powers in dealing with urban decline.

Verba, Sidney, et al. *Elites and the Idea of Equality: A Comparison of Japan, Sweden, and the United States.* Cambridge, Mass.: Harvard University Press, 1987. The authors surveyed leaders in each country representing established organizations, challenging groups, and mediating institutions to determine their views on equality and to learn how economics and politics affect the distribution of income in the modern welfare state.

Westen, Peter. *Speaking of Equality: An Analysis of the Rhetorical Force of "Equality" in Moral and Legal Discourse.* Princeton, N.J.: Princeton University Press, 1990. This philosophical treatise is not easy to read, but it has an especially useful chapter on equal opportunity, which Westen says does not mean "same opportunity."

Majoritarian or Pluralist Democracy?

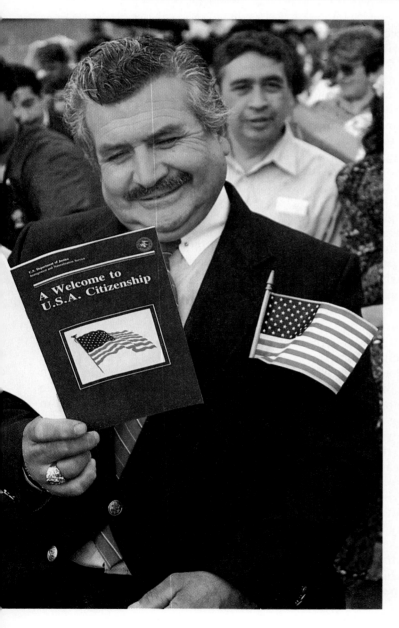

RAM CHUN'S FAMILY escaped Cambodia to search for a better life in the United States. They settled in Stockton, California, where many Cambodian families had come to start their pursuit of the American dream. Ram Chun, who was eight, attended the Cleveland Elementary School. On January 17, 1989, she was playing during recess when Patrick Purdy opened fire with his AK-47 and shot her to death.

Purdy's two-minute rampage with his semiautomatic rifle killed four other children, too. Twenty-nine students and a teacher were injured. "He was just standing there with a gun making wide sweeps," said one teacher. When he had finished firing more than one hundred rounds, Purdy took out a pistol and shot himself to death. Purdy was a drifter with an extensive criminal record, but there is no clear motive for his rampage. What is clear is that he was quite interested in things military. The day of his shooting spree, he was wearing fatigues and a flak jacket; in his hotel room were more than one hundred plastic toy figures of soldiers, tanks, and weapons.[1]

AK-47s and other semiautomatic rifles are military assault weapons. (Machine guns that fire continuously while the trigger is depressed are automatic weapons; semiautomatics require that the trigger be pulled for each shot, but they fire in rapid succession.) Purdy had purchased his AK-47 for $349.95 at a gun store in Sandy, Oregon.[2]

The Stockton massacre prompted some members of Congress to push for a ban on semiautomatic weapons such as the AK-47. The National Rifle Association (NRA) vehemently disagreed, claiming that such a ban would infringe on the constitutional right of the people to bear arms. The 3-million-member NRA is powerful because its members are vocal in communicating their impassioned views to their representatives and senators. The group has been successful in defeating gun control measures. Indeed, in 1986 the organization successfully pressured Congress to pass a law weakening a modest gun control law passed in 1968 in the wake of the assassinations of Robert Kennedy and Martin Luther King, Jr. (However, some states in the 1990s passed modest gun control measures over the objection of the NRA, and the Brady Bill approved by Congress in 1993 mandates a five-day waiting period while the backgrounds of purchasers of handguns are checked to ensure that they do not have records of mental instability or criminal activity.)

The NRA's ability to thwart gun control efforts stands in opposition to the American people's opinion on the subject. Sixty-seven percent of the

Every Boy Needs a Gun

The National Rifle Association (NRA) is a powerful organization because of its large and fervent constituency; its vocal and active members clearly love their guns. This young enthusiast samples some of the wares at a vendor's booth at the exhibition hall of an NRA convention.

public favors stricter gun control laws. Sixty-six percent favor a ban on assault rifles.[3] The Senate managed to include (by a one-vote margin) a ban on nine types of assault rifles in its 1990 anticrime bill, but the House refused to go along. In 1994 Congress struggled with assault weapons once again as part of an omnibus crime package. This time both the House and Senate passed legislation including a ban on assault weapons. However, fierce lobbying by the NRA resulted in a defeat of the House-Senate compromise on a procedural vote in the House. Public anger over Congress's failure to pass crime legislation led to a subsequent vote on a revised bill which included the assault weapons ban. It was finally passed and signed into law.[4]

These recent victories for gun control show Congress responding to majority opinion. Yet over the years Congress has regularly backed the interests of a minority, the NRA, over the preferences of the majority, which favors gun control. Is it democratic for policymakers to favor an intense minority at the expense of a less committed majority?

In Chapter 1, we discussed three basic values that underlie what government should do. In this chapter, we examine how government should decide what to do. In particular, we set forth criteria for judging whether a government's decision-making process is democratic.

THE THEORY OF DEMOCRATIC GOVERNMENT

The origins of democratic theory lie in ancient Greek political thought. Greek philosophers classified governments according to the number of citizens involved in the process. Imagine a continuum running from rule by one person, through rule by a few, to rule by many.

At one extreme is an **autocracy,** in which one individual has the power to make all important decisions. The concentration of power in the hands of one person (usually a monarch) was a more common form of government in earlier historical periods. Some countries are still ruled autocratically, such as Iraq under Saddam Hussein.

Rocky Road to Democracy
Upheaval in the Russian government has sorely tested the nation's commitment to democracy. In September of 1993, the frustrated President of Russia, Boris Yeltsin, dissolved the Parliament because of its antagonism toward his programs and called for new elections. Yeltsin's opponents in Parliament regarded his actions as illegal and said they were deposing him as head of the country. The military sided with Yeltsin, however, and a showdown came when his critics in Parliament barricaded themselves inside the White House (the Russian Parliament building). These onlookers stand amid the smoke from the shelling of the White House by tanks, which led to a surrender of those inside.

Oligarchy puts government power in the hands of an elite. At one time, the nobility or the major landowners commonly ruled as an aristocracy. Today, military leaders are often the rulers in countries governed by an oligarchy.

At the other extreme of the continuum is **democracy,** which means rule by the people. Most scholars believe that the United States, Britain, France, and other countries in Western Europe are genuine democracies. Others contend that these countries only appear to be democracies because they hold free elections but that they actually are run by wealthy business elites for their own benefit. Nevertheless, most people today agree that governments *should* be democratic.

The Meaning and Symbolism of Democracy

Americans have a simple answer to the question, "Who should govern?" It is, "The people." Unfortunately, this answer is too simple. It fails to define who *the people* are. Should we include young children? Recent immigrants? Illegal aliens? This answer also fails to tell us how the people should do the governing. Should they be assembled in a stadium? Vote by mail? Choose others to govern for them? We need to take a closer look at what "government by the people" really means.

The word *democracy* originated in Greek writings around the fifth century B.C. *Demos* referred to the common people, the masses; *kratos* meant 'power.' The ancient Greeks were afraid of democracy—rule by rank-and-file citizens. That fear is evident in the term *demagogue.* We use the term today to refer to a politician who appeals to and often deceives the masses by manipulating their emotions and prejudices.

LIBRARY
COLBY-SAWYER COLLEGE
NEW LONDON, NH 03257

Freedom, The Universal Language

These demonstrators in Beijing hoped to embarrass the authoritarian Chinese government during a state visit by former Soviet leader Mikhail Gorbachev in May 1989. Their message was, if freedom could come to the (former) Soviet Union, why not to China? Shortly after the Gorbachev visit, China erupted with massive demonstrations in Beijing's Tiananmen Square. After tolerating them for a short time, the demonstrations were brutally suppressed by the communist government.

Many centuries after the Greeks first defined democracy, the idea still carried the connotation of mob rule. When George Washington was president, opponents of a new political party disparagingly called it a *democratic* party. No one would do that in politics today. In fact, the term has become so popular that the names of more than 20 percent of the world's political parties contain some variation of democracy.[5]

In the United States, democracy has become the apple pie and motherhood of political discourse. As with *justice* and *decency*, democracy is used reverently by politicians of all persuasions. Even totalitarian regimes use it. North Korea calls itself the *Democratic People's Republic of Korea*, although by our standards it is one of the most undemocratic places on the face of the earth. Like other complex concepts, democracy means different things to different people.

There are two major schools of thought about what constitutes democracy. The first believes democracy is a form of government. It emphasizes the procedures that enable the people to govern—meeting to discuss issues, voting in elections, running for public office. The second sees democracy in the substance of government policies, in freedom of religion and the provision for human needs. The procedural approach focuses on how decisions are made; the substantive approach is concerned with what government does.

The Procedural View of Democracy

Procedural democratic theory sets forth principles that describe how government should make decisions. The principles address three distinct questions:

1. *Who* should participate in decision making?

2. *How much* should each participant's vote count?

3. *How many* votes are needed to reach a decision?

According to procedural democratic theory, all adults should participate in government decision making; everyone within the boundaries of the political community should be allowed to vote. If some people, such as recent immigrants, are prohibited from participating, they are excluded for practical or political reasons. The theory of democracy itself does not exclude any adults from participation. We refer to this principle as **universal participation.**

How much should each participant's vote count? According to procedural theory, all votes should be counted *equally.* This is the principle of **political equality.**

Note that universal participation and political equality are two distinct principles. It is not enough for everyone to participate in a decision; all votes must carry equal weight. President Abraham Lincoln reportedly once took a vote of his cabinet members and found that all opposed his position on the issue. He summarized the vote and the decision this way: "Seven noes, one aye—the ayes have it."[6] Everyone participated, but Lincoln's vote counted more than all the others combined. (No one ever said that presidents have to run their cabinets democratically.)

Finally, how many votes are needed to reach a decision? Procedural theory prescribes that a group should decide to do what the majority of its participants (50 percent plus one person) wants to do. This principle is called **majority rule.** (If participants divide over more than two alternatives and none receives a simple majority, the principle usually defaults to *plurality rule,* under which the group does what most participants want.)

A Complication: Direct Versus Indirect Democracy

The three principles—universal participation, political equality, and majority rule—are widely recognized as necessary for democratic decision making. Small, simple societies can meet the principles with a direct, or **participatory democracy,** in which all members of the group meet to make decisions while observing political equality and majority rule. The origins of participatory democracy go back to the Greek city-state, where the important decisions of government were made by its adult citizens meeting in an assembly. The people ruled for themselves rather than having a small number of notables rule on their behalf. (In Athens, the people who were permitted to attend the assemblies excluded women, slaves, and those whose families had not lived there for generations. Thus, participation was not universal. Still, the Greek city-state represented a dramatic transformation in the theory of government.)[7]

Something close to participatory democracy is practiced in some New England villages, where rank-and-file citizens gather in a town meeting, often just once a year, to make key community decisions together. A town meeting is impractical in large cities, although there are some cities which have incorporated forms of participatory democracy in the decision-making process by instituting forms of neighborhood government. For example, in Birmingham, Alabama; Dayton, Ohio; Portland, Oregon; and St. Paul, Minnesota, each area of the city is governed by a neighborhood council (see Feature 2.1). The neighborhood councils have authority over zoning and land use questions, and they usually control some funds for the development of projects within their boundaries. All adult residents of a

Hands Up for Secession

At this town meeting on Block Island, a small island off the Rhode Island coast, citizens debated whether to secede from Rhode Island and join Connecticut. Some residents were upset about a proposed state regulation limiting moped use on the island. The movement for secession failed; Block Island remains part of Rhode Island.

neighborhood may participate in the neighborhood council meetings and the larger city government respects their decisions.[8] In Chicago, the school system uses participatory democracy. Each school is primarily governed by a parents' council and not by the citywide school board.[9]

Philosopher Jean Jacques Rousseau contended that true democracy is impossible unless all citizens gather to make decisions and to supervise the government. Rousseau said that decisions of government should embody the general will, and "will cannot be represented."[10] Yet in the United States and virtually all other democracies, participatory democracy is rare. Few cities have decentralized their governments and turned power over to the neighborhoods.

Participatory democracy is commonly rejected on the ground that in large, complex societies we need professional, full-time government officials to study problems, formulate solutions, and administer programs. Moreover, the assumption is that relatively few people will take part in participatory government. This, in fact, turns out to be the case. In a study of neighborhood councils in the cities mentioned above, only 16.6 percent of residents took part in at least one meeting during a two-year period.[11] In other respects, participatory democracy works rather well on the neighborhood level. Yet even if participatory democracy is appropriate for neighborhoods or small villages, how could it work for the federal government? We cannot all gather at the Capitol in Washington to decide defense policy.[12]

The framers of the Constitution were convinced that participatory democracy on the national level was undesirable and instead instituted **representative democracy.** In such a system, citizens participate in government by electing public officials to make decisions on their behalf. Elected officials are expected to represent the voters' views and interests—that is, to serve as the agents of the citizenry and to act for them.

FEATURE 2.1

St. Paul, Minnesota: Where the Grassroots Rule

The low rate of voting by Americans has created a great deal of concern about the health of our democracy. In general, citizens do not seem to care much about becoming involved in government. They feel alienated from the political process, because they believe their participation does not make much of a difference.

In one American city, however, there is little alienation, a lot of confidence, and a lot of meaningful citizen participation in government. One reason that the government of St. Paul, Minnesota, has gained the respect of its citizens is that the city relies on a form of participatory democracy. St. Paul is officially divided into seventeen neighborhoods, each governed by a district council. The district councils are made up of residents who volunteer to serve, and a council's meetings are open to every adult who lives in the neighborhood. The city provides a small amount of financial support so each district council can rent office space and hire at least one professional staffer to do community organizing.

But money is not the most important thing the city gives the district councils; the city also gives them the authority to govern their neighborhoods. The greatest of the powers turned over to the neighborhoods is zoning. Through zoning permits and variances, a district council can regulate business development and control the physical appearance of a neighborhood. Residents are thereby given the means to make crucial decisions at a very local level, decisions that might otherwise be made by a faceless bureaucrat downtown at city hall.

When St. Paul residents were asked a standard political science survey question about confidence in government, the results were revealing. Compared to respondents in other cities, the citizens of St. Paul were much more likely to say they trusted their local government to do what is right. Of those who participate in district council meetings or activities, an astounding 86 percent said they trusted the government of St. Paul.

The district councils in St. Paul encourage residents to take responsibility for the well being of their neighborhoods. Instead of simply blaming elected officials for not representing them well, citizens can represent themselves by participating directly in the policy-making process. Residents know that if they want to have a say in government, they can go down the street and join their neighbors in deciding what is best for their community.

* *This figure comes from a survey of residents of ten medium-sized American cities. Respondents were asked about their confidence in their own local government.*

** *This figure comes from the 1987 General Social Survey (taken at about the same time as the St. Paul and ten-city surveys). Respondents were asked about their confidence in their own local government.*

• *Source: Excerpted from data in Jeffrey M. Berry, Kent E. Portney, and Ken Thomson, (Washington, D.C.: Brookings Institution, 1993).* The Rebirth of Urban Democracy *Used with permission.*

Question: How much of the time do you think you can trust the government in St. Paul [in your city] to do what is right — just about always, most of the time, or only some of the time?

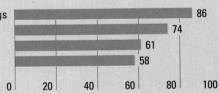

Participants in St. Paul district council meetings	86
All St. Paul residents	74
Residents of ten other cities*	61
National sample**	58

0   20   40   60   80   100

Within the context of representative democracy, we adhere to the principles of universal participation, political equality, and majority rule to guarantee that elections are democratic. But what happens after the election? The elected representatives might not make the decisions the people would have made had they gathered for the same purpose. To account for this possibility in representative government, procedural theory provides a fourth decision-making principle: **responsiveness.** Elected representatives should respond to public opinion. This does not mean that legislators simply cast their ballots on the basis of whether the people back home want alternative A or alternative B. Issues are not usually so straightforward. Rather, responsiveness means following the general contours of public opinion in formulating complex pieces of legislation.

By adding responsiveness to deal with the case of indirect democracy, we have four principles of procedural democracy:

* Universal participation

* Political equality

* Majority rule

* Government responsiveness to public opinion

The Substantive View of Democracy

According to procedural theory, the principle of responsiveness is absolute. The government should do what the majority wants, regardless of what that is. At first, this seems a reasonable way to protect the rights of citizens in a representative democracy. But think for a minute. Christians are the vast majority of the U.S. population. Suppose that the Christian majority backs a constitutional amendment to require Bible reading in public schools, that the amendment is passed by Congress, and that it is ratified by the states. From a strictly procedural view, the action would be democratic. But what about freedom of religion? What about the rights of minorities? To limit the government's responsiveness to public opinion, we must look outside procedural democratic theory, to substantive democratic theory.

Substantive democratic theory focuses on the substance of government policies, not on the procedures followed in making those policies. It argues that in a democratic government, certain principles must be incorporated in government policies. Substantive theorists would reject a law that requires Bible reading in schools, because it would violate a substantive principle, freedom of religion. The core of our substantive principles of democracy is embedded in the Bill of Rights and other amendments to the Constitution.

In defining the principles that underlie democratic government—and the policies of that government—most substantive theorists agree on a basic criterion: Government policies should guarantee civil liberties—freedom of behavior such as freedom of religion and freedom of expression—and civil rights—powers or privileges that government may not arbitrarily deny to individuals, such as protection against discrimination in employment and housing. According to this standard, the claim that

Is Housing a Right?

Some argue that a democratic government is one that promotes social and economic rights. There is little agreement in this country, however, as to what type of substantive policies in these areas qualify as rights to all who live here. This homeless man in Washington, D.C. has firm beliefs on one such issue.

the United States is a democracy rests on its record in ensuring its citizens these liberties and rights. (We look at how good this record is in Chapters 15 and 16.)

Agreement among substantive theorists breaks down when the discussion moves from civil rights to social rights (adequate health care, quality education, decent housing) and economic rights (private property, steady employment). They disagree most sharply on whether a government must promote social equality in order to qualify as a democracy. For example, must a state guarantee unemployment benefits and adequate public housing to be called *democratic*? Some insist that policies that promote social equality are essential to democratic government.[13] Others restrict the requirements of substantive democracy to those policies that safeguard civil liberties and civil rights.

The political ideology of a theorist tends to explain his or her position on what democracy really requires in substantive policies. Conservative theorists have a narrow view of the scope of democratic government and a narrow view of the social and economic rights guaranteed by that government. Liberal theorists believe that a democratic government should guarantee its citizens a much broader spectrum of social and economic rights. In later chapters, we review important social and economic policies that our government has actually followed over time. Keep in mind, however, that what the government has done is not necessarily a correct guide to what a democratic government should do.

Procedural Democracy Versus Substantive Democracy

The problem with the substantive view of democracy is that it does not provide clear, precise criteria that allow us to determine whether a government is democratic. It is, in fact, open to unending arguments over which government policies are truly democratic in the substantive sense.

Theorists are free to promote their pet values—separation of church and state, guaranteed employment, equal rights for women, whatever—under the guise of substantive democracy.

The procedural viewpoint also has a problem. Although it presents specific criteria for democratic government, those criteria can produce undesirable social policies, such as those that prey on minorities. This clashes with **minority rights**—the idea that citizens are entitled to certain things that cannot be denied by majority decisions. Opinions proliferate on what those "certain things" are, but all would agree, for example, on freedom of religion. One way to protect minority rights is to limit the principle of majority rule—requiring a two-thirds majority or some other extraordinary majority for decisions on certain subjects; another is to put the issue in the Constitution, beyond the reach of majority rule.

The issue of prayer in school is a good example of the limits on majority rule. No matter how large, majorities in Congress cannot pass a law to permit organized prayer in public schools, because the Supreme Court has determined that the Constitution forbids such a law. The Constitution could be changed so that it no longer protects religious minorities, but amending the Constitution is a cumbersome process that involves extraordinary majorities. When limits such as these are put on the principle of majority rule, the minority often rules instead.

Clearly, then, procedural democracy and substantive democracy are not always compatible. In choosing one instead of the other, we are also choosing to focus on either procedures or policies. As authors of this text, we favor a compromise. On the whole, we favor the procedural conception of democracy, because it more closely approaches the classical definition of democracy—'government by the people.' And procedural democracy is founded on clear, well-established rules for decision making. But the theory has a serious drawback: It allows a democratic government to enact policies that can violate the substantive principles of democracy. Thus, pure procedural democracy should be diluted so that minority rights guaranteeing civil liberties and civil rights are part of the structure of government. If the compromise seems familiar, it is: The approach has been used in the course of American history to balance legitimate minority and majority interests.

In the real world of politics, drawing the appropriate line between issues that should be subject to procedural democracy and those that should fall under substantive democracy is not always easy. People frequently disagree. But if we recognize that democratic government and desirable policies are not necessarily synonymous, we should be able to live with a political system that sets standards for the decision-making process, if not the decisions themselves.

INSTITUTIONAL MODELS OF DEMOCRACY

A small group can agree to make democratic decisions directly by using the principles of universal participation, political equality, and majority rule. But even the smallest nations have too many citizens to permit participatory democracy at the national level. If nations want democracy, they must achieve it through some form of representative government, electing officials to make decisions. Even then, democratic government is not guaranteed. Governments must have a way to determine what the people want, as well as some way to translate those wants into decisions. In other words, democratic government requires institutional mechanisms—established procedures and organizations—to translate public opinion into government policy and thus be responsive. Elections, political parties, legislatures, and interest groups (which we discuss in later chapters) are all examples of institutional mechanisms in politics.

Some democratic theorists favor institutions that closely tie government decisions to the desires of the majority of citizens. If most citizens want laws banning the sale of pornography, the government should outlaw pornography. If citizens want more money spent on defense and less on social welfare (or vice versa), the government should act accordingly. For these theorists, the essence of democratic government is majority rule and responsiveness.

Other theorists place less importance on the principles of majority rule and responsiveness. They do not believe in relying heavily on mass opinion; instead, they favor institutions that allow groups of citizens to defend their interests in the public policymaking process. Health care is a good example. Everyone cares about it, but it is a complex problem with many competing issues at stake. What is critical here is allowing differing interests to participate, so that all sides have the opportunity to influence the policies as they are developed.

Both schools hold a procedural view of democracy but differ in how they interpret government by the people. We can summarize the theoretical positions by using two alternative models of democracy. As a model, each is a hypothetical plan, a blueprint, for achieving democratic government through institutional mechanisms. The majoritarian model values participation by the people in general; the pluralist model values participation by the people in groups.

The Majoritarian Model of Democracy

The majoritarian model of democracy relies on our intuitive, elemental notion of what is fair. It interprets government by the people to mean government by the majority of the people. The majoritarian model tries to approximate the people's role in a direct democracy within the limitations of representative government. To force the government to respond to public opinion, the majoritarian model depends on several mechanisms that allow the people to participate directly.

The popular election of government officials is the primary mechanism for democratic government in the majoritarian model. Citizens are expected to control their representatives' behavior by choosing wisely in the first place and by reelecting or voting out public officials according to their performance. Elections fulfill the first three principles of procedural democratic theory: universal participation, political equality, and majority rule. The prospect of reelection and the threat of defeat at the polls are expected to motivate public officials to meet the fourth criterion: responsiveness.

Usually, we think of elections only as mechanisms for choosing among candidates for public office. Majoritarian theorists also see them as a means for deciding government policies. An election on a policy issue is called a referendum. When a policy question is put on the ballot by citizens circulating petitions and gathering a required minimum number of signatures, it is called an initiative. Twenty-one states allow their legislatures to put referenda before the voters and give citizens the right to place initiatives on the ballot. Five other states provide for one mechanism or the other.[14]

Statewide initiatives and referenda have been used to decide a wide variety of important questions, many of which have national implications. In 1992, Coloradans voted on an initiative designed to prohibit ordinances that ensure nondiscrimination for gays and lesbians. The majority of voters approved the measure, thus removing the civil rights protection for homosexuals that cities such as Denver and Aspen had previously put into effect. A majority of the state's voters decided that homosexuals should not be guaranteed any sort of minority rights.[15] (A Colorado court has since found the referendum unconstitutional, saying that voters cannot revoke "fundamental rights" of other citizens without a compelling state interest. Although further court challenges are likely, the measure may never take effect.[16]

In the United States, no provisions exist for referenda at the federal level, although some countries do allow policy questions to be put before the public. In Italy, national referenda made both divorce and abortion legal in that heavily Catholic country. In 1993, Italians overwhelmingly supported a national referendum that will fundamentally alter the way seats in that nation's senate are apportioned among political parties. The referendum threw out a system that facilitated representation for minor parties and endorsed a proposal that would give the large political parties most of the seats. This was designed to work against unstable coalitions of many parties and to work toward a more majoritarian form of government in which voters would exert greater control by being able to put one party in charge of the senate.[17]

Americans strongly favor a system of national referenda. In a survey, 76 percent of those queried indicated that voters should have a direct say on some national issues. Only 18 percent felt that we should leave all policy decisions to our elected representatives.[18] The most fervent advocates of majoritarian democracy would like to see modern technology used to maximize the government's responsiveness to the majority. Some have proposed incorporating public opinion polls, first used regularly in the 1930s, in government decision making. More recently, some have suggested using computers for referenda. For instance, citizens could vote on an issue by inserting plastic identification cards in computer terminals installed in all homes.[19] People disagree on the merits of "video voting," but it certainly is possible technically.

The majoritarian model contends that citizens can control their government if they have adequate mechanisms for popular participation. It also assumes that citizens are knowledgeable about government and politics, that they want to participate in the political process, and that they make rational decisions in voting for their elected representatives.

Critics contend that Americans are not knowledgeable enough for majoritarian democracy to work. They point to research that shows that only 22 percent of a national sample of voters said that they "followed what's going on" in government "most of the time." More (40 percent) said that they followed politics "only now and then" or "hardly at all."[20] Defenders of majoritarian democracy respond that while individual Americans may have only limited knowledge or interest in government, the American public as a whole still has coherent and stable opinions on the major policy questions. One 1992 study concludes that people "do not need large amounts of information to make rational voting choices."[21] Finally, some note that while the population today participates in only a limited way, Americans are actually interested in participating more. However, they need more attractive and accessible opportunities to get involved.[22]

An Alternative Model: Pluralist Democracy

For years, political scientists struggled valiantly to reconcile the majoritarian model of democracy with polls that showed widespread ignorance of politics among the American people. When only a little more than half of the adult population bothers to vote in presidential elections, our form of democracy seems to be government by some of the people.

The 1950s saw the evolution of an alternative interpretation of democracy, one tailored to the limited knowledge and participation of the real electorate, not the ideal one. It was based on the concept of *pluralism*— that modern society consists of innumerable groups that share economic, religious, ethnic, or cultural interests. Often, people with similar interests organize formal groups: the Future Farmers of America, the Chamber of Commerce, and the Rotary Club, for example. Many social groups have little contact with government, but occasionally they find themselves backing or opposing government policy. When an organized group seeks to influence government policy, it is called an **interest group.** Many interest groups regularly spend much time and money trying to influence government policy (see Chapter 10). Among them are the International Electrical Workers Union, the American Hospital Association, the Associated Milk Producers, the National Education Association (NEA), the National Association of Manufacturers, the National Organization for Women (NOW), and, of course, the NRA.

The **pluralist model of democracy** interprets government by the people to mean government by people operating through competing interest groups. According to this model, democracy exists when many (plural) organizations operate separately from the government, press their interests on the government, and even challenge the government.[23] Compared with majoritarian thinking, pluralist theory shifts the focus of democratic government from the mass electorate to organized groups. The criterion for democratic government changes from responsiveness to mass public opinion to responsiveness to organized groups of citizens.

The two major mechanisms in a pluralist democracy are interest groups and a decentralized structure of government that provides ready access to public officials and that is open to hearing the groups' arguments for or against government policies. In a centralized structure, decisions are made at one point, the top of the hierarchy. The few decision makers at the top are too busy to hear the claims of competing interest groups or to consider those claims in making their decisions. But a decentralized, complex gov-

Why They Are Called
Lobbyists

At the national level, interest groups are usually represented by paid lobbyists. These people are called lobbyists *because they often gather in the lobby outside congressional meeting rooms, positioned to contact senators and representatives coming and going. Here, lobbyists are waiting to help members of the House Ways and Means Committee understand the importance of their pet tax loopholes.*

ernment structure offers the access and openness necessary for pluralist democracy. For pluralists, the ideal system is one that divides government authority among numerous institutions with overlapping authority. Under such a system, competing interest groups have alternative points of access for presenting and arguing their claims.

Our Constitution approaches the pluralist ideal in the way it divides authority among the branches of government. When the National Association for the Advancement of Colored People (NAACP) could not get Congress to outlaw segregated schools in the South, it turned to the federal court system, which did what Congress would not. According to the ideal of pluralist democracy, if all opposing interests are allowed to organize, and if the system can be kept open so that all substantial claims are heard, the decision will serve the diverse needs of a pluralist society.

Although many scholars have contributed to the model, pluralist democracy is most closely identified with political scientist Robert Dahl. According to Dahl, the fundamental axiom of pluralist democracy is that "instead of a single center of sovereign power there must be multiple centers of power, none of which is or can be wholly sovereign."[24] Some watchwords of pluralist democracy, therefore, are *divided authority, decentralization,* and *open access.*

The Majoritarian Model Versus the Pluralist Model

In majoritarian democracy, the mass public—not interest groups—controls government actions. The citizenry must have some knowledge of government and be willing to participate in the electoral process.

Majoritarian democracy relies on electoral mechanisms that harness the power of the majority to make decisions. Conclusive elections and a centralized structure of government are mechanisms that aid majority rule. Cohesive political parties with well-defined programs also contribute to majoritarian democracy, because they offer voters a clear way to distinguish alternative sets of policies.

Pluralism does not demand much knowledge from citizens in general. It requires specialized knowledge only from groups of citizens, in particular their leaders. In contrast to majoritarian democracy, pluralist democracy seeks to limit majority action so that interest groups can be heard. It relies on strong interest groups and a decentralized government structure—mechanisms that interfere with majority rule, thereby protecting minority interests. We could even say that pluralism allows minorities to rule.

An Undemocratic Model: Elite Theory

If pluralist democracy allows minorities to rule, how does it differ from elite theory—the view that a small group (a minority) makes most important government decisions? According to elite theory, important government decisions are made by an identifiable and stable minority that shares certain characteristics, usually vast wealth and business connections.[25]

Elite theory argues that these few individuals wield power in America because they control its key financial, communications, industrial, and

The Power Elite?

This picture symbolizes the underlying notion of elite theory—that government is driven by wealth. In truth, wealthy people usually have more influence in government than do people of ordinary means. Critics of elite theory point out that it is difficult to demonstrate that an identifiable ruling elite usually sticks together and gets its way in government policy.

government institutions. Their power derives from the vast wealth of America's largest corporations and the perceived importance of the continuing success of those corporations to the growth of the economy. An inner circle of top corporate leaders provides not only effective advocates for individual companies and for the interests of capitalism in general but also supplies people for top government jobs—from which they can further promote their interests.[26]

According to elite theory, the United States is not a democracy but an oligarchy. Although the voters appear to control government through elections, elite theorists argue that the powerful few in society manage to define the issues and to constrain the outcomes of government decisions to suit their own interests. Clearly, elite theory describes a government that operates in an undemocratic fashion.

Elite theory appeals to many people, especially those who believe that wealth dominates politics. The theory also provides plausible explanations for specific political decisions. Why, over the years, has the tax code included so many loopholes that favor the wealthy? The answer, claim elitists, is that the policymakers never really change—they are all cut from the same cloth. The more liberal of the two parties, the Democrats, now control the White House. But look at who Bill Clinton's economic advisers are. By all accounts, the dominant White House adviser on economic matters is Robert Rubin, a career Wall Street investment banker. Clinton's secretary of the treasury is Lloyd Bentsen, whose long congressional career was characterized by his staunch defense of the oil industry. As chairman of the Senate Finance Committee, he was considered an advocate of a tax code partial to business. President Clinton has had little trouble getting along with Republican holdover Alan Greenspan, head of the powerful Federal Reserve Board. Elitists scoff at the idea that elections make a difference.

Political scientists have conducted numerous studies designed to test the validity of elite theory. One study, sympathetic to elite theory, tried to identify the power elite in America by defining the elite positions in the corporate, public interest, and government sectors of society. The author found 7,314 people who fit his definition of the national elite.[27] Although the figure represents only a tiny fraction of the nation's population, 7,314 seems to be too many rulers to provide coherent and coordinated leadership of government and society. Common sense suggests that a group this size is going to experience considerable disagreement.

Many studies have looked at individual cities to see whether a clearly identified elite rules across different issue areas. One influential study of New Haven, Connecticut, demonstrated that different groups won on different issues. No power elite could be found in that city.[28] Yet other studies, such as one of Atlanta, show the dominance of a downtown business elite. This group may not be a power elite that controls a broad range of important decisions across policy areas, but it nevertheless is consistently the most influential group on the key economic development decisions that are crucial to the future of the city.[29]

It is surely easier for an elite to exist on the local level than on the national level, where far more well-organized interest groups compete directly against one another on different policies. A recent study of national politics examined four broad issue areas and tried to assess whether an elite coordinated and influenced government decision making. The authors reasoned that if a power elite existed, its key leaders would communicate with the major corporations and trade associations in Washington. With thousands of business organizations represented in Washington, a power elite must have some mechanism for coordinating its demands on government. By tracking the interaction of representatives of hundreds of groups, the authors determined that there was no elite that coordinated lobbying across the four issue areas (see Figure 2.1). Their evidence supports a critical part of the pluralist argument: Each issue area has a separate set of organizations that influence government.[30]

Although not all studies come to the same conclusion, the preponderance of available evidence documenting government decisions on many different issues does not generally support elite theory—at least in the sense that an identifiable ruling elite usually gets its way. Not surprising, elite theorists reject this view. They argue that studies of decisions made on individual issues do not adequately test the influence of the power elite. Rather, they contend that much of the elite's power comes from its ability to keep things off the political agenda. That is, its power derives from its ability to keep people from questioning fundamental assumptions about American capitalism.[31]

Consequently, elite theory remains part of the debate about the nature of American government and is forcefully argued by radical critics of our political system.[32] Although we do not believe that the scholarly evidence supports elite theory, we do recognize that contemporary American pluralism favors some segments of society over others. The poor are chronically unorganized and are not well represented by interest groups. On the other hand, business is very well represented in the political system. As many interest group scholars who reject the elitist theory have documented, business is better represented than any other sector of the public.[33] Thus, one can endorse pluralist democracy as a more accurate description than elitism in American politics without believing that all groups are equally well represented.

Elite Theory Versus Pluralist Theory

The key difference between elite and pluralist theory lies in the durability of the ruling minority. In contrast to elite theory, pluralist theory does not define government conflict in terms of a minority versus the majority; instead, it sees many different interests vying with one another in each policy area. In the management of national forests, for example, many interest groups—logging companies, recreational campers, environmentalists—have joined the political competition. They press their various viewpoints on government through representatives who are well informed about how relevent issues affect group members. According to elite theory, the financial resources of big logging companies ought to win out over the arguments of campers and environmentalists, but this does not always happen.

Pluralist democracy makes a virtue of the struggle among competing interests (see Politics in a Changing America 2.1). It argues for government that accommodates the struggle and channels the result into government action. According to pluralist democracy, the public is best served if the

<table>
<tr><td>FIGURE 2.1</td><td>■ The Hollow Core</td></tr>
</table>

Using a sophisticated statistical program, the authors of a study on interest group behavior created this graphic to represent the interactions among representatives of interest groups (or lobbyists). In their research, the authors interviewed lobbyists and determined which other lobbyists their interviewees talked to in the course of doing their job. The way this statistical program works, lobbyists who talked to many different lobbyists representing a range of policy areas would be placed somewhere in the middle to symbolize their centrality in a communications network. (Each dot represents an individual lobbyist.) Lobbyists who talked primarily to lobbyists working in the same policy area would be grouped with those lobbyists in an outer sector of the graph. This indicates that their interactions are within a single policy area rather than across different policy domains. The authors' overall conclusion is that a power elite guided by lobbyists at the center of a communications network does not exist; instead, interest group representatives are dispersed by issue area.

Source: John P. Heinz, Edward O. Laumann, Robert L. Nelson, and Robert H. Salisbury, The Hollow Core (Cambridge, Mass.: Harvard University Press, 1993), p. 273.

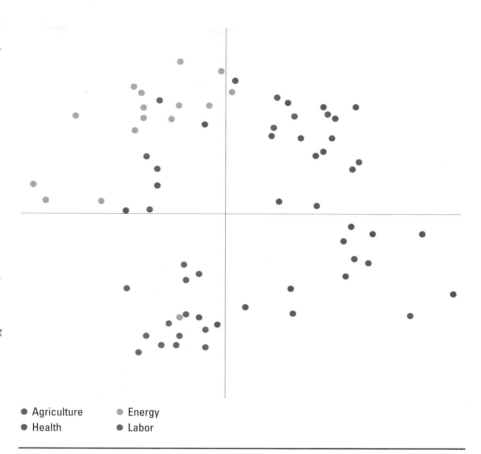

● Agriculture   ● Energy
● Health   ● Labor

government structure provides access for different groups to press their claims in competition with one another. Note that pluralist democracy does not insist that all groups have equal influence on government decisions. In the political struggle, wealthy, well-organized groups have an inherent advantage over poorer, inadequately organized groups. In fact, unorganized segments of the population may not even get their concerns placed on the agenda for government consideration, which means that what government does not discuss (its nondecisions) may be as significant as what it does discuss and decide. This is a critical weakness of pluralism, and critics relentlessly attack the theory, because it appears to justify great disparities in levels of political organization and resources among different segments of society. Pluralists contend that so long as all groups are able to participate vigorously in the decision-making process, the process is democratic.

Obviously, pluralist democracy differs from the classical, ideal conception, which is based on universal participation, political equality, and majority rule. But the pluralist reliance on access is compatible with contemporary thinking that democratic government should be open to groups

POLITICS IN A CHANGING AMERICA 2.1

Does Berkeley Discriminate Against Asian Americans?

 Affirmative action to help minority groups is a clear manifestation of pluralist government. Pluralist democracies try to satisfy the demands of different groups with public policies tailored to fit their particular needs. Affirmative action can give ethnic and racial minorities preferential treatment in such areas such as hiring and college admissions. Because such preferences typically come at the expense of the majority in this country (whites), affirmative action is highly controversial. The policies are justified, however, on the ground that they are intended to overcome the effects of systemic discrimination against minority groups in the past. But what is the justification if affirmative action helps some minority groups but works against *other* minority groups?

Such may be the case at the University of California at Berkeley. Admission to Berkeley, the state university system's flagship campus, is highly coveted. One of the finest research universities in the world, acceptance to the school is difficult with more than 20,000 applicants competing for about 3,500 freshman slots each year. Quite simply, Berkeley has many more fully qualified applicants than it has room for. In a recent year, one-fifth of the applicants who were rejected had near-perfect grade point averages.

As do virtually all colleges and universities, Berkeley pursues diversity in its student body. This should not be hard to do in California, where the population is a diverse mix of ethnic groups and where whites will be a minority in the state sometime around the year 2000. Yet, achieving diversity is difficult at Berkeley, because blacks and Hispanics meet the academic requirements for admission at much lower rates than do whites and Asian Americans. Only 6 percent of Hispanic and 4 percent of black high school graduates meet the university's standard entrance requirements. By comparison, 16 percent of whites and 26 percent of Asian Americans meet the minimum requirements. In terms of the state's population, however, Asians are just 9 percent of all California residents, while 7 percent are black and 26 percent are Hispanic.

To compensate for the lower grades and College Board scores for blacks and Hispanics,

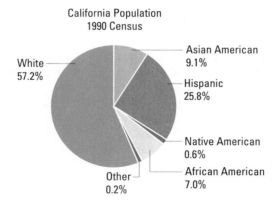

California Population
1990 Census

White 57.2%
Asian American 9.1%
Hispanic 25.8%
Native American 0.6%
African American 7.0%
Other 0.2%

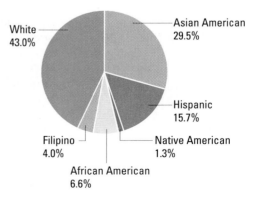

Undergraduate Enrollment
University of California, Berkeley, Fall, 1992

White 43.0%
Asian American 29.5%
Hispanic 15.7%
Native American 1.3%
African American 6.6%
Filipino 4.0%

Berkeley sets aside a certain proportion of each entering class for applicants who will be judged on additional criteria. The special admissions category includes groups such as athletes and disabled students as well as minorities. Under a revised admissions policy adopted in 1984, only 40 percent of each entering class was selected on the basis of academic criteria alone. As soon as the policy was adopted, the enrollment of Asians dropped 21 percent. Quite predictably, Asian American leaders cried foul and claimed that their students were being discriminated against. Why, they asked, should better-qualified Asian American students be refused admission so that less qualified blacks and Hispanics could attend? Asian Americans are, of course, a minority, too, and have suffered considerable discrimination. (California has a shameful history of racism toward residents of Asian ancestry.) Is it the purpose of affirmative action to hurt some minorities so that others can be helped? Asian American leaders made a simple request: Base admission to Berkeley solely on the basis of academic merit.

Merit, however, is difficult to define in such simple terms. For those blacks and Hispanics who grew up in poverty, went to poor schools, and had little exposure to life outside their neighborhood, should merit be judged on the basis of grades and SAT scores alone? If applicants have had to overcome significant obstacles—and by no means do all blacks and Hispanic applicants come from disadvantaged backgrounds—should that not be taken into account by college admissions officers? If two runners are racing and one has a free lane and the other has a series of hurdles, how do you measure who does better?

Berkeley administrators initially denied they were doing anything wrong, but continuing criticism led them to change the policy in 1990. The new policy mandates that 50 percent of each entering class be admitted solely on the basis of academic criteria. Leaders of the Asian American community were pleased, but concerns remain. At the University of California at Los Angeles (UCLA), another campus of the University of California system, an investigation of the Department of Mathematics found that Asian Americans were discriminated against in graduate admissions. The Department of Education found that the prestigious Boalt Hall law school at Berkeley had a quota system that discriminated against Asian Americans.

At Berkeley, pluralism has pitted all the major ethnic and racial groups against one another. Policies designed to help one group are seen as harmful to others. As a result, the campus is splintered and racial tensions are high (as they are on many college campuses). But if the admissions policies at Berkeley are easy to criticize, what should be done instead is not so clear. California must cope with its increasingly diverse population; so, too, must its universities, which are training the leaders of tomorrow.

Source: "New Domestic Student Enrollment by Campus and Ethnicity", Fall 1992, President's Office, University of California, Summary Population and Housing Characteristics: California *(Washington, D.C.: Bureau of the Census, 1991), p. 60; John H. Bunzel, "Choosing Freshman: Who Deserves an Edge!"* Wall Street Journal, *1 February 1988, p. 26; James S. Gibney, "The Berkeley Squeeze,"* New Republic *11 April 1988, pp. 15–17; Jack McCurdy, "Berkeley To Revise Admissions Policies,"* Chronicle of Higher Education, *31 May 1989, p. A3; Deirdre Carmody, "Berkeley Announces Plan To Overhaul Its Admissions Policy,"* New York Times, *21 April 1990, p. A26; "U.C.L.A. Program Is Found Biased Against Asians,"* New York Times, *2 October 1990, p. A21; "For Berkeley, Diversity Means Many Splinters,"* New York Times, *3, October 1990, p. B9; Kenneth J. Cooper, "Berkeley Admissions Guarantee: Some Minorities Gained, Asians Were Limited,"* Washington Post, *26 May 1991, p. A11; Michael S. Greve, "The Newest Move in Law Schools' Quota Game,"* Wall Street Journal, *5, October 1992, p. A12.*

that seek redress of grievances. The pluralist concept also fits the facts about the limited political knowledge of most American citizens. Clearly, pluralist democracy is worthy of being embraced as a rival to majoritarianism, the traditional model of procedural democracy.

| DEMOCRACIES AROUND THE WORLD | We have proposed two models of democratic government. The majoritarian model conforms with classical democratic theory for a representative government. According to this model, democracy should be a form of government that features responsiveness to majority opinion. According to the pluralist model, a government is democratic if it allows minority interests to organize and press their claims on government freely. |

No government actually achieves the high degree of responsiveness demanded by the majoritarian model. No government offers complete and equal access to the claims of all competing groups, as required by an optimally democratic pluralist model. Still, some nations approach these ideals closely enough to be considered practicing democracies.

Testing for Democratic Government

How can we determine which countries qualify as practicing democracies? A government's degree of responsiveness or access cannot be measured directly, so indirect tests must be used. One test is to look for traits normally associated with democratic government—whether defined from a procedural or from a substantive viewpoint. One scholar, for example, established five criteria for a democracy:[34]

1. *Most adults can participate in the electoral process* (embodies the principle of universal participation).

2. *Citizens' votes are secret and are not coerced* (embodies the principle of political equality).

3. *Leaders are chosen in free elections, contested by at least two viable political parties* (embodies the principle of majority rule).

4. *The government bases its legitimacy on representing the desires of its citizens* (embodies the principle of responsiveness).

5. *Citizens, leaders, and party officials enjoy basic freedoms of speech, press, assembly, religion, and organization* (substantive policies that create conditions for the practice of the other criteria).

Four of the five criteria apply to government procedures rather than to the substance of government policy. But all the criteria apply equally to the majoritarian and pluralist models of democracy. Because the United States fits all the criteria to a fairly high degree, it qualifies as a democracy. What about the other nations of the world?

Establishing Democracies

Most countries are neither majoritarian or pluralist; rather, most are governed in an authoritarian manner, or they are struggling to move out of an authoritarian tradition but are not yet true democracies. Until recently,

Christian Democracy

Fundamentalist Christians have successfully organized and become a significant force in American politics. The Christian Coalition, allied with the Reverend Pat Robertson, plays a central leadership role in mobilizing Christian conservatives and getting them involved in the political process. Critics charge that this group is trying to impose its own religious views on the rest of society by advocating a substantive theory of democracy with fundamentalist Christian values at its core. Leaders of the Christian Coalition vehemently reject this charge, arguing that they are simply empowering their constituents by informing them about issues and opportunities to influence public policy.

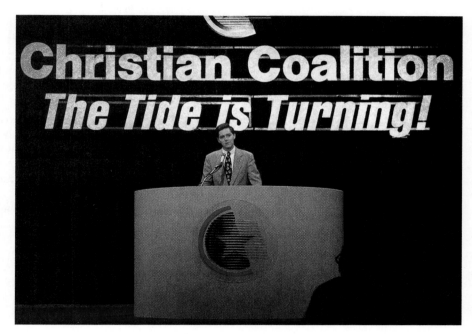

fewer than twenty countries fully met all the criteria to be judged a democracy.[35] What is encouraging, however, is that today the world is awash in countries that are trying to make a transition to democracy. In Africa alone, at least twenty countries are moving in some fashion toward a democratic form of government (see Compared with What? 2.1).[36] But democratization is a difficult process, and many efforts fail completely or succeed only in the short run and lapse into a form of authoritarianism.[37]

Russia is an example of a country struggling to make a transition to democracy. In March 1993, Russian President Boris Yeltsin, frustrated with a legislature that was largely unsympathetic to his plan for reforming the country's failed economic system, declared that he was going to rule by decree. He justified this by saying that members of the Congress of People's Deputies "refused to listen to the country's voice. They rejected the opinion of the majority of voters."[38] To try to strengthen his authority as president, Yeltsin scheduled a national referendum to allow citizens to vote on his leadership. Thus, his strategy was to rule by undemocratic means until he could fashion a majoritarian democracy through a favorable nationwide vote on his referendum. The Congress of People's Deputies threatened to impeach (remove) Yeltsin, but there were not enough votes to do this, and opponents of the president called for compromise. Failing to muster much support for his grab for more power, Yeltsin pulled back from his promise to rule by decree. He was successful in the subsequent referendum when a majority of voters endorsed his economic plan and indicated approval of his leadership. In December 1993, democracy got a split verdict from the voters in a national election. The Russian people endorsed a new constitution that strengthened the legal foundation for democracy, but parties voicing distinctly antidemocratic sentiments did well in the parliamentary elections.

COMPARED WITH WHAT? 2.1   Democratization in Africa

 The African continent is awash in democratizing countries. Although many newly democratizing nations in Africa have a long way to go to meet all the criteria of a true democracy, a number of longstanding authoritarian regimes have been replaced in recent years.

DEFINITIONS

For countries in transition to democracy, the commitment to democracy was evaluated in following manner. *Strong:* "The strength of commitment is demonstrated by substantive incorporation of democratic processes, by devolution of power, and by gradual or wholesale abandonment of party monopolies." *Moderate:* "measured, cautious and preliminary steps toward institutionalization or plu-

ralism." *Ambiguous:* "Ruling elite's commitment to democracy is at best precarious, at worst a ruse, and at most times unclear." *Directed democracy:* "A system in which formal institutions and practices of constitutional democracy are present. In practice, however, the extensive powers of the ruler, party, or regime severely limit contestation by individuals, organized groups, legislative assemblies, and the judiciary." *Contested sovereignty:* In these countries there is a dispute over what group of people or institutions constitutes the government.

Source: Africa Dēmos, *African Governance Program, The Carter Center, Emory University, July–August, 1993, p. 1 and p. 19.* Used with permission.

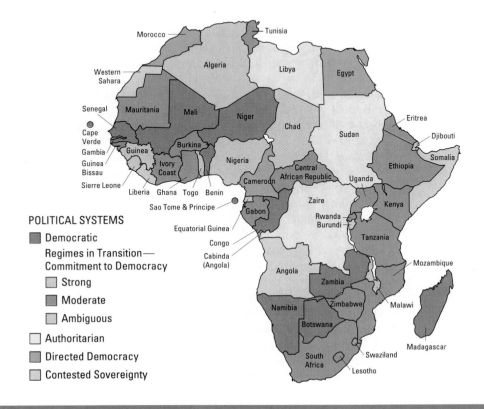

POLITICAL SYSTEMS

- Democratic

  Regimes in Transition—
  Commitment to Democracy
  - Strong
  - Moderate
  - Ambiguous
- Authoritarian
- Directed Democracy
- Contested Sovereignty

The political and economic instability that typically accompanies transitions to democracy makes new democratic governments vulnerable to attack by their opponents. The military will often revolt and take over the government on the ground that progress cannot occur until order is restored. As we noted in Chapter 1, all societies wrestle with the dilemma of freedom and order. The open political conflict that emerges in a new democracy may not be easily harnessed into a well-functioning government that tolerates opposition. Consequently, situations emerge, as in contemporary Russia, in which different factions within government regard the opposition not as a legitimate part of a democratic political system but as a fundamental threat to the well being (order) of the country.[39]

Despite such difficulties, strong forces are pushing authoritarian governments toward democratization. Nations find it difficult to succeed economically in today's world without establishing a market economy, but market economies (capitalism) give people substantial freedoms. Thus, authoritarian rulers may see economic reforms as a threat to their regime. Yet, the electronic and communications revolution has made it more difficult for authoritarian countries to keep information about democracy and capitalism from their citizens. One scholar calls the tendency toward a uniform type of government (democracy) and a uniform type of economy (capitalism) a movement toward "McWorld." Nations are being pressed "into one commercially homogeneous global network: one McWorld tied together by technology, ecology, communications, and commerce."[40]

The pressures against democratization are substantial, too. Ethnic and religious conflict is epidemic, and such conflict complicates efforts to democratize because antagonisms can run so deep that opposing groups do not want to grant political legitimacy to each other. As a result, ethnic and religious rivals are often more interested in achieving a form of government that oppresses their opponents (or, in their minds, maintains order) than in establishing a real democracy. Nowhere is this more apparent than in the new countries of the former Soviet Union and in parts of Eastern Europe. Once freedom came to the former Yugoslavia, the country split into a number of new nations. Their boundaries did not conform exactly with where various ethnic and religious groups live, and war soon broke out among Croats, Serbs, and Muslims.

Established democracies are not free of the destabilizing effects of religious and ethnic conflict, either. French-speaking Canadians have pushed for autonomy for Quebec, and India's democracy has been sorely tested by violence inspired by ethnic and religious rivalries. Democracies usually try to cope with such pressures with some form of pluralism so that different groups feel they are being treated fairly by government. Indeed, majoritarian democracy can be risky where ethnic and religious rivalries endure, because a majority faction can use its votes to suppress minorities.

More common than democracies coping with the problem of minority rights, however, are situations in which ethnic and racial minorities are subject to authoritarian rule and are excluded from or discriminated against in the governmental process. One study found 230 minority groups at risk around the globe in the early 1990s. The countries that are home to these groups have failed to establish ways to protect them from the majority or from rival minorities.[41]

American Democracy: More Pluralist Than Majoritarian

It is not idle speculation to ask what kind of democracy is practiced in the United States. The answer can help us understand why our government can be called democratic despite a low level of citizen participation in politics and despite government actions that sometimes run contrary to public opinion.

Throughout this book, we probe more deeply to determine how well the United States fits the two alternative models of democracy, majoritarian and pluralist. If our answer is not already apparent, it soon will be. We argue that the political system in the United States rates relatively low according to the majoritarian model of democracy but that it fulfills the pluralist model quite well. Yet, the pluralist model is far from a perfect representation of democracy. Its principal drawback is that it favors the well organized, and the poor are the least likely to be members of interest groups. As one advocate of majoritarian democracy once wrote, "The flaw in the pluralist heaven is that the heavenly chorus sings with a strong upper-class accent."[42]

This evaluation of the pluralist nature of American democracy may not mean much to you now. But you will learn that the pluralist model makes the United States look far more democratic than the majoritarian model does. Eventually, you will have to decide the answers to three questions: Is the pluralist model truly an adequate expression of democracy, or is it a perversion of classical ideals designed to portray America as democratic when it is not? Does the majoritarian model result in a "better" type of democracy? If so, could new mechanisms of government be devised to produce a desirable mix of majority rule and minority rights? These questions should play in the back of your mind as you read more about the workings of American government in meeting the challenge of democracy.

SUMMARY

Is the United States a democracy? Most scholars believe that it is. But what kind of democracy is it? The answer depends on the definition of *democracy*. Some believe democracy is procedural; they define democracy as a form of government in which the people govern through certain institutional mechanisms. Others hold to substantive theory, claiming a government is democratic if its policies promote civil liberties and rights.

In this book, we use the procedural concept of democracy, distinguishing between direct (participatory) and indirect (representative) democracy. In a participatory democracy, all citizens gather to govern themselves according to the principles of universal participation, political equality, and majority rule. In an indirect democracy, the citizens elect representatives to govern for them. If a representative government is elected mostly in accordance with the three principles just listed and also is usually responsive to public opinion, it qualifies as a democracy.

Procedural democratic theory has produced rival institutional models of democratic government. The classical majoritarian model—which depends on majority votes in elections—assumes that people are knowledgeable about government, that they want to participate in the political process, and that they carefully and rationally choose among candidates. But surveys of public opinion and behavior, and voter turnout, show that this is not the case for most Americans. The pluralist model of democracy—which depends on interest group interaction with government—was devised to accommodate these findings. It argues that democracy in a complex society requires only that government allow private interests to organize and to press their competing claims openly in the political arena. It differs from elite theory—the belief that America is run by a small group of powerful individuals—by arguing that different minorities win on different issues. Pluralist democracy works better in a decentralized, organizationally complex government structure than in a centralized, hierarchical one.

In Chapter 1, we talked about three political values—freedom, order, and equality. Here, we have described two models of democracy—majoritarian and pluralist. The five concepts are critical to an understanding of American government. The values discussed in the last chapter underlie the two questions with which the text began:

• Which is better: to live under a government that allows individuals complete freedom to do whatever they please or under one that enforces strict law and order?

• Which is better: to allow businesses and private clubs to choose their customers and members or to pass laws that require them to admit and serve everyone, regardless of race or sex?

The models of democracy described in this chapter lead to another question:

• Which is better: a government that is highly responsive to public opinion on all matters, or one that responds deliberately to organized groups that argue their cases effectively?

These are enduring questions, and the framers of the Constitution dealt with them, too. Their struggle is the appropriate place to begin our analysis of how these competing models of democracy have animated the debate about the nature of our political process.

Key Terms

autocracy
oligarchy
democracy
procedural democratic theory
universal participation
political equality
majority rule
participatory democracy
representative democracy
responsiveness
substantive democratic theory
minority rights
majoritarian model of democracy
referendum
initiative
interest group
pluralist model of democracy
elite theory
democratization

Selected Readings

Berry, Jeffrey M., Kent E. Portney, and Ken Thomson. The Rebirth of Urban Democracy. Washington, D.C.: Brookings Institution, 1993. An examination of neighborhood government in five American cities. The authors conclude that participatory democracy on the local level is a feasible and desirable alternative.

Dahl, Robert A. Democracy and Its Critics. New Haven, Conn.: Yale University Press, 1989. The nation's leading expert on pluralist theory examines the basic foundations of democracy. Dahl defends democracy against a variety of criticisms that have focused on its shortcomings.

Dye, Thomas R. *Who's Running America?* 5th ed. Englewood Cliffs, N.J.: Prentice-Hall, 1990. An elitist examination of power in America. Dye documents the interconnections within a wealthy establishment.

Huntington, Samuel P. *The Third Wave.* Norman: University of Oklahoma Press, 1991. A historical and comparative analysis of the democratization process, with a particular focus on the worldwide movement toward democracy that began in 1974.

Morone, James A. *The Democratic Wish.* New York: Basic Books, 1990. Morone contends that pressures for greater participation and direct citizen control over government lead to a larger and stronger central government.

Page, Benjamin I., and Robert Y. Shapiro, *The Rational Public.* Chicago: University of Chicago Press, 1992. Based on their reading of fifty years of public opinion polls, the authors contend that the United States has a responsible electorate, capable of fulfilling the requirements of majoritarian democracy.

Spitz, Elaine. *Majority Rule.* Chatham, N.J.: Chatham House, 1984. Spitz reviews the various meanings of *majority* and *rule* and the place of majority rule in democratic theory, then goes beyond the narrow definition of *majority rule,* 'as a method of deciding between policies.' She argues that majoritarianism should be viewed as a "social practice" among people who want to hold their society together when making decisions.

Foundations of American Government

CHAPTER 3

3 The Constitution

THE MIDNIGHT BURGLARS made a small mistake. They left a piece of tape over the latch they had tripped to enter the Watergate office and apartment complex in Washington, D.C. But a security guard named Frank Wills found their tampering and called police, who surprised the burglars in the offices of the Democratic National Committee at 2:30 a.m. The arrests of five men—four Cuban exiles and a former CIA agent—in the early hours of June 17, 1972, triggered a constitutional struggle that eventually involved the president of the United States, the Congress, and the Supreme Court.

The arrests took place a month before the 1972 Democratic National Convention. Investigative reporting by Carl Bernstein and Bob Woodward of the Washington Post, and a simultaneous criminal investigation by Assistant U.S. Attorney Earl J. Silbert and his staff, uncovered a link between the Watergate burglary and the forthcoming election.[1] The burglars were carrying the telephone number of another former CIA agent, who was working in the White House. At a news conference on June 22, President Richard Nixon said, "The White House has had no involvement whatsoever in this particular incident."[2]

At its convention in July, the Democratic party nominated Senator George McGovern of South Dakota to oppose Nixon in the presidential election. McGovern tried to make the break-in at the Democratic headquarters a campaign issue, but the voters either did not understand or did not care. In November 1972, Richard Nixon was reelected president of the United States, winning forty-nine of fifty states in one of the largest electoral landslides in American history.

Feature 3.1 describes the events that followed. Here we need only note that the Watergate affair posed one of the most serious challenges to the constitutional order of modern American government. The incident ultimately developed into a struggle over the rule of law between the presidency on the one hand and Congress and the courts on the other. The break-in began as an effort to impede political competition. President Nixon attempted to use the powers of his office to hide his staff's tampering with the electoral process. The cover-up quickly turned into a criminal conspiracy. Many Republicans championed their president; many Democrats opposed him. In the end, the cover-up was foiled by the Constitution and by leaders who believed in the Constitution. The constitutional principle of separation of powers among the executive, legislative, and judicial branches prevented the president from controlling the Watergate investigation. The principle of checks and balances allowed

A Witness in the Spotlight

John Dean served as special counsel to President Richard Nixon. Dean testified before the Senate Select Committee on Presidential Campaign Activities, which was created in 1973 to investigate events surrounding Watergate. Dean's claim of a presidential cover up was later verified by secret tape recordings that Nixon unsuccessfully sought to protect from release.

Congress to threaten Nixon with impeachment and removal from office. The belief that Nixon had violated the Constitution finally prompted members of his own party to support impeachment.

Nixon resigned the presidency little more than a year and a half into his second term. In 1992, twenty years after the break-in and cover-up, 70 percent of Americans still viewed Nixon's actions as having warranted his resignation.[3] In some countries, such an irregular change in government leadership provides an opportunity for a palace coup, an armed revolution, or a military dictatorship. But here, significantly, no political violence erupted after Nixon's resignation; in fact, none was expected. Constitutional order in the United States had been put to a test, and it passed with high honors.

This chapter poses several questions about the Constitution. How did it evolve? What form did it take? What values does it reflect? How can it be altered? And which model of democracy—majoritarian or pluralist—does it fit best?

THE REVOLUTIONARY ROOTS OF THE CONSTITUTION

The Constitution itself is just 4,300 words long. But those 4,300 words define the basic structure of our national government. A comprehensive document, it divides the government into three branches and describes the powers of those branches, their relationships, and the interaction between government and the governed. The Constitution makes itself the supreme law of the land and binds every government official to support it.

Most Americans revere the Constitution as political scripture. To charge that a political action is unconstitutional is to claim that it is unholy. And so the Constitution has taken on a symbolism that has strengthened its authority as the basis of American government. Strong belief in

FEATURE **3.1**

■ **Watergate**

The Watergate story did not unfold completely until after Richard Nixon's reelection in November 1972. Two months later, seven men answered in court for the break-in. They included the five burglars and two men closely connected with the president: E. Howard Hunt (a former CIA agent and White House consultant) and G. Gordon Liddy (counsel to the Committee for the Re-Election of the President, or CREEP). The burglars entered guilty pleas. Hunt and Liddy were convicted by a jury. In a letter to the sentencing judge, one burglar charged that they had been pressured to plead guilty, that perjury had been committed at the trial, and that others were involved in the break-in. The Senate launched its own investigation of the matter. It set up the Select Committee on Presidential Campaign Activities, chaired by a self-styled constitutional authority, Democratic senator Sam Ervin of North Carolina.

The testimony before the Ervin committee was shocking. The deputy director of Nixon's reelection committee, Jeb Stuart Magruder, confessed to perjury and implicated John Mitchell, Nixon's campaign manager and former attorney general, in planning the burglary. John Dean, special counsel to the president, said that the president had been a party to a cover-up of the crime for eight months. Other political burglaries and forged State Department cables intended to embarrass a potential Democratic presidential candidate, Senator Edward M. Kennedy of Massachusetts, also were disclosed.

A stunned nation watching the televised proceedings learned that the president had secretly tape recorded all his conversations in the White House. The Ervin committee asked for the tapes. Nixon refused to produce them, citing the separation of powers between the legislative and executive branches and claiming "executive privilege" to withhold information from Congress.

Meanwhile, Nixon's vice president, Spiro T. Agnew, resigned while being investigated for income tax evasion. The Twenty-fifth Amendment (1967) gave the president the power to choose a new vice president with the consent of Congress. Nixon nominated Gerald Ford, then the Republican leader in the House of Representatives. On December 6, 1973, Ford became the first appointed vice president in the nation's history.

Nixon resisted the subpoenas demanding the White House tapes. Ordered by a federal court to deliver specific tapes, Nixon proposed a compromise: He would release written summaries of the taped conversations. Archibald Cox, the special prosecutor of the attorney general's office, rejected the compromise. Nixon retaliated with "the Saturday night massacre," in which Attorney General Elliot L. Richardson and his deputy resigned, Cox was fired, and the special prosecutor's office was abolished.

The ensuing furor forced Nixon to appoint another special prosecutor, Leon Jaworski, who eventually brought indictments against Nixon's closest aides. Nixon himself was named as an unindicted co-conspirator. Both the special prosecutor and the defendants wanted the White House tapes, but Nixon continued to resist. Finally, on July 24, 1974, the Supreme Court ruled that the president had to hand over the tapes. At almost the same time, the House Judiciary Committee voted to recommend to the full House that Nixon be impeached for, or charged with, three offenses: violating his oath of office to faithfully uphold the laws, misusing and abusing executive authority and the resources of executive agencies, and defying congressional subpoenas.

The Judiciary Committee vote was decisive but far from unanimous. On August 5, however, the committee and the country finally learned the contents of the tapes released under the Supreme

(continued on p.62)

Court order. They revealed that Nixon had been aware of a cover-up on June 23, 1972, just six days after the break-in. He ordered the FBI, "Don't go any further in this case, period!"* Now, even the eleven Republican members of the House Judiciary Committee, who had opposed the first vote to impeach, were ready to vote against Nixon.

Faced with the collapse of his support and likely impeachment by the full House, Nixon resigned the presidency on August 9, 1974. Vice President Gerald Ford became the first unelected president of the United States. A month later, acting within his constitutional powers, Ford granted private citizen Richard Nixon an unconditional pardon for all crimes that he may have committed. When questioned by Congress about the circumstances surrounding the pardon, President Ford said, "There was no deal, period." Others were not so fortunate. Three members of the Nixon cabinet (two attorneys general and a secretary of commerce) were convicted and sentenced for their crimes in the Watergate affair. Nixon's White House chief of staff, H. R. Haldeman, and Nixon's domestic affairs adviser, John Ehrlichman, were convicted of conspiracy, obstruction of justice, and perjury. Other officials were tried, and most were convicted, on related charges.†

In 1992, twenty years after Watergate, the release of additional White House tapes tended to support Nixon's position that he was unaware of the break-in plan.§ Ironically, the tapes were from the set that clearly implicated Nixon in the cover-up and conspiracy that led to his resignation from office.

Watergate Postscript

John Dean served four months in jail for obstructing justice. He is now an investment banker in Beverly Hills.

John Ehrlichman served eighteen months in prison for conspiracy to obstruct justice and perjury. He lives in Atlanta and is writing a novel about the impeachment of a president.

H. R. Haldeman served eighteen months in prison for conspiracy to obstruct justice and perjury. He died in 1993.

E. Howard Hunt served thirty-three months in prison for burglary, conspiracy, and wiretapping. He lives in Miami and writes spy novels.

G. Gordon Liddy served fifty-two months in prison for burglary. Today, he hosts a popular, syndicated radio call-in talk show on WJFK-FM in the Washington, D.C. area. Liddy's car bears the vanity license plate H2O GATE.

Jeb Stuart Magruder served seven months in prison for conspiracy to obstruct justice. He is now senior minister at the First Presbyterian Church in Lexington, Kentucky.

Frank Wills, the security guard who discovered the break-in, was arrested years later for shoplifting and sentenced to a year in prison. He is unemployed and lives in South Carolina.

*The Encyclopedia of American Facts and Dates *(New York: Crowell, 1979), p. 946.*

†*Richard B. Morris, ed.,* Encyclopedia of American History *(New York: Harper & Row, 1976), p. 544.*

§*Seymour M. Hersh, "A Reporter at Large; Nixon's Last Cover-up: The Tapes He Wants the Archives To Suppress."* New Yorker, *December 14, 1992, p. 76.*

the Constitution has led many politicians to abandon party for principle when constitutional issues are in question. The power and symbolic value of the Constitution were proved once again in the Watergate affair.

The U.S. Constitution, written in 1787 for an agricultural society huddled along the coast of a wild new land, now guides the political life of a massive urban society in the post-nuclear age. The stability of the Constitution—and of the political system it created—is all the more remarkable because the Constitution itself was rooted in revolution. In fact, the U.S. Constitution (along with its immediate predecessor, the Articles of Confederation) was the first of several national constitutions that arose from revolution. Three others—the French constitution of 1791, the Mexican constitution of 1917, and the Russian constitution of 1918—were also products of revolutionary movements.

The noted historian Samuel Eliot Morison observed that "the American Revolution was not fought to obtain freedom, but to preserve the liberties that Americans already had as colonials."[4] The U.S. Constitution was designed to prevent anarchy by forging a union of states. To understand the values embedded in the Constitution, we must understand its historical roots. They lie in colonial America, in the revolt against British rule, and in the failure of the Articles of Confederation that governed the new nation after the Revolution.

Freedom in Colonial America

Although they were British subjects, American colonists in the eighteenth century enjoyed a degree of freedom denied most people in the world. In Europe, ancient custom and the relics of feudalism restricted private property, compelled support for established religion, and restricted access to trades and professions. In America, landowners could control and transfer their property at will. In America, there were no compulsory payments to support an established church. In America, there was no ceiling on wages as in most European countries and no guilds of exclusive professional associations. In America, colonists enjoyed almost complete freedom of speech, press, and assembly.[5]

By 1763, Britain and the colonies had reached a compromise between imperial control and colonial self-government. America's foreign affairs and overseas trade were controlled by the king and Parliament, the British legislature; the rest was left to home rule. But the cost of administering the colonies was substantial. The colonists needed protection from the French and their Indian allies during the Seven Years' War (1756–1763), which was an expensive undertaking. Because Americans benefited the most, their English countrymen argued, Americans should bear that cost.

The Road to Revolution

The British believed that taxing the colonies was the obvious way to meet the costs of administering the colonies; the colonists did not agree. Like most people, they did not want to be taxed. And they especially did not want to be taxed by a distant government in which they had no representation. Nevertheless, a series of taxes (including a tax on all printed matter) was imposed on the colonies by the Crown. In each instance, public opposition was widespread and immediate.

A group of citizens—merchants, lawyers, prosperous traders—created an intercolonial association, the Sons of Liberty. This group destroyed taxed items and forced their official distributors to resign. In October 1765, residents of Charleston, South Carolina, celebrated the forced resignation of the colony's stamp distributor by displaying a British flag with the word Liberty sewn across it. (They were horrified a few months later when local slaves paraded through the streets calling for "Liberty!"[6])

Women participated in the resistance to the hated taxes by joining together in symbolic and practical displays of patriotism. Young women, calling themselves the Daughters of Liberty, met in public to spin homespun cloth and thus encourage the elimination of British cloth from colonial markets. They consumed American food and drank local herbal tea as symbols of their opposition.[7]

The Founders' Nation

At the treaty negotiations that ended the Revolution, this detailed map, first drawn in 1755, was used to establish the boundaries of the United States. This was the country for which the founders fashioned a constitution in 1787. The remarkable document they created, written to govern a small society spread along the coast of a largely uncharted land, is equally powerful and authoritative today, in a society of far greater size and complexity.

On the night of December 16, 1773, colonists reacted to a British duty on tea by organizing the Boston Tea Party. A mob boarded three ships and emptied 342 chests of that valuable substance into Boston Harbor. The act of defiance and destruction could not be ignored. "The die is now cast," wrote George III. "The Colonies must either submit or triumph."[8] In an attempt to reassert British control over its recalcitrant colonists, Parliament passed the Coercive (or Intolerable) Acts (1774). One act imposed a blockade on Boston until the tea was paid for; another gave royal governors the power to quarter British soldiers in private American homes. The taxation issue became secondary; more important was the conflict between British demands for order and American demands for liberty. The Virginia and Massachusetts assemblies summoned a continental congress, an assembly that would speak and act for the people of all the colonies.

All the colonies except Georgia sent representatives to the First Continental Congress, which met in Philadelphia in September 1774. The objective was to restore harmony between Great Britain and the American colonies. In an effort at unity, all colonies were given the same voting power—one vote each. A leader, called the president, was elected. (The terms president and congress in American government trace their origins to the First Continental Congress.) In October, the delegates adopted a statement of rights and principles, many of which later found their way into the Declaration of Independence and the Constitution. For example, the congress claimed a right "to life, liberty, and property" and a right "peaceably to assemble, consider of their grievances, and petition the king." Then the congress adjourned, planning to reconvene in May 1775.

Revolutionary Action

By early 1775, however, a movement that the colonists themselves were calling a revolution had already begun. Colonists in Massachusetts were fighting the British at Concord and Lexington. Delegates to the Second Continental Congress, meeting in May, faced a dilemma: Should they prepare for war? Or should they try to reconcile with Britain? As conditions deteriorated, the Second Continental Congress remained in session to serve as the government of the colony-states.

On June 7, 1776, the Virginia delegation called on the Continental Congress to resolve "that these United Colonies are, and of right ought to be, free and Independent States, that they are absolved from all allegiance to the British Crown, and that all political connection between them and the State of Great Britain is, and ought to be, totally dissolved." The congress debated but did not immediately adopt the resolution. A committee of five men was appointed to prepare a proclamation expressing the colonies' reasons for declaring independence.

A Uniquely American Protest
Americans protested the Tea Act (1773) by holding the Boston Tea Party (see background, left) and by using a unique form of punishment—tarring and feathering. An early treatise on the subject offered the following instructions: "First, strip a person naked, then heat the tar until it is thin, and pour upon the naked flesh, or rub it over with a tar brush. After which, sprinkle decently upon the tar, whilst it is yet warm, as many feathers as will stick to it."

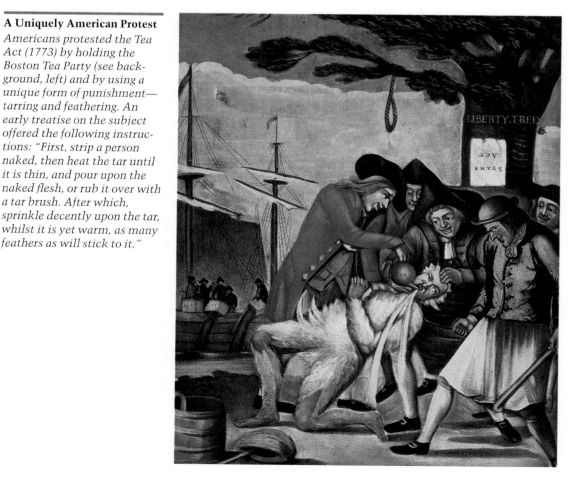

The Declaration of Independence

Thomas Jefferson, a young farmer and lawyer from Virginia, was a member of the committee. Because of his "peculiar felicity of expression," he drafted the proclamation. The document Jefferson wrote—the Declaration of Independence—was substantially unchanged by the committee and the congress. It remains a cherished statement of our heritage, expressing simply, clearly, and rationally the many arguments for separation from Great Britain.

The principles underlying the declaration were rooted in the writings of the English philosopher John Locke and had been expressed many times by speakers in the congress and the colonial assemblies. Locke argued that people have God-given, or natural, rights that are inalienable—that is, they cannot be taken away by any government. According to Locke, all legitimate political authority exists to preserve these natural rights, and the authority is based on the consent of those who are governed. The idea of consent is derived from social contract theory, which states that the people agree to establish rulers for certain purposes but that they have the right to resist or remove rulers who violate those purposes.[9]

Jefferson used similar arguments in the Declaration of Independence. His "impassioned simplicity of statement" reverberates to this day with democratic faith: "We hold these truths to be self-evident, that all men are created equal, that they are endowed by their creator with certain unalienable rights, that among these are life, liberty, and the pursuit of happiness."

The First Continental Congress had declared in 1774 that the colonists were entitled to "life, liberty, and property." Jefferson reformulated the objectives of government as "Life, Liberty, and the Pursuit of Happiness." And he continued:

> That to secure these rights, governments are instituted among men, deriving their just powers from the consent of the governed, that whenever any form of government becomes destructive of these ends, it is the right of the people to alter or to abolish it, and to institute new government, laying its foundation on such principles and organizing its powers in such form, as to them shall seem most likely to effect their safety and happiness.

He went on to list the many deliberate acts of the king that exceeded the legitimate ends of government. Finally, he declared that the colonies were "Free and Independent States," with no political connection to Great Britain.

The major premise of the Declaration of Independence is that the people have a right to revolt when they determine that their government is denying them their legitimate rights. The long list of the king's actions was evidence of that denial. And so the people had the right to rebel, to form a new government (see Compared with What? 3.1). On July 2, 1776, the Second Continental Congress finally voted for independence. The vote was by state, and the motion carried 11 to 0. (Rhode Island was not present, and the New York delegation, lacking instructions, did not cast its yea vote until July 15.) Two days later, on July 4, the Declaration of Independence was approved with few changes. Jefferson's original draft had indicted the king for allowing the slave trade to continue. But representa-

COMPARED WITH WHAT? 3.1

Exporting the American Revolution

For more than forty years, Czechoslovakia lay in the grip of the Soviet Union. But in the course of a few weeks at the end of 1989, a revolution rooted in the demand for freedom brought Czechoslovakia to independence. Here is how it began:

PRAGUE, Nov. 27—Soon after the strike began today, Zdenek Janicek, a brewery worker, rose on a platform in grimy overalls and began to speak.

"We hold these truths to be self-evident," he said, "that all men are created equal, that they are endowed by their creator with certain unalienable rights, that among these rights are life, liberty, and the pursuit of happiness."

For the nearly 1,500 workers who gathered to listen to him, today was a day of declaring independence from the stifling Communist leadership that has ruled Czechoslovakia for 40 years. Like millions of workers through-out the nation, workers here walked off their jobs at noon today in a two-hour general strike demanding greater democracy and an end to the Communist Party's monopoly on power.

"Americans understood these rights more than 200 years ago," Mr. Janicek said after reciting part of the Declaration of Independence to his co-workers. "We are only now learning to believe that we are entitled to the same rights."

Today Czechs and Slovaks have splintered into separate republics much as the early American states seemed destined to separate following the revolution that set them free from British rule.

• *Source: Esther Fein, "Millions of Czechoslovaks Increase Pressure on Party with 2-Hour General Strike,"* New York Times, *28 November 1989, p. 1. Copyright © 1989 by The New York Times Company. Reprinted by permission.*

tives from Georgia and South Carolina insisted that the phrase be deleted before they would vote for approval. Other representatives removed language they thought would incite the colonists. But, in the end, Jefferson's compelling words were left almost exactly as he had written them.

By August, fifty-five revolutionaries had signed the Declaration of Independence, pledging "our lives, our fortunes and our sacred honor" in support of rebellion against the world's most powerful nation. This was no empty pledge: An act of rebellion was treason. If they had lost the Revolutionary War, the signers would have faced a gruesome fate. The punishment for treason was hanging and drawing and quartering—the victim is first hanged until half-dead from strangulation, then disemboweled, and finally cut into four pieces while still alive. We celebrate the Fourth of July with fireworks and flag waving, parades and picnics. We sometimes forget that the Revolution was a matter of life and death.

The war imposed an agonizing choice on colonial Catholics, who were treated with intolerance by the overwhelmingly Protestant population. No other religious group found the choice so difficult. Catholics could either join the revolutionaries, who were opposed to Catholicism, or remain loyal to England and risk new hostility and persecution. But Catholics were few in number, perhaps twenty-five thousand at the time of independence (or 1 percent of the population). Anti-Catholic revolutionaries recognized that if Catholics opposed independence in Maryland and Pennsylvania, where their numbers were greatest, victory might be jeopardized. Furthermore, enlisting the support of Catholic France for the cause of independence would be difficult in the face of strong opposition from colonial Catholics. So the revolutionaries wooed Catholics to their cause.[10]

The War of Independence lasted far longer than anyone expected. It began in a moment of confusion, when a shot rang out while British soldiers approached the town of Lexington, Massachusetts, on April 19, 1775. The end came six and a half years later with Lord Cornwallis's surrender of his six thousand-man army at Yorktown, Virginia, on October 19, 1781. It was a costly war: More died and were wounded in relation to the population than in any other conflict except the Civil War.[11]

With hindsight, of course, we can see that the British were engaged in an arduous and perhaps hopeless conflict. America was simply too vast to subdue without imposing total military rule. Britain also had to transport men and supplies over the enormous distance of the Atlantic Ocean. Finally, although the Americans had neither paid troops nor professional soldiers, they were fighting for a cause—the defense of their liberty. The British never understood the power of this fighting faith.

FROM REVOLUTION TO CONFEDERATION

By declaring their independence from England, the colonists were leaving themselves without any real central government. So the revolutionaries proclaimed the creation of a republic. Strictly speaking, a republic is a government without a monarch, but the term had come to mean a government rooted in the consent of the governed, whose power is exercised by representatives who are responsible to the governed. A republic need not be a democracy, and this was fine with the founders; at that time, democracy was associated with mob rule and instability (see Chapter 2). The revolutionaries were less concerned with who would control their new government than with limiting its powers. They had revolted in the name of liberty, and now they wanted a government with strictly defined powers. To make sure they got one, they meant to define its structure and powers in writing.

The Articles of Confederation

Barely a week after the Declaration of Independence was signed, the Second Continental Congress received a committee report, "Articles of Confederation and Perpetual Union." A confederation is a loose association of independent states that agree to cooperate on specified matters. In a confederation, the states retain their sovereignty, which means that each has supreme power within its borders. The central government is weak; it can only coordinate, not control, the actions of its sovereign states. Consequently, the individual states are strong.

Voting for Independence

The Second Continental Congress voted for independence on July 2, 1776. John Adams of Massachusetts viewed the day "as the most memorable epocha [significant event] in the history of America." In this painting by John Trumbull, the drafting committee presents the Declaration of Independence to the patriots who would later sign it. The committee, grouped in front of the desk, consisted of (from left to right): Adams, Roger Sherman (Ct.), Robert Livingston (N.Y.), Thomas Jefferson (Va.), and Benjamin Franklin (Pa.).

The congress debated the Articles of Confederation, the compact among the thirteen original colonies that established a government of the United States, for more than a year. The Articles were adopted by the Continental Congress on November 15, 1777. They finally took effect on March 1, 1781, following approval by all thirteen states. For more than three years, then, Americans had fought a revolution without an effective government. Raising money, troops, and supplies for the war daunted and exhausted the leadership.

The Articles jealously guarded state sovereignty; their provisions clearly reflected the delegates' fears that a strong central government would resemble British rule. Article II, for example, stated: "Each State retains its sovereignty, freedom, and independence, and every power, jurisdiction, and right, which is not by this Confederation expressly delegated to the United States in Congress assembled."

Under the Articles, each state, regardless of its size, had one vote in the congress. Votes on financing the war and other important issues required the consent of at least nine of the thirteen states. The common danger—Britain—had forced the young republic to function under the Articles, but this first effort at a government was inadequate to the task. The delegates had succeeded in crafting a national government that was largely powerless.

The Articles failed for at least four reasons. First, they did not give the national government the power to tax. As a result, the congress had to plead for money from the states to pay for the war and to carry on the affairs of the new nation. A government that cannot reliably raise revenue cannot expect to govern effectively. Second, the Articles made no provision for an independent leadership position to direct the government (the president was merely the presiding officer of the congress). The omission was deliberate—the colonists feared the reestablishment of a monarchy—but it left the nation without a leader. Third, the Articles did not allow the national government to regulate interstate and foreign commerce. (When John Adams proposed that the confederation enter into a commercial treaty with Britain after the war, he was asked, "Would you like one treaty or thirteen, Mr. Adams?")[12] Finally, the Articles could not be amended without the unanimous agreement of the congress and the assent of all the state legislatures; thus, each state had the power to veto any changes in the confederation.

The goal of the delegates who drew up the Articles of Confederation was to retain power in the states. This was consistent with republicanism, which viewed the remote power of a national government as a danger to liberty. In this sense alone, the Articles were a grand success. They completely hobbled the infant government.

Disorder Under the Confederation

Once the Revolution ended and independence was a reality, it became clear that the national government had neither the economic nor the military power to function. Freed from wartime austerity, Americans rushed to purchase goods from abroad. The national government's efforts to restrict foreign imports were blocked by exporting states, which feared retaliation from their foreign customers. Debt mounted, and for many bankruptcy followed.

The problem was particularly severe in Massachusetts, where high interest rates and high state taxes were forcing farmers into bankruptcy. In 1786, Daniel Shays, a Revolutionary War veteran, marched on a western Massachusetts courthouse with 1,500 supporters armed with barrel staves and pitchforks. They wanted to close the courthouse to prevent the foreclosure of farms by creditors. Later, they attacked an arsenal. Called Shays' Rebellion, the revolt against the established order continued into 1787. Massachusetts appealed to the confederation for help. Horrified by the threat of domestic upheaval, the congress approved a $530,000 requisition for the establishment of a national army. But the plan failed: every state except Virginia rejected the request for money. Finally, the governor of Massachusetts called out the militia and restored order.[13]

The rebellion demonstrated the impotence of the confederation and the urgent need to suppress insurrection and maintain domestic order. Proof to skeptics that Americans could not govern themselves, the rebellion alarmed all American leaders, with the exception of Jefferson. From Paris, where he was serving as American ambassador, he remarked, "A little rebellion now and then is a good thing; the tree of liberty must be refreshed from time to time with the blood of patriots and tyrants."[14]

FROM CONFEDERATION TO CONSTITUTION

Order, the original purpose of government, was breaking down under the Articles of Confederation. The "league of friendship" envisioned in the Articles was not enough to hold the nation together in peacetime.

Some states had taken halting steps toward a change in government. In 1785, Massachusetts asked the congress to revise the Articles of Confederation, but the congress took no action. In 1786, Virginia invited the states to attend a convention at Annapolis to explore revisions aimed

Farmers' Protest Stirs Rebellion

Shays' Rebellion (1786–1787) became a symbol for the urgent need to maintain order. Here, farmers led by Daniel Shays close the courthouse to prevent farm foreclosures by creditors. The uprising demonstrated the military weakness of the confederation: The national government could not muster funds to fight the insurgents.

at improving commercial regulation. The meeting was both a failure and a success. Only five states sent delegates, but they seized the opportunity to call for another meeting—with a far broader mission—in Philadelphia the next year. That convention would be charged with "devis[ing] such further provisions as shall appear . . . necessary to render the constitution of the Federal Government adequate to the exigencies of the Union." The congress later agreed to the convention but limited its mission to "the sole and express purpose of revising the Articles of Confederation."

Shays' Rebellion lent a sense of urgency to the task before the Philadelphia convention. Congress's inability to confront the rebellion was evidence that a stronger national government was necessary to preserve order and property—to protect the states from internal as well as external dangers. "While the Declaration was directed against an excess of authority," observed Supreme Court Justice Robert H. Jackson some 150 years later, "the Constitution [that followed the Articles of Confederation] was directed against anarchy."[15]

Twelve of the thirteen states named a total of seventy-four delegates to convene in Philadelphia in May 1787. (Rhode Island, derisively renamed "Rogue Island" by a Boston newspaper, was the one exception. The state legislature sulkily rejected participation, because it feared a strong national government.) Fifty-five delegates eventually showed up at the statehouse in Philadelphia, but no more than thirty were present at any one time during that sweltering spring and summer (see Feature 3.2). Although well versed in ideas, they subscribed to the view expressed by one delegate, that "experience must be our guide. Reason may mislead us." The delegates' goal was to fashion a government that would maintain order and preserve liberty.

The Constitutional Convention—at the time called the Federal Convention—officially opened on May 25. A year earlier, at Annapolis, five states had called for the convention to draft a new, stronger charter for the national government. The spirit of the Annapolis meeting seems to have pervaded the Constitutional Convention, although the delegates were authorized only to "revise" the Articles of Confederation. Within the first week, Edmund Randolph of Virginia had presented a long list of changes, suggested by fellow Virginian James Madison, that would replace the weak confederation of states with a powerful national government. The delegates unanimously agreed to debate Randolph's proposal, called the Virginia Plan. Almost immediately, then, they rejected the idea of amending the Articles of Confederation, working instead to create an entirely new constitution.

The Virginia Plan

The Virginia Plan dominated the convention's deliberations for the rest of the summer, making several important proposals for a strong central government:

- That the powers of the government be divided among three separate branches: a legislative branch, for making laws; an executive branch, for enforcing laws; and a judicial branch, for interpreting laws.

- That the legislature consist of two houses. The first would be chosen by the people, the second by the members of the first house from among candidates nominated by the state legislatures.

- That each state's representation in the legislature be in proportion to the taxes it paid to the national government, or in proportion to its free population.

- That an executive, consisting of an unspecified number of people, be selected by the legislature and serve for a single term.

- That the national judiciary include one or more supreme courts and other, lower courts, with judges appointed for life by the legislature.

- That the executive and a number of national judges serve as a council of revision, to approve or veto (disapprove) legislative acts. However, their veto could be overridden by a vote of both houses of the legislature.

- That the scope of powers of all three branches be far greater than that assigned the national government by the Articles of Confederation, and that the legislature be empowered to override state laws.

By proposing a powerful national legislature that could override state laws, the Virginia Plan clearly advocated a new form of government. It was

FEATURE
3.2

■ Behind the Scenes in 1787

When the framers of the Constitution convened . . . on May 25, 1787, to try to keep the American Union from falling to pieces, Philadelphia was the foremost city of America.

It was a place of urban culture and accomplishment. Its streets were crowded with people of diverse national origins. Sailors from many countries mixed with leather-clad frontiersmen and with Shawnee and Delaware Indians from the forest.

But the city also reflected the hard life that most Americans lived then. More than half the population existed on the edge of poverty. Prostitution and disease were widespread. Many streets were open sewers. Flies and mosquitoes added their torment to the oppressive heat of that summer, the worst in nearly 40 years. . . .

Court records revealed much child and spouse abuse. Drunkenness was pervasive. Servants of the wealthy, including those of George Washington, spent their evenings in the taverns of a rough waterfront district called Helltown.

Independence Hall, then called the Pennsylvania State House, had seen better days: Its steeple had become shaky and had to be taken down. Across Walnut Street was a four-story stone prison. Prisoners called out for alms and cursed passers-by who failed to oblige.

When George Washington arrived in Philadelphia, he perceived a radical, divisive atmosphere that reflected the country's mood at a time when dissolution of the Union seemed likely and foreign powers waited to pounce. That perception is said to have contributed to a decision to keep the Constitutional Convention's proceedings secret. . . .

There was no press coverage. The public did not learn anything about what had gone on until after the convention adjourned on Sept. 17. Two days later, the *Pennsylvania Packet* published the Constitution, devoting its entire issue to the text. Newspapers everywhere followed suit. No political story had commanded so much space until then.

Sometimes, extraordinary measures were taken to maintain the secrecy. It seemed impossible to keep Benjamin Franklin quiet, wrote Catherine Drinker

Bowen in *Miracle at Philadelphia*, a respected history of the convention. As a result, she reported, " a discreet member" of the convention attended Franklin's convivial dinners to head off the conversation whenever he appeared ready to divulge a secret.

The delegates stayed at private homes and spent many of their evenings talking and plotting strategy at the City Tavern, the Black Horse, the George and the Indian Queen. They drank a lot: The bill for one dinner party of 12 included sixty bottles of wine.

That may be one reason why so many delegates, as historians have noted, were so corpulent. Few stood more than about 5 feet 8 inches tall, but many weighed about 200 pounds or more. The most striking exception was Washington. Every inch the general at 6 feet 2 inches, with wide shoulders and narrow hips, he towered above the convention both literally and figuratively.

The framers were not demi-gods. But many historians believe that their like will not be seen again in one place. Highly educated, they typically were fluent in Latin and Greek. Products of the Enlightenment, they relied on classical liberalism for the Constitution's philosophical underpinnings.

They were also veterans of the political intrigues of their states and as such were highly practical politicians who knew how to maneuver.

Still, if it were not for Washington, some historians believe, the convention would never have succeeded. His character and authority kept the convention from flying apart.

One facet of his authority is revealed in an anecdote reported by Bowen. Gouverneur Morris, a Pennsylvania delegate who drafted the Constitution's final version, accepted a bet proposed by Alexander Hamilton. To win it, Morris had to greet Washington with a slap on the back. That was just not done. "Well, General!" Morris said, and laid his hand on Washington's shoulder. The general said nothing, but Morris later said that Washington's imperious look made him wish . . . that he could sink through the floor.

• *Copyright 1987 by The New York Times Company. Reprinted by permission.*

James Madison, Father of the Constitution

Although he dismissed the accolade, Madison deserved it more than anyone else. As do most fathers, he exercised a powerful influence in debates (and was on the losing side of more than half of them).

to be a mixed structure, with more authority over the states and new authority over the people.

Madison was a monumental force in the ensuing debate on the proposals. He kept records of the proceedings that reveal his frequent and brilliant participation and give us insight into his thinking about freedom, order, and equality.

For example, his proposal that senators serve a nine-year term reveals his thinking about equality. Madison foresaw an increase "of those who will labor under all the hardships of life, and secretly sigh for a more equal distribution of its blessings. These may in time outnumber those who are placed above the feelings of indigence."[16] Power, then, could flow into the hands of the numerous poor. The stability of the senate, however, with its nine-year terms and election by the state legislatures, would provide a barrier against the "sighs of the poor" for more equality. Although most delegates shared Madison's apprehension about equality, the nine-year term was voted down.

The Constitution that emerged from the convention bore only partial resemblance to the document Madison wanted to create. Of the seventy-one specific proposals that Madison endorsed, he ended up on the losing side on forty of them.[17] And the parts of the Virginia Plan that were ultimately adopted in the Constitution were not adopted without challenge. Conflict revolved primarily around the basis for representation in the legislature, the method of choosing legislators, and the structure of the executive branch.

The New Jersey Plan

When in 1787 it appeared that much of the Virginia Plan would be approved by the big states, the small states united in opposition. William Paterson of New Jersey introduced an alternative set of resolutions, written to preserve the spirit of the Articles of Confederation by amending rather than replacing them. His New Jersey Plan included the following proposals:

- That a single-chamber legislature have the power to raise revenue and regulate commerce.

- That the states have equal representation in the legislature and choose its members.

- That a multiperson executive be elected by the legislature, with powers similar to those proposed under the Virginia Plan but without the right to veto legislation.

- That a supreme tribunal be created with a limited jurisdiction. (There was no provision for a system of national courts.)

- That the acts of the legislature be binding on the states—that is, that they be regarded as "the supreme law of the respective states," with the option of force to compel obedience.

The New Jersey Plan was defeated in the first major convention vote, 7–3. However, the small states had enough support to force a compromise on the issue of representation in the legislature. Table 3.1 compares the New Jersey Plan with the Virginia Plan.

| TABLE 3.1 | ■ Major Differences Between the Virginia Plan and the New Jersey Plan |

Characteristic	Virginia Plan	New Jersey Plan
Legislature	Two chambers	One chamber
Legislative power	Derived from the people	Derived from the states
Executive	Unspecified size	More than one person
Decision rule	Majority	Extraordinary majority
State laws	Legislature can override	Compel obedience
Executive removal	By Congress	By a majority of the states
Courts	National judiciary	No provision
Ratification	By the people	By the states

The Great Compromise

The Virginia Plan provided for a two-chamber legislature, with representation in both chambers based on population. The idea of two chambers was never seriously challenged, but the idea of representation according to population stirred up heated and prolonged debate. The small states demanded equal representation for all states, but another vote rejected that concept for the House of Representatives. The debate continued. Finally, the Connecticut delegation moved that each state have an equal vote in the Senate. Still another poll showed that the delegations were equally divided on this proposal.

A committee was created to resolve the deadlock. It consisted of one delegate from each state, chosen by secret ballot. After working straight through the Independence Day recess, the committee reported the Great Compromise (sometimes called the Connecticut Compromise): Representation in the House of Representatives would be apportioned according to the population of each state. Initially, there would be fifty-six members. Revenue-raising acts would originate in the House. Most important, the states would be represented equally in the Senate, with two senators each. Senators would be selected by their state legislatures, not directly by the people.

The delegates accepted the Great Compromise. The small states got their equal representation, the big states their proportional representation. The small states might dominate the Senate and the big states might control the House, but because all legislation had to be approved by both chambers, neither group would be able to dominate the other.

Compromise on the Presidency

Conflict replaced compromise when the delegates turned to the executive branch. They did agree on a one-person executive—a president—but disagreed on how the executive would be selected and what the term of office would be. The delegates distrusted the people's judgment; some feared that popular election would arouse public passions. Consequently, the delegates rejected the idea. At the same time, representatives of the small states feared that election by the legislature would allow the big states to control the executive.

Once again, a committee composed of one member from each participating state was chosen to find a compromise. That committee fashioned the cumbersome presidential election system that we know today as the electoral college. The college would consist of a group of electors chosen for the sole purpose of selecting the president and vice president. Each state legislature would choose a number of electors equal to the number of its representatives in Congress. Each elector would then vote for two people. The candidate with the most votes would become president, provided that the number of votes constituted a majority; the person with the next greatest number of votes would become vice president. (The procedure was changed in 1804 by the Twelfth Amendment, which mandates separate votes for each office.) If no candidate won a majority, the House of Representatives would choose a president, each state casting one vote.

The electoral college compromise eliminated the fear of a popular vote for president. At the same time, it satisfied the small states. If the electoral college failed to elect a president—which the delegates expected to happen—an election by the House would give every state the same voice in the selection process.

Finally, the delegates agreed that the president's term of office should be four years and that the president should be eligible for reelection.

The delegates also realized that removing a president from office would be a serious political matter. For that reason, they involved both of the other two branches of government in the process. The House alone was empowered to charge a president with "Treason, Bribery, or other high Crimes and Misdemeanors" (Article II, Section 4), by a majority vote. The Senate was given the sole power to try the president on the House's charges. It could convict, and thus remove, a president only by a two-thirds vote (an extraordinary majority). And the chief justice of the United States was required to preside over the Senate trial.

THE FINAL PRODUCT

Once the delegates resolved their major disagreements, they dispatched the remaining issues relatively quickly. A committee was then appointed to organize and write up the results of the proceedings. Twenty-three resolutions had been debated and approved by the convention; these were reorganized under seven articles in the draft constitution. The preamble, which was the last section to be drafted, begins with a phrase that would have been impossible to write when the convention opened. This single sentence contains four elements that form the foundation of the American political tradition.[18]

- *It creates a people:* "We the People of the United States" was a dramatic departure from a loose confederation of states.

- *It explains the reason for the Constitution:* "in Order to form a more perfect Union" was an indirect way of saying that the first effort, under the Articles of Confederation, had been inadequate.

- *It articulates goals:* "[to] establish Justice, insure domestic Tranquility, provide for the common defence, promote the general Welfare, and se-

FEATURE **3.3**

The Intellectual Origins of the Constitution

The creation of the U.S. Constitution was a remarkable achievement for a young nation. However, only one of its four basic political principles was made in America. The other three were inspired by ideas that first sprouted on foreign soil.

- *Republicanism.* In this form of government, power resides in the people and is exercised by their elected representatives; government is the common business of all citizens, conducted for the common good. The idea of republicanism may be traced to the Greek philosopher Aristotle (384–322 B.C.), who advocated a constitution that mixed principles of democratic and oligarchic government.
- *Federalism.* The powers of a federal government are shared by a central body and territorial units.

Citizens are thus subject to two different bodies of law. Federalism is a distinctly American idea, created by the Constitutional Convention of 1787.

- *Separation of Powers.* The responsibilities of government are divided among separate branches. This idea was formulated in a fragmentary way by John Locke and other thinkers, but its fullest exposition came from French philosopher Charles-Louis de Secondat Montesquieu (1689–1755).
- *Checks and Balances.* The branches of government scrutinize and restrain each other. This idea was first advanced by two Englishmen, the statesman Henry St. John Bolingbroke (1678–1751) and the jurist William Blackstone (1723–1780).

cure the Blessings of Liberty to ourselves and our Posterity"—in other words, the government exists to promote order and freedom.

- *It fashions a government:* "do ordain and establish this Constitution for the United States of America."

The Basic Principles

In creating the Constitution, the founders relied on four political principles that together established a revolutionary new political order: republicanism, federalism, separation of powers, and checks and balances (see Feature 3.3 for a discussion of the philosophical origins of these principles).

Republicanism.   **Republicanism** is a form of government in which power resides in the people and is exercised by their elected representatives. The framers were determined to avoid aristocracy (rule by a hereditary class), monarchy (rule by one person), and direct democracy (rule by the people). A republic was both new and daring: No people had ever been governed by a republic on so vast a scale.

The framers themselves were far from sure that their government could be sustained. They had no model of republican government to follow; moreover, republican government was thought to be suitable only for small territories, where the interests of the public would be obvious and where the government would be within the reach of every citizen. After the convention ended, Benjamin Franklin was asked what sort of government the new nation would have. "A republic," the old man replied, "if you can keep it."

Federalism.   **Federalism** is the division of power between a central government and regional units. It stands between two competing government schemes. On the one side is **unitary government**, in which all power is vested in a central authority. On the other side stands confederation, a loose union with powerful states. In a confederation, the states surrender some power to a central government but retain the rest. The Articles of Confederation, as we have seen, embodied a division of power between loosely knit states and a weak central government. The Constitution also embodied a division of power but conferred substantial powers on a national government at the expense of the states.

According to the Constitution, the powers vested in the national and state governments are derived from the people, who remain the ultimate sovereign. National and state governments can exercise their powers over people and property within their spheres of authority. But at the same time by participating in the electoral process or amending their governing charters, the people can restrain both national and state governments in order to preserve liberty.

The Constitution lists the powers of the national government and the powers denied to the states. All other powers remain with the states. Generally speaking, the states are required to give up only the powers necessary to create an effective national government; the national government is limited in turn to the powers specified in the Constitution. Despite the specific lists, the Constitution does not clearly describe the spheres of authority within which the powers can be exercised. As we will discuss in Chapter 4, limits on the exercise of power by the national government and the states have evolved as a result of political and military conflict; moreover, the limits have proved changeable.

Separation of Powers.   **Separation of powers** is the assignment of the lawmaking, law-enforcing, and law-interpreting functions to independent legislative, executive, and judicial branches of government. Nationally, the lawmaking power resides in Congress, the law-enforcing power resides in the presidency, and the law-interpreting power resides in the courts. Service in one branch prohibits simultaneous service in the others. Separation of powers safeguards liberty by ensuring that all government power does not fall into the hands of a single person or group of people. But the framers' concern with protecting the liberty of the people did not extend to the election process. The Constitution constrained majority rule by limiting the direct influence of the people on that process (see Figure 3.1). In theory, separation of powers means that one branch cannot exercise the powers of the other branches. In practice, however, the separation is far from complete. One scholar has suggested that what we have instead is "separate institutions *sharing* powers."[19]

Checks and Balances.   The constitutional system of **checks and balances** is a means of giving each branch of government some scrutiny of and

FIGURE 3.1 ■ **The Constitution and the Electoral Process**

The framers were afraid of majority rule, and that fear is reflected in the electoral process for national office described in the Constitution. The people, speaking through the voters, participated directly only in the choice of their representatives in the House. The president and senators were elected indirectly, through the electoral college and state legislatures. (Direct election of senators did not become law until 1913, when the Seventeenth Amendment was ratified.) Judicial appointments are, and always have been, far removed from representative links to the people. Judges are nominated by the president and approved by the Senate.

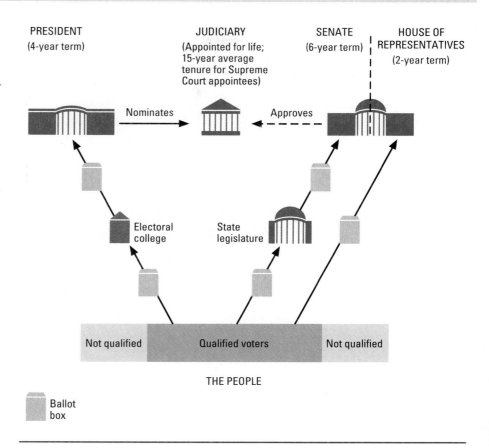

control over the other branches. The framers reasoned that checks and balances would prevent each branch from ignoring or overpowering the others.

Separation of powers and checks and balances are two distinct principles, but both are necessary to ensure that one branch does not dominate the government. Separation of powers divides government responsibilities among the legislative, executive, and judicial branches; checks and balances prevent the exclusive exercise of those powers by any one of the three branches. For example, only the Congress can enact laws. But the president (through the power of the veto) can cancel them, and the courts (by finding a law in violation of the Constitution) can nullify them. And the process goes on. In a "check on a check," the Congress can override a president's veto by an extraordinary (two-thirds) majority in each chamber. The Congress is also empowered to propose amendments to the Constitution, counteracting the courts' power to find a national law invalid. Figure 3.2 depicts the relationship between separation of powers and checks and balances.

Signing for Handgun Control
A president gives approval to legislation by signing a bill into law. On November 30, 1993 President Bill Clinton signed the Brady Handgun Violence Prevention Act. The Act imposes a five-day waiting period for handgun purchases and requires local law enforcement authorities to check the backgrounds of prospective buyers. James Brady, pictured here with the president, was White House Press Secretary for President Ronald Reagan. Brady was severely wounded in an assassination attempt on Reagan's life. Since the shooting, Brady and his wife, Sarah, have been active lobbyists for gun control. Two hundred people attended the White House signing ceremony. The extra pens (in the foreground) are keepsakes of the successful effort.

The Articles of the Constitution

In addition to the preamble, the Constitution includes seven articles. The first three establish the separate branches of government and specify their internal operations and powers. The remaining four define the relationships among the states, explain the process of amendment, declare the supremacy of national law, and explain the procedure for ratifying the Constitution.

Article I: The Legislative Article.   In structuring their new government, the framers began with the legislative branch, because they considered lawmaking the most important function of a republican government. Article I is the most detailed and therefore the longest of all the articles. It defines the **bicameral** (two-chamber) character of the Congress and describes the internal operating procedures of the House of Representatives and the Senate. Section 8 of Article I articulates the principle of enumerated powers, which means that Congress can exercise only the powers that the Constitution assigns to it. Eighteen powers are enumerated; the first seventeen are specific powers. For example, the third clause of Section 8 gives Congress the power to regulate interstate commerce. (One of the chief shortcomings of the Articles of Confederation was the lack of a means to cope with trade wars between states. The solution was to vest control of interstate commerce in the national government.)

The last clause in Section 8, known as the **necessary and proper clause** (or the elastic clause), gives Congress the means to execute the enumerated powers (see the Appendix). This clause is the basis of Congress's **implied powers**—those powers that Congress needs to execute its enumerated

FIGURE 3.2 ■ Separation of Powers and Checks and Balances

Separation of powers *is the assignment of lawmaking, law-enforcing, and law-interpreting functions to the legislative, executive, and judicial branches. The phenomenon is illustrated by the diagonal grid in the figure.* Checks and balances *give each branch some power over the other branches. For example, the executive branch possesses some legislative power, and the legislative branch possesses some executive power. These checks and balances are listed outside the diagonal grid.*

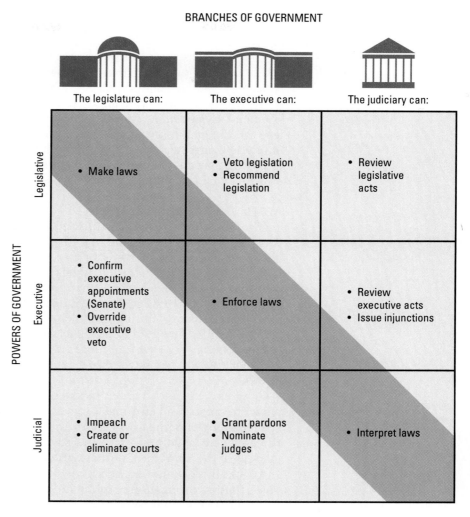

BRANCHES OF GOVERNMENT

	The legislature can:	The executive can:	The judiciary can:
Legislative	• Make laws	• Veto legislation • Recommend legislation	• Review legislative acts
Executive	• Confirm executive appointments (Senate) • Override executive veto	• Enforce laws	• Review executive acts • Issue injunctions
Judicial	• Impeach • Create or eliminate courts	• Grant pardons • Nominate judges	• Interpret laws

POWERS OF GOVERNMENT

powers. The power to levy and collect taxes (clause 1) and the power to coin money and regulate its value (clause 5), when joined with the necessary and proper clause (clause 18), imply that Congress has the power to charter a bank. Otherwise, the national government would have no means of managing the money it collects through its power to tax. Implied powers clearly expand the enumerated powers conferred on Congress by the Constitution.

Article II: The Executive Article.   Article II establishes the president's term of office, the procedure for electing a president through the electoral college, the qualifications for becoming president, and the president's duties and powers. The last include acting as commander in chief of the military; making treaties (which must be ratified by a two-thirds vote of the Senate); and appointing government officers, diplomats, and judges (again, with the advice and consent of the Senate).

The president also has legislative powers—part of the constitutional system of checks and balances. For example, the Constitution requires that the president periodically inform Congress of "the State of the Union" and of the policies and programs that the executive branch intends to advocate in the forthcoming year. Today, this is done annually, in the president's State of the Union address. Under special circumstances, the president can also convene or adjourn Congress.

The duty to "take Care that the Laws be faithfully executed" in Section 3 has provided presidents with a reservoir of power. President Nixon tried to use this power when he refused to turn over the Watergate tapes despite a judicial subpoena in a criminal trial. He claimed broad executive privilege, an extension of the executive power implied in Article II. But the Supreme Court rejected his claim, arguing that it violated the separation of powers, because the decision to release or withhold information in a criminal trial is a judicial, not an executive, function.

Article III: The Judicial Article.   The third article was left purposely vague. The Constitution established the Supreme Court as the highest court in the land. But beyond that, the framers were unable to agree on the need for a national judiciary or on its size or composition or the procedures it should follow. They left these issues to Congress, which resolved them by creating a system of federal (i.e., national) courts separate from the states.

Short of impeachment, federal judges serve for life. They are appointed to indefinite terms "during good Behaviour," and their salaries cannot be reduced while they hold office. The stipulations reinforce the separation of powers; they see to it that judges are independent of the other branches and that they do not have to fear retribution in their exercise of judicial power.

Congress exercises a potential check on the judicial branch through its power to create (and eliminate) lower federal courts. Congress can also restrict the power of the lower courts to decide cases. And, as we have noted, the president appoints—with the advice and consent of the Senate—the justices of the Supreme Court and the judges of the lower federal courts.

Article III does not explicitly give the courts the power of **judicial review,** that is, the authority to invalidate congressional or presidential actions. That power has been inferred from the logic, structure, and theory of the Constitution.

The Remaining Articles.   The remaining four articles of the Constitution cover a lot of ground. Article IV requires that the citizens, judicial acts, and criminal warrants of each state be honored in all other states. This is a provision that promotes equality; it keeps the states from treating outsiders differently from their own citizens. For example, an Illinois court awards Goldman damages against Janda for $50,000. Janda moves to Alaska to avoid payment. Rather than force Goldman to bring a new suit against Janda, the court in Alaska (Judge Berry presiding), under the full faith and credit clause of Article IV, honors the Illinois judgment and enforces it as its own. In other words, states will respect each other's judgments. The origin of this clause can be traced to the Articles of Confederation.

Article IV also allows the addition of new states and stipulates that the national government will protect the states against invasion and domestic violence.

Article V specifies the methods for amending (changing) the Constitution. We will have more to say about this shortly.

An important component of Article VI is the supremacy clause, which asserts that when they conflict, the Constitution, national laws, and treaties take precedence over state and local laws. The stipulation is vital to the operation of federalism. In keeping with the supremacy clause, Article VI also requires that all national and state officials, elected or appointed, take an oath to support the Constitution. The article also mandates that religion cannot be a qualification for holding government office.

Finally, Article VII describes the ratification process, stipulating that approval by conventions in nine states was necessary for the "Establishment" of the Constitution.

The Framers' Motives

Some argue that the Constitution is essentially a conservative document written by wealthy men to advance their own interests. One distinguished historian writing in the early 1900s, Charles A. Beard, maintained that the delegates had much to gain from a strong national government.[20] Many held government securities dating from the Revolutionary War that had become practically worthless under the Articles of Confederation. A strong national government would protect their property and pay off the nation's debts.

Beard's argument, that the Constitution was crafted to protect the economic interests of this small group of creditors, provoked a generation of historians to examine the existing financial records of the convention delegates. Their scholarship has largely discredited his once-popular view.[21] For example, it turns out that seven of the delegates who left the convention or refused to sign the Constitution held public securities worth more than twice the total of the holdings of the thirty-nine delegates who did sign. Moreover, the most influential delegates owned no securities. And only a few delegates appear to have benefited economically from the new government.[22]

What did motivate the framers? Surely economic considerations were important, but they were not the major issues. The single most important factor leading to the Constitutional Convention was the inability of the national or state governments to maintain order under the loose structure of the Articles of Confederation. Certainly, order involved the protection of property, but the framers had a broader view of property than their portfolios of government securities. They wanted to protect their homes, their families, and their means of livelihood from impending anarchy.

Although they disagreed bitterly on the structure and mechanics of the national government, the framers agreed on the most vital issues. For example, three of the most crucial features of the Constitution—the power to tax, the necessary and proper clause, and the supremacy clause—were approved unanimously without debate; experience had taught the delegates that a strong national government was essential if the United States were to survive. The motivation to create order was so strong, in fact, that the framers were willing to draft clauses that protected the most undemocratic of all institutions—slavery.

The Slavery Issue

The institution of slavery was well ingrained in American life at the time of the Constitutional Convention, and slavery helped shape the Constitution, although mentioned nowhere in it. (According to the first annual census in 1790, nearly 18 percent of the population—697,000 people—lived in slavery). It is doubtful, in fact, that there would have been a Constitution if the delegates had had to resolve the slavery issue, for the southern states would have opposed a constitution that prohibited slavery. Opponents of slavery were in the minority, and they were willing to tolerate its continuation in the interest of forging a union, perhaps believing that the issue could await another day.

The question of representation in the House of Representatives brought the slavery issue close to the surface of debate, leading to the Great Compromise. Representation in the House was to be based on population. But who counted in the population? States with large slave populations wanted all inhabitants, slave and free, counted equally; states with few slaves wanted only the free population counted. The delegates agreed unanimously that in apportioning representatives in the House and in assessing direct taxes, the population of each state was to be determined by adding "the whole Number of free Persons" and "three fifths of all other Persons" (Article I, Section 2). The phrase "all other Persons" is, of course, a substitute for slaves.

The three-fifths formula had been used by the 1783 congress under the Articles of Confederation to allocate financial assessments among the states. The rule reflected the view that slaves were less efficient producers of wealth than free people, not that slaves were three-fifths human and two-fifths personal property.[23]

The three-fifths clause gave states with large slave populations (the South) greater representation in Congress than states with small slave populations (the North). If all slaves had been included in the count, the slave states would have had 50 percent of the seats in the House. This outcome was unacceptable to the North. Had none of the slaves counted, the slave states would have had 41 percent of House seats, which was unacceptable to the South. The three-fifths compromise left the South with 47 percent of the House seats, a sizable minority, but in all likelihood a losing one on slavery issues.[24] The overrepresentation resulting from large slave populations translated into greater influence in presidential selection, because electoral votes were determined by the size of each state's congressional delegation. The three-fifths clause also undertaxed states with large slave populations.

Another issue centered around the slave trade. Several southern delegates were uncompromising in their defense of the slave trade: some delegates favored prohibition. The delegates compromised, agreeing that the slave trade would not be ended before twenty years had elapsed (Article I, Section 9). Finally, the delegates agreed, without serious challenge, that fugitive slaves be returned to their masters (Article IV, Section 2).

All Were Not Created Equal

This 1845 photograph of Isaac Jefferson, who had been one of Thomas Jefferson's slaves at Monticello, reminds us that the framers of the Constitution did not extend freedom and equality to all. Slavery was widely accepted as a social norm in the eighteenth century.

In addressing these points, the framers in essence condoned slavery. Clearly, slavery existed in stark opposition to the idea that all men are created equal. Although many slaveholders, including Jefferson and Madison, agonized over it, few made serious efforts to free their own slaves. Most Americans seemed indifferent to slavery and felt no embarrassment at the apparent contradiction between the Declaration and slavery. Do the framers deserve contempt for their toleration and perpetuation of slavery? The most prominent founders—George Washington, John Adams, and Thomas Jefferson—expected slavery to wither away. A leading colonial scholar has offered a defense: The framers were simply unable to transcend altogether the limitations of the age in which they lived. Bear in mind that the colonial period was brutal and savage. While slavery was brutal and degrading, so was much of ordinary life in the colonial period.[25]

Nonetheless, the eradication of slavery proceeded gradually in certain states. Opposition to slavery on moral or religious ground is a partial explanation. Economic forces—such as a shift in the North to agricultural production that was less labor intensive—were a contributing factor, too. By 1787, Connecticut, Massachusetts, New Jersey, New York, Pennsylvania, Rhode Island, and Vermont had abolished slavery or provided for gradual emancipation. No southern states followed suit, although several enacted laws making it easier for masters to free their slaves. The slow but perceptible shift on the slavery issue in many states masked a volcanic force capable of destroying the Constitutional Convention and the Union.

**SELLING THE
CONSTITUTION**

Nearly four months after the Constitutional Convention opened, the delegates convened for the last time, on September 17, 1787, to sign the final version of their handiwork. Because several delegates were unwilling to sign the document, the last paragraph was craftly worded to give the impression of unanimity: "done in Convention by the Unanimous Consent of the States present."

Before it could take effect, the Constitution had to be ratified by a minimum of nine state conventions. The support of key states was crucial. In Pennsylvania, however, the legislature was slow to convene a ratifying convention. Pro-Constitution forces became so frustrated at this dawdling that they broke into a local boardinghouse and hauled two errant legislators through the streets to the statehouse so the assembly could schedule the convention.

The proponents of the new charter, who wanted a strong national government, called themselves Federalists. The opponents of the Constitution were quickly dubbed Antifederalists. They claimed, however, to be the true federalists, because they wanted to protect the states from the tyranny of a strong national government. Elbridge Gerry, a vocal Antifederalist, called his opponents "rats" (because they favored ratification) and maintained that he was an "antirat."[26] Such is the Alice-in-Wonderland character of political discourse. Whatever they were called, the viewpoints of the two groups formed the bases of the first American political parties.

The *Federalist* Papers

The press of the day became a battlefield of words, filled with extravagant praise or vituperative condemnation of the proposed constitution. Beginning in October 1787, an exceptional series of eighty-five newspaper articles defending the Constitution appeared under the title *The Federalist: A Commentary on the Constitution of the United States.* The essays bore the pen name Publius (for a Roman emperor and defender of the Republic, Publius Valerius, who was later known as Publicola); they were written primarily by James Madison and Alexander Hamilton, with some assistance from John Jay. Logically and calmly, Publius argued in favor of ratification. Reprinted extensively during the ratification battle, The Federalist (also called The Federalist Papers) remains the best single commentary we have on the meaning of the Constitution and the political theory it embodies.

Not to be outdone, the Antifederalists offered their own intellectual basis for rejecting the Constitution. In several essays, the most influential published under the pseudonyms Brutus and Federal Farmer, the Antifederalists attacked the centralization of power in a strong national government, claiming it would obliterate the states, violate the social contract of the Declaration of Independence, and destroy liberty in the process. They defended the status quo, maintaining that the Articles of Confederation established true federal principles.[27]

Of all the Federalist papers, the most magnificent and most frequently cited is Federalist No. 10, written by James Madison (see the Appendix).

He argued that the proposed constitution was designed "to break and control the violence of faction": "By a faction, I understand a number of citizens, whether amounting to a majority or minority of the whole, who are united and actuated by some common impulse of passion, or of interest, adverse to the rights of other citizens, or to the permanent and aggregate interests of the community."

Madison was discussing what we described in Chapter 2 as *pluralism.* What Madison called factions today are interest groups or even political parties. According to Madison, "The most common and durable source of factions has been the various and unequal distribution of property." Madison was concerned not with reducing inequalities of wealth (which he took for granted) but with controlling the seemingly inevitable conflict stemming from them. The Constitution, he argued, was well-constructed for this purpose.

Through the mechanism of *representation,* wrote Madison, the Constitution would prevent the tyranny of the majority (mob rule). Government would not be controlled by the people directly but indirectly by their elected representatives. And those representatives would have the intelligence and the understanding to serve the larger interests of the nation. Moreover, the federal system would require that majorities form first within each state, then organize for effective action at the national level. This and the vastness of the country would make it unlikely that a majority would form "to invade the rights of other citizens."

The purpose of Federalist No. 10 was to demonstrate that the proposed government was not likely to be dominated by any faction. Contrary to conventional wisdom, Madison argued, the key to mending the evils of faction is to have a large republic—the larger, the better. The more diverse the society, the less likely it is that an unjust majority can form. Madison certainly had no intention of creating a majoritarian democracy; his view of popular government was much more consistent with the model of pluralist democracy discussed in Chapter 2.

Madison pressed his argument from a different angle in *Federalist No. 51* (see the Appendix). Asserting that "ambition must be made to counteract ambition," he argued that the separation of powers and checks and balances would control efforts at tyranny from any source. If power is distributed equally among the three branches, he argued, each branch will have the capacity to counteract the other. In Madison's words, "usurpations are guarded against by a division of the government into distinct and separate departments." Because legislative power tends to predominate in republican governments, legislative authority is divided between the Senate and the House of Representatives, with different methods of selection and terms of office. Additional protection arises from federalism, which divides power "between two distinct governments"—national and state—and subdivides "the portion allotted to each . . . among distinct and separate departments."

The Antifederalists wanted additional separation of powers and additional checks and balances, which they maintained would eliminate the threat of tyranny entirely. The Federalists believed that such protections would make decisive national action virtually impossible. But to ensure ratification, they agreed to a compromise.

TABLE 3.2	■ The Bill of Rights

The first ten amendments to the Constitution are known as the Bill of Rights. *The following is a list of those* amendments grouped conceptually. For the actual order and wording of the Bill of Rights, see the Appendix.

Guarantees	Amendment
Guarantees for Participation in the Political Process	
No government abridgement of speech or press; no government abridgement of peaceable assembly; no government abridgement of petitioning government for redress.	1
Guarantees Respecting Personal Beliefs	
No government establishment of religion; no government prohibition of free religious exercise.	1
Guarantees of Personal Privacy	
Owners' consent necessary to quarter troops in private homes in peacetime; quartering during war must be lawful.	3
Government cannot engage in unreasonable searches and seizures; warrants to search and seize require probable cause.	4
No compulsion to testify against oneself in criminal cases.	5
Guarantees Against Government Overreaching	
Serious crimes require a grand jury indictment; no repeated prosecution for the same offense; no loss of life, liberty, or property without due process; no government taking of property for public use without just compensation.	5
Criminal defendants will have a speedy public trial by impartial local jury; defendants informed of accusation; defendants confront witnesses against them; defendants use judicial process to obtain favorable witnesses; defendants have legal assistance for their defense.	6
Civil lawsuits can be tried by juries if controversy exceeds $20; in jury trials, fact-finding is a jury function.	7
No excessive bail; no excessive fines; no cruel and unusual punishment	8
Other Guarantees	
The people have the right to bear arms.	2
No government trespass on unspecified fundamental rights.	9
The states or the people reserve the powers not delegated to the national government or denied to the states.	10

A Concession: The Bill of Rights

Despite the eloquence of *The Federalist Papers,* many prominent citizens, including Thomas Jefferson, were unhappy that the Constitution did not list basic civil liberties—the individual freedoms guaranteed to citizens. The omission of a bill of rights was the chief obstacle to the adoption of the Constitution by the states. (Seven of the eleven state constitutions that were written in the first five years of independence included such a list.) The colonists had just rebelled against the British government to preserve their basic freedoms; why did the proposed Constitution not spell out those freedoms?

The answer was rooted in logic, not politics. Because the national government was limited to those powers that were granted to it and because no power was granted to abridge the people's liberties, a list of guaranteed freedoms was not necessary. In *Federalist No. 84,* Hamilton went even further, arguing that the addition of a bill of rights would be dangerous. To deny the exercise of a nonexistent power might lead to the exercise of a power that is not specifically denied. For example, to declare that the national government shall make no law abridging free speech might suggest that the national government could prohibit activities in unspecified areas, such as divorce, which is a state domain. Because it is not possible to list all prohibited powers, wrote Hamilton, any attempt to provide a partial list would make the unlisted areas vulnerable to government abuse.

But logic was no match for fear. Many states agreed to ratify the Constitution only after George Washington suggested adding a list of guarantees through the amendment process. Well in excess of one hundred amendments were proposed by the states. These were eventually narrowed to twelve, which were approved by Congress and sent to the states. Ten became part of the Constitution in 1791, after securing the approval of the required three-fourths of the states. Collectively, the ten amendments are known as the **Bill of Rights.** They restrain the national government from tampering with fundamental rights and civil liberties and emphasize the limited character of national power (see Table 3.2).

Ratification

The Constitution officially took effect upon its ratification by the ninth state, New Hampshire, on June 21, 1788. However, the success of the new government was not assured until August 1788, when the Constitution was ratified by the key states of Virginia and New York after lengthy debate.

The reflection and deliberation that attended the creation and ratification of the Constitution signaled to the world that a new government could be launched peacefully. The French observer Alexis de Tocqueville (1805–1859) later wrote:

> That which is new in the history of societies is to see a great people, warned by its lawgivers that the wheels of government are stopping, turn its attention on itself without haste or fear, sound the depth of the ill, and then wait for two years to find the remedy at leisure, and then finally, when the remedy has been indicated, submit to it voluntarily without its costing humanity a single tear or drop of blood.[28]

CONSTITUTIONAL CHANGE

The founders realized that the Constitution would have to be changed from time to time. To this end, they specified a formal amendment process—a process that was used almost immediately to add the Bill of Rights. With the passage of time, the Constitution has also been altered through judicial interpretation and changes in political practice.

FIGURE 3.3   ■ **Amending the Constitution**

There are two stages in amending the Constitution: proposal and ratification. Congress has no control over the proposal stage, but it prescribes the ratifica-tion method. Once a state has ratified an amendment, it cannot retract its action. However, a state's rejection of an amend-ment does not bar reconsideration.

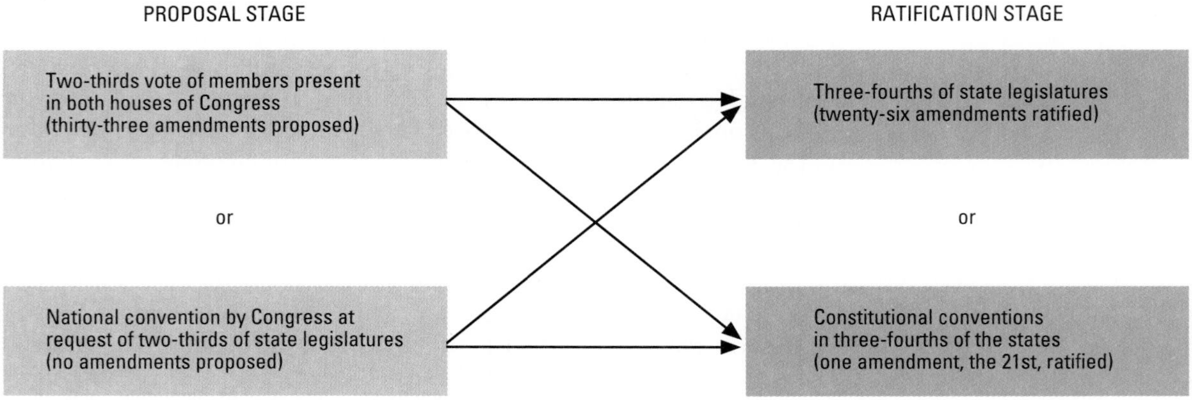

PROPOSAL STAGE

Two-thirds vote of members present in both houses of Congress (thirty-three amendments proposed)

or

National convention by Congress at request of two-thirds of state legislatures (no amendments proposed)

RATIFICATION STAGE

Three-fourths of state legislatures (twenty-six amendments ratified)

or

Constitutional conventions in three-fourths of the states (one amendment, the 21st, ratified)

The Formal Amendment Process

The amendment process has two stages, **proposal** and **ratification;** both are necessary for an amendment to become part of the Constitution. The Constitution provides two alternatives for completing each stage (see Figure 3.3). Amendments can be proposed by a two-thirds vote of the House of Representatives and of the Senate, or by a national convention, summoned by Congress at the request of two-thirds of the state legisla-tures. All constitutional amendments to date have been proposed by the first method; the second has never been used.

A proposed amendment can be ratified by a vote of the legislatures of three-fourths of the states, or by a vote of constitutional conventions held in three-fourths of the states. Congress chooses the method of ratification. It has used the state convention method only once, for the Twenty-first Amendment, which repealed the Eighteenth (prohibition of intoxicating liquors).

Note that the amendment process requires the exercise of **extraordinary majorities** (two-thirds and three-fourths). The framers purposely made it difficult to propose and ratify amendments (although nowhere near as dif-ficult as under the Articles of Confederation). They wanted only the most significant issues to lead to constitutional change. Note, too, that the pres-ident plays no formal role in the process. Presidential approval is not required to amend the Constitution, although the president's political in-fluence affects the success or failure of any amendment effort.

Calling a national convention to propose an amendment has never been tried, and the method raises several thorny questions. For example, the Constitution does not specify the number of delegates who should attend, the method by which they should be chosen, or the rules for debating and voting on a proposed amendment. Confusion surrounding the convention process tends to deter resort to it, securing the amendment process in congressional hands.[29] The major issue is the limits, if any, on the business of the convention. Remember that the convention in Philadelphia in 1787, charged with revising the Articles of Confederation, drafted an entirely new charter. Would a national convention, called to consider a particular amendment, be within its bounds to rewrite the Constitution? No one really knows.

A recent movement to convene a constitutional convention to write an amendment requiring a balanced budget was well under way when it faltered and appeared to reverse course. From 1974 to 1988, thirty-two of the required thirty-four states voted to call a convention on the budget issue. Then, in 1988, the Alabama legislature rescinded its vote. The legislators were motivated by the fear that a convention would open a Pandora's box, letting loose a whirlwind of political change and fundamentally altering the national government. Alabama's action raised additional thorny issues: May a state withdraw its support for a convention? And how long does a state's call for a convention stay in effect? In the absence of authoritative answers and political support, a constitutional convention now appears doubtful.

Most of the Constitution's twenty-seven amendments were adopted to reflect changes in political thinking. The first ten amendments (the Bill of Rights) were the price of ratification, but they have been fundamental to our system of government. The last sixteen amendments fall into three main categories: They make public policy, correct deficiencies in government structure, or they promote equality (see Table 3.3). One attempt to make public policy through a constitutional amendment was disastrous. The Eighteenth Amendment (1919) prohibited the manufacture or sale

Roll Out the Barrels

The Eighteenth Amendment, which was ratified by the states in 1919, banned the manufacture, sale, or transportation of alcoholic beverages. The amendment was spurred by moral and social reform groups, such as the Women's Christian Temperance Union, founded by Evanston, Illinois, resident Frances Willard in 1874. The amendment proved to be an utter failure. People continued to drink, but their alcohol came from illegal sources.

TABLE 3.3	■ Constitutional Amendments: 11 Through 27

No.	Proposed	Ratified	Intent	Subject
11	1794	1795	G	Prohibits an individual from suing a state in a federal court without the state's consent.
12	1803	1804	G	Requires the electoral college to vote separately for president and vice president.
13	1865	1865	E	Prohibits slavery.
14	1866	1868	E	Gives citizenship to all persons born or naturalized in the United States (former slaves); prevents states from depriving any "person of life, liberty, or property, without due process of law."
15	1869	1870	E	Guarantees that citizens' right to vote cannot be denied "on account of race, color, or previous condition of servitude."
16	1909	1913	E	Gives Congress power to collect an income tax.
17	1912	1913	E	Provides for popular election of senators, who were formerly elected by state legislatures.
18	1917	1919	P	Prohibits making and selling intoxicating liquors.
19	1919	1920	E	Gives women the right to vote.
20	1932	1933	G	Changes the presidential inauguration from March 4 to January 20 and sets January 3 for the opening date of Congress.
21	1933	1933	P	Repeals the Eighteenth Amendment.
22	1947	1951	G	Limits a president to two terms.
23	1960	1961	E	Gives citizens of Washington, D.C., the right to vote for president.
24	1962	1964	E	Prohibits charging citizens a poll tax to vote.
25	1965	1967	G	Provides for succession in event of death, removal from office, incapacity, or resignation of the president or vice president.
26	1971	1971	E	Lowers the voting age to eighteen.
27	1789	1992	G	Bars immediate pay increases to members of Congress.

P   Amendments legislating public policy.
G   Amendments correcting perceived deficiencies in government structure.
E   Amendments advancing equality.

of intoxicating beverages. Prohibition lasted fourteen years and was an utter failure. Gangsters began bootlegging liquor, people died from drinking homemade booze, and millions regularly broke the law by drinking anyway. Congress had to propose another amendment in 1933 to repeal the Eighteenth. The states ratified this amendment, the Twenty-first, in less than ten months, less time than it took to ratify the Fourteenth Amendment guaranteeing citizenship, due process, and equal protection.

Since 1787, about ten thousand constitutional amendments have been introduced; only a fraction have survived the proposal stage. Once an amendment has been approved by Congress, chances of ratification are high. The Twenty-seventh Amendment, which prevents members from voting themselves immediate pay increases, was ratified in 1992. It had been submitted to the states in 1789 but languished in a political netherworld until 1982, when a University of Texas student, Gregory D. Watson, stumbled upon the proposed amendment while researching a paper. At that time, only eight states had ratified the amendment. Watson took up the cause, prompting renewed interest in the idea. In May 1992, ratification by the Michigan legislature provided the decisive vote, 203 years after congressional approval.[30] Only six amendments submitted to the states have failed to be ratified. Two such failures occurred in the 1980s: the Equal Rights Amendment (see Chapter 16) and full congressional representation for the District of Columbia.

Interpretation by the Courts

In *Marbury v. Madison* (1803), the Supreme Court declared that the courts have the power to nullify government acts that conflict with the Constitution. (We will elaborate on judicial review in Chapter 14.) The exercise of judicial review forces the courts to interpret the Constitution. In a way, this makes a lot of sense. The judiciary is the law-interpreting branch of the government; the Constitution is the supreme law of the land, fair game then for judicial interpretation. Judicial review is the courts' main check on the other branches of government. But in interpreting the Constitution, the courts cannot help but give new meaning to its provisions. This is why judicial interpretation is a principal form of constitutional change.

What guidelines should judges use in interpreting the Constitution? For one thing, they must realize that the usage and meaning of words have changed during the last two hundred years. Judges must be careful to think about what the words meant at the time the Constitution was written. Some insist that they must also consider the original intent of the framers—not an easy task. Of course, there are records of the Constitutional Convention and the debates surrounding ratification. But there are also many questions about the completeness and accuracy of those records, even Madison's detailed notes. And, at times, the framers were deliberately vague in writing the document. This may reflect lack of agreement on, or universal understanding of, certain provisions in the Constitution. Some scholars and judges maintain that the search for original meaning is hopeless and that contemporary notions of constitutional provisions must hold sway. Critics say that this approach comes perilously close to amending the Constitution as judges see fit, transforming law interpreters into lawmakers. Still other scholars and judges maintain that judges face the unavoidable challenge of balancing two-hundred-year-old constitutional principles against the demands of modern society. Whatever the approach, judges run the risk of usurping policies of the people's representatives (see Politics in a Changing America 3.1).

POLITICS IN A CHANGING AMERICA 3.1

What the Founders Did Not Say About Sexual Orientation

 In a democracy, may a majority thwart efforts to adopt special government protections based on sexual orientation?

Survey evidence gathered in 1993 suggests that about 3 percent of American adults are homosexual or bisexual. Survey evidence also reveals that a majority of Americans look upon homosexuality with varying degrees of disfavor. These attitudes have not changed much in the past 20 years. In a 1973 National Opinion Research Center poll, 70 percent of Americans said homosexual relations were "always wrong." In 1991, 71 percent held the same view. In a 1982 Gallup poll, 51 percent of Americans opposed homosexuality as an acceptable, alternative lifestyle. In 1992, 58 percent opposed a homosexual lifestyle. But politics surrounding homosexuality has not remained fixed.

In 1992, 53 percent of Colorado voters approved a voter-initiated amendment to the state constitution. The amendment forbade state and local authorities to enact laws that would create any entitlement, minority pref-erence, or legal basis for discrimination claims by homosexuals or bisexuals.

The amendment's immediate effect was to repeal state and local government laws and regulations that barred discrimination based on sexual orientation. Its ultimate effect would be to prohibit any government body from adopting similar or more protective policies in the future, short of constitutional amendment.

Several individuals and groups challenged Colorado's new amendment in court. They argued that the amendment "fences out" from the political process gay men, lesbians, and bisexuals and singles out and prohibits them from seeking favorable government action. Consequently, the amendment denies equality of participation in the political process.

In 1993, Colorado trial judge H. Jeffrey Bayless ruled that Amendment 2 "violates the fundamental right of an identifiable group to participate in the political process." But Bayless declined to rule that gays are a disadvantaged minority worthy of special pro-

Political Practice

The Constitution is silent on many issues. It says nothing about political parties or the president's cabinet, for example, yet both parties and cabinets have exercised considerable influence in American politics. Some constitutional provisions have fallen out of use. The electors in the electoral college, for example, were supposed to exercise their own judgment in voting for president and vice president. Today, the electors function simply as a rubber stamp, validating the outcome of election contests in their states.

Meanwhile, political practice has altered the distribution of power without changes in the Constitution. The framers intended Congress to be the strongest branch of government. But the president has come to overshadow Congress. Presidents such as Abraham Lincoln and Franklin Roosevelt used their powers imaginatively to respond to national crises. And their actions paved the way for future presidents to further enlarge the powers of the office.

tection. In fact, observed Bayless, the vote demonstrated the political power of gays. Although only 4 percent of the state's population, gays gathered the support of more than 46 percent of the voters. "That is a demonstration of power, not powerlessness," Bayless wrote. The Colorado Supreme Court affirmed Bayless's decision in 1994.

Voters in 1993 banned gay rights protections in Cincinnati, repealed them in Lewiston, Maine, and rejected such a ban in Portsmouth, New Hampshire. Civil rights protections are on the books in eight states and seventy-five cities and counties.

Sources: American Demographics, *July 1993, p. 9;* Evans v. Romer, *854 P. 2d 1270 (Colo. 1993); Ann Rovin and Louis Sahagun, "Colorado's Ban on Gay Rights Laws Is Voided,"* Los Angeles Times, *15 December 1993, p. A1.*

Question: Do you feel that homosexuality should be considered an acceptable lifestyle or not?

	Should	Should not	Don't know/no answer
1982	34%	51%	15%
1992	38%	57%	6%

Question: What about sexual relations between two adults of the same sex—do you think it is always wrong?

	Always wrong
1973	70%
1991	71%

The framers could scarcely imagine an urbanized nation of 250 million people stretching across a landmass some three thousand miles wide. Never in their wildest nightmares could they have foreseen the destructiveness of nuclear weaponry or envisioned its effect on the power to declare war. The Constitution empowers Congress to consider and debate this momentous step. But with nuclear annihilation perhaps only minutes away, the legislative power to declare war must give way to the president's power to wage war as the nation's commander in chief. Strict adherence to the Constitution in such circumstances could destroy the nation's ability to protect itself.

AN EVALUATION OF THE CONSTITUTION

The U.S. Constitution is one of the world's most praised political documents. It is the oldest written national constitution and one of the most widely copied, sometimes word for word. It is also one of the shortest, consisting of about 4,300 words, not counting the amendments, which add

3,100 words. The brevity of the Constitution may be one of its greatest strengths. As we noted earlier, the framers simply laid out a structural framework for government; they did not describe relationships and powers in detail. For example, the Constitution gives Congress the power to regulate "Commerce . . . among the several States" but does not define interstate commerce. Such general wording allows interpretation in keeping with contemporary political, social, and technological developments. Air travel, for instance, unknown in 1787, now falls easily within Congress's power to regulate interstate commerce.

The generality of the U.S. Constitution stands in stark contrast to the specificity of most state constitutions. The constitution of California, for example, provides that "fruit and nut-bearing trees under the age of four years from the time of planting in orchard form and grapevines under the age of three years from the time of planting in vineyard form . . . shall be exempt from taxation" (Article XIII, Section 12). Because they are so specific, most state constitutions are much longer than the U.S. Constitution.

Freedom, Order, and Equality in the Constitution

The revolutionaries' first try at government was embodied in the Articles of Confederation. The result was a weak national government that leaned too much toward freedom at the expense of order. Deciding that the confederation was beyond correcting, the revolutionaries chose a new form of government—a *federal* government—that was strong enough to maintain order but not so strong that it could dominate the states or infringe on individual freedoms. In short, the Constitution provided a judicious balance between order and freedom. It paid virtually no attention to equality.

Consider social equality. The Constitution never mentioned slavery— a controversial issue even then. In fact, as we have seen, the Constitution implicitly condones slavery in the wording of several articles. Not until the ratification of the Thirteenth Amendment in 1865 was slavery prohibited.

The Constitution was designed long before social equality was ever even thought of as an objective of government. In fact, in *Federalist No. 10,* Madison held that protection of the "diversities in the faculties of men from which the rights of property originate" is "the first object of government." More than a century later, the Constitution was changed to incorporate a key device for the promotion of social equality—the income tax. The Sixteenth Amendment (1913) gave Congress the power to collect an income tax; it was proposed and ratified to replace a law that had been declared unconstitutional in an 1895 court case. The income tax had long been seen as a means of putting into effect the concept of **progressive taxation,** in which the tax rate increases with income. The Sixteenth Amendment gave progressive taxation a constitutional basis.[31] Progressive taxation later helped promote social equality through the redistribution of income—that is, higher-income people are taxed at higher rates to help fund social programs that benefit low-income people.

Social equality itself has never been, and is not now, a prime *constitutional* value. The Constitution has been much more effective in securing order and freedom. A poll of Americans taken during the Constitution's bicentennial in 1987 reinforces this evaluation (see Figure 3.4). Nor did the Constitution take a stand on political equality. It left voting qualifications

FIGURE 3.4 ■ **"We the People" Evaluate the Constitution**

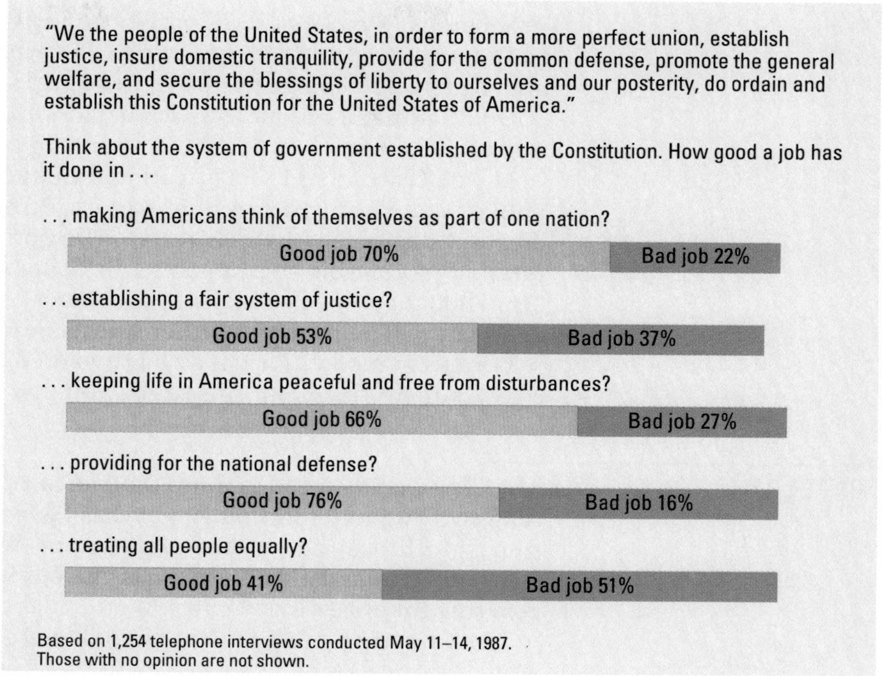

Two hundred years after the Constitutional Convention, a survey of Americans evaluated the nation's success at achieving the goals articulated in the preamble to the Constitution. According to the results, the Constitution has done a good job of forging one nation from separate states and securing an orderly and free society. Although equality was not an explicit goal in the preamble, the Constitution's success in treating all people equally received a relatively poor grade.

Source: New York Times, May 26, 1987, p. 10. Copyright © 1987 by the New York Times Company. Reprinted by permission.

"We the people of the United States, in order to form a more perfect union, establish justice, insure domestic tranquility, provide for the common defense, promote the general welfare, and secure the blessings of liberty to ourselves and our posterity, do ordain and establish this Constitution for the United States of America."

Think about the system of government established by the Constitution. How good a job has it done in . . .

. . . making Americans think of themselves as part of one nation?

| Good job 70% | Bad job 22% |

. . . establishing a fair system of justice?

| Good job 53% | Bad job 37% |

. . . keeping life in America peaceful and free from disturbances?

| Good job 66% | Bad job 27% |

. . . providing for the national defense?

| Good job 76% | Bad job 16% |

. . . treating all people equally?

| Good job 41% | Bad job 51% |

Based on 1,254 telephone interviews conducted May 11–14, 1987. Those with no opinion are not shown.

---

to the states, specifying only that people who could vote for "the most numerous Branch of the State Legislature" could also vote for representatives to Congress (Article I, Section 2). Most states at that time allowed only taxpaying or property-owning white males to vote. With few exceptions, blacks and women were universally excluded from voting. These inequalities have been rectified by several amendments (see Table 3.3).

The Constitution did not guarantee blacks citizenship until the Fourteenth Amendment was ratified (1868) and did not give them the right to vote until the Fifteenth Amendment (1870). Women were not guaranteed the right to vote until the Nineteenth Amendment (1920). Finally, the poll tax (a tax that people had to pay in order to vote and that tended to disenfranchise poor blacks) was not eliminated until the Twenty-fourth Amendment (1964). Two other amendments expanded the Constitution's grant of political equality. The Twenty-third Amendment (1961) allowed citizens of Washington, D.C., who are not residents of any state, to vote for president. The Twenty-sixth Amendment (1971) extended voting rights to all citizens who are at least eighteen years old.

THE CONSTITUTION AND MODELS OF DEMOCRACY

Think back to our discussion of the models of democracy in Chapter 2. Which model does the Constitution fit: pluralist or majoritarian? Actually, it is hard to imagine a government framework better suited to the pluralist model of democracy than the Constitution of the United

States. It is also hard to imagine a document more at odds with the majoritarian model. Consider Madison's claim, in Federalist No. 10, that government inevitably involves conflicting factions. This concept coincides perfectly with pluralist theory (see Chapter 2). Then recall his description in Federalist No. 51, of the Constitution's ability to guard against concentration of power in the majority through separation of powers and checks and balances. This concept—avoiding a single center of government power that might fall under majority control—also fits perfectly with pluralist democracy.

The delegates to the Constitutional Convention intended to create a republic, a government based on majority consent; they did not intend to create a democracy, which rests on majority rule. They succeeded admirably in creating that republic. In doing so, they also produced a government that developed into a democracy—but a particular type of democracy. The framers neither wanted nor got a democracy that fit the majoritarian model. They may have wanted, and they certainly did create, a government that conforms to the pluralist model.

SUMMARY

The U.S. Constitution is more than an antique curiosity. Although more than two hundred years old, it governs the politics of a mighty modern nation. It still has the power to force from office a president who won reelection by a landslide. It still has the power to see the country through government crises.

The Constitution was the end product of a revolutionary movement aimed at preserving existing liberties. That movement began with the Declaration of Independence, a proclamation that everyone is entitled to certain rights (among them, life, liberty, and the pursuit of happiness) and that government exists for the good of its citizens. When government denies those rights, the people have the right to rebel.

War with Britain was only part of the process of independence. A government was needed to replace the British monarchy. The Americans chose a republic and defined the structure of that republic in the Articles of Confederation. The Articles, however, were a failure. Although they guaranteed the states their coveted independence, they left the central government too weak to deal with disorder and insurrection.

The Constitution was the second attempt at limited government. It replaced a loose union of powerful states with a strong national government, incorporating four political principles: republicanism, federalism, separation of powers, and checks and balances. Republicanism is a form of government in which power resides in the people and is exercised by their elected representatives. Federalism is a division of power between the national government and the states. The federalism of the Constitution conferred substantial powers on the national government at the expense of the states. Separation of powers is a further division of the power of the national government into legislative (lawmaking), executive (law-enforcing), and judicial (law-interpreting) branches. Finally, the Constitution established a system of checks and balances, giving each branch some scrutiny of and control over the others.

When work began on ratification, a major stumbling block proved to be the failure of the Constitution to list the individual liberties the

Americans had fought to protect. With the promise of a bill of rights, the Constitution was ratified. The ten amendments guaranteed participation in the political process, respect for personal beliefs, and personal privacy. They also embodied guarantees against government overreaching in criminal prosecutions. Over the years, the Constitution has evolved through the formal amendment process, through the exercise of judicial review, and through political practice.

The Constitution was designed to strike a balance between order and freedom. It was not designed to promote social equality; in fact, it had to be amended to redress inequality. The framers had compromised on many issues, including slavery, to assure the creation of a new and workable government. The framers had not set out to create a democracy. Faith in government by the people was virtually nonexistent two centuries ago. Nevertheless, they produced a democratic form of government. That government, with its separation of powers and checks and balances, is remarkably well suited to the pluralist model of democracy. Simple majority rule, which lies at the heart of the majoritarian model, was precisely what the framers wanted to avoid.

The framers also wanted a government that would balance the powers of the national government and those of the states. The exact balance was a touchy issue, skirted by the delegates at the Constitutional Convention. Some seventy years later, a civil war was fought over that balance of power. That war and countless political battles before and since have demonstrated that the national government dominates the state governments in our political system. In Chapter 4, we will look at how a loose confederation of states has evolved into a "more perfect Union."

Key Terms

continental congress
Declaration of
  Independence
social contract theory
republic
confederation
sovereignty
Articles of
  Confederation
Shays' Rebellion
Virginia Plan
legislative branch
executive branch
judicial branch
New Jersey Plan
Great Compromise
electoral college
republicanism

federalism
unitary government
separation of powers
checks and balances
bicameral
enumerated powers
necessary and proper
  clause
elastic clause
implied powers
judicial review
supremacy clause
Bill of Rights
proposal
ratification
extraordinary
  majorities
progressive taxation

Selected Readings

Beard, Charles A. *Economic Interpretation of the Constitution of the United States.* New York: Macmillan, 1913. Beard argues that the framers' economic self-interest was the motivating force behind the Constitution.

Becker, Carl. *The Declaration of Independence: A Study in the History of Political Ideas.* New York: Alfred A. Knopf, 1942. A classic study of the theory and politics of the Declaration of Independence.

Bowen, Catherine Drinker. *Miracle at Philadelphia.* Boston: Atlantic-Little, Brown, 1966. An absorbing, well-written account of the events surrounding the Constitutional Convention.

Emery, Fred. *Watergate: The Corruption of American Politics and the Fall of Richard Nixon.* New York: Times Books, 1994. A compelling narrative of the greatest political scandal in our times.

Kammen, Michael. *A Machine That Would Go of*

Itself: The Constitution in American Culture. New York: Alfred A. Knopf, 1986. A remarkable examination of the Constitution's cultural influence. The author argues that Americans' reverence for the Constitution is inconsistent with their ignorance of its content and meaning.

Kurland, Philip B., and Ralph Lerner, eds. *The Founders' Constitution* (5 vols.) Chicago: University of Chicago Press, 1987. A thorough collection of primary documents designed to explain the Constitution, it is organized around the structure of the Constitution from preamble through the Twelfth Amendment.

McDonald, Forrest. *Novus Ordo Seclorum: The Intellectual Origins of the Constitution.* Lawrence: University Press of Kansas, 1985. An authoritative examination of the intellectual ferment surrounding the birth of the U.S. Constitution.

Norton, Mary Beth. *Liberty's Daughters.* Boston: Little Brown, 1980. This book examines the role of women before, during, and after the American Revolution. Norton argues that the Revolution transformed gender roles and set women on a course toward equality.

Rakove, Jack N. *The Beginnings of National Politics: An Interpretive History of the Continental Congress.* New York: Alfred A. Knopf, 1979. A history of the Continental Congress and the difficulties of governing under the Articles of Confederation.

Storing, Herbert J. *What the Anti-Federalists Were For.* Chicago: University of Chicago Press, 1981. An analysis of the arguments against the Constitution.

Wood, Gordon S. *The Creation of the American Republic, 1776–1787.* Chapel Hill: University of North Carolina Press, 1969. A penetrating study of political thought in the early period of the new republic.

———. *The Radicalism of the American Revolution.* New York: Knopf, 1992. A novel reexamination arguing that the revolution was not a conservative defense of American rights but a radical revolution that produced a free and democratic society far beyond that envisioned by the founders.

STEVE OLIGMUELLER, NINETEEN and a member of the Highmore High School class of 1986, had returned home to South Dakota for the summer. At night, he would get together with old friends and swap stories about freshman year at college. They would meet at The Stable, a local bar, to sit, talk, listen to music, and have a couple of beers. That spring of 1987, South Dakota was one of four states that still allowed people younger than twenty-one to drink beer. Soon, however, the cost of permitting nineteen-year-olds to drink beer would go up drastically—not just for Steve and his friends but for all the taxpayers of South Dakota. The state stood to lose nearly $10 million in federal highway funds unless it raised its minimum drinking age to twenty-one.

Just three years earlier, twenty-nine states and the District of Columbia allowed people younger than twenty-one to purchase and consume some forms of alcoholic beverages. In 1984, however, an action taken in Washington, D.C., marked the beginning of the end of legalized drinking for those younger than twenty-one. What happened? Did Congress establish a national minimum drinking age? No, at least not directly. Congress simply added a provision to a highway bill. Under that provision, states would lose 5 percent of their federal highway funds in 1986 and 10 percent every year thereafter if they allowed the purchase or consumption of alcohol by those younger than twenty-one. States would have to change their own laws or risk losing federal funds. This was a roundabout method to achieve a national objective. If the national government wanted to set twenty-one as a national drinking age, why not act directly and pass legislation to do so?

The simplest answer has to do with the federal system of government. The Constitution divides power between the national and state governments. With only one sobering exception (Prohibition under the Eighteenth Amendment), regulating liquor sales and setting minimum drinking ages had always been the responsibilities of state governments. But over the years, the national government has found ways to extend its influence into areas well beyond those originally defined in the Constitution.

How did the national government become concerned about the drinking age? Mothers Against Drunk Driving (MADD) and other interest groups had fought hard to increase public awareness of the dangers of driving drunk, and they argued that a uniform drinking age of twenty-one would

Wall of Shame

The group Mothers Against Drunk Driving (MADD) campaigns hard to get drunk drivers off the road. It supports national legislation and takes aim at state legislatures, urging tougher sanctions for driving under the influence. Here, relatives of victims of drunk drivers examine MADD's "victim board," displayed on the west steps of the U.S. Capitol to mark MADD's tenth anniversary.

reduce highway fatalities. The National Transportation Safety Board estimated that 1,250 lives could be saved each year by raising the drinking age. But campaigning for change on a state-by-state basis would be slow and might even be dangerous. So long as some states allowed teenagers to drink, young people would be able to drive across state lines in order to drink legally. The borders between states would become bloody borders, strewn with victims of teenage drinking and driving.

Supporters of the legislation believed that the national government's responsibility to maintain order justified intervention. The lives and safety of people were at stake. Opponents of the plan argued that it constituted age discrimination and infringed on states' rights. They claimed the act was an unwarranted extension of national power, that it limited the freedom of the states and of their citizens.

Despite the opposition, the bill passed handily and went to President Ronald Reagan for signing. Reagan had campaigned on a pledge to reduce the size and scope of the national government, and he strongly opposed replacing state standards with national ones. Where would he come out on this issue, which pitted order against freedom and national standards against state standards? Early on, he opposed the bill; later, he changed his position. At the signing ceremony, he said, "This problem is bigger than the individual states. It's a grave national problem and it touches all our lives. With the problem so clear cut and the proven solution at hand we have no misgiving about this judicious use of federal power. I'm convinced that it will help persuade state legislators to act in the national interest."[1]

Several states took the matter to court, hoping to have the provision declared unconstitutional under the Tenth and the Twenty-first Amendments. In June 1987, the Supreme Court reached a decision in *South Dakota* v. *Dole.* The justices conceded that direct congressional control of the drinking age in the states would be unconstitutional. Nevertheless, the Constitution does not bar the *indirect* achievement of such objectives. The seven-justice majority argued that far from being an infringement on states' rights, the law was a "relatively mild encouragement to the states to enact higher minimum drinking ages than they otherwise would choose." After all, Chief Justice William Rehnquist wrote, the goal of reducing drunk driving was "directly related to one of the main purposes for which highway funds are expended: safe interstate travel."[2] For Steve Oligmueller, the decision meant that he would have to wait two years for his next legal long neck.

Rehnquist's words show how much the role of the national government has changed since the Constitution was adopted. In the early part of the nineteenth century, chief executives routinely vetoed bills authorizing roads, canals, and other interstate improvements. They believed such projects exceeded the constitutional authority of the national government. Eventually, the national government used its authority over interstate commerce to justify a role in building roads. Witness the forty-three thousand-mile interstate highway system. In 1994, the national government planned to spend nearly $20 billion on cost-sharing projects with the states for road research, planning, and construction.[3]

The Highway Act of 1984 shows how national and state governments can interact. Congress did not challenge the constitutional power of the states to regulate the minimum drinking age (under the Twenty-first Amendment), but it used its own powers to tax and spend (see Article I, Section 8, clause 1) to encourage the states to implement a national standard. Lawmakers in Washington, D.C., believed that few states would pass up highway funds to retain power, and they were right.

An important element of federalism was at work here: the respective sovereignty of national and state governments. (Sovereignty is the quality of being supreme in power or authority.) Congress acknowledged the sovereignty of the states by not legislating a national drinking age. And the states were willing to barter their sovereignty in exchange for needed revenues. As long as this remains true, there are few areas where national power cannot reach.

Local Cops, National Cops

Local, state, and national governments share certain powers, such as law enforcement. Houston police officers enforce local criminal laws in a continuing campaign against illegal drugs (left). A SWAT team from the Federal Bureau of Investigation, the principal investigative arm of the national government, arrives to quiet a riot at a federal penitentiary in Atlanta (right).

Sovereignty also affects political leadership. A governor may not be the political equal of a president, but a governor and a president represent different sovereignties. Consequently, presidents rarely command governors; they negotiate, even plead. For example, President John F. Kennedy negotiated repeatedly—and it turned out, hopelessly—with Mississippi governor Ross Barnett to admit James Meredith as the first black student at the University of Mississippi. Kennedy lacked the power to order Barnett to admit Meredith. In the end, the U.S. Justice Department enforced a federal court order to secure Meredith's admission. Kennedy had to call out the National Guard to quell the rioting that followed.[4]

In this chapter, we examine American federalism in theory and in practice. Is the division of power between nation and states a matter of constitutional principle or practical politics? How does the balance of power between nation and states relate to the conflicts between freedom and order and between freedom and equality? Does federalism reflect the pluralist or the majoritarian model of democracy?

THEORIES OF FEDERALISM

The delegates who met in Philadelphia in 1787 were supposed to repair weaknesses in the Articles of Confederation. Instead, they tackled the problem of making one nation out of thirteen independent states by doing something much more radical. They wrote a new constitution and invented a new political form—federal government—that combined features of a confederacy with features of unitary government (see Chapter 3). Under the principle of **federalism,** two or more governments would exercise power and authority over the same people and the same territory (Table 4.1 provides instances of federalism in the Constitution). For example, the governments of the United States and Pennsylvania would share certain powers (the power to tax, for instance), while other powers would belong exclusively to one or the other. As James Madison wrote in *Federalist No. 10,* "The federal Constitution forms a happy combination . . . the great and aggregate interests being referred to the national, and the local and particular to state governments." So the power to coin money belongs to the national government; the power to grant divorces remains a state prerogative. By contrast, authority over the state militia may sometimes belong to the national government and sometimes to the state government. The history of American federalism reveals that it has not always been easy to draw a line between what is "great and aggregate" and what is "local and particular."*

Nevertheless, federalism offered a solution to the problem of diversity in America. Without a federal form of government, citizens feared they would be ruled by majorities from different regions with different interests and values. Federalism also provided a new political model. A leading scholar of federalism estimates that 40 percent of the world's population

---

* *The everyday phrase Americans use to refer to their central government—federal government— muddies the waters even more. Technically speaking, we have a federal system of government that includes both national and state governments. To avoid confusion from here on, we use the term* national government *rather than* federal government *when we are talking about the central government.*

TABLE 4.1	■ **Examples of Federalism in the U.S. Constitution**

These examples illustrate some ways in which the Constitution provides guarantees to limits on the states.

Guarantees to the States	**Limits on the States**
	1. General
Powers not delegated to the U.S. by the Constitution, or prohibited byit to the states, are reserved to the states (Amend. X)	States cannot enter into treaties, alliances, or confederations (Art. I, Sec. 10)
No division or consolidation of states without state legislative consent (Art. IV, Sec. 2)	No separate coinage (Art. I, Sec. 10)
	Constitution, all laws and treaties made under it, to be the supreme law of the land, binding every state (Art. VI)
	2. Military
Power to maintain and appoint militia officers (Art. I, Sec. 8; Amend. II)	No maintenance of standing military forces in peacetime without congressional consent (Art. I, Sec. 10)
	No levying of duties on vessels of other states (Art. I, Sec. 10)
	3. Commerce, Money, and Taxation
Equal apportionment of direct federal taxes (Art. I, Sec. 2, 9)	No legal tender other than gold or silver (Art. I, Sec. 10)
No preferential treatment for ports of one state (Art. I, Sec. 9)	
	4. Justice
Federal criminal trials to be held in state where crime was committed (Art. III, Sec. 2)	No bills of attainder or ex post facto laws (Art. I, Sec. 10)
Extradition for crimes (Art. IV, Sec. 2)	No denial of life, liberty, or property without due process of law (Amend. XIV)
	5. Representation: Congress
Members of House of Representatives chosen by voters (Art. I, Sec. 2)	Representatives must be 25 years old and U.S. citizens for seven years (Art. I, Sec. 2)
At time of elections, senators and representatives must be inhabitants of the states from which they are elected (Art. I, Sec. 2, 3)	Senators must be 30 years old and U.S. citizens for nine years (Art. I, Sec. 4)
	Congress may make or alter regulations as to the times, places, and manner of holding elections for senators and representatives (Art. I, Sec. 4)
	Representation: President
To be selected by the electors of the several states, with each allotted a number of electors equal to the total number of senators and representatives (Art. II, Sec. 1)	Congress may determine the time of choosing electors and a uniform day on which they shall cast their votes (Art. II, Sec. 1)
Each state shall have one vote if the presidential election is decided in the House of Representatives (Art. II, Sec. 1)	
	6. Amendments to the Constitution
Amendments must be ratified by three-fourths of the states (Art. V)	
Amendments can be proposed by two-thirds of the states (Art. V)	
	7. Voting
	Cannot be denied or abridged on grounds of race, color, or previous condition of servitude (Amend. XV, Sec. 1)
	Cannot be denied or abridged on account of sex (Amend. XIX, Sec. 1)
	8. Foreign Affairs
Treaties must be ratified by two-thirds of the Senate (Art. II, Sec. 2)	Treaties binding on states are the supreme law of the land (Art. VI)

Excerpted from Thomas Dye, American Federalism: Competition Among Governments *(Lexington, Mass.: Lexington Books, 1990), pp. 9–11. Reprinted by permission of Lexington Books, an imprint of Macmillan Publishing Company from* American Federalism: Competition Among Governments *by Thomas Dye. Copyright © 1990 by Lexington Books.*

live under a formal federal constitution, while another 30 percent live in polities that apply federal principles or practices without formal constitutional acknowledgment.[5] Although federalism offers an approach that unifies diverse people as nations, it also retains the elements that can lead to national disunity. Canada, the Commonwealth of Independent States, and the Russian Federation are examples of federal systems coping with the possibility of dissolution of their constituent parts (see Compared with What? 4.1)

REPRESENTATIONS OF AMERICAN FEDERALISM

The history of American federalism is full of attempts to capture its true meaning in an adjective or metaphor. By one recent reckoning, scholars have generated nearly five hundred ways to describe federalism.[6] Let us concentrate on two such representations: dual federalism and cooperative federalism.

Dual Federalism

The expression **dual federalism** sums up a theory about the proper relationship between the national government and the states. The theory has four essential parts. First, the national government rules by enumerated powers only. Second, the national government has a limited set of constitutional purposes. Third, each government unit—nation and state—is sovereign within its sphere. And fourth, the relationship between nation and states is best characterized by tension rather than cooperation.[7]

Dual federalism portrays the states as powerful components of the federal system—in some ways, the equals of the national government. Under dual federalism, the functions and responsibilities of the national and state governments are theoretically different and practically separate from each other. Dual federalism sees the Constitution as a compact among sovereign states. Of primary importance in dual federalism are **states' rights,** a concept that reserves to the states all rights not specifically conferred on the national government by the Constitution. According to the theory of dual federalism, a rigid wall separates nation and states. After all, if the states created the nation, by implication they can set limits on the activities of the national government. Proponents of states' rights believe that the powers of the national government should be interpreted narrowly. Claims of states' rights often come from opponents of a given national government policy. Their argument is that the Constitution has not delegated to the national government the power to make such policy and that the power thus remains in the states or the people. They insist that despite the elastic clause, which gives Congress the **implied powers** needed to execute its enumerated powers (see Chapter 3), the activities of Congress should be confined to the enumerated powers only. And they support their view by quoting the Tenth Amendment: "The powers not delegated to the United States by the Constitution, nor prohibited by it to the States, are reserved to the States respectively, or to the people."

Political scientists use a metaphor to describe dual federalism. They call it *layer-cake federalism.* The powers and functions of national and state

Fragmenting Federations: Canada, the Commonwealth of Independent States, and the Russian Federation

Federalism tolerates the centrifugal forces (such as different languages and religions) that can sunder a nation and provides the centripetal forces that bind it (such as the powers to raise an army and control a national economy). But federalism is no guarantee that the forces of unity will always overcome the forces of disunity. Consider several recent examples.

Canada is a federation of ten provinces. But the Canadian province of Quebec is different. Eighty percent of its population is French speaking; almost half speak little or no English. (The vast majority of Canadians outside Quebec speak only English.) Quebec has its own holidays, music videos, its own literature. By law, all signs must be in French. English is barely tolerated.

For decades, Canadians have struggled with the challenge of assimilating and differentiating Quebec. When Canada drafted a new constitution in 1982, Quebec refused to sign it. Quebecers conditioned their union with the other provinces on a constitutional amendment that would recognize Quebec as a "distinct society" within the country. The amendment had to be approved by all ten provinces. It failed when two provinces refused to ratify the Quebec agreement by the June 1990 deadline.

In October 1992, Canadians rejected another constitutional solution to the Quebec question. The reforms aimed at recognizing Quebec's special status, electing the national senate, and providing self-government for native peoples. Québecois rejected the reforms, because they did not go far enough; other provinces rejected the reforms, because they went too far. So the future of Canada, and the role of Quebec, remains in limbo. Or, as one

wit remarked, "Americans look back to their Civil War. Canadians look forward to theirs."*

The Union of Soviet Socialist Republics (USSR) was a federation of fifteen republics. In 1991, after five years of openness and political and social reform, the Soviet people had a chance to vote on a complex issue: "Do you consider it necessary to preserve the Union of Soviet Socialist Republics as a renewed federation of equal sovereign republics in which the rights and freedoms of the people of any nationality will be fully guaranteed?"

More than 80 percent of the nation's 178 million eligible voters took part; 78 percent of those who voted supported continued union. Nevertheless, disunion was just around the corner. Eight republics refused to participate in the referendum; they had already resolved to exercise greater independence from Moscow. And the Baltic republics (Estonia, Latvia, and Lithuania) had previously vowed to separate from the federation.

A failed coup in August 1991 was the final blow to the old federation. Under the leadership of Russian President Boris Yeltsin, a loose confederation of eleven republics called the *Commonwealth of Independent States* (CIS) replaced the USSR. But the CIS lacked any central power to yoke the republics for common objectives.

Russia—the largest of the fifteen republics of the former USSR—is comprised of more than seventy autonomous republics and regions, and many are trying to grab as much sovereignty as they can, while leaders in Moscow cope with economic transition and political squabbling. With sixty-seven ethnic groups, there is no shortage of disagreement.†
The new Russian constitution, approved by voters in December 1993, offered the constit-

Quebec Demonstration, 1990

uent republics some symbolic privileges, such as flags and emblems, under the banner of federalism but no significant independent power. One regional leader, the mayor of Kazan in Tatarastan, voiced his concern. "We want a confederation of equals," he declared. "In general, we like the American model of federalism." This Tatar leader was likely referring to an early federalism model, which is hardly a good match for today's American federalism.

Federalism in a diverse nation requires a delicate balance to sustain national cohesion and protect regional differences. Relaxing the cohesive forces may encourage splintering. Yet, attempts to extinguish regional differ-

ences may prompt revolution. Our own civil war remains a vivid reminder of the powerful forces contained by federalism. The Soviet Union's dissolution, Canada's fragile cohesion, and Russia's risk of rupture illustrate the continuing power of ethnic and regional differences and the allure of federalism as a way to assure continued union.

[†] *Denis J. B. Shaw, "Geographic and Historical Observations on the Future of a Federal Russia,"* Post-Soviet Geography *34 (October 1993) pp. 530–540.*

[§] *Steven Erlanger, "Heirs of the Golden Horde Reclaim a Tatar Culture,"* New York Times, *Aug. 13, 1993, p. 3.*

[*] *Robert C. Vipond, "Seeing Canada Through the Referendum: Still a House Divided,"* Publius 23 *(Summer 1993), p. 39.*

governments are separate—as separate as the layers of a cake (see Figure 4.1). Each government is supreme in its own layer, its own sphere of action; the two layers are distinct; and the dimensions of each layer are fixed by the Constitution.

Dual federalism—the theory that underlies the layer-cake metaphor—has been challenged on historical and other grounds. Some critics argue that if the national government is really a creation of the states, it is a creation of only thirteen states—those that ratified the Constitution. The other thirty-seven states were admitted after the national government came into being and were created by that government out of land it had acquired. Another challenge has to do with the ratification process. Remember, the original thirteen states ratified the Constitution in special conventions, not in state legislatures. Ratification, then, was an act of the *people,* not the *states.* Moreover, the preamble to the Constitution begins "We the People of the United States . . . ," not "We the States. . . ." The question of just where the people fit into the federal system is not handled well by dual federalism.

The concept of dual federalism—two levels of government operating on different tracks, each in control of its own activities—suited the American experience from 1789 to 1933. The demands of the Great Depression gave birth to a new federal concept: cooperative federalism.

Cooperative Federalism

Cooperative federalism, a phrase coined in the 1930s, embraces a different theory of the relationship between national and state governments. It acknowledges the increasing overlap in state and national functions and rejects the idea of separate spheres, or layers, for the states and the national government. Cooperative federalism includes three elements. First, national and state agencies typically undertake government functions jointly rather than exclusively. Second, nation and states routinely share power. And third, power is not concentrated at any government level or in any agency; the fragmentation of responsibilities gives people and groups access to many centers of influence.

The bakery metaphor used to describe this type of federalism is a *marble cake.* The national and state governments do not act in separate spheres; they are intermingled in vertical and diagonal strands and swirls. Their functions are mixed in the American federal system. Critical to cooperative federalism is an expansive view of the Constitution's supremacy clause (Article VI), which specifically subordinates state law to national law and charges every judge with disregarding state laws that are inconsistent with the Constitution, national laws, and treaties.

In contrast to dual federalism, cooperative federalism blurs the distinction between national and state powers. Some scholars argue that the layer-cake metaphor has never accurately described the American political structure.[8] National and state governments have many common objectives and have often cooperated to achieve them. In the nineteenth century, for example, cooperation—not separation—made it possible to develop transportation systems and to establish land-grant colleges. The layer cake might be a good model of what dual federalists *think* the relationship between national and state governments should be, but it does not square with the facts of recent American history.

FIGURE **4.1**   ■ **Metaphors for Federalism**

The two views of federalism can be represented graphically.

Dual Federalism:
The Layer-Cake Metaphor

Citizens cutting into the political system will find clear differences between state and national powers, functions, and responsibilities.

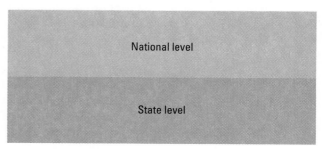

Cooperative Federalism:
The Marble-Cake Metaphor

Citizens cutting into the political system at any point will find national and state powers, functions, and responsibilities mixed and mingled.

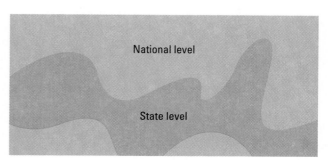

A critical difference between the theories of dual and cooperative federalism is the way they interpret two sections of the Constitution that set out the terms of the relationship between the national and state governments. Article I, Section 8, lists the enumerated powers of the Congress, then concludes with the **elastic clause,** which gives Congress the power to "make all Laws which shall be necessary and proper for carrying into Execution the foregoing Powers." The Tenth Amendment reserves to the states or the people powers not assigned to the national government or denied to the states by the Constitution. Dual federalism postulates an inflexible elastic clause and a capacious Tenth Amendment. Cooperative federalism postulates suppleness in the elastic clause and confines the Tenth Amendment to a self-evident, obvious truth. The widespread acceptance of cooperative federalism has contributed to an increasing centralization of power in the national government, often at the expense of the states.

In their efforts to limit the scope of the national government, conservatives have given much credence to the layer-cake metaphor. In contrast, liberals, believing that one function of the national government is to bring about equality, have argued that the marble-cake metaphor is more accurate.

Conservatives continue to argue that different states have different problems and resources and that returning control to state governments would give more play to diversity. States would be free to experiment with alternative ways to meet their problems. States would compete with one another. And people would be free to choose the state government they preferred by simply voting with their feet—moving to another state.

Conservatives also continue to maintain that the national government is too remote, too tied to special interests, and not responsive to the public at large. The national government overregulates, they add, and tries to promote too much uniformity. Moreover, the size and complexity of the federal system lead to waste and inefficiency. States, on the other hand, are closer to the people and better able to respond to specific local needs. If state governments were revitalized, individuals might believe that they could have a greater influence on decision making. The quality of political participation would improve. Furthermore, conservatives believe that shifting power to the states would help them achieve other parts of their political agenda. States would work harder to keep taxes down, they would not be willing to spend a lot of money on social welfare programs, and they would be less likely to pass stiff laws regulating businesses.

What conservatives hope for liberals fear. They remember that the states' rights model allowed extreme political and social inequalities and that it supported racism. Blacks and city dwellers were often left virtually unrepresented by white state legislators who disproportionately served rural interests. Liberals believe the states remain unwilling or unable to protect the rights or provide for the needs of their citizens, whether those citizens are consumers seeking protection from business interests, defendants requiring guarantees of due process of law, or poor people seeking a minimum standard of living.

These ideological conceptions of federalism reveal a simple truth. Federalism is not something written or implied in the Constitution; the Constitution is only the starting point in the debate. As one scholar observed, "To understand the condition of federalism, one needs to comprehend the functioning of the whole polity."[9]

THE DYNAMICS OF FEDERALISM

Although the Constitution establishes a kind of federalism, the actual balance of power between nation and states has always been more a matter of politics than of formal theory. A discussion of federalism, then, must do more than simply list the powers that the Constitution assigns the levels of government. The balance of power has shifted substantially since President Madison agonized over the proper role the national government should play in funding roads. Today, that government has assumed functions never dreamed of in the nineteenth century.

Why has power shifted so dramatically from the states to the national government? The answer lies in historical circumstances, not debates over constitutional theory. By far the greatest test of states' rights arose when several southern states attempted to secede from the union. The threat of secession challenged the supremacy of the national government, a supremacy that Northern armies reestablished militarily in the nation's greatest bloodbath, the Civil War. But the Civil War by no means settled all the questions about relations between governments in the United States. Many more remained to be answered, and new issues keep cropping up.

Some changes in the balance of power were the product of constitutional amendments. Several amendments have had an enormous effect, either direct or indirect, on the shape of the federal system. For example, the due process and equal protection clauses of the Fourteenth Amendment

(1868) limited states' rights, as did the income tax mandated by the Sixteenth Amendment (1913) and the Seventeenth Amendment's provision for the direct election of senators (1913).

Most of the national government's power has come to it through legislation and judicial interpretation. But political coercion has also been a factor. As Al Capone, the notorious Chicago gangster of the Prohibition era, once observed, "You can get much further with a kind word and a gun than you can with a kind word alone." The national government has used force of arms only once against the states (in the Civil War). But the states, like Capone's associates, recognize the ultimate threat of coercion.

The national government has relied primarily on two distinct legislative approaches to expand its power. Some are incentives to win state cooperation; others are sanctions (that is, mechanisms of social or economic control) designed to pinch in an effort to secure cooperation. Let us examine these tools of political change.

Legislation and the Elastic Clause

The elastic clause of the Constitution gives Congress the power to make all laws that are "necessary and proper" to carry out its responsibilities. By using this power in combination with its enumerated powers, Congress has been able to increase the scope of the national government tremendously during the last two centuries. The greatest change has come about in times of crisis and national emergency—the Civil War, the Great Depression, the world wars. The role of the national government has also grown as it has responded to needs and demands that state and local governments were unwilling or unable to meet.

Legislation is one prod the national government has used to achieve goals at the state level. The Voting Rights Act of 1965 is a good example. Section 2 of Article I of the Constitution gives the states the power to specify qualifications for voting. But the Fifteenth Amendment (1870) provides that no person shall be denied the right to vote "on account of race, color, or previous condition of servitude." Before the Voting Rights Act, states could not specifically deny blacks the right to vote, but they could require that voters pass literacy tests or pay poll taxes, requirements that virtually disenfranchised blacks in many states. The Voting Rights Act was designed to correct this political inequality (see Chapter 16).

The act gives the national government the power to decide whether individuals are qualified to vote and requires that qualified individuals be allowed to vote in all elections—including primaries and national, state, and local elections. If denials of voting rights seem to be widespread, the act authorizes the appointment of national voting examiners, who will examine and register voters for *all* elections. By replacing state election officials, the act intrudes well within the political sovereignty of the states. The constitutional authority for the act rests on the second section of the Fifteenth Amendment, which gives Congress the power to enforce the amendment through "appropriate legislation."

Judicial Interpretation

The Voting Rights Act was not a unanimous hit. Its critics used the language of dual federalism to insist that the Constitution gives the states the power to determine voter qualifications. Its supporters claimed that the

Fifteenth Amendment guarantee of voting rights takes precedence over states' rights and gives the national government new responsibilities.

The conflict was ultimately resolved by the Supreme Court, the arbiter of the federal system. The Court settles disputes over the powers of the national and state governments by deciding whether actions of the national or state governments are unconstitutional (see Chapter 14). In the nineteenth and early twentieth centuries, the Supreme Court often decided in favor of the states; since 1937, however, it has almost always supported the national government in contests involving the balance of power between nation and states.

In addition to legislation, the growth of national power has been advanced by the Supreme Court's interpretation of the Constitution's **commerce clause.** The third clause of Article I, Section 8, states that "Congress shall have Power . . . To regulate Commerce . . . among the several States. . . ." In early Court decisions, Chief Justice John Marshall (1801–1835) interpreted the word *commerce* broadly to include virtually every form of commercial activity. The clause's grant of the power to regulate commerce to the national government substantially withdrew that power from the states. Later decisions by the Court attempted to restrict national power over commerce, but events such as the Great Depression necessitated its enlargement. One scholar has gone so far as to charge that the justices have toyed with the commerce clause, treating it like a shuttlecock volleyed back and forth by changing majorities.[10] Today, the only limit on the exercise of the commerce power is Congress itself. A future Supreme Court majority may offer yet another view.

During Chief Justice Earl Warren's tenure (1953–1969), the Court used the Fourteenth Amendment to make the states subject to various provisions of the Bill of Rights, shifting power from the states to the national government. Court decisions seriously restricted the states' freedom to decide what constitutes due process of law within their jurisdictions. In the landmark *Miranda* decision, for example, the Court ordered that individuals apprehended by the police must be informed of their constitutional rights and that the arresting officer must preserve those rights.[11] Through the Supreme Court, the national government set minimum standards for due process in criminal cases, standards that the states have to meet. The standards provide equality before the law for individuals who are suspected of crimes, but critics argue that they hamper state governments in trying to maintain order.

A series of Supreme Court decisions concerning reapportionment—redrawing the boundaries of electoral districts—also eroded the power of the states in the early 1960s.[12] Until that time, states had set the boundaries of voting districts, but some had failed to adjust those boundaries to reflect shifts in population. As a result, small numbers of rural voters in certain areas were able to elect as many representatives as were large numbers of urban voters. The Court established a new standard of one person, one vote, which meant that voting districts must be apportioned on the basis of population to satisfy the equal protection clause of the Fourteenth Amendment. The new standard forced the states to redraw their districts and reapportion their legislatures.

In the due process and reapportionment cases, the Supreme Court was protecting individual rights and in the process championed political equality. But the Supreme Court is also part of the national government. When it defends the rights of an individual against a state, it also substitutes a national standard for the state standard that previously governed that relationship.

Grants-in-Aid

Since the 1960s, Washington's use of financial incentives has rivaled its use of legislation and judicial interpretation as a means of shaping relations with state governments. And state and local governments have increasingly looked to Washington for money. The principal method the national government uses to make money available to the states is grants-in-aid.

A **grant-in-aid** is money paid by one level of government to another level of government, to be spent for a specific purpose. Most grants-in-aid come with standards or requirements prescribed by Congress. Many are awarded on a matching basis; that is, a recipient must make some contribution of its own, which is then matched by the national government. Grants-in-aid take two general forms: categorical grants and block grants.

Categorical grants target specific purposes, and restrictions on their use typically leave the recipient government relatively little discretion. Recipients today include state governments, local governments, and public and private nonprofit organizations. There are two kinds of categorical grants: formula grants and project grants. As their name implies, **formula grants** are distributed according to a particular formula, which specifies who is eligible for the grant and how much each eligible applicant will receive. The formulas used to distribute grant money vary from one grant to another. They may weigh such factors as state per capita income, number of school-age children, urban population, and number of families below the poverty line. In 1991, 159 of the 543 categorical grants offered by the national government were formula grants. The remaining 384 grants were **project grants**—grants awarded on the basis of competitive applications.[13] Comparing grants since 1989 reveals a shift in policy emphasis. New grants have focused on health (substance abuse and HIV-AIDS programs), natural resources and the environment (radon, asbestos, and toxic pollution), and education, training, and employment (for the disabled, the homeless, and the aged).

In contrast to categorical grants, Congress awards **block grants** for broad, general purposes. They allow recipient governments considerable freedom to decide how to allocate money to individual programs. While a categorical grant promotes a specific activity—say, ethnic heritage studies—a block grant might be earmarked only for elementary, secondary, and vocational education. The state or local government receiving the block grant would then choose the specific educational programs to fund with it. The recipient might use some money to support ethnic heritage studies and some to fund consumer education programs. Or the recipient might choose to put all the money into consumer education programs and spend nothing on ethnic heritage studies. Figure 4.2 lists all block grants in effect from 1966 to 1991. Note that in 1966, there was only one block grant; by 1991, there were fourteen. Community development and community services block grants have been funded since 1973. Day-care assistance in

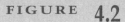

FIGURE 4.2   ■ **Block Grants in Effect, 1966–1991**

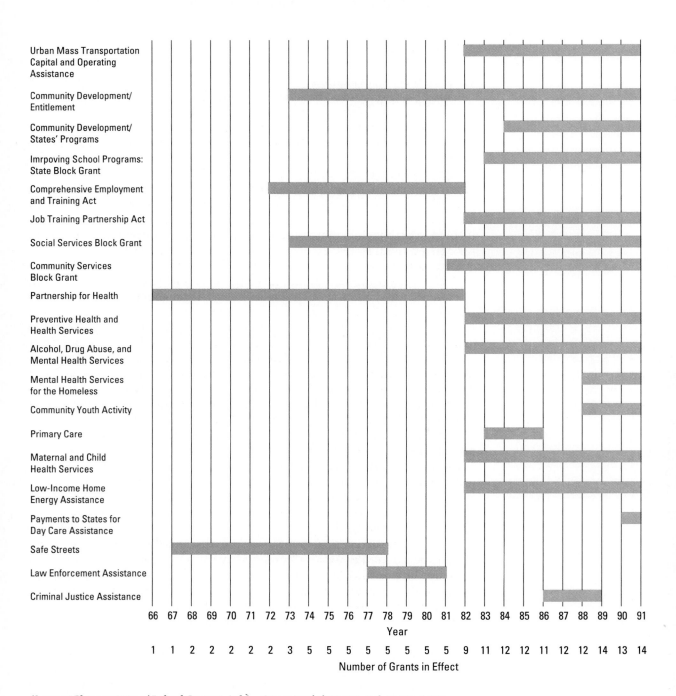

(Source: "Characteristics of Federal Grant-in-Aid   Grants Funded FY 1991. *Pub M–182. ACIR*
Programs to State and Local Governments,"   *Washington, D.C., March 1992, p. 4.)*

the form of a block grant to states has been funded only since 1990. Block grants represent about 9 percent of all national government outlays to the states.

Grants-in-aid are a method of redistributing income. Money is collected by the national government from the taxpayers of all fifty states, then allocated to other citizens, supposedly for worthwhile social purposes. Many grants have worked to reduce gross inequalities among states and their residents. But the formulas used to redistribute the income are not impartial; they are highly political, established through a process of congressional horse trading.

The dollar amount of national government grants to state and local government increased more than threefold from 1966 to 1991, from $37 billion to $119 billion (in 1982 dollars). Significant shifts in the purposes of such grants occurred in the same twenty-five-year period.[14] Figure 4.3 illustrates the distribution of grants to state and local government by policy area. Health was far more dominant in 1990 than it was in 1965; the opposite is true for transportation policy.

Whatever its form or purpose, grant money comes with strings attached. Some strings are there to ensure that the money is used for the purpose for which it was given; other regulations are designed to evaluate how well the grant is working. To this end, the national government may stipulate that recipients follow certain procedures. The national government may also attach restrictions designed to achieve some broad national goal not always closely related to the specific purpose of the grant. For example, as noted earlier, the Highway Act of 1984 reduced the funds available to states that allowed people younger than twenty-one to drink. Other grants prohibit discrimination in the activities they fund. States have been more than willing to accept the limitations. By 1988, for example, every state in the nation had approved legislation setting twenty-one as the minimum drinking age. The lure of financial aid has proved a powerful incentive for states to relinquish the freedom to set their own standards and to accept those set by the national government. In short, the growth in categorical grants has clearly increased national power and decreased state power.

| THE DEVELOPING CONCEPT OF FEDERALISM | A student of federalism once remarked that "each generation faced with new problems has had to work out its own version of federalism." Succeeding generations have used judicial and congressional power in varying degrees to shift the balance of power back and forth between national and state governments. |

McCulloch v. *Maryland*

Early in the nineteenth century, the nationalist interpretation of federalism prevailed over states' rights. In 1819, under Chief Justice John Marshall, the Supreme Court expanded the role of the national government in *McCulloch* v. *Maryland.* The Court was asked to decide whether Congress had the power to establish a national bank and, if so, whether states had the power to tax that bank. In a unanimous opinion written by

National government grants to states and localities vary substantially. In 1960, transportation programs accounted for the biggest percentage of national grants. In 1980, education and training took the biggest slice. In 1993, health programs accounted for more than one-third of all grants to state and local government. By 1995, grants for health programs may reach 45 percent of all national government spending to state and local governments.

(*Source:* Budget of the United States Government, FY 1994 *(Washington, D.C.: 1993), p. 79.)*

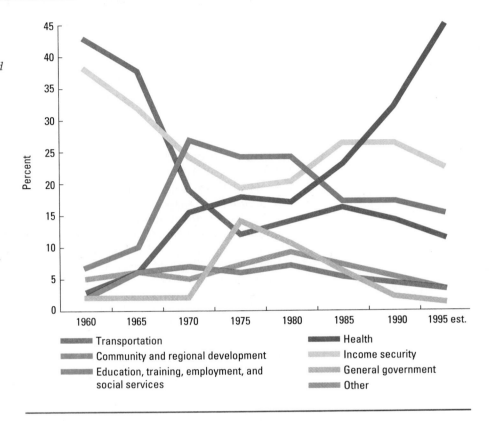

Transportation

Community and regional development

Education, training, employment, and social services

Health

Income security

General government

Other

Marshall, the Court conceded that Congress had only the powers conferred on it by the Constitution, which nowhere mentioned banks. However, Article I granted Congress the authority to enact all laws "necessary and proper" to the execution of Congress's enumerated powers. Marshall adopted a broad interpretation of this elastic clause: "Let the end be legitimate, let it be within the scope of the constitution, and all means which are appropriate, which are plainly adapted to that end, which are not prohibited, but consistent with the letter and spirit of the constitution, are constitutional."

The Court clearly agreed that Congress had the power to charter a bank. But did the states—in this case, Maryland—have the power to tax the bank? Arguing that "the power to tax is the power to destroy," Marshall insisted that states could not tax the national government, because the powers of the national government came not from the states but from the people. Marshall was embracing cooperative federalism, which sees a direct relationship between the people and the national government, with no need for the states to act as intermediaries. To assume that states had the power to tax the national government would be to give them supremacy over the national government. In that case, Marshall wrote, "The declaration that the constitution, and the laws made in pursuance thereof, shall be the supreme law of the land is an empty and unmeaning declamation."[15] The framers of the Constitution did not intend to create a meaningless document, he reasoned. Therefore, they must have meant to give the national government all the powers necessary to carry out its assigned functions, even if those powers are only implied.

States' Rights and Dual Federalism

Roger B. Taney became chief justice in 1836, and during his tenure (1836–1864) the balance of power began to shift back toward the states. The Taney Court imposed firm limits on the powers of the national government. As Taney saw it, the Constitution spoke "not only in the same words but with the same meaning and intent with which it spoke when it came from the framers." In the infamous *Dred Scott* decision (1857), for example, the Court decided that Congress had no power to prohibit slavery in the territories.[16]

Many people assume that the Civil War was fought over slavery. It was not. The real issue was the character of the federal union, of federalism itself. At the time of the Civil War, economic and cultural differences between Northern and Southern states were considerable. The Southern economy was based on labor-intensive agriculture, while mechanized manufacturing was developing in the North. Southerners' desire for cheap manufactured goods and cheap plantation labor led them to support both slavery and low tariffs on imports. Northerners, to protect their own economy, wanted high tariffs. When they sought national legislation that threatened Southern interests, Southerners invoked states' rights. They even introduced the theory of **nullification**—the idea that a state could declare a particular action of the national government null and void. The Civil War rendered the idea of nullification null and void, but it did not eliminate the tension between national and state power.

In the decades after the Civil War, the Supreme Court continued to impose limits on national power, particularly when the national government attempted to regulate industry. Early in the nineteenth century, the Court had decided that the national government possessed supreme power to regulate interstate commerce.[17] However, the Court later rejected the idea that this power could be used to justify policies not directly related to the smooth functioning of interstate commerce—such as policies setting a national minimum wage or abolishing child labor. In the late nineteenth and early twentieth centuries, the justices were influenced by laissez-faire economic theory, which called for a hands-off approach to business. Time and again, the Court ruled that congressional legislation limiting the activities of corporations was unconstitutional, because it invaded the domain of the states.

In 1918, for example, when Congress tried to use its power to regulate interstate commerce to justify legislation regulating child labor, the Court declared the law unconstitutional. The national government argued that a national child labor law was necessary because individual states would not enact such laws; to do so would increase the cost of labor in the state, making it less attractive to industry. The Court recognized this argument but was not persuaded, ruling that national legislation regulating child labor was not within the scope of the commerce clause (of Article I,

Section 8) and ran counter to the Tenth Amendment. As Justice William R. Day wrote in *Hammer* v. *Dagenhart,*

> The commerce clause was not intended to give Congress a general authority to equalize conditions [of competition between the states]. If Congress can thus regulate matters intrusted to local authority . . . all freedom of commerce will be at an end, and the power of the states over local matters may be eliminated, and thus our system of government practically destroyed.[18]

The New Deal and Its Consequences

It took the Great Depression to render dual federalism obsolete. The problems of the Depression proved too extensive for either state governments or private businesses to handle. So the national government assumed a heavy share of responsibility for providing relief and pursuing economic recovery. Under the New Deal—President Franklin D. Roosevelt's response to the Depression—Congress enacted various emergency relief programs to stimulate economic activity and help the unemployed (see Chapter 19). Many measures required the cooperation of national and state governments. For example, the national government offered money to support state relief efforts. However, to receive these funds states were usually required to provide administrative supervision or to contribute some money of their own. Relief efforts were thus wrested from the hands of local bodies and centralized. Through the regulations it attached to funds, the national government extended its power and control over the states.[19]

At first, the Supreme Court's view of the Depression was different from that of the other branches of the national government. The justices believed the Depression was an accumulation of local problems, not a national problem demanding national action. In the Court's opinion, the whole structure of federalism was threatened when collections of local troubles were treated as one national problem. Justice Owen Roberts, in *United States* v. *Butler* (1936), wrote, "It does not help that local conditions throughout the nation have created a situation of national concern; for this is but to say that whenever there is a widespread similarity of local conditions, Congress may ignore constitutional limitations on its own powers and usurp those reserved to the states."[20] In this and other decisions, the Court struck down several pieces of regulatory legislation, including the National Industrial Recovery Act, which would have regulated wages, working hours, and business competition.

In 1937, however, with no change in personnel, the Court began to alter its course. It upheld the Social Security Act and the National Labor Relations Act—both New Deal measures. Perhaps the Court was responding to the 1936 election returns (Roosevelt had been reelected in a landslide, and the Democrats commanded a substantial majority in Congress), which signified the voters' endorsement of the use of national policies to address national problems. In any event, the Court abandoned its effort to maintain a rigid boundary between national and state power. Only a few years earlier, the Supreme Court had based its thinking about federalism on a state-centered interpretation of the Tenth Amendment. But in 1941,

Made in the U.S.A.
Young boys working in a Georgia cotton mill around the turn of the century. The Supreme Court decided in 1918 that Congress had no power to limit child labor. According to the Court, that power belonged to the states, which resisted imposing limits for fear such legislation would drive businesses to other (less restrictive) states.

Chief Justice Harlan Fiske Stone referred to the Tenth Amendment as "a truism that all is retained that has not been surrendered."[21] In short, the Court agreed that the layer cake was stale and unpalatable. From then on, the division of power in the federal system became less relevant, and the relationship between levels of government became increasingly more important.

Some call the New Deal era revolutionary. There is no doubt that the period was critical in reshaping federalism in the United States. The national and state governments had cooperated before, but the extent of nation-state interaction during Franklin Roosevelt's administration clearly made the marble-cake metaphor the most accurate description of American federalism. In addition, the size of the national government and its budget increased tremendously. But perhaps the most significant change was in the way Americans thought about their problems and the role of the national government in solving them. Difficulties that at one time had been seen as personal or local were now national problems, requiring national solutions. The general welfare, broadly defined, became a legitimate concern of the national government.

In other respects, however, the New Deal was not so revolutionary. For example, Congress did not claim any new powers to address the nation's economic problems. Congress simply used its constitutional powers to suit the circumstances. And with few exceptions from the late 1930s on, the Supreme Court has upheld Congress's power on virtually every issue.[22]

The Civil Rights Revolution and the War on Poverty

During the 1950s and 1960s, the national government assumed the task of promoting social equality by combating racism and poverty (see Chapters 16 and 19). Both racism and poverty seemed impossible to solve at the state level.

Matters of race relations had generally been left to the states, which more or less ignored them despite the constitutional amendments passed after the Civil War. When the Supreme Court adopted the doctrine of separate but equal in 1896,* states were free to do as much—or as little—as they pleased about racial inequality.

In 1954, however, in *Brown* v. *Board of Education*, the Supreme Court decided that racially separate but objectively equal public schools were inherently *unequal*.[23] The decision put the national government in the position of ordering the desegregation of public schools. As the civil rights movement focused public attention on the problems of discrimination, Congress passed two important pieces of legislation: the Civil Rights Act of 1964 and the Voting Rights Act of 1965. Through these acts, the national government outlawed racial discrimination in arenas of state regulation: employment, public accommodations, and voter qualifications. The commerce clause served as a vital constitutional lever providing Congress with the power to act. The intervention by the national government was unprecedented. The acts themselves sharply limited states' rights where the effect of those rights had been to deny equality or to substantially affect interstate commerce. The enforcement of the nation's civil rights laws called for the assertion of national authority in schools, parks, hospitals, restaurants, and other public facilities. The civil rights revolution established the national government as the principal guarantor of political and social equality.

In the 1960s, President Lyndon Johnson's War on Poverty generated an enormous amount of social legislation and a massive increase in the scope of the national government. In an attempt to provide equality of opportunity and improve the quality of life throughout the United States, the national government adopted a vast array of social legislation accompanied by money inducements. The funding included vastly increased aid to higher education, aid to elementary and secondary schools, school breakfasts and lunches, food stamps, and a huge number of economic development, public service, and employment-training projects. To administer the programs, government bureaucracies expanded on both national and state levels. In fact, during the 1960s and 1970s, state bureaucracies grew even faster than the national bureaucracy.

Johnson's recipe for marble-cake federalism included some new ingredients. Before 1960, nearly all intergovernmental assistance (that is, aid from one level of government to another) had flowed from the national government to state governments. But the War on Poverty frequently bypassed state government by offering direct aid to local governments and even to community groups.

As the expansion of the national government has become more widely accepted, the focus of the debate over federalism has changed. National, state, and local governments are no longer separate and distinct; they interact. The growth of government programs has created a federal system that critics describe as overloaded and out of control. In keeping with the bakery metaphors often used to describe federalism, one writer suggested

---

* In Plessy v. Ferguson *(163 U.S. 537 [1896]), the Supreme Court upheld state-imposed racial segregation, ruling that separate facilities for blacks and whites could be maintained so long as they were "equal" (see Chapter 16).*

Reach Out and Touch Someone

The levels of government in the federal system are now intertwined. Here, in an intergovernmental conference call, New York senators Daniel Patrick Moynihan and Alfonse D'Amato discuss funding projects with the governor of New York and the mayor of New York City.

that layer-cake federalism and marble-cake federalism have given way to "fruitcake federalism"—a federalism that is dense and indestructible and offers lots of sweets for everyone.[24] The Advisory Commission on Intergovernmental Relations (ACIR), a group created by Congress to monitor the federal system concluded in 1980 that fruitcake federalism is not palatable; it just does not work. Since the 1960s, the commission said, relations between national and state governments had become "more pervasive, more intrusive, more unmanageable, more ineffective, more costly and, above all, more unaccountable."[25]

FROM NEW FEDERALISM TO NEW-AGE FEDERALISM

The new burst of national legislation aimed at curing the Great Depression stimulated governments at all levels. But while all levels of government expanded from the Great Depression through the 1970s, the national government took on substantially more responsibilities, often at the expense of the states. The concentration of power in the national government seemed easier to tolerate when the national government was prepared to foot the bill. In the 1980s, the national deficit constrained spending on state and local government. But the efforts of the national government to impose policies on the states have not diminished, despite the lack of resources to pay for the policies.

Federalism has been dusted off and given some new uses. In 1969, Richard Nixon advocated more power to state and local governments. Nixon wanted to decentralize national policies. He called this the *New Federalism*. Today, Bill Clinton proposes that the national government act as guru, guiding and encouraging states to experiment with vexing problems. We call this *New-Age Federalism*.

FIGURE 4.4 ■ The National Government's Contribution to State and Local Governments

In 1960, the national government contributed less than 15 percent of total state and local spending. By 1978, the national government had nearly doubled its contribution to state and local government spending. By 1988, the national government's contribution had declined to about 18 percent. As the national government's spending remained static or declined, state and local government spending accelerated, especially for Medicaid, welfare, prisons, and education. (The slopes of the two figures here indicate the pace of spending change.)

(*Source:* The Budget for FY 1994: Historical Tables *(Washington, D.C. Government Printing Office, 1993), Table 15.2, p. 228.)*

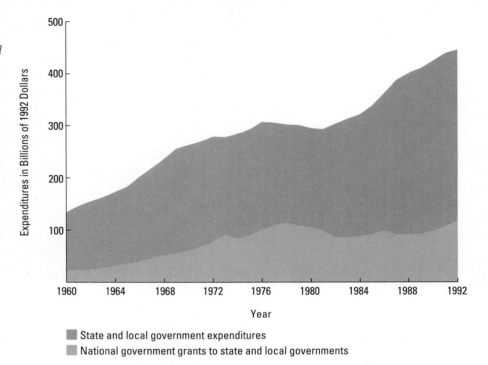

State and local government expenditures

National government grants to state and local governments

An Evolving Federalism

Every president from Nixon to Clinton has expressed disenchantment with the unmanageability of the federal system. Every president since Nixon has pledged to cut the size of the bureaucracy. When Nixon came to office in 1969, he pledged to change a national government he characterized as "overly centralized, overbureaucratized . . . unresponsive as well as inefficient." His New Federalism would channel "power, funds and authority . . . to those governments closest to the people." He expected New Federalism to help restore control of the nation's destiny "by returning a greater share of control to state and local authorities."[26]

Nixon's plan called for combining and reformulating categorical grants into block grants. The shift had dramatic implications for federalism. Block grants were a way to redress the imbalance of power among Washington and the states and localities. Conservatives in Washington wanted to return freedom to the states. New Federalism was nothing more than dual federalism in modern dress.

The perception that the federal system was bloated and out of control began to take hold. In 1976, Jimmy Carter campaigned for president as an outsider who promised to reduce the size and cost of the national government. And he did have some success. As Figure 4.4 shows, after 1978 national government aid to states and localities actually did begin to drop and then level off.

Ronald Reagan took office in 1981 charging that the federal system has been bent out of shape. Reagan promised a new New Federalism that would restore a proper constitutional relationship between the federal, state and local governments. The national government, he said, treated "elected state and local officials as if they were nothing more than administrative agents for federal authority."

Reagan's commitment to reduce taxes as well as government spending meant he could not offer the incentive of new funding to make his version of New Federalism palatable. He did resurrect an element of Nixon's New Federalism, however, in the use of block grants. To build support for the plan, Reagan emphasized the freedom state officials would have in using their block grant money. State officials were enthusiastic about the prospect of having greater control over grant money; they were less enthusiastic when they realized that the amounts they received would be cut by approximately 25 percent. The share of state and local bills footed by the national government continued to fall (see Figure 4.4). In the mid-1970s, the national government contributed about 25 percent of state and local government spending. By 1990, its contribution had declined to 20 percent.[27]

Despite presidential rhetoric from Nixon to Clinton, Congress has continued the acceleration of national power. Congressional demands on states and localities have continued in the Clinton administration. The strain on intergovernmental relations is likely to serve as the backdrop to the most important national initiative in a generation: health-care reform.

For social occasions, the president's instrument of choice is the tenor saxophone. For policies aimed at the health and welfare of Americans (a traditional state function), the congressional instrument of choice is preemption.

Bart Says, "Pay Up, Dudes!"
Californians urge their state legislators to provide more support for California's school system. In 1980, the national government shouldered more than 11 percent of public education costs. By 1991, that contribution had declined to approximately 8 percent. Because a 1 percent reduction in school aid equals nearly $3 billion, state governments are really feeling the pinch.

Preemption: Instrument of Federalism

Before 1965, increased national power and diminished state power followed from the growth in categorical grant-in-aid programs, with their attached conditions, emanating from Washington, D.C. Since 1965, Congress has used its centralizing power in new fields and in novel ways.[28]

Preemption is the power of Congress to enact laws that assume total or partial responsibility for a state government function. When the national government shoulders a new government function, it restricts the discretionary power of the states. For example, under the Age Discrimination in Employment Act of 1967, the national government stripped the states of their power to establish a compulsory retirement age for their employees. Such a policy restricts the states' hiring plans, from clerks to professors. When the states exercise their regulatory power, the different standards from state to state may cause havoc. The upshot can be a veritable tower of Babel (see Feature 4.1).

Congressional preemption statutes infringe on state powers in two ways, through mandates and restraints. A **mandate** is a requirement for a state to undertake an activity or provide a service in keeping with minimum national standards. In 1990, Congress mandated Medicaid coverage for all poor children. As a result, state Medicaid costs are expected to increase from $40 billion in 1991 to $95 billion in 1997. To pay for the Medicaid mandate, state officials face stark choices: shift scarce resources by reducing or eliminating programs or raise taxes.[29]

In contrast, a **restraint** forbids state government to exercise a power. Consider bus regulation, for example. To ensure bus service to small and remote communities, some states would condition the issuance of a bus franchise on the agreement of the bus operator to serve such communities, even if the routes lost money. But in 1982, Congress passed the Bus Regulatory Reform Act, which forbade the states from imposing such conditions. Many states now provide subsidies to bus operators to assure service to out-of-the-way areas.

Whether preemption takes the form of mandates or restraints, the result imposes additional costs on state and local government and interferes with a fundamental government task: setting priorities. Furthermore, the national government is not obliged to pay for the costs that it has imposed. As it grew in the 1980s, the national government reduced spending in the form of grants to the states. For example, the 1988 Family Support Act required states to continue Medicaid coverage for a year to families who left welfare for jobs; the states had to pick up the tab.

Despite a lack of resources, the national government seems no less determined to tell the states and local governments what to do. The national government has turned increasingly to mandates to control state and local activity without having to pay for it. Even presidential candidate Clinton commented from the stump in 1992 that the national government was "sticking it to all the states in the country and especially the poor states."[30] "If Washington is out of money, they better get out of the idea business," echoed an official of the National Governors' Association. "If the guys in Washington pass it, they'll have to pay for it. We're tired of paying their bills."[31]

FEATURE 4.1

■ Food Fight!

The multiplicity of governments that characterizes American federalism inevitably leads to regulatory proliferation and variation from state to state. When does national uniformity have priority over state regulation? Consider food labeling. In 1990, the national government proposed more information be included on labels about nutrition, serving sizes, cholesterol and fat content, and recommended daily intake. Would the new regulations nullify state labeling laws, such as warnings about cancer-causing chemicals required by California and maple syrup grading required by Vermont?

Consumer advocates argued that the states should be free to set standards stricter than the national government's. Business groups protested that food processors would have to vary their packaging to meet the requirements of each state or, more likely, to comply with the strictest state standard.

A remedy for the proliferation of rules spawned by federalism is preemption, the power of Congress to enact laws that assume total or partial responsibility for a state government function. Use of preemption has jumped dramatically in the last twenty-five years: From 1970 to 1988, Congress enacted 186 laws that preempted the states.

Initially, preemption was a device championed by liberals. During the New Deal, it was used to promote economic and labor regulations. In subsequent years, preemption benefited many other items on the liberal agenda, such as national guarantees of fair housing and voting rights, and guidelines for water quality and asbestos removal.

In the 1980s and 1990s, however, conservatives have championed the use of preemption to protect businesses from state regulations. For example, preemption conditions accompanied banking deregulation in the Reagan administration and alcoholic beverage labeling in the Bush administration. The food labeling issue illustrates the occasional willingness of conservatives to endorse the need for strong national government. As a food industry official observed, "I would rather deal with one federal gorilla than fifty state monkeys."

The food industry captured its federal gorilla in late 1990, when President Bush signed the Nutritional Labeling and Education Act. The act broadly preempted state nutritional labeling requirements, simplifying the packaging operation for food processors. However, the law not only required more nutritional information on labels, it also prohibited manufacturers from making health claims unless they are proved scientifically according to the standards of the national government's watchdog agency, the Food and Drug Administration.

• *Source: W. John Moore, "Stopping the States,"* National Journal, *21 (July 1990), pp. 1758–1762. Copyright 1990 by National Journal Inc. All rights reserved. Reprinted by permission.*

The national government is no longer a benefactor, bestowing largesse on worthy state and local units. Yet, spending pressures on state and local governments are enormous. The public demands better schools, harsher sentences for criminals (and more prisons to hold them), more and better day care for children and the elderly. Meanwhile, the sober reality of national budget deficits erases hope of increased aid. Aid to states and local communities, either in the form of grants or in direct payments for the poor (Medicaid and welfare) increased only slightly from 1982 to 1993, but its composition has changed substantially. Payments for the poor now take an increasing share of the national government's contribution to the states (see Chapter 19). The trend is likely to continue. For the first time in decades, many state and local governments are raising taxes or adopting new ones to pay for public services that were once the shared responsibility of cooperative federalism.

OTHER GOVERNMENTS IN THE FEDERAL SYSTEM

We have concentrated in this chapter on the changing roles the national and state governments play in shaping the federal system. Although the Constitution explicitly recognizes only national and state governments, the American federal system has spawned a multitude of local governments as well. A 1992 census counted nearly eighty-seven thousand.[32]

Types of Local Governments

Americans are citizens of both a nation and a state, but they also come under the jurisdiction of various local government units. These units include **municipal governments,** the governments of cities and towns. Municipalities, in turn, are located in (or may contain or share boundaries with) counties, which are administered by **county governments.** Most Americans also live in a **school district,** which is responsible for administering local elementary and secondary educational programs. They may also be served by one or more **special districts,** government units created to perform particular functions, typically when those functions—such as fire protection and water purification and distribution—spill across ordinary jurisdictional boundaries. Other examples of special districts include the Port Authority of New York and New Jersey, the Chicago Sanitation District, and the Southeast Pennsylvania Transit Authority.

Local governments are created by state governments, either in their constitutions or through legislation. This means that their organization, powers, responsibilities, and effectiveness vary considerably from state to state. About forty states endow their cities with various forms of **home rule**—the right to enact and enforce legislation in certain administrative areas. Home rule gives cities a measure of self-government and freedom of action. In contrast, county governments, which are the main units of local government in rural areas, tend to have little or no legislative power. Instead, county governments ordinarily serve as administrative units, performing the specific duties assigned to them under state law.

How can the ordinary citizen be expected to make sense of the maze of governments? And does the ordinary citizen really benefit from all the governments?

So Many Governments: Advantages and Disadvantages

In theory at least, one benefit of localizing government is that it brings government closer to the people; it gives them an opportunity to participate in the political process, to have a direct influence on policy. Localized government conjures visions of informed citizens deciding their own political fate—the traditional New England town meeting repeated across the nation. From this perspective, overlapping governments appear compatible with a majoritarian view of democracy.

Her Honor, the Mayor.
Hizzoner, the Mayor.

A mayor is the elected chief
executive and ceremonial
officer of a city. In some mod-
est-sized cities, mayors serve
part-time. Many big-city
mayors rise to national promi-
nence, though no mayor has
yet made the leap from city
hall to the White House.
These mayors are (clockwise,
from top left): Judy Chu of
Monteray Park; Rubén A.
Smith of Las Cruces, New
Mexico, Richard M. Daley of
Chicago, and Kurt Schmoke of
Baltimore, Maryland.

The reality is somewhat different, however. Studies have shown that people are much less likely to vote in local elections than national elections. In fact, voter turnout in local contests tends to be quite low, although the influence of individual votes is much greater. Furthermore, the fragmentation of powers, functions, and responsibilities among national, state, and local governments makes government as a whole seem complicated and hence incomprehensible and inaccessible to ordinary people. In addition, most people have little time to devote to public affairs, which can be very time consuming. These factors tend to discourage individual citizens from pursing politics and, in turn, enhance the influence of organized groups, which have the resources—time, money, and know-how—to influence policymaking (see Chapter 10). Instead of bringing government closer to the people and reinforcing majoritarian democracy, then, the system's enormous complexity tends to encourage pluralism.

One potential benefit of having many governments is that they enable the country to experiment with new policies on a small scale. New programs or solutions to problems can be tested in one city or state or in a few cities or states. Successful programs can then be adopted by other cities or states or by the nation as a whole. This fits President Clinton's brand of federalism. He views the states as "the laboratories of democracy." To this end, the Clinton administration has given nine states waivers from national welfare regulations so they can experiment with innovative policies such as linking children's school attendance to their family welfare benefits, restricting the time recipients are on welfare, and requiring recipients to take public service jobs while receiving government support.[33]

The states are also harbingers of important political change. The sheer number of local contests gives many citizens a chance to test their ability as elected officials. This valuable experience offers some local officials a steppingstone to higher office (see Politics in a Changing America 4.1).

The large number of governments also makes it possible for government to respond to the diversity of conditions in different parts of the country. States and cities differ enormously in population, size, economic resources, climate, and other characteristics—the diverse elements that French political philosopher Montesquieu argued should be taken into account in formulating laws for a society. Smaller political units are better able to respond to particular local conditions and can generally do so quickly. On the other hand, smaller units may not be able to muster the economic resources to meet challenges.

Of course, the United States remains one nation no matter how many local governments there are. The question of how much diversity the nation should tolerate in the way different states treat their citizens is important. For example, thirty-six states impose the death penalty for capital crimes. Even the execution methods vary (lethal injection, electrocution, lethal gas, hanging, and firing squad). As Feature 4.2 shows, public opinion is split on the general issue of state diversity. Also important is the question of whether the national government (and, indirectly, the citizens of other states) should be called on to foot the bill for problems specific to a particular region. States turn to the national government for assistance to meet national disasters such as earthquakes and floods. States expect similar assistance when confronted with such social disasters as urban riots, crime, and poverty.

Throughout American history, the national government has used its funds for regional development, to equalize disparities in wealth and development among states. The development of the Sunbelt (the southern and southwestern regions of the country), for example, has been and continues to be helped considerably by national policies and programs: The national government funded Tennessee Valley Authority (TVA) electrification, and western irrigation projects; national funding formulas designed to aid poorer areas of the country helped enormously, the South, in particular; and national largesse in the form of huge defense contracts has benefited California. (Defense cutbacks today contribute to California's high unemployment.) Overall, the government has poured more money into the Sunbelt states than they have paid in taxes.

CONTEMPORARY FEDERALISM AND THE DILEMMAS OF DEMOCRACY

To what extent were conservative hopes and liberal fears realized as federalism developed from the 1980s to the 1990s? Neither were fully realized under the various renditions of federalism. Federalism of the Reagan-Bush variety was used as a tool for cutting the national budget by offering less money to the states. Contrary to the expectations of conservatives and lib-

POLITICS IN A CHANGING AMERICA 4.1 States Lead the Way for Women's Political Power

When the 103d Congress convened in January 1993, there were a record number of women in the United States Senate (six women, or 6 percent) and in the House of Representatives (forty-seven women, or 11 percent). But these achievements pale in relation to the electoral success of women in state legislatures. By 1994, one-fifth of all state legislators were women. The growth in state officeholding has been steady and impressive for nearly twenty years. The state of Washington ranks at the top: 40 percent of its legislators were women in 1994. Alabama ranks at the bottom: 5 percent of its legislators are women.

Will women officeholders make a difference? Because more than 60 percent are Democrats, it is likely that equity issues will get higher priority. Whether Democrats or Republicans, women are sure to give more attention to public policies that have the effect of restricting women to traditional roles as caregivers in the family and society.

A federal structure provides more opportunities for citizens to participate in government. In a unitary system with fewer elected officials, competition discourages newcomers from entering the political arena. Spurred by state and local electoral success, women will vie increasingly for congressional and national offices.

- *Source: "Women in State Legislatures," a fact sheet; Center for the American Woman and Politics, Rutgers University. Used with permission.*

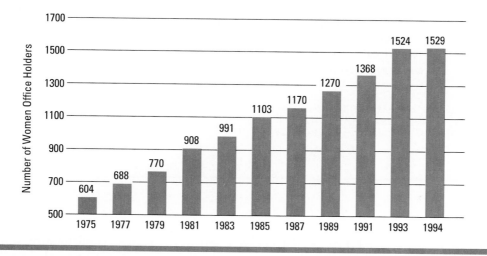

erals alike, however, states approved tax increases to pay for social services and education. In 1990–1991, thirty-seven states raised one or more major taxes (on income, sales, and motor fuels).[34] To be sure, this was risky business for politicians. Raising taxes stirs voter ire; reducing vital services (such as education) stirs voter ire. In an era when Washington was less willing to enforce antitrust legislation, civil rights laws, and affirmative action plans, state governments were more likely to do so. At a time when a conservative national government put little emphasis on the value of equality, state governments did more to embrace it.[35]

FEATURE 4.2

Who Should Make the Rules? Federalism and Public Opinion

Where do American citizens stand on the question of the distribution of power between national and state governments? What areas do they believe require uniform national standards? A CBS/New York Times poll taken in May 1987 put such questions to 1,254 people and found some deep divisions on the issues.

Only a few respondents (5 percent) believed that the states have too much power; most (47 percent) thought the balance between states and nation is about right; a sizable minority (39 percent) claimed that the national government has too much power.

When it came down to deciding whether national or state standards are better, here's how opinion divided (respondents with no opinion are not shown).

Ironically, this evidence says that Americans want the national government to assume greater responsibility for such things as penalties for murder, registration and voting, and safety standards, matters traditionally within the states' domain. Yet, most Americans hold to the view that the national government already has either enough or too much power.

- *Source: William K. Stevens, "Pagentry and the Ideals of 200 Years," New York Times, May 26, 1987, pp. A1 and A20. Copyright 1987 by The New York Times Company. Reprinted by permission.*

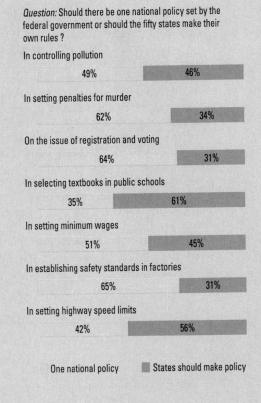

Question: Should there be one national policy set by the federal government or should the fifty states make their own rules ?

In controlling pollution
49% 46%

In setting penalties for murder
62% 34%

On the issue of registration and voting
64% 31%

In selecting textbooks in public schools
35% 61%

In setting minimum wages
51% 45%

In establishing safety standards in factories
65% 31%

In setting highway speed limits
42% 56%

One national policy ■ States should make policy

Conservatives had thought that the value of freedom would be emphasized if more matters were left to the states. Traditionally, state governments had been relatively small, lacking the wherewithal to limit large corporate interests, for example. But since the 1970s, state governments have changed. Their legislatures have become more professional. They meet regularly, and they maintain larger permanent staffs. Governors have proved willing to support major programs to enhance the skills of the work force, to promote research and development, and to subsidize new industries. State governments have become big governments themselves. They are better able to tackle problems, and they are not afraid to use their power to promote equality.

To the surprise of liberals, who had originally looked to the national government to protect individuals by setting reasonable minimum standards

Riverboat Revenue

Legalized gambling flourishes in every state except Utah and Hawaii. Governments today resist raising new revenue through increased property, sales, and income taxes. Gambling provides a new and lush source of income. Americans spend well in excess of $300 billion a year on gambling (lotteries, casinos, bingo, parimutuels). After deducting the winnings, governments and gaming establishments split the remaining revenue, which in 1992 was $30 billion, or more than six times what Americans spent on movie tickets. But gambling may exact a high social cost in ruined lives and organized crime that seem to follow in its wake.

for product safety, welfare payments, and employee benefits, states are now willing to set higher standards than the national government.

When Clinton came to the White House, liberals were delighted. His conservative predecessors Reagan and Bush had sought to reinstate layer-cake federalism and dismantle the national government's welfare-state efforts to promote social and political equality. But Clinton's experience as a governor is likely to create a strange brew when joined with liberal social welfare policies. Thus far, the Clinton administration has been silent on its brand of federalism; no coherent theory of federalism has emerged.[36] President Clinton is sympathetic to states burdened by new and costly mandates and restraints. His support for state experimentation in the big domestic problems—health care, crime, and welfare—will buy time and may provide evidence for a liberal, "one-size-fits-all" program for America.

The relationship of the federal system, political ideology, and the values of freedom, order, and equality is no longer as simple as it appeared in the 1960s. Then, liberals looked to the national government and marble-cake federalism to help secure equality. Conservatives argued for a return to small government, states' rights, and layer-cake federalism. In the 1980s, conservatives gave lip service to the ideals of federalism but were often reluctant to give up the national power that helped them achieve their vision of order. Meanwhile, the states began to promote equality more vigorously than freedom. As one prominent conservative put it, "The Great Society may be over in Washington, but it has just begun in the states."[37]

FEDERALISM AND PLURALISM

Our federal system of government was designed to allay citizens' fears that they might be ruled by majorities who were residents of distant regions and with whom they did not necessarily agree or share interests. By recognizing the legitimacy of the states as political divisions, the federal system

A River Runs Over It

For a while in 1993, the Mississippi River and its tributaries took over where once these highways overlapped. Record-breaking floods devastated the midwest from North Dakota to Missouri, soaking millions of acres of farmland and leaving tens of thousands of people homeless. The damage was mind-boggling: about $12 billion. Federalism provided a solution. The national government came to the aid of flood-ravaged states by allocating resources to rebuild or repair vital infrastructure (roads, water and sewage systems, schools, etc.). Flood victims received grants and loans to rebuild once the mighty Mississippi receded to its banks.

also recognizes the importance of diversity. The existence and cultivation of diverse interests are hallmarks of pluralism.

Each of the two competing theories of federalism supports pluralism but in somewhat different ways. Dual federalism aims to decentralize government, to shift power to the states. It recognizes the importance of local rather than national standards and applauds the diversity of those standards. The variety allows people, if not a voice in policymaking, at least the choice of policy under which to live.

In contrast, cooperative federalism is perfectly willing to override local standards for a national standard in the interests of promoting equality. Yet, this view of federalism also supports pluralist democracy. It is highly responsive to all manner of group pressures, including pressure at one level from groups unsuccessful at other levels. By blurring the lines of national and state responsibility, this type of federalism encourages petitioners to try their luck at whichever level of government offers the best chance of success.

SUMMARY

The government framework outlined in the Constitution was the product of political compromise, an acknowledgment of the states' fear of a powerful central government. The division of powers sketched in the Constitution was supposed to turn over "great and aggregate" matters to the national government, leaving "local and particular" concerns to the states. The Constitution did not explain what was great and aggregate and what was local and particular.

Federalism comes in many varieties. Two stand out, because they capture valuable differences between the original and modern vision of a national government. Dual, or layer-cake, federalism wants to retain power in the states and to keep the levels of government separate. Cooperative, or marble-cake, federalism emphasizes the power of the national government and sees national and state government working together to solve national problems. In its own way, each view supports the pluralist model of democracy.

Over the years, the national government has used both its enumerated and its implied powers to become involved in virtually every area of human activity. The tools of political change include direct legislation, judicial interpretation, and grants-in-aid to states and localities. In the absence of financial incentives, the national government may use its preemption power, imposing mandates or restraints on the states without necessarily footing the cost.

As its influence grew, so did the government. Major events, such as the Civil War and the Great Depression, mark major shifts in the growth in size and power of the national government. To alter course, conservatives offered New Federalism and argued for cutting back on the size of the national government, reducing federal spending, and turning programs over to the states in order to solve the problem of unwieldy government. Liberals worried that in the haste to decentralize and cut back, New Federalism would turn over important responsibilities to states that were unwilling or unable to assume them. Rather than being too responsive, government would become unresponsive. But neither happened in the 1980s. Congressional preemption forced states to meet national standards with or without financial inducements. The states proved ready to tackle some major problems. More than this, they were prepared to fund many programs that promoted equality.

The debate over federalism is continuing in the 1990s and will endure. Today's version of cooperative federalism will surely be replaced by another theory of intergovernmental relations, and the ghost of dual federalism may still return. One truth emerges from this overview of federalism: The balance of power between the national and state governments will be settled by political means, not by theory.

Key Terms

federalism	block grant
dual federalism	nullification
states' rights	preemption
implied powers	mandate
cooperative federalism	restraint
elastic clause	municipal government
commerce clause	county government
grant-in-aid	school district
categorical grant	special district
formula grant	home rule
project grant	

Selected Readings

Beer, Samuel H. *To Make a Nation: The Rediscovery of American Federalism.* Cambridge, Mass.: Harvard University Press, 1993. A historical examination of federalism and nationalism in American political philosophy.

Bennett, Linda L. M., and Stephen Earl Bennett. *Living with Leviathan: Americans Coming to Terms with Big Government.* Lawrence: University Press of Kansas, 1990. An invaluable study tracing American ambivalence toward national power through a half-century of public opinion data.

Berger, Raoul. *Federalism: The Founder's Design.* Norman: University of Oklahoma Press, 1987. Berger, a constitutional historian, argues that the states preceded the nation and that the states and the national government were to have mutually exclusive spheres of sovereignty.

Dye, Thomas R. *American Federalism: Competition Among Governments.* Lexington, Mass.: Lexington Books, 1990. Presents a theory of competitive federalism that encourages rivalry among states and local governments to offer citizens the best array of public services at the lowest cost.

Hall, Kermit L., ed. *Federalism: A Nation of States.* New York: Garland, 1987. A collection of the most important historical and political science scholarship on federalism.

Rivlin, Alice. *Reviving the American Dream: The Economy, the States, and the Federal Government.* Washington, D.C.: Brookings Institution, 1992. A lucid examination of economic performance and government performance resting on a reexamination of the division of responsibilities between the nation and the states.

Zimmerman, Joseph F. *Contemporary American Federalism: The Growth of National Power.* New York: Praeger, 1992. Argues that the expansion of preemption power has altered the allocation of power between nation and states.

PART

III

Linking People with Government

5 Public Opinion and Political Socialization

FRIDAYS ARE DIFFERENT in Saudi Arabia. After prayers, criminals are paraded in the streets, then punished publicly. Murderers are beheaded, adulterers are flogged, and thieves have their hands chopped off. The Saudi government wants its citizens to get the message: Crime will not be tolerated. However, what constitutes a crime in Saudi Arabia may not be a crime in the United States. Members of the U.S. armed forces sent there in 1990 during the Persian Gulf crisis learned this when their mail from home was opened to keep out alcohol and sexually oriented magazines, both of which are illegal. It is also illegal for a woman to drive a car. Saudi Arabia, which claims the lowest crime rate in the world, is a country that greatly values order.

In contrast, the United States has one of the highest crime rates in the world. Its homicide rate, for example, is three to ten times that of most other Western countries. Although no one is proud of this record, our government would never consider beheading, flogging, or dismembering to lower the crime rate. First, the Eighth Amendment to the Constitution forbids "cruel and unusual" punishment. Second, the public would not tolerate such punishment.

However, the American public definitely is not squeamish about the death penalty (capital punishment), at least for certain crimes. The Gallup Organization has polled the nation on this issue for more than fifty years. Except in 1966, most respondents have consistently supported the death penalty for murder.[1] In fact, public support for capital punishment has increased dramatically since the late 1960s. In 1992, 79 percent of all respondents were in favor of the death penalty for murder, while only 18 percent opposed it.[2] Other research has shown that substantial segments of the public have also favored the death penalty for attempting to assassinate the president (63 percent), rape (51 percent), and hijacking an airplane (49 percent).[3]

Government has been defined as the legitimate use of force to control human behavior. We can learn much about the role of public opinion in politics by reviewing the government's use of force to punish crime. During most of American history, the execution of people who threaten the social order has been a legal practice of government. In colonial times, capital punishment was imposed not just for murder but for antisocial behavior—for denying the "true" God, cursing one's parents, adultery, witchcraft, or being a rebellious child.[4] In the late 1700s, some writers, editors, and clergy argued for abolishing the death sentence. The campaign

Women Should Be Heard and Not Seen

The culture of a nation shapes public attitudes and opinions. In Saudi Arabia, women completely cover their heads and bodies when out in public in strict accordance with Islamic principles. The Saudi culture also prohibits women from engaging in many activities (such as driving automobiles) typically enjoyed by women in the United States.

intensified in the 1840s, and a few states responded by eliminating capital punishment. Interest in the cause waned until 1890, when New York State adopted a new technique, electrocution, as the instrument of death. By 1917, twelve states had passed laws against capital punishment. But the outbreak of World War I fed the public's fear of foreigners and radicals, leading to renewed support for the death penalty. Reacting to this shift in public opinion, four states restored it.

The security needs of World War II and postwar fears of Soviet communism fueled continued support for capital punishment. After the anticommunist hysteria subsided in the late 1950s, public opposition to the death penalty increased. But public opinion was neither strong enough nor stable enough to force state legislatures to outlaw the death penalty. In keeping with the pluralist model of democracy, abolition efforts shifted from the legislative arena to the courts.

The abolitionists argued that the death penalty is cruel and unusual punishment and therefore unconstitutional. Certainly, the public in the 1780s had not considered capital punishment either cruel or unusual. But two hundred years later, opponents contended that execution by the state was cruel and unusual by contemporary standards. Their argument apparently had some effect on public opinion; in 1966, a plurality of respondents opposed the death penalty for the first (and only) time since the Gallup surveys began.

The states responded to the shift in public opinion by reducing the number of executions until, in 1968, they stopped completely in anticipation of a Supreme Court decision. By then, however, public opinion had again reversed in favor of capital punishment. Nevertheless, in 1972, the Court ruled in a 5–4 vote that the death penalty as imposed by existing state laws was unconstitutional.[5] The decision was not well received in many states, and thirty-five state legislatures passed new laws to get around the ruling.

The Death Gurney
This grim-looking contraption at the prison in Huntsville, Texas, restrains a criminal condemned to death so that a lethal injection can be administered. It exemplifies the ultimate power that the government has to control behavior. Capital crimes may draw capital punishment.

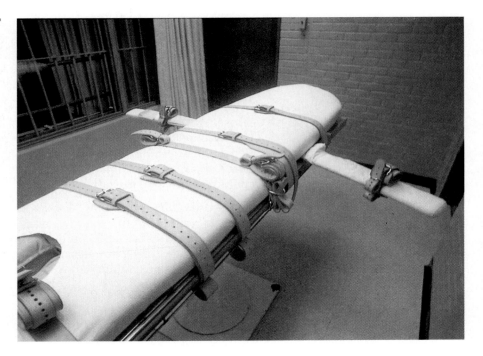

Meanwhile, as the nation's homicide rate increased, public approval of the death penalty jumped almost ten points and began climbing.

In 1976, the Supreme Court changed its position and upheld three new state laws that provided for consideration of the defendant and the offense before imposing the death sentence.[6] The Court also rejected the argument that punishment by death itself violates the Constitution while noting that public opinion favored the death penalty. Through the end of the 1970s, however, few states applied the penalty: Only three criminals were executed. Eventually, the states began to heed the clamor, executing about twenty criminals a year by the 1990s.

Does the death penalty deter people from killing? A majority of the public thinks it does.[7] What do people think is the most humane method of execution? Opinion polls tell us that most people favor lethal injection (66 percent) over electrocution (10 percent). The gas chamber has more support (6 percent) than the old-fashioned firing squad or hanging (both 3 percent).[8] Presumably, no respondents regarded beheading as humane.

The history of public thinking on the death penalty reveals several characteristics of public opinion:

1. *The public's attitudes toward a given government policy can vary over time, often dramatically.* Opinions about capital punishment tend to fluctuate with threats to the social order. The public is more likely to favor capital punishment in times of war and fear of foreign subversion and when crime rates are high.

2. *Public opinion places boundaries on allowable types of public policy.* Chopping off a hand is not acceptable to the American public (and surely to courts interpreting the Constitution) as a punishment for theft, but electrocuting a murderer is.

3. *If asked by pollsters, citizens are willing to register opinions on matters outside their expertise.* People clearly believe execution by lethal injection is more humane than electrocution, asphyxiation in the gas chamber, or hanging. How can the public know enough about execution to make these judgments?

4. *Governments tend to respond to public opinion. State laws for and against capital punishment have reflected swings in the public mood.* The Supreme Court's 1972 decision against capital punishment came when public opinion on the death penalty was sharply divided; the Court's approval of capital punishment in 1976 coincided with a rise in public approval of the death penalty.

5. *The government sometimes does not do what the people want.* Although public opinion overwhelmingly favors the death penalty for murder, few states actually punish murderers with execution. The United States averaged more than twenty thousand homicides annually in the 1980s but executed fewer than twenty murderers a year.

The last two conclusions bear on our discussion of the majoritarian and pluralist models of democracy in Chapter 2. Here, we probe more deeply into the nature, shape, depth, and formation of public opinion in a democratic government. What is the place of public opinion in a democracy? How do people acquire their opinions? What are the major lines of division in public opinion? How do individuals' ideology and knowledge affect their opinions? What is the relationship between public opinion and ideological type?

PUBLIC OPINION AND THE MODELS OF DEMOCRACY

Public opinion is simply the collected attitudes of citizens on a given issue or question. Opinion polling, which involves interviewing a sample of citizens to estimate public opinion as a whole (see Feature 5.1), is such a common feature of contemporary life that we often forget it is a modern invention, dating only from the 1930s (see Figure 5.1). In fact, survey methodology did not become a powerful research tool until the advent of computers in the 1950s.

Before polling became an accepted part of the American scene, politicians, journalists, and everyone else could argue about what "the people" wanted, but no one really knew. Observers of America before the 1930s had to guess at national opinion by analyzing newspaper stories, politicians' speeches, voting returns, and travelers' diaries. What if pollsters had been around when the colonists declared their independence from Britain in July 1776? We might learn (as some historians estimate) that "40 percent of Americans supported the Revolution, 20 percent opposed it, and 40 percent tried to remain neutral."[9] When no one really knows what the people want, it is impossible for the national government to be responsive to public opinion. As we discussed in Chapter 3, the founders wanted to build public opinion into our government structure by allowing the direct election of representatives to the House and apportioning representation there according to population. Attitudes and actions in the House of Representatives, the framers thought, would reflect public opinion, especially on the crucial issues of taxes and government spending.

FEATURE 5.1

Sampling a Few, Predicting to Everyone

How can a pollster tell what the nation thinks by talking to only a few hundred people? The answer lies in the statistical theory of sampling. Briefly, the theory holds that a sample of individuals selected by chance from any population is "representative" of that population. This means that the traits of individuals in the sample—their attitudes, beliefs, sociological characteristics, and physical features—reflect the traits of the whole population. Sampling theory does not claim that a sample exactly matches the population, only that it reflects the population with some predictable degree of accuracy.

Three factors determine the accuracy of a sample. The most important is how the sample is selected. For maximum accuracy, the individuals in the sample must be chosen randomly. *Randomly* does not mean at 'whim'; it means that every individual in the population has the same chance of being selected.

For a population as large and widespread as that of the United States', pollsters first divide the country into geographic regions. Then, they randomly choose areas and sample individuals who live within those areas. This departure from strict random sampling does decrease the accuracy of polls but only by a relatively small amount. Today, most polls conducted by the mass media are done by telephone, with computers randomly dialing numbers within predetermined calling areas. (Random dialing ensures that even people with unlisted numbers are called.)

The second factor that affects accuracy is the size of the sample. The larger the sample, the more accurately it represents the population. For example, a sample of four hundred individuals predicts accurately for a population within six percentage points (plus or minus), 95 percent of the time. A sample of six hundred is accurate within five percentage points. (Surprising, the size of sample has essentially no effect on accuracy of most samples. A sample of, say, six hundred individuals reflects the traits of a city, a state, or even the nation with equal accuracy, within five percentage points. Why this is so is better discussed in a course on statistics.)

The final factor that affects the accuracy of sampling is the amount of variation in the population. If there were no variation, every sample would reflect the population's characteristics with perfect accuracy. The greater the variation within the population, the greater is the chance that one random sample will be different from another.

The Gallup Poll and most other national opinion polls usually survey about 1,500 individuals and are accurate within three percentage points, 95 percent of the time. As shown in Figure 5.1, the predictions of the Gallup Poll for fourteen presidential elections since 1936 have deviated from the voting results by an average of only 2.2 percentage points. Even this small margin of error can mean an incorrect prediction in a close election. But for the purpose of estimating public opinion on political issues, a sampling error of three percentage points is acceptable.

Poll results can be wrong because of problems that have nothing to do with sampling theory. For example, question wording can bias the results. In surveys during the 1980s concerning aid to the Nicaraguan Contras fighting the Sandinista government, questions that mentioned President Reagan's name produced more support for increased aid by almost five percentage points.* Survey questions are also prone to random error, because interviewers are likely to obtain superficial responses from busy respondents who say anything, quickly, to get rid of them. Recently, some newspaper columnists have even urged readers to lie to pollsters outside voting booths, to confound election-night television predictions. Despite its potential for abuse or distortion, modern polling has told us a great deal about public opinion in America.

---

* *Brad Lockerbie and Stephen A. Borrelli, "Question Wording and Public Support for Contra Aid, 1983–1986,"* Public Opinion Quarterly *54 (Summer 1990), p. 200.*

FIGURE 5.1 ■ **Gallup Poll Accuracy**

One of the nation's oldest polls was started by George Gallup in the 1930s. The accuracy of the Gallup Poll in predicting presidential elections over nearly fifty years is charted here. Although not always on the mark, its predictions have been fairly close to election results. The poll was most notably wrong in 1948, when it predicted that Thomas Dewey, the Republican candidate, would defeat the Democratic incumbent, Harry Truman, underestimating Truman's vote by 5.4 percentage points. In 1992, the Gallup Poll substantially overestimated Bill Clinton's vote while underestimating Ross Perot's showing, resulting in an even greater error than in 1948. Unlike 1948, however, the 1992 Gallup Poll correctly predicted the winner.

Source: Gallup Report, *November 1992. Used by permission of The Gallup Poll.*

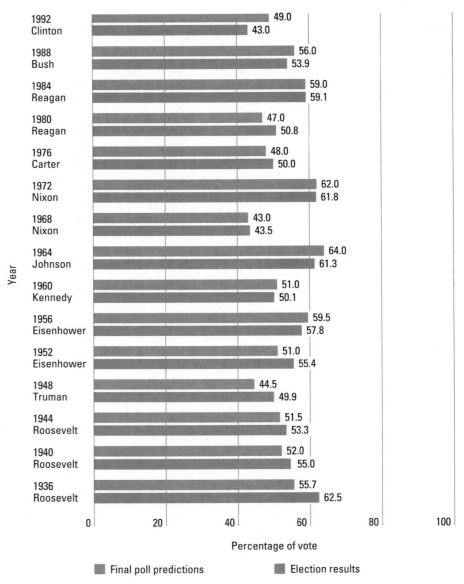

In practice, bills passed by a majority of elected representatives do not necessarily reflect the opinions of a majority of citizens. This would not have bothered the framers, because they never intended to create a full democracy, a government completely responsive to majority opinion. Although they wanted to provide for some contribution of public opinion, they had little faith in the ability of the masses to make public policy.

The majoritarian and pluralist models of democracy differ greatly in their assumptions about the role of public opinion in democratic government. According to the classic majoritarian model, the government should do what a majority of the public wants. In contrast, pluralists argue

Stop the Presses! Oops, Too Late . . .

As the 1948 election drew near, few people gave President Harry Truman a chance to defeat his Republican opponent, Thomas E. Dewey. Polling was still new, and virtually all the early polls showed Dewey far ahead. Most organizations simply stopped polling weeks before the election. The Chicago Daily Tribune *believed the polls and proclaimed Dewey's victory before the votes were counted. Here, the victorious Truman triumphantly displays the most embarrassing headline in American politics. Later, it was revealed that the few polls taken closer to election day showed Truman catching up to Dewey. Clearly, polls estimate the vote only at the time they are taken.*

that the public as a whole seldom demonstrates clear, consistent opinions on the day-to-day issues of government. At the same time, pluralists recognize that subgroups within the public do express opinions on specific matters—often and vigorously. The pluralist model requires that government institutions allow the free expression of opinions by these "minority publics." Democracy is at work when the opinions of many different publics clash openly and fairly over government policy.

Sampling methods and opinion polling have altered the debate about the majoritarian and pluralist models of democracy. Now that we know how often government policy runs against majority opinion, it becomes harder to defend the U.S. government as democratic under the majoritarian model. Even at a time when Americans overwhelmingly favored the death penalty for murderers, the Supreme Court decided that existing state laws applying capital punishment were unconstitutional. Even after the Court approved new state laws as constitutional, relatively few murderers were actually executed. Consider, too, the case of prayer in public schools. The Supreme Court has ruled that no state or local government can require the reading of the Lord's Prayer or Bible verses in public schools. Yet, surveys continually show that a clear majority of Americans (about 60 percent) does not agree with that ruling.[10] Because government policy sometimes runs against settled majority opinion, the majoritarian model is easily attacked as being an inaccurate description of reality.

The two models of democracy make different assumptions about public opinion. The majoritarian model assumes that a majority of people holds clear, consistent opinions on government policy. The pluralist model insists that public opinion is often divided, and opinion polls certainly give credence to that claim. What are the bases of these divisions? What principles, if any, do people use to organize their beliefs and attitudes about politics? Exactly how do individuals form their political opinions? We will look for answers to these questions in this chapter. In later chapters, we assess the effect of public opinion on government policies. The results should help you make up your own mind about the viability of the majoritarian and pluralist models in a functioning democracy.

THE DISTRIBUTION OF PUBLIC OPINION

A government that tries to respond to public opinion soon learns that people seldom think alike. To understand, then to act on the public's many attitudes and beliefs, governments must pay attention to the way public opinion distributes among the choices on an issue. In particular, government must analyze the shape and the stability of the distribution.

Shape of the Distribution

The results of public opinion polls are often displayed on charts such as those in Figure 5.2. The height of the columns indicates the percentage of those polled who gave each response, identified along the baseline. The shape of the opinion distribution depicts the pattern of all the responses when counted and plotted. The figure depicts three patterns of distribution—normal, skewed, and bimodal.

Figure 5.2a shows how respondents to a national survey in 1992 distributed along a liberal-conservative continuum. The most frequent response, called the *mode*, was "moderate." Progressively fewer people classified themselves in each category toward the liberal and conservative extremes. The shape of the graph resembles what statistical theory calls a **normal distribution**—a symmetrical, bell-shaped distribution around a single mode. Public opinion that is normally distributed tends to support moderate government policies. At the same time, it tolerates government policies that range to either side of the center position, shifting from liberal to conservative and back again, so long as they do not stray too far from the moderate center.

Figure 5.2b plots the percentages of those who agreed or disagreed with the statement "The private business system in the United States works better than any other system yet devised for industrial countries."[11] The shape of this graph is very different from the symmetrical distribution of liberal-conservative attitudes in Figure 5.2a. In Figure 5.2b, the mode (containing the vast majority that agrees with the statement) lies to one side, leaving a "tail" (the few who disagree) on the other. Such asymmetrical distribution is called a **skewed distribution.**

In a skewed distribution, the opinions of the majority cluster on one side of the issue. A skewed distribution indicates less diversity of opinion than does a normal distribution. The skewed distribution in Figure 5.2b tells us that most Americans are happy with capitalism as an economic system. Obviously, then, a candidate would have little hope of winning an election by denouncing free enterprise. When consensus on an issue is this strong, in fact, those with minority opinions risk social ostracism and even persecution if they persist in voicing their opinions. If the public does not feel intensely about an issue, however, politicians can sometimes discount a skewed distribution of public opinion. This is what has happened with the

FIGURE **5.2** ■ **Three Distributions of Opinion**

We have superimposed three hypothetical patterns of distribution—normal, skewed, and bimodal—on three actual distributions of responses to survey questions. Although the actual responses do not match the shapes exactly, the match is close enough that we can describe the distribution of (a) ideological attitudes as approximately normal, (b) belief in capitalism as skewed, and (c) opinions on the causes of homosexuality as bimodal.

Sources: (a) 1992 National Election Survey, Center for Political Studies, University of Michigan. The total sample size was 2,487, but Figure 5.2a excludes about 25 percent who "haven't thought much" about ideology or did not know. (b) 1981 survey by Civic Service, Inc., reported in Public Opinion *5 (October/November 1982), 21. (c) 1993 New York Times/CBS News Poll, which asked "Do you think being homosexual is something people choose to be, or do you think it is something they cannot change?" Jeffrey Schmalz, "Poll Finds an Even Split on Homosexuality's Cause,"* New York Times, *5 March 1993, p. A11.*

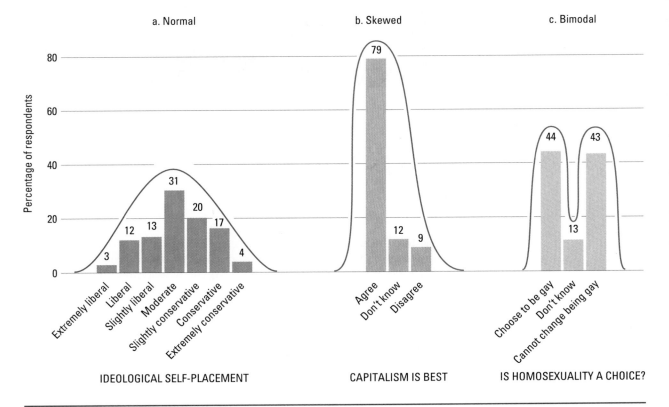

death penalty. Although most people favor capital punishment, it is not a burning issue for them. This means politicians can discount public opinion on the issue without serious consequences.

Figure 5.2c plots responses to the question of whether homosexuality is a matter of choice.[12] These responses fall into a **bimodal distribution:** Respondents chose two categories with nearly equal frequency—dividing almost evenly over whether being homosexual is a matter of choice or

Polling Booth

No, this person is not voting in an election. He is conducting a survey for the Gallup poll, the nation's best-known public opinion survey organization. To cut down on research costs, many polls are now done by telephone, and responses are entered directly into a computer to speed analysis. This methodology allows national surveys to be launched and completed literally overnight.

something that a person cannot change. Because they split the electorate in nearly equal parts, bimodal distributions of opinion present the greatest potential for political conflict, especially if both sides feel strongly.

Stability of the Distribution

A **stable distribution** shows little change over time. Public opinion on important issues can change, but it is sometimes difficult to distinguish a true change in opinion from a difference in the way a question is worded. When different questions on the same issue produce similar distributions of opinion, the underlying attitudes are stable. When the same question (or virtually the same question) produces significantly different responses over time, an actual shift in public opinion probably has occurred.

Consider Americans' attitudes toward capitalism. In the 1981 survey plotted in Figure 5.2b, 79 percent of the respondents chose capitalism over all alternative economic systems. Forty years earlier, in 1941, respondents had been asked whether they "would be better off if the concern you worked for were taken over and operated by the federal government." The responses at that time were also heavily skewed: 81 percent said that they preferred "business management." The nation's support for capitalism is very stable; it barely changed in the course of four decades.[13]

People's self-descriptions of themselves in ideological terms is another distribution that has remained surprisingly stable. Chapter 1 argued for using a two-dimensional ideological typology based on the trade-offs of freedom for equality and freedom for order. However, most opinion polls have only asked respondents to place themselves on a single liberal-conservative dimension, which tends to force libertarians and populists into the middle category. Nevertheless, we find relatively little change in respondents' self-placement on the liberal-conservative continuum over time. Even in 1964, when liberal Lyndon Johnson won a landslide victory over conservative Barry Goldwater in the presidential election, more voters described themselves as conservative than liberal. Indeed, this has been the public's ideological self-classification in every presidential election year since 1964.[14] Despite all the talk about the nation's becoming conservative in recent years, the fact is that most people did not describe themselves as liberal at any time during the last thirty years. People's self-descriptions have shifted about 5 percentage points toward the right since 1964, but more considered themselves conservative than liberal to begin with.

However, public opinion in America is capable of massive change over time. Moreover, dramatic change can occur on issues that were once highly controversial. A good example is race relations, specifically integrated schools. A national survey in 1942 asked whether "white and Negro students should go to the same schools or separate schools."[15] Only 30 percent of white respondents said that the students should attend schools together. When virtually the same question was asked in 1984 (substituting *black* for *Negro*), 90 percent of the white respondents endorsed integrated schools (see Politics in a Changing America 5.1). However, the scholars who did this research note that white Americans have not become "color-blind."[16] Despite their endorsement of integrated schools, only 23 percent of the whites surveyed in 1984 were in favor of busing to achieve racial balance. And whites were more willing to bus their children to a school with a few blacks than to one that was mostly black.[17] So white opinion changed dramatically with regard to the principle of desegregated schools, but whites seemed divided on how that principle should be implemented. Trying to explain how political opinions in general are formed and how they change, political scientists cite the process of political socialization, the influence of cultural factors, and the interplay of ideology and knowledge. In the next several sections, we examine how these elements combine to create and influence public opinion.

POLITICAL SOCIALIZATION

Public opinion is grounded in political values. People acquire their values through **political socialization,** a complex process through which individuals become aware of politics, learn political facts, and form political values. Think for a moment about your political socialization. What is your earliest memory of a president? When did you first learn about political parties? If you identify with a party, how did you decide to do so? If you do not, why don't you? Who was the first liberal you ever met? The first conservative? How did you first learn about nuclear bombs? About capitalism and communism?

Obviously, the paths to political awareness, knowledge, and values vary among individuals, but most people are exposed to the same sources of influence, or agents of socialization, especially from childhood through young adulthood. These influences are family, school, community, peers, and—of course—television.

POLITICS IN A CHANGING AMERICA 5.1

Attitudes Toward Integrated Schools

Race relations in the United States are far from perfect, but there have been important changes in public attitudes over time on key issues. This graph dramatically shows how much public opinion on the issue of school integration has changed during four decades. Scholars writing on this trend in racial attitudes have commented on "(1) its massive magnitude, moving from a solid pro-segregation majority to an overwhelming pro-integration consensus; (2) its long duration, continuing over four decades; and (3) its steady relentless pace."* Similarly, growth in the public's acceptance of integrated housing and racial intermarriage has been consistent. Nevertheless, these important attitudinal changes have not eliminated racial problems in the United States, as discussed in the text.

* *Source: Survey conducted by the National Opinion Research Center; reported in and recalculated from Tom W. Smith and Paul B. Sheatsley, "American Attitudes Toward Race Relations," Public Opinion 7 (October-November 1984): 15. Free, Lloyd A. and Hadley Cantril, The Political Beliefs of Americans. Copyright © 1968 by Rutgers University. Used with permission.*

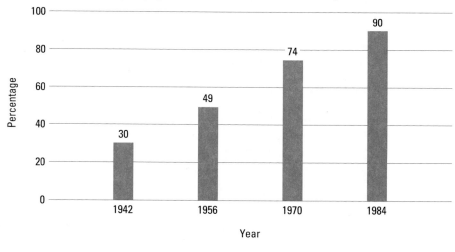

Changing Opinions on School Integration
Percentage saying that white and black students should go to same schools

The Agents of Early Socialization

Like psychologists, scholars of political socialization place great emphasis on early learning. Both groups point to two fundamental principles that characterize early learning:[18]

- *The primacy principle.* What is learned first is learned best.

- *The structuring principle.* What is learned first structures later learning.

Because most people learn first from their family, the family tends to be an important agent of early socialization. The extent of family influence—and of the influence of other socializing agents—depends on the extent of our exposure, communication, and receptivity to them.[19]

Family. In most cases, exposure, communication, and receptivity are highest in parent-child relationships, although parental influence has declined with the rise of single-parent families. Especially in two-parent homes, children learn a wide range of values—social, moral, religious, economic, and political—that helps shape their opinions. It is not surprising, then, that most people link their earliest memories of politics with their families. Moreover, when parents are interested in politics and maintain a favorable home environment for studying public affairs, they influence their children to become more politically interested and informed.[20]

One of the most politically important things that many children learn from their parents is party identification. Party identification is learned in much the same way as religion. Children (very young children, anyway) imitate their parents. When parents share the same religion, children are almost always raised in that faith. When parents are of different religions, their children are more likely to follow one or the other than to adopt a third. Similarly, parental influence on party identification is greater when both parents strongly identify with the same party.[21] Overall, about half of young American voters identify with the political party of their parents. Moreover, those who change their partisanship are more likely to shift from being partisan to independent or from independent to partisan than to convert from one party to the other.[22]

Two crucial differences between party identification and religion may explain why youngsters are socialized into a religion much more reliably

American Government 101

These teenagers in a mock government workshop at the Texas legislature in Austin are learning about the legislative process. They are also being socialized into politics, acquiring attitudes toward government that will affect their political behavior throughout their lives

than into a political party. The first is that most parents care a great deal more about their religion than about their politics. So they are more deliberate about exposing their children to religion. The second is that religious institutions recognize the value of socialization; they offer Sunday schools and other activities that reinforce parental guidance. American political parties, on the other hand, sponsor few activities to win the hearts of little Democrats and Republicans, which leaves children open to counterinfluences in the school and community.

School.   According to some researchers, schools have an influence on political learning that is equal to or greater than that of parents.[23] Here, however, we have to distinguish between elementary and secondary schools on the one hand and institutions of higher education on the other. Elementary schools prepare children in a number of ways to accept the social order. They introduce authority figures outside the family—the teacher, the principal, the police officer. They also teach the nation's slogans and symbols—the Pledge of Allegiance, the national anthem, national heroes and holidays. And they stress the norms of group behavior and democratic decision making (respecting the opinions of others, voting for class officers). In the process, they are teaching youngsters about the value of political equality.

Children do not always understand the meaning of the patriotic rituals and behaviors they learn in elementary school (see Feature 5.2). In fact, much of this early learning—in the United States and elsewhere—is more indoctrination than education. By the end of the eighth grade, however, children begin to distinguish between political leaders and government institutions. They become more aware of collective institutions, such as Congress and elections, than younger children, who tend to focus on the president and other single figures of government authority.[24] In sum, most children emerge from elementary school with a sense of national pride and an idealized notion of American government.[25]

Although newer curricula in many secondary schools emphasize citizens' rights in addition to their responsibilities, high schools also attempt to build "good citizens." Field trips to the state legislature or the city council impress students with the majesty and power of government institutions. But secondary schools also offer more explicit political content in their curricula, including courses in recent U.S. history, civics, and American government. Better teachers challenge students to think critically about American government and politics; others limit themselves to teaching civic responsibilities. The end product is a greater awareness of the political process and the most prominent participants in that process (see Figure 5.3).[26] Despite teachers' efforts to build children's trust in the political process, outside events can erode that trust as children grow up. For example, urban adolescents have been found to have views more cynical of both the police and the president than nonurban youth.[27]

Political learning at the college level can be much like that in high school or quite different. The degree of difference is greater if professors (or the texts they use) encourage their students to question authority. Questioning dominant political values does not necessarily mean rejecting them. For example, this text encourages you to recognize that freedom and equality—two values idealized in our culture—often conflict. It also

FEATURE 5.2

■ With Liberty and Blimp Rides for All

Elementary schools provide the first contact with American government for many children. Sometimes, youngsters fail to get the message right away. How many of you pledged allegiance to an "invisible" rather than an "indivisible" nation? In the excerpt that follows, playwright Arthur Miller recounts his own misunderstanding of the Pledge of Allegiance.

ROXBURY, Conn. I no longer remember how many years it took for me to realize I was making a mistake in the Pledge of Allegiance. With high passion, I stood beside my seat in my Harlem grammar school and repeated the Pledge to the Flag, which always drooped next to the teacher's desk. My feelings were doubtless warmed by my having two uncles who had been in the Great War, one in the Navy, the other as a mule driver in the Army who brought ammunition up to the front in France.

Dirigibles were much in the news in the early 20's, and the Navy, as far as I was able to make out, owned them. Thus, the patriotic connection, which was helped along by the fact that nobody I had ever heard speaking English had ever used the word Indivisible. Or Divisible either, for that matter.

None of which inhibited me from rapping out the Pledge each and every morning: ". . . One Nation in a Dirigible, with Liberty and Justice for All." I could actually see in my mind's eye hordes of faces looking down at Earth through the windows of the Navy's airships. The whole United States was up there, all for one and one for all—and the whole gang in that Dirigible. One day, maybe I could get to ride in it, too, for I was deeply patriotic, and the height of Americanism, as I then understood it, was to ride in a Dirigible.

• *Source: Arthur Miller, "School Prayer: A Political Dirigible," New York Times, 12 March 1984. Copyright © 1984 by The New York Times Company. Reprinted by permission.*

invites you to think of democracy in terms of competing institutional models, one of which challenges the idealized notion of democracy. The alternative perspectives are meant to teach you about American political values, not to subvert those values. College courses that are intended to stimulate critical thinking have the potential to introduce students to political ideas that are radically different from those they bring to class. Most high school courses do not. Still, specialists in socialization contend that taking particular courses in college has little effect on attitude change, which is more likely to come from sustained interactions with classmates who hold different views.[28]

Community and Peers.   Your community and your peers are different but usually overlapping groups. Your community is the people of all ages with whom you come in contact because they live or work near you. Your peers are friends, classmates, and coworkers. Usually, they are your age and live within your community.

The makeup of the community has a lot to do with how political opinions are formed. Homogeneous communities—those whose members are

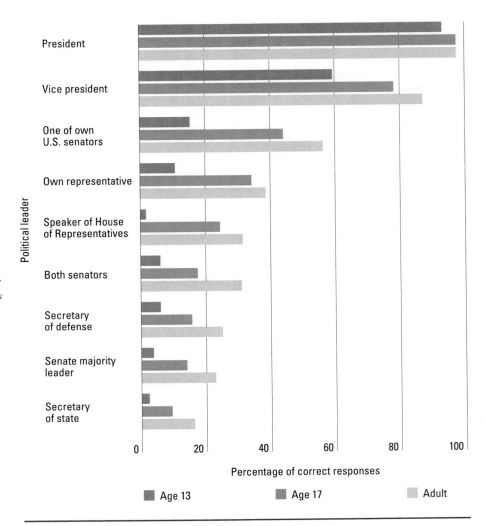

FIGURE **5.3**   ■ **Knowledge of Political Leaders, By Age Groups**

Do people actually learn any-thing about politics during high school? They seem to, according to a study that asked high school students at ages 13 and 17 and young adults for the last names of individuals who held the public offices listed here. (Respondents were not penal-ized for spelling errors.) The percentage of correct re-sponses was consistently higher with increasing age, but the greatest increases occurred during the high school years, between ages 13 and 17.

Source: Fred I. Greenstein, "What the President Means to Americans," in Choosing the President, ed. James D. Barber, p. 125. New York: The American Assembly, 1974. Used by permission.

similar in ethnicity, race, religion, or occupational status—can exert strong pressures on both children and adults to conform to the dominant attitude. For example, if all your neighbors praise the candidates of one party and criticize the candidates of the other, it is difficult to voice or even hold a dissenting opinion.[29] Communities made up of one ethnic group or religion may also voice negative attitudes about other groups. Although community socialization is usually reinforced in the schools, schools sometimes introduce students to ideas (one example is sex educa-tion) that run counter to community values.

For both children and adults, peer groups sometimes represent a defense against community pressures. Adolescent peer groups are particularly effective protection against parental pressures. In adolescence, children rely on their peers to defend their dress and lifestyle, not their politics. At the college level, however, peer group influence on political attitudes often grows substantially, sometimes fed by new information that clashes with parental beliefs. A classic study of students at Bennington College in the 1930s found that many became substantially more liberal than their affluent and conservative parents. Two follow-up studies twenty-five and fifty years later showed that most retained their liberal attitudes, in part because their spouses and friends (peers) supported their views.[30] Other evidence shows that the baby boomers who went to college during the late 1960s and became the affluent yuppies of the 1980s (perhaps your parents) became more liberal on social issues than their high school classmates who did not go to college. However, yuppies were about as conservative as nonyuppies on economic matters.[31]

Continuing Socialization

Political socialization continues throughout life. As parental and school influences wane in adulthood, peer groups (neighbors, coworkers, club members) assume a greater importance in promoting political awareness and in developing political opinions.[32] Because adults usually learn about political events from the mass media—newspapers, magazines, television, and radio—the media emerge as socialization agents. The role of television is especially important: Nearly three-quarters of adult Americans report regularly watching news on television.[33] (The mass media are so important in the political socialization of both children and adults that we devote a whole chapter—Chapter 6—to a discussion of their role.)

Regardless of how people learn about politics, they gain perspective on government as they grow older. They are apt to measure new candidates (and new ideas) against those they remember. Their values also change, increasingly reflecting their own self-interest. As voters age, for example, they begin to see more merit in government spending for Social Security than they did when they were younger. Finally, political education comes simply through exposure and familiarity. One example is the simple act of voting, which people do with increasing regularity as they grow older.

SOCIAL GROUPS AND POLITICAL VALUES

No two people are influenced by precisely the same socialization agents in precisely the same way. Each individual experiences a unique process of political socialization and forms a unique set of political values. Still, people with similar backgrounds do share learning experiences; this means they tend to develop similar political opinions. In this section, we examine the ties between people's social backgrounds and their political values. In the process, we will examine the ties between background and values by looking at responses to two questions posed by the 1992 National Election Survey by the University of Michigan's Center for Political Studies.

The first question deals with abortion. The interviewer said, "There has been some discussion about abortion during recent years. Which opinion on this page best agrees with your view? You can just tell me the number of the opinion you choose":

1. By law, abortion should never be permitted. [Ten percent agreed.]

2. The law should permit abortion only in case of rape, incest, or when the woman's life is in danger. [28 percent]

3. The law should permit abortion for reasons other than rape, incest, or danger to the woman's life, but only after the need for the abortion has been clearly established. [14 percent]

4. By law, a woman should be able to obtain an abortion as a matter of personal choice. [47 percent][34]

Those who chose the last category most clearly value individual freedom over order imposed by government. Moreover, the prochoice respondents do not view the issue as restricted to freedom of choice in reproduction. Evidence shows that they also have concerns about broader issues of social order, such as the role of women and the legitimacy of alternative life styles.[35]

The second question posed by the 1992 National Election Survey by the University of Michigan's Center for Political Studies, pertains to the role of government in guaranteeing employment:

> Some people feel the government in Washington should see to it that every person has a job and a good standard of living. Suppose that these people are at one end of the scale. . . . Others think the government should just let each person get ahead on his own. Suppose these people were at the other end. . . . Where would you put yourself on this scale, or haven't you thought much about this?

To Have and Have Not

Everyone feels uneasy at the sight of poverty in the presence of wealth. The question is, what should be done about poverty? Should the government step in to reduce income differences between the rich and the poor, perhaps by taxing the wealthy at higher rates and supplementing the income of the poor? Or should the government take no more from the wealthy than it does from the middle class, or even from the lower class?

COMPARED WITH WHAT? 5.1

Opinions on Government Provision of a Job

Compared with citizens in other industrial countries, Americans are much less likely to demand that the government guarantee employment. Respondents from twelve countries (as well as the former East Germany) were asked in 1991 whether they agreed or disagreed with this statement: "The government should provide a job for everyone who wants one." Not surprising, respondents in formerly communist countries still overwhelmingly considered this an appropriate role for government, but more than two-thirds of the respondents in Japan, West Germany, and the United Kingdom also felt that government should guarantee employment. Only in the United States were citizens equally divided on this issue.

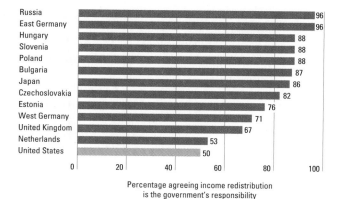

Percentage agreeing income redistribution is the government's responsibility

- *Source: International Social Justice Project, a collaborative international research effort. The data for this chart, which were kindly provided by Antal Örkény at Eotvos Lorand University in Budapest came from national surveys conducted in 1991 that were supported in whole or in part by the Institute for Social Research, University of Michigan; the Economic and Social Research Council (United Kingdom); the Deutsche Forschungsgemeinschaft; Institute of Social Science, Chuo University (Japan); and the Dutch Ministry of Social Affairs.*

Excluding those people who "haven't thought much" about this question, 30 percent wanted government to provide every person with a living and 22 percent were undecided. That left 48 percent who wanted the government to leave people alone to "get ahead" on their own. These respondents, who oppose government efforts to promote equality, apparently value freedom over equality.

Overall, the responses to each of these questions were divided approximately equally. Somewhat less than half the respondents (47 percent) felt that government should not set restrictions on abortion and nearly half (48 percent) thought the government should not guarantee a job and good standard of living. To learn about public opinion on government guarantees of jobs in other countries, see Compared with What? 5.1. However, sharp differences in attitudes on both issues emerged when American respondents were grouped by socioeconomic factors—education, income, region, origin, race, and religion. The differences are shown in Figure 5.4 as

| FIGURE | 5.4 | ■ **Group Deviations from National Opinion on Two Questions** |

Two questions—one on the dilemma of freedom versus order (opinions on abortion) and the other on the dilemma of freedom versus equality (government role in guaranteeing employment)—were asked of a national sample in 1992. Public opinion for the nation as a whole was sharply divided on each question. These two graphs show how respondents in several social groups deviated from overall public opinion. The longer the bars next to each group, the more its

respondents deviated from the expression of opinion for the entire sample. Bars that extend to the left show group opinions that deviate toward freedom. Bars that extend to the right show deviations away from freedom, toward order (part a) or equality (part b).

Source: Data from 1992 National Election Survey, Center for Political Studies, University of Michigan. Reprinted with permission.

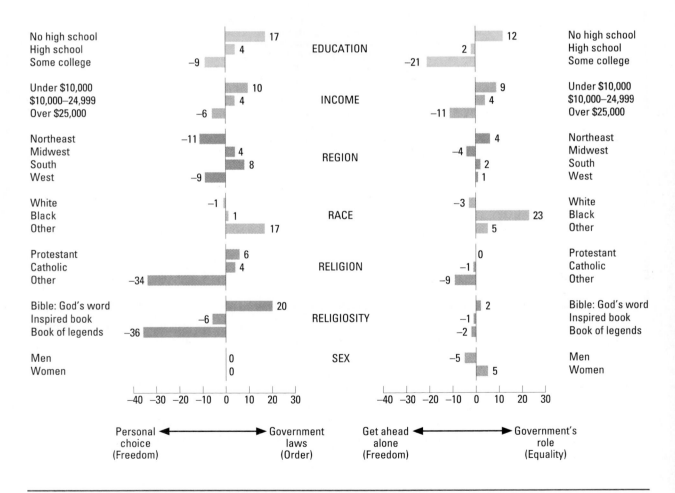

positive and negative deviations from the national averages. Bars that extend to the right identify groups that are more likely than most Americans to sacrifice freedom for a given value of government, either equality or order. Next, we examine the opinion patterns more closely for each socioeconomic group.

Education

Education increases citizens' awareness and understanding of political issues. Higher education also promotes tolerance of unpopular opinions and behavior and invites issues to be seen in terms of civil rights and liberties. This result is clearly shown in Figure 5.4a, where those with more education are more likely to view abortion as a matter of a woman's choice.[36] When confronted with issues that involve a choice between personal freedom and social order, college-educated respondents tend to choose freedom.

With regard to the role of government in reducing income inequality, Figure 5.4b shows that more education also produces opinions that favor freedom over equality. The higher their level of education, the less likely respondents were to support government-guaranteed jobs and living standards. You might expect better-educated people to be humanitarian and to support government programs to help the needy. However, because educated people tend to be wealthier, they would be taxed more heavily for such government programs. Moreover, they may believe that it is unrealistic to expect government to make such economic guarantees.

Income

In many countries, differences in social class—based on social background and occupational status—divide people in their politics.[37] In the United States, we have avoided the uglier aspects of class conflict, but here wealth sometimes substitutes for class. As Figure 5.4 shows, wealth is consistently linked to opinions favoring a limited government role in promoting order and equality. Those with higher incomes are more likely to favor personal choice in abortion and to oppose government guarantees of employment and living conditions. In both cases, wealth and education have a similar effect on opinion: The groups with more education and higher income opt for freedom.

Region

Early in our country's history, regional differences were politically important—important enough to spark a civil war between the North and South. For nearly a hundred years after the Civil War, regional differences continued to affect politics. The moneyed Northeast was thought to control the purse strings of capitalism. The Midwest was long regarded as the stronghold of "isolationism" in foreign affairs. The South was virtually a one-party region, almost completely Democratic. And the individualistic West pioneered its own mixture of progressive politics.

In the past, differences in wealth fed cultural differences among regions. In recent decades, however, the movement of people and wealth away from the Northeast and Midwest to the Sunbelt states in the South and Southwest has equalized the per capita income of the various regions. One result of the equalization is that the formerly "Solid South" is no longer solidly Democratic. In fact, the South has tended to vote for Republican presidential candidates since 1968.

Figure 5.4 shows more striking differences in public opinion of social issues than economic issues in the four major regions of the United States. Respondents in the Northeast and West are more likely to support personal choice than residents of the South, where they are more likely to favor restricting abortion. People in the Midwest are somewhat more likely to oppose government efforts to equalize income than are people in the Northeast. Despite the differences, regional effects on public opinion are weaker than the effects of most other socioeconomic factors.

The "Old" and "New" Ethnicity: European Origin and Race

At the turn of the century, the major ethnic minorities in America were immigrants from Ireland, Italy, Germany, Poland, and other European countries who came to the United States in waves during the late 1800s and early 1900s. The immigrants entered a nation that had been founded by British settlers more than a hundred years earlier. They found themselves in a strange land, usually without money and unable to speak the language. Moreover, their religious backgrounds—mainly Catholic and Jewish—differed from the predominant Protestantism of the earlier settlers. Local politicians saw the newcomers, who were concentrated in low-status jobs in urban areas of the Northeast and Midwest, as a new source of votes and soon mobilized them in politics. The urban ethnics and their descendants became part of the great coalition of Democratic voters that President Franklin Roosevelt forged in the 1930s. And for years after, the European ethnics supported liberal candidates and causes more strongly than the original Anglo-Saxon immigrants.[38] More recent studies of public opinion show the differences are disappearing.[39] But if this **"old" ethnicity**—of European origin—is giving way to assimilation, a **"new" ethnicity**—race—is taking its place.

For many years after the Civil War, the issue of race in American politics was defined as "how the South should treat the Negro." The debate between North and South over this issue became a conflict between civil rights and states' rights—a conflict in which blacks were primarily objects, not participants, in those years. But with the rise of black consciousness and the grassroots civil rights movement in the late 1950s and 1960s, blacks secured genuine voting rights in the South and exercised those rights more vigorously in the North. Although they made up only about 12 percent of the total population, blacks comprised sizable voting blocs in southern states and in northern cities. As were the European ethnics before them, American blacks were courted for their votes; finally, their opinions were politically important.

Blacks constitute the biggest racial minority in American politics but not the only significant one. Asians, American Indians (Native Americans), and other nonwhites account for another 5 percent of the population. People of Latin American and Spanish origin—Hispanics—are often commonly but inaccurately regarded as a racial group, for they consist of

Ethnicity in Elections

Irish-Americans, Italian-Americans, Polish-Americans, and members of other ethnic groups have gained political power through elections for local offices. Margaret Chin followed tradition by running in the Democratic primary for the New York City Council in 1991 and 1993. Although she lost both times to the incumbent councilwoman, her contests probably raised the political consciousness of Chinese-Americans in her district.

both whites and nonwhites. Hispanics make up about 9 percent of the nation's population, according to the 1990 census, but they comprise as much as 26 percent of the population in California and Texas and 38 percent in New Mexico.[40] Although they are politically strong in some communities, Hispanics (comprised of groups as different as Cubans, Mexicans, Haitians, and Puerto Ricans) have lagged behind blacks in mobilizing across the nation. However, Hispanics are being wooed by non-Hispanic candidates and are increasingly running for public office themselves.

Blacks and members of other minorities display somewhat similar political attitudes on questions pertaining to equality issues. The reasons are twofold.[41] First, racial minorities (excepting second-generation Asians) tend to have low **socioeconomic status,** a combination of education, occupational status, and income. Second, all racial minorities have been targets of racial prejudice and discrimination and have benefited from government actions in support of equality. Figure 5.4b clearly shows the effects of race on the freedom-equality issue. Blacks strongly favor government action to improve economic opportunity, while other minorities also favor government action but to a lesser degree. On the abortion issue, however, blacks differ little from whites, whereas other minorities favor government restrictions.

Religion

Since the last major wave of European immigration in the 1930s and 1940s, the religious makeup of the United States has remained fairly stable. Today, almost 65 percent of the population are Protestant, about 25 percent are Catholic, only about 2 percent are Jewish, and about 10 percent deny any religious affiliation or choose some other faith.[42] For many years, analysts found strong and consistent differences in the political opinions of Protestants, Catholics, and Jews.[43] Protestants were more conservative than Catholics, and Catholics tended to be more conservative than Jews.

Some such differences have remained, especially on questions of freedom versus order (e.g., the abortion question), but they are less marked than one might expect. Protestants oppose personal choice on abortion slightly more than Catholics, despite the Pope's strong opposition to abortion. Those in the "other" group, which includes mostly nonreligious persons but also includes Jews, are much more likely to favor personal choice on abortion and somewhat more inclined toward government job guarantees.

Even greater differences on the order issue emerge when respondents are classified by their "religiosity," which was measured by their attitudes toward the Bible. About 40 percent of the sample responded that it should be taken literally as the actual word of God. Almost 50 percent regarded it as an inspired book but not to be taken literally. The remaining 13 percent viewed it as an ancient book of fables, legends, history, and moral precepts recorded by humans. As Figure 5.4 indicates, religiosity has little effect on attitudes toward economic equality but powerful influence on attitudes toward social order. Those who believed that the Bible is the word of God strongly favor more government action in regulating abortion. The minority, who do not think the Bible is inspired, is far more inclined to value freedom over order. This method of classifying respondents reveals that political opinions in the United States do differ sharply according to religious beliefs. As one noted scholar in the field says, "Religion matters. It matters politically."[44]

Gender

Differences in sex, which has become known as *gender* in American politics, are often related to political opinions, primarily on the issue of freedom versus equality. As shown in Figure 5.4b, women are more likely to favor government actions to promote equality. However, men and women usually differ less on issues of freedom versus order. Even on the abortion issue, women and men are equally likely to favor personal choice (see Figure 5.4a) over government restrictions. Still, on many issues of government policy, the "gender gap" in American politics is noticeable, with women more supportive than men of government spending for social programs.

FROM VALUES TO IDEOLOGY

We have just seen that differences in groups' responses to two survey questions reflect value choices between freedom and order and between freedom and equality. But to what degree do opinions on specific issues reflect explicit political ideology (the set of values and beliefs people hold about the purpose and scope of government)? Political scientists generally agree that ideology influences public opinion on specific issues; they have much less consensus on the extent to which people explicitly think in ideological terms.[45] They also agree that the public's ideological thinking cannot be categorized adequately in conventional liberal-conservative terms.[46]

The Degree of Ideological Thinking in Public Opinion

In an early but important study of public opinion, respondents were asked to describe the parties and candidates in the 1956 election.[47] Only about 12 percent of the sample volunteered responses that contained ideological terms (such as *liberal, conservative,* and *capitalism*). Most respondents (42 percent) evaluated the parties and candidates in terms of "benefits to groups" (farmers, workers, or businesspeople, for example). Others (24 percent) spoke more generally about "the nature of the times" (for example, inflation, unemployment, and the threat of war). Finally, a good portion of the sample (22 percent) gave answers that contained no classifiable issue content. Other studies have found that the vast majority of the electorate is confused by ideological terms. Consider this response from a resident of the San Francisco Bay Area in 1972 to the question "What do the terms *liberal* and *conservative* mean to you?"

> Oh conservative. Liberal and conservative. Liberal and conservative. I haven't given it much thought. I wouldn't know. I don't know what those would mean! Liberal . . . liberal . . . liberal. And conservative. Well, if a person is liberal with their money they squander their money? Does it fall in that same category? If you're conservative you don't squander so much, you save a little, huh?[48]

A woman in Utica, New York, who participated in a separate in-depth study of how people think about politics, replied when asked if she had an idea about the meaning of *liberal* and *conservative,* "No. I read it. I read it in the paper. I read the editorials sometimes and sometimes it's just a little over my head. And I'd like to know more, but then I'll say why bother."[49]

Subsequent research found somewhat greater ideological awareness within the electorate, especially during the 1964 presidential contest between Lyndon Johnson, a Democrat and ardent liberal, and Barry Goldwater, a Republican who was then considered an archconservative.[50] But more recent research has questioned whether American voters have really changed in their ideological thinking.[51] The tendency to respond to questions by using ideological terms increased with increasing education, which helps people understand political issues and relate them to one another. Personal experiences in the socialization process can also lead people to think ideologically. For example, children raised in strong union households may be taught to distrust private enterprise and to value collective action through the government.

True ideologues hold a consistent set of values and beliefs about the purpose and scope of government, and they tend to evaluate candidates in ideological terms.[52] Some people respond to questions in ways that seem ideological but are not, because they do not understand the underlying principles. For example, most respondents dutifully comply when asked to place themselves somewhere on a liberal-conservative continuum. The result, as shown earlier in Figure 5.2, is an approximately normal distribution centering on "moderate," the modal category. But many people settle on moderate when they do not clearly understand the alternatives, because it is a safe choice. A study in 1992 gave respondents another choice—the statement "I haven't thought much about it"—which allowed them to avoid placing themselves on the liberal-conservative continuum. In this study, 25 percent of the respondents acknowledged that they had not thought much about ideology.[53] The extent of ideological thinking in America, then, is considerably less than it might seem from responses to questions that ask people to describe themselves as liberals or conservatives.[54]

The Quality of Ideological Thinking in Public Opinion

What people's ideological self-placement means in the 1990s also is not clear. Originally, the liberal-conservative continuum represented a single dimension: attitudes toward the scope of government activity. Liberals were in favor of more government action to provide public goods, and conservatives were in favor of less. The simple distinction is not as useful today. Many people who call themselves *liberals* no longer favor government activism in general, and many self-styled *conservatives* no longer oppose it in principle. As a result, many people have difficulty deciding whether they are liberal or conservative, while others confidently choose identical points on the continuum for entirely different reasons. People describe themselves as liberal or conservative because of the symbolic value of the terms as much as for reasons of ideology.[55]

Studies of the public's ideological thinking find that two themes run through people's minds when they are asked to describe liberals and conservatives. People associate liberals with change and conservatives with tradition. The theme corresponds to the distinction between liberals and conservatives on the exercise of freedom and the maintenance of order.[56]

The other theme has to do with equality. The conflict between freedom and equality was at the heart of President Roosevelt's New Deal economic policies (social security, minimum wage legislation, farm price supports) in the 1930s. The policies expanded the interventionist role of the national government in order to promote greater economic equality. And attitudes toward government intervention in the economy served to distinguish liberals from conservatives for decades after.[57] Attitudes toward government interventionism still underlie opinions about domestic economic policies.[58] Liberals support intervention to promote economic equality; conservatives favor less government intervention and more individual freedom in economic activities.

In Chapter 1, we proposed an alternative ideological classification based on people's relative evaluations of freedom, order, and equality. We described liberals as people who believe that government should promote equality, even if some freedom is lost in the process, but who oppose surrendering freedom to government-imposed order. Conservatives do not oppose equality in and of itself but put a higher value on freedom than equality when the two conflict. Yet, conservatives are not above restricting freedom when threatened with the loss of order. So both groups value freedom, but one is more willing to trade freedom for equality, and the

FIGURE 5.5 ■ Respondents Classified by Ideological Tendencies

Two survey questions presented choices between freedom and order and between freedom and equality by asking respondents whether abortion should be a matter of personal choice or of government regulation, and whether government should guarantee a job and good standard of living or people should get ahead on their own. (The questions are given verbatim on page 156.) People's responses to the questions showed no correlation, demonstrating that these value choices cannot be explained by a simple liberal-conservative continuum. Instead, their responses can be more usefully analyzed according to four different ideological types. (The one-point difference in the percentage of responses for the "government guarantee jobs" question from that given on page 158 is the result of losing a few cases when the questions are cross tabulated.)

Source: 1992 National Election Study, Center for Political Studies, University of Michigan.

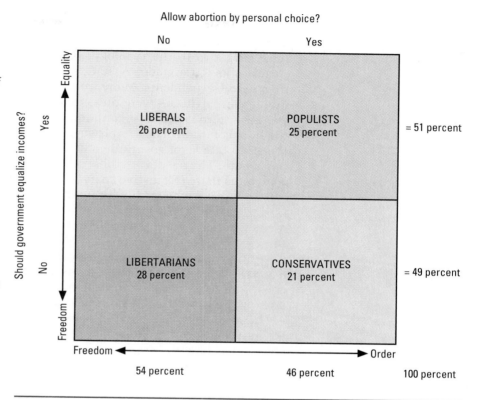

other is more inclined to trade freedom for order. If you have trouble thinking about these tradeoffs on a single dimension, you are in good company. The liberal-conservative continuum presented to survey respondents takes a two-dimensional concept and squeezes it into a one-dimensional format.[59]

Ideological Types in the United States

Our ideological typology in Chapter 1 (see Figure 1.2) classifies people as liberals if they favor freedom over order and equality over freedom. Conversely, conservatives favor freedom over equality and order over freedom. Libertarians favor freedom over both equality and order—the opposite of populists. By cross-tabulating people's answers to the two questions about freedom versus order (abortion) and freedom versus equality (government job guarantees), we can classify respondents according to their ideological tendencies. As shown in Figure 5.5, people's responses to the two questions are virtually unrelated—that is, the responses fall about equally within each of the quadrants. This finding indicates that people do not decide about government activity according to a one-dimensional ideological standard. Figure 5.5 also classifies the sample according to the two dimensions in our ideological typology. Using only two issues to classify people in an ideological framework leaves substantial room for error. Still, if the typology is worthwhile, the results should be meaningful, and they are.

It is striking that the ideological tendencies of the respondents in the 1992 sample depicted in Figure 5.5 are divided almost equally among the four categories of the typology. (Remember, however, that these categories—like letter grades A, B, C, and D—are more rigid in the typology than in the respondents. Many would cluster toward the center of the figure, if their attitudes were measured more sensitively.) The populist response pattern is the most common by a small margin and the libertarian the least common. The sample suggests that more than three-quarters of the electorate favor government action to promote order, increase equality, or both. The results resemble earlier findings by other researchers who conducted more exhaustive analyses involving more survey questions.[60]

Respondents who readily locate themselves on a single dimension running from liberal to conservative often go on to contradict their self-placement when answering questions that trade freedom for either order or equality.[61] A two-dimensional typology such as that in Figure 5.5 allows us to analyze responses more meaningfully.[62] A slight majority of respondents (52 percent) expresses opinions that are either liberal (26 percent) or conservative (26 percent), but almost as many express opinions that deviate from these familiar ideological types.

The ideological tendencies illustrate important differences among different social groups. Populists are prominent among minorities and among people with little education and low income, groups that tend to look favorably on the benefits of government in general. Libertarians are concentrated among respondents with more education and with higher income, who tend to be suspicious of government interference in their lives. People in the southern states tend to be Populists, those in the Midwest tend to be Conservatives, and those in the Northeast are inclined to be Liberals. Men are more likely to be conservative or libertarian than women, who tend to be liberal or populist.

This more refined analysis of political ideology explains why even Americans who pay close attention to politics find it difficult to locate themselves on the liberal-conservative continuum. Their problem is that they are liberal on some issues and conservative on others. Forced to choose along just one dimension, they opt for the middle category, moderate. However, our analysis also indicates that many respondents who classify themselves as liberals and conservatives do conform to our typology. There is value, then, in the liberal-conservative distinction, so long as we understand its limitations.

THE PROCESS OF FORMING POLITICAL OPINIONS

We have seen that people acquire their values through socialization and that different social groups develop different sets of political values. We also have learned that some people, but only a minority, think about politics ideologically, holding a consistent set of political attitudes and beliefs. Now let us look at how people form opinions on a particular issue. In particular, how do those who are not ideologues—in other words, most citi-

From the California Assembly to the U.S. Congress

Democrat Maxine Waters was elected to the House of Representatives in 1990, succeeding Augustus Hawkins, who retired after serving Los Angeles for fourteen terms. Representative Waters is expected to be a forceful advocate of women's rights and social programs, reflecting the interests of her low-income, largely black and Hispanic district.

MAXINE WATERS

zens—form political opinions? Four factors—self-interest, political information, opinion schemas, and political leadership—play a part in the process.

Self-interest

The **self-interest principle** states that people choose what benefits them personally.[63] The principle plays an obvious role in how people form opinions on government economic policies. Taxpayers tend to prefer low taxes to high taxes; farmers tend to favor candidates who promise them more support over those who promise them less. The self-interest principle also applies, but less clearly, to some government policies outside economics. Members of minority groups tend to see more personal advantage in government policies that promote social equality than do members of majority groups; teenage males are more likely to oppose compulsory military service than are older people of either sex. Group leaders often cue group members, telling them what policies they should support or oppose. (In the context of pluralist democracy, this often appears as grassroots support for or opposition to policies that affect only particular groups.)[64]

For many government policies, however, the self-interest principle plays little or no role for the majority of citizens, because the policies directly affect relatively few people. Outlawing prostitution is one example; doctor-assisted suicide is another. When moral issues are involved in government policy, people form opinions based on their underlying values.[65]

When moral issues are not in question and when individuals do not benefit directly from a policy, many people have trouble relating to the policy and forming an opinion. This tends to be true of the whole subject of foreign policy, which few people interpret in terms of personal benefits. Here, many people have no opinion, or their opinions are not firmly held and are apt to change quite easily, given almost any new information.

Political Information

In the United States today, education is compulsory (usually to age sixteen), and the literacy rate is relatively high. The country boasts an unparalleled network of colleges and universities entered by two-thirds of all high school graduates. American citizens can obtain information from a variety of daily and weekly news publications. They can keep abreast of national and international affairs through nightly television news, which brings live coverage of world events via satellite from virtually anywhere in the world. Yet, the average American displays an astonishing lack of political knowledge.[66]

Citizens' knowledge of politics just after an election is low enough to make the basis of their vote questionable. After the 1992 election, for example, only 27 percent of a national sample could correctly identify even one of their candidates for the House of Representatives, and only 40 percent correctly named either of their candidates for the Senates.[67] In June 1990, the Supreme Court made news by overturning an act of Congress that outlawed flag burning. The Court affirmed that flag burning is a means of expression protected by the Constitution. Despite the great publicity given the decision, 31 percent of a national sample incorrectly thought the Court had supported the anti–flag-burning law, and 17 percent acknowledged that they did not know. Only 52 percent of the public knew (guessed?) what the Court had decided on this highly charged issue.[68]

But Americans do not let lack of information stop them from expressing their opinions. They readily offer opinions on issues ranging from capital punishment to nuclear power to the government's handling of the economy. When opinions are based on little information, however, they change easily in the face of new information. The result is a high degree of instability in public opinion poll findings, depending on how questions are worded and on recent events that bear on the issue. Nevertheless, some researchers hold that the *collective* opinion of the public can be interpreted as rational. Page and Shapiro analyzed the public's responses to 1,128 questions that were repeated in one or more surveys between 1935 and 1990.[69] They found that responses to more than half of the repeated policy questions "showed no significant change at all"—that is, no more than six percentage points.[70] Moreover, Page and Shapiro concluded that when the public's collective opinion on public policy changes, it changes in "understandable, predictable ways."[71] Other scholars have contended that even collective public opinion may be misleading when the issues involve core beliefs (especially opposing beliefs) or when there is a sharp division in the quality of respondents' information (as more knowledgeable respondents impart their upper-income bias to the findings).[72]

Researchers use the term **political sophistication** for a broad range of opinions, based on factual information, that are consistent and organized conceptually.[73] One study of political sophistication counted the number of specific political issues, public figures, and events that 143 respondents brought up in hour-long interviews on political alienation. The average number of political references was 27. The highest number was 94, and the lowest was 1—just a single reference to a political subject in an hour-long interview on politics! So what *did* people talk about? The researcher said that they talked about themselves: "Asked whether they are satisfied about the way things have been going in this country, they responded only about their job, family, friends, and other aspects of their own life."[74]

The author of this study classified the American public as three broad groups in terms of political sophistication. The least sophisticated (about 20 percent of the electorate) pay little attention to public affairs and seldom participate in politics. Most adults (about 75 percent) are only moderately sophisticated. "They half-attentively monitor the flow of political news, but they run for the most part on a psychological automatic pilot." Only a small portion of the electorate (about 5 percent) is politically sophisticated, sharing the knowledge and conceptual grasp of professional politicians, journalists, and political analysts. As expected, level of education strongly relates to political sophistication but so do participation in voluntary associations and parents' interest in politics. The author describes the development of political sophistication as a "spiral process . . . a gradual process in which interest breeds knowledge, which, in turn, breeds further interest and knowledge over time."[75]

Researchers have not found any meaningful relationship between political sophistication and self-placement on the liberal-conservative scale. That is, people with equivalent knowledge of public affairs and levels of conceptualization are equally likely to call themselves liberals or conservatives.[76] Equal levels of political understanding, then, may produce quite different political views as a result of individuals' unique patterns of political socialization.

Opinion Schemas

Even people who do not approach politics with full-blown ideologies interpret political issues in terms of some preexisting mental structure. Psychologists refer to the packet of preexisting beliefs that people apply to specific issues as an **opinion schema**—a network of organized knowledge and beliefs that guides the processing of information on a particular subject.[77] Figure 5.6 is a rendition of a partial opinion schema about Bill Clinton that might be held by a liberal Democrat. It suggests the wide range of attitudes and beliefs that affect thinking about political leaders and their policies. Our opinion schemas change as we acquire new infor-

FIGURE **5.6**   ■ **Hypothetical Opinion Schema About Bill Clinton**

People express opinions on issues, persons, or events according to preexisting attitudes and beliefs that they associate with the question being asked. Psychologists sometimes refer to this network of attitudes and beliefs, and their relationships, as an opinion schema. This is a hypothetical opinion schema that might be associated with Bill Clinton in the mind of a liberal Democrat who voted for Clinton in 1992.

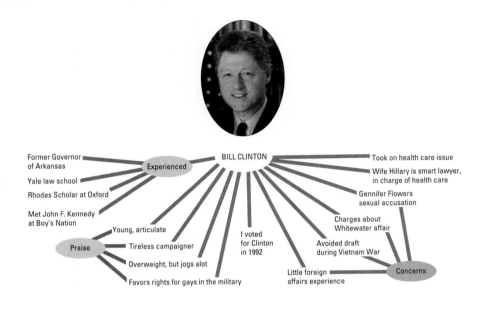

mation. A liberal embracing the opinion schema in Figure 5.6 would have been more disappointed than a conservative Republican by Clinton's backing off on his pledge to admit gays into the military.

The schema concept gives us a more flexible tool for analyzing public opinion than the more rigid concept of ideology. The main value of schemas for understanding how opinions are formed is that they remind us that opinion questions trigger many different images, connections, and values in the mind of each respondent. Given the complexity of factors in individual opinion schemas, it is surprising that researchers find as many strong correlations as they do among individuals' social backgrounds, general values, and specific opinions. Opinion schemas can pertain to any political figure and to any subject—race, economics, or international relations, for example.[78] For instance, one study found that African Americans' views on the importance of race in determining one's chances in life could be analyzed according to five different schemas.[79]

Still, the more encompassing concept of ideology is hard to escape. Researchers have found that people's personal schemas tend to be organized in ways that parallel broader ideological categories. In other words, a conservative's opinion schema about Clinton may not differ factually from a liberal's, but it will differ considerably in its evaluation of those facts.[80] Clinton's tax increases to help balance the budget, for example, might evoke anger in the conservative's schema and acceptance in the liberal's schema.

Some scholars argue that most citizens, in their efforts to make sense of politics, pay less attention to government policies than to their leaders' "style" in approaching political problems—for instance, whether they are seen as tough, compassionate, honest, or hard working.[81] When a leader behaves in a manner of which style-oriented citizens approve, they view his or her policies favorably. In this way, citizens can relate the complexities of politics to their personal experiences. If many citizens view politics in terms of governing style, the role of political leadership becomes a more important determinant of public opinion than the leader's actual policies.

Political Leadership

Public opinion on specific issues is molded by political leaders, journalists, and policy experts. Because of the attention given to the presidency by the media, presidents are uniquely positioned to shape popular attitudes. Consider Ronald Reagan and the issue of nuclear disarmament. In 1987, President Reagan and Mikhail Gorbachev signed a treaty banning intermediate-range nuclear forces (INF) from Europe and the Soviet Union. Soon afterward, a national survey found that 82 percent of the sample approved of the treaty, and 18 percent opposed it. As might be expected, those who viewed the Soviet Union as highly threatening ("hard-liners") were least enthusiastic about the INF treaty. Respondents were then asked to agree or disagree with this statement: "President Reagan is well known for his anticommunism, so if he thinks this is a good deal, it must be." Analysis of the responses showed that hard-liners who agreed with the statement were nearly twice as likely to approve of the treaty as those who were unmoved by Reagan's involvement. The researcher concluded that "a highly conciliatory move by a president known for long-standing opposition to just such an action" can override expected sources of opposition among the public.[82] The implication is that another president, such as Jimmy Carter or even George Bush, could not have won over the hard-liners—much less the anti-war protester, Bill Clinton.

The ability of political leaders to influence public opinion has been enhanced enormously by the growth of the broadcast media, especially television.[83] The majoritarian model of democracy assumes that government officials respond to public opinion, but evidence is substantial that the causal sequence is reversed: that public opinion responds to the actions of government officials.[84] If this is true, how much potential is there for public opinion to be manipulated by political leaders through the mass media? We examine the manipulative potential of the mass media in the next chapter.

SUMMARY

Public opinion does not rule in America. On most issues, it merely sets general boundaries for government policy. The shape of the distribution of opinion (normal, skewed, or bimodal) indicates how sharply the public is divided. Bimodal distributions harbor the greatest potential for political conflict. The stability of a distribution over time indicates how settled people are in their opinions. Because most Americans' ideological opinions are normally distributed around the moderate category and have been for decades, government policies can vary from left to right over time without provoking severe political conflict.

People form their values through the process of political socialization. The most important socialization agents in childhood and young adulthood are family, school, community, and peers. Members of the same social group tend to experience similar socialization processes and thus to adopt similar values. People in different social groups, who hold different values, often express vastly different opinions. Differences in education, race, and religion tend to produce sharper divisions of opinion today on questions of order and equality than do differences in income, region, and ethnicity.

Most people do not think about politics in ideological terms. When asked to do so by pollsters, however, they readily classify themselves along a liberal-conservative continuum. Many respondents choose the middle category, moderate, because the choice is safe. Many others choose it because they have liberal views on some issues and conservative views on others. Their political orientations are better captured by a two-dimensional framework for analyzing ideology based on the values of freedom, order, and equality. Responses to the survey questions we used to establish our ideological typology divide the American electorate almost equally as liberals, conservatives, libertarians, and populists. The quarter of the public that gave liberal responses, favoring government action to promote equality but not to impose order, was matched by an equal portion who gave the opposite, conservative responses. Similarly, the somewhat larger group of populists, who wanted government to impose both order and equality, was opposed by a smaller group of libertarians, who wanted government to do neither.

In addition to ideological orientation, many other factors enter the process of forming political opinions. When individuals stand to benefit or suffer from proposed government policies, they usually base their opinions on self-interest. When citizens lack information on which to base their opinions, they usually respond anyway, which leads to substantial fluctuations in poll results, depending on how questions are worded and intervening events. The various factors that impinge on the process of forming political opinions can be mapped out within an opinion schema, a network of beliefs and attitudes about a particular topic. The schema imagery helps us visualize the complex process of forming opinions. This process, however, is not completely idiosyncratic: People tend to organize their schemas according to broader ideological thinking. In the absence of information, respondents are particularly susceptible to cues of support or opposition from political leaders, communicated through the mass media.

Which model of democracy, the majoritarian or the pluralist, is correct in its assumptions about public opinion? Sometimes, the public shows clear and settled opinions on government policy, conforming to the majoritarian model. However, public opinion is often not firmly grounded in knowledge and may be unstable on given issues. Moreover, powerful groups often divide on what they want government to do. The lack of consensus leaves politicians with a great deal of latitude in enacting specific policies, a finding that conforms to the pluralist model. Of course, politicians' actions are closely scrutinized by journalists reporting in the mass media. We turn to the effect on politics of this scrutiny and of the mass media in Chapter 6.

Key Terms

public opinion
normal distribution
skewed distribution
bimodal distribution
stable distribution
political socialization

"old" ethnicity
"new" ethnicity
socioeconomic status
self-interest principle
political sophistication
opinion schema

Selected Readings

Asher, Herbert. *Polling and the Public: What Every Citizen Should Know.* Washington, D.C.: Congressional Quarterly Press, 1988. A concise text on polling methodology that gives special attention to election polls.

Herbst, Susan. *Numbered Voices: How Opinion Polling Has Shaped American Politics.* Chicago: University of Chicago Press, 1993. Herbst explores the history of public opinion in the United States, illustrated with case studies. She argues that the use of opinion polls often narrows the political debate, slighting other, important issues.

Ichilov, Orit. *Political Socialization, Citizenship Education, and Democracy.* New York: Teachers College Press, 1990. A collection of studies on how people acquire political attitudes, with special attention to childhood processes and with examples drawn from other cultures.

Margolis, Michael, and Gary A. Mauser, eds. *Manipulating Public Opinion: Essays on Public Opinion as a Dependent Variable.* Pacific Grove, Calif.: Brooks/Cole, 1989. Studies the abilities of political elites to manage public opinion in election campaigns, in shaping public policies, and in political socialization.

Mayer, William G. *The Changing American Mind: How and Why American Public Opinion Changed Between 1960 and 1988.* Ann Arbor: University of Michigan Press, 1992. The subtitle describes the book. Mayer finds that the public has become more liberal on some issues and more conservative on others. Most changes, he contends, are simply due to people changing their minds on reflection on the issues and the politics.

Niemi, Richard G., John Mueller, and Tom W. Smith. *Trends in Public Opinion: A Compendium of Survey Data.* New York: Greenwood, 1989. This handy volume collects some fifty years of polling data, with heavy concentration on annual data from the General Social Surveys, begun in 1972. The survey data are organized in fifteen chapters, each preceded by a useful descriptive essay.

Page, Benjamin I., and Robert Y. Shapiro. *The Rational Public.* Chicago: University of Chicago Press, 1992. Two experts in the field analyze more than one thousand poll questions on public policy that were repeated in identical form in at least two national surveys. After aggregating the individual responses and studying overall patterns of public opinion, they conclude that the public is indeed rational and demonstrate strong evidence for their claim.

Rinehart, Sue Tolleson. *Gender Consciousness and Politics.* New York: Routledge, 1992. Reviews literature on women and politics with special reference to the socialization process.

Sanders, Arthur. *Making Sense of Politics.* Ames: Iowa State University Press, 1990. Sanders interviewed at length twenty-six citizens of Ithaca, New York, about their thoughts on politics. In contrast to the short responses gathered from many people in opinion polls, this study reports at length on the thinking that average citizens devote to politics. It concludes that more people try to make sense of politics by focusing on the style of decision making than on the content of government policies.

Stimson, James A. *Public Opinion in America: Mood, Cycles, & Swings.* Boulder, CO: Westview, 1992. The result of a massive study of more than one thousand survey questions from 1956 to 1989, this book charts the drift of public opinion from liberal in the 1950s to conservative at the end of the 1970s and moving toward liberal in the 1980s.

CHAPTER 6

The Mass Media

IN OCTOBER 1993, the whole world watched the body of an American soldier being dragged through the streets of Mogadishu, Somalia. The unidentified soldier was killed in a disastrous attempt to capture General Farah Aidid, the Somali warlord wanted for his role in killing twenty-four U.N. troops stationed there to keep peace among the warring factions. The grisly pictures of the American corpse flashed across a global satellite network with a television interview of another American soldier captured in the raid on Aidid's hideout. Viewers saw the bloody face and heard the fearful voice of Chief Warrant Officer Michael Durant, held prisoner somewhere in Mogadishu. Reacting to these images of death and injury in a far-away land, the American public clamored for removing U.S. soldiers from Somalia. Also moved by the television coverage, President Bill Clinton said, "I'm just not going to have those kids killed for nothing,"[1] and he revamped his policy on Somalia, promised to remove U.S. troops in six months, and did so.

The public and the president were not the only ones who drew conclusions from the humiliating television images. Our friends abroad feared that the United States would lapse into isolationism, no longer playing the role of a superpower.[2] Our foes saw the United States as lacking the stomach for military confrontation, and they openly defied U.S. policies and taunted the government. Later that October, when troops were sent to assist Haiti's return to democracy, armed supporters of the military government prevented the U.S. ship from landing, threatening to repeat our Somalia experience. Early the next month, the speaker of the Iranian parliament told an anti-American rally in Iran, "You saw the American soldier bound and dragged down the street. This is a sign of a United States humiliated and stuck in a quagmire."[3]

The political power of television, once largely limited to national audiences, now has a global range. Via satellite, Americans can watch the world—and the world can watch America. In the formerly communist country of Hungary, for example, viewers have a choice of several American news programs. Cable News Network (CNN) International broadcasts news twenty-four hours a day in Hungary and more than two hundred other countries. Citizens in Budapest can also watch the CBS "Evening News" and ABC News's "Nightline" (both taped the previous night and broadcast every morning on Britain's Sky News channel), and the NBC "Nightly News" (rerun the next morning on Britain's Super Channel, owned by NBC).[4] Before global television, the president and

As Seen on TV
In the fall of 1993, television viewers all over the world saw the battered face of Chief Warrant Officer Michael Durant, who was being held prisoner after a failed U.S. military raid on the headquarters of a local warlord in Mogadishu, Somalia. His captors forced Durant to appear on camera to pressure the U.S. to withdraw its forces from Somalia. The television image helped to do just that.

Congress only had to deal with news media in the United States. Now they must confront the international implications of the media.

There is no doubt that the media affected American foreign policy in Somalia. After all, President George Bush had sent U.S. troops there in 1991 in response to heart-rending pictures of children starving during the civil war. Two years later, frightful pictures of U.S. soldiers killed and captured put pressure on President Clinton to pull them out. Decades earlier, the freewheeling television coverage of the horrors of the Vietnam War contributed to antiwar sentiment and pressures for withdrawal. Learning how images of war can sway public opinion, the military subsequently developed policies for controlling media coverage of combat zones and used them in dealing with reporters during the Persian Gulf conflict of 1991.

When the ground war began, the Pentagon restricted news coverage, even suspending regular press briefings. To get around these restrictions, some journalists began traveling with Saudi and Egyptian forces to cover the war. Other journalists tried to operate on their own and were captured by Iraqi forces (but eventually released). Ultimately, the ground campaign was such a success that the military repealed its blackout to spread the good news. If the fighting had been fierce, the public would have been told less and told later. Many journalists claim that our government infringed on freedom of the press in the last three international conflicts. Is this a cause for public concern, or does open press coverage of foreign conflict unduly hamper the military conduct of war and the pursuit of order?

Freedom of the press is essential to democratic government, but the news media also complicate the governing process. What is the nature of the mass media in America? Who uses the media, and what do they learn? Do the media promote or frustrate democratic ideals? Does freedom of the press conflict with the values of order or equality? In this chapter, we describe the origin and growth of the media, assess their objectivity, and examine their influence on politics.

PEOPLE, GOVERNMENT, AND COMMUNICATIONS

"We never talk anymore" is a common lament of couples who are not getting along very well. In politics, too, citizens and their government need to communicate in order to get along well. **Communication** is the process of transmitting information from one individual or group to another. **Mass communication** is the process by which information is transmitted to large, heterogeneous, and widely dispersed audiences. The term **mass media** refers to the means for communicating to large, heterogeneous, and widely dispersed audiences. The mass media are commonly divided into two types:

- **Print media** communicate information through the publication of words and pictures. Prime examples of print media are daily newspapers and popular magazines. Because books seldom have large circulations relative to the population, they are not typically classified as a mass medium.

- **Broadcast media** communicate information electronically through sounds and images. Prime examples of broadcast media are radio and television. Although telephones also transmit sounds and computer networks can transmit words, sounds, and images, both are usually used for more targeted communications and so are not typically included in the term *mass media*.

In the United States, the mass media are in business to make money, which they do mainly by selling advertising. To sell advertising, they provide entertainment on a mass basis, which is their general function. We are more interested in the five specific functions the mass media serve for the political system: *reporting* the news, *interpreting* the news, *influencing* citizens' opinions, *setting the agenda* for government action, and *socializing* citizens about politics.

Our special focus is on the role of the mass media in promoting communication from a government to its citizens *and* from citizens to their government. In totalitarian governments, information flows more freely in one direction (from government to people) than the other. In democratic governments, information must flow freely in both directions; a democratic government can respond to public opinion only if its citizens can make their opinions known. Moreover, the electorate can hold government officials accountable for their actions only if voters know what the government has done, is doing, and plans to do. Because the mass media provide the major channels for this two-way flow of information, they have the dual capability of reflecting and shaping our political views.

Mass media are not the only means of communication between citizens and government. As we discussed in Chapter 5, various agents of socialization (especially schools) function as "linkage mechanisms" that promote such communication. In the next four chapters we will discuss other mechanisms for communication: voting, political parties, campaigning in elections, and interest groups. Certain linkage mechanisms communicate better in one direction than in the other. Primary and secondary schools, for example, commonly instruct young citizens about government rules and symbols, whereas voting sends messages from citizens to government. Parties, campaigns, and interest groups foster communications in both directions. The mass media, however, are the only linkage mechanisms that *specialize* in communication.

Although this chapter concentrates on political uses of the four most prominent mass media—newspapers, magazines, radio, and television—political content can also be transmitted through other mass media, such as recordings and motion pictures. Rock acts such as Peter Gabriel and U2 often express political ideas in their music—as do rappers such as Tupac Shakur and Gangsta N.I.P.[5]

And motion pictures often convey particularly intense political messages. The 1976 film *All the President's Men*, about the two *Washington Post* reporters who doggedly exposed the Watergate scandal, dramatized a seamy side of political life that contrasted sharply with an idealized view of the presidency. Although the 1992 film *J.F.K.* promoted the discredited theory that John F. Kennedy's assassination was a plot involving the CIA and President Lyndon B. Johnson, the controversy it generated prompted Congress to make public nearly all the investigative files on Kennedy's assassination.

THE DEVELOPMENT OF THE MASS MEDIA IN THE UNITED STATES

Although the record and film industries sometimes convey political messages, they are primarily entertainment. Our focus is on mass media in the news industry—on print and broadcast journalism. The growth of the country, technological inventions, and shifting political attitudes about the scope of government—and also by trends in entertainment—have shaped the development of the news media in the United States.

Newspapers

When the Revolutionary War broke out in 1775, thirty-seven newspapers (all weeklies) were publishing in the colonies.[6] Most supported the colonists, and they played an important part in promoting the Revolution. However, these weekly papers were not instruments of mass communication. Their circulations were small (usually a thousand copies or so), and they were expensive. Printers had to set type by hand, the presses printed quite slowly, transportation was costly, and advertisers to defray the costs of publication were few. Still, politicians quickly saw the value of the press and founded papers that expressed their own views. During George Washington's administration, for example, the Federalists published the *Gazette of the U.S.*, and the Antifederalists published the *National Gazette*.

The first newspapers were mainly political organs, financed by parties and advocating party causes. Newspapers did not move toward independent ownership and large circulations until the 1830s, with the publication of two successful dailies (the *New York Sun* and the *New York Herald*) that sold for just a penny. Various inventions spurred the growth of the news industry. The telegraph (invented in 1837) eventually replaced the use of car-

The Origin of Yellow Journalism

The term yellow journalism *means sleazy, sensational reporting. It derives from the "Yellow Kid," a popular cartoon character in the* New York World, *one of the first newspapers to use color for cartoons and comic strips in the late 1800s. The* World *also boosted its circulation by emphasizing entertainment over straight news and by crusading for political causes, some of which were manufactured.*

TRAINING FOR THE FOOTBALL CHAMPIONSHIP GAME IN HOGAN'S ALLEY.

rier pigeons for transmitting news and allowed the simultaneous publication of news stories by papers across the country. The rotary press (1847) soon enabled publishers to print much more quickly and cheaply.

According to the 1880 census, 971 daily newspapers and 8,633 weekly newspapers and periodicals were then published in the United States. Most larger cities had a number of newspapers—New York had 29 papers; Philadelphia, 24; San Francisco, 21; and Chicago, 18. Competition for readers grew fierce among the big-city dailies. Toward the latter part of the nineteenth century, imaginative publishers sought to win readers by entertaining them with photographs, comic strips, sports sections, advice to the lovelorn, and stories of sex and crime. The sensational reporting of that period came to be called **yellow journalism**—after the "Yellow Kid," a comic-strip character featured in the lurid *New York World*, published by Joseph Pulitzer (the same man who established the Pulitzer Prizes for distinguished journalism).[7] Contests calculated to sell papers were also popular with publishers. Some promotional schemes had lasting political consequences. Pulitzer raised money to put the Statue of Liberty on its pedestal after Congress refused to do so. (Contributors' names were printed in the *New York World*'s list of donors.) And William Randolph Hearst, publisher of the rival *New York Journal*, helped get the nation into a war with Spain. When the U.S. battleship *Maine* blew up mysteriously in Havana harbor in February 1898, Hearst proclaimed it the work of enemy agents, charging his readers to "Remember the Maine!"

By the 1960s, intense competition among big-city dailies had nearly disappeared. New York, which had twenty-nine papers in 1880, had only three by 1969. This pattern was repeated in every large city; by 1993, only thirty-six U.S. towns or cities had two or more competing dailies under separate ownership.[8] The net result is that the number of newspapers per person has dropped about 30 percent since 1950.[9]

The daily paper with the biggest circulation at the start of the 1990s (almost 2 million copies) was the *Wall Street Journal*, which appeals to a national audience because of its extensive coverage of business news and its close analysis of political news. The *New York Times*, which many journalists consider the best newspaper in the country, sells about a million copies, placing it fourth in national circulation. In comparison, the weekly *National Enquirer*, which carries stories about people who return from the dead or marry aliens from outer space, sells about 4 million copies. Neither the *Times* nor the *Wall Street Journal* carries comic strips, which no doubt limits their mass appeal. They also print more political news and news analyses than most readers want to confront.

Magazines

Magazines differ from newspapers not only in the frequency of their publication but in the nature of their coverage. Even news-oriented magazines cover the news in a more specialized manner than do daily newspapers. Many magazines are forums for opinion, not strictly for news. However, magazines dealing with public affairs have had relatively small circulations and select readerships, making them questionable as mass media. The earliest public affairs magazines, such as the *Nation, McClure's*, and *Harper's*, were founded in the mid-1800s. These magazines were often politically influential—especially in framing arguments against slavery and later in publishing exposés of political corruption and business exploitation by such writers as Lincoln Steffens and Ida Tarbell. These writers, derisively called **muckrakers** (a term derived from a special rake used to collect manure), practiced an early form of investigative reporting that emphasized unsavory facts about government and business. Because their writings were lengthy critiques of the existing political and economic order, muckrakers found a more hospitable outlet in magazines of opinion than in newspapers with big circulations. Yet, magazines that have limited readerships can wield political power. Magazines may influence **attentive policy elites**—group leaders who follow news in specific areas—and thus influence mass opinion indirectly through a **two-step flow of communication.** As scholars originally viewed the two-step flow, it conformed ideally to the pluralist model of democracy. Magazines informed group leaders (for instance, union or industry leaders) about relevant developments or political thought; the leaders in turn informed their more numerous followers, mobilizing them to apply pressure on government. Today, according to a revised interpretation of the two-step flow, policy elites are more likely to influence public opinion (not necessarily their "followers") and other leaders by airing their views in the media.

Three weekly news magazines—*Time* (founded in 1923), *Newsweek* (1933), and *U.S. News & World Report* (1933)—enjoy big circulations (2.5 million to 4.5 million copies in 1990). The audiences of these magazines, however, are tiny compared with the 17 million readers of *TV Guide* or the 16 million readers of *Reader's Digest*.[10] In contrast to these mainstream

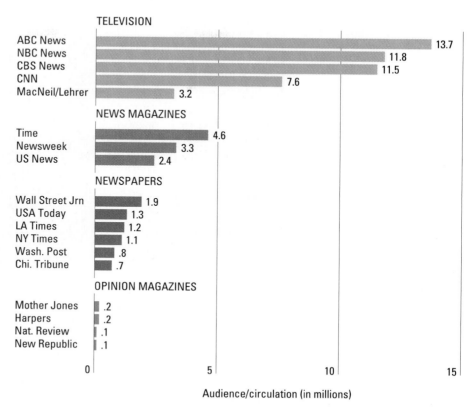

FIGURE 6.1 ■ **Audiences of Selected Media Sources**

Television, newspapers, and magazines differ sharply in their appeal to mass audiences as news sources. The difference shows clearly when the figures for the average number of homes that are tuned nightly to one of the three major network news programs are compared with the circulation figures for the three top news magazines, the eight top newspapers, and the two biggest opinion magazines. Clearly, television news enters many more homes than does news from the other media. All three news magazines (which are published weekly) have more readers than any daily newspaper, and opinion magazines reach only a small fraction of the usual television news audiences.

Sources: Average television news audiences from the New York Times, *29 November 1990, p. B4, and from Nielsen Homevideo Index, "Daily Cumulative Analysis," July 1990; magazine circulations are from* Standard Periodical Directory, 1990; *newspaper circulations are from* Editor & Publisher, *3 November 1990, p. 14.*

"capitalist" publications, a newer "alternative" press is more critical of the prevailing power structure. Such periodicals as *Mother Jones* and the *Utne Reader* have spearheaded investigations into potential government malfeasance, such as the arms-for-hostages deal in the 1985 Iran-Contra affair.[11] As shown in Figure 6.1, some of these publications have bigger readerships than mainstream opinion magazines such as the *National Review* and the *New Republic*.

Radio

Regularly scheduled and continuous radio broadcasting began in 1920 on stations KDKA in Pittsburgh and WWJ in Detroit. Both stations claim to be the first commercial station, and both broadcast returns of the 1920 election of President Warren G. Harding. The first radio network, the National Broadcasting Company (NBC), was formed in 1926. Soon four networks were on the air, which transformed radio into a national medium by linking thousands of local stations. Millions of Americans were able to hear President Franklin D. Roosevelt deliver his first "fireside chat" in 1933. However, the first coast-to-coast broadcast did not occur

Listening to the President on Radio

Before television, friends often gathered around a radio to hear the president make an important address. In 1941, American soldiers, friends, and visiting relatives gathered in the Army YMCA on Governors Island in New York to hear President Franklin Roosevelt warn of the approaching war. Of course, the message had a special meaning for this group. Still, see how intently they are listening to what the president is saying. Maybe we should consider using radio instead of television for critically important speeches.

until 1937, when listeners were shocked by an eyewitness report of the explosion of the dirigible *Hindenburg* in New Jersey.

Because the public could sense reporters' personalities over radio in a way they could not in print, broadcast journalists quickly became national celebrities. Edward R. Murrow, one of the most famous radio news personalities, broadcast news of the merger of Germany and Austria by short-wave from Vienna in 1938 and later gave stirring reports of German air raids on London during World War II.

Television

Experiments with television began in France in the early 1900s. By 1940, twenty-three television stations were operating in the United States, and—repeating the feat of radio twenty years earlier—two stations broadcast the returns of a presidential election, Roosevelt's 1940 reelection.[12] The onset of World War II paralyzed the development of television technology, but growth in the medium exploded after the war. By 1950, ninety-eight stations were covering the major population centers of the country, although only 9 percent of American households had television sets.

The first commercial color broadcast came in 1951, as did the first coast-to-coast broadcast—President Harry Truman's address to delegates at the Japanese peace treaty conference in San Francisco. That same year, Democratic senator Estes Kefauver of Tennessee called for public television coverage of his committee's investigation into organized crime. For weeks, people with television sets invited their neighbors to watch underworld crime figures answering questions before the camera. And Kefauver became one of the first politicians to benefit from television coverage. Previously unknown and representing a small state, he nevertheless won many of the 1952 Democratic presidential primaries and became the Democrats' vice presidential candidate in 1956.

**Watching the President
on Television**

*Television revolutionized
presidential politics by allowing millions of voters to look
closely at the candidates'
faces and to judge their personalities in the process. This
close-up of John Kennedy
during a debate with Richard
Nixon in the 1960 campaign
showed Kennedy to good
advantage. Close-ups of
Nixon, on the other hand,
made him look as though he
needed a shave. Kennedy won
one of the closest elections in
history; his good looks on
television may have made the
difference.*

By 1960, 87 percent of households had television sets. By 1990, the
United States had more than one thousand commercial and three hundred
public television stations, and virtually every household (98 percent) had
TV. Today, television claims by far the biggest news audiences of the mass
media (see Figure 6.1). From television's beginning, most stations were
linked into networks founded by three of the four major radio networks.
Many early anchormen of network news programs (among them, Walter
Cronkite) came to the medium with years of experience as radio broadcast
journalists. Now that the news audience could actually see the broadcasters as well as hear them, news personalities became even greater celebrities. When he retired from anchoring the "CBS Evening News" in 1981,
Walter Cronkite was one of the most trusted people in America.

Just as the appearance of the newscaster became important for television viewers, so did the appearance of the news itself. Television's great advantage over radio—that it *shows* people and events—accounts for the
influence of television news coverage. It also determines, to some extent,
the news that television chooses to cover. However, television is not alone
among the mass media in focusing on news that appeals to its audience's
emotions. The 1890s newspapers that engaged in yellow journalism also
played on emotions. In fact, private ownership of the mass media ensures
that news is selected for its audience appeal.

PRIVATE OWNERSHIP OF THE MEDIA

In the United States, people take private ownership of the media for
granted. Indeed, most Americans would regard government ownership of
the media as an unacceptable threat to freedom that would interfere with
the "marketplace of ideas" and result in one-way communication, from
government to citizens. When the government controls the news flow, the
people may have little chance to learn what the government is doing or to

pressure it to behave differently. Certainly that was true in the former Soviet Union. China offers another illustration of how arbitrary government control of the media can be. The Chinese government permitted televised coverage of protests for democracy in Bejing's Tiananmen Square in 1989 and then harshly reimposed censorship overnight to smother the democracy movement. Private ownership of the media offers a more stable, continuing forum for government criticism.

In other Western democracies, the print media (both newspapers and magazines) are privately owned, but the broadcast media often are not. Before the 1980s, the government owned and operated the major broadcast media in most of these countries. Now, in Western Europe, government radio and television stations compete with private stations.[13] In the United States, except for about 300 public television stations (out of about 1,400) and 300 public radio stations (out of about 5,000), the electronic media are privately owned.

The Consequences of Private Ownership

Private ownership of both print and broadcast media gives the news industry in America more political freedom than any other in the world, but it also makes the media more dependent on advertising revenues to cover their costs and make a profit. Because advertising rates are tied to audience size, the news operations of mass media in America must appeal to the audiences they serve.

Of the four hours or so that the average American spends watching television every day, only about ninety minutes are devoted to news or documentaries; the remainder goes to entertainment, movies, and sports.[14] More than 60 million copies of newspapers circulate daily, but more than 60 percent of their content is advertising.[15] For the space remaining, news must compete with fashions, comics, movie and restaurant reviews, and so on. Only a portion of newspaper space is devoted to news of any sort, and only a fraction of that news—excluding stories about fires, robberies, murder trials, and the like—can be classified as "political." The news function of the mass media in the United States cannot be separated from their entertainment function. Entertainment increases audiences, which increases advertising revenues. The profit motive creates constant pressure to increase the ratio of entertainment news programs or to make the news itself more "entertaining."

You might think that a story's political significance, educational value, or broad social importance determines whether the media cover it. The sad truth is that most potential news stories are not judged by such grand criteria. The primary criterion of a story's **newsworthiness** is usually its audience appeal, as judged by its high impact on readers or listeners; its sensationalist aspect (as exemplified by violence, conflict, disaster, or scandal); its treatment of familiar people or life situations; its close-to-home character, and its timeliness.[16]

Reliance on audience appeal has led the news industry to calculate its audience carefully. (The bigger the audience, the higher the advertising rates.) The print media can easily determine the size of their circulations through sales figures, but the broadcast media must estimate their audiences through various sampling techniques. Because both print and broad-

| FIGURE 6.2 | ■ Local Television: No News Is Happy News |

To determine the political content of local television news broadcasts, Robert Entman analyzed the content of local news on two television stations in Raleigh-Durham, North Carolina, during two full weeks in 1986. He found that reporting on local policy issues averaged less than two minutes per half-hour program. That amounts to about 250 words. The stations devoted more time to weather and twice as much time to sports. "Happy talk," previews of forthcoming programs, and credits accounted for the biggest portion of the half-hour programs. The total coverage of all substantive policy or political matters averaged about seven minutes per broadcast. Unfortunately, far more people regularly watch local than national news in the evening (77 percent to 60 percent).

Sources: Robert M. Entman, Democracy Without Citizens *(New York: Oxford University Press, 1989), p. 111. Copyright © 1989 by Robert M. Entman. Reprinted by permission of Oxford University Press, Inc. The stations were WRAL and WTVD in Raleigh-Durham, North Carolina. Also "Talk Radio,"* American Enterprise, *September/October 1993, p.96.*

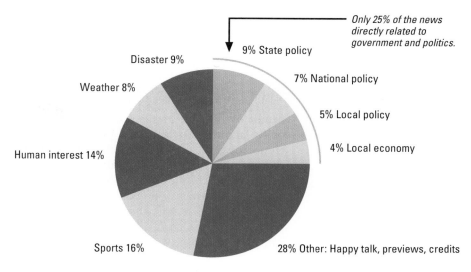

Only 25% of the news directly related to government and politics.

9% State policy
7% National policy
5% Local policy
4% Local economy
Disaster 9%
Weather 8%
Human interest 14%
Sports 16%
28% Other: Happy talk, previews, credits

AVERAGE TIME DEVOTED TO NINE NEWS CATEGORIES

cast media might be tempted to inflate their estimated audiences (to tell advertisers that they reach more people than they actually do), a separate industry has developed to rate audience size impartially. The ratings reports have resulted in a "ratings game," in which the media try to increase ratings by adjusting the delivery or content of their news. Some local television stations favor "happy talk" on their news broadcasts—breezy on-the-air exchanges among announcers, reporters, sportscasters, and meteorologists. Other stations use the "eyewitness" approach, showing a preponderance of film with human interest, humorous, or violent content. Many stations combine the two, often pleasing viewers (most of whom watch local news more regularly than national news) but perhaps not informing them properly, as illustrated in Figure 6.2. Even the three mighty television networks have departed from their traditionally high journalistic standards, following their acquisition in the 1980s by other conglomerate corporations: Capital Cities acquired ABC, General Electric bought NBC, and Loews purchased one-quarter of CBS.

From 1980 to 1990, ABC, CBS, and NBC suffered severe losses in their prime-time audiences, dropping from nearly 90 to only 63 percent of all television viewers.[17] Increasingly, viewers have been watching cable stations or videotapes instead of network programs. Audience declines brought declining profits and cutbacks in network news budgets. As their parent corporations demanded that news programs "pay their way," the networks succumbed to **infotainment**—mixing journalism with theater—in such programs as "Hard Copy" and "Inside Edition." Sometimes, these programs play fast and loose with the truth, as "Dateline NBC" did in a

1992 broadcast on vehicle gas tanks that explode in collisions. The program staff rigged a General Motors pickup truck with an incendiary device to ensure that the truck would ignite in the filmed collision. It did, but an investigation by General Motors uncovered the fraud and forced NBC to apologize on the air. Instances of poor journalism and outright fraud have increased as network executives have demanded that television news become more profitable.

The Concentration of Private Ownership

Media owners can make more money either by increasing their audiences or by acquiring additional publications or stations. There is a decided trend toward concentrated ownership of the media, enhancing the risk that a few owners could control the news flow to promote their own political interests—much as political parties influenced the content of the earliest American newspapers. In fact, the number of *independent* newpapers has declined as newspaper chains (owners of two or more newspapers in different cities) have acquired more newspapers. Most of the more than 150 newspaper chains are small, owning fewer than ten papers.[18] Some, however, are very big. The Gannett chain, which owns *USA Today* with the second biggest circulation in the nation, also owns more than eighty newspapers in thirty-six states. Only about four hundred dailies are still independent, and many of these papers are too small and unprofitable to invite acquisition.

At first glance, ownership concentration in the television industry does not seem to be a problem. Although there are only three major networks, the networks usually do not own their affiliates. About half of all the communities in the United States have a choice of ten or more stations.[19] This figure suggests that the electronic media offer diverse viewpoints and are not characterized by ownership concentration. As with newspapers, however, chains sometimes own television stations in different cities. In 1990, for example, the Capital Cities/ABC group owned eight television stations—in New York, Los Angeles, Chicago, Philadelphia, San Francisco, Houston, Fresno, and Raleigh-Durham—serving 24 percent of the national television market.[20]

Ownership concentration can also occur across the media. Sometimes, the same corporation owns a television station, a radio station, and a newspaper in the same area. For example, the Gannett Company also operates 10 television, 9 FM, and 7 AM broadcasting stations. Some people fear the concentration of media under a single owner, and government has addressed those fears by regulating media ownership, as well as other aspects of media operation. Feature 6.1 describes what can happen as a result of cross ownership.

GOVERNMENT REGULATION OF THE MEDIA

Although most of the mass media in the United States are privately owned, they do not operate free of government regulation. The broadcast media operate under more stringent regulations than the print media, initially because of technical aspects of broadcasting. In general, government regulation of the mass media addresses three aspects of their operation: technical considerations, ownership, and content.[21]

FEATURE 6.1

Cross Ownership = Cross Censorship?

 Is there good reason to fear the growth of cross media ownership by a few giant corporations? If the Federal Communication Commission no longer regulates who can own what media, more owners will acquire different types of media. Those who extol the benefits of ownership deregulation contend that competition in the information marketplace will guarantee that the public has access to a diversity of information sources. Critics argue that the information may be controlled by the governing corporation, whether it is owned by Americans or foreigners. Consider some examples.

Robert Hilliard, professor of mass communications at Boston's Emerson College, was invited by the Boston Herald in 1987 to review two new television programs, "Married . . . with Children" and "The Tracey Ullman Show," that launched the debut of the Fox Network. He initially refused because the network's creator, Rupert Murdoch, owned both the newspaper and the local Fox television channel. But Hilliard agreed to be one of the outside experts when the Herald's editors told him that they wanted an honest review. He did not like the programs, even calling "Married . . . with Children" one of the "worst sitcoms" he had ever seen. None of his prepared remarks, nor those of any non-Herald employee who screened the programs, was published by the newspaper, which headlined a review by its regular critic, "Fox Network Offers New, Lively Variety."

Peter Karl, an investigative reporter for Chicago's NBC affiliate, WMAQ-TV, prepared a story for the "Today" show in 1989 about the faulty nuts and bolts used in important construction projects such as bridges, airplane engines, nuclear missile silos, and in the NASA space program. Karl also cited the General Electric Corp., which builds airplane engines, as a user of shoddy nuts and bolts. NBC broadcast the story in November 1989, but it was edited to delete all references to General Electric, which happens to own NBC.

When Matsushita Electric bought MCA in 1990, its president, Akio Tanii, held a news conference. He sought to quell American fears of Japanese censorship of movies made by MCA's Universal Studios by announcing that he would retain MCA's American chairman. Then, a reporter asked whether the new company would "be willing to produce a movie about the wartime role of the late Emperor Hirohito." Tanii seemed agitated and said, "I could never imagine such a case, so I cannot answer such a question." Would Matsushita permit the making of movies that criticized Japanese society or economic practices? Again, he said, "I never dreamed of hearing such a question."

• Sources: Paul Starobin, "Murdoch v. Murdoch," Congressional Quarterly Weekly Report, 3 June 1989, p. 1316; James Warren, " 'Today' Edited GE from News Story," Chicago Tribune, 2 December 1989, p. 3; and David E. Sanger, "Politics and Multinational Movies," New York Times, 27 November 1990, p. C5.

Technical and Ownership Regulations

In the early days of radio, stations that operated on similar frequencies in the same area often jammed each other's signals, and no one could broadcast clearly. At the broadcasters' insistence, Congress passed the Federal Radio Act (1927), which declared that the public owned the airwaves and that private broadcasters could use them only by obtaining a license from the Federal Radio Commission. So, government regulation of broadcasting was not forced on the industry by socialist politicians; capitalist owners sought it to impose order on the use of the airwaves (thereby restricting others' freedom to enter broadcasting).

The Federal Communications Act (1934) forms the basis for current regulation of the broadcasting industry. It created the **Federal Communications Commission (FCC),** which has seven members (no more than four from the same political party) chosen by the president for terms of seven years. The commissioners can be removed from office only through impeachment and conviction. Consequently, the FCC is considered an independent regulatory commission: It is insulated from political control by either the president or Congress. (We discuss independent regulatory commissions in Chapter 13.) Today, the FCC is charged with regulating interstate and international communication by radio, television, telephone, telegraph, cable, and satellite.

The FCC also regulates the ownership structure of the electronic media. When radio began broadcasting to millions of citizens, the FCC became concerned about the concentration of too much power in the hands of single owners. In 1943, the FCC ordered the National Broadcasting Company to sell one of its two radio networks, leading to the creation of the American Broadcasting Company. Also during the 1940s, the FCC prohibited any company from owning more than one AM, one FM, or one television station in a single community.[22]

In the early 1950s, the FCC ruled that a single company could own no more than seven AM, seven FM, and seven television stations across the nation. By 1984, as the number of television stations quadrupled and the number of radio stations tripled, a majority of FCC commissioners (Ronald Reagan's appointees) opted to relax regulations by increasing the ownership limit from seven to twelve of each type of broadcast media. Now pressure is increasing to remove all numerical restrictions on media ownership.

A source of the pressure is technological; the growth of cable television has lessened the need to parcel out frequencies for television broadcasts. With more than half of all homes wired for cable television, cable firms have become powerhouses in the television industry.[23] One firm, Tele-Communications, Inc., has more than 20 percent of the nation's cable subscribers, and traditional media companies are increasing their cross ownership by acquiring cable stations. In 1989, the merger of Time, Inc., and Warner Communications not only linked these firms' publishing activities (magazines, books) and their film and record subsidiaries but also their extensive cable interests (HBO, Cinemax, Warner Cable). Then, in 1993, Tele-Communications, Inc., and Bell Atlantic, the telephone company that serves the mid-Atlantic region, announced the biggest media merger up to that point, a $33 billion deal between two companies that together reach 40 percent of all U.S. homes with cable. Such mergers between giant companies in alternative media are inevitable on the way to the so-called information highway, the national network that will unite television and computer technology. Nevertheless, TCI and Bell called off the merger, partly because an FCC decision in 1994 to cut basic cable television rates limited TCI's future revenues.[24] That consequence of the FCC's decision illustrates the complexities of government regulation of evolving technologies.

Because of the challenges that such mergers of alternative technologies pose to the broadcast industry, it has pressured the FCC to relax its restrictions on media ownership. The industry also argues that diversity among media news sources is great enough to provide citizens with a wide range of political ideas.

Regulation of Content

The First Amendment to the Constitution prohibits Congress from abridging the freedom of the press. Over time, the *press* has come to mean all the mass media, and the courts have decided many cases that define how far freedom of the press extends under the law. Chapter 15 discusses the most important of these cases, which are often quite complex. Usually, the courts have struck down government attempts to restrain the press from publishing or broadcasting the information, events, or opinions that it finds newsworthy. One notable exception concerns strategic information during wartime; the courts have supported censorship of such information as the sailing schedules of troop ships or the movements of troops in battle. Otherwise, the courts have recognized a strong constitutional case against press censorship. This stand has given the United States some of the freest, most vigorous news media in the world.

Because the broadcast media are licensed to use the public airwaves, they are subject to some regulation of the content of their news coverage that is not applied to the print media. The basis for the FCC's regulation of content lies in its charge to ensure that radio (and, later, television) stations would "serve the public interest, convenience, and necessity." For more than fifty years, broadcasters operated under three constraints rooted in the 1934 Federal Communications Act. Two of these constraints are still in effect; one has been revoked. In its **equal opportunities rule,** the FCC requires that a broadcast station that gives or sells time to a candidate for any public office make an equal amount of time under the same conditions available to all other candidates for that office. The **reasonable access rule** requires that stations make their facilities available for the expression of conflicting views on issues by all responsible elements in the community. Until 1987, the **fairness doctrine** obligated broadcasters to discuss public issues and to provide fair coverage of all views on those issues.

The regulations seem unobjectionable to most people, but they have been at the heart of a controversy about the deregulation of the broadcast media. Note that *none* of these regulations is imposed on the print media, which has no responsibility to give equal treatment to political candidates, to give fair coverage to all sides of an issue, or to express conflicting views from all responsible elements of the community. In fact, one aspect of a free press is its ability to champion causes that it favors (such as erecting the Statue of Liberty or starting a war with Spain) without having to argue the case for the other side. The broadcast media have traditionally been treated differently, because they were licensed by the FCC to operate as semimonopolies.[25] With the rise of one-newspaper cities and towns, however, competition among television stations is greater than among newspapers in virtually every market area. Advocates of dropping FCC content regulations argue that the broadcast media should be just as free as the print media to decide which candidates they endorse and which issues they support.

Under President Reagan in 1987, the FCC itself moved toward this view of unfettered freedom for broadcasters by repealing the fairness doctrine on the grounds that it chilled freedom of speech. One media analyst noted that the FCC acted in the belief that competition in the supply of news among broadcasters, cable, radio, newspapers, and magazines would provide a vibrant marketplace of ideas. However, he feared that the FCC overestimated the public's demand for high-quality news and public affairs broadcasting. Without that demand, the media are unlikely to compete to supply the news coverage needed to sustain a genuine marketplace.[26]

REPORTING AND FOLLOWING THE NEWS

"News," for most journalists, is an important event that has happened within the past twenty-four hours. A presidential news conference or an explosion in the Capitol qualifies as news. And a national political convention certainly qualifies as news, although it may not justify the thousands of media representatives at the 1992 party conventions. Who decides what is important? The media, of course. In this section, we discuss how the media cover political affairs, what they choose to report (which then becomes "news"), and who follows the news and what they remember and learn.

Covering National Politics

All the major news media seek to cover political events through firsthand reports from journalists on the scene. Because so many significant political events occur in the nation's capital, Washington has by far the biggest press corps of any city in the world—almost 6,000 accredited reporters: 2,500 from newspapers, 1,025 from magazines, and 2,400 from radio and television.[27] Only a small portion of these reporters cover the presidency—only about seventy-five "regular" journalists are in the White House press corps.[28] Since 1902, when President Theodore Roosevelt first provided a special room in the White House for reporters, the press has had special access to the president. As recently as the Truman administration, reporters enjoyed informal personal relationships with the president. Today, the media's relationship with the president is mediated primarily through the Office of the Press Secretary.

To meet their daily deadlines, White House correspondents rely heavily on information they receive from the president's staff, each piece carefully crafted in an attempt to control the news report. The most frequent form is the news release—a prepared text distributed to reporters in the hope that they will use it verbatim. A daily news briefing at 11:30 A.M. enables reporters to question the press secretary about news releases and allows television correspondents time to prepare their stories and film for the evening newscast. A news conference involves questioning high-level officials in the executive branch—including the president on occasion. News conferences appear to be freewheeling, but officials tend to carefully rehearse precise answers to anticipated questions.

Occasionally, information is given on background, meaning that the information can be quoted but reporters cannot identify the source. A vague reference—"a senior official says"—is all right. (When he was secretary of state, Henry Kissinger himself was often the "senior official" quoted on foreign policy developments.) Information disclosed off the record cannot

**Feeding Time in the
Press Room**

*President Clinton's press
secretary, Dee Dee Myers,
conducts a daily briefing for
the White House press corps.
Both print and broadcast
journalists depend on getting
the White House's views on
the news to frame their reporting for the day.*

even be printed. Journalists who violate these well-known rules risk losing their welcome at the White House. In a sense, the press corps is captive
to the White House, which feeds reporters information they need to meet
deadlines and frames events so they are covered on the evening news.[29]
Beginning in the Nixon White House, press secretaries have obliged photographers with "photo opportunities," a few minutes to take pictures or
shoot film, often with a visiting dignitary or a winning sports team. The
photographers can keep their editors supplied with visuals, and the press
secretary ensures that the coverage is favorable by controlling the environment.

Most reporters in the Washington press corps are accredited to sit in the
House and Senate press galleries, but only about four hundred cover
Congress exclusively.[30] Most news about Congress comes from innumerable press releases issued by its 535 members and from an unending supply of congressional reports. A journalist, then, can report on Congress
without inhabiting its press galleries.

Not so long ago, individual congressional committees allowed radio and
television coverage of their proceedings only on special occasions—such
as the Kefauver committee's investigation of organized crime in the 1950s
and the Watergate investigation in the 1970s. Congress banned micro-
phones and cameras from its chambers until 1979, when the House permitted live coverage while insisting on controlling the shots being
televised. Nevertheless, televised broadcasts of the House were surprisingly successful, thanks to C-SPAN (the Cable Satellite Public Affairs
Network), which feeds to 90 percent of the cable systems across the country and has a cultlike following among hundreds of thousands of regular
viewers.[31] To share in the exposure, the Senate began television coverage
in 1986. C-SPAN coverage of Congress has become important to professionals in government and politics in Washington—perhaps more so than

to its small, devoted audience across the country. Even members of the Washington press corps watch C-SPAN.

In addition to these recognized sources of news, selected reporters occasionally benefit from leaks of information released by officials who are guaranteed anonymity. Officials may leak news to interfere with others' political plans or to float ideas (trial balloons) past the public and other political leaders to gauge their reactions. At times, one carefully placed leak can turn into a gusher of media coverage through the practice of pack journalism—the tendency of journalists to adopt similar viewpoints toward the news simply because they hang around together, exchanging information and defining the day's news.

Presenting the News

Media executives, news editors, and prominent reporters function as **gatekeepers** in directing the news flow: They decide which events to report and how to handle the elements in those stories. Only a few individuals—no more than twenty-five on the average newspaper or news magazine and fifty on each of the major television networks—qualify as gatekeepers, defining the news for public consumption.[32] They are usually highly selective in choosing what goes through the gate.

The media cannot communicate everything about public affairs. There is neither space in newspapers or magazines nor time on television or radio to do so. Time limitations impose especially severe constraints on television news broadcasting. Each half-hour network news program devotes only about twenty minutes to the news. (The rest of the time is taken up by commercials, and there is even less news on local television; see Figure 6.2.) The average story lasts about one minute, and few stories run longer than two minutes. The typical script for an entire television news broadcast would fill less than two columns of one page of the *New York Times*.[33]

A parade of unconnected one-minute news stories, flashing across the television screen every night, would boggle the eyes and minds of the viewers. To make the news understandable and to hold viewers' attention, television editors and producers carefully choose their lead story and group stories together by theme. The stories themselves concentrate on individuals, because individuals have personalities; political institutions do not—except for the presidency. A careful content analysis of a year's network news coverage of the president, Congress, and the Supreme Court found that the average television news program devotes seven and a half minutes to the president compared with one minute for Congress and only a half a minute for the Court.[34] When television covers Congress, moreover, it tries to personify the institution by focusing on prominent quotable leaders, such as the speaker of the House or the Senate majority leader. Such personification for the purpose of gaining audience acceptability tends to distort the character of an institution that harbors competing views by powerfully placed members.

During elections, personification encourages **horse race journalism,** in which media coverage becomes a matter of "who's ahead in the polls, who's raising the most money, who's got TV ads and who's getting endorsed."[35] Stung by criticism of their 1988 coverage, the networks in 1992 deliberately cut back on covering the horse race and won praise for more

Live (and Sometimes Colored): Election News on Television in Three Countries

Compared with television reporters in Britain and Germany, reporters in the United States were more likely to color campaign news through commentary before and after the story. This finding comes from a cross national study of television coverage of elections in the United States and Britain in 1992 and in Germany in 1990. Stories about the candidates' activities were coded for reporters' comments in statements that preceded or followed film of the candidates' appearance. The comments were coded as "deflating," "straight or neutral," "mixed,"

or "reinforcing." Nearly one quarter of all U.S. reporters' comments were deflating—nearly three times the incidence in Britain and more than ten times that in Germany. In fact, only about half the comments in the United States were straight or neutral, compared with more than two-thirds in Britain and nearly all in Germany.

• *Source: These data were calculated from Table 7 in Holli A Semetko, "American Election News in Comparative Perspective," paper presented at the annual meeting of the American Political Science Association, Washington, D.C., September 1993.*

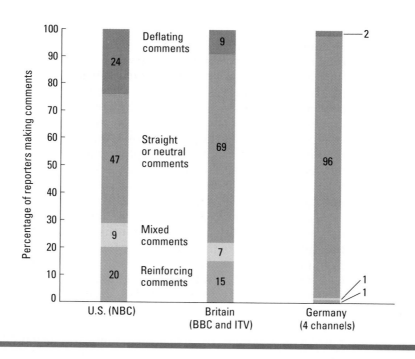

emphasis on issues.[36] Nevertheless, American television still gives less attention to issues in its election coverage than television in other countries, as Compared With What? 6.1 shows. Consequently, television presents U.S. elections as contests between individuals rather than as confrontations between parties and platforms.

Campaigning for office is a type of political news that lends itself to media coverage, especially if the candidates create a **media event**—a situation that is too "newsworthy" to pass up. One tried-and-true method is to conduct a statewide walking campaign. Newspapers and television can take pictures of the candidate on the highway and conduct interviews with local folks who just spoke with the political hiker. (See Chapter 9 for further discussion of media in political campaigns.) Television is particularly partial to events that have visual impact. Organized protests and fires, for example, "show well" on television, so television tends to cover them. Violent conflict of any kind, especially unfolding dramas that involve weapons, rate especially high in visual impact.

Where the Public Gets Its News

Until the early 1960s, most people reported getting more of their news from newspapers than from any other source. Television nudged out newspapers as the public's major source of news in the early 1960s. At the end of the 1980s, about two-thirds of the public cited television as their main news source, compared with less than one-half who named newspapers and less than one-fifth who relied on radio. Not only was television the public's most important source of news but those polled rated television news as more trustworthy than newspaper news—by a margin of nearly 2 to 1.[37] However, these frequently cited data may overstate both public reliance on television for news and people's trust in the medium. In a series of national surveys, nearly 75 percent of the respondents vowed they regularly watched news on television, yet only 52 percent said that they had actually watched "yesterday."[38] In another study, people again identified television as their most common news source, but they named newspapers more frequently as the source of specific news stories.[39] Finally, a study of believability and the press found that respondents were more likely to trust the major national newspapers and news magazines than *local* television and that people trusted news anchors more than the television networks they represented.[40] So television may not be as dominant a news medium as it might seem, and we should inquire into the public's specific sources of news.

One major study of American news media usage, based on nearly five thousand interviews during four months in 1990, found that 84 percent of the public said that they had read or heard the news yesterday through print or broadcast media: newspaper, television, or radio. However, only a bare majority (51 percent) used a national rather than a local news source.[41] The study further divided those who regularly used national news sources into four categories, as Figure 6.3 illustrates. The small group of news sophisticates read specialized opinion magazines and listened to news programs on National Public Radio or public television. The much bigger group of serious news consumers read a weekly news magazine, a major metropolitan daily newspaper, or watched Sunday morning interview shows or CNN. A slightly bigger group of moderate consumers read or watched news but not from a national source. The smallest group, the nonusers, did not regularly read or watch any news.

As one would expect, level of education is strongly related to these categories of news attentiveness, and nearly half the news sophisticates are

FIGURE **6.3** ■ **Typology of News Consumers**

In a major study of the American media, the Times Mirror Center classified respondents according to the types of news sources they used regularly. News sophisticates regularly followed news programs on National Public Radio, public television's "MacNeil/Lehrer Newshour," or read opinion magazines such as the Atlantic, Harpers, or the New Yorker. Serious consumers did not follow these sources but did read a news magazine or a major metropolitan daily newspaper, the Wall Street Journal, or USA Today, or watched Sunday morning interview shows or CNN. Moderate consumers read some other daily paper or watched or listened to news regularly. Nonusers followed no news source on a regular basis.

Surveys conducted from 1941 to 1975 showed that Americans younger than thirty followed news stories, such as Watergate and Vietnam, about as closely as their elders and knew almost as much about public affairs. But since then, they have been much less attentive, even to major developments. The opening of the Berlin Wall, ending the division between East and West Germany, was followed very closely by only 42 percent of those younger than thirty compared with 58 percent of those older than fifty.

Leaders in the world of government, business, and higher education stand at the extreme end of news consumption. Virtually none of these leaders fails to follow the news, and from 40 to 60 percent report spending from one to two hours per day reading, listening, or watching the news. In fact, from one-third to one-half say that they spend from two to five hours per day following the news.

Source: Used by permission of The Times Mirror Center for The People & The Press.

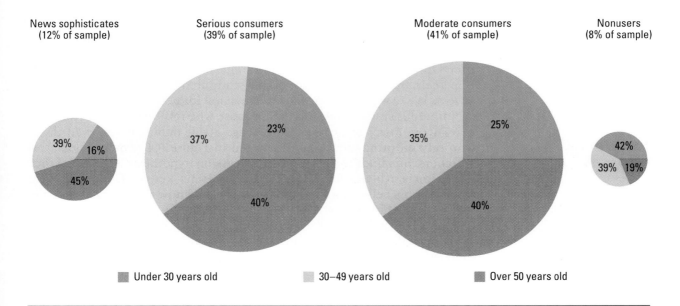

college graduates. Figure 6.3 shows that age is also related to attentiveness, with nearly half of the news sophisticates aged fifty or older and nearly half of the nonusers younger than thirty. Race bears no relationship to news attentiveness (nonwhites are as likely as whites to be news sophisticates[42]), but sex has a decided effect, with news sophisticates more likely to be male (56 percent) and nonusers to be female (60 percent). Researchers have attributed this finding and others on women's low interest in politics to what is taught at home and in school, saying that "changes in girls' early learning experiences" must occur before such gender differences evaporate.[43]

What People Remember and Know

If 84 percent of the public read or heard the news the previous day, and if nearly 75 percent say they regularly watch the news on television, how much political information do they absorb? By all accounts, not much. When a national sample was asked in the summer of 1992 (an election year) which party controlled the House of Representatives, fewer than half correctly identified the Democrats, but when asked to name the television show that Vice President Dan Quayle had criticized for glamorizing unwed motherhood, two-thirds correctly said "Murphy Brown."[44]

Those who are more attentive to news answer more political knowledge questions correctly than those who are less attentive—as expected. Given the enormous improvements in television news coverage and the increasing reliance of the public on TV for news, we might also expect the public to know more than it did twenty years ago.[45] Unfortunately, that is not so. Similar surveys in 1967 and in 1987 asked respondents to name their state governor, representative in the House, and head of the local school district. Only 9 percent failed to name a single official in 1967 compared with 17 percent in 1987. The author of this study attributed the lower performance in 1987 to greater reliance on television for news.[46]

Numerous studies have found that those who rely on television for their news score lower on tests of knowledge about public affairs than those who rely on print media, as illustrated in Figure 6.4. Among media researchers, this finding has led to the television hypothesis—the belief that television is to blame for the low level of citizens' knowledge about public affairs.[47] This belief has a reasonable basis. We know that television tends to squeeze public policy issues into one-minute or, at most, two-minute fragments, which makes it difficult to explain candidates' positions. Television also tends to cast abstract issues in personal terms to generate the visual content that the medium needs.[48] Thus, viewers may become more adept at visually identifying the candidates and describing their personal habits than at outlining their positions on issues. Finally, the television networks, with content regulated by the FCC, are concerned about being fair and equal in covering the candidates, which may result in their failing to critique the candidates' positions. Newspapers, which are not regulated, enjoy more latitude in choosing which candidates they cover and how. Whatever the explanation, the technological wonders of television may have contributed little to citizens' knowledge of public affairs. Indeed, electronic journalism may work against the informed citizenry that democratic government requires.

FIGURE **6.4**   ■ **Reading Versus Watching the News**

Study after study has demonstrated that people who rely on television for their news score lower in tests of knowledge of public affairs than those who rely on print media. This study, done in early 1993, yielded familiar results when respondents were asked, "How have you been getting most of your news about national and international issues?" Because such studies do not control for interest in the news, they do not necessarily mean that television communicates information poorly. But the better informed seem to prefer getting their news through print media.

Source: The Times Mirror Center for the People & the Press, Washington, D.C. Report dated 13 January 1993. Used with permission.

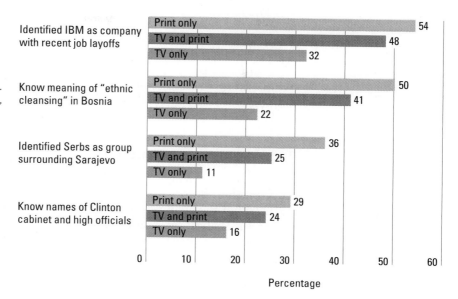

Recent research has questioned the hypothesis that television is a poor medium for disseminating information on public affairs. Neuman, Just, and Crigler studied how citizens "construct political meaning" from news gained from television, newspapers, and news magazines about five different issues prominent in 1987 and 1988: the 1987 stock market crash, AIDS, drugs, the Strategic Defense Initiative (SDI), and political change in South Africa.[49] Conceding that people who rely on television for news score lower on political knowledge tests than people who rely on print media, they argued that this was because those who knew more tended to select the print media in the first place. In a series of experiments that presented the same information via all three media, the researchers found that television was actually *more* successful in communicating abstract and distant political issues (SDI and South Africa), whereas the print media did better on the stock market crash, drugs, and AIDS.[50] The researchers also found that respondents learned differently from the media according to their cognitive skills, or ability to learn. People with high cognitive skills learned equally well from all three media, but those with average and low skills learned the most from television, next from magazines, and least from newspapers.[51] The authors' key finding was that "television was more successful in communicating information about topics that were of low salience [significance] to the audience, while print media were superior in conveying information about topics that had high salience."[52]

The authors also found that people tend to construct meaning from news reports in the media according to five different conceptual schemas, which are illustrated in Chapter 5, p. 169, and Feature 6.2. Despite their finding that television news has value for topics of low salience and for people with limited cognitive skills, the point remains that people with high cognitive skills prefer newspapers. They must know something that the others don't.

| THE POLITICAL EFFECTS OF THE MEDIA | Virtually all citizens must rely on the mass media for their political news. This endows the media with enormous potential to affect politics. To what extent do the media deliver on their potential? In this section, we probe the media's effects on public opinion, the nation's political agenda, and political socialization. |

Influencing Public Opinion

Americans overwhelmingly believe that the media exert a strong influence on their political institutions, and nearly nine out of ten Americans believe that the media strongly influence public opinion.[53] However, measuring the extent of media influence on public opinion is difficult.[54] Because few of us learn about political events except through the media, it could be argued that the media create public opinion simply by reporting events. Consider the dismantling of the Berlin Wall in 1989. Surely the photographs of joyous Berliners demolishing that symbol of oppression affected American public opinion about the reunification of Germany.

Studies of opinion change have found television coverage of particular events to have systematic, and in some cases dramatic, effects, as shown in Figure 6.5. Documenting the effects of media on opinions about standard issues in the news is harder still. One study analyzed polls on eighty issues in foreign and domestic affairs at two points in time. For nearly half of these issues, public opinion changed over time by about six percentage points. The researchers compared these changes with policy positions taken by ten different sources of information: commentators on television network news, including the president; members of the president's party; members of the opposition party; and members of interest groups. The authors found the news commentators to have the most dramatic effect—they could link a single commentary for or against an issue to a significant corresponding change in opinion (more than four percentage points).[55] A parallel study of the effects of newspapers on public opinion of fifty-one foreign and domestic issues found that a single story in a leading paper (the study used the *New York Times*) accounted for almost two percentage points of opinion change toward the story's position, which fits with the public's lesser reliance on newspapers as a source of information.[56]

Setting the Political Agenda

Despite the media's potential for influencing public opinion, most scholars believe that the media's greatest influence on politics is found in their power to set the **political agenda**—a list of issues that people identify as needing government attention. Those who set the political agenda define which issues government decision makers should discuss and debate. Like the tree that falls in the forest without anyone hearing it, an issue that does not get on the political agenda will not have anyone in government working on it.

FEATURE

6.2

■ Schemas for Understanding the News

In Chapter 5 (page 138), we encountered the view that highly individualized schemas—networks of organized knowledge and beliefs—guide the formation of people's opinions on political topics. Through in-depth interviews with forty-eight people who followed the news on five issues—the 1987 stock market crash, AIDS, drugs, the Strategic Defense Initiative (SDI), and political change in South Africa—researchers found that people tend to interpret news through five types of schemas or conceptual frames:

The Economic Frame: This schema "reflects the preoccupation with 'the bottom line,' profit and loss, and wider values of the culture of capitalism." Many interviewees used this frame but in a way that emphasized human influence, values, or moral judgments.

The Conflict Frame: The media often stress (or create) conflict between protagonists in a story to highlight drama, but people use this frame far less often than the media. "Perhaps the most dramatic use of a polarized us/them frame by individuals occurs on the topic of race and racism."

The Powerlessness Frame: This schema interprets events in terms of dominant forces—such as AIDS or the government—affecting weak individuals or groups. It appeared "in approximately half of the interviews and was used more frequently by women than by men."

The Human Impact Frame: The media frequently frame stories by focusing on specific people or groups likely to be affected by an issue. "Inter-

viewees were even more likely than the media to discuss issues in terms of the effects they have on people."

The Morality Frame: Perhaps because of the professional norm of objectivity, the media tend to avoid referring directly to moral values. However, "virtually all of the interviewees used moral and value-laden statements to talk about the five political issues. Public discourse, unlike media discourse, employed many references to morality, God and other religious tenets, and values such as equality, freedom, and peace." AIDS was especially likely to be discussed in these terms.

According to the authors, the "most dramatic difference" between the media's framing of the five issues and the mass audience's was the media's heavy emphasis on conflict, which was not central to the public's view. On the other hand, the public emphasized the human effect and morality frames more often. Media coverage is heavy with factual material and is "cleansed of much of the morality, empathy, and compassion of the political discourse of private conversations." In contrast, "people frame issues in a more visceral and moralistic (and sometimes racist and xenophobic) style. They actively filter, sort, and reorganize information in personally meaningful ways in the process of constructing an understanding of public issues."

• *Source: W. Russell Neuman, Marion R. Just, Ann N. Crigler,* Common Knowledge: News and the Construction of Political Meaning *(Chicago: University of Chicago Press, 1992), pp. 63–77. Used with permission of the publisher and authors.*

The mass media in the United States have traditionally played an influential role in defining the political agenda. As noted earlier, newspaper publisher William Randolph Hearst helped put war with Spain on the political agenda in 1898. Radio helped identify the Nazis' rise to power as a political problem in the late 1930s. Television, which reaches into virtually every home, has an even greater potential for setting the political

FIGURE 6.5 ■ The NAFTA Debate on "Larry King Live"— Not Just Talk

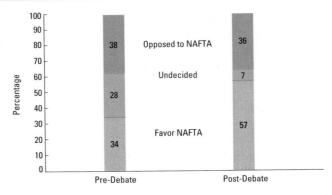

The Clinton administration was strongly in favor of the North American Free Trade Agreement (NAFTA), but the House of Representatives seemed ready to defeat the agreement in its scheduled vote on November 17, 1993. Despite Clinton's backing, most House Democrats opposed NAFTA, and the public was confused and divided. Moreover, Ross Perot was campaigning vigorously against NAFTA, saying that passage would cause a "giant sucking sound" as U.S. jobs were lured to Mexico. About two weeks before the crucial vote in the House, the administration had Vice President Al Gore challenge Perot to debate the issue on CNN's "Larry King Live." Perot accepted. For ninety minutes on November 9, Gore and Perot traded arguments, facts, and charges. Contrary to Perot's claim, Gore contended that the free trade agreement would actually create more jobs than were lost. Who won the debate on the TV talk show, and did it matter? USA Today polled 357 viewers for their positions on NAFTA both before and after the debate. By 59 to 32 percent, the respondents thought that Gore had won the debate, and the shift of opinion in favor of NAFTA was almost as strong, with the greatest change occurring among the "undecided." Many commentators claimed that Gore's strong showing turned the tide in NAFTA's favor. Indeed, the House passed the bill by the surprising margin of 34 votes, 234 to 200. Here at least, the media seemed to have a definite influence.

Source: USA Today, 10 November 1993.

agenda. As a careful study designed to isolate and examine television's effects on public opinion concluded, "By attending to some problems and ignoring others, television news shapes the American public's political priorities."[57] Indeed, the further the viewer is removed from public affairs, "the stronger the agenda-setting power of television news."[58]

Today's newspapers also heighten the public's concern about particular social issues. Crime is a good example. Certain types of crime—particularly murder—are especially attractive to the media, which therefore tend to distort perceptions of the incidence of crime. A study of newspaper coverage of crime in nine cities found more attention given to violent crimes (murder, rape, and assault) than was justified by official police statistics. In addition, the study found that newspapers in recent years have given increased attention to political crimes—such as assassinations or kidnappings—and to violent crimes committed outside the metropolitan areas served by the papers.[59] In recent years, the overall U.S. crime rate has actually decreased, but one would never know it from the media.[60]

One study found varying correlations between media coverage and what the public sees as "the most important problem facing this country today," depending on the type of event. Crises such as the Vietnam War, racial unrest, and energy shortages drew extensive media coverage, and each additional news magazine story per month generated almost one percentage point increase in citations of the event as an important problem. But public opinion was even more responsive to media coverage of recurring problems such as inflation and unemployment. Although these events received less extensive coverage, each magazine story tended to increase public concern by almost three percentage points.[61] What's more, evidence shows that television networks, at least, tend to give greater coverage to bad economic news (which is more dramatic) than to good economic news.[62] This tendency can have serious consequences for an incumbent president (ask George Bush).

The media's ability to influence public opinion by defining "the news" makes politicians eager to influence media coverage. Politicians attempt

Who Says 'Seeing is Believing'?

Not Sergeant Stacy Koon of the Los Angeles Police Department. Sgt. Koon was one of the four officers charged in the beating of black motorist, Rodney King, whom they stopped for a traffic violation. The blows were filmed by an amateur cameraman and viewed nationwide before the trial began. In court, Sgt. Koon argued that what most viewers saw as unrestrained brutality was actually controlled force. The jury apparently agreed, acquitting the officers of the charges. In response to the verdict, black neighborhoods in Los Angeles erupted in rioting and burning. Tried again on federal charges of depriving Rodney King of his civil rights, Sgt. Koon and a second officer were found guilty and sentenced to prison for two and a half years each.

to affect not only public opinion but the opinions of other political leaders.[63] The president receives a daily digest of news and opinion from many sources, and other top government leaders closely monitor the major national news sources. Even journalists work hard at following the news coverage in alternative sources. In a curious sense, the mass media have become a network for communicating among attentive elites, all trying to influence one another or to assess others' weaknesses and strengths. Suppose the White House is under pressure on some policy matter and is asked to send a representative to appear for fifteen minutes of intensive questioning on the "MacNeil/Lehrer Newshour." The White House complies as much to influence the thinking of other insiders (who faithfully watch the program) as to influence opinions among the relatively few news sophisticates in the public who watch public television. Criticisms of the president's policies, especially by members of his own party, embolden others to be critical in their comments to other media. In this way, opposition spreads and may eventually be reflected in public opinion.[64]

Socialization

The mass media act as important agents of political socialization, at least as influential as those described in Chapter 5.[65] Young people who rarely follow the news by choice nevertheless acquire political values through the entertainment function of the broadcast media. Years ago, children learned from radio programs; now they learn from television: The average American child has watched about nineteen thousand hours of television by the end of high school.[66] What children learned from radio, however, was quite different from what they are learning now. In the golden days of radio, youngsters listening to the popular radio drama "The Shadow" heard repeatedly that "crime does not pay . . . the *Shadow* knows!" In program after program—"Dragnet," "Junior G-Men," "Gangbusters"—the message never varied: Criminals are bad; the police are good; criminals get caught and are severely punished for their crimes.

Needless to say, television today does not portray the criminal justice system in the same way, even in police dramas. Consider programs such as "Cop Rock" and "Gabriel's Fire," which have portrayed police and prison guards as killers. Other series, such as "Law and Order" and "Against the Law," also portray a tainted criminal justice system and institutional corruption.[67] Perhaps years of television messages about distrust of law enforcement, disrespect for the criminal justice system, and violence shape impressionable youngsters. Certainly, one cannot easily argue that television's entertainment programs help prepare law-abiding citizens.

Some scholars argue that the most important effect of the mass media, particularly television, is to reinforce the hegemony, or dominance, of the existing culture and order. According to this argument, social control functions not through institutions of force (police, military, and prisons) but through social institutions, such as the media, that cause people to accept "the way things are."[68] By displaying the lifestyles of the rich and famous, for example, the media induce the public to accept the unlimited accumulation of private wealth. Similarly, the media socialize citizens to value "the American way," to be patriotic, to back their country "right or wrong." Ironically, when former Vice President Dan Quayle criticized "Murphy Brown" for undermining family values, he was really making a similar argument—that the media shape popular values through the cultural messages they convey—except that Quayle was criticizing the media for *undermining* the old cultural order.

So the media play contradictory roles in the process of political socialization. On one hand, they promote popular support for government by joining in the celebration of national holidays, heroes' birthdays, political anniversaries, and civic accomplishments. On the other hand, the media erode public confidence by publicizing citizens' grievances, airing investigative reports of official malfeasance, and even showing dramas about crooked cops. Some critics contend that the media also give too much coverage to government opponents, especially to those who engage in unconventional opposition (see Chapter 7). However, strikes, sit-ins, violent confrontations, and hijackings draw large audiences and thus are newsworthy by the mass media's standards.

EVALUATING THE MEDIA IN GOVERNMENT

Are the media fair or biased in reporting the news? What contributions do the media make to democratic government? What effects do they have on the pursuit of freedom, order, and equality?

Is Reporting Biased?

News reports are presented as objective reality, yet critics of modern journalism contend that news is filtered through the ideological biases of the owners and editors (the gatekeepers) and of the reporters themselves.

The argument that news reports are politically biased has two sides. On one hand, news reporters are criticized for tilting their stories in a liberal direction, promoting social equality and undercutting social order. On the other hand, wealthy and conservative media owners are suspected of preserving inequalities and reinforcing the existing order by serving a relentless round of entertainment that numbs the public's capacity for critical analysis. Let's evaluate the argument first from the reporters' side.

Although the picture is far from clear, available evidence seems to confirm the charge of liberal leanings among reporters in the major news media. Studies of the voting behavior of hundreds of reporters and broadcasters show that they voted overwhelmingly for Democratic candidates in presidential elections from 1964 through 1980.[69] Moreover, a 1992 survey of 1,400 journalists found that 44 percent called themselves Democrats versus 16 percent Republicans.[70] But do reporters' personal opinions color news coverage?

A study of television coverage during the 1992 presidential campaign found that the candidates alternated in the spotlight before Labor Day. In the weeks before and during the Democratic convention, Clinton had 454 minutes on network news shows to Bush's 400. But between the Republican convention and Labor Day, Bush drew about 2.6 minutes per newscast versus Clinton's 1.6.[71] Of course, reporters can "spin" the news so that coverage is good or bad. As shown in Compared with What? 6.1, American reporters are far more likely to spin or slant the news than reporters in Britain or Germany. When Bush chose Texas to announce that he would sell fighter jets to Taiwan to save jobs, ABC's Brit Hume reported that Bush was using foreign policy to help his campaign in his home state. After Labor Day, the Times Mirror Center for Media & Public Affairs analyzed all interviews about the candidates on the ABC, CBS, and NBC evening news broadcasts. It classified 69 percent of the comments about Bush as negative, compared with 63 percent about Clinton and only 54 percent about Perot.[72] Even 55 percent of the journalists interviewed during the campaign felt that press coverage had hurt Bush, while only 11 percent thought the coverage hurt Clinton. But most of the journalists felt that they were objectively reporting on Bush's record and the state of the economy.[73]

Although most journalists have classified themselves as liberal or Democrats, more of them described the newspapers for which they worked in 1985 as conservative (pro-Reagan and probusiness) than liberal (42 percent to 28 percent).[74] To some extent, working journalists are at odds with their own editors, who tend to be more conservative. The editors, in their function as gatekeepers, tend to tone down reporters' liberal leanings by editing their stories or not placing them well in the medium. And, newspapers are far more likely to endorse Republican than Democratic presidential candidates. This was certainly true in 1988, when newspapers favored George Bush over Michael Dukakis by nearly three to one.[75] Although 45 more papers endorsed Clinton than Bush in 1992, nearly two-thirds of the 884 papers surveyed—many of which had endorsed Bush before—declined to make an endorsement. (Only four papers endorsed Perot.)[76]

If media owners and their editors are indeed conservative supporters of the status quo, we might expect them to favor officeholders over challengers in elections, regardless of party. However, the evidence tends in the other direction. Let's compare 1980 (when Jimmy Carter, a liberal Democrat, was president and Ronald Reagan, a conservative Republican, was his challenger) with 1984 (when President Reagan faced Walter Mondale, a liberal Democrat). A comparison of television news in 1980

POLITICS IN A CHANGING AMERICA 6.1

¡Se habla español!

Hispanics constitute the fastest growing segment among the major minority groups in the U.S. Although accounting for only 9 percent of the population according to the 1990 census, Hispanics are projected to rise to 21 percent by 2050.[1] At present, nearly half of all Hispanics do not speak English and another 40 percent understand English but prefer to communicate in Spanish.[2] In an effort to tap this expected market of over 30 million in the next century, advertisers increased their spending in Hispanic markets by nearly 30 percent from 1989 to 1993.[3] This increase in advertising revenues has sparked a growth in Spanish-language mass media in areas of the U.S. with heavy concentrations of Hispanics. This growth can be seen in the

The main headline reads "Political asylum denied for boat people. They will be detained at the camp sites for an indefinite amount of time."

The caption accompanying the large photo reads "A group of Cuban refugees on board the rescue boat Courageous *wave upon arrival at Guantanamo Sunday. Later, the refugees were detained in barracks and many mothers bathed their children at faucets installed at the base. Some of the refugees displayed frustration at not be able to reach Miami."*

main Spanish-language new media: newspapers, radio, and television.

Newspapers: The big story in Spanish-language newspapers is the battle between smaller Hispanic publishers, which have served local markets for years, and mainstream Anglo publishers seeking to enter the expanding market. Tito Duran, the president of the National Association of Hispanic Publishers, estimated the nationwide circulation of 329 Hispanic papers at about 10 million.[4] In recent years, established metropolitan papers have launched Spanish-language papers to compete for many of these readers. Examples include the Chicago Tribune Company, which started *Exito* in Miami and then published a sister paper in Chicago; the New York Times Company, which publishes *El Nuevo Tiempo* in Santa Barbara; the *Fort-Worth Star-Telegram*'s *La Estrella*; and the *Miami Herald*'s *El Nuevo Herald*.

Radio: In several communities, Spanish floods the airwaves, sometimes beating English-language stations in Arbitron Company ratings. In the summer of 1993, for example, these Hispanic stations had climbed to or near the top of their markets (rankings are in brackets): KXTN [1] in San Antonio; KLAX [1] in Los Angeles; WAQI [2] and WRTO [4] both in Miami; KIWW [3], KGBT [4], and KKPS [7] all in McAllen-Brownsville-Harlingen, Texas; XEMO [6] in San Diego North, California; and KLAX [9] in Anaheim-Santa Ana, California.[5] Although most of these stations feature entertainment in their programming, many also broadcast news obtained from several networks: Cadena Radio Centro, UPI's Radio Noticias, the Spanish Information Service, and CNN's Radio Noticias For example, CNN's Radio Noticias offers nearly six minutes of newscast at the top of each hour and separate regional reports for the eastern and western halves of the U.S. to some 60 stations in 43 cities.[6]

Television: Two major networks—Univision and Telemundo—dominate Hispanic television. Univision, the larger of the two, claims an audience of nearly 25 million, which it reaches through 37 broadcast and 670 cable affiliates.[7] In late 1992, the two networks spent some $16 million for the Nielsen rating service to provide authoritative measurement of Hispanic viewers, and the more credible rating information led to increased advertising. Univision relies more on foreign-produced Spanish-language entertainment programs, while Telemundo produces more domestic programming specifically designed for Hispanics in the U.S. As yet, Hispanic television features relatively little news programming. A recent Ford Foundation study, however, reports that Hispanics are even more likely to get their news from television than the general U.S. population, for which television is already the most important news source.[8] So expect more news on Spanish-language television.

1 *Steve Coe, "Hispanic Broadcasting and Cable"* Broadcasting and Cable, *15 November 1993, p. 40.*

2 *Jim Cooper, "Advertisers rush into growing market,"* Broadcasting and Cable, *15 November 1993: p. 46.*

3 *Christy Fisher, "Hispanic media see siesta ending,"* Advertising Age, *24 January 1994: S1.*

4 *M.L. Stein, "Boast of Success,"* Editor & Publisher, *12 February 1994, p.13.*

5 *Susan Taras, "Hispanic radio heats up the airwaves,"* Advertising Age, *24 January 1994: S8.*

6 *Peter Viles, "Spanish radio news: is there room for another network?* Broadcasting and Cable, *15 November 1993, pp. 42–43.*

7 *Tim Jones, "New vision likely for Channel 66,"* Chicago Tribune, *14 March 1994, Section 4, p. 1.*

8 *Ibid., p. 2.*

and 1984 found more negative coverage of the incumbent president both times.[77] The researcher concluded that virtually no *continuing* ideological or partisan bias exists on the evening news. Instead, what was seen as ideological or partisan bias in 1980 and 1984 was actually a bias against presidential *incumbents* and *front-runners* for the presidency.[78]

According to this reasoning, if journalists have any pronounced bias, it is against office-holding politicians. When an incumbent runs for reelection, journalists may feel a special responsibility to counteract his or her advantage by putting the opposite partisan spin on the news.[79] When Clinton became president, he began to feel the sting of media criticism. One study in mid-1993 found that 64 percent of all references to Clinton by network news reporters was negative, compared with 41 percent negative references to Bush during the first six months of 1989.[80] Indeed, more than 40 percent of the public in June 1993 felt that the press was unfair to the Clinton administration, more unfair than for previous administrations.[81] Thus, whether the media coverage of campaigns is seen as pro-Democratic (and therefore liberal) or pro-Republican (and therefore conservative) depends on which party is in office at the time.

Of course, the media affect voting behavior simply by reporting daily news, which publicizes officeholders throughout the year. Noncampaign news coverage leads to greater incumbent name recognition at election time, particularly for members of Congress (see Chapter 11). This coverage effect is independent of any bias in reporting on campaigns. Moreover, bias in reporting is not limited to election campaigns, and different media may reflect different biases on political issues. A study of stories on nuclear energy carried in the media during a period of ten years found that stories in the *New York Times* were well balanced between pronuclear and antinuclear sources. In contrast, the major newsmagazines and television tended to favor antinuclear sources and to slant their stories against nuclear energy.[82]

Contributions to Democracy

As noted earlier, the communication in a democracy must move in two directions: from government to citizens and from citizens to government. In fact, political communication in the United States seldom goes directly from government to citizens without passing through the media. The point is important because, as just discussed, news reporters tend to be highly critical of politicians; they consider it their job to search for inaccuracies in fact and weaknesses in argument. Some observers have characterized the news media and the government as adversaries—each mistrusting the other, locked in competition for popular favor while trying to get the record straight. To the extent that this is true, the media serve both the majoritarian and the pluralist models of democracy well by improving the quality of information transmitted to people about their government.

The mass media transmit information in the opposite direction by reporting citizens' reactions to political events and government actions. The press has traditionally reflected public opinion (and often created it) in the process of defining the news and suggesting courses of government action. But the media's role in reflecting public opinion has become much more refined in the information age. Since the 1820s, newspapers had conducted "straw polls" of dubious quality that matched their own partisan inclinations.[83] After commercial polls (such as the Gallup and Roper polls) were established in the 1930s, newspapers began to report more reliable readings of public opinion. By the 1960s, the media (both national and local) began to conduct their own surveys. In the 1970s, some news organizations acquired their own survey research divisions. Occasionally, print and electronic media have joined forces to conduct major national surveys.

The media now have the tools to do a better job of reporting mass opinion than ever before, and they use those tools extensively, doing "precision journalism" with sophisticated data collection and analysis techniques. The well-respected New York Times/CBS News Poll conducts surveys that are aired first on the "CBS Evening News" then analyzed at length in the *Times*. After heavy criticism for relying too heavily on polls in their election coverage, most major newspapers and the television networks cut down on reporting polls in their election coverage in 1992. *USA Today* and CNN went the other way and reported a fresh poll every day from September 30 to the election.[84]

Citizens and journalists alike complain that heavy reliance on polls during election campaigns causes the media to emphasize the horse race and slights the discussion of issues.[85] But the media also use their polling expertise for other purposes, such as gauging support for going to war against Iraq and for balancing the budget. Although polls sometimes create opinions just by asking questions, their net effect has been to generate more accurate knowledge of public opinion and to report that knowledge back to the public. Although widespread knowledge of public opinion does not guarantee government responsiveness to popular demands, such knowledge is necessary if government is to function according to the majoritarian model of democracy.

Effects on Freedom, Order, and Equality

The media in the United States have played an important role in advancing equality, especially racial equality. Throughout the civil rights movement of the 1950s and 1960s, the media gave national coverage to conflict in the South, as black children tried to attend white schools or civil rights workers were beaten and even killed in the effort to register black voters. Partly because of the media coverage, civil rights moved up on the political agenda, and coalitions formed in Congress to pass new laws promoting racial equality. Women's rights have also been advanced through the media, which have reported allegations of blatant sexual discrimination exposed by groups working for sexual equality, such as the National Organization for Women (NOW). In general, the mass media offer spokespersons for any disadvantaged group an opportunity to state their case before a national audience and to work for a place on the political agenda.

Although the media are willing to encourage government action to promote equality at the cost of some personal freedom, they resist government's attempts to infringe on freedom of the press to promote order. The media, far more than the public, believe freedom of the press is sacrosanct.

FEATURE 6.3

▪ Today's News: Sex and Scandal

 In 1990, books published about President John F. Kennedy and Dr. Martin Luther King, Jr., accused them of womanizing. In Kennedy's case, the evidence is abundant—reputed liaisons with Marilyn Monroe, accounts of women procured for him by the Secret Service, and an established relationship with Judith Exner, a girlfriend of a Mafia boss. In King's case, the documentation is contested but credible. In both cases, it is significant that reporters covering these men suppressed their inside knowledge and suspicions.

Thirty years ago, the media limited coverage of political candidates and officeholders to their public acts. Today, the media accept no limits to coverage of politicians' private lives, and exposing marital infidelity is standard journalism. In 1988, reporters from the Miami Herald staked out Gary Hart's home in Washington, D.C., to get the goods on his relationship with model Donna Rice. The front-page story helped drive front-runner Hart from the race for the Democratic nomination for president. Later the same year, Henry Cisneros, the mayor of San Antonio, left office over stories about his affair with a woman staff member. In 1990, Jon Grunseth, the Republican candidate for governor in Minnesota, dropped out of the race just before the election because of reports of a lengthy extramarital relationship.

If the media acted properly in exposing these affairs, did it fail the public by not reporting on Kennedy and King? Publicizing Kennedy's sexual appetite surely would have cost him his razor-thin victory over Richard Nixon in 1960, and reports of King's indiscretions would certainly have impaired his leadership of the civil rights movement. Would the nation have been better off without these unfaithful husbands? Might Hart, Cisneros, or Grunseth also have made outstanding government leaders?*

Reporters pursue these stories of sex and scandal because they increase media audiences, raise company profits, and help make journalistic careers. The media cloak their private motives with public values: First, reporters defend their investigations into private lives as justifiable assessments of the candidate's "character." Because anything may reveal character, there is no limit to what reporters feel entitled to investigate.

Second, the media raise the shield of "freedom of the press" against all attempts to limit their coverage of "news." Consider Madonna's music video, "Justify My Love," which celebrated "voyeurism, masturbation, group sex, soft-core sadomasochism and bisexuality." Even MTV refused to air it, saying, "This one is just not for us." ABC's "Nightline" rode to the rescue, showing the steamy video in its entirety to a nationwide audience while soberly treating it as an issue of freedom of expression. The news-starved public responded by giving the program its highest rating of 1990.

Not many businesses can camouflage their private interests—making money—under the guise of public interest. Now that the media are learning to exploit this position, look for more sizzling infotainment.

* In fact, Henry Cisneros made a comeback after resigning as mayor of San Antonio; he became secretary of Housing and Urban Development in the Clinton administration.

• Sources: C. David Heymann, A Woman Named Jackie (New York: New American Library, 1990); Ralph David Abernathy, And the Walls Came Tumbling Down (New York: Harper and Row, 1989); Joan Beck, "Sex, Hype and Videotape Drown Out Voices of Reason," Chicago Tribune, 6 December 1990, p. 21.

For example, 98 percent of 2,703 journalists surveyed by the Los Angeles Times opposed allowing a government official to prevent the publication of a story the government claims is inaccurate, compared with only 50 percent of the public. Whereas a majority of the public believes that certain types of news should never be published—"exit polls saying who will win an election, secret documents dealing with national security issues, the names of CIA spies, photographs that invade people's privacy"—journalists are more reluctant to draw the line anywhere, as discussed in Feature 6.3.[86] Although reporters covering the Persian Gulf crisis chafed at restrictions imposed by the military, a survey during the war found that 57 percent of the public thought that the military "should exert more control" over reporting.[87] Finally, more citizens favor curbing news reports about racial or ethnic insults than publicizing them.[88]

To protect their freedom, the media operate as an interest group along pluralist lines. They have an interest in reporting whatever they wish, whenever they wish, which certainly erodes government's efforts to maintain order. Three examples illustrate this point.

- The media's sensational coverage of airline hijackers and other terrorist activities gives terrorists exactly what they want, making it more difficult to reduce terrorist threats to order.

- The portrayal of brutal killings and rapes on television, often under the guise of entertainment, has produced "copycat" crimes admittedly committed "as seen on TV."

- The national publicity given in 1982 to deaths from Tylenol capsules laced with cyanide has ghoulishly prompted similar tampering with other products. (The bizarre claims of syringes found in cans of Pepsi Cola in 1993 proved to be "copycat tampering."[89]).

Freedom of the press is a noble value and one that has been important to democratic government. But we should not ignore the fact that democracies sometimes pay a price for pursuing it without qualification.

SUMMARY

The mass media transmit information to large, heterogeneous, and widely dispersed audiences through print and broadcasts. The main function of the mass media is entertainment, but the media also perform the political functions of reporting news, interpreting news, influencing citizens' opinions, setting the political agenda, and socializing citizens about politics.

The mass media in the United States are privately owned and in business to make money, which they do mainly by selling space or air time to advertisers. Both print and electronic media determine which events are newsworthy, largely on the basis of audience appeal. The rise of mass-circulation newspapers in the 1830s produced a politically independent press in the United States. In their aggressive competition for readers, those newspapers often engaged in sensational reporting, a charge sometimes leveled at today's media.

The broadcast media operate under technical, ownership, and content regulations set by the government, which tend to promote more even-handed treatment of political contests on radio and television than in newspapers and news magazines.

The major media maintain staffs of professional journalists in major cities around the world. Washington, D.C., hosts the biggest press corps in the world, but only a portion of those correspondents concentrate on the presidency. Because Congress is a more decentralized institution, it is covered in a more decentralized manner. All professional journalists recognize rules for citing sources that guide their reporting. What actually gets reported in the media depends on the media's gatekeepers, the publishers and editors.

Although Americans today get more news from television than newspapers, newspapers usually do a more thorough job of informing the public about politics. Despite heavy exposure to news in the print and electronic media, the ability of most people to retain much political information is shockingly low—and lower than it was in the mid-1960s. The problem appears to be not with the media's inability to supply quality news coverage but the lack of demand for it by the public. The media's most important effect on public opinion is setting the political agenda. The role of the news media may be more important for affecting interactions among attentive policy elites than in influencing public opinion. More subtle, the media plays contradictory roles in political socialization, both promoting and undermining certain political and cultural values.

The media's elite, including reporters from the major television networks, tend to be more liberal than the public, as judged by the journalists' tendency to vote for Democratic candidates and by their own self-descriptions. Journalists' liberal leanings are checked somewhat by conservative inclinations of their editors and publishers. However, if the media systematically demonstrate any pronounced bias in their news reporting, it is a bias against incumbents and frontrunners, regardless of their party, rather than in favor of liberal Democrats.

From the standpoint of majoritarian democracy, one of the most important roles of the media is to facilitate communication from the people to the government through the reporting of public opinion polls. The media zealously defend the freedom of the press, even to the point of encouraging disorder through the granting of extensive publicity to violent protests, terrorist acts, and other threats to order.

Key Terms

communication
mass communication
mass media
print media
broadcast media
yellow journalism
muckrakers
attentive policy elites
two-step flow of
  communication
newsworthiness
infotainment

Federal Communications Commission (FCC)
equal opportunities rule
reasonable access rule
fairness doctrine
gatekeepers
horse race journalism
media event
political agenda

Selected Readings

Ansolabehere, Stephen, Roy Behr, and Shanto Iyengar. *The Media Game: American Politics in the Television Age.* New York: Macmillan, 1993. A recent text on media's influence in politics that explores how the media can filter, alter, distort, or even ignore what politicians have to say.

Bozell, L. Brent, II, and Brent H. Baker, eds. *And That's the Way It Isn't.* Alexandria, Va.: Media Research Center, 1990. Prepared by a conservative research group, this study documents the liberal bias of the media. Contrast this book with that by Kellner.

Eastland, Terry, ed. *Forbes Media Guide 500.* New

York: Forbes, 1994. A handbook of the previous year's major stories and an assessment of their coverage in the print media, including ratings of journalists. This critical source evaluates the alternative press as well as the main stream media.

Entman, Robert. *Democracy Without Citizens: Media and the Decay of American Politics.* New York: Oxford University Press, 1989. A penetrating study of the "supply" side of news reporting and the "demand" side of news consumption. Entman concludes that the media do not do a better job of reporting news because the public does not demand it.

———— *Media Power and Politics.* 2d ed. Washington, D.C.: Congressional Quarterly Press, 1990. A collection of seminal essays on political journalism and empirical studies of media effects.

Kellner, Douglas. *Television and the Crisis of Democracy.* Boulder, Colo.: Westview, 1990. A critical, leftist account of the role mass media play in controlling the limits of political discussion by extending the hegemony of the dominant culture. Serves as a counterpoint to the book by Bozell and Baker.

Lavrakas, Paul J., and Jack K. Holley, eds. *Polling and Presidential Election Coverage.* Newbury Park, Calif.: Sage, 1991. Studies of the media's use of public opinion surveys in covering the 1988 presidential election.

Neuman, W. Russell, Marion R. Just, and Ann N. Crigler. *Common Knowledge: News and the Construction of Political Meaning.* Chicago: University of Chicago Press, 1992. Studied how people construct meaning from news they received on five topics in 1987: the stock market crash, drugs, racial politics in South Africa, the Strategic Defense Initiative, and AIDS.

Rosenblum, Mort. *Who Stole the News?: Why We Can't Keep Up with What Happens in the World and What We Can Do About It.* New York: Wiley, 1993. Blames the American news media system for reporting less and less overseas news because of efforts to cut costs and increase profits.

Serfaty, Simon, ed. *The Media and Foreign Policy.* New York: St. Martin's Press, 1990. A collection of short accounts, mostly anecdotal, by insiders who were in a position to observe the relationship of the media to the White House during foreign policy crises.

Participation
and Voting

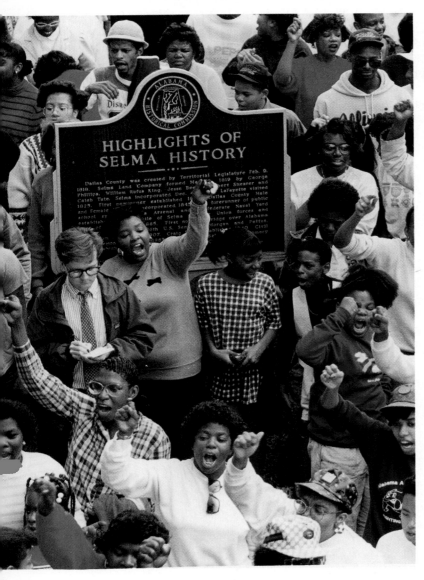

"**SOCIAL PROTEST** is at the heart of what America stands for, and has been since the Boston Tea Party," said Joseph Scheidler, the leader of an interest group protesting U.S. law.[1] Scheidler might cite demonstrations by women for the right to vote, acts of civil disobedience by African-Americans pressing for civil rights, and organized protests by college youth against the Vietnam War. As executive director of the Pro-Life Action League, however, Scheidler's protests were aimed at abortion clinics.

Outraged by the 1973 court decision that protected women's right to an abortion, the antiabortion movement was targeting abortion clinics in localized actions by the early 1980s. One of the earliest attempts to coordinate the protests was Scheidler's Pro-Life Nonviolent Action Project (PNAP), which produced flyers and provided training in nonviolent protest throughout the country. At the 1984 National Right to Life convention in Kansas City, Scheidler himself had led a demonstration at the city's abortion clinics.[2]

The actions of Randall Terry, the founder of Operation Rescue, propelled antiabortion protests into the national spotlight. Terry worked for two years to organize the "Siege on Atlanta," in which 1,200 demonstrators blocked entrances to the city's abortion clinics during the 1988 Democratic nominating convention.[3] Benefiting from coverage from the thousands of media people at the convention, Operation Rescue gained support and expanded its activities: "By early 1989 Operation Rescue claimed that it had over 35,000 members in 200 cities and had performed more than 250 'rescues.' "[4]

Although protests at abortion clinics sometimes erupted into violence, the tactics of Operation Rescue itself followed the passive resistance approach of Mahatma Gandhi and Martin Luther King, Jr. (see Feature 7.1). In the 1990s, clinic protests turned uglier. In 1992 and 1993, 123 family planning clinics were bombed or burned.[5] Doctors' families were harassed on the streets and received threatening phone calls at home. Then, on March 10, 1993, a doctor was shot and killed during a demonstration in Pensacola, Florida. Less than five months later, another doctor was shot and wounded outside a clinic in Wichita, Kansas.

Seeking legal protection, the National Organization for Women sued Joseph Scheidler and other antiabortion leaders, charging that they were orchestrating a national campaign of violence and intimidation against abortion clinics. In a surprise move in 1994, the Supreme Court unanimously declared in *National Organization for Women* v. *Scheidler* that abortion clinics could sue antiabortion protest groups under the

Debating the Issues
There is little evidence of rational debate when pro-life and pro-choice demonstrators come into contact, as they did here outside an abortion clinic in Amherst, New York.

Racketeer-Influenced and Corrupt Organizations Act (RICO). RICO prohibits any enterprise from operating in ways that violate certain state or federal criminal statutes, including those outlawing intimidation, threats, trespassing, and vandalism. If prochoice groups could prove that antiabortion groups engaged in criminal conspiracy under the RICO law, they could claim triple damages, which might bankrupt any antiabortion groups convicted. Protesting the decision as a curb on legitimate political protest and free speech, Randall Terry declared, "Under this decision, Martin Luther King, Jr., would have been a racketeer."[6]

Although most people think of political participation primarily in terms of voting, there are other forms of political participation, some more effective than voting. Did the antiabortion protesters exceed the boundaries of political participation, or were they simply following an American tradition? How politically active are Americans in general? How do they compare with citizens of other countries? And how much and what kind of participation is necessary to sustain the pluralist and majoritarian models of democracy?

In this chapter, we try to answer these and other important questions about popular participation in government. We begin by studying participation in democratic government, distinguishing between conventional and unconventional participation. Then we evaluate the nature and extent of both types of participation in American politics. Next, we study the expansion of voting rights and voting as the major mechanism for mass participation in politics. Finally, we will examine the extent to which the various forms of political participation serve the values of freedom, equality, and order and the majoritarian and pluralist models of democracy.

DEMOCRACY AND POLITICAL PARTICIPATION

"Government ought to be run by the people." That is the democratic ideal in a nutshell. But how much and what kind of citizen participation is necessary for democratic government? Neither political theorists nor politicians, neither idealists nor realists, can agree on an answer. Champions of

FEATURE 7.1

■ Even Protesters Have Rules

 This is a form that Operation Rescue of Central Virginia provides to those who participate at the site of a protest, usually at an abortion clinic.

As described in *Abortion and American Politics,*

The aim is to blockade abortion clinics and prevent those seeking abortion from entering. Demonstrators are coached ahead of time and warned not to push or shove, not to bring posters, and to lie or stand tightly together in a wall of bodies so that no one can pass. As one news account described their actions: "They move in a human sludge, on their knees, not standing, to make confrontation possible." When the police attempt to move them, participants go limp, forcing the officers to carry or drag them away. If arrested, they are supposed to continue their noncooperation by refusing to give their names or pay any fines—a strategy that usually lands them in jail.

• *Source: Barbara Hinkson Craig, and David M. O'Brien, Abortion and American Politics (Chatham, N.J.: Chatham House, 1993), pp. 58, 60–61.*

I UNDERSTAND the critical importance of Operation Rescue being unified, peaceful, and free of any actions or words that would appear violent or hateful to those watching the event on TV, or reading about it in the paper.

I REALIZE that some of the pro-abortion elements of the media would love to discredit this event (and the entire prolife movement) and focus on a side issue in order to avoid the central issue at hand: murdered children and exploited women.

HENCE, I UNDERSTAND that for the children's sake, this gathering must be orderly and above reproach.

THEREFORE . . .

(1) As an invited guest, I will cooperate with the spirit and goals of Operation Rescue, as explained in this pamphlet.

(2) I commit to be peaceful, prayerful, and non-violent in both word and deed.

(3) Should I be arrested, I will not struggle with police in any way (whether deed or word), but remain polite and passively limp, remembering that mercy triumphs over judgement.

(4) I will listen and follow the instructions of Operation Rescue's leadership and crowd control marshall.

(5) I understand that certain individuals will be appointed to speak to the media, the police, and the women seeking abortion. I will not take it upon myself to yell to anyone, but will continue singing and praying with the main group as directed.

I SIGN THIS PLEDGE, HAVING SERIOUSLY CONSIDERED WHAT I DO, WITH THE WILL AND DETERMINATION TO PERSEVERE BY THE GRACE OF GOD.

_____
DATE

_____
SIGNATURE

CIRCLE ONLY ONE ITEM

(1) I am prepared to risk arrest in order to rescue children from the violent death of abortion.

(2) I will be present to pray, picket, and show support for this rescue.

direct democracy believe that if citizens do not participate directly in government affairs, making government decisions among themselves, they should give up all pretense of democracy. More practical observers contend that people can govern indirectly through their elected representatives. And they maintain that choosing leaders through **elections**—formal procedures for voting—is the only workable approach to democracy in a large, complex nation.

We talked about the distinction between direct and indirect democracy in Chapter 2. In a direct democracy, citizens meet and make decisions themselves. In an indirect democracy, citizens participate in government by electing representatives to make decisions for them. Voting is central to the majoritarian model of government, but it is not the only means of political participation. In fact, the pluralist model of democracy relies less on voting and more on other forms of participation.

Elections are a necessary condition of democracy, but they do not guarantee democratic government. Before the collapse of communism, the former Soviet Union regularly held elections in which more than 90 percent of the electorate turned out to vote, but the Soviet Union certainly did not function as a democracy. Both the majoritarian and pluralist models of democracy rely on voting to varying degrees, but both models expect citizens to take part in other forms of political behavior as well. For example, they expect citizens to discuss politics, to form interest groups, to contact public officials, to campaign for political parties, to run for office, and even to protest government decisions.

We define **political participation** as "those actions of private citizens by which they seek to influence or to support government and politics."[7] This definition embraces both conventional and unconventional forms of political participation. In plain language, *conventional behavior* is behavior that is acceptable to the dominant culture in a given situation. Wearing a swimsuit at the beach is conventional; wearing one at a formal dance is not. Displaying campaign posters in front yards is conventional; spray-painting political slogans on buildings is not.

Things Change

When he was a student at Cornell University, Tom Jones was a nineteen-year-old leader of an armed takeover of the administration building during campus protests in the spring of 1969 against the Vietnam War and for black power. Now he is Thomas W. Jones, in his mid-forties, and president and chief executive officer of TIAA-CREF, the college teachers' retirement fund, the world's biggest private pension fund ($115 billion). He is also a member of Cornell's board of trustees. He told the New York Times *that he "made the best decisions I could make under the circumstances, and I will not repudiate that twenty-five years later," but he regrets the incidents of potential violence. Things change.*

At times, figuring out whether a particular political act is conventional or unconventional is difficult. We find the following distinction useful in analyzing political participation:

- **Conventional participation** is relatively routine behavior that uses the established institutions of representative government, especially campaigning for candidates and voting in elections.

- **Unconventional participation** is relatively uncommon behavior that challenges or defies established institutions or the dominant culture (and thus is personally stressful to participants and their opponents).

Voting and writing letters to public officials are examples of conventional political participation; staging sit-down strikes in public buildings and chanting slogans outside officials' windows are examples of unconventional participation. Demonstrations can be conventional (carrying signs outside an abortion clinic) or unconventional (linking arms to prevent entrance). Various forms of unconventional participation are often used by powerless groups to gain political benefits while also working within the system.[8]

Voting and other methods of conventional participation are important to democratic government. So are unconventional forms of participation. Let us look at both kinds of political participation in the United States.

UNCONVENTIONAL PARTICIPATION

On Sunday, March 7, 1965, a group of about six hundred people attempted to march fifty miles from Selma, Alabama, to the state capitol at Montgomery. The marchers were demonstrating in favor of voting rights for blacks. (At the time, Selma had fewer than five hundred registered black voters, out of fifteen thousand who were eligible.[9]) Alabama governor George Wallace declared the march illegal and sent state troopers to stop it. The two groups met at the Edmund Pettus Bridge over the Alabama River at the edge of Selma. The peaceful marchers were disrupted and beaten by state troopers and deputy sheriffs—some on horseback—using clubs, bullwhips, and tear gas. The day became known as *Bloody Sunday*.

The march from Selma was a form of unconventional political participation. Marching fifty miles in a political protest is certainly not common; moreover, the march challenged existing institutions, which prevented blacks from voting. From the beginning, the marchers knew they were putting themselves in a dangerous situation, that they certainly would be taunted by whites along the way and could be physically hurt as well. But they had been prevented from participating conventionally—voting in elections—for many decades, and they chose this unconventional method to dramatize their cause.

The march ended in violence because Governor Wallace would not allow even this peaceful mode of unconventional expression. In contrast to some later demonstrations against the Vietnam War, this civil rights march posed no threat of violence. The brutal response to the marchers helped the rest of the nation understand the seriousness of the civil rights problem in the South. Unconventional participation is stressful and occasionally violent but sometimes is worth the risk.

Antiwar Protest, 1968

In August 1968, thousands of youthful antiwar protesters gathered in Chicago, where the Democrats were holding their national convention. Protests against the war had already forced president Lyndon Johnson not to seek re-election. Mayor Richard Daley vowed that the protesters would not disturb the impending nomination of Hubert Humphrey, Johnson's vice president. Daley's police kept the youths from demonstrating at the convention, but the resulting violence did not help Humphrey, who lost to Richard Nixon in an extremely close election.

SUPPORT FOR UNCONVENTIONAL PARTICIPATION

Unconventional political participation has a long history in the United States. The Boston Tea Party in 1773, in which American colonists dumped three cargoes of British tea into Boston Harbor, was only the first in a long line of violent protests against British rule that eventually led to revolution. Yet, we know less about unconventional than conventional participation. The reasons are twofold: First, because collecting data on conventional practices is easier, they are studied more frequently. Second, political scientists are simply biased toward "institutionalized," or conventional, politics. In fact, some basic works on political participation explicitly exclude any behavior that is "outside the system."[10] One major study of unconventional political action asked people whether they had engaged in or approved of ten types of political participation outside of voting.[11] As shown in Figure 7.1, of the ten activities, only signing petitions was clearly regarded as conventional, in the sense that the behavior was nearly universally approved and widely practiced.

The conventionality of two other forms of behavior was questionable. Nearly a quarter of the respondents disapproved of lawful demonstrations, and only one in ten had ever participated in such a demonstration. What is and is not "lawful" is hard to determine, however. The marchers in Selma, although peaceful, violated Governor Wallace's decree, which itself may have violated their rights. If we measure conventionality in terms of the proportion of people who disapprove of an action and those who actually practice it, we might argue that all demonstrations border on the unconventional. The same reasoning could be applied to boycotting products— for example, refusing to buy lettuce or grapes picked by nonunion farm workers. Lawful demonstrations and boycotts are problem cases in deciding what is and is not conventional political participation.

The other political activities listed in Figure 7.1 are clearly unconventional. In fact, when political activities interfere with daily living (block-

| FIGURE | 7.1 | ■ **What Americans Think Is Unconventional Political Behavior** |

A survey asked Americans whether they "have done" or approved or disapproved of ten different forms of participation outside the electoral process. The respondents disapproved of most of the ten forms, often overwhelmingly. Only signing petitions was rarely disapproved of—and also widely done. Even attending lawful demonstrations (a right guaranteed in the Constitution) was disapproved of by 24 percent of the respondents and rarely practiced. Boycotting products was more objectionable but more widely practiced. Attending demonstrations and boycotting products are only marginally conventional. The other seven forms are clearly unconventional.

Source: Samuel H. Barnes and Max Kaase, eds., Political Action: Mass Participation in Five Western Democracies *(Beverly Hills, Calif.: Sage, 1979), p. 545.*

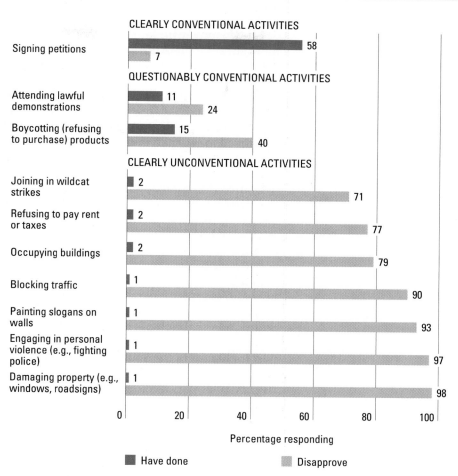

ing traffic) or involve harm to property (painting slogans on walls, breaking windows) or physical violence, disapproval is nearly universal. Americans usually disapprove of unconventional political behavior. When protesters demonstrating against the Vietnam War disrupted the 1968 Democratic National Convention in Chicago, they were clubbed by the city's police. Although the viewing public saw graphic videotape of the confrontations and heard reporters' criticisms of police behavior, most viewers condemned the demonstrators, not the police.

The Effectiveness of Unconventional Participation

Antiabortion protests discourage many doctors from performing abortions, but they have not led to outlawing abortions. Does unconventional participation ever work, especially when it provokes violence? Yes. Antiwar protesters helped convince President Lyndon Johnson not to seek reelection in 1968, and they heightened public concern about U.S. participation in the Vietnam War. American college students who disrupted campuses in the late 1960s and early 1970s helped end the military draft in 1973 and, although it was not one of their stated goals, sped up the passage of the Twenty-sixth Amendment, which lowered the voting age to eighteen.

The unconventional activities of the civil rights workers also had notable success. Dr. Martin Luther King, Jr., led the 1955 Montgomery bus boycott (prompted by Rosa Parks's refusal to surrender her seat to a white man) that sparked the civil rights movement. He used **direct action** to challenge specific cases of discrimination, assembling crowds to confront businesses and local governments and demanding equal treatment in public accommodations and government. The civil rights movement organized more than one thousand such newsworthy demonstrations nationwide—387 in 1965 alone.[12] And, like the march in Selma, many protests provoked violent confrontations between whites and blacks.

Denied the usual opportunities for conventional political participation, the civil rights movement used unconventional politics to pressure Congress to pass a series of civil rights laws in 1957, 1960, 1964, and 1968—each one in some way extending national protection against discrimination by reason of race, color, religion, or national origin. (The 1964 act also prohibited discrimination in employment on the basis of sex.)

In addition, the Voting Rights Act of 1965 placed some state electoral procedures under federal supervision, protecting the registration of black voters and increasing the rate of black voter turnout—especially in the South, where much of the violence occurred. Black protest activity (both violent and nonviolent) has also been credited with increased welfare support for blacks in the South.[13] The civil rights movement shows that social change can occur, even when it faces violent opposition at first. In 1990, twenty-five years after law enforcement officers beat civil rights marchers in Selma, some of the same marchers walked peacefully to commemorate Bloody Sunday, with a few police there to ensure they would not be disturbed. Twenty-five years after the assassination of Dr. Martin Luther King, Jr., however, racial divisions still persisted across the nation (see Politics in a Changing America 7.1).

Although direct political action and the politics of confrontation can work, using them requires a special kind of commitment. Studies show that direct action appeals most to those who both (1) distrust the political system and (2) have a strong sense of political efficacy—the feeling that they can do something to affect political decisions.[14] Whether this combination of attitudes produces behavior that challenges the system depends on the extent of organized group activity.[15] The civil rights movement involved many organized groups: King's Southern Christian Leadership Conference (SCLC); the Congress of Racial Equality (CORE), headed by James Farmer; and the Student Non-Violent Coordinating Committee (SNCC), led by Stokely Carmichael, to mention but a few.

The decision to use unconventional behavior also depends on the extent to which individuals develop a group consciousness—identification with the group and awareness of its position in society, its objectives, and its intended course of action.[16] These characteristics were present among blacks and young people in the mid-1960s and are strongly present today among blacks and to a lesser degree among women. Indeed, some researchers contend that black consciousness has heightened both African

POLITICS IN A CHANGING AMERICA **7.1**   **Race Relations Still Not Good, but Getting Better**

 Twenty-five years after Dr. Martin Luther King, Jr.'s assassination on April 4, 1968, the *New York Times* conducted a poll on racial relations in the United States. Although most black and white respondents thought that race relations were "bad" rather than "good," a clear majority of whites and a plurality of blacks felt that race relations were better than they had been twenty-five years before. Moreover, an overwhelming majority of both whites and blacks thought

that significant progress had been made toward "Martin Luther King's dream of equality." Finally, about 40 percent of blacks *and* whites supported the use of nonviolent protest as "the best way" for blacks to gain their rights, which indicates the acceptability of unconventional participation in American politics.

• Source: Peter Applebone, "Racial Divisions Persist 25 Years After King Killing," New York Times, 4 April 1993, p. 12. Copyright © 1993 The New York Times Company. Reprinted by permission.

Question: Do you think race relations in the United states are generally good or generally bad?

	Good	Bad
Total	37%	56%
Whites	38%	55%
Blacks	27%	66%

Question: Compared to 25 years ago, do you think race relations in the United States are better now, worse or about the same

	Better	Worse	Same
Total	52%	16%	28%
Whites	54%	16%	26%
Blacks	45%	15%	37%

Question: Do you believe that where there has been job discrimination in the past, preference in hiring or promotion should be given to blacks today?

	Should be given	Should not
Total	33%	53%
Whites	28%	58%
Blacks	66%	24%

Question: Do you think there has been significant progress toward Martin Luther King's dream of equality, or don't you think so?

	Progress	No Progress
Total	63%	28%
Whites	64%	27%
Blacks	62%	34%

Question: What's the best way for blacks to try to gain their rights — use laws and persuasion, use nonviolent protests, or be ready to use violence?

	Laws	Nonviolence	Violence
Total	45%	41%	2%
Whites	47%	39%	
Blacks	38%	45%	7%

When Teachers Get Angry

As might be expected, when teachers protest against low pay for educators, they make signs. Members of the local PTA in Austin, Texas, join with members of the American Federation of Teachers in a night vigil at the Texas State Capitol. Political protest isn't just for those outside the system.

Americans' distrust of the political system and their sense of individual efficacy, generating more and more varied political participation by poor blacks than by poor whites.[17] The National Organization for Women (NOW) and other women's groups have also heightened women's group consciousness, which may have contributed to their increased participation in politics, in both conventional and unconventional ways.

Unconventional Participation in America

Although most Americans disapprove of using certain forms of participation to protest government policies, U.S. citizens are about as likely to take direct action in politics as citizens of European democracies. Surveys in Britain, Germany, and France in 1981 found that Americans claim to have participated as much or more than British, German, and French citizens in unconventional actions, such as lawful demonstrations, boycotts, unlawful strikes, occupying buildings, damaging property, and even engaging in personal violence.[18] Contrary to the popular view that Americans are apathetic about politics, a recent study suggests that they are more likely to engage in political protests of various sorts than citizens in other democratic countries.[19]

Is something wrong with our political system if citizens resort to unconventional—and widely disapproved of—methods of political participation? To answer this question, we must first learn how much Americans use conventional methods of participation.

CONVENTIONAL PARTICIPATION

A practical test of the democratic nature of any government is whether citizens can affect its policies by acting through its institutions—meeting with public officials, supporting candidates, voting in elections. If people must operate outside government institutions in order to influence policymaking—as civil rights workers had to do in the South—the system is not democratic. Citizens should not have to risk life and property to participate in politics, and they should not have to take direct action to force government to hear their views. The objective of democratic institutions is to make political participation conventional—to allow ordinary citizens to engage in relatively routine, nonthreatening behavior to cause government to heed their opinions, interests, and needs.

In a democracy, for a group to gather at a statehouse or city hall to dramatize its position on an issue—say, a tax increase— is not unusual. Such a demonstration is a form of conventional participation. The group is not powerless, and its members are not risking their personal safety by demonstrating. But violence can erupt between opposing groups demonstrating in a political setting, such as between antiabortion and prochoice groups. Circumstances, then, often determine whether organized protest is or is not conventional. In general, the less that participants anticipate a threat, the more likely it is that the protest is conventional.

Conventional political behaviors fall into two major categories: actions that show support for government policies and those that try to change or *influence* policies.

Supportive Behavior

Supportive behaviors are actions that express allegiance to country and government. When we recite the Pledge of Allegiance or fly the American flag on holidays, we are showing support for the country and, by implication, its political system. Such ceremonial activities usually require little effort, knowledge, or personal courage; that is, they demand little initiative on the part of the citizen. The simple act of turning out to vote is in itself a show of support for the political system. Other supportive behaviors—serving as an election judge in a nonpartisan election or organizing a holiday parade—demand greater initiative.

At times, their perception of patriotism moves people to cross the line between conventional and unconventional behavior. In their eagerness to support the American system, they break up a meeting or disrupt a rally of a group they believe is radical or somehow "un-American." Radical groups may threaten the political system with wrenching change, but superpatriots pose their own threat. Their misguided excess of allegiance denies non-violent means of dissent to others.[20]

Influencing Behavior

Citizens use **influencing behaviors** to modify or even reverse government policy to serve political interests. Some forms of influencing behavior seek particular benefits from government; other forms have broad policy objectives.

Particular Benefits   Some citizens try to influence government to obtain benefits for themselves, their immediate families, or close friends. Two examples of influence attempts that do not require much initiative are voting to elect a relative to local office and voting against an increase in school taxes when the voter's own children have already left school.

Serving one's self-interest through the voting process is certainly acceptable to democratic theory. Each individual has only one vote, and no single voter can wangle particular benefits from government through voting unless a majority of voters agrees.

Political actions that require considerable knowledge and initiative are another story. Individuals or small groups who influence government officials to advance their self-interests—for instance, to obtain a lucrative government contract—may benefit without others knowing about it. Those who quietly obtain particular benefits from government pose a serious challenge to a democracy. Pluralist theory holds that groups ought to be able to make government respond to their special problems and needs. On the other hand, majoritarian theory holds that government should not do what a majority does not want it to do. A majority of citizens might very well not want the government to do what any particular person or group seeks, if it is costly to other citizens.

What might individual citizens or groups ask of their government, and how might they go about asking? Some citizens ask for special services from their local government. Such requests may range from contacting the city forestry department to remove a dead tree in front of a house to calling the county animal control center to deal with a vicious dog in the neighborhood. Studies of such "contacting behavior" as a form of political participation find that it tends not to be empirically related to other forms of political activity. In other words, people who complain to city hall do not necessarily vote. Contacting behavior is related to socioeconomic status: People of higher socioeconomic status are more likely to contact public officials.[21]

Americans demand much more of local government than of national government. Although many people value self-reliance and individualism in national politics, most people expect local government to solve a wide range of social problems. A study of residents of Kansas City, Missouri, found that more than 90 percent thought the city had a responsibility to provide services in thirteen areas, including maintaining parks, setting standards for new home construction, demolishing vacant and unsafe buildings, ensuring that property owners clean up trash and weeds, and providing bus service. The researcher noted that "it is difficult to imagine a set of federal government activities about which there would [be] more consensus."[22] Citizens can also mobilize against a project. The 1980s saw emergence of the "not-in-my-back-yard," or NIMBY, phenomenon, as citizens pressured local officials to stop undesired projects from being located near their homes.

Finally, contributing money to a candidate's campaign is another form of influencing behavior. Here, too, the objective can be particular or broad benefits, although determining which is which sometimes can be difficult. An example: As discussed in Chapter 9, national law limits the amount of money that an individual can contribute directly to a Democrat or Republican candidate's campaign for president, but, during the 1992 campaign, there was no limit on the amount that could be contributed to either of the *parties.* The biggest contributor of so-called soft money in 1992 was the Archer-Daniels-Midland Company (ADM), which "directly and through its chairman, Dwayne O. Andreas," contributed nearly $1 million to the Republican party and more than $100,000 to the Demo-

A Line of Argument

Tension may fill the air when citizens turn out in large numbers at local political meetings, and speaking out in such meetings requires high personal initiative. Knowledge of the issues involved helps, too. Residents attending this public transportation hearing in Austin, Texas, have come prepared to state their views. Looks like a long evening ahead.

cratic party.[23] ADM of Decatur, Illinois, is the major supplier of ethanol, alcohol made from corn that is mixed with gasoline. Andreas had an interest in retaining the tax exemptions for making ethanol and the price supports for corn, especially given that the Environmental Protection Agency was considering restricting the use of ethanol in gasoline. No doubt he also had an interest in the fate of the nation.

Several points emerge from this review of "particularized" forms of political participation. First, approaching government to serve one's particular interests is consistent with democratic theory, because it encourages participation from an active citizenry. Second, particularized contact may be a unique form of participation, not necessarily related to other forms of participation, such as voting. Third, such participation tends to be used more by citizens who are advantaged in terms of knowledge and resources. Fourth, particularized participation may serve private interests to the detriment of the majority.

Broad Policy Objectives   We come now to what many scholars have in mind when they talk about political participation: activities that influence the selection of government personnel and policies. Here, too, we find behaviors that require little initiative (such as voting) and high initiative (attending political meetings, persuading others how to vote).

Even voting intended to influence government policies is a low-initiative activity. Such policy voting differs from voting to show support or to gain special benefits by its broader influence on the community or the society. Obviously, this distinction is not sharp: Citizens vote for a number of reasons, a mix allegiance, particularized benefits, and policy concerns. In addition to policy voting, many other low-initiative forms of conventional participation—wearing a campaign button, watching a party convention on television, posting a bumper sticker—are also connected with selections. In the next section, we focus on elections as a mechanism for participation. For now, we simply note that voting to influence policy is usually a low-initiative activity. As we discuss later, it actually requires more initiative to *register* to vote in the United States than to cast a vote on election day.

Other types of participation to affect broad policies require high initiative. Running for office requires the most (see Chapter 9). Some high-initiative activities, such as attending party meetings and working in campaigns, are associated with the electoral process; others, such as attending legislative hearings and writing letters to Congress, are not. The nonelectoral activities are a form of contacting, but their objective is to obtain government benefits for some group of people—farmers, the unemployed, children, oil producers. In fact, studies of citizen contacts in the United States show that about two-thirds deal with broad social issues and only one-third are for private gain.[24]

Few people realize that using the court system is a form of political participation, a way for citizens to press their rights in a democratic society. Although most people use the courts to serve their particular interests, some also use them, as we discuss shortly, to meet broad objectives. Going to court demands high personal initiative.[25] It also demands a knowledge of the law and the financial resources to afford a lawyer.

People use the courts for both personal benefit and broad policy objectives. A person or group can bring **class action suits** on behalf of other people in similar circumstances. Lawyers for the National Association for the Advancement of Colored People pioneered this form of litigation in the famous school desegregation case *Brown* v. *Board of Education* (1954).[26] They succeeded in getting the Supreme Court to outlaw segregation in public schools, not just for Linda Brown, who brought suit in Topeka, Kansas, but for all others "similarly situated"—that is, for all other black students who want to attend desegregated schools. Participation through the courts is usually beyond the means of individual citizens, but it has proved effective for organized groups, especially those who have been unable to gain their objectives through Congress or the executive branch.

Individual citizens can also try to influence policies at the national level by participating directly in the legislative process. One way is to attend congressional hearings, which are open to the public and occasionally held outside Washington. Especially since the end of World War II, the national government has sought to increase citizen involvement in creating regulations and laws by making information on government activities available to interested parties. For example, government agencies are required to publish all proposed and approved regulations in the daily *Federal Register* and to make government documents available to citizens on request.

Conventional Participation in America

You may know someone who has testified at a congressional or administrative hearing but the odds are that you do not. Such participation is high-initiative behavior. Relatively few people—only those with high stakes in the outcome of a decision—are willing to participate this way. How often do Americans contact government officials and engage in other forms of conventional political participation, compared with citizens in other countries?

The most common political behavior reported in a study of five countries was voting for candidates (see Compared with What? 7.1). Americans are less likely to vote than citizens in the other four countries. On the other hand, Americans are as likely (or substantially more likely) to engage in all other forms of conventional political participation. As we have seen, the same pattern holds true for unconventional behaviors. Americans, then, are more apt to engage in nearly all forms of unconventional and conventional political participation, except voting.

Other researchers noted this paradox and wrote, "If, for example, we concentrate our attention on national elections we will find that the United States is the least participatory of [all] five nations." But looking at the other indicators, they found that "political apathy, by a wide margin, is lowest in the United States. Interestingly, the high levels of overall involvement reflect a rather balanced contribution of both . . . conventional and unconventional politics."[27] Clearly, low voter turnout in the United States constitutes a puzzle, to which we will return.

PARTICIPATING THROUGH VOTING

The heart of democratic government lies in the electoral process. Whether a country holds elections and, if so, what kind constitute the critical differences between democratic and nondemocratic government. Elections institutionalize mass participation in democratic government according to the three normative principles of procedural democracy discussed in Chapter 2: Electoral rules specify *who* is allowed to vote, *how much* each person's vote counts, and *how many* votes are needed to win.

Again, elections are formal procedures for making group decisions. **Voting** is the act in which individuals engage when they choose among alternatives in an election. **Suffrage** and **franchise** both mean the right to vote. By formalizing political participation through rules for suffrage and

Worth Waiting For

Soweto, South Africa, was for many years the center of black protests against the white minority government. Denied the right to vote in elections for all their lives, these thousands of voters in Soweto did not mind waiting several hours and longer in April 1994 to cast their first ballot in South Africa's first free multiracial elections.

COMPARED WITH WHAT? 7.1   **Conventional Political Participation**

A survey of respondents in five democratic industrialized nations found that Americans are far more likely than citizens in the other countries to engage in various forms of conventional political behavior—except voting. The findings clearly contradict the idea that Americans are politically apathetic. Citizens of the United States simply do not vote as much in national elections, which says more about the nature of U.S. elections than about American citizens, who are active politically in other ways.

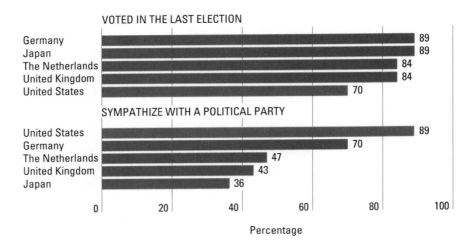

VOTED IN THE LAST ELECTION

Country	Percentage
Germany	89
Japan	89
The Netherlands	84
United Kingdom	84
United States	70

SYMPATHIZE WITH A POLITICAL PARTY

Country	Percentage
United States	89
Germany	70
The Netherlands	47
United Kingdom	43
Japan	36

Percentage

counting ballots, electoral systems allow large numbers of people, who individually have little political power, to wield great power. Electoral systems decide collectively who governs and, in some instances, what government should do.

The simple fact of holding elections is less important than the specific rules and circumstances that govern voting. According to democratic theory, everyone should be able to vote. In practice, however, no nation grants universal suffrage. All countries have age requirements for voting, and all disqualify some inhabitants on various grounds: lack of citizenship, a

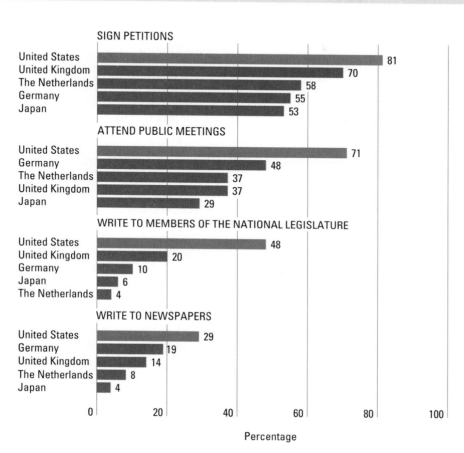

SIGN PETITIONS

United States	81
United Kingdom	70
The Netherlands	58
Germany	55
Japan	53

ATTEND PUBLIC MEETINGS

United States	71
Germany	48
The Netherlands	37
United Kingdom	37
Japan	29

WRITE TO MEMBERS OF THE NATIONAL LEGISLATURE

United States	48
United Kingdom	20
Germany	10
Japan	6
The Netherlands	4

WRITE TO NEWSPAPERS

United States	29
Germany	19
United Kingdom	14
The Netherlands	8
Japan	4

Percentage

• *Source: International Social Justice Project, a collaborative international research effort. The data for this chart, which were kindly provided by Antal Orkeny at (ELTE) Eötvös Lorand University in Hungary, came from national surveys conducted in 1991 that were supported in whole or in part by the Institute for Research, University of Michigan; the Economic and Social Research Council (United Kingdom); the Deutsche Forschungsgemeinschaft; Institute of Social Science, Chuo University (Japan); and the Dutch Ministry of Social Affairs. (The voting turnout for The Netherlands came from election reports.)*

criminal record, mental incompetence, and so forth. What is the record of enfranchisement in the United States?

Expansion of Suffrage

The United States was the first country to provide for general elections of representatives through "mass" suffrage, but the franchise was far from universal. When the Constitution was framed, the idea of full adult suffrage was too radical to consider seriously. Instead, the framers left the issue of enfranchisement to the states, stipulating only that individuals who could vote for "the most numerous Branch of the State Legislature" could also vote for their representatives to the U.S. Congress (Article I, Section 2).

Initially, most states established taxpaying or property-holding requirements for voting. Virginia, for example, required ownership of twenty-five acres of settled land or five hundred acres of unsettled land. The original thirteen states began to lift such requirements after 1800. Expansion of the franchise accelerated after 1815, with the admission of new "western" states (Indiana, Illinois, Alabama), where land was more plentiful and widely owned. By the 1850s, the states had eliminated virtually all taxpaying and property-holding requirements, thus allowing the working class—at least its white male members—to vote. Extending the vote to blacks and women took longer.

The Enfranchisement of Blacks   The Fifteenth Amendment to the Constitution, adopted shortly after the Civil War, prohibited the states from denying the right to vote "on account of race, color, or previous condition of servitude." However, the Southern states of the old Confederacy worked around the amendment by reestablishing old voting requirements (poll taxes, literacy tests) that worked primarily against blacks. Some southern states also cut blacks out of politics through a cunning circumvention of the amendment. Because the amendment said nothing about voting rights in private organizations, these states denied blacks the right to vote in the "private" Democratic *primary* elections held to choose the party's candidates for the general election. Because the Democratic party came to dominate politics in the South, the "white primary" effectively disenfranchised blacks despite the Fifteenth Amendment. Finally, in many areas of the South, the threat of violence kept blacks from the polls.

The extension of full voting rights to blacks came in two phases, separated by twenty years. In 1944, the Supreme Court decided in *Smith* v. *Allwright* that laws preventing blacks from voting in primary elections were unconstitutional, holding that party primaries are part of the continuous process of electing public officials.[28] The Voting Rights Act of 1965, which followed Selma's Bloody Sunday by less than five months, suspended discriminatory voting tests against blacks. The act also authorized federal registrars to register voters in seven southern states, where less than half of the voting-age population had registered to vote in the 1964 election. For good measure, in 1966 the Supreme Court ruled in *Harper* v. *Virginia State Board of Elections* that state poll taxes are unconstitutional.[29] Although long in coming, these actions by the national government to enforce political equality within the states dramatically increased the registration of southern blacks (see Figure 7.2).

The Enfranchisement of Women   The enfranchisement of women in the United States is a less sordid story but nothing to be proud of. Women had to fight long and hard to win the right to vote. Until 1869, women could not vote anywhere in the world.[30] American women began to organize to obtain suffrage in the mid-1800s. Known then as *suffragettes*,* the early feminists initially had a limited effect on politics. Their first major

---

* *The term* suffragist *applied to a person of either sex who advocated extending the vote to women, while* suffragette *was reserved primarily for women who did so militantly.*

FIGURE 7.2 ■ **Voter Registration in the South, 1960, 1980, and 1992**

As a result of the Voting Rights Act of 1965 and other national actions, black voter registration in the eleven states of the old Confederacy nearly doubled between 1960 and 1980. In 1992, there was little difference between the voting registration rates of white and black voters in the deep South.

Sources: *Data for 1960 and 1980 are from U.S. Bureau of the Census,* Statistical Abstract of the United States, 1982–1983 *(Washington, D.C.: U.S. Government Printing Office, 1983), p. 488; data for 1992 are computed from Bureau of the Census,* Current Population Reports, Series P20–466, Voting and Registration in the Election of November 1992 *(Washington, D.C.: U.S. Government Printing Office, 1993), pp. 10–11.*

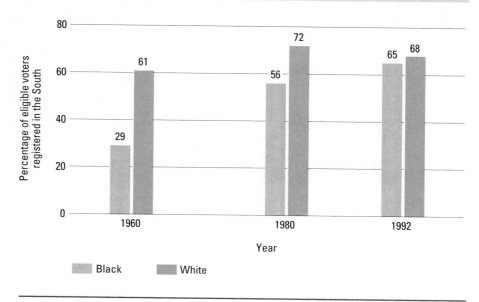

victory did not come until 1869, when Wyoming, while still a territory, granted women the right to vote. No state followed suit until 1893, when Colorado enfranchised women.

In the meantime, the suffragettes became more active. In 1884, they formed the Equal Rights party and nominated Belva A. Lockwood, a lawyer who could not herself vote, as the first woman candidate for president.[31] Between 1896 and 1918, twelve other states gave women the vote. Most of these states were in the West, where pioneer women often departed from traditional women's roles. Nationally, the women's suffrage movement intensified, often resorting to unconventional political behaviors (marches, demonstrations), which occasionally invited violent attacks from men and even other women. In 1919, Congress finally passed the Nineteenth Amendment to the Constitution, which prohibits states from denying the right to vote "on account of sex." The amendment was ratified in 1920, in time for the November election.

Evaluating the Expansion of Suffrage in America   The last major expansion of suffrage in the United States took place in 1971, when the Twenty-sixth Amendment to the Constitution lowered the voting age to eighteen. For most of its history, the United States has been far from the democratic ideal of universal suffrage. The United States initially restricted voting rights to white male taxpayers or property owners, and wealth requirements lasted until the 1850s. Through demonstrations and a constitutional amendment, women won the franchise just seventy-four years ago. Through civil war, constitutional amendments, court actions, massive demonstrations, and congressional action, blacks finally achieved full voting rights only three decades ago. Our record has more than a few blemishes.

The Fights for Women's Suffrage . . . and Against It

Young people and minorities are not the only groups that have resorted to unconventional means of political participation. In the late 1800s and early 1900s, women marched and demonstrated for equal voting rights, sometimes encountering strong opposition. Their gatherings were occasionally disrupted by men—and other women—who opposed extending the right to vote to women.

But compared with other countries, the United States looks pretty democratic.[32] Women did not gain the vote on equal terms with men until 1921 in Norway; 1922 in the Netherlands; 1944 in France; 1946 in Italy, Japan, and Venezuela; 1948 in Belgium; and not until 1971 in Switzerland. Comparing the enfranchisement of minority racial groups is difficult, because most other democratic nations do not have comparable racial make-ups. We should, however, note that the indigenous Maori population in New Zealand won suffrage in 1867, but the aborigines in Australia were not fully enfranchised until 1961. And, of course, in notoriously undemocratic South Africa, blacks—who outnumber whites by more than four to one—were not allowed to vote freely in elections until 1994. With regard to voting age, nineteen of twenty-seven countries that allow free elections also have a minimum voting age of eighteen (none has a lower age), and eight have higher age requirements.

When judged against the rest of the world, then, the United States—which originated mass participation in government through elections—has as good a record of providing for political equality in voting rights as other democracies and a better record than many.

Voting on Policies

Disenfranchised groups have struggled to gain voting rights because of the political power that comes with suffrage. Belief in the ability of ordinary citizens to make political decisions and to control government through the power of the ballot box was strongest in the United States during the Progressive Era, which began around 1900 and lasted until about 1925. **Progressivism** was a philosophy of political reform that trusted the goodness and wisdom of individual citizens and distrusted "special interests" (railroads, corporations) and political institutions (traditional political parties, legislatures).

The leaders of the Progressive movement were prominent politicians (former president Theodore Roosevelt, Senator Robert La Follette of Wisconsin) and eminent scholars (historian Frederick Jackson Turner, philosopher John Dewey). Not content to vote for candidates chosen by party leaders, the Progressives championed the **direct primary**—a preliminary election, run by the state government, in which the voters choose the party's candidates for the general election. Wanting a mechanism to remove elected candidates from office, the Progressives backed the **recall**—a special election initiated by petition signed by a specified number of voters. Although about twenty states provide for recall elections, this device is rarely used. Only a few statewide elected officials have actually been unseated through recall.[33]

Progressives also championed the voting power of the masses to propose and pass laws, thus approximating citizen participation in policymaking that is the hallmark of direct democracy. They developed two voting mechanisms for policymaking that are still in use:

- A **referendum** is a direct vote by the people either on a proposed law or on an amendment to the state constitution. The measures subject to vote are known as **propositions.** About twenty-five states permit popular referenda on laws, and all but Delaware require a referendum for a constitutional amendment. Most referenda are placed on the ballot by legislatures, not voters.

- The **initiative** is a procedure by which voters can propose a measure to be decided by the legislature or by the people in a referendum. The procedure involves gathering a specified number of signatures from registered voters (usually 5 to 10 percent of the total in the state), then submitting the petition to a designated state agency. About twenty states provide for some form of voter initiative.

Figure 7.3 shows the West's affinity for these democratic mechanisms. One scholar estimates that there have been more than 17,000 referenda since 1898 and more than 2,300 between 1968 and 1978 alone.[34] Almost 250 statewide propositions were on the ballots in each general election during the 1980s, although relatively few (usually less than fifty) got there by the initiative.[35] Among 238 ballot propositions in the 1994 elections were proposals in seven states to limit the terms of U.S. senators and representatives (typically to twelve years for senators and six to twelve years for representatives). Six of the seven passed, raising to twenty-one the number of states restricting congressional terms.[36]

At times, politicians strongly oppose the initiatives that citizens propose and approve. This is true, for example, of term limits, which many members of Congress contend are unconstitutional. A referendum can also work to the advantage of politicians, freeing them from taking sides on a hot issue. In 1994, for example, voters in Oregon and Idaho defeated measures that would have limited protection of gay rights. The most controversial initiative, however, was Proposition 187 in California, which banned the provision of social services—such as education and basic health care—to illegal immigrants. The measure easily passed by a margin of 3 to 2, despite the belief by many legal experts that it was unconstitutional. Like other matters of policy enacted by angry voters, this awaits decision by the courts.[37]

What conclusion can we draw about the Progressives' legacy of mechanisms for direct participation in government? One scholar who studied use of the initiative and referendum paints an unimpressive picture. He notes that an expensive "industry" developed in the 1980s that makes money circulating petitions, then managing the large sums of money needed to run a campaign to approve (or defeat) a referendum.[38] In 1990,

FIGURE 7.3   ■ Westward Ho!

This map shows quite clearly the western basis of the initiative, referendum, and recall mechanisms that were intended to place government power directly in the hands of the people. Advocates of "direct legislation" sought to bypass entrenched powers in state legislatures. Established groups and parties in the East dismissed them as radicals and cranks, but they gained the support of farmers and miners in the Midwest and West. The Progressive forces usually aligned with Democrats in western state legislatures to enact their proposals, often against Republican opposition.

Reprinted by permission of the publishers from Direct Democracy: The Politics of Initiative, Referendum, and Recall *by Thomas E. Cronin, Cambridge, Mass.: Harvard University Press, Copyright © 1989 by the Twentieth Century Fund.*

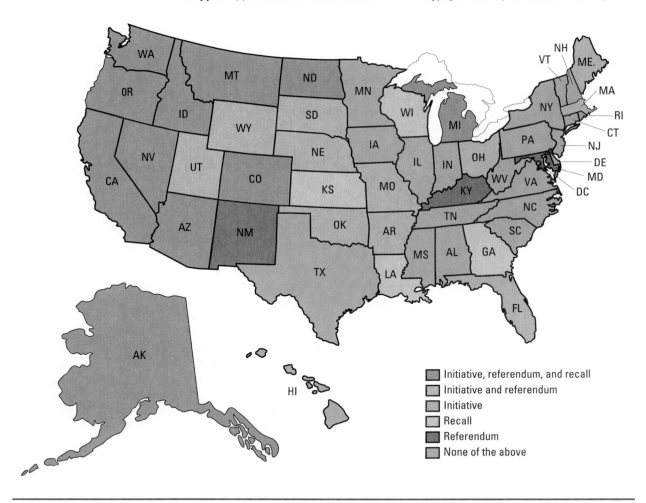

- Initiative, referendum, and recall
- Initiative and referendum
- Initiative
- Recall
- Referendum
- None of the above

various industries conducted a $10 million campaign to defeat "Big Green," a sweeping California environmental initiative that would have imposed restrictions on offshore drilling, pesticide use, and air pollutants.[39] The money required to mount a statewide campaign has increased the involvement of special interest groups in referendum politics. Moreover, most voters confess they do not know enough about most ballot propositions to vote intelligently on them. The 1990 election in California contained seventeen initiatives and constitutional amendments that were described in a ballot pamphlet more than two hundred pages long.[40] Another major study concluded that direct democracy devices "worked better at the state and local levels than most people realize" but also proposed fourteen safeguards "to ensure that they serve the larger and longer-term public interest" at the state and local levels.[41] Noting that the United States is one of the few democracies that does not permit a national referendum, the study nevertheless opposed adopting the initiative and referendum at the national level.[42]

Clearly, citizens can exercise great power over government policy through the mechanisms of the initiative and referendum. What is not clear is whether these forms of direct democracy improve on the policies made by representatives elected for that purpose.

Voting for Candidates

We have saved for last the most visible form of political participation: voting to choose candidates for public office. Voting for candidates serves democratic government in two ways. First, citizens can choose the candidates they think will best serve their interests. If citizens choose candidates "like themselves" in personal traits or party affiliation, elected officials should tend to think as their constituents do on political issues and automatically reflect the majority's views when making public policy.

Second, voting allows the people to reelect the officials they guessed right about and to kick out those they guessed wrong about. This function is very different from the first. It makes public officials accountable for their behavior through the reward-and-punishment mechanism of elections. It assumes that officeholders are motivated to respond to public opinion by the threat of electoral defeat. It also assumes that the voters (1) know what politicians are doing while they are in office and (2) participate actively in the electoral process. We look at the factors that underlie voting choice in Chapter 9. Here, we examine Americans' reliance on the electoral process.

In national politics, voters seem content to elect just two executive officers—the president and vice president—and to trust the president to appoint a cabinet to round out his administration. But at the state and local levels, voters insist on selecting all kinds of officials. Every state elects a governor (and forty-two elect a lieutenant governor). Forty-three elect an attorney general; thirty-eight, a treasurer and a secretary of state; twenty-five, an auditor. The list goes on, down through the superintendent of education, secretary of agriculture, controller, board of education, and public utilities commissioners.[43] Elected county officials commonly include commissioners, a sheriff, a treasurer, a clerk, a superintendent of schools,

FEATURE 7.2

■ If It Moves in Office, Elect It

No other country requires its voters to make so many ballot decisions in a general election. Here is just a portion of the official ballot confronting voters in the city of Evanston at the 1992 election in Cook County, Illinois. It listed 14 different types of offices, for which voters were asked to elect 38 candidates from 101 lines of names. In addition, voters were presented with the names of 32 judges of lesser courts and asked to decide, yes or no, whether "each judge shall be retained in his present office." For good measure, the ballot also contained 1 countywide referendum, 2 city referenda, an advisory referendum for the State of Illinois, and 2 constitutional amendments. Most ballots in other states are comparably complex. If citizens feel unable to vote intelligently when facing such a ballot, they can hardly be blamed.

and a judge (often several). Even at the local level, voters elect all but about 600 of 15,300 school boards across the nation.[44] Instead of trusting state and local chief executives to appoint lesser administrators (as we do for more important offices at the national level), we expect voters to choose intelligently among scores of candidates they meet for the first time on a complex ballot in the polling booth (see Feature 7.2).

In the American version of democracy, the laws recognize no limit to voters' ability to make informed choices among candidates and thus to control government through voting. The reasoning seems to be that elections are good; therefore, more elections are better, and the most elections are best. By this thinking, the United States clearly has the best and most democratic government in the world, because it is the undisputed champion at holding elections. The author of a study that compared elections in the United States with elections in twenty-six other democracies concluded:

> No country can approach the United States in the frequency and variety of elections, and thus in the amount of electoral participation to which its citizens have a right. No other country elects its lower house as often as every two years, or its president as frequently as every four years. No other country popularly elects its state governors and town mayors; no other has as wide a variety of nonrepresentative offices (judges, sheriffs, attorneys general, city treasurers, and so on) subject to election. . . . The average American is entitled to do far more electing—probably by a factor of three or four—than the citizen of any other democracy.[45]

However, we learn from Compared with What? 7.2 that the United States ranks at the bottom of twenty-seven countries in voter turnout in national elections. How do we square low voter turnout with Americans' devotion to elections as an instrument of democratic government? To complicate matters further, how do we square low voter turnout with the findings we mentioned earlier, which establish the United States as the

FOR PRESIDENT (PARA PRESIDENTE) **AND** Y **VICE PRESIDENT** (VICE PRESIDENTE) — **VOTE FOR ONE GROUP** VOTE POR UN GRUPO

BILL CLINTON	and (y)	**AL GORE**	DEMOCRATIC	**55**	→
GEORGE BUSH	and (y)	**DAN QUAYLE**	REPUBLICAN	**56**	→
ANDRE MARROU	and (y)	**NANCY LORD**	LIBERTARIAN	**57**	→
LENORA B. FULANI	and (y)	**MARIA ELIZABETH MUNOZ**	NEW ALLIANCE	**58**	→
JAMES MAC WARREN	and (y)	**WILLIE MAE REID**	SOCIALIST WORKERS	**59**	→
JAMES "BO" GRITZ	and (y)	**CY MINETT**	POPULIST	**60**	→
JOHN HAGELIN	and (y)	**MIKE TOMPKINS**	NATURAL LAW	**61**	→
ROSS PEROT	and (y)	**JAMES B. STOCKDALE**	INDEPENDENT	**62**	→

FOR UNITED STATES SENATOR (PARA SENADOR DE LOS ESTADOS UNIDOS) — **VOTE FOR ONE** VOTE POR UNO

CAROL MOSELEY BRAUN	DEMOCRATIC	**66**	→
RICHARD S. WILLIAMSON	REPUBLICAN	**67**	→
ANDREW B. SPIEGEL	LIBERTARIAN	**68**	→
ALAN J. PORT	NEW ALLIANCE	**69**	→
KATHLEEN KAKU	SOCIALIST WORKERS	**70**	→
JOHN JUSTICE	POPULIST	**71**	→
CHARLES A. WINTER	NATURAL LAW	**72**	→
CHAD KOPPIE	THE CONSERVATIVE PARTY OF ILLINOIS	**73**	→

FOR TRUSTEES OF THE UNIVERSITY OF ILLINOIS (PARA SINDICOS DE LA UNIVERSIDAD DE ILLINOIS) — **VOTE FOR THREE** VOTE POR TRES

ADA LOPEZ	DEMOCRATIC	**80**	→
JUDITH CALDER	DEMOCRATIC	**81**	→
JEFF GINDORF	DEMOCRATIC	**82**	→
DAVE DOWNEY	REPUBLICAN	**83**	→
CRAIG BURKHARDT	REPUBLICAN	**84**	→
GAYL ANNE SIMONDS PYATT	REPUBLICAN	**85**	→
STEVEN I. GIVOT	LIBERTARIAN	**86**	→
KATHERINE M. KELLEY	LIBERTARIAN	**87**	→
MICHAEL R. LINKSVAYER	LIBERTARIAN	**88**	→
SANDRA JACKSON-OPOKU	NEW ALLIANCE	**89**	→
BONITA M. BISHOP	NEW ALLIANCE	**90**	→
STEPHEN J. JACKSON	NEW ALLIANCE	**91**	→
PATRICIA SMITH CHILOANE	SOCIALIST WORKERS	**92**	→
MARGARET SAVAGE	SOCIALIST WORKERS	**93**	→
JOHN VOTAVA	SOCIALIST WORKERS	**94**	→
IRVIN E. THOMPSON	POPULIST	**95**	→
THOMAS NASH	POPULIST	**96**	→
ELDON WEDER	POPULIST	**97**	→
MERRILL M. BECKER	NATURAL LAW	**98**	→
JUDY LANGSTON	NATURAL LAW	**99**	→
LESIA WASYLYK	NATURAL LAW	**100**	→
BARBARA MARY QUIRKE	THE CONSERVATIVE PARTY OF ILLINOIS	**101**	→
ANN M. SCHEIDLER	THE CONSERVATIVE PARTY OF ILLINOIS	**102**	→
HIRAM CRAWFORD, JR.	THE CONSERVATIVE PARTY OF ILLINOIS	**103**	→

FOR REPRESENTATIVE IN CONGRESS (PARA REPRESENTANTE EN EL CONGRESO)
9TH CONGRESSIONAL DISTRICT (9NO DISTRITO CONGRESIONAL) — **VOTE FOR ONE** VOTE POR UNO

SIDNEY R. YATES	DEMOCRATIC	**118**	→
HERB SOHN	REPUBLICAN	**119**	→
SHEILA A. JONES	ECONOMIC RECOVERY	**120**	→

VOTE FOR ONE VOTE POR UNO — **FOR STATE SENATOR** (PARA SENADOR DEL ESTADO)
9TH LEGISLATIVE DISTRICT (9NO DISTRITO LEGISLATIVO)

←	105	**ARTHUR L. BERMAN**	DEMOCRATIC
		NO CANDIDATE (NINGUN CANDIDATO)	REPUBLICAN

VOTE FOR ONE VOTE POR UNO — **FOR REPRESENTATIVE IN THE GENERAL ASSEMBLY** (PARA REPRESENTANTE EN LA ASAMBLEA GENERAL)
18TH REPRESENTATIVE DISTRICT (18AVO DISTRITO REPRESENTATIVO)

←	122	**JANICE D. "JAN" SCHAKOWSKY**	DEMOCRATIC
←	123	**BRUCE W. HAFFNER**	REPUBLICAN
←	124	**THEODORE C. BECKMAN**	LIBERTARIAN

OFFICIAL BALLOT (BALOTA OFICIAL)

FOR STATE'S ATTORNEY (PARA FISCAL DEL ESTADO) — **VOTE FOR ONE** VOTE POR UNO

PATRICK J. O'CONNOR	DEMOCRATIC	**131**	→
JOHN M. "JACK" O'MALLEY	REPUBLICAN	**132**	→

FOR RECORDER OF DEEDS (PARA REGISTRADOR DE LAS PROPIEDADES) — **VOTE FOR ONE** VOTE POR UNO

JESSE C. WHITE, JR.	DEMOCRATIC	**135**	→
SUSAN CATANIA	REPUBLICAN	**136**	→

FOR CLERK OF THE CIRCUIT COURT (PARA SECRETARIO DE LA CORTE DE CIRCUITO) — **VOTE FOR ONE** VOTE POR UNO

AURELIA MARIE PUCINSKI	DEMOCRATIC	**139**	→
HERBERT T. SCHUMANN, JR.	REPUBLICAN	**140**	→
DOLORIS "DEE" JONES	HAROLD WASHINGTON	**141**	→

FOR COMMISSIONER OF THE METROPOLITAN WATER RECLAMATION DISTRICT
(PARA COMISIONADO DEL DISTRITO METROPOLITANO DE RECLAMACION DE AGUAS) — **VOTE FOR THREE** VOTE POR TRES

NANCY DREW SHEEHAN	DEMOCRATIC	**144**	→
GLORIA ALITTO MAJEWSKI	DEMOCRATIC	**145**	→
PATRICIA YOUNG	DEMOCRATIC	**146**	→
JOHN J. HOLOWINSKI	REPUBLICAN	**147**	→
SUSAN L. KELSEY	REPUBLICAN	**148**	→
SHIRLEY ANN STREET	REPUBLICAN	**149**	→

SUPREME COURT (CORTE SUPREMA)

FOR JUDGE OF THE SUPREME COURT (PARA JUEZ DE LA CORTE SUPREMA)
FIRST JUDICIAL DISTRICT (1er DISTRITO JUDICIAL)
(To fill the vacancy of the Hon. William G. Clark) (Para llenar la vacante del Hon. William G. Clark) — **VOTE FOR ONE** VOTE POR UNO

MARY ANN GROHWIN McMORROW	DEMOCRATIC	**152**	→
ROBERT CHAPMAN BUCKLEY	REPUBLICAN	**153**	→

VOTE FOR ONE VOTE POR UNO — **FOR JUDGE OF THE APPELLATE COURT** (PARA JUEZ DE LA CORTE DE APELACIONES)
FIRST JUDICIAL DISTRICT (1er DISTRITO JUDICIAL)
(To fill the vacancy of the Hon. Michael A. Bilandic) (Para llenar la vacante del Hon. Michael A. Bilandic)

←	133	**CARL McCORMICK**	DEMOCRATIC
←	134	**GERALD T. ROHRER**	REPUBLICAN

VOTE FOR ONE VOTE POR UNO — **FOR JUDGE OF THE APPELLATE COURT** (PARA JUEZ DE LA CORTE DE APELACIONES)
FIRST JUDICIAL DISTRICT (1er DISTRITO JUDICIAL)
(To fill the vacancy of the Hon. Charles E. Freeman) (Para llenar la vacante del Hon. Charles E. Freeman)

←	137	**ROBERT CAHILL**	DEMOCRATIC
		CANDIDATE WITHDRAWN (CANDIDATO RETIRADO)	REPUBLICAN

VOTE FOR ONE VOTE POR UNO — **FOR JUDGE OF THE APPELLATE COURT** (PARA JUEZ DE LA CORTE DE APELACIONES)
FIRST JUDICIAL DISTRICT (1er DISTRITO JUDICIAL)
(To fill the vacancy of the Hon. Francis S. Lorenz) (Para llenar la vacante del Hon. Francis S. Lorenz)

←	142	**WILLIAM COUSINS, JR.**	DEMOCRATIC
		NO CANDIDATE (NINGUN CANDIDATO)	REPUBLICAN

VOTE FOR ONE VOTE POR UNO — **FOR JUDGE OF THE CIRCUIT COURT** (PARA JUEZ DE LA CORTE DE CIRCUITO)
COOK COUNTY JUDICIAL CIRCUIT (CIRCUITO JUDICIAL DEL CONDADO DE COOK)
(To fill the vacancy of the Hon. John M. Breen, Jr.) (Para llenar la vacante del Hon. John M. Breen, Jr.)

←	150	**DONALD J. O'BRIEN, JR.**	DEMOCRATIC
←	151	**DAVID E. PETERS**	REPUBLICAN

VOTE FOR ONE VOTE POR UNO — **FOR JUDGE OF THE CIRCUIT COURT** (PARA JUEZ DE LA CORTE DE CIRCUITO)
COOK COUNTY JUDICIAL CIRCUIT (CIRCUITO JUDICIAL DEL CONDADO DE COOK)
(To fill the vacancy of the Hon. Ronald J. Crane) (Para llenar la vacante del Hon. Ronald J. Crane)

←	154	**DENISE MARGARET O'MALLEY**	DEMOCRATIC
		NO CANDIDATE (NINGUN CANDIDATO)	REPUBLICAN

FOR JUDGE OF THE CIRCUIT COURT (PARA JUEZ DE LA CORTE DE CIRCUITO)
COOK COUNTY JUDICIAL CIRCUIT (CIRCUITO JUDICIAL DEL CONDADO DE COOK)
(To fill the vacancy of the Hon. Cornelius F. Dore, Jr.) (Para llenar la vacante del Hon. Cornelius F. Dore, Jr.) — **VOTE FOR ONE** VOTE POR UNO

DANIEL E. JORDAN	DEMOCRATIC	**157**	→
JOSEPH G. KAZMIERSKI, JR.	REPUBLICAN	**158**	→

FOR JUDGE OF THE CIRCUIT COURT (PARA JUEZ DE LA CORTE DE CIRCUITO)
COOK COUNTY JUDICIAL CIRCUIT (CIRCUITO JUDICIAL DEL CONDADO DE COOK)
(To fill the vacancy of the Hon. Arthur N. Hamilton) (Para llenar la vacante del Hon. Arthur N. Hamilton) — **VOTE FOR ONE** VOTE POR UNO

MICHAEL JAMES MURPHY	DEMOCRATIC	**161**	→
NO CANDIDATE (NINGUN CANDIDATO)	REPUBLICAN		

FOR JUDGE OF THE CIRCUIT COURT (PARA JUEZ DE LA CORTE DE CIRCUITO)
COOK COUNTY JUDICIAL CIRCUIT (CIRCUITO JUDICIAL DEL CONDADO DE COOK)
(To fill the vacancy of the Hon. Robert G. Mackey) (Para llenar la vacante del Hon. Robert G. Mackey) — **VOTE FOR ONE** VOTE POR UNO

JOHN J. MORAN	DEMOCRATIC	**165**	→
RONALD D. BABB	REPUBLICAN	**166**	→

FOR JUDGE OF THE CIRCUIT COURT (PARA JUEZ DE LA CORTE DE CIRCUITO)
COOK COUNTY JUDICIAL CIRCUIT (CIRCUITO JUDICIAL DEL CONDADO DE COOK)
(To fill the vacancy of the Hon. Lester D. McCurrie) (Para llenar la vacante del Hon. Lester D. McCurrie) — **VOTE FOR ONE** VOTE POR UNO

JOHN A. WARD	DEMOCRATIC	**169**	→
NO CANDIDATE (NINGUN CANDIDATO)	REPUBLICAN		

FOR JUDGE OF THE CIRCUIT COURT (PARA JUEZ DE LA CORTE DE CIRCUITO)
COOK COUNTY JUDICIAL CIRCUIT (CIRCUITO JUDICIAL DEL CONDADO DE COOK)
(To fill the vacancy of the Hon. Jill K. McNulty) (Para llenar la vacante del Hon. Jill K. McNulty) — **VOTE FOR ONE** VOTE POR UNO

NANCY SIDOTE SALYERS	DEMOCRATIC	**173**	→
EDWARD R. JORDAN	REPUBLICAN	**174**	→

FOR JUDGE OF THE CIRCUIT COURT (PARA JUEZ DE LA CORTE DE CIRCUITO)
COOK COUNTY JUDICIAL CIRCUIT (CIRCUITO JUDICIAL DEL CONDADO DE COOK)
(To fill the vacancy of the Hon. Angelo D. Mistretta) (Para llenar la vacante del Hon. Angelo D. Mistretta) — **VOTE FOR ONE** VOTE POR UNO

DEBORAH MARY DOOLING	DEMOCRATIC	**177**	→
EDWARD N. PIETRUCHA	REPUBLICAN	**178**	→

FOR JUDGE OF THE CIRCUIT COURT (PARA JUEZ DE LA CORTE DE CIRCUITO)
COOK COUNTY JUDICIAL CIRCUIT (CIRCUITO JUDICIAL DEL CONDADO DE COOK)
(To fill the vacancy of the Hon. Gerald S. Murphy) (Para llenar la vacante del Hon. Gerald S. Murphy) — **VOTE FOR ONE** VOTE POR UNO

VINCENT MICHAEL GAUGHAN	DEMOCRATIC	**181**	→
NO CANDIDATE (NINGUN CANDIDATO)	REPUBLICAN		

VOTE FOR ONE VOTE POR UNO — **FOR JUDGE OF THE CIRCUIT COURT** (PARA JUEZ DE LA CORTE DE CIRCUITO)
COOK COUNTY JUDICIAL CIRCUIT (CIRCUITO JUDICIAL DEL CONDADO DE COOK)
(To fill the vacancy of the Hon. Irving R. Norman) (Para llenar la vacante del Hon. Irving R. Norman)

←	159	**JULIA MARGARET NOWICKI**	DEMOCRATIC
←	160	**DON R. SAMPEN**	REPUBLICAN

VOTE FOR ONE VOTE POR UNO — **FOR JUDGE OF THE CIRCUIT COURT** (PARA JUEZ DE LA CORTE DE CIRCUITO)
COOK COUNTY JUDICIAL CIRCUIT (CIRCUITO JUDICIAL DEL CONDADO DE COOK)
(To fill the vacancy of the Hon. Benjamin E. Novoselsky) (Para llenar la vacante del Hon. Benjamin E. Novoselsky)

←	163	**LESLIE ELAINE SOUTH**	DEMOCRATIC
←	164	**JOHN D. TOURTELOT**	REPUBLICAN

VOTE FOR ONE VOTE POR UNO — **FOR JUDGE OF THE CIRCUIT COURT** (PARA JUEZ DE LA CORTE DE CIRCUITO)
COOK COUNTY JUDICIAL CIRCUIT (CIRCUITO JUDICIAL DEL CONDADO DE COOK)
(To fill the vacancy of the Hon. Anthony J. Scotillo) (Para llenar la vacante del Hon. Anthony J. Scotillo)

←	167	**JOAN M. CORBOY**	DEMOCRATIC
←	168	**MARIA T. BURNETT**	REPUBLICAN

VOTE FOR ONE VOTE POR UNO — **FOR JUDGE OF THE CIRCUIT COURT** (PARA JUEZ DE LA CORTE DE CIRCUITO)
COOK COUNTY JUDICIAL CIRCUIT (CIRCUITO JUDICIAL DEL CONDADO DE COOK)
(To fill the vacancy of the Hon. David J. Shields) (Para llenar la vacante del Hon. David J. Shields)

←	171	**SHEILA MURPHY**	DEMOCRATIC
←	172	**ALLAN R. SPECTOR**	REPUBLICAN

VOTE FOR ONE VOTE POR UNO — **FOR JUDGE OF THE CIRCUIT COURT** (PARA JUEZ DE LA CORTE DE CIRCUITO)
COOK COUNTY JUDICIAL CIRCUIT (CIRCUITO JUDICIAL DEL CONDADO DE COOK)
(To fill the vacancy of the Hon. Pasquale A. Sorrentino) (Para llenar la vacante del Hon. Pasquale A. Sorrentino)

←	175	**SHARON MARIE SULLIVAN**	DEMOCRATIC
←	176	**DONALD M. DEVLIN**	REPUBLICAN

VOTE FOR ONE VOTE POR UNO — **FOR JUDGE OF THE CIRCUIT COURT** (PARA JUEZ DE LA CORTE DE CIRCUITO)
COOK COUNTY JUDICIAL CIRCUIT (CIRCUITO JUDICIAL DEL CONDADO DE COOK)
(To fill the vacancy of the Hon. James E. Sullivan) (Para llenar la vacante del Hon. James E. Sullivan)

←	179	**CHEYRL D. INGRAM**	DEMOCRATIC
←	180	**JOSEPH N. RATHNAU**	REPUBLICAN

FOR JUDGE OF THE CIRCUIT COURT (PARA JUEZ DE LA CORTE DE CIRCUITO)
COOK COUNTY JUDICIAL CIRCUIT (CIRCUITO JUDICIAL DEL CONDADO DE COOK)
(To fill the vacancy of the Hon. John P. Tully) (Para llenar la vacante del Hon. John P. Tully) — **VOTE FOR ONE** VOTE POR UNO

DOROTHY KIRIE KINNAIRD	DEMOCRATIC	**183**	→
NO CANDIDATE (NINGUN CANDIDATO)	REPUBLICAN		

FOR JUDGE OF THE CIRCUIT COURT (PARA JUEZ DE LA CORTE DE CIRCUITO)
COOK COUNTY JUDICIAL CIRCUIT (CIRCUITO JUDICIAL DEL CONDADO DE COOK)
(To fill the vacancy of the Hon. Alfred T. Walsh) (Para llenar la vacante del Hon. Alfred T. Walsh) — **VOTE FOR ONE** VOTE POR UNO

SUSAN RUSCITTI GRUSSEL	DEMOCRATIC	**187**	→
JAMES GREGORY SMITH	REPUBLICAN	**188**	→

FOR JUDGE OF THE CIRCUIT COURT (PARA JUEZ DE LA CORTE DE CIRCUITO)
COOK COUNTY JUDICIAL CIRCUIT (CIRCUITO JUDICIAL DEL CONDADO DE COOK)
OUTSIDE THE CITY OF CHICAGO (AFUERA DE LA CIUDAD DE CHICAGO)
(To fill the vacancy of the Hon. Robert L. Skiodowski) (Para llenar la vacante del Hon. Robert L. Skiodowski) — **VOTE FOR ONE** VOTE POR UNO

RICHARD R. ROCHESTER	DEMOCRATIC	**191**	→
DANIEL J. SULLIVAN	REPUBLICAN	**192**	→

VOTE FOR ONE VOTE POR UNO — **FOR JUDGE OF THE CIRCUIT COURT** (PARA JUEZ DE LA CORTE DE CIRCUITO)
(To fill additional judgeship A) (9th Subcircuit) (Para llenar magistratura adicional A) (9no Subcircuito)

←	199	**ALLEN S. GOLDBERG**	DEMOCRATIC
←	200	**JEANNE R. CLEVELAND**	REPUBLICAN

VOTE FOR ONE VOTE POR UNO — **FOR JUDGE OF THE CIRCUIT COURT** (PARA JUEZ DE LA CORTE DE CIRCUITO)
(To fill additional judgeship B) (9th Subcircuit) (Para llenar magistratura adicional B) (9no Subcircuito)

←	203	**RONALD A. HIMEL**	DEMOCRATIC
←	204	**NATHAN G. BRENNER, JR.**	REPUBLICAN

COMPARED WITH WHAT? 7.2

Voter Turnout in Democratic Nations

 Americans participate as much as or more than citizens of other nations in all forms of conventional political behavior except voting. Voter turnout in American presidential elections ranks at the bottom of voting rates for twenty-seven countries with competitive elections. As discussed in the text, the facts are correct, but the comparison is not as damning as it appears.

• *Source: Congressional Research Service, "Voter Participation Statistics from Recent Elections in Selected Countries," report to U.S. Rep. Mario Biaggi, 18 November 1987.*

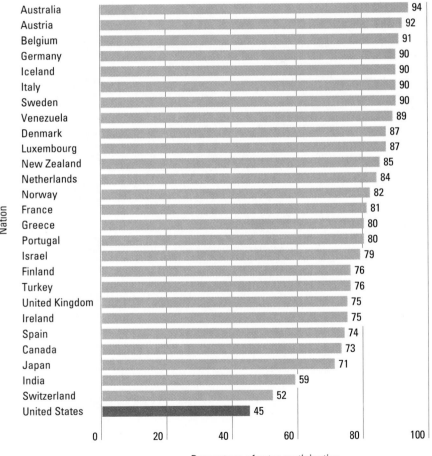

Nation	Percentage
Australia	94
Austria	92
Belgium	91
Germany	90
Iceland	90
Italy	90
Sweden	90
Venezuela	89
Denmark	87
Luxembourg	87
New Zealand	85
Netherlands	84
Norway	82
France	81
Greece	80
Portugal	80
Israel	79
Finland	76
Turkey	76
United Kingdom	75
Ireland	75
Spain	74
Canada	73
Japan	71
India	59
Switzerland	52
United States	45

Percentage of voter participation in elections, 1969–1986

| FIGURE 7.4 | ■ Electoral Participation in the United States over Time |

Participation patterns from five decades show that in the 1980s Americans participated in election campaigns about as much or more than in the 1950s on every indicator except voting. The turnout rate dropped more than ten percentage points from 1952 to 1988. The turnout for 1992 was 55 percent, a sharp rise. The decline before 1992 runs counter to the rise in educational level, a puzzle that is discussed in the text.

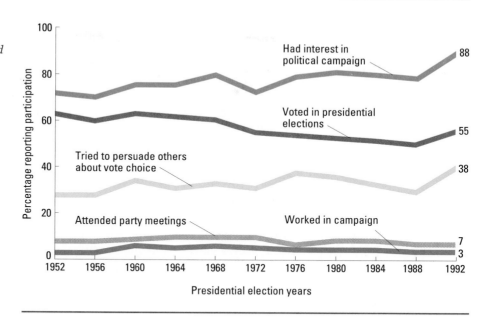

Reprinted by permission of the publishers from American National Election Studies Data Sourcebook, 1952–1978 edited by Warren Miller, Cambridge, Mass.: Harvard University Press, Copyright © 1980 by the President and Fellows of Harvard College. Data after 1978 comes from subsequent National Election Studies.

leader among five Western democratic nations in both conventional and unconventional political participation? Americans seem to participate at high levels in everything except elections.

EXPLAINING POLITICAL PARTICIPATION

As you have seen, political participation can be unconventional or conventional, can require little or much initiative, and can serve to support the government or influence its decisions. Researchers have found that people who take part in some form of political behavior often do not take part in others. For example, citizens who contact public officials to obtain special benefits may not vote regularly, participate in campaigns, or even contact officials about broader social issues. In fact, because particularized contacting serves individual rather than public interests, it is not even considered *political* behavior by some people.

This section examines some factors that affect the more obvious forms of political participation, with particular emphasis on voting. The first task is to determine how much patterns of participation vary within the United States over time.

Patterns of Participation over Time

Have Americans become more politically apathetic in the 1990s than they were in the 1960s? The answer lies in Figure 7.4, which plots several measures of participation from 1952 through 1992. The graph shows a mixed pattern of participation over the years, with upward spurts in 1992 because of the Ross Perot phenomenon. Participation was stable across time in the percentage of citizens who worked for candidates (3 to 6 percent) and who attended party meetings (6 to 9 percent) and more varied for persuading people how to vote during presidential election years (29 to 38 percent). Even interest in campaigns increased across time by 20 percentage points. Except for 1992, when voting turnout "soared" to 55 percent, participation has tended to decrease over time—*but only when measured as voter turnout in presidential elections.* The plot has thickened. Not only is voter turnout low in the United States compared with that in other countries but turnout has basically declined over time. Moreover, while voting has decreased, other forms of participation have remained stable or even increased. What is going on? Who votes? Who does not? Why? And does it really matter?

The Standard Socioeconomic Explanation

Researchers have found that socioeconomic status is a good indicator of most types of conventional political participation. People with more education, higher incomes, and white-collar or professional occupations tend to be more aware of the effect of politics on their lives, to know what can be done to influence government actions, and to have the necessary resources (time, money) to take action. So they are more likely to participate in politics than are people of lower socioeconomic status. This relationship, between socioeconomic status and conventional political involvement, is called the **standard socioeconomic model** of participation.[46]

Unconventional political behavior is less clearly related to socioeconomic status. Studies of unconventional participation in other countries have found that protest behavior is related to low socioeconomic status and especially to youth.[47] However, scattered studies of unconventional participation in the United States have found that protesters (especially blacks) are often higher in socioeconomic status than those who do not join in protests.[48]

Obviously, socioeconomic status does not account for all the differences in the ways people choose to participate in politics, even for conventional participation. Another important variable is age. As just noted, young people are more likely to take part in political protests, but they are less likely to participate in conventional politics. Voting rates tend to increase as people grow older until about age sixty-five, when physical infirmities begin to lower rates again.[49]

Two other variables—race and gender—have been related to participation in the past, but as times have changed, so have those relationships. Blacks, who had very low participation rates in the 1950s, now participate at rates comparable to whites', when differences in socioeconomic status are taken into account.[50] Women also exhibited low participation rates in the past, but gender differences in political participation have virtually disappeared.[51] (The one exception is in attempting to persuade others how to vote, which women are less likely to do than men.[52]) Recent research on the social context of voting behavior has shown that married men and women are more likely to vote than those of either sex living without spouses.[53]

Of all the social and economic variables, education is the strongest single factor in explaining most types of conventional political participation.

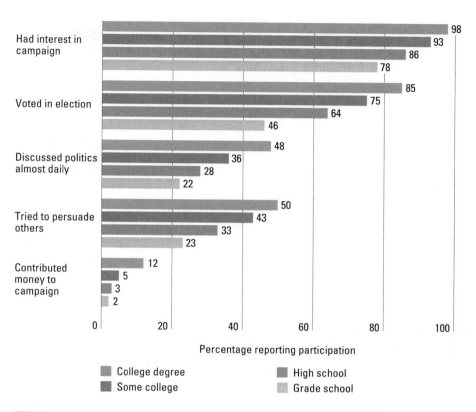

FIGURE 7.5 ■ **Effects of Education on Political Participation in 1992**

Education has a powerful effect on political participation in the United States. These data from a 1992 sample show that level of education is directly related to five different forms of conventional political participation.

Source: This analysis was based on the 1992 National Election Study done by the Center for Political Studies, University of Michigan, and distributed by the Inter-University Consortium for Political and Social Research, Ann Arbor, Michigan.

Figure 7.5 shows the striking relationship between level of formal education and various types of conventional political behaviors. The strong link between education and electoral participation raises questions about low voter turnout in the United States both over time and relative to other democracies. The fact is that the proportion of individuals with college degrees is greater in the United States than in other countries. Moreover, that proportion has been increasing steadily. Why, then, is voter turnout in elections so low? And why is it dropping over time?

Low Voter Turnout in America

Voting is a low-initiative form of participation that can satisfy all three motives for political participation—showing allegiance to the nation, obtaining particularized benefits, and influencing broad policy. How then do we explain the decline in voting within the United States over time and the low voter turnout in this country?

The Decline in Voting over Time   The graph of voter turnout in Figure 7.6 shows that the sharpest drop (five percentage points) occurred between the 1968 and 1972 elections. It was during this period (in 1971, actually) that Congress proposed and the states ratified the Twenty-sixth

FIGURE **7.6**   ■ **The Decline of Voting Turnout: An Unsolved Puzzle**

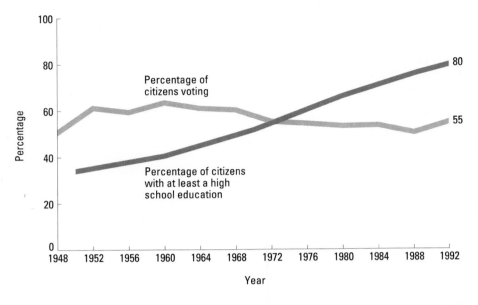

Level of education is one of the strongest predictors of a person's likelihood of voting in the United States, and the percentage of citizens older than twenty-five with a high school education or more has grown steadily since the end of World War II. Nevertheless, the overall rate of voting turnout has gone down almost steadily in presidential elections since 1960, except for the spurt in 1992 inspired by Ross Perot's campaign. The phenomenon is recognized as an unsolved puzzle in American voting behavior.

Sources: "Percentage voting" data up to 1988 come from Michael Nelson, ed., Congressional Quarterly's Guide to the Presidency *(Washington, D.C.: Congressional Quarterly, Inc., 1989), p. 170; voting turnout for 1992 and "percentage with four years of high school" come from U.S. Bureau of the Census,* Statistical Abstract of the United States, 1993 *(Washington, D.C.: U.S. Government Printing Office, 1993), pp. 284 and 153.*

Amendment to the Constitution, which expanded the electorate by lowering the voting age from twenty-one to eighteen. Because people younger than twenty-one are much less likely to vote, their eligibility actually reduced the overall national turnout rate (the percentage of those eligible to vote who actually vote). Some observers estimate that the enfranchisement of eighteen-year-olds accounts for about one or two percentage points in the total decline in turnout since 1952, but that still leaves more than ten percentage points to be explained.[54]

Researchers have not been very successful in solving the puzzle of the decline in voting turnout since 1968.[55] Some scholars attribute most of the decline to changes in voters' attitudes toward politics. One major factor is the growing belief that government is not responsive to citizens and that voting does no good. One scholar refers to "a generalized withdrawal or disconnection from the political world, manifested most dramatically by declining psychological involvement in politics and a declining belief in government responsiveness."[56] Another is a change in attitude toward political parties, along with a decline in the extent and strength of party identification.[57] According to these psychological explanations, voting turnout in the United States is not likely to increase until the government does something to restore people's faith in the effectiveness of voting—with or without political parties. According to the age explanation, turnout in the United States is destined to remain a percentage point or two below its highs in the 1960s because of the lower voting rate of citizens younger than twenty-one.

U.S. Turnout Versus Turnout in Other Countries   Scholars cite two factors to explain the low voter turnout in the United States compared with that in other countries. First are the differences in voting laws and administrative machinery.[58] In a few countries, voting is compulsory, and obviously, turnout is extremely high. But other methods can encourage voting—declaring election days to be public holidays, providing a two-day voting period, making it easy to cast absentee ballots. The United States does none of these things.

Furthermore, nearly every other democratic country places the burden of registration on the government rather than on the individual voter. This is important. Voting in the United States is a two-stage process, and the first stage—going to the proper officials to register—has required more initiative than the second stage—going to the polling booth to cast a ballot. In most American states, the registration process has been separate from the voting process by both time (usually weeks in advance of the election) and geography (often at the county courthouse, not the polling place). Studying three states (Minnesota, Maine, and Wisconsin) that allowed citizens to register and vote on the same day, one researcher estimated that such nationwide practices alone would add five points to the turnout rate.[59] Moreover, registration procedures often have been obscure, requiring calling around to find out what to do. Furthermore, people who move (and roughly one-third of the U.S. population moves between presidential elections) have had to reregister. In short, although voting requires little initiative, registration usually has required high initiative. If we compute voter turnout on the basis of those who are registered to vote, about 87 percent of Americans vote—a figure that moves the United States to the middle (but not the top) of all democratic nations.[60] Beginning in 1996, we should see somewhat higher voting turnout from enactment of the so-called motor-voter law, which requires states to allow citizens to register by mail (similar to renewing drivers' licenses) and at certain agencies that provide public assistance. The measure had been opposed since 1989 by Republicans who believed they benefited from the relationship between high socioeconomic status and voting turnout. Congress approved it in 1993, soon after Bill Clinton was elected president, and he signed it into law.[61]

The second factor usually cited to explain low turnout in American elections is the lack of political parties that mobilize the vote of particular social groups, especially lower-income and less-educated people. American parties do make an effort to get out the vote, but neither party is as closely linked to specific groups as parties are in many other countries, where certain parties work hand in hand with ethnic, occupational, or religious groups. Research shows that strong party-group links can significantly increase turnout.[62] However, recent research suggests that while well-funded, vigorous campaigns mobilize citizens to vote, the effect depends on the type of citizens. Highly educated, low-income citizens are more likely to be stimulated to vote than less-educated, higher-income citizens.[63]

To these explanations for low voter turnout in the United States—the traditional burden of registration and the lack of strong party-group links—we add another. Although the act of voting requires low initiative, the process of learning about the scores of candidates on the ballot in American elections requires a great deal of initiative. Some people undoubtedly fail to vote simply because they feel inadequate to the task of deciding among candidates for the many offices on the ballot in U.S. elections.

Teachers, newspaper columnists, and public affairs groups tend to worry a great deal about low voter turnout in the United States, suggesting that it signifies some sort of political sickness—or at least that it gives us a bad mark for democracy. Some others who study elections closely seem less concerned.[64] One scholar argues:

> Turnout rates do not indicate the amount of electing—the frequency . . . , the range of offices and decisions, the "value" of the vote—to which a country's citizens are entitled. . . . Thus, although the turnout rate in the United States is below that of most other democracies, American citizens do not necessarily do less voting than other citizens; most probably, they do more.[65]

Despite the words of assurance, the nagging thought remains that turnout ought to be higher, so various organizations mount get-out-the-vote campaigns before elections. Civic leaders often back the campaigns, because they value voting for its contribution to political order.

PARTICIPATION AND FREEDOM, EQUALITY, AND ORDER

As we have seen, Americans do participate in government in a variety of ways and to a reasonable extent, compared with citizens of other countries. What is the relationship of political participation to the values of freedom, equality, and order?

Participation and Freedom

From the standpoint of normative theory, the relationship between participation and freedom is clear. Individuals should be free to participate in government and politics the way they want and as much as they want. And they should be free not to participate as well. Ideally, all barriers to participation (such as restrictive voting registration and limitations on campaign expenditures) should be abolished—as should any schemes for compulsory voting. According to the normative perspective, we should not worry about low voter turnout, because citizens should have the freedom not to vote as well as to vote.

In theory, freedom to participate also means that individuals should be able to use their wealth, connections, knowledge, organizational power (including sheer numbers in organized protests), or any other resource to influence government decisions, provided they do so legitimately. Of all these resources, the individual vote may be the weakest—and the least important—means of exerting political influence. Obviously, then, freedom as a value in political participation favors those with the resources to advance their own political self-interest.

Participation and Equality

The relationship between participation and equality is also clear. Each citizen's ability to influence government should be equal to that of every other citizen, so that differences in personal resources do not work against the poor or otherwise disadvantaged. Elections, then, serve the ideal of equality better than any other means of political participation. Formal

America's Biggest Civil Rights Demonstration

On August 28, 1963, more than 200,000 blacks and whites participated in a march on Washington, D.C., to rally for jobs and freedom. Martin Luther King, Jr., one of the march's leaders, delivered his electrifying "I Have a Dream" speech from the steps of the Lincoln Memorial. The demonstrators pressed for legislation ensuring full civil rights for blacks, and President John F. Kennedy welcomed their leaders at the White House.

rules for counting ballots—in particular, one person, one vote—cancel differences in resources among individuals.

At the same time, groups of people who have few individual resources can combine their votes to wield political power. Various European ethnic groups exercised this power in the late nineteenth and early twentieth centuries, when their votes won them entry to the sociopolitical system and allowed them to share in its benefits (see Chapter 5). More recent, blacks, Hispanics, homosexuals, and the disabled have used their voting power to gain political recognition. However, minorities often have had to use unconventional forms of participation to win the right to vote. As two major scholars of political participation put it, "Protest is the great equalizer, the political action that weights intensity as well as sheer numbers."[66]

Participation and Order

The relationship between participation and order is complicated. Some types of participation (pledging allegiance, voting) promote order and so are encouraged by those who value order; other types promote disorder and so are discouraged. Many citizens (men and women alike) even resisted giving women the right to vote for fear of upsetting the social order by altering the traditional roles of men and women.

Both conventional and unconventional participation can lead to the ouster of government officials, but the regime—the political system itself—is threatened more by unconventional participation. To maintain order, the government has a stake in converting unconventional participation to conventional participation whenever possible. We can easily imagine this tactic's being used by authoritarian governments, but democratic governments also use it.

Think about the student unrest on college campuses during the Vietnam War. In private and public colleges alike, thousands of students stopped traffic, occupied buildings, destroyed property, struck classes, disrupted lectures, staged guerrilla theater, and behaved in other unconventional ways to protest the war, racism, capitalism, the behavior of their college presidents, the president of the United States, the military establishment, and all other institutions. (We are not exaggerating here. For example, students did all these things at Northwestern University in Evanston, Illinois, after members of the National Guard shot and killed four students at a demonstration at Kent State University in Ohio on May 4, 1970.)

Confronted by civil strife and disorder in the nation's institutions of higher learning, Congress took action. On March 23, 1971, it enacted and sent to the states the proposed Twenty-sixth Amendment, lowering the voting age to eighteen. Three-quarters of the state legislatures had to ratify the amendment before it became part of the Constitution. Astonishingly, thirty-eight states (the required number) complied by July 1, establishing a new speed record for ratification, cutting the old record nearly in half.[67] (Ironically, voting rights were not high on the list of students' demands.)

Testimony by members of Congress before the Judiciary Committee stated that the eighteen-year-old vote would "harness the energy of young people and direct it into useful and constructive channels," to keep students from becoming "more militant" and engaging "in destructive activities of a dangerous nature."[68] As one observer argued, the right to vote was extended to eighteen-year-olds not because young people demanded it but because "public officials believed suffrage expansion to be a means of institutionalizing youths' participation in politics, which would, in turn, curb disorder."[69]

PARTICIPATION AND THE MODELS OF DEMOCRACY

Ostensibly, elections are institutional mechanisms that implement democracy by allowing citizens to choose among candidates or issues. But elections also serve several other important purposes:[70]

- *Elections socialize political activity.* They transform what might otherwise consist of sporadic citizen-initiated acts into a routine public function. That is, the opportunity to vote for change encourages citizens to refrain from demonstrating in the streets. This helps preserve government stability by containing and channeling away potentially disruptive or dangerous forms of mass political activity.

- *Elections institutionalize access to political power.* They allow ordinary citizens to run for political office or to play an important role in selecting political leaders. Working to elect a candidate encourages the campaign worker to identify problems or propose solutions to the new official.

- *Elections bolster the state's power and authority.* The opportunity to participate in elections helps convince citizens that the government is responsive to their needs and wants, which reinforces its legitimacy.

Participation and Majoritarianism

Although the majoritarian model assumes that government responsiveness to popular demands comes through mass participation in politics, majoritarianism does not view participation broadly. It favors conventional, institutionalized behavior—primarily, voting in elections. Because majoritarianism relies on counting votes to determine what the majority wants, its bias toward equality in political participation is strong. Clearly, a class bias in voting exists because of the strong influence of socioeconomic status on turnout. Simply put, better-educated, wealthier citizens are more likely to participate in elections, but get-out-the-vote campaigns tend to counter this subtle class bias.[71] Favoring collective decisions formalized through elections, majoritarianism does not consider it valid for motivated, resourceful individuals to exercise private influence over government actions.

Majoritarianism also limits individual freedom in another way: Its focus on voting as the major means of mass participation narrows the scope of conventional political behavior by defining which political actions are "orderly" and acceptable. By favoring equality and order in political participation, majoritarianism goes hand in hand with the ideological orientation of populism (see Chapter 1).

Participation and Pluralism

Resourceful citizens who want the government's help with problems find a haven in the pluralist model of democracy. A decentralized and organizationally complex form of government allows many points of access and accommodates various forms of conventional participation in addition to voting. For example, wealthy people and well-funded groups can afford to hire lobbyists to press their interests in Congress. In one view of pluralist democracy, citizens are free to ply and wheedle public officials to further selfish visions of the public good. From another viewpoint, pluralism offers citizens the opportunity to be treated as individuals when dealing with the government, to influence policymaking in special circumstances, and to fulfill (insofar as is possible in representative government) their social potential through participation in community affairs.

SUMMARY

To have "government by the people," the people must participate in politics. Conventional forms of participation—contacting officials and voting in elections—come most quickly to mind. However, citizens can also participate in politics in unconventional ways—staging sit-down strikes in public buildings, blocking traffic, and so on. Most citizens disapprove of most forms of unconventional political behavior. Yet, blacks and women used unconventional tactics to win important political and legal rights, including the right to vote.

People are motivated to participate in politics for various reasons: to show support for their country, to obtain particularized benefits for themselves or their friends, or to influence broad public policy. Their political actions may demand either little political knowledge or personal initiative, or a great deal of both.

The press often paints an unflattering picture of political participation in America. Clearly, the proportion of the electorate that votes in general elections in the United States has dropped and is far below that in other nations. When compared with other nations on a broad range of conventional and unconventional political behavior, however, the United States tends to show as much or more citizen participation in politics. Voter turnout in the United States suffers by comparison with that of other nations' because of differences in voter registration here and elsewhere. We also lack institutions (especially strong political parties) that increase voter registration and help bring those of lower socioeconomic status to the polls.

The tendency to participate in politics strongly relates to socioeconomic status. Education, one component of socioeconomic status, is the single strongest predictor of conventional political participation in the United States. Because of the strong effect of socioeconomic status, the political system is potentially biased toward the interests of higher-status people. Pluralist democracy, which provides many avenues for resourceful citizens to influence government decisions, tends to increase the potential bias. Majoritarian democracy, which relies heavily on elections and the concept of one person, one vote, offers citizens without great personal resources the opportunity to control government decisions through elections.

Elections also serve to legitimize government simply by involving the masses in government through voting. Whether the vote means anything depends on the nature of the voters' choices in elections. The range of choice is a function of the nation's political parties, the topic of the next chapter.

Key Terms

election
political participation
conventional
  participation
unconventional
  participation
direct action
supportive behavior
influencing behavior
class action suit
voting

suffrage
franchise
progressivism
direct primary
recall
referendum
proposition
initiative
standard socioeconomic
  model

Selected Readings

Conway, M. Margaret. *Political Participation in the United States,* 2d ed. Washington, D.C.: Congressional Quarterly Press, 1991. An excellent review of survey data on conventional political participation.

Craig, Stephen C. The Malevolent Leaders: Popular Discontent in America. Boulder, Colo.: Westview, 1993. This book uses in-depth interviews with citizens and members of Congress to look at the rise of popular discontent with and disengagement from politics.

Cronin, Thomas E. *Direct Democracy: The Politics of Initiative, Referendum, and Recall.* Cambridge, Mass.: Harvard University Press, 1989. A sweeping study of three mechanisms of direct democracy; the data come from a national survey commissioned specifically for this study.

Dalton, Russell J. *Citizen Politics in Western Democracies.* Chatham, N.J.: Chatham House, 1988. Studies public opinion and behavior in the United States, Britain, Germany, and France. Two chapters compare conventional citizen action and protest politics in these countries.

Gant, Michael M., and Norman R. Luttbeg. *American Electoral Behavior: 1952–1988.* Itasca, Ill.: F. E. Peacock, 1991. Chapter 3 provides a concise, up-to-date analysis of trends in political participation in the United States.

Ginsberg, Benjamin. *Do Elections Matter?* 2nd ed. Armonk, N.Y.: M. E. Sharpe, 1991. Argues that the growth of the bureaucracy, the increasing activities of the judiciary, and the unmanageable budget deficit have made elections of limited consequence in American politics.

Grofman, Bernard, and Chandler Davidson, eds. Controversies in Minority Voting: The Voting Rights Act in Perspective. Washington, D.C.: Brookings Institution, 1992. Reviews the aims and accomplishments of the 1965 law that enforced voting rights for blacks in the South and some of its unintended consequences.

Jennings, M. Kent, Jan W. van Deth, et al. Continuities in Political Action: A Longitudinal Study of Political Orientations in Three Western Democracies. New York: Walter de Gruyter, 1990. The three democracies are the United States, West Germany, and the Netherlands. This study also compares political participation across time, drawing on panel studies in the 1970s and the 1980s.

Marone, James A. The Democratic Wish: Popular Participation and the Limits of American Government. New York: Basic Books, 1990. A reflective study arguing that in their search for more direct democracy, Americans have built up a weaker but more bureaucratic and intrusive government.

Rosenstone, Steven, and John Mark Hansen. Mobilization, Participation, and Democracy in America. New York: Macmillian, 1993. Explores the political meaning of citizens' declining participation in voting.

Teixeira, Ruy A. The Disappearing American Voter. Washington, D.C.: Brookings Institution, 1992. An empirical analysis of why many people do not vote, how that affects politics, and reflections on what can be done about it.

8 Political Parties

IN EARLY 1992, H. ROSS PEROT THREW A SCARE into the
Republican and Democratic parties. A prominent, successful, and outspoken businessman, Perot told CNN talk show host Larry King in February that he would run for president if his name were placed on the ballot in all fifty states. Perot's challenge struck a chord with citizens across the nation who did not like George Bush or any of the Democratic candidates seeking the nomination. Thousands of citizens called in to volunteer their assistance. By March 12, Perot's phone bank was taking six thousand calls a day. By March 23, Perot volunteers had succeeded in placing his name on the ballot in Tennessee. He was on the ballot in five more states by May, in some thirty states by July, and in every state by mid-September.

Perot's candidacy also enjoyed broad support among the general electorate. In a Gallup poll of voters' preferences taken in early June, Perot led with 39 percent, compared with 31 percent for Bush and 25 percent for Clinton.[1] At that time, many people believed that the race for the presidency would narrow into a two-way contest between Perot and Bush, leaving the Democratic candidate a dismal third. But most informed observers predicted that Perot's candidacy would fade as the election approached and that Bush and the Democratic nominee between them would take most of the votes in the election.

Given the boom for Perot in early summer, why did knowledgeable observers dismiss his ability to win the election? Why did Perot himself decide that he could not win, withdrawing from the race on July 16? (When he reentered on October 1, it was not to win but to address issues.) There were two reasons. First was the example of a similar independent candidacy a decade earlier. In early 1980, John Anderson, a Republican leader in Congress, ran for president as an independent after it became clear that his party would nominate former actor Ronald Reagan to run against the unpopular incumbent Jimmy Carter. The country's mood then was much like that in 1992. In announcing his candidacy, Anderson answered the charge that he would be only a spoiler by asking, "What's to spoil? The chances of two men whom at least half of the country does not want?"[2] Like Perot, Anderson was popular in early June, favored by 26 percent of the voters.[3] Like Perot, Anderson's dedicated volunteers placed him on the ballot in all fifty states (at a time when ballot laws were even more restrictive). But Anderson's support eroded as the election neared, and he won less than 7 percent of the popular vote, failing to carry a single state.

The second reason for discounting Perot's candidacy actually accounts for the first. Perot (like Anderson) was destined to failure as an independent candidate, because America's two-party system is too strong to be

The Populist Billionaire

H. Ross Perot promised to buy the presidency for the American people, and he made a valiant effort. Perot spent more than $60 million and won nearly 20 percent of the popular vote, but he failed to carry a single state and won no electoral votes. Nevertheless, he profoundly affected the 1992 presidential campaign and the election outcome. His hard-hitting attacks on President Bush complemented Clinton's campaign, and Perot's snappy style played well on television and helped raise voting turnout to 55 percent, the highest level since 1972.

upset by a third-party challenger. Although Perot, by winning 19 percent of the vote, fared much better than Anderson in the voting, running a strong third for president still leaves the outsider frozen out of government. The Democratic and Republican parties have dominated national and state politics in the United States for more than 125 years. Their domination is more complete than that of any other pair of parties in any other democratic government. Indeed, few democracies even have a two-party system—Britain and New Zealand are the most notable exceptions, as shown in Compared with What? 8.1—although all have some form of multiparty politics. Most people take our two-party system for granted, not realizing that it is arguably the most salient aspect of American government.

Why do we have political parties? What functions do they perform? How did we become a nation of Democrats and Republicans? Do these parties truly differ in their platforms and behavior? Are parties really necessary for democratic government, or do they just interfere in the relationship between citizens and government? In this chapter, we will answer these questions by examining political parties, perhaps the most misunderstood element in American politics.

POLITICAL PARTIES AND THEIR FUNCTIONS

According to democratic theory, the primary means by which citizens control their government is voting in free elections. Most Americans agree that voting is important: Of those surveyed after the 1992 presidential campaign, 87 percent felt that elections make the government "pay attention to what the people think."[4] However, Americans are not nearly as supportive of the role played by political parties in elections. An overwhelming majority (73 percent) surveyed in 1980 believed that "the best way to vote is to pick a candidate regardless of party label." A clear majority (56 percent) thought that "parties do more to confuse the issues than to provide a clear choice on issues." In fact, 49 percent took the extreme position: "It would be better if in all elections, we put no party labels on the ballot."[5]

On the other hand, Americans are quick to condemn as "undemocratic" countries that do not regularly hold elections contested by political parties. In truth, Americans have a love-hate relationship with political parties. They believe that parties are necessary for democratic government; at the same time, they think parties are somehow obstructionist and not to be trusted. This distrust is particularly strong among younger voters. To better appreciate the role of political parties in democratic government, we must understand exactly what parties are and what they do.

What Is a Political Party?

A **political party** is an organization that sponsors candidates for political office *under the organization's name.* The italicized part of this definition is important. True political parties hold **nominations** for candidates for election to public office to designate official candidates of the party. This function distinguishes the Democratic and Republican parties from interest groups. The AFL-CIO and the National Association of Manufacturers are interest groups. They often support candidates, but they do not nominate them to run as their avowed representatives. If they do, the interest groups become transformed into political parties. In short, the sponsoring of candidates, designated as representatives of the organization, is what defines an organization as a party.

Most democratic theorists agree that a modern nation-state could not practice democracy without at least two political parties that regularly contest elections. In fact, the link between democracy and political parties is so firm that many people define *democratic government* in terms of competitive party politics.

Party Functions

Parties contribute to democratic government through the functions they perform for the **political system**—the set of interrelated institutions that links people with government. Four of the most important party functions are nominating candidates for election to public office, structuring the voting choice in elections, proposing alternative government programs, and coordinating the actions of government officials.

Nominating Candidates　　In the absence of parties, voters would confront a bewildering array of self-nominated candidates, each seeking votes on the basis of personal friendships, celebrity status, or name. Parties can provide a form of quality control for their nominees through the process of peer review. Party insiders, the nominees' peers, usually know potential candidates much better than the average voter does and thus can judge their suitability for representing the party.

In nominating candidates, parties often do more than pass judgment on potential office seekers; sometimes, they go so far as to recruit talented individuals to become candidates. In this way, parties help not only to ensure a minimum level of quality among candidates who run for office but also to raise the quality of those candidates.

COMPARED
WITH WHAT? 8.1

Only Two to Tangle

Compared with other countries, the two-party system in the United States is unusual indeed. First, most democracies have multiparty systems, in which four or five parties win enough seats in the legislature to contest for government power. Even those countries classified as having two-party systems, such as the United Kingdom and New Zealand, really have some minor parties that regularly gain seats and thus complicate government politics. The purity of the U.S. pattern shows clearly in these graphs of party strength over time in the U.S. House compared with the British House of Commons and the New Zealand House of Representatives.*

* In the New Zealand graph, data for the New Zealand Democratic party, formed in 1985 to succeed the Social Credit party, are included in the segment for the Social Credit party.

• *Source: Dick Leonard,* World Atlas of Elections *(London: The Economist Publications, 1986), pp. 102 and 130. Used by permission.*

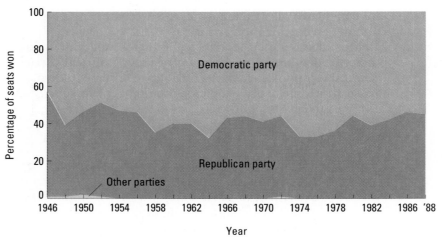

U.S. HOUSE OF REPRESENTATIVES

Percentage of seats won

Democratic party

Republican party

Other parties

1946 1950 1954 1958 1962 1966 1970 1974 1978 1982 1986 '88

Year

Structuring the Voting Choice   Political parties also help democratic government by structuring the voting choice—reducing the number of candidates on the ballot to those who have a realistic chance of winning. Established parties—those with experience in contesting elections—acquire a following of loyal voters who guarantee the party's candidates a predictable base of votes. Established parties' ability to mobilize their

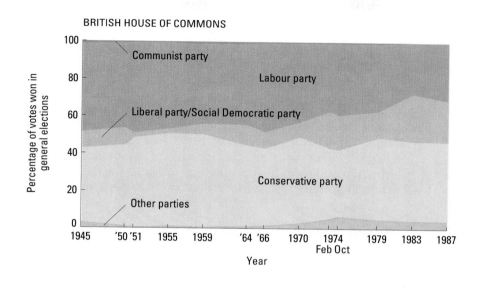

BRITISH HOUSE OF COMMONS

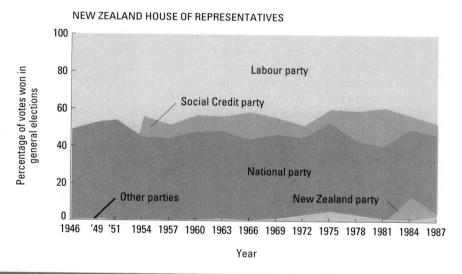

NEW ZEALAND HOUSE OF REPRESENTATIVES

electorate has the effect of discouraging nonparty candidates from running for office and of discouraging new parties from forming. Consequently, the realistic choice is between candidates offered by the major parties. This choice focuses the election on the contest between parties and on candidates with established records, reducing the amount of new information that voters need in order to make a rational decision.

Proposing Alternative Government Programs   Parties also help voters choose among candidates by proposing alternative programs of government action—general policies that party candidates will pursue if they win control of government. Even if voters know nothing about the qualities of the parties' candidates, they can vote rationally for the candidates of the party that has policies they favor. The specific policies advocated vary from candidate to candidate and from election to election. However, the types of policies advocated by candidates of one party tend to differ from those proposed by candidates of other parties. Although there are exceptions, candidates of the same party tend to favor policies that fit their party's underlying political philosophy, or ideology.

In many countries, parties' names—such as Conservative and Socialist—reflect their political stance. The Democrats and Republicans have issue-neutral names, but many minor parties in the United States have used their names to advertise their policies: the Prohibition party, the Farmer-Labor party, and the Socialist party, for example. The neutrality of the two major parties' names suggests that they are also undifferentiated in their policies. This is not true. As we shall see, they regularly adopt very different policies in their platforms.

Coordinating the Actions of Government Officials   Finally, party organizations help coordinate the actions of public officials. A government based on the separation of powers, as is that of the United States, divides responsibilities for making public policy. The president and the leaders of the House and Senate are not required to cooperate with one another. Political party organizations are the major means for bridging the separation of powers to produce coordinated policies that can govern the country effectively, which they do in two ways. First, their political fortunes are linked in a party organization that can bestow and withhold favors. Second, and perhaps more important in the United States, members of the same party in the presidency, the House, and the Senate tend to share political principles and thus often voluntarily cooperate in making policy.

A History of U.S. Party Politics

The two major U.S. parties are among the oldest in the world. In fact, the Democratic party, founded in 1828 but with roots reaching back to the late 1700s, has a strong claim to being the oldest party in existence. Its closest rival is the British Conservative party, formed in 1832, two decades before the Republican party was organized in 1854. Several generations of citizens have supported both the Democratic and Republican parties, and are part of American history. They have become institutionalized in our political process.

THE PREPARTY PERIOD   Today we think of party activities as normal, even essential, to American politics. It was not always so. The Constitution makes no mention of political parties, and none existed when the Constitution was written in 1787. It was common then to refer to groups pursuing some common political interest as *factions*. Although factions were seen as inevitable in politics, they were also considered dangerous. One argument for adopting the Constitution—proposed in *Federalist* 10 (see Chapter 3 and the Appendix)—was that its federal system would prevent factional influences from controlling the government.

Factions existed even under British rule. In colonial assemblies, supporters of the governor (and thus of the Crown) were known as *Tories* or *Loyalists*, and their opponents were called *Whigs* or *Patriots*. After independence, the arguments over whether to adopt the Constitution produced a different alignment of factions. Those who backed the Constitution were loosely known as *federalists*, their opponents as *antifederalists*. At this stage, the groups could not be called *parties*, because they did not sponsor candidates for election.

Elections then were vastly different from elections today. The Constitution provided for the president and vice president to be chosen by an **electoral college**—a body of electors who met in the capitals of their respective states to cast their ballots. Initially, the state legislatures, not the voters, chose the electors (one for each senator and representative in Congress). Presidential elections in the early years of the nation, then, actually were decided by a handful of political leaders. (See Chapter 9 for a discussion of the electoral college in modern presidential politics.) Often they met in small, secret groups, called **caucuses,** to propose candidates for public office. And often these were caucuses of like-minded members of state legislatures and Congress. This was the setting for George Washington's election as the first president in 1789.

We can classify Washington as a federalist, because he supported the Constitution, but he was not a factional leader and actually opposed factional politics. His immense prestige, coupled with his political neutrality, left Washington unopposed for the office of president, and he was elected unanimously by the electoral college. During Washington's administration, however, the political cleavage sharpened between those who favored a stronger national government and those who wanted a less powerful, more decentralized national government.

The first group, led by Alexander Hamilton, proclaimed themselves *Federalists.* The second group, led by Thomas Jefferson, called themselves *Republicans.* (Although they used the same name, they were not Republicans as we know them today.) The Jeffersonians chose the name Republicans to distinguish themselves from the "aristocratic" tendencies of Hamilton's Federalists. The Federalists countered by calling the Republicans the *Democratic Republicans,* attempting to link Jefferson's party to the disorder (and beheadings) spawned by the "radical democrats" in France during the French Revolution of 1789.

The First Party System: Federalists and Democratic Republicans

Washington was reelected president unanimously in 1792, but his vice president, John Adams, was opposed by a candidate backed by the Democratic Republicans. This brief skirmish foreshadowed the nation's first major-party struggle over the presidency. Disheartened by the political split in his administration, Washington spoke out against "the baneful effects" of parties in his farewell address in 1796. Nonetheless, the party concept was already firmly entrenched in the political system, as Figure 8.1 shows. In the election of 1796, the Federalists supported Vice Presi-

FIGURE 8.1 ■ Two-Party Systems in American History

Over time, the American party system has undergone a series of wrenching transformations. Since 1856, the Democrats and the Republicans have alternated irregularly in power, each party enjoying a long period of dominance.

1789 Washington unanimously elected president			PREPARTY PERIOD	
1792 Washington unanimously reelected				
1796	Federalist *Adams*	Democratic Republican		
1800	—	*Jefferson*	FIRST PARTY SYSTEM	
1804	—	*Jefferson*		
1808	—	*Madison*		
1812	—	*Madison*		
1816	—	*Monroe*		
1820		*Monroe*	"ERA OF GOOD FEELING"	
1824		*J.Q. Adams*		
1828		Democratic *Jackson*		National Republican
1832		*Jackson*		Whig
1836	SECOND PARTY SYSTEM	*Van Buren*		
1840		—		*Harrison*
1844		*Polk*		—
1848		—		*Taylor*
1852		*Pierce*		—
1856		*Buchanan*		Republican
1860	Constitutional Union Southern Democrat	—		*Lincoln*
1864		—		*Lincoln*
1868		—		*Grant*
1872	THIRD PARTY SYSTEM	—		*Grant*
1876		—		*Hayes*
1880		—		*Garfield*
1884		*Cleveland*		—
1888	Rough Balance	—		*Harrison*
1892		*Cleveland*		—
1896		—	Populist	*McKinley*
1900		—		*McKinley*
1904		—		*T. Roosevelt*
1908		—		*Taft*
1912	Republican Dominance	*Wilson*	Progressive	—
1916		*Wilson*		—
1920		—		*Harding*
1924		—		*Coolidge*
1928		—		*Hoover*
1932		*F.D. Roosevelt*		—
1936		*F.D. Roosevelt*		—
1940		*F.D. Roosevelt*		—
1944		*F.D. Roosevelt*		—
1948	Democratic Dominance	*Truman*	States' Rights	—
1952		—		*Eisenhower*
1956		—		*Eisenhower*
1960		*Kennedy*		—
1964		*Johnson*		—
1968		—	American Independent	*Nixon*
1972		—		*Nixon*
1976		*Carter*		—
1980		—	Independent	*Reagan*
1984		—		*Reagan*
1988		—		*Bush*
1992		*Clinton*	Independent	—

dent John Adams to succeed Washington as president. The Democratic Republicans backed Thomas Jefferson for president but could not agree on a vice presidential candidate. In the electoral college, Adams won 71 votes to Jefferson's 68, and both ran ahead of other candidates. At that time, the Constitution provided that the presidency went to the candidate who won the most votes in the electoral college and the vice presidency went to the runner-up. So Adams, a Federalist, had to accept Jefferson, a Democratic Republican, as his vice president. Obviously, the Constitution did not anticipate a presidential contest between candidates from opposing political parties.

The party function of nominating candidates emerged more clearly in the election of 1800. Both parties caucused in Congress to nominate candidates for president and vice president.[6] The result was the first true party contest for the presidency. The Federalists nominated John Adams and Charles Pinckney; the Democratic Republicans nominated Thomas Jefferson and Aaron Burr. This time, the Democratic Republican candidates won. However, the new party organization worked too well. The Democratic Republican electors unanimously cast all their votes for both Jefferson and Burr. Unfortunately, the presidency was to go to the candidate with the most votes, and the top two candidates were tied.

Although Jefferson was the party's presidential candidate and Burr its vice presidential candidate, the Constitution empowered the House of Representatives to choose one of them as president. After seven days and thirty-six ballots, the House decided in favor of Jefferson.

The Twelfth Amendment, ratified in 1804, prevented a repeat of the troublesome election outcomes of 1796 and 1800. It required the electoral college to vote separately for president and vice president, implicitly recognizing that parties would nominate different candidates for the two offices.

The election of 1800 marked the beginning of the end for the Federalists, who lost the next four elections. By 1820, the Federalists were no more. The Democratic Republican candidate, James Monroe, was reelected in the first presidential contest without party competition since Washington's time. (Monroe received all but one electoral vote, which reportedly was cast against him so that Washington would remain the only president ever elected unanimously.) Ironically, the lack of partisan competition under Monroe, dubbed "the Era of Good Feelings," also fatally weakened his party, the Democratic Republicans. Lacking competition, the Democratic Republicans neglected their function of nominating candidates. In 1824, the party caucus's nominee was challenged by three other Democratic Republicans, including John Quincy Adams and Andrew Jackson, who proved to be more popular candidates among the voters in the ensuing election.

Before 1824, the parties' role in structuring the popular vote was relatively unimportant, because relatively few people were entitled to vote. But the states began to drop restrictive requirements for voting after 1800, and voting rights for white males expanded even faster after 1815 (see Chapter 7). With the expansion of suffrage, more states began to allow voters to choose presidential electors. The 1824 election was the first in which voters selected presidential electors in most states. Still, the role of political parties in structuring the popular vote had not yet developed fully.

Although Jackson won a plurality of both the popular vote and the electoral vote in 1824, he did not win the necessary majority in the electoral college. The House of Representatives again had to decide the winner. It chose the second-place John Quincy Adams (from the established state of Massachusetts) over the voters' choice, Jackson (from the frontier state of Tennessee). The factionalism among the leaders of the Democratic Republican party became so intense that the party split in two.

The Second Party System: Democrats and Whigs

The Jacksonian faction of the Democratic Republican party represented the common people in the expanding South and West, and its members took pride in calling themselves, simply, *Democrats.* Jackson ran again for the presidency as a Democrat in 1828, a milestone that marked the beginning of today's Democratic party. That election was also the first "mass" election in U.S. history. Although the voters had chosen many presidential electors in 1824, the total votes cast in that election numbered fewer than 370,000. By 1828, relaxed requirements for voting (and the use of popular elections to select presidential electors in more states) had increased the vote by more than 300 percent, to more than 1.1 million.

As the electorate expanded, the parties changed. No longer could a party rely on a few political leaders in the state legislatures to control the votes cast in the electoral college. Parties now needed to campaign for votes cast by hundreds of thousands of citizens. Recognizing this new dimension of politics, parties responded with a new method for nominating presidential candidates. Instead of selecting candidates in a closed caucus of party representatives in Congress, the parties devised the **national convention.** At these gatherings, delegates from state parties across the nation would choose candidates for president and vice president and adopt a statement of policies called a **party platform.** The Anti-Masonic party, which was the first "third" party in American history to challenge the two major parties for the presidency, called the first national convention in 1831. The Democrats adopted the convention idea in 1832 to nominate Jackson for a second term, as did their new opponents that year, the National Republicans.

The label *National Republicans* applied to John Quincy Adams's faction of the former Democratic Republican party. However, the National Republicans did not become today's Republican party. Adams's followers called themselves National Republicans to signify their old Federalist preference for a strong national government, but the symbolism did not appeal to the voters, and the National Republicans lost to Jackson in 1832.

Elected to another term, Jackson began to assert the power of the nation over the states (acting more like a National Republican than a Democrat). His policies drew new opponents, who started calling him "King Andrew." A coalition made up of former National Republicans, Anti-Masons, and Jackson haters formed the Whig party in 1834.[7] The name harked back to the English Whigs, who opposed the powers of the British throne; the implication was that Jackson was governing like a king. For the next thirty years, Democrats and Whigs alternated in the presidency. However, the issues of slavery and sectionalism eventually destroyed the Whigs. Although the party had won the White House in 1848 and had taken 44 percent of the vote in 1852, the Whigs were unable to field a presidential candidate in the 1856 election.

The Current Party System: Democrats and Republicans

In the early 1850s, antislavery forces (including some Whigs and antislavery Democrats) began to organize. At meetings in Jackson, Michigan, and Ripon, Wisconsin, they recommended the formation of a new party, the Republican party, to oppose the extension of slavery into the Kansas and Nebraska territories. It is this party, founded in 1854, that continues as today's Republican party.

The Republican party entered its first presidential election in 1856. It took 33 percent of the vote, and its candidate (John Fremont) carried eleven states—all in the North. Then, in 1860, the Republicans nominated Abraham Lincoln. The Democrats were deeply divided over the slavery issue and actually split into two parties. The northern wing kept the Democratic party label and nominated Stephen Douglas. The Southern Democrats ran John Breckinridge. A fourth party, the Constitutional Union party, nominated John Bell. Lincoln took 40 percent of the popular vote and carried every northern state. Breckinridge won every southern state. But all three of Lincoln's opponents together still did not win enough electoral votes to deny him the presidency.

The election of 1860 is considered the first of three critical elections under the current party system.[8] A **critical election** produces a sharp change in the existing patterns of party loyalties among groups of voters. Moreover, this change in voting patterns, which is called an **electoral realignment,** does not end with the election but persists through several subsequent elections.[9] The election of 1860 divided the country politically between the northern states, which mainly voted Republican, and the southern states, which were overwhelmingly Democratic. The victory of the North over the South in the Civil War cemented Democratic loyalties in the South.

For forty years, from 1880 to 1920, no Republican presidential candidate won even one of the eleven states of the former Confederacy. The South's solid Democratic record earned it the nickname "the Solid South." The Republicans did not puncture the Solid South until 1920, when Warren G. Harding carried Tennessee. Republicans also won five southern states in 1928, when the Democrats ran the first Catholic candidate, Al Smith. Republican presidential candidates won no more southern states until 1952, when Dwight Eisenhower broke the pattern of Democratic dominance in the South—ninety years after that pattern had been set by the Civil War.

Eras of Party Dominance Since the Civil War

The critical election of 1860 established the Democratic and Republican parties as the dominant parties in our **two-party system.** In a two-party system, most voters are so loyal to one or the other of the major parties that candidates from a third party—which means any minor party—have little chance of winning office. Certainly that is true in presidential elections, as Perot found out. Third-party candidates tend to be most successful at the local or state level. Since the current two-party system was

William Jennings Bryan: When Candidates Were Orators

Today, televised images of a candidate waving his hands and shouting to an audience would look silly. But candidates once had to resort to such tactics to be effective with large crowds. One of the most commanding orators around the turn of the century was William Jennings Bryan (1860–1925), whose stirring speeches extolling the virtues of the free coinage of silver were music to the ears of thousands of westerners and southern farmers.

established, relatively few minor-party candidates have won election to the U.S. House, even fewer have won election to the Senate, and none has won the presidency.

Although voters in most states divide in their loyalties between the Republicans and the Democrats, they have not always been equally divided. In some states, counties, and communities, voters typically favor the Republicans, while voters in other areas prefer the Democrats. When one party in a two-party system *regularly* enjoys support from most voters, it is called the **majority party;** the other is called the **minority party.** Since the inception of the current two-party system, three periods have characterized the balance between the two major parties.

A Rough Balance: 1860–1894   From 1860 through 1894, the Grand Old Party (or GOP, as the Republican party is sometimes called) won eight of ten presidential elections, which would seem to qualify it as the majority party. However, some of its success in presidential elections came from its practice of running Civil War heroes and from the North's domination of southern politics. Seats in the House of Representatives are a better guide to the breadth of national support. An analysis shows that the Republicans and Democrats won an equal number of congressional elections, each controlling the chamber for nine sessions between 1860 and 1894.

A Republican Majority: 1896–1930   A second critical election, in 1896, transformed the Republican party into a true majority party. Grover Cleveland, a Democrat, occupied the White House, and the country was in a severe depression. The Republicans nominated William McKinley, governor of Ohio and a conservative, who stood for a high tariff against foreign goods and sound money tied to the value of gold. Rather than tour the country seeking votes, McKinley ran a dignified campaign from his Ohio home.

FIGURE **8.2**   ■ **The Critical Election of 1896**

In the presidential election of 1896, voters in the populous and industrial East and Midwest elected Republican William McKinley (who was probusiness) over Democrat William Jennings Bryan (advocate of the rural West and South). The Republicans emerged as the majority party in national elections that followed this election.

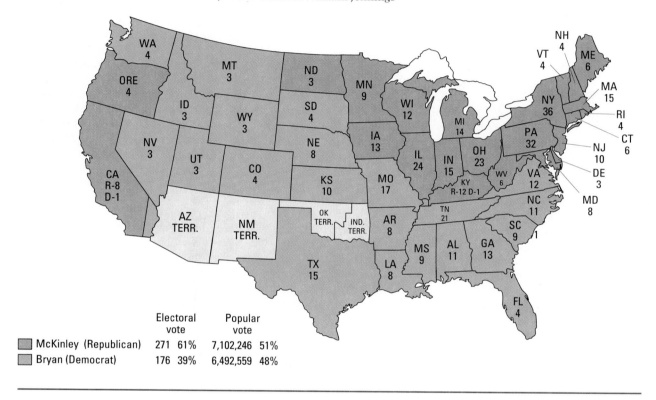

	Electoral vote		Popular vote	
McKinley (Republican)	271	61%	7,102,246	51%
Bryan (Democrat)	176	39%	6,492,559	48%

The Democrats, already in trouble because of the depression, nominated the fiery William Jennings Bryan. In stark contrast to McKinley, Bryan advocated the free and unlimited coinage of silver—which meant cheap money and easy payment of debts through inflation. Bryan was also the nominee of the young Populist party, an agrarian protest party that had proposed the free-silver platform that Bryan adopted. Feature 8.1 explains that the book *The Wonderful Wizard of Oz,* which you probably know as a movie, was actually a Populist political fable.[10] Conservatives, especially businesspeople, were aghast at the Democrats' radical turn, and voters in the heavily populated Northeast and Midwest surged toward the Republican party, many of them permanently. McKinley carried every northern state east of the Mississippi, as Figure 8.2 shows. The Republicans also won the House and continued to control it for the next six elections.

The election of 1896 helped solidify a Republican majority in industrial America and forged a link between the Republican party and business. In

FEATURE 8.1

■ The Wizard of Oz: A Political Fable

Most Americans are familiar with *The Wizard of Oz* through the children's books or the 1939 motion picture, but few realize that the story was written as a political fable to promote the Populist movement around the turn of the century. Next time you see or read it, try interpreting the Tin Woodsman as the industrial worker, the Scarecrow as the struggling farmer, and the Wizard as the president, who is powerful only as long as he succeeds in deceiving the people. (Sorry, but in the book Dorothy's ruby slippers were only silver shoes.)

The Wonderful Wizard of Oz was written by Lyman Frank Baum in 1900, during the collapse of the Populist movement. Through the Populist party, Midwestern farmers, in alliance with some urban workers, had challenged the banks, railroads, and other economic interests that squeezed farmers through low prices, high freight rates, and continued indebtedness.

The Populists advocated government ownership of railroads, telephone, and telegraph industries. They also wanted silver coinage. Their power grew during the 1893 depression, the worst in U.S. history until then, as farm prices sank to new lows and unemployment was widespread. . . .

In the 1894 congressional elections, the Populist party got almost 40 percent of the vote. It looked forward to winning the presidency, and the silver standard, in 1896. But in that election, which revolved around the issue of gold versus silver, Populist Democrat William Jennings Bryan lost to Republican William McKinley by 95 electoral votes. Bryan, a congressman from Nebraska and a gifted orator, ran again in 1900, but the Populist strength was gone.

Baum viewed these events in both rural South Dakota—where he edited a local weekly—and urban Chicago—where he wrote *Oz.* He mourned the destruction of the fragile alliance between the Midwestern farmers (the Scarecrow) and the urban industrial workers (the Tin Woodsman). Along with Bryan (the Cowardly Lion with a roar but little else), they had been taken down the yellow brick road (the gold standard) that led nowhere. Each journeyed to Emerald City seeking favors from the Wizard of Oz (the President). Dorothy, the symbol of Everyman, went along with them, innocent enough to see the truth before the others.

Along the way they meet the Wicked Witch of the East who, Baum tells us, had kept the little Munchkin people "in bondage for many years, making them slave for her night and day." She also had put a spell on the Tin Woodsman, once an independent and hardworking man, so that each time he swung his axe, it chopped off a different part of his body. Lacking another trade, he "worked harder than ever," becoming like a machine, incapable of love, yearning for a heart. Another witch, the Wicked Witch of the West, clearly symbolizes the large industrial corporations.

. . .The small group heads toward Emerald City where the Wizard rules from behind a papier-mâché façade. Oz, by the way, is the abbreviation for ounce, the standard measure for gold.

Like all good politicians, the Wizard can be all things to all people. Dorothy sees him as an enormous head. The Scarecrow sees a gossamer fairy. The Woodsman sees an awful beast, the Cowardly Lion "a ball of fire so fierce and glowing he could scarcely bear to gaze upon it."

Later, however, when they confront the Wizard directly, they see he is nothing more than "a little man, with a bald head and a wrinkled face."

"I have been making believe," the Wizard confesses. "I'm just a common man." But the Scarecrow adds, "You're more than that . . . you're a humbug."

"It was a great mistake my ever letting you into the Throne Room," admits the Wizard, a former ventriloquist and circus balloonist from Omaha.

This was Baum's ultimate Populist message. The powers-that-be survive by deception. Only people's ignorance allows the powerful to manipulate and control them. Dorothy returns to Kansas with the magical help of her Silver Shoes (the silver issue), but when she gets to Kansas she realizes her shoes "had fallen off in her flight through the air, and were lost forever in the desert." Still, she is safe at home with Aunt Em and Uncle Henry, simple farmers.

• *Source: Peter Dreier,* Today Journal, *14 February 1986, p. 11. Copyright Pacific News Service. Reprinted by permission.*

the subsequent electoral realignment, the Republicans emerged as a true majority party. The GOP dominated national politics—controlling the presidency, the Senate, and the House—almost continuously from 1896 until the Wall Street crash of 1929, which burst big business's bubble and launched the Great Depression.*

A Democratic Majority: 1932 to the Present   The Republicans' majority status ended in the critical election of 1932 between incumbent president Herbert Hoover and the Democratic challenger, Franklin Delano Roosevelt. Roosevelt promised new solutions to unemployment and the economic crisis of the Depression. His campaign appealed to labor, middle-class liberals, and new European ethnic voters. Along with Democratic voters in the Solid South, urban workers in the North, Catholics, Jews, and white ethnic minorities formed "the Roosevelt coalition." (The relatively few blacks who voted at that time tended to remain loyal to the Republicans—"the party of Lincoln.")

Roosevelt was swept into office in a landslide, carrying huge majorities into the House and Senate to enact his liberal activist programs. The electoral realignment reflected by the election of 1932 made the Democrats the majority party. Not only was Roosevelt reelected in 1936, 1940, and 1944, but Democrats held control of both houses of Congress from 1933 through 1980—interrupted by only two years of Republican control in 1953 and 1954, during the Eisenhower administration. Moreover, at the state level, the Democrats held about 60 percent or more of the total legislative seats and controlled about two-thirds or more of the legislative chambers through the 1992 election.

In presidential elections, however, the Democrats have not fared so well since Roosevelt. In fact, they have won only five elections (Truman, Kennedy, Johnson, Carter, and Clinton), compared with the Republicans' seven victories (Eisenhower twice, Nixon twice, Reagan twice, and Bush once). It is significant that no Democratic president has been reelected since Roosevelt—a precedent that President Clinton must surely ponder for 1996.

Signs are strong that the coalition of Democratic voters forged by Roosevelt in the 1930s has already cracked. Certainly the South is no longer solid for the Democrats. Since 1952, in fact, it has voted more consistently for Republican presidential candidates than for Democrats. The party system in the United States does not seem to be undergoing another realignment; rather, we seem to be in a period of **electoral dealignment,** in which party loyalties have become less important in the decisions of voters when they cast their ballots. We examine the influence of party loyalty on voting in the next chapter, after we look at the operation of our two-party system.

THE AMERICAN TWO-PARTY SYSTEM   Our review of party history has focused on the two dominant parties in U.S. politics. But we should not ignore the special contributions of certain minor parties, among them the Anti-Masonic party, the Populists, and the Progressives of 1912. In this section, we study the fortunes of minor, or

* *The only break in GOP domination was 1912, when Teddy Roosevelt's Progressive party split from the Republicans, allowing Democrat Woodrow Wilson to win the presidency and giving the Democrats control of Congress.*

third, parties in American politics. We also will look at why we have only two major parties, explain how federalism helps the parties survive, and describe voters' loyalties toward the major parties today.

Minor Parties in America

Minor parties have always figured in party politics in America. The National Unity campaign that promoted John Anderson's candidacy in 1980 and Perot's United We Stand organization in 1992 should not be regarded as parties, for both candidates ran as independents in most states.* Most true minor parties in our political history have been one of four types:[12]

- **Bolter parties** are formed by factions that have split off from one of the major parties. Six times in the thirty-one presidential elections since the Civil War, disgruntled leaders have "bolted the ticket" and challenged their former parties. Bolter parties have occasionally won significant proportions of the vote. However, with the exception of Teddy Roosevelt's Progressive party in 1912 and the possible exception of George Wallace's American Independent party in 1968, bolter parties have not affected the outcome of presidential elections.

- **Farmer-labor parties** represent farmers and urban workers who believe that they, the working class, are not getting their share of society's wealth. The People's party, founded in 1892 and nicknamed "the Populist party," was a prime example of a farmer-labor party. The Populists won 8.5 percent of the vote in 1892 and also became the first third party since 1860 to win any electoral votes. Flush with success, it endorsed William Jennings Bryan, the Democratic candidate, in 1896. When he lost, the party quickly faded. Farm and labor groups revived many Populist ideas in the Progressive party in 1924, which nominated Robert La Follette for the presidency. Although the party won 16.6 percent of the popular vote, it carried only La Follette's home state of Wisconsin. The party died in 1925, although Populist ideals—most notable a commitment to order and equality over freedom—still play a part in today's political system (see Chapter 7). To illustrate how political labels get mixed up in politics, ex-Ku Klux Klansman David E. Duke—who opposes social equality—ran for president under the Populist party banner in 1988, receiving fewer than 50,000 votes out of more than 91 million cast. His antiblack platform fits better under the next category of minor parties.

- **Parties of ideological protest** go further than farmer-labor parties in criticizing the established system. These parties reject prevailing doctrines and propose radically different principles, often favoring more government activism. The Socialist party has been the most successful party of ideological protest. Even at its high point in 1912, however, it garnered only 6 percent of the vote, and Socialist candidates for president have never won a single state. In recent years, the sound of ideo-

---

* Although Perot vowed to continue his organization, which anyone could join for $15, by early 1993 many state chapters of United We Stand were wracked with dissent and loss of members who complained that they had no voice within the organization. In 1994, the New York chapter even fought with Perot's Dallas headquarters over the use of the name "United We Stand," and the purpose of the national organization was also in doubt. [11]

logical protest has come more from rightist parties, arguing for the radical disengagement of government from society. Such is the program of the Libertarian party, which stresses freedom over order and equality. This party has run candidates for president in every election since 1972 and has emerged as the most active and fastest-growing minor party. Its presidential candidate for 1992, Andre Marrou, was on the ballot in all fifty states. But the party never has won more than 1 percent of the total votes cast.[13]

* **Single-issue parties** are formed to promote one principle, not a general philosophy of government. The Anti-Masonic parties of the 1820s and 1830s, for example, opposed Masonic lodges and other secret societies. The Free Soil party of the 1840s and 1850s worked to abolish slavery. The Prohibition party, the most durable example of a single-issue party, opposed the consumption of alcoholic beverages. Prohibition candidates consistently won from 1 to 2 percent of the vote in nine presidential elections between 1884 and 1916, and the party has run candidates in every presidential election since.

Third parties, then, have formed primarily to express discontent with the choices offered by the major parties and to work for their own objectives within the electoral system.[14] How have they fared? As vote getters, minor parties have not performed well, with two exceptions. First, bolter parties have twice won more than 10 percent of the vote; no other type has ever won as much. Second, the Republican party originated in 1854 as a single-issue third party opposed to slavery in new territories; in its first election, in 1856, the party came in second, displacing the Whigs. (Undoubtedly, the Republican exception to the rule has inspired the formation of other hopeful third parties.)

As policy advocates, minor parties have a slightly better record. At times, they have had a real effect on the policies adopted by the major parties. Women's suffrage, the graduated income tax, and the direct election of senators all originated in third parties.[15] Of course, third parties may fail to win more votes because their policies lack popular support. This was a lesson the Democrats learned in 1896, when they adopted the Populists' free-silver plank in their own platform. Both candidate and platform went down to a defeat that hobbled the Democratic party for decades.

Most important, minor parties function as safety valves. They allow those who are unhappy with the status quo to express their discontent within the system, to contribute to the political dialogue. Surely this was the function of Perot's candidacy. If minor parties and independent candidates are indicators of discontent, what should we make of the numerous minor parties, as detailed in Figure 8.3, in the 1992 election? Not much. The number of third parties that contest elections is less important than the total number of votes they receive. Despite the presence of numerous minor parties in every presidential election, the two major parties usually collect more than 99 percent of the vote. Because of Perot's candidacy, 1992 was an exception. He won 19 percent of the total vote, more than any other candidate outside the two major parties since Theodore Roosevelt ran as a Progressive in 1912. It remains to be seen whether Perot will run again in 1996 or whether his candidacy will turn out to have been another one-shot affair, like George Wallace's in 1968 and John Anderson's in 1980.

FIGURE 8.3 ■ Candidates and Parties in the 1992 Election

Most people think of Ross Perot as the "third candidate" in the 1992 election, but twenty other candidates, representing fifteen different parties, also ran. All of them together, however, failed to capture even 1 percent of the total vote. Here is the complete accounting.

Source: Federal Election Commission, "55.9 Percent Turnout in 1992 Presidential Election Highest Since 1968," press release of January 14, 1992, 2.

CANDIDATE AND PARTY	POPULAR TOTAL VOTE	PERCENTAGE OF POPULAR VOTE RECEIVED
Bill Clinton (Democrat)	44,908,233	42.95
George Bush (Republican)	39,102,282	37.40
Ross Perot (Independent)	19,721,433	18.86
Andre Marrou (Libertarian)	291,612	.28
James "Bo" Gritz (Populist/America First)	98,918	.09
Lenora Fulani (New Alliance)	73,248	.07
Howard Phillips (U.S. Taxpayers)	42,960	.04
John Hagelin (Natural Law)	37,137	.04
Ron Daniels (Independent)	27,396	.03
Lyndon LaRouche (Independent)	25,863	.02
James MacWarren (Socialist Workers)	22,883	.02
Drew Bradford (Independent)	4,749	.00
Jack Herer (Grassroots)	3,275	.00
Helen Halyard (Workers League)	3,050	.00
John Quinn Brisben (Socialist)	2,909	.00
John Yiamouyiannis (Independent)	2,199	.00
Delbert Ehlers (Independent)	1,149	.00
Jom Boren (Apathy)	956	.00
Earl Dodge (Prohibition)	935	.00
Eugene Hem (Third Party)	405	.00
Isabelle Masters (Looking Back Group)	327	.00
Robert J. Smith (American)	292	.00
Gloria Estella La Riva (Workers World)	181	.00
Write-In	177,207	.17
None of the above (Nevada)	2,537	.00
Total	104,552,736	100%

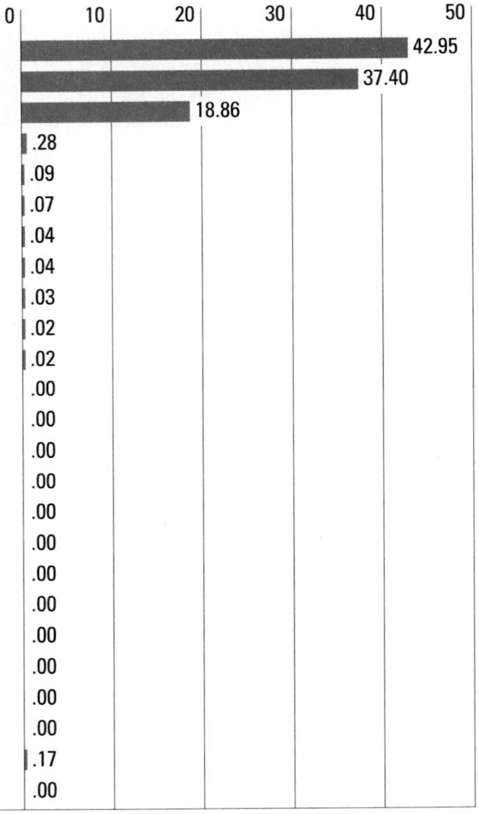

Why a Two-Party System?

The history of party politics in the United States is essentially the story of two parties alternating control of the government. With relatively few exceptions, Americans conduct elections at all levels within the two-party system. This pattern is unusual in democratic countries, where multiparty systems are more common. Why does the United States have only two major parties? The two most convincing answers to this question stem from the electoral system in the United States and the process of political socialization here.

In the typical U.S. election, two or more candidates contest each office, and the winner is the single candidate who collects the most votes, whether those votes constitute a majority or not. When these two principles of *single winners* chosen by a *simple plurality* of votes govern the election of members of a legislature, the system (despite its reliance on pluralities rather than majorities) is known as **majority representation.** Think about how the states choose representatives to Congress. A state entitled to ten representatives is divided into ten congressional districts; each district elects one representative. Majority representation of voters through single-member districts is also a feature of most state legislatures.

Alternatively, a legislature might be chosen through a system of **proportional representation,** which awards legislative seats to each party in proportion to the vote it won in an election. Under this system, the state might hold a single statewide election for all ten seats, with each party presenting its rank-ordered list of ten candidates. Voters could vote for the party list they preferred, and the party's candidates would be elected from the top of each list according to the proportion of votes won by the party. Thus, if a party got 30 percent of the vote in this example, its first three candidates would be elected.

Although this form of election may seem strange, many democratic countries (e.g., The Netherlands, Israel, and Denmark) use it. Proportional representation tends to produce (or to perpetuate) several parties, each of which can win enough seats nationwide to wield some influence in the legislature. In contrast, our system of elections forces interest groups of all sorts to work within one of the two major parties, for only one of their candidates stands a chance to be elected under plurality voting. Therefore, the system tends to produce only two parties. Moreover, the two major parties benefit from state laws that automatically list candidates on the ballot if their party won some minimum percentage of the vote in the previous election. These laws discourage minor parties, which must petition before every election for a place on the ballot.[16]

The rules of our electoral system may explain why only two parties tend to form in specific election districts. But why do the same two parties (Democratic and Republican) operate within each state? The contest for the presidency is the key to this question. A candidate can win a presidential election only by amassing a majority of electoral votes from across the entire nation. Presidential candidates try to win votes under the same party label in each state in order to pool their electoral votes in the electoral college. The presidency is a big enough political prize to induce parties to harbor uncomfortable coalitions of voters (southern white Protestants allied with northern Jews and blacks in the Democratic party, for example) just to win the electoral vote and the presidential election.

The American electoral system may force party politics into a two-party mold, but why must the same parties reappear from election to election? In fact, they do not. The earliest two-party system pitted the Federalists against the Democratic Republicans. A later two-party system involved the Democrats and the Whigs. More than 130 years ago, the Republicans replaced the Whigs in what is our two-party system today. But with modern issues so different from the issues then, why do the Democrats and Republicans persist? This is where political socialization comes into play. The two parties persist simply because they have persisted. After more

Not White Man but Whitman

In November 1993, Republican candidate Christine Todd Whitman was elected governor of New Jersey, defeating the Democratic incumbent, Jim Florio. Only one year earlier, New Jersey voted for Clinton for president in 1992. Whitman's victory demonstrates the federal structure of the party system: One party may win executive office at the national level, while another party wins executive office at the state level. In 1994, approximately 60 percent of the nation's governors were Democrats.

than one hundred years of political socialization, the two parties today have such a head start in structuring the vote that they discourage challenges from new parties. Of course, third parties still try to crack the two-party system from time to time, but most have had little success.

The Federal Basis of the Party System

Studying the history of American parties by focusing on contests for the presidency is convenient and informative, but it also oversimplifies party politics to the point of distortion. By concentrating only on presidential elections, we tend to ignore electoral patterns in the states, where elections often buck national trends. Even during its darkest defeats for the presidency, a party can still claim many victories for state offices. The victories outside the arena of presidential politics give each party a base of support that keeps its machinery oiled and ready for the next contest.

The Republican victory in the 1984 presidential election helps illustrate how the states serve as a refuge for parties defeated for the presidency. Ronald Reagan swept forty-nine states in 1984—winning everywhere but the District of Columbia and Minnesota, the home of his opponent, Walter Mondale. Even in the wake of Reagan's stunning victory, however, the Democrats kept control of the House of Representatives. They also wound up with thirty-four state governorships to the Republicans' sixteen (unchanged from before the election) and 65 percent of the state legislatures. They controlled the governorship, the upper house, and the lower house in eighteen states; the Republicans dominated only four states.[17]

Reagan's victory in 1980, his 1984 landslide, and Bush's win in 1988 might have suggested to some that the Democrats were doomed to extinction in presidential politics. Perhaps in an earlier time, when the existing parties were not so well institutionalized, that would have been so.

However, the Democratic party not only remains alive but thrives within most states in our federal system. The separation of state politics from national trends affords each party a chance to lick its wounds after a presidential election debacle and return to campaign optimistically in the next election, as Democrat Bill Clinton did in 1992.

Party Identification in America

The concept of **party identification** is one of the most important in political science. It signifies a voter's sense of psychological attachment to a party, which is not the same thing as voting for the party in any given election. Scholars measure party identification simply by asking, "Do you usually think of yourself as a Republican, a Democrat, an independent, or what?"[18] Voting is a behavior; identification is a state of mind. For example, millions of southerners voted for Eisenhower for president in 1952 and 1956 but continued to consider themselves Democrats. Across the nation, more people identify with one of the two major parties than reject a party attachment. The proportions of self-identified Republicans, Democrats, and independents (no party attachment) in the electorate since 1952 are shown in Figure 8.4. Three significant points stand out:

* The number of Republicans and Democrats combined far exceeds the independents in every year.

* The number of Democrats consistently exceeds that of Republicans.

* The number of Democrats has shrunk somewhat over time, to the benefit of both Republicans and independents.

Although party identification predisposes citizens to vote for their favorite party, other factors may convince them to choose the opposition candidate. If they vote against their party often enough, they may rethink their party identification and eventually switch. Apparently, this rethinking has gone on in the minds of many southern Democrats over time. In 1952, about 70 percent of white southerners thought of themselves as Democrats, and fewer than 20 percent thought of themselves as Republicans. By 1992, white southerners were only 34 percent Democratic—30 percent were Republican and 36 percent independent. Much of the nationwide growth in the proportion of Republicans and independents (and the parallel drop in the number of Democrats) stems from changes in party preferences among white southerners.

Who are the self-identified Democrats and Republicans in the electorate? Figure 8.5 shows party identification by social groups in 1992. The effects of socioeconomic factors are clear. People who have lower incomes and less education are more likely to think of themselves as Democrats than as Republicans. But the cultural factors of religion and race produce even sharper differences between the parties. Jews are strongly Democratic compared with other religious groups, and African-Americans are also overwhelmingly Democratic. Finally, American politics has a "gender gap": Women tend to be more Democratic than men.

The influence of region on party identification has changed over time. Because of the high proportion of blacks in the South, it is still the most heavily Democratic region, followed closely by the Northeast. The

POLITICS IN A CHANGING AMERICA 8.1

The Changing Relationship Between Age and Party Identification

The relationship between age and party identification has changed dramatically during the last forty years. We can visualize this change in comparing Gallup surveys taken in 1952 and 1992. Both graphs show the percentage of Democratic identifiers minus the percentage of Republican identifiers for 17 four-year age groupings—ranging from 18–21-year-olds to those 82 years of age and older. In 1952, the percentage of Democratic identifiers exceeded Republican identifiers by about fifteen points or more among younger and middle-aged voters, while the older age groups had far more Republicans than Democrats. By 1992, this pattern was reversed, with younger voters more likely to be Republicans and older voters (those who were young in 1952) retaining their Democratic sentiments. Note also that the overall relationship between age and party identification was substantially weaker in 1992 than in 1952.

• Source: Everett Carll Ladd, "Age, Generation, and Party ID," Public Perspective (July–August 1992), 15–16.

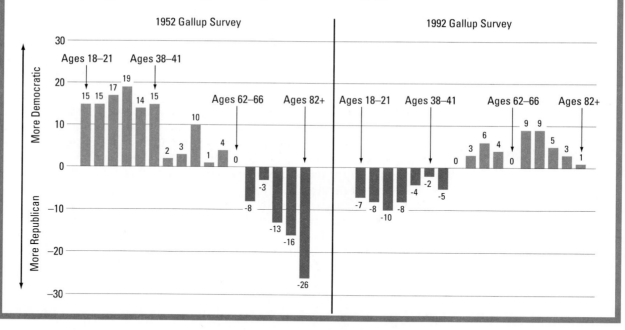

Midwest and West have proportionately more Republicans. Despite the erosion of Democratic strength in the South, we still see elements of Roosevelt's old Democratic coalition of socioeconomic groups. Perhaps the major change in that coalition has been the replacement of white European ethnic groups by blacks, attracted by the Democrats' backing of civil rights legislation in the 1960s.

Studies show that about half of all Americans adopt their parents' party. But it often takes time for party identification to develop. The youngest

FIGURE **8.4**

■ **Distribution of Party Identification, 1952–1992**

In every presidential election since 1952, voters across the nation have been asked, "Generally speaking, do you usually think of yourself as a Republican, a Democrat, an independent, or what?" Most voters readily admit to thinking of themselves as either Republicans or Democrats, but the proportion of those who think of themselves as independents has increased over time. The size of the Democratic party's majority has also shrunk. Nevertheless, most Americans today still identify with one of the two major parties, and Democrats still outnumber Republicans.

Sources: Warren E. Miller, Arthur H. Miller, and Edward J. Schneider, American National Election Studies Data Sourcebook, 1952–1978 *(Cambridge, Mass.: Harvard University Press, 1980, 1981), supplemented by data from the 1980 and 1984 National Election Survey conducted at the Center for Political Studies, University of Michigan, and distributed by the Inter-University Consortium for Political and Social Research. Data for 1988 come from the General Social Survey, provided by Dr. Tom W. Smith, National Opinion Research Center, and the 1992 data come from the September survey by Times Mirror Center for the People and the Press.*

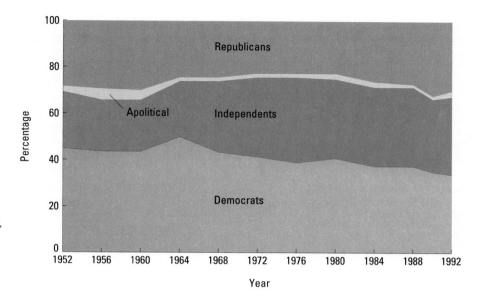

group of voters is most likely to be independent, but they also identified more than the rest of the population with Republicans during the Reagan years. The oldest group shows the most partisan commitment, reflecting the fact that citizens become more interested in politics as they mature. Also, the youngest and oldest age groups are most evenly divided between the parties. Some analysts believe this ratio of party identification among the young will persist as they age, contributing to further erosion of the Democratic majority and perhaps greater electoral dealignment.

Still, Americans tend to find their political niche and stay there.[19] The enduring party loyalty of American voters tends to structure the vote even before the election is held, even before the candidates are chosen. In Chapter 9 we will examine the extent to which party identification determines voting choice. But first we will look to see whether the Democratic and Republican parties have any significant differences.

PARTY IDEOLOGY AND ORGANIZATION

George Wallace, a disgruntled Democrat who ran for president in 1968 on the American Independent party ticket, complained that "there isn't a dime's worth of difference" between the Democrats and Republicans. Humorist Will Rogers said, "I am not a member of any organized political party—I am a Democrat." Wallace's comment was made in disgust, Rogers's in jest. Wallace was wrong; Rogers was close to being right. Here we will dispel the myth that the parties do not differ significantly on issues and explain how they are organized to coordinate the activities of party candidates and officials in government.

FIGURE 8.5 ■ Party Identification by Social Groups

Respondents to a 1992 survey were grouped by seven different social criteria—income, education, religion, race, sex, region, and age—and analyzed according to their self-descriptions as Democrats, independents, or Republicans. Region was found to have the least effect on party identification; religion and race had the greatest effects.

Source: 1992 National Election Survey, Center for Political Studies, University of Michigan.

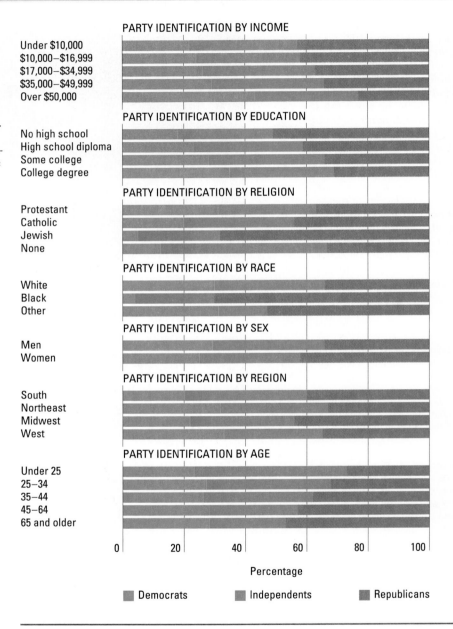

Differences in Party Ideology

George Wallace notwithstanding, there *is* more than a dime's worth of difference between the two parties. In fact, the difference amounts to many billions of dollars, the cost of the different government programs supported by each party. Democrats are more disposed to government spending to advance social welfare (and hence to promote equality) than are Republicans. And social welfare programs cost money, a lot of money.

Politics Makes Strange Bedfellows

During the 1992 presidential campaign, Mary Matalin served as campaign manager for George Bush, while James Carville—her "significant other"—was campaign manager for Bill Clinton. Although differing in their politics, they made America happy by getting married in New Orleans on November 25, 1993. Both Clinton and Bush attended the wedding, and news reports say that both occupants of the Oval Office embarrassed themselves in toasting the politically incorrect couple.

(You will see how much money in Chapters 18 and 19.) Republicans, on the other hand, are not averse to spending billions of dollars for the projects they consider important, among them, national defense. Ronald Reagan portrayed the Democrats as big spenders, but the defense buildup during his first administration alone cost the country more than $1 trillion—to be more precise, $1,007,900,000,000.[20] And Reagan's Strategic Defense Initiative (the "Star Wars" space defense), which Bush supported, cost many billions more, even by conservative estimates. The differences in spending patterns reflect some real philosophical differences between the parties.

Voters and Activists   One way to examine the differences is to compare party identifiers (those who identify themselves as Democrats or Republicans) with activists. As the middle portion of Figure 8.6 shows, 23 percent of those who identified themselves as Democrats in 1992 described themselves as conservatives, compared with more than 40 percent of those who identified themselves as Republicans. As we discussed in Chapter 5, few ordinary voters think about politics in strangely ideological terms, but party activists often do. The ideological gap between the parties looms even larger when we focus on the party activists on the left- and right-hand sides of the figure. Only 3 percent of the delegates to the 1992 Democratic convention considered themselves conservatives, compared with 70 percent of the delegates to the Republican convention.

Platforms: Freedom, Order, and Equality.   Surveys of voters' ideological orientations may merely reflect differences in personal self-image rather than actual differences in party ideology. For another test of party philosophies, we can look to the platforms adopted in party conventions. Although many people feel that party platforms don't matter very much,

| FIGURE **8.6** | ■ **Ideologies of Party Identifiers and Delegates in 1992** |

Contrary to what many people think, the Democratic and Republican parties differ substantially in their ideological centers of gravity. When citizens were asked to classify themselves on an ideological scale, more Republican than Democratic identifiers described themselves as conservative. When delegates to the parties' national conventions were asked to classify themselves, even greater ideological differences appeared.

Sources: *"Who Are the Delegates?"* Washington Post, *12 July 1992, p. A13; and "Delegates: Who They Are?"* Washington Post, *16 August 1992, p. A19.*

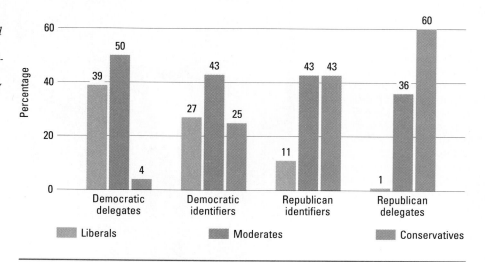

several scholars using different approaches have demonstrated that winning parties tend to carry out much of their platforms when in office.[21] One study matched the parties' platform statements from 1948 to 1985 against subsequent fund allocations in the federal budget. Spending priorities turned out to be quite closely linked to platform emphases of the winning party, especially if the party also controlled the presidency.[22]

Party platforms also matter a great deal to delegates at conventions. The wording of a platform plank often means the difference between victory and defeat for factions within the party (such as prochoice and pro-life groups concerning the party's position on abortion). Delegates fight not only over ideas but also over words and even punctuation in a plank. Platforms, then, give a good indication of policy preferences among party activists. A study of activists in both parties during the 1980s, for example, indicated that "the Reagan revolution" polarized their attitudes, increasing the conservatism of Republicans and causing Democrats to take more liberal positions on defense spending, abortion, and affirmative action.[23]

The platforms adopted by the Democratic and Republican conventions in 1992 were strikingly different in style and substance. The Democrats, who met first, produced a document of only about nine thousand words that reflected Clinton's moderate philosophy and a shift toward the center of the ideological spectrum compared with previous Democratic platforms. Whereas the party's 1988 platform had begun, "We believe that all Americans have a fundamental right to economic justice"—a phrase usually interpreted as a commitment to equality—the 1992 platform was "about restoring America's economic greatness." Whereas four years earlier the party had pledged "equal access" for all citizens to education, government services, employment, housing, business, and so on, the Democrats now promised only "opportunity" that comes from economic growth: "Our party's first priority is opportunity—broad-based, non-inflationary economic growth and the opportunity that flows from it.

Democrats in 1992 hold nothing more important for America than an economy that offers growth and jobs for all."

Meanwhile, the Republicans moved further right than perhaps President Bush wanted in their lengthy platform of 35,000 words. The Republicans quoted Lincoln that "government ought not to interfere" in things that people can individually do well for themselves, and it offered other expressions of their traditional philosophy: "Republicans have always believed that economic prosperity comes from individual enterprise, not government programs. . . . We believe that individual freedom, hard work and personal responsibility—basic to free society—are also basic to effective government."

The differences between the two 1992 party platforms emerged more clearly in their specific proposals. The Democrats supported a woman's right to an abortion without exception, whereas the Republicans would outlaw abortion through a constitutional amendment. The Democrats favored gun control, whereas the Republicans opposed it. Democrats favored redistributing funds for public education to equalize funding in different districts; Republicans favored using government funds for tuition subsidies for private schools. Democrats defended homosexual rights; Republicans opposed treating homosexuals as a protected minority. As for medical care, the Democrats favored guarantees of universal access to health care; the Republicans opposed more government control.

These statements of values clearly distinguish the two parties on the values of freedom, order, and equality that underlie the dilemmas of government discussed in Chapter 1. According to the typology presented the Republicans' 1992 platform positions on abortion, homosexual rights, education, and medical care places their party firmly in the conservative category, whereas the Democrats' platform puts their party squarely into the liberal category—despite downplaying the rhetoric of equality.

Different but Similar   The Democrats and the Republicans have very different ideological orientations. Yet, many observers claim that the parties are really quite similar in ideology when compared with other countries' parties. Specifically, both support capitalism; that is, both reject government ownership of the means of production (see Chapter 1). A study of Democratic and Republican positions on four economic issues—ownership of the means of production, the government's role in economic planning, redistribution of wealth, and providing for social welfare—found that Republicans consistently oppose increased government activity. Comparing these findings with data on party positions in thirteen other democracies, the researchers found about as much difference between the American parties as is usual within two-party systems. However, both American parties tend to be more conservative on economic matters than parties in other two-party systems. In most multiparty systems, the presence of strong socialist and antisocialist parties ensures a much greater range of ideological choice than we find in our system, despite genuine differences between the Democrats and Republicans.[24]

National Party Organization

Most political observers would agree with Will Rogers's description of the Democrats as an unorganized political party. It used to apply to the

Republicans, too, but this has changed since the 1970's—at least at the national level. Bear in mind the distinction between levels of party structure. American parties parallel our federal system: They have separate national and state organizations (and virtually separate local organizations, in many cases).

At the national level, each major party has four main organizational components:

- *National convention.* Every four years, each party assembles thousands of delegates from the states and U.S. territories (such as Puerto Rico and Guam) in a national convention for the purpose of nominating a candidate for president. This presidential nominating convention is also the supreme governing body of the party. It determines party policy through the platform, formulates rules to govern party operations, and designates a national committee, which is empowered to govern the party until the next convention.

- *National committee.* The **national committee,** which governs each party between conventions, is composed of party officials representing the states and territories, including the chairpersons of their party organizations. In 1994, the Republican National Committee (RNC) had 155 members, consisting of the national committeeman, national committeewoman, and a chairperson from each state and from the District of Columbia, Guam, Puerto Rico, and the Virgin Islands. The Democratic National Committee (DNC) had 426 members, including, in addition to the national committee members and party chairs, other members representing auxiliary organizations.[25] The chairperson of each national committee is chosen by the party's presidential nominee, then duly elected by the committee. If the nominee loses the election, the national committee usually replaces the nominee's chairperson.

- *Congressional party conferences.* At the beginning of each session of Congress, the Republicans and Democrats in each chamber hold separate **party conferences** (the House Democrats call theirs a *caucus*) to select their party leaders and to decide committee assignments. (Bernard Sanders, the lone independent member of Congress in 1991, asked to join the House Democratic Caucus but was excluded.) The party conferences deal only with congressional matters and have no structural relationship to each other and no relationship to the national committee.

- *Congressional campaign committees.* Democrats and Republicans in the House and Senate also maintain separate **congressional campaign committees,** each of which raises its own funds to support its candidates in congressional elections. The separation of these organizations from the national committee tells us that the national party structure is loose; the national committee seldom gets involved with the election of any individual member of Congress. Moreover, even the congressional campaign organizations merely supplement the funds that senators and representatives raise on their own to win reelection.

It is tempting to think of the national party chairperson as sitting at the top of a hierarchical party organization that not only controls its members in Congress but issues orders to the state committees and down to the local level. Few ideas could be more wrong.[26] The national committee has virtually no voice in congressional activity, and it exercises very little direction of and even less control over state and local campaigns. In fact, the RNC and DNC do not even really direct or control presidential campaigns. Candidates hire their own campaign staffs during the party primaries to win delegates who will support them for nomination at the party conventions. Successful nominees then keep their winning staffs to contest the general election. The main role of a national committee is to support its candidate's personal campaign staff in the effort to win.

In this light, the national committees appear to be relatively useless organizations. For many years, their role was essentially limited to planning for the next party convention. The committee would select the site, invite the state parties to attend, plan the program, and so on. In the 1970s, however, the roles of the DNC and RNC began to expand—but in different ways.

In response to street rioting by Vietnam War protesters during the 1968 Democratic convention, the Democrats created a special commission to introduce party reforms. In an attempt to open the party to broader participation and to weaken local party leaders' control over the process of selecting delegates, the McGovern-Fraser Commission formulated new guidelines for the selection of delegates to the 1972 Democratic convention. Included in these guidelines was the requirement that state parties take "affirmative action"—that is, see to it that their delegates included women, minorities, and young people "in reasonable relationship to the group's presence in the population of the state."[27] Many state parties rebelled at the imposition of quotas by sex, race, and age. But the DNC threatened to deny seating to any state delegation at the 1972 convention that did not comply with the guidelines.

Never before had a national party committee imposed such rules on a state party organization, but it worked. Even the powerful Illinois delegation, led by Chicago mayor Richard Daley, was denied seating at the convention for violating the guidelines. And overall, women, blacks, and young voters gained dramatically in representation at the 1972 Democratic convention. Although the party has since reduced its emphasis on quotas, the gains by women and blacks have held up fairly well. The representation of young people, however, has declined substantially (as the young activists grew older). Many "regular" Democrats feared that the political activists who had taken over the 1972 convention would cripple the party organization. But most challengers were socialized into the party within a decade and became more open to compromise and more understanding of organizational needs to combat developments within the Republican party.[28]

While the Democrats were busy with *procedural* reforms, the Republicans were making *organizational* reforms.[29] The RNC did little to open up its delegate selection process; Republicans were not inclined to impose quotas on state parties through their national committee. Instead, the RNC strengthened its fund-raising, research, and service roles. Republicans acquired their own building and their own computer system, and in 1976 they hired the first full-time chairperson in the history of either national party. (Until then, the chairperson had worked part time.) As RNC chairman, William Brock (formerly a senator from Tennessee) expanded the party's staff, launched new publications, held seminars, conducted election analyses, and advised candidates—things that national party committees in other countries had been doing for years.

The vast difference between the Democratic and Republican approaches to reforming the national committees shows in the funds raised by the DNC and RNC during election campaigns. During Brock's tenure as chairman of the RNC, the Republicans raised three to four times as much money as the Democrats. Although the margin has narrowed, Republican party fund-raising efforts are still superior. In 1992, for example, the Republicans' national, senatorial, and congressional committees raised $192 million, compared with $104 million for the comparable Democratic committees.[30] Although Republicans have traditionally raised more campaign money than Democrats, they no longer rely on a relatively few wealthy contributors. In fact, the Republicans received more of their funds in small contributions (of less than $100), mainly through direct-mail solicitation. In short, the RNC has recently been raising far more money than the DNC from many more citizens, in a long-term commitment to improving its organizational services. Its efforts have also made a difference at the level of state party organizations.

State and Local Party Organizations

At one time, both major parties were firmly anchored in powerful state and local party organizations. Big-city party organizations, such as the Democrats' Tammany Hall in New York City and the Cook County Central Committee in Chicago, were called *party machines*. A **party machine** was a centralized organization that dominated local politics by controlling elections—sometimes by illegal means, often by providing jobs and social services to urban workers in return for their votes. These patronage and social service functions of party machines were undercut as government expanded its role in providing unemployment compensation, aid to families with dependent children, and other social services. As a result, most local party organizations lost their ability to deliver votes and thus to determine the outcome of elections. However, machines are still strong in certain areas. In Nassau County, New York, for example, suburban Republicans have shown that they can run a machine as well as urban Democrats.[31]

The state organizations of both parties vary widely in strength, but Republican state organizations tend to be stronger than Democratic organizations. The Republicans are likely to have bigger budgets and staffs and tend to recruit candidates for more offices. Republicans also differ from Democrats in the help that the national organization gives to state organizations. A survey of forty Republican and thirty Democratic state chairpersons revealed that 70 percent of the Republican organizations received financial aid from the national organization, compared with only 7 percent of the Democratic organizations.[32] Republicans at the state level also received more candidate training, poll data and research, and campaign instruction from the national organization. The only service that the DNC supplied more often than the RNC was "rule enforcement"—enforcing guidelines for selecting convention delegates.[33] Otherwise, the dominant pattern in both parties was for the national organization not to intervene in state activities unless asked and then only to supply services. However, national-state-county linkages may actually be growing stronger.[34] Indeed, in a reversal of form in 1992, the DNC transferred more money to state party committees than the RNC, which continued to provide services to state and local parties and candidates.[35]

Decentralized but Growing Stronger

If strong party organization means that control is vested in the national headquarters, both the Democrats and Republicans are, in Will Rogers's phrase, unorganized political parties. Far from exercising centralized power from Washington, American political parties are among the most decentralized parties in the world.[36] Not even the president can count on loyalty from the members or even the officers of his party. Consider the problem that confronted President Clinton in his first term in office. Clinton was pushing hard in the House of Representatives for passage of the North American Free Trade Agreement (NAFTA), only to be opposed by both the Democratic majority leader, Richard Gephardt, and the party whip, David Bonior—whose chief job was to mobilize party votes. The House approved NAFTA in late 1993 but only because Republicans voted for it overwhelmingly. Most Democrats rejected it. President Bush experienced a similar situation in 1990, when the Republican party whip, Newt Gingrich, opposed Bush's carefully crafted budget package to deal with the deficit. Although Bush lost his key vote, Gingrich easily won reelection as party whip in 1991.

The absence of centralized power has always been the most distinguishing characteristic of American political parties. Only a few years ago, scholars wrote that these were weak parties in further decline.[37] But there is evidence that our political parties today are enjoying a period of resurgence. As Figure 8.7 shows, more voters see genuine differences between the parties in election years now than during the previous four decades. And more votes in Congress are being decided along party lines—despite the Gephardt/Bonior and Gingrich mutinies. (See Chapter 11 for a discussion of the rise of party voting in Congress since the 1970s.) In fact, a specialist in congressional politics has concluded, "When compared to its predecessors of the last half-century, the current majority party leadership is more involved and more decisive in organizing the party and the chamber, setting the policy agenda, shaping legislation, and determining legislative outcomes."[38] However, the American parties have traditionally been so weak that these positive trends have not altered their basic character. American political parties are still so organizationally diffuse and decentralized that they raise questions about how well they link voters to government.

THE MODEL OF RESPONSIBLE PARTY GOVERNMENT	According to the majoritarian model of democracy, parties are essential to making the government responsive to public opinion. In fact, the ideal role of parties in majoritarian democracy has been formalized in the four principles of **responsible party government:**[39]

1. Parties should present clear and coherent programs to voters.

2. Voters should choose candidates on the basis of party programs.

3. The winning party should carry out its program once in office.

FIGURE 8.7   ■ Evidence of Party Resurgence

Contrary to the comment by former Alabama governor George Wallace, that there isn't "a dime's worth of difference" between Democrats and Republicans, most voters have consistently seen differences between the two major parties. In every election year since 1952, a national survey has asked which party would do a better job of "keeping the country prosperous" and "keeping the U.S. out of war." Figure 8.7a shows that most respondents have always seen differences between the parties on both issues, particularly on prosperity. In the last three elections, more voters have perceived party differences on these issues than at any time since the surveys began. Figure 8.7b, which subtracts the percentage that favored the Republican party on each issue from the percentage that favored the Democrats, shows that the public rather consistently thought the Democrats were better at promoting prosperity but the Republicans were better at keeping peace.

Source: Data are reported in Gallup Poll Monthly, September 1990, p. 32, and October 1992, p. 27.

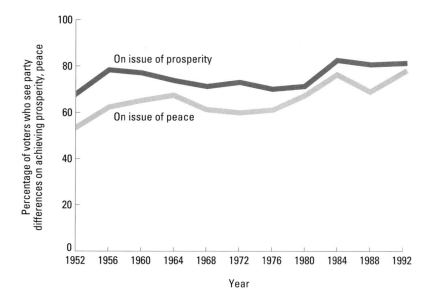

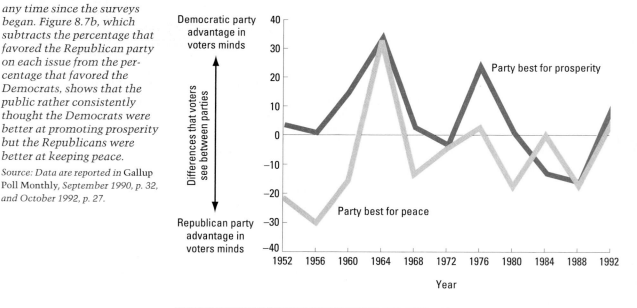

4. Voters should hold the governing party responsible at the next election for executing its program.

How well do these principles describe American politics? You've learned that the Democratic and Republican platforms are different and that they are much more ideologically consistent than many people believe. So the first principle is being met fairly well. To a lesser extent, so is the third principle: Once parties gain power, they usually try to do what they say they would do. From the standpoint of democratic theory, the real question involves principles 2 and 4: Do voters really pay attention to party platforms and policies when they cast their ballots? If so, do voters hold the governing party responsible at the next election for delivering, or failing to deliver, on its pledges? To answer these questions, we must consider in greater detail the parties' role in nominating candidates and in structuring the voters' choices in elections. At the conclusion of Chapter 9, we will return to evaluating the role of political parties in democratic government.

SUMMARY

Political parties perform four important functions in a political system: nominating candidates, structuring the voting choice, proposing alternative government programs, and coordinating the activities of government officials. Political parties have been performing these functions longer in the United States than in any other country. The Democratic party, founded in 1828, is the world's oldest political party. When the Republican party emerged as a major party after the 1856 election, our present two-party system emerged—the oldest party system in the world.

America's two-party system has experienced three critical elections, each of which realigned the electorate for years and affected the party balance in government. The election of 1860 established the Republicans as the major party in the North and the Democrats as the dominant party in the South. Nationally, the two parties remained roughly balanced in Congress until the critical election of 1896. This election strengthened the link between the Republican party and business interests in the heavily populated Northeast and Midwest and produced a surge in voter support that made the Republicans the majority party nationally for more than three decades. The Great Depression produced the conditions that transformed the Democrats into the majority party in the critical election of 1932, giving them almost uninterrupted control of Congress since then.

Minor parties have not enjoyed much electoral success in America, although they have contributed ideas to the Democratic and Republican platforms. The two-party system is perpetuated in the United States by the nature of our electoral system and the political socialization process, which results in most Americans' identifying with either the Democratic or the Republican party. The federal system of government has also helped the Democrats and Republicans survive defeats at the national level by sustaining them with electoral victories at the state level. The pattern of party identification has been changing in recent years: As more people are becoming independents and Republicans, the number of Democratic identifiers is dropping. Nonetheless, Democrats consistently outnumber Republicans, and together both far outnumber the independents.

The two major parties differ in their ideological orientations. Democratic identifiers and activists are more likely to describe themselves as liberal; Republican identifiers and activists tend to be conservative. The party platforms also reveal substantive ideological differences. The 1992 Democratic party platform showed a more liberal orientation by stressing equality over freedom; the Republican platform was more conservative, concentrating on freedom but also emphasizing the importance of restoring social order. Organizationally, the Republicans have recently become the stronger party at both national and state levels, and both parties are showing signs of resurgence. Nevertheless, both parties are very decentralized compared with parties in other countries.

In keeping with the model of responsible party government, American parties do tend to enact their platform positions into government policy if elected to power. But we must see in Chapter 9 whether citizens pay much attention to parties and policies when casting their votes. If not, American parties do not fulfill the majoritarian model of democratic theory.

Key Terms

political party
nomination
political system
electoral college
caucus
national convention
party platform
critical election
electoral realignment
two-party system
majority party
minority party
electoral dealignment
bolter party

farmer-labor party
party of ideological protest
single-issue party
majority representation
proportional representation
party identification
national committee
party conference
congressional campaign
  committee
party machine
responsible party
  government

Selected Readings

Beck, Paul Allen, and Frank J. Sorauf. *Party Politics in America.* New York: HarperCollins, 1992. The seventh edition of a comprehensive textbook on political parties.

Goldman, Ralph M. *The National Party Chairmen and Committees: Factionalism at the Top.* Armonk, N.Y.: M. E. Sharpe, 1990. A sweeping historical survey from the origins of both parties to the 1960s.

Jewell, Malcolm E., and David M. Olson. *Political Parties and Elections in American States.* 3d ed. Chicago: Dorsey Press, 1988. Compares the political party and electoral systems in the fifty states, drawing on generalizations backed by empirical research and years of experience.

Maisel, L. Sandy, ed. *The Parties Respond: Changes in the American Party System.* 2nd ed. Boulder, Col.: Westview, 1994. Essays on state party organization, parties in the electoral arena, the relationship between parties and voters, and parties in government.

Milkis, Sidney M. *The President and the Parties: The Transformation of the American Party System Since the New Deal.* New York: Oxford University Press, 1993. Argues that the modern conception of presidential power has changed party politics by making parties less important in government.

Rosenstone, Steven J., Roy L. Behr, and Edward H. Lazarus. *Third Parties in America: Citizen Response to Major Party Failure.* Princeton, N.J.: Princeton University Press, 1984. The authors not only provide an excellent review of the history of third-party movements in American politics but also analyze the factors that lead third-party voters and candidates to abandon the two major parties. They conclude that third-party efforts improve the performance of the party system.

Schattschneider, E. E. *Party Government.* New York: Holt, 1942. A clear and powerful argument for the central role of political parties in a democracy according to the model of responsible party government; a classic book in political science.

White, John Kenneth, and Jerome M. Mileur, eds. *Challenges to Party Government.* Carbondale, Ill.: Southern Illinois University Press, 1992. Examines the prospects and potential of party government fifty years after Schattschneider published his seminal study.

Sorauf, Frank J. *Money in American Elections.* Glenview, Ill.: Scott, Foresman, 1988. Surveys receipts and expenditures in presidential and congressional campaigns, including financing by individuals, political action committees, parties, and government.

Wattenberg, Martin P. *The Decline of American Political Parties, 1952–1992.* Cambridge, Mass.: Harvard University Press, 1994. Argues that the American electorate has lessened its attachment to parties because people now believe that candidates, not parties, solve governmental problems.

9 Nominations, Elections, and Campaigns

AS EARLY AS NOVEMBER 23, 1991—months before convention delegate selection began—the media settled on Bill Clinton as the favorite among five candidates seeking the Democratic nomination for president. Clinton had just impressed an audience of state Democratic chairpersons in Illinois, and national reporters began to describe him as the frontrunner.[1] Less than two months later, "Before a vote was cast, and even though polls showed that more than half of all rank-and-file Democrats didn't know who he was," one writer observed, "Clinton was hailed on the covers of *Time,* the *New Republic,* and *New York* magazine."[2] The conventional media were beginning to define the presidential campaign for the American people.

But by January 23, the *unconventional* media started to unravel the plan. The *Star,* a supermarket tabloid, published a story it purchased from Gennifer Flowers, an Arkansas state employee who claimed she had carried on an affair for years with Governor Bill Clinton. Most of the conventional national media disdained the story, but reporters pounced on Clinton as he campaigned in New Hampshire and asked him pointed questions. A reporter observed that most of the attention came from "the counterelite 'new news' media—local TV newscasts, radio and cable call-in shows, newspaper tabloids, and tabloid TV shows like 'A Current Affair' and 'Hard Copy.' "[3] Clinton's presidential campaign seemed destined to collapse as Gary Hart's did in 1988, when reporters from the *Miami Herald* exposed his liaison with model Donna Rice.

The *Star* story appeared on a Thursday. By Sunday, Clinton had decided to appear with his wife on "60 Minutes," denying Flowers's story but acknowledging that he and Hillary Clinton had survived some marital problems. Once he had appeared on prime time to discuss the story, it became "legitimate," and the journalistic dam broke. The next day hundreds of reporters covered a press conference organized by the *Star* for its cover girl, Flowers. One questioner even asked her, "Did Governor Clinton use a condom?"[4] From that point on, the "character issue" began to plague Bill Clinton, who found it difficult to turn the discussion to substantive issues. Although Clinton continued to win delegates and outpace the other candidates, his electability in November was in doubt.

A turning point in Clinton's campaign came in early April, just before the important New York primary, when he appeared on Phil Donahue's popular daytime talk show. Donahue badgered Clinton with questions about his alleged affairs, until Clinton had had enough and told him, "We're going to sit here a long time in silence, Phil. I'm not going to answer any more of these questions. I've answered them until I'm blue in the

Flowers Show and Tell
Gennifer Flowers appears at a press conference organized by the Star, *the supermarket tabloid that bought and published her story claiming a sustained affair with Bill Clinton while he was governor of Arkansas.*

face. You are responsible for the cynicism in this country. You don't want to talk about the real issues."[5]

Donahue's studio audience had had enough, too, and roundly applauded Clinton's position. One woman rose to address Donahue: "Given the pathetic state of most of the United States at this point, I can't believe you spent half an hour of airtime attacking this man's character. I'm not even a Clinton supporter, but I think this is ridiculous."[6]

After that exchange, the character issue, although it never went away, was no longer the critical issue in Clinton's campaign.[7] After winning the New York primary, he had 30 percent of the delegates he needed for the nomination.[8] By the end of the final round of primaries on June 2, Clinton had accumulated nearly 60 percent of the delegates, and his nomination at the Democratic National convention in July was merely a formality.

The story of Clinton's successful campaign for the presidency illustrates two points about contemporary campaigns for election in the United States. First, election campaigns, particularly for the presidency, are largely conducted through the mass media, especially television. Second, political parties have little control over election campaigns, which are typically conducted by ad hoc organizations built by the candidates. A candidate's campaign organization handles the candidate's media appearances and television advertising, which—in turn—are widely believed to influence the outcome of elections for major offices.[9]

In this chapter, we consider how election campaigns have changed over time, how candidates get nominated in the United States, what factors are important in election campaigns, and why voters choose one candidate over another. We also address these important questions: What roles do political parties play today in campaigns and nominations? Do election campaigns function more to inform or to confuse voters? How important is money in conducting a winning election campaign? What are the roles of party identification, issues, and candidate attributes in influencing voters' choices and thus election outcomes? How do campaigns, elections, and parties fit into the majoritarian and pluralist models of democracy?

THE EVOLUTION OF CAMPAIGNING

Voting in free elections to choose leaders is the primary way that citizens control government. As discussed in Chapter 8, political parties help structure the voting choice by reducing the number of candidates on the ballot to those who have a realistic chance of winning or who offer distinctive policies. An **election campaign** is an organized effort to persuade voters to choose one candidate over others competing for the same office. An effective campaign requires sufficient resources to acquire and analyze information about voters' interests, to develop a strategy and matching tactics for appealing to these interests, to deliver the candidate's message to the voters, and to get them to cast their ballots.[10]

Historically, political parties have conducted all phases of the election campaign. As recently as the 1950s, just forty years ago, state and local party organizations "felt the pulse" of their rank-and-file members to learn what was important to voters. They chose the candidates and then lined up leading officials to support the candidates and to ensure big crowds at campaign rallies. They also prepared buttons, banners, and newspaper advertisements that touted their candidates, proudly named under the prominent label of the party. Finally, candidates relied heavily on the local precinct and county party organizations to contact voters before elections, to mention their names, to extol their virtues, and—most important—to make sure they voted and voted correctly.

Today, candidates seldom rely much on political parties. How do candidates learn about voters' interests today? By contracting for public opinion polls, not by asking the party. How do candidates plan their campaign strategy and tactics now? By hiring political consultants to devise clever "soundbites" (brief, catchy phrases) that catch voters' attention through television footage, not by consulting party headquarters. How do candidates deliver their messages to voters? By conducting media campaigns, not by counting on party leaders to canvass the neighborhoods.

Increasingly, election campaigns have evolved from being party centered to being candidate centered.[11] This is not to say that political parties no longer have a role to play in campaigns, for they do. As noted in Chapter 8, the Democrats now exercise more control over the delegate selection process than they did before 1972. Since 1976, the Republicans have greatly expanded their national organization and fund-raising capacity. But whereas parties virtually ran election campaigns in the past, now they exist mainly to support candidate-centered campaigns by providing services or funds to party candidates. Nevertheless, we will see that the party label is usually a candidate's prime attribute at election time.

Perhaps the most important change in electoral campaigning is that candidates don't campaign just to get elected anymore. It is now necessary to campaign for *nomination* as well. As we saw in Chapter 8, nominating candidates to run for office under the party label is one of the main functions of political parties. Party organizations once controlled that func-

The Dixie Two-Step

When Bill Clinton, the demo-cratic nominee for president, chose fellow southerner, Al Gore, to be his vice-presiden-tial running mate, he fash-ioned an unusual ticket. With their young wives, Hillary and Tipper, Bill and Al (the first pair of candidates born after World War II) pitched their campaign to baby boomers. Despite its lack of regional balance, the Democratic ticket ran well across the nation, carrying 33 states with 370 electoral votes and actu-ally doing better in the North than in the South.

tion. Even Abraham Lincoln served only one term in the House before the party transferred the nomination to someone else.[12] For most important offices today, however, candidates are no longer nominated *by* the party organization but *within* the party. That is, party leaders seldom choose candidates; they merely organize and supervise the election process by which party *voters* choose the candidates. Because almost all aspiring candidates must first win a primary election to gain the party's nomina-tion, those who would campaign for election must first campaign for the nomination.

NOMINATIONS

The distinguishing feature of the nomination process in American party politics is that it usually involves an election by party voters. National party leaders do not choose the party's nominee for president or even the party's candidates for House and Senate seats. Virtually no other political parties in the world nominate candidates to the national legislature through party elections.[13] In more than half the world's parties, local party leaders choose legislative candidates—and the national party organization must usually approve even these choices. In fact, in more than one-third of the world's parties, the national organization itself selects the candidates, as described in Compared with What? 9.1.[14]

Democrats and Republicans nominate their candidates for national and statewide offices in varying ways across the country, because each state is entitled to make its own laws governing the nomination process. (This is significant in itself, for political parties in most other countries are largely free of laws stating how they must select their candidates.) We can classify nomination practices by the types of party elections and by the level of of-fice sought.

COMPARED WITH WHAT? 9.1

Choosing Legislative Candidates

In the United States, we believe that primary elections are the normal way to nominate candidates. Compared with the practice in other countries, however, our approach is not "normal" at all. Most competitive political parties in Western democracies exercise far more control over who is allowed to represent the party in elections. As this graph shows, the most common method of selection, used by thirty-two parties in nine European countries, is to have a group of party activists interview the candidates and then select among them in committees or conventions. (Some parties use a combination of methods and are thus counted twice in the tabulation.) A few parties allow all enrolled party members to hear the candidates and then vote on them in party meetings, but more parties exercise even greater control, having national executive committees choose the candidates. This is evidence of how weak our parties are compared with those elsewhere.

Source: Data are tabulated from Table 11.1 in Michael Gallagher, "Conclusion," on Candidate Selection in Comparative Perspective: The Secret Garden of Politics, Michael Gallagher and Michael Marsh, eds., (London: Sage, 1988), p. 237.

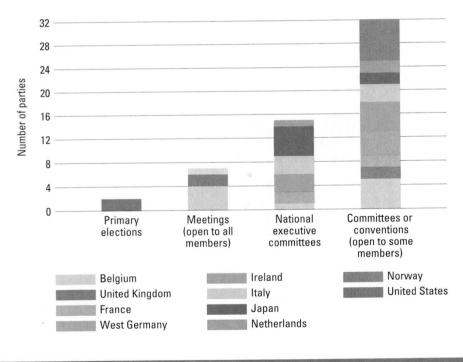

Nomination for Congress and State Offices

In the United States, most aspiring candidates for major offices are nominated through a **primary election,** a preliminary election conducted within the party to select its candidates. Thirty-seven states use primary elections alone to nominate candidates for all state and national offices, and primaries figure in the nomination process in the other states.[15] The nomination process, then, is highly decentralized, resting on the decisions of thousands, perhaps millions, of the party rank and file who participate in primary elections.

In both parties, only about half of the regular party voters (about one-quarter of the voting-age population) bother to vote in a given primary, although the proportion varies greatly by state and contest.[16] Early research on primary elections concluded that Republicans who voted in their primaries were more conservative than those who did not, while Democratic primary voters were more liberal than other Democrats. This finding led to the belief that primary voters tend to nominate candidates who are more ideologically extreme than the party as a whole preferred. But more recent research, which matches primary voters against those who missed the primary but voted in the general election, reports little evidence that primary voters are unrepresentative of the ideological orientations of other party voters.[17]

States hold different types of primary elections for state and congressional offices. The most common type (used by about forty states) is the **closed primary,** in which voters must declare their party affiliation before they are given the primary ballot, which lists the party's potential nominees. A handful of states uses the **open primary,** in which voters may choose either party's ballot to take into the polling booth. In a **blanket primary,** currently used in only two or three states, voters receive a ballot listing both parties' potential nominees and can vote in both parties' primaries.

Most scholars believe that closed primaries strengthen party organization, whereas open primaries (and certainly blanket primaries) weaken it by allowing voters to "cross over" to elect candidates that might embarrass the opposition party. But the differences among types of primaries are much less important than the fact that the parties hold elections to choose their candidates. Placing the nomination of party candidates in the hands of voters rather than party leaders is a key factor in the decentralization of power in American parties, which contributes more to pluralist than majoritarian democracy.

Nomination for President

The decentralized nature of American parties is readily apparent in campaigns for the party nomination for president. Delegates attending national conventions held the summer before the presidential election in November nominate presidential candidates. In the past, they chose the nominee right at the convention, sometimes after repeated balloting over several candidates who divided the vote and kept anyone from getting the majority needed to win the nomination. In 1920, for example, the Republican convention deadlocked over two leading candidates after nine ballots. Party leaders then met in the storied smoke-filled room and compromised on Warren G. Harding, who won on the tenth. Harding was not among the leading candidates and had won only one primary (in his native Ohio). The last time that either party needed more than one ballot to nominate its presidential candidate was in 1952, when the Democrats took three ballots to nominate Adlai E. Stevenson. Although the Republicans

FEATURE 9.1

■ Changes in the Presidential Nomination Process

 When President Lyndon Johnson abruptly announced in late March 1968 that he would not run for reelection, the door opened for his vice president, Hubert Humphrey. Humphrey felt it was too late to campaign in primaries against other candidates already in the race; nevertheless, he commanded enough support among party leaders to win the Democratic nomination. The stormy protests outside the party's convention against the "inside politics" of his nomination led to major changes in the way both parties have nominated their presidential candidates since 1968.

Presidential Nominating Process

Before 1968	***Since 1968***
Party Dominated	**Candidate Dominated**
The nomination decision is largely in the hands of party leaders. Candidates win by enlisting the support of state and local party machines.	Campaigns are independent of party establishments. Endorsements by party leaders have little effect on nomination choice.
Few Primaries	**Many Primaries**
Most delegates are selected by state party establishments, with little or no public participation. Some primaries are held, but their results do not necessarily determine the nominee. Primaries are used to indicate candidate's "electability."	Most delegates are selected by popular primaries and caucuses. Nominations are determined largely by voters' decisions at these contests.
Short Campaigns	**Long Campaigns**
Candidates usually begin their public campaign early in the election year.	Candidates begin laying groundwork for campaigns three or four years before the election. Candidates who are not well organized at least eighteen months before the election may have little chance of winning.

took only one ballot that year to nominate Dwight Eisenhower, his nomination was contested by Senator Robert Taft, and Eisenhower won his nomination on the floor of the convention.

According to a leading scholar of convention politics, 1952 was the last year that each party constructed "a nominating majority inside the convention hall."[18] The Democratic convention in 1960 and the Republican convention in 1964 also made genuine choices, but otherwise the selection now is all but official before the convention begins. Since 1968, both parties' nominating conventions have simply ratified the results of the complex process for selecting the convention delegates, as described in Feature 9.1.

Selecting Convention Delegates.   No national legislation specifies how state parties must select delegates to their national conventions. Instead, state legislatures have enacted a bewildering variety of procedures that often differ for Democrats and Republicans in the same state. The most important distinction in delegate selection is between the presidential primary and the local caucus.

A **presidential primary** is a special primary to select delegates to attend the party's national nominating convention. In *presidential preference*

Before 1968

Easy Money

Candidates frequently raise large amounts of money quickly by tapping a handful of wealthy contributors. No federal limits on spending by candidates.

Limited Media Coverage

Campaigns are followed by print journalists and, in later years, by television. But press coverage of campaigns is not intensive and generally does not play a major role in influencing the process.

Late Decisions

Events early in the campaign year, such as the New Hampshire primary, are not decisive. States that pick delegates late in the year, such as California, frequently are important in selecting the nominee. Many states enter the convention without making final decisions about candidates.

Open Conventions

National party conventions sometimes begin with the nomination still undecided. The outcome is determined by maneuvering and negotiations among party factions, often stretching over multiple ballots.

Since 1968

Difficult Fund Raising

Campaign contributions are limited to $1,000 per person, so candidates must work endlessly to raise money from thousands of small contributors. PAC contributions are important in primaries. Campaign spending is limited by law, both nationally and for individual states.

Media Focused

Campaigns are covered intensively by the media, particularly television. Media treatment of candidates plays a crucial role in determining the nominee.

"Front Loaded"

Early events, such as the Iowa caucuses and New Hampshire primary, are important. The nomination may be decided even before many major states vote. Early victories attract great media attention, which gives winners free publicity and greater fund-raiser ability.

Closed Conventions

The nominee is determined before the convention, which does little more than ratify the decision made in primaries and caucuses. Convention activities focus on creating a favorable media image of the candidate for the general election campaign.

• *Source: Michael Nelson (ed.),* Congressional Quarterly's Guide to the Presidency *(Washington, D.C.: Congressional Quarterly, Inc., 1989), p. 201. Copyright © 1989 by Congressional Quarterly, Inc. Used by permission.*

primaries (used in all Democratic primaries and in thirty-four Republican primaries in 1992), party supporters vote directly for the person they favor as their party's nominee for president, and the primary candidates win delegates according to a variety of formulas. In *delegate selection primaries* (used only by Republicans in five states in 1992), party voters directly elect convention delegates, who may or may not have declared for a presidential candidate.

The **local caucus** method of delegate selection has several stages. It begins with local meetings, or caucuses, of party supporters to choose delegates to attend a larger subsequent meeting, usually at the county level. Most delegates selected in the local caucuses openly back one of the presidential candidates. The county meetings, in turn, select delegates to a higher level. The process culminates in a state convention, which actually selects the delegates to the national convention. About fifteen states used the caucus process in 1992 (a few states combined caucuses with primaries), and Democrats used caucuses more than Republicans did.

Primary elections (which were stimulated by the Progressive movement discussed in Chapter 7) were first used to select delegates to nominating conventions in 1912. Figure 9.1 shows the growth of presidential primaries over time and the increase in the proportion of convention

FIGURE 9.1   ■ **Growth of Primaries for Delegate Selection**

Progressive forces early in this century championed the use of primary elections to select delegates to national conventions to nominate the party's presidential candidate. By 1916, nearly half the states used primaries to select more than half the delegates to both party conventions. As progressivism waned in the 1930s, however, so did presidential primaries. They regained popularity during the reform movement of the 1970s, which sought to broaden participation in the nominating process. In 1992, approximately 70 percent of the Democratic convention delegates and 80 percent of the Republican delegates came from primary states.

Source: Harold W. Stanley and Richard G. Niemi, Vital Statistics on American Politics, second edition (Washington, D.C.: C Q Press, 1990), p. 134. Used by permission. The 1992 data were kindly provided by Rhodes Cook of Congressional Quarterly.

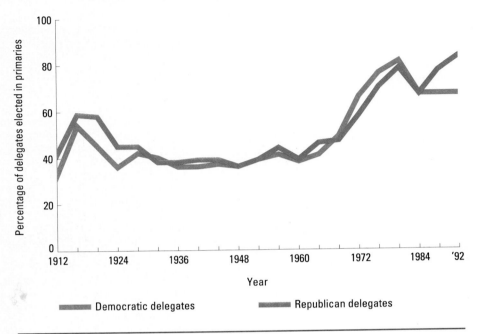

delegates selected through primaries. Now parties in nearly forty states rely on presidential primaries, which generate more than 80 percent of the delegates.

Campaigning for the Nomination.   The process of nominating party candidates for president is a complex, drawn-out affair that has no parallel in any other nation. Would-be presidents announce their candidacies and begin campaigning many months before the first convention delegates are selected. The selection process in 1992 began in early February with the Iowa caucuses, closely followed by the New Hampshire primary. By historical accident, these two small states have become the first tests of candidates' popularity with party voters. Accordingly, each basks in the media spotlight once every four years. The Iowa and New Hampshire legislatures are now committed to leading the delegate selection process, ensuring their states' share of national publicity and their bids for political history.

The Iowa caucuses and the New Hampshire primary have served different functions in the presidential nominating process.[19] The contest in Iowa has traditionally tended to winnow out candidates rejected by the party faithful. The New Hampshire primary, held one week later, has tested the Iowa frontrunners' appeal to ordinary party voters, which foreshadows their likely strength in the general election. Because voting takes little effort by itself, more citizens are likely to vote in primaries than to attend caucuses, which can last for hours. In 1992, less than 5 percent of the voting-age population participated in the Iowa caucuses, whereas more than 40 percent voted in the New Hampshire primary. Presidential aspirants have sought a favorable showing in Iowa to help them in New Hampshire. Between the 1976 and 1988 elections, several candidates in the party out of power began their run for the presidency more than a year in advance of the Iowa contest. But President George Bush, riding the crest of the Persian Gulf War, was so popular in 1991 that the first Democratic challenger, former Massachusetts senator Paul Tsongas, did not announce his candidacy until April. The other major candidates—Jerry Brown (former governor of California), Bob Kerrey (senator from Nebraska), Tom Harkin (senator from Iowa), and Bill Clinton—did not announce until early fall. By then, the field had virtually conceded the Iowa caucuses to favorite son Harkin, who won handily there but nowhere else, so the state played only a small role in the 1992 race.

New Hampshire traditionally is more important in presidential nominations. Although President Bush won the New Hampshire primary, he had to fight off a strong challenge from Pat Buchanan, a political commentator who had never run for any office. That Buchanan took 37 percent of the vote in this rural state revealed unhappiness with Bush within his own party. For the Democrats, Tsongas's primary victory over his four rivals proved to be an exception to the rule. In thirteen of the previous sixteen nominating contests in both parties since 1960, the candidate who won New Hampshire also won the party nomination. Moreover, since 1952 no candidate had won the presidency without first winning the New Hampshire primary. Despite the blemish on its record in 1992 (when Clinton became president without winning New Hampshire), future aspiring presidential candidates in both parties will no doubt spend weeks of their lives and millions of dollars trudging through snow, appealing for votes in a tiny northeastern state.

In fact, the 1996 race for the Republican nomination opened in New Hampshire two and a half years before the snowy primary season. In early fall of 1993, a parade of Republican aspirants, including senators Robert Dole, Phil Gramm, and Richard Luger and at least five others who were testing the political climate, visited the state.[20] In the absence of a Republican president and vice president, the nomination seemed to be up for grabs. New Hampshire looked like a good place to start—and sooner rather than later.

Almost 35 million citizens voted in both parties' presidential primaries in 1992, and another half million participated in party caucuses. Requiring prospective presidential candidates to campaign before many millions of party voters in primaries and hundreds of thousands of party activists in caucus states has several consequences:

- The uncertainty of the nomination process attracts a half-dozen or so plausible candidates, especially when the party does not have a president seeking reelection. That accounts for the nine Republicans visiting New Hampshire in the fall of 1993.

- Candidates usually cannot win their parties' nomination unless favored by most party identifiers. There have been only two exceptions to this rule since 1936, when poll data first became available: Adlai E. Stevenson in 1952 and George McGovern in 1972.[21] Both were Democrats; both lost impressively in the general election.

- Candidates who win the nomination do so largely on their own and owe little or nothing to the national party organization, which usually does not promote a candidate. In fact, Jimmy Carter won the nomination in 1976 against a field of nationally prominent Democrats, although he was a party outsider with few strong connections in the national party leadership.

ELECTIONS

By national law, all seats in the House of Representatives and one-third of the seats in the Senate are filled in a **general election** held in early November in even-numbered years. Every state takes advantage of the national election to fill some of the nearly 500,000 state and local offices across the country, which makes the election even more "general." When the president is chosen, every fourth year, the election is identified as a *presidential election.* The intervening years' elections are known as *congressional, midterm,* or *off-year elections.*

Presidential Elections

In contrast to almost all other offices in the United States, the presidency does not go automatically to the candidate who wins the most votes. Instead, a two-stage procedure specified in the Constitution decides elections for president; it requires selection of the president by a group (college) of electors representing the states.

The Electoral College.   Voters choose the president only indirectly; they actually vote for a little-known slate of electors (their names are rarely even on the ballot) pledged to one of the candidates. Occasionally, electors break their pledges when they cast their written ballots at their state capitols in December. This happened as recently as 1988, when Margaret Leach, chosen as a Democratic elector in West Virginia, abandoned Dukakis and voted for his running mate, Senator Lloyd Bentsen.[22] But usually the electors are faithful, especially when their votes are needed to determine the winner. The fundamental principle of the electoral college is that the outcome of the popular vote determines the outcome of the electoral vote. Whether a candidate wins a state by 5 votes or 500,000 votes, he or she wins all that state's electoral votes.*

In the electoral college, each state is accorded one vote for each of its senators (100 votes total) and representatives (435 votes total), adding up to 535 votes. In addition, the Twenty-third Amendment to the Constitution awarded three electoral votes to the District of Columbia, although it elects no voting members of Congress. So the total number of electoral votes is 538, and a candidate needs a majority of 270 electoral votes to win the presidency.†

---

* *The two exceptions are Maine and Nebraska, where two and three of the states' electoral votes, respectively, are awarded by congressional district. The presidential candidate who carries each district wins a single electoral vote, and the statewide winner gets two votes.*

† *If no candidate receives a majority when the electoral college votes, the election is thrown into the House of Representatives. The House votes by state, with each state casting one vote. The candidates in the House election are the top three finishers in the general election. A presidential election has gone to the House only twice in American history, in 1800 and 1824, before a stable two-party system had developed.*

FIGURE **9.2** ■ **Distribution of Electoral Votes in 1992**

The 1990 census produced some major changes in congressional reapportionment with implications for presidential elections. Remember that each state has as many electoral votes as its combined representation in the Senate (always two) and in the House (which depends on population). As the map shows, states in the South and West gained population and thus picked up seats in the House of Representatives, mainly at the expense of the Northeast. Thus, California, with two senators and fifty-two representatives, now has fifty-four electoral votes— or more than 10 percent of the total of 538. (Washington, D.C., has three electoral votes—equal to the smallest state— although it has no representation in Congress.)

Source: Congressional Quarterly Weekly Report, *23 March 1991, p. 765.*

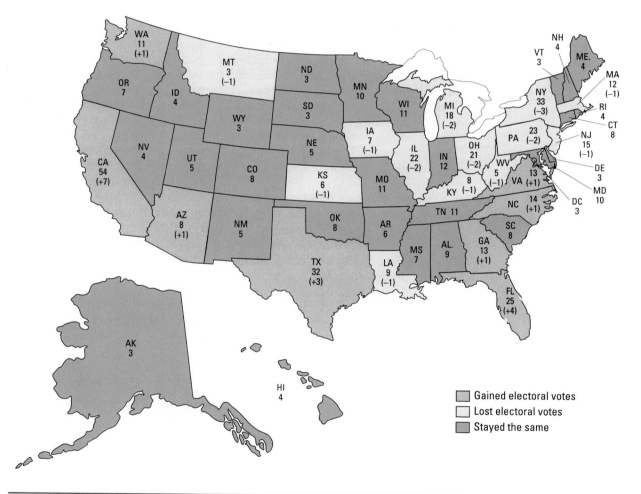

These electoral votes are apportioned among the states according to their representation in Congress, which depends, in turn, on their population. Because of population changes recorded by the 1990 census, the distribution of electoral votes among the states changed between the 1988 and 1992 presidential elections, as shown in Figure 9.2. California, the most populous state in 1980, grew even more by 1990 and now claims fifty-four electoral votes for its fifty-two representatives and two senators. The greatest population growth occurred in the so-called Sunbelt states: For example, Florida and Texas picked up additional representatives at the expense of Frostbelt states such as New York, Pennsylvania, Illinois, Michigan, and Ohio.

The most troubling aspect of the electoral college is the possibility that despite winning a plurality or even a majority of popular votes, a candidate could lose the election in the electoral college. This could happen if one candidate wins certain states by very wide margins, while the other candidate wins other states by slim margins. Indeed, it has happened in three elections, the most recent in 1888, when Grover Cleveland received 48.6 percent of the popular vote to Benjamin Harrison's 47.9 percent. Cleveland nevertheless lost to Harrison in the electoral college, 168 to 233.

Abolish the Electoral College?   Reformers argue that it is simply wrong to have a system that allows a candidate who receives the most popular votes to lose the election. They favor a purely majoritarian means of choosing the president, direct election by popular vote. Defenders of the electoral college point out that the existing system, warts and all, has been a stable one. It might be riskier to replace it with a new arrangement that could alter our party system or the way presidential campaigns are conducted. Tradition has in fact prevailed, and recent proposals for fundamental reform have not come close to adoption.

For the last one hundred years, fortunately, the candidate winning a plurality of the popular vote has also won a majority of the electoral vote. In fact, the electoral college operates to magnify the victory margin, as Figure 9.3 shows. Some scholars argue that this increases the legitimacy of the president-elect. For instance, John F. Kennedy defeated Richard Nixon by less than 1 percent of the popular vote in 1960, but he won 56 percent of the electoral vote, strengthening his claim on the presidency. Bill Clinton also benefited from the electoral college, which magnified his 43 percent of the popular vote to 69 percent of the electoral vote. In any event, since 1888 our indirect method of electing the president has produced the same outcome as a direct method of popular election, with the exception that presidential candidates must plan their campaign strategies to win states, not just votes.

Congressional Elections

The candidates for the presidency are listed at the top of the ballot in a presidential election, followed by candidates for other national, state, and local offices. A voter is said to vote a **straight ticket** when she or he chooses the same party's candidates for all the offices. A voter who chooses candidates from different parties is said to vote a **split ticket.** About half of all voters admit to splitting their tickets, and the proportion of voters who chose a presidential candidate from one party and a congressional candidate from the other has increased from about 13 percent in 1952 to 25 percent in 1992.[23] The most common pattern in recent years has been to choose a Republican for president but to reelect Democratic incumbents in the House and Senate. The net effect has been to produce divided government, in which Republicans control the presidency and Democrats the Congress (see Chapter 12).

FIGURE 9.3 ■ Popular Vote and the Electoral Vote

The electoral vote, not the popular vote, decides elections for president. Although a candidate could win a plurality of the popular vote but not the majority of the electoral vote needed to be elected president, this has not happened since 1888. More common is for candidates who win a plurality of the popular vote to win an even larger majority of the electoral vote, as shown here. Even when Richard Nixon won only 43 percent of the vote in 1968 against Hubert Humphrey, the Democratic candidate, and George Wallace of the American Independent party, he took 56 percent of the electoral vote. Similarly in 1992, Bill Clinton won only 43 percent of the popular vote but took 69 percent of the electoral votes. In general, the effect of choosing our presidents through the electoral vote system is to magnify the winner's victory and increase the legitimacy of the president-elect.

Source: Harold W. Stanley and Richard G. Niemi, Vital Statistics on American Politics, 2d ed. (Washington, D.C.: Congressional Quarterly Press, 1990), pp. 104–106 and "Presidential Election," Congressional Quarterly Weekly Report, November 1992, p. 3549.

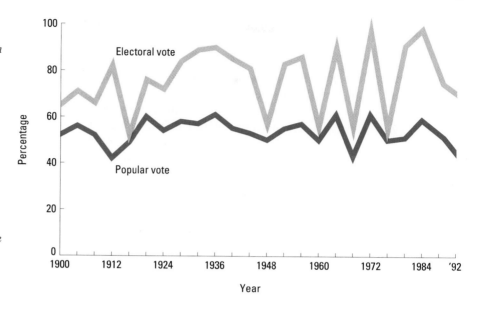

If Republicans have dominated the presidency in recent years, Democrats seem to have a lock on congressional elections. They have not only won a majority of House seats every year since 1955, but have controlled the Senate for all but six years during that period. Republicans complain that inequitable districts drawn by Democrat-dominated state legislatures have denied Republicans their fair share of votes. For example, the Republicans won 46 percent of the congressional vote in 1992, but they won only 40 percent of the seats.[24] Since 1954, Republicans have won a smaller percentage of seats than votes (on average, 6.8 percent fewer) in *every* House election. Despite the Republicans' complaint, election specialists point out that this is the inevitable consequence of **first-past-the-post elections**—a British term for elections conducted in single-member districts that award victory to the candidate with the most votes. In all such elections around the world, the party that wins the most votes tends to win more seats than projected by its percentage of the vote. The same process operates in the electoral college, which, as discussed, awards a bigger majority in electoral votes than the candidate won in popular votes.[*]

The fact remains that, historically, voters have favored Democratic candidates for both the House and the Senate, even when electing Republican candidates for president. Some analysts see special significance in that voting pattern. They credit citizens for consciously voting to produce divided government, with a Republican executive pushing one way and a Democratic legislature the other.[25] If so, voters behave quite rationally in

---

[*] *If you have trouble understanding this phenomenon, think of a basketball team that scores, on average, 51 percent of the total points in all the games it plays. Such a team usually wins far more than just 51 percent of its games, for it wins systematically and tends to win the close ones.*

making their ballot choices, favoring a weaker, pluralist government rather than a stronger, majoritarian one. It remains to be seen whether the evidence of voting choice in general elections can support such a rational interpretation of electoral behavior.

CAMPAIGNS	As Barbara Salmore and Stephen Salmore have observed, election campaigns have been studied more through anecdotes than through systematic analysis.[26] These writers developed a framework of analysis that emphasizes the political context of the campaign, the financial resources available for conducting the campaign, and the strategies and tactics that underlie the dissemination of information about the candidate.

The Political Context

The two most important structural factors that face each candidate planning a campaign are the office the candidate is seeking and whether he or she is the **incumbent,** the current officeholder running for reelection, or the **challenger,** who seeks to replace the incumbent. Alternatively, the candidate can be running in an **open election,** which lacks an incumbent because of a resignation or death. Incumbents usually enjoy great advantages over challengers, especially in elections to Congress. As explained in Chapter 11, incumbents in the House of Representatives are almost impossible to defeat, historically winning more than 95 percent of the time. However, incumbent senators are somewhat more vulnerable. An incumbent president is also difficult to defeat—but not impossible, as George Bush learned in 1992.

Every candidate organizing a campaign must also examine the characteristics of the district, including its physical size and the sociological makeup of its electorate. In general, the bigger and more populous the district and the more diverse the electorate, the more complicated and costly the campaign. Obviously, running for president means conducting a huge, complicated, and expensive campaign. After being nominated at their conventions, Bill Clinton and George Bush immediately embarked on campaign trips, Clinton and Gore on a bus tour of the Midwest and Bush flying to four southern cities.[27]

Despite comments in the news about the decreased influence of party affiliation on voting behavior, the party preference of the electorate is an important factor in the context of a campaign. It is easier for a candidate to get elected when her or his party matches the electorate's preference, in part because raising the money needed to conduct a winning campaign is easier. Challengers for Congress, for example, get far less money from organized groups than do incumbents and must rely more on their personal funds and on raising money from individuals.[28] So where candidates are of the minority party, they not only have to overcome a voting bias but also a funding bias. Finally, significant political issues—such as economic recession, personal scandals, and war—not only affect a campaign but can dominate it and even negate such positive factors as incumbency and normal inclinations of the electorate. For example, the Watergate affair overshadowed the 1974 congressional elections, resulting in the loss of

Political Campaigning: The Inside Story

Actually, it's not all that exciting. Conducting a successful campaign usually involves a careful statistical analysis of voting trends and various social and economic characteristics of the electorate. The sign in Republican strategist Karl Rove's office in Austin, Texas, says a lot: These days computers may be everything.

thirty-six seats of Republican representatives seeking reelection, mostly in Republican districts, regardless of the quality of their campaigns.

Financing

In talking about election campaigns, former House speaker Thomas ("Tip") O'Neill once said, "As it is now, there are four parts to any campaign. The candidate, the issues of the candidate, the campaign organization, and the money to run the campaign with. Without money you can forget the other three."[29] Money pays for office space, staff salaries, telephone bills, postage, travel expenses, campaign literature, and, of course, advertising in the mass media. Although a successful campaign requires a good campaign organization and a good candidate, enough money will buy the best campaign managers, equipment, transportation, research, and consultants—making the quality of the organization largely a function of money.[30] Although the equation is not quite as strong, when party sources promise ample campaign funds, good candidates become available. So from a cynical but practical viewpoint, campaign resources boil down to campaign funds.

Campaign financing is now heavily regulated by national and state governments, and regulations vary according to the level of the office—national, state, or local. Even at the national level, differences in financing laws for presidential and congressional elections are significant.

Regulating Campaign Financing.   Strict campaign financing laws are relatively new to American politics. Early laws to limit campaign contributions and to control campaign spending were flawed in one way or another, and none clearly provided for enforcement. In 1971, during the period of party reform, Congress enacted the Federal Election Campaign Act (FECA), which imposed stringent new rules for full reporting of campaign contributions and expenditures. The weakness of the old legislation soon became apparent. In 1968, before FECA was enacted, House and Senate candidates had reported spending $8.5 million for their campaigns. With FECA in force, the same number of candidates confessed to spending $88.9 million in 1972.[31]

FECA has been amended several times since 1971 and usually strengthened. For example, the original law legalized political action committees, but a 1974 amendment limited the amounts that they could contribute to election campaigns. (Political action committees are discussed in Chapter 10.) The 1974 amendment also created the **Federal Election Commission (FEC)** to implement the law. The FEC now enforces limits on financial contributions to national campaigns and requires full disclosure of campaign spending. The FEC also administers the public financing of presidential campaigns, which began with the 1976 election.

Financing Presidential Campaigns.   Presidential campaigns have always been expensive, and at times the methods of raising funds to support them were open to question. In the presidential election of 1972, the last election before the FEC took over the funding of presidential campaigns and the regulating of campaign expenditures, President Richard Nixon's campaign committee spent more than $65 million, some of it obtained illegally (for which campaign officials went to jail). In 1974, a new campaign finance law made public funds available to presidential candidates under certain conditions.

Candidates for each party's nomination for president can qualify for federal funding by raising at least $5,000 (in private contributions no greater than $250 each) in each of twenty states. The FEC then matches these contributions up to one-half of the spending limit. Originally under the 1974 law, the FEC limited spending in presidential primary elections to $10 million. But by 1992 cost-of-living provisions had raised the limit to $27.6 million (plus $5.5 million for fund-raising activities).

The presidential nominees of the Democratic and Republican parties receive twice the primary election limit in public funds for the general election campaign ($55.2 million in 1992), provided that they spend only the public funds. Each of the two major parties also receives public funds to pay for its convention ($11 million in 1992). Every major candidate since 1976 has accepted public funding, holding the costs of presidential campaigns well below Nixon's record expenditures in 1972.

Public funds go directly to each candidate's campaign committee, not to either party. But the FEC also limits what the national committees can spend on behalf of the nominees. In 1992, that limit was $10.3 million. And the FEC limits the amount individuals ($1,000) and organizations ($5,000) can contribute to presidential candidates during the nomination phase and to House and Senate candidates for the primary and general elections. Individuals or organizations are not limited, however, in the

amount of *expenses* they can incur to promote candidates of their choice. *
Independent spending by individuals or groups in the 1984 presidential
campaign amounted to more than $15 million, with about 80 percent
spent to elect Ronald Reagan. Such spending declined substantially in
1988, and it amounted to less than $5 million in 1992, although most in-
dependent expenditures again benefited the Republican candidate.[32]

Public funding has had several effects on campaign financing. Obviously, it has limited campaign expenditures. Also, it has helped equalize
the amounts spent by major party candidates in general elections, and it
has strengthened the trend toward "personalized" presidential campaigns,
because federal funds are given to the candidate, not to the party organization. Finally, public funding has forced candidates to spend a great deal of
time seeking $1,000 contributions—a limit that has not changed since
1974, despite the inflation that has more than doubled the FEC's spending
limits. In the 1980s, however, both parties began to exploit a loophole in
the law that allowed them to raise a virtually unlimited amount of "soft
money," funds to be spent for the entire ticket on party mailings, voter registration, and get-out-the-vote campaigns. In 1992, the Democrats managed to outspend the Republicans in soft money, which was uncommon.
The Clinton team spent about $40 million to Bush's $25 million.[33] The national committees channeled the soft money to state and local party committees for registration drives and other activities not exclusively devoted
to the presidential candidates but that nonetheless helped them.[34] The net
effect of these "coordinated campaigns" was to enhance the role of both
the national and state parties in presidential campaigns.

You might think that a party's presidential campaign would be closely
coordinated with the campaigns of the party's candidates for Congress. But
remember that campaign funds go to the presidential candidate, not the
party, and that the national party organization does not run the presidential campaign. Presidential candidates may join congressional candidates in public appearances for mutual benefit, but presidential campaigns
are usually isolated—financially and otherwise—from congressional
campaigns.

Strategies and Tactics

In a military campaign, strategy is the overall scheme for winning the war,
whereas tactics involve the conduct of localized hostilities.[35] In an election campaign, strategy is the broad approach used to persuade citizens to
vote for the candidate, and tactics determine the content of the messages
and the way they are delivered. Three basic strategies, which campaigns
may blend in different mixes, are:

- a party-centered strategy, which relies heavily on voters' partisan identification as well as on the party's organization to provide the resources necessary to wage the campaign;

---

* *The distinction between contributions and expenses hinges on whether funds are spent as part of a
coordinated campaign (a contribution) or spent independent of the candidate's campaign (an expense). The 1974 amendment to FECA established limits on both campaign contributions and independent expenditures by interested citizens. In* Buckley v. Valeo *(1976), the Supreme Court struck
down the limits on citizens' expenditures as an infringement on the freedom of speech, protected
under the First Amendment.*

Democratic War Room

Democrats have a reputation for informality. James Carville, Bill Clinton's 1992 campaign strategist, fulfills that reputation as he talks politics (what else?) in his office on the day before the presidential election.

- an issue-oriented strategy, which seeks support from groups that feel strongly about various policies;

- an image-oriented strategy, which depends on the candidate's perceived personal qualities, such as experience, leadership ability, integrity, independence, trustworthiness, and the like.[36]

The campaign strategy must be tailored to the political context of the election. Obviously, a party-centered strategy is inappropriate in a primary, because all contenders have the same party affiliation. Research suggests that a party-centered strategy is best suited to voters with little political knowledge.[37] How do candidates learn what the electorate knows and thinks about politics, and how can they use this information? Candidates today usually turn to pollsters and political consultants, of whom there are hundreds.[38] Well-funded candidates can purchase a "polling package" that includes

- a benchmark poll that provides "campaign information about the voting preferences and issue concerns of various groups in the electorate and a detailed reading of the image voters have of the candidates in the race"

- focus groups, consisting of ten to twenty people "chosen to represent particular target groups the campaign wants to reinforce or persuade . . . , led in their discussion by persons trained in small-group dynamics," giving texture and depth to poll results

- a trend poll "to determine the success of the campaigns in altering candidate images and voting preferences"

- tracking polls that begin in early October "conducting short nightly interviews with a small number of respondents, keyed to the variables that have assumed importance"[39]

Professional campaign managers can use information from such sources to settle on a strategy that mixes party affiliation, issues, and images in its messages. In major campaigns, the mass media disseminates these messages to voters through news coverage and advertising.[40]

Making the News.   Campaigns value news coverage by the media for two reasons: The coverage is free, and it seems objective to the audience. If news stories do nothing more than report the candidate's name, that is important, for name recognition by itself often wins elections. To get favorable coverage, campaign managers cater to reporters' deadlines and needs.[41] Getting free news coverage is yet another advantage that incumbents enjoy over challengers, for incumbents can command attention simply by announcing political decisions—even if they had little to do with them. Members of Congress are so good at this, says one observer, that House members have made news organizations their "unwitting adjuncts."[42]

Campaigns vary in the effectiveness with which they transmit their messages via the news media. Effective tactics recognize the limitations of both the audience and the media. The typical voter is not deeply interested in politics and has trouble keeping track of multiple themes supported with details. By the same token, television is not willing to air lengthy statements from candidates. A study of all weekday network newscasts from Labor Day to Election Day in 1968 found that the average statement from a candidate ran forty-two seconds; during the same period in 1988, the average utterance from a candidate was a soundbite of only ten seconds.[43]

Reacting to criticism about their coverage of the campaigns, the networks tried harder to lengthen soundbites in 1992, and CBS made the decision in July to make them at least thirty seconds.[44] Of course, the networks run much longer visuals of the candidates, but reporters' voice-over comments often are not as positive as the images in the visuals. According to a comparative study of national and local news broadcasts in 1992, all three major networks and CNN presented both Bush and Clinton "significantly more favorably in the visuals than . . . in the overall story," whereas Perot was usually presented favorably in visuals and spared criticism in commentary.[45] In contrast, the tone of the local TV news was better for the president than for Clinton and even more favorable for Perot.[46]

The media often use the metaphor of a horse race in covering politics in the United States. One long-time student of the media contends that reporters both enliven and simplify a campaign by describing it in terms of four basic scenarios: *bandwagon, losing ground, frontrunner,* and *likely loser.*[47] Once the opinion polls show weakness or strength in a candidate, reporters dust off the appropriate storyline. Accordingly, the press used the bandwagon in portraying Bill Clinton in mid-summer of 1992, while it described Bush as the likely loser in a vivid example of how the press colors the news:

In its article on the first presidential debate of 1992, *Newsweek* dismissed Bush's chances of reelection even as it dismissed his appearance: "George Bush seemed reluctant to look the camera in the eye—even though 70 million Americans were waiting to be convinced that he should be president for another four years. Whatever was said in St. Louis Sunday night in the first, and probably the most pivotal presidential debate, it was the body language that had a story to tell: Bush, often staring down at his lectern, smiling his oddly apologetic smile, had not convinced himself, and therefore could not convince the country."[48]

Given the media's preoccupation with horse race journalism, it is not surprising that television news contains little information about the issues in the campaign. In fact, studies of recent campaigns have found that most voters get their campaign information from political ads rather than television news programs.[49]

Advertising the Candidate.   In all elections, the first objective of paid advertising is name recognition. The next is to promote candidates by extolling their virtues. Finally, campaign advertising can have a negative objective, attacking the opponent to promote the candidate. But name recognition is usually the most important. Studies show that many voters cannot recall the names of their U.S. senators or representatives, but they can recognize their names on a list—as on the ballot. Researchers attribute the high reelection rate for members of Congress mainly to high levels of name recognition (see Chapter 11). Even in presidential campaigns, name recognition is the key objective during the primary elections, but other objectives become salient in advertising for the general election.

At one time, candidates for national office relied heavily on newspaper advertising; today, they overwhelmingly use the electronic media. A study of campaign spending in the 1990 congressional elections found that House candidates spent about 25 percent of their budgets for advertising and media consultants combined, whereas Senate candidates spent about 35 percent.[50] Darrell West found that both George Bush and Bill Clinton spent about 60 percent of their 1992 presidential campaign budgets on radio and television ads, whereas Ross Perot devoted up to 75 percent.[51] This emphasis on electronic media, particularly television, has raised concern about the promotion of candidates by developing a "video style" for them that helps win elections but is irrelevant to performance in office.

In cultivating a candidate's video style, consultant and candidate arrive at a campaign theme by anticipating audiences' reactions by using focus groups. Then the consultant coaches the candidate on how to deliver the theme quickly and effectively in a thirty-second commercial. A scholar who analyzed television use by six candidates in three Senate campaigns found that audiences do not usually spend time dissecting the message in a television spot; instead, they form impressions from the mood, which the producer creates using "background music, the sharpness of the visual images, and the persuasiveness of the verbal content."[52] In 1992, Clinton used the advertising firm of Greer, Margolis, Mitchell, and Grunwald (GMMG) for both the primary and general election campaigns, the Bush campaign put together a team of professionals called the November Company, and Perot created the 270 Group (for the 270 electoral votes needed to win) from the Dallas firm of Temerlin-McClain.[53]

Political ads convey more substantive information than many people believe. West's study found that presidential campaign ads since 1984 contained more specific policy content than personal qualities and had more policy content than ads in the 1950s and early 1960s.[54] However, other scholars have pointed out that the "policy content" of ads may be misleading, if not downright deceptive.[55] West also found that 1992 set a record for negative advertising. Nearly two-thirds of most prominent ads were negative.[56] And the most substantive content—on both foreign policy and domestic policy—actually appeared in negative ads. West explained, "Negative commercials are more likely to have policy-oriented content because campaigners need a clear reason to attack the opponent."[57]

The media often inflate the effect of prominent ads by reporting them as news, which means that citizens are about as likely to see controversial ads during the news as in the paid time slot.[58] This may have accounted for the public's pronounced view of negative campaigning in 1992. When surveyed in September, more respondents (46 to 31 percent) thought Bush concentrated on attacking Clinton than thought he focused on explaining his own views. Meanwhile, Clinton got more credit than Bush for explaining his views (37 to 24 percent). By late October, respondents named Bush as being responsible for negative campaigning by a whopping margin of 60 to 13 percent.[59] Some of this imbalance may be because the media were sympathetic to Clinton (see Chapter 6, page 174), and some of it may have been a legacy of Bush's negative ads in 1988 (in particular the "Willie Horton" ad) that attacked Michael Dukakis. (See Feature 9.2, which discusses negative ads.) Early in the campaign, the Democratic strategists warned about Republican media attacks and organized more effectively than Dukakis had in order to counteract them. Their efforts seemed to have paid off in the public's negative response to Bush's campaign in 1992.

Using New Media.   A major development in campaigning in 1992 was the strategic use of new media, including talk shows, entertainment shows, and Perot's half-hour "infomercials." Bill Clinton started the trend in January by appearing on "60 Minutes" to respond to Gennifer Flowers's claim of infidelity. In February, Ross Perot launched his campaign with an appearance on "Larry King Live." But no one used the new media heavily until June, when Clinton found himself behind both Bush and Perot in the polls, as detailed in Figure 9.4, and treated by the conventional news media as the third candidate in a race between Bush and Perot. From June 2 to June 30, Clinton appeared on ten talk shows, and by the end of the month he had gained seven points in the polls and moved into first place among the candidates.[60]

While Clinton went the talk show route to go over the heads of the journalists, Perot, who was less comfortable with people asking him questions, relied on buying thirty-minute time slots to present his views (with charts) to the American people, who watched his infomercials in surprisingly large numbers. President Bush engaged only sparingly in such new media campaigning. One observer counted thirty-nine separate appearances by all three candidates on "soft-format" TV programs such as "Larry King Live," "CBS This Morning," "Good Morning America," "Today," and syndicated talk shows from September 1 to October 19.[61] Most observers have concluded that these soft-format programs (watched by many people) represented an alternative form of campaigning that provided

---

FIGURE 9.4   ■ **Tracking Presidential Preferences During the Campaign**

From May to June in the 1992 presidential campaign, Bill Clinton ran a poor third to both George Bush and Ross Perot, who actually led both candidates in early June. Support for Clinton soared when he was nominated at the Democratic convention, July 13–16, which coincided with Perot's dropping out on July 16. Bush enjoyed a brief "bounce" in support during the Republican convention, August 17–20, but Clinton remained clearly ahead. When Perot reentered the race on October 1, his support was nowhere near what it had been when he dropped out, but it steadily rose under his advertising barrage and his strong performance in the debates of October 11, 15, and 19.

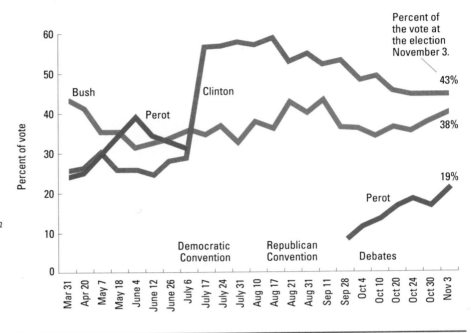

viewers with important information on the candidates' characters and policies. Even Clinton's appearance on MTV drew high marks for the quality of questions posed by the young anchor and the studio audience.

EXPLAINING VOTING CHOICE

Why do people choose one candidate over another? That is not easy to determine, but there are ways to approach the question. Individual voting choices can be analyzed as products of both long-term and short-term forces. Long-term forces operate throughout a series of elections, predisposing voters to choose certain types of candidates. Short-term forces are associated with particular elections; they arise from a combination of the candidates and the issues of the time. Party identification is by far the most important long-term force affecting U.S. elections. The most important short-term forces are candidates' attributes and their policy positions.

Party Identification

When voters in 1988 were asked at what point they had decided for whom to vote in the presidential election, nearly half (49 percent) said that they "knew all along" or had decided before the conventions.[62] In 1992, only 15 percent of the voters said that, and 56 percent said they decided only after Ross Perot withdrew in July.[63] In other presidential elections since 1952, about 40 percent of the voters reported making up their minds before the candidates squared off in the general election campaign. And voters

FEATURE 9.2

■ Two Controversial Ads: Both Parties Do It

The "Daisy" ad was run in 1964 by Lyndon Johnson's campaign against his opponent, Barry Goldwater. Kathleen Hall Jamieson, an expert on political advertising, called it "arguably the most controversial ad in the history of political broadcasting," although "it never mentions either Goldwater's name or any statement he has made about anything." As she describes it,

> It opens on a female child dressed in a jump suit standing on an open field plucking the petals from a daisy as she counts "1, 2, 3, 4, 7, 6, 6, 8, 9." The authenticity of the child derives in large part from the fact that she counts as children do—with numbers out of proper order. . . . When she reaches "9," a Cape Canaveral voice begins a countdown of its own—no longer innocent but ominous. Here is the efficient, straightforward, willful act of an adult: "10, 9, 8, 7, 6, 5, 4, 3, 2, 1, zero." At zero the camera, which throughout this second countdown has been closing on the child's face, dissolves from her eye to a mushroom cloud that expands until it envelops the screen. Lyndon Johnson's voice is heard stating a lesson that could be drawn from the Sermon on the Mount: "These are the stakes. To make a world in which all of God's children can live, or to go into the dark. We must either love each other or we must die."

The Daisy ad ran only once on one network before Johnson yanked it because of adverse reaction. As news, all three networks repeated it.

The notorious "Willie Horton" ad run in 1988 against Michael Dukakis was not produced by Bush's campaign organization but by the National Security Political Action Committee, which used an advertising agency long tied to the Republican party. As described by Jamieson, the ad linked Dukakis with William Horton, a black murderer who had jumped furlough in Massachusetts and gone on to rape a Caucasian Maryland woman and attack her Caucasian fiancee. . . .

> The ad opens with side-by-side pictures of Dukakis and Bush. Dukakis' hair is unkempt, the photo dark. Bush, by contrast is smiling and bathed in light. As the pictures appear an announcer says "Bush and Dukakis on crime." A picture of Bush flashes on the screen. "Bush supports the death penalty for first-degree murderers." A picture of Dukakis. "Dukakis not only opposes the death penalty, he allowed first-degree murderers to have weekend passes from prison." A close-up mug shot of Horton flashes onto the screen. "One was Willie Horton, who murdered a boy in a robbery, stabbing him, nineteen times." A blurry black and white photo of Horton apparently being arrested. "Despite a life sentence, Horton received ten weekend passes from prison." The words "kidnapping" "stabbing" and "raping" appear on the screen with Horton's picture as the announcer adds "Horton fled, kidnapping a young couple, stabbing the man and repeatedly raping his girlfriend." The final photo again shows Michael Dukakis. The announcer notes "Weekend prison passes. Dukakis on crime."

This ad ran nationally on cable television for twenty-eight days before the election and attracted a storm of criticism, in part because a furloughed convict in California also had killed someone when Ronald Reagan was governor.

● *Source: Kathleen Hall Jamieson,* Packaging the Presidency, *2d ed. (New York: Oxford University Press, 1992), pp. 198, 471.*

Sweeping Indictment
This sign of the times implies that incumbent officeholders were targets of voter discontent in the 1994 elections. But in a remarkable display of sharpshooting, the voters destroyed only Democratic targets. Every Republican incumbent governor, senator, or representative running for re-election was victorious, while voters threw out scores of prominent Democratic incumbents seeking to return to the governor's mansion or Congress. It was not a good year for Democratic office-holders.

who make an early voting decision generally vote according to their party identification.

Despite frequent comments in the media about the decline of partisanship in voting behavior, party identification had a substantial effect on the presidential vote in 1992, as Figure 9.5 shows. Seventy-seven percent of avowed Democrats voted for Clinton, and 73 percent of the Republicans voted for Bush. A plurality of the independents also voted for Clinton. This is a common pattern in presidential elections. The winner holds nearly all the voters who identify with his party. The loser also holds most of his fellow Democrats or Republicans, but some percentage defects to the winner, a product of the short-term forces—the candidates' attributes and the issues—surrounding the election. The winner usually gets most of the independents, who split disproportionately for him, also because of short-term forces.

Because Democrats outnumber Republicans, the Democrats should benefit. Why, then, have Republican candidates won seven out of ten presidential elections since 1952? For one thing, Democrats do not turn out to vote as consistently as Republicans do. For another, Democrats tend to defect more readily from their party. Defections are sparked by the candidates' attributes and the issues, which have usually favored Republican presidential candidates since 1952. In 1992, however, Republican identifiers defected from their party's candidate at the highest rate since reliable survey data became available in 1952.[64] Although Democratic identifiers were less likely than Republicans to defect in 1992, Democrats also de-

FIGURE **9.5**   ■ **Effect of Party Identification on the Vote, 1992**

The 1992 presidential election showed that party identification still plays a key role in voting behavior—even with an independent candidate in the contest. This chart shows the results of an exit poll of 15,490 voters as they left three hundred polling places across the nation on election day. Voters were asked what party they identified with and how they voted for president. Those who identified with one of the two parties voted strongly for their party's candidate, whereas independent voters divided roughly into thirds for Clinton, Bush, and Perot. Republicans were slightly more likely to defect to Perot than were Democrats, but independents were more than twice as likely to vote for Perot than were those who identified with either party.

Source: *"Portrait of the Electorate,"* New York Times, *5 November 1992, p. B9.*

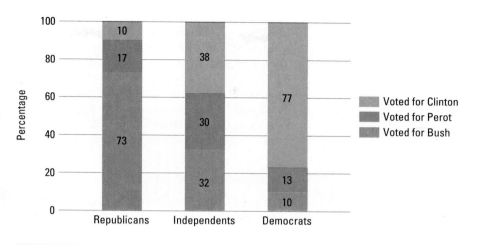

fected more than usual—because of the candidacy of Ross Perot. In fact, both Republican and Democratic defectors were more likely to vote for Perot than to cross over and support the candidate of the other major party.[65]

Issues and Policies

Throughout the 1992 campaign, the Clinton forces exploited the popular perception of a weak economy. Clinton's campaign manager, James Carville, even had a sign in his headquarters that said, "It's the economy, Stupid." Ironically, the economy was not that bad, according to the indicators. Although economic growth had slowed since 1988 and unemployment had risen, inflation had fallen, interest rates were low, and the nation was not technically in a recession, defined as two consecutive quarters of negative economic growth.[66] In fact, the same economic models that had been successful in predicting the outcome of past presidential elections uniformly predicted a *Bush* victory in 1992.[67]

Despite the objective indicators, about three-quarters of the voters thought that the nation as a whole had serious economic problems.[68] Their concerns were fed not only by the Clinton campaign but also by Perot, who focused on the growing budget deficit. After analyzing the effects of economic issues on the vote, Arthur Miller, a survey analyst, concluded that the budget deficit was the most important economic issue influencing the choice for Bush or Clinton: "Those who thought that the Bush and Reagan administrations were responsible for the deficit . . . overwhelmingly (80%) supported Clinton, while those who blamed the deficit on the Democratic congress . . . voted heavily for Bush (64%)."[69] The other economic issues linked to voting for Clinton were government spending (citizens usually favor increased spending for social programs), health care costs, and concern about America's position in the global economy.

Ironically, Miller found that voters' personal financial and employment situations were not significantly related to their choice for president. He concluded that voters in 1992 did not vote their pocketbooks as much as their worries about bigger economic problems.[70]

Miller also found that the social issues—"abortion, lifestyles, family values, ethnic differences, crime, affirmative action, and patriotism"— that had contributed to Republican victories in the 1980s backfired in 1992.[71] Bush's campaign was hurt by the strident statements of evangelist Pat Robertson and talk-show host (and former Bush opponent) Patrick Buchanan that aired on national television during the Republican National Convention. Their extreme pro-life and socially intolerant positions seemed to turn off more voters than they turned on.

Candidates' Attributes

Candidates' attributes are especially important to voters who lack good information about a candidate's past performance and policy stands—which means most of us. Without such information, voters search for clues about the candidates to try to predict their behavior in office.[72] Some fall back on their personal beliefs about religion, gender, and race in making political judgments. Such stereotypic thinking accounts for the patterns of opposition and support met by a Catholic candidate for president (John Kennedy), a woman candidate for vice president (Geraldine Ferraro in 1984), and a black contender for a presidential nomination (Jesse Jackson in 1984 and 1988). In recent years, voters have been more willing to elect candidates other than white males to public office, see Politics in a Changing America 9.1.

In 1992, much of the presidential campaign centered on Clinton's "character"—interpreted by many to involve extramarital affairs, avoidance of the draft, and use of marijuana in college. On this moral dimension of the character issue, more than half of all voters saw Bush to be more honest and trustworthy.[73] But Miller found that Clinton was perceived more favorably than Bush on two other major dimensions of candidate character. On leadership, Clinton scored with his spirited defenses against attacks on his morals, whereas voters saw Bush (who violated his "no new taxes" pledge) as vacillating and indecisive. On caring about others, Clinton was far ahead of Bush, whom voters perceived as not understanding the lives of ordinary people.

Evaluating the Voting Choice

Choosing among candidates according to personal attributes might be understandable, but it is not rational voting, according to democratic theory. According to that theory, citizens should vote according to the candidates' past performance and proposed policies. Voters who choose between candidates on the basis of their policies are voting on the issues, which fits the idealized conception of democratic theory. However, issues, candidates' attributes, and party identification all figure in the voting decision. Their relative influence, although difficult to sort out, can be estimated using multivariate statistical models.

POLITICS IN A CHANGING AMERICA 9.1

Who Makes State Laws?

 The fifty states together elect nearly 7,500 members to state legislatures. Historically, most of these seats have been contested and won by white males, and that is still true today. Times are slowly changing, however, as we can see from the trends to elect women and minorities to state houses and senates since 1971. Over the past two decades women have quintupled their representation in state legislatures, from 4 to 20 percent. Moreover, the percentage of seats won by women in state legislative races in 1992 was twice the 10 percent won by women running for the U.S. Congress (see p. 000). The difference in electoral opportunities for women is more obvious when discussing numbers rather than percentages. In the 1992 election, women won only 54 seats in Congress but 1,503 seats in state legislatures. Although blacks more than tripled their election victories at the state level since 1971, the 7 percent of seats they won in 1992 was just equal to their percentage won in Congress.

Ironically, blacks (who constitute about 12 percent of the population) are closer to the goal of equal representation than women (who constitute about 51 percent). Hispanics began with such a low base of representation in state legislatures in 1971 that the 2 percent of seats that they won in 1992 cannot be easily evaluated. Still, it was only about half of the 3.5 percent of Hispanics in the U.S. Congress, and it was far below the percentage of Hispanics in the population (about 9 percent). As electoral opportunities expand for women, blacks, and Hispanics, we can expect even more social diversity in American state legislatures.

- *Source: Albert J. Nelson,* Emerging Influentials in State Legislatures: Women, Blacks, and Hispanics *(New York: Praeger, 1991), pp. 24–25; Karl T. Kurtz, "The Election in Perspective,"* State Legislatures *(January, 1993), pp. 16–17; Rich Jones, "The State Legislatures," in* The Book of the States, 1992–93 Edition *(Lexington, Kentucky: The Council of State Governments, 1992), p. 130; and "Minorities in Congress,"* Congressional Quarterly Special Report, *16 January 1993, p. 12.*

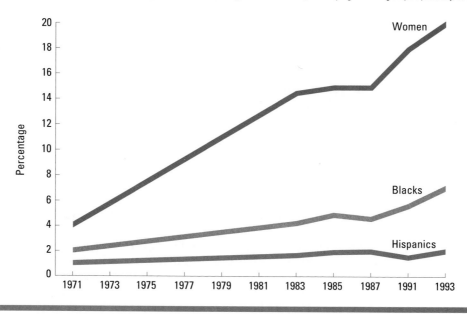

When Arthur Miller combined economic factors and character factors in his multivariate analysis, he found the two most important predictors of the vote to be "evaluations of which candidate was more caring and concerns about the deficit."[74] Given that Perot took 19 percent of the vote in 1992 (mostly from Republicans and Democrats), the role of party identification in explaining voting choice for all three candidates was necessarily less than in two-party contests. Some scholars contend that issues had already played a more important role in the voting decisions in the 1980s than in the 1950s.[75] Unfortunately for democratic theory, most studies of presidential elections show that issues are less important than either party identification or the candidates' attributes when people cast their ballots. Only in 1972, when voters perceived George McGovern as too liberal for their tastes, did issue voting exceed party identification in importance.[76] Even that year, issues were less important than the candidate's image. According to polls taken at the time, voters saw McGovern as weak and uncertain, Nixon as strong and (ironically) high principled.[77]

Although party voting has declined somewhat since the 1950s, the alignment of voters' positions on the issues and their party identification is closer today. For example, Democratic party identifiers are now more likely than Republican identifiers to describe themselves as liberal, and they are more likely than Republican identifiers to favor government spending for social welfare and abortions. The more closely party identification is aligned with ideological orientation, the more sense it makes to vote by party. In the absence of detailed information about candidates' positions on the issues, party labels are a handy indicator of those positions.[78]

Campaign Effects

If party identification is the most important factor in the voting decision and is also resistant to short-term changes, there are definite limits to the capacity of a campaign to influence the outcome of elections.[79] In a close election, however, just changing a few votes means the difference between victory and defeat, so a campaign can be decisive even if it has little overall effect.

The Television Campaign.   It is not surprising that campaigns are most effective when one side has weapons that the other side lacks, which sometimes happens in races for lower offices. In presidential elections, however, the capacity of image makers and campaign consultants to influence the outcome is minimized, because they regularly offset one another by working on both sides. In 1992, both major presidential candidates hired professional campaign consultants and advertising firms. Although Perot hired an experienced advertising firm, he essentially managed his own campaign. So all the campaigns used professionals, but how they were run was notably different.

Most observers judged that Clinton's team used the media much more effectively than Bush's. GMMG, Clinton's advertising firm, concentrated on twenty states for the general election. GMMG invested virtually no advertising funds in states such as New York and California, which polls showed to be safe for Clinton, but invested heavily in local spots in key competitive states, such as Ohio. In fact, Clinton's campaign spent an unprecedented 75 percent of its advertising budget on local rather than national spots. GMMG's strategy paid off, winning nineteen of the twenty targeted states.[80]

In contrast, the Bush campaign organization, which had steamrolled Michael Dukakis in 1988, lost its two masterminds. (Lee Atwater died of cancer and Roger Ailes declined to serve again.) The campaign never seemed to define a positive theme for the next Bush presidency. One veteran of Republican presidential advertising campaigns described the effort as "the worst one I've ever been involved in. . . . Ailes or an Atwater should have been [there]. . . . We needed some heavy hitters this time and we didn't have them."[81]

Because Perot had withdrawn from the race in July and reentered only on October 1, Perot's advertising team had a special challenge. It also had to deal with Perot's tight-fisted budgeting, which demanded that a TV spot be produced for $50,000 instead of the $400,000 normally charged for a first-class commercial.[82] Nevertheless, in only a month of campaigning, it spent almost $40 million in television advertising, about as much as each of the other two candidates had spent after their parties' conventions.[83] Placing "more advertising minutes than had any other campaign in U.S. history"—and campaigning almost exclusively on television—Perot won 19 percent of the vote, much more than expected."[84]

The Presidential Debates.   The first televised debate between presidential candidates was between John F. Kennedy and Richard Nixon in 1960, and it was thought to benefit Kennedy. Presidential debates were not held again until 1976. In one form or another, they have been a regular feature of presidential elections since. Sitting presidents have been reluctant to debate except on their own terms, and Bush favored a traditional format with a panel of reporters asking questions. But after Clinton surpassed him in the polls, Bush agreed to three presidential debates in October with questions posed successively by a panel of journalists, a group of ordinary citizens, and a combination of moderator and journalists. For different reasons, both candidates agreed to include Ross Perot. Bush though that Perot would undercut Clinton's voting base, whereas Clinton expected Perot to attack Bush's economic record.[85]

Packing four debates into eight days (there was a vice presidential debate, too) tested both voters' interest and stamina. Nevertheless, the three-cornered debates generally attracted higher audiences than the Bush-Dukakis debates in 1988. The third debate, which had the highest ratings, was seen by an estimated 88 million people.[86] When viewers were asked who won the debates, the results were mixed. Clinton and Perot virtually tied on winning the first and third (each chosen by about 30 percent), but Clinton clearly won the town hall format that he had sought, chosen as winner by 54 percent of the respondents. In none of the formats did Bush come out first.[87] Accordingly, Bush was the big loser in this phase of the campaign. Despite Clinton's strong showing in the second debate, Perot emerged as the big winner. The debates jacked up his favorability ratings and made him a more credible candidate.

Voter Satisfaction.   In 1992, voters had a choice of three major candidates for president, compared with only two in 1988. Nevertheless, in both elections only about 60 percent of the electorate were satisfied with their choice of candidates.[88] Otherwise, the 1992 election campaign was, in most respects, judged more favorably by the electorate than previous campaigns, as shown in Figure 9.6. Compared with 1988, more voters in 1992 said that they "learned enough" during the campaign to make an informed choice, and more found the presidential debates "helpful in deciding which candidate to vote for." Compared generally with past campaigns, a majority of voters also thought that there was more discussion of the issues (although a majority also found more "mud slinging"). Given the surprisingly warm reception for Perot's half-hour infomercials, which were viewed by almost 60 percent of the electorate, and the effect of campaigning in new media, we can expect longer ads and more informal appearances in 1996.[89]

CAMPAIGNS, ELECTIONS, AND PARTIES

Election campaigns today tend to be highly personalized, candidate centered, and conducted outside the control of party organizations. The increased use of electronic media, especially television, has encouraged candidates to personalize their campaign messages; at the same time, the decline of party identification has decreased the power of party-related appeals. Although the party affiliations of the candidates and the party identifications of the voters jointly explain a good deal of electoral behavior, party organizations are not central to elections in America, which has implications for democratic government.

Parties and the Majoritarian Model

According to the majoritarian model of democracy, parties link people with their government by making government responsive to public opinion. Chapter 8 outlined the model of responsible party government in a majoritarian democracy. This model holds that parties should present clear and coherent programs to voters, that voters should choose candidates according to the party programs that the winning party should carry out its programs once in office, and that voters should hold the governing party responsible at the next election for executing its program. As noted in Chapter 8, the Republican and Democratic parties do follow the model to the extent that they do formulate different platforms and do tend to pursue their announced policies when in office. The weak links in this model of responsible party government are those that connect candidates to voters through campaigns and elections.

You have not read much about the role of the party platform in nominating candidates, in conducting campaigns, or in explaining vote choice. In nominating presidential candidates, basic party principles (as captured in the party platform) do interact with the presidential primary process, and the candidate who wins enough convention delegates through the primaries will surely be comfortable with any platform that her or his delegates adopt. But House and Senate nominations are rarely fought over the party platform. And in general, thoughts about the party platforms are virtually absent from campaigning and from voters' minds when casting their ballots.

| FIGURE 9.6 | ■ Public Satisfaction with the 1992 Presidential Campaign |

No one has said that the 1992 presidential election campaign was perfect, but most people felt that they learned more about the candidates than in previous campaigns and encountered more discussion of issues (as well as more mudslinging). The public also had definite ideas about which candidate had the most informative advertisements.

Source: *"Voters Say 'Thumbs Up' to Campaign, Process, and Coverage," press release of the Times Mirror Center for the People & the Press (Washington, D.C.), 15 November 1992, pp. 22, 24.*

Learned enough about the candidates to make an informed choice
1992 77%
1988 59%

Presidential debates were helpful in deciding which candidates to vote for
1992 70%
1988 48%

Compared to past presidential elections, there was more discussion of issues
1992 59%

Compared to past presidential campaigns, there was more mud slinging
1992 68%

Which candidate ran the most informative commercials?
Perot 55%
Clinton 20%
Bush 8%

The fact is that voters do *not* choose between candidates according to party programs, and they do not hold the governing party responsible at the next election for executing its program. It has proved largely impossible to hold the governing party responsible, because no party is "governing" when the president is of one party and Congress is controlled by the other—which has occurred most of the time since the end of the Second World War (and in ten of thirteen congresses since 1969). When voters elect Republican presidents and Democratic congresses, there is little hope for the majoritarian model of party government. It is difficult enough when both branches are controlled by the same party, as President Clinton is finding out.

Parties and the Pluralist Model

The way parties in the United States operate is more in keeping with the pluralist model of democracy than the majoritarian model. Our parties are not the basic mechanism through which citizens control their government; instead, they function as two giant interest groups. The parties' interests lie in electing and reelecting their candidates to enjoy the benefits of public office. Except in extreme cases, the parties care little about the issues or ideologies favored by candidates for Congress and statewide offices. One exception that proves the rule is the Republican party's rejection of David E. Duke, the former Ku Klux Klan leader who in 1990 emerged as the party's nominee for senator in Louisiana. In a highly unusual move, national party leaders disowned Duke, and he lost the election. Otherwise, the parties are grateful for victories by almost any candidate. In turn, individual candidates operate as entrepreneurs, running their own campaigns as they like without party interference.

Some scholars believe that stronger parties would strengthen democratic government, even if they could not meet all the requirements of the responsible party model. Our parties already perform valuable functions in structuring the vote along partisan lines and in proposing alternative government policies, but stronger parties might also be able to play a more important role in coordinating government policies after elections. At present, the decentralized nature of the nominating process and campaigning for election offers many opportunities for organized groups outside the party to identify and back candidates who favor their interests. This is in keeping with pluralist theory, although it is certain to frustrate majority interests on occasion.

SUMMARY

Campaigning has evolved from a party-centered to a candidate-centered process. The successful candidate for public office usually must campaign first to win the party nomination, then to win the general election. A major factor in the decentralization of American parties is their reliance on primary elections to nominate candidates. Democratic and Republican nominations for president are no longer actually decided in the party's national conventions but are determined in advance of the convention through the complex process of selecting delegates pledged to particular candidates. Although candidates cannot win the nomination unless they have broad support within the party, the winners can legitimately say that they captured the nomination through their own efforts and that they owe little to the party organization.

The need to win a majority of votes in the electoral college structures presidential elections. Although a candidate can win a majority of the popular vote but lose in the electoral college, that has not happened in more than one hundred years. The electoral college operates to magnify the victory margin of the winning candidate. Since World War II, Republicans have usually won the presidency, whereas Democrats appear to have a lock on Congress, certainly on the House of Representatives.

In the general election, candidates usually retain the same staffs that helped them win the nomination. The dynamics of campaign financing also force candidates to rely mainly on their own resources or—in the case of presidential elections—on public funds. Party organizations contribute relatively little toward campaign expenses, and candidates must raise most of the money themselves. Money is essential in conducting a modern campaign for a major office, to conduct polls and to advertise the candidate's name, qualifications, and issue positions through the media. Candidates seek free news coverage whenever possible, but most must rely on paid advertising to get their messages across. Ironically, voters also get most of their campaign information from advertisements. The trend in recent years has been toward negative advertising, which seems to work, although it contributes to voters' distaste for politics.

Voting choice can be analyzed in terms of party identification, candidates' attributes, and policy positions. Party identification is still the most important long-term factor in shaping the voting decision, but few candidates rely on party in their campaigns. Most candidates today run personalized campaigns that stress their attributes and policies. Both Clinton and Perot used television more effectively than Bush in the 1992 presidential campaign, and the televised debates were especially helpful to Perot and harmful to Bush.

The way that nominations, campaigns, and elections are conducted in America is out of keeping with the ideals of responsible party government that fit the majoritarian model of democracy. In particular, campaigns and elections do not function to link parties strongly to voters, as the model posits. American parties are better suited to the pluralist model of democracy, which sees them as major interest groups competing with lesser groups to further their own interests. At least political parties aspire to the noble goal of representing the needs and wants of most people. As we see in the next chapter, interest groups do not even pretend as much.

Key Terms

election campaign
primary election
closed primary
open primary
blanket primary
presidential primary
local caucus
general election

straight ticket
split ticket
first-past-the-post election
incumbent
challenger
open election
Federal Election
  Commission (FEC)

Selected Readings

Buchanan, Bruce. *Electing a President: The Report on the Markle Commission on the Media and the Electorate.* Austin: University of Texas Press, 1991. Analyzes the 1988 presidential election using a special set of surveys designed to measure media effects.

Jamieson, Kathleen Hall. *Dirty Politics: Deception, Distraction, and Democracy.* New York: Oxford University Press, 1992. Dissects campaign advertisements—such as the 1988 Willie Horton ad—to show how they can mislead without being outright false.

Mableby, David B., and Candice J. Nelson. *The Money Chase: Congressional Campaign Finance Reform.* Washington, D.C.: Brookings Institution, 1990. Reviews problems in campaign finance and issues in reform; also provides valuable data on campaign receipts and expenditures.

McCubbins, Mathew D., ed. *Under the Watchful Eye: Managing Presidential Campaigns in the Television Era.* Washington, D.C.: Congressional Quarterly Press, 1992. Most of the essays argue that the changes in presidential campaigns because of television have alienated voters and made democracy less stable, but the editor argues that the changes have not materially affected the quality of the candidates or their ideological positions.

Patterson, Thomas E. *Out of Order.* New York: Alfred A. Knopf, 1993. This study of mass media's influence in presidential elections from 1960 to 1992 argues that the media, and particularly television, have replaced parties in choosing presidential candidates, with woeful results.

Pomper, Gerald M., Arterton, F. Christopher, Baker, Ross K., Burnham, Walter Dean, Frankovic, Kathleen A., Hershey, Marjorie Randon, and McWilliams, Wilson Carey. *The Election of 1992.* Chatham, N.J.: Chatham House, 1993. A group of experts thoroughly analyzes the presidential nomination and election campaigns and the congressional elections.

Salmore, Barbara G., and Stephen A. Salmore. *Candidates, Parties, and Campaigns: Electoral Politics in America,* 2d ed. Washington, D.C.: Congressional Quarterly Press, 1989. The best textbook treatment of election campaigning.

Shafer, Byron E. *Bifurcated Politics: Evolution and Reform in the National Party Convention.* Cambridge, Mass.: Harvard University Press, 1988. Explains how the conventions lost the nominating function, which now resides in the primary process. The convention is bifurcated, because delegates experience one convention while television viewers see another.

Sorauf, Frank J. *Money in American Elections.* Glenview, Ill.: Scott, Foresman, 1988. Surveys receipts and expenditures in presidential and congressional campaigns, including financing by individuals, PACs, parties, and government.

Twentieth Century Fund. *1–800 PRESIDENT: Report on the Task Force on Television and the Campaign of 1992.* New York: Twentieth Century Fund Press, 1993. This study by a group of journalists and academics concludes that television coverage in the 1992 race was dramatically better than the coverage in 1988, but there is still room for improvement.

West, Darrell M. *Air Wars: Television Advertising in Election Campaigns, 1952–1992.* Washington, D.C.: Congressional Quarterly Press, 1993. A wide-ranging analysis that concludes that, yes, television ads are becoming more negative, but voters still learn much about policy from ads, even negative ads.

10 Interest Groups

ITS DEATH WAS SLOW AND PAINFUL. The cause: a thousand cuts followed by a hemorrhage. Sadly, when the BTU tax was finally buried, no one would claim to be the parent of the proposal. Just about everyone wanted to take credit for the murder though.

The BTU proposal—a tax levied on the amount of heat in an energy source as measured by British thermal units (BTUs)—was part of President Bill Clinton's deficit reduction package introduced at the beginning of his administration in the winter of 1993. Deficit reduction had been an issue in the fall campaign, pushed especially hard by the independent presidential candidate Ross Perot. Shortly after the election, when Clinton assembled business leaders to talk about repairing the stagnant American economy, they strongly urged him to attack the deficit. And he did. Using a combination of spending cuts and tax increases, the deficit reduction proposal was designed to cut the deficit in half within five years.

A broad-based energy tax does not affect everyone the same way. Industries that use a lot of energy are going to pay more. People who live in some areas of the country are going to be affected more because of their dependence on a particular fuel. Interest groups seized on the inequities they saw in the BTU tax and pressed Congress to exempt them. Congress cooperated.

The bill was first taken up in the House, and the farm lobby was fast off the mark in getting it to reduce the tax on diesel fuel used by tractors. The steel industry got an exemption for metallurgical coal, used in great quantities in their factories. Aluminum producers and chlorine producers argued that because their manufacturing processes use so much energy, they needed a reduction in their BTU tax, too. The administration agreed, and more exemptions went into the bill. Firms that made products for the export market were upset because an energy tax would make their goods more expensive on the world market. The administration mollified these lobbies by promising a rebate on the tax for energy-intensive export products such as chemicals. The oil lobby got an exemption for fuel used by ships and jets. The farm lobby went back for a double scoop, asking that ethanol, a fuel made from corn, be exempted. Here, the House Ways and Means Committee, which is responsible for initially writing tax legislation, finally drew the line and said no. Not to worry—leading senators promised to put an ethanol exemption in when they got the bill.

By the time the legislation passed the House, interest groups had won so many exemptions that it was hard for most people to understand what the

BTU tax still covered. The *New York Times* described the bill as "one of the most exemption-loaded, head-scratchingly complicated, brow-furrowing revenue raisers in history."[1] What was left of the tax came under immediate attack in the Senate. Energy producers, especially oil companies, asked their senators to try to block the tax. With a narrow majority in the Senate, the administration could not afford many defections, because all the Republicans were promising to vote against the bill, no matter what was in it. With the BTU proposal already so badly shredded by all the exemptions, it was hardly worth fighting for. The Clinton administration quickly threw in the towel, promising to introduce another tax instead.[2] The bill that finally passed Congress included a modest tax on gasoline.

Although Americans tell pollsters they believe strongly in deficit reduction, the BTU tax was a clear example of pluralism triumphing over majoritarianism. The majority wants the deficit reduced, but no majority favors any particular method of paring down the deficit. People may grudgingly accept the need for new taxes in any deficit reduction package, but they are not going to demand that their representatives and senators vote for a tax when a specific tax plan comes before Congress. At the same time, interest groups push hard for exemptions, because their members are intensely upset about some aspect of the tax.

In this chapter, we look at the central dynamic of pluralist democracy: the interaction of interest groups and government. In analyzing the process by which interest groups and lobbyists come to speak on behalf of different groups, we focus on a number of questions. How do interest groups form? Who do they represent? What tactics do they use to convince policymakers that their views are best for the nation? Is the interest group system biased to favor certain types of people? If so, what are the consequences?

INTEREST GROUPS AND THE AMERICAN POLITICAL TRADITION

An **interest group** is an organized body of individuals who share some political goals and try to influence public policy decisions.[3] Among the most prominent interest groups in the United States are the AFL-CIO (representing labor union members), the American Farm Bureau Federation (representing farmers), the Business Roundtable (representing big business), and Common Cause (representing citizens concerned with reforming government). Interest groups are also called **lobbies,** and their representatives are referred to as **lobbyists.**

Interest Groups: Good or Evil?

A recurring debate in American politics concerns the role of interest groups in a democratic society. Are interest groups a threat to the well being of the political system, or do they contribute to its proper functioning? A favorable early evaluation of interest groups can be found in the writings of Alexis de Tocqueville, a French visitor to the United States in the early nineteenth century. During his travels, Tocqueville marveled at the array of organizations he found, and he later wrote that "Americans of all ages, all conditions, and all dispositions, constantly form associations."[4] Tocqueville was suggesting that the ease with which we form organizations reflects a strong democratic culture.

Yet, other early observers were concerned about the consequences of interest group politics. Writing in the *Federalist,* James Madison warned of the dangers of "factions," the major divisions in American society. In *Federalist* 10, written in 1787, Madison said it was inevitable that substantial differences would develop between factions. It was only natural for farmers to oppose merchants; tenants, landlords; and so on. Madison further reasoned that each faction would do what it could to prevail over other factions, that each basic interest in society would try to persuade government to adopt policies that favored it at the expense of others. He noted that the fundamental causes of faction were "sown in the nature of man."[5]

But Madison argued against trying to suppress factions. He concluded that factions can be eliminated only by removing our freedoms: "Liberty is to faction what air is to fire."[6] Instead, Madison suggested that relief from the self-interested advocacy of factions should come only through controlling the effects of that advocacy. The relief would be provided by a democratic republic in which government would mediate between opposing factions. The size and diversity of the nation as well as the structure of government would ensure that even a majority faction could never come to suppress the rights of others.[7]

How we judge interest groups—"good" or "evil"—may depend on how strongly we are committed to freedom or equality (see Chapter 1). People dislike interest groups in general, because they do not offer equal representation to all—some sectors of society are better represented than others. A 1990 survey of the American public showed that almost two-thirds of those polled regarded lobbying as a threat to American democracy.[8] Yet another survey showed that when asked about specific organizations, Americans were mostly positive about individual groups. The organizations mentioned in the survey were primarily citizen lobbies, which are probably more likely to gain approval from the public (see Figure 10.1).

FIGURE 10.1	■ Special Interest Groups: We Just Love 'Em

Despite some anxiety about the power of special interest groups, the results of this Gallup Poll show that Americans applaud the work of most individual lobbying organizations. Still, the approval ratings vary substantially, and the low score for the Tobacco Institute indicates that some organizations are seen in a less-than-positive light.

Source: *Gallup Report, May 1989, pp. 25–27. Used by permission.*

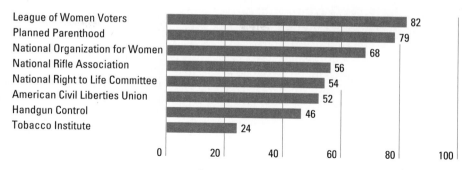

Percentage of respondents with favorable opinion

League of Women Voters	82
Planned Parenthood	79
National Organization for Women	68
National Rifle Association	56
National Right to Life Committee	54
American Civil Liberties Union	52
Handgun Control	46
Tobacco Institute	24

Yet, the two polls are not so much contradictory as they are indicative of our ambivalence toward interest groups. We distrust interest groups as a whole, but we like those that we believe represent views we support. Stated more bluntly, we hate lobbies—except those that represent us.

The Roles of Interest Groups

The "evil" side of interest group politics is all too apparent. Each group pushes its selfish interests, which, despite the group's claims to the contrary, are not always in the best interest of other Americans. The "good" side of interest group advocacy may not be so clear. How do the actions of interest groups benefit our political system?[9]

Representation.   Interest groups represent people before their government. Just as a member of Congress represents a particular constituency, so does a lobbyist. A lobbyist for the National Association of Broadcasters, for example, speaks for the interests of radio and television broadcasters when Congress or a government agency is considering a relevant policy decision.

Whatever the political interest—the cement industry, social security, endangered species—it helps to have an active lobby operating in Washington. Members of Congress represent a multitude of interests— some of them conflicting—from their own districts and states. Government administrators, too, are pulled in different directions and have their own policy preferences. Interest groups articulate their members' concerns, presenting them directly and forcefully in the political process (see Politics in a Changing America 10.1).

Participation.   Interest groups are also vehicles for political participation. They provide a means by which like-minded citizens can pool their resources and channel their energies into collective political action. People band together because they know it is much easier to get government to listen to a group than to an individual. One farmer fighting for

POLITICS IN A CHANGING AMERICA 10.1

A Political Voice for Christians

The new political movements organized in recent years represent diverse interests and constituencies. What their members have in common, however, is a feeling of being marginalized within our political system. Members share a belief that unless they are highly mobilized and aggressive in pursuing their political objectives, policymakers will ignore their concerns. This is certainly the attitude of fundamentalists—evangelical Christians whose religious beliefs are based on a literal interpretation of the Bible.

Fundamentalist Christians believe that modern society has turned away from basic moral principles, leading to serious social problems. In their eyes, liberal and moderate politicians have mistakenly tried to solve these problems with expensive, wasteful, and counterproductive social programs. Christian fundamentalists feel that what is needed instead is a return to strong family values.

In the political arena, many groups claim to represent fundamentalists, but the Christian Coalition plays a central leadership role. Based in Virginia, this conservative group is closely allied with the Reverend Pat Robertson. Robertson, who ran unsuccessfully for the Republican presidential nomination in 1988, is probably best known for his TV show, "The 700 Club," which is shown around the country on the Christian Broad-

casting Network. The Christian Coalition has roughly 350,000 members, 750 chapters, and an annual budget in excess of $10 million.

In the past few years the Christian Coalition has redirected the efforts of the religious right away from Washington politics and toward local politics. In a sophisticated and well-planned approach, the Christian Coalition and its affiliates are trying to change America from the bottom up. By running candidates for school boards, city councils, and the like, the group hopes to influence policies while building the organization through the grass-roots involvement of local adherents. This has brought about some visible successes. In San Diego, California, for example, the Christian Coalition played a critical role in putting 90 candidates on the ballot in a recent local election. Of the 90, 60 won their races.

The issues that have most animated the Christian Coalition include abortion, homosexuality, prayer in school, and the decline of the traditional nuclear family. The influence of the religious right over these issues is often exaggerated, but the movement has certainly had an impact on public policy. One of the most controversial areas is the efforts of Christian conservatives to change school textbooks so that they will more closely reflect traditional values. In Texas, Christian activists on the state Board of Education told

more generous price supports probably will not get very far, but thousands of farmers united in an organization stand a much better chance of getting policymakers to consider their needs.

Education.   As part of their efforts to lobby government and to increase their membership, interest groups help educate their members, the public at large, and government officials. When the Clinton administration proposed the BTU tax, the conservative group Citizens for a Sound Economy swung into action. One focus of their efforts was a study that made the case that such a tax would damage the competitiveness of some American publishers wishing to sell a health text to high schools that they had to remove some clinical illustrations and delete toll-free telephone numbers for gay and lesbian organizations. Critics charged censorship, but those on the school board who wanted such changes replied that the books "were promoting homosexuality as an acceptable life style and promoting sex as being OK if you use a condom."

Many liberals are antagonistic to these groups, not simply because they hold competing political views, but because they believe that the Christian right is trying to impose its particular brand of religion on the rest of the country. Yet in America political activism can also be found in black churches, synagogues, mainline Protestant congregations, and Catholic parishes. Nevertheless, it is Christian conservatives that are the best organized among all religious sects in the United States. Also, churches embracing the beliefs of the Christian right are the most rapidly growing denominations in this country. Pentecostals, an evangelical denomination whose followers are generally sympathetic to Christian conservatism, grew in membership from about 1.9 million in 1960 to 9.9 million in 1990, an increase of 423 percent.

What is especially impressive about the Christian Coalition and other groups associated with the religious right, is their success in involving rank-and-file citizens in politics and government. Senator Nancy Kassebaum of Kansas says of the religious right, "It's a voice that in many ways comes from people who feel that they've never been part of the process." As many Christians who dislike the religious right point out, the Christian Coalition does not speak for all Christians. But for those Christians it does represent, the Christian Coalition is a powerful and passionate advocate.

• *Sources: Randall Balmer,* Mine Eyes Have Seen the Glory: A Journey into the Evangelical Subculture in America *(New York: Oxford University Press, 1989); David Broder, "Christian Coalition, Shifting Tactics, To Lobby Against Clinton Budget,"* Washington Post, *18 July 1993, p. A7; Sam Dillon, "Publisher Pulls a Textbook in Furor on Sexual Content,"* New York Times, *17 March 1994, p. B10; Allen D. Hertzke,* Echoes of Discontent *(Washington, D.C.: Congressional Quarterly, 1993); Ted G. Jelen and Clyde Wilcox, "The Christian Right in the 1990s,"* Public Perspective *(March/April 1993): 10–12; Benton Johnson, "The Denominations: The Changing Map of Religious America,"* Public Perspective *(March/April 1993): 3–7; Barry A. Kosmin and Seymour Lachman,* One Nation Under God *(New York: Harmony Books, 1993); Kim Lipton, "The New Face(s) of the Religious Right,"* Christianity Today, *20 July 1992, pp. 42–45; "The Christian Coalition: Moral Majority of the 1990s,"* People for the American Way Action Fund, *September 11, 1992; Robert Sullivan, "An Army of the Faithful,"* New York Times Magazine, *25 April 1993, p. 33ff; and Michael Weisskopf, "'Gospel Grapevine' Displays Strength in Controversy Over Military Gay Ban,"* Washington Post, *1 February 1993, p. A1.*

businesses. Interest groups give only their side of the "facts," but they do serve to bring more information to the public to digest and evaluate. To gain the attention of policymakers they are trying to educate, interest groups need to provide them with information that is not easily obtained from other sources.[10]

Agenda Building. In a related role, interest groups bring new issues into the political limelight through a process called **agenda building.** American society has many problem areas, but public officials are not addressing all of them. Through their advocacy, interest groups make the

FIGURE **10.2**   ■ **Pay Attention!**

Women's interest groups have played a crucial role in gaining the public's attention for issues that once were ignored. In comparison with the executive branch and Congress, the women's movement initiates many more events that get coverage by the New York Times *(used here as a barometer of national press coverage). The news stories measured in this figure are such "events" as demonstrations, action on legislation in Congress, and lawsuits.*

Source: *Anne N. Costain,* Inviting Women's Rebellion. *The Johns Hopkins University Press, Baltimore/London, 1992, p. 101. Reprinted with permission.*

government aware of problems, then try to see to it that something is done to solve them. Women's groups have played a critical role in gaining attention for problems, such as unequal pay for women and men doing similar jobs, that were being systematically ignored. As Figure 10.2 shows, the women's movement (especially women's interest groups) generated the most news coverage of issues of concern to women.[11]

Program Monitoring.   Finally, interest groups engage in **program monitoring.** Lobbies follow government programs important to their constituents, keeping abreast of developments in Washington and in local communities, where policies are implemented. When a program is not operating as it should, concerned interest groups push administrators to change them in ways that promote the group's goals. They draw attention to agency officials' transgressions and even file suit to stop actions they consider unlawful. When the United Auto Workers felt that the Occupational Safety and Health Administration (OSHA) was not doing enough to protect workers when they cleaned dangerous machinery, the group took the agency to court. The union documented some gruesome deaths, but the court found no violation of OSHA program guidelines.

Interest groups do, then, play some positive roles in their pursuit of self-interest. But we should not assume that the positive side of interest groups neatly balances the negative. Questions remain to be answered about the overall influence of interest groups on public policymaking. Most important, are the effects of interest group advocacy being controlled, as Madison believed they should be?

**HOW INTEREST
GROUPS FORM**

Do some people form interest groups more easily than others? Are some factions represented while others are not? Pluralists assume that when a political issue arises, interest groups with relevant policy concerns begin to lobby. Policy conflicts are ultimately resolved through bargaining and negotiation between the involved organizations and government. Unlike Madison, who dwelled on the potential for harm by factions, pluralists believe interest groups are a good thing, that they further democracy by broadening representation within the system.

An important part of pluralism is the belief that new interest groups form as a matter of course when the need arises. David Truman outlines this idea in his classic work, *The Governmental Process.*[12] He says that when individuals are threatened by change, they band together in an interest group. For example, if government threatens to regulate a particular industry, the firms comprising that industry will start a trade association to protect their financial well being. Truman sees a direct cause-and-effect relationship in all of this: Existing groups stand in equilibrium until some type of disturbance (such as falling wages or declining farm prices) forces new groups to form.

Truman's thinking on the way interest groups form is like the "invisible hand" notion of laissez-faire economics: Self-correcting market forces will remedy imbalances in the marketplace. But in politics, no invisible hand, no force, automatically causes interest groups to develop. Truman's disturbance theory paints an idealized portrait of interest group politics in America. In real life, people do not automatically organize when they are adversely affected by some disturbance. A good example of "nonorganization" can be found in Herbert Gans's book *The Urban Villagers.*[13] Gans, a sociologist, moved into the West End, a low-income neighborhood in Boston, during the late 1950s. The neighborhood had been targeted for urban redevelopment; the city was planning to replace old buildings with modern ones. This meant that the people living there—primarily poor Italian-Americans who very much liked their neighborhood—would have to move.

Being evicted is a highly traumatic experience, so the situation in the West End certainly qualified as a bonafide disturbance in Truman's scheme of interest group formation. Yet, the people of the West End barely put up a fight to save their neighborhood. They started an organization, but it attracted little support. Residents remained unorganized; soon, they were moved and buildings were demolished.

Disturbance theory clearly fails to explain what happened in Boston's West End. An adverse condition or change does not automatically mean that an interest group will form. What, then, is the missing ingredient? Political scientist Robert Salisbury says that the quality of interest group leadership may be the crucial factor.[14]

Interest Group Entrepreneurs

Salisbury likens the role of an interest group leader to that of an entrepreneur in the business world. An entrepreneur is someone who starts new enterprises, usually at considerable personal financial risk. Salisbury says that an **interest group entrepreneur,** or organizer, succeeds or fails for many of the same reasons a business entrepreneur succeeds or fails. The

There Goes the Neighborhood
When the city of Boston targeted its West End for urban renewal, residents did not organize to fight the decision. Wrecking balls soon demolished the neighborhood, clearing the way for various redevelopment projects, including high-rise housing.

interest group entrepreneur must have something attractive to "market" in order to convince people to join.[15] Potential members must be persuaded that the benefits of joining outweigh the costs. Someone starting a new union, for example, must convince workers that the union can win them wages high enough to offset their membership dues. The organizer of an ideological group must convince potential members that the group can effectively lobby the government to achieve their particular goals.

The development of the United Farm Workers Union shows the importance of leadership in the formation of an interest group. The union is made up of men and women who pick crops in California and other parts of the country. The work is backbreaking, performed in the hot growing season. The pickers are predominantly poor, uneducated Mexican Americans.

Their chronically low wages and deplorable living conditions made the farm workers prime candidates for organization into a labor union. And throughout the twentieth century, various unions tried to organize the pickers. Yet for many reasons, including distrust of union organizers, intimidation by employers, and lack of money to pay union dues, all failed. Then, in 1962, the late Cesar Chavez, a poor Mexican American, began to crisscross the central valley of California, talking to workers and planting the idea of a union. Chavez had been a farm worker himself (he first worked as a picker at the age of ten), and he was well aware of the difficulties that lay ahead for his newly organized union.

After a strike against grape growers failed in 1965, Chavez changed his tactics of trying to build a stronger union merely by recruiting a larger membership. Copying the civil rights movement, Chavez and his followers marched 250 miles to the state capitol in Sacramento to demand help from the governor. The march and other nonviolent tactics began to draw sympathy from people who had no direct involvement in farming. Seeing the movement as a way to help poor members of the church the Catholic clergy was a major source of support. This support, in turn, gave the charismatic Chavez greater credibility, and his followers cast him in the role of spiritual as well as political leader. At one point, he fasted for twenty-five days to show his commitment to nonviolence. Democratic senator Robert Kennedy of New York, one of the most popular politicians of the day, joined Chavez when he broke his fast at a mass conducted on the back of a flatbed truck in Delano, California.[16]

Chavez subsequently called for a boycott, and a small but significant number of Americans stopped buying grapes. The growers, who had bitterly fought the union, were finally hurt economically. Under this and other economic pressures, they eventually agreed to recognize and bargain with the United Farm Workers. The union, in turn, helped its members through the wage and benefit agreements it was able to negotiate.

Who Is Being Organized?

Cesar Chavez is a good example of the importance of leadership in the formation of a new interest group. Despite many years of adverse conditions, efforts to organize the farm workers had failed. The dynamic leadership of Cesar Chavez is what seems to have made the difference.

But another important element is at work in the formation of interest groups. The residents of Boston's West End and the farm workers in California were poor, uneducated or undereducated, and politically inexperienced—factors that made it extremely difficult to organize them into interest groups. If they had been well to do, educated, and politically experienced, they probably would have banded together immediately. People who have money, are educated, and know how the system operates are more confident that their actions can make a difference. Together, these attributes give people more incentive to devote their time and ample resources to organizing and supporting interest groups (see Figure 10.3).

Every existing interest group has its history, but the three variables just discussed help explain why groups may or may not become fully organized. First, an adverse change or disturbance can contribute to people's

Lobbying to the Extreme

Some interest groups feel that policymakers are generally opposed or indifferent to their cause and that there is little to be gained by conventional lobbying. Instead, they use unusual and even extreme tactics to draw media attention to their side of an issue. On the left, the Reverend Rob Schenk of Operation Rescue holds up an aborted fetus outside a Buffalo, New York abortion clinic. Members of Operation Rescue believe that abortion is murder and that they must do whatever they can to shut down abortion clinics. On the right is a casket carrying the body of AIDS victim Tim Bailey. Bailey told friends in Act Up, an AIDS protest group, that he wanted a political funeral in Washington D.C. Activists from the organization tried to take the coffin out of this van to carry it into the Capitol, but Capitol police kept shoving it back in. Finally, the protesters gave up and took Bailey's body back home with them to New York.

FIGURE 10.3   ■ **Social Class and Interest Group Membership**

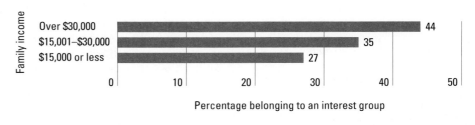

Membership in interest groups is clearly linked to social class. The higher their total family income, the more likely it is that individuals will belong to at least one political interest group. The data here come from a survey of citizens in five American cities (Birmingham, Alabama; Dayton, Ohio; Portland, Oregon; St. Paul, Minnesota; and San Antonio, Texas).

Source: Based on The Case for Participatory Democracy *by Jeffrey M. Berry, Kent E. Portney, and Ken Thomson. Copyright © Brookings Institution. Used with permission.*

awareness that they need political representation. However, change alone does not ensure that an organization will form, and organizations have formed in the absence of a disturbance. Second, the quality of leadership is critical in the organization of interest groups. Some interest group entrepreneurs are more skilled than others at convincing people to join their organizations. Finally, the higher the socioeconomic level of potential members, the more likely they are to know the value of interest groups and to participate in politics by joining them.

Because wealthy and better-educated Americans are more likely to form and join lobbies, they seem to have an important advantage in the political process. Nevertheless, as the United Farm Workers' case shows, poor and uneducated people are also capable of forming interest groups. The question that remains, then, is not *whether* various opposing interests are represented but *how well* they are represented. Or, in terms of Madison's premise in *Federalist* 10, are the effects of faction—in this case, the advantages of the wealthy and well educated—being controlled? Before we can answer this question about how interest groups affect the level of political equality in our society, we need to turn our attention to the resources available to interest groups.

INTEREST GROUP RESOURCES

The strengths, capabilities, and influence of an interest group depend in large part on its resources. A group's most significant resources are its members, lobbyists, and money, including funds that can be contributed to political candidates. The sheer quantity of a group's resources is important, and so is the wisdom with which its resources are used.

Members

One of the most valuable resources an interest group can have is a large, politically active membership. If a lobbyist is trying to convince a legislator to support a particular bill, having a large group of members who live in the legislator's home district or state is tremendously helpful. A legislator who has not already taken a firm position on a bill might be swayed by the knowledge that voters back home are kept informed by interest groups of votes on key issues.

Critical Condition

Opposition to the Clinton administration's health care reform plan was spearheaded by a phalanx of interest groups. Many of the lobbies which worked successfully to defeat the proposal were health care organizations, like insurance groups, which stood to lose financially from the reforms being considered. Conservative citizens groups also lobbied against the Clinton plan. Here are some conservative members of the House to help launch the American Conservative Union's Health Care Truth Tour, a nationwide effort to kill the proposed legislation. The ACU believed the reforms would increase the size of government, raise taxes, and ruin the American health care system.

Members give an organization not only the political muscle to influence policy but also financial resources. The more money an organization can collect through dues and contributions, the more people it can hire to lobby government officials and monitor the policymaking process. The American Medical Association has considerable resources, because its members—physicians—have high incomes and can pay expensive dues. The organization's wealth helped to make it a major player when President Clinton put comprehensive health care reform at the top of his agenda.

Greater resources also allow the organization to communicate with its members more and to inform them better. And funding helps the group maintain its membership and attract new members.

Maintaining Membership.   To keep the members it already has, an organization must persuade them that it is doing a good job in its advocacy. Most lobbies use a newsletter to keep members apprised of developments in government that relate to issues of concern to them. However, newsletters are more than a means of communicating news to members. Interest groups use them as a public relations tool to try to keep members believing that their lobby is playing a critical role in protecting their interests. Thus, the role the organization is playing in trying to influence government always receives prominent coverage in the newsletters.

Business, professional, and labor associations generally have an easier time holding onto members than do citizen groups—groups whose basis of organization is a concern for issues that are not directly related to the members' jobs. In many corporations, membership in a trade group constitutes only a minor business expense. Big individual corporations have no memberships as such, but they often open their own lobbying offices in

Washington. They have the advantage of being able to use institutional financial resources; they do not have to rely on voluntary contributions.[17] Labor unions are helped in states that require workers to affiliate with the union that is the bargaining agent with their employer. On the other hand, citizen groups base their appeal on members' ideological sentiments. These groups face a difficult challenge: Issues can blow hot and cold, and a particularly hot issue one year may not hold the same interest to citizens the next.

Attracting New Members.   All membership groups are constantly looking for new adherents to expand their resources and clout. Groups that rely on ideological appeals have a special problem, because the competition in most policy areas is intense. People concerned about the environment, for example, can join a seemingly infinite number of local, state, and national groups. The National Wildlife Federation, Environmental Action, the Environmental Defense Fund, the Natural Resources Defense Council, Friends of the Earth, the Wilderness Society, the Sierra Club, and the Environmental Policy Center are just some of the national organizations that lobby on environmental issues. Groups try to distinguish themselves from competitors by concentrating on a few key issues and developing a reputation as the most involved and knowledgeable about them.[18] The Sierra Club, one of the oldest environmental groups, has long had a focus on protecting national parks. The names of newer groups, such as Clean Water Action and the National Toxins Campaign, reveal their substantive focus (and marketing strategy). Still, organizations in a crowded policy area must go beyond such differentiation and aggressively market themselves to potential contributors.

One common method of attracting new members is **direct mail**—letters sent to a selected audience to promote the organization and appeal for contributions. The key to direct mail is a carefully targeted audience. An organization can purchase a list of people who are likely to be sympathetic to its cause or trade lists with a similar organization. A group trying to fight abortion, for instance, might use a subscription list from the conservative magazine *National Review,* while a prochoice lobby might use that of the liberal *New Republic.* The main drawbacks to direct mail are its expense and low rate of return. A response rate of 2 percent of those newly solicited is considered good. Groups usually lose money when prospecting for members from a mailing list they have rented from a direct mail broker, but they hope to recoup the money as the new members contribute again and again over time. Still, they have no assurance of this. To maximize the chances of a good return, care and thought are given to the design and content of letters (see Feature 10.1). Letters often try to play on the reader's emotions, to create the feeling that the reader should be personally involved in the struggle.[19]

The Free-Rider Problem.   The need for aggressive marketing by interest groups suggests that getting people who sympathize with a group's goals actually to join and support it with their contributions is difficult. Economists call this difficulty the **free-rider problem,** but we might call it, more colloquially, the "let-George-do-it problem".[20] The funding for public television stations illustrates the dilemma. Almost all agree that public television, which survives in large part through viewers' contributions, is of great value. But only a fraction of those who watch public television contribute on a regular basis. Why? Because people can watch the programs whether they contribute or not. The free rider has the same access to public television as the contributor.

The same problem crops up for interest groups. When a lobbying group wins benefits, those benefits are not restricted to members of the organization. For instance, if the American Business Conference wins a tax concession from Congress for capital expenditures, all businesses that fall within the provisions of the law can take advantage of the tax break. Thus, many business executives might not support their firms' joining the American Business Conference, even though they might benefit from the group's efforts; they prefer instead to let others shoulder the financial burden.

The free-rider problem increases the difficulty of attracting paying members, but it certainly does not make the task impossible. Many people realize that if everyone decides to let George do it, the job simply will not get done. Millions of Americans contribute to interest groups because they are concerned about an issue or feel a responsibility to help organizations that work on their behalf. Also, many organizations offer membership benefits that have nothing to do with politics or lobbying. Business **trade associations,** for example, are a source of information about industry trends and effective management practices; they organize conventions at which members can learn, socialize, and occasionally find new customers or suppliers. An individual firm in the electronics industry may not care that much about the lobbying done by the Electronics Industries Association, but it may have a vital interest in the information about marketing and manufacturing that the organization provides. Successful interest groups are adept at supplying the right mix of benefits to their target constituency.[21]

LOBBYISTS

Part of the money raised by interest groups is used to pay lobbyists, who represent the organizations before government. Lobbyists make sure that people in government know what their members want and that their organizations know what government is doing. For example, when an administrative agency issues new regulations, lobbyists are right there to interpret the content and implications of the regulations for rank-and-file members. The Washington representative of an oil trade association was reading the *Federal Register* (a daily compendium of all new regulations issued by the government) as part of his daily routine when he noticed that the Federal Aviation Administration planned to issue new regulations requiring detailed flight plans by noncommercial aircraft. The policy would make rescue efforts for noncommercial planes easier, but the lobbyist realized that it could compromise the confidentiality surrounding the flights of company planes for aerial exploration for oil and gas. Anyone could obtain the filed flight plans. He notified the member companies, and their lobbying prevented the implementation of the regulations, precluding the possibility of competitors' getting hold of such secret data.[22]

FEATURE **10.1**

■ Throw the Bums Out

People are flooded with direct mail from interest groups, candidates, and charities. Whatever the cause, all the letters are trying to do the same thing: to get you to part with your hard-earned cash. In this competitive environment, letters not only must be distinctive, they must pull at your emotions so that your desire to help overcomes your desire to save your money. Look at how the conservative National Taxpayers Union (NTU) designed an appeal to get prospective members to join the organization to help it fight for a constitutional limit on the number of terms that members of Congress can serve.

The first goal of a direct-mail package is to get people to open it rather than just toss it unopened into the wastebasket with other junk mail. Consequently, envelopes must entice the reader. The envelope for this appeal gives its recipients many reasons—twenty-four to be exact—to see what is inside. The direct mail consultants who designed this envelope hope that when people glance at it, items such as "23 Straight Unbalanced Budgets" (#7) and "$375,000 Beauty Shop Renovation" (#11) will remind them how angry Congress makes them.

---

24 reasons for TERM LIMITS

Canoe 1800s
Additional Nonprofit
Postage Paid
US.05

1. SAVINGS AND LOAN CRISIS
2. $4 TRILLION FEDERAL DEBT
3. CHECK BOUNCING
4. MILLION DOLLAR PENSIONS
5. TED KENNEDY
6. AUTOMATIC PAY RAISES
7. 23 STRAIGHT UNBALANCED BUDGETS
8. FRANKED MAILING ABUSES
9. PANDERING TO SPECIAL INTERESTS
10. EXPENSIVE CAR LEASES
11. $375,000 BEAUTY SHOP RENOVATION
12. LOW COST HEALTH AND FITNESS CLUB
13. $21,000 MARBLE ELEVATOR FLOORS
14. EXEMPT FROM LAWS THEY PASS
15. FREE AIRPORT PARKING
16. FREE PHARMACEUTICALS
17. UNCONTROLLED SPENDING
18. 98% RE-ELECTED IN 1990
19. COVER-UPS
20. PAC INFLUENCE
21. POLITICAL INCOMPETENCE
22. PORK BARREL PROJECTS
23. KICKBACKS
24. POWER DRUNK POLITICIANS

Direct-mail letters must engage the reader. The goal is to make you care about the issue discussed. The first page of this letter tells readers that in addition to high salaries, members of Congress have free medical care, free prescriptions, taxpayer-subsidized meals, and lucrative pensions (averaging over $1 million). The NTU hopes that this gets your blood boiling. There's no attempt at a balanced discussion. All direct mail tells only the side of the story that the lobbying group wants to communicate. Letters are typically long—this one is four oversized pages. By the end of the letter, readers should be so moved or outraged that they pull out the checkbook.

Groups often try to validate their appeal by reprinting something from an outside source that confirms the point they are trying to make. The NTU uses a copy of a letter from former President Ronald Reagan, a hero among conservatives, that praises the organization for its work to lower taxes.

TERM LIMITS ARE THE ANSWER

NATIONAL TAXPAYERS UNION

325 Pennsylvania Avenue, S.E., Washington D.C. 20003

Dear Friend,

CHECKBOUNCING, GREED, PAYRAISES AT WILL, SIX-FIGURE SALARIES . . . .

. . . . . HOW ABOUT A MILLION DOLLAR PENSION WHEN YOU RETIRE?

If you're wondering where jobs like this exist, look no further . . .

. . . YOU'RE THE EMPLOYER!

That's right. You and I pay every nickel of our politicians salaries, benefits, expense accounts, pensions. YOU NAME IT!

But, there's something even more insidious . . .

. . . Because the politicians are in charge of the national purse strings, they've greased their own palms so generously that no matter what economic catastrophe hits us so-called "lesser men", THEY CONTINUE TO SURVIVE LIKE ROYALTY.

Here's what I'm talking about . . . .

* Annual salaries of $129,500 per year - plus they can increase this any time they want.

* Big expense accounts. Typically, each Senator gets $611,000 a year. Each House Member gets an average of $199,000 a year.

* Free medical.

* Free prescriptions.

* Taxpayer subsidized meals.

* A special congressional tax deduction for $3,000 each year for living expenses.

* Free long-distance calls, free picture framing and decorating, free satellite hook-ups, and low cost health spas.

* Use of government barbers, hair salons, stationery, cameras, film and video equipment.

* Pensions fit for a king . . . the average retiring Congressman can expect to receive over $1 million

Over, please.

(continued)

NTU — A LEADER IN WASHINGTON

For the last 20 years the National Taxpayers Union has been the citizens lobby in Washington.

By keeping up to date on the activities of the Congress, NTU has reported evidence of overspending and out of control budgets to the American people.

In addition, NTU has been the leader in the fight against higher taxes and increasing deficits.

NTU has led the battle for a Balanced Budget Amendment in both Congress and the states, for which it has been highly acclaimed.

Here's what the
LOS ANGELES TIMES
had to say about
THE NATIONAL TAXPAYERS UNION. .

"James Davidson's longtime crusade to save America from Spending itself into oblivion is racing toward a historic milestone."

"National Taxpayers Union is our BEST HOPE for the future. . ."

James D. Davidson
Chairman

JOIN NTU NOW   JOIN NTU NOW   JOIN NTU NOW

TERM LIMITATION IS THE ANSWER

Now, once again, the National Taxpayers Union is ready to lead the fight to limit congressional spending.

NTU is putting together the most effective lobbying effort ever demonstrated to reform congressional spending habits and limit the terms of the members of Congress.

Certainly, no one ever dreamed that Congress would abandon the responsibilities to the taxpayers and levy taxes beyond reason on the people who elected them.

In a sense, they have created an elitism in this country and taken the rights of the citizens away.

Only with a Term Limitation Amendment can the power to govern this nation be returned to the people.

"The National Taxpayers Union has been hard at work for years in a modest turn-of-the-century red brick building a few blocks from the Capitol . . .

For Jim Davidson (chairman of The National Taxpayers Union) the need for a balanced budget is not a "liberal" or "conservative" issue . . .

. . . instead, the idea is "that the earth belongs to the living" as Thomas Jefferson said. In other words, we have no right to saddle future generations with a runaway national debt."

Detroit News

Quote from the San Francisco Chronicle. .

" The National Taxpayers Union . . . is the granddaddy of the tax revolt organizations."

**AMERICA'S FIRST ALL CITIZENS' LOBBY
NATIONAL TAXPAYERS UNION**

325 Pennsylvania Avenue, SE
Washington, D.C. 20003

WARNING: FAILURE TO ACT COULD BE HAZARDOUS TO YOUR WEALTH

Congress was never intended to be an elite club of professional politicians.

It was meant to represent real people, who did real work, held real jobs, and had a real interest in the future . . . not just in the next election.

No decent or sensible group of citizens would mortgage their own future . . . or their children's future. But that's what professional politicians have done, and it gets worse every year . . .

But one thing is for certain in this uncertain world.

Do nothing and that's exactly what you'll get. Nothing.

That's why you and I must do something NOW to take control of our government. Ultimately the power to change rests with us . . . all we need is the courage and determination to use it. But we must use it . . . while we still have the chance.

James Dale Davidson
Chairman
National Taxpayers Union

Dear American Taxpayer:

The state of this great nation is truly in your hands now.

We can continue our plunge towards economic disaster or reach into our reserves of AMERICAN PRIDE and INTEGRITY. DRAW THE LINE AND FIGHT.

The decision is yours alone to make.

Choose NOW and join NTU. That one single act will add more strength and clout to America's foremost taxpayer organization than any single thing you can do.

The objectives are clear . . . The outcome irrevocable. Join NTU and together let's take back what belongs to you. Balance the Federal Budget, do away with wild spending, throw out the scoundrels who made this ECONOMIC MESS, and make AMERICA FIRST AGAIN. We need to pass a Term Limitation Amendment as soon as possible.

Your help is needed. Pitch in now by joining the National Taxpayers Union Today.

THE WHITE HOUSE
Washington, D.C.

Dear Jim:

My administration came to Washington to achieve many of the goals shared by the National Taxpayers Union — reduction of income tax rates, control of government spending and, most importantly, ratification of the Balanced Budget Constitutional Amendment. I am deeply grateful for NTU's work in behalf of this measure. Due to the tireless efforts of NTU and others, the legislatures of 32 states have demanded that Congress propose this amendment or convene a limited Constitutional Convention for that sole purpose.

Your organization's support for the across-the-board tax rate reduction and income tax indexing helped pave the way for Congressional adoption of these important reforms during the first years of this Administration.

Congratulations on your first 15 years of service to the American Taxpayer. May you have many more.

Sincerely,

Ronald Reagan

TERM LIMITATION IS THE ANSWER!
JOIN NATIONAL TAXPAYERS
UNION NOW

A payment card is enclosed to ensure that donors are properly entered into the group's computerized records. The best prospects for a direct mailing are those who have given to the group before, so once a name goes on the house list, that person is solicited frequently by the organization.

The name of the recipient of this letter did not come from the house list. When recruiting new members, like-minded organizations often trade or rent their members' names to each other. Commercial brokers also provide lists for a fee. Note the source code *2269E* on the address label of the payment card. This is used to track how well this acquired list works. If the list produces a strong response rate, it will be used again.

A return envelope rounds out the package. The NTU wants to make it easy for you. Just write a check!

• *Source: Mailing by the National Taxpayers Union.*

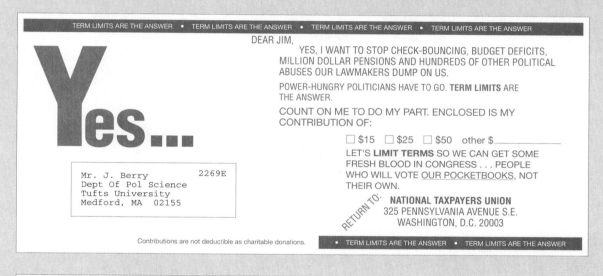

DEAR JIM,

YES, I WANT TO STOP CHECK-BOUNCING, BUDGET DEFICITS, MILLION DOLLAR PENSIONS AND HUNDREDS OF OTHER POLITICAL ABUSES OUR LAWMAKERS DUMP ON US.

POWER-HUNGRY POLITICIANS HAVE TO GO. **TERM LIMITS** ARE THE ANSWER.

COUNT ON ME TO DO MY PART. ENCLOSED IS MY CONTRIBUTION OF:

☐ $15   ☐ $25   ☐ $50   other $_____

LET'S **LIMIT TERMS** SO WE CAN GET SOME FRESH BLOOD IN CONGRESS . . . PEOPLE WHO WILL VOTE <u>OUR POCKETBOOKS</u>, NOT THEIR OWN.

RETURN TO: **NATIONAL TAXPAYERS UNION** 325 PENNSYLVANIA AVENUE S.E. WASHINGTON, D.C. 20003

Mr. J. Berry   2269E
Dept Of Pol Science
Tufts University
Medford, MA 02155

Contributions are not deductible as charitable donations.

TERM LIMITS ARE THE ANSWER • TERM LIMITS ARE THE ANSWER

Your stamp will save us much needed funds!

BUSINESS REPLY MAIL

FIRST CLASS   PERMIT NO. 10763   WASHINGTON, D.C.

POSTAGE WILL BE PAID BY ADDRESSEE

National Taxpayers Union
Att: Membership Division
325 Pennsylvania Avenue, S.E.
Washington, D.C. 20077 – 1064

NO POSTAGE
NECESSARY
IF MAILED
IN THE
UNITED STATES

The Son Also Rises

It is no surprise that Tommy Boggs has built a career in the political world. His father, Hale Boggs, was a Democratic member of the House of Representatives and served as Majority Leader. After the senior Boggs died in a plane crash, his wife Lindy succeeded him in the House. Tommy Boggs, however, turned away from electoral politics and pursued a career as a lawyer-lobbyist in Washington. Enormously skillful and highly intelligent, Boggs has attracted many corporate clients to Patton, Boggs, and Blow, a law firm known for its lobbying prowess. Although he's done well no matter who has been in office, his family's close identification with the Democrats made Bill Clinton's election especially sweet for Boggs. Shortly before the 1992 election, a Washington-based magazine, the National Journal, *embarrassed Boggs by putting his picture on its cover with the caption "Ready to Cash in on Clinton."*

Lobbyists can be full-time employees of the organization or employees of public relations or law firms who are hired on retainer. When hiring a lobbyist, an interest group looks for someone who knows her or his way around Washington. Lobbyists are valued for their experience in and knowledge of how government operates. Often, they are people who have served in the legislative or executive branches, where they have had first-hand experience with government. When they left Congress in 1992, former Democratic representatives Beryl Anthony of Arkansas and Dennis Eckart of Ohio joined the law firm of Winston and Strawn to work as lobbyists. Their lucrative list of clients includes the American Hospital Association, the American Insurance Association, and Walt Disney.[23] (When legislators and staffers leave Capitol Hill, there is a one-year "cooling off" period before they can directly lobby their former colleagues. Nothing stops them from directing others in their firms in what to do or who to call.)

Anthony and Eckart are far from exceptions. More than half of all lobbyists have some experience in government. The value of experience in the legislative or executive branch is knowledge of the policymaking process, expertise in particular issues, and contacts with those still in government.[24] Contacts with former colleagues can be invaluable. As one lobbyist said of her former associates on Capitol Hill, "They know you, and they return your phone calls."[25] Lobbying is a lucrative profession. One study of Washington representatives from a variety of organizations found that the average yearly salary was just in excess of $90,000.[26]

Many lobbyists have law degrees and find their legal backgrounds useful in the bargaining and negotiation over laws and regulations. Because of their location, many Washington law firms are drawn into lobbying. Corporations without their own Washington offices rely heavily on law firms to lobby for them before the national government. For example, NEC, the big Japanese electronics firm, has a vital interest in trade issues. It has the Washington office of Manatt, Phelps & Phillips on retainer to represent it on trade matters.

Some lobbyists and firms are known for their connections to one of the two major political parties. Manatt, Phelps & Phillips benefited when Bill Clinton was elected president, because one of its partners, Charles Manatt, is a former national chairman of the Democratic party. Another partner, Mickey Kantor, was a high-ranking official in the Clinton campaign and resigned from the firm when the new president appointed him to the post of Special Trade Representative.[27] Often, a firm that becomes identified closely with one party will go out of its way to hire a prominent member of the opposition party so that it will be seen as having clout regardless of who is in the White House.

The most common image of a lobbyist is that of arm twister, someone who spends most of the time trying to convince a legislator or administrator to back a certain policy. The stereotype of lobbyists also portrays them as people of dubious ethics, because they trade on their connections and many have campaign donations to hand out to candidates for office. One lobbyist noted, "My mother has never introduced me to her friends as 'my son, the lobbyist.' . . . I can't say I blame her. Being a lobbyist has long been synonymous in the minds of many Americans with being a glorified pimp."[28]

Unfortunately, there is an unsavory element to lobbying. (The role of campaign contributions is discussed later.) Yet, lobbying is a much maligned profession. The lobbyists' primary job is not to trade on favors or campaign contributions but to pass information on to policymakers. Lobbyists provide government officials and their staffs with a constant flow of data that support their organizations' policy goals. Lobbyists also try to build a compelling case for their goals, showing that the "facts" dictate that a change be made. What lobbyists are really trying to do, of course, is to convince policymakers that their data deserve more attention and are more accurate than those presented by other lobbyists.

POLITICAL ACTION COMMITTEES

One of the organizational resources that can make a lobbyist's job easier is a **political action committee (PAC).** PACs pool campaign contributions from group members and donate the money to candidates for political office. Under federal law, a PAC can give up as much as $5,000 for each separate election to a candidate for Congress. A change in campaign finance law in 1974 led to a rapid increase in the number of PACs, and nearly 4,200 PACs were active in the 1992 election.[29] The greatest growth came from corporations, most of which had been prohibited from operating political action committees. There was also rapid growth in the number of nonconnected PACs, largely ideological groups that have no parent lobbying organization and are formed solely for the purpose of raising and channeling campaign funds. (Thus, a PAC can be the campaign-wing affiliate of an ex-

Bitter Defeat

As the percentage of the work-force enrolled in unions has declined, labor's position in Congress has declined as well. Nothing is more symbolic of labor's weakened state than the NAFTA accord. Labor was bitterly opposed to the free trade agreement because it believed that NAFTA would lead to job losses in this country as American companies moved manufacturing jobs to Mexico where labor costs are much lower. Labor's public relations campaign, which used tactics such as this bill-board, and its direct lobbying in Washington failed to stem the tide in favor of free trade. The union movement suffered a humiliating defeat when Congress passed the measure.

isting interest group or a wholly independent, unaffiliated group.) Most PACs are rather small, and most give less than $50,000 in total contributions during a two-year election cycle. Some, however, are enormous. The Realtors Political Action Committee gave $3 million in the 1992 election, and the American Medical Association's PAC donated a similar amount. Overall, PACs contributed $188.7 million to candidates during 1991–1992, and corporate PACs were the biggest contributors (see Figure 10.4).[30]

Why do interest groups form PACs? The chief executive officer of one manufacturing company said his corporation had a PAC because "the PAC gives you access. It makes you a player."[31] Lobbyists believe that campaign contributions help significantly when they are trying to gain an audience with a member of Congress. Members of Congress and their staffers generally are eager to meet with representatives of their constituencies, but their time is limited. However, a member of Congress or an assistant would find it difficult to turn down a lobbyist's request for a meeting if the PAC of the lobbyist's company had made a significant campaign contribution in the last election.

Typically, PACs, like most other interest groups, are highly pragmatic organizations; pushing a particular political philosophy takes second place to achieving immediate policy goals. Although many corporate executives have strong beliefs in a free-market economy, for example, their company PACs tend to hold congressional candidates to a much more practical standard. As a group, corporate PACs gave 78.5 percent of their contributions to incumbent members of Congress—many of them liberal and moderate Democrats—during the 1991–1992 election cycle.[32] Although they might prefer a more conservative, probusiness Republican, business PACs are hesitant to contribute to an incumbent Democrat's opponent. The incumbent is probably going to win, and having access to the people who control the committees and subcommittees is much more important than supporting the candidates they regard as best.

| FIGURE | 10.4 | ■ **Shake the Money Tree** |

Over the years, most PAC contributions have come from corporations and business and professional associations (included in the "Trade/ Membership/Health" category). Another significant contributor has been labor. However, nonconnected groups have contributed comparatively little, although they raise an enormous amount. Many ideological groups raise their money through direct mail, which is so expensive that much of the money raised goes to repay the cost of solicitation.

Source: Federal Election Commission reports.

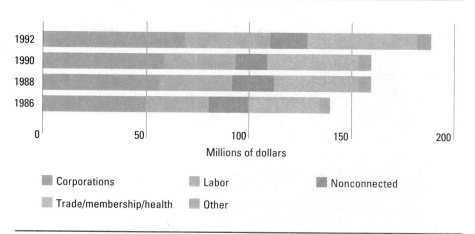

The growing role of PACs in financing congressional campaigns has become the most controversial aspect of interest group politics. Approximately half the money raised by House incumbents comes from PACs.[33] The money may not simply bring access but favoritism as well. Critics also charge that PAC money can lead to corruption; as an example, they point to the savings and loan scandal, which will cost taxpayers hundreds of billions of dollars. The savings and loan industry gave more than $11 million in donations to members of Congress during the 1980s.[34] Some influential legislators who were PAC money recipients intervened with federal regulators, asking them to go easy on some Savings and Loans that were in financial difficulty, before the shady dealings in the industry became fully apparent.

Political scientists have not been able to document any consistent link between campaign donations and the way members of Congress vote on the floor of the House and Senate. Even if we find that members of Congress vote the way the PACs that have contributed to them want them to vote, their votes do not prove that the PAC donations caused the voting decisions. It is just as plausible to suspect that PAC contributions are rewards given to those who already vote the right way. Still, influence can be felt before bills get to the floor of the full House or Senate for a vote. Some recent, sophisticated research shows that PAC donations do seem to influence what goes on in congressional committees. As will be discussed in Chapter 11, committees are where the bulk of the work on legislation takes place. Lobbies with PACs have an advantage in the committee process and appear to gain influence because of the additional access they receive.[35]

Whatever the research shows, it is clear that the American public is suspicious of political action committees and regards them as a problem in our governmental system. PACs are seen as a means of privilege for those sectors in society with the resources to purchase additional access to Congress. But in a democracy, influence should not be a function of money; some citizens have little to give, yet their interests need to be protected. From this perspective, the issue is political equality—the freedom to give should not outweigh the need for equality in political access for all sectors of society. In the words of Republican senator Robert Dole, "there aren't any Poor PACs or Food Stamp PACs or Nutrition PACs or Medicare PACs."[36]

Strong arguments can also be made for retaining PACs. They offer a means for people to participate in the political system. They allow small givers to pool their resources and to fight the feeling that one person cannot make a difference. Finally, PAC defenders also point out that prohibiting PACs would amount to a restriction on the freedom of political expression. (We take up the question of PACs and potential reforms at the end of this chapter.)

LOBBYING TACTICS

When an interest group decides to try to influence government on an issue, its staff and officers must develop a strategy, which may include a number of tactics aimed at various officials or offices. Together, these tactics should use the group's resources as effectively as possible.

Keep in mind that lobbying extends beyond the legislative branch. Groups can seek help from the courts and administrative agencies as well as from Congress. Moreover, interest groups may have to shift their focus from one branch of government to another. After a bill becomes a law, for example, a group that lobbied for the legislation will probably try to influence the administrative agency responsible for implementing the new law. Some policy decisions are left unresolved by legislation and are settled through regulations. The lobby wants to make sure regulatory decisions are as close to the group's preferences as possible.

We discuss three types of lobbying tactics here: those aimed at policymakers and implemented through interest group representatives (direct lobbying), those that involve group members (grassroots lobbying), and those directed at the public (information campaigns). We also examine the cooperative efforts of interest groups to influence government through coalitions.

Direct Lobbying

Direct lobbying relies on personal contact with policymakers. One survey of Washington lobbyists showed that 98 percent use direct contact with government officials to express their groups' views.[37] This interaction occurs when a lobbyist meets with a member of Congress, an agency official, or a staff member. In their meetings, lobbyists usually convey their arguments in the form of data about a specific issue. If a lobbyist from, for example, the Chamber of Commerce meets with a member of Congress about a bill the organization backs, the lobbyist does not say (or even suggest), "Vote for this bill, or our people in the district will vote against you in the next election." Instead, the lobbyist might say, "If this bill is passed, we're going to see hundreds of new jobs created back home." The representative has no trouble at all figuring out that a vote for the bill can help in the next election.

Personal lobbying is a day-in, day-out process. It is not enough simply to meet with policymakers just before a vote or a regulatory decision. Lobbyists must maintain contact with congressional and agency staffers,

**Friendly Skies,
Friendly Senator**

Lobbyists rely heavily on key representatives and senators who are willing to work hard on issues of particular concern to them. Here two lobbyists representing commercial aviation—Nancy Van Duyne of Continental Airlines and Peter Pike of the Air Transport Association of America— meet with Senator Slade Gorton, Republican of Washington. Gorton wants to do what he can to promote commercial aviation because Boeing is located in his state. When the airlines are doing well, Boeing does well.

constantly providing them with pertinent data. Lobbyists for the American Gas Association, for instance, keep a list of 1,200 agency personnel who are "called frequently to share informally in association intelligence." The director of the group's lobbying efforts has a shorter list of 104 key administrators with whom he has met personally and who can "be counted on to provide information on agency decision making."[38]

A tactic related to direct lobbying is testifying at committee hearings when a bill is before Congress. This tactic allows the interest group to put its views on record and make them widely known when the hearing testimony is published. Although testifying is one of the most visible parts of lobbying, it is generally considered window dressing. Most lobbyists believe that testimony usually does little by itself to persuade members of Congress.

Another direct but somewhat different approach is legal advocacy. Using this tactic, a group tries to achieve its policy goals through litigation. Claiming some violation of law, a group will file a law suit and ask that a judge make some change that will benefit the organization. In some policy areas, lobbies can also file formal complaints with administrative agencies. Lawyers working for an interest group will petition an agency with documents that purport to show that some law or set of regulations is not being followed. Lawyers for American steel companies often file complaints with the Commerce Department, claiming that various foreign steel producers are subsidized by their governments and are thus selling their steel at unfairly low prices.[39]

Grassroots Lobbying

Grassroots lobbying involves an interest group's rank-and-file members and may include people outside the organization who sympathize with its goals. Grassroots tactics, such as letter-writing campaigns and protests, are often used in conjunction with direct lobbying by Washington representatives. Letters, telegrams, faxes, and telephone calls from a group's members to their representatives in Congress or agency administrators add to a lobbyist's credibility in talks with these officials. Policymakers are more concerned about what a lobbyist says when they know that constituents are really watching their decisions.

Group members—especially influential members (corporation presidents, local civic leaders)—occasionally go to Washington to lobby. But the most common grassroots tactic is letter writing. "Write your representative" is not just a slogan for a civics test. Legislators are highly sensitive to the content of their mail. Interest groups often launch letter-writing campaigns through their regular publications or special alerts. They may even provide sample letters and the names and addresses of specific policymakers.

If people in government seem unresponsive to conventional lobbying tactics, a group might resort to some form of political protest. A protest or demonstration, such as picketing or marching, is designed to attract media attention to an issue. Protesters hope that television and newspaper coverage will help change public opinion and make policymakers more receptive to the group's demands. In one protest near the Capitol, an anti-abortion group created a mock "cemetery of the innocents," with 4,400 white crosses stuck in the ground to symbolize the number of abortions performed each day.[40] The goal was to create a striking visual that would attract media attention; if reporters covered the protest, people around the country would be exposed to the abortion opponents' belief that an abortion is the death of a living human being.

The main drawback to protest activity is that policymaking is a long-term incremental process, whereas a demonstration is short lived. It is difficult to sustain the anger and activism of group supporters—to keep large numbers of people involved in protest after protest—simply to keep the group's demands in the public eye. A notable exception was the civil rights demonstrations of the 1960s, which were sustained over a long period. National attention focused not only on the widespread demonstrations but also on the sometimes violent confrontations between protesters and white law enforcement officers. For example, the use of police dogs and high-power fire hoses against blacks marching in Alabama in the early 1960s angered millions of Americans who saw films of the confrontations on television programs. The protests were a major factor in stirring public opinion, which in turn hastened the passage of the Civil Rights Act of 1964 and the Voting Rights Act of 1965.

Information Campaigns

As the strategy of the civil rights movement shows, interest groups generally feel that public backing adds strength to their lobbying efforts. And because all interest groups believe they are absolutely right in their policy orientations, they believe that they will get that backing if they make the public aware of their positions and the evidence that supports them. To this end, interest groups launch **information campaigns,** organized efforts to gain public backing by bringing group views to the public's attention. The underlying assumption is that public ignorance and apathy are as much a problem as the views of competing interest groups. Various means are used to combat apathy. Some are directed at the larger public, others at smaller audiences with longstanding interest in an issue.

Public relations is one information tactic. A public relations campaign might involve sending speakers to meetings in various parts of the country, producing pamphlets and handouts, or taking out newspaper and magazine advertising. During the fight over the North American Free Trade Agreement (NAFTA) in 1992, the opposing sides put commercials on television. Businesses backing the treaty because they wanted expanded trade with Mexico and Canada ran ads touting the virtues of the agreement. Labor unions produced ads warning of job losses to workers in this country. Television commercials are an expensive form of public relations, as is newspaper and magazine advertising. Consequently, few groups rely on these options as their primary weapons.

Sponsoring research is another way interest groups press their cases. When a group believes that evidence has not been fully developed in a certain area, it may commission research on the subject. Groups working for the rights of the disabled have protected programs from would-be budget cutters by providing "lawmakers with abundant research findings demonstrating that it costs much more to keep people in institutions . . . than it does to utilize home and community living programs."[41]

Some groups believe that publicizing voting records of members of Congress is an effective way to influence public opinion. These interest groups simply publish in their newsletters a record of how all members of Congress voted on issues of particular concern to the organization. Other groups prepare statistical indexes that compare the voting records of all members of Congress on selected key issues. Each member is graded (from 0 to 100 percent) according to how often he or she voted in agreement with the group's views. Thus, the owners of small businesses who belong to the National Federation of Independent Business can assume that those lawmakers who scored well on the group's scorecard have usually voted in sympathy with their interests.

Coalition Building

A final aspect of lobbying strategy is **coalition building,** in which several organizations band together for the purpose of lobbying. This joint effort conserves or makes more effective use of the resources of groups with similar views. Most coalitions are informal, ad hoc arrangements that exist only for the purpose of working on a single issue. Coalitions form most often among groups that work in the same policy area and have similar constituencies, such as environmental groups or feminist groups. When an issue arises that such groups agree on, they are likely to develop a coalition.

Yet, coalitions often extend beyond organizations with similar constituencies and similar outlooks. Environmental groups and business groups are often thought of as dire enemies. Yet, some businesses support the same goals as environmental lobbies, because it is in their self-interest. For example, companies that are in the business of cleaning up toxic waste sites work with environmental groups for a strengthening of the Superfund program, the government's primary weapon for dealing

An Image That Angered a Nation

Demonstrations by blacks during the early 1960s played a critical role in pushing Congress to pass civil rights legislation. This photo of vicious police dogs attacking demonstrators in Birmingham, Alabama, is typical of the scenes shown on network news broadcasts and in newspapers that helped build public support for civil rights legislation.

with dangerous waste dumps.[42] Lobbyists see an advantage in having a diverse coalition. In the words of one health and education lobbyist, "If you have three hundred associations on a list, that's a pretty strong message."[43]

IS THE SYSTEM BIASED?

As we noted in Chapter 2, our political system is more pluralist than majoritarian. Policymaking is determined more by the interaction of groups with government than by elections. The great advantage of majoritarianism is that it is built around the most elemental notion of fairness: What government does is determined by what most people want.

How, then, do we justify decisions made in a pluralist system? How do we determine whether policy decisions in a pluralist system are fair? There is no precisely agreed upon formula, but most would support two simple notions. First, all significant interests in the population should be adequately represented by lobbying groups. That is, if a significant number of people with similar views have a stake in the outcome of policy decisions in a particular area, they should have a lobby to speak for them. If government makes policy that affects farmers who grow corn, for example, the farmers should have a corn lobby.

Second, government should listen to the views of all major interests as it develops policy. Lobbies are of little value unless policymakers are willing to listen to them. We should not require that decisions perfectly represent a balancing of all interests, because some interests are diametrically opposed. Moreover, because elections offer some majoritarianism in our system, the party that has won the last election is going to have more say in public policymaking than its opponent.

Membership Patterns

Public opinion surveys of Americans and surveys of interest groups in Washington can be used to determine who is represented in the interest group system. A clear pattern is evident: Some sectors of society are much better represented than others. As noted in the earlier discussions of the Boston West Enders and the United Farm Workers, who is being organized makes a big difference. Those who work in business or in a profession, those with a high level of education, and those with high incomes are the most likely to belong to interest groups (recall Figure 10.3). But even middle-income people are much more likely to join interest groups than those who are poor.

For example, one-third of those receiving veterans' benefits belong to an organization that works to protect and enhance veterans' benefits. A quarter of social security recipients are members of a group working for that program. By contrast, less than 1 percent of food stamp recipients belong to a group that represents their interests in regard to this program. Only about 2 percent of recipients of Aid to Families with Dependent Children (AFDC) are members of welfare rights groups.[44] Clearly, a **membership bias** is part of the pattern of who belongs to interest groups: Certain types of people are much more likely to belong to interest groups than others.

The Public Interest Movement

Because the bias in interest group membership is unmistakable, should we conclude that the interest group system is biased? Before reaching that conclusion, we should examine another set of data. The actual population of interest groups in Washington will surely reflect the class bias in membership, but that bias may be modified in an important way. Some interest groups derive support from sources other than membership. Thus, although they have no food stamp recipients as members, the Washington-based Food Research and Action Committee and the Community Nutrition Institute have been effective long-term advocates of the Food Stamp program. The Center for Budget and Policy Priorities and the Children's Defense Fund have no members who are welfare recipients, but they are highly respected Washington lobbies working on the problems of poor people. Poverty groups gain their financial support from philanthropic foundations, government grants, corporations, and wealthy individuals.[45] In our pluralist system, poor people need to be represented by interest groups, even though they have no resources of their own to establish such groups.

Groups such as these have played an important role in influencing policy on poor people's programs.[46] Given the large numbers of Americans who are on such programs as food stamps and AFDC, poor people's lobbies are not numerous enough. Nevertheless, the poor are represented by these and other organizations (such as labor unions and health lobbies) that regard the poor as part of the constituency they must protect. In short, some bias exists in the representation of the poor, but it is not nearly so bad as membership patterns would suggest.

Another part of the problem of membership bias has to do with free riders. The interests that are most affected by free riders are broad societal problems, such as the environment and consumer protection, in which literally everyone can be considered as having a stake in the outcome. We are all consumers, and we all care about the environment. But the greater the number of people who are potential members of a group, the more likely it is that any individual will decide to be a free rider, because she or he believes that plenty of others can offer financial support to the organization. As noted earlier, business trade associations and professional associations do not have the same problem, because they can offer many benefits that cannot be obtained without paying for membership.

Environmental and consumer interests have been chronically underrepresented in the Washington interest group community. In the 1960s, however, a strong public interest movement emerged. **Public interest groups** are citizen groups that have no economic self-interest in the policies they pursue.[47] For example, the members of environmental groups fighting for stricter pollution control requirements receive no financial gain from the enactment of environmental protection policies. The benefits to its members are largely ideological and esthetic. In contrast, a corporation fighting the same stringent standards is trying to protect its economic interests. A law that requires a corporation to install expensive antipollution devices can reduce stockholders' dividends, depress salaries, and postpone expansion. Although both the environmental group and the corporation have valid reasons for their stands, their motives are different. The environmental lobby is a public interest group; the corporation is not.

Today, many public interest groups are important players in Washington politics (see Compared with What? 10.1). Most are environmental and consumer groups, but other public interest groups work on corporate accountability, good government, and, as discussed previously, poverty and nutrition. Common Cause is one of the best-known public interest groups because of its work on campaign finance and other government reforms.[48] As discussed earlier, many conservative public interest groups exist as well, working in areas such as abortion and family values. Overall, the public interest movement has broadened interest group representation in national politics and made the pluralist system more democratic.

Business Mobilization

Because of the emergence of a strong public interest movement that has become an integral part of Washington politics, an easy assumption is that the bias in interest group representation in favor of business has been largely overcome. What must be factored in is that business has become increasingly mobilized as well.[49] The 1970s and 1980s saw a vast increase in the number of business lobbies in Washington. Many corporations opened up Washington lobbying offices, and many trade associations headquartered elsewhere either moved to Washington or opened up branch offices there.[50]

This mobilization was partly a reaction to the success of the liberal public interest movement, which business tended to view as hostile to the free-enterprise system. The reaction of business also reflected the expanded scope of national government. As the Environmental Protection Agency, the Consumer Product Safety Commission, OSHA, and other reg-

Well-Fed Lobbyists

At first glance, the restaurant business may not seem to be an industry with serious political problems. Yet government regulation and taxation policies can significantly affect restaurant operations and profits. The National Restaurant Association, which employs these five lobbyists, is the trade association that represents restaurant owners, food and equipment manufacturers, and distributors. Headquartered in Washington with a staff of 115 and a budget of $16 million, it is just one of the thousands of trade groups working to influence public policy in Washington.

ulatory agencies were created, many more companies found they were affected by federal regulations. And many corporations often found that they were reacting to policies already made rather than participating in their making. They saw representation in Washington—where the policy-makers are—as necessary if they were to obtain information on pending government actions soon enough to act on it. Finally, the competitive nature of business lobbying fueled the increase in business advocacy in Washington. Competition exists because legislation and regulatory decisions never seem to apply uniformly to all businesses; rather, they affect one type of business or one industry more than others.[51]

Where has the growth in various types of lobbying groups left the interest group system? One study identified the groups active in four major policy areas: agriculture, energy, health, and labor. As Figure 10.5 shows, it is clear that corporations and business trade associations dominate agriculture and energy. These are two large business domains and it is not surprising that the most active interest groups are industry related. Note, however, the significant number of citizen groups that are active. The health field has the most dispersion, with many different types of groups having a strong presence in Washington. Labor unions and trade associations are the biggest players in the labor field.

The number of organizations is far from a perfect indicator of interest group strength. The AFL-CIO, which represents millions of union members, is more influential than a two-person corporate listening post in Washington. Nevertheless, as a rough indicator of interest group influence, the data show that business has an advantage in this country's interest group system. At the same time, other types of organizations are represented too, and some policy areas (such as health) have a diverse set of interest groups.

COMPARED WITH WHAT? 10.1   Citizen Groups Paint the World Green

The world's industrialized democracies face many of the same policy problems, but they often approach the issues in different ways and at different times. Political scientist David Vogel wanted to know what explains the different responses to environmental problems by various advanced industrialized nations. He decided to look specifically at one of the most common explanations for problem-solving differences between the United States and other democracies. In the United States, we have a government with separation of powers. Most other democracies use parliamentary systems; they do not separate the legislative and executive branches. In such countries, the prime minister is a member of the legislature and is a leader of the majority party (or a leader of the party that heads a coalition of parties controlling government).

Many critics of American government argue that our separation of powers system makes it difficult for the United States to solve many of its basic problems. Because the White House and Congress are often controlled by different parties, the two institu-

tions frequently are at loggerheads. Even when the same party is in charge of both branches, the majority party in Congress is quite independent of the White House. By contrast, in a parliamentary system the fate of the prime minister and the majority party are intertwined.

To see whether our separation of powers system made any difference in the case of environmental policymaking, Vogel compared the United States with two parliamentary-style governments, Great Britain and Japan. To organize his research, he looked at three periods, beginning with the period of 1945 (the end of World War II) to 1967 (when environmental policy started to become highly visible). Despite the similarity in the structures of their governments, Britain and Japan were quite different in their attention to environmental affairs during this stretch of more than two decades. Of the three countries, Great Britain was the most aggressive in addressing environmental problems. Although its pollution problems were much worse than England's, Japan showed little interest in environmental issues. The United States seemed to fall between the two parlia-

Access

At the outset of this discussion of interest group bias, we noted the importance of finding out not only which types of constituencies are represented by interest groups but whether those in government listen to the various groups that approach them. The existence of an interest group makes little difference if the government systematically ignores it. Evidence shows that any particular policymaker or office of government can be highly selective in granting access to interest groups. The Reagan White House, for example, worked directly with only a small proportion of interest groups. Wealthy, conservative groups had much more access than others.[52]

The ideological compatibility between any given interest group and the policymaker it approaches certainly affects the likelihood that the policymaker will grant it access and listen to what the organization has to say.

mentary systems in terms of taking up pollution issues. Vogel notes that one major difference during this period was that Britain had an extensive network of environmental groups, while Japan saw little organization around the issue. Japan, of course, was also consumed with rebuilding its economy.

The second period Vogel studied was 1968 to 1973. During this time, environmental issues became highly visible in all the industrialized countries. In Japan there was considerable mobilization at the grassroots level by citizens concerned about the environment. The government responded with significant changes aimed at protecting the environment. The United States also saw dramatic growth in environmental organizations and enacted sweeping new environmental protection laws. In Britain, too, the movement was toward even more environmental legislation. In sum, all three countries moved in the same direction, regardless of the structure of their government.

During the last period he studied, 1975–1988, Vogel found a cooling of the environmental fervor. Both Britain (in 1979) and the United States (in 1980) turned to conservatives in their national elections, and the elected leaders were more sympathetic to business and less concerned about the environment. The environmental issue faded in Japan as well.

Overall, Vogel concludes that the structure of government does not seem to make much difference in environmental policy. Our separation of powers system is no better or worse at responding to the preferences of the citizenry. But if the structure of government is not a critical factor in environmental policy, what is? Vogel sees public opinion—what the people want—as the most important factor. And public opinion is expressed in many significant ways by the citizen groups that have worked on environmental issues in all three countries. Over time, the degrees to which people organized to push for environmental protection influenced the actions of their governments. The bottom line? Organizing into citizen groups makes a difference.

• Source: David Vogel, *"Representing Diffuse Interests in Environmental Policymaking,"* in R. Kent Weaver and Bert A. Rockman, eds., Do Institutions Matter? *(Washington, D.C.: Brookings Institution, 1993), pp. 237–271.*

However, pluralists are convincing when they argue that the national government has many points of access, and virtually all lobbying organizations can find some part of that government to listen to them. If liberal poverty lobbies are shut out of a conservative White House, liberal members of Congress will work with them. All forms of access are not of equal importance, and some organizations have wider access than others. Nevertheless, American government is generally characterized by the broad access it grants to interest groups.

Reform

If the interest group system is biased, should the advantages somehow be eliminated or reduced? This is hard to do. In an economic system marked by great differences in income, great differences in the degree to which

FIGURE 10.5   ■ Interest Groups in Four Policy Areas

Different types of interest groups predominate in different policy areas. Overall, however, corporations and business trade associations are the most common lobbying organizations in Washington.

Source: John P. Heinz, Edward O. Laumann, Robert L. Nelson, and Robert H. Salisbury, The Hollow Core *(Cambridge, Mass.: Harvard University Press, 1993), p. 63.*

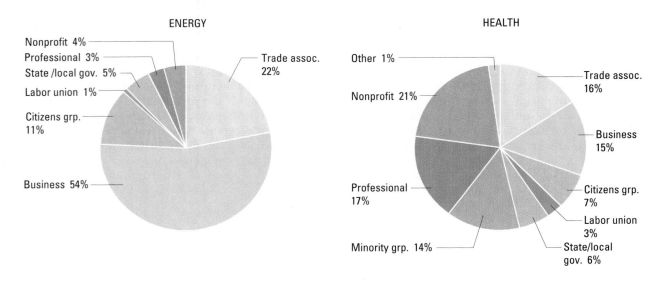

ENERGY

Nonprofit 4%
Professional 3%
State /local gov. 5%
Labor union 1%
Citizens grp. 11%
Business 54%
Trade assoc. 22%

HEALTH

Other 1%
Nonprofit 21%
Professional 17%
Minority grp. 14%
Trade assoc. 16%
Business 15%
Citizens grp. 7%
Labor union 3%
State/local gov. 6%

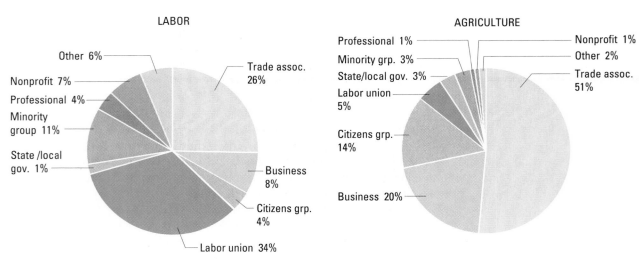

LABOR

Other 6%
Nonprofit 7%
Professional 4%
Minority group 11%
State /local gov. 1%
Trade assoc. 26%
Business 8%
Citizens grp. 4%
Labor union 34%

AGRICULTURE

Professional 1%
Minority grp. 3%
State/local gov. 3%
Labor union 5%
Citizens grp. 14%
Business 20%
Nonprofit 1%
Other 2%
Trade assoc. 51%

people are organized are inevitable. Moreover, as Madison foresaw, limiting interest group activity without limiting fundamental freedoms is difficult. The First Amendment guarantees Americans the right to petition their government, and lobbying, at its most basic level, is a form of organized petitioning.

Still, some sectors of the interest group community may enjoy advantages that are unacceptable. If it is felt that the advantages of some groups are so great that they affect the equality of opportunity to be heard in the political system, then restrictions on interest group behavior can be justified on the ground that the disadvantaged must be protected. Pluralist democracy is justified on exactly this ground: All constituencies must have the opportunity to organize, and the competition between groups as they press their case before policymakers must be fair.

Some critics charge that a system of campaign finance that relies so heavily on political action committees, undermines our democratic system. They claim that access to policymakers is purchased through the wealth of some constituencies. In the 1992 election, twenty-seven PACs contributed at least $1 million in campaign funds to congressional candidates.[53] Almost two-thirds of PAC contributions come from corporations, business trade associations, and professional associations (recall Figure 10.4).[54] It is not merely a matter of wealthy interest groups showering incumbents with donations; members of Congress aggressively solicit donations from PACs. Although observers disagree on whether the money actually influences policy outcomes, agreement is widespread that the PAC donations give donors better access to members of Congress. (As noted earlier, donors certainly believe that their chances of getting to see legislators or their staffers improve with donations.)

Campaign finance is one area in which government has enacted restrictions on interest group behavior. During the 1970s, Congress put some important reforms into effect. Strong disclosure requirements now exist— the source of all significant contributions to candidates for national office is a matter of public record. Legislation also provides for public financing of presidential campaigns; taxpayer money goes in equal amounts to the presidential nominees of the major parties.

Reformers have called for public financing of congressional elections to reduce the presumed influence of PACs on Congress. Public financing would effectively reduce people's freedom to give to whom they want; the trade-off is that it also would reduce political inequality. Other proposed approaches include reducing the amounts that individual PACs can give; limiting the overall amount of money any one candidate can accept from PACs; reducing the costs of campaigning by subsidizing the costs of commercials, printing, and postage; and giving tax incentives to individuals to contribute to candidates.[55] Yet, incumbents usually find it easier to raise money from PACs than their electoral challengers do, so the incentive to leave the status quo intact is strong. And Republicans and Democrats have sharp, partisan differences over campaign finance reforms, because each party believes that the other is trying to fashion a reform that will somehow handicap the opposing party.[56]

SUMMARY

Interest groups play many important roles in our political process. They are a means by which citizens can participate in politics, and they communicate their members' views to those in government. Interest groups differ greatly in the resources at their disposal and in the tactics they use to influence government. The number of interest groups has grown sharply in recent years.

Despite the growth and change in the nature of interest groups, the fundamental problem identified by Madison more than two hundred years ago endures. In a free and open society, groups form to pursue policies that favor them at the expense of the broader national interest. Madison hoped that the solution to the problem would come from the diversity of the population and the structure of our government.

To a certain extent, Madison's expectations have been borne out. The natural differences between groups have prevented the tyranny of any one faction. Yet, the interest group system remains unbalanced, with some segments of society (particularly business, the wealthy, and the educated) considerably better organized than others. The growth of citizen groups has reduced the disparity somewhat, but significant inequalities remain in how well different interests are represented in Washington.

The inequities point to flaws in pluralist theory. There is no mechanism to automatically ensure that interest groups will form to speak for those who need representation. Likewise, when an issue arises and policymakers meet with interest groups with a stake in the outcome, those groups may not equally represent all the constituencies that the policy changes will affect. The interest group system clearly compromises the principle of political equality as stated in the maxim "one person, one vote." Formal political equality is certainly more likely to occur outside interest group politics, in elections between candidates from competing political parties—which better fits the majoritarian model of democracy.

Despite the inequities of the interest group system, little general effort has been made to restrict interest group activity. Madison's dictum to avoid suppressing political freedoms, even at the expense of permitting interest group activity that promotes the selfish interests of narrow segments of the population, has generally guided public policy. Yet, as the problem of PACs demonstrates, government has had to set some restrictions on interest groups. Permitting PACs to give unlimited amounts to political candidates would undermine confidence in the system. Where to draw the line on PAC activity remains a thorny issue, because there is little consensus on how to balance the conflicting needs of our society. Congress is one institution that must try to balance our diverse country's conflicting interests. In the next chapter, we will see how difficult this part of Congress's job is.

Key Terms

interest group	entrepreneur	committee (PAC)	membership bias
lobby	direct mail	direct lobbying	public interest group
lobbyist	free-rider problem	grassroots lobbying	
agenda building	trade association	information campaign	
program monitoring	political action	coalition building	

Selected Readings

Berry, Jeffrey M. *Lobbying for the People.* Princeton, N.J.: Princeton University Press, 1977. A study of eighty-three public interest groups active in national politics.

———. *The Interest Group Society.* 2d ed. Glenview, Ill.: Scott, Foresman/Little, Brown, 1989. An analysis of the growth of interest group politics.

Cigler, Allan J., and Burdett A. Loomis, eds. *Interest Group Politics.* 3d ed. Washington, D.C.: Congressional Quarterly, 1991. This reader includes eighteen essays on lobbying groups.

Costain, Anne N. *Inviting Women's Rebellion.* Baltimore: Johns Hopkins University Press, 1992. A careful and original examination of the origins of the women's movement and its development into a political force.

Heinz, John P., Edward O. Laumann, Robert L. Nelson, and Robert H. Salisbury, *The Hollow Core.* Cambridge, Mass.: Harvard University Press, 1993. The best study available of large-scale issue networks in national politics.

Schlozman, Kay Lehman, and John T. Tierney. *Organized Interests and American Democracy.* New York: Harper & Row, 1986. A valuable and comprehensive study that draws on an original survey of Washington lobbyists.

Walker, Jack L. *Mobilizing Interest Groups in America.* Ann Arbor: University of Michigan Press, 1991. Walker looks at how groups support themselves and examines their access to those in government.

Woliver, Laura. *From Outrage to Action.* Urbana: University of Illinois Press, 1993. Four incisive case studies of ad hoc grassroots advocacy groups.

Institutions of Government

11 Congress

AS A CRITICAL VOTE LOOMED on the fate of the North American Free Trade Agreement (NAFTA) in the House of Representatives in the fall of 1993, legislators considered what was best for the country and what was best for their districts. For some representatives, the interests of the nation and the district appeared to be the same. For others, the two were seemingly in conflict.

The NAFTA agreement was designed to facilitate trade for Canada, Mexico, and the United States. Although economists are overwhelmingly of the opinion that the United States will benefit from free trade, many members of the House were concerned, because increased foreign competition would damage particular industries in their districts. This was an especially difficult issue for Democrats. Labor unions, a traditional mainstay of the party, were against the agreement, because they believed it would facilitate the flight of American manufacturing jobs to Mexico, where labor costs are substantially less expensive. Increased foreign trade, however, would be good for other sectors of the economy and for consumers.

Labor's opposition also made NAFTA a difficult issue for President Bill Clinton. During the summer of 1993, Clinton spoke perfunctorily in favor of NAFTA—it had been largely completed before he became president— but did little to push the agreement. As the vote grew closer and it became seen as a test of Clinton's leadership, the White House geared up to fight for NAFTA. The president began to speak passionately about how free trade was an investment in the future and called on Congress to do the right thing. Congress, however, wanted to deal.

Many members of the House who claimed to be undecided on the fate of the treaty told the White House of their concern about the adverse impact of NAFTA on some of their constituents. How were Florida representatives supposed to explain to orange growers that free trade would be good for the district, even though it meant that tariffs on orange juice imported from Mexico would be phased out? Less expensive imports mean that prices (and profits) for competing home-grown juice would have to fall. White House officials said they understood and made a deal that would reimpose tariffs if prices on American orange juice fall.

This process was repeated on a variety of crops and manufactured goods. Wheat farmers got limits on Canadian wheat imports. Additional protections were negotiated to protect American tomatoes, asparagus, peppers, wine, home appliances, flat glass, and cucumbers. There was so much vote trading that it became an issue. One Mexican businessman aptly described

Doonesbury

the process as a "bazaar" way of legislating. In the end, NAFTA passed by a vote of 234 to 200. Seventy-five percent of all Republicans in the House voted for NAFTA. Only about 40 percent of the Democrats voted for the agreement. Shortly after the House vote, the Senate passed the agreement and it soon became law.

Although the sheer amount of deal making for NAFTA may have been unusual, members of Congress often have to balance the best interests of the country against the best interests of their district or state. The diversity of the country meant that NAFTA would affect various constituencies in different ways. This led to the pluralist bargaining that paved the way for a NAFTA victory.[1]

But if NAFTA is a prime example of pluralist politics, it is also fair to say that this fight also had at least some elements of majoritarianism. The sharp division in Congress reflected the same division within the country at large. The two political parties in Congress, chief instruments for offering voters distinct ideological choices in the direction of their legislature, differed in their response to NAFTA in predictable ways. Republicans, more committed to free-market principles than Democrats, voted their ideology, although doing so helped a Democrat in the White House. House Democrats, more philosophically attuned to the preferences of working-class people, voted more in line with what organized labor wanted. In doing so, these Democrats were true to the promises they made in their election campaigns, to look out for the interests of working people. The president, who is also a Democrat, was in no way committed to going along with the majority of his congressional party. This illustrates another critical feature of the American political system. Our Constitution provides for separation of powers, and the two branches make policy together and often in a bipartisan manner.

In this chapter and throughout Part IV of this book, we emphasize the tension between pluralist and majoritarian visions of democracy. In the pages that follow, we'll examine more closely the relationship between members of Congress and their constituents, as well as the forces (such as political parties) that push legislators toward majoritarianism. We'll also focus on Congress's relations with the executive branch and analyze how the legislative process affects public policy. A starting point is asking how the framers envisioned the Congress.

THE ORIGIN AND POWERS OF CONGRESS

The framers of the Constitution wanted to keep power from being concentrated in the hands of a few, but they were also concerned with creating a union strong enough to overcome the weaknesses of the government that operated under the Articles of Confederation. They argued passionately about the structure of the new government. In the end, they produced a legislative body that was as much an experiment as the new nation's democracy was.

The Great Compromise

The U.S. Congress has two separate and powerful chambers: the House of Representatives and the Senate. A bill cannot become law unless it is passed in identical form by both chambers. When drafting the Constitution during the summer of 1787, "the fiercest struggle for power" centered on representation in the legislature.[2] The small states wanted all states to have equal representation. The more populous states wanted representation based on population; they did not want their power diluted. The Great Compromise broke the deadlock: The small states received equal representation in the Senate, but the House, where the number of each state's representatives would be based on population, retained the sole right to originate revenue-related legislation.

According to the Constitution, each state has two senators, each of whom serves for six years. Terms of office are staggered, so that one-third of the Senate is elected every two years. When it was ratified, the Constitution directed that senators be chosen by the state legislatures. However, the Seventeenth Amendment, adopted in 1913, provided for the election of senators by popular vote. From the beginning, the people have elected members of the House of Representatives. They serve two-year terms, and all House seats are up for election at the same time.

Because each state's representation in the House is in proportion to its population, the Constitution provides for a national census every ten years. Until the first census, the Constitution fixed the number of representatives at 65. As the nation's population grew and new states joined the Union, new seats were added to the House. (There were already 213 representatives after the census of 1820.[3]) At some point, however, a legislative body becomes too unwieldy to be efficient, and in 1929, the House decided to fix its membership at 435. Population shifts are handled by the **reapportionment** (redistribution) of seats among the states after each census is taken. Recent population growth has been centered in the Sunbelt as California, Texas, and Florida have gained the most seats, whereas the industrial Northeast and Midwest have lost seats in the House.

Each representative is elected from a particular congressional district within his or her state, and each district elects only one representative. Before a series of Supreme Court rulings in the 1960s, the states were not required to draw the boundaries of their districts in such a way that the districts had approximately equal populations. As a result, some sparsely populated rural districts had more representation in Congress than their number of residents warranted. The Court ruled that House districts, and all districts in state legislatures, had to be drawn so as to be reasonably equal in population.[4]

The Capitol

The Capitol sits on a site city planner Pierre L'Enfant called "a pedestal waiting for a monument." This is what the building looked like from 1825 to 1856.

Duties of the House and Senate

Although the Great Compromise provided considerably different schemes of representation for the House and Senate, the Constitution gives them essentially similar legislative tasks. They share many important powers, among them the powers to declare war, raise an army and navy, borrow and coin money, regulate interstate commerce, create federal courts, establish rules for the naturalization of immigrants, and "make all Laws which shall be necessary and proper for carrying into Execution the foregoing Powers."

Of course, the constitutional duties of the two chambers are different in at least a few important ways. As noted earlier, the House alone has the right to originate revenue bills, which apparently was coveted at the Constitutional Convention. In practice, this function is of limited consequence, because the House and Senate must approve all bills—including revenue bills. The House also has the power of **impeachment,** the power formally to charge the president, vice president, or other "civil Officers" of the national government with "Treason, Bribery, or other high Crimes and Misdemeanors." The Senate is empowered to act as a court to try impeachments; a two-thirds majority vote of the senators present is necessary for conviction. Only one president—Andrew Johnson—has ever been impeached, and in 1868 the Senate came within a single vote of finding him guilty. More recent, the House Judiciary Committee voted to impeach President Richard Nixon for his role in the Watergate cover-up, but he resigned in August 1974 before the full House could vote. A small number of federal judges, however, have been impeached, convicted, and removed from the bench.

The Constitution gives the Senate the power to approve major presidential appointments (such as to federal judgeships, ambassadorships, and cabinet posts) and treaties with foreign nations. The president is empowered to make treaties, but he must submit them to the Senate for approval

Bad Hair Day?

Congressman Jim Nussle, Republican of Iowa, appeared on the House floor with a bag over his head because he wanted to show voters back home how embarrassed he was by the House banking scandal. (Unlike many of his colleagues, Representative Nussle did not overdraw an account at the House bank.) Nussle's juvenile antics are a little unusual, but it is common for members of the House and Senate to tell their constituents how awful the Congress is. They do this because voters are cynical about the Congress, and incumbents don't want to appear to be defending the institution.

by a two-thirds majority. Because of this requirement, the executive branch generally considers the Senate's sentiments when it negotiates a treaty.[5] At times, however, a president must try to convince a doubting Senate of the worth of a particular treaty. Shortly after World War I, President Woodrow Wilson submitted to the Senate the Treaty of Versailles, which contained the charter for the proposed League of Nations. Wilson had attempted to convince the Senate that the treaty deserved its support; when the Senate refused to approve the treaty, Wilson suffered a severe setback.

Despite the long list of congressional powers in the Constitution, the question of what powers are appropriate for Congress has generated substantial controversy. For example, although the Constitution gives Congress the sole power to declare war, many presidents have initiated military action on their own. And at times, the courts have found that congressional actions have usurped the rights of the states.

ELECTING CONGRESS

If Americans are not happy with the job Congress is doing, they can use their votes to say so. With a congressional election every two years, the voters have frequent opportunities to express themselves.

The Incumbency Effect

Congressional elections offer voters a chance to show their approval of Congress's performance by reelecting **incumbents** or "throwing the rascals out." The voters do more reelecting than rascal throwing. The reelection rate is astonishingly high; in the majority of elections since 1950,

FIGURE **11.1** ■ **The Incumbency Advantage**

As these two figures illustrate, incumbents enjoy a considerable advantage in the electoral process. Despite the public's dissatisfaction with Congress in general, incumbent representatives win reelection at an exceptional rate. Incumbent senators aren't quite as successful but still do well in reelection races. The success of incumbents in raising campaign money is an important part of the reason for their success at the polls.

Sources: For the reelection rates, Norman J. Ornstein, Thomas E. Mann, and Michael J. Malbin (eds.), Vital Statistics on Congress, 1993–1994 *(Washington, D.C.: Congressional Quarterly, 1994), pp. 58–59. Used by permission. The campaign finance figures for 1978–1990 come from Frank J. Sorauf,* Inside Campaign Finance *(New Haven, Conn.: Yale University Press, 1992), p. 17. For 1992, the figures come from the Federal Election Commission, "1992 Congressional Spending Jumps 52% to $678 Million," 4 March 1993, p. 4.*

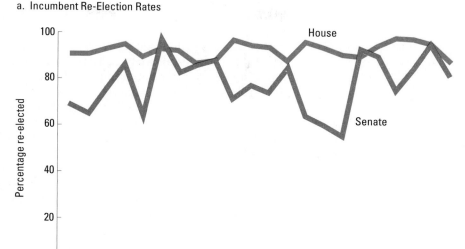

a. Incumbent Re-Election Rates

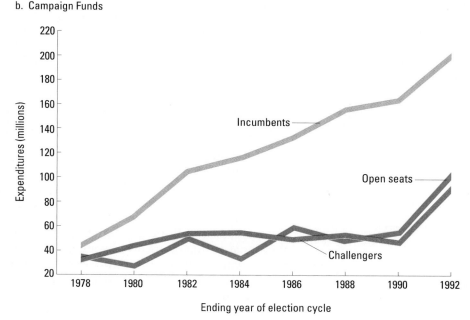

b. Campaign Funds

Ending year of election cycle

NOTE: Challengers *are candidates who are running against incumbents. The figure for "open seats" represents the spending by candidates vying for seats that have no incumbent seeking reelection.*

more than 90 percent of all House incumbents have held their seats (see Figure 11.1a). In some years, as few as a half-dozen incumbents have been defeated in the general election. Most House elections aren't even close; in recent elections, most House incumbents have won at least 60 percent of the vote. Senate elections are more competitive, but incumbents still have a high reelection rate.[6]

These findings may seem surprising. The public does not hold Congress as a whole in particularly high esteem. In a 1993 poll, only 7 percent of the public said they had a "great deal of confidence" in Congress.[7] A majority of Americans believes that at least half of all members of Congress are personally corrupt, a harsh indictment of the institution (see Figure 11.2). Yet, Americans distinguish the institution of Congress from their own members of Congress. Only 15 percent believe that their own representative is financially corrupt.[8] It is not entirely clear why Americans hate the Congress so much despite their satisfaction with their own members of the House and the Senate. Tough economic times and various scandals have surely influenced public attitudes. Campaign finance practices, especially the central role of political action committee (PAC) contributions, is another problem. Finally, American culture has traditionally held politicians in low esteem: We don't expect much from politicians, and we react sharply to their failings.

Term Limits

One manifestation of Americans' antagonism toward legislators is the movement toward **term limits.** Fifteen states have passed laws that mandate a limit on the number of years legislators can serve in office. These laws are aimed at both state legislatures and Congress. Term limits vary from state to state, but typically members of a state house of representatives can serve eight years, and a member of a state senate can serve eight to twelve years.[9]

Despite overwhelming support from voters on state initiatives, term limits for members of Congress may never take effect. The Supreme Court has yet to make a definitive ruling, but a lower federal court has determined that it is unconstitutional for a state to place term limits on members of Congress. The legal reasoning is simple: The Constitution specifically sets qualifications for representatives and senators.[10] (A representative must be at least twenty-five years of age and a citizen for at least seven years; a senator must be at least thirty and a citizen for nine years. Both must be inhabitants of the state that elects them.) Accordingly, if a state sets a term limit for members of Congress, it is in effect amending the Constitution on its own by adding qualifications. The Supreme Court has, however, ruled term limits on state legislators to be constitutional.

Although the public is enthusiastic about term limits, scholars disagree as to the wisdom of this reform. One line of argument is that "Congress has become an elaborate reelection machine" and that term limits are desirable.[11] With fewer incumbents running, national voting trends would be more influential, and political parties would become more responsive.[12] Opponents argue that term limits would reduce expertise in Congress by forcing those who are most knowledgeable about a given policy area to retire. This development could enhance the power of interest

FIGURE 11.2 ■ The Public's Verdict: "They're Crooks!"

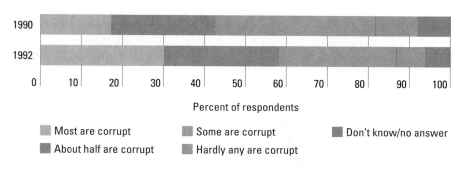

As these figures demonstrate, there is an extraordinarily high level of cynicism toward the institution of Congress. The increase in cynicism for 1992 was surely driven by the deteriorating economy and the check-kiting scandal that involved many members of the House. The question read to respondents was: "Now think about all the members of the U.S. House and Senate. How many of them do you think are financially corrupt?"

Source: "The Critique of Congress," American Enterprise 3 (May/June 1992), p. 101.

groups or that of the presidency. Others are concerned that term limits would reduce the influence of minority and women legislators.[13]

Because term limits may never be implemented on the national level, we must assume that the paradox of voters' mistrusting the Congress but reelecting their own incumbents will persist. Just what explains the electoral success of incumbents? We'll look at four plausible explanations: redistricting, name recognition, campaign financing, and the quality of challengers to incumbents.

Redistricting. One explanation of the incumbency effect centers on redistricting, the way House districts are redrawn after a census-based reapportionment. It is entirely possible for state legislatures to draw new districts to benefit the incumbents of one or both parties. Altering district lines for partisan advantage is commonly called **gerrymandering.**

But redistricting does not explain the incumbency effect in the House as a whole. Statistics show that redistricted and unredistricted seats end up approximately the same in terms of competitiveness.[14] Redistricting may be very helpful for some incumbents, but it does not explain why more than 90 percent of House incumbents are routinely reelected. Nevertheless, politicians regard gerrymandering as an important factor in elections, and the political parties put considerable effort into trying to make sure that new boundaries are drawn in the most advantageous way.

Name Recognition. Holding office brings with it some important advantages. First, incumbents develop significant name recognition among voters simply by being members of Congress. Congressional press secretaries help the name recognition advantage along through their efforts to get publicity for the activities and speeches of their bosses. The primary focus of such publicity seeking is on the local media back in the district—that's where the votes are.[15] The local press, in turn, is eager to cover what local members of Congress are saying about the issues.

Another resource available to members of Congress is the **franking privilege**—the right to send mail free of charge. Mailings work to make constituents aware of their legislators' names, activities, and accomplishments. Periodic newsletters, for example, almost always highlight success at securing funds and projects for the district, such as money to construct a highway or a new federal building. Newsletters also "advertise for business," encouraging voters to phone or visit legislators' district offices if they need help with a problem. When members of Congress visit their districts and states, making appearances in public, on TV, or on radio, they also encourage people to contact their offices for any help they may need. First term Democratic senator Barbara Boxer goes back to California frequently and always tells people to write to her with their opinions or problems. Boxer receives ten thousand letters a day from her constituents.[16]

Much of the work performed by the large staffs of members of Congress is **casework**—that is, such services for constituents as tracking down a social security check or directing the owner of a small business to the appropriate federal agency. Constituents who are helped in this way usually remember who assisted them.

Campaign Financing.   It should be clear that anyone who wants to challenge an incumbent needs solid financial backing. Challengers must spend large sums of money to run a strong campaign with an emphasis on advertising—an expensive but effective way to bring their names and records to the voters' attention. But here, too, the incumbent has the advantage. Challengers find raising campaign funds difficult, because they have to overcome contributors' doubts about whether they can win. In the 1992 elections, incumbents raised about 51 percent of all money contributed to campaigns for election to the House. Only 23 percent went to challengers. (Those running for open seats received the rest.) Challengers to Senate incumbents do better—they raised about a third of all money contributed to Senate candidates for the 1992 elections (see Figure 11.1b).[17]

PACs show a strong preference for incumbents (see Chapter 10). They tend not to want to risk offending an incumbent by giving money to a longshot challenger. The attitude of the American Medical Association's PAC is fairly typical. "We have a friendly incumbent policy," says its director. "We always stick with the incumbent if we agree with both candidates."[18] But along with their pragmatism, PACs also have an ideological side. Although corporate PACs, which tend to favor conservative economic policies, will not hesitate to give to liberal Democratic incumbents to whom they need access, they decidedly favor Republican candidates in contests in which no incumbent is running.[19]

Successful Challengers.   Although it is very difficult for a challenger to defeat an incumbent (particularly a member of the House), it is not impossible. The opposing party and unsympathetic PACs may target incumbents who seem vulnerable because of age, lack of seniority, a scandal, or unfavorable redistricting. The result is a flow of campaign contributions to the challenger, increasing the chance of victory. Vulnerable incumbents also bring out higher quality challengers—individuals who have held elective office and are capable of raising adequate campaign funds.[20]

In 1992, a number of incumbent representatives were vulnerable because of revelations that they had kited checks at a special House bank

Republicans Ascendant

Mike DeWine of Ohio is one of the many new Republican senators swept into office by the GOP landslide in the 1994 congressional elections. He replaces liberal Democrat Howard Metzenbaum, who retired. In his campaign against Democrat Joel Hyatt, DeWine stressed adopting tough measures to fight crime, reforming the Senate to make it work better, and balancing the budget.

that served them as a convenience. (Check kiting is writing a check against funds not yet deposited in the account.) The House bank covered the checks until money was subsequently deposited. Of those incumbents who were among the worst offenders and whose challengers had experience and ample campaign funds, more than half lost. Among the worst offenders whose challengers were inexperienced and poorly funded, only 14 percent lost.[21]

One reason Senate challengers have a higher success rate than House challengers is that they are higher quality candidates. Often they are governors or members of the House who enjoy high name recognition and attract significant campaign funds, because they are regarded as credible candidates.[22]

But incumbents can also fall victim to general dissatisfaction with their party. Members of the president's party almost always lose seats in the midterm elections, as voters take out their disappointments with the president on the House candidates of his party. In the 1994 elections voters dealt the Democrats a stunning defeat. Negative feelings about President Clinton fueled a Republican takeover of both the House and the Senate. Thirty-five Democratic House incumbents were defeated and the Republicans gained 53 seats overall to become the majority in the House for the first time since the 1952 elections. The vote indicated a movement by voters toward the conservative side of the political spectrum. There was no one central issue at the heart of the debate during the campaign, but voters told pollsters that they didn't think government worked very well and that it was time for a change. Ironically, "change" was what Bill Clinton promised in the 1992 presidential campaign.

For proponents of majoritarian democracy, the success rate of incumbents running for reelection, especially in the House, is disconcerting. If, however, the new Republican majority acts on its campaign promises, which it called a "Contract with America," it will inject an important element of majoritarianism into congressional elections.

Whom Do We Elect?

The people we elect (then reelect) to Congress are not a cross section of American society. Most members of Congress are professionals—primarily lawyers and businesspeople.[23] Although nearly a third of the American labor force works in blue-collar jobs, someone currently employed as a blue-collar worker rarely wins a congressional nomination.

Women and minorities have long been underrepresented in elected office, although both groups recently have significantly increased their representation in the Congress (see Politics in a Changing America 11.1). Other members of Congress don't necessarily ignore the concerns of women and minorities—there are many white men, for example, who have championed equal rights. Yet, many women and minorities believe that only members of their own group—people who have experienced what they have experienced—can truly represent their interests. This is a belief in **descriptive representation,** the view that a legislature should resemble the demographic characteristics of the population it represents.[24]

During the 1980s, both Congress and the Supreme Court provided support for the principle of descriptive representation for blacks and Hispanic Americans. When Congress amended the Voting Rights Act in 1982, it encouraged states to draw districts that concentrated minorities so that black and Hispanic Americans would have a better chance of being elected to office. Supreme Court decisions also pushed the states to concentrate minorities in House districts.[25] After the 1990 census, states redrew House boundaries with the intent of creating districts with majority or near majority minority populations. Some districts were very oddly shaped, snaking through a state to pick up black neighborhoods in various cities but leaving adjacent white neighborhoods to other districts. This effort led to a roughly 50 percent increase in the number of blacks elected to the House. Hispanic representation in the House also increased, from 10 to 17 members, after redistricting created new districts with large concentrations of Hispanic American voters.

In a decision that surprised many, the Supreme Court ruled in 1993 that states' efforts to increase minority representation through **racial gerrymandering** could violate the rights of whites. In *Shaw* v. *Reno*, the majority in a split decision ruled that a North Carolina district that meandered 160 miles from Durham to Charlotte was an example of "political apartheid" (see Figure 11.3). (In some places, the Twelfth District is no wider than Interstate 85.) In effect, the Court ruled that racial gerrymandering segregated blacks from whites instead of creating districts built around contiguous communities. The ruling sent the case back to a North Carolina court to reconsider the district's legality in light of the Court's decision.[26]

The dissenting justices' opinion noted that even with two racially gerrymandered districts, whites still represented ten of the twelve North Carolina districts, giving whites 83 percent of the congressional delegation with only 76 percent of the population. "Surely [whites] cannot com-

FIGURE	**11.3**	■ **"Political Apartheid" or Racial Equality?**

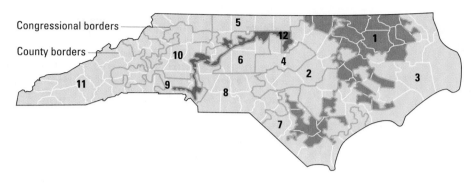

To create districts in which African American candidates were likely to win, the boundaries of two North Carolina congressional districts, 1 and 12, had to weave across the state to incorporate enough neighborhoods with concentrated minority populations. Justice Sandra Day O'Connor, writing for the Supreme Court, called these districts examples of political apartheid. Others contend that without such gerrymandering, few minorities would be elected to Congress.

plain of discriminatory treatment," remarked Justice Byron R. White. This is a difficult issue: If equality requires descriptive representation, a step away from racial gerrymandering is a retreat from equality in the Congress. On a more pragmatic level, some observers question whether packing selected districts with minorities actually reduces their influence in the Congress. If black and Hispanic populations were spread around many districts, wouldn't more representatives be supportive of the interests of those minorities?[27] But as Politics in a Changing America 11.1 points out, minority representatives do not simply vote as their constituents want (which white representatives might do as well); they also play a leadership role in initiating policy and in sensitizing the rest of the institution to the special needs of minority populations.

HOW ISSUES GET ON THE CONGRESSIONAL AGENDA

The formal legislative process begins when a member of Congress introduces a **bill,** a proposal for a new law. In the House, members drop new bills in the "hopper," a mahogany box near the rostrum where the Speaker presides. Senators give their bills to a Senate clerk or introduce them from the floor.[28] But before a bill can be introduced to solve a problem, someone must perceive that a problem exists or that an issue needs to be resolved. In other words, the problem or issue somehow must find its way onto the congressional agenda. *Agenda* actually has two meanings in the vocabulary of political scientists. The first is that of a narrow, formal agenda, such as a calendar of bills to be voted on. The second meaning refers to the broad, imprecise, and unwritten agenda that consists of all issues an institution is considering. Here we use the term in the second, broader sense.

Many issues Congress is working on at any given time seem to have been around forever. Foreign aid, the national debt, and social security have come up in just about every recent session of Congress. Yet, all issues begin at some point in time. There has always been violence on TV, for example, but only recently has it become a political issue. Although legislation regulating TV violence has yet to be enacted, criticism by Congress

POLITICS IN A CHANGING AMERICA 11.1

If Congress Looks Different, Will It Act Different?

 African Americans were first elected to Congress during the Reconstruction era after the Civil War. After the military occupation of the South ended, the number of African Americans in Congress dwindled to a single representative by the end of the nineteenth century. (Blacks were systematically disenfranchised by southern whites after they resumed control of their state governments.) George White, the last African American legislator of this period, stood on the floor of the House in 1901 and prophesised of the black man in Congress, "Phoenix-like he will rise up some day and come again."

The phoenix has indeed risen. Thirty-nine African Americans were sent to Congress in the 1992 election. This is a substantial number of legislators, but does it make any difference? Does descriptive representation bring about more effective representation for a particular sector of society?

Because the sharp increase in African American representation is so recent, there is no definitive answer. Still, early indications are that the Congressional Black Caucus—the organization of African Americans in the House—is gaining leverage in the legislative process. The leader of the Black Caucus, Kweisi Mfume, a Democrat from Maryland, can bargain with a considerable number of votes when he negotiates with the House leadership. (All but one of the blacks in the House are Democrats.) On issues directly affecting African Americans, the Black Caucus has been influential with the administration,

too. President Clinton wanted to nominate John Payton, a District of Columbia government lawyer, as head of the civil rights division in the Justice Department. Members of the Black Caucus objected privately, because Payton refused to commit himself to the racial gerrymandering that has brought more blacks into Congress. Clinton bowed to the Black Caucus's wishes and did not go forward with the nomination.

African Americans have also enhanced their clout by moving up the seniority ladder. Three blacks chair House committees and thirteen chair subcommittees. John Lewis of Georgia serves as chief deputy whip, an important position in the congressional party hierarchy. This leadership cohort of African Americans is in a strong position to initiate policy and advance the interests of their constituents.

The same questions about descriptive representation can be asked about women representatives, who also increased sharply in number in the House. (Progress is also being made in the Senate. There are seven women senators, up from two only a few years ago.) Although research on women in Congress has been hampered by their low numbers, interesting studies have been done on women in state legislatures.

In many respects, female state legislators act very similarly to male legislators of the same party. In some areas, however, women do operate differently. They are more likely than their male counterparts to introduce bills on issues pertaining to women, children, and the

has prompted the networks to issue warnings before they air violent programs. The issue is now on Congress's agenda, and Congress may take action in the future.[29]

New issues reach the congressional agenda in many ways. Sometimes a highly visible event focuses national attention on a problem. When an explosion in a West Virginia mine in 1968 killed seventy-eight miners, Congress promptly went to work on laws to promote miners' safety.[30]

family. They are also likely to make such bills their priorities—the ones they work hardest to get passed. Men and women state legislators are equally successful in getting their priority bills passed, but women's emphasis on these issues means that more such legislation gets passed and signed into law.

Simply put, women bring different concerns to a legislature. Their presence influences the mix of issues on the table and brings new perspectives on how problems may be solved. As one scholar puts it, "Leaving any group out of policy formulation and legitimation necessarily means that the range of ideas is artificially limited."

• *Source: Elizabeth Adell Cook, Sue Thomas, and Clyde Wilcox,* The Year of the Woman *(Boulder, Colo.: Westview, 1994); Kitty Cunningham, "Black Caucus Flexes Muscle on Budget—And More,"* Congressional Quarterly Weekly Report, *3 July 1993, pp. 1711–1715; John Harwood, "Kweisi Mfume Builds Black Caucus's Clout, Wins Notice in Capital,"* Wall Street Journal, *29 June 1993, A1; Wil Haygood,* King of the Cats *(Boston: Houghton Mifflin, 1993); Neil A. Lewis, "Clinton's Choice for Rights Chief Is Withdrawing,"* New York Times, *18 December 1993, p. 1; Norman J. Ornstein, Thomas E. Mann, and Michael J. Malbin (eds.),* Vital Statistics on Congress, 1993–1994 *(Washington, D.C.: Congressional Quarterly, 1994), pp. 38–39; Paula Ries and Anne J. Stone (eds.),* The American Woman, 1992–93 *(New York: W. W. Norton, 1992); Sue Thomas,* How Women Legislate *(New York: Oxford University Press, 1994).*

Presidential support can also move an issue onto the agenda quickly. The media attention paid to the president gives him enormous opportunity to draw the nation's attention to problems he believes need some form of government action.

Within Congress, party leaders and committee chairs have the opportunity to move issues onto the agenda, but they rarely act capriciously, seizing upon issues without rhyme or reason. They often bide their time,

**Congress Smokes
Tobacco Execs**

*Congressional hearings are
often structured like dramas,
staged to portray villains at
the witness table whose evil
doings are uncovered by the
crusading heroes on the committee. The villains in this bit
of congressional theater are
the chief executive officers
from the nation's largest tobacco companies. They de-
fended the cigarette industry
and refused to acknowledge
that smoking causes cancer.
The prop at the right was set
there by congressional staffers
so that television pictures and
still photographs of the executives together would include
this easel. The placards on the
easel were periodically
changed from charts with
statistics documenting the
health risks of tobacco to
gruesome photos of oral
cancer.*

waiting for other members of Congress to learn about an issue, as they attempt to gauge the level of support for some kind of action. At times, the
efforts of an interest group spark support, or at least an awareness, of an
issue. When congressional leaders—or, for that matter, rank-and-file
members—sense that the time is ripe for action on a new issue, they often
are spurred on by the knowledge that sponsoring an important bill can enhance their own image. In the words of one observer, "Congress exists to
do things. There isn't much mileage in doing nothing."[31]

THE DANCE OF LEGISLATION: AN OVERVIEW

The process of writing bills and getting them enacted is relatively simple,
in the sense that it follows a series of specific steps. What complicates the
process is the many different ways legislation can be treated at each step.
Here, we examine the straightforward process by which laws are made. In
the next few sections, we discuss some of the complexities of that process.

After a bill is introduced in either house, it is assigned to the committee
with jurisdiction over that policy area (see Figure 11.4).[32] A banking bill,
for example, would be assigned to the Banking, Finance, and Urban Affairs
Committee in the House or, in the Senate, to the Banking, Housing, and
Urban Affairs Committee depending on where it was introduced. When a
committee actively considers a piece of legislation assigned to it, the bill
is usually referred to a specialized subcommittee. The subcommittee may
hold hearings, and legislative staffers may do research on the bill. The original bill usually is modified or revised; if passed in some form, it is sent
back to the full committee. A bill approved by the full committee is reported (that is, sent) to the entire membership of the chamber, where it
may be debated, amended, and either passed or defeated.

Bills coming out of House committees go to the Rules Committee before going before the full House membership. The Rules Committee at-
taches a rule to the bill that governs the coming floor debate, typically
specifying the length of the debate and the types of amendments that

FIGURE 11.4 ■ The Legislative Process

The process by which a bill becomes law is subject to much variation. This diagram depicts the typical process a bill might follow. It is important to remember that a bill can fail at any stage because of lack of support.

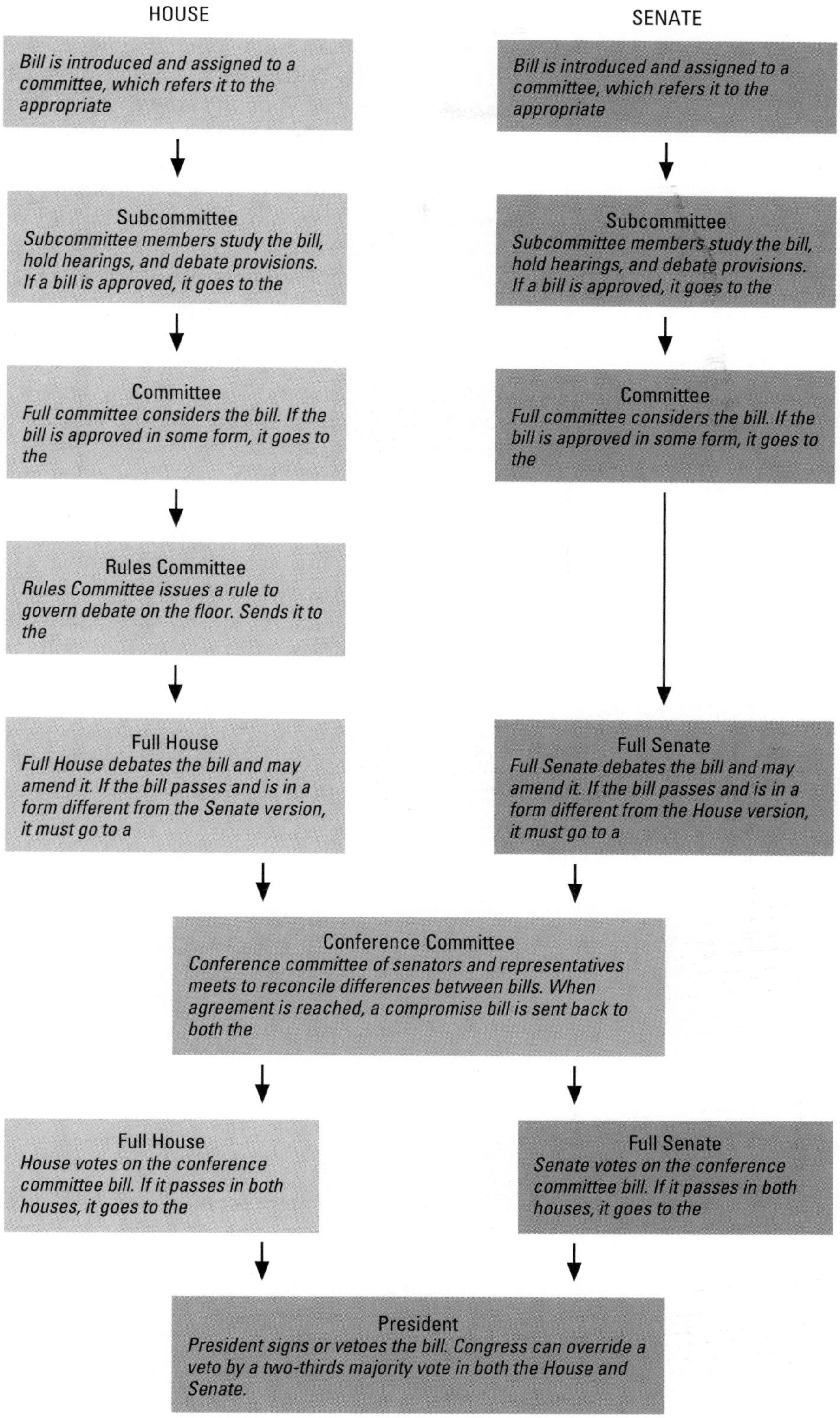

HOUSE

Bill is introduced and assigned to a committee, which refers it to the appropriate

Subcommittee
Subcommittee members study the bill, hold hearings, and debate provisions. If a bill is approved, it goes to the

Committee
Full committee considers the bill. If the bill is approved in some form, it goes to the

Rules Committee
Rules Committee issues a rule to govern debate on the floor. Sends it to the

Full House
Full House debates the bill and may amend it. If the bill passes and is in a form different from the Senate version, it must go to a

SENATE

Bill is introduced and assigned to a committee, which refers it to the appropriate

Subcommittee
Subcommittee members study the bill, hold hearings, and debate provisions. If a bill is approved, it goes to the

Committee
Full committee considers the bill. If the bill is approved in some form, it goes to the

Full Senate
Full Senate debates the bill and may amend it. If the bill passes and is in a form different from the House version, it must go to a

Conference Committee
Conference committee of senators and representatives meets to reconcile differences between bills. When agreement is reached, a compromise bill is sent back to both the

Full House
House votes on the conference committee bill. If it passes in both houses, it goes to the

Full Senate
Senate votes on the conference committee bill. If it passes in both houses, it goes to the

President
President signs or vetoes the bill. Congress can override a veto by a two-thirds majority vote in both the House and Senate.

House members can offer. The Senate does not have a comparable committee, although restrictions on the length of floor debate can be reached through unanimous consent agreements (see page 382).

Even if both houses of Congress pass a bill on the same subject, the Senate and House versions are typically different from each other. In that case, a conference committee, composed of legislators from both houses, works out the differences and develops a compromise version. This version goes back to both houses for another floor vote. If both chambers approve the bill, it goes to the president for his signature or veto.

When the president signs a bill, it becomes law. If the president **vetoes** (disapproves) the bill, he sends it back to Congress with his reasons for rejecting it. The bill becomes law only if Congress overrides the president's veto by a two-thirds vote of each house. If the president neither signs nor vetoes the bill within ten days (Sundays excepted) of receiving it, the bill becomes law. There is an exception here: If Congress adjourns within the ten days, the president can let the bill die through a **pocket veto,** by not signing it.

The content of a bill can be changed at any stage of the process in either house. Lawmaking (and thus policymaking) in Congress has many access points for those who want to influence legislation. This openness tends to fit within the pluralist model of democracy. As a bill moves through the dance of legislation,[33] it is amended again and again, in a search for a consensus that will get it enacted and signed into law. The process can be tortuously slow and often fruitless. Derailing legislation is much easier than enacting it. The process gives groups frequent opportunities to voice their preferences and, if necessary, to thwart their opponents. One foreign ambassador stationed in Washington aptly described the twists and turns of our legislative process: "In the Congress of the U.S., it's never over until it's over. And when it's over, it's still not over."[34]

COMMITTEES: THE WORKHORSES OF CONGRESS

Woodrow Wilson once observed that "Congress in session is Congress on public exhibition, whilst Congress in its committee-rooms is Congress at work."[35] His words are as true today as when he wrote them more than one hundred years ago. A speech on the Senate floor, for example, may convince the average citizen, but it is less likely to influence other senators. Indeed, few of them may even hear it. The real nuts and bolts of lawmaking go on in the congressional committees.

The Division of Labor Among Committees

The House and Senate are divided into committees for the same reason that other large organizations are broken into departments or divisions—to develop and use expertise in specific areas. At IBM, for example, different groups of people design computers, write software, assemble hardware, and sell the company's products. Each task requires an expertise that may have little to do with the other tasks that the company performs. Likewise, in Congress, decisions on weapons systems require a special knowledge that is of little relevance to decisions on reimbursement formulas for health insurance, for example. It makes sense for some members of Congress to spend more time examining defense issues, becoming increasingly expert as they do so, while others concentrate on health matters.

Eventually, all members of Congress have to vote on each bill that emerges from the committees. Those who are not on a particular committee depend on committee members to examine the issues thoroughly, to make compromises as necessary, and to bring forward a sound piece of legislation that has a good chance of being passed. Each member decides individually on the bill's merits. But once it reaches the House or Senate floor, members may get to vote on only a handful of amendments (if any at all) before they must cast their yeas and nays for the entire bill.

Standing Committees. There are several different kinds of congressional committees, but the **standing committee** is predominant. Standing committees are permanent committees that specialize in a particular area of legislation—for example, the House Judiciary Committee or the Senate Environment and Public Works Committee. Most of the day-to-day work of drafting legislation takes place in the seventeen standing Senate committees and twenty-two standing House committees. Typically, seventeen to twenty senators serve on each standing Senate committee and about forty-five members on each standing committee in the House. The proportions of Democrats and Republicans on a standing committee generally reflect party proportions in the full Senate or House, and each member of Congress serves on only a small number of committees.

With a few exceptions, standing committees are further broken down into subcommittees. The House Agriculture Committee, for example, has six subcommittees, among them one on specialty crops and natural resources and another on livestock. Subcommittees exist for the same reason parent committees exist: Members acquire expertise by continually working within the same fairly narrow policy area. Typically, members of the subcommittee are the dominant force in the shaping of the content of a bill.[36]

Other Congressional Committees. Members of Congress can also serve on joint, select, and conference committees. **Joint committees** are made up of members of both the House and the Senate. Like standing committees, the small number of joint committees is concerned with particular policy areas. The Joint Economic Committee, for instance, analyzes the country's economic policies. Joint committees operate in much the same way as standing committees, but they are almost always restricted from reporting bills to the House or Senate.

A **select committee** is a temporary committee created for a specific purpose. Congress establishes select committees to deal with special circumstances or with issues that either overlap or fall outside the areas of expertise of standing committees. The Senate committee that investigated the Watergate scandal was a select committee, created for that purpose only.

A **conference committee** is also a temporary committee, created to work out differences between the House and Senate versions of a specific piece of legislation. Its members are appointed from the standing committees or

Pat Schroeder, Defense Specialist

Schroeder, a Colorado Democrat, is a leader among House liberals on defense issues. She chairs a subcommittee of the House Armed Services Committee.

Sam Nunn, Defense Specialist

The cerebral Democrat from Georgia, extremely knowledgeable on defense policy, exerts a great deal of influence as the chair of the Senate Armed Services Committee.

subcommittees in each house that originally handled and reported the legislation. Depending on the nature of the differences and the importance of the legislation, a conference committee may meet for hours or for weeks on end. The conference committee for a recent defense bill had to resolve 2,003 separate differences between the two versions.[37] When the conference committee reaches a compromise, it reports the bill to both houses. Each house may either approve or disapprove the compromise; they cannot amend or change it in any way. Only about 15 to 25 percent of all bills that eventually pass Congress go to a conference committee (although virtually all important or controversial bills do).[38] Committee or subcommittee leaders of both houses reconcile differences in other bills through informal negotiation.

Congressional Expertise and Seniority

Once appointed to a committee, a representative or senator has great incentive to remain on it and to gain expertise over the years. Influence in Congress increases with a member's expertise. Influence also grows in a more formal way, with **seniority,** or years of consecutive service on a committee. In the quest for expertise and seniority, members tend to stay on the same committees. However, sometimes they switch places when they are offered the opportunity to move to one of the high-prestige committees (such as Ways and Means in the House or Finance in the Senate) or to a committee that handles legislation of vital importance to their constituents.

In a committee, the senior member of the majority party usually becomes the committee chair. (The majority party in each house controls committee leadership.) Other high-seniority members of the majority party become subcommittee chairs, whereas their counterparts from the minority party gain influence as ranking minority members. The 120 subcommittees in the House and 90 in the Senate offer multiple opportunities for power and status.

Unlike seniority, expertise does not follow simply from length of service. Ability and effort are critical factors, too. When Georgia Democrat Sam Nunn entered the Congress, he single-mindedly devoted himself to mastering the intricacies of defense policy. By the time he became chair of the Senate Armed Services Committee, he was already a respected expert on defense matters. When President Clinton proposed allowing gays to serve openly in the military, Nunn's opposition was critical in killing the plan. He then became a key figure in the "don't ask, don't tell" compromise that later emerged.

The role of seniority and the powers of committee chairs once were stronger than they are today. In the 1970s, there was a rebellion against the House establishment led by liberal, junior members who "chafed under the restrictions on their participation and policy influence that the old committee-dominated regime imposed. The committee chair, often in collaboration with the ranking minority member, dominated the panel."[39] The House adopted new rules that held that seniority did not have to be followed in the selection of committee chairs. In 1975, House Democrats voted out three aging, unpopular committee chairmen, serving notice to all committee chairs that they would not tolerate autocratic rule.

The Lawmaking Process

The way in which committees and subcommittees are organized within Congress is ultimately significant because much public policy decision making takes place there. The first step in drafting legislation is to collect information on the issue. Committee staffers research the problem, and committees hold hearings to take testimony from witnesses who have some special knowledge of the subject.

At times, committee hearings are more theatrical than informational, to draw public attention to them. When the House Judiciary Subcommittee on Administrative Law held hearings on alleged malpractice in military hospitals, it did not restrict its list of witnesses to the experts who had done relevant research. Instead, it called witnesses such as Dawn Lambert, a former member of the navy, who sobbed as she told the subcommittee that she had been left sterile by a misdiagnosis and a botched operation that had left a sponge and a green marker inside her. It was an irresistible story for the evening news and brought the malpractice problem to light.[40]

The meetings at which subcommittees or committees actually debate and amend legislation are called *markup sessions.* The process by which committees reach decisions varies. Many committees have a strong tradition of decision by consensus. The chair, the ranking minority member, and others in these committees work hard, in formal committee sessions and in informal negotiations, to find a middle ground on issues that divide committee members. In other committees, members exhibit strong ideological and partisan sentiments. However, committee and subcommittee leaders prefer to find ways to overcome the inherent ideological and partisan divisions so that they can build compromise solutions that will appeal to the broader membership of their house.

Although there is considerable bargaining at markup sessions, negotiation over significant or controversial policies will precede the formal committee meetings. Sometimes these negotiations can be quite protracted. In the late 1980s, Congress was having a difficult time reaching agreement on welfare reform legislation. Liberals and conservatives were far apart, and the House and Senate had substantial differences in their approach to the problem. Paraphrasing Dickens, the *New York Times* said, "It was the best of bills, it was the worst of bills. It was a bill everybody wanted, it was a bill nobody wanted." The deal that was struck in the end gave each side its main priority but also made each side accept a lot of things with which it was uncomfortable. The Republicans got a "workfare" provision—which forces one parent in two-parent welfare families to work sixteen hours a week in community service. Liberal Democrats got expanded benefit coverage for Medicaid and child care for welfare families. The bill was still a tough pill to swallow, because each side strongly disliked what the other side got. To build consensus for the compromise, Daniel Moynihan, the Democratic senator from New York, lobbied each of his 99 colleagues. The chief House negotiator, Thomas Downey, also a Democrat from New

York, talked individually to about 150 other members of the House. In the end, the bill was enacted.[41]

Committees: The Majoritarian and Pluralist Views

It makes sense to bring as much expertise as possible to the policymaking process, and the committee system does just that. But government by committee vests a tremendous amount of power in the committees and subcommittees of Congress—especially in their leaders. This is particularly true of the House, which is more decentralized than the Senate in its patterns of influence and more restrictive in the degree to which members can amend legislation on the floor. Committee members can bury a bill by not reporting it to the full House or Senate. The influence of committee members extends even further, to the floor debate. And many of them make up the conference committee that is charged with developing a compromise version of the bill.

In some ways, the committee system enhances the force of pluralism in American politics. Representatives and senators are elected by the voters in particular districts and states, and they tend to seek membership on the committees that make the decisions most important to their constituents. Members from farm areas, for example, want membership on the House and Senate Agriculture committees. Westerners like to serve on the committees that deal with public lands and water rights. Urban liberals like the committees that handle social programs. As a result, those committees that have a membership that represents constituencies that have an unusually strong interest in their policy area are predisposed to writing legislation favorable to those districts or states.

The committees have a majoritarian aspect as well. Although some committees have an imbalance of legislators from particular kinds of districts or states, the memberships of most committees tend to resemble the general profiles of the two parties' congressional contingents. For example, Republicans on individual House committees tend to vote like all Republicans in the House. Moreover, even if a committee's views are not in line with those of the full membership, it is constrained in the legislation it writes, because bills cannot become law unless they are passed by the parent chamber and by the other house. Consequently, in formulating legislation, committees anticipate what other representatives and senators will accept. The parties within each chamber also have means of rewarding members who are the most loyal to party priorities. Party committees and the party leadership within each chamber make committee assignments and respond to requests for transfers from less prestigious to more prestigious committees. Those whose voting is the most in line with the party get better assignments.[42]

LEADERS AND FOLLOWERS IN CONGRESS	Above the committee chairs is another layer of authority in the organization of the House and Senate. The Democratic and Republican leaders in each house work to maximize the influence of their own party while trying to keep their chamber functioning smoothly and efficiently. The operation of the two houses is also influenced by the rules and norms that each chamber has developed over the years.

The Johnson Treatment

When he was Senate majority leader in the 1950's, Lyndon Johnson was well known for his style of interaction with other members. In this unusual set of photographs, we see him applying the "Johnson treatment" to Democrat Theodore Francis Green of Rhode Island. Washington journalists Rowland Evans and Robert Novak offered the following description of the treatment: "Its tone could be supplication, accusation, cajolery, exuberance, scorn, tears, complaint, the hint of threat. It was all of these together. It ran the gamut of human emotions. Its velocity was breathtaking and it was all in one direction. Interjections from the target were rare. Johnson anticipated them before they could be spoken. He moved in close, his face a scant millimeter from his target, his eyes widening and narrowing, his eyebrows rising and falling. From his pockets poured clippings, memos, statistics. Mimicry, humor, and the genius of analogy made The Treatment an almost hypnotic experience and rendered the target stunned and helpless." (Rowland Evans and Robert Novak, Lyndon B. Johnson: The Exercise of Power. *New York: New American Library, 1966. p. 104.)*

The Leadership Task

Each of the two parties in each of the two houses elects leaders. In the House of Representatives, the majority-party leader is the **Speaker of the House,** who, gavel in hand, chairs sessions from the ornate rostrum at the front of the chamber. The counterpart in the opposing party is the minority leader. The Speaker is a constitutional officer, but the Constitution does not list the Speaker's duties. The minority leader is not mentioned in the Constitution, but that post has evolved into an important party position in the House.

The Constitution makes the vice president of the United States the president of the Senate. But in practice the vice president rarely visits the Senate chamber, unless there is a possibility of a tie vote, in which case he can break the tie. The *president pro tempore* (president "for the time"), elected by the majority party, is supposed to chair the Senate in the vice president's absence, but by custom this constitutional position is entirely honorary.

The real power in the Senate resides in the **majority leader.** As in the House, the top position in the opposing party is that of minority leader. Technically, the majority leader does not preside (members rotate in the president pro tempore's chair), but the majority leader does schedule legislation in consultation with the minority leader. More broadly, party leaders play a critical role in getting bills through Congress. The most significant function that leaders play is steering the bargaining and negotiating over the content of legislation. When an issue divides their party, their house, the two houses, or their house and the White House, the leaders must take the initiative to work out a compromise.

Day in, day out, much of what leaders do is meet with other members of their house to try to strike deals that will yield a majority on the floor. It is often a matter of finding out whether one faction is willing to give up a policy preference in exchange for another concession. Beyond trying to engineer trade-offs that will win votes, the party leaders must persuade others (often powerful committee chairs) that theirs is the best deal possible. Senator Robert Dole of Kansas aptly described himself as the "majority

pleader" when he served as Senate majority leader.[43] (His party's victories in the 1994 elections will again make Dole majority leader; he lost the post in 1986 when the Democrats took back the Senate.)

Party leaders today are coalition builders, not autocrats. Gone are the days when leaders ruled the House and the Senate with iron fists. Even as recently as the 1950s, strong leaders dominated the legislative process. When he was Senate majority leader, Lyndon Johnson made full use of his intelligence, parliamentary skills, and forceful personality to direct the Senate. When he approached individual senators for one-on-one persuasion, "no one subjected to the 'Johnson treatment' ever forgot it."[44] In today's Congress, rank-and-file representatives and senators would not stand for this kind of leadership. But contemporary leaders clearly have an effect on policy outcomes in Congress. As one expert concluded, "Although leadership contributions may be marginal, most important political choices are made at the margins."[45]

Rules of Procedure

The operation of the House and Senate is structured by both formal rules and informal norms of behavior. Rules in each chamber are mostly matters of parliamentary procedure. For example, they govern the scheduling of legislation, outlining when and how certain types of legislation can be brought to the floor. Rules also govern the introduction of floor amendments. In the House, amendments must be directly germane (relevant) to the bill at hand; in the Senate, except in certain, specified instances, amendments that are not germane to the bill at hand can be proposed.

As noted earlier, an important difference between the two chambers is the House's use of its Rules Committee to govern floor debate. Lacking a similar committee to act as a "traffic cop" for legislation approaching the floor, the Senate relies on unanimous consent agreements to set the starting time and length of debate. If one senator objects to such an agreement, it does not take effect. Senators do not routinely object to unanimous consent agreements, however, because they need them when bills of their own await scheduling by the leadership. The rules facilitate cooperation among the competing interests and parties in each house so that legislation can be voted on. However, the rules are not neutral: they are a tool of the majority party and help it control the legislative process.[46]

If a senator wants to stop a bill badly enough, she or he may start a **filibuster,** trying to talk the bill to death. By historical tradition, the Senate gives its members the right of unlimited debate. During a 1947 debate, Idaho Democrat Glen Taylor "spoke for 8 1/2 hours on fishing, baptism, Wall Street, and his children." The record for holding the floor belongs to Republican Senator Strom Thurmond of South Carolina, for a twenty-four-hour, eighteen-minute marathon.[47] In the House, no member is allowed to speak for more than an hour without unanimous consent.

After a 1917 filibuster by a small group of senators killed President Wilson's bill to arm merchant ships—a bill favored by a majority of senators—the Senate finally adopted **cloture,** a means of limiting debate. A petition signed by sixteen senators initiates a cloture vote. It now takes the votes of sixty senators to invoke cloture. Senators successfully invoked cloture when a filibuster by southern senators threatened passage of the far-reaching Civil Rights Act of 1964. Three-quarters of senators recently

FEATURE 11.1

■ Maybe They Ought to Make Crocodile Dundee Speaker

 We wouldn't expect a legislature with members named "Toecutter" Williams, "Dingo" Dawkins, and "Ironbar" Tuckey to be a quiet, formal, contemplative body. And the Australian Parliament is not. In fact, the Australian Parliament makes the boisterous British Parliament—after which it is modeled—seem almost subdued.

Name calling has rarely reached the heights of imagination heard in the hallowed chambers of the Parliament Down Under. Cries of "harlot," "sleazebag," "mug," "boxhead," "fop," "sucker," and "thug" are hurled back and forth among members as they debate the bills before them. For the record, it's only fair to point out that the body's rules actually forbid such language. Indeed, the Senate handbook explicitly states that it's wrong to call other senators such names as "arrant humbug" or "yahoo from Tasmania." But when an Australian senator gets angry, no handbook is going to stop him from calling a yahoo from Tasmania a "yahoo from Tasmania."

The Australian Parliament does have a rich sense of tradition. Legislators are called to impending votes by bells that ring for two minutes. There is no clock on the wall of the chambers; time is measured with an hourglass. And attendants who work in the chambers are dressed in wigs and gowns.

One of the traditions is freely speaking one's mind. When they have something to say, Australian legislators can be quite persistent. Unlike Representative Barney Frank, who was content to sit down after a single insult, Brian Howe, an Australian representative, was only warming up when he called a colleague "something of a grub if I could put it that way." When the Speaker told Howe no, that he couldn't put it that way, Howe responded, "I will withdraw that term and substitute the term *parasite*." Again, the Speaker objected. Howe then substituted the phrase "this leech over there," which led the Speaker to reprimand him.

- *Source: Adapted from Geraldine Brooks, "In This Parliament, Decorum Often Sinks Down Under Insults,"* Wall Street Journal, *14 November 1986, p. 1. Reprinted by permission of the* Wall Street Journal, *Dow Jones Company, Inc., 1986. All rights reserved worldwide.*

surveyed professed some support for making it more difficult to filibuster, but apparently sentiment is not intense enough to propel reform forward because no changes are now being actively considered.[48]

Norms of Behavior

Both houses have codes of behavior that help keep them running. These codes are largely unwritten norms, although some have been formally adopted as rules. Members of Congress recognize that they must eliminate (or minimize) personal conflict, lest Congress dissolve into bickering factions unable to work together. One of the most celebrated norms is that members show respect for their colleagues in public deliberations. During floor debate, bitter opponents still refer to one another in such terms as "my good friend, the senior senator from . . ." or "my distinguished colleague."

Members of Congress are only human, of course, and tempers occasionally flare (see Feature 11.1). For example, when Democrat Barney Frank of Massachusetts was angered by what he thought were unusually harsh charges against the Democratic party, made by Republican Robert Walker of Pennsylvania, Frank rose to ask the presiding officer if it was permissible to refer to Walker as a "crybaby." When he was informed that it was not, Frank sat down, having made his point without technically violating the House's code of behavior.[49]

Probably the most important norm of behavior in Congress is that individual members should be willing to bargain with one another. Policymaking is a process of give and take; it demands compromise. And the cost of not compromising is high. When Republican Richard Armey of Texas first came to Congress in 1985, he was a strident conservative ideologue who enjoyed trying to disrupt the Democratic-controlled House to prevent it from passing legislation that it favored. Consequently, other representatives ignored him; they never included him in the bargaining over legislation, and he had no real influence on the lawmaking process. By his next term in office, Armey realized that if he was going to have any influence on public policy, he had to stop thinking of the Democrats as liberal heathens and be willing to negotiate. Now, he's a "player" in the process.[50]

It is important to point out that members of Congress are not expected to violate their consciences on policy issues simply to strike a deal. They are expected, however, to listen to what others have to say and to make every effort to reach a reasonable compromise. Obviously, if they all stick rigidly to their views, they will never agree on anything. Moreover, few policy matters are so clear cut that compromise destroys one's position.

Recent years have seen an important evolution in some norms of behavior. Legislators have shown less patience toward the norms of apprenticeship and committee autonomy. Junior members have become much more assertive and now refuse to spend a long time as apprentices, gaining experience before playing a major role in the development of legislation. As one scholar notes, "The apprenticeship norm . . . has disappeared in both chambers."[51]

Members also have less respect for the primacy of committees. Committees continue to be a dominant force in Congress, but members not serving on a committee are no longer content to grant it autonomy over its policy area. Today, members not serving on committees offer more amendments on the floor to try to change the policy thrust of the committee's bill.[52] This trend has worked against pluralism and enhanced majoritarianism in Congress, because it makes more of the specifics of legislation subject to the influence of the entire chamber.

The unrelenting ambition of the members of Congress fuel these changing norms. One does not get to Congress without being ambitious.[53] Once there, new members look for ways to build their careers. With the help of the reforms of the 1970s, these changing norms have allowed new members of Congress to be more entrepreneurial. They search for issues they can make their mark on without strictly following the jurisdictions of their committees and without having to wait until they have attained seniority.[54]

THE LEGISLATIVE ENVIRONMENT

After legislation emerges from committee, it is scheduled for floor debate. How do legislators make up their minds on how to vote? In this section, we examine the broader legislative environment that affects decision

Friendly Enemies

After a White House meeting, President Clinton makes small talk with Republican congressional leaders Bob Dole of Kansas and Newt Gingrich of Georgia. With the GOP takeover of both houses of Congress, Dole will become majority leader in the Senate and Gingrich will become Speaker of the House. In our system of government, policy-making in Congress usually incorporates some element of bipartisanship. Amenities aside, as Figure 11.5 demonstrates, partisanship has been rising over time.

making in Congress. More specifically, we look at the influence on legislators of political parties, the president, constituents, and interest groups. The first two influences, parties and the president, push Congress toward majoritarian democracy. The other two, constituents and interest groups, are pluralist influences on congressional policymaking.

Political Parties

The national political parties might appear to have limited resources at their disposal to influence lawmakers. They do not control the nominations of House and Senate candidates. Candidates receive the bulk of their funds from individual contributors and political action committees, not from the national parties. Nevertheless, parties are strong forces in the legislative process. The party leaders and various committees within each house can help or hinder the efforts of rank-and-file legislators to get on the right committees, get their bills and amendments considered, and climb onto the leadership ladder themselves. Moreover, as we saw earlier, the Democrats and Republicans on a given committee tend to reflect the views of the entire party membership in the chamber. Thus, party members on a committee tend to act as agents of their party as they search for solutions to policy problems.[55]

FIGURE **11.5**	■ **Rising Partisanship**

The figures here show the percentages of representatives and senators who voted with a majority of their party on party unity votes. (Party unity votes are those in which a majority of one party votes one way and a majority of the other party votes the opposite way.) The rising percentage of party unity votes indicates that congressional parties are more frequently at odds with each other. In a true majoritarian system, parties vote against each other on all key issues.

Sources: Norman J. Ornstein, Thomas E. Mann, and Michael J. Malbin (eds.), Vital Statistics on Congress, 1993–1994 (Washington, D.C.: Congressional Quarterly, 1994), p. 200; and Kitty Cunningham, "With Democrats in White House, Partisanship Hits New High," Congressional Quarterly Weekly Report, 18 December 1993, p. 3432.

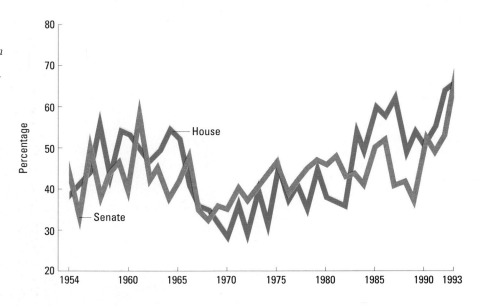

The most important reason that parties are important in Congress is, of course, that Democrats and Republicans have different ideological views. Both parties have diversity, but as Figure 11.5 illustrates, Democrats increasingly tend to vote one way and Republicans the other. Partisanship in Congress has risen for a number of reasons. One is greater party loyalty among southern Democrats. The issue of race no longer dominates southern politics as it once did. Also, since the Voting Rights Act of 1965, southern blacks have registered in large numbers. They now comprise a large share of the Democratic coalition in the South and act as a moderating influence on the traditionally conservative southern Democratic party. At the same time, Republican party strength has grown in the South, siphoning white conservatives from the Democrats. Another reason is that the presidency of Ronald Reagan in the 1980s sharpened the ideological differences between the parties. As Figure 11.5 shows, Reagan's highly conservative agenda worked to unite both parties, as Republicans voted together to support him while Democrats fought the Reagan program. When the Democrats reclaimed the White House after twelve years, partisan differences were again heightened.[56]

Some applaud this rising partisanship, because it is a manifestation of majoritarianism. When congressional parties are more unified, it gives voters a stronger means of influencing public policy choices through their selection of representatives and senators. Others are skeptical of majoritarianism, believing that Congress is more productive and responsible when it relies on bipartisanship. In their view, parties that cooperate in searching for consensus will serve the nation better.[57]

Collins and Staffer

The staff in each legislator's office is responsible for a variety of tasks, including handling casework and press relations, doing research, monitoring legislation, writing speeches, and meeting with constituents and interest group representatives. Here, Democratic representative Cardiss Collins of Illinois goes over some paperwork with one of her assistants.

The President

Unlike members of Congress, the president is elected by voters across the entire nation. The president has a better claim, then, to representing the nation than does any single member of Congress. But it can also be argued that Congress as a whole has a better claim than the president to representing the majority of voters. In fact, when Congress and the president differ, opinion surveys sometimes show that Congress's position on a given bill more closely resembles the majority view; at other times, these surveys show that the president's position accords with the majority. Nevertheless, presidents capitalize on their popular election and usually act as though they are speaking for the majority.

During the twentieth century, the public's expectations of what a president can accomplish in office have grown enormously. We now expect the president to be our chief legislator: to introduce legislation on major issues and to use his influence to push bills through Congress.[58] This is much different from our early history, when presidents felt constrained by the constitutional doctrine of separation of powers and had to have members work confidentially for them during legislative sessions.[59]

Today, the White House is openly involved not only in the writing of bills but also in their development as they wind their way through the legislative process. If the White House does not like a bill, it tries to work out a compromise with key legislators in order to have the legislation amended. On issues of the greatest importance, the president himself may meet with individual legislators to persuade them to vote a certain way. To monitor daily congressional activities and lobby for the broad range of administration policies, hundreds of legislative liaison personnel work for the executive branch.

Although members of Congress grant presidents a leadership role in proposing legislation, they jealously guard their power to debate, shape, pass, or defeat any legislation the president proposes. Congress often clashes sharply with the president when his proposals are seen as ill advised.

Constituents

Constituents are the people who live and vote in a legislator's district or state. Their opinions on an issue are a crucial part of the legislative decision-making process. As much as members of Congress want to please the party leadership or the president by going along with their preferences, legislators have to think about what the voters back home want. If they displease enough people by the way they vote, they might lose their seats in the next election.

Constituency influence contributes to pluralism, because the diversity of America is mirrored in the geographical basis of representation in the House and Senate. A representative from Los Angeles, for instance, may need to be sensitive to issues of particular concern to constituents whose backgrounds are Korean, Vietnamese, Hispanic, African American, or Jewish. A representative from Montana will have few such constituents but must pay particular attention to issues involving minerals and mining. A senator from Nebraska will give higher priority to agricultural issues than to urban issues. Conversely, a senator from New York will be hypersensitive to issues involving the cities. All these constituencies, enthusiastically represented by legislators who want to do a good job for the people back home, push and pull Congress in many different directions.

At all stages of the legislative process, the interests of the voters are on the minds of members of Congress. As they decide what to spend time on and how to vote, they weigh how different courses of action will affect their constituents' views of them.[60]

Interest Groups

As we pointed out in Chapter 10, interest groups are a means of constituency influence in the Congress. Because they represent a vast array of vocational, regional, and ideological groupings within our population, interest groups exemplify pluralist politics. Interest groups press members of Congress to take a particular course of action, believing sincerely that what they prefer is also best for the country. Legislators, in turn, are attentive to interest groups, not because of an abstract commitment to pluralist politics but because these organizations represent citizens, some of whom live back home in the district or state. Lobbies are also sources of useful information and potentially of political support (and in some instances, campaign contributions) to members of Congress.

Because the four external sources of influence on Congress—parties, the president, constituents, and interest groups—push legislators in both majoritarian and pluralist directions, Congress exhibits aspects of both pluralism and majoritarianism in its operations. We'll return to the conflict between pluralism and majoritarianism at the end of this chapter.

OVERSIGHT: FOLLOWING THROUGH ON LEGISLATION

It is often said in Washington that "knowledge is power." For Congress to retain its influence over the programs it creates, it must be aware of how the agencies responsible for them are administering them. To that end, legislators and their committees engage in **oversight,** the process of reviewing agency operations to determine whether the agency is carrying out policies as Congress intended.

As the executive branch has grown and policies and programs have become increasingly complex, oversight has become more difficult. The sheer magnitude of executive branch operations is staggering. On a typical weekday, for example, agencies issue more than a hundred pages of new regulations. Even with the division of labor in the committee system, determining how good a job an agency is doing in implementing a program is no easy task.

Congress performs its oversight function in a number of different ways. The most visible is the hearing. Hearings may be part of a routine review or the by-product of information that reveals a major problem with a program or with an agency's administrative practices. Another way Congress keeps track of what departments and agencies are doing is by requesting reports on specific agency practices and operations. A good deal of congressional oversight also takes place informally. There is ongoing contact between committee and subcommittee leaders and agency administrators, and between committee staffers and top agency staffers.

Congressional oversight of the executive branch has increased sharply since the early 1970s.[61] A primary reason for this increase was that Congress gave itself the staff necessary to watch over the growing federal government.[62] In addition to sizable growth in the staffs of individual legislators and of House and Senate committees, Congress created two new specialized offices in the 1970s—the Congressional Budget Office and the Office of Technology Assessment—to do sophisticated analyses of agency operations and proposals. The older Government Accounting Office (GAO) and the Congressional Research Service of the Library of Congress also do in-depth studies for Congress. Finally, the Nixon administration's attempts to dominate the legislative branch goaded Congress into a more aggressive oversight stance.

Oversight is often stereotyped as a process whereby angry legislators bring some administrators before the hot lights and TV cameras at a hearing and proceed to dress them down for some recent scandal or mistake. Some of this does go on, but the pluralist side of Congress makes it likely that at least some members of a committee are advocates of the programs they oversee, because those programs serve constituents back home. Members on the Agriculture committees, Democrat and Republican, want farm programs to succeed. Thus, most oversight is aimed at trying to find ways to improve programs and is not directed at efforts to discredit them.[63]

Congress was long criticized for doing too little oversight. Today, many critics charge that Congress's frequent intervention in administrative policymaking amounts to **micromanagement.** These critics argue that Congress is violating the spirit of the separation of powers by not giving agencies the flexibility to administer programs as they see fit. For example, the Veterans committees of Congress intervene constantly in the deliberations of the Veterans Administration. Pressure from individual members of Congress has prevented the agency from taking an action that affected only ten of its 240,000 employees.[64]

Particularly interesting is the increasing aggressiveness of Congress in the area of foreign policy, long the preserve of the presidency. In 1970, the Nixon administration refused to tell Congress its negotiating position until just before the start of arms limitation talks with the Russians. By the 1980s, however, the Reagan administration felt compelled to allow congressional participation in its arms negotiating. When the United States was developing an arms proposal in 1983, senators William Cohen and Sam Nunn went to the White House to hammer out a proposal with Chief of Staff James Baker.[65]

THE DILEMMA OF REPRESENTATION

When candidates for the House and Senate campaign for office, they routinely promise to work hard for their district's or state's interests. When they get to Washington, though, they all face a troubling dilemma: What their constituents want may not be what the people across the nation want.

Presidents and Shopping Bags

In doing the research for his book *Home Style,* political scientist Richard Fenno accompanied several representatives as they worked, interacting with constituents in their home districts. On one of Fenno's trips, he was in an airport with a congressional aide, waiting for the representative's plane from Washington to land. When the representative arrived, he said, "I spent fifteen minutes on the telephone with the president this afternoon. He had a plaintive tone in his voice and he pleaded with me." His side of the issue had prevailed over the president's, and he was elated by the victory. When the three men reached the aide's car, the representative saw the back seat piled high with campaign paraphernalia: shopping bags printed with his name and picture. "Back to this again," he sighed.[66]

Every member of Congress lives in two worlds: the world of presidents and the world of personalized shopping bags. A typical week in the life of a representative means working in Washington, then boarding a plane and flying back to the district. There the representative spends time meeting with individual constituents and talking to civic groups, church gatherings, business associations, labor unions, and the like. A survey of House members during a nonelection year showed that each made an average of thirty-five trips back to her or his district, spending an average of 138 days there.[67]

Members of Congress are often criticized for being out of touch with the people they are supposed to represent. This charge does not seem justified.

Power Broker

With the increase in the number of African American representatives, the Black Caucus has become a significant force among House Democrats. Kweisi Mfume of Baltimore (center), the leader of the Black Caucus, has proven to be a deft bargainer with both House leaders and the Clinton administration. Mfume has not hesitated to leverage the votes of the Black Caucus for concessions on various policy issues.

Legislators work extraordinarily hard at keeping in touch with voters, at finding out what is on their constituents' minds. The difficult problem is how to act on that knowledge.

Trustees or Delegates?

Are members of Congress bound to vote the way their constituents want them to vote, even if it means voting against their conscience? Some say no. They argue that legislators must be free to vote in line with what they think is best. This view has long been associated with the eighteenth-century English political philosopher Edmund Burke (1729–1797). Burke, who served in Parliament, told his constituents in Bristol that "you choose a member, indeed; but when you have chosen him, he is not a member of Bristol, but he is a member of *Parliament*."[68] Burke reasoned that representatives are sent by their constituents to vote as they think best. As **trustees,** representatives are obligated to consider the views of constituents, but they are not obligated to vote according to those views if they think they are misguided.

Others hold that legislators are duty bound to represent the majority view of their constituents, that they are **delegates** with instructions from the people at home on how to vote on critical issues. And delegates, unlike trustees, must be prepared to vote against their own policy preferences. When he faced a decision on how to vote on the proposed constitutional amendment to ban flag burning, Representative Peter Hoagland knew that his constituents back in Nebraska favored the amendment. As a Democrat in a seat traditionally held by Republicans, Hoagland also knew that a vote against the flag-burning amendment would be used against him in the upcoming 1990 fall election. His aides strongly advised him to vote for the amendment, because of the political damage a no vote would do with the generally conservative voters in his district. In the end, Hoagland voted against the amendment, because his conscience would not let him do otherwise.[69] (Hoagland won reelection despite the flag vote.)

Members of Congress are subject to two opposing forces, then. While the interests of the district encourage them to act as delegates, their interpretation of the larger national interest calls on them to be trustees. Given these conflicting role definitions, it is not surprising that Congress is not clearly a body of delegates or of trustees. Research has shown, however, that members of Congress are more apt to take the delegate role on issues that are of great concern to constituents.[70] But much of the time, what the constituency really wants is not clear. Many issues are not highly visible back home, they may cut across the constituency to affect it in different ways, or constituents only partially understand them. For such issues, no delegate position is obvious.

PLURALISM, MAJORITARIANISM, AND DEMOCRACY

The dilemma that individual members of Congress face in adopting the role of either delegate or trustee has broad implications for the way our country is governed. If legislators tend to act as delegates, congressional policymaking is more pluralistic, and policies reflect the bargaining that goes on among lawmakers who speak for different constituencies. If, instead, legislators tend to act as trustees and vote their consciences, policymaking becomes less tied to the narrower interests of districts and states. But even here there is no guarantee that congressional decision making reflects majority interests. True majoritarian legislatures require a paramount role for political parties.

We end this chapter with a short discussion of pluralism versus majoritarianism in Congress. But first, to establish a frame of reference, we need to take a quick look at a more majoritarian type of legislature—the parliament.

Parliamentary Government

In our legislative system, the executive and legislative functions are divided between a president and a congress, each elected separately. Most other democracies—for example, Britain and Japan—have parliamentary governments. In a **parliamentary system,** the chief executive is the legislative leader whose party holds the most seats in the legislature after an election or whose party forms a major part of the ruling coalition. For instance, in Great Britain, voters do not cast a ballot for prime minister. They vote only for their member of Parliament and thus must influence the choice of prime minister indirectly, by voting for the party they favor in the local district election. Parties are unified, and in Parliament legislators vote for the party position, giving voters a strong and direct means of influencing public policy.

In a parliamentary system, government power is highly concentrated in the legislature, because the leader of the majority party is also the head of government. Moreover, parliamentary legislatures are usually composed of only one house or have a second chamber that is much weaker than the other. (In the British Parliament, the House of Commons makes the decisions of government; the other chamber, the House of Lords, is largely an honorary debating club for distinguished members of society.) And parliamentary governments usually do not have a court that can invalidate acts of the parliament. Under such a system, the government is in the hands of

COMPARED WITH WHAT? 11.1   Women in Parliament

The percentage of women in the legislature differs considerably from one democracy to the other. The pattern shown in the figure here does not seem to be a function of the structure of the legislature or the party system. Instead, the differences in the representation of women seem to have more to do with the cultures of these Western democracies and the progress women have made in pressing for a role in the political process. Clearly, the Scandinavian countries have the best record of electing women to their parliaments.

The United States lags behind many of the European democracies, although the rapid gain in the number of women in the Congress suggests that the percentage of women representatives and senators will continue to rise. Particularly striking is the tiny percentage of women in the French Parliament. In the 1993 parliamentary elections, only 6.1 percent of all seats went to women candidates. Feminists in France are so frustrated with the lack of progress in the representation of women that they are calling for a law to require that all seats in the lower house of Parliament be equally divided between men and women.

• *Source: Alan Riding, "Frenchwomen Say It's Time to Be a 'Bit Utopian,' " New York Times, 31 December 1993, p. A5.*

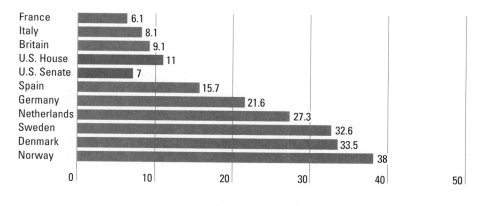

Country	Percentage
France	6.1
Italy	8.1
Britain	9.1
U.S. House	11
U.S. Senate	7
Spain	15.7
Germany	21.6
Netherlands	27.3
Sweden	32.6
Denmark	33.5
Norway	38

the party that controls the parliament. With no separation of government powers, checks on government action are few. Parliamentary systems can differ in many respects, as described in Compared with What? 11.1, but overall these governments fit the majoritarian model of democracy to a much greater extent than a separation-of-powers system.

Pluralism Versus Majoritarianism in Congress

The U.S. Congress is often criticized for being too pluralist and not majoritarian enough. The federal budget deficit is a case in point. Americans are deeply concerned about the big deficits that have plagued our national budgets in recent years. And both Democrats and Republicans in Congress repeatedly call for reductions in those deficits. But when spending bills come before Congress, legislators' concern turns to what the bills will or will not do for their districts or states. Appropriations bills usually include "pork barrel" projects that benefit specific districts or states and further add to the deficit. In one recent spending bill, Democrat Daniel Akaka got a $250,000 appropriation for pig and plant control at the Haleakala National Park in Hawaii. And Republican Ted Stevens delivered $2.6 million to the Fisheries Promotional Fund in Alaska.[71]

Projects such as these get into the budget through bargaining among members; as you saw earlier in the chapter, congressional norms encourage it. Members of Congress try to win projects and programs that will benefit their constituents and thus help them at election time. To win approval of such a project, a member must be willing to vote for other legislators' projects. Such a system obviously promotes pluralism (and spending).

Some feel that Congress has to be less pluralistic if it is going to attack such serious problems as the national deficit.[72] Yet, those who favor pluralism are quick to point out Congress's merits. For example, many different constituencies are well served by the spending deliberations described earlier. For Alaska's fishermen, an appropriation to promote new markets for its industry is not frivolous spending. It is vital to their livelihood. They pay taxes to fund the government, and they have a right to expect the government to care about their problems and try to help them.

Proponents of pluralism also argue that the makeup of Congress generally reflects that of the nation, that different members of Congress represent farm areas, oil and gas areas, low-income inner cities, industrial areas, and so on. They point out that America itself is pluralistic, with a rich diversity of economic, social, religious, and racial groups, and that even if our own representatives and senators don't represent our particular viewpoint, it's likely that someone in Congress does.[73]

This chapter has argued that the contemporary Congress has strong elements of pluralism and majoritarianism, although scholars have long regarded it as more pluralistic than majoritarian. The voting patterns illustrated in Figure 11.5 show increasing majoritarianism in one important respect, but it is far from certain that this will be a long-term trend. Some believe that we need to make a real break with pluralism in Congress and establish a true majoritarian legislature. For such a system to work, we would need strong parties—as described by the principles of responsible party government (see Chapter 8). That is, congressional candidates for each party would have to stand united on the major issues, as they would in a parliamentary system. Then, the majority party in Congress would act on a clear mandate from the voters—at least on the major issues discussed in the preceding election campaign. This would be very different from the system we now have, which facilitates the influence of interest groups and local constituencies in national policymaking. But which is better, a pluralistic or majoritarian Congress?

SUMMARY   Congress writes the laws of the land and attempts to oversee their implementation. It helps to educate us about new issues as they appear on the political agenda. Most important, members of Congress represent us, working to see to it that interests from home and from around the country are heard throughout the policymaking process.

We count on Congress to do so much that criticism about how well it does some things is inevitable. But certain strengths are clear. The committee system fosters expertise; representatives and senators who know the most about particular issues have the most influence over them. And the structure of our electoral system keeps legislators in close touch with their constituents.

Bargaining and compromise play important roles in the congressional policymaking process. Some find this disquieting. They want less deal making and more adherence to principle. This thinking is in line with the desire for a more majoritarian democracy. Others defend the current system, arguing that the United States is a large, complex nation and the policies that govern it should be developed through bargaining among various interests.

There is no clear-cut answer to whether a majoritarian or a pluralist legislative system provides better representation for voters. Our system is a mix of pluralism and majoritarianism. It serves minority interests that might otherwise be neglected or even harmed by an unthinking or uncaring majority. At the same time, congressional parties work to represent the broader interests of the American people.

Key Terms

reapportionment
impeachment
incumbent
term limits
gerrymandering
franking privilege
casework
descriptive
 representation
racial gerrymandering
bill
veto
pocket veto
standing committee

joint committee
select committee
conference committee
seniority
Speaker of the House
majority leader
filibuster
cloture
constituents
oversight
micromanagement
trustee
delegate
parliamentary system

Selected Readings

Aberbach, Joel D. *Keeping a Watchful Eye*. Washington, D.C.: Brookings Institution, 1990. A careful examination of the growth of congressional oversight.

Arnold, R. Douglas. *The Logic of Congressional Action*. New Haven, Conn.: Yale University Press, 1990. Arnold offers a theory of congressional policymaking, closely linking legislators' perceptions of constituent opinion to the policy decisions they make.

Fenno, Richard F., Jr. *Home Style*. Boston: Little, Brown, 1978. A classic analysis of how House members interact with constituents during visits to their home districts.

Fowler, Linda L., and Robert D. McClure. *Political Ambition*. New Haven, Conn.: Yale University Press, 1989. An engaging, highly readable study of the recruitment of congressional candidates.

Loomis, Burdett. *The New American Politician*. New York: Basic Books, 1988. A study of how the ambition and entrepreneurship of legislators is changing Congress.

Mann, Thomas E., and Norman J. Ornstein. *Renewing Congress: A First Report* (1992), and *Renewing Congress: A Second Report* (1993). Washington, D.C.: American Enterprise Institute and the Brookings Institution. These two monographs outline a variety of reform proposals to streamline and improve the congressional process.

Swain, Carol M. *Black Faces, Black Interests*. Cambridge, Mass.: Harvard University Press, 1993. Swain looks at a variety of districts that have elected African American representatives and outlines a strategy for electing more that goes beyond racial gerrymandering.

Thomas, Sue. *How Women Legislate*. New York: Oxford University Press, 1994. Using surveys of state legislators, the author details the ways in which women are different from men in the way they do their job.

12 The Presidency

BILL CLINTON PROMISED to hit the ground running when he came to Washington. He had ambitious plans to reorient the country's priorities— "putting people first," as he had stressed in his campaign. His strategy for reviving the lagging economy was to create an investment program that would improve the nation's infrastructure, increase educational opportunities, and enhance training for those whose skills were not adequate for the demands of today's job market.

Clinton's first step was a modest $16.3 billion economic stimulus package, introduced less than a month after he took office. The legislation was intended to give a jump start to an economy that had performed poorly for the previous three years. The increased spending was not concentrated in any one area but had additional money for a variety of programs, including summer youth employment, AIDS care, child immunization, highway construction, Pell grants for college students, water projects, and Head Start. The biggest component of the package was simply a continuation of unemployment compensation.

Republicans in Congress were hostile to the plan. They wondered why Clinton was proposing more spending when he was about to introduce a deficit reduction package. Less partisan critics suggested that given the aggregate size of our economy, $16.3 billion wasn't enough to get the economy moving. Democrats countered that the bill would directly create 200,000 jobs and that another 150,000 jobs would result from the increased economic activity generated by the new spending. For the unemployed, this proposal hardly represented frivolous spending. Moreover, the Democrats, with their traditional commitment to equality and social justice, felt that they needed to begin reversing the twelve years of Reagan-Bush cutbacks on social programs.

The big Democratic majority in the House easily approved the bill in mid-March. In the Senate, Appropriations Committee chair Robert Byrd, a Democrat, was so eager to demonstrate his support to the president that he devised a complicated legislative strategy to get the bill through without any Republican amendments. Byrd's actions incensed the Republicans, who began a filibuster. The Democrats needed three Republican votes to break the filibuster, but the Republicans held firm in their unanimous opposition to the bill. Although polls showed that Americans supported the stimulus package, public sentiment did not appear to be intensely held, and Republicans weren't worried about adverse public reaction to their efforts to scuttle the bill. Clinton resisted compromise at first, and by the

**Maybe Some Day
You'll Grow Up
to be President**

A seminal event in young Bill Clinton's life was when he shook hands with his idol, President John F. Kennedy in the White House's Rose Garden. When Clinton became president, he traveled to Russia and, in one of his Moscow public appearances, held a televised town meeting. A precocious young Muscovite, Alexander Fyodorov, asked Clinton about the time he got to shake Kennedy's hand. Fyodorov was rewarded not only with an answer but he was invited on the stage where Clinton shook his hand for posterity. Maybe some day Fyodorov will grow up and . . . who knows?

time he reluctantly realized that the bill could not get through without concessions to the Republicans, Senate minority leader Bob Dole knew that his party had beaten the president. At the end of April, Clinton finally gave up on the economic stimulus package; Congress later enacted a narrowly focused bill extending unemployment benefits.

The new president had gone eyeball to eyeball with Bob Dole and had suffered a humiliating defeat. It was not merely that Clinton had been sabotaged by Byrd, who had been too eager to help; Clinton himself bore much of the responsibility for the bill's failure. He never convinced the American people that the bill was vital. (The economy did, in fact, sharply improve in the months to come, despite the lack of a stimulus package.) The Republicans had made Clinton understand that without bipartisan support, he wouldn't be able to get much through the Congress. It was a cruel lesson for the new president. Rather than hitting the ground running, Bill Clinton had simply hit the ground.[1]

As we analyze the various facets of the presidency, bear in mind one recurring question: Is the presidency primarily an instrument of pluralist democracy, serving small but vocal constituencies, or does the office promote majoritarian democracy by responding primarily to public opinion? In the case we have just discussed, President Clinton thought that both pluralist and majoritarian politics would work in his favor. In fact, neither did. That is, he thought the public would back him, but it was apathetic, and he thought that interest groups benefiting from the bill would help him get the legislation through, but these organizations had little influence with the Republicans. In addition to examining the majoritarian and pluralist sides of presidential politics, we focus in this chapter on a number of other important questions. What are the powers of the presidency? How is the president's advisory system organized? How does the separation of powers between the executive and legislative branches affect public policymaking? Finally, what are the particular issues and problems that presidents face in foreign affairs?

THE CONSTITUTIONAL BASIS OF PRESIDENTIAL POWER

When the presidency was created, the colonies had just fought a war of independence; their reaction to British domination had focused on the autocratic rule of King George III. Thus, the delegates to the Constitutional Convention were extremely wary of unchecked power and were determined not to create an all-powerful, dictatorial presidency.

The delegates' fear of a powerful presidency was counterbalanced by their desire for strong leadership. The Articles of Confederation—which did not provide for a single head of state—had failed to bind the states together in a unified nation (see Chapter 3). In addition, the governors of the individual states had generally proved to be inadequate leaders, because they had few formal powers. The new nation was conspicuously weak; its congress had no power to compel the states to obey its legislation. The delegates knew they had to create some type of effective executive office. Their task was to provide for national leadership without allowing opportunity for tyranny.

Initial Conceptions of the Presidency

Debates about the nature of the office began. Should there be one president or a presidential council or committee? Should the president be chosen by Congress and remain largely subservient to that body? The delegates gave initial approval to a plan that called for a single executive, chosen by Congress for a seven-year term and ineligible for reelection.[2] But some delegates continued to argue for a strong president who would be elected independent of the legislative branch.

The final structure of the presidency reflected the "checks and balances" philosophy that shaped the entire Constitution. In the minds of the delegates, they had imposed important limits on the presidency through the powers specifically delegated to the Congress and the courts. Those counterbalancing powers would act as checks, or controls, on presidents who might try to expand the office beyond its proper bounds.

The Powers of the President

The requirements for the presidency are set forth in Article II of the Constitution: A president must be a U.S.-born citizen, at least thirty-five years old, who has lived in the United States for a minimum of fourteen years. Article II also sets forth the responsibilities of presidents. In view of the importance of the office, the constitutional description of the president's duties is surprisingly brief and vague. This vagueness has led to repeated conflict about the limits of presidential power.

The delegates undoubtedly had many reasons for the lack of precision in Article II. One likely explanation was the difficulty of providing and at the same time limiting presidential power. Furthermore, the framers of the Constitution had no model—no existing presidency—on which to base their description of the office. And, ironically, their description of the presidency might have been more precise if they had had less confidence in George Washington, the obvious choice for the first president. According to one account of the Constitutional Convention, "when Dr. Franklin predicted on June 4 that 'the first man put at the helm will be a good one,' every delegate knew perfectly well who that first good man would be."[3] The delegates had great trust in Washington; they did not fear that he would try to misuse the office.

The Commanders and the Commander in Chief

During World War II, President Franklin Roosevelt visited the troops at an American base in Sicily. There, the commander in chief met with General Dwight Eisenhower (to FDR's left), who would himself win the presidency in 1952. At the far left is the legendary General George Patton.

The major duties and powers that the delegates listed for Washington and his successors can be summarized as follows:

- *Serve as administrative head of the nation.* The Constitution gives little guidance on the president's administrative duties. It states merely that "the executive Power shall be vested in a President of the United States of America" and that "he shall take Care that the Laws be faithfully executed." These imprecise directives have been interpreted to mean that the president is to supervise and offer leadership to various departments, agencies, and programs created by Congress. In practice, a chief executive spends much more time making policy decisions for his cabinet departments and agencies than trying to enforce existing policies.

- *Act as commander in chief of the military.* In essence, the Constitution names the president as the highest-ranking officer in the armed forces. But it gives Congress the power to declare war. The framers no doubt intended Congress to control the president's military power; nevertheless, presidents have initiated military action without the approval of Congress. The entire Vietnam War was fought without a congressional declaration of war. (Congress did enact a resolution authorizing the use of force in the Persian Gulf before the American-led coalition began its military campaign.)

- *Convene Congress.* The president can call Congress into special session on "extraordinary Occasions," although this has rarely been done. He must also periodically inform Congress of "the State of the Union."

- *Veto legislation.* The president can **veto** (disapprove) any bill or resolution enacted by Congress, with the exception of joint resolutions that propose constitutional amendments. Congress can override a presidential veto with a two-thirds vote in each house.

- *Appoint various officials.* The president has the authority to appoint federal court judges, ambassadors, cabinet members, other key policy-makers, and many lesser officials. Many appointments are subject to Senate confirmation.

- *Make treaties.* With the "Advice and Consent" of at least two-thirds of those senators voting at the time, the president can make treaties with foreign powers. The president is also to "receive Ambassadors," a phrase that presidents have interpreted as the right to formally recognize other nations.

- *Grant pardons.* The president can grant pardons to individuals who have committed "Offenses against the United States, except in Cases of Impeachment."

THE EXPANSION OF PRESIDENTIAL POWER

The framers' limited conception of the president's role has given way to a considerably more powerful interpretation. In this section, we look beyond the presidential responsibilities explicitly listed in the Constitution and examine the additional sources of power that presidents have used to expand the authority of the office. First, we look at the claims that presidents make about "inherent" powers implicit in the Constitution. Second, we turn to congressional grants of power to the executive branch. Third, we discuss the influence that comes from a president's political skills. Finally, we analyze how a president's popular support affects his political power.

The Inherent Powers

Several presidents have expanded the power of the office by taking actions that exceeded commonly held notions of the president's proper authority. These men justified what they had done by saying that their actions fell within the **inherent powers** of the presidency. From this broad perspective, presidential power derives not only from those duties clearly outlined in Article II but also from inferences that may be drawn from the Constitution.

When a president claims a power that has not been considered part of the chief executive's authority, he forces Congress and the courts to acquiesce to his claim or to restrict it. When presidents succeed in claiming a new power, they leave to their successors the legacy of a permanent expansion of presidential authority. One early use of the inherent power of the presidency occurred during George Washington's tenure in office. The British and the French were at war, and Washington was under some pressure from members of his own administration to show favoritism toward the French. Instead, he issued a proclamation of strict neutrality, angering many who harbored anti-British sentiments; the ensuing controversy provoked a constitutional debate. Washington's critics noted that the Constitution does not include a presidential power to declare neutrality. His defenders said that the president had inherent power to conduct diplomatic relations. In the end, Washington's decision was not overturned by Congress or the courts and thus set a precedent in the area of foreign

A Time of Crisis

Abraham Lincoln's courage and decisiveness during the Civil War has become a model of heroic leadership for the American presidency. All presidents since the Civil War have aspired to be like Lincoln, but few come close (see Figure 12.4). Today, Lincoln's words at Gettysburg still inspire us. Standing at the battlefield cemetery, he hoped "that these dead shall not have died in vain—that this nation, under God, shall have a new birth of freedom— and that government of the people, by the people, for the people, shall not perish from the earth."

affairs. (Later, Congress enacted legislation affirming Washington's decision.[4])

Claims of inherent powers often come at critical points in the nation's history. During the Civil War, for example, Abraham Lincoln issued a number of orders that exceeded the accepted limits of presidential authority. One order increased the size of the armed forces well beyond the congressionally mandated ceiling, although the Constitution gives only Congress the power "to raise and support Armies." And because military expenditures would then have exceeded military appropriations, Lincoln clearly had also acted to usurp the taxing and spending powers constitutionally conferred on Congress. In another order, Lincoln instituted a blockade of Southern ports, thereby committing acts of war against the Confederacy without the approval of Congress.

Lincoln said the urgent nature of the South's challenge to the Union forced him to act without waiting for congressional approval. His rationale was simple: "Was it possible to lose the nation and yet preserve the Constitution?"[5] In other words, Lincoln circumvented the Constitution in order to save the nation. Subsequently, Congress and the Supreme Court approved Lincoln's actions. That approval gave added legitimacy to the theory of inherent powers—a theory that over time has transformed the presidency.

Any president who lays claim to new authority runs the risk of being rebuffed by Congress or the courts and suffering political damage. After Andrew Jackson vetoed a bill reauthorizing a national bank, for example, he ordered William Duane, his secretary of the treasury, to withdraw all federal deposits and to place them in state banks. Duane refused, claiming that he was under the supervision of both Congress and the executive branch; Jackson responded by firing him. The president's action angered many members of Congress who believed that Jackson had overstepped his constitutional bounds; the Constitution does not actually state that a president may remove his cabinet secretaries. Although that prerogative is now taken for granted, Jackson's presidency was weakened by the controversy. His censure by the Senate was a slap in the face, and he was denounced even by members of his own party. It took many years for the president's right to remove cabinet officers to become widely accepted.[6]

Congressional Delegation of Power

Presidential power grows when presidents successfully challenge Congress, but in many instances Congress willingly delegates power to the executive branch. As the American public pressures the national government to solve various problems, Congress, through a process called **delegation of powers,** gives the executive branch more responsibility to administer programs that address those problems. One example of delegation of legislative power occurred in the 1930s, during the Great Depression, when Congress gave Franklin Roosevelt's administration wide latitude to do what it thought was necessary to solve the nation's economic ills.

When Congress concludes that the government needs flexibility in its approach to a problem, the president is often given great freedom in how or when to implement policies. Richard Nixon was given discretionary authority to impose a freeze on wages and prices in an effort to combat escalating inflation. If Congress had been forced to debate the timing of the freeze, merchants and manufacturers would surely have raised their prices in anticipation of the event. Instead, Nixon was able to act suddenly, imposing the freeze without warning. (We discuss congressional delegation of authority to the executive branch in more detail in Chapter 13.)

However, at other times Congress believes that too much power is accumulating in the executive branch, and it enacts legislation reasserting congressional authority. During the 1970s, many representatives and senators agreed that Congress's role in the American political system was declining, that presidents were exercising power that rightfully belonged to the legislative branch. The most notable reaction was the enactment of the War Powers Resolution (1973), which was directed at ending the president's ability to pursue armed conflict without explicit congressional approval.

The President's Power to Persuade

A president's influence in office comes not only from his assigned responsibilities but also from his political skills and how effectively he uses the resources of his office. A classic analysis of the use of presidential resources is offered by Richard Neustadt in his book *Presidential Power.* Neustadt develops a model of how presidents gain, lose, or maintain their influence. This initial premise is simple enough: "Presidential power is the power to persuade."[7] Presidents, for all their resources—a skilled staff, extensive media coverage of presidential actions, the great respect for the office—must depend on others' cooperation to get things done. Harry Truman echoed Neustadt's premise when he said, "I sit here all day trying

Comfort and Commemoration

An unwritten part of the presidential job description is to act as a symbol of unity in times of tragedy or turmoil. Here President Reagan comforts grieving relatives of the astronauts killed in 1986 when the space shuttle Challenger *exploded shortly after takeoff.*

to persuade people to do the things they ought to have sense enough to do without my persuading them. . . . That's all the powers of the President amount to."[8]

The abilities displayed in bargaining, dealing with adversaries, and choosing priorities, according to Neustadt, separate above-average presidents from mediocre ones. A president must make wise choices about which policies to push and which to put aside until he can find more support. He must decide when to accept compromises and when to stand on principles. He must know when to go public and when to work behind the scenes.

Often, a president faces a dilemma in which all the alternatives carry some risk. After Dwight Eisenhower took office in 1953, he had to decide how to deal with Joseph McCarthy, the Republican senator from Wisconsin who had been largely responsible for creating national hysteria over allegations about communists in government. McCarthy had made many wild, reckless charges, damaging a number of innocent people's careers by accusing them of communist sympathies. Many people expected Eisenhower to control McCarthy—not only because he was president but also because he was a fellow Republican. Yet Eisenhower, worrying about his own popularity, chose not to confront him. He used a "hidden hand" strategy, working behind the scenes to weaken McCarthy. Politically, Eisenhower seems to have made the right choice; McCarthy soon discredited himself.[9] However, Eisenhower's performance can be criticized as weak moral leadership. If he had publicly denounced the senator, he might have ended the McCarthy witch hunt sooner.

A president's political skills can be important in affecting outcomes in Congress. The chief executive cannot intervene in every legislative struggle. He must choose his battles carefully, then try to use the force of his personality and the prestige of his office to forge an agreement among differing factions. In terms of getting members to vote a certain way, presidential influence is best described as taking place "at the margins." That is, presidents do not have the power to consistently move large numbers of votes one way or the other. They can, however, affect some votes—perhaps enough to affect the outcome of a closely fought piece of legislation.[10]

Neustadt stresses that a president's influence is related to his professional reputation and prestige. When a president pushes hard for a bill that Congress eventually defeats or emasculates, the president's reputation is hurt. The public perceives him as weak or showing poor judgment, and Congress becomes even less likely to cooperate with him in the future. President Clinton was clearly damaged by his defeat on the economic stimulus package described at the beginning of this chapter. Yet, presidents cannot easily avoid controversial bills, especially those that deliver on campaign promises. Clinton took risks with his strong backing for controversial issues such as NAFTA and handgun control legislation but gained considerable respect for his efforts when the bills were enacted. If a president backs only sure things, he will be credited with little initiative and perceived as too cautious.[11]

The President and the Public

Neustadt's analysis suggests that a popular president is more persuasive than an unpopular one. A popular president has more power to persuade, because he can use his public support as a resource in the bargaining process.[12] Members of Congress who know that the president is highly popular back home have more incentive to cooperate with the administration. If the president and his aides know that a member of Congress does not want to be seen as hostile to the president, they can apply more leverage to achieve a favorable compromise in a legislative struggle.

A familiar aspect of the modern presidency is the effort of its incumbents to mobilize public support for their programs. (Chief executives in other Western democracies have the same problems with public approval; see Compared with What? 12.1.) A president uses televised addresses and the media coverage that surround his speeches, remarks to reporters, and public appearances to speak directly to the American people and convince them of the wisdom of his policies. It may seem only sensible for a president to seek popular endorsement of particular bills or broad initiatives, but public appeals have not always been a part of the presidency. Our first fifteen presidents averaged fewer than ten speeches a year. It was not simply that the lack of modern communications made attempts to mobilize the public more difficult; early presidents felt constrained in the way they interacted with the public. The founders' fear that the executive office might be used to inflame popular passions led early presidents to be reserved in their communications.[13]

In recent years, presidents have increased their direct communication with the American people. As Figure 12.1 illustrates, the number of presidential public appearances has grown sharply since World War II. Obviously, modern technology has contributed to this growth. Nonetheless, the increase in public appearances represents something more than increased visibility for the president and his views. The power of the presidency also has changed fundamentally. The decline of party and congressional leadership has hastened the rise of the public president; at the same time, the president's direct communication with the American people has

COMPARED WITH WHAT? 12.1   Tough Job

It didn't take long for Bill Clinton to realize he was playing to an awfully tough audience. Soon after taking office, he found that his deficit reduction plan was unpopular with the American people and a number of policy gaffes had reduced the public's confidence in him. By June 1993, after five months in office, he had the second-lowest popularity rating of any president at a comparable period since presidential polling began on a systematic basis in the Truman years. (Gerald Ford was the only president lower in popularity at the five-month mark.)

It may have not been much comfort to Clinton, but low popularity ratings seem to be an occupational hazard for leaders of Western democracies. Later that summer, when he went off to Tokyo for an economic summit of the leading industrialized (or "G-7") countries, Clinton may have been surprised to find out that he and President François Mitterrand of France had the highest approval ratings among the heads of state

gathered there. None of the seven leaders had an approval rating greater than 50 percent.

Why were these leaders so unpopular? The primary reason is economics. In today's world, the Western economies are closely linked. If the economies of France and Germany are ailing, it's bad news for the American economy: Weak economies there hurt our export industries. At the time of the G-7 summit all these countries had suffered some degree of economic slowdown. There were, of course, other reasons peculiar to each country. In Japan and Italy, for example, scandals had undermined confidence in government.

- Source: "Democracies' Discontents," American Enterprise 4 (July/August 1993), 86. The rating for Helmut Kohl comes from Rich Thomas and Jolie Solomon, "No Stuff to Strut," Newsweek, 12 July 1993, p. 38. The wording differs from country to country, but polls generally ask whether the respondent approves, is satisfied, or supports the leader in power. The commentary updating what has happened to these officials since the polling was current as of September 1, 1994.

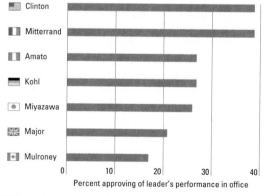

Clinton — *His popularity increased modestly in the latter half of 1993 and the first part of the year, but dropped back down in the summer of 1994.*

Mitterrand — *Remains in office as President of France.*

Amato — *Amato resigned as Cabinet President of Italy in April 1993, but continued on for some time as head of a caretaker government. In the 1994 elections his party lost control of the government.*

Kohl — *Remains in office as Chancellor of Germany.*

Miyazawa — *After a no confidence vote in the Japanese Diet in June, 1993, he resigned as Prime Minister. A month later his party lost in the elections, the first time ever that it fell from power.*

Major — *Remains as the British Prime Minister but is very unpopular.*

Mulroney — *Resigned from office in the summer of 1993. His party suffered a catastrophic defeat in the next election.*

Percent approving of leader's performance in office

---

made it more difficult for political parties and Congress to reinvigorate themselves.[14]

Presidential popularity is typically at its highest during a president's first year in office. This "honeymoon period" affords the president a particularly good opportunity to use public support to get some of his programs through Congress.[15] When Ronald Reagan made a televised appeal

FIGURE 12.1 ■ **Going Public**

This graph depicts the average number of public appearances made in a year by presidents from 1929 to 1990. The increase in presidential public appearances is driven in large part by the efforts of presidents to rally public support for their proposals and policies.

Source: Kernell, Samuel, Going Public, *Second Edition. Copyright © 1993 by CQ Press, 1993, p. 102. Used with permission.*

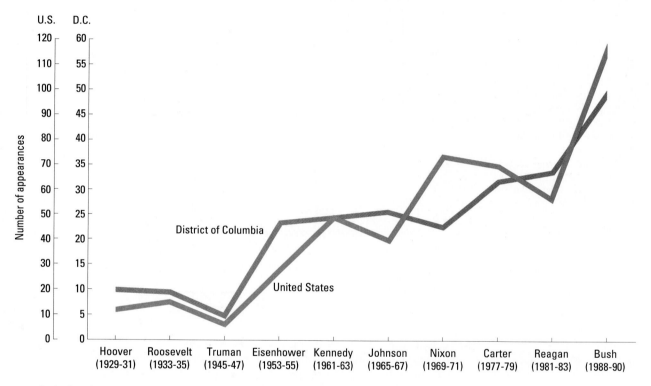

* *Only the first three years of their first terms were examined; the fourth year was not tabulated in order to exclude appearances arranged with an eye toward an upcoming election. Gerald Ford's term also is excluded for this reason. The Bush figures are for his first two years only.*

for support for a legislative proposal during his first year in office, some congressional offices received calls and letters that ran 10 to 1 in favor of the president. At the beginning of his second term, typical congressional offices received an equal number of negative and positive responses after a Reagan appeal.[16] Perhaps the positions he advocated were less attractive, but it was also clear that the public viewed Reagan with a more skeptical eye than it had four years earlier.

Because unpopular policies can quickly erode public support, not all presidents get a honeymoon. Gerald Ford's popularity evaporated when he pardoned Richard Nixon before any legal action could be taken against the former president. The public's indifference toward the economic stimulus package was only one of the problems that bedeviled President Clinton at

FIGURE 12.2   ■ **Bad Economy, Bad Poll Ratings**

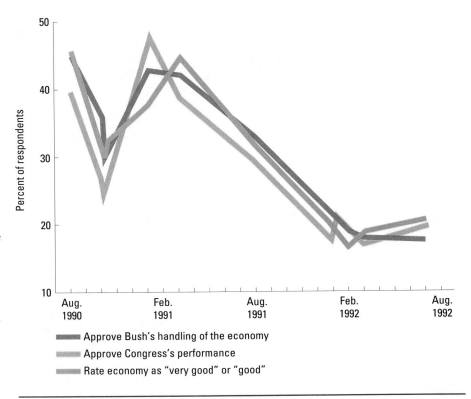

As the public's perception of economic conditions declined during the Bush years, people's confidence in the president's handling of the economy declined in tandem. Notice that confidence in Congress's performance took a similar tumble. Yet in the 1992 elections, most congressional incumbents were re-elected while President Bush was voted out of office. As we discussed in Chapter 11, people judge the Congress as a whole much differently than they judge their own members of the House and Senate.

Source: Gary C. Jacobson, "Congress: Unusual Year, Unusual Election," in The Elections of 1992, Michael Nelson, ed. (Washington, D.C.: Congressional Quarterly Press, 1993), p. 163. Copyright © 1993 by CQ Press. Used with permission.

the beginning of his term. His promise to allow gays to serve openly in the military, two botched nominations for attorney general, and Republican attacks on the taxes he proposed as part of his deficit reduction package all took their toll on Clinton's popularity.

Several factors generally explain the rise and fall in presidential popularity. First, public approval of the job done by a president is affected by economic conditions, such as inflation and unemployment as Figure 12.2 shows.[17] Voters hold presidents responsible for the state of the economy, although much of what happens in the economy is beyond their control. Second, a president is affected by unanticipated events of all types that occur during his administration.[18] When American embassy personnel were taken hostage in Teheran by militantly anti-American Iranians, Jimmy Carter's popularity soared. This "rally 'round the flag" support for the president eventually gave way to frustration with his inability to gain the hostages' release, and Carter's popularity plummeted. The third factor that affects presidential popularity is American involvement in a war, which can affect public approval. Lyndon Johnson, for example, suffered a loss of popularity during his escalation of the American effort in Vietnam.[19]

Presidents closely monitor their popularity, because it is widely regarded as a basic report card on how well they are performing their duties.

First-term presidents are especially concerned about their popularity, because they are worried about their reelection prospects. Carter, Ford, and Bush, all unpopular at the time of the election, were defeated in their efforts to win another term. A president's popularity can change dramatically during the course of a term. In the aftermath of the Gulf War, roughly 9 in 10 Americans approved of President Bush's performance in office. A month before the 1992 election, fewer than 4 in 10 Americans approved of Bush.

Presidents and their political advisers rely heavily on polls to tell them how they are doing with the American public. They not only read the Gallup Poll in the newspaper but commission in-depth polling for their own purposes. The Democratic party commissions three or four polls a month for President Clinton, and the pollster, Stanley Greenberg, analyzes how different segments of the population view the president and his policies.[20] This obsessive concern with public popularity can be defended as a means of furthering majoritarian democracy: The president tries to gauge what the people want so that he can offer policies that reflect popular preferences. Some believe that presidents are too concerned about popularity and are unwilling to champion unpopular causes or take principled stands that may affect their poll ratings. Commenting on the presidential polls that first became widely used during his term, Harry Truman said, "I wonder how far Moses would have gone if he'd taken a poll in Egypt?"[21]

THE ELECTORAL CONNECTION

In his farewell address to the nation, Jimmy Carter lashed out at the interest groups that had bedeviled his presidency. Interest groups, he said, "distort our purposes because the national interest is not always the sum of all our single or special interests." Carter noted the president's singular responsibility: "The president is the only elected official charged with representing all the people."[22] Like all other presidents, Carter quickly recognized the dilemma of majoritarianism versus pluralism after he took office. The president must try to please countless separate constituencies while trying to do what is best for the whole country.

It is easy to stand on the sidelines and say that presidents should always try to follow a majoritarian path—pursuing policies that reflect the preferences of most citizens. However, simply by running for office candidates align themselves with particular segments of the population. As a result of their electoral strategy, their identification with activists in their party, and their own political views, candidates come into office with an interest in pleasing some constituencies more than others.

Each candidate attempts to put together an electoral coalition that will provide at least the minimum 270 (out of 538) electoral votes needed for election. As the campaign proceeds, the candidate tries to win votes from different groups of voters through his stand on various issues. He promises that once he is in office, he will take certain actions that appeal to people holding a particular view on an issue. Just as each presidential candidate attracts voters with his stand on particular issues, he offends others who are committed to the opposite side of those issues. In 1992, George Bush emphasized that environmental protection can cost jobs, surely making the Republican ticket more attractive to many businesspeople and workers in industries in which environmental regulation is an issue. On the

**Time Runs Out on the
Bush Presidency**

*During the second straight
debate of 1992 in which he
performed poorly, the TV
camera caught George Bush
looking at his watch. The
scene poignantly evoked the
end of the Bush presidency, as
the three presidential debates
did little to turn around
Bush's faltering campaign.*

other hand, Bush's stand gave environmentalists more reason to vote for Clinton.

Because issue stances can cut both ways—attracting some voters and driving others away—candidates may try to finesse an issue by being deliberately vague. Candidates sometimes hope that voters will put their own interpretations on ambiguous stances. If the tactic works, the candidate will attract some voters without offending others. During the 1968 campaign, Nixon said he was committed to ending the war in Vietnam but gave few details about how he would accomplish that end. He wanted to appeal not only to those who were in favor of military pressure against the North Vietnamese but also to those who wanted quick military disengagement.[23]

But candidates cannot be deliberately vague about all issues. A candidate who is noncommittal on too many issues appears wishy-washy. And future presidents do not build their political careers without working strongly for and becoming associated with important issues and constituencies.

Elections and Mandates

Presidents-elect inevitably claim that they have been given a **mandate,** or endorsement, by the voters to carry out the policies they campaigned on. They equate the approval of the voters with approval for the major policies they promised to pursue. Newly chosen presidents make a majoritarian interpretation of the electoral process, claiming that their selection is an expression of the direct will of the people and they are a superior embodiment of national sentiment, compared with the 535 individual members of Congress. Members of the House and Senate are, after all, elected from much smaller constituencies, and their election often turns on local or statewide issues.

Mandates tend to be more rhetoric than reality.[24] Although presidents claim that the vote they received at the polls is an expression of support for their policy proposals, more dispassionate observers usually find it difficult to document concrete evidence of broad public support for the range of specific policies a winning candidate wants to pursue. In the 1992 presidential race, for example, it was hard to discern a clear sense of what the public wanted. The vote split three ways, and Bill Clinton received only 43 percent of the popular vote. Clinton saw his victory as a strong endorsement of his policies, but many neutral observers regarded the election as more of a repudiation of George Bush because of the poor performance of the economy.[25] Still, Clinton was right in claiming that the election results indicated a desire for economic revival and some action on health care. As Clinton learned when he got to Washington, voters had not endorsed any specific course of action on either front and rallying public support for what he had in mind was difficult.

Divided Government

A central reason why it is difficult to read the political tea leaves of election campaigns is that the election of the president is independent of the election of the Congress. Often this leads to **divided government,** one party controlling the White House and the other party controlling at least one house of Congress. President Bush, for example, had to work with a Democratic-controlled House and Senate throughout all four years of his term. This may seem politically schizophrenic, with the electorate saying one thing by electing a president and another by electing a majority in Congress that opposes his policies. This does not appear to bother the American people: Polls often show that the public feels it's desirable for control of the government to be divided between Republicans and Democrats.[26]

During the twentieth century, the votes for president and Congress have shown less and less of a relationship.[27] In the election of 1900, only 3 percent of all House districts were carried by a presidential candidate of one party and a congressional candidate of another. Recent elections have seen split results in as much as 44 percent of the districts, as illustrated in Figure 12.3. Although partisan identification remains important, American voters have become less loyal to political parties and today vote more on the basis of candidate appeal and issues.

Voters appear to use quite different criteria when choosing a president than they do when choosing congressional representatives. As one scholar has noted, "Presidential candidates are evaluated according to their views on national issues and their competence in dealing with national problems. Congressional candidates are evaluated on their personal character and experience and on their devotion to district services and local issues."[28]

This congressional independence is at the heart of why contemporary presidents work so hard to gain public support for their policies.[29] Without a strong base of representatives and senators who feel their election was tied to his, a president often feels that he needs to win in the court of pub-

---

FIGURE   **12.3**   ■ **Split Voting**

The percentage of House districts carried by a congressional candidate of one party and the presidential candidate of the other party has risen dramatically during the twentieth century. Consequently, members of Congress increasingly see their electoral fortunes as being independent of those of their presidential candidates.

Source: Ornstein, Norman J., et al., Vital Statistics on Congress, 1993–94. *Copyright © 1994 by CQ Press. Used with permission. Note that data for every district are not available before 1952.*

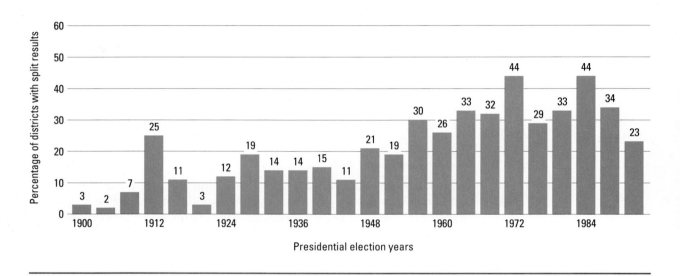

lic opinion. Favorable public opinion can help him build consensus in a highly independent legislative branch.

THE EXECUTIVE BRANCH ESTABLISHMENT

As a president tries to maintain the support of his electoral coalition for the policies he pursues, he draws on the extensive resources of the executive branch of government. The president has a White House staff that helps him formulate policy. The vice president is another resource; his duties within the administration vary according to his relationship with the president. The president's cabinet secretaries—the heads of the major departments of the national government—play a number of roles, including the critical function of administering the programs that fall within their jurisdictions. Effective presidents think strategically about how best to use the resources available. Each must find ways to organize structures and processes that best suit his management style.[30]

The White House Staff

A president depends heavily on key aides. They advise him on crucial political choices, devise the general strategies the administration follows in pursuing congressional and public support, and control access to the president to ensure that he has enough time for his most important tasks. Consequently, he needs to trust and respect these top staffers; many in a president's inner circle of assistants are long-time associates.

Presidents typically have a chief of staff, who may be a first among equals or, in some administrations, the unquestioned leader of the staff. H. R. Haldeman, Richard Nixon's chief of staff, played the stronger role. He ran a highly disciplined operation, frequently prodding staff members to work harder and faster. Haldeman also felt that part of his role was to take the heat for the president by assuming responsibility for many of the administration's unpopular decisions: "Every president needs a son of a bitch, and I'm Nixon's."[31] Hamilton Jordan, President Carter's chief of staff, was at the other end of the spectrum: Carter did not give him the authority to administer the White House with a strong hand.

Presidents also have a national security adviser to provide daily briefings on foreign and military affairs and longer-range analyses of issues confronting the administration. The Council of Economic Advisers is also located in the White House. Senior domestic policy advisers help determine the administration's basic approach to such areas as health, education, and social services.

Below these top aides are large staffs that serve them and the president. These staffs are organized around certain specialties. Some staff members work on political matters, such as liaison with interest groups, relations with ethnic and religious minorities, and party affairs. One staff deals exclusively with the media, and a legislative liaison staff lobbies the Congress for the administration. The large Office of Management and Budget (OMB) analyzes budget requests, is involved in the policymaking process, and examines agency management practices. This extended White House executive establishment is known as the **Executive Office of the President.** The Executive Office employs about 1,750 individuals and has an annual budget of nearly $200 million.[32]

No one agrees about a "right way" for a president to organize his White House staff. Dwight Eisenhower, for example, a former general, wanted clear lines of authority and a hierarchical structure that mirrored a military command. One factor that influences how a president uses his senior staff is the degree to which he delegates authority to them. Carter immersed himself in the policymaking process to ensure that he made all significant decisions. Early in his administration, he told his staff, "Unless there's a holocaust, I'll take care of everything the same day it comes in."[33]

Ronald Reagan was the opposite: He saw his role as setting a general direction for the administration but delegated wide-ranging authority to his staff to act on his behalf. Critics charge that Reagan went too far in delegating. In his second term, his top aides even decided who his chief of staff would be. James Baker, who had been chief of staff during Reagan's first term, and Donald Regan, who had been the secretary of the treasury, decided they wanted to switch jobs. After another aide informed the president of their desire to do this, Reagan treated it as an irreversible decision rather than a choice that was actually his to make.[34] The loose rein Reagan used on his staff is, in fact, seen as a key cause of the Iran-Contra scandal.[35] There is no shortage of examples of staff members who have performed poorly and even embarrassed the presidents they served. As President Harding put it, "I have no trouble with my enemies, but my damn friends . . . they're the ones that keep me walking the floor at night."[36]

Panetta to the Rescue

As criticism of the White House staff operations mounted, President Clinton tapped his Office of Management and Budget director, Leon Panetta, to replace Mack McLarty as Chief of Staff. Panetta has received praise for redefining the jobs of a number of White House staffers and establishing clearer lines of administrative authority. Yet early in Panetta's tenure, Clinton resisted his advice for replacing a few of the president's key aides, and some Washington observers continue to criticize Clinton for trying to "micromanage" the White House.

The Clinton staff structure has shown both strengths and weaknesses. The President made a surprising (and questionable) choice for his chief of staff, Mack McLarty. McLarty, a friend of Clinton's since childhood and a successful Arkansas businessman, had no Washington experience. This appointment seemed to suggest that Clinton really wanted to be his own chief of staff, deeply involved in the nuts and bolts of White House policy-making. Indeed, as the White House planned the President's program during the first year, "Clinton found no detail too small for his attention."[37] The president's own undisciplined style and tendency to take too much on were initially reflected in a free-wheeling staff structure.[38] Sharp criticism of White House operations led to a staff shake-up in June 1994. McLarty was moved aside to become a senior adviser to Clinton, and Leon Panetta, the President's budget director, became the new chief of staff.[39] Panetta served in Congress for many years and was widely seen as someone who could improve White House operations. The President's wife, Hillary Rodham Clinton, is also a key adviser, which we discuss in Politics in a Changing America 12.1.

The Vice President

The vice president's primary function is to serve as standby equipment, only a heartbeat from the presidency itself. Feature 12.1 discusses this aspect of the vice presidency. Traditionally, vice presidents have not been used in any important advisory capacity. Instead, presidents tend to give them political chores—campaigning, fund raising, and "stroking" the party faithful. This is often the case because vice presidential candidates are chosen for reasons that have more to do with the political campaign than with governing the nation. Richard Nixon chose the little-known governor of Maryland, Spiro Agnew, to be his vice presidential candidate and assigned Agnew to play the same role Nixon had under Dwight Eisenhower—that of a political hatchet man who went after the Democrats.

President Carter broke the usual pattern of vice presidents' being relegated to political chores; he relied heavily on his vice president, Walter Mondale. Carter was wise enough to recognize that Mondale's experience in the Senate could be of great value to him, especially because Carter had never served in Congress. Neither Ronald Reagan's vice president, George Bush, nor George Bush's vice president, Dan Quayle, played as central a role as Mondale. Still, they were more a part of the White House inner circle than vice presidents had been before the Carter-Mondale years.

President Clinton has given Al Gore a considerable amount of responsibility, and Gore has taken a leadership role in the administration on telecommunications, environment, and government reform. Gore's central position in the administration has been facilitated by the personal chemistry between him and the president. "They are buddies," concluded one analysis.[40]

The Cabinet

The president's **cabinet** is composed of the heads of the departments in the executive branch and a small number of other key officials, such as the head of the Office of Management and Budget and the ambassador to the United Nations. The cabinet has expanded greatly since George Washington formed his first cabinet, which included an attorney general and the secretaries of state, treasury, and war. Clearly, the growth of the cabinet to fourteen departments reflects the growth of government responsibility and intervention in areas such as energy, housing, and transportation.

In theory, the members of the cabinet constitute an advisory body that meets with the president to debate major policy decisions. In practice, however, cabinet meetings have been described as "vapid non-events in which there has been a deliberate non-exchange of information as part of a process of mutual nonconsultation."[41] One Carter cabinet member called meetings "adult Show-and-Tell."[42] Why is this so? First, the cabinet has become rather large. Counting department heads, other officials of cabinet rank, and presidential aides, it is a body of at least twenty people—a size that many presidents find unwieldy for the give and take of political decision making. Second, most cabinet members have limited areas of expertise and simply cannot contribute much to deliberations in areas they know little about. The secretary of defense, for example, would probably be a poor choice to help decide important issues of agricultural policy. Third, although cabinet members have impressive backgrounds, they may not be personally close to the president or easy for him to work with. Cabinet choices are not necessarily made on the basis of personal relationships. The president often chooses cabinet members because of their reputations, or he may be guided by a need to give his cabinet some racial, ethnic, geographic, sexual, or religious balance.

Finally, modern presidents do not rely on the cabinet to make policy because they have such large White House staffs, which offer most of the advisory support they need. In contrast to cabinet secretaries, who may be

POLITICS IN A CHANGING AMERICA 12.1   A Different Kind of First Lady

 Hillary Rodham Clinton is not the first first lady to play a prominent political role in her husband's administration. Edith Wilson was said to have made decisions for her husband Woodrow after he was debilitated by a stroke. Eleanor Roosevelt was a visible and tireless advocate for causes she believed in. (Republicans were critical of her, some calling the liberal first lady "Lenin in skirts.") But just as Rosie the Riveter returned to the kitchen after World War II, the first ladies who followed Mrs. Roosevelt, Bess Truman and Mamie Eisenhower, were content to stand in the background and play the role of dutiful wife and mother.

A significant change in the role of the first lady came with Lady Bird Johnson. Her predecessor, the youthful Jackie Kennedy, had captivated the American public with her beauty, charm, and elegance. Lady Bird Johnson shrewdly staked out her own territory, choosing an issue with which to identify herself (beautification of America) and playing a visible role in working for relevant policy changes. Since that time, most first ladies have also selected an uncontroversial issue to work on. Nancy Reagan's "Just Say No" antidrug campaign was typical.

Despite these important historical antecedents, there's never been a first lady quite like Hillary Rodham Clinton. She is the first woman of her generation to occupy the White House, and the change from the grandmotherly Barbara Bush was startling. The new first lady grew up in suburban Chicago and attended Wellesley College where she was president of the student body. After Wellesley came Yale Law School (where she met Bill Clinton) and work as a congressional staffer, law professor, and corporate lawyer for Little Rock, Arkansas's most prestigious law firm. While working as an attorney, she did volunteer work, notably chairing the Children's Defense Fund, a Washington-based advocacy group, and spearheading an educational reform drive in Arkansas.

When the Clintons arrived in Washington, the president announced that Hillary Rodham Clinton would be in charge of developing a plan to restructure the nation's health care. The president had made health care a central issue in the campaign, promising to reform the system so that it would provide insurance for the uninsured and to reduce the sharply rising expenditures for all. Never had a first lady been given such a controversial and visible leadership position. The initial reaction of the American public was generally positive about Hillary Clinton as a person but cautious as to her role. A poll at the beginning of the administration showed that 74 percent believed she was "a positive role model for American women," but only 47 percent said it was appropriate for her "to be involved in the development of major policy positions." Forty-five percent said she shouldn't be involved.

The first lady's early efforts on health care were successful, and members of Congress were highly impressed with her comprehensive grasp of the intricacies of this complex issue. Her successive appearances before five congressional committees were, in the words of one journalist, "widely perceived as virtuoso."

Yet not all has gone well for Hillary Clinton in the White House. The plan she and her task force devised for restructuring the health care system fared poorly with Congress and the American people. In the fall of 1994, Congress backed away from comprehensive

health care reform and began focusing on more limited policy changes. Many attribute to her the Clintons' initial resistance to a special prosecutor to investigate the Whitewater matter. Politically, it would have been much wiser to have accepted early on what became inevitable. The Clintons' opposition looked to many like a cover-up. The first lady's finances also became an embarrassment when it was revealed that in 1979 she turned a $1,000 investment into $100,000 in a short time by trading cattle futures and other commodities. Commodities are an extremely risky investment, and it is unlikely that a novice could do so well the first time out. She subsequently acknowledged that a leading Arkansas businessman had made many of the trades for her, and there were allegations (unproved at this writing) that her broker had manipulated the trades to enhance her winnings.

All these factors have contributed to a modest drop in her popularity, but the first lady remains a much-admired political figure. The president relies on her advice and counsel, and together they are a formidable team. Beyond the ties of their marriage is a common commitment to social change. As a close friend of the Clintons' put it, "They both passionately share the sense that they're supposed to make a difference in this world."

• *Sources: James M. Perry and Jeffrey H. Birnbaum, "New First Lady Shows Washington She, Too, Is Now at the Helm,"* Wall Street Journal, *28 January 1993, p. A1; Michael Kelly, "Saint Hillary,"* New York Times Magazine, *23 May 1993, pp. 22ff; Gwen Ifill, "Role in Health Expands Hillary Clinton's Power,"* New York Times, *22 September 1993, p. A24, and "Hillary Clinton Tackles Questions on Whitewater,"* New York Times, *23 April 1994, p.1; James K. Glassman, "Hillary's Cows,"* New Republic, *16 May 1994, pp. 18–22; Connie Bruck, "Hillary the Pol,"* New Yorker, *30 May 1994, pp. 58–96; "Hillary Rodham Clinton,"* American Enterprise, *5 (May/June 1994), pp. 81–83; and Leslie Bennetts, "Pinning Down Hillary,"* Vanity Fair, *June 1994, pp. 104ff.*

■ Who's President When the President Can't Be?

What happens if a president dies in office? The vice president, of course, becomes the new president. But what happens if the vice president has died or left office for some reason? What happens if the president becomes senile or is disabled by illness? These are questions that the authors of the Constitution failed to resolve.

The nuclear age made these questions more troubling. When Woodrow Wilson suffered a stroke in 1919, it meant that the country was without effective leadership for a time, but the lack of an active president during that period did not endanger the lives of all Americans. Today national security dictates that the nation have a commander in chief at all times. The Twenty-fifth Amendment, ratified in 1967, specifies a mechanism for replacing a living president in case he cannot carry out the duties of his office. A president can declare himself unable to carry on, or the vice president and the cabinet can decide collectively that the president is incapacitated. In either case, the vice president becomes acting president and assumes all powers of the office. In 1981, when Ronald Reagan was seriously wounded in an assassination attempt and had to undergo emergency surgery, the vice president and the cabinet did not invoke the Twenty-fifth Amendment. Four years later, when Reagan underwent cancer surgery, he sent a letter to Vice President George Bush that transferred the power of the office to him at the moment the president was anesthetized. Eight hours later, Reagan reclaimed his authority. Under the Twenty-fifth Amendment, if the president and the cabinet disagree about whether he is able to resume his duties, Congress must decide.

The Twenty-fifth Amendment also provides that the president select a new vice president in the event that office becomes vacant; the president's choice must be approved by a majority of both houses of Congress. In 1973, Gerald Ford became vice president in this manner when Spiro Agnew resigned after pleading no contest to charges of income tax evasion and accepting bribes. Later, when Richard Nixon resigned and Ford became president, he chose Nelson Rockefeller as his vice president.

pulled in different directions by the wishes of the president and the wishes of their department's clientele groups, White House staffers are likely to see themselves as responsible to the president alone. Thus, despite periodic calls for the cabinet to be a collective decision-making body, cabinet meetings seem doomed to be little more than academic exercises. In practice, presidents prefer the flexibility of ad hoc groups, specialized White House staffs, and the advisers and cabinet secretaries with whom they feel most comfortable.

More broadly, presidents use their personal staffs and the large Executive Office of the President to centralize control over the entire executive branch. The vast size of the executive branch and the number and complexity of decisions that must be made each day pose a challenge for the White House. Each president must be careful to appoint people to top administration positions who are not merely competent but passionately share the president's goals and are skillful enough to lead others in the executive branch to fight for the president's program instead of their own agendas.[43] Ronald Reagan was especially good at infusing his top appointees with clear ideological principles that they were to follow in shaping administration policy.[44] To fulfill more of their political goals and policy preferences, modern presidents have given their various staffs more responsibility for overseeing decision making throughout the executive branch.[45]

THE PRESIDENT AS NATIONAL LEADER

With an election behind him and the resources of his office at hand, a president is ready to lead the nation. Each president enters office with a general vision of how government should approach policy issues. During his term, a president spends much of his time trying to get Congress to enact legislation that reflects his general philosophy and specific policy preferences.

From Political Values . . .

Presidents differ greatly in their views of the role of government. Lyndon Johnson had a strong liberal ideology concerning domestic affairs. He believed that government has a responsibility to help disadvantaged Americans. Johnson described his vision of justice in his inaugural address:

> . . . Justice was the promise that all who made the journey would share in the fruits of the land.
>
> In a land of wealth, families must not live in hopeless poverty. In a land rich in harvest, children just must not go hungry. In a land of healing miracles, neighbors must not suffer and die untended. In a great land of learning and scholars, young people must be taught to read and write.
>
> For [the] more than thirty years that I have served this nation, I have believed that this injustice to our people, this waste of our resources, was our real enemy. For thirty years or more, with the resources I have had, I have vigilantly fought against it.[46]

Johnson used *justice* and *injustice* as code for *equality* and *inequality*. He used them six times in his speech; he used *freedom* only twice. Johnson used his popularity, his skills, and the resources of his office to press for a "just" America, which he termed the "Great Society".

To achieve his Great Society, Johnson sent Congress an unprecedented package of liberal legislation. He launched such projects as the Job Corps (which created centers and camps offering vocational training and work experience to youths aged sixteen to twenty-one), Medicare (which provided medical care for the elderly), and the National Teacher Corps (which paid teachers to work in impoverished neighborhoods). Supported by huge Democratic majorities in Congress during 1965 and 1966, he had tremendous success getting his proposals through. Liberalism was in full swing.

In 1985, exactly twenty years after Johnson's inaugural speech, Ronald Reagan took his oath of office for the second time, then addressed the nation. Reagan reasserted his conservative philosophy. He emphasized freedom, using the term fourteen times, and failed to mention justice or equality once. In the following excerpts, we have italicized the term freedom for easy reference:

> By 1980, we knew it was time to renew our faith, to strive with all our strength toward the ultimate in individual *freedom* consistent with an orderly society. . . . We will not rest until every American enjoys the fullness of *freedom*, dignity, and opportunity as our birthright. . . . Americans . . .

turned the tide of history away from totalitarian darkness and into the warm sunlight of human *freedom*. . . . Let history say of us, these were golden years—when the American Revolution was reborn, when *freedom* gained new life, when America reached for her best. . . . *Freedom* and incentives unleash the drive and entrepreneurial genius that are at the core of human progress. . . . From new *freedom* will spring new opportunities for growth. . . . Yet history has shown that peace does not come, nor will our *freedom* be preserved by good will alone. There are those in the world who scorn our vision of human dignity and *freedom*. . . . Human *freedom* is on the march, and nowhere more so than in our own hemisphere. *Freedom* is one of the deepest and noblest aspirations of the human spirit. . . . America must remain *freedom's* staunchest friend, for *freedom* is our best ally. . . . Every victory for human *freedom* will be a victory for world peace. . . . One people under God, dedicated to the dream of *freedom* that He has placed in the human heart.[47]

Reagan turned Johnson's philosophy on its head, declaring that "government is not the solution to our problem. Government is the problem." During his presidency, Reagan worked to undo many welfare and social service programs and cut funding for such programs as the Job Corps and the food stamp program. By the end of his term, there had been a fundamental shift in federal spending, with sharp increases in defense spending and "decreases in federal social programs [which] served to defund Democratic interests and constituencies."[48]

Although Johnson and Reagan had well-defined political philosophies and communicated a clear vision of where they wanted to lead the country, not all presidents bring such ideological passion to their position. George Bush was much more comfortable as the "faithful son" of Reaganism, trying to uphold and improve upon its programs rather than articulate a vision of his own.[49] Indeed, Bush derided what he called "the vision thing." In the end, his administration's timid domestic initiatives helped to create an impression of a president comfortable with the status quo. Recognizing Bush's vulnerability on this score, his two opponents, Clinton and Perot, preached change during the 1994 campaign. Looking back, one Bush aide concluded that "the absence of ideology coming from the Oval Office signaled an Administration lacking in direction."[50]

. . . To Policy Agenda

The roots of particular policy proposals, then, can be traced to the more general political ideology of the president. Presidential candidates outline that philosophy of government during their campaigns for the White House. But when the hot rhetoric of the presidential campaign meets the cold reality of what is possible in Washington, the newly elected president must make some hard choices about what to push for during the coming term. These choices are reflected in the bills the president submits to Congress, as well as in the degree to which he works for their passage. The president's bills, introduced by his allies in the House and Senate, always receive a good deal of initial attention. In the words of one Washington lobbyist, "When a president sends up a bill, it takes first place in the queue. All other bills take second place."[51]

The president's role in legislative leadership is largely a twentieth-century phenomenon. Not until the Budget and Accounting Act of 1921 did executive branch departments and agencies have to clear their proposed budget bills with the White House. Before this, the president did not even coordinate proposals for how much the executive branch would spend on all the programs it administered. Later, Franklin Roosevelt required that all major legislative proposals by an agency or department be cleared by the White House. No longer could a department submit a bill without White House support.[52]

Roosevelt's influence on the relationship between the president and Congress went far beyond this new administrative arrangement. With the nation in the midst of the Great Depression, Roosevelt began his first term in 1933 with an ambitious array of legislative proposals. During the first hundred days Congress was in session, it enacted fifteen significant laws, including the Agricultural Adjustment Act, the Civilian Conservation Corps, and the National Industrial Recovery Act. Never had a president demanded—and received—so much from Congress. Roosevelt's legacy was that the president would henceforth provide aggressive leadership for Congress through his own legislative program.

A handful of presidents have entered office after a serious upheaval or a general decline of a dominant political coalition, situations that they can use to their advantage. The economic collapse that preceded Roosevelt's entry into office ended an era of conservative Republicanism that had steadfastly ruled the country for many years. Andrew Jackson and Abraham Lincoln also had fortuitous chances to redefine the terms of political debate and move the country toward a new political agenda.[53] But times of upheaval and decline merely present opportunities; presidents must be skillful enough to exploit the chances for large-scale change. And, as Figure 12.4 shows, history has taught us that presidents differ greatly in their skills.

Chief Lobbyist

When Franklin Roosevelt and Harry Truman first became heavily involved in preparing legislative packages, political scientists typically described the process as one in which "the president proposes and the Congress disposes." In other words, once the president sent his legislation to Capitol Hill, Congress decided what to do with it. Over time, though, presidents have become increasingly active in all stages of the legislative process. The president is expected not only to propose legislation but also to make sure that it passes (see Figure 12.5).

The president's efforts to influence Congress are reinforced by the work of his legislative liaison staff. All departments and major agencies have legislative specialists as well. These department and agency people work with the White House liaison staff to coordinate the administration's lobbying on major issues.

The **legislative liaison staff** is the communications link between the White House and Congress. As a bill slowly makes its way through Congress, liaison staffers advise the president or a cabinet secretary on the problems that emerge. They specify what parts of a bill are in trouble and

FIGURE 12.4 ■ Presidential Greatness

In 1982, *the* Chicago Tribune *asked forty-nine leading historians and political scholars to rate all past presidents on a descending scale from 5 (best) to 0 (worst) in five categories: leadership qualities, accomplishments and crisis management, political skills, quality of appointments, and character and integrity. Lincoln ranked at the top, and Franklin Roosevelt edged out Washington for second place. Among more recent presidents, Eisenhower, Johnson, and Kennedy all rated far higher than Ford, Carter, and Nixon. Nixon's ranking suffered from his extraordinarily low score for character and integrity—the lowest that the scholars gave to any president in history.*

Source: *Copyrighted Chicago Tribune Company. All rights reserved. Used with permission.*

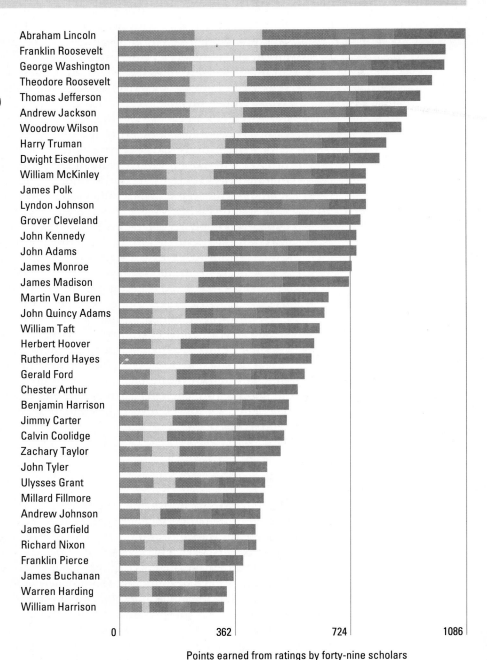

Points earned from ratings by forty-nine scholars

- Leadership qualities
- Accomplishments/crisis management
- Political skills
- Appointments
- Character/integrity

FIGURE **12.5**   ■ **Legislative Success**

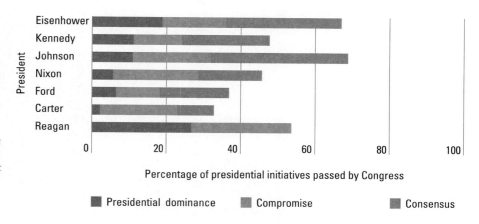

Percentage of presidential initiatives passed by Congress

■ Presidential dominance   ■ Compromise   ■ Consensus

Presidents vary considerably in their ability to convince Congress to enact the legislation that they send to Capitol Hill. Eisenhower and Johnson got about two-thirds of their proposals enacted, whereas Jimmy Carter was successful only a third of the time. There is also substantial variation in the degree to which presidents have had to compromise to get their bills enacted. The category "presidential dominance" refers to those initiatives that opponents failed to defeat or alter. "Compromise" represents the percentage of presidential initiatives that Congress significantly changes and then enacts. "Consensus" indicates that there was no real opposition to a president's bill. All remaining legislation for each president failed to pass Congress.

Source: *Adapted and reprinted by permission of the publishers from* Legislating Together: The White House And Capitol Hill From Eisenhower To Reagan *by Mark A. Peterson, Cambridge, Mass.: Harvard University Press, Copyright © 1990 by the President and Fellows of Harvard College.*

may have to be modified or dropped. They tell their boss what amendments are likely to be offered, which members of Congress need to be lobbied, and what the bill's chances for passage are with or without certain provisions. Decisions on how the administration will respond to such developments must then be reached. For example, when the Reagan White House realized that it was still a few votes short of victory on a budget bill in the House, it reversed its opposition to a sugar price-support bill. This attracted the votes of representatives from Louisiana and Florida, two sugar-growing states, for the budget bill. The White House would not call what happened a "deal" but noted that "adjustments and considerations" had been made.[54]

A certain amount of the president's job is stereotypical arm twisting—pushing reluctant legislators to vote a certain way. Yet most day-in, day-out interactions tend to be more subtle, as the liaison staff tries to build consensus by working cooperatively with members of Congress. When a congressional committee is working on a bill, liaison people talk to committee members individually to see what concerns they have and to help fashion a compromise if some differ with the president's position.

The White House also works directly with interest groups in its efforts to build support for legislation.[55] Presidential aides hope key lobbyists will activate the most effective lobbyists of all: the voters back home. Interest groups can quickly reach the constituents who are most concerned about a bill. One White House aide said with admiration, "The Realtors can send out half a million Mailgrams within 24 hours."[56] There are so many interest groups in our pluralist political system that interest groups could easily overload the White House with their demands. Consequently, except for those groups most important to the president, lobbies tend to be granted access only when the White House needs them to mobilize public opinion.[57]

Although much of the liaison staff's work with Congress is done in a cooperative spirit, agreement cannot always be reached. When Congress

The Nation's Top Lobbyists

President Clinton's "power to persuade" was sorely tested by his deficit reduction package, which Republicans refused to support. Needing all the Democratic votes he could get, the president lobbied strenuously to get the bill through the House and the Senate. Here Clinton and Vice President Gore meet with some members of Congress at the White House to try to convince them to vote for the bill. Passage of the legislation in 1993 is one of the administration's most important accomplishments.

passes a bill the president opposes, he may veto it and send it back to Congress; as we noted earlier, Congress can override a veto with a two-thirds majority of those voting in each house. Presidents use their veto power sparingly, but the threat that a president will veto an unacceptable bill increases his bargaining leverage with members of Congress. We have also seen that a president's leverage with Congress is related to his standing with the American people. The ability of the president and his liaison staff to bargain with members of Congress is enhanced when he is riding high in the popularity polls and hindered when the public is critical of his performance.

Party Leader

Part of the president's job is to lead his party. This is very much an informal duty, with no prescribed tasks. In this respect, American presidents are considerably different from European prime ministers, who are the formal leaders of their party in the national legislature as well as the heads of government. Because political parties in Europe tend to have strong national organizations, prime ministers have more reason to lead the party organization. In the United States, national party committees play a relatively minor role in national politics, although they are active in raising money for their congressional candidates (see Chapter 8).

The simple fact is that presidents can operate effectively without the help of a national party apparatus. Lyndon Johnson was contemptuous of the Democratic National Committee. He saw to it that the committee's budget was cut and refused some advisers' request that he replace its ineffectual head. Johnson thought a weak national committee would allow him to control party affairs from the White House. As other modern presidents, Johnson believed he would be most effective communicating directly with the American people and did not see the need for national, state, or local party officials to be intermediaries in the process of coalition building.[58]

Work with the party may be more important for gaining the presidency than actually governing. George Bush worked tirelessly on the "rubber chicken" circuit while he was vice president and built up a hefty billfold of IOUs by campaigning for Republican candidates and appearing at their fund-raising dinners. When he and his main competitor for the 1988 Republican nomination, Robert Dole, faced each other in the critical Super Tuesday primaries in 1988, Bush had enormous strength among state and local party leaders; those individuals formed the backbone of his campaign organization. Yet such party work is not absolutely essential. In 1976, Carter not only won the nomination without much of a record of party work, he campaigned as an outsider, claiming that he would be a better president without having ties to those who had long been in power.

THE PRESIDENT AS WORLD LEADER

The president's leadership responsibilities extend beyond Congress and the nation to the international arena. Each administration tries to further what it sees as the country's best interests in its relations with allies, adversaries, and the developing countries of the world. In this role, the president must be ready to act as diplomat and crisis manager.

Foreign Relations

From the end of World War II to the beginning of the Bush administration, presidents were preoccupied with containing communist expansion around the globe (see Chapter 20). Truman and South Korea, Kennedy and Cuba, Johnson and Nixon and South Vietnam, and Reagan and Nicaragua are just some examples of presidents and the communist crosses they had to bear. Presidents not only used overt and covert military means to fight communism but tried to reduce tensions through negotiations. President Nixon made particularly important strides in this regard, completing an important arms control agreement with the Soviet Union and beginning negotiations with the Chinese, with whom the United States had had no formal diplomatic relations.

With the collapse of communism in the Soviet Union and Eastern Europe, American presidents are entering a new era in international relations. The new presidential job description places much more emphasis on managing economic relations with the rest of the world. Trade relations are an especially difficult problem, because presidents must balance the conflicting interests of foreign countries (many of which are our allies), the interests of particular American industries, the overall needs of the American economy, and the demands of the legislative branch. Although they know the virtues of free trade, presidents must often accommodate political realities at home. Recall from Chapter 11 the concessions to various interest groups that President Clinton had to make to get the NAFTA trade accord passed. Still, the pluralist deal making enabled the legislation to get through Congress and NAFTA has already increased trade between the United States and Mexico.[59]

Our American Friend

As a young politician, Richard Nixon was notorious for his staunch anticommunism. As president, however, he achieved a stunning reversal of U.S. policy toward the People's Republic of China. His trip there in 1972 signaled an end to the Cold War hostility between the United States and the communist regime.

However, the decline of communism has not enabled the president to ignore security issues. The world remains a dangerous place, and regional conflicts can still embroil the United States. When Iraq invaded and quickly conquered Kuwait in August 1990, President Bush felt he had no choice but to respond firmly to protect our economic interests and to stand beside our Arab allies in the area. Bush worked the phones hard to try to get both Western and Arab leaders to join the United States in a co-ordinated military buildup in the area surrounding Kuwait. He had laid the groundwork for cooperation with the heavy emphasis he placed in the early months of his administration on building personal relationships with many important heads of state. It was, said one journalist, a "dazzling performance. In roughly four days, Bush organized the world against Saddam Hussein."[60]

Bush's impressive leadership of the twenty-eight-nation coalition continued in the months that followed. The coalition remained unified even through the difficult decision to go to war in January, when the air campaign began. Bush played a key role in convincing the Israelis, who were not part of the coalition, to refrain from retaliating against Iraq after Israel came under attack from Scud missiles. (Iraq had hoped that by drawing Israel into the war, the United States's Arab allies would withdraw their support for the war because of their opposition to the Jewish state.) The successful ground war against Iraqi forces was a capstone to a remarkable foreign policy achievement.

Crisis Management

Periodically, the president faces a grave situation in which conflict is imminent or a small conflict threatens to explode into a larger war. Handling such episodes is a critical part of the president's job. Voters may make the candidates' personal judgment and intelligence primary considerations in how they cast their ballots. A major reason for Barry Goldwater's crushing defeat in the 1964 election was his warlike image. Goldwater's bellicose rhetoric scared many Americans, who, fearing that he would be too quick to resort to nuclear weapons, voted for Lyndon Johnson.

A president must be able to exercise good judgment and remain cool in crisis situations. John Kennedy's behavior during the Cuban missile crisis of 1962 has become a model of effective crisis management. When the United States learned that the Soviet Union had placed missiles containing nuclear warheads in Cuba, U.S. government leaders saw those missiles as an unacceptable threat to this country's security. Kennedy asked a group of senior aides, including top people from the Pentagon, to advise him on feasible military and diplomatic actions. An armed invasion of Cuba and air strikes against the missiles were two options considered. In the end, Kennedy decided on a less dangerous response: implementing a naval blockade of Cuba. The Soviet Union thought better of prolonging its challenge to the United States and soon agreed to remove its missiles. For a short time, though, the world held its breath over the very real possibility of a nuclear war.

Are there guidelines for what a president should do in times of crisis or at other important decision-making junctures? Drawing on a range of advisers and opinions is certainly one.[61] Not acting in unnecessary haste is another. A third is having a well-designed, formal review process that promotes thorough analysis and open debate.[62] A fourth guideline is rigorously examining the chain of reasoning that has led to the option chosen, ensuring that presumptions have not been subconsciously equated with what is actually known to be true. When Kennedy decided to back a CIA plan to sponsor a rebel invasion of Cuba by expatriates hostile to Fidel Castro, he never really understood that its chances for success were based on unfounded assumptions of immediate uprisings by the Cuban population.[63]

Still, these are rather general rules and provide no assurance that mistakes will not be made. Almost by definition, each crisis is a unique event.

Sometimes all alternatives carry substantial risks. And almost always, time is of the essence. This was the situation when Cambodia captured the American merchant ship *Mayaguez* off its coast in 1975. Not wanting to wait until the Cambodian government moved the sailors inland, where there would be little chance of rescuing them, President Gerald Ford immediately sent in the marines. Unfortunately, forty-one American soldiers were killed in the fighting, "all in vain because the American captives had shortly before the attack been released and sent across the border into Thailand."[64] Even so, Ford can be defended for making the decision he did; he did not know what the Cambodians would do. World events are unpredictable, and in the end presidents must rely on their own judgment in crisis situations.

PRESIDENTIAL CHARACTER

How does the public assess which presidential candidate has the best judgment and whether a candidate's character is suitable to the office? Americans must make a broad evaluation of the candidates' personalities and leadership styles. The character issue emerged in 1992 when the Bush campaign harshly attacked Bill Clinton for evasiveness about how he had avoided the Vietnam draft. Questions about Clinton's marital fidelity had materialized earlier in the year, during the primaries, and many interpreted his acknowledgment on "60 Minutes" that he was responsible for "causing pain in my marriage" as an indirect admission of infidelity.[65] The economy seemed to weigh more heavily on the voters' minds, however, and Clinton won despite the harsh attacks on his character by the Bush campaign.

The character issue has continued to dog Clinton in the White House. Questions have been raised about an investment that he and Hillary Rodham Clinton made in the Whitewater land development project. The complicated allegations, fueled by Republican charges of a cover-up, led to the appointment of a special prosecutor to investigate the matter. The issue of infidelity was raised again when a former Arkansas state government employee, Paula Jones, said she was sexually harassed by Clinton when he was governor. Clinton unequivocally denied her claim. Much of what has been said about Clinton may be unfair, but it has clearly taken its toll. Polls showed that after fifteen months in office, the percentage of people who believed the terms *honest* and *trustworthy* apply to Bill Clinton had dropped from 76 percent to 48 percent.[66]

A president's character is clearly relevant to his performance in office. His actions in office reflect something more than ideology and politics; they also reflect the moral, ethical, and psychological forces that comprise his character. Much of any person's character is formed in childhood, and many individual traits can be traced to early experiences. Lyndon Johnson had a troubled relationship with his father, who questioned his son's masculinity. Johnson recalled that when he ran away from home after wrecking his father's car, his father phoned him and said that people in town were calling Lyndon "yellow" and a coward.[67] Johnson biographer Robert Caro notes another crucial episode in young Lyndon's life—a humiliating beating at the hands of a dance partner's jealous boyfriend. In front of family and friends, "blood was pouring out of Lyndon's nose and mouth, running down his face and onto the crepe-de-chine shirt."[68]

What History Teaches

During a January 1994 trip to Eastern Europe, President Clinton took time to visit this Jewish cemetery in Prague with National Security Council staffer Richard Schifter (rear), whose parents died during the Holocaust. Clinton had been subjected to criticism for the United States' inability to stop the killing in Bosnia, where the Serbs' strategy of "ethnic cleansing" was a chilling reminder of the Third Reich's effort to exterminate European Jewry. Clinton could not help but think of the criticism President Roosevelt received for doing so little to stop the Nazi horror against the Jews. Clinton did, however, make a concerted endeavor to bring peace to the area, which paid dividends later in the year.

Was Johnson overly concerned about his masculinity? Did this psychological problem make it difficult for him to extricate the United States from the Vietnam War? Another Johnson biographer, Doris Kearns, argues that Johnson wanted to make sure he "was not forced to see himself as a coward, running away from Vietnam."[69] Nonetheless, it is almost impossible to establish the precise roots of Johnson's behavior as president, and some might find connections between childhood humiliations and presidential policy decisions rather speculative. Others, however, feel that psychobiography—the application of psychological analysis to historical figures—has enormous potential as an approach to studying political leaders, as discussed in Feature 12.2.

Whatever their roots, the personality characteristics of presidents clearly have an important effect on their success or failure in office. Richard Nixon had such an exaggerated fear of what his "enemies" might try to do to him that he created a climate in the White House that nurtured the Watergate break-in and subsequent cover-up. Franklin Roosevelt, on the other hand, was certainly aided in office by his relaxed manner and self-confidence.[70]

■ Portrait of the Young President as a Complete and Utter Monster

Few presidential biographies have so thoroughly altered our perception of a chief executive as much as Robert Caro's volumes on Lyndon Johnson. The publication of the second of a projected four-volume biography of Johnson stoked the controversy about what we can learn by examining the personalities of presidents and would-be presidents. *Means of Ascent* covers the years between 1941, when Johnson lost a bid for the Senate, and 1948, when he won his second Senate race. What is remarkable—and troubling—about this book is that the young Johnson is portrayed as an entirely evil person. There are no shades of gray; Johnson is depicted as an utter monster who will stop at nothing to achieve his goals. For Lyndon Johnson, the ends always justified the means.

The means documented by Caro were Johnson's lying, stealing, and cowardice. As he campaigned for the Senate in 1941, he told voters that if war came he would leave that body to be "in the trenches, in the mud and blood with your boys." When war did come, Johnson did his best to avoid a combat assignment, even going so far as to visit the White House to ask President Roosevelt to make him an administrator of a Washington-based agency that would provide war-related training to youths. He didn't get that job but was eventually given a position in the navy that took him to the South Pacific as an observer.

Yet when he campaigned for the Senate again in 1948, Johnson showed no shame in claiming that he was an experienced combat veteran of World War II. His campaign made a consistent effort to find veterans who were amputees to introduce Johnson at campaign rallies to emphasize his status as a war veteran. Johnson never let on that he was just an observer and that his only exposure to combat was passage on a single B-26 flight that engaged the enemy for a total of thirteen minutes.

Johnson lied about other things as well. He claimed he had no role in his wife's broadcasting business, but that was not true. He accused his opponent in the 1948 race of being a communist sympathizer, but he had no evidence of that. Most

Lyndon Johnson, 1948

revealing of Johnson's character, according to Caro, is that Johnson and his operatives stole the 1948 Senate election. Stealing votes was nothing new in Texas at that time, but Johnson's flagrant abuse of the democratic process was truly breathtaking. The campaign paid large sums of money to various political bosses to ensure that they would produce sizable pluralities on election day. When election day came and it turned out that Johnson was trailing his opponent, Coke Stevenson, Johnson's man swung into action to change the vote tallies by claiming mistakes had been made and by "discovering" votes that had supposedly not been counted. The final vote in Duval County shows just how far Johnson's vote stealing went. There were 4,679 people eligible to cast ballots on election day. Of that number, 4,662 were reported to have voted, and

4,622 (or 99.1 percent) were reported as voting for Johnson.

After days of corrections and the addition of the new votes, Johnson was still behind by a handful of votes. This led Johnson lieutenants in Jim Wells County to phone the election bureau to say that a mistake had been made in Precinct 13 there and that Johnson had actually received 965 votes rather than 765. On the tally sheet, someone simply added a loop to the 7 to turn it into a 9. This put Johnson over the top, giving him victory by 87 votes out of close to 1 million cast by Texas voters.

Caro is quite clear in explaining why he has focused so much on Johnson's personality in the two books he has completed so far. "Lyndon Johnson's personality and character bore an unusually heavy weight" on the evolution of his administration. "To understand that history, we have to understand that personality." Caro sums up what he found

about Johnson's character this way: "The pattern of pragmatism, cynicism and ruthlessness that pervaded Lyndon Johnson's entire early political career was marked by a lack of any discernible limits."

Yet, there is a mystery in all of this. If Johnson was such a ruthless person, why did he do so much good as president? He compiled a remarkable record on civil rights, and his War on Poverty demonstrated an unusual commitment and compassion for the less fortunate in society. What, then, has all this psychobiography told us? If much of a president's behavior in office can be predicted by his earlier experiences, it also seems to be the case that there is much that can't be predicted.

• *Source: Robert A. Caro,* Means of Ascent *(New York: Alfred A. Knopf, 1990). Copyright 1990 by Alfred A. Knopf, Publisher. The first volume of the Caro biography is* The Path to Power *(New York: Alfred A. Knopf, 1982).*

Candidates don't come neatly labeled as having healthy or unhealthy presidential characters. Although voters make their own estimations of how presidents will behave in office, there is no guarantee that those evaluations will turn out to be accurate. And a candidate's character must still be weighed along with other factors, including ideology, party affiliation, and stances on specific issues.

SUMMARY

When the delegates to the Constitutional Convention met to design the government of this new nation, they had trouble shaping the office of the president. They struggled to find a balance—an office that was powerful enough to provide unified leadership but not so strong that presidents could use their powers to become tyrants or dictators. The initial conceptions of the presidency have slowly been transformed over time, as presidents have adapted the office to meet the nation's changing needs. The trend has been to expand presidential power. Some expansion has come from presidential actions under claims of inherent powers. Congress has also delegated a great deal of power to the executive branch, further expanding the role of the president.

Because the president is elected by the entire nation, he can claim to represent all citizens when proposing policy. This broad electoral base equips the presidency to be an institution of majoritarian democracy—compared with Congress's structural tendencies toward pluralist democracy. Whether the presidency actually operates in a majoritarian manner depends on several factors—the individual president's perception of public opinion on political issues, the relationship between public opinion and the president's political ideology, and the extent to which the president is committed to pursuing his values through his office.

The executive branch establishment has grown rapidly, and the White House has become a sizable bureaucracy. New responsibilities of the twentieth-century presidency are particularly noticeable in the area of legislative leadership. Now a president is expected to be a policy initiator for Congress, as well as a lobbyist who guides his bills through the legislative process.

The presidential "job description" for foreign policy has changed considerably. Post–World War II presidents had been preoccupied with containing the spread of communism, but with the collapse of communism in the Soviet Union and Eastern Europe, international economic relations now loom even larger as a priority for presidents. However, national security issues remain, because regional conflicts can directly involve the interests of the United States.

Key Terms

veto
inherent powers
delegation of powers
mandate
divided government

Executive Office of the
  President
cabinet
legislative liaison staff

Selected Readings

Brace, Paul, and Barbara Hinckley. *Follow the Leader.* New York: Basic Books, 1992. The authors examine the role that polls play in the modern presidency.

Jones, Charles O. *The Presidency in a Separated System.* Washington, D.C.: Brookings Institution, 1994. Jones argues that ours is not a presidency-centered system and that policy initiation in Congress is more independent of the executive branch than most scholars realize.

Kernell, Samuel. *Going Public,* 2d ed. Washington, D.C.: Congressional Quarterly Press, 1993. A study of how modern presidents rely more and more on direct communication with the American people as a way of trying to expand their influence.

Milkis, Sidney M. *The President and the Parties.* New York: Oxford University Press, 1993. An in-depth look at the influence of the New Deal on the relationship between presidents and political parties.

Neustadt, Richard E. *Presidential Power,* rev. ed. New York: John Wiley, 1980. Neustadt's classic work examines the president's power to persuade.

Peterson, Mark A. *Legislating Together.* Cambridge, Mass.: Harvard University Press, 1990. A well-documented study of the interaction between the White House and Congress.

Skowronek, Stephen. *The Politics Presidents Make.* Cambridge, Mass.: Harvard University Press, 1993. A sweeping, magisterial analysis of the cycles of presidential history.

Woodward, Bob. *The Agenda.* New York: Simon & Schuster, 1994. An inside, behind-the-scenes look at economic policymaking during the first year of the Clinton administration.

13

The Bureaucracy

THE FEDERAL COMMUNICATIONS COMMISSION (FCC) is a classic regulatory agency. It balances the interests of consumers—literally everyone who has a telephone, radio, or TV—against the interests of the companies that provide telephone, radio, or TV products and services. It must weigh majoritarian interests against pluralistic interests as it makes policy on issues of importance to both couch potatoes and chief executive officers of major telecommunications conglomerates. Its decisions affect the bottom lines of family budgets and corporate balance sheets. The FCC giveth and the FCC taketh away.

Consider cable TV rates. Following the strong movement toward deregulation that began in the 1970s, government decided in 1986 to give up the authority for setting cable TV rates. Cable TV operators were free to charge whatever the market would bear. Theoretically, prices would be kept down by competition within the industry. Cable TV executives also claimed that the consumer would be better served, because the increased capital that companies would raise through any rate increases would be plowed back into better programming and better service.

But deregulation brought skyrocketing rates. Between 1986 and 1992, the price for basic cable service nearly doubled. Competition may have held down prices for premium channels or pay per view, but there really is no competition for basic service and expanded tier service (popular channels such as MTV, ESPN, and CNN). Congress started to hear consumers complain that they were being ripped off and enacted legislation instructing the FCC to reregulate cable TV prices. In 1993, the FCC responded and ordered a rollback of rates of about 10 percent. Cable TV executives were outraged and consumers were pleased.[1]

Yet, one tiny little problem emerged: For many consumers, cable rates went up, not down.

How was it that Congress wrote a law, the FCC wrote five hundred pages of regulations implementing the law, and the actual effect of the new policy was the opposite of what was intended? Clearly, regulating business markets is not a simple task. Regulations often allow flexibility and include various loopholes so that they will not create inequities for some businesses in the industry. Whether an individual cable system was overcharging customers depended on complicated calculations designed to measure the degree to which that system deviated from what the FCC had determined was a "reasonable rate." But different systems offer different packages, and many companies based what was "reasonable" on assump-

Bureaucrats, Planners, Auctioneers.

The Federal Communications Commission plays a central role in overseeing the nation's telecommunications industry. These FCC bureaucrats did the planning that led to the 1994 sale of airwave licenses for paging and data transmission services. The successful auction yielded $617 million for the federal government.

tions different from those that a disinterested party would have made. Another problem is that enforcement of regulations is often highly complex and requires the cooperation of another level of government. Monitoring compliance with cable TV rules is complicated because eleven thousand communities are subject to the regulations. It was impossible for the FCC to monitor all of them, so it left it to individual communities to take the first step in the monitoring process. Many small towns and cities were intimidated by the complexity of the process and took no initiative; others were successfully lobbied by cable companies arguing that a rate reduction would be counterproductive in terms of the services offered.

Finally, the regulations failed, because they did not adequately anticipate how the cable companies would try to get around them. In Los Angeles, for example, most customers paying $16.30 for the basic package found that *after* reregulation, they were required to pay $24.67, a 51 percent increase. The cable company, Century Communications, raised rates by adding eight channels to the basic twenty-three-channel package. The new rates were said to reflect the added costs of the new channels.

Embarrassed by the ineffectiveness of its regulations, and under pressure from Congress and consumers, the FCC went back to the drawing board and issued a new set of regulations in February 1994. The FCC believes these regulations will work and will bring an average decrease of 17 percent from the rates charged before the 1993 regulations.[2] Will the new regulations work better than the first set? Stay tuned.

This chapter examines agencies such as the FCC, or more broadly, the bureaucracies of the executive branch of government. We will focus on how the conflict between pluralism and majoritarianism animates bureaucratic politics. The cable regulation issue is a classic case involving a bureaucracy that has to balance the legitimate needs of a single industry to grow and thrive with the need to look out for the interests of consumers.

The role of the bureaucracy in shifting policy toward freedom, order, or equality will be examined as well. We also will try to determine who controls the bureaucracy in our government. In the cable case, Congress and public opinion prompted the FCC to act. But it often seems as though bureaucracies are unresponsive towwhat the public wants. Finally, we will analyze why people are so dissatisfied with bureaucracy and discuss reforms that might make government work better.

ORGANIZATION MATTERS

A nation's laws and policies are administered, or put into effect, by a variety of departments, agencies, bureaus, offices, and other government units, which together are known as its *bureaucracy.* **Bureaucracy** actually means any large, complex organization in which employees have specific job responsibilities and work within a hierarchy of authority. The employees of these government units, who are quite knowledgeable within their narrow areas, have become known somewhat derisively as **bureaucrats.**

We study bureaucracies because they play a central role in the governments of modern societies. Yet, organizations are a crucial part of any society, no matter how elementary. For example, a preindustrial tribe is an organization. It has a clearly defined leader (a chief), senior policymakers (elders), a fixed division of labor (some hunt, some cook, some make tools), an organizational culture (religious practices, initiation rituals), and rules of behavior (what kind of property belongs to families and what belongs to the tribe). How that tribe is organized is not merely a quaint aspect of its evolution but is critical to the survival of its members in a hostile environment.

The organization of modern government bureaucracies also reflects their need to survive. The environment of modern bureaucracies, filled with conflicting political demands and the ever-present threat of budget cuts, can be no less hostile. The way a given government bureaucracy is organized also reflects the particular needs of its clients. The bottom line, however, is that the manner in which any bureaucracy is organized affects how well it is able to accomplish its tasks.

A recent study of America's schools vividly demonstrates the importance of organization. After studying a large number of high schools around the country, two political scientists tried to determine what makes some better than others. They used the test scores of students to measure the achievement level of each school. Because some high schools' students are much better prepared than others, the authors compared similar schools. In other words, schools in low-income neighborhoods with students who enter high school with average or below-average reading scores were compared with other, similar schools, not to schools in wealthy suburban neighborhoods where entering students have above-average reading scores. When similar schools were compared in terms of improvements in student performance, it was evident that the students in some schools achieved more. Why?

The authors' statistical tests led them to conclude that the difference in the performance of students attending similar schools is a result of the way the schools are organized. And the biggest influence on the effective-

The Genius Was in the Logistics

The U.S. victory over Iraq in 1991 was not simply a military conquest; it was also a spectacular organizational achievement. The unsung heroes of the campaign were the men and women who equipped the different components of this extraordinarily complex operation and kept each supplied and functioning at all times.

ness of a school's organization is its level of autonomy. Schools that have more control over hiring, curriculum, and discipline do better in terms of student achievement. This freedom seems to allow for strong leadership, which helps schools develop coherent goals and build staffs strongly supportive of those goals.[3]

Clearly, organization matters. The ways in which bureaucracies are structured to perform their work directly affect their ability to accomplish their tasks. Unfortunately, "if organization matters, it is also the case that there is no one best way of organizing."[4] Although greater autonomy may improve the performance of public schools, it may not improve other kinds of organizations. If a primary goal of a state social welfare agency, for example, is treating its clients equally, providing the same benefits to people with the same needs and circumstances, then giving local offices a lot of individual autonomy is not a good approach. The study of bureaucracy, then, centers around finding solutions to the many different kinds of problems faced by large government organizations.

THE DEVELOPMENT OF THE BUREAUCRATIC STATE

A common complaint voiced by Americans is that the national bureaucracy is too big and tries to accomplish too much. To the average citizen, the national government may seem like an octopus—its long arms reach just about everywhere.

The Growth of American Government

American government seems to have grown unchecked during this century. As one observer noted wryly, "The assistant administrator for water and hazardous materials of the Environmental Protection Agency presided over a staff larger than Washington's entire first administration."[5] Yet, even during George Washington's time, bureaucracies were necessary. No one argued then about the need for a postal service to deliver mail or a department of the treasury to maintain a system of currency. However, government at all levels (national, state, and local) has grown enormously in the twentieth century. There are a number of major reasons for this.

Science and Technology.   One reason government has grown so much is the increasing complexity of society. George Washington did not have an assistant administrator for water and hazardous materials because he had no need for one. The National Aeronautics and Space Administration (NASA) was not necessary until rockets were invented.

Even longstanding departments have had to expand the scope of their activities to keep up with technological and societal changes. Consider the changes brought about by genetic engineering. The Patent and Trademark Office in the U.S. Department of Commerce has responded to requests that new life forms—such as the geep, a species derived from the fusion of goat and sheep embryos—be patented to protect manufacturers' interests.[6]

Business Regulation.   Another reason government has grown is that the public's attitude toward business has changed. Throughout most of the nineteenth century, there was little or no government regulation of business. Business was generally autonomous, and any government intervention in the economy that might limit that autonomy was considered inappropriate. This attitude began to change toward the end of the nineteenth century, as more Americans became aware that the end product of a laissez-faire approach was not always highly competitive markets that benefited consumers. Instead, business sometimes formed oligopolies such as the infamous "sugar trust," a small group of companies that controlled virtually the entire sugar market.

Gradually, government intervention came to be accepted as necessary to protect the integrity of markets. And if government was to police unfair business practices effectively, it needed administrative agencies. During the twentieth century, new bureaucracies were organized to regulate specific industries. Among them are the Securities and Exchange Commission (SEC), which oversees securities trading; the Food and Drug Administration (FDA), which tries to protect consumers from unsafe food, drugs, and cosmetics; and the Occupational Safety and Health Administration (OSHA), which tries to protect workers from exposure to unnecessary or unacceptable risks at their places of employment.

Through bureaucracies such as these, government has become a referee in the marketplace, developing standards of fair trade, setting rates, and licensing individual businesses for operation. As new problem areas have emerged, government has added new agencies, further expanding the scope of its activities. During the 1960s, for instance, Ralph Nader made the public aware that certain design flaws in automobiles made them unnecessarily dangerous. For example, sharp, protruding dashboard knobs caused a car's interior to be dangerous on impact. Congress responded to public demands for change by creating the National Highway Traffic Safety Administration (originally called the National Safety Agency) in 1966. Recent years have seen a general movement toward lessening the government's role in the marketplace. Yet, as the discussion of the cable

TV rates suggests, the pressures pushing government toward more regulation can be substantial.

Social Welfare.   General attitudes about government's responsibilities in the area of social welfare have changed, too. An enduring part of American culture has been a belief in self-reliance. People are expected to overcome adversity on their own, to succeed on the basis of their own skills and efforts. Yet, certain segments of our population are believed to deserve government support, because we so value their contribution to society or have come to believe that they cannot realistically be expected to overcome adversity on their own.[7]

As far back as the nineteenth century, the government provided pensions to Civil War veterans, because they were judged to deserve financial support. Later, programs to help mothers and children were developed.[8] Further steps toward income security came in the wake of the Great Depression when the Social Security Act became law, creating a fund that workers pay into, then collect income from, during old age. In the 1960s, the government created programs designed to help minorities. As the government made these new commitments, it made new bureaucracies or expanded existing ones.

A Belief in Progress.   A larger, stronger central government can also be traced to Americans' firm belief in the idea of progress. Another thread that runs through the fabric of American culture is faith in our ability to solve problems. No problem is too big or too complicated. This attitude was typified by President John F. Kennedy's commitment in 1961 to put a man on the moon by 1970. As difficult as the task seemed when he made the pledge, a man walked on the moon on July 20, 1969. The same spirit leads politicians to declare war on poverty or war on cancer through massive programs of coordinated, well-funded activities. When an undertaking is too large or the financial risks too high, people look to the government to step in and produce progress. Although some drug companies are searching for an AIDS vaccine, the problem is so great and the research is so expensive that the government has committed significant funds for scientific work analyzing the AIDS virus.

Ambitious Administrators.   Finally, government has grown because agency officials have expanded their organizations and staffs to take on added responsibilities. Imaginative, ambitious agency administrators look for ways to serve their clients. Each new program leads to new authority. Larger budgets and staffs, in turn, are necessary to support that authority. When, for example, the collapse of communism in the Soviet bloc threatened the budgets of the defense and security bureaucracies, the Department of Defense started to think about taking on research tasks relating to serious worldwide environmental problems.[9] The Central Intelligence Agency (CIA), which had resisted efforts to join the fight against drugs, changed its mind and announced that "narcotics is a new priority."[10] Faced with choosing between a smaller budget or an expanded mission, in both cases administrators chose the expanded mission.

FIGURE   **13.1**   ■ **We Hate Government (in General)**

Americans demonstrate little confidence in government when asked about its general capabilities. Poll results show that citizens believe government creates more problems than it solves and are dissatisfied with its performance.

Source: American Enterprise, March/April 1993, p. 89.

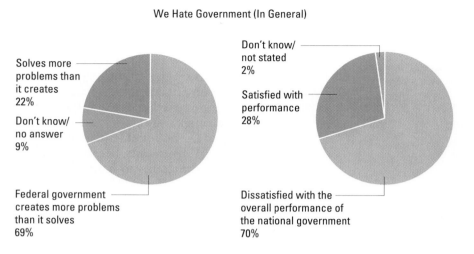

We Hate Government (In General)

Solves more problems than it creates
22%

Don't know/ no answer
9%

Federal government creates more problems than it solves
69%

Don't know/ not stated
2%

Satisfied with performance
28%

Dissatisfied with the overall performance of the national government
70%

Can We Reduce the Size of Government?

When candidates for Congress and the presidency campaign, they typically run against the government—even if they are incumbents. Government is unpopular, and Americans have little confidence in its capabilities, feel that it wastes money, and that it is out of touch with the American people (see Figure 13.1). Americans want a smaller government that costs less and performs better.

Most of the national government is composed of large bureaucracies, so if government is to become smaller, bureaucracies will have to be eliminated or reduced in size. Yet, presidents and members of Congress face a tough job when they try to reduce the size of the executive branch. Each government bureaucracy performs a service of value to some sector of society. For example, bankers as a group favor laissez-faire capitalism, the principles of a free market, and minimal government intervention. Few bankers voiced those principles when the savings and loan industry collapsed in the late 1980s. A noninterventionist government could have stood by and done nothing, but inaction would have had a disastrous effect on the U.S. financial system, and free-market economics looked like a very unattractive option. Bankers became more concerned about order than freedom and were happy to have government mount a rescue effort. A new bureaucracy, the Resolution Trust Corporation, was created to administer the medicine to the sick patient. Big government got even bigger.

Bankers are far from the only group that wants to be protected by the national government. Farmers want the price supports of the U.S. Department of Agriculture. Builders profit from programs offered by the U.S. Department of Housing and Urban Development. And labor unions want a vigorous Occupational Safety and Health Administration. Interest groups that have a stake in an agency almost always resist efforts to cut back its scope.

FIGURE 13.2 ■ We Like Government (in Particular)

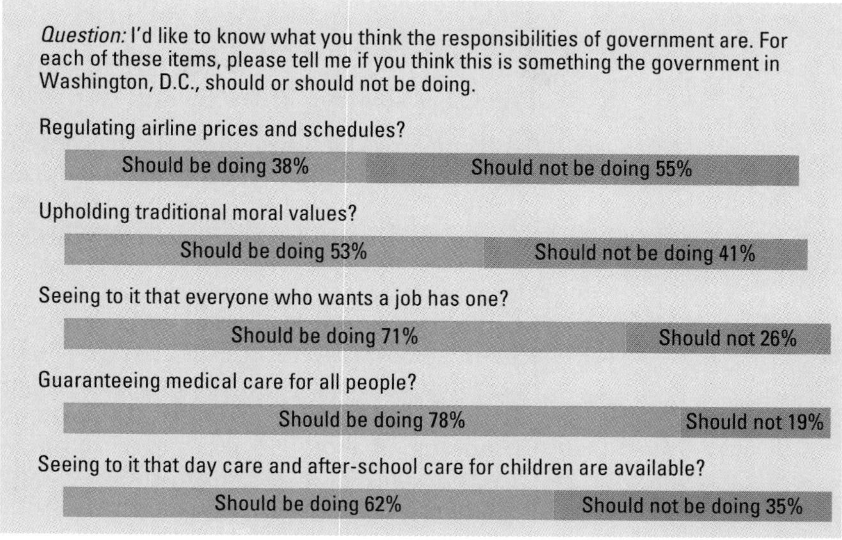

Americans are critical of government, believing that it tries to do too much, has become too powerful, and wastes a lot of money. When asked about specific programs, however, they tend to be much more supportive of what government is doing.

Source: *Adapted from a November 1987 New York Times/CBS News poll. Berman, Larry, ed.* Looking Back on the Reagan Presidency. *The Johns Hopkins University Press, Baltimore/London, 1990, p. 307. Reprinted with permission.*

Question: I'd like to know what you think the responsibilities of government are. For each of these items, please tell me if you think this is something the government in Washington, D.C., should or should not be doing.

Regulating airline prices and schedules?
Should be doing 38% | Should not be doing 55%

Upholding traditional moral values?
Should be doing 53% | Should not be doing 41%

Seeing to it that everyone who wants a job has one?
Should be doing 71% | Should not 26%

Guaranteeing medical care for all people?
Should be doing 78% | Should not 19%

Seeing to it that day care and after-school care for children are available?
Should be doing 62% | Should not be doing 35%

As for the public, people's attitudes toward government in general tell only part of the story. When asked about specific programs or functions of government, citizens tend to be highly supportive. As Figure 13.2 shows, public support for expensive government endeavors (including guaranteeing a job for all who want one, which would be a significant expansion of government's reach into the economy) is considerable.

Given interest group and public support, it is rare for the government to abolish a department or agency. But agencies are not immune to change. Major reorganizations, in which programs are consolidated and the size and scope of activities are reduced, are not uncommon. During the Reagan administration, changes at the Department of the Interior were profound. In Reagan's first term, thirty-nine thousand employees left Interior, some voluntarily, but others were forced out, because the administration's priorities were different from the preceding administration's. The Bureau of Land Management, which is part of Interior, emphasized developing government-owned land in the West for business purposes; environmental protection activities got less attention than in the Carter administration. This, in turn, affected which jobs were eliminated and which offices grew in staffing.[11]

The tendency for big government to endure reflects the tension between majoritarianism and pluralism. Even when the public wants a smaller national government, that sentiment can be undermined by the strong preferences of different segments of society for government to perform some valuable function for them. Lobbies that represent these segments work strenuously to convince Congress and the administration that their agency's particular part of the budget is vital and that any cuts ought to come out of some other agency's budget. At the same time, that other agency is also working to protect itself and to garner support.

BUREAUS AND BUREAUCRATS

We often think of the bureaucracy as a monolith. In reality, the bureaucracy in Washington is a disjointed collection of departments, agencies, bureaus, offices, and commissions—each of these a bureaucracy in its own right.

The Organization of Government

By examining the basic types of government organizations, we can better understand how the executive branch operates. In our discussion, we pay particular attention to the relative degree of independence of these organizations and their relationship to the White House.

Departments.   **Departments** are the biggest units of the executive branch, covering broad areas of government responsibility. As noted in Chapter 12, the secretaries (heads) of the departments, along with a few other key officials, form the president's cabinet. The current cabinet departments are State, Treasury, Defense, Interior, Agriculture, Justice, Commerce, Labor, Health and Human Services, Housing and Urban Development, Transportation, Energy, Education, and Veterans Affairs. Each of these massive organizations is broken down into subsidiary agencies, bureaus, offices, and services.

Independent Agencies.   Within the executive branch are many **independent agencies,** which are not part of any cabinet department. Instead, they stand alone and are controlled to varying degrees by the president. Some, among them the CIA, are directly under the president's control. Others, such as the FCC, are structured as **regulatory commissions.** Each commission is run by a small number of commissioners (usually an odd number, which helps to prevent tie votes) appointed to fixed terms by the president. Some commissions were formed to guard against unfair business practices. Others were formed to protect the public from unsafe products. Regulatory commissions are outside the direct control of the White House, so they have less pressure from the political process and the partisan considerations that influence other agencies.

Still, regulatory commissions are not immune to political pressure. Client groups lobby them fervently, and they must take the demands of those groups into account when they make policy. When low-cost foreign carbon steel began to seriously erode the sales of American steel manufacturers, the U.S. International Trade Commission (ITC) was under significant pressure from the steel companies to rule that the imports were causing economic harm to an American industry. The ITC resisted the pressure and ruled against the American steel industry. Later, however, President Reagan forced a change in policy by having the White House's special trade representative (an office separate from the ITC) negotiate a trade agreement that restricted carbon steel imports. The result saved American jobs, but consumers had to pay more for products containing carbon steel. In the end, consumers paid $113,600 extra for each job saved.[12]

Government Corporations.   Finally, Congress has also created a small number of **government corporations.** The services these executive branch

Anybody Home?

Census workers called enumerators try to find people who did not receive a census questionnaire through the mail. During the 1990 census, big city mayors pressured the Census Bureau to locate and count the homeless. Because funding for many national grants-in-aid programs is based on per capita formulas, an undercount of a city's homeless population could lessen the amount of federal aid the city receives.

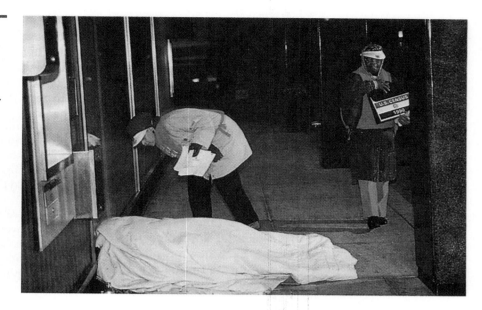

agencies perform theoretically could be provided by the private sector, but Congress has decided that the public would be better served if the agencies have some link with the government. For example, the national government maintains a postal service, because it feels that Americans need low-cost, door-to-door service for all kinds of mail, not just for mail on profitable routes or mail that requires special services. In some instances, the private sector does not have enough financial incentive to provide an essential service. This is the case with the financially troubled Amtrak train line.[13]

The Civil Service

The national bureaucracy is staffed by about 3 million civilian employees, who account for about 2.3 percent of the U.S. work force.[14] Americans have a tendency to stereotype all government workers as faceless paper pushers, but the work force is actually quite diverse. Government workers include forest rangers, FBI agents, typists, foreign service officers, computer programmers, policy analysts, public relations specialists, security guards, librarians, administrators, engineers, plumbers, and people from literally hundreds of other occupations.

An important feature of the national bureaucracy is that most of its workers are hired under the requirements of the **civil service.** The civil service was created after the assassination of President James Garfield, who was killed by an unbalanced and dejected job seeker. Congress responded by passing the Pendleton Act (1883), which established the Civil Service Commission (now the Office of Personnel Management). The objective of the act was to reduce patronage—the practice of filling government positions with the president's political allies or cronies. The civil service fills jobs on the basis of merit and sees to it that workers are not fired for political reasons. Over the years, job qualifications and selection procedures have been developed for most government positions.

POLITICS IN A CHANGING AMERICA 13.1   Does Gender Make a Difference?

 When the U.S. Forest Service was sued for discriminating against women employees, it signed a consent decree pledging to hire enough women at each level of the organization so that its employment mix would be similar to the gender composition of the rest of the American work force. It moved quickly to hire more women in all types of jobs.

It is easy to applaud the Forest Service for tackling discrimination within its ranks to create more opportunities for women. Clearly, it makes a difference for women who can now compete more fairly for better jobs with increased responsibility and better pay. But does it make a difference in how the Forest Service operates? Does employing more women have an impact on the Forest Service's policy decisions? After all, the primary job of the Forest Service is to manage publicly owned forests—is there a distinctly "feminine" approach to managing trees?

Recent research demonstrates that men andwwomen in the Forest Service are different in important ways. A survey of those working for the agency shows that women are decidedly more concerned about environmental protection. Women in the Forest Service are more likely to believe that there are limits to the number of people the earth can support, that the balance of nature is easily upset, that economic growth should be "steady-state," and that humans are abusing the environment.

The Forest Service must balance the needs of consumers for wood products with the desire of Americans to have our forests preserved for generations to come. But if a larger percentage of employees entering the Forest Service believes we need to do more to protect the environment, then the existing balance between development and preservation is likely to be challenged.

The influx of women into the agency is too recent to measure whether these attitudes have carried over into new policies. Furthermore, basic policy is set by Congress and by the president's appointees who run the agency. Inevitably, though, the different mix of men and women within the Forest Service is going to affect policy, just as adding a lot more liberals or conservatives to an agency would change it. The National Forest Products Association, a trade group of businesses that develop or use public forest resources, has warned its members that "the sharp changes in the demographic character-

About 88 percent of the national government's workers are employed outside Washington.[15] One reason for this decentralization is to make government offices accessible to the people they serve. The Social Security Administration, for example, has to have offices within a reasonable distance of most Americans, so that its many clients have somewhere to take their questions, problems, and paperwork. Decentralization is also a way to distribute jobs and income across the country. The government's Centers for Disease Control could easily have been located in Washington, but it is in Atlanta. Likewise, NASA's headquarters for space flights is located in Houston. Members of Congress, of course, are only too happy to place some of the "pork" back home, so that their constituents will credit them with the jobs and money that government installations create.

Given the enormous variety of government jobs, employees come from all walks of life. Like most large organizations, the federal government has

istics of Forest Service employees will lead to further de-emphasis on commodity production and to increasing emphasis accorded to non–timber resource values." In other words, more women in the agency means a different outlook on how to manage the nation's forests.

• *Source: Greg Brown and Charles C. Harris, "The Implications of Work Force Diversification in the U.S. Forest Service,"* Administration and Society 25 *(May 1993), 85–113.*

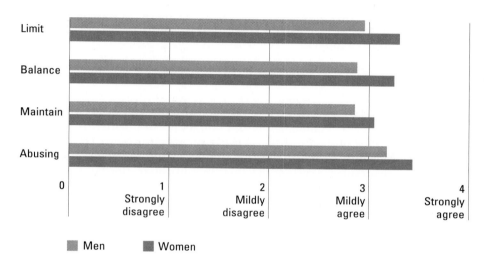

Men   Women

Average response based on placement of respondents on the four-point scale.
Limit = We are approaching the limit of the number of people the earth can support.
Balance = The balance of nature is very delicate and easily upset.
Maintain = To maintain a healthy economy we will have to develop a "steady-state" economy where industrial growth is controlled.
Abusing = Humankind is severely abusing the environment.

taken steps to try to make its work force mirror the larger population in terms of race and gender (on gender, see Politics in a Changing America 13.1). Minorities have substantial representation (27.3 percent) within the federal government's work force. However, at the highest level of the civil service, minorities are woefully underrepresented, and in recent years there has been little progress in placing more blacks, Hispanics, and other minorities into top civil service positions.[16]

Presidential Control over the Bureaucracy

Civil service and other reforms effectively insulate the vast majority of government workers from party politics. An incoming president can appoint about three thousand people to jobs in his administration—fewer than 1 percent of all executive branch employees.[17] Still, presidential appointees fill the top policymaking positions in government. Each new president, then, establishes an extensive personnel review process to find appointees who are both politically compatible and qualified in their field. Although the president selects some people from his campaign staff, most political appointees have not been campaign workers. Instead, cabinet secretaries, assistant secretaries, agency heads, and the like tend to be drawn directly from business, universities, and government itself.

Because so few of their own people are in each department and agency, presidents often believe that they do not have enough control over the bureaucracy. Republican presidents have also worried that the civil service would be hostile to their objectives, because they assume that career bureaucrats have a liberal Democratic bias.

Recent presidents have tried repeatedly to centralize power by tightening the reins on the rest of the executive branch. During his term in office, Ronald Reagan and his White House staff were effective at gaining control over the bureaucracy.[18] Through two key strategies, the Reagan White House was able to infuse the bureaucracy with greater ideological direction. First, the administration required that all major regulations formulated by executive branch departments and agencies be approved by the Office of Management and Budget (OMB), which is part of the Executive Office of the President. OMB used its authority to push the bureaucracy to develop policies more in line with the president's strong, conservative principles. Second, the Reagan administration also made a concerted effort to ensure that its top appointees were steadfast in their support of the president's program. Reagan's appointments were far more partisan in nature than those of either of his immediate Republican predecessors, Richard Nixon and Gerald Ford.[19]

When George Bush became president, he placed less emphasis on appointing "true believers" than Ronald Reagan did, and he selected many Republican moderates who lacked the ideological zeal of those in the previous administration. Bush's head of the National Endowment for the Arts (NEA), John Frohnmayer, had not even voted for Bush for president, and he repeatedly clashed with conservative Republicans in Congress who believed the NEA was funding artists whose work was obscene. The NEA, for example, gave grants to performance artist Karen Finley, who as part of her art sometimes symbolically defiles her partially nude body by smearing chocolate over it. Frohnmayer was far more concerned about protecting artistic freedom than in rooting out obscenity in the art world, and he resisted efforts in Congress to legislate anti-obscenity guidelines for projects funded with taxpayer dollars. In his eyes, artistic freedom was much more important than the order Congress wanted to impose. Frohnmayer became such a political liability that he was fired.[20]

Bush also pulled back from the regulatory review conducted by OMB and gave agencies more flexibility in writing regulations. After complaints from business that they were being hurt by regulations issued by Bush appointees, the president set up a Council on Competitiveness chaired by Vice President Dan Quayle. The Quayle council began to review regulations, as OMB had done earlier, and it was in frequent conflict with the Environmental Protection Agency (EPA), where another Bush-appointed moderate, John Reilly, was ruffling conservative feathers by pursuing policy compromises that environmentalists might buy into.[21]

Your Tax Dollars at Work
Karen Finley is one of the artists whose work ignited a debate about government funding of the arts during the Bush years. The National Endowment of the Arts has supported Finley's work, which some regard as offensive if not obscene and wonder why it is that taxpayers must subsidize her work. Others defend such government grants on the grounds of artistic freedom. Finley appears here with her painting, Holy Family on Acid.

Bush was slow to learn that presidents must be aggressive in taking control of the executive branch. The scope of what it does is staggering, and presidents must be strategic in marshalling their resources to get the bureaucracy moving in the direction they want. Appointing loyal people and developing mechanisms for White House control of agencies are means by which presidents try to get the individual parts of the executive branch to be responsive to their goals.[22]

The obstacle to getting agencies to respond to the White House agenda is not civil servants' opposition to the president's program. Research shows that civil servants work well with their politically appointed superiors and are loyal to the administration, even when they do not share the ideology of the president and his appointees.[23] Rather, the problem of maximizing responsiveness springs from two other sources. First, presidents typically appoint people to cabinet and agency positions for a variety of reasons instead of sticking strictly to those who are "ideologically correct." The Quayle council fought with the EPA because Bush said he wanted to be the "environmental president" and appointed a pro-environment moderate to head the agency. Yet, his most important constituency was the business community. Inevitably, Bush's probusiness side clashed with his pro-environment side.

Likewise, when Bill Clinton began to put together his cabinet, he kept in mind his campaign promise to put in place "an administration that looks like America."[24] Thus, he emphasized diversity as well as loyalty and ideological compatibility (see Figure 13.3).

Agencies also are not perfectly responsive to the president's goals because they frequently have constituencies pushing them in another direction. OSHA in a Republican administration may want to reduce the regulatory burdens on businesses but will be under pressure from labor unions that do not want any relaxation of standards designed to prote t workers on the job. OSHA cannot simply ignore labor, because unions have liberal allies in Congress who will cajole and threaten the agency.

| FIGURE | 13.3 | ■ **A Cabinet That Looks Like America** |

President Clinton pledged to have an administration that looked like America. His cabinet may not look exactly like America, but it certainly has more diversity to it than those of previous administrations.

Source: Data compiled by the authors.

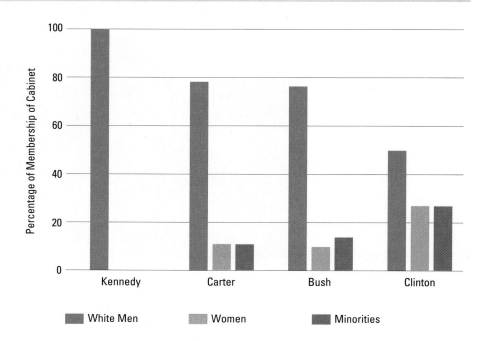

For purposes of this graph, the cabinet includes those positions defined as cabinet-level by the Clinton White House. Not all positions existed in earlier administrations. The number of cabinet and cabinet-level positions for each administration is Kennedy (14), Carter (18), Bush (21), and Clinton (22).

Unions will also go to court when they think the agency is violating some labor law. As a result, the agency administrator will often look for ways to broker compromises between unions and business lobbies. Yet, such accommodation, which may make sense from the agency head's perspective, dilutes the president's program.[25]

ADMINISTRATIVE POLICYMAKING: THE FORMAL PROCESSES

Many Americans wonder why agencies sometimes actually *make* policy rather than merely carry it out. Administrative agencies are, in fact, authoritative policymaking bodies, and their decisions on substantive issues are legally binding on the citizens of this country.

Administrative Discretion

What are executive agencies set up to do? To begin with, cabinet departments, independent agencies, and government corporations are creatures of Congress. Congress creates a new department or agency by enacting a law that describes each organization's mandate, or mission. As part of that mandate, Congress grants to the agency the authority to make certain policy decisions. Congress long ago recognized that it has neither the time nor the technical expertise to make all policy decisions. Ideally, it sets general guidelines for policy and expects agencies to act within those guidelines. The latitude that Congress gives agencies to make policy in the spirit of their legislative mandate is called **administrative discretion.** When discretion is granted to agencies, it is indirectly granted to the White House, because it is the president who appoints agency heads.

In 1988, the Department of Health and Human Services (HHS) finalized regulations that forbade family planning clinics that receive federal money to provide "counseling concerning the use of abortion as a method of family planning" or even to provide referrals to those that would discuss abortion as a method of family planning. Antiabortion Republicans at both the White House and HHS believed they had the authority to issue such regulations, because Congress had given HHS the administrative discretion to write regulations governing the dispersal of grants under Title X of the Public Health Services Act.[26] When the Clinton administration came into office, the new HHS secretary, Donna Shalala, in turn used her administrative discretion to rescind the so-called gag rule that prohibited discussion of the abortion option at federally funded family planning clinics.

Critics of bureaucracy frequently complain that agencies are granted too much discretion. In his book *The End of Liberalism,* Theodore Lowi argues that Congress commonly gives vague directives in its initial enabling legislation instead of truly setting guidelines.[27] Congress charges agencies with protecting "the public interest" but leaves them to determine on their own what policies best serve the public. Lowi and other critics believe that members of Congress delegate too much of their responsibility for difficult policy choices to appointed administrators.

Congress often is vague about its intent when setting up a new agency or program. At times, a problem is clear cut, but the solution is not; yet,

Goring the Bureaucracy

Under the direction of Vice President Gore, the Clinton administration promised to "reinvent government" through streamlining administrative procedures, reducing the number of bureaucrats, and delivering better service to the public. After the first year of this effort, the Brookings Institute, a respected Washington think tank, issued an evaluation that gave the Gore initiative mixed grades. It criticized the reform program for focusing too much on short-term savings rather than on long-term management issues. On the other hand, the reinventing government campaign was praised for cutting red tape, simplifying rules, and improving procurement practices.

Congress is under pressure to act. So it creates an agency or program to show that it is concerned and responsive and leaves it to administrators to develop specific solutions. For example, the 1934 enabling legislation that established the FCC recognized a need for regulation in the burgeoning radio industry. The growing number of stations and overlapping frequencies would soon have made it impossible to listen to the radio. But Congress avoided tackling several sticky issues by giving the FCC the ambiguous directive that broadcasters should "serve the public interest, convenience, and necessity."[28] In other cases, a number of obvious solutions to a problem may be available, but lawmakers cannot agree on which is best. Thus, compromise wording is often ambiguous, papering over differences and ensuring conflict over the administrative regulations that try to settle the lingering policy disputes.

The wide latitude Congress gives administrative agencies often leads to charges that the bureaucracy is out of control, a power unto itself. But the claims are frequently exaggerated. Administrative discretion is not a fixed commodity. Congress has the power to express its displeasure by reining in agencies with additional legislation. If Congress is unhappy with an agency's actions, it can pass laws invalidating specific policies. This method of control may seem cumbersome, but Congress does have periodic opportunities to amend the original legislation that created an agency or program. Over time, Congress makes increasingly detailed policy decisions, often affirming or modifying agency decisions.[29] A second, powerful tool is Congress's control over the budget. Congress can influence an agency because it has the power to cut budgets and to reorder agency priorities through its detailed appropriations legislation.

Informal contacts with members of Congress also influence administrators. Through these communications, legislators can clarify exactly which actions they want administrators to take. And administrators listen, because they are wary of offending members of the committees and subcommittees that oversee their programs and, particularly, their budgets. In addition to providing a better idea of congressional intent, contacts with legislators allow administrators to explain the problems their agencies are facing, justify their decisions, and negotiate compromises on unresolved issues. When the Pentagon was developing its plan to allow gays to serve in the military, Defense Secretary Les Aspin kept in close touch with Sam Nunn, chairman of the Senate Armed Services Committee and Congress's most respected expert on defense matters. Aspin knew that Nunn was a bellwether of what would be acceptable to Congress. The compromise policy that the Pentagon recommended to the president was what Nunn had recommended to the military.[30]

In general, then, the bureaucracy is not out of control. But Congress has chosen to limit its own oversight in one area—domestic and international security. Both the Federal Bureau of Investigation (FBI) and CIA have enjoyed a great deal of freedom from formal and informal congressional constraints because of the legitimate need for secrecy in their operations. (For an example of how security needs were met in communist East Germany, see Compared with What? 13.1.) During the years that the legendary J. Edgar Hoover ran the FBI (1924–1972), it was something of a rogue elephant, independent of both Congress and presidents. Politicians were afraid of Hoover, who was not above keeping files on them and using those

The Man with the Secrets

Even presidents were afraid of what FBI Director J. Edgar Hoover had in his files. Although the Nixon administration wasn't fond of him, Hoover let it know that if its criticism of his agency didn't stop, he would testify before Congress about some wiretapping done by a secret White House investigation unit. Hoover remained secure in his job. The White House wiretapping was later revealed as part of the Watergate scandal.

files to increase his power. At Hoover's direction, the FBI spied on Martin Luther King, Jr., and once sent King a tape recording with embarrassing revelations gathered by bugging his hotel rooms. The anonymous letter accompanying the tape suggested that King save himself further embarrassment by committing suicide.[31]

Over the years, the CIA has also abused its need for privacy by engaging in covert operations that should never have been carried out. Congress, however, has increased its oversight of the agency and has enacted legislation designed to force the administration to share more information with it. Still, members of Congress complain that they are often misled by the CIA and administration officials. Said one representative, "They treat us like mushrooms. Keep us in the dark and feed us a lot of manure."[32]

Rule Making

Agencies exercise the policymaking discretion that Congress grants them through formal administrative procedures, usually rule making. **Rule making** is the administrative process that results in the issuance of regulations. **Regulations** are rules that govern the operation of government programs. When an agency issues regulations, it is using the discretionary authority granted to it by Congress to implement a program or policy enacted into law.

Because they are authorized by congressional statutes, regulations have the effect of law. The policy content of regulations is supposed to follow from the intent of enabling legislation. After Congress enacted the

COMPARED WITH WHAT? 13.1   No Tears for the *Staatsicherheit*

 Every society needs to maintain order, but in many countries of the world, the bureaucratic apparatus designed to maintain order is really a mechanism for ensuring the survival of an autocratic regime. Nowhere was this more vividly illustrated than in the formerly communist regimes in Eastern Europe. The state security agencies there were instruments of terror, enforcing control by making any opposition to the government extremely dangerous.

The East German secret police, the *Staatsicherheit* (or Stasi), was an enormous bureaucracy that reached into every part of society. It had 85,000 full-time employees, including 6,000 people whose sole task was to listen in on telephone conversations. Another 2,000 steamed open mail, read it, resealed the letters, and sent them on to the intended recipients. The Stasi also employed 150,000 active informers and hundreds of thousands of part-time snitches. Files were kept on an estimated 4 to 5 million people in a country that had a total population, including children, of just 17 million. Although East Germany had a large standing army, the Stasi kept its own arsenal of 250,000 weapons.

The Stasi infiltrated the top echelons of government, business, and universities in East Germany, placing two thousand agents in positions of importance. The Stasi's primary job was to make East Germans too scared to threaten the communist dictatorship that ran the country. Eventually, of course, the East German government did fall when a largely peaceful revolution swept through the Eastern bloc countries. After a democratic transition government was installed, angry East Germans ransacked the Stasi building, piling up old uniforms that would later be sold and smashing glass and office equip-

ment. Protesters said that they were worried that the Stasi was trying to find a role in the new government.

East Germans were understandably appalled at the idea of a secret police in a unified, democratic Germany. But democracies do have legitimate security needs that require that the bureaucracies in charge of security be allowed to operate largely in private. The United States has a sizable internal security establishment, including the FBI and the Secret Service. As the treatment of Martin Luther King, Jr., by the FBI demonstrates, however, the internal security bureaucracies of this country have at times acted in a highly irresponsible and sometimes illegal manner. A society's need for police powers to help it maintain order must be balanced by mechanisms of accountability.

• *Sources: Steven Emerson, "Keeping Watch on the Stasi Machine,"* San Francisco Chronicle, *August 15, 1990, p. Br. 1; Serge Schemann, "East Berlin Faults Opposition on Raid,"* New York Times, *January 17, 1990, p. A9; and Craig R. Whitney, "East Europeans Are Making Big Brother Smaller,"* New York Times, *January 22, 1991, p. A1.*

Nutrition Labeling and Education Act, for example, the FDA drew up regulations to implement the policy guidelines set forth in the law. One part of the law says that producers of foods and food supplements can make health claims for their products only when "significant scientific agreement" exists. Following that principle, the FDA proposed regulations requiring manufacturers of vitamins and dietary supplements to substantiate the health claims made for their products on the labels. Clearly, the FDA was following the intent of a law enacted by Congress.

When agencies draft regulations, they are first published as proposals to give all interested parties an opportunity to comment on them and to try to persuade the agency to adopt, alter, or withdraw them. When the FDA issued its proposed regulations on vitamins and health supplements, the industry fought them vigorously. Aware that many health claims could not be substantiated, and that it would be expensive to finance scientific studies to try to prove their assertions, the manufacturers asked Congress for relief. Although it had originated the legislation authorizing the regulations, Congress passed a one-year moratorium on the proposed rules. Congress seemed to want to have it both ways, ensuring the integrity of food and drugs while protecting the business interests of industry constituents. When the moratorium expired, however, the FDA announced plans to reissue the regulations.[33]

The regulatory process is controversial because regulations often require individuals and corporations to act against their own self-interest. In this case, the producers of vitamins and dietary supplements resented the implication that they were making false claims and reminded policymakers that they employ many people to make products that consumers want. The FDA must, however, balance its desire not to put people out of work by overregulation with its concern that people are not misled or harmed by false labeling.

ADMINISTRATIVE POLICYMAKING: INFORMAL POLITICS

When an agency is considering a new regulation, and all the evidence and arguments have been presented, how does an administrator reach a decision? Because policy decisions typically address complex problems that lack a single satisfactory solution, they rarely exhibit mathematical precision and efficiency.

The Science of Muddling Through

In a classic analysis of policymaking, "The Science of Muddling Through," Charles Lindblom compared the way policy ideally should be made with the way it is formulated in the real world.[34] The ideal, rational decision-making process, according to Lindblom, begins with an administrator tackling a problem by ranking values and objectives. After the objectives are clarified, the administrator thoroughly considers all possible solutions to the problem. The administrator comprehensively analyzes alternative solutions, taking all relevant factors into account. Finally, the administrator chooses the alternative that is seen as the most effective means of achieving the desired goal and solving the problem.

Lindblom claimed that this "rational-comprehensive" model is unrealistic. To begin with, policymakers have great difficulty defining precise values and goals. Administrators at the U.S. Department of Energy, for example, want to be sure that supplies of home heating oil are sufficient each winter. At the same time, they want to reduce dependence on foreign oil. Obviously, the two goals are not fully compatible. How do administrators decide which is more important? And how do they relate them to the other goals of the nation's energy policy?

Real-world decision making parts company with the ideal in another way: The policy selected cannot always be the most effective means to the desired end. Even if a tax at the pump is the most effective way to reduce gasoline consumption during a shortage, motorists' anger would make this theoretically "right" decision politically difficult. So the "best" policy is often the one on which most people can agree. However, political compromise may mean that the government is able to solve only part of a problem.

Finally, critics of the rational-comprehensive model point out that policy making can never be based on truly comprehensive analysis. A secretary of energy could not possibly find the time to read a comprehensive study of all alternative energy sources and relevant policy considerations for the future. A truly thorough investigation of the subject would produce thousands of pages of text. Instead, administrators usually rely on short staff memos that outline a limited range of feasible solutions to immediate problems. Time is of the essence, and problems are often too pressing to wait for a complete study.

In short, policymaking tends to be characterized by **incrementalism,** with policies and programs changing bit by bit, step by step.[35] Decision makers are constrained by competing policy objectives, opposing political forces, incomplete information, and the pressures of time. They choose from a limited number of feasible options that are almost always modifications of existing policies rather than wholesale departures from those policies.

Because policymaking proceeds with small modifications of existing policies, it is easy to assume that incrementalism describes a process that is intrinsically conservative, sticking close to the status quo. Yet even if policymaking moves in small steps, those steps may all be in the same direction. Over time, a series of incremental changes can significantly alter a program.[36]

The Culture of Bureaucracy

How an organization makes decisions and performs its tasks is greatly affected by the people who work there—the bureaucrats. Americans often find their interactions with bureaucrats are frustrating, because bureaucrats are inflexible (they go by the book) or lack the authority to get things done. Top administrators, too, can become frustrated with the bureaucrats who work for them.

Why do people act bureaucratically? Individuals who work for large organizations cannot help but be affected by the culture of bureaucracy, even in their everyday speech (see Feature 13.1). Modern bureaucracies develop explicit rules and standards in order to make operations more efficient and

FEATURE 13.1

■ Praise the Lord and Pass the Projectiles

One rather maddening characteristic of bureaucracies is their reliance on jargon, the specialized language that people in an organization or vocation develop over time. The use of jargon is not restricted to government, but government bureaucrats seem to excel at using bizarre terminology.

Why does jargon rear its ugly head in organizations? Some people assume that jargon is a sign of professionalism, and that using specialized terms reflects a command of their subject. Another reason is the decline of writing skills. It's much easier to write several long, complex, jargon-laden sentences than it is to write one that is short and crystal clear.

Although the use of jargon is ubiquitous throughout government, nowhere is it worse than in the Department of Defense. There's no close second; the military has debased the English language in ways that seem unimaginable. Some samples of Pentagonese:

Pentagonese	English
Frame-supported tension structure	Tent
Aerodynamic personnel decelerator	Parachute
Interlocking slide fastener	Zipper
Projectile	Bullet
Hexiform rotatable surface compressor unit	Nut
Universal obscurant	Smoke
The missile impacted with the ground prematurely.	The missile crashed.
A forcible ejection of the internal bomb components	The bomb blew up.
Ambient noncombatant personnel	Refugees
Pre-dawn vertical insertion	Invasion

• *Source: Excerpt from* Doublespeak *by William Lutz. Copyright © 1989 by William Lutz. Reprinted by permission of HarperCollins Publisher, Inc.*

to guarantee fair treatment of their clients. But within each organization, **norms** (informal, unwritten rules of behavior) also develop and influence the way people act on the job. At the CIA, for example, rules not only mandate secrecy for sensitive intelligence activities but a norm enshrines secrecy for virtually everything that the employees do. In the wake of the collapse of the Cold War, a 1992 internal assessment at the CIA concluded that excessive secrecy fed public misunderstanding of what the agency did and a lack of appreciation for what it accomplished. The report found that the passion for secrecy had meant that documents analyzing troop movements at the beginning of World War I still were classified for national security reasons.[37]

Bureaucracies are often influenced in their selection of policy options by the prevailing customs, attitudes, and expectations of the people working within them. Departments and agencies commonly develop a sense of mission where a particular objective or a means for achieving it is emphasized. The Army Corps of Engineers, for example, is dominated by engineers who define the bureaucracy's objective as protecting citizens from floods by building dams. There could be other objectives, and there are certainly other methods of achieving this one, but the engineers promote the solutions that fit their conception of what the agency should be doing. As one study concluded, "When asked to generate policy proposals for review by their political superiors, bureaucrats are tempted to bias the search for alternatives so that their superiors wind up selecting the kind of program the agency wants to pursue."[38]

At first glance, bureaucrats seem to be completely negative sorts of creatures. They do have their positive side, however. Those agencies with a clear sense of mission are likely to have a strong esprit de corps that adds to the bureaucrats' motivation. Also, bureaucrats' caution and close adherence to agency rules offer a measure of consistency. It would be unsettling if government employees interpreted rules as they pleased. Simply put, bureaucrats "go by the book" because the "book" consists of the laws and regulations of this country as well as the internal rules and norms of a particular agency. Americans expect to be treated equally before the law, and bureaucrats work with that expectation in mind.

PROBLEMS IN IMPLEMENTING POLICY

The development of policy in Washington is the end of one phase of the policymaking cycle and the beginning of another. After policies have been developed, they must be implemented. **Implementation** is the process of putting specific policies into operation. Ultimately, bureaucrats must convert policies on paper into policies in action. It is important to study implementation because policies do not always do what they were designed to do.

Implementation may be difficult because the policy to be carried out is not clearly stated. Policy directives to bureaucrats sometimes lack clarity and leave them with too much discretion. We noted earlier that when John Frohnmayer headed the National Endowment for the Arts, he fought legislation intended to prohibit federal funding for obscene art. After a bitter fight in Congress, a compromise required that NEA grants be restricted to works that fall within "general standards of decency." But what exactly is a "general standard of decency"? It was left to the NEA, and to an administrator hostile to the very idea of a decency standard, to figure it out.[39]

Implementation can also be problematic because of the sheer complexity of some government endeavors. Take, for example, the government's Superfund program to clean up toxic waste sites. When the EPA cleans up a site itself, the cleanup takes an average of eight years to complete. Yet, this is not a program that works badly because of malfeasance by administrators. Toxic cleanups pose complex engineering, political, and financial problems. Inevitably, regional EPA offices and key actors on the local level engage in considerable negotiations at each stage of the process.[40] The more organizations and levels of government involved, the more difficult it is to coordinate implementation.

Policymakers can create implementation difficulties by ignoring the administrative capabilities of an agency they have chosen to carry out a program. This happened in 1981 when the Reagan administration and Congress instructed the Social Security Administration to expand its review of those citizens receiving disability insurance benefits. The disability program had grown during the 1970s when eligibility requirements

Gagged with a Regulation

When the White House cannot get Congress to pass what it wants, it may try to accomplish certain of its goals through the administrative powers of a relevant agency. The Reagan administration, sympathetic to the aims of the antiabortion movement, instituted the so-called "gag rule" to stop federally funded family planning units from discussing abortion with clients. The rule was rescinded by the Clinton administration.

were broadened to take in younger people and those with shorter-term disabilities.

The increased costs associated with the changes made the program a target of the Reagan administration's effort to cut domestic spending. Eligibility reviews were increased dramatically as a means of assessing whether people were still disabled and merited continued payment of their benefits. The state agencies that carried out the reviews had been doing 20,000 to 30,000 cases a quarter. The same agencies were ordered to review 100,000 to 150,000 cases a quarter. As the number of people terminated increased, so did the legal appeals to reverse the terminations, and the backlog of unresolved cases grew sharply. With tens of thousands of individuals believing they had been unfairly removed from the disability rolls and the administrative system inundated with more cases than it could handle, the problems with the program reached crisis proportions.

The lesson of this episode was that policymakers were so eager to cut costs that they made wholly unrealistic assumptions about the administrative capacities of the state agencies implementing the program. Because those agencies were given a huge increase in work without a significant increase in resources to hire additional people, they inevitably buckled under the expanded case load.[41]

Obstacles to effective implementation can create the impression that nothing the government does succeeds, but programs can and do work. Problems in implementation demonstrate why patience and continual analysis are necessary ingredients of successful policymaking. To return to a term we used earlier, implementation is by its nature an incremental process, in which trial and error eventually lead to policies that work.

REFORMING THE BUREAUCRACY: MORE CONTROL OR LESS?

As we saw at the outset, organization matters. How bureaucracies are designed directly affects how effective they are in accomplishing their tasks.[42] People in government constantly tinker with the structure of bureaucracies, trying to find ways to improve their performance. Administrative reforms have taken many different approaches in recent years while criticism of government has mounted.[43] Like those before it, the Clinton administration has proposed many management changes to save the taxpayers money and to streamline the bureaucracy. Led by Vice President Al Gore, the Reinventing Government initiative encompasses eight hundred proposals, "ranging from a top-to-bottom overhaul of the civil-service system to elimination of the subsidy for mohair."[44]

A central question that overrides much of the debate over bureaucratic reform is whether we need to establish more control over the bureaucracy or less. There is no magic bullet that will work for every type of bureaucracy: Less control may be best for public schools, but the National Endowment for the Arts may need more direction by Congress if it is to retain the public's confidence. Those who advocate less government control of public policy extol the virtues of letting consumer preferences and popular opinion play more of a role in the workings of government and the economy. Those who believe that the problem is to reform government without reducing its role look for a way to enhance government performance by improving management. We will look at both broad approaches.

Deregulation

Many people believe that government is too involved in **regulation,** intervening in the natural working of business markets to promote some social goal. For example, government might regulate a market to ensure that products pose no danger to consumers. Through **deregulation,** the government reduces its role and lets the natural market forces of supply and demand take over. Conservatives have championed deregulation, because they see freedom in the marketplace as the best route to an efficient and growing economy. Indeed, nothing is more central to capitalist philosophy than the belief that the free market will efficiently promote the balance of supply and demand. Considerable deregulation took place in the 1970s and 1980s, notably in the airline, trucking, financial services, and telecommunications industries.[45]

In the case of the airlines, the Civil Aeronautics Board (CAB) had been determining fares and controlling access to routes. The justification for its regulatory efforts was that they would prevent overloads, both in the sky and at airport facilities, and would ensure some service to all parts of the nation. But regulation had a side effect: It reduced competition among the airlines, which worked to the disadvantage of consumers. Congress responded by enacting a law in 1978 that mandated deregulation of fares and routes, and the airlines became more competitive. New carriers entered lucrative markets, fares dropped, and price wars broke out. In smaller cities, which major carriers no longer were required to serve, commuter airlines offered essential services. In retrospect, government clearly had been overregulating the airline industry. Nevertheless, in the past few years there has been a trend toward dominance of the industry by a few large carriers. Open competition has forced the mergers and bankruptcies of a number of airlines, and just what the air travel market will look like in the future is unclear.

Deciding on an appropriate level of deregulation is particularly difficult for health and safety issues. Companies within a particular industry may have legitimate claims that health and safety regulations are burdensome, making it difficult for them to earn sufficient profits or compete effectively with foreign manufacturers. But the drug-licensing procedures used by the Food and Drug Administration illustrate the potential danger of deregulating such policy areas. The thorough and lengthy process the FDA uses to evaluate drugs has as its ultimate validation the thalidomide case. The William S. Merrill Company purchased the license to market this sedative, already available in Europe, and filed an application with the FDA in 1960. The company then began a protracted fight with an FDA bureaucrat, Dr. Frances Kelsey, who was assigned to evaluate the thalidomide application. She demanded that the company abide by all FDA drug-testing requirements, despite the fact that the drug was already in use in other countries. She and her superiors resisted pressure from the company to bend the rules a little and expedite approval. Before Merrill had conducted all the FDA tests, news came pouring in from Europe that some women who had taken thalidomide during pregnancy were giving birth to babies without arms, legs, or ears. Strict adherence to government regulation protected Americans from the same tragic consequences.

Nevertheless, the pharmaceutical industry has been highly critical of the FDA, claiming that the licensing procedures are so complex that drugs of great benefit are kept from the marketplace for years, while people suffering from a particular disease are denied access to new treatments. Manufacturers claim that there is a "drug lag," citing the fact that many more new medicines are introduced in Great Britain than in the United States. They have encouraged the FDA to adopt faster procedures to save the industry substantial research and development costs and to speed valuable drugs into the hands of seriously ill Americans. The FDA has resisted doing anything that would compromise what it sees as necessary precautions.

In recent years, however, the AIDS epidemic has brought about some concessions from the FDA. Although AIDS is incurable, drugs have been found to help patients deal with various symptoms and to lengthen their lives. The FDA has issued new rules expediting the availability of experimental drugs, and more generally, the FDA has adopted a somewhat speedier timetable for clinical tests of new drugs.[46]

Monitoring, Accountability, and Responsiveness

There is substantial sentiment to make government smaller by reducing government supervision of various industries and business activities. Yet, reducing government's regulatory role can entail serious risks. Nowhere are those risks more evident than in the collapse of the savings and loan industry.

Savings and loan institutions, which were primarily designed to provide mortgages for a growing housing market, were tightly regulated by the federal government. As the financial markets became much more complex and much more competitive, and the need for savings and loans to provide

It Might Have Been Better if Big Government Had Been a Little Bit Bigger

The Savings and Loan crisis illustrates the tradeoff between the desire to reduce government and the desire to have government protect citizens from unfair or fraudulent business practices.

Among the major reasons for the collapse of so many S&Ls was that after deregulation, there were too few government auditors to monitor the risky investments and shady business dealings that came to characterize the industry. However, these worried depositors, waiting outside their failed bank, came out all right. The Federal Deposit Insurance Corporation (FDIC) reimbursed them for the money they had in the bank.

mortgages lessened, a good case was made for loosening the reins on the industry so that it could compete more effectively in the marketplace. Between 1980 and 1983, Congress approved a number of changes that significantly deregulated savings and loans. For example, Congress lifted the ceiling on the amount of interest savings and loans could pay on deposits, thus enabling them to attract deposits that were going to other types of financial institutions. Subsequently, they attracted considerably more money, but the money cost them a lot more in interest and thus had to earn much more when lent out. Legislation also expanded the range of investments available to the savings and loans, allowing them to make loans for commercial real estate, for example. In addition, insurance on deposits was raised from $40,000 to $100,000.

While these changes were being made, the Reagan administration refused to allow the Federal Home Loan Bank Board, which then supervised the industry, to hire the bank examiners it felt it needed to monitor the health of the individual savings and loans. The administration was trying to shrink the size of government and did not believe that so much money should be spent to police business practices. As the real estate market cooled off, the savings and loans got into serious trouble. So many commercial real estate developers ran into problems and could not repay their loans that many savings and loans plunged into insolvency. The federal bailout of the failed savings and loans will cost taxpayers hundreds of billions of dollars.

The savings and loan debacle illustrates the tension between trying to reduce the size and costs of government and the continuing need for accountability and monitoring.[47] Two constant functions of government are to audit what it is doing and to protect the integrity of business markets. When government deemphasizes those roles, it takes the risk that taxpayers' money may be squandered and that people will be taken advantage of in the marketplace. Ironically, when waste, fraud, and abuse surface, the calls for reform usually involve adding new layers of bureaucracy.[48]

The conflict over how far to take deregulation reflects the traditional dilemma between freedom and order. A strong case can be made for deregulated business markets, in which free and unfettered competition benefits consumers and promotes productivity. The strength of capitalist economies comes from the ability of individuals and firms to compete freely in the marketplace, and the regulatory state places restrictions on this freedom. But without regulation, nothing ensures that marketplace participants will act responsibly.

Good management of government involves far more than auditing spending and policing markets. Bureaucracies must also strive to be responsive to the public, providing services in an efficient and accessible manner. In the past few years, a management reform program known as **total quality management (TQM)** has increasingly gotten attention. Although initially directed at improving the quality of manufacturing, it is now being adapted to organizations (such as government bureaucracies) that provide services as their "product." Some principles of TQM are listening to the customer, relying on teamwork, focusing on continually improving quality, breaking down barriers between parts of organizations, and participatory management.[49]

Most Americans believe that government has a long way to go in treating its clients like "customers." As one manual on TQM in government puts it, "When was the last time you felt like a valued customer" when you encountered a government bureaucracy?[50] Government, of course, does not have to treat people as customers, because its customers cannot go to the competition—government has a monopoly over most everything it does.

Yet in an era when people are highly antagonistic toward government and budgets are tight, government bureaucrats know they need to do better. TQM has shown some promise. After hearing a lecture on TQM, Mayor Joseph Sensenbrenner of Madison, Wisconsin, thought about the long delays the city was experiencing in getting its motor vehicles repaired. Squad cars, dump trucks, garbage trucks, and road scrapers were often unavailable while the city garage waited for a part. Because TQM preaches that managers need to break down barriers to solve problems, the mayor went to the garage himself. He talked to the parts manager and found out that the city owned 440 different models of motor vehicles in a total fleet of only 765 units. It was impossible to stock such a large inventory; repairs had to await the arrival of parts.

The mayor asked why the city owned so many different kinds of cars and trucks. The parts manager told him the city had a policy to save money by requiring the purchase of whatever appropriate vehicle had the lowest sticker price on the day it was ordered. When Sensenbrenner asked the city's central purchasing office whether the policy could be changed, the purchaser replied that the city comptroller would not allow it. The mayor went to see the comptroller, but he could not approve such a change, because the city attorney would not allow it. Sensenbrenner went to see the city attorney, who told him, "Why, of course you can do that" and told him how to make the simple changes. Once instituted, the new purchasing policy reduced the average turnaround time for car and truck repairs from nine days to three.[51]

Yet, TQM has no shortage of problems. The single most important rule of TQM is to listen to your customers in an effort to serve them better. But

---

FIGURE **13.4**   ■ **Should Government Listen to Its Customers?**

When a Washington-based think tank analyzed the allocation of resources within the Environmental Protection Agency, it found that EPA spends only about 20 percent of its funds on the pollution problems that present the most serious risks to either public health or the environment. The study concluded that EPA spending was driven by the public's perception of what was important. (Hazardous Waste Management was not ranked according to actual risk.)

Source: *Jeff Bailey and Timothy Noah, "EPA Spending Is Off Target, Study Says,"* The Wall Street Journal, *May 24, 1993, p. B1. Reprinted by permission of The Wall Street Journal, © 1993 by Dow Jones & Company, Inc. All Rights Reserved Worldwide.*

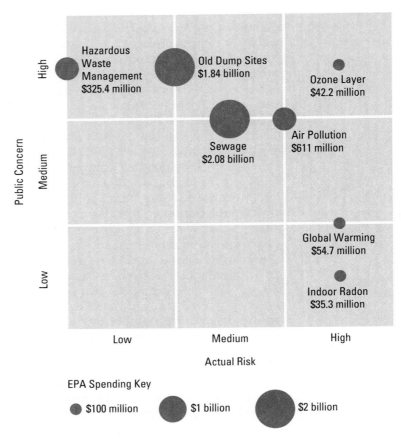

for a government agency, who is the customer? Are the Department of Agriculture's customers the farmers who want it to spend a lot of money providing them with services and subsidies, or are its customers the taxpayers who want it to minimize the amount of money they spend? TQM does not solve this basic conflict between pluralism and majoritarianism. More broadly, evidence suggests that following public opinion may lead bureaucracies to make poor choices in setting priorities. A study of the EPA shows that it favors spending money on problems characterized by high public concern rather than on problems that pose high risks to public health (see Figure 13.4).

SUMMARY

As the scope of government activity has grown during the twentieth century, so has the bureaucracy. The executive branch has evolved into a complex set of departments, independent agencies, and government corporations. The way in which the various bureaucracies are organized matters a great deal because their structure affects their ability to carry out their tasks.

Through the administrative discretion granted them by Congress, these bodies make policy decisions by making rules that have the force of law. In making policy choices, agency decision makers are influenced by their external environment, especially the White House, Congress, and interest groups. Internal norms and the need to work cooperatively with others both within and outside their agencies also influence decision makers.

The most serious charge facing the bureaucracy is that it is unresponsive to the will of the people. In fact, the White House, Congress, interest groups, and public opinion act as substantial controls on the bureaucracy. Still, to many Americans, the bureaucracy seems too big, too costly, and too intrusive. Reducing the size and scope of bureaucratic activity is difficult, because pluralism characterizes our political system. The entire executive branch may appear too large, and each of us can point to agencies that we believe should be reduced or eliminated. Yet each bureaucracy has its supporters. The Department of Agriculture performs vital services for farmers. Unions care a great deal about the Department of Labor. Scholars want the National Science Foundation protected. And home builders do not want Housing and Urban Development programs cut back. Bureaucracies survive because they provide important services to groups of people, and those people—no matter how strong their commitment to less government—are not willing to sacrifice their own needs to that commitment.

Reform plans for making the bureaucracy work better are not in short supply. Proponents of deregulation believe our economy would be more productive if we freed the marketplace from the heavy hand of government supervision. Opponents believe that deregulation involves considerable risk and that we ought to be careful in determining which markets and business practices can be subjected to less government supervision. To prevent disasters such as the thalidomide episode and the savings and loan scandal, government bureaucracies must be able to monitor the behavior of people inside and outside government, and supervise business practices in a wide range of industries. However, most people continue to believe that the overall management of bureaucracies is poor and that government needs to be more customer driven.

Key Terms

bureaucracy
bureaucrat
department
independent agency
regulatory commission
government corporation
civil service
administrative discretion
rule making

regulations
incrementalism
norms
implementation
regulation
deregulation
total quality management
  (TQM)

Selected Readings

Derthick, Martha, and Paul J. Quirk. *The Politics of Deregulation.* Washington, D.C.: Brookings Institution, 1985. An interesting look at why some industries have undergone deregulation while others have not.

  Durant, Robert F. *The Administrative Presidency Revisited.* Albany: State University of New York Press, 1992. Durant provides an excellent analysis of the effect of the Reagan revolution on one government agency, the Bureau of Land Management.

Eisner, Marc Allen. *Regulatory Politics in Transition.* Baltimore: Johns Hopkins University Press, 1993. Eisner offers an overview of regulation in different periods of American history.

Gormley, William T., Jr. *Taming the Bureaucracy: Muscles, Prayers, and Other Strategies.* Princeton, N.J.: Princeton University Press, 1989. An incisive look at competing strategies for reform, with particular emphasis on whether the instruments for change should be mandatory controls or informal persuasion.

Harris, Richard A., and Sidney M. Milkis. *The Politics of Regulatory Change.* New York: Oxford University Press, 1989. A study of how the regulatory regime of the Reagan years affected policymaking at the Federal Trade Commission and the Environmental Protection Agency.

Kerwin, Cornelius M. *Rulemaking: How Government Agencies Write Law and Make Policy.* Washington, D.C.: Congressional Quarterly, 1994. An inside look at how agencies write regulations to carry out the laws they must administer.

Osborne, David, and Ted Gaebler. *Reinventing Government.* Although it makes the process of administrative reform seem too simple, this is a valuable guide to making government more entrepreneurial and customer driven.

Wilson, James Q. *Bureaucracy.* New York: Basic Books, 1989. A comprehensive look at the operations of large, complex government organizations.

CHAPTER 14

The Courts

WHEN CHIEF JUSTICE Fred M. Vinson died unexpectedly in September 1953, Justice Felix Frankfurter commented, "This is the first solid piece of evidence I've ever had that there really is a God."[1] Frankfurter despised Vinson as a leader and disliked him as a person. Vinson's sudden death would bring a new colleague—and perhaps new hope—to the school segregation cases known collectively as *Brown* v. *Board of Education*.

The issue of segregated schools had arrived in the Supreme Court in late 1951. Although the Court had originally scheduled argument for October 1952, the justices elected a postponement until December and merged several similar cases. When a law clerk expressed puzzlement at the delay, Frankfurter explained that the Court was holding the cases for the outcome of the national election in 1952. "I thought the Court was supposed to decide without regard to the elections," declared the clerk. "When you have a major social political issue of this magnitude," replied Frankfurter, "we do not think this is the time to decide it."[2]

The justices were at loggerheads following the December argument, with Vinson unwilling to invalidate racial segregation in public education. Because the justices were still not ready to reach a decision, they scheduled the cases for reargument the following year. The justices asked the attorneys to address the history of the adoption of the Fourteenth Amendment and the potential remedies if the Court ruled against segregation.

Frankfurter's caustic remark about Vinson's death reflected the critical role Vinson's replacement would play when the Court again tackled the desegregation issue. In his first appointment to the nation's highest court, President Dwight D. Eisenhower chose California governor Earl Warren as chief justice. The president would later regret his choice.

When the Court heard the reargument of *Brown* v. *Board of Education* in late 1953, the new chief justice led his colleagues from division to unanimity on the issue of school segregation. Unlike his predecessor, Warren began the secret conference to decide the segregation issue with a strong statement: that segregation was contrary to the Thirteenth, Fourteenth, and Fifteenth Amendments to the Constitution. "Personally," remarked the new chief justice, "I can't see how today we can justify segregation based solely on race."[3] Moreover, if the Court were to uphold segregation, he argued, it could do so only on the theory that blacks were inherently inferior to whites. As the discussion proceeded, Warren's opponents were cast in the awkward position of appearing to support racism.

Central Force on the Top Court

Earl Warren (1891–1974) served as the fourteenth chief justice of the United States. A true liberal, Warren led the Supreme Court by actively preferring equality to freedom and freedom to order. The decisions occasionally brought calls from Congress for Warren's impeachment. He retired in 1968 after sixteen years of championship (critics might say controversial) activity.

Five justices were clearly on Warren's side, making six votes; two were prepared to join the majority if Warren's reasoning satisfied them. With only one clear holdout, Warren set about the task of responding to his colleagues' concerns. In the months that followed, he met with them individually in their chambers, reviewing the decision and the justification that would accompany it. Finally, in April 1954, Warren approached Justice Stanley Reed, whose vote would make the opinion unanimous. "Stan," said the chief justice, "you're all by yourself in this now. You've got to decide whether it's really the best thing for the country." Ultimately, Reed joined the others. On May 17, 1954, the Supreme Court unanimously ruled against racial segregation in public schools, signaling the end of legally created or government-enforced segregation of the races in the United States.[4]

Judges confront conflicting values in the cases before them, and in crafting their decisions, judges—especially Supreme Court justices—make policy. Their decisions become the precedents other judges use to rule in similar cases. One judge in one court makes public policy to the extent that she or he influences other decisions in other courts.

The power of the courts to shape policy creates a difficult problem for democratic theory. According to that theory, the power to make law resides only in the people or in their elected representatives. When judges undo the work of elected majorities, judges risk depriving the people of the right to make the laws to govern themselves.

Court rulings—especially Supreme Court rulings—extend far beyond any particular case. Judges are students of the law, but they remain human beings. They have their own opinions about the values of freedom, order, and equality. And although all judges are constrained by statutes and precedents from expressing their personal beliefs in their decisions, some judges are more prone than others to interpret laws in light of those beliefs.

America's courts are deeply involved in the life of the country and its people. Some courts, such as the Supreme Court, make fundamental policy decisions vital to the preservation of freedom, order, and equality. Through checks and balances, the elected branches link the courts to democracy, and the courts link the elected branches to the Constitution. But does it work? Can the courts exercise political power within the pluralist model? Or are judges simply sovereigns in black robes, making decisions independent of popular control? In this chapter, we try to answer these questions by exploring the role of the judiciary in American political life.

NATIONAL JUDICIAL SUPREMACY

Section 1 of Article III of the Constitution created "one supreme Court." The founders were divided on the need for other national courts, so they deferred to Congress the decision to create a national court system. Those who opposed the creation of national courts believed that the system would usurp the authority of the state courts.[5] Congress considered the issue in its first session and, in the Judiciary Act of 1789, gave life to a system of federal, i.e. national, courts that would coexist with the courts in each state but be independent of them. Federal judges would also be independent of popular influences, because the Constitution provided for their virtual lifetime appointment.

In the early years of the Republic, the federal judiciary was not a particularly powerful branch of government. It was especially difficult to recruit and keep Supreme Court justices. They spent much of their time as individual traveling judges ("riding circuit"); disease and poor transportation were everyday hazards. The justices met as the Supreme Court only for a few weeks in February and August.[6] John Jay, the first chief justice, refused to resume his duties in 1801, because he concluded that the Court could not muster the "energy, weight, and dignity" to contribute to national affairs.[7] Several distinguished statesmen refused appointments to the Court, and several others, including Oliver Ellsworth, the third chief justice, resigned. But a period of profound change began in 1801 when President John Adams appointed his secretary of state, John Marshall, to the position of chief justice.

Judicial Review of the Other Branches

Shortly after Marshall's appointment, the Supreme Court confronted a question of fundamental importance to the future of the new Republic: If a law enacted by Congress conflicts with the Constitution, which should prevail? The question arose in the case of *Marbury* v. *Madison* (1803), which involved a controversial series of last-minute political appointments.

Chief Justice John Marshall

John Marshall (1755–1835) clearly ranks as the Babe Ruth of the Supreme Court. Both Marshall and the Bambino transformed their respective games and became symbols of their institutions. Scholars now recognize both men as originators—Marshall of judicial review, and Ruth of the modern age of baseball.

The case began in 1801, when an obscure Federalist, William Marbury, was designated as a justice of the peace in the District of Columbia. Marbury and several others were appointed to government posts created by Congress in the last days of John Adams's presidency, but the appointments were never completed. The newly arrived Jefferson administration had little interest in delivering the required documents; qualified Jeffersonians would welcome the jobs.

To secure their jobs, Marbury and the other disgruntled appointees invoked an act of Congress to obtain the papers. The act authorized the Supreme Court to issue orders against government officials. Marbury and the others sought such an order in the Supreme Court against the new secretary of state, James Madison, who held the crucial documents.

Marshall observed that the act of Congress invoked by Marbury to sue in the Supreme Court conflicted with Article III, which did not authorize such suits. In February 1803, the Court delivered its opinion.*

Must the Court follow the law or follow the Constitution? The high Court held, through Marshall's forceful argument, that the Constitution was "the fundamental and paramount law of the nation" and that "an act of the legislature repugnant to the constitution is void." In other words, when the Constitution—the nation's highest law—conflicts with an act of the legislature, that act is invalid. Marshall's argument vested in the judiciary the power to weigh the validity of congressional acts:

> It is emphatically the province and duty of the judicial department to say what the law is. Those who apply the rule to particular cases, must of necessity expound and interpret that rule. . . . If a law be in opposition to the constitution, if both the law and the constitution apply to a particular case, so that the court must either decide that case conformably to the law, disregarding the constitution; or conformably to the constitution, disregarding the law; the court must determine which of these conflicting rules governs the case. This is the very essence of judicial duty.[8]

The decision in *Marbury* v. *Madison* established the Supreme Court's power of **judicial review**—the power to declare congressional acts invalid if they violate the Constitution.** Subsequent cases extended the power to presidential acts.[9]

Marshall expanded the potential power of the Supreme Court to equal or exceed that of the other branches of government. Should a congressional act or, by implication, a presidential act conflict with the Constitution, the Supreme Court claimed the power to declare the act void. The judiciary would be a check on the legislative and executive branches, con-

---

* *Courts publish their opinions in volumes called* reporters. *Today, the* United States Reports *is the official reporter for the U.S. Supreme Court. For example, the Court's opinion in the case of* Brown v. Board of Education *is cited as 347 U.S. 483 (1954). This means that the opinion in* Brown *begins on page 483 of Volume 347 in* United States Reports. *The citation includes the year of the decision, in this case 1954.*

Before 1875, the official reports of the Supreme Court were published under the names of private compilers. For example, the case of Marbury v. Madison *is cited as 1 Cranch 137 (1803). This means that the case is found in Volume 1, compiled by reporter William Cranch, starting on page 137, and that it was decided in 1803.*

** *The Supreme Court had earlier* upheld *an act of Congress in* Hylton v. United States *(3 Dallas 171 [1796]).* Marbury v. Madison *was the first exercise of the power of a court to* invalidate *an act of Congress.*

sistent with the principle of checks and balances embedded in the Constitution. Although Congress and the president may wrestle with the constitutionality of their actions, judicial review gave the Supreme Court the final word on the meaning of the Constitution.

The exercise of judicial review—an appointed branch's checking of an elected branch in the name of the Constitution—appears to run counter to democratic theory. In two hundred years of practice, however, the Supreme Court has invalidated fewer than 150 provisions of national law, and only a small number have had great significance for the political system.[10] Moreover, there are mechanisms to override judicial review (constitutional amendment) and to control the excesses of the justices (impeachment). In addition, the Court can respond to the continuing struggle among competing interests (a struggle that is consistent with the pluralist model) by reversing itself.

Judicial Review of State Government

The establishment of judicial review of national laws made the Supreme Court the umpire of the national government. When acts of the national government conflict with the Constitution, the Supreme Court can declare those acts invalid. But what about state laws? If they conflict with the Constitution, national laws, or treaties, can the Court invalidate them as well?

The Supreme Court answered in the affirmative in 1796. *Ware* v. *Hylton* involved a British creditor who was trying to collect a debt from the state of Virginia.[11] Virginia law canceled debts owed to British subjects, yet the Treaty of Paris (1783), in which Britain formally acknowledged the independence of the colonies, guaranteed that creditors could collect such debts. The Court ruled that the Constitution's supremacy clause (Article VI) nullified the state law.

The states continued to resist the yoke of national supremacy. Although advocates of strong states' rights conceded that the supremacy clause obligates state judges to follow the Constitution when it conflicts with state law, they maintained that the states were bound only by their own interpretation of the Constitution. The Supreme Court said no, ruling in *Martin* v. *Hunter's Lessee* that it had the authority to review state court decisions that called for the interpretation of national law.[12] National supremacy required the Supreme Court to impose uniformity on national law; otherwise, the Constitution's meaning would vary from state to state. The people, not the states, had ordained the Constitution, and the people had subordinated state power in order to establish a viable national government. In time, the Supreme Court would use its judicial review power in nearly 1,200 instances to invalidate state and local laws on issues as diverse as abortion, the death penalty, rights of the accused, and reapportionment.[13]

The Exercise of Judicial Review

The decisions in *Marbury*, *Ware*, and *Martin* established the components of judicial review:

- The power of the courts to declare national, state, and local laws invalid if they violate the Constitution

- The supremacy of national laws or treaties when they conflict with state and local laws

- The role of the Supreme Court as the final authority on the meaning of the Constitution

But this political might—the power to undo decisions of the representative branches of national and state governments—lay in the hands of appointed judges, people who were not accountable to the electorate. Did judicial review square with democratic government?

Alexander Hamilton had foreseen and tackled the problem in *Federalist* 78. Writing during the ratification debates surrounding the adoption of the Constitution (see Chapter 3), Hamilton maintained that despite the power of judicial review, the judiciary would be the weakest of the three branches of government, because it lacked "the strength of the sword or the purse." The judiciary, wrote Hamilton, had "neither FORCE nor WILL, but only judgment."

Although Hamilton was defending legislative supremacy, he argued that judicial review was an essential barrier to legislative oppression.[14] He recognized that the power to declare government acts void implied the superiority of the courts over the other branches. But this power, he contended, simply reflects the will of the people, declared in the Constitution, as compared with the will of the legislature, declared in its statutes. Judicial independence, embodied in life tenure and protected salaries, minimizes the risk of judges' deviating from the law established in the Constitution by freeing the judiciary from executive and legislative control. And if judges make a mistake, the people or their elected representatives have the means to correct the error, through constitutional amendment and impeachment.

Their life tenure does free judges from the direct influence of the president and Congress. And although mechanisms to check judicial power are in place, these mechanisms require extraordinary majorities and are rarely used. When they exercise the power of judicial review, then, judges can and occasionally do operate counter to majoritarian rule by invalidating the actions of the people's elected representatives (see Compared with What? 14.1 for a discussion of the nature of judicial review in other governments, democratic and nondemocratic). Are the courts out of line with majority sentiment? Or are the courts simply responding to pluralist demands—the competing demands of interest groups that turn to the courts to make public policy? We will return to these questions later in this chapter.

THE ORGANIZATION OF COURTS

The American court system is complex, a function in part of our federal system of government. Each state runs its own court system and no two states are identical. In addition, we have a system of courts for the national government. The national, or federal, courts coexist with the state courts (see Figure 14.1). Individuals fall under the jurisdiction of both court systems. They can sue or be sued in either system, depending mostly on what their case is about. Litigants file nearly all cases (99 percent) in state courts.[15]

COMPARED WITH WHAT? 14.1   Judicial Review

The U.S. Constitution does not explicitly give the Supreme Court the power of judicial review. In a controversial interpretation, the Court inferred this power from the text and structure of the Constitution. Other countries, trying to avoid political controversy over the power of the courts to review legislation, explicitly define that power in their constitutions. For example, Japan's constitution, inspired by the American model, went beyond it in providing that "the Supreme Court is the court of last resort with power to determine the constitutionality of any law, order, regulation, or official act."

The basic objection to the American form of judicial review is an unwillingness to place judges, who are usually appointed for life, above representatives elected by the people. Some constitutions explicitly deny judicial review. For example, Article 28 of the Belgian constitution (1831) firmly asserts that "the authoritative interpretation of laws is solely the prerogative of the Legislative authority."

The logical basis of judicial review—that government is responsible to higher authority—can take interesting forms in other countries. In some, judges can invoke an authority higher than the constitution—God, an ideology, or a code of ethics. For example, both Iran and Pakistan provide for an Islamic review of all legislation. (Pakistan also has the American form of judicial review.)

By 1985, sixty-five countries—most in Western Europe, Latin America, Africa, and the Far East—had adopted some form of judicial review. Australia, Brazil, Burma, Canada, India, Japan, and Pakistan give their courts a full measure of judicial review power. Australia and Canada come closest to the American model of judicial review, but the fit is never exact. And wherever courts exercise judicial review, undoing it calls for extraordinary effort. For example, in Australia, the Federal Parliament has no recourse after a law is declared unconstitutional by the High Court but to redraft the offending act in a manner prescribed by the court. In the United States, overruling judicial review by the Supreme Court requires a constitutional amendment.

Governments with a tradition of judicial review share some common characteristics: stability, competitive political parties, distri-

Some Court Fundamentals

Courts are full of mystery to citizens uninitiated in their activities. Lawyers, judges, and seasoned observers understand the language, procedures, and norms associated with legal institutions. Let's start with some fundamentals.

Criminal and Civil Cases.   Crime is a violation of a law that forbids or commands an activity. Criminal laws are defined in each state's penal code, as are punishments for violations. Some crimes—murder, rape, arson—are on the books of every state. Others—sodomy between consenting adults is one example—are considered crimes in certain states but not all. Because crime is a violation of public order, the government prosecutes **criminal cases.** Maintaining public order through the criminal law is largely a state and local function. Criminal cases brought by the national

bution of power (akin to separation of powers), a tradition of judicial independence, and a high degree of political freedom. Is judicial review the cause or the consequence of these characteristics? More likely than not, judicial review contributes to stability, judicial independence, and political freedom. And separation of powers, judicial independence, and political freedom contribute to the effectiveness of judicial review.

Some constitutional courts possess extraordinary power compared with the American model. The German constitutional court, for example, has the power to invalidate the failure of the lawmakers to act. In 1975, for example, the German constitutional court nullified the legalization of abortion and declared that the government had a duty to protect unborn human life against all threats. The court concluded that the constitution required the legislature to enact legislation protecting the fetus.

The Supreme Court of India offers an extreme example of judicial review. In 1967, the court held that the parliament could not change the fundamental rights sections of the constitution, even by constitutional amendment! The parliament then amended the constitution to secure its power to amend the constitution. The Supreme Court upheld the amendment but declared that any amendments that attacked the "basic structure" of the constitution would be invalid. In India, the Supreme Court is supreme.

Switzerland's Supreme Federal Tribunal is limited by its constitution to ruling on the constitutionality of cantonal laws (the Swiss equivalent of our state laws). It lacks the power to nullify laws passed by the national assembly. Through a constitutional initiative or a popular referendum, the Swiss people exercise the sovereign right to determine the constitutionality of federal law. In Switzerland, the people are truly supreme.

• *Sources: Henry J. Abraham,* The Judicial Process, *6th ed. (New York: Oxford University Press, 1993), pp. 291–330; Chester J. Antineau,* Adjudicating Constitutional Issues *(London: Oceana, 1985), pp. 1–6; Jerold L. Waltman and Kenneth M. Holland,* The Political Role of Law Courts in Modern Democracies *(New York: St. Martin's Press, 1988), pp. 46, 99–100; and Robert L. Hardgrave, Jr., and Stanley A. Kochanek,* India: Government and Politics in a Developing Nation, *4th ed. (New York: Harcourt Brace Jovanovich, 1986), p. 93.*

government represent only a small fraction of all criminal cases prosecuted in the United States. The national penal code is specialized. It does not cover ordinary crimes, just violations of national laws, such as tax fraud or possession of controlled substances banned by Congress.

The definition of *crime* rests with the legislative branch. And the definition is dynamic, that is, it is subject to change. For example, desktop publishing has given a big boost to the counterfeiting of stock certificates, bank checks, purchase orders, even college transcripts. As a result, government has made it illegal to own computers and laser printers for counterfeiting purposes.

Courts decide both criminal and civil cases. **Civil cases** stem from disputed claims to something of value. Disputes arise from accidents, contractual obligations, and divorce, for example. Often, the parties disagree over tangible issues (the possession of property, the custody of children),

FIGURE 14.1 ■ The Federal and State Court Systems, 1993

The federal courts have three tiers: district courts, courts of appeals, and the Supreme Court. The Supreme Court was created by the Constitution; all other federal courts were created by Congress. Most litigation occurs in state courts. The structure of state courts varies from state to state; usually, there are minor trial courts for less serious cases, major trial courts for more serious cases, intermediate appellate courts, and supreme courts. State courts were created by state constitutions.

Sources: National Center for State Courts, "State Court Caseload Statistics," Annual Report, 1992 *(Williamsburg, Va.: National Center for State Courts, 1994); Administrative Office of the United States Courts, Statistics Division, Analysis and Reports Branch; Lee Epstein, Jeffrey A. Segal, Harold J. Spaeth, and Thomas G. Walker,* The Supreme Court Compendium *(Washington, D.C.: Congressional Quarterly, Inc., 1994), pp. 70–73; Clerk's Office, Supreme Court of the United States.*

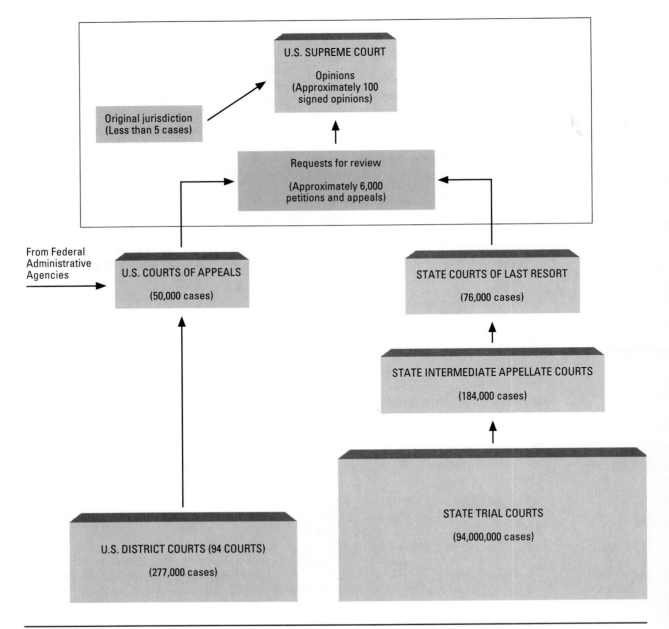

but civil cases can involve more abstract issues, too (the right to equal accommodations, damages for pain and suffering). The government can be a party to civil disputes, called on to defend or to allege wrongs.

Procedures and Policymaking. Most civil and criminal cases never go to trial. In a criminal case, a defendant's lawyer and a prosecutor will **plea bargain,** which means they will negotiate the severity and number of charges to which the defendant will plead guilty in return for a reduction in the more serious charges or for a promise to seek less severe punishment. In a civil case, one side may be using a lawsuit as a threat to exact a concession from the other. Often, the parties settle their dispute. Less frequently, cases end with **adjudication,** a court judgment resolving the parties' claims and ultimately enforced by the government. When trial judges adjudicate cases, they may offer written reasons to support their decisions. When the issues or circumstances of cases are novel, judges may publish **opinions,** explanations justifying their rulings.

Judges make policy in two different ways. Occasionally, in the absence of legislation, they use rules from prior decisions. We call this body of rules the **common,** or **judge-made, law.** The roots of the common law lie in the English legal system. Contracts, property, and torts (an injury or wrong to the person or property of another) are common-law domains. The second area of judicial lawmaking involves the application of statutes enacted by legislatures. The judicial interpretation of legislative acts is called *statutory construction.* The application of a statute is not always clear from its wording. To determine how a statute should be applied, judges first look for the legislature's intent, reading reports of committee hearings and debates. If these sources do not clarify the statute's meaning, the court does so. With or without legislation to guide them, judges look to the relevant opinions of higher courts for authority to decide the issues before them.

The federal courts are organized in three tiers, as a pyramid. At the bottom of the pyramid are the **U.S. district courts,** where litigation begins. In the middle are the **U.S. courts of appeals.** At the top is the U.S. Supreme Court. To *appeal* means to take a case to a higher court. The courts of appeals and the Supreme Court are appellate courts; with few exceptions, they review cases that have been decided in lower courts. Most federal courts hear and decide a wide array of civil and criminal cases.

The U.S. District Courts

There are ninety-four federal district courts in the United States. Each state has at least one district court, and no district straddles more than one state.[16] In 1993, 554 full-time federal district judges received almost 277,000 new criminal and civil cases.[17]

The district courts are the entry point for the federal court system. When trials occur in the federal system, they take place in the federal district courts. Here is where witnesses testify, lawyers conduct cross-examinations, and judges and juries decide the fate of litigants. More than one judge may sit in each district court, but each case is tried by a single judge, sitting alone. Federal magistrates assist district judges, but they lack independent judicial authority. In 1993, there were 345 full-time magistrates.

A Great Justice

Oliver Wendell Holmes, Jr. (1841–1935) is a towering figure in American Law. Born to a prominent Boston family, Holmes became a fervent abolitionist and served coura- geously with the Twentieth Massachusetts Volunteers in the Civil War. Holmes was seriously wounded three times. He was a distinguished scholar, a state judge, and a Supreme Court Justice. His considerable ability hardly dimmed with age, though he served on the high Court until he was ninety-one. Holmes's opinions were remarkable for his poetic gift of metaphor, his brevity, and his freedom from legal jargon. He was said to employ a simple rule of thumb when judging the constitu- tionality of legislation. Asked Holmes: "Does it make you puke?"

Sources of Ligitation.   Today, the authority of U.S. district courts ex- tends to

- criminal cases authorized by national law (for example, robbery of a na- tionally insured bank or interstate transportation of stolen securi- ties),

- civil cases brought by individuals, groups, or government that allege vi- olation of national law (for example, failure of a municipality to imple- ment pollution-control regulations required by a national agency),

- civil cases brought against the national government (for example, a ve- hicle manufacturer sues the motor pool of a government agency for its failure to take delivery of a fleet of new cars), and

- civil cases between citizens of different states when the amount in con- troversy exceeds $50,000 (for example, when a citizen of New York sues a citizen of Alabama in a United States district court in Alabama for damages stemming from an auto accident that occurred in Alabama).

The U.S. Courts of Appeals

All cases resolved by final judgments in the U.S. district courts and all decisions of federal administrative agencies can be appealed to one of the thirteen U.S. courts of appeals. These courts, with a corps of 158 full-time judges, received fifty thousand new cases in 1993.[18] Each appeals court hears cases from a geographic area known as a *circuit.* The U.S. Court of Appeals for the Seventh Circuit, for example, is located in Chicago; it hears appeals from the U.S. district courts in Illinois, Wisconsin, and Indiana. The United States is divided into twelve circuits.*

Appellate Court Proceedings.   Appellate court proceedings are public, but they usually lack courtroom drama. There are no jurors, witnesses, or cross-examinations; these are features only of the trial courts. Appeals are based strictly on the rulings made and procedures followed in the trial courts. Suppose, for example, that in the course of a criminal trial, a U.S. district judge allows the introduction of evidence that convicts a defendant but was obtained in questionable circumstances. The defendant can appeal on the ground that the evidence was obtained in the absence of a valid search warrant and so was inadmissible. The issue on appeal is the admissibility of the evidence, not the defendant's guilt or innocence. If the appellate court agrees with the trial judge's decision to admit the evidence, the conviction stands. If the appellate court disagrees with the trial judge and rules that the evidence is inadmissible, the defendant must be retried without the incriminating evidence or be released.

It is common for litigants to try to settle their dispute while it is on appeal. For example, when Pennzoil won an $11 billion state court judgment against Texaco Oil Company in 1985 (the dispute was over Texaco's questionable purchase of another company), settlement discussions began immediately. Texaco settled with Pennzoil in 1988 for $3 billion. Occasionally, litigants abandon their appeals for want of resources or resolve. Most of the time, however, appellate courts adjudicate the cases.

The courts of appeals are regional courts. They usually convene in panels of three judges to render judgments. The judges receive written arguments known as **briefs** (which are also sometimes submitted in trial courts). Often, the judges hear oral arguments and question the lawyers to probe their arguments.

Precedents and Making Decisions.   Following review of the briefs and, in many appeals, oral argument, the three-judge panel will meet to reach a judgment. One judge attempts to summarize the panel's views, although each judge remains free to disagree with the reasons or with the judgment. When an appellate opinion is published, its influence can reach well beyond the immediate case. For example, a lawsuit turning on the meaning of the Constitution produces a ruling that then serves as a **precedent** for subsequent cases; that is, the decision becomes a basis for deciding similar cases in the same way. Although district judges sometimes publish their

---

* *The thirteenth court, the U.S. Court of Appeals for the Federal Circuit, is not a regional court; it specializes in appeals involving patents, contract claims against the national government, and federal employment cases.*

opinions, it is the exception rather than the rule. At the appellate level, however, precedent requires that opinions be written.

Decision making according to precedent is central to the operation of our legal system, providing continuity and predictability. The bias in favor of existing decisions is captured by the Latin expression *stare decisis,* which means 'let the decision stand.' But the use of precedent and the principle of stare decisis do not make lower court judges cogs in a judicial machine. "If precedent clearly governed," remarked one federal judge, "a case would never get as far as the Court of Appeals: the parties would settle."[19]

Judges on the courts of appeals direct their energies to correcting errors in district court proceedings and interpreting the law (in the course of writing opinions). When judges interpret the law, they often modify existing laws. In effect, they are making policy. Judges are politicians in the sense that they exercise political power, but the black robes that distinguish judges from other politicians signal constraints on their exercise of power.

Uniformity of Law.   Decisions by the courts of appeals ensure a measure of uniformity in the application of national law. For example, when similar issues are dealt with in the decisions of different district judges, the decisions may be inconsistent. The courts of appeals harmonize the decisions within their region so that laws are applied uniformly.

The regional character of the courts of appeals undermines uniformity somewhat, because the courts are not bound by the decisions of other circuits. A law in one court of appeals may be interpreted differently in another. For example, the Internal Revenue Code imposes identical tax burdens on similar individuals. But thanks to the regional character of the courts of appeals, national tax laws may be applied differently throughout the United States. The percolation of cases up through the federal system of courts virtually guarantees that, at some point, two or more courts of appeals, working with similar sets of facts, are going to interpret the same law differently. However, the problem of conflicting decisions in the intermediate appellate courts can be corrected by review in the Supreme Court, where policymaking, not error correcting, is the paramount goal.

THE SUPREME COURT

Above the west portico of the Supreme Court building are inscribed the words EQUAL JUSTICE UNDER LAW. At the opposite end of the building, above the east portico, are the words JUSTICE THE GUARDIAN OF LIBERTY (see Feature 14.1). The mottos reflect the Court's difficult task: achieving a just balance among the values of freedom, order, and equality. Consider how the values came into conflict in two controversial issues the Court has faced in recent years.

Flag burning as a form of political protest pits the value of order—the government's interest in maintaining a peaceful society—against the value of freedom—the individual's right to vigorous and unbounded political expression. In the recent flag-burning cases (1989 and 1990), the Supreme Court affirmed constitutional protection for unbridled political expression, including the emotionally charged act of desecrating a national symbol.[20]

School desegregation pits the value of equality—equal educational opportunities for minorities—against the value of freedom—the right of parents to send their children to neighborhood schools. In *Brown v. Board of Education,* the Supreme Court carried the banner of racial equality by striking down state-mandated segregation in public schools. The decision helped launch a revolution in race relations in the United States. The justices recognized the disorder their decision would create in a society accustomed to racial bias, but in this case, equality clearly outweighed freedom. Twenty-four years later, the Court was still embroiled in controversy over equality when it ruled that race could be a factor in university admissions (to diversify the student body), in the *Bakke* case.[21] In securing the equality of blacks, the Court then had to confront the charge that it was denying the freedom of whites to compete for admission.

The Supreme Court makes national policy. Because its decisions have far-reaching effects on all of us, it is vital that we understand how it reaches those decisions. With this understanding, we can better evaluate how the Court fits within our model of democracy.

Access to the Court

There are rules of access that must be followed to bring a case to the Supreme Court. Also important is a sensitivity to the interests of the justices. The idea that anyone can take a case all the way to the Supreme Court is true only in theory, not fact.

The Supreme Court's cases come from two sources. A few (one case in 1994[22]) arrive under the Court's **original jurisdiction,** conferred by Article III, Section 2, of the Constitution, which gives the Court the power to hear and decide "all Cases affecting Ambassadors, other public Ministers and Consuls, and those in which a State shall be Party." Cases falling under the Court's original jurisdiction are tried and decided in the Court itself; the cases begin and end there. For example, the Court is the first and only forum in which legal disputes between states are resolved. The Court hears few original jurisdiction cases today, however, usually referring them to a special master, often a retired judge, who reviews the parties' contentions and recommends a resolution that the justices are free to accept or reject.

Most cases enter the Supreme Court from the U.S. Courts of Appeals or the state courts of last resort. This is the Court's **appellate jurisdiction.** These cases have been tried, decided, and reexamined as far as the law permits in other federal or state courts. The Court exercises judicial power under its appellate jurisdiction only because Congress gives it the authority to do so. Congress may change (and, perhaps, eliminate) the Court's appellate jurisdiction. This is a powerful but rarely used weapon in the congressional arsenal of checks and balances.

Litigants in state cases who invoke the Court's appellate jurisdiction must satisfy two conditions: First, the case must reach the end of the line in the state court system. Litigants cannot jump at will from state to national arenas of justice. Second, the case must raise a **federal question,** an issue covered under the Constitution, federal laws, or treaties. However, even most cases that meet these conditions do not reach the High Court. Since 1925, the Court has exercised substantial (today, nearly complete) control over its **docket,** or agenda (see Figure 14.2). The Court selects a handful of cases (about 100) for consideration from the six thousand or

FEATURE 14.1

■ The Marble Palace

The Supreme Court of the United States sits east of the Capitol in a building designed both to embrace the majesty of the law and to elevate its occupants to the status of Platonic guardians. The Corinthian-style marble building was completed in 1935 at a cost of $10 million. Until it settled in its permanent home, the Court had occupied makeshift, hand-me-down quarters in nearly a dozen places (including two taverns) since its first session in February 1790.

Each justice has a suite of offices, including space for several law clerks—top graduates from the nation's elite law schools, who serve for a year or two.

The courtroom is 82 feet by 91 feet, with a 44-foot-high ceiling and twenty-four columns of Italian marble. The room is dominated by marble panels, which were sculpted by Adolph A. Weinman. Directly above the mahogany bench, which is angled so that all the justices can see and hear one another, are two marble figures depicting Majesty of Law and Power of Government. A tableau of the Ten Commandments is between the figures.

The Court begins its official work year on the first Monday of October, known as the October Term. During its public sessions, when appeals are argued or the justices announce opinions, the court mar-shal (dressed in a cutaway) pounds the gavel at exactly 10:00 A.M., directs everyone in the courtroom to stand, and announces:

> The honorable, the chief and the associate justices of the Supreme Court of the United States: Oyez. Oyez. Oyez. All persons having business before the honorable, the Supreme Court of the United States, are admonished to draw near and give their attention, for the Court is now sitting. God save the United States and this honorable Court.

Then the justices enter in black robes from behind a velvet curtain. In the front is the chief justice; the other justices follow in order of seniority.

Contrary to popular impression, most of the 100 or so cases that the Court hears annually do not involve provocative constitutional issues. The Constitution provides for the Supreme Court to hear cases "arising under . . . the laws of the United States." These cases call for the interpretation of federal statutes, which may or may not be interesting to the public at large.

Oral argument is usually limited to thirty minutes for each side. Few attorneys argue appeals regularly before the Court, so the significance of the moment can overwhelm even seasoned advocates. The jus-

more requests filed each year. For the vast majority of the cases left unreviewed by the Court, the decision of the lower court stands. No explanations accompany cases that are denied review, so they have little or no value as court rulings.

The Court grants review only when four or more justices agree that a case warrants full consideration. This unwritten rule is known as the **rule of four.** With advance preparation by their law clerks, who screen petitions and prepare summaries, all nine justices make these judgments at secret conferences held twice a week. During the conferences, justices vote on previously argued cases and consider which new cases to add to the docket. The chief justice circulates a "discuss list" of worthy petitions. Cases on the list are then subject to the rule of four. Since the retirement of Justice William J. Brennan in 1990, no justice personally scans requests for review. The clerks review and summarize the petitions.[23]

tices constantly question the attorneys, attempting to poke holes in every argument.

Sometimes the intensity of an argument before the court was too much for a lawyer to endure. Solicitor General Stanley Reed once fainted while arguing a case before his brethren-to-be. One day a private practitioner completely lost the thread of his argument and began to babble incoherently. [Chief Justice Charles Evans] Hughes tried to aid him by asking simple questions about the case. Seeing that this further bewildered the lawyer, Hughes took the brief and completed the argument that counsel was unable to make. . . .

There were other occasions when the utmost restraint was necessary to maintain the dignity of the court. . . . A New York attorney argued so vehemently that his false teeth popped out of his mouth. With amazing dexterity he scooped up the errant dentures almost before they hit the counsel's table in front of him and flipped them back into his mouth, with scarcely a word interrupted. Not a smile ruffled the dignity of the bench, but the Justices' pent-up mirth broke into gales of laughter when they reached safe havens of privacy.*

* *Merlo J. Pusey,* Charles Evans Hughes, *vol. 2. (New York: Macmillan, 1951), pp. 674–675.*

• *Source:* Congressional Quarterly's Guide to the U.S. Supreme Court, *2d ed. (Washington: Congressional Quarterly, 1990),. pp. 739–740, 780–781. Reprinted by permission.*

The Solicitor General

Why does the Court decide to hear certain cases but not others? The best evidence scholars have adduced suggests that agenda-setting depends on the justices, who vary in their decision making, and on the issues raised by the cases. Occasionally, justices will weigh the ultimate outcome of a case when granting or denying review. At other times, justices will grant or deny review based on disagreement among the lower courts or because delay in resolving the issues would impose alarming economic or social costs.[24] The solicitor general plays a vital role in the Court's agenda setting.

The **solicitor general** represents the national government before the Supreme Court. Appointed by the president, the solicitor general is the third-ranking official in the U.S. Department of Justice (after the attorney general and deputy attorney general). President Bill Clinton's choice for

**The Supreme Court,
1994 Term:
The Starting Lineup**

*The justices of the Supreme
Court of the United States,
pictured in uniform from left
to right. Sitting: Antonin
Scalia, John Paul Stevens,
William H. Rehnquist (chief
justice), Sandra Day
O'Connor, and Anthony M.
Kennedy. Standing: Ruth
Bader Ginsburg, David H.
Souter, Clarence Thomas, and
Stephen G. Breyer.*

FIGURE **14.2**   ■ **Access to and Decision Making in the U.S.
Supreme Court**

*State and national appeals courts churn
out thousands of decisions each year.
Only a fraction ends up on the Supreme
Court's docket. This chart sketches the
several stages leading to a decision from
the high Court.*

*Sources: Administrative Office of the United
States Courts, Statistics Division, Analysis and
Reports Branch; Lee Epstein, Jeffrey A. Segal,
Harold J. Spaeth, and Thomas G. Walker,* The
Supreme Court Compendium *(Washington, D.C.:
Congressional Quarterly, Inc., 1994), pp. 70–73.*

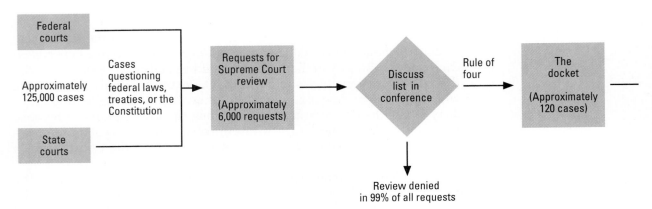

the position was Yale law school professor Drew Days. His duties include determining whether the government should appeal lower court decisions; reviewing and modifying, when necessary, the briefs filed in government appeals; and deciding whether the government should file an **amicus curiae brief*** in any appellate court.[25] His objective is to create a cohesive program for the executive branch in the federal courts.

Solicitors general play two different, occasionally conflicting, roles. First, they are advocates for the president's policy preferences; second, as an officer of the Court, they traditionally defend the institutional interests of the national government. Sometimes, the institutional interests prevail. For example, the Reagan administration was committed to returning power to the states. But Solicitor General Rex E. Lee argued for the exercise of national power in his defense of a national law that set wage requirements for a city-owned mass transit system. In a sharp blow to the administration, the Court held that the Constitution places no specific limit on congressional power to interfere in state and local affairs.[26]

Solicitors general usually act with considerable restraint in recommending to the Court that a case be granted or denied review. By recommending only cases of general importance, they increase their credibility and their influence. Lee, who was solicitor general from 1981 to 1985, acknowledged in an unusually candid interview that he had refused to make arguments that members of the Reagan administration had urged on him: "I'm not the pamphleteer general; I'm the solicitor general. My audience is not 100 million people; my audience is nine people. . . . Credibility is the most important asset that any solicitor general has."[27]

By contrast, President Bush's solicitor general, Kenneth Starr, reluctantly but vigorously argued that the justices should uphold an act of Congress designed to curb flag burning, although the Court had struck down a similar Texas law the year before. "There was no doubt at all in my mind that the constitutionality of the statute could appropriately be defended," recalled Starr. "Once Congress passes a law, our duty is to defend

---

* *Amicus curiae is Latin for 'friend of the court.' Amicus briefs can be filed with permission of the court. They allow groups and individuals who are not parties to the litigation but have an interest in it to influence the court's thinking and, perhaps, its decision.*

Decision-making process

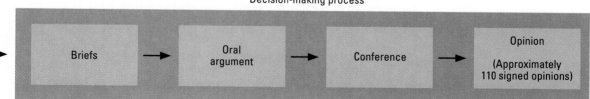

Briefs → Oral argument → Conference → Opinion (Approximately 110 signed opinions)

it. That is perhaps the most fundamental duty of this office."[28] Starr lost; the Court struck down the prohibition.

Solicitors general are a "formidable force" in the process that results in the Supreme Court's agenda.[29] Their influence in bringing cases to the Court and arguing them there has earned them the informal title of "the tenth justice."

Decision Making

Once the Court grants review, attorneys submit written arguments (briefs). Oral arguments, limited to thirty minutes for each side, usually follow. From October through April, the justices spend four hours a day, five or six days a month, hearing arguments. The justices like crisp, concise, and conversational presentations; they disapprove of attorneys who read from a prepared text. Some justices are aggressive and relentless questioners who frequently interrupt the lawyers; others are more subdued. In a recent free speech case, an attorney who offered an impassioned plea on the facts of the case was soon "awash in a sea of judicial impatience that at times seemed to border on anger. . . . 'We didn't take this case to determine who said what in the cafeteria,' " snapped one justice.[30]

Court protocol prohibits justices from addressing one another directly during oral argument, but justices often debate obliquely through the questions they pose to the attorneys. The justices reach no collective decision at oral argument. They reach a tentative decision only after they have met in conference.

Our knowledge of the dynamics of decision making on the Supreme Court is all secondhand. What evidence we have suggests that the assignment lately calls for a tough ego (see Feature 14.2). Only the justices attend the Court's Wednesday and Friday conferences. By tradition, the justices first shake hands, a gesture of harmony. The chief justice then begins the presentation of each case with a combined discussion and vote, followed in order of seniority by the discussion and vote of the other justices. Justice Antonin Scalia, who joined the Court in 1986, remarked that "not much conferencing goes on." By *conferencing,* Scalia meant efforts to persuade others to change their views by debating points of disagreement. "To call our discussion of a case a conference," he said, "is really something of a misnomer. It's much more a statement of the views of each of the nine Justices, after which the totals are added and the case is assigned" for an opinion.[31]

How do the justices decide how to vote on a case? According to some scholars, legal doctrines and previous decisions explain their votes. This explanation, which is consistent with the majoritarian model, anchors the justices closely to the law and minimizes the contribution of their personal values. This view is embodied in the concept of **judicial restraint,** which maintains that legislators, not judges, should make the laws. Other scholars contend that the value preferences and resulting ideologies of the justices provide a more powerful interpretation of their voting.[32] This view is embodied in the concept of **judicial activism**, which maintains that judges should interpret laws loosely, using their power to promote their preferred social and political goals (see Feature 14.3). Judicial activism, which is consistent with the pluralist model, sees the justices as

FEATURE **14.2**

■ Name Calling in the Supreme Court: When the Justices Vent Their Spleen, Is There a Social Cost?

The Supreme Court begins business on the first Monday in October. Refreshed and renewed, the justices shake hands in good fellowship and sit down around the conference table to begin the work of the new term. The vituperative and personal tone that marked some of the major opinions of recent terms, however, raises the question whether the justices will be able to look one another in the eye, let alone get back to work.

What do you say to someone after you have told her in public that her views are "irrational" and "cannot be taken seriously"? (Justice Antonin Scalia to Justice Sandra Day O'Connor in Webster v. Reproductive Health Services, the Missouri abortion case.) Or after you have accused someone of "an Orwellian rewriting of history"? (Justice Anthony M. Kennedy to Justice Harry A. Blackmun in County of Allegheny v. American Civil Liberties Union, the Pittsburgh case that permitted the government to display a Hanukkah menorah but barred a Nativity scene.) Or after you have dismissed someone's opinions as "a regrettably patronizing civics lecture"? (Chief Justice William H. Rehnquist to Justice William J. Brennan, Jr., in Texas v. Johnson, the flag-burning case.)

The questions go beyond the Court's mood to its credibility. Unlike the other branches, which replenish their political capital periodically when officeholders face the voters, the Court's credibility depends on the public's belief that its members are engaged in principled judging rather than personal one-upmanship.

While this is hardly the first, or even the most, stressful period in the Court's history—it was Justice Oliver Wendell Holmes who described the Supreme Court half a century ago as "nine scorpions in a bottle"—the 1988 Term was the nastiest in years. Can the venom that was splattered across the pages of opinions really fade in the summer sun like so much disappearing ink?

It may not be easy to rattle Justice O'Connor. A former clerk for another Justice expressed doubt the other day that Justice O'Connor was particularly perturbed by Justice Scalia's verbal slings.

Shortly after Justice Scalia joined the Court in 1986, the ex-clerk recalled, the Justices met to discuss a pending case called Johnson v. Santa Clara County, which concerned the legality of an affirmative action program intended to benefit women. Justice Scalia treated his new colleagues to a 15-minute lecture on the evils of affirmative action, particularly affirmative action for women. When he finished, Justice O'Connor smiled and, addressing him by his nickname, said, "Why, Nino, how do you think I got my job?" Her eventual opinion supported the program; Justice Scalia attacked it in a long dissent.

Students of the Court note that even when it is running smoothly, it has not been a very collegial place in recent years. A generation has passed since Chief Justice Earl Warren cajoled his colleagues to produce the unanimous opinion that marked the end of the era of segregation. Scholars now view the unanimity of Brown v. Board of Education as an indispensable element that gave the decision its moral weight.

"The country holds an ideal of the Court as a place where people sit down and reason together," [said] Martha Minow, a Harvard law professor who clerked on the Court.... "That's not true now even in the best of times. It's really nine separate courts. The Justices lead separate, even isolated lives. They deal with each other only in quite formalized settings. They vote the way they want to and then retreat to their own chambers."

With law clerks serving as ambassadors between the Justices' chambers, "the Justices have learned to run a Court quite well without talking to one another," another ex-clerk said.

The machinery works well enough to weather stormy periods like this one. The Court can get by. Can it also inspire and lead? That is a question as important as any asked in the briefs now accumulating . . . and only the Justices have the answer.

• *Source: Linda Greenhouse, "At the Bar," New York Times, 28 July 1989, p. 21. Copyright © 1989 by The New York Times Company. Reprinted by permission.*

FEATURE 14.3

■ Judicial Restraint and Judicial Activism

The terms *judicial restraint and judicial activism* describe the relative assertiveness of judicial power. Judges are said to exercise judicial restraint when they hew closely to statutes and previous cases in reaching their decisions. Judges are said to exercise judicial activism when they are apt to interpret existing laws and rulings more loosely and to interject their own values in court decisions.

Judges acting according to an extreme model of judicial restraint would decide nothing at all, deferring to the superiority of other government institutions in construing the law. Judges acting according to an extreme model of judicial activism would be an intrusive and ever-present force that dominated other government institutions. Actual judicial behavior lies somewhere between the two extremes.

In recent history, many activist judges have tended to opt for equality over freedom in their decisions, a tendency that has linked the concept of judicial activism with liberalism. However, there is no necessary connection between judicial activism and liberalism. If judges interpret existing statutes and precedents more loosely in favor of order over freedom, they are still activists—conservative activists.

actively promoting their value preferences. In a recent study of the legal versus the ideological approach to judicial voting, the legal model required tempering by political forces and the ideological approach required legal constraints. These shortcomings suggest an integrated model of decision making that takes into account both law and politics to explain judicial decisions.[33]

A Power Player . . .

Antonin Scalia, the 103d justice appointed to the Supreme Court, began his tenure in 1986 after four years as a federal appellate court judge. The confirmation hearings and subsequent Senate vote on his appointment were remarkably unanimous for this most conservative justice. Scalia has lived up to his reputation as a brilliant scholar, using his personal computer to write incisive, and occasionally scornful, opinions.

Judgment and Argument.   The voting outcome is the **judgment,** the decision on who wins and who loses. Justices often disagree, not only on winners and losers but also on the reasons for their judgments. This should not be surprising, given nine independent minds and issues that can be approached in several ways. Voting in the conference does not end the work or resolve the disagreements. Votes remain tentative until the Court issues an opinion announcing its judgment.

After voting, the justices in the majority must draft an opinion setting out the reasons for their decision. The **argument** is the kernel of the opinion, its logical content, as distinct from facts, rhetoric, and procedure. If all justices agree with the judgment and the reasons supporting it, the opinion is unanimous. Agreement with a judgment, but for different reasons than those set forth in the majority opinion, is called a **concurrence.** Or a justice can **dissent** if she or he disagrees with a judgment. Both concurring and dissenting opinions may be drafted in addition to the majority opinion.

The Opinion.   After the conference, the chief justice writes the majority opinion or assigns that responsibility to another justice in the majority. If the chief justice is not in the majority, the writing or assignment of responsibility rests with the most senior associate justice in the majority. The assigning justice may consider several factors in allocating the crucial opinion-writing task: workload, expertise, public opinion, and, above all, the author's ability to hold the majority together. (Remember, at this point, votes are only tentative.) If the drafting justice holds an extreme view on the issues in a case and is not able to incorporate the views of more moderate colleagues, those justices may withdraw their votes. On the other hand, assigning a more moderate justice to draft an opinion could weaken the argument on which the opinion rests. Opinion-writing assignments can also be punitive. Justice Harry Blackmun once commented, "If

. . . And a Junior Member of His Team

*Supreme Court justices use recent law school graduates as short-term clerks. Here, Larry Lessig, one of Scalia's four clerks, divides his time between one of the thousands of petitions for review that arrive at the Court each year and the final draft of a dissent by Scalia concerning the length of time a person can be held in custody without a hearing. The Court majority established a forty-eight-hour limit; Scalia argued that the limit should be set at twenty-four hours (*County of Riverside v. McLaughlin *[1991]).*

one's in the doghouse with the Chief [former Chief Justice Warren Burger], he gets the crud."[34]

Opinion writing is the justices' most critical function. It is not surprising, then, that they spend much of their time drafting opinions. The justices usually call on their law clerks—top graduates of the nation's elite law schools—to help them prepare opinions and carry out other tasks. The commitment can be daunting. Justice Blackmun's four clerks typically worked twelve hours a day, seven days a week. They wrote detailed memos outlining the facts and issues in each appeal, they prepared memos for each case before oral argument, and they prepared draft opinions that Blackmun eventually completed. According to one close Court observer, the clerks shoulder much of the writing responsibility for most of the justices.[35]

On the occasion of his eightieth birthday, after more than thirty years of service on the Court, Justice William J. Brennan, Jr., offered a rare account of the process of preparing and exchanging memoranda and drafts that leads to a final opinion: "It's startling to me every time I read these darned things to see how much I've had in the way of exchanges and how the exchanges have resulted in changes of view both of my own and of colleagues. And all of a sudden at the end of the road, we come up with an agreement on an opinion of the Court."[36]

The writing justice distributes a draft opinion to all the justices; the other justices read it, then circulate criticisms and suggestions. An opinion may have to be rewritten several times to accommodate colleagues who remain unpersuaded by the draft. Justice Felix Frankfurter was a perfectionist; some of his opinions went through thirty or more drafts. Justices can change their votes, and perhaps alter the judgment, up until the decision is officially announced. And the justices announce their decisions only when they are ready. Often, the most controversial cases pile up as the coalitions on the Court vie for support or sharpen their criticisms. When the Court announces decisions, the justices who have written opinions read or summarize their views in the courtroom (see Feature 14.4). Printed and electronic copies of the opinions, known as *slip opinions*, are then distributed to interested parties and the press.

Justices in the majority frequently try to muffle or stifle dissent in order to encourage institutional cohesion. Since the mid-1940s, however, unity has been more difficult to obtain.[37] Gaining agreement from the justices today is akin to negotiating with nine separate law firms. It may be more surprising that the justices ever agree. Nevertheless, the justices must be keenly aware of the slender foundation of their authority, which rests largely on public respect. That respect is tested whenever the Court ventures into areas of controversy. Banking, slavery, and Reconstruction policies embroiled the Court in controversy in the nineteenth century. Freedom of speech and religion, racial equality, and the right of privacy have led the Court into controversy in this century.

Strategies on the Court

The Court is more than the sum of its formal processes. The justices exercise real political power. If we start with the assumption that the justices are attempting to stamp their own policy views on the cases they review, we should expect typical political behavior from them. Cases that reach

FEATURE 14.4

Supremely Sheltered

More than almost any other public officials, the people who embody the Supreme Court put themselves on display day after day. A Senator may visit the Senate floor to cast a vote or read a speech, but the chamber is often nearly deserted even when the Senate is in session.

In the Court, by contrast, every public session is a working session, requiring the Justices to perform without a safety net. Power and vulnerability exist side by side. No aides hand the Justices follow-up questions to ask lawyers; no chairman gavels a recess when things get sticky. The atmosphere is businesslike. The Justices make nothing so clear as that every second counts. Showmanship is disfavored; when an inexperienced lawyer makes a florid presentation, a chill almost visibly settles on the bench.

An argument session can be an occasion for enlightenment when the lawyers are skilled. But sometimes they are not; or the Justices are distracted, domineering, or rude; or the argument just gets off on the wrong foot. . . .

The Justices are not only on view, they are accountable. They explain themselves. Congress and the White House can put off decisions indefinitely; entire agendas sink without a trace. But the court publicly disposes of everything on its docket, every petition, every motion. Every case argued in a term gets some resolution that term.

Issuing decisions is a bureaucratic function in most courts, handled by a faceless clerk's office. But at the Supreme Court, the author of a majority opinion announces it personally.

The announcements are rarely high drama, but they are riveting in their modest way. For example, Chief Justice Rehnquist's announcements of decisions in criminal cases almost invariably recount the crime in all its excruciating detail. On he goes in a conversational tone: the date, scene, weapon, everyone's names, fact after damning fact. His presentation makes clear that what matters most to the Chief Justice is that a crime has been committed. Someone should have to pay.

Back when liberal Justices occasionally . . . got to make these announcements, their emphasis was the opposite. An announcement by Justice William J. Brennan Jr. would leave listeners virtually in the dark about who did what to whom. But no one would come away uninformed about why some part of the Bill of Rights made the conviction invalid. . . .

- *Source: Linda Greenhouse, "Endpaper: Life and Times," New York Times Magazine, 7 March 1993, p. 84. Copyright © 1993 by The New York Times Company. Reprinted by permission.*

the Supreme Court's docket pose difficult choices. Because the justices are grappling with conflict on a daily basis, they probably have well-defined ideologies that reflect their values. Scholars and journalists have attempted to pierce the veil of secrecy that shrouds the Court from public view and analyze the justices' ideologies.[38]

The beliefs of most justices can be located on the two-dimensional model of political values discussed in Chapter 1 (see Figure 1.2). Liberal justices, such as John Paul Stevens and Ruth Bader Ginsburg, choose freedom over order and equality over freedom. Conservative justices—Antonin Scalia and Clarence Thomas, for example—choose order over freedom and freedom over equality. The choices translate into policy preferences as the justices struggle to win votes and retain coalitions.

May I Have This Dance?

Ruth Bader Ginsberg became the nation's 107th Supreme Court Justice in August 1993. Chief Justice William H. Rehnquist administered the judicial oath of office and then shared the limelight on the Court plaza with his new colleague.

As in any group of people, the justices also vary in intellectual ability, advocacy skills, social graces, temperament, and the like. For example, Chief Justice Charles Evans Hughes (1930–1941) had a photographic memory and came to each conference armed with well-marked copies of Supreme Court opinions. Few justices could keep up with him in debate. Then as now, justices argue for the support of their colleagues, offering information in the form of drafts and memoranda to explain the advantages and disadvantages of voting for or against an issue. And justices make occasional, if not regular, use of friendship, ridicule, and appeals to patriotism to mold their colleagues' views.

A justice might adopt a long-term strategy of influencing the appointment of like-minded colleagues in order to marshal additional strength on the Court. Chief Justice (and former President) William Howard Taft, for example, bombarded President Warren G. Harding with recommendations and suggestions whenever a Court vacancy was announced. Taft was especially determined to block the appointment of anyone who might side with the "dangerous twosome," Justices Oliver Wendell Holmes and Louis D. Brandeis. Taft said he "must stay on the Court in order to prevent the Bolsheviki from getting control."[39]

The Chief Justice

The chief justice is only one of nine justices, but he has several important functions based on his authority.[40] Apart from his role in docket-control decisions and his direction of the conference, the chief justice can also be a social leader, generating solidarity within the group. Sometimes, a chief justice can embody intellectual leadership. Finally, the chief justice can provide policy leadership, directing the Court toward a general policy position. Perhaps only John Marshall could lay claim to social, intellectual, and policy leadership. (Docket control did not exist during Marshall's time.) Warren E. Burger, who resigned as chief justice in 1986, was reputed to be a lackluster leader in all three areas.[41]

When presiding at the conference, the chief justice can control the discussion of issues, although independent-minded justices are not likely to acquiesce to his views. At the end of the conference on *Brown* v. *Board of Education*, for example, Chief Justice Warren had six firm votes for his position, that segregated public schools were unconstitutional. By April 1954, only one holdout remained, and he eventually joined the others. Warren's patriotic appeals had made both the decision and the opinion unanimous.[42]

JUDICIAL RECRUITMENT	Neither the Constitution nor national law imposes formal requirements for appointment to the federal courts. Once appointed, district and appeals judges must reside in the district or circuit to which they are appointed.

The president appoints judges to the federal courts, and all nominees must be confirmed by the Senate. Congress sets, but cannot lower, a judge's compensation. In 1994, salaries were

Chief justice of the Supreme Court	$171,500
Associate Supreme Court justices	164,100
Courts of appeals judges	141,700
District judges	133,600
Magistrates	122,912

State courts operate somewhat similarly. Governors appoint judges in more than half the states. In many of these states, voters decide whether judges should be retained in office. Other states select their judges by partisan, nonpartisan, or (rarely) legislative election.[43] In some states, nominees must be confirmed by the state legislature. Contested elections for judgeships are unusual. In Chicago, where judges are elected, even highly publicized and widespread criminal corruption in the courts in the 1980s failed to unseat incumbents. Most voters paid no attention whatsoever.

The Appointment of Federal Judges

The Constitution states that federal judges hold their commissions "during good Behaviour," which in practice means for life.* A president's judicial appointments, then, are likely to survive his administration, a kind of political legacy. The appointment power assumes that the president is free to identify candidates and appoint judges who favor his policies. President

---

* Only eleven federal judges have been impeached. Of these, seven have been convicted in the Senate and removed from office. Three judges were removed by impeachment in the Senate in the 1980s. In 1992, Alcee Hastings became the first such judge to serve in Congress.

Chicago Justice

From the age of four, Bertina Lampkin accompanied her father, a criminal defense attorney, to court. Today, she is a judge in Cook County, Illinois, assigned to night narcotics court. "I don't think there is a better job. I love to hear the arguments. If the lawyers come prepared and give good arguments, it is the best day I can have." (Anne Keegan, "Women on the Bench," Chicago Tribune Magazine, *12 May 1991, p. 11.)*

Franklin Roosevelt had appointed nearly 75 percent of all the sitting federal judges by the end of his twelve years in office. In contrast, President Ford appointed fewer than 13 percent in his three years in office. And Presidents Reagan and Bush together appointed more than 60 percent of all federal judges.

Judicial vacancies occur when sitting judges resign, retire, or die. Vacancies also arise when Congress creates new judgeships to handle increasing caseloads. In both cases, the president nominates a candidate, who must be confirmed by the Senate. The president has the help of the Justice Department, which screens candidates before the formal nomination, subjecting serious contenders to FBI investigation. The department and the Senate vie for control in the appointment of district and appeals judges.

The "Advice and Consent" of the Senate.   For district and appeals vacancies, the appointment process hinges on the nominee's acceptability to the senior senator in the president's party from the state in which the vacancy arises. The senator's influence is greater for appointments to district court than for appointments to the courts of appeals.

This practice, called **senatorial courtesy,** forces presidents to share the nomination power with members of the Senate. The Senate will not confirm a nominee who is opposed by the senior senator from the nominee's state, if that senator is a member of the president's party. The Senate does not actually reject the candidate. Instead, the chairman of the Senate Judiciary Committee, which reviews all judicial nominees, will not schedule a confirmation hearing, effectively killing the nomination.

Although the Justice Department is still sensitive to senatorial prerogatives, senators can no longer submit a single name to fill a vacancy. The department searches for acceptable candidates and polls the appropriate senator for her or his reaction to them. President Bush asked Republican senators to seek more qualified female and minority recommendations. Bush made progress in developing a more diverse bench of judges, and President Clinton is accelerating the change.[44]

The Senate Judiciary Committee conducts a hearing for each judicial nominee. The chairman exercises a measure of control in the appointment process that goes beyond senatorial courtesy. If a nominee is objectionable to the chairman, he or she can delay a hearing or hold up other appointments until the president and the Justice Department find an alternative. Such behavior does not win a politician much influence in the long run, however. So committee chairmen are usually loathe to place obstacles in a president's path, especially when they may want presidential support for their own policies and constituencies.

The American Bar Association.   The American Bar Association (ABA), the biggest organization of lawyers in the United States, has been involved in screening candidates for the federal bench since 1946.[45] Its role is defined by custom, not law. At the president's behest, the ABA's Standing Committee on the Federal Judiciary routinely rates prospective appointees, using a four-value scale ranging from "exceptionally well qualified" to "not qualified."

Presidents do not always agree with the committee's judgment, in part because its objections can mask disagreements with a candidate's political views. Occasionally, a candidate deemed "not qualified" is nominated and even appointed, but the overwhelming majority of appointees to the federal bench since 1946 has had the ABA's blessing.

Recent Presidents and the Federal Judiciary

President Jimmy Carter had two objectives in his judicial appointments. First, Carter wanted to base judicial appointments on merit, to appoint judges of higher quality than had his predecessors. Whether he succeeded is a question that only time and scholarship can answer. But he did meet his second objective, to make the judiciary more representative of the general population. Carter appointed substantially more blacks, women, and Hispanics to the federal bench than did any of his predecessors or his immediate successors. Here, his actions were consistent with the pluralist model, at least in a symbolic sense.

Early in his administration, it was clear that President Reagan did not share Carter's second objective. Although Reagan generally heeded senatorial recommendations for the district courts and, like Carter, held a firm rein on appointments to the appeals courts, the differences were strong. Only 2 percent of Reagan's appointments were blacks and only 8 percent were women; in contrast, 14 percent of Carter's appointments were blacks and 16 percent were women (see Figure 14.3). Four percent of Reagan judges were Hispanics, compared to 6 percent of Carter judges. Bush's record on women and minority appointments was better than Reagan's. President Clinton's appointments stand in stark contrast to his conservative predecessors'. In his first eighteen months in office, nearly a third of Clinton's judicial nominees were women and a quarter were black.

FIGURE **14.3** ■ **Diversity on the Federal Courts**

To what extent should the courts reflect the diverse character of the population? President Jimmy Carter sought to make the federal courts more representative of the population by appointing more blacks, Hispanics, and women. Ronald Reagan's appointments reflected neither the lawyer population nor the population at large. Bush's appointments were somewhat more representative than Reagan's on race and gender criteria. Clinton's nominees represent a dramatic departure in appointments, especially on race and gender.

Sources: Sheldon Goldman, "Bush's Judicial Legacy: The Final Imprint," Judicature 76, pp. 282–302 (1993); "Clinton Faces 113 Federal Court Vacancies," Daily Report for Executives (BNA), 3 January 1994 (LEXIS); Felicity Barringer, "Census Shows Profound Change in Racial Makeup for the Nation," New York Times, 11 March 1991, p. A1; U.S. Bureau of the Census, Statistical Abstract of the United States, 1993 (Washington, D.C., 1993), Table No. 644; Alliance For Justice, Judicial Selection Project Mid-Year Report 1994.

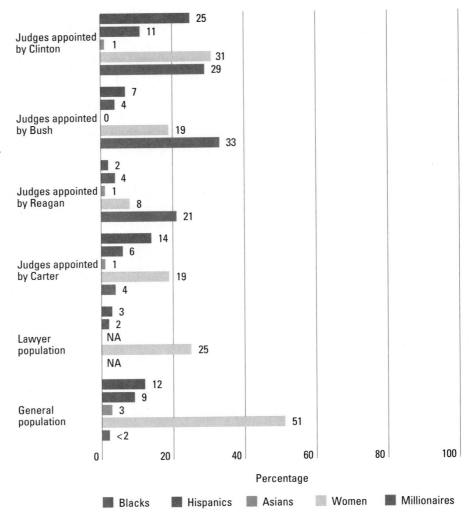

Clinton's chief judge-picker, Assistant Attorney General Eleanor Acheson, is following through on Clinton's campaign pledge to make his appointees "look like America."

It seems clear that political ideology, not demographics, lies at the heart of judicial appointments. Reagan and Bush sought nominees with particular policy preferences in order to leave their stamp on the judiciary well into the twenty-first century. The Reagan-Bush legacy is considerable: They appointed nearly two-thirds of all judges sitting today.[46] Clinton's quest for greater ethnic and gender diversity on the bench distinguishes his nominees from those of his predecessors. On another criterion, personal wealth, 29 percent of Clinton's judges possessed millionaire status, falling between Reagan's (21 percent) and Bush's (33 percent) judges. Whatever their experience or wealth, presidents are likely to appoint men and women who share similar value preferences.

Appointment to the Supreme Court

The announcement of a vacancy on the high Court usually causes quite a stir. Campaigns for Supreme Court seats are commonplace, although the public rarely sees them. Hopefuls contact friends in the administration and urge influential associates to do the same on their behalf. Some candidates never give up hope. Judge John J. Parker, whose nomination to the Court was defeated in 1930, tried in vain to rekindle interest in his appointment until he was well past the age—usually the early sixties—that appointments are made.[47]

The president is not shackled by senatorial courtesy when it comes to nominating a Supreme Court justice. However, appointment to the Court attracts more intense public scrutiny than do lower-level appointments, effectively narrowing the president's options and focusing attention on the Senate's advice and consent.

Of the 146 men and 2 women nominated to the Court, 28—or about 1 in 5—have failed to receive Senate confirmation. Only six such fumbles have come in this century, the last two during the Reagan administration. The most important factor in the rejection of a nominee is partisan politics. Thirteen candidates lost their bids for appointment because the presidents who nominated them were lame ducks: The party in control of the Senate anticipated victory for its candidate in an upcoming presidential race and sought to deny the incumbent president an important political appointment.[48] The most recent nominee to be rejected, on partisan and ideological grounds, was Judge Robert H. Bork.

Since 1950, twenty-one of twenty-three Supreme Court nominees have had prior judicial experience in federal or state courts. This "promotion" from within the judiciary may be based on the idea that a judge's previous opinions are good predictors of future opinions on the high Court. After all, a president is handing out a powerful lifetime appointment; it makes sense to want an individual who is sympathetic to his views. Federal or state court judges holding lifetime appointments are likely to state their views frankly in their opinions. In contrast, the policy preferences of high Court candidates who have been in legal practice or in political office must be based on the conjecture of professional associates or on the text of a speech to the local Rotary Club or on the floor of the legislature.

The resignation of Chief Justice Warren Burger in 1986 gave Reagan the chance to elevate Associate Justice William H. Rehnquist to the position of chief justice. Elevation within the Court to the chief justice position is not routine. Sixteen chief justices have served, but only four were elevated from positions as associate justices. Rehnquist faced stern questioning from critics during his Senate confirmation hearings. (The testimony of Supreme Court nominees is a relatively recent phenomenon; it began in 1925 when Harlan Fiske Stone was nominated to the high Court.) Reagan then nominated Antonin Scalia, who was a judge in a federal court of appeals, as Rehnquist's replacement. Rehnquist and Scalia did not try to defend their judicial records; they argued that judicial independence meant that they could not be called to account before the Senate. Both judges also ducked discussing issues that might come to the Court for fear of compromising their impartiality. Rehnquist's opponents were unable to stop his confirmation. The Republican-controlled Senate voted to confirm, 65 to 33. The same day, the Senate confirmed Scalia unanimously, 98–0.[49]

In 1987, when Justice Lewis F. Powell, Jr., resigned, Reagan had an opportunity to shift the ideological balance on the Court toward a more conservative consensus. He nominated Bork, a conservative, to fill the vacancy. Although Bork advocated judicial restraint, some of Bork's critics maintained that he was really a judicial activist draped in the robes of judicial restraint. Bork's critics charged that his true purpose, spelled out in his prodigious writings, was to advance his conservative ideology from the high Court.

The hearings concluded after several days of televised testimony from Judge Bork and a parade of witnesses. Liberal interest groups formed a temporary, anti-Bork coalition representing abortion rights, civil rights, feminist, labor, environmental, and senior citizen organizations. They put aside their disagreements and mounted a massive campaign to defeat the nomination, overwhelming conservative efforts to buttress Bork. At first, the public was undecided on Bork's confirmation; by the time the televised hearings ended, public opinion had shifted against him. Although his defeat was a certainty, Bork insisted that the Senate vote on his nomination, hoping for a sober discussion of his record. But the rancor never abated. Bork was defeated by a vote of 58–42, the biggest margin by which the Senate has ever rejected a Supreme Court nominee.

The rules of the game for appointment to the high Court appeared to have changed in 1990 when President Bush plucked David Souter from relative obscurity to replace liberal Justice William J. Brennan, Jr., who retired because of failing health. Souter fit the model of other nominees: He had extensive judicial experience as a justice on the New Hampshire Supreme Court and had recently been appointed to the federal court of appeals. But there was one significant difference: Souter was a "Stealth" candidate. His views on provocative topics were undetectable, because he had written little and spoken less on privacy, abortion, religious liberty, and equal protection. To elicit his views, some members of the Senate Judiciary Committee tried sparring with Souter at his confirmation hearings; he successfully avoided or deflected the most controversial topics. Souter was confirmed by the Senate, 90–9.

In 1991, George Bush nominated a black conservative judge, Clarence Thomas, to replace ailing Thurgood Marshall.[50] Thomas weathered days of questioning from the Senate Judiciary Committee. He declined to express opinions about policies or approaches to constitutional interpretation, which stymied his opponents. Thomas's nomination seemed assured until a last-minute witness, Professor Anita Hill, came forward with charges that Thomas had harassed her sexually when she worked for him ten years earlier.

A transfixed nation watched the riveting testimony of Hill, then Thomas, and a parade of corroborating witnesses. The coverage preempted soap operas and competed for World Series viewers. Thomas's critics heaved charges of sexism; his champions leveled charges of racism. After a marathon hearing, the committee failed to unearth convincing proof

Supreme Court nominee Clarence Thomas proved a substantial target for criticism from liberals frustrated by successive conservative judicial appointments during the Reagan and Bush presidencies.

of Hill's allegations. In the end, the Senate voted 52 to 48 to confirm Thomas's nomination.[51]

President Clinton made his mark on the Court in 1993 when Associate Justice Byron R. White announced his retirement. Clinton chose Ruth Bader Ginsburg for the vacancy; she was an active civil rights litigator, a law professor, and a federal judge. Some Court watchers described her as the Thurgood Marshall of women's rights because of her tireless efforts to alter the legal status of women. In the 1970s, she argued several key cases in the Supreme Court. Ginsburg's Senate confirmation hearing revealed little of her constitutional philosophy beyond her public record. Some Republican senators tried to encourage specificity in her broad affirmation of constitutional principles. Ginsburg declined the implicit invitation to reveal her constitutional value preferences. She cruised through to a 96–3 confirmation vote in the Senate.

Justice Harry Blackmun's resignation in 1994 gave Clinton a second opportunity to leave his imprint on the Court. After six weeks of deliberation, Clinton chose federal appellate judge Stephen G. Breyer for the coveted appointment. Breyer's moderate pragmatic views made him a consensus candidate. He sailed through tame confirmation hearings to take his place as the 108th justice.

THE LEGAL PROFESSION

We have noted that judges bring their beliefs, values, and experiences to bear on their judicial responsibilities. We have argued that the judiciary is a vital link between law and politics. It follows that the legal profession is the raw material from which that link is forged. To better understand judges and the power they wield, we have to understand lawyers and the nature of their craft.[52]

Growth of the Profession

Today, the number of lawyers in the United States exceeds 755,000.[53] This translates to one lawyer for every 340 people. Thirty years ago, there was one lawyer for every seven hundred people. The rate at which the legal profession is growing will probably continue to outpace the rate of population growth through the end of the century.

Once a bastion of white men, the legal profession has undergone profound change in gender and, to a lesser extent, in minority composition. More than 43 percent of law students today are women, and nearly 17 percent are minority group members.[54]

Legal careers remain popular despite a real downturn in the demand for legal talent. Why is a career in law so popular? We know that in 1988 the average salary of experienced lawyers in private practice was $110,000. The figure for all lawyers, whatever their experience, would probably be much lower, certainly well below the $108,000 average salary of physicians. But lawyers' salaries are still substantially greater than those of many other professionals'.[55] Salaries for newly minted lawyers heading for big New York City law firms approached $82,000 in 1993.[56] Some firms offered additional bonuses for clerkship experience in the federal courts and state supreme courts. The glamor of legal practice contributes to the attraction of its financial rewards.

What Lawyers Do

Lawyers perform four major functions:

- **Lawyers counsel.** This means that lawyers offer advice, even if it is advice their clients would prefer not to hear. Of course, lawyers regularly counsel clients before and during negotiation and litigation.

- **Lawyers negotiate.** This means that they mediate competing interests, aiming for results that will prove advantageous to their clients and, if possible, satisfactory to their opponents. Because the vast majority of cases settle out of court, attorneys necessarily spend a significant portion of their time negotiating.

- **Lawyers draft documents.** This is probably their most intellectually challenging function, because the objective is to compose documents (such as a contract or a will) to which all parties will agree and that will withstand any challenges.

- **They litigate.** This is the skill most people associate with lawyers. Ironically, only a small fraction of all lawyers devotes much time to courtroom activities. In fact, the majority of attorneys never ventures into a courthouse except to file legal papers with a clerk.[57]

In the endless debate over the role of lawyers in society, some scholars claim that lawyers are social architects, trained to design their vision of a better society. An alternative view proposes that we regard lawyers "not as the architects of society but as its janitors."[58] After all, lawyers tidy up and repair the wear and tear that society creates. Whether lawyers are architects or janitors, demand for the legal profession's services seem boundless. One explanation is that the materialism and individualism of American culture encourage disputes. Furthermore, federalism gives us separate legal systems for each state plus the national government; thus, the structure of American government provides a number of judicial outlets. Also, advertising by law firms can now create demand for legal services, acting as tinder for disputes that might otherwise die on their own. Finally, the principles of separation of powers and of checks and balances help generate lawsuits by making governing difficult and sometimes impossible.

When political institutions act, they often are forced to compromise, deflecting critical issues to the courts. Pluralist democracy permits groups to press their interests on, and even challenge, the government. The expression of group demands in a culture that encourages lawsuits thrusts on the courts all manner of disputes and interests. Is it any wonder that America finds work for the many lawyers it trains?[59]

U.S. Attorneys

The Justice Department is responsible for the faithful execution of the laws. The attorney general, who is a member of the president's cabinet, supervises and directs the activities of the department. The regional administrators of national law enforcement are the ninety-four U.S. attorneys, who are appointed by the president with the advice and consent of the Senate. Unlike federal judges, these appointees serve at the pleasure of the president and are expected to relinquish their positions when the government changes hands.

There is a U.S. attorney in each federal judicial district. Their staffs of assistant attorneys vary in size with the amount of litigation in the district. U.S. attorneys have considerable discretion, which makes them powerful political figures. Their decision to prosecute or not affects the wealth, freedom, rights, and reputation of the individuals and organizations in the districts. There is evidence of substantial variation in prosecution policies from district to district. In a study of the offices of seven U.S. attorneys, investigators found that each office prosecuted certain offenses, such as bank fraud, when a minimum amount of money was involved, but the amount varied a good deal from office to office for the same offense.[60]

U.S. attorneys are political appointees who often harbor political ambitions.[61] Their position commands media attention and can serve political goals. For example, Republican William F. Weld is a former U.S. attorney who ran successfully for governor in Massachusetts in 1990. Weld earned a reputation—and valuable visibility—as a tough prosecutor, notching his briefcase with convictions of members of Boston's organized crime family and of top Democrats in Boston city government. Facing a more conservative Democratic opponent, Weld appeared moderate, enabling him to eke out a victory in a decidedly Democratic state.

THE CONSEQUENCES OF JUDICIAL DECISIONS

Lawsuits are the tip of the iceberg of disputes; most disputes never surface in the courts. Of all the lawsuits begun in the United States, the overwhelming majority ends without a court judgment. Many civil cases are settled, or the parties give up, or the courts dismiss the claims, because they are beyond the legitimate bounds of judicial resolution. Most criminal cases end with a plea bargain, the defendant's admission of guilt in exchange for a less severe punishment. Only about 10 percent of criminal cases in the federal district courts are tried; an equally small percentage of civil cases is adjudicated.

Furthermore, the fact that a judge sentences a criminal defendant to ten years in prison or that a court holds a company liable for $11 billion in damages does not guarantee that the defendant or the company will give up either freedom or assets. In the case of the criminal defendant, the grounds for appeal following trial and conviction are well traveled and, if nothing else, serve to delay the day when no alternative to prison remains. In civil cases, the immediate consequence of a judgment may also be an appeal, which delays the day of reckoning.

Supreme Court Rulings: Implementation and Impact

When the Supreme Court makes a decision, it relies on others to implement it, to translate policy into action. How a judgment is implemented rests in good measure on how it was crafted. Remember that the justices, in preparing opinions, are working to hold their majorities together, to gain greater, if not unanimous, support for their arguments. This forces them to compromise in their opinions, to moderate their arguments, and introduces ambiguity into many policies they articulate. Ambiguous opinions affect the implementation of policy. For example, when the Supreme Court issued its order in 1955 to desegregate public school facilities "with all deliberate speed,"[62] judges who opposed the Court's policy dragged their feet in implementing it. In the early 1960s, the Supreme Court prohibited prayers and Bible reading in public schools. Yet, state court judges and attorneys general reinterpreted the High Court's decision to mean that only compulsory prayer or Bible reading was unconstitutional, that state-sponsored voluntary prayer or Bible reading was acceptable.[63]

Because the Supreme Court confronts issues freighted with deeply felt social values or fundamental political beliefs, its decisions have influence beyond the immediate parties in a dispute. The Court's decision in *Roe* v. *Wade*, legalizing abortion, generated heated public reaction. The justices were barraged with thousands of angry letters. Groups opposing abortion vowed to overturn the decision; groups favoring the freedom to obtain an abortion moved to protect the right they had won. Within eight months of the decision, more than two dozen constitutional amendments had been introduced in Congress, although none managed to carry the extraordinary majority required for passage. Still, the antiabortion faction achieved a modest victory with the passage of a provision forbidding the use of national government funds for abortions except when the woman's life is in jeopardy. Since 1993, the exception includes victims of rape or incest.

Opponents of abortion have also directed their efforts at state legislatures, hoping to load abortion laws with enough regulations to discourage women from terminating their pregnancies. For example, one state required that women receive detailed information about abortions, then wait at least twenty-four hours before consenting to the procedure. The information listed every imaginable danger associated with abortion and included a declaration that fathers are liable to support their children financially. In 1989, the Court abandoned its strong defense of abortion rights. It continued to support a woman's right to abortion but now recognized the government's power to further limit the exercise of that right.[64]

Public Opinion and the Supreme Court

Democratic theorists have a difficult time reconciling a commitment to representative democracy with a judiciary that is not accountable to the electorate yet has the power to undo legislative or executive acts. The difficulty may simply be a problem for theorists, however. The policies coming from the Supreme Court, although lagging years behind public opinion, rarely seem out of line with the public's ideological choices.[65] Surveys in several controversial areas reveal that an ideologically balanced Court seldom departs from majority sentiment or the trend toward such sentiment.[66]

The evidence supports the view that the Supreme Court reflects public opinion at least as often as other elected institutions. In a comprehensive study matching 146 Supreme Court rulings with nationwide opinion polls from the mid-1930s through the mid-1980s, the Court reflected public opinion majorities or pluralities in more than 60 percent of its rulings.[67] The fit is not perfect, however. The Court parted company with public opinion in a third of its rulings. For example, the Court has clearly defied the wishes of the majority for decades on the issue of school prayer. Most Americans today do not agree with the Court's position. And so long as the public continues to want prayer in schools, the controversy will continue.

There are at least three explanations for the Court's consistency with majority sentiment. First, the modern Court has shown deference to national laws and policies, which typically echo national public opinion. Second, the Court moves closer to public opinion during periods of crisis. And, third, rulings that reflect the public view are subject to fewer changes than rulings that depart from public opinion.

Finally, the evidence also supports the view that the Court seldom influences public opinion. The Court enjoys only moderate popularity, and its decisions are not much noticed by the public. With few exceptions, there is no evidence of shifting public opinion before and after its rulings.[68]

THE COURTS AND MODELS OF DEMOCRACY

How far should judges stray from existing statutes and precedents? Supporters of the majoritarian model would argue that the courts should adhere to the letter of the law, that judges must refrain from injecting their own values into their decisions. If the law places too much (or not enough) emphasis on equality or order, the elected legislature, not the courts, can change the law. In contrast, those who support the pluralist model maintain that the courts are a policymaking branch of government. It is thus legitimate for the individual values and interests of judges to mirror group

Courtly Demeanor

The New York Court of Appeals is the highest court in the state. Although it is bound by the decisions of the U.S. Supreme Court when defining and limiting national constitutional rights, it may rely on provisions of the state constitution to extend protections to individuals beyond those granted by the Supreme Court. For example, the New York court requires police to follow stricter procedures during car searches than those implemented by the U.S. Supreme Court.

interests and preferences and for judges to consciously attempt to advance group interests as they see fit.

The argument that our judicial system fits the pluralist model gains support from a legal procedure called **class action.** Class action is a device for assembling the claims or defenses of similarly situated individuals so that they can be tried as a single lawsuit. A class action makes it possible for people with small individual claims and limited financial resources to aggregate their claims and resources in order to make a lawsuit viable. The class action also permits the case to be tried by representative parties, with the judgment binding on all. Decisions in class action suits can have broader impact than decisions in other types of cases. Since the 1940s, class action suits have been the vehicles through which groups have asserted claims involving civil rights, legislative apportionment, and environmental problems. For example, schoolchildren have sued (through their parents) under the banner of class action to rectify claims of racial discrimination on the part of school authorities, as in *Brown* v. *Board of Education.*

Abetting the class action is the resurgence of state supreme courts in fashioning policies consistent with group preferences. Informed Americans often look to the U.S. Supreme Court for the protection of their rights and liberties. In many circumstances, the expectation is correct. But state courts may serve as the staging areas for legal campaigns to change the law in the nation's highest court. They also exercise substantial influence over policies that affect citizens daily, including the rights and liberties enshrined in their state constitutions, statutes, and common law (see Politics in a Changing America 14.1).[69]

Furthermore, state judges need not look to the U.S. Supreme Court for guidance on the meaning of similar state rights and liberties. If a state court chooses to rely solely on national law in deciding a case, that case is

POLITICS IN A CHANGING AMERICA 14.1 — Finding the Right Case

 A new body of "gay rights" law is developing as judges across the country become less tolerant of government policies that discriminate against homosexuals.

The goal of gay rights lawyers is the Supreme Court, where they hope the justices will rule that the constitution protects homosexuals from discrimination.

Toward that end, activists are coordinating their legal efforts nationally and pursuing cases with the most sympathetic plaintiffs they can find. The approach is similar to the strategy behind the civil rights movement of the 1950s and 1960s and the women's movement after that.

In the past 15 months [late 1992–late 1993] the Hawaii Supreme Court opened the door to gay marriages, the Kentucky Supreme Court invalidated a law against sodomy, and a federal appeals court ruled that the military cannot exclude people solely because of homosexuality.

[In December 1993], a Colorado district judge struck down a state ballot initiative that stopped cities from writing laws that protect homosexuals from job and housing bias. The judge said the voter-approved initiative—Amendment 2—breached the Constitution's guarantee of equal protection of the laws.

"Lesbians and gay men are looking for their *Brown* v. *Board of Education*," said William B. Rubenstein, director of the ACLU's [American Civil Liberties Union] national Lesbian and Gay Rights Project, referring to the landmark 1954 opinion declaring segregation in public schools unconstitutional.

"We would very much like a Supreme Court ruling . . . saying that discrimination based on prejudice against gay people violates the Constitution," he said. "It is something we are all building towards, trying to find the right test case." . . .

Court cases are being launched across the country: over local anti-discrimination ordinances and ballot initiatives that try to stop such homosexual-sympathetic measures; pressing job discrimination complaints; and regarding privacy and family-law conflicts (for example, whether a lesbian mother is less fit than a heterosexual father to care for a child).

The significant rulings so far apply only in local contexts and individual situations, but they are creating a legal climate more favorable to homosexuals than ever before—one that eventually could influence the Supreme Court.

The gay rights legal strategy mirrors the approach taken by Thurgood Marshall and other civil rights activists in their efforts to outlaw school segregation and by Ruth Bader Ginsburg and women's advocates to persuade the justices to make it harder for governments to discriminate on the basis of sex. . . .

- *Source: Joan Biskupic, "Gay Rights Activists Seek a Supreme Court Test Case,"* Washington Post, *19 December 1993, p. A1. © 1993 The Washington Post. Reprinted with permission.*

reviewable by the U.S. Supreme Court. But a state court can avoid review by the U.S. Supreme Court by basing its decision solely on state law or by plainly stating that its decision rests on both state and federal law. If the U.S. Supreme Court is likely to render a restrictive view of a constitutional right, and the judges of a state court are inclined to a more expansive view, the state judges can use the state ground to avoid Supreme Court review. In a period when the nation's highest court is moving in a decidedly moderate direction, some state courts have become safe havens for liberal values. And individuals and groups know where to moor their policies.

The New Jersey Supreme Court has been more aggressive than most state supreme courts in following its own liberal constitutional path. It has gone further than the U.S. Supreme Court in promoting equality at the expense of freedom by prohibiting discrimination against women by private employers and by striking down the state system of public school finance, which maintained vast disparities in public education within the state. The court has also preferred freedom to order by protecting the right to terminate life-support systems and by protecting free speech against infringement.[70] The New Jersey judges have charted their own path, despite the similarity in language between sections of the New Jersey Constitution and the U.S. Constitution. The New Jersey judges have parted company with their national "cousins," even when the constitutional provisions at issue are identical.

For example, the U.S. Supreme Court ruled in 1988 that warrantless searches of curbside garbage were constitutionally permissible. Both the New Jersey Constitution and the U.S. Constitution bar unreasonable searches and seizures. Yet, in a 1990 decision expanding constitutional protections, the New Jersey court ruled that police officers need a search warrant before they can rummage through a person's trash. The court claimed that the New Jersey Constitution offers a greater degree of privacy than the U.S. Constitution. Because the decision rested on an interpretation of the state constitution, the existence of a similar right in the national charter had no bearing. New Jersey cannot act in a more restrictive manner than the guidelines established by the U.S. Supreme Court, but it can be—and is—less restrictive in its practices.[71]

When judges reach decisions, they pay attention to the views of other courts, and not just to those above them in the judicial hierarchy. State and federal court opinions are the legal storehouse from which judges regularly draw their ideas. Often the issues that affect individual lives—property, family, contracts—are grist for state courts, not federal courts. For example, when a state court faces a novel issue in a contract dispute, it will look at how other state courts have dealt with the problem. (Contract disputes are not a staple of the federal courts.) And if courts in several states have addressed an issue and the direction of the opinion is largely one-sided, the weight and authority of those opinions may move the court in that direction.[72] Courts that confront new issues with cogency and clarity are likely to become leaders of legal innovation.

State courts have become renewed arenas for political conflict with litigants, individually or in groups, vying for their policies. The multiplicity of court systems, with their overlapping state and national responsibilities, provides alternative points of access for individuals and groups to present and argue their claims. This description of the courts fits the pluralist model of government.

SUMMARY

The power of judicial review, claimed by the Supreme Court in 1803, placed the judiciary on an equal footing with Congress and the president. The principle of checks and balances can restrain judicial power through several means, such as constitutional amendment and impeachment. But restrictions on that power have been infrequent, leaving the federal courts to exercise considerable influence through judicial review and statutory construction.

The federal court system has three tiers. At the bottom are the district courts, where litigation begins and most disputes end. In the middle are the courts of appeals. At the top is the Supreme Court. The ability of judges to make policy increases as one moves up the pyramid from trial courts to appellate courts.

The Supreme Court, free to draft its agenda through the discretionary control of its docket, harmonizes conflicting interpretations of national law and articulates constitutional rights. It is helped at this crucial stage by the solicitor general, who represents the executive branch of government before the high Court. The solicitor general's influence with the justices affects their choice of cases to review.

From the nation's lawyers come the nation's judges, whose political allegiance and values are usually a necessary condition of appointment by the president. The president and senators from the same party share the power of appointment of federal district and appellate judges. The president has more leeway in the nomination of Supreme Court justices, although nominees must be confirmed by the Senate.

Courts inevitably fashion policy for each of the states and for the nation. They provide multiple points of access for individuals to pursue their preferences and so fit the pluralist model of democracy. Furthermore, the class action enables people with small individual claims and limited financial resources to pursue their goals in court, reinforcing the pluralist model.

Judges confront the original and modern dilemmas of government. The impact of their decisions can extend well beyond a single case. Some democratic theorists are troubled by the expansion of judicial power. But today's courts fit within the pluralist model and usually are in step with what the public wants.

As the U.S. Supreme Court heads in a more moderate direction, state supreme courts have become safe havens for more liberal policies on civil rights and civil liberties. The state court systems have overlapping state and national responsibilities, offering groups and individuals many access points to present and argue their claims.

Key Terms

judicial review
criminal case
civil case
plea bargain
adjudication
opinion
common (judge-made) law
U.S. District Court
U.S. Court of Appeals
brief
precedent
stare decisis
original jurisdiction
appellate jurisdiction
federal question
docket
rule of four
solicitor general
amicus curiae brief
judicial restraint
judicial activism
judgment
argument
concurrence
dissent
senatorial courtesy
class action

Selected Readings

Baum, Lawrence. *American Courts: Process and Policy.* 3d ed. Boston: Houghton Mifflin, 1994. A comprehensive review of trial and appellate courts in the United States that addresses their activities, describes their procedures, and explores the processes that affect them.

Bork, Robert H. *The Tempting of America.* New York: Free Press, 1990. This nationwide best seller offers Judge Bork's view on the current state of legal scholarship and the political agenda he claims it masks. Bork also offers his candid view of the events surrounding his unsuccessful battle for a seat on the nation's highest court.

Coffin, Frank M. *The Ways of a Judge: Reflections from the Federal Appellate Bench.* Boston: Houghton

Mifflin, 1980. A close look at the workings of a federal appellate court and the ways in which its chief judge reaches decisions.

Ely, John Hart. *Democracy and Distrust.* Cambridge, Mass.: Harvard University Press, 1980. An appraisal of judicial review that attempts to identify and justify the guidelines for the Supreme Court's application of a two-hundred-year-old constitution to conditions of modern life.

Friedman, Lawrence M. *American Law: An Introduction.* New York: Norton, 1984. A clear, highly readable introduction to the bewildering complexity of the law that explains how law is made and administered.

Jacob, Herbert. *Law and Politics in the United States.* 2nd edition. New York: HarperCollins, 1994. An introduction to the American legal system with an emphasis on links to the political arena.

O'Brien, David M. *Storm Center: The Supreme Court in American Politics.* 3d ed. New York: Norton, 1993. A primer on the Supreme Court, its procedures, personalities, and political influence.

Posner, Richard A. *The Federal Courts: Crisis and Reform.* Cambridge, Mass.: Harvard University Press, 1985. A provocative, comprehensive, and lucid analysis of the institutional problems besetting the federal courts. Written by a distinguished law professor, now a federal appellate judge.

Salokar, Rebecca Mae. *The Solicitor General: The Politics of Law.* Philadelphia: Temple University Press, 1992. A timely and well-researched empirical assessment of one of the least known but most important offices in the national government.

Wasby, Stephen L. *The Supreme Court in the Federal Judicial System.* 3d ed. Chicago: Nelson-Hall, 1988. A thorough study of the Supreme Court's internal procedures, its role at the apex of the national and state court systems, and its place in the political system.

Wice, Paul. *Judges & Lawyers: The Human Side of Justice.* New York: HarperCollins, 1991. A thoughtful overview of the legal profession based on hundreds of interviews with lawyers and judges and on courtroom observations in fifteen cities.

PART

V

Civil Liberties and Civil Rights

15 Order and Civil Liberties

THE PHOTOGRAPHS BY ROBERT MAPPLETHORPE, a critically acclaimed photographer who died in 1989, were shocking. His subjects included still lifes, celebrities, nudes, children, and models in graphic sexual poses. The technique of the photographs was flawless. The content of some disturbed and offended many viewers, who saw them as degrading, humiliating, and painful images.

An exhibition of Mapplethorpe's work traveled to several museums without incident. Then, in 1990, local officials charged Cincinnati's Contemporary Arts Center and its director with pandering obscenity and illegal use of a minor. At issue were seven photographs out of the 175 in the exhibit. Five photographs depicted homoerotic and sadomasochistic acts (one was a self-portrait of the artist with a bull whip in his rectum), which the city claimed were obscene. Two photographs showed nude or partially nude children (one captured a toddler with her dress raised and her genitals exposed), which the city contended violated laws against child pornography. If convicted, the museum faced up to $10,000 in fines and its director faced up to a year in jail and $2,000 in fines.

Cincinnati has no adult bookstores, no X-rated theaters, no peep shows, no nude dancing clubs, no massage parlors. Residents cannot buy hardcore sex magazines nor can they rent X-rated videos. Cincinnati law enforcement officials had a long history of restricting anything perceived as sexually provocative, including Broadway shows such as *Hair!* and *Oh! Calcutta.* If Cincinnati could declare such forms of expression off limits, then surely it could punish the display of photographs that it deemed offensive. In defense of social order, the city pursued a criminal prosecution.

The museum and its director—and countless others who came to their aid—responded with a vigorous defense of free expression. They maintained that the Mapplethorpe images were art and the Constitution protects artistic expression from government interference and censorship. Ultimately, a court had to decide between the conflicting values of freedom and order. (The verdict is discussed later in this chapter.)

How well do the courts respond to clashes that pit freedom against order in some cases and freedom against equality in others? Are freedom, order, or equality ever unconditional? In this chapter, we explore some value conflicts that the judiciary has resolved. You will be able to judge from the decisions in these cases whether American government has met the challenge of democracy by finding the appropriate balance between freedom and order and between freedom and equality.

No Sin in Cincinnati
Many residents of Cincinnati, Ohio, take pride in the absence of X-rated theaters and topless bars in their city; activities and forms of expression that might not raise an eyebrow in other communities are banned there. Nevertheless, not every citizen agrees with the city's self-imposed standards of conduct. Here, demonstrators show their support for the Contemporary Arts Center, which was prosecuted for exhibiting the work of photographer Robert Mapplethorpe.

The value conflicts described in this chapter revolve around claims or entitlements that rest on law. Although we concentrate here on conflicts over constitutional issues, the Constitution is not the only source of people's rights. Government at all levels can—and does—create rights through laws written by legislatures and regulations issued by bureaucracies.

We begin this chapter with the Bill of Rights and the freedoms it protects. Then we take a closer look at the role of the First Amendment in the original conflict between freedom and order. Next we turn to the Fourteenth Amendment and the limits it places on the states. Then we examine the Ninth Amendment and its relationship to issues of personal autonomy. Finally, we will examine the threat to the democratic process when judges transform policy issues into constitutional issues. In Chapter 16, we will look at the Fourteenth Amendment's promise of equal protection, which sets the stage for the modern dilemma of government: the struggle between freedom and equality.

THE BILL OF RIGHTS

You may remember from Chapter 3 that at first the framers of the Constitution did not include a list of individual liberties—a bill of rights—in the national charter. They believed that a bill of rights was not necessary, because the Constitution spelled out the extent of the national government's power. But during the ratification debates, it became clear that the omission of a bill of rights was the most important obstacle to the adoption of the Constitution by the states. Eventually, the First Congress approved twelve amendments and sent them to the states for ratification. In 1791, the states ratified ten of the twelve amendments and the nation had a bill of rights.

The Bill of Rights imposed limits on the national government but not on the state governments.* During the next seventy-seven years, litigants repeatedly pressed the Supreme Court to extend the amendments' restraints to the states, but the Court refused until well after the adoption of the Fourteenth Amendment in 1868. Before then, protection from repressive state government had to come from state bills of rights.

The U.S. Constitution guarantees Americans numerous liberties and rights. In this chapter we explore a number of them. We will define and distinguish civil liberties and civil rights. (On some occasions, we will use the terms interchangeably.) **Civil liberties** are freedoms that are guaranteed to the individual. The guarantees take the form of restraints on government. For example, the First Amendment declares that "Congress shall make no law . . . abridging the freedom of speech." Civil liberties declare what the government cannot do; in contrast, civil rights declare what the government must do or provide.

Civil rights are powers and privileges that are guaranteed to the individual and protected against arbitrary removal at the hands of the government or other individuals. The right to vote and the right to jury trial in criminal cases are civil rights embedded in the Constitution. Today, civil rights also embrace laws that further certain values. The Civil Rights Act of 1964, for example, furthered the value of equality by establishing the right to nondiscrimination in public accommodations and the right to equal employment opportunity. Civil liberties are the subject of this chapter; we discuss civil rights and their ramifications in Chapter 16.

The Bill of Rights lists both civil liberties and civil rights. When we refer to the rights and liberties of the Constitution, we mean the protections enshrined in the Bill of Rights and in the first section of the Fourteenth Amendment.[1] The list includes freedom of religion, freedom of speech and the press, the right to peaceable assembly and petition, the rights of the criminally accused, the requirement of due process, and the equal protection of the laws.

FREEDOM OF RELIGION

Congress shall make no law respecting an establishment of religion, or prohibiting the free exercise thereof.

Religious freedom was important to the colonies and later to the states. That importance is reflected in its position among the ratified amendments that we know as the Bill of Rights: first, in the very first amendment. The amendment guarantees freedom of religion in two clauses: The **establishment clause** prohibits laws establishing religion; the **free-exercise clause** prevents the government from interfering with the exer-

---

* *Congress considered more than one hundred amendments in its first session. One that was not approved would have limited the power of the states to infringe on the rights of conscience, speech, press, and jury trial in criminal cases. James Madison thought this amendment was the "most valuable" of the list, but it failed to muster a two-thirds vote in the Senate.*

Sacrificing Rights
Animal sacrifice is a central ritual in the Afro-Carribean-based religion of Santeria. The Miami suburb of Hialeah banned such sacrifices. A Santeria church in Hialeah challenged the local law. In a 1993 ruling, the Supreme Court sided with the church. Animal sacrifice for religious purposes is protected by the First Amendment free exercise clause.

cise of religion. Together, they ensure that government can neither promote nor inhibit religious beliefs or practices.

At the time of the Constitutional Convention, many Americans, especially in New England, maintained that government could and should foster religion, specifically Protestantism. However, many more Americans agreed that this was an issue for state governments, that the national government had no authority to meddle in religious affairs. The religion clauses were drafted in this spirit.[2]

The Supreme Court has refused to interpret the religion clauses definitively. The result is an amalgam of rulings, the cumulative effect of which is that freedom to believe is unlimited, but freedom to practice a belief can be limited. Religion cannot benefit directly from government actions (for example, government cannot make contributions to churches or synagogues), but it can benefit indirectly from those actions (for example, government can supply books on secular subjects for use in all schools —public, private, and parochial).

Most Americans identify with a particular religious faith, and 40 percent attend church in a typical week. The vast majority believe in God, a judgment day, and life after death. America is the most religious nation in the developed world.[3] Majoritarians might argue, then, that government should support religion. They would agree that the establishment clause bars government support of a single faith, but they might maintain that government should support all faiths. Such support would be consistent with what the majority wants and true to the language of the Constitution. In its decisions, the Supreme Court has rejected this interpretation of the establishment clause, leaving itself open to charges of undermining democracy. Those charges may be true with regard to majoritarian democracy, but the Court can justify its protection in terms of the basic values of democratic government.

The Establishment Clause

The provision that "Congress shall make no law respecting an establishment of religion" bars government sponsorship or support of religious activity. The Supreme Court has consistently held that the establishment clause requires government to maintain a position of neutrality toward religions and to maintain that position in cases that involve choices between religion and nonreligion. However, the Court never has interpreted the clause as barring all assistance that incidentally aids religious institutions.

Government Support of Religion. In 1879, the Supreme Court contended, quoting Thomas Jefferson's words, that the establishment clause erected "a wall of separation between church and state."[4] That wall was breached somewhat in 1947, when the justices upheld a local government program that provided free transportation to parochial school students.[5] The breach seemed to widen in 1968, when the Court held constitutional a government program in which parochial school students borrowed state-purchased textbooks.[6] The objective of the program, reasoned the majority, was to further educational opportunity. The students, not the schools, borrowed the books, and the parents, not the church, realized the benefits.

But in 1971, in **Lemon v. Kurtzman,** the Court struck down a state program that would have helped pay the salaries of teachers hired by parochial schools to give instruction in secular subjects.[7] The justices proposed a three-pronged test for constitutionality under the establishment clause:

- The law must have a secular purpose (such as lending books to parochial school students).

- The primary effect of the law must not be to advance or inhibit religion.

- The law must not entangle the government excessively with religion.

A law missing any prong would be unconstitutional.

The program at issue in *Lemon* failed on the last ground: To be certain that they did not include religious instruction in their lessons, the state would have to constantly monitor the secular teachers. For example, the state would be required to monitor mathematics lessons to ensure that the instruction did not reinforce religious dogma. Such supervision would entangle the government in religious activity, violating the Constitution's prohibition.

Does the display of religious artifacts on public property violate the establishment clause? In *Lynch* v. *Donnelly* (1984), the Court said no, by a vote of 5–4.[8] At issue was a publicly funded nativity scene on public property, surrounded by commercial symbols of the Christmas season such as Santa and his sleigh. While conceding that a crèche has religious significance, Chief Justice Warren E. Burger, writing for the majority, maintained that the display had a legitimate secular purpose: the celebration of a national holiday. Second, the display did not have the primary effect of benefiting religion; the religious benefits were "indirect, remote and incidental." And third, the display led to no excessive entanglement of religion and government. The justices hinted at a relaxation of the establishment clause by asserting their "unwillingness to be confined to any single test or criterion in this sensitive area." The upshot of *Lynch* was an "acknowledgment" of the religious heritage of the majority of Americans, although the Christmas holiday is a vivid reminder to religious minorities and the nonreligious of their separateness from the dominant Christian culture.

The *Lynch* decision led to a proliferation of cases testing the limits of government-sponsored religious displays. In 1989, a divided Court approved the display of a menorah while rejecting the display of a crèche.[9] The menorah appeared on the steps of the main entrance to a government building alongside a Christmas tree and a sign reading "Salute to Liberty." The crèche appeared alone in a courthouse during the Christmas season. A majority found that the crèche display violated the second prong of the *Lemon* test but could not agree on the reasons for validating the menorah display. In such circumstances, the justices become vulnerable to the charge that they serve as constitutional "interior designers," imposing their own value preferences when they cannot fully explain why one religious image passes muster but another does not.

In the latest test of the establishment clause, the Court in 1994 struck down a New York law that created a public school district for the benefit of a village of ultra-Orthodox Jews. The district's sole purpose was to provide special education in a sheltered environment for children of the Satmar Hasidim. The parents had refused to send their children to the nearby public school program for fear that their Yiddish-speaking children with their unusual deportment would make them targets of ridicule.

Justice David H. Souter wrote the majority opinion for a sharply divided bench in *Board of Education* v. *Grumet*.[10] The existence of the new district violated the principle at the heart of the Establishment Clause, declared Souter: "Government should not prefer one religion to another, or religion to irreligion."

Interestingly, the court avoided its own *Lemon* test, neither endorsing nor repudiating it. A majority of the justices have expressed doubt about the test's utility, but they evidently have not agreed on an appropriate replacement.

The cautious but fragmented approach employed by the majority suggested a new avenue for the New York State legislature. Within two weeks of the Court's decision, the legislature enacted a slightly different law to accomplish the same objective. A new legal challenge seems certain.[11]

School Prayer.   The Supreme Court has consistently equated prayer in public schools with government support of religion. In 1962, it struck down the daily reading of this twenty-two-word nondenominational prayer in New York's public schools: "Almighty God, we acknowledge our dependence upon Thee, and we beg Thy blessings upon us, our parents, our teachers, and our country." Justice Hugo L. Black, writing for a 6–1 majority, held that official state approval of prayer was an unconstitutional attempt on the part of the state to establish a religion. This decision, in *Engle* v. *Vitale,* drew a storm of protest that has yet to subside.[12]

The following year, the Court struck down a state law calling for daily Bible reading and recitation of the Lord's Prayer in Pennsylvania's public schools.[13] The district defended the reading and recitation on the grounds

Contested Rights

In 1993 students at Wingfield High School in Jackson, MS, with the approval of the principal read short nondenominational prayers over the school intercom. The school superintendent fired the principal, citing a 1962 Supreme Court ruling which banned school prayer. Hundreds of students and parents staged protests and vigils (pictured here). The principal was reinstated six months later.

that they taught literature, perpetuated traditional institutions, and inculcated moral virtues. But the Court held that the state's involvement violated the government's constitutionally imposed neutrality in matters of religion.

A new school prayer issue arose in 1992 when the Court struck down the offering of nonsectarian prayers at official public school graduations. In a 5–4 decision, the Court held that government involvement creates "a state-sponsored and state-directed religious exercise in a public school."[14] The justices said that the establishment clause means that government may not conduct a religious exercise in the context of a school event.

Thus, the Constitution bars school prayer. Does it also bar silent meditation in school? In *Wallace* v. *Jaffree* (1985), the Court struck down a series of Alabama statutes requiring a moment of silence for meditation or voluntary prayer in elementary schools.[15] In a 6–3 decision, the Court renewed its use of the *Lemon* test and reaffirmed the principle of government neutrality between religion and nonreligion. The Court found that the purpose of the statute was to endorse religion; however, a majority of the justices hinted that a straightforward moment-of-silence statute that steered clear of religious endorsements might pass constitutional muster.

In yet another response to the school prayer controversy, Congress enacted the Equal Access Act in 1984. The act declares that no public secondary school receiving federal funds may bar after-school meetings on school property by student religious or political groups if it extends the same privileges to other noncurriculum groups. In an 8–1 decision in 1990, the Court upheld the validity of the act, opening the door to the Bible Society as well as the Chess Club, and making room for the Witches' Coven too.[16]

The establishment clause creates a problem for government. Support for all religions at the expense of nonreligion seems to pose the least risk to

POLITICS IN
A CHANGING
AMERICA   **15.1**   **Freedom Versus Order: A Holiday Dilemma**

Pity the public school principal in December. With Hanukkah, Christmas, and Kwanzaa, this long last month lays a minefield of grand proportions for educators trying to acknowledge the holidays without bridging the separation of church and state.

Every decoration is fraught with peril. Every lesson and every song must pass the "does not promote religion" test. Red and green cookies? Maybe. "A Christmas Carol"? Maybe. "Silent Night"? Definitely not.

With parents who want their religion in the schools, parents who want less of some other religion in the schools, and parents who want no religion at all in the schools, school officials in the New York Metropolitan area know that come December, their phones will be jingling. They also have to deal with such cultural events as Kwanzaa, a black American holiday that celebrates family and community and is based on African harvest festivals, and the Chinese New Year, a month or so later.

"At this time of year, emotions run so high," said Ralph Lieber, superintendent of the South Orange–Maplewood School District in New Jersey. Most districts in the region try to chart a middle course though the holidays, relying on the U.S. Supreme Court and copious suggestions from parents, religious groups, and the American Civil Liberties Union (ACLU). Some districts, for example, draw heavily on a pair of 1989 Supreme Court rulings that upheld a display of a menorah next to a Christmas tree on the steps of the Pittsburgh City Hall but said a crèche standing alone at the county courthouse was unconstitutional.

The key, said William Olds, executive director of the Connecticut chapter of the ACLU, is to teach religion without celebrating it and to treat all religions and atheism equally. The policy of the West Hartford public schools, for example, is to recognize Buddhism, Christianity, Hinduism, Islam, and Judaism and their holidays without celebrating their beliefs in any way. "We do not object to the teaching of various religions in the historical sense," Olds said. "But too many school districts have used Christmas in what seems to be an attempt to teach religion instead of

social order. Tolerance of the dominant religion at the expense of other religions risks minority discontent, but support for no religion (neutrality between religion and nonreligion) risks majority discontent, as illustrated in Politics in a Changing America 15.1.

The Free-Exercise Clause

The free-exercise clause of the First Amendment states that "Congress shall make no law . . . prohibiting the free exercise [of religion]." The Supreme Court has struggled to avoid absolute interpretations of this restriction so as not to violate its complement, the establishment clause. An example: Suppose Congress grants exemptions from military service to individuals who have religious scruples against war. These exemptions could be construed as a violation of the establishment clause, because they favor some religious groups over others. But if Congress forced conscientious objectors to fight—to violate their religious beliefs—the government would run afoul of the free-exercise clause. In fact, Congress has granted

teaching about religion."

Two years ago, school officials in Voorhees, New Jersey, decided they needed a policy to guide them through the holiday season. Until that point, the district had been operating mostly on a squeaky-wheel basis. "Someone would complain about this, so we would eliminate it. Someone would complain about that, so we would eliminate it," said Geri Borbe, a spokeswoman for the district. "We were at the point where people were objecting to red and green sprinkles on cookies, and to St. Valentine's Day," she said. "And it was forming a backlash."

The school board had scarcely begun work on the policy when one member of the school-parent association issued a memo for parents interested in organizing spring parties. She suggested that to avoid problems, party designers steer clear of Easter baskets, the colors purple and yellow, and jelly beans.

"I think the jelly beans did it," Borbe said. Frustrated Christian parents held a meeting and began a petition drive. Jewish parents rallied to prevent the pendulum from swinging the other way. The issue threatened to divide the three-thousand-student district.

But in the end, the event seemed to serve as a sort of catharsis, said Nancy Siegle, a parent. It revealed tensions, people spoke their minds, and the district created a policy that seems to be working. Christmas trees are permissible; religious decorations and nativity scenes are not. Menorahs are permitted, but not the daily lighting of candles. Educators preface concerts and parties with the words *holiday* or *winter* instead of *Christmas.* "The majority feeling was that one of the reasons many parents moved into the area was because of the diverse, multicultural aspect," Siegle said. "It reassured those of us who feel strongly about having multiculturalism embraced."

Source: Kimberly J. McLarin, "Holiday Dilemma at Schools: Is That a Legal Decoration?" New York Times, 16 December 1993, p. 192. Copyright © 1993 by The New York Times Company. Reprinted by permission.

military draftees such exemptions. But the Supreme Court has avoided a conflict between the establishment and free-exercise clauses by equating religious objection to war with any deeply held humanistic opposition to it. This solution leaves unanswered a central question: Does the free-exercise clause require government to grant exemptions from legal duties that conflict with religious obligations, or does it guarantee only that the law will be applicable to religious believers without discrimination or preference?[17]

In the free-exercise cases, the justices have distinguished religious beliefs from actions based on those beliefs. Beliefs are inviolate, beyond the reach of government control. But the First Amendment does not protect antisocial actions. Consider conflicting values about saluting the flag, working on the sabbath, and using drugs as religious sacraments.

Saluting the Flag.   The values of order and religious freedom clashed in 1940, when the Court considered the first of two cases involving compulsory flag saluting in the public schools. In *Minersville School District* v.

Gobitis, a group of Jehovah's Witnesses challenged the law on the ground that the action forced them to worship graven images, which their faith forbids.[18] Order won, in an 8–1 decision. The "mere possession of religious convictions," wrote Justice Felix Frankfurter, "which contradict the relevant concerns of a political society does not relieve the citizen from the discharge of political responsibilities." The reaction in Minersville and elsewhere was brutal and swift: People jeered the Gobitises on the streets, schoolmates beat up one of the children, and local churches led a boycott of the family business. In other communities, Witnesses were forced to swallow castor oil when they refused to salute the flag; others were tarred, feathered, even castrated for following the dictates of their faith.[19]

Three years later, the Court reversed itself in **West Virginia State Board of Education v. Barnette.** This time, the Court saw a larger issue: Can an individual be forced to salute the flag against his or her will? The Court had decided *Gobitis* on the narrower issue of religious belief versus saluting the flag. In *Barnette,* the justices chose to focus instead on the broader issue of freedom of expression. In stirring language, Justice Robert H. Jackson argued in the majority opinion that no one could be compelled by the government to declare any belief:

> If there is any fixed star in our constitutional constellation, it is that no official, high or petty, can prescribe what shall be orthodox in politics, nationalism, religion, or other matters of opinion or force citizens to confess by word or act their faith therein. If there are any circumstances which permit an exception, they do not now occur to us.[20]

Working on the Sabbath.   The modern era of free-exercise thinking begins with **Sherbert v. Verner** (1963). Adeil Sherbert, a Seventh-Day Adventist, lost her mill job because she refused to work on Saturday, her sabbath. She filed for unemployment compensation and was referred to a job, which she declined, because it also required Saturday work. By declining the job, the state disqualified her from unemployment benefits. In a 7–2 decision, the Supreme Court ruled that the disqualification imposed an impermissible burden on Sherbert's free exercise of religion. The First Amendment, declared the majority, protects observance as well as belief. A neutral law that burdens the free exercise of religion is subject to **strict scrutiny.** This means that the law may be upheld only if the government can demonstrate that the law is justified by a "compelling governmental interest" and is the least restrictive means for achieving that interest.[21] And only rarely can government muster enough evidence to demonstrate a compelling interest.

The *Sherbert* decision prompted religious groups and individual believers to challenge laws that conflict with their faiths. We have seen how conflicts arise from the imposition of penalties for refusing to engage in religiously prohibited conduct. But conflicts may also arise from laws that impose penalties for engaging in religiously motivated conduct.[22]

Using Drugs as Sacrament.   Partaking of illegal substances as part of a religious sacrament forces believers to violate the law. For example, the Rastafarians and members of the Ethiopian Zion Coptic church smoke marijuana in the belief that it is the body and blood of Christ. Obviously, taking to an extreme the freedom to practice religion can be a license for illegal conduct. But even when that conduct stems from deeply held convictions, government resistance to it is understandable. The inevitable result is a clash between religious freedom and social order.

The courts used the compelling government interest test for many years and invalidated most laws subject to the test. But in 1990, the Supreme Court abruptly and unexpectedly rejected its longstanding rule, tipping the balance in favor of social order. In *Employment Division* v. *Smith*, two members of the Native American Church sought an exemption from an Oregon law that made the possession or use of peyote a crime.[23] (Peyote is a cactus that contains the hallucinogen mescaline. Native Americans have used it for centuries in their religious ceremonies.) Oregon did not prosecute the two church members for use or possession of peyote. Rather, the state rejected their applications for unemployment benefits after they were dismissed from their drug-counseling jobs for using peyote. Oregon believed it had a compelling interest in proscribing the use of certain drugs according to its own drug laws.

Justice Antonin Scalia, writing for the 6–3 majority, examined the conflict between freedom and order through the lens of majoritarian democratic thought. He observed that the Court has never held that an individual's religious beliefs excuse him or her from compliance with an otherwise valid law prohibiting conduct that government is free to regulate. Allowing exceptions to every state law or regulation affecting religion "would open the prospect of constitutionally required exemptions from civic obligations of almost every conceivable kind." Scalia cited as examples compulsory military service, payment of taxes, vaccination requirements, and child-neglect laws. Government restrictions on religion were acceptable, he argued, so long as they were not aimed at religious groups alone.

The decision brought in its wake scores of government actions infringing on religious exercise. One such case involved unauthorized autopsy. Several religions proscribe the mutilation of the human body; they view autopsy as a form of mutilation. Many Jews, Navajo Indians, and the Hmong, an immigrant group from Laos, hold this belief. For the Hmong, an autopsy means that the deceased's spirit will never be free. Yet, Rhode Island performed an autopsy on a Hmong without regard to the family's religious beliefs. Because the autopsy rule did not target a religious group, the family had no recourse against the shame of government mutilation of their loved one. The demands of social order triumphed over the spirit of religious freedom.

The political response to *Employment Division* v. *Smith* was an example of pluralism in action. An unusual coalition of religious and nonreligious groups (including the National Association of Evangelicals, the American Civil Liberties Union, the National Islamic Prison Foundation, and B'nai B'rith) organized to restore the more restrictive test of compelling government interest. At first, the coalition failed to rouse much public interest in a case involving the use of hallucinogenic drugs. But as government infringements on religious practice mounted, public interest and legislative reaction soon meshed.

Spanning the theological and ideological spectrum, the alliance established in Congress what it had lost in the Supreme Court. In 1993,

President Bill Clinton signed into law the Religious Freedom Restoration Act. The law once again requires government to satisfy the strict scrutiny standard before it can institute measures that interfere with religious practices. Voicing wonder at this alliance of groups so often at odds across religion and ideology, Clinton observed, "The power of God is such that even in the legislative process miracles can happen."[24]

FREEDOM OF EXPRESSION

Congress shall make no law . . . abridging the freedom of speech, or of the press, or the right of the people peaceably to assemble, and to petition the Government for a redress of grievances.

James Madison introduced the original versions of the speech clause and the press clause of the First Amendment in the House of Representatives in June 1789. One early proposal provided that "the people shall not be deprived of their right to speak, to write, or to publish their sentiments, and the freedom of the press, as one of the great bulwarks of liberty, shall be inviolable." That version was rewritten several times, then merged with the religion and peaceable assembly clauses to yield the First Amendment.

The original House debates on the proposed speech and press clauses are not informative. There is no record of debate in the Senate or in the states during ratification. But careful analysis of other records supports the view that the press clause prohibited only the imposition of **prior restraint**—censorship before publication. Publishers could not claim protection from punishment if works they had already published were later deemed improper, mischievous, or illegal.

The spare language of the First Amendment seems perfectly clear: "Congress shall make no law . . . abridging the freedom of speech, or of the press." Yet, a majority of the Supreme Court has never agreed that this "most majestic guarantee" is absolutely inviolable.[25] Historians have long debated the framers' intentions regarding these **free-expression clauses,** the press and speech clauses of the First Amendment. The dominant view is that the clauses confer the right to unrestricted discussion of public affairs.[26] Other scholars, examining much the same evidence, conclude that few, if any, of the framers clearly understood the clause; moreover, they insist that the First Amendment does not rule out prosecution for seditious statements (statements inciting insurrection).[27]

The Sedition Act of 1798 lends credibility to the latter claim. The act punished "false, scandalous and malicious writings against the government of the United States," seemingly in direct conflict with the free-expression clauses. President John Adams's administration used the Sedition Act to punish its political opponents for expressing contempt for the government and its officials. Thomas Jefferson and his allies attacked Adams's use of the act; they supported a broad view of the protection afforded by the First Amendment. An act of Congress later repaid the fines imposed on Adams's critics under the Sedition Act, and Jefferson, as Adams's successor, pardoned those who had been convicted and sentenced under the law.

The license to speak freely does not move multitudes of Americans to speak out on controversial issues. Americans have woven subtle restrictions into the fabric of our society: the risk of criticism or ostracism by family, peers, or employers tends to reduce the number of people who test the limits of free speech to individuals ready to bear the burdens. As Mark Twain once remarked, "It is by the goodness of God that in our country we have three unspeakably precious things: freedom of speech, freedom of conscience, and the prudence never to practice either of them."[28]

Jefferson's libertarian view remains the basis for the modern perspective on the First Amendment free-expression clauses. Today, the clauses are deemed to bar most forms of prior restraint (consistent with their initial understanding) as well as after-the-fact prosecution for political and other discourse.

The Supreme Court has evolved two approaches to the resolution of claims based on the free-expression clauses. First, government can regulate or punish the advocacy of ideas but only if it can prove that the goal is to promote lawless action and that a high probability exists that such action will occur. Second, government may impose reasonable restrictions on the means for communicating ideas, restrictions that can incidentally discourage free expression.

Suppose, for example, that a political party advocates nonpayment of personal income taxes. Government cannot regulate or punish that party for advocating tax nonpayment, because the standards of proof—that the act be directed at inciting or producing imminent lawless action and that the act be likely to produce such action—do not apply. But government can impose restrictions on the way the party's candidates communicate what they are advocating. Government can bar them from blaring messages from loudspeakers in residential neighborhoods at 3 A.M. As Feature 15.1 describes, free expression has limits when it comes to loud music.

Freedom of Speech

The starting point for any modern analysis of free speech is the **clear and present danger test,** formulated by Justice Oliver Wendell Holmes in the Supreme Court's unanimous decision in *Schenck* v. *United States* (1919). Charles T. Schenck and his fellow defendants were convicted under a federal criminal statute for attempting to disrupt World War I military recruitment by distributing leaflets claiming that conscription was unconstitutional. The government believed this behavior threatened the public order. At the core of the Court's opinion, Holmes wrote,

> The character of every act depends upon the circumstances in which it is done. . . . The most stringent protection of free speech would not protect a man in falsely shouting fire in a theatre and causing a panic. . . . The question in every case is whether the words used are used in such circumstances and are of such a nature as to create *a clear and present danger* that they will bring about the substantive evils that Congress has a right to prevent. It is a question of proximity and degree. When a nation is at war many things that might be said in time of peace are such a hindrance to its effort that their utterance will not be endured so long as men fight and that no court could regard them as protected by any constitutional right.[29] [Emphasis added.]

■ The Freedom To Be Loud

Here's a question that will strike a resonant chord with parents, apartment dwellers, and dorm residents: May government limit the volume of rock music? At issue before the U.S. Supreme Court in 1989 was the constitutionality of a New York City noise-control regulation requiring musical performances in Central Park to use a city-supplied sound system and sound technician. The regulation was a response to nearby residents' worries about excessive noise and performers' need for high-quality amplification equipment.

Rock musicians and civil libertarians objected. They claimed that the city's imposition of restrictions in a public forum interfered with their artistic creativity and their message. A lower court had held that government has the right to limit the sound level at concerts but that it must use the least restrictive means available. The court struck down the regulation, concluding that city control of sound mixing was simply too intrusive. This thunderous issue reached the Supreme Court when Big Apple officials appealed.

The justices seemed bemused at the lively oral argument. Justice Anthony Kennedy asked whether the sound technician responsible for the mix was as important as the conductor of a symphony. Leonard J. Koerner, who represented New York City, claimed the technician was just a technician. But William M. Kunstler, who represented an organiza-tion of musical groups that challenged the regulation, was of a different mind. "A conductor and the man that does the mix are very comparable," he declared. The substitution of the city's technician for the band's own was "as if the city said that we're going to put George Solti [former music director of the Chicago Symphony] in there instead of Zubin Mehta [former music director of the New York Philharmonic] because Solti plays *andante* and *dolce* and Mehta always plays loud."

Justice Antonin Scalia observed at one point that "when I was a young man occasionally I was at parties that got a little loud." Kunstler leaned forward and interjected, "Is this a confession?"

Four months later, the Court upheld the regulation in a 6–3 decision. Writing for the majority, Justice Kennedy said that "so long as the means chosen are not substantially broader than necessary to achieve the government's interest, the regulation will not be invalid simply because a court concludes that the government's interest could be adequately served by some less-speech-restrictive alternative." The government's hand now rests on the volume control. (Justice Scalia joined in the majority opinion.)

• *Sources: Linda Greenhouse, "Supreme Court Accord: Music is Loud," New York Times, 28 February 1989, Section A, p. 1; Linda Greenhouse, "High Court Upholds Noise Rule for Central Park Bandshell," New York Times, 23 June 1989, Section B, page 1; Ward v. Rock Against Racism, 491 U.S. 781 (1989).*

Because the actions of the defendants in *Schenck* were deemed to create a clear and present danger to the United States at that time, the Supreme Court upheld the defendants' convictions. The clear and present danger test helps to distinguish the advocacy of ideas, which is protected, from incitement, which is not. However, Holmes later frequently disagreed with a majority of his colleagues in applying the test.

In an often-quoted dissent in *Abrams* v. *United States* (1919), Holmes revealed his deeply rooted resistance to the suppression of ideas. The majority had upheld Jacob Abrams's criminal conviction for distributing leaflets that denounced the war and U.S. opposition to the Russian Revolution. Holmes wrote,

When men have realized that time has upset many fighting faiths, they may come to believe . . . that the ultimate good desired is better reached by free trade in ideas—that the best test of truth is the power of the thought to get itself accepted in the competition of the market, and that truth is the only ground upon which their wishes safely can be carried out. That at any rate is the theory of our Constitution.[30]

In 1925, the Court issued a landmark decision in *Gitlow* v. *New York*.[31] Benjamin Gitlow was arrested for distributing copies of a "left-wing manifesto" that called for the establishment of socialism through strikes and working-class action of any form. Gitlow was convicted under a state criminal anarchy law; Schenck and Abrams had been convicted under a federal law. For the first time, the Court held that the First Amendment speech and press provisions applied to the states through the due process clause of the Fourteenth Amendment. Still, a majority of the justices affirmed Gitlow's conviction. Justices Holmes and Louis D. Brandeis argued in dissent that Gitlow's ideas did not pose a clear and present danger. "Eloquence may set fire to reason," conceded the dissenters. "But whatever may be thought of the redundant discourse before us, it had no chance of starting a present conflagration."

The protection of advocacy faced yet another challenge in 1948, when eleven members of the Communist party were charged with violating the Smith Act, a federal law making the advocacy of force or violence against the United States a criminal offense. The leaders were convicted, although the government introduced no evidence that they had actually urged people to commit specific violent acts. The Supreme Court mustered a majority for its decision to uphold the convictions under the act, but it could not get a majority to agree on the reasons in support of that decision. The biggest bloc, of four justices, announced the plurality opinion in 1951, arguing that the government's interest was substantial enough to warrant criminal penalties.[32] The justices interpreted the threat to government to be the gravity of the advocated action "discounted by its improbability." In other words, a single soap-box orator advocating revolution stands little chance of success. But a well-organized, highly disciplined political movement advocating revolution in the tinderbox of unstable political conditions stands a greater chance of success. In broadening the meaning of "clear and present danger," the Court held that the government was justified in acting preventively rather than waiting until revolution is about to occur.

By 1969, the pendulum had swung back in the other direction: The justices began to put more emphasis on freedom. That year, in ***Brandenburg v. Ohio,*** a unanimous decision extended the freedom of speech to new limits.[33] Clarence Brandenburg, the leader of the Ohio Ku Klux Klan, had been convicted under a state law for advocating racial strife at a Klan rally. His comments, which had been filmed by a television crew, included threats against government officials.

The Court reversed Brandenburg's conviction, because the government failed to prove that the danger was real. The Court went even further and declared that threatening speech is protected by the First Amendment, unless the government can prove that such advocacy is "directed to inciting or producing imminent lawless action" and is "likely to produce such action." The ruling offered wider latitude for the expression of political ideas than ever before in the nation's history.

Symbolic Expression.   Symbolic expression, or nonverbal communication, generally receives less protection than pure speech. But the courts have upheld certain types of symbolic expression. ***Tinker v. Des Moines Independent County School District*** (1969) involved three public school students who wore black arm bands to school to protest the Vietnam War. Principals in their school district had prohibited the wearing of arm bands on the ground that such conduct would provoke a disturbance: the district suspended the students. The Supreme Court overturned the suspensions. Justice Abe Fortas declared for the majority that the principals had failed to show that the forbidden conduct would substantially interfere with appropriate school discipline:

> Undifferentiated fear or apprehension is not enough to overcome the right to freedom of expression. Any departure from absolute regimentation may cause trouble. Any variation from the majority's opinion may inspire fear. Any word spoken, in class, in the lunchroom, or on the campus, that deviates from the views of another person may start an argument or cause a disturbance. But our Constitution says we must take this risk.[34]

The flag is an object of deep veneration in our society, yet its desecration is also a form of symbolic expression protected by the First Amendment. In 1989, a divided Supreme Court struck down a Texas law that barred the desecration of venerated objects. Congress then enacted the Flag Protection Act of 1989 in an attempt to overcome the constitutional flaws of the Texas decision. Gregory Johnson, whose 1984 flag-burning behavior in Texas led to the Court's 1989 decision, joined other protesters and burned an American flag on the steps of the Capitol in October 1989, in a test of the new national law.

The Supreme Court nullified the federal flag-burning statute in ***United States v. Eichman*** (1990). The Court was unpersuaded that the new law was distinguishable from its Texas cousin. By a vote of 5–4, the justices reaffirmed First Amendment protection for all expressions of political ideas. The vote was identical to the Texas case, with conservative justices Anthony M. Kennedy and Scalia joining with the liberal wing to forge an unusual majority. The majority applied the same emphasis on freedom it used in the Texas case, including a quotation from its earlier opinion: " 'If there is a bedrock principle underlying the First Amendment, it is that the Government may not prohibit the expression of an idea simply because society finds the idea itself offensive or disagreeable.' Punishing desecration of the flag dilutes the very freedom that makes this emblem so revered, and worth revering."[35]

In this opinion, the Court majority relied on the substantive conception of democratic theory, which embodies the principle of freedom of speech. Yet, a May 1990 poll revealed that most people wanted to outlaw flag burning as a means of political expression and that a clear majority favored a constitutional amendment to that end.[36] (Such an amendment won Senate approval in 1990, but it fell 34 votes shy of the required two-thirds majority in the House.) The procedural interpretation of democratic theory holds that government should do what the people want. In the case of flag burning, the people are apparently willing to abandon the principle of freedom of speech embodied in the substantive view of democracy.

Although offensive to the vast majority of Americans, flag burning is a form of political expression. But suppose the conduct in question does not embody a political idea. May government ever legitimately ban that conduct? Consider the case of three nude dancers in JR's Kitty Kat Lounge, a South Bend, Indiana, strip joint, who sought to block the enforcement of an Indiana law that bans all public nudity. If nude dancing is merely conduct, government has the latitude to control, even ban, it. But if nude dancing is expression, government action to prohibit it runs afoul of the First Amendment.

The distinction between conduct and expression masks underlying value conflicts. Control advocates who sought to promote social order argued that the statute attempted to promote public decency and morality. Expression advocates who sought to promote a form of freedom argued that the dancers provided entertainment, communicating eroticism and sensuality. In 1991, a sharply divided Supreme Court upheld the state pro-

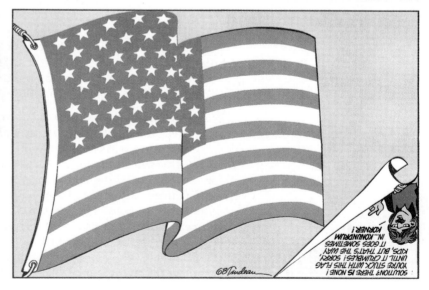

hibition in the interest of "protecting order and morality" so long as the prohibition does not target the erotic message of the performance, a form of expression entitled to some protection under the First Amendment.[37]

Order Versus Free Speech: Fighting Words.   Fighting words are a notable exception to the protection of free speech. In *Chaplinsky* v. *New Hampshire* (1942), a Jehovah's Witness, convicted under a state statute for calling a city marshal a "God-damned racketeer" and "a damned fascist" in a public place, appealed to the Supreme Court.[38] The Supreme Court upheld Chaplinsky's conviction on the theory that **fighting words**—words that "inflict injury or tend to incite an immediate breach of the peace"— do not convey ideas and thus are not subject to First Amendment protection.

The Court sharply narrowed the definition of *fighting words* just seven years later. Arthur Terminiello, a suspended Catholic priest from Alabama and a vicious anti-Semite, addressed the Christian Veterans of America, a right-wing extremist group, in a Chicago hall. Terminiello called the jeering crowd of fifteen hundred angry protesters outside the hall "slimy scum" and ranted on about the "Communistic Zionistic" Jews of America, evoking cries of "kill the Jews" and "dirty kikes" from his listeners. The crowd outside the hall heaved bottles, bricks, and rocks, while the police attempted to protect Terminiello and his listeners inside. Finally, the police arrested Terminiello for disturbing the peace.

Terminiello's speech was far more incendiary than Walter Chaplinsky's. Yet, the Supreme Court struck down Terminiello's conviction on the ground that provocative speech, even speech that stirs people to anger, is protected by the First Amendment. "Freedom of speech," wrote Justice William O. Douglas in the majority opinion, "though not absolute . . . is nevertheless protected against censorship or punishment, unless shown likely to produce a clear and present danger of serious substantive evil that rises far above public inconvenience, annoyance, or unrest."

This broad view of protection brought a stiff rebuke in Justice Jackson's dissenting opinion:

> The choice is not between order and liberty. It is between liberty with order and anarchy without either. There is danger that, if the Court does not temper its doctrinaire logic with a little practical wisdom, it will convert the constitutional Bill of Rights into a suicide pact.[39]

The times seem to have caught up with the idealism that Jackson criticized in his colleagues. In ***Cohen* v. *California*** (1971), a nineteen-year-old department store worker expressed his opposition to the Vietnam War by wearing a jacket emblazoned FUCK THE DRAFT. STOP THE WAR. The young man, Paul Cohen, was charged in 1968 under a California statute that prohibits "maliciously and willfully disturb[ing] the peace and quiet of any neighborhood or person [by] offensive conduct." He was found guilty and sentenced to thirty days in jail. On appeal, the U.S. Supreme Court reversed Cohen's conviction. The Court reasoned that the expletive he used, while provocative, was not directed at anyone in particular; besides, the state presented no evidence that the words on Cohen's jacket would provoke people in "substantial numbers" to take some kind of physical action. In recognizing that "one man's vulgarity is another's lyric," the Supreme Court protected two elements of speech: the emotive (the expression of emotion) and the cognitive (the expression of ideas).[40]

The latest variant of speech restrictions has arisen on university campuses. Public and private campuses have established rules barring racial or ethnic slurs on the ground that such language is a form of harassment or discrimination. But such government-authorized restrictions may go too far. When a teenager burned a cross on a black family's lawn, police officials charged him with the bias-motivated crime of "arousing anger, alarm, or resentment in others on the basis of race, color, creed, religion or gender." (They could have charged him with arson, terrorism, or trespass.) In a unanimous 1992 decision, the justices struck down the bias-motivated criminal statute on free speech grounds.[41] The justices observed that the law punished some expression (odious racial epithets) but not others (odious homophobic epithets). Such distinctions regarding expression were out of bounds. Government has no authority "to license one side of a debate to fight freestyle," wrote Justice Scalia, "while requiring the other to follow the Marquis of Queensberry rules."

Free Speech Versus Order: Obscenity.   The Supreme Court has always viewed obscene material—words, music, books, magazines, films—as outside the bounds of constitutional protection, which means that states may regulate or even ban obscenity. However, difficulties arise in determining what is obscene and what is not. In *Roth* v. *United States* (1957), Justice William J. Brennan Jr., outlined a test for judging whether a work is obscene: "Whether to the average person, applying contemporary community standards, the dominant theme of the material taken as a whole appeals to prurient interest."[42] (*Prurient* means having a tendency to incite lustful thoughts.) Yet, a definition of *obscenity* has proved elusive; no objective test seems adequate. Justice Potter Stewart will long be remembered for his solution to the problem of identifying obscene materials. He declared that he could not define it. "But," he added, "I know it when I see it."[43]

In **Miller v. California** (1973), its most recent major attempt to clarify constitutional standards governing obscenity, the Court declared that a work—a play, film, or book—is obscene and may be regulated by government if (1) the work taken as a whole appeals to prurient interest; (2) the work portrays sexual conduct in a patently offensive way; and (3) the work taken as a whole lacks serious literary, artistic, political, or scientific value.[44] Local community standards govern application of the first and second prongs of the *Miller* test.

A Cincinnati jury applied the *Miller* obscenity test in the case of the Mapplethorpe photographs discussed at the beginning of the chapter. After deliberating for less than two hours, the mostly working-class jury of four women and four men reached a unanimous verdict of acquittal. Using the *Miller* test, they concluded that the photos appealed to prurient interest in sex and were patently offensive. However, they could not assent to the third requirement: that the photographs lacked artistic merit. In conclud-

Rappin' Rights
Luther Campbell and the rap group "2 Live Crew" wrote an album, Nasty As They Wanna Be. *A federal trial judge found the album's lyrics obscene in a step to ban its sale and distribution in Florida. An appellate court overturned the ruling in 1993. The court held that artistic expression was protected by the First Amendment. The group returned for an encore in 1994 when the Supreme Court ruled that the group's parody of "Oh, Pretty Woman" did not violate copyright law.*

ing that the photographs were art, the jurors deferred to the testimony of expert witnesses. One juror's candid remarks suggested a widely shared view: "I'm not an expert. I don't understand Picasso's art. But I assume the people who call it art know what they're talking about."[45]

Feminism, Free Expression, and Equality.   Historically, civil liberties have conflicted with demands for social order. However, civil liberties can also conflict with demands for equality. In the 1980s, city officials in Indianapolis, Indiana, influenced by radical feminists, invoked equality principles to justify legislation restricting freedom of expression. Specifically, they argued that pornography is sex discrimination.[46]

The ordinance focused on pornography and its effect on women's status and treatment. It defined *pornography* as the graphic, sexually explicit subordination of women, in words or pictures, that presents women "as sexual objects who experience pleasure in being raped" and/or as "sexual objects of domination, conquest, violation, exploitation, possession, or use, or [in] postures or positions of servility or submission or display." The ordinance rested on three findings:

- That pornography is a form of discrimination that denies equal opportunities in society

- That pornography is central in creating and maintaining gender as a category of discrimination

- That pornography is a systematic practice of exploitation and subordination based on sex, imposing differential harms on women

The ordinance then banned pornographic material according to the following argument: Government interest in equality outweighs any First

Amendment interest in communication; pornography affects thoughts; it works by socializing, by establishing the expected and permissible; depictions of subordination tend to perpetuate subordination; and this leads to affront and to the maintenance of lower pay at work, insult and injury at home, and battery and rape in the streets. Hence, pornography conditions society to subordinate women impermissibly. An ordinance regulating expression will regulate and control the underlying unacceptable conduct.

According to the ordinance, works depicting sexual encounters premised on equality are lawful no matter how sexually explicit. And works that treat women in the disapproved way—as sexually submissive or as enjoying humiliation—are unlawful no matter how significant the literary, artistic, or political qualities of the work. U.S. District Judge Sarah Evans Barker declared the ordinance unconstitutional, stating that it went beyond the categories of unprotected expression (such as child pornography) to suppress otherwise protected expression.

Judge Barker thus confronted the trade-off between equality and freedom in a pluralist democracy. Interest groups that use the democratic process to carve exceptions to the First Amendment benefit at the expense of everyone's rights. Although efforts to restrict behavior that leads to humiliation and degradation of women may be necessary and desirable, "free speech, rather than being the enemy," wrote Judge Barker, "is a long-tested and worthy ally. To deny free speech in order to engineer social change in the name of accomplishing a greater good for one sector of our society erodes the freedom of all."[47]

This novel effort to recast an issue of freedom versus order as one of freedom versus equality remains a theory. Barker's decision protected freedom. Her judgment was affirmed by the U.S. Court of Appeals in 1985 and affirmed without argument by the Supreme Court in 1986. The citizens of Bellingham, Washington, in 1988 approved by referendum an ordinance similar to the one in Indianapolis, but a federal district judge invalidated it in 1989. The Massachusetts legislature introduced a narrower version in 1992. In the next confrontation—and, in a pluralist democracy, there will surely be others—equality may prove the victor. Compared with What? 15.1 describes a new censorship regime in Canada based on the equality-centered attack on pornography.

Freedom of the Press

The First Amendment guarantees that government "shall make no law . . . abridging the freedom . . . of the press." Although it originally was adopted as a restriction on the national government, since 1931 the Supreme Court has held the free press guarantee to apply to state and local governments as well.

The ability to collect and report information without government interference was (and still is) thought to be essential to a free society. The print media continue to use and defend the freedom conferred on them by the framers. However, the electronic media have had to accept government regulation that stems from the scarcity of broadcast frequencies (see Chapter 6).

COMPARED WITH WHAT? 15.1   Censorship, Canadian Style

Sometimes, a helping hand can prove more harmful than no help at all. In 1993, the Canadian Supreme Court ruled that words and images that degrade women are harmful and should be banned. Relying on the theories of Catherine MacKinnon and her associate, Andrea Dworkin, the court in *Butler* v. *Her Majesty, The Queen* established a new censorship regime in Canada.

Since the decision, customs officers have seized novels by authors David Leavitt (*The Lost Language of Cranes*), Kathy Acker (*Blood and Guts in High School*), and Bell Hooks (*Talking Back*). Canadian officials have pulled the plug on computer bulletin boards and yanked artwork from galleries. The Miss Canada pageant was canceled, because it was "degrading" to women. Lesbian and gay literature have been particular targets of the new government censorship campaign. Dworkin must have been stunned when two of her own books were caught in the government censorship net that she helped shape. (Media coverage and public uproar produced a change of heart by the authorities.) "The Supreme Court of Canada doesn't give a damn about gender equality," said the

Canadian sociologist Thelma McCormack. "It is concerned about control, and was pleased to have a feminist gloss to put on it."

On the surface, the decision appears to protect women, but what is the definition of *degrading*, and who shall decide to what it applies? Seventy years ago, U.S. Supreme Court Justice Louis Brandeis counseled Americans to be on guard when zealous officials act in well-intentioned ways, but without understanding, to curtail individual liberty. Canadian artists, writers, and scholars are learning this lesson the hard way, and they are directing their anger at MacKinnon and Dworkin and at the theory that women can benefit from censorship. As one feminist opponent of the new censorship said, "The Canadian situation has made it unambiguous that the sex wars have entered a new phase. There's nothing like a little taste of state repression to put one back in touch with reality."

- *Source: Leanne Katz, "Secrets of the Flesh: Censors' Helpers," New York Times, 4 December 1993, Section 1, p. 21; Barry Brown, "Canada's New Pornography Laws Drawing Charges of Censorship," Buffalo News, 10 January 1994, p. 7; Jeffrey Toobin, "Annals of Law: X-Rated," The New Yorker, 3 October 1994, pp. 70–78.*

Defamation of Character.   Libel is the written defamation of character.* A person who believes his or her name and character have been harmed by false statements in a publication can institute a lawsuit against the publication and seek monetary compensation for the damage. Such a lawsuit can impose limits on freedom of expression; at the same time, false statements impinge on the rights of individuals. In a landmark decision in **New York Times v. Sullivan** (1964), the Supreme Court declared that freedom of the press takes precedence—at least when the defamed individual is a public official.[48] The Court unanimously agreed that the First

* *Slander is the oral defamation of character. The durability of the written word usually means that libel is a more serious accusation than slander.*

Amendment protects the publication of all statements, even false ones about the conduct of public officials, except when statements are made with actual malice (with knowledge that they are false or in reckless disregard of their truth or falsity). Citing John Stuart Mill's 1859 treatise *On Liberty*, the Court declared that "even a false statement may be deemed to make a valuable contribution to public debate, since it brings about the clearer perception and livelier impression of truth, produced by its collision with error."

Three years later, the Court extended this protection to apply to suits brought by any public figures, whether they are public officials or not. **Public figures** are people who assume roles of prominence in society or who thrust themselves to the forefront of public controversy—including officials, actors, writers, television personalities, and others. These people must show actual malice on the part of the publication that prints false statements about them. Because the burden of proof is so great, few plaintiffs prevail. And freedom of the press is the beneficiary.

What if the damage inflicted is not to one's reputation but to one's emotional state? Government seeks to maintain the prevailing social order, which prescribes proper modes of behavior. Does the First Amendment restrict government in protecting citizens from behavior that intentionally inflicts emotional distress? This issue arose in a parody of a public figure in *Hustler* magazine. The target was the Reverend Jerry Falwell, a Baptist televangelist who founded the Moral Majority, organizing conservative Christians into a political force. The parody had Falwell—in an interview—discussing a drunken, incestuous rendezvous with his mother in an outhouse, saying, "I always get sloshed before I go out to the pulpit." Falwell won a $200,000 award for "emotional distress." When the magazine appealed, the Supreme Court confronted the issue of social order versus free speech in 1988.[49]

In a unanimous decision, the Court overturned the award. In his sweeping opinion for the Court, Chief Justice William H. Rehnquist gave a wide latitude to the First Amendment's protection of free speech. He observed that "graphic depictions and satirical cartoons have played a prominent role in public and political debate throughout the nation's history" and that the First Amendment protects even "vehement, caustic, and sometimes unpleasantly sharp attacks." Free speech protects criticism of public figures, even if the criticism is outrageous and offensive.

Prior Restraint and the Press.   In the United States, freedom of the press has primarily meant protection from *prior restraint*, or censorship. The Supreme Court's first encounter with a law imposing prior restraint on a newspaper was in *Near v. Minnesota* (1931).[50] In Minneapolis, Jay Near published a scandal sheet in which he attacked local officials, charging that they were in league with gangsters.[51] Minnesota officials obtained an injunction to prevent Near from publishing his newspaper under a state law that allowed such action against periodicals deemed "malicious, scandalous, and defamatory."

The Supreme Court struck down the law, declaring that prior restraint is a special burden on a free press. Chief Justice Charles Evans Hughes forcefully articulated the need for a vigilant, unrestrained press: "The fact that the liberty of the press may be abused by miscreant purveyors of scandal does not make any the less necessary the immunity of the press from previous restraint in dealing with official misconduct." Although the Court acknowledged that prior restraint may be permissible in exceptional circumstances, it did not specify those circumstances, nor has it yet done so.

Consider another case, which occurred during a war, a time when the tension between government-imposed order and individual freedom is often at a peak. In 1971, Daniel Ellsberg, a special assistant in the Pentagon's Office of International Security Affairs, delivered portions of a classified U.S. Department of Defense study to the *New York Times* and the *Washington Post*. By making the documents public, he hoped to discredit the Vietnam War and thereby end it. The U.S. Department of Justice sought to restrain the *Times* and the *Post* from publishing the documents, contending that publication would prolong the war and embarrass the government. The case was quickly brought before the Supreme Court, which delayed its summer adjournment to hear oral argument.

Three days later, in a 6–3 decision in **New York Times v. United States** (1971), the Court concluded that the government had not met the heavy burden of proving that immediate, inevitable, and irreparable harm would follow publication.[52] The majority expressed its view in a brief, unsigned opinion; individual and collective concurring and dissenting views added nine opinions to the decision. Two justices maintained that the First Amendment offers absolute protection against government censorship, no matter what the situation. But the other justices left the door ajar for the imposition of prior restraint in the most extreme and compelling circumstances. The result was hardly a ringing endorsement of freedom of the press, nor was it a full affirmation of the public's right to all the information that is vital to the debate of public issues.

Freedom of Expression Versus Maintaining Order.   The courts have consistently held that freedom of the press does not override the requirements of law enforcement. A grand jury called a Louisville, Kentucky, reporter, who had researched and written an article about drug activities, to identify people he had seen in possession of marijuana or in the act of processing it. The reporter refused to testify, maintaining that freedom of the press shielded him from inquiry. In a closely divided decision, the Supreme Court in 1972 rejected this position.[53] The Court declared that no exception, even a limited one, is permissible to the rule that all citizens have a duty to give their government whatever testimony they are capable of giving.

A divided Supreme Court reiterated in 1978 that journalists are not protected from the demands of law enforcement. The Court upheld a lower court's warrant to search a Stanford University campus newspaper office for photographs of a violent demonstration. The investigation of criminal conduct seems to be a special area—one in which the Supreme Court is not willing to provide the press with extraordinary protection of its freedom.[54]

The Supreme Court again confronted the conflict between free expression and order in 1988.[55] The principal of a St. Louis high school deleted articles on divorce and teenage pregnancy from the school's newspaper on the ground that the articles invaded the privacy of the students and families who were the focus of the stories. Three student editors filed suit in federal court, claiming that the principal had violated their First Amendment rights. They argued that the principal's censorship interfered with the newspaper's function as a public forum, a role protected by the First Amendment. The principal maintained that the newspaper was just an extension of classroom instruction, not protected by the First Amendment.

In a 5–3 decision, the Court upheld the principal's actions in sweeping terms. Educators may limit speech within the confines of the school curriculum and speech that might seem to bear the approval of the school, provided their actions serve "any valid educational purpose." The majority justices maintained that students in public school do not "shed their constitutional rights to freedom of expression at the schoolhouse gate," but recent Court decisions suggest that students do lose certain rights—including elements of free expression—when they pass through the public school portals.

The Right to Peaceable Assembly and Petition

The final clause of the First Amendment states that "Congress shall make no law . . . abridging . . . the right of the people peaceably to assemble, and to petition the Government for a redress of grievances." The roots of the right of petition trace to the Magna Carta, the charter of English political and civil liberties granted by King John at Runnymede in 1215. The right of peaceable assembly arose much later. Historically, this section of the First Amendment should read "the right of the people peaceably to assemble" *in order to* "petition the government."[56] Today, however, the right of peaceable assembly stems from the same root as free speech and free press; precedent has merged these rights and made them equally indivisible. Government cannot prohibit peaceful political meetings and cannot brand as criminals those who organize, lead, and attend such meetings.[57]

The rights of assembly and petition have merged with the guarantees of free speech and a free press under the more general freedom of expression. Having the right to assemble and to petition the government implies having the freedom to express one's thoughts and beliefs.

The clash of interests in cases involving these rights illustrates the continuing nature of the effort to define and apply fundamental principles. The need for order and stability has tempered the concept of freedom. And when freedom and order conflict, the justices of the Supreme Court, who are responsible only to their consciences, strike the balance. Such clashes are certain to occur again and again. Freedom and order conflict when public libraries become targets for community censors, when religious devotion interferes with military service, when individuals and groups express views or hold beliefs at odds with majority sentiment. Conflicts between freedom and order, and between minority and majority viewpoints, are part and parcel of politics and government here and abroad. How do other nations rank on the degree of civil liberties they guarantee their citizens? Is freedom increasing or declining worldwide? For some answers, see Compared with What? 15.2.

COMPARED WITH WHAT? 15.2   Freedom in Retreat

Each year, Freedom House researchers analyze the state of freedom around the world. Using a seven-point scale, they rank nations from 1 (the greatest degree of freedom) to 7 (the least degree of freedom).

In countries rated 1, the expression of political opinion has an outlet in the press, especially when the intent of that expression is to affect the legitimate political process. In addition, in these countries no major medium of expression serves as a simple conduit for government propaganda. The courts protect the individual; people cannot be punished for their opinions; there is respect for private rights and wants in education, occupation, religion, and residence; and law-abiding citizens do not fear for their lives because of their political activities.

Moving down the scale from 2 to 7, we see a steady loss of civil freedoms. Compared with nations rated 1, the police and courts in nations rated 2 have more authoritarian traditions or a less institutionalized or secure set of liberties. Nations rated a 3 or higher may have political prisoners and varying forms of censorship. Often, their security services torture prisoners. States rated 6 almost always have political prisoners. Here the legitimate media usually are completely under government supervision; there is no right to assembly; and often, narrow restrictions apply to travel, residence, and occupation. However, at level 6 there may still be relative freedom in private conversations, especially at home; illegal demonstrations can or do occur; and underground literature circulates. At 7 on the scale, there is pervasive fear; little independent expression, even in private; and almost no public expression of opposition to the government. Imprisonment and execution here are swift and sure.

In 1994, a country is considered free if it scores between 1 and 2.5 (n = 72); partly free if it scores between 3 and 5.5 (n = 63); and, not free if it scores between 5.5 and 7 (n = 55). The number of people living in free societies fell by 300 million from 1993 to 1994, while the number of people denied basic freedoms rose by 531 million. The proportion of people who are free today stands at 19 percent, the lowest level since 1976.

New entrants to the ranks of the Not Free countries are: Azerbaijan, Bahrain, Burundi, Egypt, Eritrea, Ethiopia, Guinea, Indonesia, Ivory Coast, Kenya, Mozambique, Nigeria, Oman, Swaziland, Tanzania, Tunisia, United Arab Emirates, and Yugoslavia. With the exception of Swaziland, each of these countries shares one of two critical factors: each is either (1) a multi-ethnic state in which there is no dominant majority ethnic group or the

APPLYING THE BILL OF RIGHTS TO THE STATES

The major purpose of the Constitution was to structure the division of power between the national government and the state governments. Even before it was amended, the Constitution set some limits on both the nation and the states with regard to citizens' rights. It barred both governments from passing **bills of attainder,** laws that make an individual guilty of a crime without a trial. It also prohibited them from enacting **ex post facto laws,** laws that declare an action a crime after it has been performed. And it barred both nation and states from impairing the **obligation of contracts,** the obligation of the parties in a contract to carry out its terms.

Although initially the Bill of Rights seemed to apply only to the national government, various litigants pressed the claim that its guarantees also

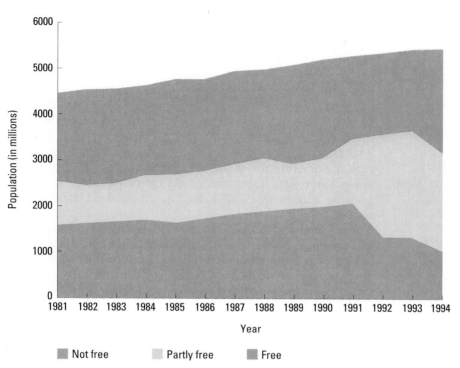

Source for figure: Freedom House, *120 Wall St., New York, NY, 10005.*

dominant ethnic group is denied power or (2) a Muslim state, usually confronting a serious challenge by fundamentalist Islamic groups.

• *Source: Adrian Karatnycky, "The Comparative Survey of Freedom: 1994" Freedom Review, 25 (No. 1), p. 4-21 (Jan-Feb 1994). Published by Freedom House, New York, NY. (for text)*

applied beyond the national government to the states. In response to one such claim, Chief Justice John Marshall affirmed what seemed plain from the Constitution's language and "the history of the day" (the events surrounding the Constitutional Convention): The provisions of the Bill of Rights served only to limit national authority. "Had the framers of these amendments intended them to be limitations on the powers of the state governments," wrote Marshall, "they would have . . . expressed that intention."[58]

Change came with the Fourteenth Amendment, which was adopted in 1868. The due process clause of that amendment is the linchpin that holds the states to the provisions of the Bill of Rights.

The Fourteenth Amendment: Due Process of Law

Section 1. . . . No State shall make or enforce any law which shall abridge the privileges or immunities of citizens of the United States; nor shall any State deprive any person of life, liberty, or property, without due process of law.

Most freedoms protected in the Bill of Rights today function as limitations on the states. And many of the standards that limit the national government serve equally to limit state governments. The changes have been achieved through the Supreme Court's interpretation of the due process clause of the Fourteenth Amendment: "nor shall any State deprive any person of life, liberty, or property, without due process of law." The clause has two central meanings. First, the due process clause requires government to adhere to appropriate procedures. For example, in a criminal trial, the government must establish the defendant's guilt beyond a reasonable doubt. Second, the due process clause forbids unreasonable government action. For example, at the turn of the century, the Supreme Court struck down a state law that forbade bakers from working more than sixty hours a week. The justices held the law unreasonable under the due process clause.

The Supreme Court has used the first meaning of the due process clause as a sponge, absorbing or incorporating the procedural specifics of the Bill of Rights and spreading or applying them to the states. The history of due process cases reveals that unlikely litigants often champion constitutional guarantees and that freedom is not always the victor.

The Fundamental Freedoms

In 1897, the Supreme Court declared that the states are subject to the Fifth Amendment's prohibition against the taking of private property without just compensation.[59] The Court reached that decision by absorbing the prohibition into the due process clause of the Fourteenth Amendment, which explicitly applies to the states. Thus, one Bill of Rights protection—but only that one—applied to the states and the national government, as illustrated in Figure 15.1. In 1925, the Court *assumed* that the due process clause protected the First Amendment speech and press liberties from impairment by the states.[60]

The inclusion of other Bill of Rights guarantees within the due process clause faced a critical test in ***Palko v. Connecticut*** (1937).[61] Frank Palko had been charged with homicide in the first degree. He was convicted instead of second-degree murder and sentenced to life imprisonment. The state of Connecticut appealed and won a new trial; this time, Palko was found guilty of first-degree murder and sentenced to death. Palko appealed the second conviction on the ground that it violated the protection against double jeopardy guaranteed to him by the Fifth Amendment. This protection applied to the states, he contended, because of the Fourteenth Amendment's due process clause.

The Supreme Court upheld Palko's second conviction. In his opinion for the majority, Justice Benjamin N. Cardozo formulated principles that were to guide the Court's actions for the next three decades. He reasoned that some Bill of Rights guarantees—such as freedom of thought and speech—are fundamental and that these fundamental rights are absorbed

FIGURE **15.1** ■ **The Incorporation of the Bill of Rights**

The Supreme Court has used the due process clause of the Fourteenth Amendment as a sponge, absorbing many—but not all—the provisions in the Bill of Rights and applying them to state and local governments. All provisions in the Bill of Rights apply to the national government.

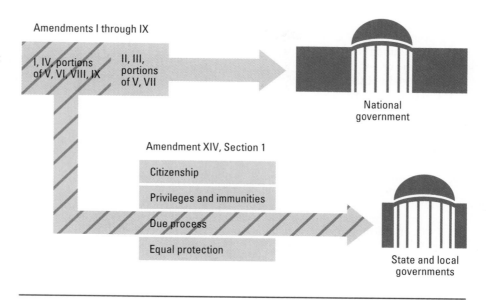

Amendments I through IX

I, IV, portions of V, VI, VIII, IX

II, III, portions of V, VII

National government

Amendment XIV, Section 1

Citizenship

Privileges and immunities

Due process

Equal protection

State and local governments

by the Fourteenth Amendment's due process clause and are applicable to the states. These rights are essential, argued Cardozo, because "neither liberty nor justice would exist if they were sacrificed." Trial by jury and other rights, although valuable and important, are not essential to liberty and justice and therefore are not absorbed by the due process clause. "Few would be so narrow or provincial," Cardozo claimed, "as to maintain that a fair and enlightened system of justice" would be impossible without these other rights. In other words, only certain provisions of the Bill of Rights—the "fundamental" provisions—were absorbed into the due process clause and made applicable to the states. Because protection against double jeopardy was not one of them, Palko died in Connecticut's gas chamber in 1938.

The next thirty years saw slow but perceptible change in the standard for determining whether a Bill of Rights guarantee was fundamental. The reference point changed from the idealized "fair and enlightened system of justice" in *Palko* to the more realistic "American scheme of justice" outlined in *Duncan* v. *Louisiana* (1968).[62] Case after case tested various guarantees that the Court found to be fundamental. By 1969, when *Palko* was finally overturned, the Court had found most of the Bill of Rights applicable to the states. Table 15.1 shows how the standards changed after 1897.

Criminal Procedure: The Meaning of Constitutional Guarantees

"The history of liberty," remarked Justice Frankfurter, "has largely been the history of observance of procedural safeguards."[63] The safeguards embodied in the Fourth through Eighth Amendments to the Constitution

TABLE 15.1 ■ Cases Applying the Bill of Rights to the States

Amendment	Case	Date
1. Congress shall make no law respecting an establishment of religion,	*Everson* v. *Board of Education*	1947
or prohibiting the free exercise thereof;	*Cantwell* v. *Connecticut*	1940
or abridging the freedom of speech,	*Gitlow* v. *New York*	1925
or of the press;	*Near* v. *Minnesota*	1931
or the right of the people peaceably to assemble,	*DeJonge* v. *Orgeon*	1937
and to petition the Government for a redress of grievances.	*DeJonge* v. *Orgeon*	1937
2. A well regulated Militia, being necessary to the security of a free State, the right of the people to keep and bear Arms, shall not be infringed.		
3. No Soldier shall, in time of peace be quartered in any house, without the consent of the Owner, nor in time of war, but in a manner to be prescribed by law.		
4. The right of the people to be secure in their persons, houses, papers, and effects, against unreasonable searches and seizures, shall not be violated,	*Wolf* v. *Colorado*	1949
and no Warrants shall issue, but upon probable cause, supported by Oath or affirmation, and particularly describing the place to be searched, and the persons or things to be seized.	*Aguilar* v. *Texas*	1964
5. No person shall be held to answer for a capital, or otherwise infamous crime, unless on a presentment or indictment of a Grand Jury,		
except in cases arising in the land or naval forces, or in the Militia, when in actual service in time of War or public danger;		
nor shall any person be subject for the same offense to be twice put in jeopardy of life or limb;	*Benton* v. *Maryland*	1969
nor shall be compelled in any criminal case to be a witness against himself,	*Malloy* v. *Hogan*	1964
nor be deprived of life, liberty, or property, without due process of law;		
nor shall private property be taken for public use, without just compensation.	*Chicago B. & Q. R.* v. *Chicago*	1897
6. In all criminal prosecutions, the accused shall enjoy the right to a speedy	*Klopfer* v. *North Carolina*	1967
and public trial	In re *Oliver*	1948
by an impartial	*Parker* v. *Gladden*	1966
jury	*Duncan* v. *Louisiana*	1968
of the State and district wherein the crime shall have been committed, which district shall have been previously ascertained by law,		
and to be informed of the nature and cause of the accusation;	*Lanzetta* v. *New Jersey*	1939
to be confronted with the witnesses against him;	*Pointer* v. *Texas*	1965
to have compulsory process for obtaining witnesses in his favor,	*Washington* v. *Texas*	1967
and to have the assistance of counsel for his defence.	*Gideon* v. *Wainwright*	1963
7. In Suits at common law, where the value of the controversy shall exceed twenty dollars, the right of trial by jury shall be preserved, and no fact tried by a jury shall be otherwise re-examined in any Court of the United States, than according to the rules of the common law.		
8. Excessive bail shall not be required,		
nor excess fines imposed,		
nor cruel and unusual punishments inflicted.	*Robinson* v. *California*	1962
9. The enumeration in the Constitution, in certain rights, shall not be construed to deny or disparage others retained by the people.	*Griswold* v. *Connecticut*	1965
10. The powers not delegated to the United States by the Constitution are reserved to the Department of Justice and Treasury, except when the states are willing to forsake federal financing.		

specify how government must behave in criminal proceedings. Their application to the states has reshaped American criminal justice in the last thirty years in two steps. The first step is a judgment that a guarantee asserted in the Bill of Rights also applies to the states. The second step requires that the judiciary give specific meaning to the guarantee. The courts cannot allow the states to define guarantees themselves without risking different definitions from state to state—and differences among citizens' rights. If rights are fundamental, their meaning cannot vary. But life is not quite so simple under the U.S. Constitution. The concept of federalism is sewn into the constitutional fabric, and the Supreme Court recognizes that there may be more than one way to prosecute the accused while heeding fundamental rights.

Consider, for example, the right to a jury trial in criminal cases, which is guaranteed by the Sixth Amendment. This right was made obligatory for the states in *Duncan* v. *Louisiana* (1968). The Supreme Court later held that the right applied to all nonpetty criminal cases, those in which the penalty for conviction was more than six months' imprisonment.[64] But the Court did not require that state juries have twelve members, the number required for federal criminal proceedings. The Court permits jury size to vary from state to state, although it set the minimum number at six. Furthermore, it did not impose on the states the federal requirement of a unanimous jury verdict. As a result, even today many states do not require unanimous verdicts for criminal convictions. Some observers question whether criminal defendants in these states enjoy the same rights as defendants in unanimous verdict states.

In contrast, the Court left no room for variation in its definition of the fundamental right to an attorney, also guaranteed by the Sixth Amendment. Clarence Earl Gideon was a penniless vagrant accused of breaking into and robbing a pool hall. (The "loot" he was charged with taking was mainly change from vending machines.) Because Gideon could not afford a lawyer, he asked the state to provide him with legal counsel for his trial. The state refused and subsequently convicted Gideon and sentenced him to five years in the Florida State Penitentiary. From his cell, Gideon appealed to the U.S. Supreme Court, claiming that his conviction should be struck down because the state had denied him his Sixth Amendment right to counsel. (Gideon was also without counsel in this appeal; he filed a hand-written "pauper's petition" with the Court after studying law texts in the prison library. When the Court agreed to consider his case, he was assigned a prominent Washington attorney, Abe Fortas, who later became a Supreme Court justice.)[65]

In its landmark decision in **Gideon v. Wainwright** (1963), the Court set aside Gideon's conviction and extended to the states the Sixth Amendment right to counsel.[66] The state retried Gideon, who this time had the assistance of a lawyer, and found him not guilty.

In subsequent rulings that stretched over more than a decade, the Court specified at which points in the course of criminal proceedings a defendant is entitled to a lawyer (from arrest to trial, appeal, and beyond). These pronouncements are binding on all states. In state as well as federal proceedings, the government must furnish legal assistance to those who do not have the means to hire their own attorney.

During this period the Court also came to grips with another procedural issue: informing suspects of their constitutional rights. Without this

A Pauper's Plea

Clarence Earl Gideon, penni-less and without a lawyer, was convicted and sent to prison for breaking into and robbing a pool hall. At his trial, Gideon pleaded with the judge: "Your Honor, the U.S. Constitution says I am enti-tled to be represented by counsel." The judge was re-quired by state law to deny Gideon's request. Undaunted, Gideon continued his quest for recognition of his Sixth Amendment right to counsel. On the basis of his penciled petition, the Supreme Court agreed to consider his case, ultimately granting Gideon the right he advocated with such conviction.

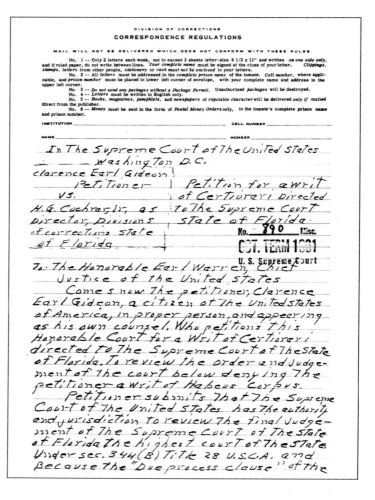

knowledge, procedural safeguards are meaningless. Ernesto Miranda was arrested in Arizona in connection with the kidnapping and raping of an eighteen-year-old woman. After the police questioned him for two hours and the woman identified him, Miranda confessed to the crime. An Arizona court convicted him on the basis of that confession—although he was never told he had the right to counsel and the right not to incriminate himself. Miranda appealed his conviction, which was overturned by the Supreme Court in 1966.[67]

The Court based its decision in *Miranda* v. *Arizona* on the Fifth Amendment privilege against self-incrimination. According to the Court, the police had forced Miranda to confess during in-custody questioning, not with physical force but with the coercion inherent in custodial inter-rogation without counsel. The Court said that warnings are necessary to dispel that coercion. The Court does not require warnings if a person is only in custody without questioning or subject to questioning without arrest. But in *Miranda,* the Court found the combination of custody and interrogation sufficiently intimidating to require warnings before ques-tioning. These statements are known today as the **Miranda warnings:**

- You have the right to remain silent.

- Anything you say can be used against you in court.
- You have the right to talk to a lawyer of your own choice before questioning.
- If you cannot afford to hire a lawyer, a lawyer will be provided without charge.

In each area of criminal procedure, the justices have had to grapple with the two steps in the application of constitutional guarantees to criminal defendants: the extension of a right to the states and the definition of that right. In *Duncan*, the issue was the right to jury trial, and the Court allowed variation from state to state. In *Gideon*, the Court applied the right to counsel uniformly from state to state. Finally, in *Miranda*, the Court declared that all governments—national, state, and local—have a duty to inform suspects of the full measure of their constitutional rights.

The problems of balancing freedom and order can be formidable. A primary function of government is to maintain order. What happens when the government infringes upon individual freedom for the sake of order? Consider the guarantee in the Fourth Amendment: "The right of the people to be secure in their persons, houses, papers, and effects, against unreasonable searches and seizures, shall not be violated." The Court made this right applicable to the states in *Wolf* v. *Colorado* (1949).[68] Following the reasoning in *Palko*, the Court found that the core of the amendment—security against arbitrary police intrusion—is a fundamental right and that citizens must be protected from illegal searches by state and local government. But how? The federal courts had long followed the **exclusionary rule,** which holds that evidence obtained from an illegal search and seizure cannot be used in a trial. And of course, if that evidence is critical to the prosecution, the appellate court must overturn the conviction. But the Court refused to apply the exclusionary rule to the state courts. Instead, it allowed the states to decide on their own how to handle the fruits of an illegal search. The upshot of *Wolf* was a declaration that the evidence used to convict the defendant had been obtained illegally, but the court confirmed his conviction on the basis of that illegal evidence.

The justices considered the exclusionary rule again twelve years later, in *Mapp* v. *Ohio*.[69] An Ohio court had found Dolree Mapp guilty of possessing obscene materials after an admittedly illegal search of her home for a fugitive. The Ohio Supreme Court affirmed her conviction, and she appealed to the U.S. Supreme Court. Mapp's attorneys argued for a reversal based on freedom of expression, contending that the First Amendment protected the confiscated materials. However, the Court elected to use the decision in *Mapp* to give meaning to the constitutional guarantee against unreasonable search and seizure. In a 6–3 decision, the justices declared that "all evidence obtained by searches and seizures in violation of the Constitution is, by [the Fourth Amendment], inadmissible in a state court." Ohio had convicted *Mapp* illegally.

The decision was historic. It placed the exclusionary rule under the umbrella of the Fourth Amendment and required all levels of government to operate according to the provisions of that amendment. Failure to do so could result in the dismissal of criminal charges against otherwise guilty defendants.

Mapp launched a divided Supreme Court on a troubled course of determining how and when to apply the exclusionary rule. For example, the

Court continued to struggle with police use of sophisticated electronic eavesdropping devices and searches of movable vehicles. In each case, the justices confront a rule that appears to handicap the police, while it offers freedom to people whose guilt has been established by the illegal evidence. In the Court's most recent pronouncements, order has triumphed over freedom.

The struggle over the exclusionary rule took a new turn in 1984, when the Court reviewed *United States* v. *Leon*.[70] In this case, the police obtained a search warrant from a judge on the basis of a tip from an informant of unproved reliability. The judge issued a warrant without firmly establishing probable cause to believe the tip. The police, relying on the warrant, found large quantities of illegal drugs. The Court, by a vote of 6–3, established the **good faith exception** to the exclusionary rule. The justices held that the state could introduce at trial evidence seized on the basis of a mistakenly issued search warrant. The exclusionary rule, argued the majority, is not a right but a remedy justified by its ability to deter illegal police conduct. The rule is costly to society. It excludes pertinent valid evidence, allowing guilty people to go unpunished and generating disrespect for the law. These costs are justifiable only if the exclusionary rule deters police misconduct. Such a deterrent effect was not a factor in *Leon:* The police acted in good faith. Hence, the Court decided, there is a need for an exception to the rule.

In 1988, the justices ruled 6–2 that police may search through garbage bags and other containers that people leave outside their houses. The case resulted from an investigation of man police suspected of narcotics trafficking. The police obtained his trash bags from the local garbage collector; the bags contained evidence of narcotics, which then served as the basis for obtaining a search warrant for his house. That search revealed quantities of cocaine and hashish and led to criminal charges. The lower courts dismissed the drug charges on the ground that the warrant was based on an unconstitutional search. By overturning that ruling, the Supreme Court further eroded the Fourth Amendment's protection of individual privacy.[71]

The exclusionary rule continues to divide the Supreme Court. In 1990, the justices again reaffirmed the rule but by a bare 5–4 majority.[72] The current Supreme Court line-up has a more conservative bent, which suggests that the battle over the exclusionary rule is not ended.

Mapp and all the cases that followed it forced the Court to confront the classic dilemma of democracy: the choice between freedom and order. If the justices tipped the scale toward freedom, guilty parties would go free, perhaps break the law again. If they chose order, they would be giving government approval to police conduct that violates the Constitution.

THE NINTH AMENDMENT AND PERSONAL AUTONOMY

The enumeration in the Constitution, of certain rights, shall not be construed to deny or disparage others retained by the people.

The wording and history of the Ninth Amendment remain an enigma; the evidence supports two different views. The amendment may protect rights that are not enumerated, or it may simply protect state governments against the assumption of power by the national government.[73] The

The Supreme Court: Where the Twain Meets

While the justices of the Supreme Court sit inside a magisterial marble and mahogany courtroom, opposing groups of demonstrators hurl taunts across the plaza outside. Both justices and protesters have been divided over the issue of abortion. In 1992, the Court upheld a woman's right to choose abortion but it also upheld new restrictions on the exercise of that right.

meaning of the amendment was not an issue until 1965, when the Supreme Court used it to protect privacy, a right that is not enumerated in the Constitution.

Controversy: From Privacy to Abortion

In ***Griswold* v. *Connecticut*** (1965), the Court struck down, by a vote of 7–2, a seldom-used Connecticut statute that made the use of birth control devices a crime.[74] Justice Douglas, writing for the majority, asserted that the "specific guarantees in the Bill of Rights have prenumbras [partially illuminated regions surrounding fully-lit areas]" that give "life and substance" to broad, unspecified protections in the Bill of Rights. Several specific guarantees in the First, Third, Fourth, and Fifth Amendments create a zone of privacy, Douglas argued, and this zone is protected by the Ninth Amendment and is applicable to the states by the due process clause of the Fourteenth Amendment.

Three justices gave further emphasis to the relevance of the Ninth Amendment, which, they contended, protects fundamental rights derived from those specifically enumerated in the first eight amendments. This view contrasted sharply with the position expressed by the two dissenters, justices Black and Stewart. In the absence of some specific prohibition, they argued, the Bill of Rights and the Fourteenth Amendment do not allow judicial annulment of state legislative policies, even if those policies are abhorrent to a judge or justice.

Griswold established the principle that the Bill of Rights as a whole creates a right to make certain intimate, personal choices, including the right of married people to engage in sexual intercourse for reproduction or pleasure. This zone of personal autonomy, protected by the Constitution, was the basis of a 1973 case that sought to invalidate state antiabortion laws. But rights are not absolute, and in weighing the interests of the individual against the interests of the government, the Supreme Court found itself caught up in a flood of controversy that has yet to subside.

In **Roe v. Wade** (1973), the Court in a 7–2 decision declared unconstitutional a Texas law making it a crime to obtain an abortion except for the purpose of saving the woman's life.[75] Justice Harry A. Blackmun, who wrote the majority opinion, could not point to a specific constitutional guarantee to justify the Court's ruling. Instead, he based the decision on the right to privacy protected by the due process clause of the Fourteenth Amendment. In effect, state abortion laws were unreasonable and hence unconstitutional. The Court declared that in the first three months of pregnancy, the abortion decision must be left to the woman and her physician. In the interest of protecting the woman's health, states may restrict but not prohibit abortions in the second three months of pregnancy. Finally, in the last three months of pregnancy, states may regulate or even prohibit abortions to protect the life of the fetus, except when medical judgment determines that an abortion is necessary to save the woman's life. In all, the Court's ruling affected the laws of forty-six states.

The dissenters—Justices Bryon R. White and Rehnquist—were quick to assert what critics have frequently repeated since the decision: The Court's judgment was directed by its own dislikes, not by any constitutional compass. In the absence of guiding principles, they asserted, the majority justices simply substituted their views for the views of the state legislatures whose abortion regulations they invalidated.[76] In a 1993 television interview, Blackmun insisted that *"Roe versus Wade* was decided . . . on constitutional grounds."[77] It was as if Blackmun was trying, by sheer force of will, to turn back twenty years of stinging objections to the opinion he crafted.

The composition of the Court shifted under President Ronald Reagan. His elevation of Rehnquist to chief justice in 1986 and his appointments of Scalia in 1986 and Kennedy in 1988 raised new hope among abortion foes and old fears among advocates of choice.

A perceptible shift away from abortion rights materialized in **Webster v. Reproductive Health Services** (1989). The case was a blockbuster, attracting voluminous media coverage. *Webster* also set a record for the number of amicus briefs submitted on behalf of individuals and organizations with an interest in the outcome. (The number of briefs—seventy-eight—surpassed the old record of fifty-eight set in the landmark affirmative action case *Regents of the State of California* v. *Bakke* in 1978.)

In *Webster,* the Supreme Court upheld the constitutionality of a Missouri law that denied the use of public employees or publicly funded facilities in the performance of an abortion unless the woman's life was in danger.[78] Furthermore, the law required doctors to perform tests to determine whether fetuses twenty weeks and older could survive outside the womb. This was the first time that the Court upheld significant government restrictions on abortion.

The justices issued five opinions, but no single opinion captured a majority. Four justices (Blackmun, Brennan, Thurgood Marshall, and John Paul Stevens) voted to strike down the Missouri law and hold fast to *Roe.* Four justices (Kennedy, Rehnquist, Scalia, and White) wanted to overturn *Roe* and return to the states the power to regulate abortion. The remaining justice—Sandra Day O'Connor—avoided both camps. Her position was that state abortion restrictions are permissible provided they are not "unduly burdensome." She voted with the conservative plurality to uphold the restrictive Missouri statute on the ground that it did not pose an undue burden on women's rights. But she declined to reconsider (and overturn) *Roe.*

The Court has since moved cautiously down the road toward greater government control of abortion policy. In 1990, the justices split on two state parental notification laws. The Court struck down a state requirement that compelled unwed teenagers to notify both parents before an abortion. In another case, the Court upheld a state requirement that a physician notify one parent of a pregnant minor of her intent to have an abortion. In both cases, the justices voiced widely divergent opinions, revealing continuing division over the abortion issue.[79]

Abortion pits freedom against order. The decision to bear or beget children should be free from government control. Yet, government has a legitimate interest in protecting and preserving life, including fetal life, as part of its responsibility to maintain an orderly society. Rather than choose between freedom and order, the majority on the Court has withdrawn constitutional protection from abortion rights and cast the politically divisive issue into the state legislative process, where elected representatives can thrash out the conflict.

Many groups defending and opposing abortion have now turned to state legislative politics to advance their policies. This approach will force candidates for state office to debate the abortion issue and then translate the electoral outcome into new legislation that restricts or enlarges abortion policy. If the abortion issue is deeply felt by Americans, pluralist theory would argue that the strongest voices for or against abortion will mobilize support in the political arena.

With a clear conservative majority, the Court seemed poised to reverse *Roe* in 1992. But a new coalition—forged by Reagan and Bush appointees O'Connor, David Souter, and Kennedy—reaffirmed *Roe* yet tolerated additional restrictions on abortions. In *Planned Parenthood* v. *Casey,* a bitterly divided bench opted for the O'Connor "undue burden" test. The Court apparently remains deeply divided on abortion.[80]

Presidential values, as reflected in the appointment process, have left an imprint on the abortion controversy. Justices appointed by presidents Reagan and Bush weakened abortion as a constitutional right. But President Clinton's appointment of Ruth Bader Ginsburg as associate justice in 1993 added a liberal vote to a conservative Court and made good on a Clinton campaign promise to protect a woman's right to choose from further assault. (Ginsburg replaced White, who had opposed *Roe* v. *Wade* from its inception.) Although Ginsburg ducked most questions at her confirmation hearings, she was forthright in her judgment that the Constitution protects a woman's right to choose. But Ginsburg offered objections of her own to the Court's abortion reasoning. She seemed unpersuaded by the "right to privacy" roots of *Roe.* Instead, she saw a woman's right to abortion as rooted in the equal protection clause of the Fourteenth Amendment.[81]

President Clinton appointed Stephen G. Breyer to succeed Harry Blackmun as the nation's 108th Supreme Court justice in 1994. A self-described pragmatist, Breyer made clear his view that a woman's right to an abortion was now settled law. Ironically, Breyer's research as a Supreme Court law clerk in 1965 contributed to the right-to-privacy decision in *Griswold* v. *Connecticut*.

Personal Autonomy and Sexual Orientation

The right-to-privacy cases may have opened a Pandora's box of divisive social issues. Does the right to privacy embrace private homosexual acts between consenting adults? Consider the case of Michael Hardwick, who was arrested in 1982 in his Atlanta bedroom while having sex with another man. In a standard approach to prosecuting homosexuals, Georgia charged him under a state criminal statute with the crime of sodomy, which means oral or anal intercourse. The police said that they had gone to his home to arrest him for failing to pay a fine for drinking in public. Although the prosecutor dropped the charges, Hardwick sued to challenge the law's constitutionality. He won in the lower courts, but the state pursued the case.

The conflict between freedom and order lies at the core of the case. "Our legal history and our social traditions have condemned this conduct uniformly for hundreds and hundreds of years," argued Georgia's attorney. Constitutional law, he continued, "must not become an instrument for a change in the social order." Hardwick's attorney, a noted constitutional scholar, said that government must have a more important reason than "majority morality to justify regulation of sexual intimacies in the privacy of the home." He maintained that the case involved two precious freedoms: the right to engage in private sexual relations and the right to be free from government intrusion in one's home.[82]

More than half the states have eliminated criminal penalties for private homosexual acts between consulting adults. The rest still outlaw homosexual sodomy, and many outlaw heterosexual sodomy as well. As a result, homosexual rights groups and some civil liberties groups followed Hardwick's case closely. Fundamentalist Christian groups and defenders of traditional morality expressed deep interest in the outcome, too.

In a bitterly divided ruling in 1986, the Court held in **Bowers v. Hardwick** that the Constitution does not protect homosexual relations between consenting adults, even in the privacy of their own homes.[83] The logic of the privacy cases involving contraception and abortion seemed to compel a right to personal autonomy—to make personal choices unconstrained by government. But the 5–4 majority maintained that only heterosexual choices—whether and whom to marry, whether to conceive a child, whether to have an abortion—fall within the zone of privacy established by the Court in its earlier rulings. "The judiciary necessarily takes to itself further authority to govern the country without express constitutional authority" when it expands the list of fundamental rights "not rooted in the language or design of the Constitution," wrote Justice White, the author of the majority opinion.

The arguments on both sides of the privacy issue are compelling. This makes the choice between freedom and order excruciating for ordinary citizens and Supreme Court justices alike. At the preliminary conference to decide the merits of the *Hardwick* case, Justice Lewis Powell cast his vote to extend privacy rights to homosexual conduct. Later, he joined with his

What's in a Name?

A generation of young homosexuals has adopted with pride the term queer, *which was once a degrading slur. Despite a new militancy on the part of gay and lesbian activists, the quest for national constitutional protection of homosexual rights halted with the Supreme Court's 1986 decision upholding state laws against sodomy. In response, many activists have shifted their efforts from the national level to state and local arenas.*

conservative colleagues, fashioning a new majority. Four years after the *Hardwick* decision, Powell revealed another change of mind. "I probably made a mistake," he declared, speaking of his decision to vote with the conservative majority.[84]

The appointments of conservatives to replace liberals on the Court cast freedom-preferring policies such as gay rights in continued jeopardy. Powell, who was ambivalent on the issue of homosexual rights, retired in 1987; Reagan appointed moderate conservative Anthony Kennedy as Powell's replacement. Liberal justice William J. Brennan stepped down in 1990; President Bush appointed a conservative unknown, David Souter, as a replacement. And when liberal stalwart Thurgood Marshall resigned in poor health in 1991, Bush turned to conservative judge Clarence Thomas to assure a new conservative majority on the High Court. But the conservative juggernaut appears over for now. Clinton's appointments of Ginsburg and Breyer signal movement toward a liberal view: Ginsburg did not evade or hedge on her support for the constitutional rights of homosexuals in her confirmation hearings.

That the Court will soon reverse course on matters of personal autonomy is unlikely. It will take several more liberal Court appointments and the right cases to create the conditions for a change in direction. The conservative justices are among the youngest on the bench, and today they command a clear majority. However, this does not foreclose successful advocacy, as we saw in Politics in a Changing America 14.1.

The direction of personal autonomy has shifted toward the states, where various groups continue to assert their political power. For example, the Hawaii Supreme Court opened the door to homosexual marriages when it ruled in 1993 that the state's ban on same-sex marriages is presumed to be unconstitutional, unless state government can show that compelling government interests justify the ban. All fifty states ban same-sex marriages. Should the Hawaii decision stand, every state will have to recognize same-sex marriages in Hawaii. (The Constitution's full faith and credit clause

■ The Bill o' Rights Lite

With quiet efficiency, our understanding of the first 10 amendments to the Constitution has been profoundly revised by the state and Federal judiciary during the last couple decades, sparing us the untidy political melee of a constitutional convention. In light of these changes, a new Bill of Rights, based on current case law, might look something like what follows.

AMENDMENT I.

Congress shall encourage the practice of Judeo-Christian religion by its own public exercise thereof and shall make no laws abridging the freedom of *responsible* speech, unless such speech is in a digitized form or contains materials that are copyrighted, classified, proprietary or deeply offensive to non-Europeans, non-males, differently-abled or alternatively preferenced persons; or the right of the people to peaceably assemble, unless such assembly is taking place on corporate or military property or within an electronic environment; or to petition the Government for a redress of grievances, unless those grievances relate to national security.

AMENDMENT II.

A well-regulated Militia having become irrelevant to the security of the State, the right of the people to keep and bear arms against each other, shall nevertheless remain uninfringed; excepting such arms as may be afforded by the poor or those preferred by drug pushers, terrorists and organized criminals, which shall be banned.

AMENDMENT III.

No soldier shall, in time of peace, be quartered in any house, without the consent of the owner, unless that house is thought to have been used for the distribution of illegal substances.

AMENDMENT IV.

The right of the people to be secure in their persons, houses, papers, and effects, against unreasonable searches and seizures, may be suspended to protect public welfare. Upon the unsupported suspicion of law enforcement officials, any place or conveyance shall be subject to immediate search, and any such places or conveyances or property within them may be permanently confiscated without further judicial proceeding.

AMENDMENT V.

Any person may be held to answer for a capital, or otherwise infamous crime involving illicit substances, terrorism or upon any suspicion whatever; and may be subject for the same offense to be twice put in jeopardy of life or limb, once by the state courts and again by the Federal judiciary; and may be compelled by various means, including the forced submission of breath samples, bodily fluids or encryption keys to be a witness against himself, refusal to do so constituting an admission of guilt, and may be deprived of life, liberty, or property without further legal delay; and any private property thereby forfeited shall be dedicated to the discretionary use of law enforcement agents without just compensation.

AMENDMENT VI.

In all criminal prosecutions, the accused shall enjoy the right to a speedy and private plea bargaining session before pleading guilty. He is entitled to the assistance of underpaid and indifferent counsel to negotiate his sentence, except where such sentence falls under Federal mandatory sentencing requirements.

AMENDMENT VII.

In suits at common law, where the contesting parties have nearly unlimited resources to spend on legal fees, the right of trial by jury shall be preserved.

AMENDMENT VII.

Sufficient bail may be required to insure that dangerous criminals will remain in custody, where cruel and unusual punishments are usually inflicted.

AMENDMENT IX.

The enumeration in the Constitution, of certain rights, shall not be construed to deny or disparage others which may be retained by the Government to preserve public order, family values or national security.

AMENDMENT X.

The powers not delegated to the United States by the Constitution are reserved to the Departments of Justice and Treasury, except when the states are willing to forsake Federal financing.

• *Source: John Perry Barlow, New York Times, 27 January 1993, p. A11. Copyright © 1993 by The New York Times Company. Reprinted by permission.*

assures this outcome.) The pluralist model, then, gives us one solution to dissatisfaction with rulings from the nation's highest court. State courts and state legislatures have demonstrated their receptivity to positions that are probably untenable in the federal courts. However, state-by-state decisions offer little comfort to Americans who believe the Constitution protects them in their most intimate decisions and actions, regardless of where they reside.

CONSTITUTIONAL-IZING PUBLIC POLICIES

The issues embedded in *Griswold* and *Roe* are more fundamental and disturbing for democracy than the surface issues of privacy and personal autonomy. By enveloping a policy in the protection of the Constitution, the courts remove that policy from the legislative arena, where the people's will can be expressed through the democratic process. One social commentator has revised the Bill of Rights to incorporate the changes; his article appears as Feature 15.3.

As the abortion controversy demonstrates, the courts can place under the cloak of the Constitution a host of public policies that the democratic process once debated and resolved. By giving a policy constitutional protection (as the Court did with abortion), judges assume responsibilities that have traditionally been left to the elected branches to resolve. If we trust appointed judges to serve as guardians of democracy, we have no reason to fear for the democratic process. But if we believe that democratic solutions are necessary to resolve such questions, our fears may well be grounded. The controversy will continue as the justices wrestle among themselves and with their critics over whether the Constitution authorizes them to fill the due process clause with fundamental values that cannot easily be traced to constitutional text, history, or structure.

Although the courts may be "the chief guardians of the liberties of the people," they ought not have the last word, argued the great jurist Learned Hand, because

> a society so riven that the spirit of moderation is gone, no court can save; . . . a society where that spirit flourishes, no court need save; . . . in a society which evades its responsibilities by thrusting upon the courts the nurture of that spirit, that spirit in the end will perish.[85]

SUMMARY

In establishing a new government, the states and the people compelled the framers, through the Bill of Rights, to protect their freedoms. In this interpretation of these ten amendments, the courts, especially the Supreme Court, have taken on the task of balancing freedom and order.

The First Amendment protects several freedoms: religion, speech and press, peaceable assembly, and petition. The establishment clause demands government neutrality toward religions and between the religious and nonreligious. According to judicial interpretations of the free-exercise clause, religious beliefs are inviolate, but the Constitution does not protect antisocial actions in the name of religion. Extreme interpretations of the religion clauses could bring the clauses into conflict with each other.

Freedom of expression encompasses freedom of speech and of the press and the right to peaceable assembly and petition. Freedoms of speech and of the press have never been held to be absolute, but the courts ruled that the Bill of Rights gives them far greater protection than other freedoms. Exceptions to free speech protections include some forms of symbolic expression, fighting words, and obscenity. Press freedom has enjoyed broad constitutional protection, because a free society depends on the ability to collect and report information without government interference. The rights of peaceable assembly and petition stem from the freedoms of speech and press. Each freedom is equally fundamental, but the right to exercise them is not absolute.

The adoption of the Fourteenth Amendment in 1868 extended the guarantees of the Bill of Rights to the states. The due process clause became the vehicle for applying specific provisions of the Bill of Rights, one at a time, case after case, to the states. The designation of a right as fundamental also called for a definition of that right. The Supreme Court has tolerated some variation from state to state in the meaning of certain constitutional rights. The Court has also imposed a duty on government to inform citizens of their rights so that they are equipped to exercise them.

As it has fashioned new fundamental rights from the Constitution, the Supreme Court has become embroiled in controversy. The right to privacy served as the basis for the right of women to terminate a pregnancy, which in turn suggested a right to personal autonomy. The abortion controversy is still raging, and the justices appear to have called a halt to the extension of personal privacy in the name of the Constitution.

In the meantime, judicial decisions raise a basic issue. By offering constitutional protection to certain public policies, the courts may be threatening the democratic process, the process that gives the people a say in government through their elected representatives. One thing is certain: The challenge of democracy requires the constant balancing of freedom and order.

Key Terms

civil liberties
civil rights
establishment clause
free-exercise clause
strict scrutiny
prior restraint
free-expression clauses
clear and present danger
  test

fighting words
public figures
bill of attainder
ex post facto law
obligation of contracts
Miranda warning
exclusionary rule
good faith exception

Brandenburg v. *Ohio*
Tinker v. *Des Moines Independent County School District*
United States v. *Eichman*
Cohen v. *California*
Miller v. *California*
New York Times v. *Sullivan*
New York Times v. *United States*
Palko v. *Connecticut*
Gideon v. *Wainwright*
Griswold v. *Connecticut*
Roe v. *Wade*
Webster v. *Reproductive Heath Services*
Bowers v. *Hardwick*

Key Cases

Lemon v. *Kurtzman*
West Virginia State Board of Education v. *Barnette*
Sherbert v. *Verner*

Selected Readings

Baker, Liva. *Miranda: Crime, Law and Politics.* New York: Atheneum, 1983. Baker uses *Miranda* as a vehicle for explaining the American legal system. She traces the case from its origin to its landmark resolution.

Barnett, Randy E., ed. *The Rights Retained by the People: The History and Meaning of the Ninth Amendment.* Fairfax, Va.: George Mason University Press, 1989. An excellent collection of writings on the Ninth Amendment, including a set of primary documents and a summary of the competing theories in this controversial area of constitutional jurisprudence.

Carter, Stephen L. *The Culture of Disbelief: How American Law and Politics Trivialize Religious Devotion.* New York: Basic Books, 1993. In this wide-ranging, thoughtful work, Carter argues that Americans can simultaneously preserve separation of church and state, embrace American spirituality, and avoid treating believers with disdain.

Downs, Donald Alexander. *The New Politics of Pornography.* Chicago: University of Chicago Press, 1990. An exploration of the controversial modern antipornography movement. Downs analyzes similar ordinances in Minneapolis and Indianapolis, which were rooted in the radical feminist thought of Catherine MacKinnon and Andrea Dworkin.

Garrow, David. *Liberty & Sexuality: The Right to Privacy and the Making of* Roe *v.* Wade. New York: Macmillan, 1994. This is a comprehensive, historical narrative of the fundamental right to sexual privacy.

Levy, Leonard W. *The Emergence of a Free Press.* New York: Oxford University Press, 1985. This work revises Levy's original scholarship, *The Legacy of Suppression*, which caused a stir when it was published in 1960. Levy originally maintained that the generation that adopted the Constitution and the Bill of Rights did not believe in a broad view of freedom of expression, especially in the area of politics. His new position, based both on new evidence and on continued criticism of his original thesis, is that Americans were more tolerant of government criticism but that the Revolutionary generation did not intend to wipe out seditious libel with the adoption of the First Amendment.

———. *The Establishment Clause: Religion and the First Amendment.* New York: Macmillan, 1986. This searching study of the establishment clause claims that the view that government can assist all religions is historically groundless. Levy argues that it is unconstitutional for government to provide aid to any religion.

Lewis, Anthony. *Make No Law: The* Sullivan *Case and the First Amendment.* New York: Random House, 1991. This is an enlightening study of a great constitutional decision. Lewis illuminates the history and evolution of the First Amendment guarantees of free expression and free press.

Polenberg, Richard. *Fighting Faiths.* New York: Alfred A. Knopf, 1987. By focusing on the famous case of *Abrams* v. *United States,* a noted historian examines anarchism, government surveillance, freedom of speech, and the effect of the Russian Revolution on American liberals.

Smolla, Rodney A. *Free Speech in an Open Society.* New York, Alfred A. Knopf, 1993. A lucid examination covering a wide range of contemporary problems in free speech, such as flag burning, hate speech, and new technologies.

Tribe, Laurence H. *Abortion: The Clash of Absolutes.* New York: W. W. Norton, 1990. Tribe seeks an accommodation in the clash of absolutes in the abortion debate through a historical, political, and legal analysis of the issues.

CHAPTER

16

Equality and Civil Rights

DIANE JOYCE AND PAUL JOHNSON worked hard patching holes, shoveling asphalt, and opening culverts for the Santa Clara County (California) Transportation Agency. In 1980, a skilled position as road dispatcher opened up; it meant less strenuous work and higher pay. Joyce and Johnson competed along with ten other applicants for the job. At the time, men held all of the agency's 238 skilled positions.

Seven of the applicants, including Joyce and Johnson, passed an oral exam. Next, the agency conducted a round of interviews. Johnson tied for second with a score of 75; Joyce ranked third with a score of 73. After a second round of interviews with the top contenders, the agency gave the job to Paul Johnson.

Diane Joyce didn't let the matter rest. She filed a complaint with the head of the agency, invoking the county government's affirmative action policy. **Affirmative action** is a commitment by an employer, school, or other public or private institution to expand opportunities for women, blacks, Hispanic Americans, and members of other minority groups. Affirmative action embraces a wide range of policies, from special recruitment efforts to numerical goals and quotas.

The county's affirmative action policy was an effort to remedy the effects of prior practices, intentional or not, that had restricted work opportunities for women, minorities, and the disabled. Its goal was the employment of individuals from these groups in upper-level jobs in proportion to their representation in the area's total work force. After reviewing its decision in light of the county's policy, the agency took the job away from Johnson and gave it to Joyce. A government-imposed equality policy thus thwarted Paul Johnson's freedom to climb the ladder of success. Angered by the lost promotion, he sued.

Johnson argued that he was the victim of sex discrimination. **Discrimination** is the act of making or recognizing distinctions. When making distinctions between people, discrimination may be benign (that is, harmless) or invidious (harmful). The national government has enacted policies to prohibit invidious discrimination, which is often rooted in prejudice. Johnson invoked Title VII of the 1964 Civil Rights Act, which bars employment discrimination based on race, religion, national origin, or sex. He won the first round in a federal district court; Joyce's employer appealed and won a reversal. They fought the final round in the Supreme Court in 1987.[1] Diane Joyce emerged the victor.

In an emotion-filled ceremony before 2,000 disabled visitors and their families, President George Bush autographs one of the most important laws of his administration, the Americans with Disabilities Act of 1990.

Laws and policies that promote equality inevitably come into conflict with demands for freedom. The conflict intensifies when we recognize that Americans advocate competing conceptions of equality.

TWO CONCEPTIONS OF EQUALITY

Americans want equality, at least in principle. Public support for the principle of equal treatment has increased dramatically from the 1940s to the 1980s. Today, more than nine in ten Americans espouse equal treatment for all in schools, public accommodations, housing, employment, and public transportation. However, Americans are far less united in their support for how to implement this principle.[2]

Most Americans support **equality of opportunity,** the idea that people should have an equal chance to develop their talents and that effort and ability should be rewarded. This form of equality offers all individuals the same chance to get ahead; it glorifies personal achievement through free competition and allows everyone to climb the ladder of success, starting at the first rung. Special recruitment efforts aimed at identifying qualified minority or female job applicants, for example, ensure that everyone has the same chance starting out. The initial competition for promotion between Joyce and Johnson illustrates equality of opportunity.

Americans are less committed to **equality of outcome,** which means greater uniformity in social, economic, and political power. For example, schools and businesses aim at equality of outcome when they allocate admissions or jobs on the basis of race, gender, or disability, which are unrelated to ability. (Some observers refer to these allocations as *quotas,* while others call them *goals.* The difference is subtle. A quota requires proportional shares of some benefit to a favored group. A goal aims for proportional shares without requiring it.) But the vast majority of Americans

FIGURE **16.1**   ■ **Public Attitudes Toward Preferential Treatment**

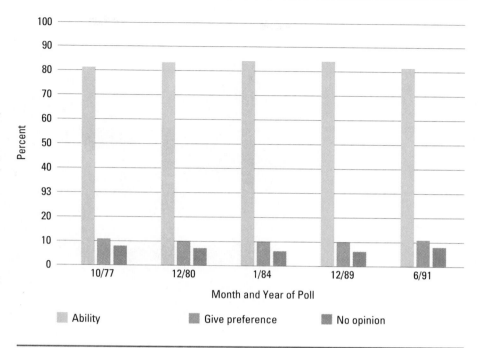

Polling results since 1977 show a clear rejection of preferential treatment for minorities and women in employment and college admissions. More than 80 percent of Americans consistently favor ability as the only criterion for jobs and college entrance. The results for women and men are identical.

[QUESTION: Some people say that to make up for past discrimination, women and members of minority groups should be given preferential treatment in getting jobs and places in colleges. Others say that ability, as determined in test scores, should be the main consideration. Which point of view comes closer to how you feel on the subject?]

Source: *The Gallup Monthly Poll, August 1991, p. 56. Used with permission. Additional data provided by the Roper Center for Public Opinion Research and the Gallup Organization.*

consistently favors merit-based admissions and employment over preferential treatment,[3] as Figure 16.1 shows.

Equality of outcome can occur only if we restrict the free competition that is the basis of equality of opportunity. One restriction takes the form of a limit on personal achievement. Preferential treatment in hiring is an apt example. That treatment gave Joyce the advancement and prevented Johnson from climbing the ladder of success.

Quota policies generate the most opposition, because they confine competition. Quotas limit advancement for some individuals and ensure advancement for others. They alter positions on the ladder of success by taking into account factors unrelated to ability. Equal outcomes policies that benefit minorities or women or the disabled at the expense of whites or men or the able bodied create strong opposition, because quotas seem to be at odds with individual initiative. In other words, freedom clashes with equality. To understand the ways government resolves this conflict, we have to understand the development of civil rights in this country.

The history of civil rights in the United States is primarily the story of the search for social and economic equality. This search has persisted for more than a century and is still going on today. It began with the civil rights of black citizens, whose subjugation roused the passions of a nation and brought about its bloodiest conflict, the Civil War. The struggle of blacks has been a beacon lighting the way for Native Americans, Hispanic Americans, women, and the disabled. Each of these groups has confronted discrimination, sometimes subtle, sometimes overt, sometimes from other minorities. Each has achieved a measure of success by pressing its

Separate and Unequal

The Supreme Court gave constitutional protection to racial separation on the theory that states could provide "separate but equal" facilities for blacks. But racial separation meant unequal facilities, as these two water fountains dramatically illustrated. The Supreme Court struck a fatal blow against the "separate but equal" doctrine in its landmark 1954 ruling, Brown *v.* Board of Education.

interests on government, even challenging government. These challenges and government's responses to them have helped shape our democracy.

Remember that **civil rights** are powers or privileges guaranteed to the individual and protected from arbitrary removal at the hands of the government or other individuals. (Rights need not be confined to humans. Some advocates claim that animals have rights, too.) In this chapter, we will concentrate on the rights guaranteed by the constitutional amendments adopted after the Civil War and by laws passed to enforce those guarantees. Prominent among them is the right to equal protection of the laws. This right remained a promise rather than a reality well into the twentieth century.

THE CIVIL WAR AMENDMENTS

The Civil War amendments were adopted to provide freedom and equality to black Americans. The Thirteenth Amendment, ratified in 1865, provided that

> Neither slavery nor involuntary servitude . . . shall exist within the United States, or any place subject to their jurisdiction.

The Fourteenth Amendment was adopted three years later. It provides first that freed slaves are citizens:

> All persons born or naturalized in the United States, and subject to the jurisdiction thereof, are citizens of the United States and of the State wherein they reside.

As we saw in Chapter 15, it also prohibits the states from abridging the "privileges or immunities of citizens of the United States" or depriving "any person of life, liberty, or property, without due process of law." The amendment then goes on to protect equality under the law, declaring that no state shall

> deny to any person within its jurisdiction the equal protection of the laws.

The Fifteenth Amendment, adopted in 1870, added a measure of political equality:

> The right of citizens of the United States to vote shall not be denied or abridged by the United States or by any State on account of race, color, or previous condition of servitude. American blacks were thus free and politically equal—at least according to the Constitution. But for many years, the courts checked the efforts of other branches to protect these constitutional rights.

Congress and the Supreme Court: Lawmaking Versus Law Interpreting

In the years after the Civil War, Congress went to work to protect the rights of black citizens. In 1866, lawmakers passed a civil rights act that gave the national government some authority over the treatment of blacks by state courts. This legislation was a response to the **black codes,** laws enacted by the former slave states to restrict the freedom of blacks. For example, vagrancy and apprenticeship laws forced blacks to work and denied them a free choice of employers. One section of the 1866 act that still applies today grants all citizens the rights to make and enforce contracts, sue or be sued, give evidence, and inherit, purchase, lease, sell, hold, or convey property. Later, in the Civil Rights Act of 1875, Congress attempted to guarantee blacks equal access to public accommodations (streetcars, inns, parks, theaters, and the like).

While Congress was enacting laws to protect the civil rights of black citizens, the Supreme Court seemed intent on weakening those rights. In 1873, the Court ruled that the Civil War amendments had not changed the relationship between the state and national governments.[4] State citizenship and national citizenship remained separate and distinct. According to the Court, the Fourteenth Amendment did not obligate the states to honor the rights guaranteed by U.S. citizenship. In effect, the Court stripped the amendment of its power to secure the Bill of Rights' guarantees for black citizens.

In subsequent years, the Court continued to shrink constitutional protections for blacks. In 1876, the justices crippled congressional attempts to enforce the rights of blacks.[5] A group of Louisiana whites had used violence and fraud to prevent blacks from exercising their basic constitutional rights, including the right of peaceable assembly. The justices held that the rights allegedly infringed on were not nationally protected rights and that therefore Congress was powerless to punish those who violated them. On the very same day, the Court ruled that the Fifteenth Amendment did not guarantee all citizens the right to vote; it simply listed grounds that could not be used to deny that right.[6] And in 1883, the Court struck down the public accommodations section of the Civil Rights

Act of 1875.[7] The justices declared that the national government could prohibit only government action that discriminated against blacks; private acts of discrimination or acts of omission by a state were beyond the reach of the national government. For example, a state law excluding blacks from jury service was an unlawful abridgment of individual rights. However, a person who refused to serve blacks in a private club was outside the control of the national government, because the discrimination was a private—not a governmental—act. The Court refused to see racial discrimination as an act that the national government could prohibit. In case after case, the justices tolerated racial discrimination. In the process they abetted **racism,** a belief that inherent differences among races determine achievement and that one's own race is superior to and thus has a right to dominate others.

The Court's decisions gave the states ample room to maneuver around civil rights laws. In the matter of voting rights, for example, states that wanted to bar black men from the polls simply used nonracial means to do so. One popular tool was the **poll tax,** first imposed by Georgia in 1877. This was a tax of $1 or $2 on every citizen who wanted to vote. The tax was not a burden for most whites. But many blacks were tenant farmers, deeply in debt to white merchants and landowners; they just did not have any extra money for voting. Other bars to black suffrage included literacy tests, minimum education requirements, and a grandfather clause that restricted suffrage to men who could establish that their grandfathers were eligible to vote before 1867 (three years before the Fifteenth Amendment declared that race could not be used to deny the right to vote).[8] White southerners also used intimidation and violence to keep blacks from the polls.

The Roots of Racial Segregation

Well before the Civil War, **racial segregation** was a way of life in the South: Blacks lived and worked separately from whites. After the war, southern states began to enact Jim Crow laws that enforced segregation. (*Jim Crow* was a derogatory term for a black person.) Once the Supreme Court nullified the Civil Rights Act of 1875, such laws proliferated. They required blacks to live in separate and generally inferior areas and restricted them to separate and inferior sections of hospitals, separate cemeteries, separate drinking and toilet facilities, and separate sections of streetcars, trains, schools, jails, and parks. Each day, in countless ways, they were reminded of the inferior status accorded them by white society.

In 1892, Homer Adolph Plessy—who was seven-eighths Caucasian—took a seat in a "whites-only" car of a Louisiana train. He refused to move to the car reserved for blacks and was arrested. Plessy argued that Louisiana's law mandating racial segregation on its trains was an unconstitutional infringement on both the privileges and immunities and the equal protection clauses of the Fourteenth Amendment. The Supreme Court disagreed. The majority in **Plessy v. Ferguson** (1896) upheld state-imposed racial segregation.[9] They based their decision on what came to be known as the **separate-but-equal doctrine,** that separate facilities for blacks and whites satisfied the Fourteenth Amendment so long as they were equal. The lone dissenter was John Marshall Harlan (the first of two distinguished justices with the same name). Harlan, who envisioned a "color-blind Constitution," wrote:

> We boast of the freedom enjoyed by our people above all other peoples. But it is difficult to reconcile that boast with a state of the law which, practically, puts the brand of servitude and degradation upon a large class of our fellow citizens—our equals before the law. The thin disguise of "equal" accommodations for passengers in railroad coaches will not mislead any one, nor atone for the wrong this day done.[10]

Three years later, the Supreme Court extended the separate-but-equal doctrine to the schools.[11] The justices ignored the fact that black educational facilities (and most other "colored-only" facilities) were far from equal to those reserved for whites.

By the end of the nineteenth century, racial segregation was firmly and legally entrenched in the American South. Although constitutional amendments and national laws to protect equality under the law were in place, the Supreme Court's interpretation of those amendments and laws rendered them ineffective. Several decades would pass before any change was discernible.

THE DISMANTLING OF SCHOOL SEGREGATION

Denied the right to vote and be represented in government, blacks sought access to power in other parts of the political system. The National Association for the Advancement of Colored People (NAACP), founded in 1909 by W. E. B. Du Bois and others, both black and white, with the goal of ending racial discrimination and segregation, took the lead in the campaign for black civil rights. The plan was to launch two-pronged legal and lobbying attacks on the separate-but-equal doctrine: first by pressing for fully equal facilities for blacks, then by proving the unconstitutionality of segregation. The process would be a slow one, but the strategies involved did not require a large organization or heavy financial backing; at the time, the NAACP had neither.*

Pressure for Equality . . .

By the 1920s, the separate-but-equal doctrine was so deeply ingrained in American law that no Supreme Court justice would dissent from its continued application to racial segregation. But a few Court decisions offered hope that change would come. In 1935, Lloyd Gaines graduated from Lincoln University, a black college in Missouri, and applied to the state law school. The law school rejected him because he was black. Missouri refused to admit blacks to its all-white law school; the state's policy was to pay the costs of blacks who were admitted to out-of-state law schools. With the support of the NAACP, Gaines appealed to the courts for admission to the University of Missouri Law School. In 1938, the United States Supreme Court ruled that he must be admitted.[12] Under the *Plessy* doctrine, Missouri could not shift to other states its responsibility to provide an equal education.

---

* *In 1939, the NAACP established an offshoot, the NAACP Legal Defense and Education Fund, to work on legal challenges, whereas the parent organization concentrated on lobbying.*

Two later cases helped reinforce the requirement that segregated facilities must be equal in all major respects. One was brought by Heman Sweatt, again with the help of the NAACP. The all-white University of Texas Law School had denied Sweatt entrance because of his race. A federal court ordered the state to provide a black law school for him; the state responded by renting a few rooms in an office building and hiring two black lawyers as teachers. Sweatt refused to attend the school and took his case to the Supreme Court.[13]

The second case raised a related issue. A doctoral program in education at the all-white University of Oklahoma had refused George McLaurin admission because he was black. The state had no equivalent program for blacks. McLaurin sought a federal court order for admission, but under pressure from the decision in *Gaines*, the university amended its procedures and admitted McLaurin "on a segregated basis." It restricted the sixty-eight-year-old McLaurin to hastily designated "colored-only" sections of a few rooms. With the help of the NAACP, McLaurin appealed this obvious lack of equal facilities to the Supreme Court.[14]

The Court ruled on *Sweatt* and *McLaurin* in 1950. The justices unanimously found that the facilities in each case were inadequate: The separate "law school" provided for Sweatt did not approach the quality of the white state law school, and the restrictions placed on McLaurin's interactions with other students would result in an inferior education. Their respective state universities had to give both Sweatt and McLaurin full student status. But the Court avoided reexamination of the separate-but-equal doctrine.

. . . And Pressure for Desegregation

These decisions—especially *McLaurin*—suggested to the NAACP that the time was right for an attack on segregation itself. In addition, public attitudes toward race relations were slowly changing from the predominant racism of the nineteenth and early twentieth centuries. Black groups had fought with honor—albeit in segregated military units—in World War II. Blacks and whites were working together in unions and in service and religious organizations. Social change and court decisions suggested that government-imposed segregation was vulnerable.

President Harry S Truman risked his political future with his strong support of black civil rights. In 1947, he established the President's Committee on Civil Rights. The committee's report, issued later that year, became the agenda for the civil rights movement during the next two decades. It called for national laws prohibiting racially motivated poll taxes, segregation, and brutality and for guarantees of voting rights and equal employment opportunity. In 1948, Truman ordered the **desegregation** (the dismantling of authorized racial segregation) of the armed forces.

In 1947, the U.S. Department of Justice had begun to submit briefs to the courts in support of civil rights. The department's most important intervention probably came in ***Brown v. Board of Education***.[15] This case was the culmination of twenty years of planning and litigation on the part of the NAACP to invalidate racial segregation in public schools.

Linda Brown was a black child whose father tried to enroll her in a white public school in Topeka, Kansas. The school was close to Linda's home,

Anger Erupts in Little Rock

In 1957, the school board in Little Rock, Arkansas, attempted to implement court-approved desegregation. The first step called for admitting nine blacks to Central High School on September 3, but the governor sent in the national guard to bar their attendance. On September 23, when the black students again attempted entry, police escorts could not control the mob that gathered at the school. Two days later, under the protection of federal troops ordered by President Eisenhower, the students were finally admitted. Although hostility and violence led the school board to seek a postponement of the desegregation plan, the Supreme Court, meeting in special session, affirmed the Brown *decision and ordered the plan to proceed.*

and the walk to the black school meant that she had to cross a dangerous set of railroad tracks. Brown's request was refused because of Linda's race. A federal district court found that the black public school was, in all major respects, equal in quality to the white school; therefore, according to the *Plessy* doctrine, Linda was required to go to the black public school. Brown appealed the decision.

Brown v. *Board of Education* reached the Supreme Court in late 1951. The justices delayed argument on the sensitive race issue until after the 1952 national election. The Court merged *Brown* with four similar cases into a class action, a device for combining the claims or defenses of similar individuals so that they can be tried in a single lawsuit (see Chapter 14). And all were supported by the NAACP and coordinated by Thurgood Marshall, who would later become the first black justice to sit on the Supreme Court. The five cases squarely challenged the separate-but-equal doctrine. By all tangible measures (standards for teacher licensing, teacher-pupil ratios, library facilities), the two school systems in each case—one white, the other black—were equal. The issue was legal separation of the races.

On May 17, 1954, Chief Justice Earl Warren, who had recently joined the Court, delivered a single opinion covering four of the cases. (Chapter 14 describes how he approached them.) Warren spoke for a unanimous Court when he declared that "in the field of public education the doctrine of 'separate but equal' has no place. Separate educational facilities are inherently unequal,"[16] depriving the plaintiffs of the equal protection of the laws. Segregated facilities generate in black children "a feeling of inferiority . . . that may affect their hearts and minds in a way unlikely ever to be undone."[17] In short, the nation's highest court found that state-imposed public school segregation violated the equal protection clause of the Fourteenth Amendment.

A companion case to *Brown* challenged the segregation of public schools in Washington, D.C.[18] Segregation there was imposed by Congress. The equal protection clause protected citizens only against state violations; no equal protection clause restrained the national government. It was unthinkable for the Constitution to impose a lesser duty on the national government than on the states. In this case, the Court unanimously decided that the racial segregation requirement was an arbitrary deprivation of liberty without due process of law, a violation of the Fifth Amendment. In short, the concept of liberty embraced the idea of equality.

The Court deferred implementation of the school desegregation decisions until 1955. Then, in **Brown v. Board of Education II,** it ruled that school systems must desegregate "with all deliberate speed" and assigned the process of supervising desegregation to the lower federal courts.[19]

Some states quietly implemented the *Brown* decree. Others did little to desegregate their schools. And many communities in the South defied the Court, sometimes violently. Some white business and professional people formed "white citizens councils." The councils put economic pressure on blacks who asserted their rights by foreclosing on mortgages and denying blacks credit at local stores. Georgia and North Carolina resisted desegregation by paying the tuition of white students who attended private schools. Virginia and other states ordered that desegregated schools be closed.

This resistance, along with the Supreme Court's "all deliberate speed" order, placed a heavy burden on federal judges to dismantle what were by now fundamental social institutions in many communities.[20] Gradual desegregation under *Brown* was in some cases no desegregation at all. By 1969, a unanimous Supreme Court ordered that the operation of segregated school systems must stop "at once."[21]

Two years later, the Court approved several remedies to achieve integration, including busing, racial quotas, and the pairing or grouping of non-contiguous school zones. In *Swann* v. *Charlotte-Mecklenburg County Schools,* the Supreme Court affirmed the right of lower courts to order the busing of children to ensure school desegregation.[22] But these remedies applied only to **de jure segregation,** government-imposed segregation (for example, government assignment of whites to one school and blacks to another within the same community). Court-imposed remedies did not apply to **de facto segregation,** segregation that is not the result of government action (for example, racial segregation resulting from residential patterns).

The busing of schoolchildren came under heavy attack in both the North and the South. Desegregation advocates saw busing as a potential remedy in many northern cities, where schools had become segregated as white families left the cities for the suburbs. This "white flight" left inner-city schools predominantly black and suburban schools almost all white. Public opinion strongly opposed the busing approach, and Congress sought to impose limits on busing as a remedy. In 1974, a closely divided Court ruled in **Milliken v. Bradley** that lower courts could not order busing across school district boundaries, unless each district had practiced racial discrimination or unless school district lines had been deliberately drawn to achieve racial segregation.[23] This ruling meant an end to large-scale school desegregation in metropolitan areas.

Dishonoring Old Glory

The struggle for racial equality in Boston in the 1970s divided the city and generated hatred and resentment between blacks and whites. Federal court orders mandating school desegregation touched off particularly violent reactions. In 1976, a white protester marching toward the federal courthouse tried to impale a black passerby with a flagstaff. This photograph captured the ugliness of the city's conflicts more powerfully than words could.

THE CIVIL RIGHTS MOVEMENT

Although the NAACP concentrated on school desegregation, it also made headway in other areas. The Supreme Court responded to the NAACP's efforts in the late 1940s by outlawing whites-only primary elections in the South, declaring them to be in violation of the Fifteenth Amendment. The Court also declared segregation on interstate bus routes to be unconstitutional, and desegregated restaurants and hotels in the District of Columbia. Despite these and other decisions that chipped away at existing barriers to equality, states still were denying black citizens political power, and segregation remained a fact of daily life, as Feature 16.1 describes.

Dwight D. Eisenhower, who became president in 1953, was not as concerned about civil rights as his predecessor had been. He chose to stand above the battle between the Supreme Court and those who resisted the Court's decisions. He even refused to reveal whether he agreed with the Court's decision in *Brown* v. *Board of Education.* "It makes no difference," Eisenhower declared, because "the Constitution is as the Supreme Court interprets it."[24]

Eisenhower did enforce school desegregation when the safety of schoolchildren was involved, but he appeared unwilling to do much more to advance racial equality. That goal seemed to require the political mobilization of the people—black and white—in what is now known as the **civil rights movement.**

Black churches served as the crucible of the movement. More than places of worship, they served hundreds of other functions. In black communities, the church was "a bulletin board to a people who owned no organs of communication, a credit union to those without banks, and even a

FEATURE 16.1

■ American Racism: An International Handicap

 In August 1955, the ambassador from India, G. L. Mehta, walked into a restaurant at the Houston International Airport, sat down, and waited to order. But Texas law required service of whites and blacks in separate dining facilities. The dark-skinned diplomat, who had seated himself in a whites-only area, was told to move. The insult stung deeply and was not soon forgotten. From Washington, Secretary of State John Foster Dulles telegraphed his apologies for this blatant display of racism, fearing that the incident would injure relations with a nation whose allegiance the United States was seeking in the Cold War.

Such embarrassments were not uncommon in the 1950s. A Columbus, Ohio, restaurant refused to serve Burma's minister of education, and a Howard Johnson's restaurant just outside the nation's capital turned away the finance minister of Ghana. Secretary Dulles complained that segregationist practices were becoming a "major international hazard," a threat to U.S. efforts to gain the friendship of developing countries. Americans stood publicly condemned as a people who did not honor the ideal of equality.

Thus, when the attorney general [James P. McGranery] appealed to the Supreme Court to strike down segregation in public schools, his introductory remarks [in the government's amicus brief] took note of the international implications. "It is in the context of the present world struggle between freedom and tyranny that the problem of racial discrimination must be viewed," he warned. The humiliation of dark-skinned diplomats in Washington, D.C., "the window through which the world looks into our house," was damaging to American interests. Racism "furnished grist for the Communist propaganda mills."

- *Source: Mary Beth Norton et al.,* A People and a Nation: A History of the United States, *3d ed. (Boston: Houghton Mifflin, 1990), p. 869. Copyright © 1990 by Houghton Mifflin Company. Adapted with permission.*

kind of people's court." Some of its preachers were motivated by fortune, others by saintliness. One would prove to be a modern-day Moses.[25]

Civil Disobedience

Rosa Parks, a black woman living in Montgomery, Alabama, sounded the first call to action. That city's Jim Crow ordinances were tougher than those in other southern cities, where blacks were required to sit in the back of the bus and whites in the front, both races converging as the bus filled with passengers. In Montgomery, however, bus drivers had power to define and redefine the floating line separating blacks and whites: Drivers would order blacks to vacate an entire row to make room for one white or order blacks to stand even when some seats were vacant. Blacks could not walk through the white section to their seats in the back; they had to leave the bus after paying the fare and reenter through the rear.[26] In December 1955, Parks boarded a city bus on her way home from work and took an available seat in the front of the bus; she refused to give up her seat when the driver asked her to do so and was arrested and fined $10 for violating the city ordinance.

Montgomery's black community responded to Parks's arrest with a boycott of the city's bus system. A **boycott** is a refusal to do business with a company or individual as an expression of disapproval or means of coercion. Blacks walked or car-pooled or made no trips that were not absolutely necessary. As the bus company moved closer to bankruptcy and downtown merchants suffered from the loss of black business, city officials began to harass blacks, hoping to frighten them into ending the boycott. But Montgomery's black citizens now had a leader—a charismatic twenty-six-year-old Baptist minister named Martin Luther King, Jr.

King urged the people to hold out, and they did. A year after the boycott began, a federal court ruled that segregated transportation systems violated the equal protection clause of the Constitution. The boycott proved to be an effective weapon.

In 1957, King helped organize the Southern Christian Leadership Conference (SCLC) to coordinate civil rights activities. King was totally committed to nonviolent action to bring racial issues into the light. To that end, he advocated **civil disobedience,** the willful but nonviolent violation of unjust laws.

One nonviolent tactic was the sit-in. On February 1, 1960, four black freshmen from North Carolina Agricultural and Technical College in Greensboro sat down at a whites-only lunch counter. They were refused service by the black waitress, who said, "Fellows like you make our race look bad." The freshmen stayed all day and promised to return the next morning to continue what they called a "sit-down protest." Other students soon joined in, rotating shifts so that no one missed classes. Within two days, eighty-five students had flocked to the lunch counter. Although abused verbally and physically, the students would not move. Finally, they were arrested. Soon people held similar sit-in demonstrations throughout the South and then in the North.[27] The Supreme Court upheld the actions of the demonstrators, although the unanimity that had characterized its earlier decisions was gone. (In this decision, three justices argued that even bigots had the right to call on the government to protect their property interests.)

The Civil Rights Act of 1964

In 1961, a new administration headed by President John F. Kennedy came to power. At first, Kennedy did not seem to be committed to civil rights. His stance changed as the movement gained momentum and as more and more whites became aware of the abuse being heaped on sit-in demonstrators, freedom riders (who tested unlawful segregation on interstate bus routes), and those who were trying to help blacks register to vote in southern states. Volunteers were being jailed, beaten, and killed for advocating activities that whites took for granted.

In late 1962, President Kennedy ordered federal troops to ensure the safety of James Meredith, the first black to attend the University of Mississippi. In early 1963, Kennedy enforced the desegregation of the University of Alabama. In April 1963, television viewers were shocked to see marchers in Birmingham, Alabama, attacked with dogs, fire hoses, and cattle prods. (The idea of the Birmingham march was to provoke confrontations with white officials in an effort to compel the national government to intervene on behalf of blacks.) Finally, in June 1963, Kennedy asked Congress for legislation that would outlaw segregation in public accommodations.

A Modern-Day Moses

Martin Luther King, Jr., was a Baptist minister who believed in the principles of nonviolent protest practiced by India's Mahatma Gandhi. This photograph, taken in 1963 in Baltimore, captures the crowd's affection for King, the man many thought would lead them to a new Canaan of racial equality. King, who won the Nobel Peace Prize in 1964, was assassinated in 1968 in Memphis, Tennessee.

Two months later, Martin Luther King, Jr., joined in a march on Washington, D.C. The organizers named their activity, "A March for Jobs and Freedom," signaling the economic goals of black America. More than 250,000 people, black and white, gathered peaceably at the Lincoln Memorial to hear King speak. "I have a dream," he told them, "that my little children will one day live in a nation where they will not be judged by the color of their skin but by the content of their character,"[28] (Feature 16.2 describes events surrounding the speech.) Congress had not yet enacted Kennedy's public accommodations bill when he was assassinated on November 22, 1963. His successor, Lyndon B. Johnson, considered civil rights his top legislative priority. Within months, Congress enacted the Civil Rights Act of 1964, which included a vital provision barring segregation in most public accommodations. Congressional action was, in part, a reaction to Kennedy's death. But it was also almost certainly a response to the brutal treatment of blacks throughout the South.

Congress had enacted civil rights laws in 1957 and 1960, but they dealt primarily with voting rights. The 1964 act was the most comprehensive legislative attempt ever to erase racial discrimination in the United States. Congress acted after the longest debate in Senate history and only after the first successful use of a procedure to end a civil rights filibuster.

Among its many provisions, the act

- entitled all persons to "the full and equal enjoyment" of goods, services, and privileges in places of public accommodation without discrimination on the grounds of race, color, religion, or national origin.

- established the right to equality in employment opportunities.

- strengthened voting rights legislation.

FEATURE 16.2

■ A Preacher's Afterthought: A Dream of Freedom from Inequality

 The Rev. Martin Luther King, Jr., gave Americans a vision of a society free from racial inequality in his famous "I Have a Dream" speech. But King's most memorable lines on the steps of the Lincoln Memorial in Washington, D.C., were not part of his prepared text. King ad-libbed.

King was the last speaker that day in Washington. He recited his prepared text until shortly near the end, when he decided not to deliver what one historian has labeled the lamest and most pretentious section. ("And so today, let us go back to our communities as members of the international association for the advancement of creative dissatisfaction.") Instead, he extemporized, urging his audience to believe that change would come "somehow" and that they could not "wallow in the valley of despair."

Voices from behind urged King on. Mahalia Jackson, the great gospel singer, added her voice: "Tell 'em about the dream, Martin." The dream device was one King had used in the past, in speeches and at the pulpit. It's not clear whether he heard Jackson's words or simply reached instinctively for a familiar and effective piece of oratory.

After the powerful "dream" sequence, King returned to a few sentences from his prepared text. But then he was off on his own again, reciting the first stanza from "My Country 'Tis of Thee," ending with "let freedom ring." King continued: "And if America is to be a great nation, this must become true. So let freedom ring." King concluded with an old vision from the pulpit, born of enslavement but new to a world now riveted to his words: "And when this happens . . . we will be able to speed up that day when all God's children, black men and white men, Jews and Gentiles, Protestants and Catholics, will be able to join hands and sing in the words of the old Negro spiritual, 'Free at last! Free at last! Thank God Almighty, we are free at last!' "

• *Source: Taylor Branch,* Parting the Waters: America in the King Years, 1954–63 *(New York: Simon & Schuster, 1988), chap. 22. Copyright 1988 by Taylor Branch. Reprinted by permission of Simon & Schuster, Inc.*

• created the Equal Employment Opportunity Commission (EEOC), charging it to hear and investigate complaints of job discrimination.*

• provided that funds could be withheld from federally assisted programs that were administered in a discriminatory manner.

The last of these provisions had a powerful effect on school desegregation when Congress enacted the Elementary and Secondary Education Act in 1965. That act provided for billions of federal dollars in aid for the nation's schools; the threat of losing that money spurred local school boards to formulate and implement new plans for desegregation.

The 1964 act faced an immediate constitutional challenge. Its opponents argued that the Constitution does not forbid acts of private discrimination—the position the Supreme Court itself had taken in the late nineteenth century. But this time, a unanimous Court upheld the law, declaring that acts of discrimination impose substantial burdens on interstate commerce and thus are subject to congressional control.[29] In a

---

* *Since 1972, the EEOC has had the power to institute legal proceedings on behalf of employees who allege that they have been victims of illegal discrimination.*

companion case, Ollie McClung, the owner of a small restaurant, had refused to serve blacks. McClung maintained that he had the freedom to serve whomever he wanted in his own restaurant. The justices, however, upheld the government's prohibition of McClung's racial discrimination on the ground that a substantial portion of the food served in his restaurant had moved in interstate commerce.[30] Thus, the Supreme Court vindicated the Civil Rights Act of 1964 by reason of the congressional power to regulate interstate commerce rather than on the basis of the Fourteenth Amendment. Since 1937, the Court had approved ever-widening authority to regulate state and local activities under the commerce clause. It was the most powerful basis for the exercise of congressional power in the Constitution.

President Johnson's goal was a "great society." Soon a constitutional amendment and a series of civil rights laws were in place to help him meet his goal:

- The Twenty-fourth Amendment, ratified in 1964, banned poll taxes in primary and general elections for national office.

- The Economic Opportunity Act of 1964 provided education and training to combat poverty.

- The Voting Rights Act of 1965 empowered the attorney general to send voter registration supervisors to areas in which fewer than half the eligible minority voters had been registered. This act has been credited with doubling black voter registration in the South in only five years.[31]

- The Fair Housing Act of 1968 banned discrimination in the rental or sale of most housing.

The Continuing Struggle over Civil Rights

However, civil rights on the books do not ensure civil rights in action. This was the case in 1984, when the Supreme Court was called on to interpret a law forbidding sex discrimination in schools and colleges receiving financial assistance from the national government. Must the entire institution comply with the regulations or only those portions of it that receive assistance?

In *Grove City College* v. *Bell*, the Court ruled that government educational grants to students implicate the institution as a recipient of government funds; therefore, it must comply with government nondiscrimination provisions. However, only the specific department or program receiving the funds (in Grove City's case, the financial aid program), not the whole institution, was barred from discriminating.[32] Athletic departments rarely receive such government funds, so colleges had no obligation to provide equal opportunity for women in their sports programs.

The *Grove City* decision had widespread effects, because three other important civil rights laws were worded similarly. The implication was that any law barring discrimination on the basis of race, sex, age, or disability would be applicable only to programs receiving federal funds, not to the entire institution. So a university laboratory that received federal research grants could not discriminate, but other departments that did not receive federal money could. The effect of *Grove City* was to frustrate enforcement of civil rights laws. In keeping with pluralist theory, civil rights and women's groups shifted their efforts to the legislative branch.

Congress reacted immediately, exercising its lawmaking power to check the law-interpreting power of the judiciary. Congress can revise decisions that interpret national laws; in this political chess game, the Court's move is hardly the last move. Legislators protested that the Court had misinterpreted the intent of the antidiscrimination laws, and they forged a bipartisan effort to make that intent crystal clear: If any part of an institution gets federal money, no part can discriminate. Their work led to the Civil Rights Restoration Act, which became law in 1988 despite a presidential veto by Ronald Reagan.

While Congress tried to restore and expand civil rights enforcement, the Supreme Court weakened it again. The Court restricted minority contractor set-asides of state public works funds, an arrangement it had approved in 1980. (A set-aside is a purchasing or contracting provision that allocates a certain percentage of business to minority-owned companies.) The five-person majority held that past societal discrimination alone cannot serve as the basis for rigid quotas.[33]

Buttressed by Republican appointees, the Supreme Court continued to narrow the scope of national civil rights protections in a string of 1989 decisions that suggested the ascendancy of a new conservative majority more concerned with freedom than equality.[34] Because the issues hinged on the Court's interpretation of civil rights laws, liberal advocates turned to Congress to restore and enlarge the earlier decisions by writing them into law. The result was a comprehensive new civil rights bill. President George Bush vetoed a 1990 version, asserting that it would impose quotas in hiring and promotion. But a year later, after months of debate, Bush signed a similar measure. The Civil Rights Act of 1991 reversed or altered six Court decisions that had narrowed civil rights protections. The new law clarified and expanded earlier legislation and increased the costs to employers for intentional, illegal discrimination. The likely result will be more awards to women and the disabled who sue for deliberate job bias and sexual harassment. The act gave some support to freedom-favoring advocates by barring "race norming" of test scores. (Race norming is the practice of adjusting test scores according to the test taker's race. The U.S. Labor Department encouraged race norming to give minority applicants a break on employment aptitude tests.) This issue has not yet reached the Supreme Court.

Racial Violence and Black Nationalism

Increased violence on the part of those who demanded their civil rights and those who refused to relinquish them marked the middle and late 1960s. Violence against civil rights workers was confined primarily to the South, where volunteers continued to work for desegregation and to register black voters. Among the atrocities that incensed even complacent whites were the bombing of dozens of black churches; the slaying of three young civil rights workers in Philadelphia, Mississippi, in 1964 by a group of whites, among them deputy sheriffs; police violence against demonstrators marching peacefully from Selma, Alabama, to Montgomery in 1965; and the assassination of Martin Luther King, Jr., in Memphis in 1968.

Black violence took the form of rioting in the black ghettos of northern cities. Civil rights gains had come mainly in the South. Northern blacks had the vote and were not subject to Jim Crow laws, yet most lived in poverty. Unemployment was high, work opportunities at skilled jobs were limited, and earnings were low. The segregation of blacks in inner-city ghettos, although not sanctioned by law, was nevertheless real; their voting power was minimal, because they constituted a small minority of the northern population. The solid gains made by southern blacks added to their frustration. Beginning in 1964, northern blacks took to the streets, burning and looting. Riots in 168 cities and towns followed King's assassination in 1968.

The lack of progress toward equality for northern blacks was an important factor in the rise of the black nationalist movement in the 1960s. The Nation of Islam, or Black Muslims, called for separation from whites rather than integration and for violence in return for violence; Malcolm X was their leading voice, until he distanced himself from the Muslims shortly before his assassination by fellow Muslims in 1965. The militant Black Panther Party generated fear with its denunciation of the values of white America. In 1966, Stokely Carmichael, then chairman of the Student Nonviolent Coordinating Committee (SNCC), called on blacks to assert "We want black power" in their struggle for civil rights. Organizations that had espoused integration and nonviolence now argued that blacks needed power more than white friendship.

The movement had several positive effects. Black nationalism promoted and instilled pride in black history and culture. By the end of the decade, colleges and universities were beginning to institute black studies programs for their students. More black citizens were voting than ever before, and their voting power was evident: Increasing numbers of blacks were winning election to public office. In 1967, Cleveland's voters elected Carl Stokes the first black major of a major American city. And by 1969, black representatives were able to form the Congressional Black Caucus. These achievements were incentives for other groups that also faced barriers to equality.

CIVIL RIGHTS FOR OTHER MINORITIES

Recent civil rights laws and court decisions protect members of all minority groups. The Supreme Court underscored the breadth of this protection in an important decision in 1987.[35] The justices ruled unanimously that the Civil Rights Act of 1866 (known today as *Section 1981*) offered broad protection against discrimination to all minorities. Previously, members of white ethnic groups could not invoke the law in bias suits. Under the decision, members of any ethnic group—Italian, Iranian, Chinese, Norwegian, or Vietnamese, for example—can recover money damages if they prove they have been denied jobs, excluded from rental housing, or subjected to other forms of discrimination prohibited by the law. The 1964 Civil Rights Act offers similar protections but specifies strict procedures for filing suits that tend to discourage litigation. Moreover, the remedies in most cases are limited. In job discrimination, for example, back pay and

Righting a Wrong

During World War II, Congress authorized the quarantine of Japanese residents in the western United States. The Supreme Court upheld the Congressional action in 1944. More than 110,000 men, women, and children—including native-born U.S. citizens—were incarcerated simply because they were of Japanese ancestry. The men pictured here were confined to the Japanese Evacuation Colony at Manzanar, California. In 1988, Congress passed legislation that offered apologies and $20,000 tax-free to each surviving internee. The cost to the government: $1.25 billion.

reinstatement are the only remedies. Section 1981 has fewer hurdles and allows litigants to seek punitive damages (damages awarded by a court as additional punishment for a serious wrong). In some respects, then, the older law is a more potent weapon than the newer one in fighting discrimination.

Clearly, the civil rights movement has had an effect on all minorities. However, the United States has granted equality most slowly to nonwhite minorities. Here we examine the civil rights struggles of three groups—Native Americans, Hispanic Americans, and the disabled.

Native Americans

During the eighteenth and nineteenth centuries, the U.S. government took Indian lands, isolated Native Americans on reservations, and denied them political and social rights. The government's dealings with the Indians were often marked by violence and broken promises. The agency system for administering Indian reservations kept Native Americans poor and dependent on the national government.

The national government switched policies at the turn of the century, promoting assimilation instead of separation. The government banned the use of native languages and religious rituals; it sent Indian children to boarding schools and gave them non-Indian names. In 1924, Indians received U.S. citizenship. Until that time, they were considered members of tribal nations whose relations with government were subject to treaties made with the United States. The Native American population suffered badly during the Depression, primarily because the poorest Americans were affected most but also because of the inept administration of Indian reservations. Poverty persisted on the reservations well after the Depression was over, and Indian landholdings continued to shrink through

Bury My Heart

Native American mourners gathered at Wounded Knee, South Dakota, on December 29, 1990, to remember a tragedy. On that site a hundred years earlier, Seventh Cavalry soldiers massacred two hundred Sioux—including women and children. Descendants of the survivors traveled by foot and horseback to mark the anniversary and honor their heritage.

the 1950s and into the 1960s—despite signed treaties and the religious significance of portions of those lands. In the 1960s, for example, a part of the Hopi Sacred Circle, which is considered the source of all life in tribal religion, was strip-mined for coal.

Anger bred of poverty, unemployment, and frustration with an uncaring government exploded in militant action in late 1969, when several American Indians seized Alcatraz Island, an abandoned island in San Francisco Bay. The group cited an 1868 Sioux treaty that entitled them to unused federal lands; they remained on the island for a year and a half. In 1973, armed members of the American Indian Movement seized eleven hostages at Wounded Knee, South Dakota, the site of an 1890 massacre of two hundred Sioux (Lakota) by troops of the U.S. cavalry. They remained there, occasionally exchanging gunfire with federal marshals, for seventy-one days, until the government agreed to examine the treaty rights of the Oglala Sioux.[36]

In 1946, Congress had enacted legislation establishing an Indian claims commission to compensate Native Americans for land that had been taken from them. In the 1970s, the Native American Rights Fund and other groups used that legislation to win important victories in the courts. The tribes won the return of lands in the Midwest and in the states of Oklahoma, New Mexico, and Washington. In 1980, the Supreme Court ordered the national government to pay the Sioux $117 million plus interest for the Black Hills of South Dakota, which had been stolen from them a century before. Other cases, involving land from coast to coast, are still pending.

The fight for lost lands and for survival of ancient native cultures continues. However, the preservation of Native American culture and the exercise of Native American rights sometimes create conflict with the interests of the majority. For example, the Chippewa in northern Wisconsin engage in an annual battle with local anglers on the shores of Lake

Minocqua. The Indians wish to exercise their acknowledged right to spear-fish for walleyed pike. Anglers fear that the Indians will deplete the stock and drive sport fishing away. The Chippewa voluntarily limit their annual catch, but they are offended that their ancestral rights are envied as government concessions.

In other instances, economic necessity may overwhelm ancient ways. One Alaskan tribe desperate for funds has been forced into unsettling choices: Sign away logging rights, permit oil drilling in a wildlife area, or allow the construction of an airfield in a vast habitat for Kodiak bears. Some tribes have allowed the use of their reservations for dumps and waste disposal, only to face land and water contamination as a consequence.

Throughout American history, Native Americans have been coerced physically and pressured economically to assimilate into the mainstream of white society. The destiny of Native Americans as viable groups with separate identities depends in no small measure on curbing their dependence on the national government.[37] Litigation on behalf of Native Americans may prove to be their most effective weapon in retaining and regaining their heritage.

Hispanic Americans

Many Hispanic Americans have a rich and deep-rooted heritage in America, but until the 1920s that heritage was largely confined to the southwestern states and California. Then, unprecedented numbers of Mexican and Puerto Rican immigrants came to the United States in search of employment and a better life. Businesspeople who saw in them a source of cheap labor welcomed them. Many Mexicans became farm workers, but both groups settled mainly in crowded, low-rent, inner-city districts: the Mexicans in the Southwest, the Puerto Ricans primarily in New York City. Both groups formed their own barrios, or neighborhoods, within the cities, where they maintained the customs and values of their homelands.

Like blacks who had migrated to northern cities, most new Latino immigrants found poverty and discrimination. And, like poor blacks and Native Americans, the Depression hit them hard. About one-third of the Mexican American population (mainly those who had been migratory farm workers) returned to Mexico during the 1930s.

World War II gave rise to another influx of Mexicans, who this time were courted to work farms primarily in California. But by the late 1950s, most farm workers—blacks, whites, and Hispanics—were living in poverty. Those Hispanic Americans who lived in cities fared little better. Yet, millions of Mexicans continued to cross the border into the United States, both legally and illegally. The effect was to depress wages for farm labor in California and the Southwest.

In 1965, Cesar Chavez led a strike of the United Farm Workers Union against growers in California. The strike lasted several years but eventually, in combination with a national boycott, resulted in somewhat better pay, working conditions, and housing for workers.

In the 1970s and 1980s, the Hispanic American population continued to grow. The 20 million Hispanics living in the United States in the 1970s were still mainly Puerto Rican and Mexican American, but they were joined by immigrants from the Dominican Republic, Colombia, Cuba, and Ecuador. Although civil rights legislation helped them to an extent, they were among the poorest and least-educated groups in the United States. Their problems were similar to those faced by other nonwhites, but most also had to overcome the further difficulty of learning and using a new language.

One effect of the language barrier is that voter registration and voter turnout among Latinos are lower than among other groups. The creation of nine Hispanic majority congressional districts now assures a measure of representation. With few or no Spanish-speaking voting officials, low registration levels may be inevitable. Voter turnout, in turn, depends on effective political advertising, and Hispanics are not targeted as often as other groups with political messages that they can understand. Despite these stumbling blocks, Latinos have started to exercise a measure of political power.

Hispanics occupy positions of power in national and local arenas. Hispanics constitute 9 percent of the population and 4 percent of Congress. The 103d Congress (1993–95) convened with the biggest class of Latino freshmen ever. The Congressional Hispanic Caucus now numbers nineteen (including delegates from the U.S. Virgin Islands and Puerto Rico). Hispanic Americans have won the mayoralties of San Antonio, San Diego, Denver, and Miami. President Clinton appointed two Hispanics to his cabinet: Henry G. Cisneros, secretary of the Department of Housing and Urban Development, and Frederico F. Peña, secretary of Transportation. Cuban Americans look with pride as two of their own serve in Congress. Hispanics have also increased their access to political power; in 1994, three Hispanic Americans were serving on the powerful House Appropriations Committee.[38]

Although race-based redistricting has brought more blacks and Latinos to Congress, voting turnout in minority districts remains low. Such districting assures minority representation but provides little incentive to vote. Fostering a culture of political participation calls for more work to bring uninvolved minorities into the mainstream of the political process.[39]

Disabled Americans

Minority status is not confined to race or ethnicity. After more than two decades of struggle, 43 million disabled Americans gained recognition in 1990 as a protected minority with the enactment of the Americans with Disabilities Act (ADA).

The law extends the protections embodied in the Civil Rights Act of 1964 to people with physical or mental disabilities, including people with AIDS and recovering alcoholics and drug abusers. It guarantees access to employment, transportation, public accommodations, and communication services.

The roots of the disabled rights movement stem from the period after World War II. Thousands of disabled veterans returned to a country and a society that were inhospitable to their needs. Institutionalization seemed the best way to care for the disabled, but this approach came under increasing fire as the disabled and their families sought care at home.

Advocates for the disabled found a ready model in the existing civil rights laws. Opponents argued that the changes mandated by the 1990 law (such as access for those confined to wheelchairs) could cost billions of dollars, but supporters replied that the costs would be offset by an equal or greater reduction in federal aid to disabled people who would rather be working.

The law's enactment set off an avalanche of job discrimination complaints filed with the national government's watchdog agency, the EEOC. By mid-1993, the EEOC had received more than twelve thousand ADA-related complaints. Curiously, most complaints came from already-employed people, both previously and recently disabled. They charged that their employers failed to provide reasonable accommodations as required by the new law. The disabilities cited most frequently were back problems, mental illness, heart trouble, neurological disorders, and diabetes.[40]

A change in the law, no matter how welcome, does not assure a change in attitudes. Laws that end racial discrimination do not extinguish racism, and laws that ban biased treatment of the disabled will not mandate acceptance of the disabled. But rights advocates predict that bias against the disabled, like similar biases against other minorities, will wither as the disabled become full participants in society.

GENDER AND EQUAL RIGHTS: THE WOMEN'S MOVEMENT

The ballot box and the lawsuit have brought minorities in America a measure of equality. The Supreme Court—once responsible for perpetuating inequality for blacks—has expanded the array of legal weapons available to all minorities to help them achieve social equality. Women, too, have benefited from this change.

Protectionism

Until the early 1970s, laws that affected the civil rights of women were based on traditional views of the relationship between men and women. At the heart of these laws was **protectionism**—the notion that women must be sheltered from life's harsh realities. Thomas Jefferson, author of the Declaration of Independence, believed that "were our state a pure democracy there would still be excluded from our deliberations women, who, to prevent deprivation of morals and ambiguity of issues, should not mix promiscuously in gatherings of men."[41] And "protected" they were, through laws that discriminated against them in employment and other areas. With few exceptions, women were also "protected" from voting until early in the twentieth century.

The demand for women's rights arose from the abolition movement and later was based primarily on the Fourteenth Amendment's prohibition of laws that "abridge the privileges or immunities of citizens of the United States." However, the courts consistently rebuffed challenges to protectionist state laws. In 1873, the Supreme Court upheld an Illinois statute that prohibited women from practicing law. The justices maintained that the Fourteenth Amendment had no bearing on a state's authority to regulate admission of members to the bar.[42] In a concurring opinion, Justice Joseph P. Bradley articulated the common protectionist belief that women were unfit for certain occupations: "Man is, or should be, woman's protector and defender. The natural and proper timidity and delicacy which belongs to the female sex evidently unfits it for many of the occupations of civil life."

Protectionism reached a peak in 1908, when the Court upheld an Oregon law limiting the number of hours that women could work.[43] The decision was rife with assumptions about the nature and role of women, and it gave wide latitude to laws that protected the "weaker sex." It also led to protectionist legislation that barred women from working more than forty-eight hours a week and from jobs that required workers to lift more than thirty-five pounds. (The average work week for men was sixty hours or longer.) In effect, women were locked out of jobs that called for substantial overtime (and overtime pay); instead, they were shunted to jobs that men believed suited their abilities.

Protectionism can take many forms. Some employers hesitate to place women at risk in the workplace. One such policy excluded women capable of bearing children from exposure to toxic substances that could harm a developing fetus. Usually, these jobs offered more pay as a consequence of higher risk. Although they faced similar reproductive risks, men faced no exclusions.

In 1991, the Supreme Court struck down a fetal protection policy in strong terms. The Court relied on amendments to the 1964 Civil Rights Act that provide for very few narrow exceptions to the principle that unless some workers differ from others in their ability to work, they must be treated the same as other employees. "In other words," declared the majority, "women as capable of doing their jobs as their male counterparts may not be forced to choose between having a child and having a job."[44]

Political Equality for Women

With a few exceptions, women were not allowed to vote in this country until 1920. In 1869, Francis and Virginia Minor sued a St. Louis, Missouri, registrar for not allowing Virginia Minor to vote. In 1875, the Supreme Court held that the Fourteenth Amendment's privileges and immunities clause did not confer the right to vote on all citizens or require that the states allow women to vote.[45]

The decision clearly slowed the movement toward women's suffrage, but it did not stop it. In 1878, Susan B. Anthony, a women's rights activist, convinced a U.S. senator from California to introduce a constitutional amendment requiring that "the right of citizens of the United States to vote shall not be denied or abridged by the United States or by any State on account of sex." The amendment was introduced and voted down a number of times through the next twenty years. Meanwhile, as noted in Chapter 7, a number of states—primarily in the Midwest and West—did grant limited suffrage to women.

The movement for women's suffrage had now become a political battle to amend the Constitution. In 1917, police arrested 218 women from twenty-six states when they picketed the White House demanding the right to vote. Nearly one hundred went to jail, some for days, others for months. Hunger strikes and force feedings followed. The movement culminated in the adoption in 1920 of the **Nineteenth Amendment,** which gave women the right to vote. Its wording was that first suggested by Anthony.

Meanwhile, the Supreme Court continued to act as the benevolent protector of women. Women had entered the work force in significant numbers during World War I, and they did so again during World War II, but they received lower wages than the men they replaced. Again, the justification was the "proper" role of women as mothers and homemakers. Because society expected men to be the principal providers, it followed that women's earnings were less important to the family's support. This thinking perpetuated inequalities in the workplace. Economic equality was closely tied to social attitudes. Because society expected women to stay at home, the assumption was that they needed less education than men. Therefore, they tended to qualify only for low-paying, low-skill jobs with little chance of advancement.

Prohibiting Sex-Based Discrimination

The movement to provide equal rights to women advanced a step with the passage of the Equal Pay Act of 1963. That act requires equal pay for men and women doing similar work. However, state protectionist laws still had the effect of restricting women to jobs that men usually did not want. Where employment was stratified by sex, equal pay was an empty promise. To remove the restrictions of protectionism, women needed equal opportunity for employment. They got it in the Civil Rights Act of 1964 and later legislation.

The objective of the Civil Rights Act of 1964 was to eliminate racial discrimination in America. The original wording of Title VII of the act prohibited employment discrimination based on race, color, religion, and national origin—but not gender. In an effort to scuttle this provision during House debate, Democrat Howard W. Smith of Virginia proposed an

Free to Choose

Gloyce Qualls celebrates an important victory for women. In 1982, her employer, the Johnson Controls battery plant in Milwaukee, Wisconsin, had instituted a mandatory protection policy that placed women of child-bearing age in less hazardous (and often lower-paying) jobs. On behalf of women such as Qualls, several workers challenged the "fetal protection" policy. In 1991, the Supreme Court unanimously declared such policies unconstitutional.

amendment barring job discrimination based on sex. Smith's intention was to make the law unacceptable; his effort to ridicule the law brought gales of laughter to the debate. But Democrat Martha W. Griffiths of Michigan used Smith's strategy against him. With her support, Smith's amendment carried, as did the act.[46] Congress extended the jurisdiction of the Equal Employment Opportunity Commission to cover cases of invidious sex discrimination, or **sexism.**

Presidential authority also played a crucial role in the effort to eliminate sexism. In 1965, President Johnson issued an executive order that bound federal contractors to nondiscrimination and affirmative action in hiring and employment without regard to race, color, religion, or national origin. Three years later, he amended the order to apply to gender as well. The result was new opportunity for women.

Subsequent women's rights legislation was motivated by the pressure for civil rights, as well as a resurgence of the women's movement, which had subsided in 1920 after the adoption of the Nineteenth Amendment. One particularly important law was Title IX of the Education Amendments of 1972, which prohibited sex discrimination in federally aided education programs. Another boost to women came from the Revenue Act of 1972, which provided tax credits for child care expenses. In effect, the act subsidized parents with young children so that women could enter or remain in the work force. However, the high watermark in the effort to secure women's rights was the Equal Rights Amendment, as we shall explain shortly.

Stereotypes Under Scrutiny

After nearly a century of protectionism, the Supreme Court began to take a closer look at gender-based distinctions. In 1971, it struck down a state law that gave men preference over women in administering the estate of a person who died without naming an administrator.[47] The state maintained that the law reduced court workloads and avoided family battles; however, the Court dismissed those objections, because they were not important enough to sustain the use of gender distinctions. Two years later, the justices declared that paternalism operated to "put women not on a pedestal, but in a cage."[48] They then proceeded to strike down several gender-based laws that either prevented or discouraged departures from "proper" sex roles. In 1976, the Court finally developed a workable standard for reviewing such laws: Gender-based distinctions are justifiable only if they serve some important government purpose.[49]

The objective of the standard is to dismantle laws based on sexual stereotypes while fashioning public policies that acknowledge relevant differences between men and women. Perhaps the most controversial issue is the idea of "comparable worth," which would require employers to pay comparable wages for different jobs that are of about the same worth to an employer, even if one job is filled predominantly by women and another mainly by men. Absent new legislation, the courts remain reluctant and ineffective vehicles for ending wage discrimination.[50]

The courts have not been reluctant to extend to women the *constitutional* guarantees won by blacks. In 1994, the Supreme Court extended the Constitution's equal protection guarantee by forbidding the exclusion of potential jurors on the basis of their sex. In a 6-to-3 decision, the justices held that gender, like race, is an unconstitutional proxy for juror competence and impartiality. "Discrimination in jury selection," wrote Justice Harry A. Blackmun for the majority, "whether based on race or gender, causes harm to the litigants, the community and the individual jurors who are wrongfully excluded from participation in the judicial process."[51] The 1994 decision completed a constitutional revolution in jury selection that began in 1986 with a bar to jury exclusion on the basis of race.

The Equal Rights Amendment

Policies protecting women, based largely on sexual stereotypes, have been woven into the legal fabric of American life. That protectionism limited the freedom of women to compete with men socially and economically on an equal footing. However, the Supreme Court has been hesitant to extend the principles of the Fourteenth Amendment beyond issues of race. If constitutional interpretation imposes such a limit, only a constitutional amendment can overcome it.

The National Women's Party, one of the few women's groups that did not disband after the Nineteenth Amendment was enacted, first introduced the proposed **Equal Rights Amendment (ERA)** in 1923. The ERA declared that "equality of rights under the law shall not be denied or abridged by the United States or any State on account of sex." It remained bottled up in committee in every Congress until 1970, when Representative Martha Griffiths filed a discharge petition to bring it to the House floor for a vote. The House passed the ERA, but the Senate scuttled it by attaching a section calling for prayer in the public schools.

A national coalition of women's rights advocates generated enough support to get the ERA through Congress in 1972. Its proponents then had seven years in which to get the amendment ratified by thirty-eight state legislatures, as required by the Constitution. By 1977, they were three states short of that goal, and three states had rescinded earlier ratification. Then, in an unprecedented action, Congress extended the ratification deadline. It didn't help. The ERA died in 1982, still three states short of adoption.

Why did the ERA fail? There are several explanations. Its proponents mounted a national campaign to generate approval, while its opponents organized state-based anti-ERA campaigns. ERA proponents hurt their cause by exaggerating the amendment's effects; such claims only gave ammunition to the amendment's opponents. For example, the puffed-up claim that the amendment would make wife and husband equally responsible for their family's financial support caused alarm among the undecided. As the opposition grew stronger, especially from women who wanted to maintain their traditional role, state legislators began to realize that supporting the amendment involved risk. Given the exaggerations and counterexaggerations, lawmakers ducked. It takes an extraordinary majority to amend the Constitution, which is equivalent to saying that it takes only a committed minority to thwart the majority's will.

Despite its failure, the movement to ratify the ERA produced real benefits. It raised the consciousness of women about their social position, it spurred the formation of the National Organization for Women (NOW) and other large organizations, it contributed to women's participation in politics, and it generated important legislation affecting women.[52]

The failure to ratify the ERA stands in stark contrast to the quick enactment of many laws that now protect women's rights. Such legislation had little audible opposition. If years of racial discrimination called for government redress, then so did years of gender-based discrimination. Furthermore, laws protecting women's rights required only the amending of civil rights bills or enactment of similar bills.

In contrast, the constitutional effects of an equal rights amendment are unclear. It would certainly raise gender to the same status as race in evaluating the validity of government policies. The courts have ruled that policies based on race are valid only when they are essential to achieve a compelling goal. Presumably, under an equal rights amendment, government policies based on gender classifications would be valid only when they were essential to achieve a compelling goal. Today, for example, many government policies concerning the armed services make gender distinctions. The validity of these policies would be open to question with the enactment of an equal rights amendment.

Some scholars argue that, for practical purposes, the Supreme Court has implemented the equivalent of the ERA through its decisions. It has struck down distinctions based on sex and held that stereotyped generalizations about sexual differences must fall.[53] In recent rulings, the Court has held that states may require employers to guarantee job reinstatement to women returning from maternity leave, that sexual harassment in the workplace is illegal, and that a hostile work environment will be judged by a reasonable perception of abuse rather than a demonstration of psychological injury.[54]

But the Supreme Court can reverse its decisions, and legislators can repeal statutes. Without an equal rights amendment, argue some feminists, the Constitution will continue to bear the sexist imprint of a document written by men for men. Until the ERA becomes part of the Constitution, said veteran feminist Betty Friedan, "We are at the mercy of a Supreme Court that will interpret equality as it sees fit."[55]

AFFIRMATIVE ACTION: EQUAL OPPORTUNITY OR EQUAL OUTCOME?

In his vision of the Great Society, President Johnson linked economic rights with civil rights and equality of outcome with equality of opportunity. "Equal opportunity is essential, but not enough," he declared. "We seek not just legal equity but human ability. Not just equality as a right and a theory but equality as a fact and equality as a result."[56] This commitment led to affirmative action programs to expand opportunities for women, minorities, and the disabled.

Affirmative action, as we have seen, aims to overcome the present effects of past discrimination. It embraces a range of public and private programs, policies, and procedures, including special recruitment, preferential treatment, and quotas in job training and professional education, employment, and awards of government contracts. The point of these programs is to move beyond equality of opportunity to equality of outcome.

No Marathons But Tennis Would Be Okay

In the landmark 1978 Bakke *decision, the Supreme Court approved the use of carefully crafted affirmative action programs aimed at redressing long-standing unfair minority exclusions from the practice of medicine. The number of minority physicians doubled in the decade following the decision. And these physicians tended to serve larger proportions of poor patients.*

Numerical goals (such as designating a specific number of places in a law school for minority candidates or specifying that 10 percent of the work on a government contract must be subcontracted to minority-owned companies) are the most aggressive form of affirmative action, and they generate more debate and less agreement than any other aspect of the civil rights movement. Advocates claim that such goal setting for college admissions, training programs, employment, and contracts will move minorities, women, and the disabled out of second-class status. President Johnson explained why aggressive affirmative action was necessary:

> You do not take a person who for years has been hobbled by chains, liberate him, bring him up to the starting line of a race, and then say, "You are free to compete with all the others," and still justly believe that you have been completely fair. Thus, it is not enough just to open the gates of opportunity; all our citizens must have the ability to walk through those gates.[57]

Arguments for affirmative action programs (from increased recruitment efforts to quotas) tend to reduce to the following reasoning: Certain groups have historically suffered invidious discrimination, denying them educational and economic opportunities. To eliminate the lasting effects of such discrimination, the public and private sectors must take steps to provide access to good education and jobs. If the majority once discriminated to hold groups back, discriminating to benefit those groups is fair. Therefore, quotas are a legitimate means to provide a place on the ladder to success.[58]

Affirmative action opponents maintain that quotas for designated groups necessarily create invidious discrimination (in the form of reverse discrimination) against individuals who are themselves blameless. Moreover, they say, quotas lead to admission, hiring, or promotion of the less qualified at the expense of the well qualified. In the name of equality, such policies thwart an individual's freedom to succeed.

Government-mandated preferential policies probably began in 1965 with the creation of the Office of Federal Contract Compliance. Its purpose was to ensure that all private enterprises doing business with the federal government complied with nondiscrimination guidelines. Because so many companies do business with the federal government, a large portion of the American economy became subject to these guidelines. In 1968, the guidelines required "goals and timetables for the prompt achievement of full and equal employment opportunity." By 1971, they called for employers to eliminate "underutilization" of minorities and women, which meant that employers must hire minorities and women in proportion to the government's assessment of their availability.[59]

Preferential policies are seldom explicitly legislated. More often, such policies are the result of administrative regulations, judicial rulings, and initiatives in the private sector as remedial responses to specific discrimination and to new legal standards of proof. Quotas or goals enable administrators to assess changes in hiring, promotion, and admissions policies. Racial quotas are an economic fact of life today. Employers engage in race-conscious preferential treatment to avoid litigation. Cast in value terms, equality trumps freedom.

Reverse Discrimination

The Supreme Court confronted an affirmative action quota program for the first time in ***Regents of the University of California* v. *Bakke*.**[60] Allan Bakke, a thirty-five-year-old white man, had twice applied for admission to the University of California Medical School at Davis. He was rejected both times. The school had reserved sixteen places in each entering class of one hundred for qualified minority applicants, as part of the university's affirmative action program, in an effort to redress longstanding and unfair minority exclusions from the medical profession. Bakke's qualifications (college grade-point average and test scores) exceeded those of any of the minority students admitted in the two years his applications were rejected. Bakke contended, first in the California courts, then in the Supreme Court, that he was excluded from admission solely on the basis of race. He argued that the equal protection clause of the Fourteenth Amendment and the Civil Rights Act of 1964 prohibited this reverse discrimination.

The Court's decision in *Bakke* contained six opinions and spanned 154 pages. But even after careful analysis of the decision, discerning what the Court had decided was difficult: No opinion had a majority. One bloc of four justices opposed the Davis plan, contending that any racial quota system endorsed by government violated the Civil Rights Act of 1964. A second bloc of four justices supported the Davis plan, arguing that government may use a racial classification scheme, provided it does not demean or insult any racial group and only to remedy minority disadvantages imposed by racial prejudice. Justice Lewis F. Powell, Jr., agreed with parts of both arguments. With the first bloc, he argued that the rigid use of racial quotas as used by the school violated the equal protection clause of the Fourteenth Amendment. With the second bloc, he contended that the use of race was permissible as one of several admissions criteria. Powell cast the deciding vote ordering the medical school to admit Bakke. Despite the confusing multiple opinions, the Court signaled its approval of affirmative action programs that use race as a preferential factor. Thus, the Court managed to minimize white opposition to the goal of equality (by finding for Bakke) while extending gains for racial minorities through affirmative action.

Although the Court sent a mixed message, *Bakke* did have tangible benefits. The number of minority physicians doubled in the decade after the decision. Moreover, minority physicians tended to relocate to areas that had critical health care shortages. They also tended to serve significantly larger proportions of poor patients, regardless of race or ethnicity.[61]

Other cases followed. In 1979, the Court upheld a voluntary affirmative action plan giving preferences to blacks in an employee training program.[62] Five years later, however, the Court held that affirmative action did not exempt minorities (typically the most recently hired employees) from traditional work rules, which specify that the last hired are the first fired. Layoffs must proceed by seniority, declared the Court, unless minority employees can demonstrate that they are actual victims of their employer's discrimination.[63]

The Supreme Court has thus greeted reverse discrimination claims with a mixture of approval and disapproval. Do preferential policies in other nations offer lessons for us? See Compared with What? 16.1 to learn the answer.

Victims of Discrimination

The 1984 layoff decision raised a troublesome question: Do all affirmative action programs apply solely to actual victims of past discrimination? The Supreme Court delivered a partial answer in 1986, when it struck down a school board's layoff plan that gave preference to members of minority groups.[64] The layoff plan favored black teachers in an effort to redress general social discrimination and to retain sufficient role models for black students. But the Supreme Court ruled that these objectives were insufficient to force certain individuals to bear the severe effect of layoffs. Hiring goals impose a diffuse burden on society, argued Justice Powell for the Court. But layoffs of innocent whites, he continued, "impose the entire burden of achieving racial equality on particular individuals."

Thus, remedies for general racial discrimination had to avoid harming innocent whites. Another troubling issue was whether remedies for repeated and outrageous forms of specific discrimination confer benefits on individuals who were not themselves the victims of that discrimination. The local chapter of a construction union in New York City practiced egregious racial discrimination for more than seventy-five years, barring most blacks and Hispanics at every turn. The list of ruses to block the entry of nonwhites seemed endless. The local required special examinations and a high school diploma for entrance; neither had any bearing on job performance. The union used its funds to provide special tutoring for members' friends and relatives who were taking the entrance exams. The local refused to keep records on the racial composition of its membership, in an attempt to avoid charges of discrimination.

Americans are not alone in their disagreements over affirmative action. Controversies, and even bloodshed, have been the order of the day in countries where certain groups receive government-sanctioned preferences over others.

India, Sri Lanka, Malaysia, Nigeria, Australia, and Canada are among the nations with affirmative action policies of their own. The phraseology of these policies may differ somewhat from the American model. Although Australia and Canada use the American label *affirmative action*, India refers to its policy as *positive discrimination*. Nigeria's preferential policy is designed to "reflect the federal character of the country." In Malaysia, the constitution recognizes the "special position" of the Malays (the dominant group) and reserves a share of public benefits (including government jobs, educational scholarships, and land) for them.

The particular problems created by affirmative action policy in India recently claimed international attention. The untouchables, a pariah group, have long been the chief beneficiary of the nation's preferential policies. In 1990, the government of India decided to strengthen its policy of positive discrimination by reserving more than half of all government jobs for members of the lower castes.

Although the job quota proved popular among the lower castes, who make up well over half of India's population, it generated deep resentment among the higher castes. Students from the higher castes have traditionally viewed government jobs as a way to secure their middle-class expectations. The new ruling made government jobs much more difficult for them to obtain. Regardless of their academic success, many high-caste students will be passed over for government jobs. In a singularly gruesome form of protest, scores of young upper-caste men and women have set themselves ablaze. And when the Indian courts issued a temporary injunction that halted the government's affirmative action plan, terrorists who supported the plan protested by bombing a train, killing dozens of people. Tension is likely to remain high in Indian society, given the country's ethnic heterogeneity and an economy that is not expanding rapidly enough to satisfy every interest.

One recent study of preferential policies has aimed to generalize from the experiences of many nations. The cultures, politics, and economies of nations with preferential policies vary enormously. The groups benefiting from these policies also vary; they may be locally or nationally dominant or poor and relatively powerless politically.

Despite these variables, nations with affirmative action policies seem to share some common patterns. First, although often defined as temporary, preferential policies tend to persist and even expand to embrace more individuals and groups. Second, benefits tend to flow disproportionately to members of recipient groups who are already more fortunate. Third, antagonism among groups tends to increase in the wake of implementation of preferential policies. The reactions of groups that do not benefit from such policies range from a change in voting behavior to violence, even civil war. And fourth, false claims of membership in designated beneficiary groups increase.

These observations have implications for majoritarian and pluralist models of democracy. All governments broker conflict in varying degrees. Under a majoritarian model, group demands could lead quickly to conflict and instability, because majority rule leaves little room for compromise. A pluralist model allows different groups to get a piece of the pie. By parceling out benefits, pluralism mitigates disorder in the short term. But in the long term, repeated demands for increased benefits can spark instability. A vigorous pluralist system should provide acceptable mechanisms (legislative, executive, bureaucratic, judicial) to vent such frustrations and yield a new allocation of benefits.

• Sources: Donald L. Horowitz, Ethnic Groups in Conflict *(Berkeley: University of California Press, 1985);* Facts on File, *19 October 1990, pp. 784–785; Edward W. Desmond, "Fatal Fires of Protest,"* Time, *15 October 1990, p. 63; and Thomas Sowell,* Preferential Policies: An International Perspective *(New York: William Morrow, 1990).*

Headline News: Joyce Dispatches Johnson

Diane Joyce gained a promotion from laborer to road dispatcher by invoking a government affirmative action policy. Paul Johnson, who had been given the dispatcher job initially, sued; he claimed he was the victim of sex discrimination, which the Civil Rights Act of 1964 forbids. Johnson lost his case in the Supreme Court in 1987.

In litigation that stretched over a decade, a federal court concluded in 1975 that the union local had violated Title VII of the Civil Rights Act of 1964. The court ordered the establishment of a minority membership goal to end the union's discriminatory practices. The union continued to resist several court orders to end its discriminatory practices. In a last gambit, the union took its case to the Supreme Court. The union argued that the membership goal ordered by the lower courts was unlawful, because it extended race-conscious preferences to individuals who were not identified victims of the local's admittedly unlawful discrimination. In 1986, the Court voted 6 to 3 in support of affirmative action that would benefit individuals who were not the actual victims of discrimination.[65] The majority held that the courts may order unions to use quotas to overcome a history of egregious discrimination and that black and Hispanic applicants can benefit from affirmative action, even if they themselves were not the victims of earlier bias.

Another issue is whether affirmative action policies must be limited to concerns about racial inequality. What about the conflict between Diane Joyce and Paul Johnson described at the beginning of this chapter? Johnson took his case all the way to the Supreme Court to argue that he was the victim of sex discrimination under Title VII of the Civil Rights Act of

POLITICS IN A CHANGING AMERICA 16.1

Do Americans Change Their Minds on Racial Equality?

Many Americans express qualified and conflicted commitment to racial equality. This is not surprising, given the cluster of values and concerns raised by race-related issues from affirmative action to welfare dependency. Yet it is not customary to think of white Americans as pliable when it comes to racial issues.

Social scientists Paul Sniderman and Thomas Piazza have examined the extent to which white American beliefs about race are conditional or contingent. To test Americans' commitment or opposition to racial equality, Sniderman and Piazza developed an ingenious strategy to measure *pliability:* the degree

to which people can be dislodged from positions they have taken by calling their attention directly to a counter-argument.

In a 1986 random telephone poll of adults in the San Francisco Bay area, Sniderman and Piazza obtained results contrasting support for various racial policies before and after they introduced counter-arguments in an attempt to change their respondents' minds.

The four pie charts contrast two situations: on the left, when no pressure on either side of the issue was exerted, and, on the right, when arguments on both sides of the issue were presented. In the unpressured condition, three of the four policies generated liberal majorities; only one policy drew a conservative majority.

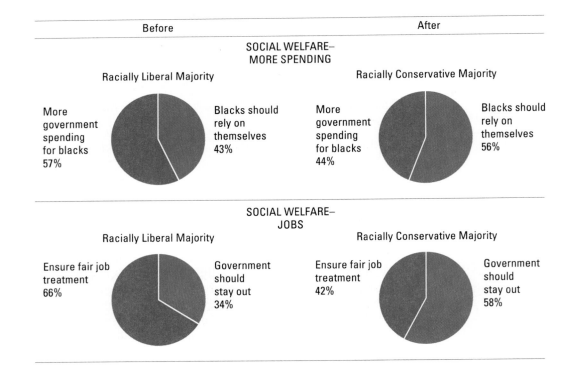

After presenting arguments for and against each policy, some majorities shifted while others remained the same.

- On the issues of more government spending for blacks and government assurance of fair treatment in employment for blacks, racially liberal majorities switched to racially conservative majorities following the introduction of arguments to persuade respondents on both sides of the issue.
- In contrast, an initial liberal majority on fair housing was unmoved by counter-arguments on both sides. And an initial conservative majority opposed to racial quotas in college admissions remained a majority (though somewhat smaller) when confronted with counter-arguments on both sides.

The results suggest that a current liberal majority favoring government activism to assist blacks harbors within it a counter-majority which is more likely to emerge as advocates articulate strong arguments both for and against social welfare assistance and fair job treatment for blacks. When equality and freedom conflict in these areas, freedom-preferring arguments appear more persuasive than equality-preferring arguments.

- *Source: Reprinted by permission of the publishers from* The Scar Of Race, *Paul M. Sniderman and Thomas Piazza, Cambridge, Mass.: Harvard University Press, Copyright © 1993 by the President and Fellows of Harvard College.*

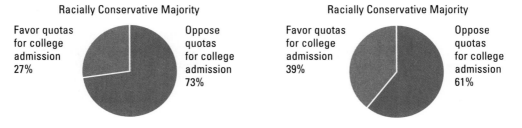

Before	After

EQUAL TREATMENT

Racially Liberal Majority — Homeowners cannot refuse to sell because of race 74% / Homeowners can decide 26%

Racially Liberal Majority — Homeowners cannot refuse to sell because of race 73% / Homeowners can decide 27%

RACE CONSCIOUS

Racially Conservative Majority — Favor quotas for college admission 27% / Oppose quotas for college admission 73%

Racially Conservative Majority — Favor quotas for college admission 39% / Oppose quotas for college admission 61%

1964, the provision that employers cannot "limit, segregate or classify" workers so as to deprive "any individual of employment opportunities."

The justices decided ***Johnson v. Transportation Agency, Santa Clara County*** in 1987.[66] They ruled, 6–3, that if women and minorities are underrepresented in the workplace, employers can act to remedy the imbalance. The decision was significant for at least two reasons. First, employers with affirmative action plans do not have to admit to a history of past discrimination. And second, employees who are passed over for promotions are nearly powerless to sue for reverse discrimination. The upshot of the decision is to encourage the adoption of affirmative action programs.

In hindsight, Paul Johnson's belief that he was the better-qualified candidate failed to acknowledge the full range of legitimate interests considered by employers when they make hiring and promotion decisions. After all, both Johnson and Joyce were deemed qualified for the dispatcher's position; the fact that Johnson scored a few points higher on a test hardly demonstrates clear and unequivocal superiority, as college students know all too well. Given two equally matched candidates for the job, forcing a choice on the basis of a higher exam or interview score seems excessively rigid when other factors may have a legitimate bearing on the outcome. Affirmative action was such a factor, according to the decision's defenders.

In a scathing dissent, Justice Antonin Scalia saw the issue in a different light. He focused on two familiar themes: values in conflict and models of democracy. Scalia declared that the majority was converting "a guarantee that race or sex will not be the basis for employment determination, to a guarantee that it often will." The Court, continued Scalia, was replacing the goal of a society free from discrimination with the incompatible goal of proportionate representation by race and by sex in the workplace. In simpler terms, equality prevailed over freedom.

Scalia then offered his observations on pluralism. The Court's decision would be pleasing to elected officials, he said, because it "provides the means of quickly accommodating the demands of organized groups to achieve concrete, numerical improvement in the economic status of particular constituencies. The only losers in the process," he concluded, are the Paul Johnsons of the country, "predominantly unknown, unaffluent, unorganized—[who] suffer this injustice at the hands of a Court fond of thinking itself the champion of the politically impotent."

The conflict between Paul Johnson and Diane Joyce is over, but the conflict between freedom and equality continues as other individuals and groups press their demands through litigation and legislation. The choice depends on whether and to what extent Americans are prepared to change their minds on these thorny issues, questions we explored in Politics in a Changing America 16.1.

SUMMARY

Americans want equality, but they disagree on the extent to which government should guarantee it. At the heart of this conflict is the distinction between equal opportunities and equal outcomes.

Congress enacted the Civil War amendments—the Thirteenth, Fourteenth, and Fifteenth amendments—to provide full civil rights to black Americans. In the late nineteenth century, however, the Supreme Court interpreted the amendments very narrowly, declaring that they did not restrain individuals from denying civil rights to blacks and that they did not apply to powers that were reserved to the states. The Court's rulings had the effect of denying the vote to most blacks and of institutionalizing racial segregation, making racism a fact of daily life.

Through a series of court cases spanning two decades, the Court slowly dismantled segregation in the schools. The battle for desegregation culminated in the *Brown* cases in 1954 and 1955, in which a now-supportive Supreme Court declared segregated schools to be inherently unequal and therefore unconstitutional. The Court also ordered the desegregation of all schools and upheld the use of busing to do so.

Gains in other spheres of civil rights came more slowly. The motivating force was the civil rights movement, led by Martin Luther King, Jr., until his assassination in 1968. King believed strongly in civil disobedience and nonviolence, strategies that helped secure for blacks equality in voting rights, public accommodations, higher education, housing, and employment opportunity.

Civil rights activism and the civil rights movement worked to the benefit of all minority groups, in fact, of all Americans. Native Americans obtained some redress for past injustices. Hispanic Americans came to recognize the importance of group action to achieve economic and political equality. Disabled Americans won civil rights protections enjoyed by African Americans and others. And civil rights legislation removed the protectionism that was, in effect, legalized discrimination against women in education and employment.

Despite legislative advances in the area of women's rights, the states did not ratify the Equal Rights Amendment. Still, the struggle for ratification produced several positive results, heightening awareness of the role of women and mobilizing the political power of women. And legislation and judicial rulings implemented much of the amendment in practice.

Government and business instituted affirmative action programs to counteract the results of past discrimination. These provide preferential treatment for women, minorities, and the disabled in a number of areas that affect economic opportunity and well being. In effect, such programs discriminate to remedy earlier discrimination. A conservative majority on the Supreme Court emerged to roll back the equality-preferring policies of a more liberal bench. Congress objected to the tide of conservative policies from the Court, reversing some key cases and adding a measure of additional protection besides.

We can guarantee equal outcomes only if we restrict the free competition that is an integral part of equal opportunity. Many Americans object to quotas and policies that restrict individual freedom, that arbitrarily change positions on the ladder of success. The challenge of pluralist democracy is to balance these conflicting values.

Key Terms

affirmative action	racism	de jure segregation	Nineteenth Amendment
discrimination	poll tax	de facto segregation	sexism
equality of opportunity	racial segregation	civil rights movement	Equal Rights Amendment
equality of outcome	separate-but-equal	boycott	(ERA)
civil rights	doctrine	civil disobedience	
black codes	desegregation	protectionism	

Key Cases

Plessy v. *Ferguson*
Brown v. *Board of Education*
Brown v. *Board of Education II*
Milliken v. *Bradley*
Regents of the University of California v. *Bakke*
Johnson v. *Transportation Agency, Santa Clara County*

Selected Readings

Berger, Raoul. *Government by Judiciary: The Transformation of the Fourteenth Amendment.* Cambridge, Mass.: Harvard University Press, 1977. This provocative work argues that the framers of the Fourteenth Amendment had narrow aims and that the Supreme Court, especially since 1954, has disregarded this historical legacy in its promotion of freedom and equality.

Branch, Taylor. *Parting the Waters: America in the King Years, 1954–1963.* New York: Simon & Schuster, 1988. A riveting, Pulitzer Prize–winning narrative history and biography of the King years.

Browning, Rufus P., Dale Rogers Marshall, and David H. Tabb. *Racial Politics in American Cities.* New York: Longman, 1990. This collection of essays documents the continuing struggle for minority access to political power in cities across the United States.

Deloria, Vine, Jr., and Clifford M. Lytle. *The Nations Within.* New York: Pantheon, 1984. A thorough discussion of Native American policies from the New Deal to the present; examines the drive for Indian self-determination and self-government.

Greenberg, Jack. *Crusaders in the Courts.* New York: Basic Books, 1994. This readable narrative describes how a small but dedicated band of lawyers fought for the Civil Rights revolution. The author was a principal architect of that revolution.

Hampton, Henry, and Steve Fayer with Sarah Flynn. *Voices of Freedom: An Oral History of the Civil Rights Movement from the 1950s Through the 1980s.* New York: Bantam, 1990. Chronologically arranged interview excerpts recorded during the production of "Eyes on the Prize," the widely acclaimed public television series.

Jackson, Donald W. *Even the Children of Strangers: Equality Under the U.S. Constitution.* Lawrence: University Press of Kansas, 1992. A readable examination of the complex issues surrounding equal protection under the law, including a valuable multinational perspective.

Kluger, Richard. *Simple Justice.* New York: Alfred A. Knopf, 1975. A monumentally detailed history of the desegregation cases; it examines the legal, political, and sociological events culminating in *Brown* v. *Board of Education.*

Lyons, Oren, et al. *Exiled in the Land of the Free: Democracy, Indian Nations, and the U.S. Constitution.* Santa Fe, N.M.: Clear Light, 1992. A collection of essays exploring the relationship of Indians to the Constitution, how Indian traditions influenced the Constitution's creation, and how constitutional interpretation has affected Indian lives.

Mansbridge, Jane J. *Why We Lost the ERA.* Chicago: University of Chicago Press, 1986. A valuable case study of organizations pitted for and against the Equal Rights Amendment in Illinois.

Pearson, Hugh. *The Shadow of the Panther: Huey Newton and the Price of Black Power in America.* New York: Addison-Wesley Publishing Company, 1994. This fascinating history of the Black Panther Party explains how the Party instilled fear in middle-class America while it won the support from many white liberals. Huey Newton, the brilliant and loathsome Party co-founder and leader, routinely relied on violence to achieve his objectives.

Sniderman, Paul M., and Thomas Piazza. *The Scar of Race.* Cambridge, Mass.: Belknap Press of Harvard University Press, 1993. The authors of this insightful study argue that the problems of race cannot be reduced to racism. On many racial issues, white Americans are open to argument and persuasion, even though they disagree on racial policies.

Urofsky, Melvin I. *A Conflict of Rights: The Supreme Court and Affirmative Action.* New York: Scribner's, 1991. An absorbing case study of the events, participants, and issues surrounding the landmark affirmative action decision of *Joyce* v. *Johnson.*

Verba, Sidney, and Gary R. Orren. *Equality in America: The View From the Top.* Cambridge, Mass.: Harvard University Press, 1985. Two political scientists isolate different meanings of equality, then analyze the opinions of American leaders on the application of equality of opportunity and equality of outcome across a range of policy areas.

Williams, Juan. *Eyes on the Prize: America's Civil Rights Years, 1954–1965.* New York: Viking, 1987. A lucid account of black Americans' struggle for social and political equality; it contains vivid portraits of courageous blacks and the violence they had to endure in their fight for desegregation and the right to vote in the South.

PART VI

Making Public Policy

17 Policymaking

KIMBER REYNOLDS RETURNED HOME to Fresno, California, from her fashion design college to take part in a friend's wedding. She was walking out of a trendy restaurant after meeting a friend for dessert when two men on motorcycles stopped her on the way to her car. One man grabbed her purse; Reynolds grabbed it back. The man put a .357 Magnum in her ear and shot her to death.

The Fresno police quickly identified two suspects. The gunman, Joe Davis, died in a shootout when the police tried to apprehend him. The other, Doug Walker, was captured and pleaded guilty as an accessory to the crime. He was sentenced to nine years in prison. Both Davis and Walker were recent parolees. When Reynolds's father Mike, a wedding photographer, found out that with "good behavior" Walker could be paroled after serving less than half of his sentence, he knew he had to do something.

After meeting with some judges and attorneys he knew, Mike Reynolds launched a campaign to put a "three strikes and you're out" initiative on the statewide ballot. The measure was designed to require anyone convicted of a third serious crime be sentenced to a minimum of twenty-five years in prison. Fed up with violent crime, Californians responded enthusiastically to Reynolds's crusade. "Three strikes" has a gut-level appeal to people, because its intent is to take career criminals off the street and put them in prison until they die or become too old to be much of a threat.

Caught off guard by an issue that seemed to have sprung from nowhere, state legislators rushed to introduce legislation that would accomplish much the same goals as Reynolds's initiative. In March 1994, three strikes and you're out passed the legislature and was signed into law in California, although many judges, district attorneys, and criminologists think it is a bad idea. Their concerns are that it will overwhelm prison capacity, that it will reduce the incentives to plea bargain for those charged with crimes (thus increasing the demand for time-consuming and expensive trials), and that it does nothing to get at the root causes of crime.

But Mike Reynolds and millions of other Californians are sick of revolving door justice, which paroles violent criminals after they have served only part of their sentences. Nearly 60 percent of California prisoners who are released are back in prison within just two years. Reynolds hit a raw nerve and became the focus of much media attention, including appearances on "20/20" and "Today" and profiles in the *New York Times* and *People.* Although three strikes was not a new idea—other states had already adopted it—Mike Reynolds helped to place it on the national agenda.[1] In his 1994 State of the Union address, President Bill Clinton pro-

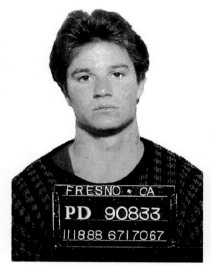
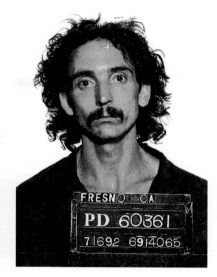

A Death, Then Outrage

After Kimber Reynolds (left) was brutally murdered, her father was grief-stricken. Reminiscing about her childhood, Mike Reynolds described her as his "little buddy." His grief turned to political advocacy, however, and three strikes is now law in California. Ironically, three strikes would not have kept Kimber's murderer, Joe Davis (middle) off the streets prior to his assault on her. Davis had only two prior felonies before he shot her to death. Doug Walker (right) was convicted as an accessory and sentenced to nine years in prison.

posed making three strikes part of federal law. (Most crimes, however, are violations of state rather than national law.) Nevertheless, the president's endorsement was a recognition of the priority Americans place on dealing with the issue of career criminals.

In this case, an issue arose because of a gruesome homicide and because a political activist effectively capitalized on the anger of other citizens. But how do issues usually reach the political agenda? And what happens to them once they are there? Previous chapters have focused on individual institutions of government. Here we focus on the government more broadly and ask how policymaking takes place *across* institutions. We first identify different types of public policies and then analyze the stages in the policymaking process. Because different institutions and different levels of government (national, state, and local) frequently work on the same issues, policymaking is often fragmented. How can better coordination be achieved? We then turn from the general to the specific by focusing on one policy area: telecommunications. In particular, we will examine how policy is made when many competing interest groups are trying to influence the outcome and how the relationships between those groups, and between groups and different parts of government, structure the policymaking process.

GOVERNMENT PURPOSES AND PUBLIC POLICIES

In Chapter 1, we noted that virtually all citizens are willing to accept limitations on their personal freedom in return for various benefits of government. We defined the major purposes of government as maintaining order, providing public benefits, and promoting equality. Different governments place different values on each broad purpose, and those differences are reflected in their public policies. A **public policy** is a general plan of action adopted by a government to solve a social problem, counter a threat, or pursue an objective.

At times, governments choose not to adopt a new policy to deal with a troublesome situation; instead, they just "muddle through," hoping the problem will go away or diminish in importance. This, too, is a policy decision, because it amounts to a choice to maintain the status quo. Sometimes, government policies are carefully developed and effective. Sometimes, they are hastily drawn and ineffective, even counterproductive. But careful planning is no predictor of success. Well-constructed policies may result in total disaster, and quick fixes may work just fine.

Whatever their form and effectiveness, however, all policies have this in common: They are the means by which government pursues certain goals within specific situations. People disagree about public policies, because they disagree about one or more of the following elements: the goals that government should have, the means it should use to meet them, and the perception of the situation.

How do policymakers attempt to achieve their goals? As a starting point, we will divide all government approaches to solving problems into four broad types. We can analyze public policies according to whether they prohibit, protect, promote, or provide.

Some policies are intended to prohibit behaviors that endanger society. All governments outlaw murder, robbery, and rape. Governments that emphasize order tend to favor policies of prohibition, which instruct people in what they must not do (drink liquor, have abortions, use illegal drugs).

Government policies can also protect certain activities, business markets, or special groups of citizens. For example, taxes were once levied on colored margarine (a butter substitute) to reduce its sales and protect the dairy industry from competition. Regulations concerning the testing of new drugs are intended to protect citizens from harmful side effects; government rules about safety in the workplace are enacted to protect workers. Although governments argue that these kinds of regulations serve the public good, some people believe that most protective legislation is unwarranted government interference.

Policies can also promote social activities that are important to the government. One way that government promotes is by persuasion. For instance, our government has used advertising to urge people to buy bonds or to join the army. When policymakers really want to accomplish a goal they have set, they can be quite generous. To promote railroad construction in the 1860s, Congress granted railroad companies huge tracts of public land as rights-of-way through western states.

The government also promotes activities through favorable treatment within the tax structure. Because it amounts to a loss of government revenue, the technical term for this form of government promotion is *tax expenditure*. For example, the government encourages people to buy their own homes by allowing them to deduct mortgage payments from their taxable income. In 1993, this tax expenditure cost the national government nearly $45 billion.[2] And of course, churches and private educational institutions typically pay no property taxes to state and local governments.

Finally, public policies can provide benefits directly to citizens, either collectively or selectively. Collective benefits are facilities or services that all residents share (mail service, roads, schools, street lighting, libraries, parks). Selective benefits go to certain groups of citizens (poor people, farmers, veterans, college students). Collective benefits are more difficult to deliver, because they require either the construction of facilities (roads, dams, sewer systems) or the creation of organizations (transportation agencies, power companies, sanitation departments) to provide them. Selective benefits are simply payments to individuals in the form of food stamps, subsidies, pensions, and loans. The payments are made because the recipients are particularly needy or politically powerful, or both.

In sum, the notion of policy is a many splendored thing. Government has many different means at its disposal for pursuing particular goals. Those means and goals, in turn, are shaped by the specific situations that surround a problem at the time. Policies aimed at specific problems are not static; means, goals, and situations change.

THE POLICYMAKING PROCESS

We distinguish government policies according to their approaches, not simply to create an inventory of problem-solving methods but also to emphasize the relationship between policy and process. By *process* we mean the configuration of participants involved, the procedures used for decision making, and the degree of cooperation or conflict usually present. The premise is simple: Different kinds of policies are going to affect the political process in different ways.

The Effect of Policy

One basic reason for the various policymaking processes is that different approaches to public policy affect people in different ways. If a policy proposal affects a well-organized constituency adversely, that constituency will fight it aggressively. When Secretary of the Interior Bruce Babbitt proposed legislation to raise fees on the use of federal land for grazing, western ranchers who wanted to maintain the relatively low rates they were paying resisted bitterly. (Ostensibly, the existing policy was a tax expenditure aimed at promoting the beef industry. However, in Babbitt's eyes, the industry did not need promotion and the policy was little more than a way to provide direct benefits to ranchers.) The ranchers' anger led sympathetic senators to successfully filibuster the proposal, but Babbitt announced plans to put it into effect anyway, through his administrative powers.[3]

Other policies pit well-organized groups against each other. The North American Free Trade Agreement (NAFTA) was designed to facilitate trade and investment for Canada, the United States, and Mexico (see Chapter 11). Concerned about low-cost Mexican labor, labor unions in the United States fought the measure. Many businesses liked NAFTA because they wanted greater access to Mexico's market for services and consumer goods. In our framework, it was a choice between promoting exports and protecting labor. Caught between the proverbial rock and a hard place in this lobbying war, Congress finally voted for NAFTA and against labor's position in 1993.

Whether a policy is intended to prohibit, protect, promote, or provide does not fully predict the level of public involvement, the degree of mobilization by affected constituencies, or the degree of competition between organizations working on different sides of the same issue. But by being aware of the kind of approach the government is proposing on an issue, we can begin to understand which factors are going to influence policymaking. If a well-entrenched set of interest groups is ready to fight a policy to prohibit, a solution emphasizing promotion might be more feasible politically.

A government may use more than one approach to a problem, not only because some alternatives engender less opposition than others but because public policy problems can be quite complex. One approach will not always ameliorate all manifestations of a problem. Let us return to the subject of career criminals. Even the most ardent backers of three strikes and you're out would not pretend that it will completely stop paroled convicts from committing additional crimes. Shouldn't we have counseling and job training for those convicted of a single crime? How about youthful offenders who might be saved by combining education with punishment? Boot camps might work for them. But why wait for a first crime to be committed? At-risk populations must receive the support from social service agencies if we are to minimize the problems associated with broken homes and poverty. And can any progress really be made against repeat offenders when so much crime is associated with drugs? Getting people off drugs and into treatment programs has to be part of any serious effort to reduce the crime problem in America.

When officials have choices in the means for addressing a problem, they consider how each approach would affect policymaking. Is the best approach one that is likely to generate a lot of conflict between opposing groups? If so, will it be possible to enact a new policy, or is the conflict likely to scuttle a new proposal and leave the status quo? In short, when policymakers weigh new policy options, they carefully consider the effect of each approach on those most directly affected.

A Policymaking Model

Clearly, different approaches to solving policy problems affect the policymaking process, but common patterns do underlie most processes. Political scientists have produced many models of the policymaking process to distinguish the different types of policy, such as our framework of policies that prohibit, protect, promote, or provide.[4] They also distinguish different stages of the policymaking process and try to identify patterns in the way people attempt to influence decisions and in the way decisions are reached.

We can separate the policymaking process into four stages: agenda setting, policy formulation, implementation, and policy evaluation.[5] Figure 17.1 shows the four stages in sequence. Note, however, that the process does not end with policy evaluation. As you will see, policymaking is a circular process; the end of one phase is really the beginning of another.

Agenda Setting   **Agenda setting** is the part of the process during which problems are defined as political issues. Many problems confront Americans in their daily lives, but government is not actively working to solve them all. Today, for example, social security seems a hardy perennial of American politics, but the old age insurance program was not created until the New Deal (see Chapter 19). The problem of poverty among the elderly did not suddenly emerge during the 1930s—there have always been

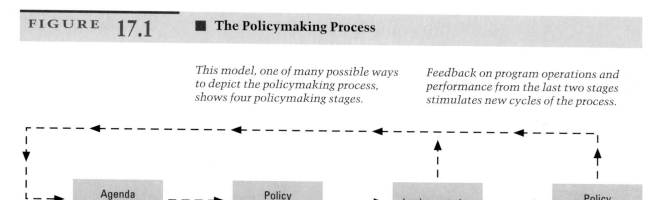

FIGURE **17.1** ■ **The Policymaking Process**

This model, one of many possible ways to depict the policymaking process, shows four policymaking stages.

Feedback on program operations and performance from the last two stages stimulates new cycles of the process.

poor people of all ages; rather, that is when inadequate incomes for the elderly became defined as a political problem (see Politics in a Changing America 17.1 for a discussion of how a problem came to be defined as a political issue). During this time people began arguing that it was government's responsibility to create a system of income security rather than leaving old people to fend for themselves.

When the government begins to consider action on an issue it had previously ignored, we say that the issue has become part of the political agenda. Usually when we use *agenda* in this context, we are simply referring to the entire set of issues before all institutions of government. (There is no formal list of issues for the entire political system; the concept of an agenda for the system is merely a useful abstraction.[6])

Why does an existing social problem become redefined as a political problem? There is no single reason; many different factors can stimulate new thinking about a problem. Sometimes, highly visible events or developments push issues onto the agenda. Examples include great calamities (such as a terrible oil spill showing a need for safer tankers), technological changes (such as the pollution that comes from automobiles), or irrational human behavior (such as airline hijackings).[7] The probability that problems will move onto the agenda is also affected by who controls the government and broad ideological shifts in attitudes. The women's movement had a great deal of success in getting issues on the agenda in the 1970s, but when the conservative Reagan administration came into office in 1981, it had considerably more difficulty.[8]

Issues may also be placed on the agenda through the efforts of scholars and activists to get more people to pay attention to a condition of which the public is generally unaware. The problem of child abuse was long hidden in America. It goes on behind closed doors, and it is difficult for the victims to ask for assistance. However, in 1962 a group of pediatricians who were studying child abuse published an article in a medical journal on the "battered child syndrome." This article stimulated popular treatments of the subject that ran in widely circulated magazines such as *Time* and the *Saturday Evening Post*, articles that played a major role "in creating a sense of an urgent national problem."[9]

POLITICS IN A CHANGING AMERICA 17.1   The Politics of Breast Cancer

One in every eight American women will get breast cancer during her lifetime. Of those diagnosed with breast cancer, one in four will die from it. It is an epidemic, and it is getting worse, not better.

In the past few years, breast cancer has gone from being just a medical problem to becoming a full-fledged political issue. But why has breast cancer been placed on the nation's political agenda? It hardly seems an issue that divides people. After all, who is in favor of cancer?

Breast cancer is a political problem in a number of ways. One controversy is about the responsibilities of health insurers to pay for various treatments, ranging from initial baseline mammograms for younger women to expensive bone marrow transplant therapy for women with advanced breast cancer. Many state governments have adopted legislation that requires insurance companies to cover certain kinds of treatments. President Bill Clinton has proposed a major overhaul of health care; should it pass the Congress it is not clear what the standard package of benefits will include for mammography. A recent National Cancer Institute study rejected the American Cancer Society's guideline that says all women older than forty should have a yearly mammogram. The study concludes that yearly mammograms do not save lives for women without high-risk factors until age fifty.

Under our current health system, breast cancer reflects the unfortunate differences in access to care for those who are poor and those who are middle income. The government's Medicaid program, which pays for medical care for the poor, does not pay for mammograms in all states. At Miami's Jackson Memorial Hospital, the city's only public hospital, a woman must wait two months for an appointment for an evaluation. After that session, the wait for a mammogram is two months more. If the mammogram shows a potential malignancy, the woman would wait at least two months more before undergoing a biopsy. That's at least six months simply to get to the stage at which treatment might start, six months while cancer cells could be multiplying. For a middle-income woman who has a private physician, the same steps are likely to take a month. Research has shown that women with private insurance learn about their breast cancer at an earlier stage and live longer once diagnosed than do women who have Medicaid or no insurance at all.

Some see the politics of breast cancer as symptomatic of discrimination against women. One breast cancer sufferer whose insurance company paid for a mammogram only every other year, said bitterly, "If you could do a mammogram on the testes—a testegram—you'd be goddam sure that men would be having them every year and that insurance would pay."

The national government has begun to pay considerably more attention to this deadly disease. Medical research on all diseases is largely supported by the national government, and for years women's groups have argued that breast cancer research is not adequately funded. In 1990, breast cancer research received $77 million in funding from Congress. For 1994, funding was set at $263 million.

Congress also reacted to the problem of a lack of federal standards for mammography machines and licensing requirements for the technicians who conduct mammograms. Sadly, there have been many instances of incorrect evaluations of mammograms. The

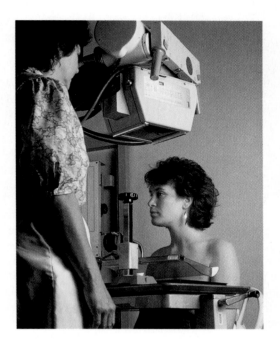

Mammography Quality Standards Act of 1992 establishes national standards for equipment, requires licensing of technicians, mandates board certification and continuing education for physicians who interpret mammograms, and sets up accreditation procedures for mammography facilities.

Ironically, advocates for breast cancer issues have been so successful at getting government to respond that some are saying the disease is getting an undue share of the research dollars distributed by government. Critics point out that forty-six thousand women die of breast cancer each year while fifty-six thousand women die from lung cancer. Yet, research on lung cancer, a disease that strikes men as well as women, receives only about a third of the funding for breast cancer. Prostate cancer, a disease that strikes only men and

kills thirty-five thousand yearly, receives only $51 million in federal research funds. What explains the differences? The differences in funding reflect the changing nature of women in politics. Advocates of breast cancer research are organized; those concerned about lung cancer and prostate cancer have not mobilized to the same degree.

Organizations such as the National Breast Cancer Coalition not only pushed the issue to the top of the nation's health agenda but have been effective at getting a disproportionate share of medical research dollars. The Coalition's Fran Visco, who has led the lobbying on breast cancer issues, rejects the criticism of growing favoritism. "For too long, funding decisions have been made at the expense of women's lives," she says. "We have to make up for being ignored so long, and we believe the best way to do that is to target funds." What Visco left unsaid is that the best way to get Congress to target funds is to get organized.

• *Sources: Dorothy J. Gaiter, "Although Cures Exist, Poverty Fells Many Afflicted with Cancer,"* Wall Street Journal, *May 1, 1991, p. A1; Melinda Beck et al., "The Politics of Breast Cancer,"* Newsweek, *December 10, 1990, pp. 62–65; Pat Towell, "Pentagon as Cancer Fighter,"* Congressional Quarterly Weekly Report, *September 26, 1992, p. 2954; "Effective Lobbying Increases Federal Funds for Breast Cancer,"* New York Times, *October 19, 1992, p. A15; The Mammography Quality Standards Act of 1992, Pub. L. No. 102-539; Stephen Burd, "Clinton's Budget Increase for Breast-Cancer Research Divides Scientists and Activists and Satisfies No One,"* Chronicle of Higher Education, *June 9, 1993, p. A22; "Insurance Linked to Early Diagnosis,"* New York Times, *July 29, 1993, p. A16; Gina Kolata, "Weighing Spending on Breast Cancer,"* New York Times, *October 20, 1993, p. C14; Kolata, "Avoiding Mammogram Guidelines,"* New York Times, *December 5, 1993, p. 30; Jerry Adler, "The Killer We Don't Discuss,"* Newsweek, *December 27, 1993, pp. 40–41.*

It's Difficult to Talk About
The sexual abuse of children was long a problem without being on the policymaking agenda of government. As awareness grew, however, government began to consider ways of addressing the issue. This little girl was being treated at the Village of Childhelp USA in Beaumont, California, at the time this picture was taken. She was a victim of severe sexual abuse before she was taken out of her home and sent to the Beaumont facility. There she received treatment for three years before being placed in foster care.

Agenda building is not only bringing new issues to the attention of government but also the process of redefining an issue so that people look at it in a different way. For years, the nuclear power industry convinced Congress that the primary issue concerning nuclear power was America's growing energy demand. Beginning in the mid-1960s, some activists began to charge that nuclear power plants were unsafe. Over time, more and more people began to take the charge seriously, and Congress responded with more hearings, which were largely critical of the safety practices within the industry.[10] Criticism of the industry peaked after a dangerous accident at the Three Mile Island nuclear facility in Pennsylvania in 1979 (see Figure 17.2).

Policy Formulation   **Policy formulation** is that stage of the policymaking process in which formal policy proposals are developed and officials decide whether to adopt one. The most obvious kind of policy formulation is the proposal of a measure by the president or the development of legislation by Congress. Administrative agencies also formulate policy through the regulatory process. Courts formulate policy, too, when their decisions establish new interpretations of the law. We usually think of policy formulation as a formal process in which a published document (a statute, a regulation, or a court opinion) is the final outcome. In some instances, however, policy decisions are not published or otherwise made explicit. Presidents or secretaries of state may not always fully articulate their foreign policy decisions, for example, because they want some wiggle room for adapting policy to changing conditions.

Although policy formulation is depicted in Figure 17.1 as one stage, it can actually take place over a number of separate stages. For example, the Americans with Disabilities Act of 1990 was enacted by Congress to protect the civil rights of those who are blind, deaf, use a wheelchair, are otherwise physically disabled, or are mentally ill. In 1991, the Architectural and Transportation Barriers Compliance Board issued administrative reg-

FIGURE **17.2**   ■ **Power Failure**

The change in tone at congressional hearings held to discuss nuclear power vividly illustrates the appearance of nuclear safety on the political agenda. Hearings that were generally supportive of the industry were roughly equal in number to those negative in tone until the late 1960s. Since then, congressional hearings have sharply increased in number and have been largely critical of safety practices in the industry.

Source: Frank R. Baumgartner and Bryan D. Jones, Agendas and Instability in American Politics *(Chicago: University of Chicago Press, 1993), p. 75. Reprinted with permission of the publisher.*

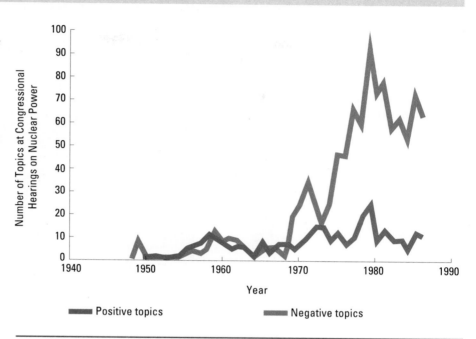

ulations that set some highly specific standards. For instance, at least 5 percent of tables in a restaurant must be accessible to those with disabilities and at least half the drinking fountains on every floor in an office building must be accessible to those in wheelchairs.[11] And the Justice Department has issued guidelines for those who want to bring legal complaints against the government for failing to properly implement the act.[12]

Keep in mind that policy formulation is only the development of proposals designed to solve a problem. Some issues reach the agenda and stimulate new proposals but then fail to win enactment because political opposition mobilizes. In the early 1980s, for example, a movement arose to freeze the development of nuclear weapons. Although a freeze resolution gained significant support in Congress, it never gained enough votes to pass and was not adopted. The nuclear freeze movement quickly withered away and disappeared from sight. Thus, the move from proposal to policy requires the approval of some authoritative, policymaking body.

Implementation   Policies are not self-executing; **implementation** is the process by which they are carried out. When regulations are issued by agencies in Washington, some government bodies must then put those policies into effect. This may involve notifying the intended targets of agency actions that program regulations have changed. In the case of the regulations promulgated under the 1990 Disabilities Act, the owners of an office building would probably not reposition water fountains simply because Washington published new regulations. Administrative bodies at the state or local level have to inform the owners that the rule exists, give

A Winning Team

The Supreme Court's power to formulate policy has never been illustrated more dramatically than when it declared in 1954 that segregation in public schools is unconstitutional. The team of litigators that won this momentous case was (left to right) George E. C. Hayes, Thurgood Marshall, and James Nabrit, Jr.

them a timetable for compliance, communicate the penalties for noncompliance, be available to answer questions that emerge, and report to Washington on how well the regulations are working.

As pointed out in Chapter 13, one of the biggest problems at the implementation stage of policymaking is coordination. After officials in Washington enact a law and write the subsequent regulations, people outside Washington typically are designated to implement the policy. The agents may be local officials, state administrators, or federal bureaucrats headquartered in regional offices around the country. Those who implement programs are often given considerable discretion as to how to apply general policies to specific, local situations. The discretion can give agents flexibility to tailor situations to local conditions, but it can also mean that people affected by the programs are treated differently depending on where they live. Some polluters, for example, may be treated more leniently than others, depending on which regional office of the Environmental Protection Agency (EPA) is handling their case.[13]

Often, state and local officials are asked to carry out policies they had no hand in writing. This is a source of conflict between them and officials in Washington, and it can be a cause of implementation failure. A case in point is the national government's efforts in 1990 to improve the quality of care provided by nursing homes. One regulation was designed to reduce the number of patients who are routinely sedated. Many nursing homes regard sedating patients as a relatively cheap way to take care of those who are not compliant. The state of California did not like the national government's new standards. (California's nursing homes sedate 65 percent of their patients, compared with a national average of 40 percent.) Declaring that the care provided by its homes was excellent, and federal busybodies were simply adding unwarranted costs to the price of nursing care, California refused to implement the new standards. Its authority challenged outright, the national government first sent health inspectors to

California to examine nursing homes for compliance with the new regulations. Facing determined resistance and political pressure from Republican governor Pete Wilson (an ally of President Bush's), federal regulators subsequently backed down and indicated that they would change the regulations.[14]

Although it may sound highly technical, implementation is very much a political process. It involves a great deal of bargaining and negotiation among different groups of people in and out of government. The difficulty of implementing complex policies in a federal system, with multiple layers of government, and in a pluralistic system, with multiple competing interests, seems daunting. Yet, there are incentives for cooperation, not the least of which is avoiding blame if the policy fails. (We will discuss coordination in more detail later in the chapter.)

Policy Evaluation   How does government know whether a policy is working? In some cases, success or failure may be obvious, but at other times experts in a specific field must tell government officials how well a policy is working. **Policy evaluation** is the analysis of public policy. Although there is no one method of evaluating policy, evaluation tends to draw heavily on approaches used by academics, including cost-benefit analysis and various statistical methods designed to provide concrete measurements of the effects of a program. Although technical, the studies can be quite influential in decisions on whether to continue, expand, alter, reduce, or eliminate programs. The continuing stream of negative evaluations of programs designed to bring jobs to the unemployed has clearly reduced political support for such policies.[15]

Policy evaluation tries not only to analyze which parts of a program are working and which are not, but also usually specifies alternate approaches that might improve a program's success. In the area of pollution control,

Rolling Toward Equality

These demonstrators gathered to call for the passage of the Americans with Disabilities Act of 1990. Once the law was enacted, new regulations had to be formulated before the statute could be fully implemented.

for example, studies have tried to establish the optimum level of pollution. Although it might seem that the optimum level of pollution is no pollution, in the real world this is not possible. Rather, "to have a perfectly clean environment would probably bring the nation's (even the world's) economy to a standstill."[16] Thus, evaluational research in this area specifies trade-offs in various approaches to decreasing pollution. Studies use rigorous research methods to determine whether prohibiting pollution by legally restricting certain kinds of emissions, or promoting pollution control with tax breaks, is the more efficacious for pollution control and economic growth.

Evaluating public policy is extremely difficult. The most pertinent data are not always available, predicting trends may require making problematic assumptions, and policy analysts may have biases that influence their research. Sometimes, the data are unclear and subject to differing interpretations. One interesting case involves initial efforts to evaluate the success of school busing. As discussed in Chapter 16, a primary objective of school integration was to improve the quality of education for poor blacks who were isolated by residential segregation. One major policy evaluation by a prominent sociologist concluded that none of the research that had been done demonstrated that integration had an effect on the educational achievement of students who were bused.[17] Working from the same data, another respected scholar concluded that "the achievement effects of 'busing' [were] more complex and positive than [previously] reported."[18] Two equally adept analysts, using the same data, had arrived at different conclusions.

Evaluation is part of the policymaking process, because the knowledge gained from it helps to identify problems and issues that arise from current policy. In other words, evaluation studies provide **feedback** to policymakers on program performance. (The dotted line in Figure 17.1 represents a feedback loop. Problems that emerge during the implementation stage also provide feedback to policymakers.) By drawing attention to emerging problems, policy evaluation influences the political agenda. For instance, you may recall our discussion of oversight in Chapter 11. When congressional committees perform oversight duties, they are evaluating policy with an eye to identifying issues they will have to deal with in subsequent legislation. Thus, we have come full circle. The end of the process—evaluating whether the policy is being implemented as it was envisioned when it was formulated—is the beginning of a new cycle of public policymaking.

A MULTIPLICITY OF PARTICIPANTS	The policymaking process encompasses many different stages and many different participants at each stage. Here we examine some forces that pull the government in different directions and make problem solving less coherent than it might otherwise be. In the next section, we look at some structural elements of American government that work to coordinate competing and sometimes conflicting approaches to the same problem.

Multiplicity and Fragmentation

A single policy problem may be attacked in different and sometimes competing ways by government for many reasons. At the heart of this **fragmentation** of policymaking is the fundamental nature of government in

America. Separation of powers divides authority among the branches of the national government; federalism divides authority among the national, state, and local levels of government. The multiple centers of power are, of course, a primary component of pluralist democracy. Different groups try to influence different parts of government; no one entity completely controls policymaking. Consequently, groups rebuffed by one part of government can lobby another that might be more sympathetic. And as a result, separate parts of government may make conflicting decisions in the same policy area.

Policy directed at ensuring the rights of Native Americans illustrates how the structure of government both benefits a segment of the population and fails to produce a unified approach to its problems. Native Americans have had limited success at lobbying Congress. For the most part, constituents back home are not eager to cede land or special freedoms to Native Americans; this reluctance influences their members of Congress. However, Native Americans have been more successful at convincing the courts of their property claims to various areas. Nevertheless, their legal victories often anger people. After a court decided that members of one tribe did not have to pay local taxes, the government of Ledyard, Connecticut, prohibited tribe members from using the town library.[19]

Fragmentation exists both because of conflict between branches or levels of government and because of lack of coordination within a branch of government. Despite the furor over the need to do more to combat drug use in America, the executive branch of the national government has been beset by chronic infighting among the more than thirty agencies involved in one way or another. In the area of drug enforcement alone, nineteen agencies share responsibility. The Customs Service and the Drug Enforcement Administration (DEA) regard each other with suspicion, although they ostensibly are working toward the same goal. Neither wants the other to encroach on what it regards as its territory. One consequence of these attitudes is that the DEA will not give the Customs Service direct access to DEA intelligence files.[20]

Congress is characterized by the same diffusion of authority over drug policy. Seventy-five separate House and Senate committees and subcommittees claim some jurisdiction for drug legislation. The committees jealously guard their prerogatives.[21]

The multiplicity of institutional participants is partly the product of the complexity of public policy issues. Controlling illegal drugs is not one problem but a number of different, interrelated problems. Drug treatment questions, for example, have little in common with questions related to the smuggling of drugs into the country. Still, the responsibilities of agencies and committees do overlap. Why are responsibilities not parceled out more precisely to clarify jurisdictions and eliminate overlap? Such reorganizations create winners and losers, and agencies fearing the loss of jurisdiction over an issue become highly protective of their turf.

The Pursuit of Coordination

How does government overcome fragmentation so that it can make its public policies more coherent? Coordination of different elements of government is not impossible, and fragmentation often creates a productive pressure to rethink jurisdictions.

One common response to the problem of coordination is the formation of interagency task forces within the executive branch. Their common goal is to develop a broad policy response that all relevant agencies will endorse. Such task forces include representatives of all agencies claiming responsibility for a particular issue. They attempt to forge good policy as well as good will among competing agencies. Because of its frustration with the lack of progress in the development of drugs to combat AIDS, the Clinton administration formed a task force. A primary goal of the Task Force on AIDS Drug Development is to make sure that red tape does not delay approval of promising AIDS drugs.[22]

Sometimes, the executive branch attempts to reassign jurisdictions among its agencies, although certain players may resist the loss of their turf. Reorganization of jurisdiction is more common within than across agencies. A shift across agencies is likely to require White House involvement. Nevertheless, the president and his aides sometimes orchestrate such restructurings, which may involve creating a new agency to assume control over other, existing agencies or programs. With congressional approval, President Richard Nixon created the Environmental Protection Agency in 1970 to better coordinate fifteen programs administered by five other parts of the executive branch.[23]

The Office of Management and Budget (OMB) also fosters coordination in the executive branch. The OMB can do much more then review budgets and look for ways to improve management practices. The Reagan administration used OMB to clear regulations before they were proposed publicly by the administrative agencies. It initiated OMB's regulatory review role to centralize control of the executive branch. The Bush administration used the President's Council on Competitiveness in a comparable way to review regulations before agencies implemented them. Under Vice President Dan Quayle, the council rejected regulations that it regarded as detrimental to the economy.[24] Vice President Al Gore is responsible for meeting with agency heads to set regulatory priorities for the Clinton administration.[25] The virtue of centralized control by the White House through such instruments as the OMB and the Council on Competitiveness is that the administration can ensure that its objectives are carried out, not compromised by agencies eager to please interest groups that give them political support. Critics say that such White House control excludes many relevant groups from the policymaking process. Clearly, central clearance of regulations is an instrument to promote majoritarianism and to work against pluralist politics.

Congress has moved in some limited ways toward greater coherence and coordination in its policymaking. More unified party voting and stronger leadership have led to some recentralization of authority after a period of decentralization of power.[26] At the same time, Congress finds it difficult to eliminate overlapping jurisdictions through reorganization. Committee reorganizations are rare, and the proliferation of subcommittees has made the problem of competing jurisdictions worse. The leadership in Congress does not have the same authority to enforce coordination that the president has.

Finally, the fragmentation of policy created by federalism may be solved when an industry asks the national government to develop a single regulatory policy. Often, the alternative is for that industry to try to accommodate different regulatory approaches used in various states. Although an industry may prefer no regulation at all, it generally prefers one master to fifty. (Recall the "Food Fight!" feature in Chapter 4.)

The effect of pluralism on the problem of coordination is all too evident. In a decentralized, federal system of government, which has large numbers of interest groups, fragmentation is inevitable. Beyond the structural factors is the natural tendency of people and organizations to defend their base of power. Government officials understand, however, that mechanisms of coordination are necessary so that fragmentation does not overwhelm policymaking. Such mechanisms as interagency task forces, reorganizations, and White House review can bring some coherence to policymaking.

ISSUE NETWORKS

So far, we have emphasized how different kinds of issues can affect the policymaking process in different ways and how government officials cope with the problems of fragmentation and coordination. We want to extend these themes by focusing more closely on interest groups. Within any issue area, a number—often a very large number—of interest groups are trying to influence policy decisions. Representatives from these organizations interact with each other and with government officials on a recurring basis. The ongoing interaction produces both conflict and cooperation.

Government by Policy Area

We noted earlier that policy formulation takes place across different institutions. Participants from these institutions do not patiently wait their turn as policymaking proceeds from one institution to the next. Rather, they try to influence policy at whatever stage they can. Suppose that Congress is considering amendments to the Clean Air Act. Because Congress does not function in a vacuum, the other parts of government that will be affected by the legislation participate in the process, too. The EPA has an interest in the outcome, because it will have to administer the law. The White House is concerned about any legislation that affects such vital sectors of the economy as the steel and coal industries. As a result, officials from both the EPA and the White House work with members of Congress and the appropriate committee staffs to try to ensure that their interests are protected. At the same time, lobbyists representing corporations, trade associations, and environmental groups are doing their best to influence Congress, agency officials, and White House aides. Trade associations might hire public relations firms to sway public opinion toward industry's point of view. Experts from think tanks and universities might be asked to testify at hearings or to serve in an informal advisory capacity in regard to the technical, economic, and social effects of the proposed amendments.[27]

What the participants have in common is membership in an **issue network,** "a shared-knowledge group having to do with some aspect . . . of public policy."[28] The form of an issue network is fuzzy, but in general terms networks include members of Congress, committee staffers, agency officials, lawyers, lobbyists, consultants, scholars, and public relations specialists who interact frequently as they work to influence policies in a particular issue area. This makes for a large number of participants—in a broad policy area, the number of interest group organizations alone is usually in the dozens, if not hundreds.[29]

Not all participants in an issue network have a working relationship with all others. Indeed, some may be chronic antagonists. Others tend to be allies. For example, environmental groups will coalesce in trying to influence a clean air bill but are likely to be in opposition to business groups. The common denominator for friends and foes in an issue network is technical mastery of a particular policy area.

Iron Triangles

Examining politics in Washington by looking at policy area rather than at individual institutions is not new. Research by an earlier generation of political scientists and journalists described a system of subgovernments, each dominating policymaking in an issue area. For example, journalist Douglass Cater wrote about the sugar subgovernment of the late 1950s:

> Political power within the sugar subgovernment is largely vested in the Chairman of the House Agricultural Committee who works out the schedule of quotas. It is shared by a veteran civil servant, the director of the Sugar Division of the U.S. Department of Agriculture, who provides the necessary "expert" advice for such a complex marketing arrangement. Further advice is provided by Washington representatives of the domestic beet and sugar cane growers, the sugar refineries, and the foreign producers.[30]

According to Cater, the subgovernment had three components:

- Key members of the congressional committees and subcommittees responsible for the policy area (in this case, the chairman of the House Agriculture Committee)

- Officials from the agency or bureau that administers the policy (the director of a division of the U.S. Department of Agriculture)

- Lobbyists who represent the agency's clients (growers, refineries, and foreign producers)

These policymaking communities were called **iron triangles.** The word *iron* describes important properties of the subgovernments: They were largely autonomous and closed; outsiders had a great deal of difficulty penetrating them. Even presidents had difficulty influencing iron triangles, which endured from one administration to another. And job changes did not usually affect them. An individual who left one component of the triangle often would move to another. Iron triangles worked because participants shared similar policy views and tried to reach a consensus that would benefit all of them.

The iron triangle model was popular with political scientists.[31] Although some used different terms (*subgovernments, cozy little triangles*) and some developed more sophisticated frameworks than the simplified version offered here, the basic ideas were the same. Typically, a small group of individuals dominated policymaking in their issue area, the policy communities were largely autonomous, and they favored those who were well organized. The model was used not only to describe the American political process but also to show what was wrong with our policymaking system.[32]

The Case of Telecommunications

In recent years, it has become increasingly clear that iron triangles are no longer typical policymaking systems. The telecommunications industry provides a useful illustration of the changing nature of politics in Washington. Once a harmonious iron triangle, telecommunications today is a large issue network filled with conflict.

Until fairly recently, the telecommunications industry was dominated by American Telephone & Telegraph (AT&T), which, with its affiliated Bell System telephone companies around the country, constituted a monopoly.[33] Customers had no choice but to use the phone lines and phone equipment of "Ma Bell." It was easy for AT&T executives to defend their company's control of the industry. The United States had an impressive system with low-cost, reliable service to residential customers. Moreover, the AT&T network was a mainstay of our defense communications system. Within the telecommunications iron triangle—a policymaking community made up of some key members of Congress, the Federal Communications Commission, and AT&T—policymaking was usually consensual and uncontroversial.

At one time, AT&T was the world's biggest corporation, and it seemed invulnerable. But in 1968, the Federal Communications Commission (FCC) ruled that other companies could compete against AT&T in the "terminal" equipment market. This meant that a customer could buy a telephone (or more complex telephone equipment) from a company other than AT&T and attach it to AT&T phone lines. This jolt of competition was followed a year later by a second blow to AT&T, when the FCC ruled that MCI, a small start-up company marketing microwave technology, could sell a limited form of long-distance service to business clients.

As significant as the changes were, the greatest challenge to AT&T lay ahead. In 1974, the U.S. Department of Justice brought a lawsuit against the corporation, charging it with illegal monopolistic behavior in the telecommunications industry. The eventual outcome of the suit was an out-of-court settlement that required AT&T to give up control over local operating service. The Bell System was broken up into seven independent regional telephone companies. AT&T was allowed to retain its long-distance service, but it would have to compete against other long-distance carriers. (AT&T did win the right to enter the computer industry, which was one of its major goals.) All in all, AT&T lost three-quarters of its assets.[34] The giant telephone company had fallen victim to a growing belief among academics and policymakers that government regulation was hampering the economy by restricting competition and lessening the incentives for innovation, as well as limiting the price and product choices available to consumers. Thus, telecommunications was deregulated by the changes that introduced more business competition.[35]

Toll Taker on the Information Superhighway

John Malone, the chief executive officer of TCI, is a shrewd business visionary who is one of the most influential leaders in the telecommunications industry. He built the Denver-based TCI into the largest operator of cable television franchises around the country and created strategic business alliances with a number of important telecommunications companies.

Today, policymaking in telecommunications bears no resemblance to an iron triangle. After the AT&T divestiture, competition among businesses selling various services and equipment became even more intense. Many new companies emerged to join the highly fractious issue network. Much of the political conflict that ensued had its origins in the consent agreement, which tried to define major markets (such as local telephone service) and specify who could participate. Various companies made repeated attempts to get the government to change the rules of the consent agreement so that they could compete in more markets. Thus, typical conflicts involved fights between the Baby Bells and long-distance carriers, each side wanting to expand into new markets while protecting their current markets from encroachment by would-be competitors.[36]

The government did make some changes in the initial consent agreement to expand competition even further. The Clinton administration supports replacing the divestiture agreement with further deregulation to permit virtually all kinds of firms to participate in all kinds of markets.[37]

More important, however, are three further developments that have brought even more change to the telecommunications issue network. First are the technological innovations either not anticipated by the consent decree or excluded from it, because commercial markets for the technology had not yet matured. One example is cellular phones and other forms of wireless communication. Second, various technologies began to converge in many significant ways. One of the more significant changes in this respect is that telephone lines have become more important to computer users as the electronic transmission of data and digital communications became more feasible. As technologies converged, new business opportunities beckoned in reconfigured markets.

Third, entrepreneurs began to see the future as one in which the strongest companies—or at least those that survived the tumultuous changes in the marketplace—would be those which were alliances of many different businesses with expertise in individual products. The alliances could produce an array of services to customers through integrated technology. For example, John Malone of TCI (Tele-Communications Inc.), the nation's biggest operator of cable TV services in the country, is one business visionary who sees the future of cable TV as a five hundred-channel center of home life.[38] Over telephone lines, people will be able to order movies on demand, purchase airline tickets, watch sporting events of their choice, take part in interactive programming with a hand-held console, and do countless other things.

As Figure 17.3 shows, the changes have led to an issue network characterized not so much by political alliances as business alliances. Mergers, acquisitions, joint ventures, and cross ownership arrangements have created many firms with far-reaching interests.[39] Issue network politics is characterized by rapidly changing coalitions as partners on one issue become opponents on the next. Conflict within the network is chronic. No one controls telecommunications policymaking, but many organizations and individuals have a say in it. Europe is grappling with many of the same issues relating to development of the telecommunications industry (see Compared with What? 17.1).

Not all policymaking communities in Washington have evolved into issue networks.[40] Some policy domains are relatively small with few interest group participants. Policymaking is not necessarily consensual in smaller issue areas, but fewer participants usually means that patterns of interactions among interest groups and between groups and government are more stable than is the case with big issue networks, in which coalitions are ever changing.

Broader policy areas, such as health care and agriculture, are distinguished by large numbers of participants and high degrees of conflict.[41] Why have so many iron triangles rusted through and larger, more conflicted issue networks evolved? Deregulation and technological change have been the reasons not only in telecommunications but in other areas as well. Another source of change has been the rapid growth in the number of interest groups. As more and more new lobbying groups set up shop in Washington, they demanded the attention of policymakers. The new groups brought with them new concerns, and their interests were usually at odds with at least some groups active in the same policy area. The growth of groups was not simply a reflection of new businesses starting up. The increasing number of groups was also a manifestation of existing constituencies that had become better organized. Part of the growth of interest groups also stems from the public interest movement. The groups that evolved from that movement were natural adversaries of business, so new conflicts emerged in many issue areas.

POLICY EXPERTISE

Although contemporary issue networks may be much more open to new participants than iron triangles, there is still a significant barrier to admission. One must have the necessary expertise to enter the community of activists and politicians that influences policymaking in an issue area. Expertise has always been important, but "more than ever, policy-making is becoming an intramural activity among expert issue watchers."[42]

Oil companies, for example, are crucial to our economy, and lobbyists for the major firms have always had easy access to policymakers in government. Yet, there are lots of oil lobbyists in Washington, and not all have the same influence. They compete for the attention and respect of those in government by offering solutions that are technically feasible as well as politically palatable. Consider the issues addressed during a period of expanding regulation of the domestic oil industry. Seemingly obscure and complicated policy questions were unending. How were "original costs" to be distinguished from "reproduction costs"? Was it fair for "secondary and tertiary production" to be exempted from "base-period volumes"? Did drilling that yielded "new pays" or "extensions" qualify as "new" oil or "old" oil for pricing purposes?[43]

Those in an issue network speak the same language. They can participate in the negotiation and compromise of policymaking because they can offer concrete, detailed solutions to the problems at hand. They understand the substance of policy, the way Washington works, and one another's viewpoints.

One reason participants in an issue network have such a good understanding of the needs and problems of others in the network is that job switches within policy communities continue to be common. When

---

FIGURE 17.3   ■ The Telecommunications Issue Network

There is no one way to draw an issue network. This graphic illustrates the different types of relationships between different private sector groups involved in the telecommunications industry. Recent trends in the industry are toward more and more mergers and acquisitions as companies try to expand into integrated, large-scale entities that provide a range of services that will be popular in the future. The congressional commit- *tees and units of the executive branch specified in this figure are those with primary responsibility for telecommunications policymaking.*

Source: Jeffrey M. Berry, "The Dynamic Qualities of Issue Networks," paper delivered at the annual meeting of the American Political Science Association, September 1994, New York City. Used with permission.

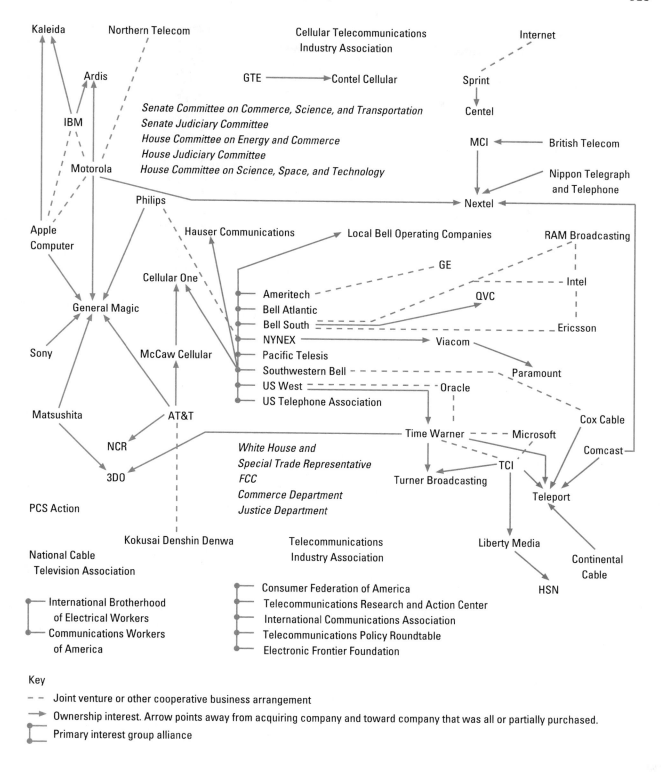

Key

- - - Joint venture or other cooperative business arrangement

→ Ownership interest. Arrow points away from acquiring company and toward company that was all or partially purchased.

⊢ Primary interest group alliance

COMPARED WITH WHAT? 17.1   Rewiring Europe

As complex as the transformation of the American telecommunications industry is, it is even more complicated in Europe. Government-run or government-sanctioned monopolies in Europe are having to change, just as AT&T had to when faced with deregulation and divestiture. The breakup of AT&T involved one large company and one (albeit) large market. However, in Europe today the deregulation of a telephone company in one country cannot really be independent of what is going on in the other countries of Europe.

European telecommunications companies have had to respond to technological, economic, and political imperatives. In terms of technology, the digital revolution has required European phone companies to think of themselves as part of one large, integrated, electronic network. If a business in Berlin wants to send a fax (which is transmitted over telephone lines) to a company in Paris, the electronic impulses sent from Berlin must be carried by a compatible technology once they enter French phone lines. The fax machine in the Paris office must also be able to understand the electronic language in which the fax was sent. Without standardized technology, Europe would be an electronic tower of Babel.

This technological requirement may seem all too obvious. Yet, as one observer has noted, "Historically [telecommunication] network developments in Europe were largely independent of one another. Each country developed its own infrastructure with its national specifications and services." This has changed because leaders in government and in the telecommunications industry recognized that the failure to integrate telecommunications services in Europe would be an economic disaster for all concerned. An equipment manufacturer in Amsterdam who could sell only to other companies in the Netherlands would have a relatively small market in which to operate. If that company could sell in all of Europe, it would have the incentives to invest more in research and development. The Europeans were also facing competition from AT&T and other American firms in areas that were already deregulated, such as the transmission of data over telephone lines around the world. An integrated Europe will lead to more effective competition against American companies.

The political push for deregulation and integration came from the European Union (EU). The EU is a regional organization composed of twelve countries of Western Europe and is committed to the integration of European economies. The EU has significant powers over its member states, and it was responsible for catalyzing the deregulation of telecommunications markets and the movement toward standardizing technology. Modernization of equipment and services in Europe is occurring at a rapid pace, and the twelve member countries will soon be the single market for telecommunications that the EU envisions.

• *Sources: Reinhard Ellger, "Telecommunications in Europe: Law and Policy of the European Community in a Key Industrial Sector," in* Singular Europe, *ed. William James Adams (Ann Arbor: University of Michigan Press), pp. 203–250; Gerald Fuchs, "ISDN— the Telecommunications Highway for Europe after 1992!"* Telecommunications Policy *(November 1992), 635–645; Wayne Sandholtz, "Institutions and Collective Action: The New Telecommunications in Western Europe,"* World Politics *45 (January 1993), 242–270; Jacques Arlandis, "Trading Telecommunications,"* Telecommunications Policy *(April 1993), 171–185.*

FIGURE **17.4**	■ **Government Service: A Useful Credential**

Individuals who have held high-level government jobs become very attractive to the private sector. This survey of political appointees to top executive branch positions shows that only a little more than one-fourth came to those jobs directly from business or law. When they left their appointed positions, however, nearly two-thirds took jobs with corporations or law firms.

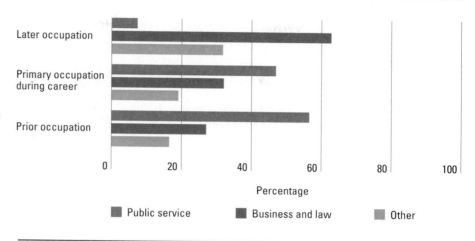

Source: Linda L. Fisher, "Fifty Years of Presidential Appointments," in The In-and-Outers, *ed. G. Calvin Mackenzie (Baltimore: Johns Hopkins University Press, 1987), p. 27. Used by permission.*

someone wants to leave her or his current position but remain in Washington, the most obvious place to look for a new job is within the same policy field. For these **in-and-outers,** knowledge and experience remain relevant to a particular issue network, no matter which side of the fence they are on.

A common pattern of job switching—one that is the focus of much criticism—is to work in government for a number of years, build up knowledge of a policy area, and then take a lobbying job (see Figure 17.4). Law firms, consulting firms, public relations firms, and trade associations generally pay much higher salaries than the government. And they pay not just for experience and know-how but for connections with government.[44] When the Washington lobbying firm of Black, Manafort, Stone & Kelly hired James C. Healy, a former aide to the Democratic chairman of the House Ways and Means Committee, it knew that this in-and-outer would give them better access to that critical tax-writing unit. Corporations that want to influence the committee can choose from among many Washington firms, but Black, Manafort, Stone & Kelly can make a convincing case to prospective clients that Healy's phone calls to the House Democratic leadership are returned.[45]

Some congressional staffers and high-ranking executive branch officials start their own firms rather than go to work for an existing firm. Despite the competition, those with valuable government experience and the respect of their peers can quickly establish themselves as the people with the right expertise and the right contacts in a particular policy field. During his seven-year stint as a high-ranking official in the Defense Department, for example, Richard Perle acquired great expertise on a variety of subjects, including military assistance to Turkey. A few years after leaving the government, Perle founded International Advisers, Inc. Before he actually established the company, he convinced the government of

Worth a Million!

Despite President Clinton's promise to stop the revolving door, his chief legislative liaison aide, Howard Paster, left the White House to work for the Washington office of Hill and Knowlton. The lobbying and public relations firm has a lucrative list of clients including Boeing, Exxon, and Mazda. The New York Times *reported that in his new position as chief executive of Hill & Knowlton, Paster will probably be making close to $1 million a year.*

Turkey that he could help it in its efforts to gain military and economic assistance from Washington. Turkey pays International Advisers an annual retainer of $875,000 a year.[46]

In short, participation in an issue network not only gives government employees expertise but can also endow them with contacts that make them attractive to business clients. Personal familiarity with policymakers can be of value in and of itself, but it is of greatest utility when coupled with the expertise that comes from extensive work on specific issues.

Although spectacular fees and salaries for those going from government to the private sector are hardly representative of what happens to in-and-outers, many do receive substantial financial incentive to leave government work. Indeed, people who take high-level government jobs often do so at some cost to their income. One survey of political appointees to top government jobs showed that 55 percent said they had made a financial sacrifice to move into government. Yet, roughly 50 percent indicated that government service had enhanced their subsequent earning power.[47]

One constraint on in-and-outers is the Ethics in Government Act of 1978, which specifies that senior executive branch officials cannot lobby their former agency for a year after leaving the government. Critics have complained, however, that in-and-outers have not found it much of an inhibition and that some executive branch officials have had little trouble getting around it. To counter this problem, Bill Clinton issued a new, seemingly tougher standard of ethics for those joining his administration. Eleven hundred top administration appointees were required to sign a pledge not to lobby their former agencies for five years after they leave government and to promise to never lobby on behalf of foreign clients.[48] The president-elect announced that the new rules would "stop the revolving door from public service to private enrichment."[49]

After less than a year in office, the Clinton administration's ethics rules proved to be embarrassingly ineffective. Clinton's congressional liaison chief, Howard Paster, resigned from the administration to take a job as head of Hill & Knowlton, a public relations and lobbying firm, at a reported salary of $1 million a year. Roy Neel, deputy chief of staff at the White House, resigned to take a job as president of the United States Telephone Association, a lobbying arm of the Baby Bells (see Figure 17.3). Neel's salary is estimated at $500,000, quadruple his White House salary. Both Paster and Neel told the press that they would not lobby the White House in their new jobs.[50] Yet, nothing prevents them from directing other lobbyists or from using their knowledge of how the White House operates to their firm's advantage.

ISSUE NETWORKS AND DEMOCRACY

Are issue networks making the government too fragmented? Are some issue networks beyond popular control? Has the increasing complexity of public policy given technical experts too much policymaking authority?

These questions relate to the broad issues raised in Chapter 2. For many years, political scientists have described American democracy as a system in which different constituencies work energetically to influence policies of concern to them. Policymaking is seen as a response to these groups rather than to majority will. This is a considerably different conception of democracy than the more traditional view, that policies reflect what most people want. It is a pluralist, not a majoritarian, view of American government.

When iron triangles were considered typical of the policymaking process, they were the target of much criticism. Some argued that the type of pluralism that they represented did not promote democracy through group politics but engendered closed systems that favored the status quo. The groups that were part of the iron triangles found government highly responsive, but these groups did not represent all the interests that should have been at the bargaining table. Consumer groups and environmental groups pledged to protect the public interest were not there to participate. Business groups that dominated the iron triangles used their position to try to stifle new competition through regulatory restrictions, as AT&T did in the telecommunications field.

In a number of ways, issue networks are an improvement over iron triangles as a model of pluralist democracy. They are open systems, populated by a much wider range of interest groups. Decision making is not centralized in the hands of a few key players; policies are formulated in a much more participatory fashion. But there is still no guarantee that all relevant interests are represented, and those with greater financial resources have an advantage. Nevertheless, issue networks come much closer to meeting the objectives of pluralist democracy than do iron triangles.[51]

For those who prefer majoritarian democracy, however, issue networks are an obstacle to achieving their vision of how government should operate. The technical complexity of contemporary issues makes it especially difficult for the public at large to exert control over policy outcomes.

When we think of the complexity of nuclear power, toxic wastes, air pollution, poverty, drug abuse, and so on, it is easy to understand why majoritarian democracy is so difficult to achieve. The more complex the issue, the more elected officials must depend on a technocratic elite for policy guidance. And technical expertise, of course, is a chief characteristic of participants in issue networks.

At first glance, having technical experts play a key role in policymaking may seem highly desirable. After all, who but the experts should be making decisions about toxic wastes? But a dependence on technocrats works to the advantage of interest groups, which use policy experts to maximize their influence with government. Seen in this light, issue networks become less appealing. Interest groups—at least those with which we do not personally identify—are seen as selfish. They pursue policies that favor their constituents rather than the national interest.

Although expertise is an important factor in bringing interest groups into the decision-making process, it is not the only one. Americans have a fundamental belief that government should be open and accessible to people. If some constituency has a problem, they reason, government ought to listen to it. The practical consequence of this view is a government that is open to interest groups.

Finally, although issue networks promote pluralism, keep in mind that majoritarian influences on policymaking are still significant. The broad contours of public opinion can be a dominant force on highly visible issues. Policymaking on civil rights, for example, has been sensitive to shifts in public opinion. Elections, too, send messages to policymakers about the most widely discussed campaign issues. What issue networks have done, however, is facilitate pluralist politics in policy areas in which majoritarian influences are weak.

SUMMARY

Government tries to solve problems through a variety of approaches. Some public policies prohibit, some protect, some promote, and some provide. The approach chosen can significantly affect the policymaking process.

Although there is much variation in the policymaking process, we can conceive of it as consisting of four stages. The first stage is agenda setting, the process by which problems become defined as political issues worthy of government attention. Once people in government feel that they should be doing something about a problem, an attempt at policy formulation will follow. All three branches of the national government formulate policy. Once policies have been formulated and ratified, administrative units of government must implement them. Finally, once policies are being carried out, they need to be evaluated. Implementation and policy evaluation influence agenda building, because program shortcomings become evident during these stages. Thus, the process is really circular, with the end often marking the beginning of a new round of policymaking.

Our policymaking system is also characterized by forces that push it toward fragmentation and by institutional structures intended to bring some element of coordination to government. The multiplicity of participants in policymaking, the diffusion of authority within both Congress and the executive branch, the separation of powers, and federalism are chief causes of conflict and fragmentation in policymaking.

Policymaking in many areas can be viewed as an ongoing process of interaction through issue networks of those in government and those outside it. Each network is a way to communicate and exchange information and ideas about a particular policy area. In a network, lobbying coalitions form easily and dissolve rapidly as new issues arise. Generally, contemporary policy communities are more open to new participants than were the old iron triangles. Issue networks place a high premium on expertise as public policy problems grow ever more complex.

Political scientists view issue networks with some concern. The networks unquestionably facilitate the representation of many interests in the policymaking process, but they do so at a price. They allow well-organized, aggressive constituencies to prevail over the broader interests of the nation. Once again, the majoritarian and pluralist models of democracy conflict. It is easy to say that the majority should rule. But in the real world, the majority tends to be far less interested in issues than are the constituencies most directly affected by them. It is also easy to say that those most affected by issues should have the most influence. But experience teaches us that such influence leads to policies that favor the well represented at the expense of those who should be at the bargaining table but are not.

Key Terms

public policy	feedback
agenda setting	fragmentation
policy formulation	issue network
implementation	iron triangle
policy evaluation	in-and-outer

Selected Readings

Anderson, James E. *Public Policymaking.* 2nd ed. Boston: Houghton Mifflin, 1994. A brief overview of the policymaking system.

Baumgartner, Frank R., and Bryan D. Jones. *Agendas and Instability in American Politics.* Chicago: University of Chicago Press, 1993. A systematic analysis of how issues arise and how they fall off the national agenda.

Cater, Douglass. *Power in Washington.* New York: Vintage Books, 1964. A classic statement of the iron triangle thesis by a veteran Washington reporter.

Church, Thomas W., and Robert T. Nakamura. *Cleaning Up the Mess.* Washington, D.C.: Brookings Institution, 1993. The authors focus on different strategies for implementing the Superfund program for cleaning up hazardous waste sites.

Ingram, Helen, and Steven Rathgeb Smith. *Public Policy for Democracy.* Washington, D.C.: Brookings Institution, 1993. An interesting array of articles that focus on how different policy choices affect our conception of ourselves as citizens.

Mackenzie, G. Calvin, ed. *The In-and-Outers.* Baltimore: Johns Hopkins University Press, 1987. A collection of essays examining the problems associated with the movement of people between the private sector and the executive branch.

Portney, Kent. *Approaching Public Policy Analysis.* Englewood Cliffs, N.J.: Prentice-Hall, 1986. A sophisticated but highly readable introduction to policy evaluation.

Weir, Margaret. *Politics and Jobs.* Princeton, N.J.: Princeton University Press, 1992. An excellent case study of how one issue (employment policy) has evolved.

18

Economic Policy

IN THE SUMMER OF 1993, President Bill Clinton's economic program to reduce the national debt of more than $4 trillion appeared headed toward defeat in the House of Representatives. To reduce the debt by nearly $500 billion by 1998, Clinton had proposed a budget that combined new taxes on the rich with less government spending. Its higher taxes departed sharply from the low-tax policies initiated by President Ronald Reagan in the 1980s, and Newt Gingrich, the House Republican whip from Georgia, warned that the new taxes would prompt business to eliminate jobs.[1] When the House was ready to vote on the budget on August 5, Clinton could count on only 212 votes, 6 short of the 218 needed to guarantee passage.[2] Not one of the 175 House Republicans supported the budget bill.

The Democrats had a majority in the House, but many moderates and conservatives in the party thought the bill did not go far enough in cutting spending—whereas some liberal Democrats thought that it had already cut too many programs. At the last moment, the decisive vote was cast by freshman Democrat Marjorie Margolies-Mezvinsky, who the day before had told her constituents in a wealthy section of metropolitan Philadelphia that she would vote against the plan's higher taxes. But when President Clinton himself called her minutes before the vote, Representative Margolies-Mezvinsky supported the president, and the bill passed 218 to 216. Afterwards she said, "The Republicans are calling me spineless and sinister, and the Democrats are calling me a heroine."[3] The next day, the bill went to the Senate, where it again faced united opposition from Republicans and again lacked enough Democratic votes to guarantee passage. The tide turned when Democratic senator Bob Kerrey of Nebraska announced his support of the bill in a dramatic statement on the floor of the Senate. Addressing Clinton, he said, "I could not and should not cast a vote that brings down your presidency."[4] Even with Kerrey's support, the vote was 50–50, and the bill passed only when Vice President Al Gore broke the tie.

The passage of Clinton's deficit reduction plan was historic in several respects. First, only a few other important issues in public policy have been decided by such bare voting margins. (One was the one-vote failure in the Senate to convict President Andrew Johnson of impeachment charges in 1868; another was the one-vote House passage of the extension of the military draft in 1941.[5]) Second, probably no other critically important legislation has ever been passed without a single vote from the opposition party. Then, too, the adoption of Clinton's plan swung the nation not only away from the low-tax policies of the Reagan administration but also from

We Told You So!

Leon Panetta, who was Budget Director in August, 1993, when Congress narrowly passed Clinton's first budget, testified before Congress in early 1994 that the deficit reduction proposals in that budget were working as intended. The deficit had been sharply reduced and — despite claims that jobs would be lost—unemployment was falling. Later in 1994, Panetta would be elevated to Clinton's chief of staff.

the traditional spending-oriented policies of Democratic presidents and congresses.[6]

Although Clinton had to make many compromises with individual Democrats to secure passage of his economic program, it passed essentially as outlined in his February budget message following his November election. Clinton proposed to reduce the deficit mainly through a program of higher taxes on the wealthy and spending cuts in defense, Medicare, and overall limits on appropriations.[7] Whether Clinton's deficit reduction program would actually work over the long haul, remained to be seen. One year after the program's passage the deficit had been cut substantially and the economy was growing.

Nevertheless, Clinton's economic program faced two major problems that were largely beyond his control. First, it assumed that lowering the deficit would lower interest rates. However, interest rates are only indirectly affected by the size of the deficit. They are more directly determined by actions of the Federal Reserve Board (the Fed), which by law is independent of presidential control. Historically, the Fed has adjusted interest rates to combat inflation rather than to stimulate economic growth.[8] A former Fed chairman once described its task as being "to remove the punch bowl when the party gets going."[9] Beginning in early 1994, the Fed raised rates by small margins four times in four months in an effort to ward off *future* inflation expected from economic growth, and some politicians and economists worried that its actions would strangle the very growth it expected. Representative Lee Hamilton (Democrat from Indiana and former chair of the Joint Economic Committee) said, "The Fed holds in its hands the future of President Clinton—to exaggerate it just a little."[10]

The second problem is the relatively small portion of government spending that the president can control in the budget. Most government spending (such as for social security and health care) is determined by law and not reducible by the president without congressional support. Some established government spending programs (such as social security) have broad public support and are vigorously defended by members of Congress who fear election defeat if benefits are cut. Other areas of spending (as for health care) are strongly entwined with special interests that oppose overhauling government programs from which they benefit, and these programs also have vigorous defenders in Congress.

Although President Clinton's run for reelection in 1996 may be decided largely by the state of the economy, his powers as president do not enable him to determine interest rates or really to control spending. In this respect, Clinton suffers the same restrictions as his twentieth-century predecessors. All have had to work with a Fed that was made independent of the president and Congress and to deal with a Congress that ultimately controlled spending. A president running for reelection may not appreciate the theoretical point that these restrictions on presidential authority are in keeping with the pluralist model of democracy.

How much control can government really exercise over the economy through judicious usage of economic theory? How is the national budget formulated, and why has the deficit grown so large and proved so difficult to control? What effects do government taxing and spending policies have on the economy and on economic equality? We grapple with these and other questions in this chapter on the economics of public policy.

THEORIES OF ECONOMIC POLICY

Clinton's budget, like any national budget, relied on theories about how the economy responds to government taxing and spending policies. How policymakers tax and spend depends on their beliefs about (1) how the economy functions, and (2) the proper role of government in the economy. The American economy is so complex that no policymaker knows exactly how it works. Policymakers have to rely on economic theories to explain its functioning, and there are nearly as many theories as economists, as discussed in Feature 18.1. Unfortunately, different theories (and economists) often predict quite different outcomes. One source of differing predictions is the assumptions that underlie every economic theory, for these differ from theory to theory. Another problem is the difference between an abstract theory and the real world. Still, despite the disagreement among economists, a knowledge of basic economics is necessary to understand how government approaches public policy.

We are concerned here with economic policy in a market economy—one in which the prices of goods and services are determined through the interaction of sellers and buyers (that is, through supply and demand). This kind of economy is typical of the consumer-dominated societies of Western Europe and the United States. A nonmarket economy relies on government planners to determine both the prices of goods and the amounts that are produced. The old Soviet economy is a perfect example. In a nonmarket economy, the government owns and operates the major means of production.

Market economies are loosely called *capitalist economies:* They allow private individuals to own property, sell goods for profit in a free, or open, markets, and accumulate wealth, called *capital.* Market economies often exhibit a mix of government and private ownership. For example, Britain has considerably more government-owned enterprises (railroads, broadcasting, and housing) than the United States. The competing theories of

FEATURE **18.1**

■ Economics: The Dismal Science

Thomas Carlyle, a nineteenth-century British social critic, called economics "the dismal science." Although Carlyle was speaking in a different context, his phrase has stuck. If being a science requires agreement on fundamental propositions among practitioners, economics certainly is a dismal science. When twenty-seven standard propositions in economic theory were put to almost a thousand economists in five Western countries, they did not agree on a single one. Consider this example: "Reducing the role of regulatory authorities (for instance, in air traffic) would improve the efficiency of the economy." About 33 percent of the economists "generally disagreed," 30 percent "generally agreed," and 34 percent "agreed with provisions." When learned economists cannot agree on basic propositions in economic theory, politicians are free to choose theories that fit their views of the proper role of government in the economy.

- *Source: Adapted from Bruno S. Frey et al., "Consensus and Dissension Among Economists: An Empirical Inquiry,"* American Economic Review 74 *(December 1984): 986–994.*

THE ECONOMISTS

market economies differ largely on how free the market should be—in other words, on the role of government in directing the economy.

Laissez-Faire Economics

The French term *laissez faire,* introduced in Chapter 1 and discussed again in Chapter 13, describes the absence of government control. The economic doctrine of laissez faire likens the operation of a free market to the process of natural selection. Economic competition weeds out the weak and preserves the strong. In the process, the economy prospers and everyone eventually benefits.

Advocates of laissez-faire economics are fond of quoting Adam Smith's

The Wealth of Nations. In this 1776 treatise, Smith argued that each individual, pursuing his own selfish interests in a competitive market, was "led by an invisible hand to promote an end which was no part of his intention." Smith's "invisible hand" has been used for two centuries to justify the belief that the narrow pursuit of profits serves the broad interests of society. Strict advocates of laissez faire maintain that government interference with business tampers with the laws of nature, obstructing the workings of the free market.

Keynesian Theory

One problem with laissez-faire economics is its insistence that government should do little about **economic depressions** (periods of high unemployment and business failures) or about raging **inflation** (price increases that decrease the value of currency). Inflation is ordinarily measured by the Consumer Price Index (CPI), which Feature 18.2 explains. Since the beginning of the Industrial Revolution, capitalist economies have suffered through many cyclical fluctuations. The United States has experienced more than fifteen of these **business cycles**—expansions and contractions of business activity, the first stage accompanied by inflation and the second stage by unemployment. No one had a theory that really explained these cycles until the Great Depression of the 1930s.

That was when John Maynard Keynes, a British economist, theorized that business cycles stem from imbalances between aggregate demand and productive capacity. **Aggregate demand** is the income available to consumers, business, and government to spend on goods and services. **Productive capacity** is the total value of goods and services that can be produced when the economy is working at full capacity. The value of the goods and services actually produced is called the **gross national product (GNP).** When demand exceeds productive capacity, people are willing to pay more for available goods, which leads to price inflation. When produc-

We Make Money the Old-Fashioned Way: We Print It

The U.S. Mint stamps out coins, but paper money is produced by the Bureau of Engraving and Printing, which also prints Treasury notes and other U.S. securities. Imagine how frustrating it might be to work among these sheets of money.

FEATURE **18.2**

■ The Consumer Price Index

Inflation in the United States is usually measured in terms of the Consumer Price Index, which is calculated by the U.S. Bureau of Labor Statistics. The CPI is based on prices paid for food, clothing, shelter, transportation, medical services, and other items necessary for daily living. Data are collected from eighty-five areas across the country, from nearly sixty thousand homes and almost twenty thousand businesses.

The CPI is not a perfect yardstick. One problem is that it does not differentiate between inflationary price increases and other price increases. A Ford sedan bought in 1985, for instance, is not the same as a Ford sedan bought in 1995. To some extent, the price difference reflects improvements in quality as well as a decrease in the value of the dollar. The CPI is also slow to reflect changes in purchasing habits. Wash-and-wear clothes were tumbling in the dryer for several years before the government agreed to include them as an item in the index.

These are minor issues compared with the weight given over time to the cost of housing. Until 1983, 26 percent of the CPI was attributed to the cost of purchasing and financing a home. This formula neglected the realities that many people rent and that few people buy a home every year. A better measure of the cost of shelter is the cost of renting equivalent housing. Using this method of calculating, the cost of shelter dropped the weighting given to housing in the CPI from 26 percent to 14 percent.

The government uses the CPI to make cost-of-living adjustments in civil service and military pension payments, social security benefits, and food stamp allowances. Moreover, many union wage contracts with private businesses are indexed (tied) to the CPI. Because the CPI tends to rise each year, so do payments that are tied to it. In a way, indexing payments to the CPI promotes both the growth of government spending and inflation itself. The United States is one of the few nations that also ties its tax brackets to a price index, which reduces government revenues by eliminating the effect of inflation on taxpayer incomes.

The last overhaul of the CPI was in 1987, and new versions are planned for 1995. The Bureau of Labor Statistics estimates that the current measure overestimates the true amount of inflation by about one-fourth. Thus, people whose incomes are tied to the index, such as retirees on social security, may actually be enjoying an increasing standard of living, but few politicians would attempt to tell that to voters older than sixty-five.

Despite its faults, the CPI is at least a consistent measure of prices and is likely to continue as the basis for adjustments to wages, benefits, and payments affecting millions of people.

• *Source: Adapted from David S. Moore,* Statistics: Concepts and Controversies, *2d ed. (New York: Freeman, 1985), pp. 238–241. Used by permission of W. H. Freeman. Also see U.S.* Bureau of the Census, U.S. Department of Commerce Statistical Abstract of the United States, 1990 *(Washington, D.C.: U.S. Government Printing Office, 1990), pp. 465–466; and Robert D. Hershey, Jr., "An Inflation Index Is Said to Overstate the Case,"* New York Times, *11 January 1994, C1–C2.*

tive capacity exceeds demand, producers cut back their output of goods, which leads to unemployment. When many people are unemployed for an extended period, the economy is in a depression. Keynes theorized that government could stabilize the economy (and smooth out or eliminate business cycles) by controlling the level of aggregate demand.

Keynesian theory holds that aggregate demand can be adjusted through a combination of fiscal and monetary policies. **Fiscal policies,** which are enacted by the president and Congress, involve changes in government spending and taxing. When demand is too low, according to Keynes, government should either spend more itself—hiring people and thus giving them money—or cut taxes, giving people more of their own money to spend. When demand is too great, the government should either spend less or raise taxes, giving people less money to spend. **Monetary policies**, which are largely determined by the Federal Reserve Board, involve changes in the money supply and operate less directly on the economy. Increasing the amount of money in circulation increases aggregate demand and thus increases price inflation. Decreasing the money supply decreases aggregate demand and inflationary pressures.

Despite some problems with the assumptions of Keynesian theory, capitalist countries have widely adopted it in some form.[11] At one time or another, virtually all have used the Keynesian technique of **deficit financing**—spending in excess of tax revenues—to combat an economic slump. The objective of deficit financing is to inject extra money into the economy to stimulate aggregate demand. Most deficits are financed with funds borrowed through the issuing of government bonds, notes, or other securities. The theory holds that deficits can be paid off with budget surpluses after the economy recovers.

Because Keynesian theory requires government to play an active role in controlling the economy, it runs counter to laissez-faire economics. Before Keynes, no administration in Washington would shoulder responsibility for maintaining a healthy economy. In 1946, the year in which Keynes died, Congress passed an employment act establishing under law "the continuing responsibility of the national government to . . . promote maximum employment, production and purchasing power." It also created the **Council of Economic Advisers (CEA)** within the Executive Office of the President to advise the president on maintaining a stable economy. The CEA normally consists of three economists (usually university professors) appointed by the president with Senate approval. Aided by a staff of about twenty-five people (mostly economists), the CEA helps the president prepare his annual economic report, also a provision of the 1946 act. The chair of the CEA is usually a prominent spokesperson for the administration's economic policy. Under Clinton, the chair is Dr. Laura D'Andrea Tyson, formerly a professor of economics at the University of California at Berkeley.

The Employment Act of 1946, which reflected Keynesian theory, had a tremendous effect on government economic policy. Many people believe it was the primary source of "big government" in America. Even Richard Nixon, a conservative president, acknowledged that "we are all Keynesians now."

Monetary Policy

Although most economists accept Keynesian theory in its broad outlines, they disagree on its political utility. Some especially question the value of fiscal policies in controlling inflation and unemployment. They argue that government spending programs take too long to enact in Congress and to implement through the bureaucracy. As a result, jobs are created not when they are needed but years later, when the crisis may have passed and government spending needs to be reduced.

Also, government spending is easier to start than to stop, because the groups that benefit from spending programs tend to defend them even when they are no longer needed. A similar criticism applies to tax policies. Politically, it is much easier to cut taxes than to raise them. In other

**Mr. Economic Growth and
Mr. Low Inflation**

*Secretary of the Treasury
Lloyd Bentsen and Alan
Greenspan, chairman of the
Federal Reserve Board, try to
present a unified front on
economic policy, but they
sometimes differ. Secretary
Bentsen, who holds office at
the pleasure of President
Clinton, is primarily concerned with the state of the
economy and favors economic
growth. Chairman Greenspan,
on the other hand, heads an
independent central bank that
is primarily worried about
controlling inflation. The rub
is that growth usually brings
inflation.*

words, Keynesian theory requires that governments be able to begin and
end spending quickly and to cut and raise taxes quickly. But in the real
world, these fiscal tools are easier to use in one direction than the other.
Ronald Reagan gained popularity by cutting taxes, whereas George Bush
may have lost the 1992 election by raising them. Clinton gambled heavily
in his 1995 deficit reduction plan, for it both raised taxes and cut spending.

Recognizing these limitations of fiscal policies, **monetarists** argue that
government can control the economy's performance effectively only by
controlling the nation's money supply. Monetarists favor a long-range policy of small but steady growth in the amount of money in circulation
rather than frequent manipulation of monetary policies.

Monetary policies in the United States are under the control of the
Federal Reserve System, which acts as its central bank. Established in
1914, the Fed is not a single bank but a system of banks. At the top of the
system is the board of governors, seven members appointed by the president for staggered terms of fourteen years. The president designates one
member of the board to be its chairperson, serving a four-year term that extends beyond the president's term of office. This complex arrangement
was intended to make the board independent of the president and even of
Congress. An independent board, the reasoning went, would be able to
make financial decisions for the nation without regard to their political
implications.

The Fed controls the money supply, which affects inflation, in three
ways. *It can change the reserve requirement,* which is the amount of cash
that member banks must keep on deposit in a regional Federal Reserve
Bank. An increase in the reserve requirement reduces the amount of
money a bank has available to lend. *The Fed can also change its discount
rate,* the interest rate that member banks have to pay to borrow money
from a Federal Reserve Bank. A lower rate encourages a member bank to
borrow and lend more freely. *Finally, the Fed can buy and sell government
securities* (such as U.S. Treasury notes and bonds) on the open market.

When it buys securities, it pays out money, putting more money into circulation; when it sells securities, the process works in reverse. These transactions influence the federal funds rate, which banks charge one another for overnight loans. Again, a lower federal funds rate encourages borrowing and lending money.

The Fed's activities are essential parts of the overall economic policy, but they lie outside the direct control of the president. This can create problems in coordinating economic policy. For example, the president might want the Fed to lower interest rates to stimulate the economy, but the Fed might resist for fear of inflation. Such policy clashes can pit the chair of the Federal Reserve Board directly against the president. This happened early in 1991, when President Bush publicly criticized the Fed for not taking action to lower interest rates. When the Fed finally did cut its discount rate to encourage banks to lower interest rates in the spring of 1991, some analysts felt that the cut came partly in response to Bush's criticisms.[12] Clinton carefully courted the same Fed chairman, Alan Greenspan, even inviting him to sit next to Hillary Rodham Clinton when the president announced his economic plan to Congress in a televised address.[13] Clinton had good reason for courting Greenspan, for the Fed's low interest rates were credited in 1993 with pulling the economy out of its depression, underscoring the importance of monetary policy.[14]

Although the Fed's economic policies are not perfectly insulated from political concerns, they are sufficiently independent that the president is not able to control monetary policy without the Fed's cooperation. This means that the president cannot be held completely responsible for the state of the economy—despite the Employment Act of 1946. Moreover, economic theories that predict the outcomes of various moves by the Fed are sometimes proved incorrect. For example, when the Fed attempted to raise interest rates slightly in February 1994, the market did not respond as predicted: Short-term rates moved less than the Fed wanted and long-term rates moved more. As one analyst said, "None of this was forecast, either by the Fed or by most private economists."[15] Of course, academic theories interact with investor psychology, and according to one Nobel Prize-winning economist, "The markets just aren't sophisticated about economics."[16] Nor, perhaps, are politicians.

Supply-Side Economics

When Reagan came to office in 1981, he embraced a school of thought called **supply-side economics** to deal with the double-digit inflation that the nation was experiencing. Keynesian theory argues that inflation results when consumers, businesses, and governments have more money to spend than there are goods and services to buy. The standard Keynesian solution is to reduce demand (for example, by increasing taxes). Supply-siders argued that inflation could be lowered more effectively by increasing the supply of goods. (That is, they stressed the supply side of the economic equation.) Specifically, they favored tax cuts to stimulate investment (which, in turn, would lead to the production of more goods) and less government regulation of business (again, to increase productivity—which they held would yield more, not less, government revenue).

To support their theory, supply-side economists point to a 1964 tax cut that was initiated by President Kennedy. It stimulated investment and

Ticking Time Bomb

"Say buddy, can you tell me the deficit?" If you were in Manhattan on a day in October 1992, you would have seen that your family's share of the national debt was $61,851, give or take a dollar. And, second by second, it continues to increase.

raised the total national income. As a result, the government took in as much tax revenue under the tax cut as it had before taxes were cut. Supply-siders also argue that the rich should receive larger tax cuts than the poor, because the rich have more money to invest. The benefits of increased investment then "trickle down" to working people in the form of additional jobs and income.

In a sense, supply-side economics resembles laissez-faire economics in preferring less government regulation and less taxation. Supply-siders believe that government interferes too much with the efforts of individuals to work, save, and invest. Inspired by supply-side theory, Reagan proposed (and got) massive tax cuts in the Economic Recovery Tax Act of 1981. It reduced individual tax rates by 23 percent over a three-year period and cut the tax rate for the highest income group from 70 to 50 percent. Reagan also launched a program to deregulate business. According to supply-side theory, these actions would generate extra government revenue, making spending cuts unnecessary. Nevertheless, Reagan also cut funding for some domestic programs, including Aid to Families with Dependent Children and the food stamp program (see Chapter 19). Contrary to supply-side theory, he also proposed hefty increases in military spending. This blend of tax cuts, deregulation, cuts in spending for social programs, and increases in spending for defense became known, somewhat disparagingly, as *Reaganomics*.

How well did Reaganomics work? Annual price inflation fell substantially during Reagan's administration and so did unemployment. The Reagan administration also largely fulfilled its plans to deregulate the economy. According to a study by economist Clifford Winston, about 17 percent of GNP came from regulated industries in 1977, but after "ten years of partial and complete economic deregulation of large parts of the transportation, communications, energy, and financial industries," the total was cut to 6.6 percent of GNP.[17] Winston also contends that deregulation fulfilled theoretical predictions of enhanced efficiency in delivering services to the public. He calculates a saving to the public of about $40 billion annually (in 1990 dollars) from economic deregulation.[18] But Winston excludes the tremendous losses that followed deregulation of savings and loan associations, saying, "Deregulation per se cannot be blamed."[19] Others would argue with his judgment,[20] and they might also point out the overall negative effect of deregulation on the airline industry.[21]

Although Reaganomics reduced inflation and unemployment (aided by a sharp decline in oil prices) and worked largely as expected in industry deregulation, it failed massively to reduce the budget deficit. Contrary to supply-side theory, the 1981 tax cut was accompanied by a massive drop in tax revenues. Shortly after taking office, Reagan promised that his economic policies would balance the national budget by 1984, but lower tax revenues and higher defense spending produced the largest budget deficits ever, as shown in Figure 18.1.[22]

PUBLIC POLICY AND THE BUDGET

To most people—college students included—the national budget is B-O-R-I-N-G. To national politicians, it is an exciting script for high drama. The numbers, categories, and percentages that numb normal minds cause politicians' nostrils to flare and their hearts to pound. The budget is a battlefield on which politicians wage war over the programs they support.

Today, the president prepares the budget and Congress approves it. This was not always the case. Before 1921, Congress prepared the budget under its constitutional authority to raise taxes and appropriate funds. The budget was formed piecemeal by enacting a series of laws that originated in the many committees involved in the highly decentralized process of raising revenue, authorizing expenditures, and appropriating funds. Executive agencies even submitted their budgetary requests directly to Congress, not to the president. No one was responsible for the big picture—the budget as a whole. The president's role was essentially limited to approving revenue and appropriations bills, just as he approved other pieces of legislation.

Congressional budgeting (such as it was) worked well enough for a nation of farmers but not for an industrialized nation with a growing population and an increasingly active government. Soon after World War I, Congress realized that the budget-making process needed to be centralized. With the Budgeting and Accounting Act of 1921, it thrust the responsibility for preparing the budget onto the president. The act established the Bureau of the Budget to help the president write "his" budget, which had to be submitted to Congress each January. Congress retained its constitutional authority to raise and spend funds, but now Congress would begin its work with the president's budget as its starting point. And all executive agencies' budget requests had to be funneled through the Bureau of the Budget (which became the Office of Management and Budget in 1970) for review; those consistent with the president's overall economic and legislative program were incorporated in the president's budget.

The Nature of the Budget

The national budget is complex. But its basic elements are not beyond understanding. We begin with some definitions. The *Budget of the United*

FIGURE 18.1 ■ Budget Deficits Over Time

In his first inaugural address, President Reagan said, "You and I, as individuals, can, by borrowing, live beyond our means, but only for a limited period of time. Why, then, should we think that collectively, as a nation, we're not bound by that same limitation?" But borrow he did. Reagan's critics charged that the budget deficits under his administra- *tion—more than $1.3 trillion—exceeded the total deficits of all previous presidents. But this charge does not take inflation into account. A billion dollars in the 1990s is worth much less than it was a century ago or even ten years ago.*
A fairer way to calculate deficits is in constant dollars—dollars whose value has been standardized to a given year.

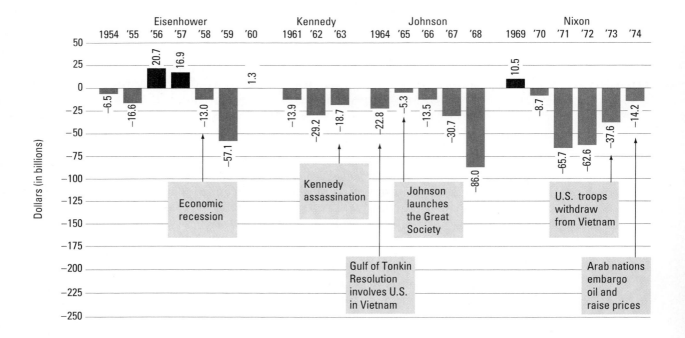

States Government is the annual financial plan that the president is required to submit to Congress at the start of each year. It applies to the next **fiscal year (FY),** the interval the government uses for accounting purposes. Currently, the fiscal year runs from October 1 to September 30. The budget is named for the year in which it *ends,* so the FY 1995 budget applies to the twelve months from October 1, 1994, to September 30, 1995.

Broadly, the budget defines **budget authority** (how much government agencies are authorized to spend on programs), **budget outlays** or expenditures (how much they are expected to spend), and **receipts** (how much is expected in taxes and other revenues). Figure 18.2 diagrams the relationship of authority to outlays. President Clinton's FY 1995 budget contained authority for expenditures of $1,537 billion, but it provided for outlays of

This chart shows the actual deficits in 1987 dollars incurred under presidential administrations from Eisenhower to Clinton. Even computed this way, Reagan's deficits were enormous—especially for a president who claimed to oppose government borrowing. The deficit grew to be as large under Bush before being reduced under Clinton.

Source: Executive Office of the President, Budget of the United States Government, Fiscal Year 1995: Historical Tables (Washington, D.C.: U.S. Government Printing Office, 1994) p. 17.

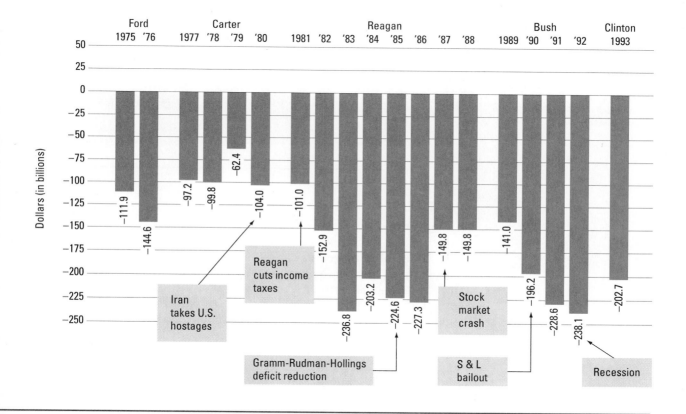

"only" $1,519 billion. The budget anticipated receipts of $1,354 billion, leaving an estimated deficit of $165 billion—the difference between receipts and outlays. Clinton's proposed budget deficit, however, was the lowest since 1989.

Clinton's FY 1995 printed budget (with appendices) was more than fifteen hundred pages long and weighed more than four pounds. (The budget document contains more than numbers. It also explains individual spending programs in terms of national needs and agency objectives, and it analyzes proposed taxes and other receipts.) Each year, the publication of the budget is anxiously awaited by reporters, lobbyists, and political analysts eager to learn the president's plan for government spending in the coming year.

FIGURE 18.2   ■ Relationship of Budget Authority to Budget Outlays

The national budget is a complicated document. One source of confusion for people studying the budget for the first time is the relationship of budget authority to budget outlay. These two amounts differ because of sums that are carried over from previous years and to future years. The diagram helps explain the relationship (all amounts are in billions of dollars).

Source: Executive Office of the President; Budget of the United States Government, Fiscal Year 1995: Analytical Perspectives (Washington, D.C.: U.S. Government Printing Office, 1994), p. 268.

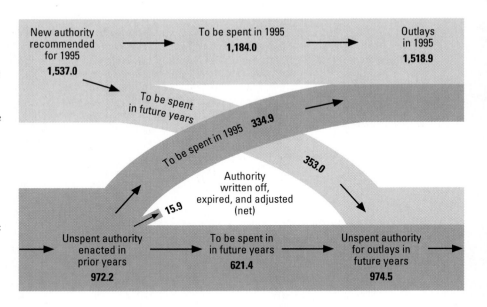

Preparing the President's Budget

The budget that the president submits to Congress each winter is the end product of a process that begins the previous spring under the supervision of the **Office of Management and Budget (OMB).** OMB is located within the Executive Office of the President and is headed by a director who is appointed by the president with the approval of the Senate. The OMB, with a staff of more than five hundred, is the most powerful domestic agency in the bureaucracy, and its director, who attends meetings of the president's cabinet, is one of the most powerful figures in government. Clinton originally chose Leon E. Panetta, formerly Democratic chair of the House Budget Committee, as his budget director. When Panetta became Clinton's White House chief of staff in 1994, Alice Rivlin, once head of the Congressional Budget Office, became director of OMB.

The OMB initiates the budget process each spring by meeting with the president to discuss the economic situation and his budgetary priorities. It then sends broad economic guidelines to every government agency and requests their initial projections of how much money each needs for the next fiscal year. The OMB assembles this information and makes recommendations to the president, who settles on more precise guidelines as to how much each is likely to get. By summer, the agencies are asked to prepare budgets based on the new guidelines. By fall, they submit their formal budgets to the OMB, where budget analysts scrutinize agency requests for both costs and consistency with the president's legislative program. A lot of politicking goes on at this stage, as agency heads try to circumvent the OMB by pleading for their pet projects with presidential advisers and perhaps even the president himself. Unlike presidents Reagan and Bush, who basically delegated economic policy to others in their administrations,

Budgeting! What Fun!

Alice Rivlin, Director of the Office of Management and Budget, suggests the serious side of budgeting in testifying before Congress. Dr. Rivlin was hired in 1975 to be the first director of the Congressional Budget Office and quickly established her independence in providing economic advice to Congress. Appointed by President Clinton as Deputy Director of OMB, she was named director when her predecessor, Leon Panetta, became Clinton's chief of staff in June, 1994.

Clinton has been more involved in the process and makes more of the big decisions himself. Although often criticized for his lack of understanding of foreign policy, Clinton appears to have a genuine grasp of economic policy. According to his chief assistant on economic matters, Robert E. Rubin, "He understands this, he really does. I don't mean he just read a paper on some topic or other. He has a feel for these economic issues."[23]

Political negotiations over the budget may extend into the early winter—often until it goes to the printer. The voluminous document looks very much like a finished product, but the figures it contains are not final. In giving the president the responsibility for preparing the budget, Congress has simply provided itself with a starting point for its own work.

Passing the Congressional Budget

Congress must approve the president's budget. Its process for doing so is a creaky conglomeration of traditional procedures overlaid with structural reforms from the 1970s, external constraints from the 1980s, and hasty changes introduced by the 1990 Budget Enforcement Act. The cumbersome process has had difficulty producing a budget according to Congress's own timetable.

The Traditional Procedure: The Committee Structure.   Traditionally, the tasks of budget making were divided among a number of committees—a process that has been retained. Three types of committees are involved in budgeting:

- **Tax committees** are responsible for raising the revenues to run the government. The Ways and Means Committee in the House and the Finance Committee in the Senate consider all proposals for taxes, tariffs, and other receipts contained in the president's budget.

- **Authorization committees** (such as the House Armed Services Committee and the Senate Banking, Housing, and Urban Affairs Committee) have jurisdiction over particular legislative subjects. The House has about twenty committees that can authorize spending, and the Senate about fifteen. Each pores over the portions of the budget that pertain to its area of responsibility. However, in recent years power has shifted from the authorization committees to the appropriations committees.

- **Appropriations committees** decide which of the programs approved by the authorization committees will actually be funded (that is, given money to spend). For example, the House Armed Services Committee might decide to build a new line of tanks for the army and succeed in getting its decision enacted into law. But the tanks will never be built unless the appropriations committees appropriate funds for that purpose. Thirteen distinct appropriations bills are supposed to be enacted each year to fund the nation's spending.

Two serious problems are inherent in a budgeting process that involves three distinct kinds of congressional committees. First, the two-step spending process (first authorization, then appropriation) is complex; it offers wonderful opportunities for interest groups to get into the budgeting act in the spirit of pluralist democracy. Second, because one group of legislators in each house plans for revenues and many other groups plan for spending, no one is responsible for the budget as a whole. In the 1970s, Congress added a new committee structure that combats the pluralist politics inherent in the old procedures and allows budget choices to be made in a more majoritarian manner, by votes in both chambers.

Reforms of the 1970s: The Budget Committee Structure.   In 1921, when Congress gave the president the responsibility to prepare the budget, it surrendered considerable authority. During the next fifty years, attempts by Congress to regain control of the budgeting process failed because of jurisdictional squabbles between the revenue and appropriations committees.

Overall control of the budget is important to Congress for several reasons. First, members of Congress are politicians, and politicians want to wield power, not watch someone else wield it. Second, the Constitution established Congress, not the president, as the "first branch" of government and the people's representatives. Third, Congress as a body often disagrees with presidential spending priorities, but it has been unable to mount a serious challenge to his authority by presenting a coherent alternative budget.

After bitter spending fights with President Nixon in the late 1960s and early 1970s, Congress finally passed the Budget and Impoundment Control Act of 1974. That act fashioned a typically political solution to the problem of wounded egos and competing jurisdictions that had frustrated previous attempts to change the budget-making procedure. All the tax and appropriations committees (and chairpersons) were retained, and new House and Senate budget committees were superimposed on the old committee structure. The **budget committees** supervised a comprehensive budget review process, aided by the Congressional Budget Office. The **Congressional Budget Office (CBO),** with a staff of more than two hundred, acquired a budgetary expertise equal to that of the president's OMB so it could prepare credible alternative budgets for Congress.

At the heart of the 1974 reforms was a timetable for the congressional budget process. The original timetable has since been modified several times, and its deadlines are often missed. Still, it is a useful means of guiding the process. The budget committees are supposed to propose an initial budget resolution that sets overall revenue and spending levels, broken down into twenty-one different "budget functions," among them national defense, agriculture, and health. By April 15, both houses are supposed to have agreed on a single budget resolution to guide their work on the budget during the summer. The appropriations committees are supposed to begin drafting the thirteen appropriations bills by May 15 and to complete them by June 30. Throughout, the levels of spending set by majority vote on the budget resolution are supposed to constrain pressures by special interests to increase spending in the context of pluralist politics.

Congress implemented this process (or one very much like it) in 1975, and it worked reasonably well for the first few years. Congress was able to work on and structure the budget as a whole rather than change pieces of it. But the process broke down during the Reagan administration, as the president submitted annual budgets with huge deficits. For its part, a Democratic Congress adjusted Reagan's priorities away from military spending and toward social spending but refused to propose a tax increase to reduce the deficit without the president's cooperation. At loggerheads with the president, Congress encountered increasing difficulty in enacting its budget resolutions according to its own timetable.

External Constraints of the 1980s: Gramm-Rudman.   Alarmed by the huge deficits in Reagan's budgets, frustrated by his refusal to raise taxes, and stymied by their own inability to cut the deficit, members of Congress were ready to try almost anything. Republican senators Phil Gramm of Texas and Warren Rudman of New Hampshire were joined by Democrat Ernest Hollings of South Carolina in proposing drastic action to force a balanced budget. Officially titled the Balanced Budget and Emergency Deficit Control Act (1985), their bill became known simply as Gramm-Rudman-Hollings, or **Gramm-Rudman** for short.

In its original form, Gramm-Rudman mandated that the budget deficit be lowered to a specified level each year until the budget was balanced in FY 1991. If Congress did not meet the mandated deficit level in any year, across-the-board budget cuts were to be made automatically. Senator Rudman described his own bill as "a bad idea whose time has come," but congressional members' frustration was so great that Gramm-Rudman sailed through both houses on a wave of exasperation. The bill was not reviewed by congressional committees in the usual manner, nor was it subjected to formal economic, procedural, or legal analysis. No one really knew what the legislation would do—except give Congress an out in deciding which programs to cut or whose taxes to raise in order to reduce the deficit.

An excess in the budget deficit triggered Gramm-Rudman in 1986, the first year after it was passed. The president and Congress saw 4.3 percent sliced from every domestic and defense program (except for those specifically exempted, such as social security) without regard to their value for the nation, thus weakening most programs through underfunding. Thereafter, Gramm-Rudman was a brooding threat over congressional decision making and the budgetary process. Again unable to make the deficit meet the law in 1987, Congress and the president simply changed the law

No Dough, No Show

In October 1990, an impasse between the president and Congress over the national budget created a shortage of operating funds that shut down most of the government. Many museums, monuments, and agencies (including the Washington Monument and the White House) were closed to the public. The resulting publicity put pressure on both sides to settle the argument.

to match the deficit. But when the 1990 recession threatened another huge deficit for FY 1991 that would again trigger even the relaxed Gramm-Rudman targets, Congress and the president agreed on a new package of reforms and deficit targets in the Budget Enforcement Act of 1990.

Reforms of 1990: The Budget Enforcement Act.   This law divided government spending into two types and imposed certain restrictions on both. It defined **mandatory spending** as expenditures required by legal commitments. For example, spending is mandatory for **entitlement** programs (such as social security and veterans' benefits) that provide benefits to individuals legally entitled to them (see Chapter 19). For the first time, the law established **pay-as-you-go** restrictions on mandatory spending. Under PAYGO, any proposal to expand coverage of an entitlement program must be offset by other savings or a tax increase. Similarly, any tax cut must be offset by another tax increase or other savings.[24] That drastically altered the significance of the new deficit targets. The law defined **discretionary spending** as authorized expenditures from annual appropriations (such as the personnel budget for the military). For the first time, the law imposed limits, or "caps," on discretionary spending—for example, some $540 million in FY 1995.

Significantly, the 1990 law, with its caps on spending and its PAYGO requirements, removed most of the pressure to reduce the deficit to meet the Gramm-Rudman targets. Under earlier rules, any economic downturn that caused the government to spend more or to raise less revenue than expected might cause the deficit to exceed the Gramm-Rudman target and thus trigger across-the-board cuts. But now these unexpected external events (including war and the massive costs of the S&L bailout) are—like acts of God—regarded as "outside" the budgetary agreement, which requires only that everyone keep their part of the bargain on spending caps and pay-as-you-go restrictions.

A failure to limit discretionary spending in any category to its cap in any year or a violation of pay-as-you-go restrictions by Congress, will trigger a **sequestration**—an across-the-board spending cut in the overspent category or in nonexempt entitlement programs. These sequesters (cuts) would occur automatically fifteen days after Congress adjourns. Whether these new changes in the budget process will make it any more workable in the future remains to be seen. What does seem likely is that the new process will increase the power of the appropriations committees at the expense of the authorizing committees, which will have less latitude in spending, and the budget committees, which will find caps already set on overall spending.[25]

TAX POLICIES

So far, we have been concerned mainly with the spending side of the budget, for which appropriations must be enacted each year. The revenue side of the budget is governed by overall tax policy, which is designed to provide a continuous flow of income without annual legislation. On occasion, however, tax policy is significantly changed to accomplish one or more of several objectives:

- To adjust overall revenue to meet budget outlays

- To make the tax burden more equitable for taxpayers

- To help control the economy by raising taxes (thus decreasing aggregate demand) or by lowering taxes (thus increasing demand)[26]

The Reagan administration had engineered a significant change in the nation's tax policies in the 1980s. In Reagan's first three years, personal income taxes were lowered by 23 percent, resulting in a total revenue loss of $500 billion over the next five years.[27] According to supply-side economic theory, that massive tax cut should have stimulated the economy and yielded even more revenue than was lost—if not in the first year, then soon afterward. It didn't happen. Revenues lagged badly behind spending, and the deficit grew.

Although the Reagan administration enacted various tax increases in 1982 and 1984 to offset the lost revenue, few politicians in the 1980s dared mention a hike in income tax rates. Democratic presidential candidate Walter Mondale tried it in the 1984 election and was beaten badly. The Democratic leadership in Congress and many leading Republicans believed that taxes had to be raised to cut the deficit, but no one was willing to propose an increase. Reagan went further. He urged Congress to enact sweeping tax reform that would (1) lower still further the rate for those in the highest income tax bracket, (2) reduce the number of tax brackets, (3) eliminate virtually all the tax loopholes through which many wealthy people and corporations avoided paying taxes, and (4) be revenue neutral, in the sense that it would bring in no more and no less revenue than existing tax policy.

Tax Reform

Tax reform proposals are usually so heavily influenced by interest groups looking for special benefits that they end up working against their original purpose. However, Reagan's proposals met with relatively few major changes, and in 1986 Congress passed one of the most sweeping tax reform laws in history. The new policy reclaimed a great deal of revenue by eliminating many deductions for corporations and wealthy citizens. That revenue was supposed to pay for a general reduction in tax rates for individual citizens. By eliminating many tax brackets, the new tax policy approached the idea of a flat tax—one that requires everyone to pay at the same rate. A flat tax has the appeal of simplicity, but it violates the principle of **progressive taxation,** by which the rich pay proportionately higher taxes than the poor. The ability to pay has long been a standard of fair taxation, and governments can use progressive taxation to redistribute wealth and thus promote economic equality.

In general, the greater the number of tax brackets, the more progressive a tax can be. Before Reagan proposed his tax reforms in 1986, there were fourteen tax brackets, ranging from 11 percent to 50 percent. After the law became effective in 1988, there were only two rates—15 and 28 percent. Campaigning for the presidency in 1988, Bush quickly allied himself with Reagan's tax policy and promised the Republican convention and the nation that he would tell Congress: "Read my lips: No new taxes." As president, however, he found that existing taxes did not produce enough revenue to control the deficit. By 1990, his pledge began to stick in his throat, and he acknowledged the need for "tax revenue increases" and reopened the issue of tax policy.

Many Republicans were furious with Bush for reneging on his promise, and key members of his party failed to support the new tax package that he negotiated with the Democratic leadership in a budget summit. Democratic leaders soon forced the president to accept their own hastily constructed deficit reduction plan, which established a third tax rate of 31 percent for those with the highest incomes. Even with both houses of Congress controlled by the Democrats in 1993, Clinton only narrowly

Representation without Taxation!

Across the nation, citizens are up in arms about high taxes, although the United States has one of the lowest tax burdens in the world. Taxes are not perceived as high at just the national level. This demonstration against state taxes is for the benefit of the Texas legislature.

managed to raise taxes to meet the deficit. His plan, which created a fourth level with a maximum tax rate of 40 percent, signaled a move toward a more progressive tax structure at the national level, although still less progressive than before 1986. As the national government moved away from the supply-side assumption that reduced taxes on the wealthy would actually produce more revenue, so did many states. Unable to fund state services, one-fourth raised taxes on the wealthy in the early 1990s.[28]

Comparing Tax Burdens

No one likes to pay taxes, so it is politically popular to attack taxation—which Reagan and Bush did with stunning success. Is the tax burden too heavy on American citizens? One way to compare tax burdens is to examine taxes over time in the same country; another is to compare taxes in different countries at the same time. By comparing taxes over time in the United States, we find that the total tax burden of U.S. citizens has indeed been growing. For the average family, the percentage of income that went to all national, state, and local taxes doubled to 23 percent between 1953 and 1993.[29]

However, neither the national government nor the national income tax accounts for the bulk of that increase. First, national taxes as a percentage of the gross national product have changed very little during the last thirty years; it is the state and local tax burden that has doubled in size.[30] Second, the income tax has not been the main culprit in the increasing tax bite at the national level; the proportion of national budget receipts contributed by income tax has remained fairly constant since the end of World War II. The largest increases have come in social security taxes, which have risen steadily to pay for the government's single largest social welfare program, aid to the elderly (see Chapter 19).

Another way to compare tax burdens is to examine tax rates in different countries. As you can see in Compared with What? 18.1, Americans enjoy very low taxes on gasoline. Despite complaints about high taxes, the U.S. tax burden is not large compared with taxes in other democratic nations. As shown in Compared with What 18.2, Americans' taxes in general are quite low compared with those in twenty-one other democratic nations. Primarily because they provide their citizens with more generous social benefits (such as health care and unemployment compensation), *every* nation ranked above the United States.

SPENDING POLICIES

The national government spends hundreds of billions of dollars every year. Where does the money go? Figure 18.3 shows the $1.5 trillion in outlays in President Clinton's FY 1995 budget according to eighteen major budgetary functions. The largest amount (22 percent of the total budget) was earmarked for social security. Until FY 1993, the largest spending category was national defense, but military spending dropped into second place after the collapse of communism. The third largest category, income security, encompasses a variety of programs that provide a "social safety net": unemployment compensation, food for low-income parents and children, aid to families with dependent children, help for the blind and disabled, and assistance for the homeless. The fourth largest outlay was interest on the accumulated national debt, which alone consumes about 14 percent of all government spending. Medicare and health, the next largest categories, together account for more than 18 percent of all budgetary outlays, which underscores the urgency of Clinton's attempt to control health care costs.

To understand current expenditures, it is a good idea to examine national expenditures over time, as in Figure 18.4. The effect of World War II is clear: Spending for national defense rose sharply after 1940, peaked at about 90 percent of the budget in 1945, and fell to about 30 percent in peacetime. The percentage allocated to defense rose again in the early 1950s, reflecting rearmament during the Cold War with the Soviet Union. Thereafter, the share of the budget devoted to defense decreased steadily (except for the bump during the Vietnam War in the late 1960s), until the trend was reversed by the Reagan administration in the 1980s. Defense spending significantly decreased under Bush, continued down under Clinton's FY 1995 budget, and Congress further trimmed Clinton's allocation for defense by about $0.2 billion.[31]

Government payments to individuals (social security checks) consistently consumed less of the budget than national defense until 1971. Since then, payments to individuals have accounted for the largest portion of the national budget, and they have been increasing. Net interest payments have also increased substantially in recent years, reflecting the rapidly growing national debt. Pressure from payments for national defense, individuals, and interest on the national debt has squeezed all other government outlays.

Because of continuing price inflation, we would expect government expenditures to increase steadily in dollar amounts. However, national spending has far outstripped inflation. Figure 18.5 graphs government receipts and outlays as a percentage of GNP, which eliminates the effect of inflation. It shows that national spending has increased from about 15 percent of GNP soon after World War II to nearly 25 percent, most recently at the price of a growing national deficit. There are two major explanations for this steady increase in government spending. One is bureaucratic, the other political.

COMPARED WITH WHAT? 18.1   **Gasoline Prices and Taxes in Fifteen Countries**

Chapter 10 opened by discussing the slow death of President Clinton's attempt to levy a BTU tax, a new type of tax based on the amount of heat in energy sources as measured by British thermal units (BTUs). When that tax was killed, Clinton had to settle for a 4.3-cent-a-gallon tax on gasoline. This modest tax generated much less revenue than his proposed BTU tax, but it was still bitterly opposed by legislators in farm states and in the West, where residents drive longer distances. Nevertheless, Americans enjoy very low gasoline taxes and low gas prices in comparison with people in other countries. Even with the added 4.3-cent tax on gasoline, the United States has both the lowest average price per gallon of unleaded gasoline and the lowest tax rate.

• *Source: Paul F. Horvitz, "U.S. Learns a Lesson From Gasoline Tax,"* International Herald Tribune, *18 May 1994, 19.*

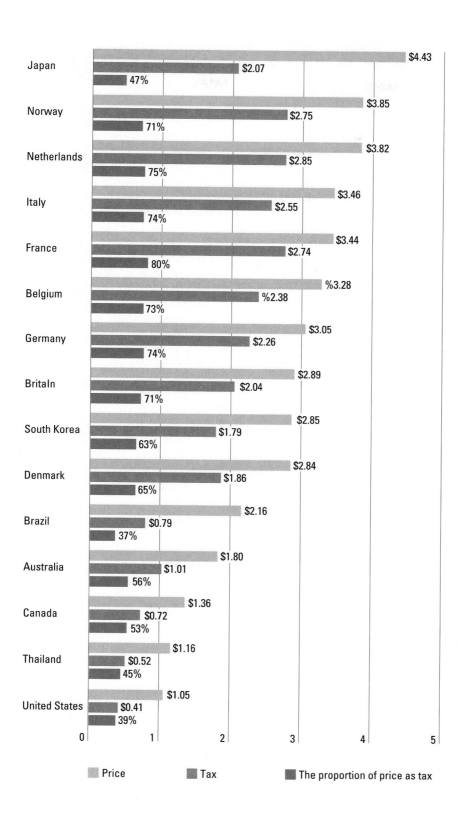

Japan — $4.43, $2.07, 47%
Norway — $3.85, $2.75, 71%
Netherlands — $3.82, $2.85, 75%
Italy — $3.46, $2.55, 74%
France — $3.44, $2.74, 80%
Belgium — %3.28, %2.38, 73%
Germany — $3.05, $2.26, 74%
Britaln — $2.89, $2.04, 71%
South Korea — $2.85, $1.79, 63%
Denmark — $2.84, $1.86, 65%
Brazil — $2.16, $0.79, 37%
Australia — $1.80, $1.01, 56%
Canada — $1.36, $0.72, 53%
Thailand — $1.16, $0.52, 45%
United States — $1.05, $0.41, 39%

Price · Tax · The proportion of price as tax

COMPARED WITH WHAT? 18.2

Tax Burdens in Twenty-Two Countries

All nations tax their citizens, but some nations impose a heavier tax burden than others. This graph compares tax burdens in 1990 as a percentage of gross domestic product (GDP), which is a country's GNP minus the value of goods produced outside the country. The percentages include national, state, and local taxes and social security contributions. By this measure, the U.S. government extracts less in taxes from its citizens than the governments of virtually all democratic nations. At the top of the list stands Sweden, well known as a state that provides heavily for social welfare, which consumes nearly 60 percent of its gross domestic product in taxes.

• *Source: U.S. Bureau of the Census, U.S. Department of Commerce* Statistical Abstract of the United States, *1993 (Washington, D.C.: U.S. Government Printing Office, 1993), p. 857.*

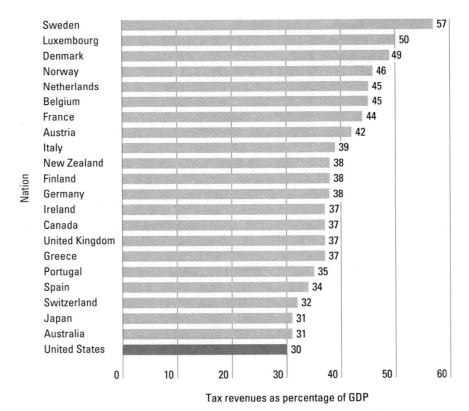

Tax revenues as percentage of GDP

Nation	Percentage
Sweden	57
Luxembourg	50
Denmark	49
Norway	46
Netherlands	45
Belgium	45
France	44
Austria	42
Italy	39
New Zealand	38
Finland	38
Germany	38
Ireland	37
Canada	37
United Kingdom	37
Greece	37
Portugal	35
Spain	34
Switzerland	32
Japan	31
Australia	31
United States	30

Incremental Budgeting . . .

The bureaucratic explanation for spending increases involves **incremental budgeting:** Bureaucrats, in compiling their funding requests for next year, ask for the amount they got this year plus some increment to fund new projects. Because Congress has already approved the agency's budget for

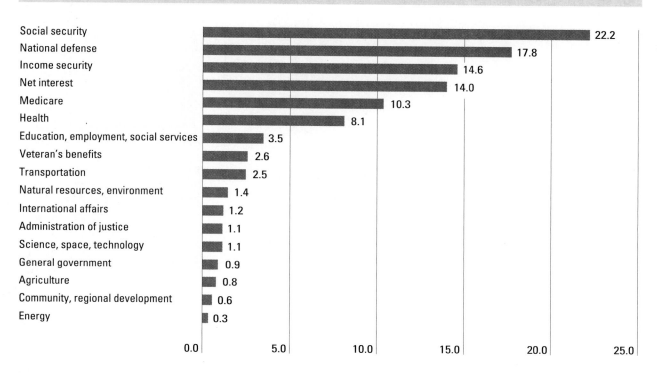

| FIGURE 18.3 | ■ President Clinton's FY 1995 Budget by Function |

Federal budget authorities and outlays are organized into about twenty categories, some of which are mainly for bookkeeping purposes. This graph shows expected outlays for each of seventeen substantive functions in Clinton's FY 1995 budget. The final budget differed somewhat from this distribution, because Congress amended some of the president's spending proposals, but the proportions remained nearly the same. The graph makes clear the huge differences among spending categories. Nearly 40 percent of government outlays are for social security and income security—that is, payments to individuals. Health costs (including Medicare) account for nearly 20 percent more, slightly more than national defense, and net interest consumes almost 15 percent. This leaves relatively little for transportation, agriculture, justice, science, and energy—matters often regarded as the object of government activity.

Source: From Congressional Quarterly Weekly Report, *12 February 1994, pp. 312–313. Copyright © 1994 by Congressional Quarterly. Used with permission.

the current year, members pay little attention to its size (the largest part of that budget), focusing instead on the extra money (the increment) requested for next year. As a result, few agencies are ever cut back, and spending continually goes up.

Incremental budgeting produces a sort of bureaucratic momentum that continually pushes up spending. Once an agency is established, it attracts a clientele that defends its existence and supports the agency's requests for extra funds to do more year after year. Because budgeting is a two-step process, agencies that get cut back in the authorizing committees sometimes manage (assisted by their interest group clientele) to get funds restored in the appropriations committees—and if not in the House then

FIGURE **18.4**   ■ **National Government Outlays over Time**

This chart plots the percentages of the annual budget devoted to four major expense categories. It shows that significant changes have occurred in national spending since 1940. In the 1940s, spending for World War II consumed more than 80 percent of the national budget. Defense again accounted for most national expenditures during the Cold War of the 1950s. Since then, the military's share of expenditures has declined, while payments to individuals (mostly in the form of social security benefits) have increased dramatically. Also, as the graph shows, the proportion of the budget paid in interest on the national debt has increased substantially since the 1970s.

Source: *Executive Office of the President,* Budget of the United States Government, Fiscal Year 1995: *Historical Tables (Washington, D.C.: U.S. Government Printing Office, 1994), pp. 82–88.*

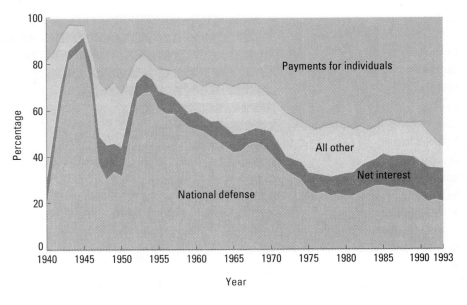

perhaps in the Senate. So incremental budgeting and the process itself is ideally suited to pluralist politics. However, the huge budget deficit has substantially checked the practice of incremental budgeting. For example, Clinton's FY 1995 budget proposed terminating about 115 programs and cutting back on another 200.[32]

Caps on discretionary spending also discourage incremental budgeting and force closer scrutiny of budgetary proposals by agencies and members of Congress alike. As a result, agencies now do more analytical budgeting, in which existing programs are justified in terms of their effectiveness (see Chapter 13). Still, any president today would find it impossible to reduce government spending enough to balance the budget, because politics has put most of the budget beyond his control.

. . . And Uncontrollable Spending

Certain spending programs are effectively immune to budget reductions, because they have been enacted into law and enshrined in politics. For example, social security legislation guarantees certain benefits to participants in the program when they retire from work. Medicare and veterans' benefits also entitle citizens to certain payments. Because these payments have to be made under existing law, they represent **uncontrollable outlays**. In Clinton's FY 1995 budget, nearly two-thirds of all budget outlays were uncontrollable or relatively uncontrollable—mainly payments to individuals under social security, Medicare, public assistance, interest on debt, and farm price supports. Most of the rest goes for defense, leaving about 15 percent in domestic discretionary spending for balancing the budget.

FIGURE 18.5 ■ Government Outlays and Receipts as a Percentage of GDP

We can see the growth of government spending—and the rising national debt—by plotting budget outlays and receipts against each other over time. In this graph, outlays and receipts are each expressed as a percentage of GNP, to control for inflation and to demonstrate that both government spending and taxes have been taking a progressively larger share of the nation's productive output. The estimated deficit for 1994 was only 2.4 percent, close to the average of 2 percent.

Source: *Executive Office of the President,* Budget of the United States Government, Fiscal Year 1995: *Historical Tables (Washington, D.C.: U.S. Government Printing Office, 1994), p. 17;* and George Hager, *"White House, CBO Both Foresee Lower Deficits for '94 and '95,"* Congressional Quarterly Weekly Report, *16 July 1994: 1911.*

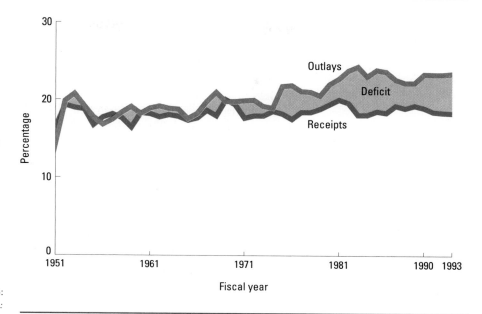

To be sure, Congress could change the laws to abolish entitlement payments, and it does modify them through the budget process. But politics argues against large-scale reductions. The only major social program that escaped cutting during the Reagan administration was social security—the single largest domestic program and, according to many surveys, the most popular one. (Even Senator Gramm, coauthor of Gramm-Rudman, acknowledged that trying to cut spending for the elderly is "not winnable." His mother, in her eighties, told her son to "keep your mouth shut" when it came to that part of the budget.)

What spending cuts would be popular or even acceptable to the public? When voters were asked in 1992 how they felt about spending cuts in twelve different areas, a majority rejected any decrease in any of the domestic programs. In fact, clear majorities of both Republicans and Democrats wanted increases in spending in three areas—fighting crime, education, and programs to fight AIDS.[33] A perplexed Congress, trying to reduce the budget deficit, faced a public that favored funding programs at even higher levels than those favored by most lawmakers.[34] Moreover, spending for the most expensive of these programs—social security and Medicare—is uncontrollable. Americans have grown accustomed to certain government benefits, but they do not like the idea of raising taxes to pay for them.

The largest controllable expenditure in the budget lies in the area of defense. Of the twelve programs in the 1992 survey, the public proposed cuts only in defense, no doubt reflecting the easing of the Soviet threat. Public sentiment for cuts in defense was reflected in Clinton's FY 1995 budget and in Congress's imposition of further cuts.

TAXING, SPENDING, AND ECONOMIC EQUALITY

As we noted in Chapter 1, the most controversial purpose of government is promoting equality, especially economic equality. Economic equality comes about only at the expense of economic freedom, for it requires government action to redistribute wealth from the rich to the poor. One means of redistribution is government tax policy, especially the progressive income tax. The other instrument for reducing inequalities is government spending through welfare programs. The goal in both cases is not to produce equality of outcome; it is to reduce inequalities by helping the poor.

The national government introduced an income tax in 1862 to help finance the Civil War. That tax was repealed in 1871, and a new tax imposed in 1893 was declared unconstitutional by the Supreme Court. The Sixteenth Amendment (1913) gave the government the power to levy a tax on individual incomes, and it has done so every year since 1914.[35] From 1964 to 1981, people who reported taxable incomes of $100,000 or more paid a top tax rate of 70 percent (except during the Vietnam War), whereas those with lower incomes paid taxes at progressively lower rates, as set forth in Figure 18.6. About the same time, the government launched the War on Poverty as part of President Johnson's Great Society initiative. His programs and their successors are discussed at length in Chapter 19. For now, let us look at the overall effect of government spending and tax policies on economic equality in America.

Government Effects on Economic Equality

We begin by asking whether government spending policies have any measurable effect on income inequality. Economists refer to government payments to individuals through social security, unemployment insurance, food stamps, and other programs, such as agricultural subsidies, as **transfer payments.** Transfer payments need not always go to the poor. In

But you MUST have a computer number!

Government programs that deal with needs of millions of citizens are inherently bureaucratic. As this unemployment office shows, people of all types sometimes lose their jobs and need help in finding new ones.

FIGURE 18.6 ■ **The Ups and Downs of National Tax Rates**

In 1913, the Sixteenth Amendment empowered the national government to collect taxes on income. Since then, the government has levied taxes on individual and corporate income and on capital gains realized by individuals and corporations from the sale of assets, such as stocks or real estate. This chart of the top tax rates shows that they have fluctuated wildly over time, from less than 10 percent to more than 90 percent. (They tend to be highest during periods of war.) During the Reagan administration, the maximum individual income tax rate fell to the lowest level since the Coolidge and Hoover administrations in the late 1920s and 1930s. The top rate increased slightly for 1991 to 31 percent as a result of a law enacted in 1990 and jumped to 39.6 percent for 1994 under Clinton's 1993 budget package.

Sources: Wall Street Journal, 18 August 1986, p. 10. Reprinted by permission of the Wall Street Journal, Dow Jones & Company, Inc., 1986. All rights reserved. Worldwide. Additional data from Congressional Quarterly Weekly Report, 3 November 1990, pp. 3714–3715; and "Tax Law Update," published by Merrill Lynch, 1993.)

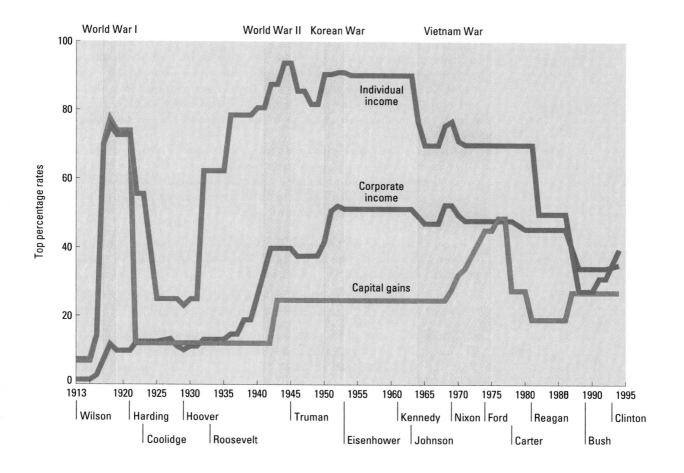

fact, one problem with the farm program is that the wealthiest farmers have often received the largest subsidies.[36] Nevertheless, most researchers have determined that transfer payments have had a definite effect in reducing income inequality.

A study of government policies from 1966 to 1985 found that families in the lowest tenth of the population in terms of income paid 33 percent of their income in national, state, and local taxes but also received payments from all levels of government that almost equaled their earned income.[37] So the lowest-income group enjoyed a net benefit from government because of transfer payments. Another study covering 1979 to 1988 found that transfer payments nearly cut in half the percentage of families with children that were below the official poverty line.[38] Both studies found that tax policies had little effect on the redistribution of income. From 1966 to 1985, ironically, families with the top 1 percent of income paid proportionately less of their income in taxes (about 28 percent) than did people in the lowest-income group.[39] The tax burden has grown even more for the younger generation, see Politics in a Changing America 18.1.

How can people in the lowest-income group pay a higher percentage of their income in taxes than those in the very highest group? The answer has to do with the combination of national, state, and local tax policies. Only the national income tax is progressive, with rates rising as income rises. The national payroll tax, which funds social security and Medicare, is highly regressive: Its effective rate decreases as income increases beyond a certain point. Everyone pays social security at the same rate (6.2 percent in 1994), but this tax is levied only up to a maximum wage ($60,600 annually in 1994). There is no tax at all on wages over that amount. So the effective rate of the social security tax is higher for lower-income groups than for the very top group.

Most state and local sales taxes are equally regressive. Poor and rich usually pay the same flat rate on their purchases. But the poor spend almost everything they earn on purchases that are taxed, whereas the rich are able to save. A study showed that the effective sales tax rate for the lowest-income group was about 7 percent, whereas that for the top 1 percent was only 1 percent.[40]

In general, the nation's tax policies at all levels have historically favored not only the wealthy but also those who draw their income from capital (wealth) rather than labor.[41] For example,

- The tax on income from the sale of real estate or stock (called *capital gains*) was typically lower than the highest tax on income from salaries.

- The tax on earned income (salaries and wages) is withheld from paychecks by employers under national law; the tax on unearned income (interest and dividends) is not.

- There is no national tax at all on investments in certain securities, including municipal bonds (issued by local governments for construction projects).

Effects of Taxing and Spending Policies over Time

In 1966, at the beginning of President Johnson's Great Society programs, the poorest fifth of American families received 4 percent of the nation's in-

18.1 The Younger You Are, The Higher Your Taxes

 According to government estimates, each succeeding generation of Americans pays taxes at a
higher rate than the preceding
generation but also gets a higher rate of
money transferred back in government benefits, such as social security and welfare payments. For example, citizens born in 1920
(who are 70 years old in 1990) will, during the
course of their lives, pay about 36 percent of
their income in national, state, and local
taxes while receiving about 7 percent of their
income back in government payments. On
the other hand, those born in 1970 (20 years
old in 1990) will, over the course of *their*
lives, pay over 50 percent of their income in
taxes, but they will receive about 14 percent
back in government payments. The *net* tax

rate (taxes paid less transfers received) for
those born in 1920 is about 29 percent compared with 36 percent for those born in 1970.
So despite the increasing rates by which taxes
are transferred back from government
through expanded social programs, students
in the 1990s, as a group, can expect to pay a
good deal more of their income in taxes during their lifetimes than their grandparents or
even their parents.

• *Source: These data are adapted from Tables 3–1 and
3–3 in Executive Office of the President,* Budget of the
United States Government, Fiscal Year 1995: Analytical
perspectives *(Washington, D.C.: U.S. Government
Printing Office, 1994), pp. 23 and 25.*

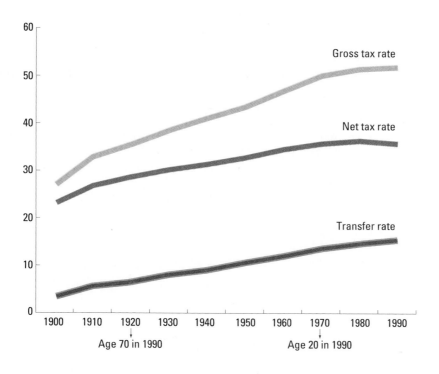

come after taxes and transfer payments, whereas the richest fifth had 46 percent. In 1991, after many billions of dollars had been spent on social programs, the poorest fifth had only 4.5 percent of the nation's income, whereas the richest fifth had 44 percent, as illustrated in Figure 18.7.[42] In short, little change had occurred in the distribution of income. (Moreover, many households in the lowest category had about one-third more earners, mainly women, going to work.)[43]

The economic policies of the Reagan administration had more effect on the truly rich than the rest of the top 20 percent, and some analysts say this owes to tax policy. This is the conclusion of Kevin Phillips, a former Republican election strategist. According to Phillips, in his book *The Politics of Rich and Poor:* "Most of the Reagan decade, to put it mildly, was a heyday for unearned income as rents, dividends, capital gains and interest gained relative to wages and salaries as a source of wealth and increasing economic inequality."[44] Phillips notes that the number of millionaires grew during the Reagan years from about 600,000 to 1.5 million. The very rich were those with $100 million, who tripled from 400 to 1,200. And the truly rich—billionaires, of whom there were thirteen in 1982—nearly quadrupled to fifty-one in 1988.[45] The approximately 20 percent inflation during this period could account for some of this growth, but the rich far outstripped the average family in income gains. While the average family actually *lost* about $1,500 in income between 1977 and 1988 after adjusting for inflation, the top 1 percent experienced nearly a 50 percent increase, from $270,053 to $404,566.[46] Phillips notes that these newly rich made their money in large part through deregulation of financial markets and speculative investments encouraged by the administration, and they were allowed to keep much of what they made by a large net reduction in overall national tax rates during the period.[47] The Congressional Budget Office calculated that families with annual incomes in excess of $200,000 owed 9 percent less in taxes each year than they would have without the tax law changes in the 1980s.[48] Still, many economists believe that the main cause of the growth of income inequality in the 1980s was declining wages at the bottom of the income scale and stagnating salaries in the middle.[49]

In a capitalist system, some degree of inequality is inevitable. Is there some mechanism that limits how much economic equality can be achieved and that would prevent government policies from further equalizing income, no matter what was tried? To find out, we should look to other democracies to see how much equality they have been able to sustain. A 1985 study of six other countries found that only in France is as much as 46 percent of total income received by the top fifth of the population. In Canada, Italy, West Germany, Britain, and Sweden that percentage runs from 42 down to 37 percent.[50] The comparison suggests that our society has measurably more economic inequality than others. The question is why?

Democracy and Equality

Although the United States is a democracy that prizes political equality for its citizens, its record in economic equality is not as good. In fact, its distribution of wealth—which includes not only income but ownership of savings, housing, automobiles, stocks, and so on—is strikingly unequal.

FIGURE 18.7   ■ Distribution of Family Income over Time

During the last quarter century, the 20 percent of U.S. families with the highest incomes received about 45 percent of all income, even after subtracting taxes and adding government payments to individuals. This distribution of income is one of the most unequal among Western nations. At the bottom end of the scale, the poorest 20 percent of families received 5 percent or less of total family income.

Sources: *For the 1966 data,* Joseph A. Pechman, Who Paid the Taxes, 1966–1985? *(Washington, D.C.: Brookings Institution, 1985), p. 74; for the 1991 data,* U.S. Bureau of the Census, U.S. Deapartment of Commerce, Statistical Abstract of the United States, *1993 (Washington, D.C.: U.S. Government Printing Office, 1993) p. 463.*

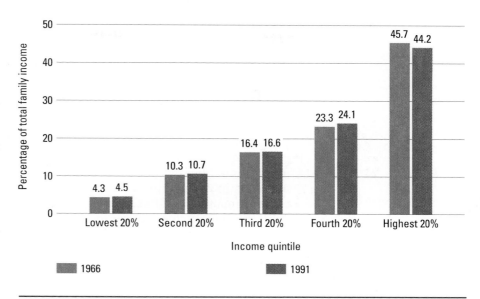

According to the Census Bureau, the top 12 percent of American families control almost 40 percent of household wealth. Moreover, the distribution of wealth by ethnic groups is alarming. The typical white family—whose annual income is more than 1.7 times that of blacks and 1.5 times that of Hispanics—has more than ten times the accumulated wealth of black families and nearly eight times the wealth of Hispanic families.[51] If democracy means government "by the people," why aren't the people sharing more equally in the nation's wealth? If one of the purposes of government is to promote equality, why are government policies not working that way?

One scholar theorizes that interest group activity in a pluralist democracy distorts government's efforts to promote equality. His analysis of pluralism sees "corporations and organized groups with an upper-income slant as exerting political power over and above the formal one-man-one-vote standard of democracy."[52] As you learned in Chapters 10 and 17, the pluralist model of democracy rewards those groups that are well organized and well funded.

An example: As we have already noted, national income tax is withheld by law from earned income (salaries and wages), not from unearned income (interest and dividends). Early in his first term, President Reagan surprised the financial world by proposing to withhold taxes from unearned income, and Congress made the plan law in 1982. Financial institutions were given a year to devise procedures for withholding 10 percent of dividend and interest payments for income tax (the withholding was to begin in mid-1983). Led by the American Bankers' Association, the banking interests urged their depositors to write legislators protesting the law; they even handed out sample letters that could be sent to members of Congress.

Washington was flooded with mail stimulated by local banks and savings and loan associations. Congress had to hire temporary workers to answer letters from angry high-income taxpayers (who are also high-turnout voters). Some people, who apparently had never declared their bank interest as income, indignantly protested this "new" tax. The president and many members of Congress were furious at the American Bankers' Association, which spent more than $300,000 in its effort to have the law repealed. Democratic representative Thomas J. Downey of New York said that repeal of withholding would "send a signal that the Congress of the United States is a group of patsies to every well-organized group in America."[53] But Congress did back down, and withholding from unearned income was repealed only weeks before it was to go into effect.

What would happen if national tax policy were determined according to principles of majoritarian rather than pluralist democracy? Perhaps not much—if public opinion is any guide. The people of the United States are not eager to redistribute wealth by increasing the only major progressive tax, the income tax. If national taxes must be raised, Americans strongly favor a national sales tax over increased income taxes.[54] But a sales tax is a flat tax, paid by rich and poor at the same rate; it would have a regressive effect on income distribution, promoting inequality. The public also prefers a weekly $10 million national lottery to an increase in the income tax.[55] Because the poor are willing to chance more of their income on winning a fortune through lotteries than are rich people, lotteries (run by more than half the states) also contribute to income inequality.[56]

The newest tax on the horizon is a type of national retail sales tax called the *value-added tax* (VAT), which is applied to the value added to a product at each stage of production and distribution. The VAT is levied by all countries in the European Economic Community, and—with the potential of a 5 percent VAT to raise about $100 billion annually in revenue—it is certain to be a subject of debate in the United States.[57] But if a VAT is adopted in place of raising the income tax rate, it, like all sales taxes, will be regressive.

Majoritarians might argue that most Americans fail to understand the inequities of the national tax system. However, majoritarians *cannot* argue that the public demands "fairer" tax rates that take from richer citizens to help poorer ones. If it did, the lowest-income families might receive a greater share of the national income than they do. Instead, economic policy is determined mainly through a complex process of pluralist politics that preserves nearly half the national income in the hands of the wealthiest 20 percent of families.

SUMMARY

There are conflicting theories about how market economies work best. Laissez-faire economics holds that the government should keep its hands off the economy. Keynesian theory holds that government should take an active role in dealing with inflation and unemployment, using fiscal and monetary policies to produce desired levels of aggregate demand. Monetarists believe fiscal policies are unreliable, opting instead to use the money supply to control aggregate demand. Supply-side economists, who had an enormous influence on economic policy during the Reagan administration, focus on controlling the supply of goods and services rather than the demand for them.

Congress alone prepared the budget until 1921, when it thrust the responsibility on the president. After World War II, Congress tried unsuccessfully to regain control of the process. Later, Congress managed to restructure the process under House and Senate Budget committees. The new process worked well until it confronted the huge budget deficits in the 1980s. Because so much of the budget involves military spending and uncontrollable payments to individuals, it is virtually impossible to balance the budget by reducing what remains—mainly spending for nonentitlement domestic programs. Unwilling to accept responsibility for a tax increase, Congress accepted the Gramm-Rudman antideficit law in 1985. Under that law, deficits were to be reduced in stages, through automatic across-the-board cuts if necessary, until the budget was balanced by FY 1991. The deficit problem proved so intractable that Congress had to amend the law in 1987 to extend the deadline to 1993. Although President Bush promised "no new taxes" when he was campaigning for office in 1988, he had to acknowledge the need for revenue increases to cut the deficit and was forced to accept the Budget Enforcement Act of 1990, which raised the income tax. This act modified the budget procedure and made it easier to meet the Gramm-Rudman targets, but Bush suffered for breaking his pledge.

That act also amended the sweeping tax reform of 1986, which had eliminated tax loopholes and drastically reduced the number of tax brackets. The new law added a third bracket at 31 percent, which was much lower than the top rate before 1986. In an effort to reduce the deficit, President Clinton formulated a budget that created a fourth bracket set at 40 percent. Nevertheless, current U.S. tax rates are lower than taxes in most other major countries and lower than they have been in the United States since the Depression. But even with the heavily progressive tax rates of the past, the national tax system did little to redistribute income. Government transfer payments to individuals have helped reduce income inequalities. Nevertheless, the distribution of income is less equal in the United States than in most major Western nations.

Pluralist democracy as practiced in the United States has allowed well-organized, well-financed interest groups to manipulate tax and spending policies to their benefit. The result is that a larger and poorer segment of society is paying the price. Taxing and spending policies in the United States are tipped in the direction of freedom rather than equality.

Key Terms

economic depression
inflation
business cycle
aggregate demand
productive capacity
gross national product (GNP)
appropriations committees
Keynesian theory

fiscal policies
monetary policies
deficit financing
Council of Economic Advisers (CEA)
monetarists
Federal Reserve System
supply-side economics
fiscal year (FY)
budget authority

budget outlays
receipts
Office of Management and Budget (OMB)
tax committees
authorization committees
budget committees
Congressional Budget Office (CBO)

Gramm-Rudman
mandatory spending
entitlement
pay-as-you-go
discretionary spending
sequestration
progressive taxation
incremental budgeting
uncontrollable outlay
transfer payment

Selected Readings

Axelrod, Donald. *Budgeting for Modern Government, Second Edition.* New York: St. Martin's Press, 1995. Thorough explanation of the process of public budgeting from agency requests to the budget message. Excellent in evaluating criticisms and in proposing reforms.

Levy, Frank. *Dollars and Dreams: The Changing American Income Distribution.* New York: Russell Sage Foundation, 1987. Ties government economic policies to various social and economic trends. Sees an increasingly unequal distribution of chances to purchase the middle-class dream.

Mishel, Lawrence, and David M. Frankel. *The State of Working America, 1990–91 Edition.* Washington, D.C.: Economic Policy Institute, 1990. A statistical cafeteria of information on income inequality, unemployment, and poverty; also contains some useful cross-national comparisons.

Peters, B. Guy. *The Politics of Taxation: A Comparative Approach.* Cambridge, Mass.: Basil Blackwell, 1991. A worldwide survey of how governments raise revenue that contains many informative tables about sources of revenue, spending policies, and attitudes toward taxation.

Phillips, Kevin. *The Politics of Rich and Poor: Wealth and the American Electorate in the Reagan Aftermath.* New York: Random House, 1990. A serious indictment of the economic policies of the Reagan administration from an unlikely source, a conservative Republican who outlined the victorious "southern strategy" for Richard Nixon in 1968.

Rubin, Irene S. *The Politics of Public Budgeting: Getting and Spending, Borrowing and Balancing.* Chatham, N.J.: Chatham House, 1990. Offers a comprehensive overview of budget politics and provides valuable case studies and examples that give life to the budget process.

Steuerle, C. Eugene. *The Tax Decade.* Washington, D.C.: Urban Institute Press, 1992. Written by a top tax official in the Reagan administration, this book not only describes the important tax laws enacted during the 1980s but also explains them in the context of previous and later administrations.

White, Joseph, and Aaron Wildavsky. *The Deficit and the Public Interest: Search for Responsible Budgeting in the 1980s.* Berkeley: University of California Press, 1989. Describes an elaborate "Madisonian," or pluralist, budget system, in which everyone's point of view has merit and in which the deficit has become a political weapon, paralyzing our political system.

19 Domestic Policy

TEN-YEAR-OLD NICHOLAS WHITIKER lost his childhood or perhaps never had one. He cooks, cleans, mediates, and takes care of his immediate and extended family. His mother, a welfare recipient, used to be a crack addict. At twenty-six, she has traveled from desperation to redemption, returning to school to seek economic salvation as a nurse. By default, Nicholas has become the family caretaker.

Nicholas lives with his four half-brothers and half-sisters, his mother, and her companion in Chicago's bleak Englewood section. A reporter described Englewood this way: "It is a forlorn landscape of burned-out tenements and long-shuttered storefronts where drunk men hang out on the corner, where gang members command more respect than police officers and where every child can tell you where the crack houses are."[1] Gunshots are common in Englewood. The murder rate is higher than the combined murder rates of Pittsburgh and Omaha.

An extended family of aunts, an uncle, cousins, and a maternal grandmother provides stability in an uncertain urban landscape. Discipline is stern and punishment predictable; "spare the rod" has no place in Nicholas's world. Their Ethiopian-based Christianity also anchors the family. As the children bundle up for school on a bitter winter day, Mom sprays each of them with a special holy oil to protect against gangs and bullets. The kids recite the rules that give structure to their existence: "Don't stop off playing." "When you hear shooting, don't stand around—run." "Why do I say run?" asks Mom. "Because a bullet don't have no eyes," reply the boys.

More than 5 million poor inner-city children lead lives similar to Nicholas's. Many youngsters routinely exposed to violence suffer nightmares, depression, and personality disorders. Some withdraw and give up hope; others become aggressive. Safety and security have vanished from many of these inner-city communities; crime and violence contrast starkly with the accepted order elsewhere.

Physical safety and psychological security are preconditions for growing up healthy. Good schools, accessible medical care, and lavish libraries are irrelevant to children who fear for their lives when they set foot on their own sidewalks. Somehow, in a land of promise and opportunity, countless Americans are living in an abyss of unimaginable urban violence, squalor, and decay.[2] Although America is one of the freest and richest countries in the world, Nicholas Whitiker, his peers, and his family take little comfort in its liberties and its wealth. Government action helped generate this contradiction, and government action aims to correct it. We call this kind

A Moving Memorial

Each 3-by-6-foot panel of the AIDS quilt was stitched in memory of a life lost to AIDS. As of August 1994, the quilt weighed 32 tons, and if the more than 28,000 panels from 29 countries were placed end to end, they would stretch nearly 32 miles. Yet the quilt represents only a fraction of those who will die of AIDS, for which there is now no cure. Organizers hope the traveling displays of portions of the quilt help raise the public's awareness of the nature and scope of the disease.

of government action **public policy:** a general plan of action adopted by government to solve a social problem, counter a threat, or pursue an objective.

In Chapter 17 we examined the policymaking process in general; in this chapter we look at specific domestic public policies, government action targeting concerns internal to the United States. We begin our inquiry by discussing policies that protect Americans from disease and policies that prohibit the sale, distribution, and use of certain drugs. Then we analyze policies that provide social insurance and public assistance. (We discussed policies that promote disadvantaged groups through affirmative action programs in Chapter 16.) Four key questions guide our inquiry: What are the origins and politics of specific policies? What are the effects of those policies once they are implemented? Why do some policies succeed and others fail? Finally, are disagreements about policy really disagreements about values?

Public policies sometimes seem as numerous as fast-food restaurants, offering something for every appetite and budget. With the wide range of policies worth exploring, you may be wondering why we plan to spend much of the chapter discussing social insurance and public assistance. These policies deserve special consideration for three reasons. First, government expenditures in these areas represent more than half the national budget and one-tenth of our gross domestic product (the total market value of all goods and services produced in this country during a year). In 1995, of every dollar spent by the national government, 48 cents will go to direct payments to individuals.[3] All citizens ought to know how their resources are allocated and why. Regrettably, the public has limited and distorted knowledge about national government spending. For example, only one in four Americans knows that the government spends more for social security than for national defense.[4] Second, one goal of social insurance and public assistance policies is to alleviate some consequences of economic inequality. Nevertheless, poverty remains a fixture of American life, and we must try to understand why. Third, these policies pose some vexing questions involving the conflicts between freedom and order, and freedom and equality.

This chapter concentrates on policies based on the authority of the national government to tax and spend for the general welfare. But it is important to recognize that state and local governments play a vital role in shaping and directing the policies that emanate from Washington. For example, the national government sets standards for the allocation of welfare benefits, but states may impose stricter standards for recipients—and some do.[5]

We begin with a discussion of public policies designed to protect health and prohibit controlled substances. Americans disagree about such policies, because they disagree about the need for government action, the goals of such action, and the means the government should use to fulfill those goals. We will focus on some of these disagreements as a means of understanding the conflicting values that underlie them.

POLICIES THAT PROTECT: AIDS

Acquired Immune Deficiency Syndrome (AIDS) kills. According to national government researchers, there have been 402,000 cases of AIDS in the United States. More than 243,000 Americans died of the disease between 1981 (when the disease was first officially recognized) and 1994.[6] In 1991, AIDS surpassed accidents as the leading cause of death among men aged twenty-five to forty-four.[7] AIDS now rivals or exceeds cancer as the most feared disease.[8] Predictably, Americans regard AIDS as the nation's "number one" health problem.[9]

Estimates vary on the spread of AIDS through the population, but one fact is certain: Most of the men, women, and children who are afflicted will die from the opportunistic infections that ravage AIDS victims. Babies who acquire the virus from their mothers before birth typically live only a couple of years. So far, most victims are either intravenous drug users or male homosexuals. There is a real possibility, however, that the disease will spread widely through the nondrug-using heterosexual population. Because the symptoms of AIDS can take seven years or more to appear, public health officials fear that the worst is yet to come.

In 1990, the national government spent $2.9 billion on AIDS research, treatment, prevention, and income-support programs for persons with AIDS who are unable to work.[10] By 1995, the national government plans to spend $7.5 billion on such programs.

Sending the Message

A startled cat is the star in a television campaign to encourage young people to protect themselves from sexually transmitted diseases. This spot and others were produced by the national government's Centers for Disease Control and Prevention and the Department of Health and Human Services.

What, in addition to research, should the government do to stop the spread of AIDS? What public policies will be both effective and widely accepted?

Protection Through Education

Public health officials are virtually certain that human immunodeficiency virus (HIV), the AIDS-causing virus, is spread only by the exchange of body fluids—blood or semen. To try to stem the spread of AIDS, the Public Health Service (the national government agency charged with protecting public health) in 1986 mounted a national campaign to educate children and young adults about the sexual practices that increase the risk of AIDS transmission. This campaign infuriated many citizens, who believed that instruction about "safe sex" infringes on a parent's freedom to guide a child's sexual education.

Some public health officials at state and local levels advocate the distribution of free condoms as a simple and relatively effective way to combat the spread of AIDS. However, some Americans believe the distribution of free condoms, like safe-sex classes, encourages sexual activity and undercuts the moral guidance offered by parents.

Opponents of the classes-and-condoms approach maintain that schools should concentrate on academic knowledge and that sex education, if offered at all, should focus on sexual abstinence. Advocates of an AIDS-awareness campaign maintain that students are already sexually active and that appeals to sexual abstinence are like medicine after death: It certainly can't harm the patient, but it will do no good.

The evidence on the effects of sex counseling in high schools remains inconclusive. AIDS has such a long latency period that reduced rates of infection resulting from consistent condom use will not be apparent for years, if at all. A few studies report a lower incidence of teen pregnancy associated with free condoms and safe-sex classes, but other studies report earlier initiation of sexual intercourse in schools where safe-sex classes are taught. (Lower rates of teen pregnancy may be viewed as a side benefit of the fight against the spread of AIDS.) The competing viewpoints pose difficult choices: parental freedom to direct children's moral and personal development without government intervention, or government-imposed intervention to prevent the spread of a dreaded disease.[11]

Testing and Protection

Another way government can intervene in the lives of citizens is to require HIV testing for everyone and mandatory reporting of positive results to public health officials. A majority of Americans supports this idea. Nearly two-thirds of college freshmen agree.[12] Those favoring testing argue that it would assist health authorities in finding and notifying the sexual and needle-sharing partners of individuals who test positive for the virus. Because the stigma attached to the disease and the behaviors associated with it (homosexuality and intravenous drug use) discourage candor, advocates of mandatory testing maintain that government has an obligation to inform the sexual partners of an infected person if he or she is unlikely to do so. Almost half the states now require that physicians report the names of people who are HIV positive to public health agencies, which may try to trace their partners.

However, mandatory testing and name reporting may deter infected individuals from seeking care. Once their identities become known, infected persons risk discrimination from their employers, who may be unsympathetic to their plight and irrationally fearful of the spread of the disease in the workplace. Discrimination may extend to housing, where irrational fears may generate eviction notices, and to health insurance carriers, which might be unwilling to bear the high costs associated with AIDS treatment.

Public policy on AIDS generates controversy, because it forces us to make difficult choices between order and freedom. Mandatory testing and reporting are adopted to preserve social order by curtailing the spread of the infection. But such policies also invade the privacy of infected people and may fuel discrimination against them. The freedom of AIDS patients may therefore be sacrificed for the good of the public health.

Government AIDS policy aims to protect. Let us consider government's policy against illegal drugs, which aims primarily to prohibit traffic and trade in addictive substances.

POLICIES THAT PROHIBIT: ILLEGAL DRUGS

A growing number of Americans identify illegal drug use as the nation's most serious problem, outdistancing the problems of AIDS, homelessness, poverty, and the federal budget deficit. In a 1989 poll, 44 percent viewed the use of illegal drugs as the major problem facing the country—more than double the number who had identified drugs as the major problem in 1988.[13]

Americans face two serious problems: the persistence of hard-core drug use and the changeable attitudes of young people toward illegal drugs.

Most Americans oppose the use of such drugs as cocaine, heroin, and marijuana. Marijuana use once had considerable public acceptance, but that acceptance has declined sharply. Thirty percent of American adults favored legalization in 1978; 18 percent favored it in 1991.[14] Similarly, more than half of the nation's college freshmen supported legalization of pot in 1977; only 23 percent favored legalization in 1992.[15]

Preliminary evidence from a variety of sources suggests that casual use of all drugs has started to decline; the number of weekly cocaine users has also dropped. By all accounts, say the experts, illegal drug use among the middle class has begun to ebb. Despite severe legal penalties, however, drug abuse persists among the inner-city poor.[16] One study estimates that Americans spend $15 to $20 billion a year on cocaine alone. A recent survey revealed that 1.5 million Americans use cocaine and crack cocaine at least once a month and that marijuana and hashish, with 12 million monthly users, are still the nation's most popular illegal "highs," [17] as described in Feature 19.1. Although the government prohibits the sale and possession of these drugs, and imposes stern penalties for breaking drug laws, the government's drug policy has been largely ineffective. Given the history of drug use and abuse in America, this ineffectiveness should not be surprising.

Historical Perspective

This is not the first time policymakers have waged war on illegal drugs.[18] In fact, this is the nation's second large-scale assault on the drug epidemic. Cocaine was first isolated from the coca plant in 1860 and quickly became a component of popular elixirs. American physicians were early enthusiasts, prescribing cocaine to cure Americans' widespread addiction to opiates (such as morphine) and alcohol. Cocaine even became the official remedy of the American Hay Fever Association because of its ability to drain the sinuses and shrink irritated mucous membranes.

By 1900, cocaine addiction was becoming widespread. States adopted laws requiring a doctor's prescription for cocaine, ending the practice of over-the-counter cocaine sales, but the national government did not regulate drugs until 1906, when Congress enacted the Pure Food and Drug Act. This act required manufacturers to list addictive ingredients on the labels of all patent medicines shipped in interstate commerce. Following its passage, sales of drug-laced medicines dropped by one-third. And as the older, medically addicted users and their opiate- and cocaine-prescribing physicians died off, fewer doctors prescribed cocaine for their patients. Cocaine consumption dropped steadily, although it never disappeared completely, especially in urban areas.

As cocaine waned in fashion, however, other drugs arose as substitutes. Opium smoking persisted, as did alcohol addiction. Urban drug addicts switched to morphine and then to the more powerful morphine derivative, heroin. By 1910, most drug users were addicted to heroin, and most were concentrated in New York.

Many states enacted narcotics-control legislation. In 1914, for example, New York enacted its first law regulating the distribution of habit-forming drugs such as heroin. As a result, the street price for an ounce of heroin rose from $6.50 to $100. Meanwhile, the underworld found that heroin was profitable—strongly addictive and easy to smuggle. Within a few years, heroin use began to spread beyond New York.

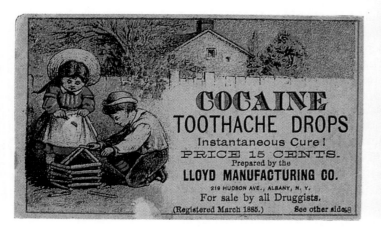

Drugs: An Old Story

Addictive substances have long been part of American life. Cocaine was once an ingredient in over-the-counter medication, as this label from 1888 shows (left). Later, inaccurate information helped shape public opinion about another drug. In 1938, this ad was part of a national campaign designed to convince Americans that marijuana use leads to insanity and criminal behavior (right).

Drug policy shifted as addiction spread. Initially, government was tolerant of addicts and their addiction. However, that approach waned with the spread of heroin and the involvement of organized crime in the distribution and sale of illegal drugs. In the 1920s, government policy switched to attempting to eliminate the drug problem entirely. Government studies cited false or misleading information, inflating the number of addicts to well over 1 million; in fact, the number was probably less than 300,000. This exaggeration confirmed the popular view that drug addiction was epidemic. By 1930, public revulsion at illegal drug use was widespread. Every state had comprehensive drug education programs aimed at impressing upon young minds the evils of drug use.

The Great Depression nearly eliminated these drug education programs. At about the same time, national policymakers took the position that any discussion of drug abuse would only generate interest in drug use. For almost two generations, this government-sponsored campaign of silence contributed to the near-total ignorance of illicit drugs. When government did disseminate information, it was often exaggerated. In 1937, for example, the FBI labeled marijuana "the killer weed" and "the assassin of youth." This policy of overstatement led to lurid exploitation films such as the 1938 classic *Reefer Madness.* The hyperbole backfired in the 1960s, however, as young men and women found that pot smoking did not lead to madness, criminality, or prostitution. The government policy of purposeful exaggeration tainted legitimate warnings about the harmful effects of more potent and addictive drugs, such as cocaine and heroin.

FEATURE **19.1**

America's Legal (and Illegal) Drug Use

A huge number of Americans use drugs, including the legally sanctioned drugs of nicotine and alcohol. In a massive survey conducted by the national government in 1992, alcohol and cigarettes had the most lifetime, past-year, and past-month users. There is some good news in the data. Use of legal and illegal drugs has been on the decline for the last decade or more in the critical eighteen-to-twenty five-year-old cohort. Still, the toll in human misery remains unacceptably high.

The economic cost of America's drug habit is staggering. One estimate calculated the cost in health care, crime, lost productivity, forfeited education, and property destruction as more than $300 billion in 1989; it is likely to reach $1 trillion by the mid-1990s.

- *Source: Joseph A. Califano, "Drug War: Fool's Errand No. 3," New York Times, 8 December 1989, p. 31. Copyright 1989 by The New York Times Company. Reprinted by permission. And 1993 Statistical Abstract of the United States, Table 208, p. 136 (1994).*

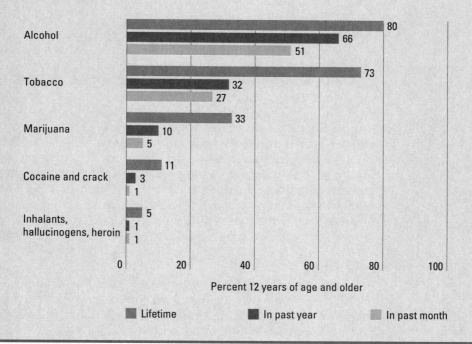

Percent 12 years of age and older

■ Lifetime   ■ In past year   ▨ In past month

Markets and Controls

Today's market in illegal drugs, like other markets, exists because of supply and demand. In theory, the elimination of the drug supply would eliminate the market, but efforts aimed at the supply side have been notably unsuccessful. Why? A partial explanation is that drug trafficking, despite the risks, is lucrative. It can be a short cut to wealth and, in some communities, social status. Penalties such as long prison terms do not act as sufficient deterrents.

The national government has also attempted to constrict or eliminate the supply and distribution network that keeps America awash in narcotics. One approach, currently in effect, is to convince drug-producing or drug-trafficking nations to act in accordance with U.S. drug policy. Under this plan, the president must certify whether twenty-four nations identified by Congress as major drug producers or transit points are cooperating with American drug-control efforts. If the president does not certify a country, U.S. foreign aid and other financial assistance to that country drop substantially. The president can push for tougher sanctions, including trade embargoes, against particularly recalcitrant countries.

In 1994, the State Department identified Nigeria as a major drug trafficker, accounting for an estimated 35 to 40 percent of the heroin entering the United States.[19] Nigeria joined other countries failing certification: Myanmar, Iran, and Syria. Ironically, the United States has no relations with these countries or only severely strained relations. No United States ally has been penalized for lack of cooperation. So far, these sanctions have not dented the supply of illegal drugs entering the United States.

Government drug policy calls for the use of military force in addition to foreign aid. For example, in Colombia, Peru, and Bolivia, the United States has agreed to fund programs aimed at substituting crops for coca, promote more Western investment in the region, and crack down on U.S. exports (such as guns and chemicals) that are essential in the drug trade. In return, the United States will send military advisers and equipment to assist in local drug-busting operations. Closer to home, the National Guard (military reserve units controlled by each state and equipped by the national government) has assisted in border patrols and customs inspections.[20]

Imposing these controls on the drug market creates costs that government must bear. In 1995, the national government will spend more than $13 billion to combat importation, distribution, and consumption of illegal drugs. The major share will go to enforcement. Meanwhile, the states spend at least half that amount on local antidrug efforts.[21] Despite all this money and an increased arrest rate, however, the government is not winning the drug war by stemming the supply of drugs.

Testing and Prohibition

If government policies have been unsuccessful in eliminating the supply of drugs, perhaps government should concentrate on reducing or eliminating the demand for drugs. Consider the policy of mandatory drug testing for certain national government employees.

The national government employs thousands of individuals in drug enforcement. Proponents of drug testing for those employees argue that the government has a strong interest in ensuring that drug enforcement officials are not drug users themselves. Under the existing policy, if a urinalysis of an employee shows traces of an illegal drug, the employee is required to undergo counseling. Workers who refuse to be tested can be dismissed.

Polls continue to report that an overwhelming majority of Americans is willing to take drug tests. In a massive 1992 survey of college freshmen, more than eight in ten favored mandatory drug testing in the workplace.[22] Opponents of mandatory drug testing argue, however, that testing would not be based on "reasonable suspicion" of drug use and that it would therefore interfere with personal liberty or privacy. Such testing, remarked one vocal opponent, would be "a comic exercise in Ty-D-Bol justice," flushing away freedom in the process.[23]

Values and Policies

The Clinton administration has opted for a balanced set of antidrug policies. Although the bulk of government spending goes to enforcement, an increasing fraction is earmarked for treatment and prevention. Nearly 80 percent of Americans support this balanced approach.[24] Some politicians acknowledge a preference for treatment and prevention policies over criminal penalties, but they fear that allocating less for enforcement will make them look soft on crime.

Will strict prohibition achieve eventual victory in our second drug war, although it has not worked so far? A few Americans who believe that it will not propose a policy of legalization, arguing that taxing and regulating drug sales would control drug use more effectively than prohibition. They assert that the money saved from futile attempts at prohibition could be more effectively spent on education, prevention, and treatment.

Legalization advocates hold to four fundamental, and sometimes controversial, views. First, they maintain that illicit drugs should be treated as a health issue, not a crime issue. As Feature 19.1 illustrates, legal drugs, such as alcohol and nicotine, are as serious a problem as illegal drugs. The government estimates that 8 percent of the population are frequent drinkers (twenty or more days per month) and 5 percent are heavy drinkers (five or more drinks on five or more occasions per month). More alarming still, 15 percent of the population smoke at least one pack of cigarettes a day.[25] The social and economic costs of these legal addictions are as sobering as those resulting from illegal addictions. Addiction is the problem, and it will not be eradicated by executing drug lords and hiring more cops.

Second, advocates of legalization believe that the drug war is unwinnable. Addictive drugs are not new to American society; their existence for well over one hundred years suggests that the problem is chronic. Moreover, our experiment with alcohol prohibition in the 1920s proved an utter failure. The same destiny, they say, awaits strict drug prohibition. Third, a policy that makes drugs illegal only creates a black market, driving prices—and drug-dealer profits—sky high. No wonder there are so many drug entrepreneurs.

Finally, advocates maintain that legalization with strict government regulation will create little or no increase in drug use. They maintain that legalization is unlikely to increase availability in areas already saturated with illegal drugs. And even if legalization produces a few more abusers, the cost of helping all addicts would still be far less than the cost of today's drug war.[26]

The debate over legalization sometimes erupts into a clash of moral positions. Opponents claim that legalization of hard drugs such as cocaine and heroin is simply immoral. Legalizers argue that alcohol use is no different than hard drug use; tolerating one but not the other is hypocritical. The gulf between these two positions is still enormous, and legalization remains an unthinkable alternative to most Americans.[27]

The choice between drug prohibition and legalization is easy for most Americans; the majority prefers order, whereas few choose freedom on

Woodstock Nation '94

Woodstock '94 marked the 25th anniversary of the 1969 concert, which for many Americans defined their generation. The 1994 event drew more than 300,000 people to hear fifty acts, from Joe Cocker and Bob Dylan to Metallica and Nine Inch Nails. Illegal drugs remain part of the pop culture celebrated by Woodstock images, then and now.

this issue. Most Americans continue to believe that the war on drugs will eventually end in victory, provided government supplies adequate resources and demonstrates ample resolve. The evidence—despite some successes, especially among the middle class—is discouraging. Meanwhile, a few Americans steadfastly maintain that the current drug war is being fought against impossible odds and that legalization is inevitable.

Although most Americans agree that illicit drugs are a serious problem that warrants government action, they disagree when the means selected to address the problem generate value conflicts or prove ineffective. Questionable or ineffective means have stirred debates about other domestic policies, including those designed to provide income, health, and welfare benefits to citizens.

GOVERNMENT POLICIES AND INDIVIDUAL WELFARE

The most controversial purpose of government is to promote social and economic equality. To do so may conflict with the freedom of some citizens, for it requires government action to redistribute income from rich to poor. This choice between freedom and equality constitutes the modern dilemma of government; it has been at the center of many conflicts in U.S. public policy since World War II. On one hand, most Americans believe that government should help the needy. On the other hand, they do not want to sacrifice their own standard of living to provide government handouts to those whom they may perceive as shiftless and lazy.

The Growth of the American Welfare State

At one time, governments confined their activities to the minimal protection of people and property—to ensuring security and order. Now, however, almost every modern nation may be characterized as a **welfare state,**

FIGURE **19.1** ■ **Government Payments to Individuals, 1960–1994**

The national government spends a large portion of its budget on payments to individuals (for example, on social security). This spending has nearly doubled since 1960.

Source: Historical Tables, Budget of the United States Government, FY 1995, *Table 11.1.*

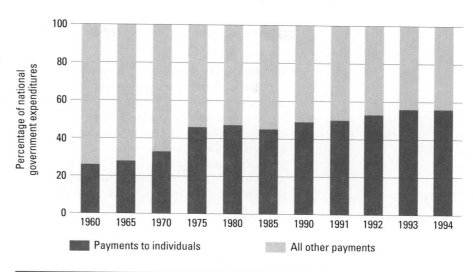

serving as the provider and protector of individual well being through economic and social programs. The term **social welfare** is used to describe government programs that provide the minimum living conditions necessary for all citizens. Income for the elderly, health care, subsidized housing, and nutrition are among the concerns addressed by government social welfare programs.

The recent history of U.S. government spending in support of social welfare policies is illustrated in Figure 19.1. In 1960, 26 cents of every dollar of national spending went to payments for individuals. In 1970, 33 cents of every dollar went to payments for individuals. And, in 1980, nearly half of each dollar went to individuals. By 1985, spending for individuals had fallen off by a few percentage points, but by 1987 it had returned to the 1980 level. The latest data for 1995 show that about half the national spending goes to direct payments to individuals. The national government clearly remains a provider of social welfare, despite changes in administrations.

The origins of social welfare policy go back to the Industrial Revolution, when the mechanization of production resulted in a shift from home manufacturing to large-scale factory production. As more and more people worked for wages, many more were subjected to the dreadful consequences of a loss of employment because of sickness, injury, old age, or economic conditions. The sick, the disabled, and the aged were tended, for the most part, by families and charities. Communities confined the destitute to poorhouses or almshouses, which were little more than warehouses for the impoverished. In the eighteenth and nineteenth centuries, poverty was viewed as a disgrace. Poor people were seen as lazy and incompetent. (Indeed, many Americans still hold this view.) Relief was made disagreeable to discourage dependence on outside assistance.

America today is far from being a welfare state on the order of Germany or Great Britain; those nations provide many more medical, educational, and unemployment benefits to their citizens. However, the United States does have several social welfare functions. To understand social welfare policies in the United States, you must first understand the significance of a major event—the Great Depression—and the two presidential plans that extended the scope of government—the New Deal and the Great Society.

The Great Depression.   Throughout its history, the U.S. economy has experienced alternating good times and hard times, generally referred to as *business cycles* (see Chapter 18). The **Great Depression** was, by far, the longest and deepest setback that the American economy has ever experienced. It began with the stock market crash of 1929 (on October 29, a day known as Black Tuesday) and did not end until the start of World War II. By 1932, one out of every four U.S. workers was unemployed, and millions more were underemployed. No other event has had a greater effect on the thinking and the institutions of government in the twentieth century.

In the 1930s, the forces that had stemmed earlier business declines were no longer operating. There were no more frontiers, no growth in export markets, no new technologies to boost employment. Unchecked, unemployment spread like an epidemic. And the crisis fueled itself. Workers who lost their source of income could no longer buy the food, goods, and services that kept the economy going. Thus, private industry and commercial farmers tended to produce more than they could sell profitably. Closed factories, surplus crops, and idle workers were the consequences.

The Great Depression generated powerful ironies. Seeking to restore profits, producers trimmed costs by replacing workers with machines, which only increased unemployment. Unemployed workers could not afford to buy goods, which drove down profits. People went hungry, because so much food had been produced that it could not be sold profitably; dumping it was cheaper than taking it to market.

The industrialized nations of Europe were also hit hard. The value of U.S. exports fell and the value of imports increased; this led Congress to impose high tariffs, which strangled trade and fueled the Depression. From 1929 to 1932, more than 44 percent of the nation's banks failed when unpaid loans exceeded the value of bank assets. Farm prices fell by more than half in the same period. Marginal farmers lost their land, and tenant farmers succumbed to mechanization. The uprooted—tens of thousands of dispossessed farm families—headed West with their possessions atop their cars and trucks in a hopeless quest for opportunity.

The New Deal.   In his speech accepting the presidential nomination at the 1932 Democratic National Convention, Franklin Delano Roosevelt (then governor of New York) made a promise: "I pledge you, I pledge myself to a new deal for the American people." Roosevelt did not specify what his **New Deal** would consist of, but the term was later applied to measures undertaken by the Roosevelt administration to stem the Depression. Some scholars regard these measures as the most imaginative burst of domestic policy in the nation's history. Others see them as the source of massive government growth without matching benefits.

President Roosevelt's New Deal was composed of two phases. The first, which ended in 1935, was aimed at boosting prices and lowering unemployment. The second phase, which ended in 1938, was aimed at aiding

A Human Tragedy

The Great Depression made able-bodied Americans idle. By 1933, when President Herbert Hoover left office, about one-fourth of the labor force was out of work. Private charities were swamped with the burden of feeding the destitute. The hopeless men pictured here await a handout from a wealthy San Francisco matron known as the "White Angel" who provided resources for a bread line.

the forgotten people: the poor, the aged, unorganized working men and women, and the farmers.

The New Deal programs were opportunistic; they were not guided by, or based on, a single political or economic theory. They aimed at relief for the needy, recovery for the nation, and long-range reform for the economy. Many New Deal programs were rooted in the concept of short-term relief to get people back on their feet without continuous dependence on government assistance. (For example, the Civilian Conservation Corps Reconstruction Relief Act of 1933 provided short-term jobs for young men.) Administering these programs called for government growth; funding them required higher taxes. Government could no longer rely on either the decentralized political structure of federalism or the market forces of laissez-faire capitalism to bring the country out of its decline. The New Deal embodied the belief that a complex economy required centralized-government control. (One of the New Deal's lasting legacies is the social security system, which we will examine in detail later in this chapter.)

The Supreme Court stymied Roosevelt's first-phase reform efforts by declaring major New Deal legislation unconstitutional, beginning in 1935. A majority of the justices maintained that in its legislation, Congress had exceeded its constitutional authority to regulate interstate commerce.

The Democrats won overwhelming popular support for their efforts at relief and recovery. The voters returned Roosevelt to office in a landslide election in 1936. But the Supreme Court continued its opposition to New Deal legislation. This prompted Roosevelt to advocate an increase in the

**Experiencing the
Great Depression**

The despair of the Depression can be seen in the faces of this desperate migrant mother and her children, waiting for work picking peas in Nipomo, CA, in 1936. She had just sold the tires from her car to buy food. Uprooted farmers, forced from their land by foreclosure, trooped from town in search of jobs or food. The health, nutrition, and shelter of millions of Americans suffered in the Great Depression's wake.

number of justices on the Court; his goal was to appoint justices sympathetic to the legislation he endorsed. However, Roosevelt's attack on the Court, coupled with increasing labor violence, alarmed conservatives and put the New Deal on the defensive. Still, within a few months of the 1936 election, the Supreme Court began to adopt an interpretation of the Constitution that permitted expanded power for the national government. In an abrupt about-face, the Court upheld the New Deal policies that comprised the second phase. (It was, said one wag, "the switch in time that saved nine.")

Poverty and unemployment persisted, however, despite the best efforts of the Democrats. By 1939, 17 percent of the work force (more than 9 million people) were still unemployed. Only World War II was able to provide the economic surge needed to yield lower unemployment and higher prices, the elusive goals of the New Deal.

Roosevelt's overwhelming popularity did not translate into irresistibly popular policy or genuine popularity for government. Public opinion polls revealed that Americans were divided over New Deal policies through the early 1940s. Eventually, the New Deal became the status quo, and Americans grew satisfied with it. But Americans remained wary of additional growth in the power of the national government.[28]

Economists still debate whether the actual economic benefits of the New Deal reforms outweighed their costs. It is clear, however, that New Deal policies initiated a long-range trend toward government expansion. And another torrent of domestic policymaking burst forth three decades later.

The Great Society.   John F. Kennedy's election in 1960 brought to Washington public servants sensitive to persistent poverty and the needs of minorities. This raised expectations that national government policies would benefit the poor and minorities. But Kennedy's razor-thin margin of victory was far from a mandate to improve the plight of the poor and dispossessed. At first, Kennedy proposed technical and financial aid for depressed areas and programs for upgrading the skills of workers in marginal jobs. But Kennedy and influential members of his administration were motivated by politics as well as poverty; in 1962, with the economy faltering again, the Kennedy administration proposed substantial tax breaks for middle- and upper-income groups. Fixing the economy took precedence over the needs of the less fortunate. Many low-income Americans remained untouched by the administration's programs.

Kennedy's assassination in November 1963 provided the backdrop and generated needed support for new policies founded on equality, proposed by his successor, Lyndon Baines Johnson. In his 1965 State of the Union address, President Johnson offered his own version of the New Deal; his vision of the **Great Society** included a broad array of programs designed to redress political, social, and economic inequality. In contrast to the New Deal, few if any of Johnson's programs aimed at short-term relief; most were targeted at chronic ills requiring long-term commitment by the national government. Some programs had already been enacted when Johnson articulated his vision, whereas others were still in the planning stage. The Civil Rights Act of 1964 was aimed at erasing racial discrimination from most areas of American life. The Voting Rights Act of 1965 had as its goal the elimination of voting restrictions that discriminated against blacks and other minorities. Both statutes prohibited conduct that was inconsistent with political and social equality (see Chapter 16).

Another part of Johnson's Great Society plan was based on the traditional American belief that social and economic equality could be attained through equality of educational opportunity. The Elementary and Secondary Education Act of 1965 provided, for the first time, direct national government aid to local school districts, based on the number of low-income families in each district. Later, the national government was able to use the threat of withholding school aid (under the 1964 Civil Rights Act) to dramatically increase the pace of school integration in the South.

Still another vital element of the Great Society was the **War on Poverty**. The major weapon in this war was the Economic Opportunity Act (1964); its proponents promised that it would eradicate poverty in ten years. The act encouraged a variety of local community programs to educate and train people for employment. Among them were college work-study programs, summer employment for high school and college students, loans to small businesses, a domestic version of the Peace Corps (called VISTA, for Volunteers in Service to America), educational enrichment for preschoolers, and legal services for the poor. It offered opportunity: a hand up, rather than a handout.

The act also established the Office for Economic Opportunity (OEO), which was the administrative center of the War on Poverty. Its basic strategy was to involve the poor themselves in administering antipoverty programs, in the hope that they would know which programs would best serve their needs. The national government channeled money directly to local community action programs. This approach avoided the vested interests of state and local government bureaucrats and political machines. But it also led to new local controversies by shifting the control of government funds from local politicians to other groups. (In one notorious example, the Blackstone Rangers, a Chicago street gang, received funds for a job-training program.)

In 1967, the Johnson administration responded to pressure from established local politicians by requiring that poverty funds be distributed through certified state and local agencies. In addition, all sectors of the community (including business, labor, and local leaders) would now be represented, along with the poor, in administering community action programs.

The War on Poverty eventually faded as funding was diverted to the Vietnam War. Although it had achieved little in the way of income redistribution, it did lead to one significant change: It made the poor aware of their political power. Some candidates representing the poor ran for political office, and officeholders paid increased attention to the poor. The poor also found that they could use the legal system to their benefit. For example, with legal assistance from the OEO, low-income litigants were successful in striking down state laws requiring a minimum period of residency before people could receive public assistance.[29]

Some War on Poverty programs remain as established features of government. (Among these is the work-study program that enables many college students to finance their education.) Yet poverty remains, and the evidence suggests that it may once again be on the rise. However, public attitudes toward poverty have changed since the Great Depression. When Americans were polled recently on the reasons for poverty, they cited in approximately equal measure circumstances beyond the control of the poor and lack of effort. Many Americans today believe that the persistence of poverty results from flawed programs that encourage dependence on government assistance.[30]

Social welfare policy is based on the premise that society has an obligation to provide for the basic needs of its members. In an unusual national survey targeting the poor and nonpoor, both sectors agreed that government should protect its citizens against the risks that they are powerless to combat. Americans expressed a clear conviction that money and wealth ought to be more evenly shared.[31] The term *welfare state* describes this protective role of government.

By meeting people's minimum needs, government welfare policies attempt to promote equality. New Deal policies were aimed at meeting the needs of the poor by redistributing income: People paid progressively higher taxes as their incomes rose—in effect, the wealthy paid to alleviate poverty. Today's liberals tend to follow the New Deal path. They are willing to curtail economic freedom somewhat to promote economic equality. As a result, their policies aim at providing direct income subsidies and government jobs. Today's conservatives avoid this government-as-provider approach, preferring economic freedom to government intervention. Their policies aim at curbing inflation and reducing government spending, on the theory that the rising tide of a growing economy lifts all boats.

The evidence from the 1980s, however, does not support the conservatives' theory. Both before-tax and after-tax income inequality grew in that decade (see Chapter 18). Changes in families and household composition suggest several plausible explanations for this increased gulf between the haves and the have-nots. For one thing, growth in the number of elderly people—who have substantially lower incomes—tends to increase income inequality. Growth in the number of persons living alone (or with nonrelatives)—who typically have much lower incomes than family households—also increases income inequality. In addition, the growth in the number of female-headed households contributes to income inequality; about half of such households are in the lowest income group, as described in Politics in a Changing America 19.1. Researchers have labeled this trend the *feminization of poverty*, the growing percentage of all poor Americans who are women or dependents of women. [32]

The Reduction of the Welfare State

A spirit of equality—equality of opportunity—motivated the reforms of the 1960s, many of which carried over to the 1970s. But Ronald Reagan's overwhelming election in 1980 and his landslide reelection in 1984 forced a reexamination of social welfare policy.

In a dramatic departure from his predecessors (Republicans as well as Democrats), Reagan shifted emphasis from economic equality to economic freedom. He questioned whether government alone should continue to be responsible for guaranteeing the economic and social well being of less fortunate citizens. And, to the extent that government should bear this responsibility, he maintained that state and local governments could do so more efficiently than the national government. Ironically, when Reagan attempted to act on his rhetoric about limited government, his political support started to evaporate. Two political scientists articulated the lesson for all post–Great Society presidents, including Reagan: "A powerful central government is here to stay, and its beneficiaries, many of whom approved of Reagan, want it that way."[33]

Reagan professed support for the "truly needy" and for preservation of a "reliable safety net of social programs," by which he meant the core programs begun in the New Deal. Nevertheless, his administration abolished a number of social welfare programs and redirected others. Reagan proposed sharp cutbacks in housing assistance, welfare, the food stamp program, and education and job-training programs. Reagan and Congress also trimmed the most basic of American social welfare programs—social security—although cuts here were less severe than in other areas.[34]

Congress blocked some of the president's proposed cutbacks, and many Great Society programs remained in force, although at lower funding levels. Overall spending on social welfare programs (as a proportion of the gross national product) fell to about mid-1970s levels. But the dramatic growth in the promotion of social welfare that began with the New Deal ended with the Reagan administration. It remained in repose during the Bush administration. And the national budget deficit—a deficit that ballooned during the Reagan and Bush administrations—will continue to restrict future efforts to expand the government's social welfare role. The enormous government debt will force Congress to avoid new and costly social welfare programs until income and expenditures approach a balance.

POLITICS IN A CHANGING AMERICA 19.1   The Feminization of Poverty

When we examine the composition of poor families, especially over the last twenty-five years, we observe a dramatic and disturbing trend. One in every two poor Americans resides in a family in which a woman is the sole householder, or head of the household (see graph). Thirty years ago, only one in every four poor people lived in such a family. What accounts for this dramatic upward shift in the proportion of female-headed poor families?

This century bears witness to extraordinary changes for women. Women won the right to vote and own property. Women also gained a measure of legal and social equality (see Chapter 16). But increases in rates of divorce, marital separation, and adolescent pregnancy have cast more and more women in the head-of-household role. Caring for children competes with commitment to work. Affordable child care is out of reach for many single parents. In the absence of a national child care policy, single women with young children face limited employment opportunities and lower wages in comparison with full-time workers. These factors and others contribute to the **feminization of poverty,** the growing percentage of all poor Americans who are women or the dependents of women.

• *Sources: Barbara Ehrenreich and Frances Fox Piven, "The Feminization of Poverty,"* Dissent *(Spring 1984), 162–170;* Harrell R. Rodgers, Jr., Poor Women, Poor Families: The Economic Plight of America's Female-Headed Households, *2d ed. (Armonk, N.Y.: M.E. Sharpe, 1990).*

Source for data: U.S. Bureau of the Census, U.S. Department of Commerce, Poverty in the United States, 1992, *Current Population Reports, Series P-60, No. 185 (Washington, D.C.: U.S. Government Printing Office, 1993).*

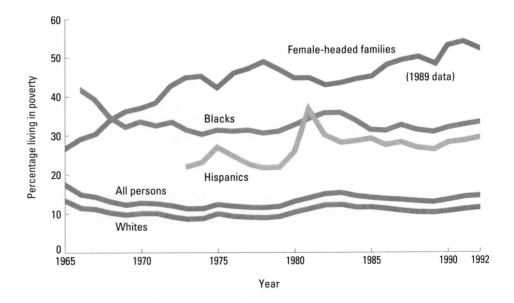

POLICIES THAT PROVIDE: SOCIAL INSURANCE

Insurance is a device for protecting against loss. Since the late nineteenth century, there has been a growing tendency for governments to offer **social insurance,** which is government-backed protection against loss by individuals, regardless of need, as described in Compared with What? 19.1. The most common forms of social insurance guard against losses from worker sickness, injury, and disability, old age, and unemployment. The first example of social insurance in the United States was workers' compensation. Beginning early in this century, most states created systems of insurance that compensated workers who lost income because they were injured in the workplace.

Social insurance benefits are distributed to recipients without regard to their economic status. Old-age benefits, for example, are paid to workers—rich or poor—provided that they have enough covered work experience and they have reached the required age. In most social insurance programs, employees and employers contribute to a fund from which employees later receive payments.*

Social insurance programs are examples of entitlements—benefits to which every eligible person has a legal right and which government cannot deny. National entitlement programs consume about half of every dollar of government spending; the largest entitlement program is social security.

Social Security

Social security is social insurance that provides economic assistance to people faced with unemployment, disability, or old age; it is financed by taxes on employers and employees. Initially, social security benefits were distributed only to the aged, the unemployed, and poor people with dependent children. Today, social security also provides medical care for the elderly and income support for the disabled.

Origins of social security. The idea of Social Security came late to the United States. As early as 1883, Germany enacted legislation to protect workers against the hazards of industrial life. Most European nations adopted old-age insurance after World War I; many provided income support for the disabled and income protection for families after the death of the principal wage earner. In the United States, however, the needs of the elderly and the unemployed were left largely to private organizations and individuals. Although twenty-eight states had old-age assistance programs by 1934, neither private charities nor state and local governments—nor both together—could cope with the prolonged unemployment and distress that resulted from the Great Depression. It became clear that a national policy was necessary to deal with a national crisis.

The first important step came on August 14, 1935, when President Franklin Roosevelt signed the **Social Security Act;** that act is the cornerstone of the modern American welfare state. The act's framers developed

* *Examine your next paycheck stub. It should indicate your contribution to Social Security Tax (SST) and Medicare Tax (MT). SST supports disability, survivors', and retirement benefits. In 1994, it was 6.2 percent of the first $60,600 earned. MT pays for Medicare benefits. In 1994, it was 1.45 percent of all wages. Employers provide matching contributions to SST and MT.*

COMPARED
WITH WHAT? **19.1**   **Social Insurance Programs, 1940-1993**

The number of countries with some form of social insurance program has nearly tripled since 1940. The most widespread type of social security measure is the work-injury program; Americans refer to this type of insurance as *workers' compensation.* Old-age and survivors programs (Americans refer to these as *social security*) are nearly as common. For example, in 1993, 156 countries had a work-injury program; 155 countries had an old-age program.

Sixty-three countries—most of them industrialized nations—now offer some form of unemployment benefits. The number of countries that offer such benefits has increased recently.

Family allowance programs provide regular cash payments to families with children, regardless of need. In some countries, these programs include grants for education and maternal and child health services. In 1993, such programs existed in eighty-two countries, including all the industrialized countries in the world, with one exception: the United States.

• *Source: U.S. Department of Health and Human Services and the Social Security Administration,* Social Insurance Programs Throughout the World—1993 *(Washington, D.C.: U.S. Department of Health and Human Services and the Social Security Administration 1994), p. xxxviii.*

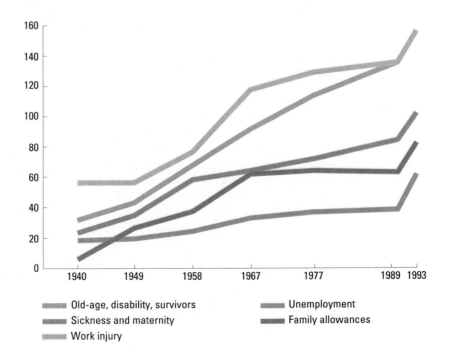

Old-age, disability, survivors

Sickness and maternity

Work injury

Unemployment

Family allowances

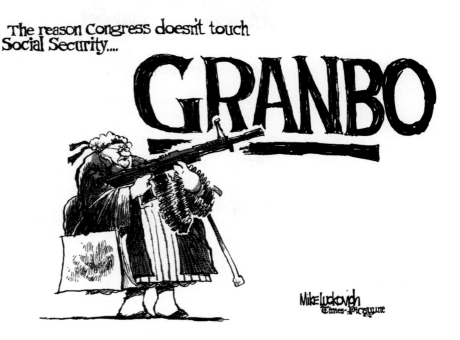

three approaches to the problem of dependence. The first provided social insurance in the form of old-age and surviving-spouse benefits, and cooperative state-national unemployment assistance. To ensure that the elderly did not retire into poverty, it created a program to provide income to retired workers. Its purpose was to guarantee that the elderly had a reliable base income after they stopped working. (Most Americans equate *social security* with this program.) An unemployment insurance program, financed by employers, was also created to provide payments for a limited time to workers who were laid off or dismissed for reasons beyond their control.

The second approach provided aid to the destitute in the form of grants-in-aid to the states. The act represented the first permanent national commitment to provide financial assistance to the needy aged, needy families with dependent children, the blind, and (since the 1950s) the permanently and totally disabled.

The third approach provided health and welfare services through federal aid to the states. Included were health and family services for disabled children and orphans and vocational rehabilitation for the disabled.

How Social Security Works.   Old-age retirement revenue goes into its own *trust fund* (each social security program has a separate fund). The fund is administered by the Social Security Administration; it became an independent government agency in 1995. Trust fund revenue can be spent only for the old-age benefits program. Benefits, in the form of monthly payments, begin when an employee reaches retirement age, which today is sixty-five. (People can retire as early as age sixty-two but with reduced benefits.) The age at which full benefits are paid will increase to sixty-seven after the year 2000.

Many Americans believe that each person's social security contributions are set aside specifically for his or her retirement, like a savings account.[35] But social security doesn't operate quite like that. Instead, the social security taxes collected today pay the benefits of today's retirees. Thus, social security (and social insurance in general) is not a form of savings; it is a pay-as-you-go tax system. Today's workers support today's elderly.

When the social security program began, it had many contributors and few beneficiaries. The program could thus provide relatively large benefits with low taxes. In 1937, for example, the tax rate was 1 percent, and the social security tax of nine workers supported each beneficiary. As the program matured and more people retired, the ratio of workers to recipients decreased. In 1993, the social security system paid benefits to 41.5 million people and collected tax revenues from 133 million, a ratio of only three workers for every beneficiary.[36]

At one time, federal workers, members of Congress, judges, even the president were omitted from the social security system. Today there are few exceptions. Universal participation is essential for the system to operate, because it is a tax program, not a savings program. If participation were not compulsory, there would not be enough revenue to provide benefits to current retirees. Government—the only institution that can coerce—requires all employees and their employers to contribute, thereby imposing restrictions on freedom.

Those people who currently pay into the system will receive retirement benefits financed by future participants. As with a pyramid scheme or a chain letter, success depends on the growth of the base. If the birthrate remains steady or grows, future wage earners will be able to support today's contributors when they retire. If the economy expands, there will be more jobs, more income, and a growing wage base to tax for increased benefits to retirees. But suppose the birthrate falls, or unemployment rises and the economy falters? Then contributions could decline to the point at which benefits exceed revenues. The pyramidal character of social security is its Achilles' heel, as Figure 19.2 shows.

Who Pays? Who Benefits?   "Who pays?" and "Who benefits?" are always important questions in government policymaking, and they continue to shape social security policy. In 1968, the Republican party platform called for automatic increases in social security payments as the cost of living rose. The theory was simple: As the cost of living rises, so should retirement benefits; otherwise, benefits are paid in "shrinking dollars" that buy less and less. Cost-of-living adjustments (COLAs) became a political football in 1969 as Democrats and Republicans tried to outdo each other by suggesting larger increases for retirees. The result was a significant expansion in benefits, far in excess of the cost of living. The beneficiaries were the retired, who were beginning to flex their political muscle. Politicians knew that alienating this constituency could change an election.[37]

In 1972, Congress adopted automatic adjustments in benefits and in the dollar amount of contributors' wages subject to tax, so that revenue would expand as benefits grew. This approach set social security on automatic pilot. When inflation exceeds 3 percent, the automatic adjustment goes into effect. (Politicians sometimes fear retribution at the polls if there is no annual adjustment. Although it appeared that inflation would fall below 3 percent in 1986, Congress authorized an adjustment for that year.)

| FIGURE 19.2 | ■ Ratio of Workers to Beneficiaries in the Social Security System |

Demographers predict a steady decline in the ratio of workers to social security beneficiaries starting in the year 2000. By 2030, there will be only two workers for every beneficiary. If current revenue continues to pay current benefits, it is a sure bet that social security taxes will increase or benefits will decrease as the worker-beneficiary ratio falls.

Source: Social Security Administration Board of Trustees, "Federal Old-Age and Survivors Insurance and Disability Insurance Trust Funds," 1985 Annual Report, *Table 29, p. 65.*

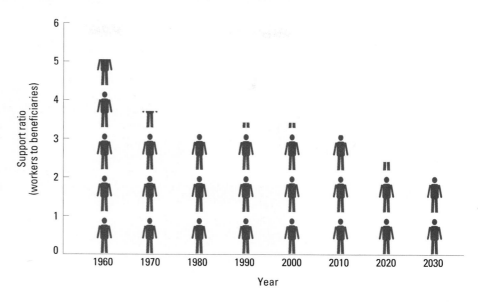

Then, when stagflation (high unemployment coupled with high inflation) took hold in the 1970s, it jeopardized the entire social security system. Stagflation gripped the social security system in an economic vise: Unemployment meant a reduction in revenue; high inflation meant automatically growing benefits. This one-two punch drained social security trust fund reserves to critically low levels in the late 1970s and early 1980s. Meanwhile, other troubling factors were becoming clear. A lower birthrate means that in the future, fewer workers will support the pool of retirees. And the number of retirees will grow as average life spans lengthen and the baby-boom generation retires. Higher taxes—an unpopular political move—loomed as one alternative. Another was to pay for social security out of general revenues, that is, income taxes. Social security would then become a public assistance program, similar to welfare. In 1983, shortly before existing social security benefit funds were exhausted, Congress and President Reagan agreed to a solution that called for two painful adjustments: increased taxes and reduced benefits.

The changes enacted in 1983 may have saved the social security system. However, future economic conditions will determine its success or failure. Despite various revenue-generating plans, higher taxes or lower benefits may be the only means for ensuring the viability of social security.[38]

Today, few argue against the need for social security. But debate surrounds the extent of coverage and the level of benefits. "The [Social Security] Act is the most successful program of the modern state," declared Nobel Prize laureate Paul Samuelson. Yet Milton Friedman, another Nobel laureate and social security opponent, labeled the act "a sacred cow that no politician can criticize." How can two renowned economists maintain such dramatically different views? Samuelson is a liberal in the Keynesian tradition; he favors equality over freedom. According to

Life Begins at Sixty-five

Old age and impoverishment used to go hand in hand but not any more. Because of social security, people aged sixty-five and older are the second-richest age group in the United States. Only Americans aged fifty-five to sixty-four are better off. One political economist recently estimated that the government spends about $350 billion on the aged, more than on national defense. Today's elderly remain vulnerable to impoverishment only if they need long-term nursing home care.

his view, social security lifted the elderly from destitution by redistributing income from workers (who have growing incomes) to the elderly (who have little or no income). Friedman is a libertarian and a monetarist; he favors freedom over equality. Because social security limits freedom in order to provide economic equality, Friedman would no doubt prefer that the program be scaled back or even eliminated. However, the political risks associated with social security cutbacks are too great for most politicians to bear.

As a group, older Americans exercise enormous political power. People at or near retirement age now comprise almost 30 percent of the potential electorate, and voter turnout among older Americans is reported to be about twice that of younger people.[39] These facts help explain the stability of social security and the expansion of health care for the elderly.

Medicare

In 1962, the Senate considered extending social security benefits to provide hospitalization and medical care for the elderly. In opposing the extension, Democratic senator Russell Long of Louisiana declared, "We are not staring at a sweet old lady in bed with her kimono and nightcap. We are looking into the eyes of the wolf that ate Red Riding Hood's grandma."[40] Long was concerned that costs would soar without limit. Other opponents echoed the fears of the American Medical Association (AMA), which saw virtually any form of government-provided medical care as a step toward government control of medicine. Long and his compatriots won the battle that day. Three years later, however, the Social Security Act was amended to provide **Medicare,** health care for all people aged sixty-five and older.

Origins of Medicare.   As early as 1945, public opinion clearly supported some form of national health insurance. However, that idea became entangled in Cold War politics—the growing crusade against communism in America.[41] The AMA, representing the nation's physicians, mounted and financed an all-out campaign to link national health insurance (so-called socialized medicine) with socialism; the campaign was so successful that the prospect of a national health policy vanished.

Both proponents and opponents of national health insurance tried to link their positions to deeply rooted American values: Advocates emphasized equality and fairness; opponents stressed individual freedom. In the absence of a clear mandate on the kind of insurance (publicly funded or private) the public wanted, the AMA was able to marshal political influence to prevent any national insurance at all.[42]

By 1960, however, the terms of the debate had changed. Its focus was no longer fixed on the clash of freedom and equality. Now the issue of health insurance was cast in terms of providing assistance to the aged, and a ground swell of support forced it onto the national agenda.[43]

The Democratic victory in 1964 and the advent of President Johnson's Great Society made some form of national health policy almost inevitable. On July 30, 1965, Johnson signed a bill that provided a number of health benefits to the elderly and the poor. Fearful of the AMA's power to punish its opponents, the Democrats had confined their efforts to a compulsory hospitalization-insurance plan for the elderly. (This is known today as Part A of Medicare.) In addition, the bill contained a version of an alternative Republican plan, which called for voluntary government-subsidized insurance to cover physician's fees. (This is known today as Part B of Medicare.) A third program, added a year later, is called *Medicaid*; it provides medical aid to the poor through federally assisted state health programs. Medicaid is need-based comprehensive medical and hospitalization program: If you are poor, you qualify. Medicaid today covers 31.1 million people at a cost in 1992 exceeding $114 billion.[44]

Medicare Today.   Part A of Medicare is compulsory insurance that covers certain hospital services for people aged sixty-five and older. Workers pay a tax; retirees pay premiums deducted from social security payments. Payments for necessary services are made by the national government directly to participating hospitals and other qualifying facilities. In 1992, more than 35 million people were enrolled in Part A, and the government paid nearly $84 billion in benefits.[45]

Part B of Medicare is a voluntary program of medical insurance for people aged sixty-five and older who pay the premiums. The insurance covers the services of physicians and other qualified providers. In 1992, nearly 34 million people were enrolled; the government spent more than $49 billion for Part B benefits of which about $15 billion came from enrollees. In 1993, the monthly premium for this insurance was $36.60.[46]

The fears that Senator Long voiced in 1962 approached reality in the 1980s: Medicare costs soared out of control. By 1986, Medicare costs exceeded $75 billion, representing a fourfold increase in ten years. For the moment, Medicare is solvent, thanks to modest payroll tax increases and low unemployment, but the program lacks a financial cushion. Spending reductions (through curtailed benefits) or income increases (through raised taxes) are still viable, although politically unpalatable, alternatives.[47]

Medicare costs continue to increase at rates well in excess of the cost of living. Consequently, government has sought to contain those costs. One attempt at cost containment makes use of economic incentives in the hospital treatment of Medicare patients. The plan seems to have had the desired economic benefits, but it raises questions about the endangerment of the health of elderly patients. Medicare payments to hospitals had been based on the length of a patient's stay; the longer the stay, the more revenue the hospitals earned. This approach encouraged longer, more expensive hospital stays, because the government was paying the bill. In 1985, however, the government switched to a new payment system under which hospitals are paid a fixed fee based on the patient's diagnosis. If the patient's stay costs more than the fee schedule allows, the hospital pays the difference. On the other hand, if the hospital treats a patient for less than the fixed fee, the hospital reaps the profit. This new system provides an incentive for hospitals to discharge patients sooner, perhaps in some cases before they are completely well.

Health Care for Everyone

Medicare provides health care for the elderly. Medicaid provides health care for the poor. Yet the United States is the only major industrialized nation without a universal health-care system. Nearly everyone maintains that the health-care system needs fixing. Let's consider the two main problems.

First, many Americans have no health insurance. In 1992, 37 million Americans—that's about 15 percent of the nonelderly population—were uninsured on any given day. They are uninsured because either their employers do not provide health insurance or the cost of health insurance is prohibitive. In 1993, the average annual family premium for employer-based group health insurance was $5,200, which was more than double the average premium in 1988. Compounding the problem is the risk that a job change or job loss may entail losing health insurance coverage.

Second, the cost of health care is rising faster by far than the cost of living. The United States spends far more money on health than any other nation. Today, we spend more than $800 billion a year on health care, or 14 percent of the gross domestic product. Without some cost containment, health-care costs will exceed 18 percent of GDP by the year 2000.

The American public remains divided on the remedy. The Clinton administration has held firm to its objective of universal coverage, but none of the various approaches to this end has the support of a majority of Americans. Moreover, there is no clear sense of how to pay for the increased cost that any plan will entail. Half the public is prepared to pay higher taxes to assure universal coverage, but the only taxes that generate strong support are "sin" taxes on alcohol and cigarettes. Yet these taxes are insufficient to pay for the comprehensive coverage Americans want. In summarizing the array of data on health care reform, a commentator remarked, "We want the government to reform our health care system, but we lack a shared vision of what that system should be or how to achieve it."[48]

The two central problems of health care give rise to two key goals and a familiar dilemma. First, any reform should democratize health care, that is, make health care available to everyone. But by providing broad access to medical care, we will increase the amount we spend on such care. Second, any reform must control the ballooning cost of health care. But controlling cost requires restricting the range of procedures and providers. Thus, the health-care issue goes to the heart of the modern dilemma of government. We must weigh greater equality in terms of universal coverage and cost controls against a loss of freedom in markets for health care and in choosing a doctor.

The Clinton Administration's effort at health care reform started boldly in September 1993 with a plan for the total overhaul of the system. Hundreds of experts under the direction of Hillary Rodham Clinton conceived the plan. It weighed in at a hefty 1,300 pages. Their version called for universal coverage and cost controls. But universal coverage necessarily meant more taxes and cost controls implied limits on consumer behavior. In short, reforming health care was no free lunch. It became an easy target for critics, and criticism there was aplenty.

The plan proved both appealing and appalling to key interest groups: small businesses, the insurance industry, and the doctors. There was something in it for each of them to support and to oppose. By August 1994—just one year following its introduction—the administration proposal was dead, a victim of the old adage that "it is easier to stop what you're against than to achieve what you are for."

POLICIES THAT PROVIDE: PUBLIC ASSISTANCE

Public assistance is what most people mean when they use the terms *welfare* or *welfare payments;* it is government aid to individuals who can demonstrate a need for that aid. Public assistance is directed toward those who lack the ability or the resources to provide for themselves or their families.

Public assistance programs instituted under the Social Security Act are known today as *categorical assistance programs.* They include (1) old-age assistance for the needy elderly not covered by old-age pension benefits, (2) aid to the needy blind, (3) aid to needy families with dependent children, and (4) aid to the totally and permanently disabled. Adopted initially as stopgap measures during the Depression, these programs have become entitlements. They are administered by the states, but the bulk of the funding comes from the national government's general tax revenues. Because the states also contribute to the funding of their public assistance programs, the benefits vary widely from state to state.

Poverty and Public Assistance

The national government imposes national standards on state welfare programs. It distributes funds to each state based on the proportion of its population living in poverty. That proportion is, in turn, determined on the basis of a national **poverty level,** or poverty threshold, which is the minimum cash income that will provide for a family's basic needs. The poverty level varies by family size and is calculated as three times the cost of an economy food plan, a market basket of food that provides a minimally nutritious diet. (The threshold is computed in this way because research sug-

Boxed In, Boxed Out

Most observers agree that homelessness is increasing, but there is little reliable information about the scope and causes of the problem. Some advocates for the homeless attribute the increase to the national economy and the lack of affordable housing; others cite the deinstitutionalization of the mentally ill. With nowhere to go, the homeless are always in sight.

gests that poor families of three or more persons spend approximately one-third of their income on food.*)

The poverty level is fairly simple to apply, but it is only a rough measure for distinguishing the poor from the nonpoor. Using it is like using a wrench as a hammer: It works but not very well. We attach importance to the poverty level, despite its inaccuracies, because measuring poverty is a means of measuring how the American promise of equality stands up against the performance of our public policies. In 1992, the government calculated that nearly 37 million people, or 14.5 percent of the population, were living in poverty in the United States.

The poverty level is adjusted each year to reflect changes in consumer prices. In 1993, the poverty threshold for a family of four was cash income below $14,350.[49] This is income *before* taxes. If the poverty threshold were defined as disposable income (income *after* taxes), the proportion of the population categorized as living in poverty would increase.

Some critics believe that factors other than income should be considered in computing the poverty level. Assets (home, cars, possessions), for example, are excluded from the definition. Also, the computation fails to

---

* *Although it has been the source of endless debate, today's definition of poverty retains remarkable similarity to its precursors. As early as 1795, a group of English magistrates "decided that a minimum income should be the cost of a gallon loaf of bread, multiplied by 3, plus an allowance for each dependent." See Alvin L. Schorr, "Redefining Poverty Levels,"* New York *Times, 9 May 1984, p. 27.*

take into account such noncash benefits as food stamps, health benefits (Medicaid), and subsidized housing. Presumably, the inclusion of these noncash benefits as income would reduce the number of individuals seen as living below the poverty level.

The graphic in Politics in a Changing America 19.1 shows that the poverty rate in the United States has declined since the mid 1960s. It rose again slightly in the early 1980s, then declined slightly and now is just shy of 15 percent. Blacks and whites have progressed about equally. Nevertheless, in 1992 poverty was still the economic condition of one in nine whites, one in three blacks, and one in four Hispanics. Poverty retains a growing hold on the American population.

Poverty was once a condition of old age. Social security changed that. Today, the likelihood of poverty is still related to age, but in the opposite direction: Poverty is largely a predicament of the young. Twenty-two percent of persons younger than eighteen live in poverty.[50]

It is relatively easy to draw a portrait of the poor; it is much more difficult to craft policies that move them out of destitution. Critics of social welfare spending argue that antipoverty policies have made poverty more attractive by removing incentives to work. They believe these policies, which aim to provide for the poor, have actually promoted poverty.

Another explanation for the failure of government policies to reduce poverty rests on changes in racial attitudes. In the 1960s, racial barriers kept the black middle class in the same urban ghettos as the poor. The middle class's presence provided social stability, role models, and community institutions and businesses. Then the decline of racial barriers allowed middle-class blacks to move out of the ghetto. As a result, the inner city became increasingly poor and increasingly dependent on welfare.[51]

Assistance to the Needy: AFDC and Food Stamps

The biggest public assistance program is **Aid to Families with Dependent Children (AFDC),** which was created by the 1935 Social Security Act. Each month, almost 4 million families (or roughly 11 million individuals) receive benefits through AFDC; it is the major source of government cash assistance to low-income children and their families. AFDC benefits are distributed in cash through the states. In 1991, the AFDC program cost $20.9 billion: $11.3 billion paid by the national government and $9.6 billion paid by the states.[52]

The typical AFDC family lives in a large urban area and consists of a mother younger than thirty and two children younger than eight. More than half of AFDC recipients are white; 40 percent are black. Eligibility for AFDC automatically qualifies recipients for Medicaid and other forms of public assistance. However, recipients must first go through a complicated qualifying process, because government is very wary of giving money to people who might in any way be regarded as undeserving. The process has four parts, which are illustrated in Figure 19.3.

- Family Composition Test. In general, an applicant for AFDC benefits must be a single parent living with at least one child younger than age eighteen. In half the states, recipients can be married, but the principal wage earner must be unemployed.

FIGURE 19.3	■ AFDC Qualification Process

A family seeking AFDC benefits must complete a four-step process. Some steps vary from state to state.
Source: Tom Joe and Cheryl Rogers, By the Few,

For the Few: The Reagan Welfare Legacy (Lexington, Mass.: Lexington Books, 1985), p. 25. © 1985, Lexington Books. Reprinted by permission of the authors.

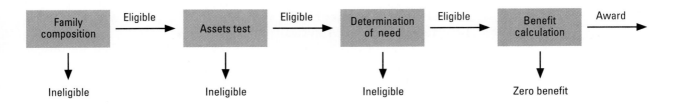

- Assets Test (varies by state). Assets are savings, clothing, and furniture. The national government sets a limit on the value of the assets an AFDC family can possess (in 1994, it was $1,000). Equity in an automobile cannot exceed $4,500. States can impose stricter asset limits.

- Determination of need (varies by state). A family is considered in need if its income is below a "need standard" set by each state. In Cook County, Illinois, for example, the need standard for a three-person family in 1994 was $890 a month. Only families with incomes below the need standard qualify for benefits.

- Benefit calculation (varies by state). Each state establishes a payment standard for determining benefits. (The payment standard is not identical to the need standard, and in half the states the payment standard is lower than the need standard.) For qualifying families, the difference between the payment standard and the family income is the AFDC benefit. In 1994, the typical AFDC grant for a one-parent family of three in Cook County, Illinois, was $377 a month (plus automatic Medicaid eligibility and a maximum of $295 in food stamps).

Inflation raises the poverty level, but eligibility for AFDC has remained stationary. In 1994, in order to qualify for AFDC (and Medicaid), a family's income could be, on average, no more than about half of the poverty level. So although many families are poor according to the poverty level, they are not poor enough to qualify for cash assistance or medical care.

The original purpose of AFDC was to provide assistance to fatherless families, enabling mothers to rear their children full time. But a growing chorus of critics argued that AFDC policies encouraged dependence on welfare. A recipient who took a job did not have to earn very much before losing all benefits. In some states, for example, full-time employment at the minimum wage meant an end to public assistance. However, re-

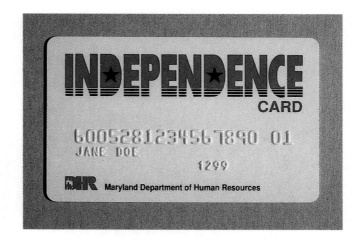

The Dole Card: Don't Be Homeless Without It

The national government is experimenting with a new means of distributing welfare benefits: ATM cards. Independence Card-holders simply use their cards in machines at banks and grocery stores to obtain cash or draw against a food stamp account. Officials hope the new system will reduce administrative costs and recipient fraud. The stigma and inconvenience traditionally associated with welfare may also be reduced; some critics view the latter result as a disadvantage, believing stigma and inconvenience serve a purpose by helping keep people off welfare.

searchers found that mandatory employment and training programs (also known as *workfare*) were moderately successful in ending welfare's grip on the poor. Model workfare programs in Massachusetts, Maryland, and California increased the average earnings of female participants, assured social contributions from recipients in return for public assistance, and may have discouraged dependence on welfare.[53] This evidence moved Congress to overhaul the nation's welfare system in 1988 by enacting the Family Support Act.

The central provision of the Family Support Act of 1988 requires most welfare recipients whose children are older than three to participate in state-approved work, education, or training programs. To smooth the transition between welfare and work, the states must provide child care and health insurance during the training period and continue this assistance for as long as one year after the recipient has found a job. The reforms will cost the states and the national government more than $3.3 billion for the first five years; the effects of the new law will take years to materialize.

Unfortunately, some preliminary evidence suggests that these effects are likely to be trivial. According to the Congressional Budget Office, the reform that was supposed to "turn the welfare system upside down" will prompt only about fifty thousand families (or about 1.3 percent of the current welfare case load) to leave the welfare system.[54]

The high expectations inherent in the law have already run afoul of brutal budget facts. Some states, such as Massachusetts and Minnesota, have found that the only way to provide mandated benefits for those on welfare is to reduce benefits for the working poor. Ironically, this has forced some working poor parents to quit their jobs and return to the welfare rolls, at

FIGURE 19.4   ■ Number of Welfare Recipients, 1970–1993

Aid to Families with Dependent Children (AFDC) is the cornerstone of the nation's welfare policy. In 1993, benefits of more than $22 billion went to more than 14 million people of which nearly 10 million were children.

Source: Data from Department of Health and Human Services, Congressional Research Service, January 1994. From Congressional Quarterly, *January 22, 1994 issue, page 121. Copyright © 1994 by Congressional Quarterly, Inc. Used with permission.*

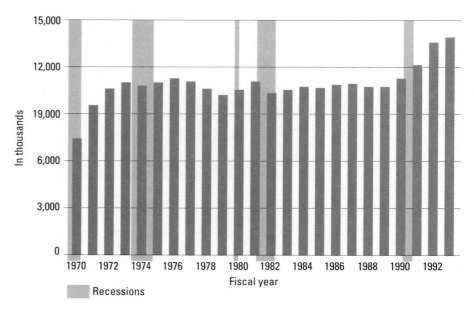

much greater public expense.[55] The average yearly enrollment in AFDC climbed from 11 million persons in 1989 to more than 14 million in 1993,[56] as shown in Figure 19.4.

What is to be done? Renewed public antipathy toward the welfare system resonated in Bill Clinton's presidential campaign. As a candidate, Clinton vowed to "end welfare as we know it." His plan, unveiled in mid-1994, would expand training programs for the adult members of the 5 million households that depend on welfare. The heart of Clinton's plan is a two-year limit on benefits. It would require those still on the welfare rolls after two years to join a work program, which would offer subsidized jobs at the prevailing minimum wage. Those who refused work would receive no further support. Can the combination of job training and time limits change the lives of welfare recipients? When he unveiled his program, the president said in a moment of candor, "Let's be honest. None of this will be easy to accomplish."[57] A skeptic of reform remarked, "We simply don't have a way to make work pay for a high school dropout with two children. It can't be done."[58]

The national government's **food stamp program** aims to improve the diets of low-income households by supplementing their food-purchasing power. The nationally funded program is administered through local agencies, which distribute the stamps to needy individuals and families. The stamps are actually coupons that can be used to purchase any food meant for human consumption.

The AFDC and food stamp programs are structured to work jointly. AFDC benefits vary from state to state, but food stamp benefits are set nationally. In states that offer lower AFDC benefits, participants receive larger food stamp allotments. In 1992, the food stamp program cost the government nearly $21 billion. More than 25 million participants (one in ten Americans) received an average of $69 a month in food stamps.[59]

BENEFITS AND FAIRNESS

Ronald Reagan once observed, "In the war on poverty, poverty won." Americans tend to agree. About half of all Americans believe the liberal welfare policies of the 1960s made things "somewhat better" for the poor; only 10 percent maintain that those policies made the poor much better off.[60] But more than 90 percent of Americans seem convinced that poverty will remain a persistent problem, partly because, more than 70 percent believe, government doesn't know enough about how to eliminate poverty.[61]

The national government provides many Americans with benefits. There are two kinds of benefits: cash, such as a retiree's social security check, or noncash, such as food stamps. Some benefits are conditional. **Means-tested benefits** impose an income test to qualify. For example, free or low-cost school lunch programs and Pell college grants are available to households that have an income that falls below a designated threshold. **Non-means-tested benefits** impose no such income test; benefits such as Medicare and social security are available to all, regardless of income.

Some Americans question the fairness of non-means-tested benefits. After all, benefits are subsidies, and some people need them more than others. If the size of the benefit pie remains fixed because of large budget deficits, imposing means tests on more benefits has real allure. For example, all elderly people now receive the same Medicare benefits, regardless of income. Fairness advocates maintain that the affluent elderly should shoulder a higher share of Medicare costs, shifting more benefits to the low-income elderly. If the idea of shifting benefits gains support in the future, debate will focus on the income level below which a program will apply.

In the long run, understanding the consequences of public policy will help reduce poverty in America. For the moment, however, debates among scholars and policymakers offer no comfort to Nicholas Whitiker and children such as he, who confront the daily reality of inner-city violence, hunger, and despair.

SUMMARY

Public policies fulfill one or more purposes: protection, prohibition, provision, and promotion. Often, disagreements about public policy are disagreements about values. Choices between freedom and order are at the heart of many policies such as mandatory AIDS or drug testing. Choices between freedom and equality are at the heart of other policies, such as those designed to ease inner-city poverty.

Many domestic policies that provide benefits to individuals and promote economic equality were instituted during the Great Depression. Today, government plays an active role in providing benefits to the poor, the elderly, and the disabled. The object of these domestic policies is to alleviate conditions that individuals are powerless to prevent. This is the social welfare function of the modern state. The call for health-care reform for all Americans is but a reflection of the modern dilemma of democracy: universal coverage and costs controls versus a loss in freedom in health-care choices.

Government confers benefits on individuals through social insurance and public assistance. Social insurance is not based on need; public assistance (welfare) hinges on proof of need. In one form of social insurance—old-age benefits—a tax on current workers pays retired workers' benefits. Aid for the poor, by contrast, comes from government's general tax revenues. Although the current welfare system has few defenders, clear solutions to the problem of welfare dependence have yet to emerge. In contrast, the food stamp program has proved successful by improving the diet of low-income Americans.

Programs to aid the elderly and the poor have been gradually transformed into entitlements, or rights that accrue to eligible persons. These government programs have reduced poverty among some groups, especially the elderly. However, poverty retains a grip on certain segments of the population. Social and demographic changes have feminized poverty, and there is little prospect of reversing that trend any time soon.

Some government subsidy programs provide means-tested benefits wherein eligibility hinges on income. Non-means-tested benefits are available to all, regardless of income. As the demand for such benefits exceeds available resources, policymakers have come to question their fairness. Subsidies for rich and poor alike are the basis for a broad national consensus. A departure from that consensus in the name of fairness may very well be the next challenge of democracy.

Key Terms

public policy	Medicare
welfare state	public assistance
social welfare	poverty level
Great Depression	"feminization of poverty"
New Deal	Aid to Families with
Great Society	Dependent Children
War on Poverty	(AFDC)
social insurance	food stamp program
entitlements	means-tested benefits
social security	non-means-tested
Social Security Act	benefits

Selected Readings

Bennett, Linda L. M., and Stephen Earl Bennett. *Living with Leviathan: Americans Coming to Terms with Big Government.* Lawrence: University Press of Kansas, 1990. An analysis of public opinion about the powers and responsibilities of national government, from Franklin Roosevelt to Ronald Reagan.

Berry, Jeffrey M. *Feeding Hungry People: Rulemaking in the Food Stamp Program.* New Brunswick, N.J.: Rutgers University Press, 1984. A thorough examination of the evolution of the food stamp program, especially the relationships among Congress, the Department of Agriculture, and interest groups.

Ellwood, David T. *Poor Support: Poverty in the American Family.* New York: Basic Books, 1988. Ellwood agrees with Murray's analysis but argues for incentives to break the grip of poverty. Ellwood's ideas are part of the Clinton's adminstration's effort "to end welfare as we know it."

Goldberg, Gertrude Schaffner, and Eleanor Kremen, eds. *The Feminization of Poverty: Only in America?* New York: Greenwood, 1990. This cohesive study of poverty among females in seven capitalist and socialist countries argues that the feminization of poverty is not unique to the United States.

Katz, Michael B. *The Undeserving Poor: From the War on Poverty to the War on Welfare.* New York: Pantheon, 1989. A historical overview of the ideas and assumptions that shaped policies toward the poor from the 1960s through the 1980s.

Kotlowitz, Alex. *There Are No Children Here: The Story of Two Boys Growing Up in the Other America* (New York: Doubleday, 1991). The riveting story of two young brothers and their family in Chicago's Henry Horner Homes, a public housing project plagued by crime, drugs, and neglect.

Maney, Ardith L. *Still Hungry After All These Years: Food Assistance Policy from Kennedy to Reagan.* Westport, Conn.: Greenwood, 1989. A carefully documented and well-reasoned analysis of one of the important legacies of the Great Society. Maney examines the motivations and consequences of food assistance policies through six presidential administrations.

Marmor, Theodore, and Jerry L. Mashaw, eds. *Social Security: Beyond the Rhetoric of Crisis.* Princeton, N.J.: Princeton University Press, 1988. This collection of essays and studies examines the future of social security in light of profound social and economic change.

Murray, Charles. *Losing Ground.* New York: Basic Books, 1985. An assessment of American social policy from 1950 to 1980. Murray argues that by attempting to remove the barriers to the good life for the poor, policymakers have created a poverty trap. Controversial in its day, Murray's analysis is taken as received wisdom today.

Starr, Paul. *The Social Transformation of American Medicine.* New York: Basic Books, 1982. The definitive work on the evolution of the American health-care system of doctors, hospitals, health plans, and government programs.

Starr, Paul. *The Logic of Health-Care Reform.* Grand Rounds Press/Whittle Direct Books, 1993. An articulate defense of the Clinton Administration's efforts by one of its principal architects.

Wilson, William Julius. *The Truly Disadvantaged: The Inner City, the Underclass, and Public Policy.* Chicago: University of Chicago Press, 1987. Wilson argues that the decay of the inner city cannot be explained by racism alone and targets the class structure of ghetto neighborhoods as the most important factor in a complex web of reasons.

CHAPTER 20

Global Policy

THE COLD WAR OFFICIALLY ENDED on November 21, 1990. On that day, leaders of thirty-four nations proclaimed the end of the "era of confrontation and division" that followed World War II. Adding his signature to the Charter of Paris for a New Europe, President George Bush said for the first time, "The Cold War is over."[1]

The **Cold War,** an intense rivalry between the U.S.-led Western alliance and Eastern European nations controlled by the former Soviet Union, had shaped global politics for more than four decades. Its end came into view late in 1988 when Soviet president Mikhail Gorbachev, squeezed by economic troubles, began military cutbacks. Soviet control over Eastern European countries soon disintegrated. One after another, the peoples of Poland, Hungary, Czechoslovakia, East Germany, and Romania ousted communist governments and proclaimed their commitment to freedom and democracy. The menacing Berlin Wall, for thirty years the most prominent symbol of East-West confrontation, came down late in 1989. East and West Germany had unified only weeks before the Paris meeting.

The leaders who gathered in Paris in 1990 signed agreements promoting human rights, democracy, the free market, and the rule of law. In addition, twenty-two nations from the opposing Cold War blocs accepted a far-reaching arms reduction agreement. This was cause for jubilation—the greatest threat to global security seemed to have passed. In the wake of the Cold War, President Bush hoped for the creation of a "new world order."

Hopes for a new era of worldwide peace and stability were short lived. Within two months of the Charter of Paris, the United States and twenty-seven other nations found themselves at war with Iraq in the Persian Gulf. Although that conflict resulted in the swift defeat of Iraqi forces, some twenty-nine other major armed conflicts still were going on around the world.[2] In the three years after the fall of communism, United Nations forces became involved in fourteen peacekeeping missions—as many as the U.N. had undertaken in the previous forty-three years.[3] By 1993, American forces sent to feed hungry Somalians had come under fire from local warlords, and President Bill Clinton found himself threatening to launch air strikes against Bosnian Serbs in the former Yugoslavia. Closer to home, the United States was frustrated in its efforts to restore democracy in Haiti. In short, the post–Cold War world seemed anything but orderly.

Although the end of the Cold War did not herald world peace, it did bring

697

The Cold War Ends

The Berlin Wall, a concrete barrier erected in 1961 by East Germany to separate East and West Berlin, symbolized the Cold War. November 9, 1989, marked the unofficial end to cold war tensions when East Germany gave its citizens the right to travel to West Berlin. Joyous demonstrators scaled the wall, which was later dismantled. The official end to the Cold War came on November 21, 1990, when President Bush signed the Charter of Paris for a New Europe.

about fundamental changes in the context of international politics. The approaches to foreign policy crafted during the Cold War no longer fit, and policymakers often appeared to be floundering as they tried to redefine Americas goals in the arena of world politics. New issues came into prominence. During the Cold War, issues of war, peace, and military security (sometimes called **high politics**) tended to dominate the nation's foreign policy agenda. In the post–Cold War world, global economic and environmental problems (or **low politics**) received more attention. Furthermore, as U.S. policymakers pondered the nation's role in world politics, they did so amid signs that Americans wanted their leaders to concentrate less on foreign affairs and more on domestic issues such as recession and unemployment.[4]

The handling of foreign policy in a democracy has long been a subject of debate. Many have argued that foreign policy, which concerns dealings with nations and peoples outside the United States, requires a degree of unity rarely found in domestic politics. People disagree about foreign policies, because they differ about the goals government should adopt, the means to reach them, and the nature of a given situation. Although vigorous discussion is usually thought to show vitality in a democracy, some people think it can lead to problems in foreign policy. Because foreign policy often involves high stakes—matters of national security and defense from outside threats—some argue that "politics should stop at the water's edge." As far back as 1837, Alexis de Tocqueville, French political thinker and observer of the American scene, noted that certain features inherent in democracies could cause problems in the area of foreign policy:

Foreign politics demand scarcely any of those qualities which are peculiar to a democracy; they require, on the contrary, the perfect use of almost all those in which it is deficient. . . . A democracy can only with great diffi-

The New World Order Begins

The Cold War stand off between the superpowers ended but world peace did not result. In fact, UN blue-helmeted peace-keeping troops were deployed in more nations than ever before. These soldiers are trying to restore order in Bosnia.

culty regulate the details of an important undertaking, persevere in a fixed design, and work out its execution in spite of severe obstacles. It cannot combine its measures with secrecy or await their consequences with patience.[5]

As Tocqueville predicted, the workings of foreign policy have challenged American democracy. During the Cold War especially, some observers insisted that foreign policy should be free of the democratic wrangling that characterized domestic policymaking. In the aftermath of World War II, faced with a communist threat spearheaded by the Soviet Union, the United States forged a foreign policy consensus built on bipartisanship and strong presidential leadership. That consensus broke down during the Vietnam era amid doubts about the nature of the threat and the means appropriate to counter it. Divided government and power struggles between the president and Congress intensified the breakdown. In the post–Cold War era, signs have already appeared that future U.S. foreign policy may be highly politicized and that the new configurations of opinion may not fall along predictable party lines. Also, as issues of low politics increase in importance, it will be hard to draw clear distinctions between domestic and foreign policy. The **North American Free Trade Agreement (NAFTA),** for instance, pertains to international relations with Mexico and Canada, but, as we noted in Chapter 11, it also involves American jobs. More and more, foreign policy issues are likely to be **intermestic**—a blend of international and domestic concerns, as discussed in Politics in a Changing America 20.1.

Does more democracy make for bad foreign policy? Is it possible for a democracy to achieve its goals around the globe without compromising its domestic political process? Specifically, can America pursue freedom, order, and equality abroad without undermining these values at home?

POLITICS IN A CHANGING AMERICA 20.1

Immigration Policy and Foreign Policy—Who Comes in the Golden Door

When Bill Clinton campaigned for the presidency, he criticized as cruel the Bush administration's policy of returning Haitian boat people to Haiti rather than allowing them to seek political asylum in the United States. As president, Clinton himself continued the Bush policy and refused to end the ban on Haitian immigration until mid-1994, when, pressured by the hunger strike of political activist Randall Robinson, he relented and ordered U.S. vessels to screen Haitian refugees and not repatriate those who had a well-founded fear of political reprisals.

Clinton's vacillation on the Haitian issue points up the fact that although the United States is a nation of immigrants, immigration policy has often been a political hot potato. It is also a classic domestic vs. global policy issue. The question of whom to let inside the "golden door" is important for both domestic and global politics. Should our support for human rights lead us to open the door wide for those fleeing political oppression? What about those fleeing poverty? What about our own citizens who fear that immigrants may take their jobs?

Until 1882, immigration was virtually unrestricted. The nation welcomed newcomers, who helped make continental expansion a reality; approximately one out of every seven people living in the United States was foreign born. In 1882, Congress enacted the first immigration law, which, among other things, excluded Chinese immigrants. In 1921, a new law established quotas on immigration from overseas. (There was no quota on immigrants from other nations in the Western hemisphere.) By setting the limit for each country at 3 percent of the number of that nationality already living in the United States, the quota act had the effect of limiting ethnic and cultural diversity. The formula heavily favored Northern and Western Europeans; it penalized Eastern and Southern Europeans; it virtually excluded Asians and Africans. This system was not changed until the 1960s.

After the United States moved to limit the number of immigrants admitted, it established a special category, outside the regular immigration quotas, for those fleeing political oppression. After World War II, under the Displaced Persons Act, the United States admitted hundreds of thousands of European refugees outside the quotas. As part of America's Cold War strategy, people fleeing communist countries could jump the quota queue and seek political asylum; among these were many Hungarians in the 1950s, Cubans in the 1960s, and Vietnamese in the 1970s.

Still, the percentage of foreign-born people living in the United States decreased. By 1970, only about one in every twenty residents had been born outside the country. But in the 1970s and 80s, immigration, legal and illegal, increased. In 1990, Congress responded with the Immigration Reform and Control Act, which provided amnesty for illegal immigrants already in the United States, eased legal immigration, and cracked down on employers who hired illegals. Today, one in every twelve U.S. residents is foreign born. Nearly 1 million immigrants and refugees

This chapter examines these questions. We focus on the foreign policy-making process in America and the strains it places on democratic government. Also, we discuss the division of responsibility for foreign policy among the branches of government and the effect this division has on the policymaking process. Finally, we consider new challenges to U.S. foreign policy in the realms of high and low politics.

enter the country legally each year. Who are today's immigrants? Until the 1950s, some two-thirds of legal immigrants came from Canada and Europe, but by the 1980s that had changed. The percentage of immigrants from Europe shrank to 14 percent, whereas Asians climbed to 44 percent and Latin Americans to 40 percent of new arrivals admitted legally.

In addition to those arriving legally, many hundreds of thousands of immigrants arrive illegally—as many as 3 million a year across the Mexican border. Yet, most of them do not expect to stay permanently. Tales of Mexicans streaming across the border and Haitians and Asians trying to sneak in by boat have captured media attention, but as much as 40 percent of the 200,000 to 300,000 illegal immigrants who take up permanent residence in the United States each year enter the country legally as visitors, then overstay their visas. Many are Europeans, who are more difficult to track and to deport than Mexicans caught at the border.

The overall pattern of new immigration is increasing America's cultural diversity. Many Americans think the new arrivals make the country better. Still, immigration is controversial. Some of the opposition is no doubt a reaction to changes in "American identity," as America becomes more Asian, more African, more Latino, and less European. Particularly in times of high unemployment, many people worry about immigrants' taking jobs from native-born Americans. A high number of complaints about immigration come from a few states, such as California, New York, Florida, and Texas, which have been the major desti-nations of new immigrants. Politicians in these states have complained that social services for immigrants have increased state and local government costs. They have begun to call for the national government to restrict the flow of immigrants or to take over some costs. There are widespread feelings that America does not have control of its borders and needs stronger police measures to keep illegal entrants out. Still others have called for drastic limitations, such as a three-year moratorium on all immigration. Such a strategy might not prove effective, however. Previous crackdowns on legal immigration usually have led to more illegal entries.

Political oppression and lack of economic opportunity in the home country tend to fuel immigration. So foreign policy may also become a tool for reducing immigration. European immigration to America declined as prosperity and stability took hold. Measures such as NAFTA, geared to increase Mexican prosperity, might also help stem the new tide of immigration. Experts estimate that if Mexico's wage rate climbs to one-quarter of America's, the number of Mexicans seeking work in the United States will decline drastically. Similarly, working to end political oppression or restore democracy in Haiti and Guatemala may also help reduce the numbers of those seeking asylum in the United States.

• *Sources: Dick Kirschten, "Catch-Up Ball,"* National Journal, *7 August 1993, pp. 1976–1979; Rodman D. Griffen, "Illegal Immigration,"* CQ Researcher, *24 April 1992; pp. 361–363; Mary H. Cooper, "Immigration Reform,"* CQ Researcher, *24 September 1993.*

U.S. VALUES AND INTERESTS: THE HISTORICAL CONTEXT

Above all else, the goal of American foreign policy is to preserve our national interests. The most important of these interests is national security. The difficulty in foreign policymaking comes in deciding just what *national interests* and *national security* mean in practice and exactly what to do to preserve them. During the Cold War, Americans interpreted their national security as a matter of preventing communist expansion. Now that the Cold War is over, such goals as promoting economic prosperity and preserving environmental quality are increasingly seen as vital to our national interest.

From Isolationism to Regionalism to Globalism

Americans have not always viewed national security interests in global terms. For most of the nineteenth century, the limits of American interests were those staked out by the Monroe Doctrine of 1823, in which the United States rejected European intervention in the western hemisphere and agreed not to involve itself in European politics. Americans remained reluctant to become enmeshed in the politics of the Old World and generally practiced a policy of isolationism, or withdrawal from the political entanglements of Europe. American isolationism was never total, however, and as the nineteenth century wore on, the United States continued its expansion from coast to coast. It also became a regional power, increasingly involved in the affairs of nations in the Pacific and Latin America. However, America's defense establishment and foreign policy commitments remained limited.

World War I was the United States' first serious foray into European politics. The rhetoric that surrounded our entry into the war in 1917—"to make the world safe for democracy"—gave an idealistic tone to America's effort to advance its own interest in freedom of the seas. Such moralism has often characterized America's approach to international politics. At

The Same in Any Language

These three World War I posters, (from Germany, Great Britain, and the United States) were used to persuade men to join the army. Interestingly, they all employed the same psychological technique—pointing at viewers to make each individual feel the appeal personally.

the Versailles Peace Conference in 1919, for instance, President Woodrow Wilson championed the League of Nations as a device for preventing future wars. When the Senate refused to ratify the Versailles Treaty, Americas brief moment of internationalism ended. Until the Second World War, America continued to define its security interests narrowly and needed only a small military establishment to defend them.

World War II dramatically changed America's orientation toward the world. The United States emerged from the war a superpower, and its national security interests became global in scope. The United States did not withdraw into a new isolationism but instead confronted a new rival in its wartime ally, the Soviet Union. In the fight against Hitler, the Soviets overran much of Eastern Europe. In the aftermath of the war, the Soviets solidified their control over these lands. Their communist ideology was spreading. To Americans, Soviet communism appeared to be destructive of freedom, while the possibility of continued Soviet expansion in Europe threatened order. European conflicts had drawn the United States into war twice in twenty-five years; the Soviets, left unchecked, might well do it again.

Cold War and Containment

To frustrate Soviet expansionist designs, Americans prepared to wage a new kind of war: not an actual shooting war, or "hot war," but a cold one in which the relationship between the superpowers was characterized by suspicion, rivalry, mutual ideological revulsion, and a military buildup but not by direct hostilities. To wage the Cold War, United States policy

Rosie the Riveter

War often stimulates social change. During World War II, more than 6 million women entered the labor force, many doing jobs—such as installing fixtures and assemblies in airplane fuselages—that had previously been done by men.

makers fashioned a foreign policy consensus around the idea of **containment.** This term, coined by State Department official George Kennan, meant holding Soviet power in check as if it were in a container. The American course of action, as sketched out by Kennan, had to be longterm, patient but firm and vigilant containment."[6] Cold War required commitment and sacrifice.

Cold War foreign policy had military, economic, and political dimensions. Militarily, the United States committed itself to high defense expenditures and maintained a large fighting force with troops stationed around the world. Economically, the United States backed the establishment of an international economic system, known as the **GATT-Bretton Woods system**, which relied on free trade, fixed currency exchange rates, and America's ability to act as banker for the world. This system, plus an aid program to rebuild Europe (the **Marshall Plan**), fueled recovery and reduced the economic appeal of communism. Politically, the United States joined in numerous alliances against Soviet aggression. The first treaty of alliance (1949) created the **North Atlantic Treaty Organization (NATO),** dedicated to the defense of member countries in Europe and North America. In addition, the United States tried to use international institutions, such as the United Nations, as instruments of containment. Because the Soviets had veto power in the U.N. Security Council, the United States was rarely able to use the U.N. as anything more than a sounding board to express anti-Soviet feelings.

In the first decades of the Cold War, the United States relied heavily on its superiority in nuclear weapons. American policy emphasized nuclear **deterrence** it discouraged Soviet expansion by threatening to use nuclear weapons to retaliate against Soviet advances. The Soviets countered with their own nuclear program. In 1962, they attempted to plant missiles in Cuba, only ninety miles from United States shores. This precipitated a crisis that brought the world to the brink of war. As the arms race continued throughout the 1950s and 1960s, the superpowers became capable of **mutual assured destruction (MAD)**—each nation could totally destroy the other. Faced with this possibility, the two superpowers began to seek new strategies. During the Kennedy administration, the United States adopted a defense policy of **flexible response,** under which America would develop its conventional (non-nuclear) military forces. In the event of Soviet provocation, the United States would have many options available short of nuclear war.

Also in the 1950s and 1960s, many parts of the developing world were seeking independence from colonial control imposed by Western nations. The Soviets began to pay attention to these developing nations. They offered to help communist forces involved in what they called **wars of national liberation**—that is, wars fought to end colonialism and install communist regimes. To counter the Soviets, the United States followed policies that aimed at **nation building.** These measures were designed to strengthen the opponents of communism in newly emerging nations by promoting democratic reforms and shoring up their economies. While United States rhetoric often emphasized the value of freedom in describing these policies, sometimes freedom took a back seat to America's desire for order. Once, while speaking about potential regimes in the Dominican Republic, President Kennedy made the priority of these values clear: "There are three possibilities in descending order of preference: a decent democratic regime, a continuation of the [right-wing dictatorship under the] Trujillo [family], or a Castro [communist] regime. We ought to aim at the first but we really can't renounce the second until we are sure that we can avoid the third."[7]

Vietnam and the Challenge to Cold War Consensus

One place where Soviet support for a war of national liberation and American nation building came into conflict was in Vietnam. The United States tried to strengthen noncommunist institutions in South Vietnam in order to prevent a takeover by Soviet-backed forces from North Vietnam and their communist allies in the South, the Viet Cong. In Vietnam, the Cold War turned hot and more than fifty thousand Americans died during the protracted fighting. This was not the first major conflict of the Cold War era. (Nearly as many Americans had been killed in a conflict in Korea between the communist North and the noncommunist South in 1950–1953.) But the Vietnam War badly damaged the Cold War consensus on containment. Critics of the American presence in Vietnam came in many varieties. Some complained that America lacked the will to use enough military force to win the war. Others argued that America relied too much on military force to solve what were really political problems. Still others objected that America was intervening in a civil war rather than blocking Soviet expansion. In short, Americans disagreed passionately on what to do in Vietnam and how to do it. Eventually, after signing a peace agreement in 1973, American forces pulled out of Vietnam, and

Making Peace With Our Past

President Bill Clinton's active opposition to the Vietnam War and his avoidance of military service generated strong feelings among veterans when, as president, Clinton visited the Vietnam Veterans Memorial in Washington D.C. The memorial is a place of national sorrow. The long chevron of black granite is etched with the names of 58,156 American soldiers who died in the nation's longest conflict. The Vietnam War cost the United States more than $3.3 trillion, divided the American people, and fragmented the Cold War foreign policy consensus.

in 1975, North and South were forceably united under a communist regime.

Not only did the Vietnam War call into question the military and political dimensions of America's foreign policy consensus, it also undermined its economic basis. The cost of the war contributed to balance of payments deficits that weakened the dollar, increased inflation, and forced an end to the system of currency exchange fashioned at Bretton Woods.

Even as the war in Vietnam wore on, President Richard Nixon and his chief foreign policy adviser (and later secretary of state), Henry Kissinger, overhauled American foreign policy. Under the **Nixon doctrine**, an attempt to scale back America's overseas commitments, America would no longer "undertake all the defense of the free nations of the world." Instead, the United States would intervene only where "it makes a real difference and is considered in our interest."[8] Kissinger had long been a student of nineteenth-century diplomatic history. He believed that peace had prevailed then because the great nations of Europe maintained a balance of power among themselves. Nixon and Kissinger sought to create a similar framework for peace among the world's most powerful nations in the late twentieth century. To this end, they pursued better relations (détente) with the Soviet Union and ended decades of United States hostility toward the communist People's Republic of China. The theory of **détente** emphasized the value of order—order based not only on military might but also on recognition of mutual interests among the superpowers. Kissinger believed that if the Soviets and the Chinese were treated as legitimate participants in the international system, they would have a vested interest in supporting world order. Specifically, they would have less incentive to promote revolutionary challenges to international stability. The brief period of détente saw the conclusion of a major arms agreement, the Strategic Arms Limitation Treaty (SALT I) limiting the growth of strategic nuclear weapons. This thaw in the Cold War also witnessed greater cooperation between the United States and Soviet Union in other spheres, including a joint space mission.

Critics have noted that détente, with its attention to U.S.-Soviet relations, did not bring about a successful end to the Vietnam War. Nor did it solve other problems such as the 1973 oil embargo, a decision by Arab nations warring with Israel not to sell oil to the West. In fact, while Kissinger concentrated on East-West politics—relations between Eastern bloc communist nations and Western capitalist nations—other issues were increasing in importance. These often pitted richer, more developed nations of the North against poorer, less developed nations of the South. Others have suggested that the Nixon-Kissinger approach to foreign policy was too cynical, paid too much attention to power and interests, and deemphasized basic American values such as human rights.

Initially, President Jimmy Carter's stance on foreign policy differed substantially from that of his predecessors. He tended to downplay the importance of the Soviet threat throughout much of his administration. He saw revolutions in Nicaragua and Iran as the products of internal forces rather than of Soviet involvement. Nonetheless, Carter did attempt to articulate national interests—in particular, America's stake in the Persian Gulf region. The United States had depended on the shah of Iran as a bulwark of support for American policies in the gulf. But the shah was deposed and ultimately succeeded by an Islamic fundamentalist rule. In late 1979, some months after the shah's ouster, the Soviets marched into Afghanistan, a country bordered by the Soviet Union and Iran. Fearing that the Soviets might see the Iranian Revolution as an opportunity, the president set forth the **Carter doctrine,** stating that "an attempt by any outside force to gain control of the Persian Gulf region will be regarded as an assault on the vital interests of the United States of America. And such an assault will be repelled by any means necessary including military force."[9]

In contrast to Nixon and Kissinger, Carter was sometimes criticized as overly idealistic. He emphasized human rights, leveling criticism—and sometimes even sanctions—at both friends and enemies with poor human rights records. He usually leaned toward open (rather than secret) diplomacy. Nonetheless, his greatest foreign policy achievement, the Camp David accords, which brought about peace between Egypt and Israel, resulted from closed negotiations he arranged between Egyptian president Anwar Sadat and Israeli premier Menachem Begin.

In many ways, Carter's foreign policy reflected the influence of the **Vietnam syndrome,** a crisis of confidence that resulted from America's failure in Vietnam and the breakdown of the Cold War consensus about America's role in the world. In particular, his administration deemphasized the use of military force. Many Americans were frustrated, however, by Carter's inability to develop effective responses when Iranians took American diplomats hostage or when the Soviets invaded Afghanistan.

Reagan and Cold War II

Carter's successor, Ronald Reagan, came to the Oval Office untroubled by the Vietnam syndrome. He believed that the Soviets were responsible for most of the evil in the world. Attributing instability in Central America, Africa, and Afghanistan to Soviet meddling, he argued that the best way to combat the Soviet threat was to renew and demonstrate American military strength.

The Reagan years witnessed a huge increase in defense spending and a new willingness to use American military muscle, in Libya and Grenada, for example. The administration argued that its massive military buildup was both a deterrent and a bargaining chip to use in talks with the Soviets. During this period, the Cold War climate grew even chillier. Things changed when Mikhail Gorbachev came to power in the Soviet Union. Gorbachev wished to reduce his nation's commitments abroad in order to concentrate its resources on needed domestic reform. By the end of Reagan's second term, the United States and Soviet Union had concluded agreements outlawing intermediate-range nuclear forces (the INF treaty) and providing for a Soviet military pullout from Afghanistan.

The Reagan administration also took a hard line at the United Nations. Until the mid-1960s, votes in the U.N. General Assembly had usually supported United States positions. Later, however, as the U.N. expanded its membership to include many newly independent states, the United States and its Western European allies frequently found themselves outvoted. Under Reagan, the United States reduced its commitment to international institutions such as the U.N. and the World Court when they acted in ways that ran counter to American interests. For example, the United States began to drag its feet on paying its U.N. assessments, withdrew from the International Labor Organization, and rejected the jurisdiction of the World Court in cases involving United States activities in Nicaragua.

As we noted at the outset of the chapter, the Cold War ended not long after Reagan left office. The conventional view is that the Cold War ended and America won.[10] How? Because of Reagan's "peace through strength" policies, some believed. Others insisted that the appeal of Western affluence, Gorbachev's own new thinking, and a shared interest in overcoming the nuclear threat led to the end of the Cold War.[11] Still others argued that both superpowers had lost by spending trillions of dollars on defense while neglecting other sectors of their economies.[12] These issues will be debated for a long time. But for now, a more important question for our purposes is what the direction of U.S. foreign policy will be. For more than forty years, the main goal of American foreign policy had been to contain the Soviet threat. With that goal apparently achieved once and for all, what will shape American foreign policy?

What New World Order? Foreign Policy Under Bush and Clinton

The Bush and Clinton administrations have had difficulty articulating firm answers to these questions. President Bush came to the White House with an excellent foreign policy résumé. He had served as U.N. ambassador, director of the Central Intelligence Agency (CIA), and ambassador to China. Often described as a "consummate cold warrior," he was faulted for his lack of vision in seeking out new directions for American foreign policy in the post–Cold War world.[13]

When Iraqs invasion of Kuwait threatened U.S. interests in the Persian Gulf (interests clearly articulated years before under the Carter doctrine), Bush responded skillfully. He emphasized multilateral action and the use of international organizations such as the U.N. in the gulf crisis. U.S. diplomats carefully built a coalition of nations, including the United States' Western allies, the Soviet Union, Eastern European states, many Arab states, and other developing countries to oppose Saddam Hussein. The United States also won U.N. Security Council approval for a series of motions against Iraq. During the Cold War, the Security Council usually proved ineffective in major crises. Most crises pitted U.S.-backed clients against those supported by the Soviet Union. As a result, one or the other superpower could usually be counted on for a veto. However, in this post–Cold War crisis, the two superpowers cooperated against Saddam. Feature 20.1 describes the structure of the U.N.

The Gulf War showed the United States continuing to act as world leader. When the agenda shifted toward such issues as international economic competition, the environment, human rights, and emerging democracy in Europe and elsewhere, American leadership was often lacking. For example, recession and federal budgetary problems made Washington slow to help underwrite Eastern Europe's development of democratic and market-oriented institutions, and America had little beyond rhetoric to offer in response to Serbian atrocities in the former Yugoslavia. At the Earth Summit on the environment in Rio de Janeiro in 1992, the United States served more as an obstructionist than as a leader.

Under Bill Clinton, too, the White House has struggled to provide clear, coherent foreign policy leadership. Clinton came to the presidency with virtually no foreign policy experience. His presidential campaign emphasized domestic concerns. Although he announced his intention to "focus like a laser beam on the economy," he soon found that crises in Somalia, Bosnia, and Haiti absorbed a good deal of his time. The difficulties Bush and Clinton have had may reflect the nature of post–Cold War problems rather than personal failures. In analyzing the situation in Somalia, for example, General Merrill A. McPeak, Air Force chief of staff, remarked, "This is really a typical post–cold war security problem. It's messy, it's ambiguous, and there's not a common agreement on goals or threats."[14] Still, the inability of presidents to exert leadership by supplying a clear rationale for foreign policy may prompt Congress—which usually takes a back seat in foreign affairs—to try to assert itself more in the foreign policy process.

FEATURE 20.1

■ The United Nations and the New World Order

At the end of World War II, the victorious Allies established the United Nations to maintain global peace and security. As the Cold War developed, United States-Soviet rivalry usually paralyzed any U.N. effort to resolve disputes when the superpowers' interests were involved. Because the two nations had worldwide interests, the scope for U.N. action was quite limited. Now that Cold War tension has faded, however, both the United States and the former Soviet Union have shown a new willingness to use the United Nations as a tool of foreign policy.

The structure of the United Nations makes it a large, complex, decentralized institution. Although its most attention-grabbing activities focus on security issues, it includes many specialized agencies geared to deal with economic and social concerns.

Each of the more than 160 member states of the United Nations has one vote in the General Assembly. The General Assembly passes non–binding resolutions and chooses members to serve in other U.N. organizations (for example, in the Security Council and the Economic and Social

Council). The General Assembly is responsible for U.N. finances; it has also created a variety of organizations to deal with specific problem areas. Among these are UNICEF (United Nations Children's Emergency Fund) and UNEP (United Nations Environment Program).

The Security Council is a fifteen-member body that has the main responsibility for keeping the peace. Its resolutions are binding on all U.N. members, and it may back up its resolutions by taking enforcement measures, including deployment of blue-helmeted U.N. peacekeeping forces. A measure must have 9 votes and no vetoes to win approval. This body is made up of five permanent members with veto power—the United States, the Soviet Union, Great Britain, France, and China—as well as ten members elected for two-year terms. Recently, Germany and Japan have sought seats on the Security Council in recognition of their economic power.

The Economic and Social Council (ECOSOC) is a fifty-four-member organization under the authority of the General Assembly, and it is responsible for coordinating the economic and social programs

---

FOREIGN POLICYMAKING: THE CONSTITUTIONAL CONTEXT

Under the Constitution, the president is clearly the dominant actor in American foreign policy. However, the framers also included checks and balances to prevent the president from conducting foreign policy without substantial cooperation from Congress. Still, presidents have found ways to sidestep these provisions when they have felt it important to do so. Congress, for its part, sometimes seeks to rein in presidential power over foreign policy.

The Formal Division of Power

The Constitution gives the president four significant foreign policymaking powers:

- The president is commander in chief of the armed forces.

- The president has the power to make treaties (subject to the consent of the Senate).

of the U.N. and its numerous specialized and affiliated agencies.

At the end of World War II, the Trusteeship Council administered some eleven trust territories. Today, all but one of these trusts has achieved independence or has become part of a neighboring country. Now only the trust territory of the Pacific Islands (Micronesia) remains.

The International Court of Justice (ICJ), or World Court, hears cases brought to it by the states involved and at the request of the Security Council or General Assembly may provide advisory opinions on matters of international law. The Security Council and General Assembly elect judges from fifteen nations. They serve nine-year terms.

The Secretariat is the executive arm of the United Nations. It administers the programs and policies set up by other U.N. bodies. To do this job, the Secretariat relies on a bureaucracy of some fourteen thousand civil servants. The head of the Secretariat is the secretary general, who serves for five years. The secretary is recommended by the Security Council and elected by the General Assembly. In addition to coordinating the U.N. bureaucracy, the secretary may also play a major role in bringing security threats to the Security Council and in resolving international disputes through personal diplomatic efforts.

In addition to these organizations, about sixteen specialized agencies are connected with the U.N. Among these are bodies that help promote smooth international transportation and communication (Universal Postal Union, International Civil Aviation Organization, International Maritime Organization, International Telecommunication Union), those that deal with agriculture (Food and Argicultural Organization, International Fund for Agricultural Development), those concerned with public health (World Health Organization), and those concerned with supporting economic development (International Monetary Fund, World Bank, United Nations Industrial Development Organization). Some agencies, such as the United Nations Educational, Scientific and Cultural Organization and the International Labor Organization, became controversial in the United States when the Reagan administration withdrew from them, arguing that they had become too "politicized."

As this list of specialized agencies suggests, the U.N. does not confine itself to narrow security issues. Many believe that instability grows out of poverty, and so, by seeking to improve the quality of life around the world, the U.N. promotes peace as well.

- The president appoints United States ambassadors and the heads of executive departments (also with the advice and consent of the Senate).

- The president receives (and may refuse to receive) ambassadors from other countries.

Congress also has specific powers in the foreign policy arena:

- Congress alone may declare war.

- Congress has the legislative power.

- Congress controls the nation's pursestrings.

- Congress is charged with raising, supporting, and maintaining the army and navy.

- Congress may call out the militia to repel invasions.

Lonely at the Top

Being commander in chief of the armed forces is an awesome responsibility. Stunned by a resurgence of enemy activity during the Vietnam War in early 1968, President Lyndon Johnson decided not to seek reelection. Here, in July 1968, the president listens to a tape-recorded message from his son-in-law, who was serving in Vietnam.

The most important foreign policy power the Constitution gives to Congress is the power to declare war, a power it has used only five times. However, Congress has become involved in foreign policy in other ways. Using its legislative power, it may create programs of international scope, such as SEED (Support for East European Democracy Act of 1989), a program to improve trade relationships with Poland and Hungary. Congress may also use the legislative power to imposed legal limits on the actions of the executive branch as it did when it restricted arms transfers under the Arms Control Export Act (1988). In addition, Congress has used its power of the purse to provide funds for activities it supports and prohibit funds to those it opposes. Finally, some foreign policy functions belong to the Senate alone:

• The Senate consents to treaties.

• The Senate gives its advice and consent to the appointment of ambassadors and various other public officials.

The Senate has not been shy about using these powers. We have already mentioned its refusal to ratify the Versailles Treaty after World War I. More recently, the United States-Soviet SALT II treaty, an arms limitation agreement negotiated under the Carter administration, was introduced in the Senate but not brought to a vote, because its supporters feared defeat.

Sidestepping the Constitution

Although the Constitution gives the executive enormous power in the foreign policy area, it also places limits on that power. Presidents and their advisers have often found ingenious ways around these constitutional limitations. Among the innovative devices they have used are executive agreements, discretionary funds, transfer authority and reprogramming, undeclared wars, and special envoys. Since the Vietnam War and the breakdown of foreign policy consensus, however, Congress has attempted to assert control over the use of these presidential tools.

An **executive agreement** is a pact between the heads of two countries. Initially, such agreements were used to work out the tedious details of day-to-day international affairs. In *U.S.* v. *Curtiss-Wright* (1936), the Supreme Court ruled that executive agreements are within the inherent powers of the president and have the legal status of treaties.[15] This ruling gave the president an enormously powerful tool. Executive agreements, like treaties, have the force of law, but unlike treaties they do not require Senate approval. Until 1972, the president did not even have to report the texts of these agreements to Congress. Legislation enacted that year now requires the president to send copies to the House and Senate Foreign Relations committees.

This requirement has not seriously affected the use of executive agreements, which has escalated dramatically since World War II. In 1986, for example, executive agreements outnumbered treaties by about 24 to 1.[16] And presidents have used these agreements to make substantive foreign policy. In fact, senators have complained that the treaties now submitted for Senate approval deal with petty, unimportant matters, whereas serious issues are handled by executive agreement. Moreover, executive agreements are subject to few limits. One observer noted that the principal limitation on their use is political in nature—the degree to which it is wise to exclude the Senate from [its] constitutional foreign policy role."[17]

Presidents have used several devices to circumvent congressional control over the nation's finances. For one, the chief executive is provided with a **discretionary fund**—large sums of cash that may be spent on unpredicted needs to further the national interest. Kennedy used discretionary funds to run the Peace Corps in its first year; Johnson used $1.5 billion of his funds to pursue the war in Southeast Asia in 1965 and 1966.[18]

The president's **transfer authority,** or the **reprogramming** of funds, allows him to take money that Congress has approved for one purpose and to spend it on something else. In 1989, the administration made an unsuccessful effort to shift $777 million from other defense accounts in order to avoid making personnel cuts.[19] The executive branch has control over the disposal of excess stocks, including surplus or infrequently used equipment. The CIA has been an important beneficiary of excess stock disposal.

The Constitution makes the president commander in chief of the armed forces. In this role, several presidents have exercised the right to involve the United States in undeclared wars by committing American troops in emergency situations. America's "undeclared" wars, police actions, and other interventions have outnumbered formal, congressionally declared wars by about 40 to 1. Since the last declared war ended in 1945, more than 100,000 American servicemen and women have died in locations ranging from Korea and Vietnam to Grenada, Panama, and the Persian Gulf.

During the Vietnam conflict, congressional opponents of that conflict passed the **War Powers Resolution** to restrict the president's ability to wage undeclared wars. Under this resolution, a president must "consult" with Congress in "every possible instance" before involving U.S. troops in hostilities. In addition, the president is required to notify Congress within forty-eight hours of committing troops to a foreign intervention. Once troops have been deployed, they may not remain there for more than sixty days without congressional approval (although the president may take up to thirty days more to remove troops "safely"). President Nixon vetoed the War Powers Resolution as an unwarranted restriction on the president's constitutional authority, but it was approved over his veto. Critics charged that the legislation, far from restricting presidential power, gives the president a free hand to wage war for as long as sixty days.* By the end of that period, a Congress might find it difficult indeed to force the president to bring the troops home. The actual effect of the War Powers Resolution is debatable. Nixon's successors in the White House have all questioned its constitutionality, and no president has ever been "punished" for violating its provisions. At the time of the Persian Gulf crisis, Congress passed a resolution authorizing the use of force and avoided a showdown between the branches over this thorny issue. More recently, as U.S. involvement in Somalia wore on and as it seemed possible that U.S. troops might be dispatched to Haiti, congressional leaders have called for a thorough-going reevaluation of the War Powers Resolution.

Although the Senate rarely rejects a presidential personnel choice, senators have used confirmation hearings as opportunities for investigating the president's foreign policy activities. For example, when Robert Gates was nominated to head the CIA, his confirmation hearings provided Congress with the opportunity to re-open the Iran-Contra affair and compel him to testify about his involvement in it.†

One way presidents get around the Senate's power over appointments is to rely heavily on the White House staff, which is accountable to no one but the president, or to use **special envoys** or "personal representatives," who may perform a wide variety of foreign policy tasks. For example,

---

* *These critics included both conservative Republican senator Barry Goldwater of Arizona and liberal Democratic senator Thomas Eagleton of Missouri. The latter's feelings were succinctly summarized in the title of his book,* War and Presidential Power: A Chronicle of Congressional Surrender *(New York: Liveright, 1974).*

† *A foreign policy debacle in which the Reagan administration attempted to obtain freedom for Americans held hostage in Lebanon by selling arms to Iran and then, despite congressional prohibitions, use the proceeds from the arms sales to aid the Contras fighting in Nicaragua.*

President Clinton appointed William Gray, a former member of Congress, as his special envoy to Haiti.

<table>
<tr><td>

FOREIGN POLICYMAKING: THE ADMINISTRATIVE MACHINERY

</td><td>

Although American foreign policy is developed and administered by the executive branch, it requires approval and funding by Congress and is subject to Congressional oversight. When America assumed a larger role in world affairs after World War II, the old foreign policy machinery proved inadequate to the demands of American superpower status. In 1947, Congress overhauled the system, enacting the National Security Act, which established three new organizations with important foreign policy roles: the Department of Defense, the National Security Council, and the CIA. These organizations joined the existing executive branch department with major foreign policymaking power and responsibility, the Department of State.

</td></tr>
</table>

The Department of State

The department most centrally responsible for the overall conduct of foreign affairs is the Department of State. It helps to formulate and then executes and monitors American policy throughout the world. Its head, the secretary of state, is the highest-ranking official in the cabinet; the secretary is also, in theory at least, the president's most important foreign policy adviser. However, some chief executives, such as John Kennedy, preferred to act as their own secretaries of state and have thus appointed relatively weak figures to the post. Others, such as Dwight Eisenhower, appointed stronger individuals to the post (John Foster Dulles). Presidents often come to the Oval Office promising to rely on the State Department and its head to play a leading role in formulating and carrying out foreign policy. The reality that emerges is usually somewhat different and prompts analysts to bemoan the chronic weakness of the department.[20] During his first term, Richard Nixon planned to control foreign policy from the White House. He appointed William Rogers as secretary of state but relied far more heavily on Henry Kissinger, whose office was located in the White House. More recently, George Bush named one of his closest advisors, James Baker, to head the State Department. Yet, when Bush's re-election effort began to run into trouble, he pulled his trusted lieutenant out of the State Department and used him instead to help with the election campaign.

Like other executive departments, the State Department is staffed by political appointees and permanent employees selected under the civil service merit system. The former include deputy secretaries and undersecretaries of state and some—but not all—ambassadors; the latter include approximately 3,500 foreign service officers at home and abroad who staff United States embassies and consulates. They have primary responsibility for representing America to the world and caring for American citizens and interests abroad. Although the Foreign Service is highly selective (fewer than two hundred of the fifteen thousand candidates who take the annual examination are appointed), the State Department is often charged with a lack of initiative and creativity. Critics claim that bright young

In the Gulf, on the Verge of War

Richard Cheney, Secretary of defense under George Bush, and General Colin Powell, then chairman of the Joint Chiefs of Staff, feel the gravity of the moment as they visit with U.S. airmen stationed in Saudi Arabia in December 1990, one month before the air campaign against the Iraqi forces began.

Foreign Service officers quickly realize that conformity is the best path to career advancement.[21] As one observer put it, "There are old foreign service officers; and there are bold foreign service officers; but, there are no old, bold foreign service officers."[22] Some presidents have complained that the department's foreign policy machinery is too slow and unwieldy. As President Kennedy remarked, "[McGeorge] Bundy [Kennedy's national security adviser] and I get more done in one day in the White House than they do in six months in the State Department. . . . They never have any ideas over there, never come up with anything new."[23]

Probably the most serious problem facing the State Department today is the lack of a strong domestic constituency to exert pressure in support of its policies. The Department of Agriculture, by contrast, can mobilize farmers to support its activities; the Department of Defense can count on help from defense industries and veterans' groups. In a pluralist democracy, the lack of a natural constituency is a serious drawback for a department. Exacerbating this problem is the changing character of global political issues. As the issues become more intermestic, executive agencies with pertinent domestic policy expertise become more involved in shaping foreign policy.

The Department of Defense

The Department of Defense replaced two cabinet-level departments, the War Department and the Department of the Navy. It was created in 1947 to provide the modern bureaucratic structure needed to manage America's much-increased peacetime military strength and to promote unity and coordination among the armed forces. In keeping with the United States tradition of civilian control of the military, the new department was given a civilian head—the secretary of defense, a cabinet member with authority over the military. Later reorganizations of the department (in 1949 and 1958) have given the secretary greater budgetary powers, control of defense research, and the authority to transfer, abolish, reassign, and consolidate functions among the military services.

The power wielded by defense secretaries often depends on the secretary's own vision of the job and willingness to use the tools available. Strong secretaries of defense, including Robert McNamara (under Kennedy and Johnson), Melvin Laird (under Nixon), James Schlesinger (under Nixon and Ford), and Caspar Weinberger (under Reagan) have wielded tremendous power.

Below the secretary are the civilian secretaries of the army, navy, and air force; below them are the military commanders of the individual branches of the armed forces. These military leaders make up the Joint Chiefs of Staff (JCS). The JCS meet to coordinate military policy; they also serve as the primary military advisers to the president, the secretary of defense, and the National Security Council, helping to shape policy positions on such matters as alliances, plans for nuclear and conventional war, and arms control and disarmament.

The CIA and the Intelligence Community

Before World War II, the United States had no permanent agency specifically charged with gathering intelligence (that is, information) about the actions and intentions of foreign powers. In 1941, poor American intelligence procedures contributed to the success of the Japanese surprise attack on Pearl Harbor. After the war, when America began to play a more internationalist role and the ice of the Cold War had begun to harden, Congress created the Central Intelligence Agency to collect such information. The departments of Defense, State, Energy, and Treasury also possess intelligence-related agencies, which, together with the CIA, make up the intelligence community.

The CIA's charter charges it with collecting, analyzing, evaluating, and circulating intelligence relating to national security matters. Most activities are relatively uncontroversial. By far, the bulk of material obtained by the CIA comes from readily available sources: statistical abstracts, books, newspapers, and the like. The agency's Intelligence Directorate is responsible for these overt (open) information-processing activities.

The charter also empowers the CIA "to perform such other functions and duties related to intelligence affecting the national security as the National Security Council shall direct." This vague clause has been used by the agency as its legal justification for the covert (secret) and sometimes illegal activities undertaken by its Operations Directorate. These activities have included espionage, coups, assassination plots, wiretaps, interception of mail, and infiltration of protest groups.

Critics sometimes point out that the CIA's intelligence gathering has not eliminated unpleasant foreign policy surprises for the United States.

As Senator Ernest Hollings put it, "Weve flunked Iran; we've flunked Angola . . . Ethiopia . . . Iraq . . . Kuwait. We've flunked the fall of the Berlin wall."[24] Some gaffes have been the result of faulty intelligence, but others were more the result of policymakers' failure to accept analyses or interpret them properly. The usual congressional response to intelligence failures is to investigate and then propose structural changes in institutions, but at least one analyst claims that "intelligence failure is political and psychological more often than it is institutional."[25] Even the best-designed intelligence network will not prevent the United States from being caught by surprise some of the time—at most, it might minimize the frequency or intensity of such surprises.

A key dilemma posed by the CIA and the intelligence community concerns the role of covert activities. Covert operations raise both moral and legal questions for a democracy. Allen Dulles, President Eisenhower's CIA director, once called these operations "an essential part of the free world's struggle against communism." But are they equally important in a post–Cold War world? Can they be reconciled with America's stated commitment to open, democratic government, free elections, and self-determination at home and abroad? Abroad, covert activities may undermine the opportunity for citizens of other nations to choose their own leaders, as has happened when the CIA secretly has tried to engineer election results favorable to United States interests. It is also difficult to reconcile such activities with basic operating principles of American government, such as the principle of checks and balances. Obviously, Americans cannot hold their government responsible for clandestine actions the public does not know about. Furthermore, although the CIA's covert activities are supposed to be approved by a subcommittee of the National Security Council, the president himself is not always briefed about them.

Is the intelligence community needed at all in the post–Cold War. One analyst argues that "the Cold War may be over, but the U.S. need for accurate information about the world remains acute."[26] Such commentators see the role of the intelligence agencies shifting away from Cold War concerns toward new issues such as terrorism, drug traffic, nuclear proliferation, and even economics. Feature 20.2 discusses how the CIA might be used to economic advantage.

The National Security Council

The National Security Council (NSC) is a permanent group of advisers created to help the president mold a coherent approach to foreign policy by integrating and coordinating the details of domestic, foreign, and military affairs as they relate to national security. The statutory members of the NSC include the president, the vice president, and the secretaries of state and defense. At the pleasure of the president, these people are advised by others, including the chairman of the Joint Chiefs of Staff, the director of the CIA, the director of the United States Information Agency, the director of the Arms Control and Disarmament Agency, and others chosen by the president. NSC discussions can cover a wide range of issues, such as how to deal with changes in Eastern Europe or what U.S. policy in the Middle East should be. In theory at least, NSC discussions offer the president an opportunity to solicit advice while allowing key participants in

■ $py vs. $py: Two Former CIA Directors on Economic Espionage

The CIA was chartered to gather intelligence affecting the national security of the United States. For most of its life, that has meant devoting considerable attention to monitoring the Soviet Union, once the principal threat to our national security. But now, with the Soviet Union gone, policymakers have begun to rethink American national security and to see it as connected directly to economic well being. Because the CIA no longer needs to direct its vast resources to Soviet watching, some have suggested that the agency should direct its attention to economic threats to our security. Two former directors of the CIA considered the possibility and reached very different conclusions.

Stansfield Turner, CIA director from 1977 to 1981, argues this way:

If the objective of collecting economic intelligence is to buttress national economic strength, then that requires making our businesses more competitive in the global marketplace.

The United States . . . would have no compunction about stealing military secrets to help it manufacture better weapons.

If economic strength should now be recognized as a vital component of national security, parallel with military power, why should America be concerned about stealing and employing economic secrets? . . . [I]n an age of increasing attention to economic strength, there needs to be a more symbiotic relationship between the worlds of intelligence and business.

Robert Gates, who ran the CIA during the Bush administration, disagrees:

As for the role of the . . . intelligence community in the world of industrial or commercial espionage, I would like to state clearly that the U.S. intelligence community does not, should not, and will not engage in industrial espionage. . . . I have serious concerns about the ethical, legal, and sources-and-methods questions surrounding the issue of industrial espionage.

Plainly put, it is the role of U.S. business to size up their foreign competitors' trade secrets, marketing strategies and bid proposals. Some years ago, one of our clandestine service officers overseas said to me: "You know, I'm prepared to give my life for my country but not for a company."

That case officer was absolutely right.

• *Source: Adapted from Rodney D. Griffin, "The New CIA." CQ Researcher (December 11, 1992), p. 1089. Used with permission.*

the foreign policymaking process to keep abreast of the policies and capabilities of other departments.

In practice, the role played by the NSC has varied considerably under different presidents. Truman and Kennedy seldom met with the NSC; Eisenhower and Nixon brought it into much greater prominence. During the Nixon administration, the NSC was critically important in making foreign policy. Much of this importance derived from Nixon's reliance on Kissinger, his assistant for national security affairs (the title held by the head of the NSC staff). Under Nixon and Kissinger, the NSC staff ballooned to more than one hundred people—in effect, a little state depart-

Presidential Adviser

Anthony Lake (center) is the national security adviser to President Bill Clinton. Lake served on the NSC staff during the Nixon administration and in the State Department during the Carter administration. Prior to his current position, Lake was a professor of international relations at Mount Holyoke College in Hadley, Massachusetts. To Lake's right is General John. M. Shalikashvili, chairman of the Joint Chiefs of Staff, America's highest ranking military officer.

ment in the White House. Kissinger also used this staff for direct diplomacy and covert operations, as did the Reagan administration. By using the NSC, which has been almost completely exempt from outside scrutiny, staffers hoped to preserve secrecy and, more important, to prevent Congress from prohibiting operations they wished to undertake.

Practitioners of international relations have traditionally valued secrecy, but democratic theory requires that citizens know what their leaders are doing. As we have seen, Tocqueville believed that democracies' weakness in foreign affairs stemmed in part from the difficulty of combining the secrecy necessary for foreign policy with the openness needed for democratic government. This dilemma continues to cause problems for American policymakers.

Other Parts of the Foreign Policy Bureaucracy

The last few decades have witnessed a proliferation in the number of players in the foreign policy game. Many departments and agencies other than those described thus far now find themselves involved in foreign policymaking. For example, the Department of Agriculture provides agricultural assistance to other countries and promotes U.S. farm products abroad. Likewise, the Department of Commerce tries to expand overseas markets for nonagricultural goods. In addition, Commerce administers export control laws to prevent other nations from gaining access to American technologies connected with national security (such as computers and military equipment). The Department of Energy monitors nuclear weapons programs internationally and works with foreign governments and international agencies such as the International Atomic Energy Agency to coordinate international energy programs. The Agency for International Development (AID) oversees programs of aid to nations around the globe. In doing so, AID works with a full range of other departments and agencies, including the Defense Department, CIA, Peace Corps, and the Department of Agriculture. The United States Information Agency, which staffs more than two hundred offices in some 120 countries, provides educational and cultural materials about the United States. An array of government corporations, independent agencies, and quasi-governmental organizations also participates in the foreign policy arena. These include the National Endowment for Democracy, an independent quasigovernmental organization established to promote democracy in other countries, the Export-Import Bank, a government corporation that subsidizes the export of American products, and the Overseas Private Investment Corporation, an independent agency that helps United States companies invest abroad.

This list of bureaucratic entities with foreign policy interests is by no means exhaustive, but it does suggest the complexity of the foreign policymaking machinery. Furthermore, as issues of low politics become more prominent on the foreign policy agenda, we can expect an increase in the involvement of other agencies not traditionally preoccupied with foreign policy. Finally, states and localities have also begun to pay attention to international matters. By 1991, most state governments in the United States had specific offices, bureaus, or divisions responsible for promoting state exports, attracting overseas investment to the state.[27] All this suggests that the line between domestic and foreign policy will become even more blurred, offering more opportunities for the practice of pluralist politics.

THE PUBLIC, THE MEDIA, AND FOREIGN POLICY

Another great difficulty Tocqueville predicted for democracies in foreign affairs stemmed from the changeable views of a mass electorate. He believed foreign relations requires patience and persistence in the pursuit of long-term goals. But the public can be fickle, unwilling to set aside short-term gains for long-term security and unable to wait long enough for a policy to bear fruit. In response to domestic pressures, leaders can be forced to act in ways that are harmful to global interests. Their democratic responsiveness might well be detrimental to the long-term success of their foreign policy.

The Public and the Majoritarian Model

When foreign policy practitioner George Kennan worried about the "erratic and subjective nature of public reaction," he echoed Tocqueville's fears.[28] For many years, political scientists played down these concerns, not because they took a more flattering view of the public but because they believed that the public had little influence on foreign policy. In general, they saw the public as uninformed about foreign affairs and uninterested in the subject. Furthermore, although public opinion about foreign policy issues tended to be volatile, the issues themselves were not very important to voters. As a result, foreign policy remained essentially an elite preserve where the general public had little influence and tended to follow the leader.[29] During much of the Cold War, this simply reinforced the consensus on containment.

The picture became more complicated during the Vietnam era, when

America's foreign policy elite split and three new groups emerged, namely, conservative interventionists, liberal interventionists, and noninterventionists.[30] Conservative interventionists, also called *Cold War internationalists*, focused on the East-West split; they emphasized the threat posed by Soviet communism and the need to keep America strong to oppose it. By contrast, liberal interventionists, or post–Cold War internationalists, emphasized the complexity of world politics and the interdependence of nations. They stressed the importance of U.S. relations with other developed, capitalist countries and with the less-developed countries of the South. Finally, noninternationalists or semiisolationists argued for the United States to scale back its international commitments and concentrate more on domestic problems. Researchers initially found this three-way division among the elite, but because further research suggested that it mirrored the attitudes of the public as well, there seemed little need to reevaluate the overall view of the public in the foreign policy area.[31]

More recently, however, some political scientists have questioned these long-held beliefs about the public's role in foreign policy. Some researchers have shown that the foreign policy attitudes of the public are actually more stable than those of the elite.[32] By examining responses to questions asked consistently in public opinion polls over the years, researchers have found no significant change in the public's response on more than half the questions asked about foreign policy. Only a minority of questions (15 percent) saw shifts of 20 percent or more. Although opinion did change more frequently on foreign policy matters than on domestic issues, these analysts argue that underlying attitudes toward foreign policy remain remarkably stable.[33] And even when abrupt opinion shifts do occur, they are not necessarily erratic but may well represent a rational response to new information or changed circumstances.[34] For example, from 1986 to 1990, the public's attitude toward the Soviet Union "warmed" (as measured by a "feeling thermometer" in which respondents are asked to express their feeling toward other nations as degrees of warmth on a thermometer) from 32° to 59°.[35] This was a huge swing but arguably an appropriate reaction to momentous political changes.

Finally, newer research on public opinion suggests that foreign policy issues are important to voters and that the public can indeed influence the policymaking process. For one thing, researchers point out that presidential candidates often give considerable attention to foreign policy issues—a strange thing to do if these issues are irrelevant to winning elections.[36] They conclude that candidates who make foreign policy appeals to voters are acting rationally because voters do in fact respond to their appeals."[37] However, opinion leadership often really consists of an effort to ride the wave of preexisting mass attitudes, not to chart new directions.[38]

Furthermore, although public opinion can and does have an influence, as Thomas Graham notes, foreign policy formulation and implementation do not take place "in a world of majority rule."[39] Public opinion may be influential, but usually it must reach consensus levels (60 percent) in order to overcome the inertia of policymakers and their innate suspicion of the general public.[40] While recent research lends more credibility to the majoritarian model, it does not fully describe the policymaking process in the United States.

Interest Groups and the Pluralist Model

Many people take an interest in foreign policy issues when they believe those issues affect them directly. Auto workers and manufacturers may favor import restrictions on Japanese cars. Jewish citizens may pay close attention to America's relations with Israel. These individuals often join organizations that present their policy positions to policymakers.

On foreign affairs issues, two of the most prominent kinds of lobbies have included businesses and unions, often seeking trade protection, and ethnic groups attempting to tailor foreign policy toward the "old country," as described in Feature 20.3. Some members of Congress have found ethnic interest groups a rich source of campaign funds. For example, the Sikhs, an ethnic minority from India, have become key contributors to Republican Representative Dan Burton. Although Burton has fewer than 120 Sikhs in his Indiana district, he received more than $61,000 in 1991–1992 for his reelection warchest from 146 Sikhs around the country.[41] During his career, Burton has emerged as an advocate for Sikh causes, supporting more than 20 legislative initiatives on behalf of the Sikhs and other ethnic minorities in India, often despite State Department opposition.

In keeping with the current lobbying boom in Washington, foreign firms and governments have hired high-powered Washington lobbying firms to represent their interests (see Feature 10.2). In 1989, Japanese companies spent about $150 million to hire Washington lawyers and lobbyists. Among other things, their lobbying efforts helped shape the U.S. government's trade agenda, held off trade penalties against Japanese consumer electronics, and blocked congressional attempts to restrict foreign investment.[42]

The influence of these groups varies with the issue. In general, however, lobbying seems to be more effective when it takes place behind the scenes and deals with noncrisis issues of little importance to the public at large. Interest groups are more effective maintaining support for the status quo than at bringing about policy changes.[43]

As is true in domestic issues, foreign policy interest groups tend to counterbalance each other. The Turkish lobby may try to offset the Greek lobby; the Arms Control Association or the Federation of American Scientists may oppose the American Legion or the Veterans of Foreign Wars on issues of détente and military spending. The result is often that foreign policy making resembles a taffy-pull: every group attempts to pull policy in its own direction while resisting the pulls of others, with the result that policy fails to move in any discernible direction. The process encourages solutions tending toward the middle of the road and maintenance of the status quo."[44]

The Media and Foreign Policy

Do the media shape foreign policy? Or do policymakers manage the medias coverage of foreign affairs? Television coverage of the Vietnam War is often credited, or blamed, for the shift in public opinion against that war. Fearing a repetition of this phenomenon, the Pentagon restricted press coverage of Operation Desert Storm in the Persian Gulf.

FEATURE 20.3

■ *Cuba, Si! Castro, No! The Cuban American Foundation in Action*

The Cold War in Europe ended, but five years later one small part of the Cold War continued on the North American continent. As the United States moved to normalize relationships with formerly communist opponents around the world, it tightened the embargo against the nearest communist state, Cuba. Why? One reason was that Fidel Castro's island nation remained avowedly communist, untouched by the reform movements that had swept most of the communist world. Another reason was the involvement of the Cuban American Foundation in shaping U.S. policy toward Cuba.

The Cuban American Foundation (CAF), a Miami-based organization of Cuban Americans founded during the 1980s lobbying boom and led by Jorge Mas Canosa, staunchly opposes any softening of the U.S. stand toward Cuba. CAF officers oversee three legally separate organizations: the Cuban American National Foundation to provide research, information, and education, the Free Cuba PAC to contribute to political campaigns, and the Cuban American Foundation to lobby public officials. The group is well heeled. It receives financial support from Cuban Americans and has also been bankrolled by U.S. corporations, including Chiquita Brands International, which provided some $200,000.

Since its founding, the group has enjoyed considerable success in winning support for its policy positions. Although its leadership is on the right of the political spectrum, the foundation plays politics on both sides of the partisan fence. From 1991 to 1992, the Free Cuba PAC dished out $250,000 to $400,000. Major recipients of its largesse have included senators Joseph Lieberman, a Democrat from Connecticut, and Orrin Hatch, the Utah Republican, as well as representatives Robert Torricelli, a Democrat from New Jersey, and Ileana Ros-Lehtinen, a Florida Republican.

Nor has the foundation focused its efforts at influence only on Congress. In 1992, the usually sympathetic Bush administration quietly opposed the so-called Cuban Democracy Act (Torricelli bill), legislation strongly supported by the foundation.

The media do help to set the foreign policy agenda (see Chapter 6). By giving play to a particular issue, policy, or crisis, the media are able to focus public opinion on it. Media attention to starvation in Somalia helped pave the way for U.S. intervention there. As in domestic affairs, the media may not tell people what to think, but they tell them what to think about.[45] Some issues lend themselves more to media coverage than do others, however. Pictures of malnourished children make better television than do technical negotiations over import quotas for agricultural products.

The relationship between policymakers and the media may often appear adversarial, but it is also highly symbiotic—that is, interdependent. Official Washington sometimes learns about breaking stories from worldwide television news networks such as CNN and ITN. Yet, despite dramatic video footage from Somalia, Bosnia, or Baghdad, news gathering in the foreign policy arena still depends heavily on official sources. Reporters make the rounds of the White House, State Department, Defense Department, and Capitol Hill. They tend to be most dependent on these sources where national security issues are involved and tend to discount

The bill proposed to increase economic pressure by prohibiting U.S. foreign subsidiaries from trading with Cuba. But 1992 was a presidential election year. When candidate Bill Clinton was asked about the Torricelli bill during a campaign stop in Florida, he said simply, "I like it." With that, the purses of Miami's Cuban Americans opened to him, and President Bush reassessed his administration's stance. Representative Torricelli toned down some of his bill's language, although not its ban on foreign subsidiary trade; the Bush administration agreed to support it, and the bill became law.

The foundation provides pamphlets and newsletters detailing the woes of Cuban society. It also tries to disseminate its views back home in Cuba through use of Radio Martí and TV Martí, stations that the foundation lobbied hard to create. Both stations are run by the United States Information Agency (USIA) with the help of the Advisory Board for Cuban Broadcasting which Mas Canosa chairs.

The foundation weighs in on other matters as well, including appointments. Recently, the foundation proved its lobbying clout when it opposed as insufficiently anti-Castro Clinton's nominee for the top Latin American job in the State Department. The foundation's leadership might expect to have an opportunity to vet appointments to other agencies that are important to it. Given the foundation's involvement with Radio and TV Martí, it pays considerable attention to who is chosen to head the USIA, for example.

The foundation has often seemed to call the shots on U.S. policy toward Cuba, but it has not done so without criticism. U.S. allies saw the proposed Cuban Democracy Act as an infringement on their sovereignty. Britain and Canada warned U.S. subsidiaries that compliance with the American measure would mean violating their laws. Both Radio and TV Martí's closeness to the foundation have been questioned. Furthermore, the General Accounting Office has criticized TV Martí for lack of balance and for failing to live up to the standards established for Voice of America broadcasts. Overall, however, the success of the foundation serves as an excellent example of pluralist politics in action.

• *Sources: Carla Anne Robbins, "Dateline Washington: Cuban-American Clout,"* Foreign Policy *(Fall 1992), pp. 162–182; Peter Stone, "Cuban Clout,"* National Journal, *20 February 1993, pp. 449–453; Dick Kirschten, "A Bridge to Cuba?"* National Journal, *11 September 1993, p. 2219.*

the qualifications of activist groups in this arena. If conflict or controversy break out among officials, the media will increase their coverage and may also turn to grassroots groups for new angles. When an official consensus prevails, however, news coverage tends to fade.

As foreign policy matters become more intermestic, news coverage may increasingly resemble that accorded to domestic political issues, with more open debate and greater reliance on a wide variety of sources. Simultaneously, the government may attempt to "mass market" foreign policy by using the media to influence opinion. The struggle over the NAFTA agreement involved considerable efforts to sway public opinion through political advertising, and the debate between vice President Al Gore and NAFTA opponent H. Ross Perot was widely credited with helping to turn the tide of public opinion in favor of NAFTA.

THE FOREIGN POLICY PROCESS   Having explained the historical context of American foreign policy and the participants, let us examine the policymaking process itself. How is foreign policy made?

Sources of Information for the Executive Branch

By virtue of constitutional position and practical control of resources, the president is the leading figure in the foreign policymaking process. A president comes to the job with a world view that helps him interpret and evaluate international events. And, as chief executive, he commands vast foreign policy resources, including information and personnel. The Pentagon, the State Department, and the CIA are among his main sources of information about the outside world, and their staffs advise him on foreign policy and its implementation. A president's sources of foreign policy advice are not limited to executive branch officials. Members of Congress can try to pressure the White House into a particular course of action. And foreign governments can also attempt to move an administration in a certain direction. The availability of so many sources of information can create a dilemma, however. Presidential advisers often present conflicting information and provide different, even contradictory, advice. Advisers may compete for a president's ear or bargain among themselves to shape administration policy. As a result of these competing pressures, the president's most important task in the foreign policymaking process is figuring out whom to believe—those who agree with his policy predispositions or those who challenge them. The wrong choice can be extremely costly. Some observers argue that President Lyndon Johnson's tendency to surround himself with yes men kept him from hearing critical analyses of the Vietnam situation until quite late.

Congress and the President

A president may carry out a policy without congressional approval, if he has a clear constitutional mandate (as, for example, when he recognizes a government or puts troops on alert). He may ask Congress for the funds or authority to carry out the policy. When his legal authority is shaky or congressional approval appears unlikely, he may use the techniques we described.

The president's command of information and personnel gives him a considerable advantage over Congress. Legislators have ample access to independent sources of information on domestic issues, but their sources on foreign affairs are more limited. Although members of Congress may go on fact-finding tours or get information from lobbyists, they have only a fraction of the president's sources of information and thus are forced to rely heavily on the executive branch.

The president may use his informational advantage to swing votes. During the 1991 congressional debate over the use of force in Iraq, CIA Director William Webster sent a letter to members of Congress providing data on the sanctions policy, along with his department's conclusion that an embargo alone would not force Saddam Hussein to leave Kuwait. The White House also fed information to Les Aspin, then the chair of the House Armed Services Committee, that was designed to convince him that American casualties would be very low in a military action against Iraq.

The chief executive's personnel resources give him considerable ability to influence events. Many analysts argue, for example, that the incidents that sparked the Gulf of Tonkin Resolution during the Vietnam War were pretexts that President Johnson seized on to expand American involvement.

Another disadvantage Congress faces in the foreign policy process is its fragmented authority over international issues. Each house has its own committees with authority over the armed services, foreign relations, intelligence oversight, foreign trade, and development. There is no equivalent of the National Security Council to coordinate congressional activities. Granted, disagreements occur within the executive branch and can even spill over into the congressional arena. For example, a Pentagon official might quietly appeal to friendly members of the Armed Services committees to restore a defense appropriations cut requested by the president. Disaffected executive branch officials might leak information. But by and large, the executive is much better equipped than Congress to mold a unified approach to foreign policy.

Faced with these disadvantages in information, personnel, and organization, the general tendency is for Congress to accede to the president's foreign policy programs.

Lobbies and the "Lobbyist in Chief"

Lobbies participate in the foreign policymaking process in many ways. When, during the Persian Gulf crisis, the Bush administration floated the possibility of putting together a $21 billion arms package for Saudi Arabia, lobbyists from the American-Israeli Public Affairs Committee, fearing future Saudi aggression, immediately began to mobilize their congressional allies; soon the administration retreated and offered only $7 billion. As fighting began in the gulf, a variety of newly organized groups geared up to express opinions on all sides of the issue. Among them were the Coalition to Stop U.S. Intervention in the Middle East, Churches for a Middle East Peace, the Citizens for a Free Kuwait, and the Coalition for America at Risk.

More recently, the NAFTA agreement brought out lobbyists in droves. Opposition to NAFTA ranged from the AFL-CIO to the Doris Day Animal League and included a variety of environmental, family farm, and consumer groups as well as Ross Perot's organization, United We Stand. NAFTA supporters, including trade associations, business coalitions and corporations, put together an umbrella group called U.S.A.*NAFTA. In addition to direct contact with legislators, both sides spent considerable sums on advertising to generate grassroots support for their positions.

However, the single most effective "lobbyist" on an issue is often not a lobbyist at all but the president, as both presidents Bush and Clinton demonstrated in recent years. When Congress began its new session on January 3, 1991, few would have guessed that only nine days later it would, in effect, vote to authorize war. Because Republicans were a minority in Congress, President Bush knew he had to win substantial support among Democrats for his gulf policy. He courted Dante Fascell, the Florida Democrat who chaired the House Foreign Affairs Committee, as well as several liberal members of Congress known for longstanding support of

Israel. He invited one hundred members to the White House for breakfast to hear his side of things. In the end, presidential arm twisting paid off in congressional approval of the resolution of support.

Because his party, the Democrats, controlled both houses of Congress, President Clinton might have expected an easy time securing passage of the NAFTA agreement. Yet, only days before the vote, NAFTA opponents confidently predicted that the measure would be defeated. Powerful interest groups aligned with the Democrats strongly opposed the pact, as did some of the party's congressional leadership. As a result, Clinton had to work hard to forge a coalition that included more Republicans than Democrats. To woo recalcitrant lawmakers, Clinton promised an array of concessions and spent hours breakfasting, lunching, dining, and golfing with fence straddlers. To win over Representative Harold Ford, a Democratic minister from Tennessee, the president prayed with him at the Olivet Baptist church in his Memphis home district. When the results were tallied, the president scored a major victory—NAFTA passed with votes to spare.

Policy Implementation

A president may decide on a course of action, and Congress may authorize it, but the policy still must be carried out. The question of who should carry out a particular policy is not always easy to answer. The functions of certain departments and agencies overlap, and agencies sometimes squabble over which should perform a particular mission. During the Cuban missile crisis, for example, the CIA and the military were disputing who should fly reconnaissance flights over Cuba. Coordination among competing bureaucracies can also be a problem. Rivalries among the various branches of the military were blamed for logistical and communications breakdowns when the United States invaded Grenada in 1983. The army and navy used different communications frequencies. One officer on the ground in Grenada, stymied by his inability to contact the navy on his army communications equipment, resorted to a long-distance calling card to telephone the Pentagon and ask to have his message relayed to the navy.[46]

Congress is responsible for overseeing the implementation of programs. That means, among other things, monitoring the correct use of funds and evaluating the effectiveness of programs. It may mean designing new legislation to deal with shortcomings. For example, in the 1980s Congress heard a great deal about military failures (such as the credit-card case in Grenada) as well as about waste in defense spending. In a famous case, Congress learned that the Pentagon had paid $500 for a hammer. To address these problems, Congress enacted the Defense Reorganization Act of 1986 (the Goldwater-Nichols Act), which gave more power to the chair of the Joint Chiefs of Staff and reduced the power of the individual services.[47]

FOREIGN POLICY ISSUE AREAS

During the Cold War, American foreign policy was preoccupied with the threat communism posed to our national security. With the end of the Cold War, the foreign policy problems the United States faces have changed. While issues of high politics, such as national security and defense, remain important, low politics issues have increased in importance. In this section we examine a few of these issues.

National Security and Defense Issues

The United States remains concerned with promoting peace and stability in Europe and with preventing nuclear proliferation. Aware that democracies seldom go to war with other democracies, United States policymakers have tried to promote democracy in Eastern Europe and the Soviet successor states by providing economic aid and technical assistance. The changes in Europe have also brought about a need to rethink NATO, America's oldest alliance. During the Cold War era, the United States relied on NATO to deter Soviet expansion into Western Europe. Lately, East European states, fearing a revival of Russian expansionism, have asked to join NATO. Reluctant to cause alarm in Russia, the NATO nations, with United States prodding, have created a special status, short of full NATO membership, for East European nations. By spring 1994, the Russians were suggesting that they, too, would like to become part of the NATO structure.

The United States has also worked to reduce the continued threat of nuclear weapons by negotiating with Soviet successor states such as Ukraine and Belarus to dismantle their nuclear arsenals and by attempting to prevent renegade states such as Iraq and North Korea from acquiring these capacities.

To protect its national interests, the United States will continue to need an adequate defense. Few disagree with that statement, but beyond that point agreement breaks down. Now that the Cold War is over, against whom are we defending ourselves? What constitutes an adequate defense?

To what extent should defense spending take priority over other kinds of spending?

During the Reagan years, the United States undertook an enormous defense buildup; the main justification was to counter the Soviet threat. As Soviet power declined, many Americans anticipated large defense cuts, a "peace dividend." Policymakers debated how far and how fast they could reduce the defense budget. This discussion slowed with the outbreak of war in the Persian Gulf, but subsequently both Bush and Clinton administration officials have continued to push for cuts in defense spending. Nonetheless, the fact that in the post–cold war world, the United States found itself involved in a full-scale war against a nation other than Russia raised new questions about future United States defense policy. In the new world order would the United States continue high levels of defense spending to be a global police officer? The Pentagon has adopted the position that the United States should have the military capacity to fight two conventional wars in different parts of the world simultaneously. The brass reasons that should the United States become involved in fighting in Korea, for example, nations in the Persian Gulf would be less likely to try to take advantage of the situation.

With the end of the Cold War, the United States armed forces have been scaled back in size. Policymakers have also begun to envision different tasks for the military services—such as providing humanitarian relief to Kurds and Somalis, fighting natural disasters, including floods and earthquakes, combating drug production and trade, and even fighting violent crime in Washington, D.C. Not all these roles have been or are likely to be adopted, but the fact that they have been entertained suggests a major shift in the way America thinks about its military.

Defense policy also requires decisions about how to use defense dollars. Should they pay for a volunteer military force, or should the United States require service by its citizens? Who should serve? Should homosexuals be permitted to serve? What about women? Compared with What? 20.1 discusses the roles of women in the military. Another issue concerns the kinds of weapons systems to build and the mix of nuclear and conventional forces. These decisions have obvious international ramifications, but they have important domestic significance. Closing a military base or stopping production of a piece of weaponry, such as a plane or submarine, can have huge economic consequences. In the short run, defense cutbacks cost jobs and may rouse domestic political opposition.

Critics of defense spending worry that the United States invests too much in sophisticated military hardware and not enough in developing "human capital." Without domestic programs for child nutrition, education, and job training, we may waste valuable human resources and end up with a population that lacks the ability to run the economy or defend the country. Other critics insist that high levels of defense spending help create budget deficits that endanger the overall performance of the United States economy. A weak economy, in turn, could make the nation more vulnerable to outside pressures.

It is important to consider the relationship between defense policy and foreign policy. Even if a strong defense is the cornerstone of foreign policy, not every foreign policy objective can be achieved by applying military force. Military might helped the United States push Iraq out of Kuwait, but

Women in Combat

 During the last two decades, women in America's all-volunteer military have found more and more job classifications open to them. Some 35,000 of the more than half-million Americans who served in the Persian Gulf War were women. Women served in dangerous spots, but they were officially banned from jobs actually defined as combat positions. After the Gulf War, the Pentagon reexamined its stance on women in combat, and in 1993, Secretary of Defense Les Aspin ordered the military to allow women to serve in combat roles in fighter planes, bombers, and armed helicopters. In allowing women to take up combat assignments, the United States followed a path already taken by some other NATO allies. Here are examples of the policies of other nations regarding women in the military.

Country	Policy	Percent of Women on Active Duty, 1992
Britain	Women may serve in combat roles in navy and air force as well as in all positions with ground forces, except armor and infantry.	6
Canada	Women serve in all combat jobs, except submarine duty. New submarines will have separate women's quarters.	11
Denmark	Women are eligible for every job, except combat aircraft.	3
Germany	Women are only allowed in medical jobs and military bands.	NA
Israel	Women are drafted but barred from serving in combat positions.	11
Netherlands	Women serve in all combat jobs, except submarine duty.	2
Norway	Women are eligible for every job in military.	2
Russia	Women are allowed in combat support and noncombat roles.	1
United States	Women are allowed in aerial combat jobs; military has been ordered to seek repeal of legislation barring women from serving on warships.	12

• *Source: Adapted from "Women in Combat: How Other Nations Rank,"* New York Times, *2 May 1993, p. 4.*

it isn't very useful, for example, in solving the debt crisis of developing nations or slowing global warming.

Economic and Environmental Issues

Some of the greatest problems the United States faces around the globe are not military but economic and environmental. During the last twenty years, the American economy has become **interdependent,** that is, much more closely tied to the economies of other nations. The United States may still be unrivalled as a military superpower, but it is certainly not without rivals as an economic power. Although America's military tools have proved impressive, American economic tools, in the areas of investment, trade, and aid, have not always performed as well. Furthermore, as new environmental issues have come to the fore, the United States has had difficulty formulating consistent, coherent policies to deal with them.

Against All Odds

For more than 27 years, the Palestine Liberation Organization headed by Yasser Arafat (second from right) fought with Israel for control of Israeli-held territory. The Israelis and the Palestinians reached an accord in September 1993, but the devil was in the details. At the diplomatic signing ceremony in May 1994 Arafat refused to sign some parts of the final deal, and Yitzhak Rabin, the Israeli Prime Minister (third from the left) threatened to walk out as U.S. Secretary of State Warren Christopher (far right) looked on. In the end, Arafat signed his name but appended remarks at each point stating his objections.

Although America began the 1980s as the world's leading creditor nation, it closed the decade as the number one debtor.[48] Some analysts in the United States and abroad have even suggested that America's military strength and its economic weakness may be related. In their view, America courted "imperial overstretch" by assuming too big a world military role. For example, whereas in 1988 the United States had a 46 percent share of the combined gross national products of the five most advanced industrial nations,* it picked up the tab for 70 percent of their combined defense expenditures. In comparison with Japan or Germany, the United States invested far more on defense research and far less on research in high-tech commercial areas.[49] As historian Paul Kennedy points out, a similar pattern of overspending on defense, combined with underspending on other areas, characterized the declines of such former great powers as Spain, the Netherlands, and Great Britain.[50]

Investment and Trade

The high level of national attention paid to the NAFTA debate in 1993 illustrates the new prominence of economic issues in foreign policy. America could not expect to retain for long the economic dominance it enjoyed immediately after World War II, but even through the 1970s the United States was able to invest heavily abroad, prompting European concern that both profits and control of European-based companies would drain away to America. In the 1980s, however, the situation began to reverse itself. A combination of tax cuts and defense spending increases created gaping deficits in the federal budget. The gaps were largely financed

---

* *France, Japan, West Germany, the United Kingdom, and the United States.*

by selling United States Treasury obligations to foreigners at high rates of interest. As investors from abroad bought up American government debts, the value of the dollar soared. This made American goods very expensive on the world market and also made foreign goods relatively inexpensive for Americans to buy. The result was a shift in our balance of trade—the United States began to import more than it exported and continued to borrow heavily. In 1985, an agreement among the industrialized nations resulted in a devaluation of the dollar in comparison with other currencies. As the dollar fell in value, American corporations and real estate became attractive investments for foreign investors. British Petroleum bought Sohio and Purina pet food. By 1988, foreigners held bonds totaling approximately $272 billion of the $1.7 trillion used to finance the national debt. They also owned $1.6 trillion in real property in America.[51] With the onset of recession and declining interest rates in the 1990s, foreign companies became less interested in investing in the United States. As the flow of foreign capital into the United States slowed, American economic problems deepened. This development underscores U.S. vulnerability in the increasingly interdependent world of international finance.

Some Americans resent the penetration of the United States economy by foreign investors. Others complain that American trading efforts have been hampered by unfair trading practices, such as the establishment of **nontariff barriers (NTBs)** by other countries. These are regulations that outline the exact specifications an imported product must meet in order to be offered for sale. The Japanese, for example, have been criticized for excessive use of NTBs. In a recent instance, American-made baby bottle manufacturers were not permitted to sell their product in Japan, because the bottles provided level marks in ounces as well as centiliters.[52] The U.S. has responded by pressuring the Japanese to reduce red tape and make it easier for American companies to compete in Japan. The Japanese have accepted some voluntary limits on exports to the U.S. and finally allowed importation of American rice to Japan. American business has not been fully satisfied with these efforts.

As we pointed out in Chapter 9, domestic pressure to adopt import restrictions can be strong. Most unions and manufacturers opposed NAFTA because they believed that if tariffs were removed, Mexico, with its low labor costs, would be able to undersell American producers, thus running them out of business (or forcing them to move their operations to Mexico). Either alternative threatened American jobs. At the same time, many Americans were eager to take advantage of new opportunities in a growing Mexican market for American goods and services. They realized that protectionism can be a double-edged sword. Countries whose products are kept out of the United States retaliate by refusing to import American goods. And protectionism complicates the foreign policymaking process enormously. It is a distinctly unfriendly move to make toward nations that may be our allies.

Still, some analysts have worried that American emphasis on free enterprise and the "magic of the marketplace" puts the nation at a disadvantage in competition with, among others, the Germans and Japanese, who have adopted national industrial policies—that is, government-sponsored coordinated plans for promoting economic expansion.[53] When Japanese makers of semiconductors threatened to drive American microchip producers out of business, the United States government responded by helping to fund Sematech, a consortium of semiconductor manufacturers whose goal was to rescue the American microchip industry and recapture its lost share of the world market. The United States did succeed in reviving the industry, and as a result other industries, such as autos and aerospace, have sought and received government backing to create similar consortia.[54]

Foreign Aid and Development Assistance

The United States has many economic tools with which to pursue its policies in the developing world. These include development aid, preferential trade agreements, debt forgiveness and loans on favorable credit terms. Assistance to developing countries also takes the form of donation of American goods and thus directly benefits American businesses that supply the products.

Inequality between rich nations and poor nations is growing. Figures show an increasing gap in income between the industrialized states of the North and the nonindustrialized states of the South.[55] This gap is a cause of concern for several reasons. Many people believe it is unjust for the developed world to enjoy great wealth while people in less developed states are deprived. Sheer self-interest may also motivate policymakers to address this problem. Great disparities in wealth between the developed and the developing worlds may lead to political instability and disorder and thus threaten the interests of industrialized democracies. Recently, Russia and the countries of Eastern Europe have begun to compete with the Third World for development dollars. As they have, U.S. lawmakers have taken into account the need to ensure political stability and bring about a successful transition to democracy in the former communist states. As a result, the first foreign aid bill enacted during the Clinton administration included $2.5 billion in aid for the former Soviet Union.

Developing states have tried to reduce inequalities by enlisting the cooperation of the developed world in a proposal for a **New International Economic Order (NIEO)**. Under the proposed NIEO, industrialized states would take a variety of steps to help less-developed nations. These measures include providing access to markets, transferring technology, and increasing foreign development aid to 0.7 percent of gross national product (GNP). On the whole, the United States has shown little interest in promoting greater global equality through NIEO. American development aid amounts to about 0.25 percent of GNP, far short of the NIEO goal, and proportionally less than that offered by most other developed nations.[56] Foreign aid serves both political and humanitarian ends, but in times of fiscal austerity, foreign aid expenditures are easy targets for budget cutters.

Sanctions and Embargoes

In addition to the rewards offered by development aid, economic measures may be used in service of high politics, for example, to punish states that do not behave as the United States would like. Sanctions, embargoes, and boycotts fall into this category. Many think the effectiveness of these tools is quite limited, but they are often a first resort in times of crisis. For example, although NATO nations were unable to agree on military action in response to Serbian aggression against Bosnia, they did impose economic sanctions. When the United States wanted to force Iraq out of Kuwait, it first tried an embargo. Under the Carter administration, the United States imposed a grain embargo against the Soviet Union—that is, the United States stopped wheat shipments to the Soviet Union—to convince the Russians to leave Afghanistan. Shortly after Castro took power in Cuba, the United States imposed a **boycott** on Cuban products—that is, it refused to allow American citizens to import Cuban sugar, cigars, and other goods.

Neither the grain embargo nor the boycott of Cuban goods has proved particularly effective in furthering foreign policy goals. The Soviets stayed in Afghanistan to the end of Reagan's presidency, and Castro's power in Cuba is still secure. American pluralist democracy helps explain why one was dropped and the other remains in effect. American grain farmers were seriously hurt by the Soviet grain embargo. They were caught without a market for huge amounts of wheat originally destined for the Soviet Union. They were a vocal minority, and the nation heard them. When the embargo became generally unpopular, President Reagan lifted it. In contrast, the boycott of Cuban sugar has helped America's domestic sugar industry. Any attempt to lift the boycott would be resisted not only by the large community of anti-Castro Cuban Americans in this country but also by the sugar industry, which would suddenly have to compete with less-expensive Cuban sugar. Because there is no strong pressure to remove the boycott, it remains in place. Pluralist politics triumph.

The Environment

The 1992 United Nations Conference on Environment and Development, popularly known as the Earth Summit, signaled the growing worldwide acknowledgement of a new and vital issue area in global politics. Nations have become increasingly aware that various human activities threaten to degrade or destroy the earth's environment. But reaching international agreement on how to deal with these challenges and crafting national policies to meet them has proved difficult.

The Earth Summit considered a wide range of environmental problems. Two of the chief among them were

- decreasing biodiversity. Humans have become increasingly dependent on a limited number of species for food and other needs. Some 80 percent of our food comes from fewer than two dozen species. In 1992, some one hundred to two hundred species became extinct, according to some environmental scientists.[57] If disease or climatic change threatened these species, the food supply could be seriously threatened. Furthermore, many species are yet unknown and could offer the opportunity for new advances in agriculture, medicine, or other fields.

- global warming. A buildup of gases, such as carbon dioxide and methane emitted by automobiles and industries, acts as a barrier that prevents heat from the sun from escaping the earth's atmosphere, creating a greenhouse effect. The result, many scientists believe, will be a gradual increase in global surface temperatures, causing the polar ice caps to melt. This would submerge vast areas of low-lying countries. In addition, increased temperature could render productive agricultural land less usable.

Although environmental problems were becoming clearer to the world at Rio, the steps put forth there to solve them were not acceptable to the United States. Nations that agreed to a biodiversity treaty offered there committed themselves to preserve habitat. Other treaty provisions called for developed nations to pay less-developed states for the right to extract biological products from rare species in protected habitat. President Bush feared that the treaty placed too many limits on U.S. patent rights in biotechnology and failed to protect intellectual property rights. Consequently, he refused to sign the biodiversity treaty. Nor did the United States agree to a timetable designed to slow global warming. In the view of the Bush administration, these measures would impose regulations that threaten the U.S. economy. When the Clinton administration came to office, the president promised to reverse his predecessor's stand on these issues, yet he too avoided asking for tough action that might crack down on major sources of carbon dioxide, emissions such as automobile exhaust and smoke from coal-burning utilities, again demonstrating that global environmental issues are likely to be closely tied to domestic politics.

Human Rights

Rhetorically, America has long championed democracy and human rights—from President Wilson's call to "make the world safe for democracy," through President Carter's claim that "human rights is the soul of our foreign policy," President Reagan's efforts to "foster the infrastructure of democracy," and presidential candidate Bill Clinton's call for the United States to back democratic change, drawing "the new map of freedom."

To an extent, the support for moral ideals such as freedom, democracy, and human rights fits in well with U.S. interests. It is enormously useful to the United States to have other nations adopt elements of the liberal political ideology that has suffused our political culture. For one thing, democracies virtually never go to war with other democracies.

Other nations may well insist on retaining their own hierarchy of values, regardless of U.S. pressure. Thus, despite criticism from human rights advocates and a presidential appeal for leniency, the government of Singapore held fast to its preference for the value of order and carried out a sentence of four strokes of a cane on Ohio teenager Michael Fay, who had been accused of vandalism.

Although the United States gives lip service to human rights, other values often take a higher priority in foreign policy. When other nations reject U.S. human rights standards, the United States does not always enforce penalties. For example, in 1993, after reviewing China's dismal record in human rights, the U.S. threatened the Chinese with withdrawal of **most favored nation** (MFN) status (which gives China the same low-tariff treatment other nations receive). In 1994, President Clinton backed away from this threat and renewed MFN for China, despite clear evidence that its leaders had done little to improve human rights. In doing so, the president "delinked" trade policy and human rights. He accorded a higher priority to other interests that the United States and China shared, including trade as well as maintaining Asian and global security and sustaining the global environment.[58] As some analysts note, he also weighed domestic considerations, namely, the American jobs that would be lost if trade with China were cut.[59]

SUMMARY

America emerged as a superpower after World War II and soon developed a consensus on foreign policy: Communism was the threat, and the goal was to contain Soviet expansion. The Vietnam War challenged that consensus. In the post–Cold War era, international issues and domestic issues have become more closely entwined, so today it seems less meaningful to suggest that politics should stop at the water's edge. With shared responsibility and no clear consensus, foreign policy can become a political football in contests between Congress and the executive and among the bureaucracies. These contests are frequently played before a mass audience on live television. It was exactly the potential for this sort of conflict that led Tocqueville to predict that democracies would not be very good at foreign politics. Increasingly, the pluralism characteristic of the rest of the political system characterizes the foreign policy arena as well.

Key Terms

Cold War
high politics
low politics
North American Free
 Trade Agreement
 (NAFTA)
intermestic
containment
GATT–Bretton Woods
 system
Marshall Plan
North Atlantic Treaty
 Organization (NATO)
deterrence
mutual assured
 destruction (MAD)
flexible response
wars of
 national liberation
nation building
Nixon doctrine
détente
Carter doctrine
Vietnam syndrome
executive agreement

discretionary funds
transfer authority
reprogramming
War Powers Resolution
special envoy
National Security
 Council (NSC)
interdependent
nontariff barrier (NTB)
New International
 Economic Order (NIEO)
boycott
most favored nation
 (MFN)

Selected Readings

Crabb, Cecil V., and Pat M. Holt. *An Invitation to Struggle*. Washington, D.C.: Congressional Quarterly Press, 1980. This work describes the interplay between Congress and the executive on foreign policy issues.

Deese, David., ed. *The New Politics of American Foreign Policy*. New York: St. Martins Press, 1994. A good collection of articles focusing on the reasons for the increased politicization of the foreign policy process.

Kennedy, Paul. *The Rise and Fall of the Great Powers*. New York: Random House, 1988. Discusses why various nations have gained and lost power in the modern world and concludes with a section called "The United States: The Problem of Number One in Relative Decline."

Nathan, James, and James Oliver. *United States Foreign Policy and World Order*, 4th ed. Boston: Little, Brown, 1989. An excellent general history of American foreign policy since World War II.

Snow, Donald, and Eugene Brown. *Puzzle Palace and Foggy Bottom: United States Foreign and Defense Policy-making in the 1990s*. New York: St. Martins Press, 1994. A study of key foreign policy institutions as they try to cope with the challenges of the post–Cold War world.

Appendices

■

The Declaration of Independence in Congress   July 4, 1776

The unanimous declaration of the thirteen United States of America

When, in the course of human events, it becomes necessary for one people to dissolve the political bands which have connected them with another, and to assume, among the powers of the earth, the separate and equal station to which the laws of nature and of nature's God entitle them, a decent respect to the opinions of mankind requires that they should declare the causes which impel them to the separation.

We hold these truths to be self-evident: That all men are created equal; that they are endowed by their Creator with certain unalienable rights; that among these are life, liberty, and the pursuit of happiness; that, to secure these rights, governments are instituted among men, deriving their just powers from the consent of the governed; that whenever any form of government becomes destructive of these ends, it is the right of the people to alter or to abolish it, and to institute new government, laying its foundation on such principles, and organizing its power in such form, as to them shall seem most likely to effect their safety and happiness. Prudence, indeed, will dictate that governments long established should not be changed for light and transient causes; and accordingly all experience hath shown that mankind are more disposed to suffer, while evils are sufferable, than to right themselves by abolishing the forms to which they are accustomed. But when a long train of abuses and usurpations, pursuing invariably the same object, evinces a design to reduce them under absolute despotism, it is their right, it is their duty, to throw off such government, and to provide new guards for their future security. Such has been the patient sufferance of these colonies; and such is now the necessity which constrains them to alter their former systems of government. The history of the present King of Great Britain is a history of repeated injuries and usurpations, all having in direct object the establishment of an absolute tyranny over these states. To prove this, let facts be submitted to a candid world.

He has refused his assent to laws, the most wholesome and necessary for the public good.

He has forbidden his governors to pass laws of immediate and pressing importance, unless suspended in their operation till his assent should be obtained; and, when so suspended, he has utterly neglected to attend to them.

He has refused to pass other laws for the accommodation of large districts of people, unless those people would relinquish the right of representation in the legislature, a right inestimable to them, and formidable to tyrants only.

He has called together legislative bodies at places unusual, uncomfortable, and distant from the depository of their public records, for the sole purpose of fatiguing them into compliance with his measures.

He has dissolved representative houses repeatedly, for opposing, with manly firmness, his invasions on the rights of the people.

He has refused for a long time, after such dissolutions, to cause others to be elected; whereby the legislative powers, incapable of annihilation, have returned to the people at large for their exercise; the state remaining, in the mean time, exposed to all the dangers of invasions from without and convulsions within.

He has endeavored to prevent the population of these states; for that purpose obstructing the laws for naturalization of foreigners; refusing to pass others to encourage their migration hither, and raising the conditions of new appropriations of lands.

He has obstructed the administration of justice, by refusing his assent to laws for establishing judiciary powers.

He has made judges dependent on his will alone, for the tenure of their offices, and the amount and payment of their salaries.

He has erected a multitude of new offices, and sent hither swarms of officers to harass our people and eat out their substance.

He has kept among us, in times of peace, standing armies, without the consent of our legislatures.

He has affected to render the military independent of, and superior to, the civil power.

He has combined with others to subject us to a jurisdiction foreign to our constitution, and unacknowledged by our laws, giving his assent to their acts of pretended legislation:

For quartering large bodies of armed troops among us;

For protecting them, by a mock trial, from punishment for any murders which they should commit on the inhabitants of these states;

For cutting off our trade with all parts of the world;

For imposing taxes on us without our consent;

For depriving us, in many cases, of the benefits of trial by jury;

For transporting us beyond seas, to be tried for pretended offenses;

For abolishing the free system of English laws in a neighboring province, establishing therein an arbitrary government, and enlarging its boundaries, so as to render it at once an example and fit instrument for introducing the same absolute rule into these colonies;

For taking away our charters, abolishing our most valuable laws, and altering fundamentally the forms of our governments;

For suspending our own legislatures, and declaring themselves invested with power to legislate for us in all cases whatsoever.

He has abdicated government here, by declaring us out of his protection and waging war against us.

He has plundered our seas, ravaged our coasts, burned our towns, and destroyed the lives of our people.

He is at this time transporting large armies of foreign mercenaries to complete the works of death, desolation, and tyranny already begun with circumstances of cruelty and perfidy scarcely paralleled in the most barbarous ages, and totally unworthy the head of a civilized nation.

He has constrained our fellow-citizens, taken captive on the high seas, to bear arms against their country, to become the executioners of their friends and brethren, or to fall themselves by their hands.

He has excited domestic insurrection among us, and has endeavored to bring on the inhabitants of our frontiers the merciless Indian savages, whose known rule of warfare is an undistinguished destruction of all ages, sexes, and conditions.

In every stage of these oppressions we have petitioned for redress in the most humble terms; our repeated petitions have been answered only by repeated injury. A prince, whose character is thus marked by every act which may define a tyrant, is unfit to be the ruler of a free people.

Nor have we been wanting in our attentions to our British brethren. We have warned them, from time to time, of attempts by their legislature to extend an unwarrantable jurisdiction over us. We have reminded them of the circumstances of our emigration and settlement here. We have appealed to their native justice and magnanimity; and we have conjured them, by the ties of our common kindred, to disavow these usurpations, which would inevitably interrupt our connections and correspondence. They, too, have been deaf to the voice of justice and of consanguinity. We must, therefore, acquiesce in the necessity which denounces our separation, and hold them, as we hold the rest of mankind, enemies in war, in peace friends.

We, therefore, the representatives of the United States of America, in General Congress assembled, appealing to the Supreme Judge of the world for the rectitude of our intentions, do, in the name and by the authority of the good people of these colonies, solemnly publish and declare, that these United Colonies are, and of right ought to be, FREE AND INDEPENDENT STATES; that they are absolved from all allegiance to the British crown, and that all political connection between them and the state of Great Britain is, and ought to be, totally dissolved; and that, as free and independent states, they have full power to levy war, conclude peace, contract alliances, establish commerce, and do all other acts and things which independent states may of right do. And for the support of this declaration, with a firm reliance on the protection of Divine Providence, we mutually pledge to each other our lives, our fortunes, and our sacred honor.

JOHN HANCOCK
and fifty-five others

Articles of Confederation

Whereas the Delegates of the United States of America in Congress assembled did on the fifteenth day of November in the Year of our Lord One Thousand Seven Hundred and Seventy seven, and in the Second

Year of the Independence of America agree to certain articles of Confederation and perpetual Union between the States of Newhampshire, Massachusetts-bay, Rhodeisland and Providence Plantations, Connecticut, New York, New Jersey, Pennsylvania, Delaware, Maryland, Virginia, North-Carolina, South-Carolina and Georgia in the Words following, viz. "Articles of Confederation and perpetual Union between the states of Newhampshire, Massachusetts-bay, Rhodeisland and Providence Plantations, Connecticut, New-York, New-Jersey, Pennsylvania, Delaware, Maryland, Virginia, North-Carolina, South-Carolina and Georgia.

Article I The Stile of this confederacy shall be "The United States of America."

Article II Each state retains its sovereignty, freedom and independence, and every Power, Jurisdiction and right, which is not by this confederation expressly delegated to the United States, in Congress assembled.

Article III The said states hereby severally enter into a firm league of friendship with each other, for their common defence, the security of their Liberties, and their mutual and general welfare, binding themselves to assist each other, against all force offered to, or attacks made upon them, or any of them, on account of religion, sovereignty, trade, or any other pretence whatever.

Article IV The better to secure and perpetuate mutual friendship and intercourse among the people of the different states in this union, the free inhabitants of each of these states, paupers, vagabonds and fugitives from Justice excepted, shall be entitled to all privileges and immunities of free citizens in the several states; and the people of each state shall have free ingress and regress to and from any other state, and shall enjoy therein all the privileges of trade and commerce, subject to the same duties, impositions and restrictions as the inhabitants thereof respectively, provided that such restriction shall not extend so far as to prevent the removal of property imported into any state, to any other state of which the Owner is an inhabitant; provided also that no imposition, duties or restriction shall be laid by any state, on the property of the united states, or either of them.

If any Person guilty of, or charged with treason, felony, or other high misdemeanor in any state, shall flee from Justice, and be found in any of the united states, he shall upon demand of the Governor or executive power, of the state from which he fled, be delivered up and removed to the state having jurisdiction of his offence.

Full faith and credit shall be given in each of these states to the records, acts and judicial proceedings of the courts and magistrates of every other state.

Article V For the more convenient management of the general interests of the united states, delegates shall be annually appointed in such manner as the legislature of each state shall direct, to meet in Congress on the first Monday in November, in every year, with a power reserved to each state, to recall its delegates, or any of them, at any time within the year, and to send others in their stead, for the remainder of the Year.

No state shall be represented in Congress by less than two, nor by more than seven Members; and no person shall be capable of being a delegate for more than three years in any term of six years; nor shall any person, being a delegate, be capable of holding any office under the united states, for which he, or another for his benefit receives any salary, fees or emolument of any kind.

Each state shall maintain its own delegates in a meeting of the states, and while they act as members of the committee of the states.

In determining questions in the united states, in Congress assembled, each state shall have one vote.

Freedom of speech and debate in Congress shall not be impeached or questioned in any Court, or place out of Congress, and the members of congress shall be protected in their persons from arrests and imprisonments, during the time of their going to and from, and attendance on congress, except for treason, felony, or breach of the peace.

Article VI No state without the Consent of the united states in congress assembled, shall send any embassy to, or receive any embassy from, or enter into any conference, agreement, or alliance or treaty with any King, prince or state; nor shall any person holding any office of profit or trust under the united states, or any of them, accept of any present, emolument, office or title of any kind whatever from any king, prince or foreign state; nor shall the united states in congress assembled, or any of them, grant any title of nobility.

No two or more states shall enter into any treaty, confederation or alliance whatever between them, without the consent of the united states in congress assembled, specifying accurately the purposes for which the same is to be entered into, and how long it shall continue.

No state shall lay any imposts or duties, which may interfere with any stipulations in treaties, entered into by the united states in congress assembled, with any king, prince or state, in pursuance of any treaties already proposed by congress, to the courts of France and Spain.

No vessels of war shall be kept up in time of peace by any state, except such number only, as shall be deemed necessary by the united states in congress assembled, for the defence of such state, or its trade; nor shall any body of forces be kept up by any state, in time of peace, except such number only, as in the judgment of the united states, in congress assembled, shall be deemed requisite to garrison the forts necessary for the defence of such state; but every state shall always keep up a well regulated and disciplined militia, sufficiently armed and accoutred, and shall provide and constantly have ready for use, in public stores, a due number of field pieces and tents, and a proper quantity of arms, ammunition and camp equipage.

No state shall engage in any war without the consent of the united states in congress assembled, unless such state be actually invaded by enemies, or shall have received certain advice of a resolution being formed by some nation of Indians to invade such state, and the danger is so imminent as not to admit of a delay, till the united states in congress assembled can be consulted: nor shall any state grant commissions to any ships or vessels of war, nor letters of marque or reprisal, except it be after a declaration of war by the united states in congress assembled, and then only against the kingdom or state and the subjects thereof, against which war has been so declared, and under such regulations as shall be established by the united states in congress assembled, unless such state be infested by pirates, in which case vessels of war may be fitted out for that occasion, and kept so long as the danger shall continue, or until the united states in congress assembled shall determine otherwise.

Article VII   When land-forces are raised by any state for the common defence, all officers of or under the rank of colonel, shall be appointed by the legislature of each state respectively by whom such forces shall be raised, or in such manner as such state shall direct, and all vacancies shall be filled up by the state which first made the appointment.

Article VIII   All charges of war, and all other expences that shall be incurred for the common defence or general welfare, and allowed by the united states in congress assembled, shall be defrayed out of a common treasury, which shall be supplied by the several states, in proportion to the value of all land within each state, granted to or surveyed for any Person, as such land and the buildings and improvements thereon shall be estimated according to such mode as

the united states in congress assembled, shall from time to time direct and appoint. The taxes for paying that proportion shall be laid and levied by the authority and direction of the legislatures of the several states within the time agreed upon by the united states in congress assembled.

Article IX   The united states in congress assembled, shall have the sole and exclusive right and power of determining on peace and war, except in the cases mentioned in the sixth article—of sending and receiving ambassadors—entering into treaties and alliances, provided that no treaty of commerce shall be made whereby the legislative power of the respective states shall be restrained from imposing such imposts and duties on foreigners, as their own people are subjected to, or from prohibiting the exportation or importation of any species of goods or commodities whatsoever—of establishing rules for deciding in all cases, what captures on land or water shall be legal, and in what manner prizes taken by land or naval forces in the service of the united states shall be divided or appropriated.—of granting letters of marque and reprisal in times of peace—appointing courts for the trial of piracies and felonies committed on the high seas and establishing courts for receiving and determining finally appeals in all cases of captures, provided that no member of congress shall be appointed a judge of any of the said courts.

The united states in congress assembled shall also be the last resort on appeal in all disputes and differences now subsisting or that hereafter may arise between two or more states concerning boundary, jurisdiction or any other cause whatever; which authority shall always be exercised in the manner following. Whenever the legislative or executive authority or lawful agent of any state in controversy with another shall present a petition to congress, stating the matter in question and praying for a hearing, notice thereof shall be given by order of congress to the legislative or executive authority of the other state in controversy, and a day assigned for the appearance of the parties by their lawful agents, who shall then be directed to appoint by joint consent, commissioners or judges to constitute a court for hearing and determining the matter in question: but if they cannot agree, congress shall name three persons out of each of the united states, and from the list of such persons each party shall alternately strike out one, the petitioners beginning, until the number shall be reduced to thirteen; and from that number not less than seven, nor more than nine names as congress shall direct, shall in the presence of congress be drawn out by lot, and the persons whose names shall be so drawn or any five of them, shall be commissioners or judges, to hear and finally determine the controversy, so always as a major part of the judges who shall hear the cause shall agree in the determination: and if either party shall neglect to attend at the day appointed, without shewing reasons, which congress shall judge sufficient, or being present shall refuse to strike, the congress shall proceed to nominate three persons out of each state, and the secretary of congress shall strike in behalf of such party absent or refusing; and the judgment and sentence of the court to be appointed, in the manner before prescribed, shall be final and conclusive; and if any of the parties shall refuse to submit to the authority of such court, or to appear to defend their claim or cause, the court shall nevertheless proceed to pronounce sentence, or judgment, which shall in like manner be final and decisive, the judgment or sentence and other proceedings being in either case transmitted to congress, and lodged among the acts of congress for the security of the parties concerned: provided that every commissioner, before he sits in judgment, shall take an oath to be administered by one of the judges of the supreme or superior court of the state, where the cause shall be tried, "well and truly to hear and determine the matter in question, according to the best of his judgment, without favour, affection or hope of reward:" provided also that no state shall be deprived of territory for the benefit of the united states.

All controversies concerning the private right of soil claimed under different grants of two or more states, whose jurisdictions as they may respect such lands, and the states which passed such grants are adjusted, the said grants or either of them being at the same time claimed to have originated antecedent to such settlement of jurisdiction, shall on the petition of either party to the congress of the united states, be finally determined as near as may be in the same manner as is before prescribed for deciding disputes respecting territorial jurisdiction between different states.

The united states in congress assembled shall also have the sole and exclusive right and power of regulating the alloy and value of coin struck by their own authority, or by that of the respective states—fixing the standard of weights and measures throughout the united states.—regulating the trade and managing all affairs with the Indians, not members of any of the states, provided that the legislative right of any state within its own limits be not infringed or violated—establishing and regulating post-offices from one state to another, throughout all the united states, and exacting such postage on the papers passing thro' the same as may be requisite to defray the expences of the said office—appointing all officers of the land forces, in the service of the united states, excepting regimental officers.—appointing all the officers of the naval forces,

and commissioning all officers whatever in the service of the united states—making rules for the government and regulation of the said land and naval forces, and directing their operations.

The united states in congress assembled shall have authority to appoint a committee, to sit in the recess of congress, to be denominated "A Committee of the States," and to consist of one delegate from each state; and to appoint such other committees and civil officers as may be necessary for managing the general affairs of the united states under their direction—to appoint one of their number to preside, provide that no person be allowed to serve in the office of president more than one year in any term of three years; to ascertain the necessary sums of Money to be raised for the service of the united states, and to appropriate and apply the same for defraying the public expences—to borrow money, or emit bills on the credit of the united states, transmitting every half year to the respective states an account of the sums of money so borrowed or emitted,—to build and equip a navy—to agree upon the number of land forces, and to make requisitions from each state for its quota, in proportion to the number of white inhabitants in such state; which requisition shall be binding, and thereupon the legislature of each state shall appoint the regimental officers, raise the men and cloath, arm and equip them in a soldier like manner, at the expence of the united states, and the officers and men so cloathed, armed and equipped shall march to the place appointed, and within the time agreed on by the united states in congress assembled: But if the united states in congress assembled shall, on consideration of circumstances judge proper that any state should not raise men, or should raise a smaller number than its quota, and that any other state should raise a greater number of men than the quota thereof, such extra number shall be raised, officered, cloathed, armed and equipped in the same manner as the quota of such state, unless the legislature of such state shall judge that such extra number cannot be safely spared out of the same, in which case they shall raise, officer, cloath, arm and equip as many of such extra number as they judge can be safely spared. And the officers and men so cloathed, armed and equipped, shall march to the place appointed, and within the time agreed on by the united states in congress assembled.

The united states in congress assembled shall never engage in a war, nor grant letters of marque and reprisal in time of peace, nor enter into any treaties or alliances, nor coin money, nor regulate the value thereof, nor ascertain the sums and expences necessary for the defence and welfare of the united states, or any of them, nor emit bills, nor borrow money on the credit of the united states, nor appropriate money, nor agree upon the number of vessels of war, to be built or purchased, or the number of land or sea forces to be raised, nor appoint a commander in chief of the army or navy, unless nine states assent to the same: nor shall a question on any other point, except for adjourning from day to day be determined, unless by the votes of a majority of the united states in congress assembled.

The congress of the united states shall have power to adjourn to any time within the year, and to any place within the united states, so that no period of adjournment be for a longer duration than the space of six Months, and shall publish the Journal of their proceedings monthly, except such parts thereof relating to treaties, alliances or military operations as in their judgment require secresy; and the yeas and nays of the delegates of each state on any question shall be entered on the Journal, when it is desired by any delegate; and the delegates of a state, or any of them, at his or their request shall be furnished with a transcript of the said Journal, except such parts as are above excepted, to lay before the legislatures of the several states.

Article X   The committee of the states, or any nine of them, shall be authorised to execute, in the recess of congress, such of the powers of congress as the united states in congress assembled, by the consent of nine states, shall from time to time think expedient to vest them with; provided that no power be delegated to the said committee, for the exercise of which, by the articles of confederation, the voice of nine states in the congress of the united states assembled is requisite.

Article XI   Canada acceding to this confederation, and joining in the measures of the united states, shall be admitted into, and entitled to all the advantages of this union: but no other colony shall be admitted into the same, unless such admission be agreed to by nine states.

Article XII   All bills of credit emitted, monies borrowed and debts contracted by, or under the authority of congress, before the assembling of the united states, in pursuance of the present confederation, shall be deemed and considered as a charge against the united states, for payment and satisfaction whereof the said united states, and the public faith are hereby solemnly pledged.

Article XIII   Every state shall abide by the determinations of the united states in congress assembled, on all questions which by this confederation are submitted to them. And the Articles of this confederation shall be inviolably observed by every state, and the union shall be perpetual; nor shall any alteration at any time hereafter be made in any of them; unless such

alteration be agreed to in a congress of the united states, and be afterwards confirmed by the legislatures of every state.

AND WHEREAS it hath pleased the Great Governor of the World to incline the hearts of legislatures we respectively represent in congress, to approve of, and to authorize us to ratify the said articles of confederation and perpetual union. KNOW YE that we the undersigned delegates, by virtue of the power and authority to us given for that purpose, do by these presents, in the name and in behalf of our respective constituents, fully and entirely ratify and confirm each and every of the said articles of confederation and perpetual union, and all and singular the matters and things therein contained: And we do further solemnly plight and engage the faith of our respective constituents, that they shall abide by the determinations of the united states in congress assembled, on all questions, which by the said confederation are submitted to them. And that the articles thereof shall be inviolably observed by the states we respectively represent, and that the union shall be perpetual. In Witness whereof we have hereunto set our hands in Congress. Done at Philadelphia in the state of Pennsylvania the ninth Day of July in the Year of our Lord one Thousand seven Hundred and Seventy-eight, and in the third year of the independence of America.

■

The Constitution of the United States of America*

(Preamble: outlines goals and effect)

We the people of the United States, in order to form a more perfect union, establish justice, insure domestic tranquility, provide for the common defense, promote the general welfare, and secure the blessings of liberty to ourselves and our posterity, do ordain and establish this Constitution for the United States of America.

Article I   (The legislative branch)

(Powers vested)

Section 1   All legislative powers herein granted shall be vested in a Congress of the United States, which shall consist of a Senate and a House of Representatives.

(House of Representatives: selection, term, qualifications, apportionment of seats, census requirement, exclusive power to impeach)

*Passages no longer in effect are printed in italic type.

Section 2 The House of Representatives shall be composed of members chosen every second year by the people of the several States, and the electors in each State shall have the qualifications requisite for electors of the most numerous branch of the State Legislature.

No person shall be a Representative who shall not have attained to the age of twenty-five years, and been seven years a citizen of the United States, and who shall not, when elected, be an inhabitant of that State in which he shall be chosen.

Representatives and direct taxes shall be apportioned among the several States which may be included within this Union, according to their respective numbers, *which shall be determined by adding to the whole number of free persons, including those bound to service for a term of years and excluding Indians not taxed, three-fifths of all other persons.* The actual enumeration shall be made within three years after the first meeting of the Congress of the United States, and within every subsequent term of ten years, in such manner as they shall by law direct. The number of Representatives shall not exceed one for every thirty thousand, but each State shall have at least one Representative; *and until such enumeration shall be made, the State of New Hampshire shall be entitled to choose three, Massachusetts eight, Rhode Island and Providence Plantations one, Connecticut five, New York six, New Jersey four, Pennsylvania eight, Delaware one, Maryland six, Virginia ten, North Carolina five, South Carolina five, and Georgia three.*

When vacancies happen in the representation from any State, the Executive authority thereof shall issue writs of election to fill such vacancies.

The House of Representatives shall choose their Speaker and other officers; and shall have the sole power of impeachment.

(Senate: selection, term, qualifications, exclusive power to try impeachments)

Section 3 The Senate of the United States shall be composed of two Senators from each State, *chosen by the legislature thereof,* for six years; and each Senator shall have one vote.

Immediately after they shall be assembled in consequence of the first election, they shall be divided as equally as may be into three classes. The seats of the Senators of the first class shall be vacated at the expiration of the second year, of the second class at the expiration of the fourth year, and of the third class at the expiration of the sixth year, so that one-third may be chosen every second year; *and if vacancies happen by resignation or otherwise, during the recess of the legislature of any State, the Executive thereof may make temporary appointments until the next meeting of the legislature, which shall then fill such vacancies.*

No person shall be a Senator who shall not have attained to the age of thirty years, and been nine years a citizen of the United States, and who shall not, when elected, be an inhabitant of that State for which he shall be chosen.

The Vice-President of the United States shall be President of the Senate, but shall have no vote, unless they be equally divided.

The Senate shall choose their other officers, and also a President *pro tempore,* in the absence of the Vice-President, or when he shall exercise the office of President of the United States.

The Senate shall have the sole power to try all impeachments. When sitting for that purpose, they shall be on oath or affirmation. When the President of the United States is tried, the Chief Justice shall preside: and no person shall be convicted without the concurrence of two-thirds of the members present.

Judgment in cases of impeachment shall not extend further than to removal from the office, and disqualification to hold and enjoy any office of honor, trust or profit under the United States: but the party convicted shall nevertheless be liable and subject to indictment, trial, judgment and punishment, according to law.

(Elections)

Section 4 The times, places and manner of holding elections for Senators and Representatives shall be prescribed in each State by the legislature thereof; but the Congress may at any time by law make or alter such regulations, except as to the places of choosing Senators.

The Congress shall assemble at least once in every year, and such meeting *shall be on the first Monday in December, unless they shall by law appoint a different day.*

(Powers and duties of the two chambers: rules of procedure, power over members)

Section 5 Each house shall be the judge of the elections, returns and qualifications of its own members, and a majority of each shall constitute a quorum to do business; but a smaller number may adjourn from day to day, and may be authorized to compel the attendance of absent members, in such manner, and under such penalties, as each house may provide.

Each house may determine the rules of its proceedings, punish its members for disorderly behavior, and with the concurrence of two-thirds, expel a member.

Each house shall keep a journal of its proceedings, and from time to time publish the same, excepting such parts as may in their judgment require secrecy; and the yeas and nays of the members of either house on any question shall, at the desire of one-fifth of those present, be entered on the journal.

Neither house, during the session of Congress, shall, without the consent of the other, adjourn for more than three days, nor to any other place than that in which the two houses shall be sitting.

(Compensation, privilege from arrest, privilege of speech, disabilities of members)

Section 6 The Senators and Representatives shall receive a compensation for their services, to be ascertained by law and paid out of the treasury of the United States. They shall in all cases except treason, felony and breach of the peace, be privileged from arrest during their attendance at the session of their respective houses, and in going to and returning from the same; and for any speech or debate in either house, they shall not be questioned in any other place.

No Senator or Representative shall, during the time for which he was elected, be appointed to any civil office under the authority of the United States, which shall have been created, or the emoluments whereof shall have been increased, during such time; and no person holding any office under the United States shall be a member of either house during his continuance in office.

(Legislative process: revenue bills, approval or veto power of president)

Section 7 All bills for raising revenue shall originate in the House of Representatives; but the Senate may propose or concur with amendments as on other bills.

Every bill which shall have passed the House of Representatives and the Senate, shall, before it become a law, be presented to the President of the United States; if he approve he shall sign it, but if not he shall return it with objections to that house in which it originated, who shall enter the objections at large on their journal, and proceed to reconsider it. If after such reconsideration two-thirds of that house shall agree to pass the bill, it shall be sent, together with the objections, to the other house, by which it shall likewise be reconsidered, and, if approved by two-thirds of that house, it shall become a law. But in all such cases the votes of both houses shall be determined by yeas and nays, and the names of the persons voting for and against the bill shall be entered on the journal of each house respectively. If any bill shall not be returned by the President within ten days (Sundays excepted) after it shall have been presented to him, the same shall be a law, in like manner as if he had signed it, unless the Congress by their adjournment prevent its return, in which case it shall not be a law.

Every order, resolution, or vote to which the concurrence of the Senate and House of Representatives may be necessary (except on a question of adjournment) shall be presented to the President of the United States; and before the same shall take effect, shall be approved by him, or being disapproved by him, shall be repassed by two-thirds of the Senate and House of Representatives, according to the rules and limitations prescribed in the case of a bill.

(Powers of Congress enumerated)

Section 8 The Congress shall have power

To lay and collect taxes, duties, imposts, and excises, to pay the debts and provide for the common defense and general welfare of the United States; but all duties, imposts and excises shall be uniform throughout the United States;

To borrow money on the credit of the United States;

To regulate commerce with foreign nations, and among the several States, and with the Indian tribes;

To establish an uniform rule of naturalization, and uniform laws on the subject of bankruptcies throughout the United States;

To coin money, regulate the value thereof, and of foreign coin, and fix the standard of weights and measures;

To provide for the punishment of counterfeiting the securities and current coin of the United States;

To establish post offices and post roads;

To promote the progress of science and useful arts by securing for limited times to authors and inventors the exclusive right to their respective writings and discoveries;

To constitute tribunals inferior to the Supreme Court;

To define and punish piracies and felonies committed on the high seas and offenses against the law of nations;

To declare war, grant letters of marque and reprisal, and make rules concerning captures on land and water;

To raise and support armies, but no appropriation of money to that use shall be for a longer term than two years;

To provide and maintain a navy;

To make rules for the government and regulation of the land and naval forces;

To provide for calling forth the militia to execute the laws of the Union, suppress insurrections, and repel invasions;

To provide for organizing, arming, and disciplining the militia, and for governing such part of them as may be employed in the service of the United States, reserving to the States respectively the appointment of the officers, and the authority of training the militia according to the discipline prescribed by Congress;

To exercise exclusive legislation in all cases whatsoever, over such district (not exceeding ten miles square) as may, by cession of particular States, and the acceptance of Congress, become the seat of government of the United States, and to exercise like authority over all places purchased by the consent of the legislature of the State, in which the same shall be, for erection of forts, magazines, arsenals, dockyards, and other needful buildings;—and

(Elastic clause)

To make all laws which shall be necessary and proper for carrying into execution the foregoing powers, and all other powers vested by this Constitution in the government of the United States, or in any department or officer thereof.

(Powers denied Congress)

Section 9 *The migration or importation of such persons as any of the States now existing shall think proper to admit shall not be prohibited by the Congress prior to the year 1808; but a tax or duty may be imposed on such importation, not exceeding $10 for each person.*

The privilege of the writ of habeas corpus shall not be suspended, unless when in cases of rebellion or invasion the public safety may require it.

No bill of attainder or ex post facto law shall be passed.

No capitation, or other direct, tax shall be laid, unless in proportion to the census or enumeration herein before directed to be taken.

No tax or duty shall be laid on articles exported from any State.

No preference shall be given by any regulation of commerce or revenue to the ports of one State over those of another; nor shall vessels bound to, or from, one State, be obliged to enter, clear, or pay duties in another.

No money shall be drawn from the treasury, but in consequence of appropriations made by law; and a regular statement and account of the receipts and expenditures of all public money shall be published from time to time.

No title of nobility shall be granted by the United States: and no person holding any office or profit or trust under them, shall, without the consent of the Congress, accept of any present, emolument, office, or title, of any kind whatever, from any king, prince, or foreign state.

(Powers denied the states)

Section 10 No State shall enter into any treaty, alliance, or confederation; grant letters of marque and reprisal; coin money; emit bills of credit; make anything but gold and silver coin a tender in payment of debts; pass any bill of attainder, ex post facto law, or law impairing the obligation of contracts, or grant any title of nobility.

No State shall, without the consent of Congress, lay any imposts or duties on imports or exports, except what may be absolutely necessary for executing its inspection laws: and the net produce of all duties and imposts, laid by any State on imports or exports, shall be for the use of the treasury of the United States; and all such laws shall be subject to the revision and control of the Congress.

No State shall, without the consent of Congress, lay any duty of tonnage, keep troops or ships of war in time of peace, enter into any agreement or compact with another State, or with a foreign power, or engage in war, unless actually invaded, or in such imminent danger as will not admit of delay.

Article II (The executive branch)

(The president: power vested, term, electoral college, qualifications, presidential succession, compensation, oath of office)

Section 1 The executive power shall be vested in a President of the United States of America. He shall hold his office during the term of four years, and, together with the Vice-President, chosen for the same term, be elected as follows:

Each State shall appoint, in such manner as the legislature thereof may direct, a number of electors, equal to the whole number of Senators and Representatives to which the State may be entitled in the Congress; but no Senator or Representative, or person holding an office of trust or profit under the United States, shall be appointed an elector.

The electors shall meet in their respective States, and vote by ballot for two persons, of whom one at least shall not be an inhabitant of the same State with themselves. And they shall make a list of all the persons voted for, and of the number of votes for each: which list they shall sign and certify, and transmit sealed to the seat of government of the United States, directed to the President of the Senate. The President of the Senate shall, in the presence of the Senate and House of Representatives, open all the certificates, and the votes shall then be counted. The person having the greatest number of votes shall be the President, if such number be a majority of the whole number of electors appointed; and if there be more than one who have such majority, and have an equal number of votes, then the House of Representatives shall immediately choose by ballot one of them for President; and if no person have a majority, then from the five highest on the list said house shall in like manner choose the President. But in choosing the President the votes shall be taken by States, the representation from each State having one vote; a quorum for this purpose shall consist of a member or members from two-thirds of the States, and a majority of all the States shall be necessary to a choice. In every case, after the choice of the President, the person having the greatest number of votes of the electors shall be the Vice-President. But if there should remain two or more who have equal votes, the Senate shall choose from them by ballot the Vice-President.

The Congress may determine the time of choosing the electors and the day on which they shall give their votes; which day shall be the same throughout the United States.

No person except a natural-born citizen, *or a citizen of the United States at the time of the adoption of this Constitution,* shall be eligible to the office of President; neither shall any person be eligible to that office who shall not have attained to the age of thirty-five years, and been fourteen years a resident within the United States.

In cases of the removal of the President from office or of his death, resignation, or inability to discharge the powers and duties of the said office, the same shall devolve on the Vice-President, and the Congress may by law provide for the case of removal, death, resignation, or inability, both of the President and Vice-President, declaring what officer shall then act as President, and such officer shall act accordingly, until the disability be removed, or a President shall be elected.

The President shall, at stated times, receive for his services a compensation, which shall neither be increased nor diminished during the period for which he shall have been elected, and he shall not receive within that period any other emolument from the United States, or any of them.

Before he enter on the execution of his office, he shall take the following oath or affirmation:—"I do solemnly swear (or affirm) that I will faithfully execute the office of the President of the United States, and will to the best of my ability preserve, protect and defend the Constitution of the United States."

(Powers and duties: as commander in chief, over advisers, to pardon, to make treaties and appoint officers)

Section 2   The President shall be commander in chief of the army and navy of the United States, and of the militia of the several States, when called into the actual service of the United States; he may require the opinion, in writing, of the principal officer in each of the executive departments, upon any subject relating to the duties of their respective offices, and he shall have power to grant reprieves and pardons for offenses against the United States, except in cases of impeachment.

He shall have power, by and with the advice and consent of the Senate, to make treaties, provided two-thirds of the Senators present concur; and he shall nominate, and by and with the advice and consent of the Senate, shall appoint ambassadors, other public ministers and consuls, judges of the Supreme court, and all other officers of the United States, whose appointments are not herein otherwise provided for, and which shall be established by law: but Congress may by law vest the appointment of such inferior officers, as they think proper, in the President alone, in the courts of law, or in the heads of departments.

The President shall have power to fill up all vacancies that may happen during the recess of the Senate, by granting commissions which shall expire at the end of their next session.

(Legislative, diplomatic, and law-enforcement duties)

Section 3   He shall from time to time give to the Congress information of the state of the Union, and recommend to their consideration such measures as he shall judge necessary and expedient; he may, on extraordinary occasions, convene both houses, or either of them, and in case of disagreement between them, with respect to the time of adjournment, he may adjourn them to such time as he shall think proper; he shall receive ambassadors and other public ministers; he shall take care that the laws be faithfully executed, and shall commission all the officers of the United States.

(Impeachment)

Section 4   The President, Vice-President and all civil officers of the United States shall be removed from office on impeachment for, and on conviction of, treason, bribery, or other high crimes and misdemeanors.

Article III   (The judicial branch)

(Power vested; Supreme Court; lower courts; judges)

Section 1   The judicial power of the United States shall be vested in one Supreme Court, and in such inferior courts as the Congress may from time to time ordain and establish. The judges, both of the Supreme and inferior courts, shall hold their offices during good behavior, and shall, at stated times, receive for their services a compensation which shall not be diminished during their continuance in office.

(Jurisdiction; trial by jury)

Section 2   The judicial power shall extend to all cases, in law and equity, arising under this Constitution, the laws of the United States, and treaties made, or which shall be made, under their authority;—to all cases affecting ambassadors, other public ministers and consuls;—to all cases of admiralty and maritime jurisdiction;—to controversies to which the United States shall be a party;—to controversies between two or more States;—*between a State and citizens of another State;*—between citizens of different States—between citizens of the same State claiming lands under grants of different States, and between a State, or the citizens thereof, and foreign states, citizens or subjects.

In all cases affecting ambassadors, other public ministers and consuls, and those in which a State shall be party, the Supreme Court shall have original jurisdiction. In all the other cases before mentioned, the Supreme Court shall have appellate jurisdiction, both as to law and fact, with such exceptions, and under such regulations, as the Congress shall make.

The trial of all crimes, except in cases of impeachment, shall be by jury; and such trial shall be held in the state where said crimes shall have been committed; but when not committed within any State, the trial shall be at such place or places as the Congress may by law have directed.

(Treason: definition, punishment)

Section 3 Treason against the United States shall consist only in levying war against them, or in adhering to their enemies, giving them aid and comfort. No person shall be convicted of treason unless on the testimony of two witnesses to the same overt act, or on confession in open court.

The Congress shall have power to declare the punishment of treason, but no attainder of treason shall work corruption of blood, or forfeiture except during the life of the person attained.

Article IV
(States' relations)

(Full faith and credit)

Section 1
Full faith and credit shall be given in each State to the public acts, records, and judicial proceedings of every other State. And the Congress may by general laws prescribe the manner in which such acts, records, and proceedings shall be proved, and the effect thereof.

(Interstate comity, rendition)

Section 2 The citizens of each State shall be entitled to all privileges and immunities of citizens in the several States.

A person charged in any State with treason, felony, or other crime, who shall flee from justice, and be found in another State, shall on demand of the executive authority of the State from which he fled, be delivered up, to be removed to the State having jurisdiction of the crime.

No person held to service or labor in one State, under the laws thereof, escaping into another, shall, in consequence of any law or regulation therein, be discharged from such service or labor, but shall be delivered up on claim of the party to whom such service or labor may be due.

(New states)

Section 3 New States may be admitted by the Congress into this Union; but no new State shall be formed or erected within the jurisdiction of any other State; nor any state be formed by the junction of two or more States, or parts of States, without the consent of the legislatures of the States concerned as well as of the Congress.

The Congress shall have power to dispose of and make all needful rules and regulations respecting the territory or other property belonging to the United States; and nothing in this Constitution shall be so construed as to prejudice any claims of the United States, or of any particular State.

(Obligations of the United States to the states)

Section 4 The United States shall guarantee to every State in this Union a republican form of government, and shall protect each of them against invasion; and on application of the legislature, or of the executive (when the legislature cannot be convened), against domestic violence.

Article V (Mode of amendment)

The Congress, whenever two-thirds of both houses shall deem it necessary, shall propose amendments to this Constitution, or, on the application of the legislatures of two-thirds of the several States, shall call a convention for proposing amendments, which, in either case, shall be valid to all intents and purposes, as part of this Constitution, when ratified by the legislatures of three-fourths of the several States, or by conventions in three-fourths thereof, as the one or the other mode of ratification may be proposed by the Congress; provided *that no amendments which may be made prior to the year one thousand eight hundred and eight shall in any manner affect the first and fourth clauses in the ninth section of the first article;* and that no State, without its consent, shall be deprived of its equal suffrage in the Senate.

Article VI (Prior debts; supremacy of Constitution; oaths of office)

All debts contracted and engagements entered into, before the adoption of this Constitution, shall be as valid against the United States under this Constitution, as under the Confederation.

This Constitution, and the laws of the United States which shall be made in pursuance thereof; and all treaties made, or which shall be made, under the authority of the United States, shall be the supreme law of the land; and the judges in every State shall be bound thereby, anything in the Constitution or laws of any State to the contrary notwithstanding.

The Senators and Representatives before mentioned, and the members of the several State legislatures, and all executive and judicial officers, both of the United States and of the several States, shall be bound by oath or affirmation to support this Constitution; but no religious test shall ever be required as a qualification to any office or public trust under the United States.

Article VII (Ratification)

The ratification of the conventions of nine States shall be sufficient for the establishment of this Constitution between the States so ratifying the same.

Done in Convention by the unanimous consent of the States present, the seventeenth day of September in the year of our Lord one thousand seven hundred and eighty-seven and of the Independence of the United States of America the twelfth. In witness whereof we have hereunto subscribed our names.

GEORGE WASHINGTON
and thirty-seven others

Amendments to the Constitution

(The first ten amendments—the Bill of Rights—were adopted in 1791.)

Amendment I (Freedom of religion, speech, press, assembly)

Congress shall make no law respecting an establishment of religion, or prohibiting the free exercise thereof; or abridging the freedom of speech, or of the press; or the right of the people peaceably to assemble, and to petition the government for a redress of grievances.

Amendment II (Right to bear arms)

A well-regulated militia being necessary to the security of a free State, the right of the people to keep and bear arms shall not be infringed.

Amendment III (Quartering of soldiers)

No soldier shall, in time of peace, be quartered in any house without the consent of the owner, nor in time of war, but in a manner to be prescribed by law.

Amendment IV (Searches and seizures)

The right of the people to be secure in their persons, houses, papers, and effects, against unreasonable searches and seizures, shall not be violated, and no warrants shall issue but upon probable cause, supported by oath or affirmation, and particularly describing the place to be searched, and the persons or things to be seized.

Amendment V (Rights of persons: grand juries; double jeopardy; self-incrimination; due process; eminent domain)

No person shall be held to answer for a capital, or otherwise infamous crime, unless on a presentment or indictment of a grand jury, except in cases arising in the land or naval forces, or in the militia, when in actual service in time of war or public danger; nor shall any person be subject for the same offense to be twice put in jeopardy of life or limb; nor shall be compelled in any criminal case to be a witness against himself, nor be deprived of life, liberty, or property, without due process of law; nor shall private property be taken for public use without just compensation.

Amendment VI (Rights of accused in criminal prosecutions)

In all criminal prosecutions, the accused shall enjoy the right to a speedy and public trial, by an impartial jury of the State and district wherein the crime shall have been committed, which district shall have been previously ascertained by law, and to be informed of the nature and cause of the accusation; to be confronted with the witnesses against him; to have compulsory process for obtaining witnesses in his favor, and to have the assistance of counsel for his defense.

Amendment VII (Civil trials)

In suits at common law, where the value in controversy shall exceed twenty dollars, the right of trial by jury shall be preserved, and no fact tried by a jury shall be otherwise reexamined in any court of the United States, than according to the rules of the common law.

Amendment VIII (Punishment for crime)

Excessive bail shall not be required, nor excessive fines imposed, nor cruel and unusual punishments inflicted.

Amendment IX   (Rights retained by the people)

The enumeration in the Constitution, of certain rights, shall not be construed to deny or disparage others retained by the people.

Amendment X   (Rights reserved to the states)

The powers not delegated to the United States by the Constitution, nor prohibited by it to the States, are reserved to the states respectively, or to the people.

Amendment XI   (Suits against the states; adopted 1798)

The judicial power of the United States shall not be construed to extend to any suit in law or equity, commenced or prosecuted against one of the United States by citizens of another state, or by citizens or subjects of any foreign state.

Amendment XII   (Election of the president; adopted 1804)

The electors shall meet in their respective States, and vote by ballot for President and Vice-President, one of whom, at least, shall not be an inhabitant of the same State with themselves; they shall name in their ballots the person voted for as President, and in distinct ballots the person voted for as Vice-President, and they shall make distinct lists of all persons voted for as President, and of all persons voted for as Vice-President, and of the number of votes for each, which lists they shall sign and certify, and transmit sealed to the seat of government of the United States, directed to the President of the Senate;—the President of the Senate shall, in the presence of the Senate and House of representatives, open all the certificates and the votes shall then be counted;—the person having the greatest number of votes for President shall be the President, if such number be a majority of the whole number of electors appointed; and if no person have such majority, then from the persons having the highest numbers not exceeding three on the list of those voted for as President, the House of Representatives shall choose immediately, by ballot, the President. But in choosing the President, the votes shall be taken by States, the representation from each State having one vote; a quorum for this purpose shall consist of a member or members from two-thirds of the States, and a majority of all the States shall be necessary to a choice. And if the House of Representatives shall not choose a President whenever the right of choice shall devolve upon them, before *the fourth day of March* next following, then the Vice-President shall act as President, as in the case of the death or other constitutional disability of the President.

The person having the greatest number of votes as Vice-President shall be the Vice-President, if such number be a majority of the whole number of electors appointed; and if no person have a majority, then from the two highest numbers on the list the Senate shall choose the Vice-President; a quorum for the purpose shall consist of two-thirds of the whole number of Senators, and a majority of the whole number shall be necessary to a choice. But no person constitutionally ineligible to the office of President shall be eligible to that of Vice-President of the United States.

Amendment XIII   (Abolition of slavery; adopted 1865)

Section 1   Neither slavery nor involuntary servitude, except as a punishment for crime whereof the party shall have been duly convicted, shall exist within the United States, or any place subject to their jurisdiction.

Section 2   Congress shall have power to enforce this article by appropriate legislation.

Amendment XIV   (Adopted 1868)

(Citizenship rights; privileges and immunities; due process; equal protection)

Section 1   All persons born or naturalized in the United States, and subject to the jurisdiction thereof, are citizens of the United States and of the State wherein they reside. No State shall make or enforce any law which shall abridge the privileges or immunities of citizens of the United States; nor shall any State deprive any person of life, liberty, or property, without due process of law; nor deny to any person within its jurisdiction the equal protection of the laws.

(Apportionment of representation)

Section 2   Representatives shall be apportioned among the several States according to their respective numbers, counting the whole number of persons in each State, excluding Indians not taxed. But when the right to vote at any election for the choice of Electors for President and Vice-President of the United States, Representatives in Congress, the executive and judicial officers of a State, or the members of the legislature thereof, is denied to any of the male inhabitants of such State, being twenty-one years of age and citizens of the United States, or in any way abridged, except for participation in rebellion, or other crime, the basis of representation therein shall be reduced in the proportion which the number of such male citizens shall bear to the whole number of male citizens twenty-one years of age in such State.

(Disqualification of Confederate officials)

Section 3   No person shall be a Senator or Representative in Congress, or Elector of President and Vice-President, or hold any office, civil or military, under the United States, or under any State, who, having previously taken an oath, as a member of Congress, or as an officer of the United States, or as a member of any State legislature, or as an executive or judicial officer of any State, to support the Constitution of the United States, shall have engaged in insurrection or rebellion against the same, or given aid or comfort to the enemies thereof. Congress may, by a vote of two-thirds of each house, remove such disability.

(Public debts)

Section 4   The validity of the public debt of the United States, authorized by law, including debts incurred for payment of pensions and bounties for services in suppressing insurrection or rebellion, shall not be questioned. But neither the United States nor any State shall assume or pay any debt or obligation incurred in aid of insurrection or rebellion against the United States, or any claim for the loss of emancipation of any slave; but all such debts, obligations, and claims shall be held illegal and void.

(Enforcement)

Section 5   The Congress shall have power to enforce, by appropriate legislation, the provisions of this article.

Amendment XV   (Extension of right to vote; adopted 1870)

Section 1   The right of citizens of the United States to vote shall not be denied or abridged by the United States or by any State on account of race, color, or previous condition of servitude.

Section 2   The Congress shall have power to enforce this article by appropriate legislation.

Amendment XVI   (Income tax; adopted 1913)

The Congress shall have power to lay and collect taxes on incomes, from whatever source derived, without apportionment among the several States, and without regard to any census or enumeration.

Amendment XVII   (Popular election of senators; adopted 1913)

Section 1   The Senate of the United States shall be composed of two Senators from each State, elected by the people thereof, for six years; and each Senator shall have one vote. The electors in each State shall have the qualifications requisite for electors of [voters for] the most numerous branch of the State legislatures.

Section 2   When vacancies happen in the representation of any State in the Senate, the executive authority of such State shall issue writs of election to fill such vacancies: Provided, that the Legislature of any State may empower the executive thereof to make temporary appointments until the people fill the vacancies by election as the Legislature may direct.

Section 3   This amendment shall not be so construed as to affect the election or term of any Senator chosen before it becomes valid as part of the Constitution.

Amendment XVIII   (Prohibition of intoxicating liquors; adopted 1919, repealed 1933)

Section 1   After one year from the ratification of this article the manufacture, sale or transportation of intoxicating liquors within, the importation thereof into, or the exportation thereof from the United States and all territory subject to the jurisdiction thereof, for beverage purposes, is hereby prohibited.

Section 2   The Congress and the several States shall have concurrent power to enforce this article by appropriate legislation.

Section 3   This article shall be inoperative unless it shall have been ratified as an amendment to the Constitution by the legislatures of the several States, as provided by the Constitution, within seven years from the date of the submission thereof to the States by the Congress.

Amendment XIX   (Right of women to vote; adopted 1920)

Section 1   The right of citizens of the United States to vote shall not be denied or abridged by the United States or by any State on account of sex.

Section 2   The Congress shall have power to enforce this article by appropriate legislation.

Amendment XX   (Commencement of terms of office; adopted 1933)

Section 1   The terms of the President and Vice-President shall end at noon on the 20th day of January, and the terms of Senators and Representatives at noon on the 3d day of January, of the years in which such terms would have ended if this article had not been ratified; and the terms of their successors shall then begin.

Section 2   The Congress shall assemble at least once in every year, and such meetings shall begin at noon on the 3d day of January, unless they shall by law appoint a different day.

(Extension of presidential succession)

Section 3 If, at the time fixed for the beginning of the term of the President, the President-elect shall have died, the Vice-President-elect shall become President. If a President shall not have been chosen before the time fixed for the beginning of his term, or if the President-elect shall have failed to qualify, then the Vice-President-elect shall act as President until a President shall have qualified; and the Congress may by law provide for the case wherein neither a President-elect nor a Vice-President-elect shall have qualified, declaring who shall then act as President, or the manner in which one who is to act shall be selected, and such persons shall act accordingly until a President or Vice-President shall have qualified.

Section 4 The Congress may by law provide for the case of the death of any of the persons from whom the House of Representatives may choose a President whenever the right of choice shall have devolved upon them, and for the case of the death of any of the persons from whom the Senate may choose a Vice-President whenever the right of choice shall have devolved upon them.

Section 5 Sections 1 and 2 shall take effect on the 15th day of October following the ratification of this article.

Section 6 This article shall be inoperative unless it shall have been ratified as an amendment to the Constitution by the Legislatures of three-fourths of the several States within seven years from the date of its submission.

Amendment XXI (Repeal of Eighteenth Amendment; adopted 1933)

Section 1 The eighteenth article of amendment to the Constitution of the United States is hereby repealed.

Section 2 The transportation or importation into any State, Territory, or Possession of the United States for delivery or use therein of intoxicating liquors, in violation of the laws thereof, is hereby prohibited.

Section 3 This article shall be inoperative unless it shall have been ratified as an amendment to the Constitution by conventions in the several States, as provided in the Constitution, within seven years from the date of submission thereof to the States by the Congress.

Amendment XXII (Limit on presidential tenure; adopted 1951)

Section 1

No person shall be elected to the office of President more than twice, and no person who has held the office

of President, or acted as President, for more than two years of a term to which some other person was elected President shall be elected to the office of President more than once. But this article shall not apply to any person holding the office of President when this article was proposed by the Congress, and shall not prevent any person who may be holding the office of President, or acting as President, during the term within which this article becomes operative from holding the office of President or acting as President during the remainder of such term.

Section 2 This article shall be inoperative unless it shall have been ratified as an amendment to the Constitution by the legislatures of three-fourths of the several States within seven years from the date of its submission to the States by the Congress.

Amendment XXIII (Presidential electors for the District of Columbia; adopted 1961)

Section 1 The District constituting the seat of Government of the United States shall appoint in such manner as the Congress may direct:

A number of electors of President and Vice-President equal to the whole number of Senators and Representatives in Congress to which the District would be entitled if it were a State, but in no event more than the least populous State; they shall be in addition to those appointed by the States, but they shall be considered for the purposes of the election of President and Vice-President, to be electors appointed by a State; and they shall meet in the District and perform such duties as provided by the twelfth article of amendment.

Section 2 The Congress shall have the power to enforce this article by appropriate legislation.

Amendment XXIV (Poll tax outlawed in national elections, adopted 1964)

Section 1 The right of citizens of the United States to vote in any primary or other election for President or Vice-President, for electors for President or Vice-President, or for Senator or Representative in Congress, shall not be denied or abridged by the United States or any State by reason of failure to pay any poll tax or other tax.

Section 2 The Congress shall have the power to enforce this article by appropriate legislation.

Amendment XXV (Presidential succession; adopted 1967)

Section 1 In case of the removal of the President from office or of his death or resignation, the Vice-President shall become President.

(Vice-presidential vacancy)

Section 2 Whenever there is a vacancy in the office of the Vice-President, the President shall nominate a Vice-President who shall take office upon confirmation by a majority vote of both Houses of Congress.

Section 3 Whenever the President transmits to the President pro tempore of the Senate and the speaker of the House of Representatives his written declaration that he is unable to discharge the powers and duties of his office, and until he transmits to them a written declaration to the contrary, such powers and duties shall be discharged by the Vice-President as Acting President.

(Presidential disability)

Section 4 Whenever the Vice-President and a majority of either the principal officers of the executive departments or of such other body as Congress may by law provide, transmit to the President pro tempore of the Senate and the Speaker of the House of Representatives their written declaration that the President is unable to discharge the powers and duties of his office, the Vice-President shall immediately assume the powers and duties of the office as Acting President.

Thereafter, when the President transmits to the President pro tempore of the Senate and the Speaker of the House of Representatives his written declaration that no inability exists, he shall resume the powers and duties of his office unless the Vice-President and a majority of either the principal officers of the executive department(s) or of such other body as Congress may by law provide, transmit within four days to the President pro tempore of the Senate and the Speaker of the House of Representatives their written declaration that the President is unable to discharge the powers and duties of his office. Thereupon Congress shall decide the issue, assembling within forty-eight hours for that purpose if not in session. If the Congress, within twenty-one days after receipt of the latter written declaration, or, if Congress is not in session, within twenty-one days after Congress is required to assemble, determines by two-thirds vote of both Houses that the President is unable to discharge the powers and duties of his office, the Vice-President shall continue to discharge the same as Acting President; otherwise, the President shall resume the powers and duties of his office.

Amendment XXVI (Right of eighteen-year-olds to vote; adopted 1971)

Section 1 The right of citizens of the United States, who are eighteen years of age or older, to vote shall not be denied or abridged by the United States or by any State on account of age.

Section 2 The Congress shall have power to enforce this article by appropriate legislation.

Amendment XXVII (Congressional pay raises; adopted 1992)

No law, varying the compensation for the services of the Senators and Representatives shall take effect, until an election of Representatives shall have intervened.

■

Federalist No. 10   1787

To the People of the State of New York: Among the numerous advantages promised by a well-constructed union, none deserves to be more accurately developed than its tendency to break and control the violence of faction. The friend of popular governments, never finds himself so much alarmed for their character and fate, as when he contemplates their propensity to this dangerous vice. He will not fail, therefore, to set a due value on any plan which, without violating the principles to which he is attached, provides a proper cure for it. The instability, injustice, and confusion introduced into the public councils, have, in truth, been the mortal diseases under which popular governments have everywhere perished; as they continue to be the favourite and fruitful topics from which the adversaries to liberty derive their most specious declamations. The valuable improvements made by the American constitutions on the popular models, both ancient and modern, cannot certainly be too much admired; but it would be an unwarrantable partiality, to contend that they have as effectually obviated the danger on this side, as was wished and expected. Complaints are everywhere heard from our most considerate and virtuous citizens, equally the friends of public and private faith, and of public and personal liberty, that our governments are too unstable; that the public good is disregarded in the conflicts of rival parties; and that measures are too often decided, not according to the rules of justice, and the rights of the minor party, but by the superior force of an interested and overbearing majority. However anxiously we may wish that these complaints had no foundation, the evidence of known facts will not permit us to deny that they are in some degree true. It will be found, indeed, on a candid review of our situation, that some of the distresses under which we labour have been erroneously charged on the operation of our governments;

but it will be found, at the same time, that other causes will not alone account for many of our heaviest misfortunes; and, particularly, for that prevailing and increasing distrust of public engagements, and alarm for private rights, which are echoed from one end of the continent to the other. These must be chiefly, if not wholly, effects of the unsteadiness and injustice, with which a factious spirit has tainted our public administrations.

By a faction, I understand a number of citizens, whether amounting to a majority or minority of the whole, who are united and actuated by some common impulse of passion, or of interest, adverse to the rights of other citizens, or to the permanent and aggregate interests of the community.

There are two methods of curing the mischiefs of faction: The one, by removing its causes; the other, by controlling its effects.

There are again two methods of removing the causes of faction: The one, by destroying the liberty which is essential to its existence; the other, by giving to every citizen the same opinions, the same passions, and the same interests.

It could never be more truly said, than of the first remedy, that it was worse than the disease. Liberty is to faction what air is to fire, an ailment without which it instantly expires. But it could not be a less folly to abolish liberty, which is essential to political life, because it nourishes faction, than it would be to wish the annihilation of air, which is essential to animal life, because it imparts to fire its destructive agency.

The second expedient is as impracticable, as the first would be unwise. As long as the reason of man continues fallible, and he is at liberty to exercise it, different opinions will be formed. As long as the connection subsists between his reason and his self-love, his opinions and his passions will have a reciprocal influence on each other; and the former will be objects to which the latter will attach themselves. The diversity in the faculties of men, from which the rights of property originate, is not less an insuperable obstacle to an uniformity of interests. The protection of these faculties is the first object of government. From the protection of different and unequal faculties of acquiring property, the possession of different degrees and kinds of property immediately results; and from the influence speculation as of practice; an attachment to different leaders ambitiously contending for preeminence and power; or to persons of other descriptions whose fortunes have been interesting to the human passions, have, in turn, divided mankind into parties, inflamed them with mutual animosity, and rendered them much more disposed to vex and oppress each other, than to cooperate for their common good. So strong is this propensity of mankind, to fall into

mutual animosities, that where no substantial occasion presents itself, the most frivolous and fanciful distinctions have been sufficient to kindle their unfriendly passions and excite their most violent conflicts. But the most common and durable source of factions, has been the various and unequal distribution of property. Those who hold, and those who are without property, have ever formed distinct interests in society. Those who are creditors, and those who are debtors, fall under alike discrimination. A landed interest, a manufacturing interest, a mercantile interest, a moneyed interest, with many lesser interests, grow up of necessity in civilized nations, and divide them into different classes, actuated by different sentiments and views. The regulation of these various and interfering interests forms the principal task of modern legislation, and involves the spirit of the party and faction in the necessary and ordinary operations of the government.

No man is allowed to be a judge in his own cause; because his interest will certainly bias his judgment, and, not improbably, corrupt his integrity. With equal, nay, with greater reason, a body of men are unfit to be both judges and parties at the same time; yet what are many of the most important acts of legislation, but so many judicial determinations, not indeed concerning the right of single persons, but concerning the rights of large bodies of citizens? And what are the different classes of legislators, but advocates and parties to the causes which they determine? Is a law proposed concerning private debts? It is a question to which the creditors are parties on one side, and the debtors on the other. Justice ought to hold the balance between them. Yet the parties are, and must be, themselves the judges; and the most numerous party, or, in other words, the most powerful faction, must be expected to prevail. Shall domestic manufactures be encouraged, and in what degree, by restrictions on foreign manufactures? are questions which would be differently decided by the landed and the manufacturing classes; and probably by neither with a sole regard to justice and the public good. The apportionment of taxes, on the various descriptions of property, is an act which seems to require the most exact impartiality; yet there is, perhaps, no legislative act, in which greater opportunity and temptation are given to a predominant party to trample on the rules of justice. Every shilling, with which they overburden the inferior number, is a shilling saved to their own pockets.

It is in vain to say, that enlightened statesmen will be able to adjust these clashing interests, and render them all subservient to the public good. Enlightened statesmen will not always be at the helm: nor, in many cases, can such an adjustment be made at all, without taking into view indirect and remote considerations, which will rarely prevail over the immediate interest which one party may find in disregarding the rights of another, or the good of the whole.

The inference to which we are brought is, that the *causes* of faction cannot be removed; and that relief is only to be sought in the means of controlling its *effects*.

If a faction consists of less than a majority, relief is supplied by the republican principle, which enables the majority to defeat its sinister views, by regular vote. It may clog the administration, it may convulse the society; but it will be unable to execute and mask its violence under the forms of the constitution. When a majority is included in a faction, the form of popular government, on the other hand, enables it to sacrifice to its ruling passion or interest, both the public good and the rights of other citizens. To secure the public good, and private rights, against the danger of such a faction, and at the same time to preserve the spirit and the form of popular government, is then the great object to which our inquiries are directed. Let me add, that it is the great desideratum, by which alone this form of government can be rescued from the opprobrium under which it has so long laboured, and be recommended to the esteem and adoption of mankind.

By what means is this object attainable? Evidently by one of two only. Either the existence of the same passion or interest in a majority, at the same time, must be prevented; or the majority, having such coexistent passion or interest, must be rendered, by their number and local situation, unable to concert and carry into effect schemes of oppression. If the impulse and the opportunity be suffered to coincide, we well know that neither moral nor religious motives can be relied on as an adequate control. They are not found to be such on the injustice and violence of individuals, and lose their efficacy in proportion to the number combined together; that is, in proportion as their efficacy becomes needful.

From this view of the subject, it may be concluded, that a pure democracy, by which I mean a society consisting of a small number of citizens, who assemble and administer the government in person, can admit of no cure for the mischiefs of faction. A common passion or interest will, in almost every case, be felt by a majority of the whole; a communication and concert, results from the form of government itself; and there is nothing to check the inducements to sacrifice the weaker party, or an obnoxious individual. Hence, it is, that such democracies have ever been spectacles of turbulence and contention; have ever been found incompatible with personal security, or the rights of property; and have in general been as short in their lives, as they have been violent in their deaths. Theoretic politicians, who have patronized this species of government, have erroneously supposed, that by reducing mankind to a perfect equality in their political rights, they would, at the same time, be perfectly equalized and assimilated in their possessions, their opinions, and their passions.

A republic, by which I mean a government in which the scheme of representation takes place, opens a different prospect, and promises the cure for which we are seeking. Let us examine the points in which it varies from pure democracy, and we shall comprehend both the nature of the cure and the efficacy which it must derive from the union.

The two great points of difference, between a democracy and a republic, are, first, the delegation of the government, in the latter, to a small number of citizens, elected by the rest; secondly, the greatest number of citizens, and greater sphere of country, over which the latter may be extended.

The effect of the first difference is, on the one hand, to refine and enlarge the public views, by passing them through the medium of a chosen body of citizens, whose wisdom may best discern the true interest of their country, and whose patriotism and love of justice, will be least likely to sacrifice it to temporary or partial considerations. Under such a regulation, it may well happen, that the public voice, pronounced by the representatives of the people, will be more consonant to the public good, than if pronounced by the people themselves, convened for the purpose. On the other hand the effect may be inverted. Men of factious tempers, of local prejudices, or of sinister designs, may by intrigue, by corruption, or by other means, first obtain the suffrages, and then betray the interest of the people. The question resulting is, whether small or extensive republics are most favourable to the election of proper guardians of the public weal; and it is clearly decided in favour of the latter by two obvious considerations.

In the first place, it is to be remarked that, however small the republic may be, the representatives must be raised to a certain number, in order to guard against the cabals of a few; and that however large it may be, they must be limited to a certain number, in order to guard against the confusion of a multitude. Hence, the number of representatives in the two cases not being in proportion to that of the constituents, and being proportionally greatest in the small republic, it follows, that if the proportion of fit characters be not less in the large than in the small republic, the former will present a greater option, and consequently a greater probability of a fit choice.

In the next place, as each representative will be chosen by a greater number of citizens in the large than in the small republic, it will be more difficult for unworthy candidates to practise with success the vicious arts, by which elections are too often carried; and the suffrages of the people being more free, will be more likely to centre in men who possess the most attractive merit, and the most diffusive and established characters.

It must be confessed, that in this, as in most other cases, there is a mean, on both sides of which inconveniences will be found to lie. By enlarging too much the number of electors, you render the representatives too little acquainted with all their local circumstances and lessers interests; as by reducing it too much, you render him unduly attached to these, and too little fit to comprehend and pursue great and national objects. The federal constitution forms a happy combination being referred to the national, the local and particular to the state legislatures.

The other point of difference is, the greater number of citizens, and extent of territory, which may be brought within the compass of republican, than of democratic government; and it is this circumstance principally which renders factious combinations less to be dreaded in the former, than in the latter. The smaller the society, the fewer probably will be the distinct parties and interests composing it; the fewer the distinct parties and interests, the more frequently will a majority be found of the same party; and the smaller the number of individuals composing a majority, and the smaller the compass within which they are placed, the more easily will they concert and execute their plans of oppression. Extend the sphere, and you take in a greater variety of parties and interests; you make it less probable that a majority of the whole will have a common motive to invade the rights of other citizens; or if such a common motive exists, it will be more difficult for all who feel it to discover their own strength, and to act in unison with each other. Besides other impediments, it may be remarked, that where there is a consciousness of unjust or dishonourable purposes, communication is always checked by distrust, in proportion to the number whose concurrence is necessary.

Hence, it clearly appears, that the same advantage, which a republic has over a democracy, in controlling the effects of faction, is enjoyed by a large over a small republic,—is enjoyed by the union over the states composing it. Does this advantage consist in the substitution of representatives, whose enlightened views and virtuous sentiments render them superior to local prejudices, and to schemes of injustice? It will not be denied that the representation of the union will be most likely to possess these requisite endowments. Does it consist in the greater security afforded by a greater variety of parties, against the event of any one party being able to outnumber and oppress the rest? In an equal degree does the increased variety of parties,

comprised within the union, increase the security? Does it, in fine, consist in the greater obstacles opposed to the concert and accomplishment of the secret wishes of an unjust and interested majority? Here, again, the extent of the union gives it the most palpable advantage.

The influence of factious leaders may kindle a flame within their particular states, but will be unable to spread a general conflagration through the other states; a religious sect may degenerate into a political faction in a part of the confederacy; but the variety of sects dispersed over the entire face of it, must secure the national councils against any danger from that source: a rage for paper money, for an abolition of debts, for an equal division of property, or for any other improper or wicked project, will be less apt to pervade the whole body of the union than a particular member of it; in the same proportion as such a malady is more likely to taint a particular county or district, than an entire state.

In the extent and proper structure of the union, therefore, we behold a republican remedy for the diseases most incident to republican government. And according to the degree of pleasure and pride we feel in being republicans, ought to be our zeal in cherishing the spirit, and supporting the character of federalists.

JAMES MADISON

■

Federalist No. 51   **1788**

To the People of the State of New York: To what expedient then shall we finally resort for maintaining in practice the necessary partition of power among the several departments, as laid down in the constitution? The only answer that can be given is, that as all these exterior provisions are found to be inadequate, the defect must be supplied, by so contriving the interior structure of the government, as that its several constituent parts may, by their mutual relations, be the means of keeping each other in their proper places. Without presuming to undertake a full development of this important idea, I will hazard a few general observations, which may perhaps place it in a clearer light, and enable us to form a more correct judgment of the principles and structure of the government planned by the convention.

In order to lay a due foundation for that separate and distinct exercise of the different powers of government, which to a certain extent, is admitted on all hands to be essential to the preservation of liberty, it is evident that each department should have a will of its own; and consequently should be so constituted, that the members of each should have as little agency as possible in the appointment of the members of the others. Were this principle rigorously adhered to, it would require that all the appointments for the supreme executive, legislative, and judiciary magistracies, should be drawn from the same fountain of authority, the people, through channels, having no communication whatever with one another. Perhaps such a plan of constructing the several departments would be less difficult in practice than it may in contemplation appear. Some difficulties however, and some additional expense, would attend the execution of it. Some deviations therefore from the principle must be admitted. In the constitution of the judiciary department in particular, it might be inexpedient to insist rigorously on the principle; first, because peculiar qualifications being essential in the members, the primary consideration ought to be to select that mode of choice, which best secures these qualifications; secondly, because the permanent tenure by which the appointments are held in that department, must soon destroy all sense of dependence on the authority conferring them.

It is equally evident that the members of each department should be as little dependent as possible on those of the others, for the emoluments annexed to their offices. Were the executive magistrate, or the judges, not independent of the legislature in this particular, their independence in every other would be merely nominal.

But the great security against a gradual concentration of the several powers in the same department, consists in giving to those who administer each department, the necessary constitutional means, and personal motives, to resist encroachments of the others. The provision for defense must in this, as in all other cases, be made commensurate to the danger of attack. Ambition must be made to counteract ambition. The interest of the man must be connected with the constitutional rights of the place. It may be a reflection on human nature, that such devices should be necessary to control the abuses of government. But what is government itself but the greatest of all reflections on human nature? If men were angels, no government would be necessary. If angels were to govern men, neither external nor internal controls on government would be necessary. In framing a government which is to be administered by men over men, the great difficulty lies in this: You must first enable the government to control the governed; and in the next place, oblige it to control itself. A dependence on the people is no doubt the primary control on the government; but experience has taught mankind the necessity of auxiliary precautions.

This policy of supplying by opposite and rival interests, the defect of better motives, might be traced through the whole system of human affairs, private as well as public. We see it particularly displayed in all the subordinate distributions of power; where the constant aim is to divide and arrange the several offices in such a manner as that each may be a check on the other; that the private interest of every individual, may be a sentinel over the public rights. These inventions of prudence cannot be less requisite in the distribution of the supreme powers of the state.

But it is not possible to give to each department an equal power of self defense. In republican government the legislative authority, necessarily, predominates. The remedy for this inconveniency is, to divide the legislature into different branches; and to render them by different modes of election, and different principles of action, as little connected with each other, as the nature of their common functions, and their common dependence on the society, will admit. It may even be necessary to guard against dangerous encroachments by still further precautions. As the weight of the legislative authority requires that it should be thus divided, the weakness of the executive may require, on the other hand, that it should be fortified. An absolute negative, on the legislature, appears at first view to be the natural defense with which the executive magistrate should be armed. But perhaps it would be neither altogether safe, nor alone sufficient. On ordinary occasions, it might not be exerted with the requisite firmness; and on extraordinary occasions, it might be perfidiously abused. May not this defect of an absolute negative be supplied, by some qualified connection between this weaker department, and the weaker branch of the stronger department, by which the latter may be led to support the constitutional rights of the former, without being too much detached from the rights of its own department?

If the principles on which these observations are founded be just, as I persuade myself they are, and they be applied as a criterion, to the several state constitutions, and to the federal constitution, it will be found, that if the latter does not perfectly correspond with them, the former are infinitely less able to bear such a test.

There are moreover two considerations particularly applicable to the federal system of America, which place that system in a very interesting point of view.

First. In a single republic, all the power surrendered by the people, is submitted to the administration of a single government; and usurpations are guarded against by a division of the government into distinct and separate departments. In the compound republic of America, the power surrendered by the people, is first divided between two distinct governments, and then the portion allotted to each, subdivided among distinct and separate departments. Hence a double security arises to the rights of the people. The different governments will control each other; at the same time that each will be controlled by itself.

Second. It is of great importance in a republic, not only to guard the society against the oppression of its rulers; but to guard one part of the society against the injustice of the other part. Different interests necessarily exist in different classes of citizens. If a majority be united by a common interest, the rights of the minority will be insecure. There are but two methods of providing against this evil: The one by creating a will in the community independent of the majority, that is, of the society itself; the other by comprehending in the society so many separate descriptions of citizens, as will render an unjust combination of a majority of the whole, very improbable, if not impracticable. The first method prevails in all governments possessing an hereditary or self appointed authority. This at best is but a precarious security; because a power independent of the society may as well espouse the unjust views of the major, as the rightful interests, of the minor party, and may possibly be turned against both parties. The second method will be exemplified in the federal republic of the United States. While all authority in it will be derived from and dependent on the society, the society itself will be broken into so many parts, interests and classes of citizens, that the rights of individuals or of the minority, will be in little danger from interested combinations of the majority. In a free government, the security for civil rights must be the same as for religious rights. It consists in the one case in the multiplicity of sects. The degree of security in both cases will depend on the number of interests and sects; and this may be presumed to depend on the extent of country and number of people comprehended under the same government. This view of the subject must particularly recommend a proper federal system to all the sincere and considerate friends of republican government: Since it shows that in exact proportion as the territory of the union may be formed into more circumscribed confederacies or states, oppressive combinations of a majority will be facilitated; the best security under the republican form, for the rights of every class of citizens, will be diminished; and consequently, the stability and independence of some mem-

ber of the government, the only other security, must be proportionally increased. Justice is the end of government. It is the end of civil society. It ever has been, and ever will be pursued, until it be obtained, or until liberty be lost in the pursuit. In a society under the forms of which the stronger faction can readily unite and oppress the weaker, anarchy may as truly be said to reign, as in a state of nature where the weaker individual is not secured against the violence of the stronger: And as in the latter state even the stronger individuals are prompted by the uncertainty of their condition, to submit to a government which may protect the weak as well as themselves: So in the former state, will the more powerful factions or parties be gradually induced by alike motives, to wish for a government which will protect all parties, the weaker as well as the more powerful. It can be little doubted, that if the state of Rhode Island was separated from the confederacy, and left to itself, the insecurity of rights under the popular form of government within such narrow limits, would be displayed by such reiterated oppressions of factious majorities, that some power altogether independent of the people would soon be called for by the voice of the very factions whose misrule had proved the necessity of it. In the extended republic of the United States, and among the great variety of interests, parties and sects which it embraces, a coalition of a majority of the whole society could seldom take place on any other principles than those of justice and the general good; and there being thus less danger to a minor from the will of the major party, there must be less pretext also, to provide for the security of the former, by introducing into the government a will not dependent on the latter; or in other words, a will independent of the society itself. It is no less certain than it is important, notwithstanding the contrary opinions which have been entertained, that the larger the society, provided it lie within a practicable sphere, the more duly capable it will be of self government. And happily for the *republican cause*, the practicable sphere may be carried to a very great extent, by a judicious modification and mixture of the *federal principle*.

JAMES MADISON

Presidents of the United States

	Party	Term
1. George Washington (1732–1799)	Federalist	1789–1797
2. John Adams (1734–1826)	Federalist	1797–1801
3. Thomas Jefferson (1743–1826)	Democratic-Republican	1801–1809
4. James Madison (1751–1836)	Democratic-Republican	1809–1817
5. James Monroe (1758–1831)	Democratic-Republican	1817–1825
6. John Quincy Adams (1767–1848)	Democratic-Republican	1825–1829
7. Andrew Jackson (1767–1845)	Democratic	1829–1837
8. Martin Van Buren (1782–1862)	Democratic	1837–1841
9. William Henry Harrison (1773–1841)	Whig	1841
10. John Tyler (1790–1862)	Whig	1841–1845
11. James K. Polk (1795–1849)	Democratic	1845–1849
12. Zachary Taylor (1784–1850)	Whig	1849–1850
13. Millard Fillmore (1800–1874)	Whig	1850–1853
14. Franklin Pierce (1804–1869)	Democratic	1853–1857
15. James Buchanan (1791–1868)	Democratic	1857–1861
16. Abraham Lincoln (1809–1865)	Republican	1861–1865
17. Andrew Johnson (1808–1875)	Union	1865–1869
18. Ulysses S. Grant (1822–1885)	Republican	1869–1877
19. Rutherford B. Hayes (1822–1893)	Republican	1877–1881
20. James A. Garfield (1831–1881)	Republican	1881
21. Chester A. Arthur (1830–1886)	Republican	1881–1885
22. Grover Cleveland (1837–1908)	Democratic	1885–1889
23. Benjamin Harrison (1833–1901)	Republican	1889–1893
24. Grover Cleveland (1837–1908)	Democratic	1893–1897
25. William McKinley (1843–1901)	Republican	1897–1901
26. Theodore Roosevelt (1858–1919)	Republican	1901–1909
27. William Howard Taft (1857–1930)	Republican	1909–1913
28. Woodrow Wilson (1856–1924)	Democratic	1913–1921
29. Warren G. Harding (1865–1923)	Republican	1921–1923
30. Calvin Coolidge (1871–1933)	Republican	1923–1929
31. Herbert Hoover (1874–1964)	Republican	1929–1933
32. Franklin Delano Roosevelt (1882–1945)	Democratic	1933–1945
33. Harry S Truman (1884–1972)	Democratic	1945–1953
34. Dwight D. Eisenhower (1890–1969)	Republican	1953–1961
35. John F. Kennedy (1917–1963)	Democratic	1961–1963
36. Lyndon B. Johnson (1908–1973)	Democratic	1963–1969
37. Richard M. Nixon (1913–1994)	Republican	1969–1974
38. Gerald R. Ford (b. 1913)	Republican	1974–1977
39. Jimmy Carter (b. 1924)	Democratic	1977–1981
40. Ronald Reagan (b. 1911)	Republican	1981–1989
41. George Bush (b. 1924)	Republican	1989–1993
42. Bill Clinton (b. 1946)	Democratic	1993–

Twentieth-Century Justices of the Supreme Court

Justice*	Term of Service	Years of Service	Life Span	Justice*	Term of Service	Years of Service	Life Span
Oliver W. Holmes	1902–1932	30	1841–1935	Wiley B. Rutledge	1943–1949	6	1894–1949
William R. Day	1903–1922	19	1849–1923	Harold H. Burton	1945–1958	13	1888–1964
William H. Moody	1906–1910	3	1853–1917	*Fred M. Vinson*	1946–1953	7	1890–1953
Horace H. Lurton	1910–1914	4	1844–1914	Tom C. Clark	1949–1967	18	1899–1977
Charles E. Hughes	1910–1916	5	1862–1948	Sherman Minton	1949–1956	7	1890–1965
Willis Van Devanter	1911–1937	26	1859–1941	*Earl Warren*	1953–1969	16	1891–1974
Joseph R. Lamar	1911–1916	5	1857–1916	John Marshall Harlan	1955–1971	16	1899–1971
Edward D. White	1910–1921	11	1845–1921	William J. Brennan, Jr.	1956–1990	34	1906–
Mahlon Pitney	1912–1922	10	1858–1924	Charles E. Whittaker	1957–1962	5	1901–1973
James C. McReynolds	1914–1941	26	1862–1946	Potter Stewart	1958–1981	23	1915–1985
Louis D. Brandeis	1916–1939	22	1856–1941	Byron R. White	1962–	—	1917–
John H. Clarke	1916–1922	6	1857–1930	Arthur J. Goldberg	1962–1965	3	1908–
William H. Taft	1921–1930	8	1857–1945	Abe Fortas	1965–1969	4	1910–1982
George Sutherland	1922–1938	15	1862–1942	Thurgood Marshall	1967–1991	24	1908–1993
Pierce Butler	1922–1939	16	1866–1939	*Warren C. Burger*	1969–1986	17	1907–
Edward T. Sandford	1923–1930	7	1865–1930	Harry A. Blackmun	1970–	—	1908–
Harlan F. Stone	1925–1941	16	1872–1946	Lewis F. Powell, Jr.	1972–1987	15	1907–
Charles E. Hughes	1930–1941	11	1862–1948	William H. Rehnquist	1972–1986	14	1924–
Owen J. Roberts	1930–1945	15	1875–1955	John P. Stevens, III	1975–	—	1920–
Benjamin N. Cardozo	1932–1938	6	1870–1938	Sandra Day O'Connor	1981–	—	1930–
Hugo L. Black	1937–1971	34	1886–1971	*William H. Rehnquist*	1986–	—	1924–
Stanley F. Reed	1938–1957	19	1884–1980	Antonin Scalia	1986–	—	1936–
Felix Frankfurter	1939–1962	23	1882–1965	Anthony M. Kennedy	1988–	—	1936–
William O. Douglas	1939–1975	36	1898–1980	David Souter	1990–	—	1939–
Frank Murphy	1940–1949	9	1890–1949	Clarence Thomas	1991–	—	1948–
Harlan F. Stone	1941–1946	5	1872–1946	Ruth Bader Ginsberg	1993–	—	1933–
James F. Byrnes	1941–1942	1	1879–1972	Stephen G. Breyer	1994–	—	1938–
Robert H. Jackson	1941–1954	13	1892–1954				

* The names of chief justices are printed in italic type.

Party Control of the Presidency, Senate, and House of Representatives   1901–1993

Congress	Years	President	Senate			House		
			D	R	Other*	D	R	Other*
57th	1901–1903	McKinley T. Roosevelt	31	55	4	151	197	9
58th	1903–1905	T. Roosevelt	33	57	—	178	208	—
59th	1905–1907	T. Roosevelt	33	57	—	136	250	—
60th	1907–1909	T. Roosevelt	31	61	—	164	222	—
61st	1909–1911	Taft	32	61	—	172	219	—
62d	1911–1913	Taft	41	51	—	228	161	1
63d	1913–1915	Wilson	51	44	1	291	127	17
64th	1915–1917	Wilson	56	40	—	230	196	9
65th	1917–1919	Wilson	53	42	—	216	10	6
66th	1919–1921	Wilson	47	49	—	190	240	3
67th	1921—1923	Harding	37	59	—	131	301	1
68th	1923–1925	Coolidge	43	51	2	205	225	5
69th	1925–1927	Coolidge	39	56	1	183	247	4
70th	1927–1929	Coolidge	46	49	1	195	237	3
71st	1929–1931	Hoover	39	56	1	167	267	1
72d	1931–1933	Hoover	47	48	1	220	214	1
73d	1933–1935	F. Roosevelt	60	35	1	319	117	5
74th	1935–1937	F. Roosevelt	69	25	2	319	103	10
75th	1937–1939	F. Roosevelt	76	16	4	331	89	13
76th	1939–1941	F. Roosevelt	69	23	4	261	164	4
77th	1941–1943	F. Roosevelt	66	28	2	268	162	5
78th	1943–1945	F. Roosevelt	58	37	1	218	208	4
79th	1945–1947	Truman	56	38	1	242	190	2
80th	1947–1949	Truman	45	51	—	188	245	1
81st	1949–1951	Truman	54	42	—	263	171	1
82d	1951–1953	Truman	49	47	—	234	199	1
83d	1953–1955	Eisenhower	47	48	1	211	221	—
84th	1955–1957	Eisenhower	48	47	1	232	203	—
85th	1957–1959	Eisenhower	49	47	—	233	200	—
86th**	1959–1961	Eisenhower	65	35	—	284	153	—
87th**	1961–1963	Kennedy	65	35	—	263	174	—
88th	1963–1965	Kennedy Johnson	67	33	—	258	177	—

Sources: Department of Commerce, Bureau of the Census, *Statistical Abstract of the United States* (Washington, D.C.: U.S. Government Printing Office, 1980), p. 509, and *Members of Congress Since 1789*, 2d ed. (Washington, D.C.: Congressional Quarterly Press, 1981), pp. 176–177. Adapted from Barbara Hinckley, *Congressional Elections* (Washington, D.C.: Congressional Quarterly Press, 1981), pp. 144–145.

* Excludes vacancies at beginning of each session.

** The 437 members of the House in the 86th and 87th Congresses is attributable to the at-large representative given to both Alaska (January 3, 1959) and Hawaii (August 2, 1959) prior to redistricting in 1962.

Party Control of the Presidency, Senate, and House of Representatives 1901–1993 *(continued)*

Congress	Years	President	Senate D	R	Other*	House D	R	Other*
89th	1965–1967	Johnson	68	32	—	295	140	—
90th	1967–1969	Johnson	64	36	—	247	187	—
91st	1969–1971	Nixon	57	43	—	243	192	—
92d	1971–1973	Nixon	54	44	2	254	180	—
93d	1973–1975	Nixon Ford	56	42	2	239	192	1
94th	1975–1977	Ford	60	37	2	291	144	—
95th	1977–1979	Carter	61	38	1	292	143	—
96th	1979–1981	Carter	58	41	1	276	157	—
97th	1981–1983	Reagan	46	53	1	243	192	—
98th	1983–1985	Reagan	45	55	—	267	168	—
99th	1985–1987	Reagan	47	53	—	252	183	—
100th	1987–1989	Reagan	54	46	—	257	178	—
101st	1989–1991	Bush	55	45	—	262	173	—
102d	1991–1993	Bush	56	44	—	276	167	—
103d	1993–1995	Clinton	56	44	—	256	178	1

Glossary

adjudication The settling of a case judicially. More specifically, formal hearings in which persons or businesses under government agency scrutiny can present their position with legal counsel present. (13, 14)

administrative discretion The latitude that Congress gives agencies to make policy in the spirit of their legislative mandate. (13)

affirmative action Programs through which businesses, schools, and other institutions expand opportunities for women and members of minority groups. (16)

agenda building The process by which new issues are brought into the political limelight. (10)

agenda setting The stage of the policymaking process during which problems get defined as political issues. (17)

aggregate demand The money available to be spent for goods and services by consumers, businesses, and government. (18)

Aid to Families with Dependent Children (AFDC) A federal public assistance program that provides cash to low-income families with children. (19)

amicus curiae brief A brief filed (with the permission of the court) by an individual or group that is not a party to a legal action but has an interest in it. (14)

anarchism A political philosophy that opposes government in any form. (1)

appellate jurisdiction The authority of a court to hear cases that have been tried, decided, or reexamined in other courts. (14)

appropriations committees Committees of Congress that decide which of the programs passed by the authorization committees will actually be funded. (18)

argument The heart of a judicial opinion; its logical content separated from facts, rhetoric, and procedure. (14)

Articles of Confederation The compact among the thirteen original states that established the first government of the United States. (3)

attentive policy elites Leaders who follow news in specific policy areas. (6)

authorization committees Committees of Congress that can authorize spending in their particular areas of responsibility. (18)

autocracy A system of government in which the power to govern is concentrated in the hands of one individual. Also called *monarchy*. (2)

bicameral Having two legislative chambers, such as the Senate and House in the U.S. Congress. (3)

bill A formal proposal for a new law. (11)

bill of attainder A law that pronounces an individual guilty of a crime without a trial. (15)

Bill of Rights The first ten amendments to the Constitution. They prevent the national government from tampering with fundamental rights and civil liberties, and emphasize the limited character of national power. (3)

bimodal distribution A distribution (of opinions) that shows two responses being chosen about as frequently as each other. (5)

black codes Legislation enacted by former slave states to restrict the freedom of blacks. (16)

blanket primary A primary election in which voters receive a ballot containing both parties' potential nominees and can help nominate candidates for all offices for both parties. (9)

block grant A grant-in-aid awarded for general purposes, allowing the recipient great discretion in spending the grant money. (4)

bolter party A political party formed from a faction that has split off from one of the major parties. (8)

boycott A refusal to do business with a firm, individual, or nation as an expression of disapproval or as a means of coercion. (16, 20)

brief A written argument submitted to a judge. (14)

broadcast media Mass media that transmit information electronically. (6)

budget authority The amounts that government agencies are authorized to spend for their programs. (18)

budget committees One committee in each house of Congress that supervises a comprehensive budget review process. (18)

budget outlays The amounts that government agencies are expected to spend in the fiscal year. (18)

bureaucracy A large, complex organization in which employees have specific job responsibilities and work within a hierarchy of authority. (13)

bureaucrat An employee of a bureaucracy, usually meaning a government bureaucracy. (13)

business cycle Expansions and contractions of business activity, the first accompanied by inflation and the second by unemployment. (18)

Cabinet A group of presidential advisers; the heads of the executive departments and other key officials. (12)

capitalism The system of government that favors free enterprise (privately owned businesses operating without government regulation). (1)

Carter Doctrine A statement asserting that attempts "by any outside force to gain control of the Persian Gulf region" would be seen "as an assault on the vital interests of the United States." (20)

casework Solving problems for constituents, especially problems involving government agencies. (11)

categorical grant A grant-in-aid targeted for a specific purpose. (4)

caucus A closed meeting of the members of a political party to decide upon questions of policy and the selection of candidates for office. (8)

challenger A candidate who seeks to replace an incumbent. (9)

checks and balances A government structure that gives each branch some scrutiny and control over the other branches. (3)

citizen group An interest group whose basis of organization is a concern for issues unrelated to the members' vocations. (10)

civil case A court case that involves a private dispute arising from such matters as accidents, contractual obligations, and divorce. (14)

civil disobedience The willful but nonviolent violation of laws that are regarded as unjust. (16)

civil liberties Freedoms guaranteed to individuals. (15)

civil rights Powers or privileges guaranteed to individuals and protected from arbitrary removal at the hands of government or individuals. (15, 16)

civil rights movement Political mobilization of the people—black and white—to promote racial equality. (16)

civil service The system by which most appointments to the federal bureaucracy are made, to ensure that government jobs are filled on the basis of merit and that employees are not fired for political reasons. (13)

class-action suit A legal action brought by a person or group on behalf of a number of people in similar circumstances. (7, 14)

clear and present danger test A means by which the Supreme Court has distinguished between speech as the advocacy of ideas, which is protected by the First Amendment, and speech as incitement, which is not protected. (15)

closed primary A primary election in which voters must declare their party affiliation before they are given the primary ballot containing that party's potential nominees. (9)

cloture The mechanism by which a filibuster is cut off in the Senate. (11)

coalition building The banding together of several interest groups for the purpose of lobbying. (10)

Cold War A prolonged period of adversarial relations between the two superpowers, the U.S. and the Soviet Union. During the Cold War, which lasted from the late 1940's to the late 1980's, many crises and confrontations brought the superpowers to the brink of war, but they avoided direct military conflict with each other. (20)

commerce clause The third clause of Article I, Section 8, of the Constitution, which gives Congress the power to regulate commerce among the states. (4)

common (judge-made) law Legal precedents derived from previous judicial decisions. (14)

communication The process of transmitting information from one individual or group to another. (6)

communism A political system in which, in theory, ownership of all land and productive facilities is in the hands of the people, and all goods are equally shared. The production and distribution of goods are controlled by an authoritarian government. (1)

concurrence The agreement of a judge with the court's majority decision, for a reason other than the majority reason. (14)

confederation A loose association of independent states that agree to cooperate on specified matters. (3)

conference committee A temporary committee created to work out differences between the House and Senate versions of a specific piece of legislation. (11)

Congressional Budget Office (CBO) The budgeting arm of Congress, which prepares alternative budgets to those prepared by the president's OMB. (18)

congressional campaign committee An organization maintained by a political party to raise funds to support its own candidates in congressional elections. (8)

conservatives Generally, those people whose political ideology favors a narrow scope for government. Also, those who value freedom more than equality but would restrict freedom to preserve social order. (1)

constituents People who live and vote in a government official's district or state. (11)

containment The idea that the Soviets had to be prevented from expanding further. (20)

Continental Congress A political assembly called to speak out and act collectively for the people of all the colonies. The First Continental Congress met in 1774 and adopted a statement of rights and principles; the Second Continental Congress adopted the Declaration of Independence in 1776 and the Articles of Confederation in 1777. (3)

conventional participation Relatively routine political behavior that uses institutional channels and is acceptable to the dominant culture. (7)

cooperative federalism A view that holds that the Constitution is an agreement among people who are citizens of both state and nation, so there is little distinction between state powers and national powers. (4)

Council of Economic Advisers (CEA) A group that works within the executive branch to provide advice on maintaining a stable economy. (18)

county government The government unit that administers a county. (4)

criminal case A court case involving a crime, or violation of public order. (14)

critical election An election that produces a sharp change in the existing pattern of party loyalties among groups of voters. (8)

Declaration of Independence Drafted by Thomas Jefferson, the document that proclaimed the right of the colonies to separate from Great Britain. (3)

de facto segregation Segregation that is not the result of government influence. (16)

deficit financing The Keynesian technique of spending beyond government income to combat an economic slump. Its purpose is to inject extra money into the economy to stimulate aggregate demand. (18)

de jure segregation Government-imposed segregation. (16)

delegate A legislator whose primary responsibility is to represent the majority view of his or her constituents, regardless of his or her own view. (11)

delegation of powers The process by which Congress gives the executive branch the additional authority needed to address new problems. (12)

democracy A system of government in which, in theory, the people rule, either directly or indirectly. (2)

democratic socialism A socialist form of government that guarantees civil liberties such as freedom of speech and religion. Citizens determine the extent of government activity through free elections and competitive political parties. (1)

democratization A process of transition as a country attempts to move from an authoritarian form of government to a democratic one. (2)

department The biggest unit of the executive branch, covering a broad area of government responsibility. The heads of the departments, or secretaries, form the president's cabinet. (13)

deregulation A bureaucratic reform by which the government reduces its role as a regulator of business. (13)

descriptive representation A belief that constituents are most effectively represented by legislators who are similar to them in such key demographic characteristics as race, ethnicity, religion, or gender. (11)

desegregation The ending of authorized segregation, or separation by race. (16)

detente A reduction of tensions. This term is particularly used to refer to a reduction of tensions between the U.S. and the Soviet Union in the early 1970's during the Nixon administration. (20)

deterrence The defense policy of American strategists during the Eisenhower administration, who believed the Soviets would not take aggressive action knowing they risked nuclear annihilation. (20)

direct action Unconventional participation that involves assembling crowds to confront businesses and local governments to demand a hearing. (7)

direct lobbying Attempts to influence a legislator's vote through personal contact with the legislator. (10)

direct mail Advertising via the mails; more specifically, a method of attracting new members to an interest group by sending letters to people in a carefully targeted audience. (10)

direct primary A preliminary election, run by the state government, in which the voters choose each party's candidates for the general election. (7)

discretionary funds Sums of money that may be spent on unpredicted needs to further national interests. (20)

discretionary spending In the Budget Enforcement Act of 1990, authorized expenditures from annual appropriations. (18)

discrimination Acts of irrational suspicion or hatred, directed toward a specific group of people. (16)

dissent The disagreement of a judge with a majority decision. (14)

divided government The situation in which one party controls the White House and the other controls the Congress. (12)

docket A court's agenda. (14)

dual federalism A view that holds the Constitution is a compact among sovereign states, so that the powers of the national government are fixed and limited. (4)

economic depression A period of high unemployment and business failures; a severe, long-lasting downturn in a business cycle. (18)

elastic clause See *necessary and proper clause.*

election A formal procedure for voting. (7)

election campaign An organized effort to persuade voters to choose one candidate over others competing for the same office. (9)

electoral college A body of electors chosen by voters to cast ballots for president and vice president. (3, 8)

electoral dealignment A lessening of the importance of party loyalties in voting decisions. (8)

electoral realignment The change in voting patterns that occurs after a critical election. (8)

elite theory The view that a small group of people actually makes most of the important government decisions. (2)

embargo A government freeze on the movement of goods or vessels to or from a specific country, as a means of coercion or of expressing disapproval. (20)

entitlement A benefit to which every eligible person has a legal right and that the government cannot deny. (18, 19)

enumerated powers The powers explicitly granted to Congress by the Constitution. (3)

equality of opportunity The idea that each person is guaranteed the same chance to succeed in life. (1, 16)

equality of outcome The concept that society must ensure that people are equal, and governments must design policies to redistribute wealth and status so that economic and social equality is actually achieved. (1, 16)

equal opportunities rule Under the Federal Communications Act of 1934, the requirement that if a broadcast station gives or sells time to a candidate for any public office, it must make available an equal amount of time under the same conditions to all other candidates for that office. (6)

Equal Rights Amendment (ERA) A failed constitutional amendment first introduced by the National Women's party in 1923, declaring that "equality of rights under the law shall not be denied or abridged by the United States or any State on account of sex." (16)

establishment clause The first clause in the First Amendment, which forbids the establishment of a national religion. (15)

excess stock disposal The selling of excess government stocks, such as surplus or infrequently used equipment. (20)

exclusionary rule The judicial rule that states that evidence obtained in an illegal search and seizure cannot be used in trial. (15)

executive agreement A pact between the heads of two countries. (20)

executive branch The law-enforcing branch of government. (3)

Executive Office of the President The president's executive aides and their staffs; the extended White House executive establishment. (12)

ex post facto law A law that declares an action to be criminal *after* it has been performed. (15)

extraordinary majorities Majorities greater than that required by majority rule, that is, greater than 50 percent plus one. (3)

fairness doctrine An FCC regulation that obligated broadcasters to discuss public issues and provide fair coverage to each side of those issues; repealed in 1987. (6)

farmer-labor party A political party that represents farmers and urban workers who believe that the working class does not get its share of society's wealth. (8)

Federal Communications Commission (FCC) An independent federal agency that regulates interstate and international communication by radio, television, telephone, telegraph, cable, and satellite. (6)

Federal Election Commission (FEC) A federal agency that oversees the financing of national election campaigns. (9)

federalism The division of power between a central government and regional governments. (3, 4)

federal question An issue covered by the constitution, national laws, or U.S. treaties. (14)

Federal Reserve System The system of banks that acts as the central bank of the United States and controls major monetary policies. (18)

feedback Information received by policymakers about the effectiveness of public policy. (17)

feminization of poverty The term applied to the fact that a growing percentage of all poor Americans are women or the dependents of women. (19)

fighting words Speech that is not protected by the First Amendment because it inflicts injury or tends to incite an immediate disturbance of the peace. (15)

filibuster A delaying tactic, used in the Senate, that involves speechmaking to prevent action on a piece of legislation. (11)

first-past-the-post election A British term for elections conducted in single-member districts that award victory to the candidate with the most votes. (9)

First, Second, and Third Worlds The terms applied to industrialized democracies (First World), the countries of Eastern Europe (Second World), and underdeveloped countries (Third World). (20)

fiscal policies Economic policies that involve government spending and taxing. (18)

fiscal year (FY) The twelve-month period from October 1 to September 30 used by the government for accounting purposes. A fiscal-year budget is named for the year in which it ends. (18)

flexible response The basic defense policy of the Kennedy administration, involving the ability to wage both nuclear and conventional war. (20)

food stamp program A federally funded program that increases the purchasing power of needy families by providing them with coupons they can use to purchase food. (19)

formula grant A grant-in-aid distributed according to a particular formula, which specifies who is eligible for the grants and how much each eligible applicant will receive. (4)

fragmentation In policymaking, the phenomenon of attacking a single problem in different and sometimes competing ways. (17)

franchise The right to vote. Also called *suffrage.* (7)

franking privilege The right of members of Congress to send mail free of charge. (11)

freedom from Immunity, as in *freedom from want.* (1)

freedom to An absence of constraints on behavior;

may also be stated as *freedom of,* as in *freedom of religion.* (1)

free-exercise clause The second clause in the First Amendment, which prevents the government from interfering with the exercise of religion. (15)

free-expression clauses The press and speech clauses of the First Amendment. (15)

free-rider problem The situation in which people benefit from the activities of an organization (such as an interest group) but do not contribute to those activities. (10)

gatekeepers Media executives, news editors, and prominent reporters who direct the flow of news. (6)

GATT-Bretton Woods system An international economic system in operation from the end of World War II until the early 1970's. (20)

general election A national election held by law in November of every even-numbered year. (9)

general revenue sharing Part of a federal program introduced by President Nixon that returned tax money to state and local governments to be spent largely as they wished. (4)

gerrymandering Redrawing a congressional district to intentionally benefit one political party. (11)

glasnost A domestic reform instituted by Mikhail Gorbachev in the Soviet Union: a greater openness in political affairs. (20)

globalism A policy of global, or worldwide, involvement, as is current U.S. foreign policy. (20)

good faith exception Established by the Supreme Court, an exception to the exclusionary rule maintaining that evidence seized on the basis of a mistakenly issued search warrant can be introduced at trial. (15)

government The legitimate use of force to control human behavior; also, the organization or agency authorized to exercise that force. (1)

government corporation A government agency that performs services that might be provided by the private sector but that involve either insufficient financial incentive or are better provided when they are somehow linked with government. (13)

Gramm-Rudman Popular name for an act passed by Congress in 1985 that, in its original form, sought to lower the national deficit to a specified level each year, culminating in a balanced budget in FY 1991. New reforms and deficit targets were agreed on in 1990. (18)

grant-in-aid Money provided by one level of government to another, to be spent for a specific purpose. (4)

grassroots lobbying Lobbying activities performed by rank-and-file interest group members and would-be members. (10)

Great Compromise Submitted by the Connecticut delegation to the Constitutional Convention of 1787, and thus also known as the *Connecticut Compromise,* a plan calling for a bicameral legislature in which the House of Representatives would be apportioned according to population and the states would be represented equally in the Senate. (3)

Great Depression The longest and deepest setback the American economy has ever experienced. It began with the stock market crash on October 12, 1929, and did not end until the start of World War II. (19)

Great Society President Lyndon Johnson's broad array of programs designed to redress political, social, and economic equality. (19)

gross national product (GNP) The total value of the goods and services produced by a country during a year. (18)

high politics A term used to describe strategic and security issues in global politics. Traditionally, policymakers involved in global politics were expected to give greater priority to these issues than to issues of low politics such as socioeconomic or welfare issues . (20)

home rule The right to enact and enforce legislation locally. (4)

horse race journalism Election coverage by the mass media that focuses on which candidate is ahead, rather than on national issues. (6)

impeachment The formal charging of a government official with "Treason, Bribery, or other High Crimes and Misdemeanors." (11)

implementation The process of putting specific policies into operation. (13, 17)

implied powers Those powers that Congress requires in order to execute its enumerated powers. (3, 4)

in-and-outer A participant in an issue network who has a good understanding of the needs and problems of others in the network and can easily switch jobs within the network. (17)

incremental budgeting A method of budget making that involves adding new funds (an increment) onto the amount previously budgeted (in last year's budget). (18)

incrementation Policymaking that moves in small steps from the existing policy. (13)

incumbent A current officeholder. (9, 11)

independent agency An executive agency that is not part of a cabinet department. (13)

inflation An economic condition characterized by price increases linked to a decrease in the value of the currency. (18)

influencing behavior Behavior that seeks to modify or reverse government policy to serve political interests. (7)

information campaign An organized effort to gain public backing by bringing a group's views to public attention. (10)

infotainment The practice of mixing journalism with theater, employed by some news programs. (6)

inherent powers Authority claimed by the president that is not clearly specified in the Constitution. Typically, these powers are inferred from the Constitution. (12)

initiative A procedure by which voters can propose an issue to be decided by the legislature or by the people in a referendum. It requires gathering a specified number of signatures and submitting a petition to a designated agency. (2, 7)

interdependent The close interrelationship of two or more states such that what happens in one state affects the other. (20)

interest group An organized group of individuals that seeks to influence public policy. Also called a *lobby.* (2, 10)

interest group entrepreneur An interest group organizer or leader. (10)

intergovernmental relations The interdependence and relationships among the various levels of government and government personnel. (4)

iron triangles The members of congressional committees, federal agencies or bureaus, and lobbies who work toward policy ends in a specific area. (17)

isolationism The policy of noninvolvement, as was the foreign policy of the United States during most of the nineteenth century. (20)

issue network A shared-knowledge group consisting of representatives of various interests involved in some particular aspect of public policy. (17)

joint committee A committee made up of members of both the House and the Senate. (11)

judgment The judicial decision in a court case. (14)

judicial activism A judicial philosophy whereby judges interpret existing laws and precedents loosely and interject their own values in court decisions. (14)

judicial branch The branch of government that interprets laws. (3)

judicial restraint A judicial philosophy whereby judges adhere closely to statutes and precedents in reaching their decisions. (14)

judicial review The power to declare congressional (and presidential) acts invalid because they violate the Constitution. (3, 14)

Keynesian theory A theory of the economy that states that aggregate demand can be adjusted through a combination of fiscal and monetary policies. (18)

laissez faire An economic doctrine that opposes any form of government intervention in business. (1)

legislative branch The lawmaking branch of government. (3)

legislative liaison staff Those people who comprise the communications link between the White House and Congress, advising the president or cabinet secretaries on the status of pending legislation. (12)

libel Written defamation of character. (15)

liberals Generally, those people whose political ideology favors a broad scope for government; those who value freedom more than order but not more than equality. (1)

libertarianism A political ideology that is opposed to all government action except as necessary to protect life and property. (1)

libertarians Those who advocate minimal government action; those who subscribe to libertarianism. (1)

linkage In international relations, the idea of using rewards and advantages in one area of negotiation to promote another country's compliance in other areas of negotiation. (20)

lobby See *interest group.*

lobbyist A representative of an interest group. (10)

local caucus A method used to select delegates to attend a party's national convention. Generally, a local meeting selects delegates for a county-level meeting, which in turn selects delegates for a higher-level meeting; the process culminates in a state convention that actually selects the national convention delegates. (9)

low politics A term used to describe socioeconomic or welfare issues. Traditionally, policymakers involved in global politics were expected to place less emphasis on these issues than on issues of high politics such as strategic and security issues. (20)

majoritarian model of democracy The classical theory of democracy in which government by the people is interpreted as government by the majority of the people. (2)

majority leader The head of the majority party in the Senate; the second highest ranking member of the majority party in the House. (11)

majority party A political party that regularly enjoys the support of the most voters. (8)

majority representation The system by which one office, contested by two or more candidates, is won by the single candidate who collects the most votes. (8)

majority rule The principle—basic to procedural democratic theory—that the decision of a group must reflect the preference of more than half of those participating; a simple majority. (2)

mandate An endorsement by voters. Presidents sometimes argue they have been given a mandate to carry out policy proposals. (4, 12)

mandatory spending In the Budget Enforcement Act of 1990, expenditures required by previous commitments. (18)

Marshall Plan A post-World War II plan to restore European economic viability. The plan sent approximately $12 billion in aid to Europe over a four-year period. (20)

mass communication The process by which individuals or groups transmit information to large, heterogeneous, and widely dispersed audiences. (6)

mass media The means employed in mass communication, often divided into print media and broadcast media. (6)

means-tested benefits Conditional benefits provided by government to individuals whose income falls below a designated threshold. (19)

media event A situation that is so "newsworthy" that the mass media are compelled to cover it; candidates in elections often create such situations to garner media attention. (6)

Medicare A health-insurance program for all persons older than sixty-five. (19)

membership bias The tendency of some sectors of society—especially the wealthy, the highly educated, professionals, and those in business—to organize more readily into interest groups. (10)

micromanagement A term applied by critics to describe Congress's constant intervention in administrative policymaking. (11)

military-industrial complex The combined interests of the military establishment and the large arms industry. The two groups are united by two common interests: war and military spending. (20)

minority party   A political party that does not have the support of the most voters. (8)

minority rights   The benefits of government that cannot be denied to any citizens by majority decisions. (2)

Miranda warnings   Statements concerning rights that police are required to make to a person before he or she is subjected to in-custody questioning. (15)

monetarists   Those who argue that government can effectively control the performance of an economy only by controlling the supply of money. (18)

monetary policies   Economic policies that involve control of, and changes in, the supply of money. (18)

most favored nation status   A trading status that allows a nation to pay the lowest tariff rates when it sells its goods in another nation. (20)

muckrakers   Writers who practiced an early form of investigative reporting, replete with unsavory details. (6)

Munich paradigm   The foreign policy view that the United States must be willing to intervene, militarily if necessary, anywhere on the globe to put down a major threat to world order and freedom. (20)

municipal government   The government unit that administers a city or town. (4)

mutual assured destruction (MAD)   The capability of the two great superpowers—the United States and the Soviet Union—to destroy each other, ensuring no winner of a nuclear war. (20)

national committee   A committee of a political party composed of party chairpersons and party officials from every state. (8)

national convention   A gathering of delegates of a single political party from across the country to choose candidates for president and vice president and to adopt a party platform. (8)

national industrial policies   The government-sponsored coordinated plans adopted by some nations, including Germany and Japan, to promote economic expansion. (20)

National Security Council (NSC)   A permanent group of advisers created to help the president integrate and coordinate the details of domestic, foreign, and military affairs as they relate to national security. (20)

nation-building policy   A policy once intended to shore up Third World countries economically and democratically, thereby making them less attractive targets for Soviet opportunism. (20)

necessary and proper clause   The last clause in Section 8 of Article I of the Constitution, which gives Congress the means to execute its enumerated powers. This clause is the basis for Congress's implied powers. Also called the *elastic clause*. (3, 4)

New Deal   The measures advocated by the Roosevelt administration to alleviate the Depression. (19)

"new" ethnicity   A newer outlook on the people comprising America's "melting pot," with focus on race. (5)

New International Economic Order (NIEO)   A proposal whereby industrialized states would help in the economic development of Third World countries. (20)

New Jersey Plan   Submitted by the head of the New Jersey delegation to the Constitutional Convention of 1787, a set of nine resolutions that would have, in effect, preserved the Articles of Confederation by amending rather than replacing them. (3)

newsworthiness   The degree to which a news story is important enough to be covered in the mass media. (6)

Nineteenth Amendment   The amendment to the Constitution, adopted in 1920, that assures women of the right to vote. (16)

Nixon Doctrine   An attempt to reduce America's foreign involvement by calling for U.S. intervention only where it made a "real difference" and was considered to be in our interest. (20)

nomination   Designation as an official candidate of a political party. (8)

nonconnected PAC   A largely ideological political action committee that has no parent lobbying organization and is formed solely for the purpose of raising and channeling campaign funds. (10)

non-means-tested benefits   Benefits provided by government to all citizens, regardless of income; Medicare and social security are examples. (19)

nontariff barrier (NTB)   A regulation that outlines the exact specifications an imported product must meet in order to be offered for sale. (20)

norm   An organization's informal, unwritten rules that guide individual behavior. (10)

normal distribution   A symmetrical bell-shaped distribution (of opinions) centered on a single mode, or most frequent response. (5)

North American Free Trade Agreement (NAFTA)   An agreement among the United States, Canada and Mexico providing for the free flow of goods and services among the three nations. (20)

North Atlantic Treaty Organization (NATO)   An organization including the nations of Western Europe, the United States and Canada created for defense purposes. Established in 1949, NATO's primary purpose was to contain Soviet expansion. (20)

nullification The declaration by a state that a particular action of the national government is not applicable to that state. (4)

obligation of contracts The obligation of the parties to a contract to carry out its terms. (15)

Office of Management and Budget (OMB) The budgeting arm of the Executive Office; prepares the president's budget. (18)

"old" ethnicity An older outlook on the people comprising America's "melting pot," with focus on religion and country of origin. (5)

oligarchy A system of government in which power is concentrated in the hands of a few people. (2)

omnibus legislation A number of different bills that are considered and passed as a single entity by Congress. (11)

open election An election that lacks an incumbent. (9)

open primary A primary election in which voters need not declare their party affiliation but must choose one party's primary ballot to take into the voting booth. (9)

opinion An explanation written by one or more judges, justifying their ruling in a court case. (14)

opinion schema A network of organized knowledge and beliefs that guides a person's processing of information regarding a particular subject. (5)

order The rule of law to preserve life and protect property. Maintaining order is the oldest purpose of government. (1)

original jurisdiction The authority of a court to hear a case before any other court does. (14)

oversight The process of reviewing the operations of an agency to determine whether it is carrying out policies as Congress intended. (11)

parliamentary system A system of government in which the chief executive is the leader whose party holds the most seats in the legislature after an election or whose party forms a major part of the ruling coalition. (11)

participatory democracy A system of government where rank-and-file citizens rule themselves rather than electing representatives to govern on their behalf. (2)

party conference A meeting to select party leaders and decide committee assignments, held at the be-ginning of a session of Congress by Republicans or Democrats in each chamber. (8)

party identification A voter's sense of psychological attachment to a party. (8)

party machine A centralized party organization that dominates local politics by controlling elections. (8)

party of ideological protest A political party that rejects prevailing doctrines and proposes racially different principles, often favoring more government activism. (8)

party platform The statement of policies of a national political party. (8)

pay-as-you-go (PAYGO) In the Budget Enforcement Act of 1990, the requirement that any tax cut or expansion of an entitlement program must be offset by a tax increase or other savings. (18)

perestroika A domestic reform instituted by Mikhail Gorbachev in the Soviet Union: an economic and political restructure. (20)

picket fence federalism A view of federalism that stresses the interactions and interrelationships among interest groups and the various levels of government. (4)

plea bargain A defendant's admission of guilt in exchange for a less severe punishment. (14)

pluralist model of democracy An interpretation of democracy in which government by the people is taken to mean government by people operating through competing interest groups. (2)

pocket veto A means of killing a bill that has been passed by both houses of Congress, in which the president does not sign the bill within ten days of Congress's adjournment. (11)

police power The authority of a government to maintain order and safeguard citizens' health, morals, safety, and welfare. (1)

policy evaluation The analysis of public policy. (17)

policy formulation The stage of the policymaking process during which formal proposals are developed and adopted. (17)

political action committee (PAC) An organization that pools campaign contributions from group members and donates those funds to candidates for political office. (10)

political agenda A list of issues that need government attention. (6)

political equality Equality in political decision making: one vote per person, with all votes counted equally. (1, 2)

political ideology A consistent set of values and beliefs about the proper purpose and scope of government. (1)

political participation Actions of private citizens by which they seek to influence or support government and politics. (7)

political party An organization that sponsors candidates for political office under the organization's name. (8)

political socialization The complex process by which people acquire their political values. (5)

political sophistication The depth and scope of a person's knowledge of public affairs. (5)

political system A set of interrelated institutions that links people with government. (8)

poll tax A tax of $1 or $2 on every citizen who wished to vote, first instituted in Georgia in 1877. Although it was no burden on white citizens, it effectively disenfranchised blacks. (16)

populists Those people whose political ideology favors government action both to reduce inequality and to ensure social order. (1)

poverty level The minimum cash income that will provide for a family's basic needs; calculated as three times the cost of a market basket of food that provides a minimally nutritious diet. (19)

precedent A judicial ruling that serves as the basis for the ruling in a subsequent case. (14)

presidential primary A special primary election used to select delegates to attend the party's national convention, which in turn nominates the presidential candidate. (9)

press clause The First Amendment guarantee of freedom of the press. (15)

primary election A preliminary election conducted within a political party to select candidates who will run for public office in a subsequent election. (9)

print media Mass media that transmits information through the publication of the written word. (6)

prior restraint Censorship before publication. (15)

procedural democratic theory A view of democracy as being embodied in a decision-making process that involves universal participation, political equality, majority rule, and responsiveness. (2)

productive capacity The total value of goods and services that can be produced when the economy works at full capacity. (18)

program monitoring Keeping track of government programs, usually by interest groups. (10)

progressive taxation A system of taxation whereby the rich pay proportionately higher taxes than the poor; used by governments to redistribute wealth and thus promote equality. (3, 18)

progressivism A philosophy of political reform based upon the goodness and wisdom of the individual citizen as opposed to special interests and political institutions. (7)

project grant A grant-in-aid awarded on the basis of competitive applications submitted by prospective recipients. (4)

proportional representation The system by which legislative seats are awarded to a party in proportion to the vote that party wins in an election. (8)

proposal The first of two stages in amending the constitution: An amendment may be proposed, or offered, either by Congress or by a national convention summoned by Congress. (3)

proposition An issue to be voted on in a referendum. (7)

protectionism The notion that women must be protected from life's cruelties; until the 1970s, the basis for laws affecting women's civil rights. (16)

public assistance Government aid to individuals who can demonstrate a need for that aid. (16)

public figures People who assume roles of prominence in society or thrust themselves to the forefront of public controversy. (15)

public goods Benefits and services, such as parks and sanitation, that benefit all citizens but are not likely to be produced voluntarily by individuals. (1)

public interest group A citizen group that generally is considered to have no economic self-interest in the policies it pursues. (10)

public opinion The collected attitudes of citizens concerning a given issue or question. (5)

public policy A general plan of action adopted by the government to solve a social problem, counter a threat, or pursue an objective. (19)

racial gerrymandering The drawing of a legislative district to maximize the chances that a minority candidate will win election. (11)

racial segregation Separation from society because of race. (16)

racism A belief that human races have distinct characteristics such that one's own race is superior to, and has a right to rule, others. (16)

ratification The second of two stages in amending the Constitution: A proposed amendment can be ratified, or accepted, either by the legislatures of the states or by constitutional conventions held in the states. (3)

reapportionment Redistribution of representatives among the states, based on population movement. Congress is reapportioned after each census. (11)

reasonable access rule An FCC rule that requires broadcast stations to make their facilities available for the expression of conflicting views or issues by all responsible elements in the community. (6)

recall The process for removing an elected official from office. (7)

receipts For a government, the amount expected or obtained in taxes and other revenues. (18)

redistricting Redrawing congressional districts after census-based reapportionment. (11)

referendum An election on a policy issue. (2, 7)

regulation Government intervention in the workings of business to promote some socially desired goal. (13)

regulations Administrative rules that guide the operation of a government program. (13)

regulatory commission An agency of the executive branch of government that controls or directs some aspect of the economy. (13)

representative democracy A system of government where citizens elect public officials to govern on their behalf. (2)

reprogramming The use for one purpose of money that Congress has approved for some other purpose. (20)

republic A government without a monarch; a government rooted in the consent of the governed, whose power is exercised by elected representatives responsible to the governed. (3)

republicanism A form of government in which power resides in the people and is exercised by their elected representatives. (3)

responsible party government A set of principles formalizing the ideal role of parties in a majoritarian democracy. (8)

responsiveness A decision-making principle, necessitated by representative government, that implies that elected representatives should do what the majority of people wants. (2)

rights The benefits of government to which every citizen is entitled. (1)

rule making The administrative process that results in the issuance of regulations by government agencies. (13)

rule of four An unwritten rule that requires at least four justices to agree that a case warrants consideration before it is reviewed by the Supreme Court. (14)

school district An area for which a local government unit administers elementary and secondary school programs. (4)

select committee A temporary congressional committee created for a specific purpose and disbanded after that purpose is fulfilled. (11)

self-interest principle The implication that people choose what benefits them personally. (5)

senatorial courtesy A practice whereby the Senate will not confirm for a lower federal court judgeship a nominee who is opposed by the senior senator in the president's party in the nominee's state. (14)

seniority Years of consecutive service on a particular congressional committee. (11)

separate-but-equal doctrine The concept that providing separate but equivalent facilities for blacks and whites satisfies the equal protection clauses of the Fourteenth Amendment. (16)

separation of powers The assignment of law-making, law-enforcing, and law-interpreting functions to separate branches of government. (3)

sequestration In the Budget Enforcement Act of 1990, an automatic across-the-board spending cut in an overspent category or in nonexempt entitlement programs. (18)

sexism Sex discrimination. (16)

Shays' Rebellion A revolt led by Daniel Shays in 1786 and 1787 in Massachusetts against the foreclosure of farms resulting from high interest rates and high state taxes. The rebellion dramatized the weakness of the newly created national government. (3)

single-issue party A political party formed to promote one principle rather than a general philosophy of government. (8)

skewed distribution An asymmetrical but generally bell-shaped distribution (of opinions); its mode, or most frequent response, lies off to one side. (5)

social contract theory The belief that the people agree to set up rulers for certain purposes and thus have the right to resist or remove rulers who act against those purposes. (3)

social equality Equality in wealth, education, and status. (1)

social insurance A government-backed guarantee against loss by individuals without regard to need. (19)

socialism A form of rule in which the central government plays a strong role in regulating existing private industry and directing the economy, although it does allow some private ownership of productive capacity. (1)

social security Social insurance that provides economic assistance to persons faced with unemployment, disability, or old age. It is financed by taxes on employers and employees. (19)

Social Security Act The law that provided for social security and is the basis of modern American social welfare. (19)

social welfare Government programs that provide the minimum living standards necessary for all citizens. (19)

socioeconomic status Position in society, based on a combination of education, occupational status, and income. (5)

solicitor general The third highest ranking official of the U.S. Department of Justice, and the one who represents the national government before the Supreme Court. (14)

sovereignty The power of self-rule. (3)

Speaker of the House The presiding officer of the House of Representatives. (11)

special district A government unit created to perform particular functions, especially when those functions are best performed across jurisdictional boundaries. (4)

special envoy A personal representative of the president to a foreign government. (20)

special revenue sharing Part of a federal program introduced by President Nixon that was to consolidate existing categorical grant programs. (4)

speech clause The part of the First Amendment that guarantees freedom of speech. (15)

split ticket In voting, candidates from different parties for different offices. (9)

stable distribution A distribution (of opinions) that shows little change over time. (5)

standard socioeconomic model A relationship between socioeconomic status and conventional political involvement: People with higher status and more education are more likely to participate than those with lower status. (7)

standing committee A permanent congressional committee that specializes in a particular legislative area. (11)

stare decisis Literally, let the decision stand; decision making according to precedent. (14)

states' rights The idea that all rights not specifically conferred on the national government by the Constitution are reserved to the states. (4)

statutory construction Judicial interpretation of legislative acts. (14)

straight ticket In voting, a single party's candidates for all the offices. (9)

Strategic Defense Initiative (SDI) A large-scale research and development effort to build a system that will defend the United States against Soviet missiles. Also called "Star Wars." (20)

substantive democratic theory The view that democracy is embodied in the substance of government policies rather than in the policymaking procedure. (2)

suffrage The right to vote. Also called the *franchise*. (7)

supply-side economics Economic policies intended to counter extreme inflation by increasing the supply of goods to match demand. (18)

supportive behavior Actions that express allegiance to government and country. (7)

supremacy clause The clause in Article VI of the Constitution that asserts that national laws take precedence over state and local laws when they conflict. (3)

symbolic expression Nonverbal communication. (15)

tax committees The two committees of Congress responsible for raising the revenue with which to run the government. (18)

term limits Legal limitations on the number of terms a member can serve in a legislative body. (11)

torts Injuries or wrongs to the person or property of another. (14)

totalitarianism A political philosophy that advocates unlimited power for the government to enable it to control all sectors of society. (1)

total quality management (TQM) A management philosophy emphasizing listening closely to customers, breaking down barriers between parts of an organization, and continually improving quality. (13)

trade association An organization that represents firms within a particular industry. (10)

transfer authority The president's power to use for one purpose money that Congress has approved for some other purpose. (20)

transfer payment A payment by government to an individual, mainly through social security or unemployment insurance. (18)

trustee   A representative who is obligated to consider the views of constituents but is not obligated to vote according to those views if he or she believes they are misguided. (11)

two-party system   A political system in which two major political parties compete for control of the government. Candidates from a third party have little chance of winning office. (8)

two-step flow of communication   The process in which a few policy elites gather information and then inform their more numerous followers, mobilizing them to apply pressure to government. (6)

uncontrollable outlay   A payment that government must make by law. (18)

unconventional participation   Relatively uncommon political behavior that challenges or defies government channels and thus is personally stressful to participants and their opponents. (7)

unitary government   A form of government in which all power is vested in a central authority. (3)

universal participation   The concept that everyone in a democracy should participate in governmental decision making. (2)

U.S. Court of Appeals   A court within the second tier of the three-tiered federal court system, to which decisions of the district courts and federal agencies may be appealed for review. (14)

U.S. district court   A court within the lowest tier of the three-tiered federal court system; a court where litigation begins. (14)

veto   The president's disapproval of a bill that has been passed by both houses of Congress. Congress can override a veto with a two-thirds vote in each house. (11, 12)

Vietnamization   President Nixon's plan for turning over more and more of the fighting in the Vietnam War to the South Vietnamese. This tactic finally led to the peace agreement in 1973. (20)

Vietnam paradigm   The foreign policy view that not all left-wing revolutionary movements are necessarily directed from Moscow, but instead can be a product of internal nationalist forces. Proponents of this paradigm also argue that military force is not the most effective way to "win the hearts and the minds" of people in other countries. (20)

Vietnam Syndrome   An attitude that rejects the use of armed force as a tool of global politics. As a result of America's failure in the Vietnam War, people affected by the Vietnam syndrome see the use of military force as ineffective or immoral or both. (20)

Virginia Plan   A set of proposals for a new government, submitted to the Constitutional Convention of 1787; included separation of the government into three branches, division of the legislature into two houses, and proportional representation in the legislature. (3)

voting   The act in which individuals engage when they formally choose among alternatives in an election. (7)

War on Poverty   A part of President Lyndon Johnson's Great Society program, intended to eradicate poverty within ten years. (19)

War Powers Resolution   An act of Congress that limits the president's ability to wage undeclared war. (20)

wars of national liberation   A term used especially by the Soviet Union to describe the struggles fought by peoples under colonial rule. The Soviets offered support for communist forces engaged in these fights.

welfare state   A nation in which the government assumes responsibility for the welfare of its citizens, redistributing income to reduce social inequality. (1, 19)

yellow journalism   The distorted, sensationalist reporting of stories that became popular toward the end of the nineteenth century. (6)

zero-sum game   In international politics, a situation in which one superpower's gain is the other's loss. (20)

References

Chapter 1 / Freedom, Order, or Equality? / pp. 2–28

1. Tom Morganthau, "Dr. Kevorkian's Death Wish," *Newsweek* 8 March 1993:48; and Jack Lessenberry, "In Tactical Change, Kevorkian Promises To Halt Suicide Aid," *New York Times* 26 December 1993:1.
2. Lessenberry, "In Tactical Change, Kevorkian Promises To Halt Suicide Aid," p. 1.
3. "Kevorkian Victory: 3rd Judge Says Suicide Law Is Unconstitutional," *New York Times* 28 January 1994:A9.
4. Center for Political Studies of the Institute for Social Research, *Election Study 1992* (Ann Arbor, Mich., University of Michigan).
5. 1977 Constitution of the Union of Soviet Socialist Republics, Article 11, in *Constitutions of Countries of the World*, ed. A. P. Blaustein and G. H. Flanz (Dobbs Ferry, N.Y.: Oceana, 1971).
6. Karl Marx and Friedrich Engels, *Critique of the Gotha Programme* (New York: International Publishers, 1938), p. 10. Originally written in 1875 but published in 1891.
7. See the argument in Amy Gutman, *Liberal Equality* (Cambridge, England: Cambridge University Press, 1980), pp. 9–10.
8. See John H. Schaar, "Equality of Opportunity and Beyond," in *Equality*, NOMOS IX, eds. J. Roland Pennock and John W. Chapman (New York: Atherton Press, 1967), pp. 228–249.
9. Jean Jacques Rousseau, *The Social Contract and Discourses*, trans. G. D. H. Cole (New York: Dutton, 1950), p. 5.
10. Sam Vincent Meddis, "Crime's No Worse, But USA's Fear Grows," *USA Today* (International Edition) 28 October 1993, p. 1. See also Wesley G. Skogan, *Disorder and Decline: Crime and the Spiral of Decay in American Neighborhoods* (New York: The Free Press, 1990), Chap. 2.
11. *Statistical Abstract of the United States 1992* (Washington, D.C.: U.S. Government Printing Office, 1992), p. 186.
12. Jill Solowe, "The Long Hard Road to Moscow," *Time*, 12 January 1987, p. 47.
13. "MN Express Poll," *Moscow News*, No. 7, February 1993, p. 1.
14. "MN Express Poll," *Moscow News*, 8 October 1993, p. 1.
15. Geoffrey Cowley, "The Future of AIDS," *Time*, 22 March 1993, p. 49; Centers for Disease Control, *HIV/AIDS Surveillance*, October 1992; and Joan Beck, "New AIDS mystery puts focus on safeguarding public," *Chicago Tribune*, 30 July 1990, p. 9.
16. *Morbidity and Mortality Weekly Report*, 43 (11 March 1994), p. 155.
17. Craig R. Whitney, "Moscow a Year Later: Rutted Streets and Despair," *New York Times*, 19 February 1990, p. A6.
18. Milton Friedman, *Capitalism and Freedom* (Chicago: University of Chicago Press, 1962).
19. "Anarchist Convention Ends With an Exercise in Rioting," *New York Times*, 29 July 1989, p. 6.
20. Lawrence Herson, *The Politics of Ideas: Political Theory and American Public Policy* (Homewood, Ill.: Dorsey Press, 1984), pp. 166–176.

Chapter 2 / Majoritarian or Pluralist Democracy / pp. 29–56

1. "Five Children Killed as Gunman Attacks a California School," *New York Times*, 18 January 1989, p. A1; and Robert Reinhold, "After Shooting, Horror but Few Answers," *New York Times*, 20 January 1989, p. B6.
2. Wayne King, "Weapon Used by Deranged Man Is Easy To Buy," *New York Times*, 20 January 1989, p. B6.
3. The Gallup Poll for *USA Today*, 30 December 1993, p. 1A. At the time of the Purdy attack, the figures were 72 percent favoring stricter gun control and 70 percent favoring a ban on assault rifles. *Gallup Report*, March–April 1989, pp. 2–5.
4. Katherine Q. Seeyle, "House Approves Bill to Prohibit 19 Assault Arms," *New York Times*, 6 May 1994, p. A1; Kathleen Q. Seeyle, "Crime Bill Fails on a House Vote, Stunning Clinton," *New York Times*, 12 August 1994, p. A1; and Adam Clymer, "Crime Bill Clears Hurdle, But Senate is Going Home Without Acting on Health," *New York Times*, 26 August 1994, p. A1.
5. Kenneth Janda, "What's in a Name? Party Labels Across the World," in *The CONTA Conference: Proceedings of the Conference of Conceptual and Terminological Analysis in the Social Sciences*, ed. F. W. Riggs (Frankfurt: Indeks Verlage, 1982), pp. 46–62.
6. Richard F. Fenno, Jr., *The President's Cabinet* (New York: Vintage, 1959), p. 29.
7. Robert A. Dahl, *Democracy and Its Critics* (New Haven: Yale University Press, 1989), pp. 13–23.
8. Jeffrey M. Berry, Kent E. Portney, and Ken Thomson, *The Rebirth of Urban Democracy* (Washington, D.C.: Brookings Institution, 1993).
9. Isabel Wilkerson, "Chicago On Brink of New School System," *New York Times*, 11 October 1989, p. A18.
10. Jean Jacques Rousseau, *The Social Contract*, 1762, Reprint (Hammondsworth, England: Penguin, 1968), p. 141.

11. Berry, Portney, and Thomson, *Rebirth*, p. 77.

12. On the possibility of infusing national politics with a dose of participatory democracy, see James S. Fishkin, *Democracy and Deliberation* (New Haven, Conn.: Yale University Press, 1991).

13. See C. B. Macpherson, *The Real World of Democracy* (New York: Oxford University Press, 1975), pp. 58–59.

14. Thomas E. Cronin, *Direct Democracy* (Cambridge, Mass.: Harvard University Press, 1989), p. 47.

15. Dirk Johnson, "Colorado Homosexuals Feel Betrayed," *New York Times*, 8 November 1992, p. 38.

16. Dirk Johnson, "Blow Dealt to Colorado Anti-Gay Law," *New York Times*, 20 July 1993, p. A8.

17. Alan Cowell, "By a Big Margin, Italians Support Political Reform," *New York Times*, 20 April 1993, p. A1.

18. Cronin, *Direct Democracy*, p. 80.

19. See F. Christopher Arterton, *Teledemocracy: Can Technology Protect Democracy?* (Newbury Park, Calif.: Sage, 1987); and Jeffrey B. Abramson, F. Christopher Arterton, and Gary B. Orren, *The Electronic Commonwealth* (New York: Basic Books, 1988).

20. M. Margaret Conway, *Political Participation in the United States*, 2d ed. (Washington, D.C.: Congressional Quarterly, 1991), p. 44.

21. Benjamin I. Page and Robert Y. Shapiro, *The Rational Public* (Chicago: University of Chicago Press, 1992), p. 387.

22. See *Citizens and Politics* (Dayton, Ohio: Kettering Foundation, 1991).

23. See Robert A. Dahl, *Dilemmas of Pluralist Democracy* (New Haven: Yale University Press, 1982), p. 5.

24. Robert A. Dahl, *Pluralist Democracy in the United States* (Chicago: Rand McNally, 1967), p. 24.

25. The classic statement on elite theory is C. Wright Mills, *The Power Elite* (New York: Oxford University Press, 1956).

26. Michael Useem, *The Inner Circle* (New York: Oxford University Press, 1984). On a broader level,

see Charles E. Lindblom, *Politics and Markets* (New York: Basic Books, 1977).

27. Thomas R. Dye, *Who's Running America? The Bush Era*, 5th ed. (Englewood Cliffs, N.J.: Prentice-Hall, 1990), p. 12.

28. The most prominent study is Robert Dahl's research on decision making in New Haven, Connecticut, in *Who Governs?* (New Haven, Conn.: Yale University Press, 1961).

29. Clarence N. Stone, *Regime Politics* (Lawrence: University of Kansas Press, 1989).

30. John P. Heinz, Edward O. Laumann, Robert L. Nelson, and Robert H. Salisbury, *The Hollow Core* (Cambridge, Mass.: Harvard University Press, 1993).

31. Peter Bachrach and Morton S. Baratz, "Two Faces of Power," *American Political Science Review*, 56 (December 1962), pp. 947–952; and John Gaventa, *Power and Powerlessness* (Urbana: University of Illinois Press, 1980).

32. See Kenneth M. Dolbeare, *Democracy at Risk* (Chatham, N.J.: Chatham House, 1984); and Edward S. Greenberg *The American Political System: A Radical Approach* (Boston: Little, Brown, 1986).

33. See Kay Lehman Schlozman and John T. Tierney, *Organized Interests and American Politics* (New York: Harper & Row, 1986).

34. Reprinted by permission of the publishers from *Contemporary Democracies: Participation, Stability, and Violence* by G. Bingham Powell, Jr. Cambridge, Mass.: Harvard University Press, Copyright 1982 by the President and Fellows of Harvard College.

35. Arend Lijphart, *Democracies* (New Haven, Conn.: Yale University Press, 1984).

36. *Africa Demos*, 3 (February 1993), pp. 1 and 19. See also Michael Bratton and Nicholas van de Walle, "Popular Protest and Political Reform in Africa," *Comparative Politics*, 24 (July 1992), pp. 419–442.

37. See generally, Samuel P. Huntington, *The Third Wave* (Norman: University of Oklahoma Press, 1991).

38. "Excerpts from Address to

Russians by Yeltsin," *New York Times*, March 21, 1993, p. 12.

39. The classic treatment of the conflict between freedom and order in democratizing countries is Samuel P. Huntington, *Political Order in Changing Societies* (New Haven, Conn.: Yale University Press, 1968).

40. Benjamin R. Barber, "Jihad vs. McWorld," *Atlantic Monthly*, March 1992, p. 53.

41. Rita Jalali and Seymour Martin Lipset, "Racial and Ethnic Conflicts: A Global Perspective," *Political Science Quarterly*, 107 (Winter 1992–93), p. 588.

42. E. E. Schattschneider, *The Semi-Sovereign People* (New York: Holt, Rinehart, & Winston, 1960), p. 35.

Chapter 3 / The Constitution / pp. 58–100

1. Carl Bernstein and Bob Woodward, *All the President's Men* (New York: Warner, 1975); Stanley I. Kutler, *The Wars of Watergate* (New York: Alfred H. Knopf, 1990).

2. Bernstein and Woodward, *All the President's Men*, p. 30.

3. Gallup Organization, *Gallup Poll Monthly*, June 1992, pp. 2–3.

4. Samuel Eliot Morison, *Oxford History of the American People* (New York: Oxford University Press, 1965), p. 182.

5. Ibid., p. 172.

6. Richard Walsh, *Charleston's Sons of Liberty: A Study of the Artisans, 1763–1789* (Columbia: University of South Carolina Press, 1959).

7. Mary Beth Norton, *Liberty's Daughters* (Boston: Little, Brown, 1980), pp. 155–157.

8. Morison, *Oxford History*, p. 204.

9. John Plamentz, (rev. ed. by M. E. Plamentz and Robert Wokler), *Man and Society*, Vol. 1: *From the Middle Ages to Locke* (New York: Longman, 1992), pp. 216–218.

10. Charles H. Metzger, S. J., *Catholics and the American Revolution: A Study in Religious Climate* (Chicago: Loyola University Press, 1962).

11. Extrapolated from U.S. Department of Defense, *Selected Manpower Statistics, FY 1982* (Washington, D.C.: U.S. Government Printing Office,

1983), Table 2-30, p. 130; and U.S. Bureau of the Census, *1985 Statistical Abstract of the United States* (Washington, D.C.: U.S. Government Printing Office, 1985), Tables 1 and 2, p. 6.

12. Joseph T. Keenan, *The Constitution of the United States* (Homewood, Ill.: Dow-Jones-Irwin, 1975).

13. David P. Szatmary, *Shays' Rebellion: The Making of an Agrarian Insurrection* (Amherst: University of Massachusetts Press, 1980), pp. 82–102.

14. As cited in Morison, *Oxford History*, p. 304.

15. Robert H. Jackson, *The Struggle for Judicial Supremacy* (New York: Alfred A. Knopf, 1941), p. 8.

16. Catherine Drinker Bowen, *Miracle at Philadelphia* (Boston: Little, Brown, 1966), p. 122.

17. Forrest McDonald, *Novus Ordo Seclorum: The Intellectual Origins of the Constitution* (Lawrence: University Press of Kansas, 1985), pp. 205–209.

18. Donald S. Lutz, "The Preamble to the Constitution of the United States," *This Constitution* 1 (September 1983), pp. 23–30.

19. Richard E. Neustadt, *Presidential Power: The Politics of Leadership* (New York: Wiley, 1960), p. 33.

20. Charles A. Beard, *An Economic Interpretation of the Constitution of the United States* (New York: Macmillan, 1913).

21. Leonard W. Levy, *Constitutional Opinions* (New York: Oxford University Press, 1986), p. 101.

22. Robert E. Brown, *Charles Beard and the Constitution* (Princeton, N.J.: Princeton University Press, 1956), Levy, *Constitutional Opinions*, pp. 103–104; and Forrest McDonald, *We the People: Economic Origins of the Constitution* (Chicago: University of Chicago Press, 1958).

23. Compare Eugene D. Genovese, *The Political Economy of Slavery: Studies in the Economics and Society of the Slave South* (Middletown, Conn.: Wesleyan University Press, 1989) and Robert William Fogel, *Without Contract or Consent: The Rise and Fall of American Slavery* (New York: W. W. Norton, 1989).

24. Robert A. Goldwin, Letter to the Editor, *Wall Street Journal*, 30 August 1993, p. A11.

25. Bernard Bailyn, *Faces of Revolution: Personalities and Themes in the Struggle for American Independence* (New York: Alfred A. Knopf, 1990), pp. 221–222.

26. Walter Berns, *The First Amendment and the Future of Democracy* (New York: Basic Books, 1976), p. 2.

27. Herbert J. Storing, ed., *The Complete Anti-Federalist*, 7 vols. (Chicago: University of Chicago Press, 1981).

28. Alexis de Tocqueville, *Democracy in America*, 1835–1839, Reprint, eds. J. P. Mayer and Max Lerner (New York: Harper & Row, 1966), p. 102.

29. Russell L. Caplan, *Constitutional Brinkmanship: Amending the Constitution by National Convention* (New York: Oxford University Press, 1988), p. 162.

30. Richard L. Berke, "1789 Amendment Is Ratified but Now the Debate Begins," *New York Times*, 8 May 1992, p. A1.

31. Jerold L. Waltman, *Political Origins of the U.S. Income Tax* (Jackson: University Press of Mississippi, 1985), p. 10.

Chapter 4 / Federalism / pp. 101–136

1. Ronald Reagan, "National Minimum Drinking Age: Remarks on Signing HR4616 into Law (17 July 1984)," *Weekly Compilation of Presidential Documents*, 23 July 1984, p. 1036.

2. South Dakota v. Dole, 483 U.S. 203 (1987).

3. *Budget of the United States Government, FY 1994*, pp. A-828 and A-829 (Government Printing Office 1993).

4. Taylor Branch, *Parting the Waters: America in the King Years, 1954–63* (New York: Simon & Schuster, 1988), Chapter 17.

5. Daniel J. Elazar, "Opening the Third Century of American Federalism: Issues and Prospects," *Annals of the American Academy of Political and Social Sciences*, 509 (May 1990), p. 14.

6. William H. Stewart, *Concepts of Federalism* (Lanham, Md.: University Press of America, 1984).

7. Corwin, *The Passing of Dual Federalism*, 36 *Va. L. Rev.* 4 (1950).

8. See Daniel J. Elazar, *The American Partnership* (Chicago: University of Chicago Press, 1962); and Morton Grodzins, *The American System* (Chicago: Rand McNally, 1966).

9. Martha Derthick, "The Enduring Features of American Federalism," *The Brookings Review* p. 35 (Summer 1989).

10. Raoul Berger, Federalism: *The Founders' Design* (Norman: University of Oklahoma Press, 1987), pp. 61–62.

11. Miranda v. Arizona, 384 U.S. 436 (1966).

12. Baker v. Carr, 369 U.S. 186 (1962); Wesberry v. Sanders, 376 U.S. 1 (1964); and Reynolds v. Sims, 377 U.S. 533 (1964).

13. Advisory Commission on Intergovernmental Relations, *Characteristics of Federal Grant-in-Aid Programs to State and Local Governments: Grants Funded FY 1991* (Washington, D.C.: U.S. Government Printing Office, 1992), Table 3, p. 8.

14. Ibid., Table 2, p. 5.

15. McCulloch v. Maryland, 4 Wheat. 316 (1819).

16. Dred Scott v. Sanford, 19 How. 393 (1857).

17. Gibbons v. Ogden, 9 Wheat. 1 (1824).

18. Hammer v. Dagenhart, 247 U.S. 251 (1918).

19. James T. Patterson, *The New Deal and the States: Federalism in Transition* (Princeton, N.J.: Princeton University Press, 1969).

20. United States v. Butler, 297 U.S. 1 (1936).

21. United States v. Darby, 312 U.S. 100 (1941).

22. A recent skirmish over state sovereignty is New York v. United States, 112 S.Ct. 2408 (1992). The dispute centered on the disposal of radioactive waste.

23. Brown v. Board of Education of Topeka, 347 U.S. 483 (1954).

24. Aaron Wildavsky, "Bare Bones: Putting Flesh on the Skeleton of American Federalism," in *The Future of Federalism in the 1980s*, Advisory Commission on Intergovernmental Relations

(Washington, D.C.: U.S. Government Printing Office, 1981), p. 80.

25. Advisory Commission on Intergovernmental Relations, *The Federal Role in the Federal System: The Dynamics of Growth* (A-86) (Washington, D.C.: U.S. Government Printing Office, 1981), p. 101.

26. Richard M. Nixon, "Speech to National Governor's Conference, September 1, 1969," in *Congressional Quarterly Almanac* (Washington, D.C.: Congressional Quarterly Press, 1969), pp. 101A–103A.

27. *Budget of the United States Government, FY 1994* (Washington, D.C.: U.S. Government Printing Office, 1993), p. 79.

28. Joseph F. Zimmerman, *Contemporary American Federalism: the Growth of National Power* (New York: Praeger, 1992), Chap. 4.

29. *The Book of the States, 1992–93* (Lexington, Ky: Council of State Governments, 1992), p. 605.

30. John Abell, "Clinton Says Bush Not Credible on Jobs Creation," *Reuter Library Report* (31 August 1992), NEXIS.

31. Ron Suskind, "Health Care Reform May Seem Like a Bitter Pill to Localities Sick of Unfunded Federal Mandates," *Wall Street Journal*, 21 December 1993, p. A14.

32. U.S. Bureau of the Census, *Statistical Abstract of the United States: 1993* (Washington, D.C.: U.S. Government Printing Office, 1993), Table 466, p. 291.

33. Chuck Raasch, "Governors' Meeting Displays Confusion Over Role of Feds," *Gannet News Service* (1 February 1994), NEXIS.

34. *Book of the States, 1992–93,* p. 246.

35. Alice Rivlin, *Reviving the American Dream: The Economy, the States, and the Federal Government* (Washington, D.C.: Brookings Institution, 1992).

36. Michael A. Pagano and Ann O'M. Bowman, "The State of American Federalism, 1992–93" *Publius* 23 (Summer 1993), pp. 1–22.

37. Paul M. Weyrich, quoted in Neal

Pierce, "Conservatives Weep as the States Make Left Turn," *National Journal,* 10 October 1987, p. 2559.

Chapter 5 / Public Opinion and Political Socialization / pp. 138–173

1. Gallup Organization, *Gallup Poll Monthly,* June 1991, p. 43.

2. American 1992 National Election Survey, conducted by the Center for Political Studies, University of Michigan.

3. Gallup Organization, *Gallup Report,* 280 (January 1989), 27.

4. *New York Times,* 3 July 1976.

5. *Furman v. Georgia,* 408 U.S. 238 (1972).

6. *Gregg v. Georgia,* 248 U.S. 153 (1976).

7. Gallup Organization, *Gallup Monthly Poll* (June 1991), p. 41.

8. Ibid., p. 42.

9. "If Pollsters Had Been Around During the American Revolution," letter to the editor of the *New York Times,* from W. Wayne Carp, 17 July 1993, p. 10.

10. Nine national surveys taken from 1971 through 1988 found that an average of 61 percent of Americans disapproved of the ruling in *Abington School District v. Schempp,* 374 U.S. 203 (1963). Niemi, G., Mueller, J. & Smith, T. *Trends in Public Opinion: A Compendium of Survey Data.* (New York: Greenwood Press, 1989), p. 263.

11. 1981 survey by Civic Service, Inc., *Public Opinion* 5 (October/ November 1982), 21.

12. Jeffrey Schmalz, "Poll Finds an Even Split on Homosexuality's Cause," *New York Times,* 5 March 1993, p. A11.

13. These questions are not ideally matched, but other survey items about private enterprise yield comparable results. See Donald J. Devine, *The Political Culture of the United States* (Boston: Little, Brown, 1972), pp. 209–214.

14. Warren E. Miller, Arthur H. Miller, and Edward J. Schneider, *American National Election Studies Sourcebook, 1952–1978* (Cambridge, Mass.: Harvard University Press, 1980), pp. 94–95. See Niemi,

Mueller, and Smith, *Trends,* p. 19, for later years.

15. Tom W. Smith and Paul B. Sheatsley, "American Attitudes Toward Race Relations," *Public Opinion* 7 (October/November 1984), p. 15.

16. Ibid.

17. Ibid., p. 83.

18. Steven A. Peterson, *Political Behavior: Patterns in Everyday Life* (Newbury Park, Calif.: Sage, 1990), pp. 28–29.

19. Paul Allen Beck, "The Role of Agents in Political Socialization," in *Handbook of Political Socialization Theory and Research,* ed. Stanley Allen Renshon (New York: Free Press, 1977), pp. 117–118.

20. W. Russell Neuman, *The Paradox of Mass Politics: Knowledge and Opinion in the American Electorate* (Cambridge, Mass.: Harvard University Press, 1986), pp. 113–114. See also Richard G. Niemi and Jane Junn, "Civics Courses and the Political Knowledge of High School Seniors," paper prepared for presentation at the annual meeting of the American Political Science Association, Washington, D.C., September, 1993. They found that a favorable home environment (e.g., having reading and reference material at home) related significantly to factual knowledge in a high school civics test.

21. M. Kent Jennings and Richard G. Niemi, *The Political Character of Adolescence: The Influence of Families and Schools* (Princeton, N.J.: Princeton University Press, 1974), p. 39. See also Stephen E. Frantzich, *Political Parties in the Technological Age* (New York: Longman, 1989), p. 152. Frantzich presents a table showing that more than 60 percent of children in homes in which both parents have the same party preference will adopt their preference. When parents are divided, the children tend to be divided among Democrats, Republicans, and independents.

22. In a panel study of parents and high school seniors in 1965 and in 1973, some years after their graduation, Jennings and Niemi found that 57

percent of children shared their parents' party identification in 1965, but only 47 percent did by 1973. See Jennings and Niemi, *Political Character*, pp. 90–91. See also Robert C. Luskin, John P. McIver, and Edward G. Carmines, "Issues and the Transmission of Partisanship," *American Journal of Political Science* 33 (May 1989), pp. 440–458. They find that children are more likely to shift between partisanship and independence than to "convert" to the other party. When conversion occurs, it is more likely to be based on economic issues than on social issues.

23. Robert D. Hess and Judith V. Torney, *The Development of Political Attitudes in Children* (Chicago: Aldine, 1967). But other researchers disagree. See Jerry L. Yeric and John R. Todd, *Public Opinion: The Visible Politics* (Itasca, Ill.: F. E. Peacock, 1989), pp. 45–47, for a summary of the issues. For a critical evaluation of the early literature on political socialization, see Pamela Johnston Conover, "Political Socialization: Where's the Politics?" in *Political Science: Looking to the Future, Volume 3: Political Behavior*, ed. William Crotty (Evanston, Ill.: Northwestern University Press, 1991), pp. 125–151.

24. David Easton and Jack Dennis, *Children in the Political System* (New York: McGraw-Hill, 1969).

25. Jarol B. Manheim, *The Politics Within* (New York: Longman, 1982), p. 83, pp. 125–151.

26. Richard Niemi and Jane Y. Junn, "Civics Courses and the Political Knowledge of High School Seniors," paper prepared for presentation at the annual meeting of the American Political Science Association, Washington, D.C., September 1993.

27. Edith J. Barrett, "The Political Socialization of Inner-City Adolescents," paper prepared for presentation at the annual meeting of the American Political Science Association, Washington, D.C., September 1993.

28. Janie S. Steckenrider and Neal E. Cutler, "Aging and Adult Political Socialization: The Importance of Roles and Transitions," *Political Learning in Adulthood: A Sourcebook of Theory and Research*, ed. Roberta S. Sigel (Chicago: University of Chicago Press, 1989), pp. 56–88.

29. See Robert Huckfeldt and John Sprague, "Networks in Context: The Social Flow of Information," *American Political Science Review* 81 (December 1987), 1197–1216. The authors' study of voting in neighborhoods in South Bend, Indiana, found that residents who favored the minority party were acutely aware of their minority status.

30. Theodore M. Newcomb, *Persistence and Social Change: Bennington College and Its Students After Twenty-Five Years* (New York: Wiley, 1967); and Duane F. Alwin, Ronald L. Cohen, and Theodore M. Newcomb, *Political Attitudes over the Life Span: The Bennington Women after Fifty Years* (Madison: University of Wisconsin Press, 1991).

31. M. Kent Jennings and Gregory Marcus, "Yuppie Politics," *Institute of Social Research Newsletter* (August 1986).

32. See Roberta S. Sigel, ed., *Political Learning in Adulthood: A Sourcebook of Theory and Research* (Chicago: University of Chicago Press, 1989).

33. Times Mirror Center for the People & the Press, "The American Media: Who Reads, Who Watches, Who Listens, Who Cares?" 15 July 1990, p. 4.

34. The wording of this question is criticized by R. Michael Alvarez and John Brehm in "When Core Beliefs Collide: Conflict, Complexity, or Just Plain Confusion?" a paper prepared for delivery at the annual meeting of the American Political Science Association, Washington, D.C., September, 1993, p. 9. They argue that using the phrase "personal choice" (which they call a core value) triggers the psychological effect of reactance, or the feeling that a freedom has been removed. But this core value is precisely our focus in this analysis. Alvarez and Brehm favor using instead the battery of six questions on abortion that have been used in the General Social Survey. Those six questions are also used in Elizabeth Adell Cook, Ted G. Jelen, and Clyde Wilcox, *Between Two Absolutes: Public Opinion and the Politics of Abortion* (Boulder, Co.: Westview, 1992). Those interested primarily in analyzing the various attitudes toward abortion probably should use data from the General Social Survey.

35. Although some people view the politics of abortion as "single issue" politics, the issue has broader political significance. In their book on the subject, Cook, Jelen, and Wilcox say, "Although embryonic life is *one* important value in the abortion debate, it is not the *only* value at stake." They contend that the politics is tied to alternative sexual relationships and traditional roles of women in the home, which are all "social order" issues. See *Between Two Absolutes*, pp. 8–9.

36. Ibid., p. 50.

37. The increasing wealth in industrialized societies may or may not be replacing class conflict with conflict over values. See the exchange between Ronald Inglehart and Scott C. Flanagan, "Value Change in Industrial Societies," *American Political Science Review* 81 (December 1987), pp. 1289–1319.

38. For a review of these studies, see Robert S. Erikson, Norman R. Luttbeg, and Kent L. Tedin, *American Public Opinion*, 3d ed. (New York: Macmillan, 1988).

39. Nathan Glazer, "The Structure of Ethnicity," *Public Opinion* 7 (October/November 1984), p. 4.

40. Felicity Barringer, "Census Shows Profound Change in Racial Makeup of the Nation," *New York Times*, 11 March 1991, pp. 1 and 12.

41. Glazer, "Structure of Ethnicity," p. 5.

42. These figures came from the 1990 General Social Survey and were kindly provided by Tom W. Smith, director of the GSS.

43. See David C. Leege and Lyman A. Kellstedt, eds., *Rediscovering the Religious Factor in American*

Politics (M. E. Sharpe: Armonk, N.Y.: 1993) for a comprehensive examination of religion in political life that goes far beyond the analysis here.

44. Lyman A. Kellstedt, "Religion, the Neglected Variable: An Agenda for Future Research on Religion and Political Behavior," in Leege and Kellstedt, *Rediscovering the Religious Factor*, p. 273.

45. John Robinson, "The Ups and Downs and Ins and Outs of Ideology," *Public Opinion* 7 (February/March 1984), p. 12.

46. For a more positive interpretation of ideological attitudes within the public, see William G. Jacoby, "The Structure of Ideological Thinking in the American Electorate," paper presented at the Annual Meeting of the American Political Science Association, Washington, D.C., September, 1993. Jacoby applies a new method to survey data for the 1984 and 1988 elections and concludes "that there is a systematic, cumulative structure underlying liberal-conservative thinking in the American public" p. 1.

47. Angus Campbell, Philip E. Converse, Warren E. Miller, & Donald E. Stokes, *The American Voter* (New York: Wiley, 1960), Chap. 10.

48. Neuman, *Paradox*, pp. 19–20.

49. Arthur Sanders, "Ideological Symbols," *American Politics Quarterly* 17 (July 1989), p. 235.

50. See Norman H. Nie, Sidney Verba, and John R. Petrocik, *The Changing American Voter*, 2d ed. (Cambridge, Mass.: Harvard University Press, 1979).

51. Some scholars believe that the methods used for classifying respondents as ideologues was too generous. See Robert C. Luskin, "Measuring Political Sophistication," *American Journal of Political Science* 31 (November 1987), pp. 878, 887–888. For a comprehensive critique, see Eric R. A. N. Smith, *The Unchanging American Voter* (Berkeley: University of California Press, 1989), especially Chap. 1.

52. See William G. Jacoby, "Levels of Conceptualization and Reliance on the Liberal-Conservative Continuum," *Journal of Politics* 48 (May 1986), pp. 423–432. We also know that certain political actors, such as delegates to national party conventions, hold far more consistent and durable beliefs than the public. See M. Kent Jennings, "Ideological Thinking Among Mass Publics and Political Elites," *Public Opinion Quarterly* 56 (Winter 1992), pp. 419–441.

53. National Election Study for 1992, election survey conducted by the Center for Political Studies at the University of Michigan.

54. However, citizens can engage in ideologically consistent behavior in attitudes toward candidates and perceptions about domestic issues without thinking about politics in explicitly liberal and conservative terms. See William G. Jacoby, "The Structure of Liberal-Conservative Thinking in the American Public," paper prepared for presentation at the annual meeting of the Midwest Political Science Association, 1990.

55. Pamela Johnston Conover, "The Origins and Meaning of Liberal-Conservative Self-identifications," *American Journal of Political Science* 25 (November 1981), pp. 621–622, 643.

56. The relationship of liberalism to political tolerance is found by John L. Sullivan et al., "The Sources of Political Tolerance: A Multivariate Analysis," *American Political Science Review* 75 (March 1981), 102. See also Robinson, "Ups and Downs," pp. 13–15.

57. Herbert Asher, *Presidential Elections and American Politics* (Homewood, Ill.: Dorsey, 1980), pp. 14–20. Asher also constructs a two-dimensional framework, distinguishing between "traditional New Deal" issues and "new lifestyle" issues.

58. John E. Jackson, "The Systematic Beliefs of the Mass Public: Estimating Policy Preferences with Survey Data," *Journal of Politics* 45 November 1983, pp. 840–865.

59. Milton Rokeach also proposed a two-dimensional model of political ideology grounded in the terminal values of freedom and equality. See *The Nature of Human Values* (New York: Free Press, 1973), especially Chap. 6. Rokeach found that positive and negative references to the two values permeate the writings of socialists, communists, fascists, and conservatives and clearly differentiate the four bodies of writing from one another (pp. 173–174). However, Rokeach built his two-dimensional model around only the values of freedom and equality; he did not deal with the question of freedom versus order.

60. William S. Maddox and Stuart A. Lilie, *Beyond Liberal and Conservative: Reassessing the Political Spectrum* (Washington, D.C.: Cato Institute, 1984), p. 68.

61. See Neuman, *Paradox*, p. 81. See also Aaron Wildavsky, "Choosing Preferences by Constructing Institutions: A Cultural Theory of Preference Formation," *American Political Science Review* 81 (March 1987), p. 13.

62. The same conclusion was reached in a major study of British voting behavior. See Hilde T. Himmelweit et al., *How Voters Decide* (New York: Academic Press, 1981), pp. 138–141. See also Wildavsky, "Choosing Preferences," p. 13.

63. But a significant literature is developing on the limitations of self-interest in explaining political life. See Jane J. Mansbridge, ed., *Beyond Self-interest* (Chicago: University of Chicago Press, 1990).

64. Wildavsky, "Choosing Preferences," pp. 3–21.

65. David O. Sears and Carolyn L. Funk, "Self-interest in Americans' Political Opinions," in Mansbridge, *Beyond Self-interest*, pp. 147–170.

66. Two researchers who compared the public's knowledge in 1989 with the same questions in the 1940s and 1950s found similar levels of knowledge across the years, but they say, "That knowledge has been stable during a period of rapid changes in education, communication, and the public role of women seems paradoxical." They suspect, but cannot demonstrate, that the increase expected did not materialize because of a decline in political

interest over time. See Michael X. Delli Carpini and Scott Keeter, "Stability and Change in the U.S. Public's Knowledge of Politics," *Public Opinion Quarterly* 55 (Winter 1991), p. 607.

67. 1992 National Election Study Center for Political Studies, University of Michigan Inter-University Consortium for Political and Social Research, Post-Election Survey.

68. Times Mirror Center for the People & the Press, "Times Mirror News Interest Index," 12 July 1990, p. 2.

69. Benjamin I. Page and Robert Y. Shapiro, *The Rational Public* (Chicago: University of Chicago Press, 1992).

70. Ibid., p. 45.

71. Ibid., p. 385. The argument for a rational quality in public opinion by Page and Shapiro was supported by Stimson's massive analysis of swings in the liberal-conservative attitudes of the U.S. public from 1956 to 1990. Analyzing more than one thousand attitude items, he found that the public mood had already swung away from liberalism when Ronald Reagan appeared on the scene to campaign for president as a conservative. See James A. Stimson, *Public Opinion in America: Moods, Cycles, & Swings* (Boulder, Colo.: Westview, 1992).

72. See R. Michael Alvarez and John Brehm, "When Core Beliefs Collide"; and Scott L. Althaus, "The Conservative Nature of Public Opinion," paper prepared for the annual meeting of the American Political Science Association, Washington, D.C., September, 1993.

73. Smith, *Unchanging American Voter*, p. 5. However, Smith later argues that the information component of the definition is more important than attitude consistency or level of conceptualization (pp. 224–227). For another attempt to measure political sophistication—by using a ten-word vocabulary test—see Lawrence Bobo and Frederick C. Licari, "Education and Political Tolerance: Testing the Effects of Cognitive Sophistication and Target Group Affect,"

Public Opinion Quarterly 53 (Fall 1989), pp. 285–308.

74. Neuman, *Paradox*, pp. 19–20.

75. Ibid., pp. 6–7. There is evidence that the educational system and parental practices hamper the ability of women to develop their political sophistication. See Linda L.M. Bennett and Stephen Earl Bennett, "Enduring Gender Differences in Political Interests," *American Politics Quarterly* 17 (January 1989), pp. 105–122.

76. Ibid., p. 81.

77. Pamela Johnston Conover and Stanley Feldman, "How People Organize the Political World: A Schematic Model," *American Journal of Political Science* 28 (February 1984), 96. For an excellent review of schema structures in contemporary psychology—especially as they relate to political science—see Reid Hastie, "A Primer of Information-Processing Theory for the Political Scientist," in *Political Cognition*, ed. Richard R. Lau and David O. Sears (Hillsdale, N.J.: Erlbaum, 1986), pp. 11–39.

78. John Hurwitz and Mark Peffley, "How Are Foreign Policy Attitudes Structured? A Hierarchical Model," *American Political Science Review* 81 (December 1987), 1099–1220.

79. Richard L. Allen, Michael C. Dawson, and Ronald E. Brown. "A Schema-Based Approach to Modeling an African-American Racial Belief System," *American Political Science Review* 83 (June 1989), 421–441.

80. See Milton Lodge and Ruth Hamill, "A Partisan Schema for Political Information Processing," *American Political Science Review* 80 (June 1986), pp. 505–519.

81. Arthur Sanders, *Making Sense Out of Politics* (Ames: Iowa State University Press, 1990).

82. Lee Sigelman, "Disarming the Opposition: The President, the Public, and the INF Treaty," *Public Opinion Quarterly* 54 (Spring 1990), p. 46.

83. Benjamin I. Page, Robert Y. Shapiro, and Glenn R. Dempsey, "What Moves Public Opinion?" *American Political Science Review* 81 (March 1987), pp. 23–43.

84. Michael Margolis and Gary A. Mauser, *Manipulating Public Opinion: Essays on Public Opinion as a Dependent Variable* (Pacific Grove, Calif.: Brooks/Cole, 1989).

Chapter 6 / The Mass Media / pp. 174–211

1. Michael Elliott, "The Making of a Fiasco," *Newsweek*, 18 October 1993, p. 34.

2. Lee Michael Katz, "Graphic Photos from Somalia Gave 'Urgency'," *USA Today (International)*, 14 October 1993, p. 7a.

3. Chris Hedges, "Iranians, Marking 1979 Crisis, Denounce U.S.," *New York Times*, 5 November 1993, p. A4.

4. Kenneth Janda was able to watch all these programs when he was in Budapest as a Fulbright scholar in 1993–1994 and was revising his chapters of this book for the fourth edition.

5. A man who shot a state trooper in Austin, Texas, in 1992 blamed his action on antipolice rap music from a Shakur album to which he was listening before he was stopped by the trooper. See "Rap Music Blamed in Trooper's Killing," *Chicago Tribune*, 3 June 1993, p. 13.

6. S. N. D. North, *The Newspaper and Periodical Press* (Washington, D.C.: U.S. Government Printing Office, 1884), p. 27. This source provides much of the information reported about newspapers and magazines before 1880.

7. Sidney Kobre, *The Yellow Press and Gilded Age Journalism* (Tallahassee: Florida State University Press, 1964), p. 52.

8. John Schmeltzer, "Iowa Towns Deliver Twice the News," *Chicago Tribune*, 1 April 1993, section 3, p. 1.

9. In 1950, a total of 1,772 daily papers had a circulation of 53.8 million; in 1989, a total of 1,642 papers had a circulation of 62.7 million. U.S. Bureau of the Census, *Statistical Abstract of the United States, 1988* (Washington, D.C.:

U.S. Government Printing Office, 1988), p. 528. The number of newspapers per capita was 0.35 in 1950 and 0.26 in 1987. See Harold W. Stanley and Richard G. Niemi (eds.), *Vital Statistics on American Politics,* 2d ed. (Washington, D.C.: Congressional Quarterly Press, 1990), p. 48.

10. Matthew Manning, (ed.), *Standard Periodical Directory,* 13th ed. (New York: Oxbridge Communications, 1990).

11. Douglas Kellner, *Television and the Crisis of Democracy* (Boulder, Colo.: Westview, 1990), pp. 225–248.

12. Dana R. Ulloth, Peter L. Klinge, and Sandra Eells, *Mass Media: Past, Present, Future* (St. Paul, Minn.: West, 1983), p. 278.

13. Steve Lohr, "European TV's Vast Growth: Cultural Effect Stirs Concern," *New York Times,* 16 March 1989, p. 1.

14. Roper Organization, *Trends in Attitudes Toward Television and Other Media* (New York: Television Information Office, 1983), p. 8.

15. U.S. Bureau of the Census, *Statistical Abstract of the United States, 1982–1983* (Washington, D.C.: U.S. Government Printing Office, 1984), p. 562.

16. Doris A. Graber, *Mass Media and American Politics* (Washington, D.C.: Congressional Quarterly Press, 1984), pp. 78–79.

17. Kenneth R. Clark, "Network Audience Share at Record Low," *Chicago Tribune,* 30 November 1990, section 3, p. 1.

18. *Editor & Publisher International Yearbook* (New York: Editor & Publisher Company 1984), pp. 435–442.

19. Christopher H. Sterling, *Electronic Media: A Guide to Trends in Broadcasting and Newer Technologies, 1920–1983* (New York: Praeger, 1984), p. 22.

20. *Broadcasting Yearbook, 1990* (Washington, D.C.: Broadcasting Publications, 1990).

21. Joseph Turow, *Media Industries: The Production of News and Entertainment* (New York: Longman, 1984), p. 18. Our discussion of government regulation draws heavily on this source.

22. Joseph R. Dominick, *The Dynamics of Mass Communication* (Reading, Mass.: Addison-Wesley, 1983), p. 331.

23. Paul Starobin, "Media-Ownership Overhaul May Divide Legislators," *Congressional Quarterly Weekly Report,* 3 June 1989, p. 1315.

24. Steve Lohr, "How Bell Atlantic and T.C.I.'s Match Went Awry," *New York Times* 23 March 1994, pp. C1 and C5.

25. Graber, *Mass Media,* p. 110.

26. Robert Entman, *Democracy Without Citizens: Media and the Decay of American Politics* (New York: Oxford University Press, 1989), pp. 103–108.

27. Michael Nelson (ed.), *Guide to the Presidency* (Washington, D.C.: Congressional Quarterly Press, 1989), p. 729.

28. Ibid., p. 729.

29. Ibid., p. 735.

30. Warren Weaver, "C-Span on the Hill: 10 Years of Gavel to Gavel," *New York Times,* 28 March 1989, p. 10.

31. Graber, *Mass Media,* p. 241.

32. Ibid., p. 72.

33. Austin Ranney, *Channels of Power: The Impact of Television on American Politics* (New York: Basic Books, 1983), p. 46.

34. Doris A. Graber, *Mass Media and American Politics,* 3d ed. (Washington, D.C.: Congressional Quarterly Press, 1989), p. 237. See also Janet Hook, "Most of Us Don't Have a Clue About How Congress Works," *Chicago Tribune,* 10 June 1993, section 1, p. 17.

35. Gregory Katz, "Issues Distant Second to 'Horse-Race' Stories," *USA Today,* 22 April 1988, p. 6A.

36. Twentieth Century Fund, *1-800 PRESIDENT: The Report of the Twentieth Century Fund Task Force on Television and the Campaign of 1992* (New York: Twentieth Century Fund Press, 1993), p. 5.

37. Harold W. Stanley and Richard G. Niemi (eds.), *Vital Statistics on American Politics,* 2d ed. (Washington, D.C.: Congressional Quarterly Press, 1989), p. 69. However, a 1994 survey found similar percentages of respondents rating newspapers and television news as "believable" (68 and 73

percent, respectively. See Times Mirror Center for the People & the Press, "Mixed Message About Press Freedom on Both Sides of the Atlantic," News Release, 16 March 1994, p. 7.

38. There was less of a difference between those who said they regularly read a newspaper and those who did so "yesterday," whereas more people (53 percent) actually listened to news on the radio the previous day than said they regularly did so (46 percent). Times Mirror Center for the People & the Press, "The American Media: Who Reads, Who Watches, Who Listens, Who Cares," press release, 15 July 1990, p. 4.

39. Doris A. Graber, *Processing the News: How People Tame the Information Tide,* 2d ed. (New York: Longman, 1988), p. 101.

40. Michael J. Robinson and Andrew Kohut, "Believability and the Press," *Public Opinion Quarterly* 52 (Summer 1988), pp. 174–189.

41. Times Mirror Center for the People & the Press, "The American Media," 15 July 1990.

42. This fits with findings by Stephen Earl Bennett in "Trends in Americans' Political Information, 1967–1987," *American Politics Quarterly* 17 (October 1989), pp. 422–435. Bennett found that race was significantly related to level of political information in a 1967 survey but not in a 1987 survey.

43. Linda L. M. Bennett and Stephen Earl Bennett, "Enduring Gender Differences in Political Interests," *American Politics Quarterly* 17 (January 1989), pp. 105–122, especially pp. 116–117.

44. Times Mirror Center for the People & the Press, press release, 8 July 1992, p. 80.

45. One seasoned journalist argues instead that the technology of minicams and satellites has set back the quality of news coverage. Now a television crew can fly to the scene of a crisis and immediately televise information without knowing much about the local politics or culture, which was not true of the old foreign correspondents. See David R. Gergen, "Diplomacy in a Television Age:

The Dangers of Teledemocracy," in *The Media and Foreign Policy*, ed. Simon Serfaty (New York: St. Martin's Press, 1990), p. 51.

46. Bennett, "Trends in Americans' Political Information." Bennett's findings are supported by a national poll in 1990 that found only 40 percent of the sample had read a newspaper "yesterday," compared with 71 percent asked the same question in 1965. Times Mirror Center for the People & the Press, "The American Media," p. 100. Two researchers who compared the public's level of knowledge in 1989 with answers to the same questions in the 1940s and 1950s found similar levels of knowledge across the years but added: "That knowledge has been stable during a period of rapid changes in education, communication, and the public role of women seems paradoxical." They suspect, but cannot demonstrate, that the lack of expected increase is because of a decline in political interest over time. See Michael X. Delli Carpini and Scott Keeter, "Stability and Change in the U.S. Public's Knowledge of Politics," *Public Opinion Quarterly* 55 (Winter 1991), pp. 583–612.

47. W. Russell Neuman, Marion R. Just, and Ann N. Crigler, *Common Knowledge: News and the Construction of Political Meaning* (Chicago: University of Chicago Press, 1992) p. 10.

48. Graber, *Processing the News*, pp. 166–169.

49. Neuman, Just, and Crigler, *News and the Contruction of Political Meaning*.

50. Ibid., pp. 86–87.

51. Ibid., pp. 106–107.

52. Ibid., p. 113.

53. Laurence Parisot, "Attitudes About the Media: A Five-Country Comparison," *Public Opinion* 10 (January/February 1988), p. 60.

54. The statistical difficulties in determining media effects owing to measurement error are discussed in Larry M. Bartels, "Messages Received: The Political Impact of Media Exposure," paper prepared for delivery at the annual meeting of the American Political Science Association, Washington, D.C.,

September 1993. According to Bartels, "More direct and convincing demonstrations of significant opinion changes due to media exposure will require data collections spanning considerably longer periods of time" (p. 27).

55. Benjamin I. Page, Robert Y. Shapiro, and Glenn R. Dempsey, "What Moves Public Opinion?" *American Political Science Review* 81 (March 1987), p. 31.

56. Donald L. Jordan, "Newspaper Effects on Policy Preferences," *Public Opinion Quarterly* 57 (Summer 1993), pp. 191–204. Interestingly, Bartels's study of media effects in the 1980 presidential election, which used very different methodology, found that "the average impact of newspaper exposure across a wide range of candidate and issue perceptions was only about half as large as the corresponding impact of television news exposure" (Bartels, "Messages Received," p. 26).

57. Shanto Iyengar and Donald R. Kinder, *News That Matters: Television and American Opinion* (Chicago: University of Chicago Press, 1987), p. 33.

58. Ibid., p. 60.

59. Herbert Jacob, *The Frustration of Policy: Responses to Crime by American Cities* (Boston: Little, Brown, 1984), pp. 47–50.

60. Sam Vincent Meddis, "Crime's No Worse, But USA's Fear Grows," *USA Today International*, 28 October 1993, p. 1. See also Jeffrey D. Alderman, "Leading the Public: The Media's Focus on Crime Shaped Sentiment," *Public Perspective* 5 (March/April 1994), pp. 26–27.

61. W. Russell Neuman, "The Threshold of Public Attention," *Public Opinion Quarterly* 54 (Summer 1990), pp. 159–176.

62. David E. Harrington, "Economic News on Television: The Determinants of Coverage," *Public Opinion Quarterly* 53 (Spring 1989), pp. 17–40.

63. Entman, *Democracy Without Citizens*, p. 86.

64. Ibid., pp. 47–48.

65. A panel study of ten- to seventeen-year-olds during the 1988 presidential campaign found that the

campaign helped these young people crystallize their party identifications and their attitudes toward the candidates but had little effect on political ideology and views on central campaign issues. See David O. Sears, Nicholas A. Valentino, and Rick Kosterman, "Domain Specificity in the Effects of Political Events on Preadult Socialization," paper prepared for delivery at the annual meeting of the American Political Science Association, Washington, D.C., September 1993.

66. Richard Zoglin, "Is TV Ruining Our Children?" *Time*, 5 October 1990, p. 75. Moreover, much of what children see are advertisements. See "Study: Almost 20% of Kid TV Is Ad-Related," *Chicago Tribune*, 22 April 1991, p. 11.

67. John J. O'Connor, "Soothing Bromides? Not on TV," *New York Times*, Arts & Leisure section, 28 October 1990, pp. 1, 35.

68. Douglas Kellner, *Television and the Crisis of Democracy* (Boulder, Colo.: Westview, 1990), p. 17.

69. For analysis of elections from 1964 to 1976, see S. Robert Lichter and Stanley Rothman, "Media and Business Elites," *Public Opinion* 5 (October/November 1981), pp. 42–46. For a study of the 1980 election, see L. Brent Bozell II and Brent H. Baker (eds.), *And That's the Way It Isn't* (Alexandria, Va.: Media Research Center, 1990), p. 32.

70. "Journalism Heavy with Democrats," *Chicago Tribune*, 18 November 1992, section 1, p. 14.

71. Elizabeth Kolbert, "For Bush, More TV News Is Also Good News," *New York Times*, 22 September 1992, p. 1.

72. Elizabeth Kolbert, "Maybe the Media DID Treat Bush a Bit Harshly," *New York Times*, 22 November 1992, p. 3E.

73. "Press Coverage of the 1992 Campaign," *American Enterprise* (May/June 1993), p. 95.

74. William Schneider and I. A. Lewis, "Views on the News," *Public Opinion* 8 (August/September 1985), pp. 6–11, 58–59.

75. Stanley and Niemi, *Vital Statistics on American Politics*, p. 73.

76. *Editor & Publisher*, 24 October 1992, 7 November 1992.

77. Michael Robinson and Margaret Sheehan, *Over the Wire and on TV: CBS and UPI in Campaign '80* (New York: Russell Sage Foundation, 1983).

78. Michael J. Robinson, "The Media in Campaign '84: Part II; Wingless, Toothless, and Hopeless," *Public Opinion* 8 (February/March 1985), p. 48.

79. Maura Clancey and Michael J. Robinson, "General Election Coverage: Part I," *Public Opinion* 7 (December/January 1985), p. 54.

80. William Glaberson, "The Capitol Press vs. the President: Fair Coverage or Unreined Adversity?" *New York Times,* 17 June 1993, p. A11.

81. Times Mirror Center for the People & the Press, news release, 18 June 1993, pp. 7 and 10.

82. Stanley Rothman and S. Robert Lichter, "Elite Ideology and Risk Perception in Nuclear Energy Policy," *American Political Science Review* 81 (June 1987), p. 393.

83. For a historical account of efforts to determine voters' preferences before modern polling, see Tom W. Smith, "The First Straw? A Study of the Origin of Election Polls," *Public Opinion Polling* 54 (Spring 1990), pp. 21–36. See also Chapter 4 in Susan Herbst, *Numbered Voices: How Opinion Polling Has Shaped American Politics* (Chicago: University of Chicago Press, 1993).

84. Philip Meyer, "The Media Reformation: Giving the Agenda Back to the People," in *The Elections of 1992,* ed. Michael Nelson (Washington, D.C.: Congressional Quarterly Press, 1993), p. 102.

85. Michael W. Traugott, "Public Attitudes About News Organizations, Campaign Coverage, and Polls," in *Polling and Presidential Election Coverage,* p. 135.

86. Schneider and Lewis, "Views on the News," p. 11. For similar findings from a 1994 study, see Times Mirror Center for the People & the Press, "Mixed Message," p. 65.

87. Times Mirror Center for the People & the Press, "The People,

the Press and the War in the Gulf," 31 January 1991, p. 1.

88. Times Mirror Center for the People & the Press, "Mixed Message," p. 65.

89. "7 Arrested for Lying About Objects in Pepsis," *Chicago Tribune,* 18 June 1993, p. 3; and Charles M. Madigan, "Canned Hoax: The Media and the Pepsi Scare," *Chicago Tribune* 20 June 1993, section 4, p. 1.

Chapter 7 / Participation and Voting / pp. 212–249

1. Tamar Lewin, "Anti-Abortion Protests To Continue, Groups Say," *New York Times* 25 January 1994, p. 1.

2. Barbara Hinkson Craig and David M. O'Brien, *Abortion and American Politics* (Chatham, N.J.: Chatham House, 1993), p. 57.

3. Ibid.

4. Ibid., p. 58.

5. Dan Baum, "Violence is driving away rural abortion providers," *Chicago Tribune* 21 August 1993, p. 1.

6. Tamar Lewin, "Anti-Abortion Protests To Continue," *Times,* p. A10.

7. Lester W. Milbrath and M. L. Goel, *Political Participation* (Chicago: Rand McNally, 1977), p. 2.

8. *New York Times,* 4 March 1985.

9. Michael Lipsky, "Protest as a Political Resource," *American Political Science Review* 62 (December 1968), p. 1145.

10. See Sidney Verba and Norman H. Nie, *Participation in America: Political Democracy and Social Equality* (New York: Harper & Row, 1972), p. 3.

11. Samuel H. Barnes and Max Kaase (eds.), *Political Action: Mass Participation in Five Western Democracies* (Beverly Hills, Calif.: Sage, 1979).

12. Jonathan D. Casper, *Politics of Civil Liberties* (New York: Harper & Row, 1972), p. 90.

13. David C. Colby, "A Test of the Relative Efficacy of Political Tactics," *American Journal of Political Science* 26 (November 1982), pp. 741–753. See also Frances Fox Piven and Richard Cloward, *Poor People's*

Movements (New York: Vintage, 1979).

14. Stephen C. Craig and Michael A. Magiotto, "Political Discontent and Political Action," *Journal of Politics* 43 (May 1981), pp. 514–522. But see Mitchell A. Seligson, "Trust Efficacy and Modes of Political Participation: A Study of Costa Rican Peasants," *British Journal of Political Science* 10 (January 1980), pp. 75–98, for a review of studies that came to different conclusions.

15. Philip H. Pollock III, "Organizations as Agents of Mobilization: How Does Group Activity Affect Political Participation?" *American Journal of Political Science* 26 (August 1982), pp. 485–503. Also see Jan E. Leighley, "Social Interaction and Contextual Influence on Political Participation," *American Politics Quarterly* 18 (October 1990), pp. 459–475.

16. Arthur H. Miller, et al., "Group Consciousness and Political Participation," *American Journal of Political Science* 25 (August 1981), p. 495. See also Susan J. Carroll, "Gender Politics and the Socializing Impact of the Women's Movement," in *Political Learning in Adulthood: A Sourcebook of Theory and Research,* ed. Roberta S. Sigel (Chicago: University of Chicago Press, 1989), p. 307.

17. Richard D. Shingles, "Black Consciousness and Political Participation: The Missing Link," *American Political Science Review* 75 (March 1981), pp. 76–91. See also Lawrence Bobo and Franklin D. Gilliam, Jr., "Race, Sociopolitical Participation, and Black Empowerment," *American Political Science Review* 84 (June 1990), pp. 377–393.

18. Russell J. Dalton, *Citizen Politics in Western Democracies* (Chatham, N.J.: Chatham House, 1988), p. 65.

19. M. Kent Jennings, Jan W. van Deth, et al., *Continuities in Political Action: A Longitudinal Study of Political Orientations in Three Western Democracies* (New York: Walter de Gruyter, 1990).

20. See James L. Gibson, "The Policy Consequences of Political Intolerance: Political Repression During the Vietnam War Era,"

Journal of Politics 51 (February 1989), pp. 13–35. Gibson found that individual state legislatures reacted quite differently in response to antiwar demonstrations on college campuses, but the laws passed to discourage dissent were not related directly to public opinion within the state.

21. See Verba and Nie, *Participation in America*, p. 69. Also see John Clayton Thomas, "Citizen-Initiated Contacts with Government Agencies: A Test of Three Theories," *American Journal of Political Science* 26 (August 1982), pp. 504–522; and Elaine B. Sharp, "Citizen-Initiated Contacting of Government Officials and Socioeconomic Status: Determining the Relationship and Accounting for It," *American Political Science Review* 76 (March 1982), pp. 109–115.

22. Elaine B. Sharp, "Citizen Demand Making in the Urban Context," *American Journal of Political Science* 28 (November 1984), pp. 654–670, especially pp. 654 and 665.

23. Stephen Labaton, "Where the 'Soft Money' Comes From," *New York Times*, 10 July 1992, p. A10.

24. Verba and Nie, *Participation in America*, p. 67; and Sharp, "Citizen Demand Making," p. 660.

25. See Joel B. Grossman, et al., "Dimensions of Institutional Participation: Who Uses the Courts and How?" *Journal of Politics* 44 (February 1982), pp. 86–114; and Frances Kahn Zemans, "Legal Mobilization: The Neglected Role of the Law in the Political System," *American Political Science Review* 77 (September 1983), pp. 690–703.

26. Brown v. Board of Education, 347 U.S. 483 (1954).

27. Max Kaase and Alan Marsh, "Political Action: A Theoretical Perspective," in *Political Action*, p. 168.

28. Smith v. Allwright, 321 U.S. 649 (1944).

29. Harper v. Virginia State Board of Elections, 383 U.S. 663 (1966).

30. Everett Carll Ladd, *The American Polity* (New York: W. W. Norton, 1985), p. 392.

31. Gorton Carruth and associates,

eds., *The Encyclopedia of American Facts and Dates* (New York: Crowell, 1979), p. 330.

32. Ivor Crewe, "Electoral Participation," in *Democracy at the Polls: A Comparative Study of Competitive National Elections*, ed. David Butler, Howard R. Penniman, and Austin Ranney (Washington, D.C.: American Enterprise Institute, 1981), pp. 219–223.

33. Thomas E. Cronin, *Direct Democracy: The Politics of Initiative, Referendum, and Recall* (Cambridge, Mass.: Harvard University Press, 1989), p. 127.

34. David B. Magleby, *Direct Legislation: Voting on Ballot Propositions in the United States* (Baltimore: Johns Hopkins University Press, 1984), p. 70.

35. Cronin, *Direct Democracy*, p. 197.

36. Robert Reinhold, "Move to Limit Terms Gathers Steam After Winning in 14 States," *New York Times*, 5 November 1992, p. B16.

37. Timothy Egan, "Ballot Measures on Term Limits and Crime Draw Wide Support," *New York Times*, 4 November 1993, p. A11.

38. Magleby, *Direct Legislation*, p. 59.

39. "Fears on Economy Doom Environment Issues, Tax Cuts," *Chicago Tribune*, 8 November 1990, Section 1, p. 22.

40. Robert Reinhold, "Complicated Ballot Is Becoming Burden to California Voters," *New York Times*, 24 September 1990, p. 1.

41. Cronin, *Direct Democracy*, p. x.

42. Cronin, *Direct Democracy*, p. 251.

43. *The Book of the States 1990–91*, vol. 28 (Lexington, Ky.: Council of State Governments, 1990), p. 85.

44. *Chicago Tribune*, 10 March 1985.

45. Crewe, "Electoral Participation," p. 232. Several scholars have successfully explained variations in voting turnout across nations with only a few institutional and contextual variables. (See G. Bingham Powell, Jr., "American Voter Turnout in Comparative Perspective," *American Political Science Review* 80 (March 1986), pp. 17–43; and Robert W. Jackman, "Political Institutions and Voter Turnout in the Industrial Democracies," *American Political Science Review* 81 (June 1987), pp. 405–423.) However, this work has

been criticized on methodological grounds and also for failing to successfully explain two deviant cases, the United States and Switzerland, both of which have low voter turnout. (See Wolfgang Hirczy, "Comparative Turnout: Beyond Cross-National Regression Models," paper prepared for presentation at the annual meeting of the American Political Science Association, Chicago, September 1992.)

46. Verba and Nie, *Participation in America*, p. 13.

47. Max Kaase and Alan Marsh, "Distribution of Political Action," in *Political Action*, p. 186.

48. Milbrath and Goel, *Political Participation*, pp. 95–96.

49. Verba and Nie, *Participation in America*, p. 148. For a concise summary of the effect of age on voting turnout, see Michael M. Gant and Norman R. Luttbeg, *American Electoral Behavior* (Itasca, Ill.: F. E. Peacock, 1991), pp. 103–104.

50. Richard Murray and Arnold Vedlitz, "Race, Socioeconomic Status, and Voting Participation in Large Southern Cities," *Journal of Politics* 39 (November 1977), pp. 1064–1072; and Verba and Nie, *Participation in America*, p. 157. See also Bobo and Gilliam, "Race, Sociopolitical Participation, and Black Empowerment." Their study of 1987 national survey data with a black oversample found that African Americans participated more than whites of comparable socioeconomic status in cities in which the major's office was held by an African American.

51. Carol A. Cassel, "Change in Electoral Participation in the South," *Journal of Politics* 41 (August 1979), 907–917.

52. Ronald B. Rapoport, "The Sex Gap in Political Persuading: Where the 'Structuring Principle' Works," *American Journal of Political Science* 25 (February 1981), pp. 32–48.

53. Bruce C. Straits, "The Social Context of Voter Turnout," *Public Opinion Quarterly* 54 (Spring 1990), pp. 64–73.

54. Stephen D. Shaffer, "A Multivariate Explanation of Decreasing Turnout in Presidential Elections,

1960–1976," *American Journal of Political Science* 25 (February 1981), pp. 68–95; and Paul R. Abramson and John H. Aldrich, "The Decline of Electoral Participation in America," *American Political Science Review* 76 (September 1981), pp. 603–620. However, one scholar argues that this research suffers because it looks only at voters and nonvoters in a single election. When the focus shifts to people who vote sometimes but not at other times, the models do not fit so well. See M. Margaret Conway and John E. Hughes, "Political Mobilization and Patterns of Voter Turnout," paper prepared for delivery at the annual meeting of the American Political Science Association, Washington, D.C., September 1993.

55. A sizable literature attempts to explain the decline in voting turnout in the United States. Some authors have claimed to account for the decline with just a few variables, but their work has been criticized for being too simplistic. See Carol A. Cassel and Robert C. Luskin, "Simple Explanations of Turnout Decline," *American Political Science Review* 82 (December 1988), pp. 1321–1330. They contend that most of the post–1960 decline is still unexplained. If it is any comfort, voting in Western European elections has seen a somewhat milder decline, and scholars have not been very successful at explaining it, either. See Richard S. Flickinger and Donley T. Studlar, "The Disappearing Voters? Exploring Declining Turnout in Western European Elections," *West European Politics* 15 (April 1992), pp. 1–16.

56. Ruy A. Teixeira, *The Disappearing American Voter* (Washington, D.C.: Brookings Institution, 1992) p. 57.

57. Abramson and Aldrich, "Decline of Electoral Participation," p. 519; and Shaffer, "Multivariate Explanation," pp. 78, 90.

58. The negative effect of registration laws on voting turnout is argued in Frances Fox Piven and Richard A. Cloward, "Government Statistics and Conflicting Explanations of Nonvoting," *PS: Political Science and Politics* 22 (September 1989), pp. 580–588. Their analysis was hotly contested in Stephen Earl Bennett, "The Uses and Abuses of Registration and Turnout Data: An Analysis of Piven and Cloward's Studies of Nonvoting in America," *PS: Political Science and Politics* 23 (June 1990), pp. 166–171. Bennett showed that turnout declined 10 to 13 percent after 1960 despite efforts to remove or lower legal hurdles to registration. For their reply, see Frances Fox Piven and Richard L. Cloward, "A Reply to Bennett," *PS: Political Science and Politics* 23 (June 1990), pp. 172–173. You can see that reasonable people can disagree on this matter.

59. Mark J. Fenster, "The Impact of Allowing Day of Registration Voting on Turnout in U.S. Elections from 1960 to 1992: A Research Note," *American Politics Quarterly* 22 (January 1994), pp. 74–87.

60. David Glass, Peverill Squire, and Raymond Wolfinger, "Voter Turnout: An International Comparison," *Public Opinion* 6 (December/January 1984), p. 52. Because of the strong effect of registration on turnout, Wolfinger says that most rational choice analyses of voting would be better suited to analyzing turnout of only registered voters. See Raymond E. Wolfinger, "The Rational Citizen Faces Election Day," *Public Affairs Report* 6 (November 1992), p. 12.

61. Richard Sammon, "Senate Kills Filibuster Threat, Clears 'Motor Voter' Bill," *CQ Weekly Report*, 15 May 1993, p. 1221.

62. Recent research finds that "party contact is clearly a statistically and substantively important factor in predicting and explaining political behavior." See Peter W. Wielhouwer and Brad Lockerbie, "Party Contacting and Political Participation, 1952–1990," paper prepared for delivery at the annual meeting of the American Political Science Association, Chicago, 1992, p. 14. Of course, parties strategically target the groups that they want to see vote in elections. See Peter W. Wielhouwer, "Mobilizing Activists and Voters: Strategic Canvassing by Political Parties, 1952–1990," paper prepared for delivery at the annual meeting of the American Political Science Association, Washington, D.C., September 1993.

63. See Robert A. Jackson, "Voter Mobilization in the 1986 Midterm Election," *Journal of Politics* 55 (November 1993), pp. 1081–1099.

64. See Charles Krauthammer, "In Praise of Low Voter Turnout," *Time*, 21 May 1990, p. 88. Krauthammer says, "Low voter turnout means that people see politics as quite marginal to their lives, as neither salvation nor ruin. . . . Low voter turnout is a leading indicator of contentment."

65. Crewe, "Electoral Participation," p. 262.

66. Barnes and Kaase, *Political Action*, p. 532.

67. *1971 Congressional Quarterly Almanac* (Washington, D.C.: Congressional Quarterly Press, 1972), p. 475.

68. Benjamin Ginsberg, *The Consequences of Consent: Elections, Citizen Control, and Popular Acquiescence* (Reading, Mass.: Addison-Wesley, 1982), p. 13.

69. Ginsberg, *Consequences of Consent*, pp. 13–14.

70. Ginsberg, *Consequences of Consent*, pp. 6–7.

71. Some people have argued that the decline in voter turnout during the 1980s served to increase the class bias in the electorate, because people of lower socioeconomic status stayed home. But recent research has concluded that "class bias has not increased since 1964" (p. 734, Jan E. Leighley and Jonathan Nagler, "Socioeconomic Class Bias in Turnout, 1964–1988: The Voters Remain the Same," *American Political Science Review* 86 [September 1992], pp. 725–736).

Chapter 8 / Political Parties / pp. 250–284

1. "The Public Opinion and Demographic Report," *Public Perspective* 3 (July/August 1992), 84.

2. John B. Anderson, fund-raising letter, 30 April 1980.

3. "The Major Election Polls," *Public Opinion* 3 (December/January 1981), 19.

4. Center for Political Studies of the Institute for Social Research, *American National Election Study 1992* (Ann Arbor, Mich.: University of Michigan, 1993, p. 997).

5. Alan R. Gitelson, M. Margaret Conway, and Frank B. Fiegert, *American Political Parties: Stability and Change* (Boston: Houghton Mifflin, 1984), p. 317.

6. Noble E. Cunningham, Jr. (ed.), *The Making of the American Party System, 1789 to 1809* (Englewood Cliffs, N.J.: Prentice-Hall, 1965), p. 123.

7. Richard B. Morris (ed.), *Encyclopedia of American History* (New York: Harper & Row, 1976), p. 209.

8. See Jerome M. Clubb, William H. Flanigan, and Nancy H. Zingale, *Partisan Realignment: Voters, Parties, and Government in American History*, vol. 108 (Beverly Hills, Calif.: Sage, 1980), p. 163.

9. See Gerald M. Pomper, "Classification of Presidential Elections," *Journal of Politics* 29 (August 1967), pp. 535–566.

10. For a more extensive treatment, see Henry M. Littlefield, "The Wizard of Oz: Parable on Populism," *American Quarterly* 16 (Spring 1964), pp. 47–58.

11. David Firestone, "Clash over Group's Name Divides Perot Followers in New York State," *New York Times*, 10 January 1994, p. A9.

12. The discussion that follows draws heavily on Austin Ranney and Willmoore Kendall, *Democracy and the American Party System* (New York: Harcourt, Brace, 1956), Chaps. 18 and 19.

13. "Libertarian Party Facts," distributed by the Ron Paul for President Committee, 1120 NASA Road, Houston, Texas (no date).

14. See Steven J. Rosenstone, Roy L. Behr, and Edward H. Lazarus, *Third Parties in America: Citizen Response to Major Party Failure* (Princeton, N.J.: Princeton University Press, 1984), pp. 5–6.

15. Ibid., p. 8.

16. State laws and court decisions may systematically support the major parties, but the U.S. Supreme Court seems to hold a more neutral position toward major and minor parties. See Lee Epstein and Charles D. Hadley, "On the Treatment of Political Parties in the U.S. Supreme Court, 1900–1986," *Journal of Politics* 52 (May 1990), pp. 413–432.

17. *Public Opinion* 7 (December/January 1985), p. 26.

18. Measuring the concept of party identification has had its problems. For recent insights into the issues, see R. Michael Alvarez, "The Puzzle of Party Identification," *American Politics Quarterly* 18 (October 1990), pp. 476–491; and Donald Philip Green and Bradley Palmquist, "Of Artifacts and Partisan Instability," *American Journal of Political Science* 34 (August 1990), pp. 872–902.

19. There is some dispute over how stable party identification really is when the question is asked of the same respondents over a period of several months during an election campaign. This literature is reviewed in Brad Lockerbie, "Change in Party Identification: The Role of Prospective Economic Evaluations," *American Politics Quarterly* 17 (July 1989), pp. 291–311. Lockerbie argues that respondents change their party identification according to whether they think that the parties will help them personally in the future. But also see Green and Palmquist, "Of Artifacts and Partisan Instability."

20. Bill Keller, "As Arms Buildup Eases, U.S. Tries to Take Stock," *New York Times*, 14 May 1985.

21. See, for example, Gerald M. Pomper, *Elections in America* (New York: Dodd, Mead, 1968); Benjamin Ginsberg, "Election and Public Policy," *American Political Science Review* 70 (March 1976), pp. 41–50; and Jeff Fishel, *Presidents and Promises* (Washington, D.C.: Congressional Quarterly Press, 1985).

22. Ian Budge and Richard I. Hofferbert, "Mandates and Policy Outputs: U.S. Party Platforms and Federal Expenditures," *American Political Science Review* 84 (March 1990), pp. 111–131.

23. Walter J. Stone, Ronald B. Rapoport, and Alan I. Abramowitz, "The Reagan Revolution and Party Polarization in the 1980s," in *The Parties Respond: Changes in the American Party System*, ed. L. Sandy Maisel (Boulder, Colo.: Westview, 1990), pp. 67–93.

24. Robert Harmel and Kenneth Janda, *Parties and Their Environments: Limits to Reform?* (New York: Longman, 1982), pp. 27–29.

25. Personal communication with DNC and RNC staff, January 24, 1994.

26. See Ralph M. Goldman, *The National Party Chairmen and Committees: Factionalism at the Top* (Armonk, N.Y.: M. E. Sharpe, 1990). The subtitle is revealing.

27. William Crotty and John S. Jackson III, *Presidential Primaries and Nominations* (Washington, D.C.: Congressional Quarterly Press, 1985), p. 33.

28. Debra L. Dodson, "Socialization of Party Activists: National Convention Delegates, 1972–1981," *American Journal of Political Science* 34 (November 1990), pp. 1119–1141.

29. John F. Bibby, "Party Renewal in the National Republican Party," in *Party Renewal in America: Theory and Practice*, ed. Gerald M. Pomper (New York: Praeger, 1980), pp. 102–115.

30. The Federal Election Commission, *The Presidential Public Funding Program* (Washington, D.C., April, 1993), p. 18.

31. Tom Watson, "Machines: Something Old, Something New," *Congressional Quarterly Weekly Report*, 17 August 1985, p. 1619.

32. Advisory Commission on Intergovernmental Relations, *The Transformation of American Politics: Implications for Federalism* (Washington, D.C.: Report A-106, August 1986), pp. 112–116; see also Cornelius P. Cotter, et al., *Party Organizations in American Politcs* (New York: Praeger, 1984), pp. 26–27.

33. Cotter, *Party Organizations*, p. 63.

34. James L. Gibson, John P. Frendreis, and Laura L. Vertz, "Party Dynamics in the 1980s: Change in County Organizational Strength,

1980–1984," *American Journal of Political Science* 33 (February 1989), pp. 67–90. See also Paul S. Herrnson, "Reemergent National Party Organizations," in *Parties Respond*, pp. 41–66.

35. The Federal Election Commission, *The Presidential Public Funding Program* (Washington, D.C., April, 1993), p. 19.

36. See the evidence presented in Harmel and Janda, *Parties and Their Environments*, Chap. 5.

37. David S. Broder, *The Party's Over: The Failure of Politics in America* (New York, Harper & Row, 1972); and William C. Crotty and Gary C. Jacobson, *American Parties in Decline* (Boston: Little, Brown, 1980).

38. Barbara Sinclair, "The Congressional Party: Evolving Organizational, Agenda-Setting, and Policy Roles," in *Parties Respond*, p. 227.

39. The model is articulated most clearly in a report by the American Political Science Association, "Toward a More Responsible Two-Party System," *American Political Science Review* 44 (September 1950). See also Gerald M. Pomper, "Toward a More Responsible Party System? What, Again?" *Journal of Politics* 33 (November 1971), pp. 916–940.

Chapter 9 / Nominations, Campaigns, and Elections / pp. 285–320

1. Ken Auletta, "On and Off the Bus: Lessons from Campaign '92," in *1-800-PRESIDENT*, ed. Twentieth Century Fund (New York: Twentieth Century Fund Press, 1993), p. 66.

2. Ibid., p. 69.

3. Ibid., p. 72.

4. Ibid., p. 74.

5. Kathleen Hall Jamieson, "The Subversive Effects of a Focus on Strategy in News Coverage of Presidential Campaigns," in *1-800-PRESIDENT*, ed. Twentieth Century Fund (New York: Twentieth Century Fund Press, 1993), p. 35.

6. Ibid.

7. Charles Leroux, "Study: Issue of Character Not Helping Bush,"

Chicago Tribune, 29 October 1992, section 1, p. 10.

8. Ross K. Baker, "Sorting Out and Suiting Up: The Presidential Nominations," in *The Election of 1992*, ed. Gerald M. Pomper et al. (Chatham: N.J.: Chatham House, 1993), p. 54.

9. Barbara G. Salmore and Stephen A. Salmore vigorously argue this position in *Candidates, Parties, and Campaigns: Electoral Politics in America*, 2d ed. (Washington, D.C.: Congressional Quarterly Press, 1989), pp. 7–9.

10. This is essentially the framework for studying campaigns that Salmore and Salmore set forth in *Candidates, Parties, and Campaigns*, pp. 10–11.

11. Martin P. Wattenberg, *The Rise of Candidate-Centered Politics: Presidential Elections of the 1980s* (Cambridge, Mass.: Harvard University Press, 1991).

12. Stephen E. Frantzich, *Political Parties in the Technological Age* (New York: Longman, 1989), p. 105.

13. Michael Gallagher, "Conclusion," in *Candidate Selection in Comparative Perspective: The Secret Garden of Politics*, eds. Michael Gallagher and Michael Marsh (London: Sage, 1988), p. 238.

14. Kenneth Janda, *Political Parties: A Cross-National Survey* (New York: Free Press, 1980), p. 112.

15. *The Book of the States, 1990–91*, vol. 28 (Lexington, Ky.: Council of State Governments, 1990), pp. 234–235.

16. Malcolm E. Jewell and David M. Olson, *Political Parties and Elections in American States*, 3d ed. (Chicago: Dorsey Press, 1988), pp. 108–112.

17. See John G. Geer, "Assessing the Representativeness of Electorates in Presidential Elections," *American Journal of Political Science* 32 (November 1988), pp. 929–945; and Barbara Norrander, "Ideological Representativeness of Presidential Primary Voters," *American Journal of Political Science* 33 (August 1989), pp. 570–587.

18. Byron E. Shafer, *Bifurcated Politics: Evolution and Reform in the National Party Convention* (Cambridge, Mass.: Harvard University Press, 1988), p. 8.

19. Gary R. Orren and Nelson W. Polsby (eds.), *Media and Momentum: The New Hampshire Primary and Nomination Politics* (Chatham, N.J.: Chatham House, 1987), p. 23.

20. Richard L. Berke, "In New Hampshire, It's Already 1996," *International Herald Tribune*, 26 October 1993, p. 3.

21. See James R. Beniger, "Winning the Presidential Nomination: National Polls and State Primary Elections, 1936–1972," *Public Opinion Quarterly* 40 (Spring 1976), pp. 22–38.

22. Michael Nelson (ed.), *Congressional Quarterly Guide to the Presidency* (Washington, D.C.: Congressional Quarterly Press, 1989), p. 1427. You can find the other exceptions there, too.

23. Harold W. Stanley and Richard G. Niemi, *Vital Statistics on American Politics*, 2d ed. (Washington, D.C.: Congressional Quarterly Press, 1990), p. 132, and the 1992 National Election Study, Center for Political Studies, University of Michigan.

24. Rhodes Cook, "House Republicans Scored a Quiet Victory in '92," *Congressional Quarterly Weekly Report*, 17 April 1993, p. 966.

25. Everett Carll Ladd, "The 1988 Elections: Continuation of the Post-New Deal System," *Political Science Quarterly* 104 (1989), pp. 1–18; and Seymour Martin Lipset, "A Reaffirming Election: 1988," *International Journal of Public Opinion Research* 1 (January 1989).

26. Salmore and Salmore, *Candidates, Parties, and Campaigns*, p. 1.

27. "Democrats Hunt Electoral Votes," *Chicago Tribune*, 26 July 1992, p. 1; Andrew Rosenthal, "Bush Pulls Close in Poll, but Not with Women," *New York Times*, 22 August 1992, p. 1.

28. John Theilmann and Al Wilhite, "The Determinants of Individuals' Campaign Contributions to Congressional Campaigns," *American Politics Quarterly* 17 (July 1989), pp. 312–333.

29. Quoted in E. J. Dionne, Jr., "On the Trail of Corporation Donations," *New York Times*, 6 October 1980.

30. Salmore and Salmore, *Candidates, Parties, and Campaigns*, p. 11.

31. Federal Election Commission, "The First Ten Years: 1975–1985" (Washington, D.C.: Federal Election Commission), 14 April 1985, p. 1.

32. "The Presidential Funding Program" (Washington, D.C.: Federal Election Commission, April, 1993), p. 17.

33. F. Christopher Arterton, "Campaign '92: Strategies and Tactics of the Candidates," in *The Election of 1992*, ed. Pomper, p. 83.

34. Paul S. Herrnson, "Political Parties, Campaign Finance Reform, and Presidential Elections," paper prepared for presentation at the annual meeting of the Midwest Political Science Association, Chicago, 5–7 April 1990, p. 11. See also Richard L. Berke, "In Election Spending: Watch the Ceiling, Use a Loophole," *New York Times*, 3 October 1988, pp. 1 and 13.

35. Janda, *Political Parties*, p. 78.

36. Salmore and Salmore, *Candidates, Parties, and Campaigns*, p. 11.

37. David Moon, "What You Use Depends on What You Have: Information Effects on the Determinants of Electoral Choice," *American Politics Quarterly* 18 (January 1990), pp. 3–24.

38. See "The Political Pages," *Campaigns & Elections* 10 (February 1990), which contain more than a hundred pages of names, addresses, and telephone numbers of people who supply "political products and services."

39. Salmore and Salmore, *Candidates, Parties, and Campaigns*, pp. 115–116.

40. Stephen Ansolabehere, Roy L. Behr, and Shanto Iyengar, "Mass Media and Elections: An Overview," *American Politics Quarterly* 19 (January 1991), pp. 109–139.

41. James Warren, "Politicians Learn Value of Sundays—Too Well," *Chicago Tribune*, 22 October 1990, p. 1.

42. Timothy E. Cook, *Making Laws and Making News: Media Strategies in the U.S. House of Representatives* (Washington, D.C.: Brookings Institution, 1989). Recent research into media effects on Senate and House elections finds that in low information elections, which characterize House more than Senate elections, the media coverage gives an advantage to incumbents, particularly among independent voters. See Robert Kirby Goidel, Todd G. Shields, and Barry Tadlock, "The Effects of the Media in United States Senate and House Elections: A Comparative Analysis," paper presented at the annual meeting of the American Political Science Association, Washington, D.C., September 1993.

43. Kiku Adatto, "The Incredible Shrinking Sound Bite," *New Republic*, 28 May 1990, p. 20.

44. Ann N. Crigler, Marion R. Just, and Timothy E. Cook, "Local News, Network News and the 1992 Presidential Campaign," paper presented at the annual meeting of the American Political Science Association, Washington, D.C., September 1993, p. 9.

45. Ibid., p. 11.

46. Ibid., p. 16.

47. Thomas E. Patterson, "News Images of Presidential Candidates: 1960–1992," paper prepared for delivery at the annual meeting of the American Political Science Association, Washington, D.C., September 1993.

48. Ibid., p. 17.

49. Montague Kern, *30-Second Politics: Political Advertising in the Eighties* (New York: Praeger, 1989), p. 57.

50. See Sara Fritz and Dwight Morris, "Burden of TV Election Ads Exaggerated, Study Finds," *Los Angeles Times*, 18 March 1991, pp. A1, A14. However, specialists warn that such averages, which include many uncontested elections, mask much higher levels of spending for media in contested elections. See Herbert E. Alexander and Monica Bauer, *Financing the 1988 Election* (Boulder, Colo.: Westview, 1991).

51. Darrell M. West, *Air Wards: Television Advertising in Election Campaigns, 1952–1992* (Washington, D.C.: Congressional Quarterly Press, 1993), p. 7.

52. Dorothy Davidson Nesbit, *Videostyle in Senate Campaigns* (Knoxville: University of Tennessee Press, 1988), p. 152.

53. L. Patrick Devlin, "Contrasts in Presidential Campaign Commercials of 1992," *American Behavioral Scientist* 37 (November 1993), pp. 272–290.

54. West, *Air Wards*, p. 40.

55. This theme runs throughout Kathleen Hall Jamieson's *Dirty Politics: Deception, Distraction, and Democracy* (New York: Oxford University Press, 1992). See also John Boiney, "You Can Fool All of the People . . . Evidence on the Capacity of Political Advertising to Mislead," paper presented at the annual meeting of the American Political Science Association, Washington, D.C., September 1993.

56. West, *Air Wards*, p. 50. West's figures are roughly comparable to data reported by Devlin, "Contrasts in Presidential Campaign Commercials," who says that both Clinton and Bush had a 50:50 positive to negative ad buying ratio and cites this as a "new high" in negative advertising, p. 287.

57. West, *Air Wards*, p. 52.

58. Ibid., p. 58.

59. Ibid., p. 143.

60. Christine F. Ridout, "News Coverage and Talk Shows in the 1992 Presidential Campaign," *PS: Political Science & Politics* 26 (December 1993), pp. 712–716.

61. Edwin Diamond, Martha McKay, and Robert Silverman, "Pop Goes Politics," *American Behavioral Scientist* 37 (November 1993), p. 258.

62. The 1988 National Election Study, Center for Political Studies, University of Michigan (data made available through the Inter-University Consortium for Political and Social Research).

63. The 1992 National Election Study and press release of the Times Mirror Center for the People & the Press (Washington, D.C.), 15 November 1992, p. 13.

64. Arthur H. Miller, "Economic, Character, and Social Issues in the 1992 Presidential Election," *American Behavioral Scientist* 37 (November, 1993), p. 317.

65. Ibid.

66. Ibid., p. 318.

67. Michael Lewis-Beck and Tom W.

Rice, *Forecasting Elections* (Washington, D.C.: 1992).

68. Gerald M. Pomper, "The Presidential Election," *The Election of 1992*, ed. Pomper, p. 145.

69. Miller, "Economic, Character, and Social Issues," p. 319.

70. Ibid., p. 321.

71. Ibid., p. 324–325.

72. Pamela Johnston Conover and Stanley Feldman, "Candidate Perception in an Ambiguous World: Campaigns, Cues, and Inference Processes," *American Journal of Political Science* 33 (November 1989), pp. 912–940.

73. Miller, "Economic, Character, and Social Issues," p. 321.

74. Ibid., p. 324.

75. Frantzich, *Political Parties*, p. 167.

76. Michael M. Gant and Norman R. Luttberg, *American Electoral Behavior* (Itasca, Ill.: Peacock, 1991), pp. 63–64. The literature on the joint effects of party, issues, and candidate is quite involved. See also David W. Romero, "The Changing American Voter Revisited: Candidate Evaluations in Presidential Elections, 1952–1984," *American Politics Quarterly* 17 (October 1989), pp. 409–421. Romero contends that research that finds a "new" American voter who votes according to issues is incorrectly looking at standardized rather than unstandardized regression coefficients.

77. Herbert Asher, *Presidential Elections and American Politics* (Homewood, Ill.: Dorsey, 1980), p. 196.

78. Conover and Feldman, "Candidate Perception," p. 938.

79. Party identification has been assumed to be relatively resistant to short-term campaign effects, but see Dee Allsop and Herbert F. Weisberg, "Measuring Change in Party Identification in an Election Campaign," *American Journal of Political Science* 32 (November 1988), pp. 996–1017. They conclude that partisanship is more volatile than we have thought.

80. Devlin, "Contrasts in Presidential Campaign Commercials," p. 282.

81. Devlin, "Contrasts in Political Campaign Commercials," p. 282.

82. Ibid., p. 290.

83. Ibid., p. 273.

84. Ibid., p. 283.

85. F. Christopher Arterton, "Campaign '92," pp. 93–95.

86. Richard L. Berke, "Debating the Debates: John Q. Defeats Reporters," *New York Times*, 21 October 1992, p. A13.

87. Kathleen A. Frankovic, "Public Opinion in the 1992 Campaign," *The Election of 1992*, ed. Pomper p. 120.

88. "Voters Say 'Thumbs Up' to Campaign, Process, & Coverage," press release of the Times Mirror Center for the People & the Press (Washington, D.C.), 15 November 1992, p. 21.

89. "1993—Priorities for the President," press release of the Times Mirror Center for the People & the Press (Washington, D.C.), 28 October 1992, p. 17.

Chapter 10 / Interest Groups / pp. 321–357

1. Michael Wines, "Congress's Twists and Turns Reshape Bill on Energy," *New York Times*, 6 June 1993, p. A1.

2. John Harwood and David Wessel, "White House Gives Ground on Energy Tax," *Wall Street Journal*, 27 May 1993, p. A3; Steven Greenhouse, "Energy Plan To Be Scaled Back, Moynihan Reports," *New York Times*, 30 May 1993, p. 1; Wines, "Congress Twists and Turns"; Timothy Noah, "BTU Tax Is Dying Death of a Thousand Cuts as Lobbyists Seem Able To Write Their Own Exemptions," *Wall Street Journal*, 8 June 1993, p. A18.

3. Jeffrey M. Berry, *The Interest Group Society*, 2d ed. (Glenview, Ill.: Scott, Foresman/Little, Brown, 1989), p. 4.

4. Alexis de Tocqueville, *Democracy in America*, 1835–1839, Reprint, ed. Richard D. Heffner (New York: Mentor Books, 1956), p. 198.

5. *The Federalist Papers* (New York: Mentor, 1961), p. 79.

6. Ibid., p. 78.

7. See Robert A. Dahl, *A Preface to Democratic Theory* (Chicago: University of Chicago Press, 1956), pp. 4–33.

8. Alan Rosenthal, *The Third House*

(Washington, D.C.: Congressional Quarterly, 1993), p. 7.

9. This follows from Berry, *The Interest Group Society*, pp. 6–8.

10. John Mark Hansen, *Gaining Access* (Chicago: University of Chicago Press, 1991), p. 11–17.

11. Anne N. Costain, *Inviting Women's Rebellion* (Baltimore: Johns Hopkins University Press, 1992).

12. David B. Truman, *The Governmental Process* (New York: Alfred A. Knopf, 1951).

13. Herbert Gans, *The Urban Villagers* (New York: Free Press, 1962).

14. Robert H. Salisbury, "An Exchange Theory of Interest Groups," *Midwest Journal of Political Science* 13 (February 1984), pp. 1–32.

15. See Mancur Olson, Jr., *The Logic of Collective Action* (New York: Schocken, 1968).

16. Peter Matthiessen, *Sal Si Puedes* (New York: Random House, 1969); and John G. Dunne, *Delano*, rev. ed. (New York: Farrar, Straus & Giroux, 1971).

17. Robert H. Salisbury, "Interest Representation: The Dominance of Institutions," *American Political Science Review* 78 (March 1984), pp. 64–76.

18. William P. Browne, "Organized Interests and Their Issue Niches: A Search for Pluralism in a Policy Domain," *Journal of Politics* 52 (May 1990), pp. 477–509.

19. R. Kenneth Godwin, *One Billion Dollars of Influence* (Chatham, N.J.: Chatham House, 1988), pp. 1–34.

20. See Olson, *Logic*.

21. David C. King and Jack L. Walker, "The Provision of Benefits by Interest Groups in the United States," *Journal of Politics* 54 (May 1992), pp. 394–426.

22. Edward O. Laumann and David Knoke, *The Organizational State* (Madison: University of Wisconsin Press, 1987), p. 3. Cited in Robert H. Salisbury, "The Paradox of Interest Groups in Washington— More Groups, Less Clout," in *The New American Political System*, 2d ed., ed. Anthony King (Washington, D.C.: American Enterprise Institute, 1990), p. 226.

23. Jackie Calmes, "Revolving Door

Between Congress and Lobbyists Spins on Despite Yearlong Cooling-Off Period," *Wall Street Journal*, 24 January 1994, p. A14.

24. John P. Heinz, Edward O. Laumann, Robert L. Nelson, and Robert H. Salisbury, *The Hollow Core* (Cambridge, Mass.: Harvard University Press, 1993), pp. 105–155.

25. Jeffrey H. Birnbaum, *The Lobbyists* (New York: Times Books, 1992), pp. 128–29.

26. Robert H. Salisbury, "Washington Lobbyists: A Collective Portrait," in *Interest Group Politics*, 2d ed., ed. Allan J. Cigler and Burdett A. Loomis (Washington, D.C.: Congressional Quarterly, 1986), p. 155.

27. Jill Abramson, "Influence of Lobbyist Groups Likely Won't Diminish," *Wall Street Journal*, 5 November 1992, p. A12; and Richard B. Schmitt, "Ties to Clinton Aid Law Firms in Washington," *Wall Street Journal*, 12 March 1993, p. B1.

28. Birnbaum, *Lobbyists*, p. 7.

29. "FEC Releases 1992 Year-End PAC Count," Federal Election Commission, 23 January 1993, p. 1.

30. "PAC Activity Rebounds in 1991–92 Election Cycle," Federal Election Commission, 29 April 1993, pp. 3, 7, and 13.

31. Dan Clawson, Alan Neustadtl, and Denise Scott, *Money Talks* (New York: Basic Books, 1992), p. 1.

32. "PAC Activity Rebounds" p. 3.

33. Frank J. Sorauf, *Inside Campaign Finance* (New Haven, Conn.: Yale University Press, 1992), p. 71.

34. Nathaniel C. Nash, "Savings Unit Donations Criticized," *New York Times*, 29 June 1990, p. D4.

35. John R. Wright, "Contributions, Lobbying, and Committee Voting in the U.S. House of Representatives," *American Political Science Review* 84 (June 1990), pp. 417–438; and Richard L. Hall and Frank W. Wayman, "Buying Time: Money Interests and the Mobilization of Bias in Congressional Committees," *American Political Science Review* 84 (September 1990), pp. 797–820.

36. Elizabeth Drew, "Politics and Money—Part I," *New Yorker*, 6 December 1982, p. 147.

37. Kay Lehman Schlozman and John T. Tierney, *Organized Interests and American Democracy* (New York: Harper & Row, 1986), p. 150.

38. John E. Chubb, *Interest Groups and the Bureaucracy* (Stanford, Calif.: Stanford University Press, 1983), p. 144.

39. Keith Bradsher, "Trade Gap Too High? Export a Few Lawyers," *New York Times*, 7 July 1992, p. D1.

40. Barbara Hinkson Craig and David M. O'Brien, *Abortion and American Politics* (Chatham, N.J.: Chatham House, 1993), p. 67.

41. Roger P. Kingsley, "Advocacy for the Handicapped," paper delivered at the annual meeting of the American Political Science Association, Washington, D.C., September 1984, p. 10.

42. Marc K. Landy and Mary Hague, "Private Interests and Superfund," *Public Interest* 108 (Summer 1992), pp. 97–115.

43. Kevin Hula, "Rounding Up the Usual Suspects: Forging Interest Group Coalitions in Washington," paper delivered at the annual meeting of the Midwest Political Science Association, Chicago, April 1993, p. 29.

44. Sidney Verba, Kay Lehman Schlozman, Henry Brady, and Norman H. Nie, "Citizen Activity: Who Participates? What Do They Say?" *American Political Science Review* 87 (June 1993), p. 311.

45. See Jack L. Walker, *Mobilizing Interest Groups in America* (Ann Arbor: University of Michigan Press, 1991).

46. Jeffrey M. Berry, *Feeding Hungry People* (New Brunswick, N.J.: Rutgers University Press, 1984).

47. Berry, *Lobbying for the People* (Princeton, N.J.: Princeton University Press, 1977), pp. 6–10.

48. Andrew S. McFarland, *Common Cause* (Chatham, N.J.: Chatham House, 1984); and Lawrence S. Rothenberg, *Linking Citizens to Government* (New York: Cambridge University Press, 1992).

49. Schlozman and Tierney, *Organized Interests*, pp. 58–87.

50. See *Public Affairs Offices and Their Functions* (Boston: Boston University School of Management, 1981), p. 8.

51. David Plotke, "The Mobilization of Business," in *The Politics of Interests*, ed. Mark P. Petracca (Boulder, Colo.: Westview, 1992), pp. 175–198; and David Vogel, *Fluctuating Fortunes* (New York: Basic Books, 1989).

52. Mark A. Peterson, "The Presidency and Organized Interests: White House Patterns of Interest Group Liaison," *American Political Science Review* 86 (September 1992), pp. 612–625.

53. "PAC Activity Rebounds," p. 13.

54. Ibid., p. 3.

55. Richard L. Berke, "Clinton Unveils Plan To Restrict PAC Influence," *New York Times*, 8 May 1993, p. 1.

56. On the need for reform, see Clawson, Neustadtl, and Scott, *Money Talks*, and Sorauf, *Inside Campaign Finance*.

Chapter 11 / Congress / pp. 359–395

1. Michael Wines, "A 'Bazaar' Method of Dealing for Votes," *New York Times*, 11 November 1993, p. A23; Keith Bradsher, "Clinton's Shopping List for Votes Has Ring of Grocery Buyer's List," *New York Times*, 17 November 1993, p. A21; and Jackie Calmes, "How a Sense of Clinton's Commitment and a Series of Deals Clinched the Vote," *Wall Street Journal*, 19 November 1993, p. A7.

2. Clinton Rossiter, *1787: The Grand Convention* (New York: Mentor, 1968), p. 158.

3. *Origins and Development of Congress* (Washington, D.C.: Congressional Quarterly Press, 1976), pp. 81–89.

4. Wesberry v. Sanders, 376 U.S. 1 (1964) (congressional districts within a state must be substantially equal in population); and Reynolds v. Sims, 377 U.S. 364 (1964) (state legislatures must be apportioned on the basis of population).

5. See James M. Lindsay and Randall B. Ripley, "How Congress Influences Foreign and Defense Policy," in *Congress Resurgent*, eds. Randall B. Ripley and James M. Lindsay (Ann Arbor: University

of Michigan Press, 1993), pp. 25–28.

6. Norman J. Ornstein, Thomas E. Mann, and Michael J. Malbin (eds.) *Vital Statistics on Congress, 1993–1994* (Washington, D.C.: Congressional Quarterly Press, 1994), pp. 58–61.

7. "Confidence in Institutions," *American Enterprise* 4 (November/December 1993), 94.

8. "Ethics," *American Enterprise* 3 (November/December 1992), p. 84.

9. Gerald Benjamin and Michael J. Malbin, "Term Limits for Lawmakers," in *Limiting Legislative Terms*, eds. Gerald Benjamin and Michael J. Malbin (Washington, D.C.: Congressional Quarterly, 1992), pp. 10–11.

10. Dan Balz, "Term Limits Drive Dealt Sharp Blow," *Washington Post*, 11 February 1994, p. A1.

11. David W. Brady and Douglas Rivers, "Term Limits Make Sense," *New York Times*, 5 October 1991, p. 21.

12. For an analysis of how term limits might improve the operation of Congress, see George Will, *Restoration* (New York: Free Press, 1992).

13. Chris Afendulis, "Concentrated Minorities, Careers, and Influence: The Dead-End of Term Limits for Minority Legislators," (paper delivered at the Workshop on Race, Ethnicity, Representation, and Governance, Harvard University, June 1993). For the opposing view, see Joel A. Thompson and Gary F. Moncrief, "The Implications of Term Limits for Women and Minorities: Some Evidence from the States," *Social Science Quarterly* 74 (June 1993), pp. 301–309.

14. John A. Ferejohn, "On the Decline of Competition in Congressional Elections," *American Political Science Review* 71 (March 1977), pp. 166–176; Norman Ornstein, "The Permanent Democratic Congress," *Public Interest* 100 (Summer 1990), pp. 24–44; and Mark E. Rush, *Does Redistricting Make a Difference?* (Baltimore: Johns Hopkins University Press, 1993).

15. Timothy E. Cook, *Making Laws and Making News* (Washington, D.C.: Brookings Institution, 1989), p. 83.

16. " 'Write Me,' Senator Says, and the People Take Heed," *New York Times* 25 October 1993, p. A15.

17. Federal Election Commission, "1992 Congressional Election Spending Jumps 52% to $678 Million," 4 March 1993, p. 4.

18. Larry Sabato, *PAC Power* (New York: W. W. Norton, 1992), p. 72.

19. Frank J. Sorauf, *Inside Campaign Finance* (New Haven, Conn.: Yale University Press, 1992), p. 84.

20. Gary C. Jacobson and Samuel Kernell, *Strategy and Choice in Congressional Elections*, 2d ed. (New Haven Conn: Yale University Press, 1983).

21. Gary C. Jacobson, "If Sleazy Politicians Are the Problem, Why Aren't Elections the Solution?" (paper delivered at the Center for American Political Studies, Harvard University, December 1993, p. 29).

22. Alan I. Abramowitz and Jeffrey S. Segal, *Senate Elections* (Ann Arbor: University of Michigan Press, 1992), pp. 228–229.

23. Ornstein, Mann, and Malbin, *Vital Statistics*, pp. 22–33.

24. Hanna Fenichel Pitkin, *The Concept of Representation* (Berkeley: University of California Press, 1967), pp. 60–91.

25. Carol M. Swain, *Black Faces, Black Interests* (Cambridge, Mass.: Harvard University Press, 1993), p. 197.

26. Shaw v. Reno (slip opinion 92–357) (28 June 1993).

27. Swain, *Black Faces*. See also David Ian Lublin, "Race, Representation, and Reapportionment" (paper presented at the Workshop on Race, Ethnicity, Representation, and Governance, Harvard University, June 1993).

28. Walter J. Oleszek, *Congressional Procedures and the Policy Process*, 3d ed. (Washington, D.C.: Congressional Quarterly, 1989), p. 81.

29. Edmund L. Andrews, "Mild Slap at TV Violence," *New York Times*, 1 July 1993, p. A1.

30. Roger W. Cobb and Charles D. Elder, *Participation in American Politics*, 2d ed. (Baltimore: Johns Hopkins University Press, 1983), pp. 64–65.

31. John W. Kingdon, *Agendas, Alternatives, and Public Policies* (Boston: Little, Brown, 1984), p. 41.

32. See David C. King, "The Nature of Congressional Committee Jurisdictions," *American Political Science Review* 88 (March 1994), pp. 48–62.

33. It was Woodrow Wilson who described the legislative process as the "dance of legislation." Eric Redman used the phrase for the title of his case study of a health bill, *The Dance of Legislation* (New York: Touchstone, 1973).

34. David Shribman, "Canada's Top Envoy to Washington Cuts Unusually Wide Swath," *Wall Street Journal*, 29 July 1985, p. 1.

35. Woodrow Wilson, *Congressional Government* (Boston: Houghton Mifflin, 1885), p. 79.

36. Richard L. Hall and C. Lawrence Evans, "The Power of Subcommittees," *Journal of Politics* 52 (May 1990), p. 342.

37. Lawrence D. Longley and Walter J. Oleszek, *Bicameral Politics* (New Haven, Conn.: Yale University Press, 1989), p. 10.

38. Ibid., p. 4.

39. Leroy Rieselbach, *Congressional Reform* (Washington, D.C.: Congressional Quarterly, 1994), p. 52.

40. Philip M. Boffey, "Lawmakers Vow a Legal Recourse for Military Malpractice Victims," *New York Times*, 9 July 1985, p. A14.

41. Martin Tolchin, "Welfare Overhaul: Right Timing for a War Dance," *New York Times*, 3 October 1988, p. A18.

42. Gary W. Cox and Mathew D. McCubbins, *Legislative Leviathan* (Berkeley: University of California Press, 1993); and Keith Krehbiel, *Information and Legislative Organization* (Ann Arbor: University of Michigan Press, 1992).

43. Andy Plattner, "Dole on the Job," *Congressional Quarterly Weekly Report*, 29 June 1985, p. 1270.

44. Roger H. Davidson, "Senate Leaders: Janitors for an Untidy Chamber?" in *Congress Reconsidered*, 3d ed., ed. Lawrence C. Dodd and Bruce I. Oppenheimer (Washington, D.C.: Congressional Quarterly Press, 1985), p. 228.

45. Robert L. Peabody, *Leadership in*

Congress (Boston: Little, Brown, 1976), p. 9.

46. Cox and McCubbins, *Legislative Leviathan.*

47. Charles O. Jones, *The United States Congress* (Homewood, Ill.: Dorsey Press, 1982), p. 322.

48. *Congress Speaks: A Survey of the 100th Congress* (Washington, D.C.: Center for Responsive Politics, 1988), p. 61. For some potential modifications of the filibuster rules, see Thomas E. Mann and Norman J. Ornstein, *Renewing Congress: A Second Report* (Washington, D.C.: American Enterprise Institute and the Brookings Institution, 1993), pp. 50–53.

49. Deborah Baldwin, "Pulling Punches," *Common Cause* (May/June 1985), p. 22.

50. Jeffrey H. Birnbaum, "Rep. Armey, Texas Firebrand, Changes Tactics and Starts Accomplishing Things in the House," *Wall Street Journal*, 2 June 1988, p. 1.

51. Steven S. Smith, *Call to Order* (Washington, D.C.: Brookings Institution, 1989), p. 138.

52. Ibid.

53. Linda L. Fowler and Robert D. McClure, *Political Ambition* (New Haven, Conn.: Yale University Press, 1989); and Linda L. Fowler, *Candidates, Congress, and the American Democracy* (Ann Arbor: University of Michigan Press, 1993).

54. Burdett A. Loomis, *The New American Politician* (New York: Basic Books, 1988).

55. Cox and McCubbins, *Legislative Leviathan*; D. Roderick Kiewiet and Mathew D. McCubbins, *The Logic of Delegation* (Chicago: University of Chicago Press, 1991); and Krehbiel, *Information and Legislative Organization.*

56. Kitty Cunningham, "With Democrat in White House, Partisanship Hits New High," *Congressional Quarterly Weekly Report*, 18 December 1993, p. 3432.

57. There are other ways to measure partisanship besides party unity votes, and some of these show decreasing partisanship. See Paul E. Peterson and Jay P. Greene, "Why Executive-Legislative Conflict in the United States Is Dwindling," *British Journal of Political Science* 24 (January 1994), pp. 33–55.

58. See Mark A. Peterson, *Legislating Together* (Cambridge, Mass.: Harvard University Press, 1990).

59. James Sterling Young, *The Washington Community* (New York: Harcourt, Brace, 1964).

60. R. Douglas Arnold, *The Logic of Congressional Action* (New Haven, Conn.: Yale University Press, 1990).

61. Joel D. Aberbach, *Keeping a Watchful Eye* (Washington, D.C.: Brookings Institution, 1990), p. 44.

62. Ornstein, Mann, and Malbin, *Vital Statistics*, pp. 128–132.

63. Aberbach, *Keeping a Watchful Eye*, pp. 162–183.

64. Jeremy Rabkin, "Micromanaging the Administrative Agencies," *Public Interest* 100 (Summer 1990), p. 120.

65. Barry M. Blechman, "The New Congressional Role in Arms Control," in *A Question of Balance*, ed. Thomas E. Mann (Washington, D.C.: Brookings Institution, 1990), pp. 109–146.

66. Richard F. Fenno, Jr., *Home Style* (Boston: Little, Brown, 1978), p. xii.

67. Ibid., p. 32.

68. Louis I. Bredvold and Ralph G. Ross (eds.), *The Philosophy of Edmund Burke* (Ann Arbor: University of Michigan Press, 1960), p. 148.

69. Dirk Johnson, "Flag Vote: The People Back Home," *New York Times*, 25 June 1990, p. A12.

70. Warren E. Miller and Donald E. Stokes, "Constituency Influence in Congress," *American Political Science Review* 57 (March 1963), pp. 45–57.

71. Julie Johnson, "Picking over the Pork in the 1988 Spending Bill," *New York Times*, 5 January 1988, p. B6.

72. For an opposing view, see John W. Ellwood and Eric M. Patashnik, "In Praise of Pork," *Public Interest* 110 (Winter 1993), pp. 19–33.

73. Robert Weissberg, "Collective vs. Dyadic Representation in Congress," *American Political Science Review* 72 (June 1978), pp. 535–547.

Chapter 12 / The Presidency / pp. 396–432

1. Jon Healey, "Spending Increases Come First in Rush to Pass Package," *Congressional Quarterly Weekly Report*, 20 February 1993, pp. 365–369; Jon Healey, "Republicans Slam the Brakes on Economic Stimulus Package," *Congressional Quarterly Weekly Report*, 3 April 1993, pp. 817–819; Gwen Ifill, "White House Trying to Trim Blocked Jobs Bill, Aides Say," *New York Times*, 8 April 1993, p. D20; Ann Devroy and David S. Broder, "Missteps Mired Clinton Package," *Washington Post*, 11 April 1993, p. A1; Jeffrey H. Birnbaum and David Rogers, "GOP Filibuster Defeats Clinton on Stimulus Package," *Wall Street Journal*, 22 April 1993, p. A2; and Bob Woodward, *The Agenda* (New York: Simon & Schuster, 1994).

2. Clinton Rossiter, *1787: The Grand Convention* (New York: Mentor, 1968), p. 148.

3. Ibid., pp. 190–91.

4. Richard M. Pious, *The American Presidency* (New York: Basic Books, 1979), pp. 51–52.

5. Wilfred E. Binkley, *President and Congress*, 3d ed. (New York: Vintage, 1962), p. 155.

6. Pious, *American Presidency*, pp. 60–63.

7. Richard E. Neustadt, *Presidential Power* (New York: John Wiley, 1980), p. 10.

8. Ibid., p. 9.

9. Fred I. Greenstein, *The Hidden-Hand Presidency* (New York: Basic Books, 1982), pp. 155–227.

10. George C. Edwards III, *At the Margins* (New Haven, Conn.: Yale University Press, 1989). See also Jon R. Bond and Richard Fleisher, *The President in the Legislative Arena* (Chicago: University of Chicago Press, 1990).

11. On the president's calculations of risks in legislative proposals, see Mark A. Peterson, *Legislating Together* (Cambridge, Mass.: Harvard University Press, 1990).

12. See Edwards, *At the Margins*, pp. 101–125.

13. Jeffrey K. Tulis, *The Rhetorical Presidency* (Princeton, N.J.:

Princeton University Press, 1987),
p. 64ff.

14. Theodore J. Lowi, *The Personal Presidency* (Ithaca, N.Y.: Cornell University Press, 1985).

15. Richard A. Brody, *Assessing the President* (Stanford, Calif.: Stanford University Press, 1991), pp. 27–44.

16. Darrell M. West, *Congress and Economic Policymaking* (Pittsburgh: University of Pittsburgh Press, 1987), p. 33.

17. Kristen Renwick Monroe, *Presidential Popularity and the Economy* (New York: Praeger, 1984).

18. Paul Brace and Barbara Hinckley, *Follow the Leader* (New York: Basic Books, 1992).

19. Charles W. Ostrom and Dennis M. Simon, "Promise and Performance: A Dynamic Model of Presidential Popularity," *American Political Science Review* 79 (June 1985), pp. 334–358.

20. James M. Perry, "Clinton Relies Heavily on White House Pollster to Take Words Right Out of the Public's Mouth," *Wall Street Journal*, 23 March 1994, p. A16.

21. Brace and Hinckley, *Follow the Leader*, p. 19.

22. "Prepared Text of Carter's Farewell Address," *New York Times*, 15 January 1981, p. B10.

23. Benjamin I. Page, *Choices and Echoes in Presidential Elections* (Chicago: University of Chicago Press, 1978).

24. Robert A. Dahl, "Myth of the Presidential Mandate," *Political Science Quarterly* 105 (Fall 1990), pp. 355–372.

25. Paul J. Quirk and Jon K. Dalager, "The Election: A 'New Democrat' and a New Kind of Presidential Campaign," in *The Elections of 1992*, ed. Michael Nelson (Washington, D.C.: Congressional Quarterly Press, 1993), pp. 57–88.

26. "Two Cheers for United Government," *American Enterprise* 4 (January/February 1993), pp. 107–108.

27. David W. Brady and Morris Fiorina, "The Ruptured Legacy: Presidential-Congressional Relations in Historical Perspective," in *Looking Back on the Reagan Presidency*, ed. Larry Berman (Baltimore: Johns Hopkins University Press, 1990), pp. 269–287.

28. Gary C. Jacobson, "Meager Patrimony: The Reagan Era and Republican Representation in Congress," in *Looking Back on the Reagan Presidency*, p. 300.

29. See generally, Charles O. Jones, *The Presidency in a Separated System* (Washington, D.C.: Brookings Institution, 1994).

30. Terry M. Moe, "Presidents, Institutions, and Theory," in *Researching the Presidency*, eds. George C. Edwards III, John H. Kessel, and Bert A. Rockman (Pittsburgh: University of Pittsburgh Press, 1993), pp. 337–385.

31. Jeb Stuart Magruder, *An American Life* (New York: Atheneum, 1974), p. 58, quoted in Benjamin I. Page and Mark Petracca, *The American Presidency* (New York: McGraw-Hill, 1983), p. 171.

32. U.S. Bureau of the Census, U.S. Department of Commerce, *Statistical Abstract of the United States, 1993* (Washington, D.C.: U.S. Government Printing Office, 1993), p. 343; and U.S. Office of Management and Budget, *Budget of the United States Government, Fiscal Year 1995* (Washington, D.C.: U.S. Government Printing Office, 1994), p. 237.

33. Paul J. Quirk, "Presidential Competence," in *The Presidency and the Political System*, 3d ed., ed. Michael Nelson (Washington, D.C.: Congressional Quarterly Press, 1990), p. 165.

34. Jane Mayer and Doyle McManus, *Landslide* (Boston: Houghton Mifflin, 1988), pp. 22–24.

35. *The Tower Commission Report* (New York: Bantam Books, 1987). See also, Samuel Kernell, "New and Old Lessons on White House Management," in *Executive Leadership in Anglo-American Systems*, eds. Colin Campbell, S.J., and Margaret Jane Wyszomirski (Pittsburgh: University of Pittsburgh Press, 1991), pp. 341–359.

36. James M. Perry, "Clinton Echoes a Familiar Lament: Good Help Is Hard to Find—Especially Among Friends," *Wall Street Journal*, 1 April 1994, p. A10.

37. Woodward, *The Agenda*, p. 127.

38. Fred I. Greenstein, "The Presidential Leadership Style of Bill Clinton: An Early Appraisal," paper delivered at the annual meeting of the American Political Science Association, Washington, D.C., September 1993.

39. Douglas Jehl, "Clinton Shuffles His Aides, Selecting Budget Director as White House Staff Chief," *New York Times*, 28 June 1994, p. A1.

40. James M. Perry and Jeffrey H. Birnbaum, "Clinton and Gore Smoothly Overcome the Perils of Their Relationship, and They're Buddies Too," *Wall Street Journal*, 3 January 1994, p. 38. See also Michael Nelson, "Vice President Gore: Not Second Fiddle," *Baltimore Sun*, 1 August 1993, p. 1C.

41. Edward Weisband and Thomas M. Franck, *Resignation in Protest* (New York: Penguin, 1975), p. 139, quoted in Thomas E. Cronin, *The State of the Presidency*, 2d ed. (Boston: Little, Brown, 1980), p. 253.

42. Griffin B. Bell with Ronald J. Ostrow, *Taking Care of the Law* (New York: Morrow, 1982), p. 45.

43. See Richard W. Waterman, "Combining Political Resources: The Internalization of the President's Appointment Power," in *The Presidency Reconsidered*, ed. Richard W. Waterman (Itasca, Ill.: Peacock, 1993), pp. 195–214.

44. Bert Rockman, "The Style and Organization of the Reagan Presidency," in *The Reagan Legacy*, ed. Charles O. Jones (Chatham, N.J.: Chatham House, 1988), pp. 172–210.

45. Terry M. Moe, "The Politicized Presidency," in *The New Direction in American Politics*, ed. John E. Chubb and Paul E. Peterson (Washington, D.C.: Brookings Institution, 1985), pp. 235–271.

46. *Public Papers of the President, Lyndon B. Johnson, 1965*, vol. 1 (Washington, D.C.: U.S. Government Printing Office, 1966), p. 72.

47. "Transcript of Second Inaugural

Address by Reagan," *New York Times*, 22 January 1985, p. 72.

48. Kevin Phillips, *The Politics of Rich and Poor* (New York: Random House, 1990), p. 88.

49. Stephen Skowronek, *The Politics Presidents Make* (Cambridge, Mass.: Harvard University Press, 1993), pp. 429–441.

50. Charles Kolb, *White House Daze* (New York: Free Press, 1994), p. 9.

51. John W. Kingdon, *Agendas, Alternatives, and Public Policies* (Boston: Little, Brown, 1984), p. 25.

52. Richard E. Neustadt, "Presidency and Legislation: The Growth of Central Clearance," *American Political Science Review* 48 (September 1954), pp. 641–671.

53. Skowronek, *The Politics Presidents Make.*

54. Seth King, "Reagan, in Bid for Budget Votes, Reported to Yield on Sugar Prices," *New York Times*, 27 June 1981, p. A1.

55. See Mark A. Peterson, "The Presidency and Organized Interests: Patterns of Interest Group Liaison," *American Political Science Review* 86 (September 1992), pp. 175–98; and Joseph A. Pika, "Reaching Out to Organized Interests: Public Liaison in the Modern White House," in *The Presidency Reconsidered*, pp. 145–168.

56. Martha Joynt Kumar and Michael Baruch Grossman, "The Presidency and Interest Groups," in *The Presidency and the Political System*, ed. Michael Nelson (Washington, D.C.: Congressional Quarterly, 1984), p. 309.

57. Jeffrey M. Berry and Kent E. Portney, "Centralizing Regulatory Control and Interest Group Access: The Quayle Council on Competitiveness," in *Interest Group Politics*, 4th ed., eds. Allan J. Cigler and Burdett A. Loomis (Washington, D.C.: Congressional Quarterly Press, 1994).

58. Sidney M. Milkis, *The President and the Parties* (New York: Oxford University Press, 1993), pp. 189–191.

59. Patrick J. Lucey, ". . .While NAFTA Speeds Right Along," *The Wall Street Journal*, 30 August 1994, p. A10.

60. Fred Barnes, "Hour of Power," *New Republic*, 3 September 1990, p. 12.

61. Alexander George, "The Case for Multiple Advocacy in Foreign Policy," *American Political Science Review* 66 (September 1972), pp. 751–782.

62. John P. Burke and Fred I. Greenstein, *How Presidents Test Reality* (New York: Russell Sage Foundation, 1989).

63. Richard E. Neustadt and Earnest R. May, *Thinking in Time* (New York: Free Press, 1986), p. 143.

64. Lowi, *Personal President*, p. 185.

65. Dan Balz, "Clinton Concedes Marital Wrongdoing," *Washington Post*, 27 January 1992, p. A1.

66. "Scandals: Whitewater," *American Enterprise* 5 (May/June 1994), p. 75.

67. Robert A. Caro, *The Path to Power* (New York: Alfred A. Knopf, 1982), p. 131.

68. Ibid., p. 135.

69. Doris Kearns, *Lyndon Johnson and the American Dream* (New York: Signet, 1977), p. 363.

70. See generally, James David Barber, *The Presidential Character*, 4th ed. (Englewood Cliffs, N.J.: Prentice-Hall, 1992).

Chapter 13 / The Bureaucracy / pp. 433–464

1. Paul Farhi, "FCC Sets Cable TV Rate Cuts," *Washington Post*, 1 April 1993, p. A1; Paul Fahri, "FCC Imposes Cable Price Restrictions," *Washington Post*, 2 April 1993, p. F1; and Jeanne Saddler and Mark Robichaux, "Billion-Dollar Rollback Is Set for Cable Rates," *Wall Street Journal*, 2 April 1993, p. B1.

2. Mark Robichaux, "How Cable-TV Firms Raised Rates in Wake of Law To Curb Them," *Wall Street Journal*, 28 September 1993, p. A1; Edmund Andrews, "Enforcement Problems May Help Cable Systems Sidestep Rules," *New York Times*, 11 November 1993, p. A1; and Elizabeth Kolbert, "F.C.C. Orders Cuts in Cable TV Rates of 7% on Average," *New York Times*, 23 February 1994, p. A1.

3. John E. Chubb and Terry M. Moe, *Politics, Markets, and America's Schools* (Washington, D.C.: Brookings Institution, 1990).

4. James Q. Wilson, *Bureaucracy* (New York: Basic Books, 1989), p. 25.

5. Bruce D. Porter, "Parkinson's Law Revisited: War and the Growth of American Government," *Public Interest* 60 (Summer 1980), p. 50.

6. Keith Schneider, "Farmers To Face Patent Fees To Use Gene-Altered Animals," *New York Times*, 6 January 1988, p. A1.

7. See Anne Schneider and Helen Ingram, "Social Construction of Target Populations: Implications for Politics and Policy," *American Political Science Review* 87 (June 1993), pp. 334–347.

8. Theda Skocpol, *Protecting Soldiers and Mothers: The Political Origins of Social Policy in the United States* (Cambridge, Mass.: Harvard University Press, 1992).

9. Philip Shabecoff, "Senator Urges Military Resources Be Turned to Environmental Battle," *New York Times*, 29 June 1990, p. A1.

10. Jeff Gerth, "C.I.A. Shedding Its Reluctance To Aid in Fight Against Drugs," *New York Times*, 25 March 1990, p. A1.

11. Robert F. Durant, *The Administrative Presidency Revisited* (Albany: State University of New York Press, 1992), pp. 51–77.

12. Pietro S. Nivola, *Regulating Unfair Trade* (Washington, D.C.: Brookings Institution, 1993), pp. 52 and 60.

13. John T. Tierney, "Government Corporations and Managing the Public's Business," *Political Science Quarterly* 99 (Spring 1984), pp. 73–92.

14. U.S. Bureau of the Census, *Statistical Abstract of the United States, 1992* (Washington, D.C.: U.S. Government Printing Office, 1992), pp. 331 and 381.

15. Ibid., p. 331.

16. Ibid., pp. 332–333.

17. Robert D. Hershey, Jr., "For Capitol Job Hunters, the Spoils of Victory are Limited," *New York Times*, 6 November 1992, p. A18.

18. See Elizabeth Sanders, "The Presidency and the Bureaucratic State," in *The Presidency and the Political System*, 3d ed., ed.

Michael Nelson (Washington, D.C.: Congressional Quarterly, 1990), pp. 409–442.

19. Joel D. Aberbach and Bert A. Rockman with Robert M. Copeland, "From Nixon's Problem to Reagan's Achievement," in *Looking Back on the Reagan Presidency*, ed. Larry Berman (Baltimore: Johns Hopkins University Press, 1990), p. 180.

20. John Frohnmayer, *Leaving Town Alive* (Boston: Houghton Mifflin, 1993).

21. Jeffrey M. Berry and Kent E. Portney, "Centralizing Regulatory Control and Interest Group Access: The Quayle Council on Competitiveness," in *Interest Group Politics*, 4th ed., ed. Allan J. Cigler and Burdett Loomis (Washington, D.C.: Congressional Quarterly, forthcoming).

22. Francis E. Rourke, "Responsiveness and Neutral Competence in American Bureaucracy," *Public Administration Review* 52 (November/December 1992), pp. 559–546.

23. Paul C. Light, "When Worlds Collide: The Political-Career Nexus," in *The In-and-Outers*, ed. G. Calvin MacKenzie (Baltimore: Johns Hopkins University Press, 1987), pp. 156–173.

24. Michael K. Frisby, "Even as Clinton Appoints Women and Minorities, Insiders Resemble Those of George (Washington)," *Wall Street Journal*, 9 April 1993, p. A12.

25. Berry and Portney, "Centralizing Regulatory Control."

26. Barbara Hinkson Craig and David M. O'Brien, *Abortion and American Politics* (Chatham, N.J.: Chatham House, 1993), pp. 188–189.

27. Theodore J. Lowi, *The End of Liberalism*, 2d ed. (New York: Norton, 1979).

28. Doris A. Graber, *Mass Media and American Politics*, 3d ed. (Washington, D.C.: Congressional Quarterly Press, 1989), p. 51.

29. Jeffrey M. Berry, *Feeding Hungry People* (New Brunswick, N.J.: Rutgers University Press, 1984).

30. Eric Schmitt, "Aspin Is Said To Pick a Conservative Tack on Gay Troop Ban," *New York Times*, 14 July 1993, p. A1.

31. David J. Garrow, *Bearing the Cross* (New York: Morrow, 1986), pp. 373–374.

32. Gregory F. Treverton, "Intelligence: Welcome to the American Government," in *A Question of Balance*, ed. Thomas E. Mann (Washington, D.C.: Brookings Institution, 1990), p. 89.

33. Marian Burros, "F.D.A. Is Again Proposing To Regulate Vitamins and Supplements," *New York Times*, 15 June 1993, p. A25.

34. Charles E. Lindblom, "The Science of Muddling Through," *Public Administration Review* 19 (Spring 1959), pp. 79–88.

35. See Michael T. Hayes, *Incrementalism and Public Policy* (White Plains, N.Y.: Longman, 1992).

36. Andrew Weiss and Edward Woodhouse, "Reframing Incrementalism: A Constructive Response to the Critics," *Policy Sciences* 25 (August 1992), pp. 255–273.

37. Elaine Sciolino, "Panel from C.I.A. Urges Curtailing of Agency Secrecy," *New York Times*, 12 January, 1992, p. A1.

38. Jonathan Bendor, Serge Taylor, and Roland Van Gaalen, "Stacking the Deck: Bureaucratic Mission and Policy Design," *American Political Science Review* 81 (Spring 1987), p. 874.

39. Frohnmayer, *Leaving Town Alive*, pp. 213 and 262.

40. Thomas W. Church and Robert T. Nakamura, *Cleaning Up the Mess* (Washington, D.C.: Brookings Institution, 1993), p. 9.

41. Martha Derthick, *Agency Under Stress* (Washington, D.C.: Brookings Institution, 1990), pp. 33–48.

42. See generally, Terry M. Moe, "The Politics of Bureaucratic Structure," in *Can the Government Govern?*, ed. John E. Chubb and Paul E. Peterson (Washington, D.C.: Brookings Institution, 1989), pp. 267–329.

43. William T. Gormley, Jr., *Taming the Bureaucracy* (Princeton, N.J.: Princeton University Press, 1989).

44. Jeffrey H. Birnbaum and Paulette Thomas, "Clinton Moves To Streamline Government," *Wall Street Journal*, 8 September 1993, p. A2.

45. Martha Derthick and Paul J. Quirk, *The Politics of Deregulation* (Washington, D.C.: Brookings Institution, 1985).

46. David Vogel, "AIDS and the Politics of Drug Lag," *Public Interest* 96 (Summer 1989), pp. 73–85.

47. Walter Williams, *Mismanaging America: The Rise of the Anti-Analytic Presidency* (Lawrence: University of Kansas Press, 1990), p. 102.

48. James A. Morone, *The Democratic Wish* (New York: Basic Books, 1990).

49. A good, short introduction to TQM in government is James E. Swiss, "Adapting Total Quality Management to Government," *Public Administration Review* 52 (July/August 1992), pp. 356–362.

50. David Osborne and Ted Gaebler, *Reinventing Government* (New York: Plume Books, 1993), p. 166.

51. Joseph Sensenbrenner, "Quality Comes to City Hall," *Harvard Business Review* 69 (March/April 1991), pp. 64–75.

Chapter 14 / The Courts / pp. 465–506

1. Philip Elman (interviewed by Norman Silber), *The Solicitor General's Office, Justice Frankfurter, and Civil Rights Litigation, 1946–1960: An Oral History*, 100 Harv. L. Rev. 817 at 840 (1987).

2. David M. O'Brien, *Storm Center*, 2d ed. (Norton, 1990), p. 324.

3. Bernard Schwartz, *The Unpublished Opinions of the Warren Court* (New York: Oxford University Press, 1985), p. 446.

4. Ibid., pp. 445–448.

5. Felix Frankfurter and James M. Landis, *The Business of the Supreme Court* (New York: Macmillan, 1928), pp. 5–14; and Julius Goebel, Jr., *Antecedents and Beginnings to 1801*, vol. 1 of *The History of the Supreme Court of the United States* (New York: Macmillan, 1971).

6. Maeva Marcus, ed., *The Justices on Circuit, 1795–1800*, vol. 3 of *The Documentary History of the Supreme Court of the United States, 1789–1800* (New York: Columbia University Press, 1990).

7. Robert G. McCloskey, *The United States Supreme Court* (Chicago: University of Chicago Press, 1960), p. 31.

8. Marbury v. Madison, 1 Cranch 137 at 177, 178 (1803).

9. Interestingly, the phrase *judicial review* dates only to 1910; it was apparently unknown to Marshall and his contemporaries. Robert Lowry Clinton, *Marbury v. Madison and Judicial Review* (Lawrence: University Press of Kansas, 1989), p. 7.

10. Henry J. Abraham, *The Judicial Process*, 6th ed. (New York: Oxford University Press, 1993), pp. 274–279.

11. Ware v. Hylton, 3 Dallas 199 (1976).

12. Martin v. Hunter's Lessee, 1 Wheat. 304 (1816).

13. *Constitution of the United States of America: Annotated and Interpreted* (Washington, D.C.: U.S. Government Printing Office, 1987).

14. Garry Wills, *Explaining America: The Federalist* (Garden City, N.Y.: Doubleday, 1981), pp. 127–136.

15. *State Justice Institute News*, 4 (Spring 1993), p. 1.

16. Charles Alan Wright, *Handbook on the Law of Federal Courts*, 3d ed. (St. Paul, Minn.: West, 1976), p. 7.

17. Administrative Office of the United States Courts, Statistics Division, Analysis and Reports Branch. (Telephone interview, March 1994).

18. Ibid.

19. Linda Greenhouse, "Precedent for Lower Courts: Tyrant or Teacher?" *New York Times*, 29 January 1988, p. B7.

20. Texas v. Johnson, 491 U.S. 397 (1989); United States v. Eichman, 496 U.S. 310 (1990).

21. Regents of the University of California v. Bakke, 438 U.S. 265 (1978).

22. Clerk's Office, Supreme Court of the United States (Telephone interview, January 1994).

23. "Reading Petitions Is for Clerks Only at High Court Now," *Wall Street Journal*, 11 October 1990, p. B7.

24. H. W. Perry, Jr., *Deciding to Decide: Agenda Setting in the United States Supreme Court* (Cambridge, Mass.: Harvard University Press, 1991); and Gregory A. Caldiera and John R. Wright, *The Discuss List: Agenda Building in the Supreme Court*, 24 LAW & SOC. REV. 807 (1990).

25. Doris M. Provine, *Case Selection in the United States Supreme Court* (Chicago: University of Chicago Press, 1980), pp. 74–102.

26. Garcia v. San Antonio Metropolitan Transit Authority, 469 U.S. 528 (1985).

27. Elder Witt, *A Different Justice: Reagan and the Supreme Court* (Washington, D.C.: Congressional Quarterly Press, 1986), p. 133.

28. Neil A. Lewis, "Solicitor General's Career Advances at Intersection of Law and Politics," *New York Times*, 1 June 1990, p. A11.

29. Perry, *Deciding to Decide*, p. 286.

30. Michael Kirkland, *Court Hears 'Subordinate' Speech Debate*, UPI, 1 December 1993, available in Internet News Bulletin Board.

31. "Rising Fixed Opinions," *New York Times*, 22 February 1988, p. 14.

32. Jeffrey A. Segal and Harold J. Spaeth, *The Supreme Court and the Attitudinal Model* (Cambridge: Cambridge University Press, 1993).

33. Jeffrey A. Segal and Albert D. Cover, "Ideological Values and the Votes of U.S. Supreme Court Justices," *American Political Science Review* 83 (1989), pp. 557–565; Tracy E. George and Lee Epstein, "The Nature of Supreme Court Decision Making," *American Political Science Review* 86 (1992), pp. 323–337.

34. Stuart Taylor, Jr., "Lifting of Secrecy Reveals Earthy Side of Justices," *New York Times*, 22 February 1988, p. A16.

35. *Chicago Tribune*, 6 June 1990, Glen Elasser, "Courting Justice," Tempo, p. 1.

36. Stuart Taylor, Jr., "Brennan: 30 Years and the Thrill Is Not Gone," *New York Times*, 16 April 1986, p. B8.

37. Thomas G. Walker, Lee Epstein, and William J. Dixon, "On the Mysterious Demise of Consensual Norms in the United States Supreme Court," *Journal of Politics* 50 (1988), pp. 361–389.

38. See, for example, Walter F. Murphy, *Elements of Judicial Strategy* (Chicago: University of Chicago Press, 1964); and Bob Woodward and Scott Armstrong, *The Brethren* (New York: Simon & Schuster, 1979).

39. Henry J. Abraham, *Justices and Presidents: A Political History of Appointments to the Supreme Court*, 2d ed. (New York: Oxford University Press, 1985), pp. 183–185.

40. Stephen L. Wasby, *The Supreme Court in the Federal Judicial System*, 3d ed. (Chicago: Nelson-Hall, 1988), p. 241.

41. Wasby.

42. Schwartz, *Unpublished Opinions*, pp. 446–447.

43. Lawrence Baum, *American Courts: Process and Policy*, 3d ed. (Boston: Houghton Mifflin, 1994), pp. 114–129.

44. Paul Barrett, "More Minorities, Women Named to U.S. Courts." *Wall Street Journal*, 23 December 1993, p. B1.

45. Wasby, *Supreme Court*, pp. 107–110.

46. Sheldon Goldman, "Bush's Judicial Legacy: The Final Imprint," *Judicature* 76 (June 1993), p. 295.

47. Peter G. Fish, "John J. Parker," in *Dictionary of American Biography*, supp. 6, 1956–1980 (New York: Scribner's, 1980), p. 494.

48. *Congressional Quarterly's Guide to the U.S. Supreme Court*, 2d ed. (Washington, D.C.: Congressional Quarterly, 1990), pp. 655–656.

49. Ibid., pp. 878–890.

50. Maureen Daud, "The Supreme Court: Conservative Black Judge, Clarence Thomas, Named to Marshall's Court Seat," *New York Times*, 2 July 1991, pp. A1, A16.

51. Timothy M. Phelps and Helen Winternitz, *Capitol Games: Clarence Thomas, Anita Hill and the Story of a Supreme Court Nomination* (New York: Hyperion, 1992); David Brock, *The Real*

Anita Hill (New York: Free Press, 1992).

52. Paul Wice, *Judges & Lawyers: The Human Side of Justice* (New York: HarperCollins, 1991).

53. American Bar Foundation, *Lawyer Statistical Report* (1990).

54. Laura Duncan, "Although Law School Enrollment is Down Slightly, Minority Numbers Increase," CH. DAILY L. BULL., 5 March 1993, p. 3.

55. Bureau of Labor Statistics, Occupational Outlook Handbook, 1986–1987 (Washington, D.C.: U.S. Government Printing Office, 1986).

56. Laura Duncan, "Law Firms 'Freeze on Associates' Starting Salaries Unabated," CH. DAILY L. BULL., 14 July 1993, p. 1.

57. Wice, *Judges & Lawyers*, pp. 99–109.

58. Ken Emerson, "When Legal Titans Clash," *New York Times Magazine,* 22 April 1990, p. 66 (statement attributed to Charles Fried).

59. Nicholas O. Berry, "Of Lawyers' Work, There Is No End," *New York Times,* 28 December 1985, p. 19.

60. Baum, *American Courts*, p. 186.

61. James Eisenstein, *Attorneys for the Government* (Baltimore: Johns Hopkins University Press, 1980), p. 204.

62. Brown v. Board of Education II, 349 U.S. 294 (1955).

63. Charles A. Johnson and Bradley C. Canon, *Judicial Policies: Implementation and Impact* (Washington, D.C.: Congressional Quarterly Press, 1984).

64. Planned Parenthood v. Casey, 112 S. Ct. 2791 (1992).

65. Alexander M. Bickel, *The Least Dangerous Branch* (Indianapolis: Bobbs-Merrill, 1962); and Robert A. Dahl, *Decision-Making in a Democracy: The Supreme Court as a National Policy-Maker,"* 6 J. PUB. L. 279 (1962).

66. William Mishler and Reginal S. Sheehan, "The Supreme Court as a Countermajoritarian Institution? The Impact of Public Opinion on Supreme Court Decisions," *American Political Science Review* 87 (1993), pp. 87–101.

67. Thomas R. Marshall, *Public Opinion and the Supreme Court*

(Boston: Unwin Hyman, 1989).

68. Ibid., pp. 192–193; Gerald N. Rosenberg, *The Hollow Hope: Can Courts Bring About Social Change?* (Chicago: University of Chicago Press, 1991).

69. William J. Brennan, Jr., *State Supreme Court Judge Versus United States Supreme Court Justice: A Change in Function and Perspective,* 19 U. FL. L. REV. 225 (1966).

70. G. Alan Tarr and M. C. Porter, *State Supreme Courts in State and Nation* (New Haven, Conn.: Yale University Press, 1988), pp. 206–209.

71. Dennis Hevesi, "New Jersey Court Protects Trash from Police Searches," *New York Times,* 19 July 1990, p. A9.

72. Baum, *American Courts,* p. 319–347.

Chapter 15/ Order and Civil Liberties / pp. 508–551

1. Learned Hand, *The Bill of Rights* (Boston: Atheneum, 1958), p. 1.

2. Leonard W. Levy, *The Establishment Clause: Religion and the First Amendment* (New York: Macmillan, 1986); Leo Pfeffer, *Church, State, and Freedom* (Boston: Beacon, 1953); and Leonard W. Levy, "The Original Meaning of the Establishment Clause of the First Amendment," in *Religion and the State,* ed. James E. Wood, Jr. (Waco, Texas: Baylor University Press, 1985), pp. 43–83.

3. Garry Wills, *Under God: Religion and American Politics* (New York: Simon & Schuster, 1990); Barry A. Kosmin and Seymour P. Lachman, *One Nation Under God: Religion in Contemporary American Society* (New York: Harmony Books, 1993).

4. Reynolds v. United States, 98 U.S. 145 (1879).

5. Everson v. Board of Education, 330 U.S. 236 (1947).

6. Board of Education v. Allen, 392 U.S. 236 (1968).

7. Lemon v. Kurtzman, 403 U.S. 602 (1971).

8. Lynch v. Donnelly, 465 U.S. 668 (1984).

9. County of Allegheny v. ACLU Greater Pittsburgh Chapter, 109 S. Ct. 3086 (1989).

10. Slip op. 93–517 (decided 27 June 1994).

11. "Bill Signed to Keep Hasidic School Open," *New York Times,* 9 July 1994, p. 16.

12. Engle v. Vitale, 260 U.S. 421 (1962).

13. Abington School District v. Schempp, 364 U.S. 203 (1963).

14. Lee v. Weisman, 505 U.S. (1992).

15. Wallace v. Jaffree, 472 U.S. 38 (1985).

16. Board of Education v. Mergens, 497 U.S. (1990).

17. Michael W. McConnell, *The Origins and Historical Understanding of Free Exercise of Religion,* 103 HAR. L. REV. 1409 (1990).

18. Minersville School District v. Gobitis, 310 U.S. 586 (1940).

19. David Margolick, "Pledge Dispute Evokes Bitter Memories," *New York Times,* 11 September 1988, p. A1.

20. West Virginia State Board of Education v. Barnette, 319 U.S. 624 at 642 (1943).

21. Sherbert v. Verner, 374 U.S. 398 (1963).

22. McConnell, *Origins and Historical Understanding.*

23. Employment Division v. Smith, 110 S. Ct. 1595 (1990).

24. Peter Steinfels, "Clinton Signs Law Protecting Religious Practices," 16 November 1993, *New York Times,* p. A18.

25. Laurence Tribe, *Treatise on American Constitutional Law,* 2d ed. (St. Paul, Minn.: West, 1988), p. 566.

26. Zechariah Chafee, *Free Speech in the United States* (Cambridge, Mass.: Harvard University Press, 1941).

27. Leonard W. Levy, *The Emergence of a Free Press* (New York: Oxford University Press, 1985).

28. Mark Twain, *Following the Equator* (Hartford, Conn.: American Publishing, 1897).

29. Schenck v. United States, 249 U.S. 46 at 52 (1919).

30. Abrams v. United States 250 U.S. 616 at 630 (1919).

31. Gitlow v. New York, 268 U.S. 652 (1925).

32. Dennis v. United States, 341 U.S. 494 (1951).

33. Brandenburg v. Ohio, 395 U.S. 444 (1969).

34. Tinker v. Des Moines Independent County School District, 393 U.S. 503 at 508 (1969).

35. United States v. Eichman, 110 S. Ct. 2404 (1990).

36. Linda Greenhouse, "Supreme Court Voids Flag Law," *New York Times*, 12 June 1990, p. A1.

37. Barnes v. Glen Theatre 111 S. Ct. 2456 (1991).

38. Chaplinsky v. New Hampshire, 315 U.S. 568 (1942).

39. Terminiello v. Chicago, 337 U.S. 1 at 37 (Jackson, J., dissenting).

40. Cohen v. California, 403 U.S. 15 (1971).

41. 403 U.S., at 25.

42. Roth v. United States, 354 U.S. 477 (1957).

43. Jacobellis v. Ohio, 378 U.S. 184 at 197 (Stewart, J., concurring).

44. Miller v. California, 415 U.S. 15 (1973).

45. "The Cincinnati Obscenity Trial and What Makes Photos Art," *New York Times*, 18 October 1990, p. B1.

46. Donald Alexander Downs, *The New Politics of Pornography* (Chicago: University of Chicago Press, 1989) pp. 95–143.

47. American Booksellers Ass'n v. Hudnut, 598 F. Supp. 1316 (1984).

48. New York Times v. Sullivan, 376 U.S. 254 (1964).

49. Hustler Magazine v. Falwell, 485 U.S. 46 (1988).

50. Near v. Minnesota, 283 U.S. 697 (1931).

51. For a detailed account of *Near*, see Fred W. Friendly, *Minnesota Rag* (New York: Random House, 1981).

52. New York Times v. United States, 403 U.S. 713 (1971).

53. Branzburg v. Hayes, 408 U.S. 665 (1972).

54. Zurcher v. Stanford Daily, 436 U.S. 547 (1978).

55. Hazelwood School District v. Kuhlmeier, 484 U.S. 280 (1988).

56. United States v. Cruikshank, 92 U.S. 542 (1876); *Constitution of the United States of America: Annotated and Interpreted* (Washington, D.C.: U.S. Government Printing Office, 1973), p. 1031.

57. DeJonge v. Oregon, 299 U.S. 353 at 364 (1937).

58. Barron v. Baltimore, 7 U.S. (1 Pet.) 243 (1833).

59. Chicago B. & O. R. v. Chicago, 166 U.S. 226 (1897).

60. *Gitlow*, 268 U.S. at 666 (1925).

61. Palko v. Connecticut, 302 U.S. 319 (1937).

62. Duncan v. Louisiana, 391 U.S. 145 (1968).

63. McNabb v. United States, 318 U.S. 332 (1943).

64. Baldwin v. New York, 399 U.S. 66 (1970).

65. Anthony Lewis, *Gideon's Trumpet* (New York: Random House, 1964).

66. Gideon v. Wainwright, 372 U.S. 335 (1963).

67. Miranda v. Arizona, 384 U.S. 486 (1966).

68. Wolf v. Colorado, 338 U.S. 225 (1949).

69. Mapp v. Ohio, 307 U.S. 643 (1961).

70. United States v. Leon, 468 U.S. 897 (1984).

71. California v. Greenwood, 486 U.S. 35 (1988).

72. James v. Illinois, 110 S. Ct. 648 (1990).

73. Paul Brest, *Processes of Constitutional Decision-making* (Boston: Little, Brown, 1975), p. 708.

74. Griswold v. Connecticut, 381 U.S. 479 (1965).

75. Roe v. Wade, 410 U.S. 113 (1973).

76. See John Hart Ely, *The Wages of Crying Wolf: A comment on Roe v. Wade*, 82 YALE. L. J. 920 (1973).

77. Interview with Justice Harry Blackmun, ABC "Nightline," 2 December 1993.

78. Webster v. Reproductive Health Services, 492 U.S. 490 (1989).

79. Hodgson v. Minnesota, 110 S. Ct. 2926 (1990); Ohio v. Akron Center for Reproductive Health, 110 S. Ct. 2972 (1990).

80. Planned Parenthood v. Casey, 505 U.S. (1992).

81. Ruth Bader Ginsburg, *Some Thoughts on Autonomy and Equality in Relation to* Roe v. Wade, 63 N. C. L. REV. 375 (1985).

82. Stuart Taylor, "Supreme Court Hears Case on Homosexual Rights," Section A, *New York Times*, 1 April 1986, p. 24.

83. Bowers v. Hardwick, 478 U.S. 186 (1986).

84. Linda Greenhouse, "Washington Talk: When Second Thoughts Come Too Late," Section A, p. 14.

New York Times, 5 November 1990, p. A9.

85. Learned Hand, "The Contribution of an Independent Judiciary to Civilization," in *The Spirit of Liberty: Papers and Addresses of Learned Hand*, ed. Irving Dilliard, 3d ed. (New York: Alfred A. Knopf, 1960), p. 164.

Chapter 16 / Equality and Civil Rights / pp. 552–590

1. Johnson v. Transportation Agency, Santa Clara County, 480 U.S. 616 (1987).

2. Howard Schuman, Charlotte Steeh, and Lawrence Bobo, *Racial Attitudes in America: Trends and Interpretations* (Cambridge, Mass.: Harvard University Press, 1985); Sidney Verba and Gary R. Orren, *Equality in America: The View from the Top* (Cambridge, Mass.: Harvard University Press, 1985), especially pp. 1–51.

3. *The Gallup Monthly Poll*, August 1991, p. 56; Paul M. Sniderman and Thomas Piazza, *The Scar of Race* (Cambridge, Mass.: Belknap Press of Harvard University Press, 1993) pp. 133–134.

4. The Slaughterhouse Cases, 68 (1 Wall.) 36 (1873).

5. United States v. Cruikshank, 92 U.S. 542 (1876).

6. United States v. Reese, 12 U.S. 214 (1876).

7. Civil Rights Cases, 109 U.S. 3 (1883).

8. Mary Beth Norton et al., *A People and a Nation: A History of the United States*, 3d ed. (Boston: Houghton Mifflin, 1990), p. 490.

9. Plessy v. Ferguson, 163 U.S. 537 (1896).

10. Plessy, 163 U.S. at 562 (Harlan, J., dissenting).

11. Cummings v. County Board of Education, 175 U.S. 528 (1899).

12. Missouri ex rel. Gaines v. Canada, 305 U.S. 337 (1938).

13. Sweatt v. Painter, 339 U.S. 629 (1950).

14. McLaurin v. Oklahoma State Regents, 339 U.S. 637 (1950).

15. Brown v. Board of Education, 347 U.S. 487 (1954).

16. Brown v. Board of Education, 347 U.S. 487, 495 (1954).

17. Brown v. Board of Education, 347 U.S. 487, 494 (1954).

18. Bolling v. Sharpe, 347 U.S. 497 (1954).
19. Brown v. Board of Education II, 349 U.S. 294 (1955).
20. Jack W. Peltason, *Fifty-Eight Lonely Men*, rev. ed. (Urbana: University of Illinois Press, 1971).
21. Alexander v. Holmes County Board of Education, 369 U.S. 19 (1969).
22. Swann v. Charlotte-Mecklenberg County Schools, 402 U.S. 1 (1971).
23. Milliken v. Bradley, 418 U.S. 717 (1974).
24. Richard Kluger, *Simple Justice* (New York: Alfred A. Knopf, 1976), p. 753.
25. Taylor Branch, Parting the Waters: America in the King Years, 1955–1963 (New York: Simon & Schuster, 1988), p. 3.
26. Ibid., p. 14.
27. Ibid., p. 271.
28. Norton, et al., *People and a Nation*, p. 943.
29. Heart of Atlanta Motel v. United States, 379 U.S. 241 (1964).
30. Katzenbach v. McClung, 379 U.S. 294 (1964).
31. But see Abigail M. Thernstrom, *Whose Vote Counts? Affirmative Action and Minority Voting Rights* (Cambridge, Mass.: Harvard University Press, 1987).
32. Grove City College v. Bell, 465 U.S. 555 (1984).
33. Richmond v. J.A. Croson Co., 488 U.S. 469 (1989).
34. Martin v. Wilks, 490 U.S. 755 (1989); Wards Cove Packing Co. v. Atonio, 490 U.S. 642 (1989); Patterson v. McLean Credit Union, 491 U.S. 164 (1989); Price Waterhouse v. Hopkins, 490 U.S. 228 (1989); Lorance v. AT&T Technologies, 490 U.S. 900 (1990); and EEOC v. Arabian American Oil Co., 499 U.S. (1991).
35. Saint Francis College v. Al-Khazraji, 481 U.S. 604 (1987).
36. Dee Brown, *Bury My Heart at Wounded Knee: An Indian History of the American West* (New York: Holt, Rinehart & Winston, 1971).
37. Francis Paul Prucha, *The Great Father: The United States Government and the American Indian*, vol. 2 (Lincoln: University of Nebraska Press, 1984).
38. Rufus P. Browning, Dale Rogers Marshall, and David H. Tabb, *Protest Is Not Enough* (Berkeley:

University of California Press, 1984); "Hispanics Gain Members, Power," *Congressional Quarterly Weekly Report*, 2 January 1993, p. 7.
39. Phil Duncan, "Minority Districts Fail to Enhance Turnout," *Congressional Quarterly Weekly Report*, 23 March 1993, p. 798.
40. Larry Reynolds, "ADA Complaints Are Not What Experts Expected," *HR Focus* 70 (November 1993), 1.
41. Cited in Martin Gruberg, *Women in American Politics* (Oshkosh, Wisc.: Academic Press, 1968), p. 4.
42. Bradwell v. State, 68 (1 8345 Wall.) 130 (1873).
43. Muller v. Oregon, 208 U.S. 412 (1908).
44. International Union, United Automobile, Aerospace and Agricultural Implement Workers of America v. Johnson Controls, Inc., 111 S. Ct. 1196 (1991).
45. Minor v. Happersett, 21 Wall. 162 88 U.S. (1875).
46. John H. Aldrich, et al., *American Government: People, Institutions, and Policies* (Boston: Houghton Mifflin, 1986), p. 618.
47. Reed v. Reed, 404 U.S. 71 (1971).
48. Frontiero v. Richardson, 411 U.S. 677 (1973).
49. Craig v. Borden, 429 U.S. 190 (1976).
50. Paul Weiler, *The Wages of Sex: The Uses and Limits of Comparable Worth*, 99 Harv. L. Rev. 1728 (June 1986); Paula England, *Comparable Worth: Theories and Evidence* (New York: Aldine de Gruyter, 1992).
51. J.E.B. v. T.B. slip op. No. 92–1239 (1994).
52. Jane J. Mansbridge, *Why We Lost the ERA* (Chicago: University of Chicago Press, 1986).
53. Melvin I. Urofsky, *A March of Liberty* (New York: Alfred A. Knopf, 1988), p. 902.
54. Harris v. Forklift Systems, 510 U.S. (1993). No. 92-1168 slip op. at (1993).
55. *Time*, 6 July 1987, p. 91.
56. *Facts on File* 206B2 (4 June 1965).
57. As quoted in Melvin I. Urofsky, *A Conflict of Rights: The Supreme Court and Affirmative Action* (New York: Scribner's, 1991), p. 17.
58. Ibid., p. 29.

59. Thomas Sowell, *Preferential Policies: An International Perspective* (New York: Morrow, 1990), pp. 103–105.
60. Regents of the University of California v. Bakke, 438 U.S. 265 (1978).
61. Steven N. Keith, Robert M. Bell, and Albert P. Williams, *Assessing the Outcome of Affirmative Action in Medical Schools* (Santa Monica, Calif.: Rand, 1987).
62. United Steelworkers of America, AFL-CIO v. Weber, 443 U.S. 193 (1979).
63. Firefighters v. Stotts, 467 U.S. 561 (1984).
64. Wygant v. Jackson Board of Education, 106 S. Ct. 1842 (1986).
65. Local 28 of the Sheet Metal Workers' International Association v. EEOC, 478 U.S. 421 (1986).
66. Johnson, 480 U.S. 616.

Chapter 17 / Policymaking / p. 593–621

1. Transcript from "20/20," January 14, 1994; Dana Wilkie, "Three Strikes and You're Out," *San Diego Union-Tribune*, 6 February 1994, p. A1; Elizabeth Glieck and Laird Harrison, "Slamming the Prison Door," *People*, 7 February 1994, p. 51; James Richardson, " 'Three Strikes' Supporters Divided," *Sacramento Bee*, 12 February 1994, p. A4; Anne Krueger, "Officials Split on 3 Strikes," *San Diego Union-Tribune*, 13 February 1994, p. B1.
2. U.S. Bureau of the Census, *Statistical Abstract of the United States*, 1993 (Washington, D.C.: U.S. Government Printing Office, 1993), p. 334.
3. Catalina Camia, "As Interior Filibuster Continues, Risks for Westerners Grow," *Congressional Quarterly Weekly Report*, 30 October 1993, pp. 2957–2959.
4. For one example, see Randall B. Ripley and Grace A. Franklin, *Congress, the Bureaucracy, and Public Policy*, 5th ed. (Pacific Grove, Calif.: Brooks/Cole, 1991).
5. The policymaking process can be depicted in many ways. One approach, a bit more elaborate than this, is James E. Anderson, *Public*

Policymaking, 2d ed. (Boston: Houghton Mifflin, 1994), p. 37.

6. Roger W. Cobb and Charles D. Elder, *Participation in American Politics*, 2d ed. (Baltimore: Johns Hopkins University Press, 1983), p. 14.

7. Ibid., p. 84.

8. Anne N. Costain, *Inviting Women's Rebellion* (Baltimore: Johns Hopkins University Press, 1992).

9. Barbara J. Nelson, *Making an Issue of Child Abuse* (Chicago: University of Chicago Press, 1984), p. 13.

10. Frank D. Baumgartner and Bryan D. Jones, *Agendas and Instability in American Politics* (Chicago: University of Chicago Press, 1993), pp. 59–82.

11. Robert Pear, "U.S. Proposes Rules To Bar Obstacles for the Disabled," *New York Times*, 22 January 1991, p. A1.

12. Peter C. Bishop and Augustus J. Jones, Jr., "Implementing the Americans with Disability Act of 1990: Assessing the Variables of Success," *Public Administration Review* 53 (March/April 1993), p. 126.

13. Thomas W. Church and Robert T. Nakamura, *Cleaning Up the Mess* (Washington, D.C.: Brookings Institution, 1993).

14. "For California: A Political Fix," *New York Times*, 18 March 1991, p. A14.

15. Margaret Weir, *Politics and Jobs* (Princeton, N.J.: Princeton University Press, 1992), p. 170.

16. Kent E. Portney, *Approaching Public Policy Analysis* (Englewood Cliffs, N.J.: Prentice-Hall, 1986), p. 46.

17. David J. Armor, "The Evidence on Busing," *Public Interest* 28 (Summer 1972), pp. 90–126.

18. Thomas F. Pettigrew et al., "Busing: A Review of the Evidence," *Public Interest* 30 (Winter 1973), p. 106.

19. W. John Moore, "Tribal Imperatives," *National Journal*, 9 June 1990, pp. 1396–1401.

20. John E. Yang and Paul M. Barrett, "Drug Issue Triggers Washington Habit: Turf Wars in Congress, Administration," *Wall Street Journal*, August 11, 1989, p. A5.

21. Ibid.

22. Philip J. Hilts, "Panel Is Created To Speed Effort on AIDS Drugs," *New York Times*, 1 December 1993, p. A18.

23. Alfred Marcus, "Environmental Protection Agency," in *The Politics of Regulation*, ed. James Q. Wilson (New York: Basic Books, 1980), p. 267.

24. Jeffrey M. Berry and Kent E. Portney, "Centralizing Regulatory Control and Interest Group Access: The Quayle Council on Competitiveness," in *Interest Group Politics*, 4th ed., eds. Allan J. Cigler and Burdett A. Loomis (Washington, D.C.: Congressional Quarterly Press, forthcoming).

25. Bob Davis, "Clinton Orders New Regulatory Process in Effort To Reduce Influence-Peddling," *Wall Street Journal*, 1 October 1993, p. A2.

26. On recentralization, see Roger H. Davidson, "The New Centralization on Capitol Hill," paper delivered at the annual meeting of the Midwest Political Science Association, Chicago, April 1988.

27. On the role of think tanks and outside experts, see James A. Smith, *The Idea Brokers* (New York: Free Press, 1991).

28. Hugh Heclo, "Issue Networks and the Executive Establishment," in *The New American Political System*, ed. Anthony King (Washington, D.C.: American Enterprise Institute, 1978), p. 103.

29. John P. Heinz, Edward O. Laumann, Robert L. Nelson, and Robert H. Salisbury, *The Hollow Core* (Cambridge, Mass.: Harvard University Press, 1993).

30. Douglass Cater, *Power in Washington* (New York: Vintage Books, 1964), p. 18.

31. Although the subgovernment concept has fallen on hard times, some political scientists have tried to adapt it to contemporary politics. See Daniel McCool, "Subgovernments as Determinants of Political Viability," *Political Science Quarterly* 105 (Summer 1990), pp. 269–293.

32. Jeffrey M. Berry, "Subgovernments, Issue Networks, and Political Conflict," in *Remaking American Politics*, ed. Richard A.

Harris and Sidney M. Milkis (Boulder, Colo.: Westview, 1989), pp. 239–260.

33. For a brief overview of the evolution of AT&T and government regulation, see Robert W. Crandall, *After the Breakup* (Washington, D.C.: Brookings Institution, 1991), pp. 16–42.

34. This account is based on Steven Coll, *The Deal of the Century* (New York: Atheneum, 1986); and Peter Temin with Louis Galambos, *The Fall of the Bell System* (New York: Cambridge University Press, 1987).

35. See Martha Derthick and Paul J. Quirk, *The Politics of Deregulation* (Washington, D.C.: Brookings Institution, 1985); and Robert Britt Horwitz, *The Irony of Regulatory Reform* (New York: Oxford University Press, 1989).

36. For an analysis of the telecommunications issue network as it existed in the late 1980s, see Jeffrey M. Berry, *The Interest Group Society*, 2d ed. (Glenview, Ill.: Scott, Foresman/Little Brown, 1989), pp. 189–193.

37. Daniel Pearl, "Gore Says Telecommunications Laws Need Easing, But 'Safety Net' To Stay," *Wall Street Journal*, 22 December 1993, p. B6.

38. Allen R. Myerson, "A Corporate Man and a Cable King," *New York Times*, 14 October 1993, p. D11.

39. Jeffrey M. Berry, "The Dynamic Qualities of Issue Networks," paper to be presented at the annual meeting of the American Political Science Association, New York, September 1994.

40. For an alternative perspective, see James A. Thurber, "Dynamics of Policy Subsystems in American Politics," in *Interest Group Politics*, 3d ed., eds. Allan J. Cigler and Burdett A. Loomis (Washington, D.C.: Congressional Quarterly Press, 1991), pp. 319–343.

41. Heinz, Laumann, Nelson, and Salisbury, *The Hollow Core*.

42. Heclo, "Issue Networks," p. 105.

43. John M. Blair, *The Control of Oil* (New York: Pantheon, 1976), pp. 354–370.

44. Robert H. Salisbury and Paul Johnson, "Who You Know Versus What You Know," *American*

Journal of Political Science 33 (February 1989), pp. 175–195.

45. Thomas B. Edsall, "Republican Lobbyists Expanding, Advantages Seen After Landslide," *Washington Post*, 16 December 1984, p. A10a.

46. John J. Fialka, "Former Defense Official Creates Firm To Lobby in Washington for Turkey," *Wall Street Journal*, 16 February 1989, p. A16.

47. Carl Brauer, "Tenure, Turnover, and Postgovernment Employment Trends of Presidential Appointees," in *The In-and-Outers*, ed. G. Calvin MacKenzie (Baltimore: Johns Hopkins University Press, 1987), pp. 181 and 189.

48. "Clinton Announces New Ethics Standards," *Congressional Quarterly Almanac, 1992* (Washington, D.C.: Congressional Quarterly Press, 1993), p. 62.

49. Richard L. Berke, "Many Will Escape Ethics Restriction," *New York Times*, 9 December 1992, p. A1.

50. Douglas Jehl, "Lobbying Rules for Ex-Officials at Issue Again," *New York Times*, 8 December 1993, p. A1.

51. Berry, "Subgovernments, Issue Networks."

Chapter 18 / Economic Policy / pp. 622–658

1. George Hager and David S. Cloud, "Democrats Tie Their Fate to Clinton's Budget Bill," *Congressional Quarterly Weekly Report*, 7 August 1993, p. 2122.

2. Ibid., p. 2127.

3. David S. Cloud, "Big Risk for Margolies-Mezvinsky," *Congressional Quarterly Weekly Report*, 7 August 1993, p. 2125.

4. David E. Rosenbaum, "Crucial Senator Backs Budget, Tipping Bill in Clinton's Favor," *New York Times*, 7 August 1993, p. A1.

5. Ibid.

6. Hager and Cloud, "Democrats Tie Their Fate," p. 2122.

7. George Hager, "1993 Deal: Remembrance of Things Past," *Congressional Quarterly Weekly Report*, 7 August 1993, p. 2131.

8. Lawrence Malkin, "In Financial Markets, All Eyes Are on the Fed," *International Herald Tribune*, 17 May 1994, pp. 1 and 4.

9. David Wessel, "Common Interest: The President and Fed Appear to Be in Step on Latest Rate Rise," *Wall Street Journal* 7 February 1994, p. A1. See also Lawrence Malkin, "Markets Satisfied as U.S. Rates Rise," *International Herald Tribune* 18 May 1994, pp. 1 and 6, and "Fed Chief Tries to Ease Fears in Senate on Rates," *International Herald Tribune*, 28–29 May 1994, p. 11.

10. Meg Vaillancourt, "Minehan Defends Fed Policy," *Boston Globe* 9 June 1994, p. A1.

11. N. Gregory Mankiw, "Symposium on Keynesian Economics Today," *Journal of Economic Perspectives*, 7 (Winter 1993), pp. 3–4. In his preface to four articles in the symposium, Mankiw says, "The literature that bears the label 'Keynesian' is broad, and it does not offer a single vision of how the economy behaves."

12. Louis Uchitelle, "Federal Reserve Trims Loan Costs to Spur Economy," *New York Times*, 1 May 1991, p. A1.

13. Wessel, "Common Interest," p. A5. See also David E. Rosenbaum, "Clinton Economic Team: An Island in a Sea of Troubles," *International Herald Tribune*, 28–29 May 1994, pp. 1 and 4.

14. Sylvia Nasar, "Economy's Happy Landing: No-Inflation Growth," *New York Times*, 27 January 1994, pp. A1 and C5.

15. Floyd Norris, "The Case of the Misbehaving Yield Curve," *International Herald Tribune*, 25 April 1994, p. 11.

16. Peter Passell, "Dollar Off, Growth Up—Go Figure: Inflation Is Unlikely," *International Herald Tribune*, 14–15 May 1994, p. 11.

17. Clifford Winston, "Economic Deregulation: Days of Reckoning for Microeconomists," *Journal of Economic Literature* 31 (September 1993), p. 1263.

18. Ibid., p. 1284.

19. Ibid., p. 1280.

20. Steven Waldman and Rich Thomas, "How Did It Happen?" *Newsweek*, 21 May 1990, p. 27.

21. Louis Uchitelle, "Off Course," *New York Times Magazine*, 1 September 1991, pp. 12ff.

22. Jonathan Rauch, Lawrence J. Haas, and Bruce Stokes, "Payment Deferred," *National Journal*, 14 May 1988, p. 1256.

23. Rosenbaum, "Clinton Economic Team," p. 4.

24. George Hager, "With Little Room to Maneuver, Bush Sets His Priorities," *Congressional Quarterly Weekly Report*, 9 February 1991, p. 336.

25. For the first point, see Lawrence J. Haas, "Unauthorized Action," *National Journal*, 2 January 1988, pp. 17–21. For the second, see George Hager, "New Rules on Taxes, Spending May Mean Budget Standoff," *Congressional Quarterly Weekly Report*, 26 January 1991, p. 237. The plight of the budget committees under the 1990 act is covered by George Hager, "Relevance of Budget Process Is Tricky Question on Hill," *Congressional Quarterly Weekly Report*, 20 April, 1991, pp. 962–968.

26. Richard A. Musgrave and Peggy B. Musgrave, *Public Finance in Theory and Practice*, 2d ed. (New York: McGraw-Hill, 1976), p. 42.

27. Kevin Phillips, *The Politics of Rich and Poor: Wealth and the American Electorate in the Reagan Aftermath* (New York: Random House, 1990), p. 78.

28. Sylvia Nasar, "Like the U.S., States Look to Affluent for More Taxes," *New York Times*, 21 March 1993, p. A18. See also, Sylvia Nasar, "Supply Side Goes by the Wayside," *New York Times*, 20 February 1993: p. A13.

29. Advisory Commission on Intergovernmental Relations, *Significant Features of Fiscal Federalism, 1981–1982* (Washington, D.C., 1983), p. 54; and David E. Rosenbaum, "A New Heave in Tax Tug-of-War," *New York Times*, 8 December 1992, p. C1.

30. Lawrence Mishel and David M. Frankel, *The State of Working America, 1990–91 Edition* (Washington, D.C.: Economic Policy Institute, 1990), p. 62. In 1994, however, many states enacted tax reductions both to improve their tax climate to attract

business and in reaction to the improving national economy. See Tom Redburn, "Many States Moving to Ease Property Tax Burdens," *New York Times,* 17 March 1994, p. A9.

31. George Hager, "House Budget Panel Leaves Clinton Plan Largely Intact," *Congressional Quarterly Weekly Report,* 5 March 1994, p. 525.

32. George Hager, "Clinton's Bid to Shift Priorities Constrained by Fiscal Limits," *Congressional Quarterly Weekly Report,* 12 February 1994, p. 287.

33. Center for Political Research, University of Michigan, *1992 National Election Study.* The twelve spending areas dealt with the environment, crime, schools, social security, food stamps, college study, the unemployed, science and technology, defense, aid to blacks, aid to the former USSR, and AIDS.

34. Fay Lomax Cook et al., *Convergent Perspectives on Social Welfare Policy: The Views from the General Public, Members of Congress, and AFDC Recipients* (Evanston, Ill.: Center for Urban Affairs and Policy Research, Northwestern University, 1988), Table 4-1.

35. B. Guy Peters, *The Politics of Taxation: A Comparative Perspective* (Cambridge, Mass.: Basil Blackwell, 1991), p. 228.

36. David S. Cloud, "Farm Bloc on the Defensive as Bills Move to Floor," *Congressional Quarterly Weekly Report,* 14 July 1990, pp. 2209–2212.

37. Joseph A. Pechman, "Who Paid the Taxes, 1966–1985? (Washington, D.C.: Brookings Institution, 1985).

38. Mishel and Frankel, *State of Working America,* pp. 178–179. The proportion of people living below the poverty line is also less if one uses the consumption of commodities as the measure of well being instead of before-tax income. See Daniel T. Slesnick, "Gaining Ground: Poverty in the Postwar United States," *Journal of Political Economy* 101 (1993), pp. 1–38.

39. But the rich received only 1 percent of their income in transfer payments, suffering a net loss from government. See Pechman, *Who Paid the Taxes?* p. 53. Families in the top 1 percent of income actually had their effective national tax rates drop from 31.7 percent in 1980 to 24.9 percent in 1985, before they were raised to 28.8 percent in 1992 after the 1990 tax increase. See Sylvia Nasar, "One Group Saw Relief: Richest 1%," *New York Times,* 1 October 1992, p. C2.

40. Pechman, *Who Paid the Taxes?,* p. 80.

41. Ibid., p. 73.

42. Ibid., p. 74.

43. Mishel and Frankel, *State of Working America,* pp. 37–39. See also Gary Burtless, ed., *A Future of Lousy Jobs? The Changing Structure of U.S. Wages* (Washington, D.C.: Brookings Institution, 1990), for discussions of the rise in women's earnings and the decline in lower-paid men's earnings. Other researchers have found that women's earnings have also accounted for increases in the "rich." See Sheldon Danziger, Peter Gottschalk, and Eugene Smolensky, "How the Rich Have Fared, 1973–87," *American Economic Association, Papers and Proceedings* 79 (May 1989), pp. 310–314.

44. Phillips, *Politics of Rich and Poor,* p. 11.

45. Ibid., p. 157. Somewhat different figures showing the same trend were reported by Sylvia Nasar, "The Rich Get Richer, But Never the Same Way Twice," *New York Times,* 16 August 1992, p. E3. She says there were 21 billionnaires in 1982 and 71 in 1991.

46. Phillips, *Politics of Rich and Poor,* p. 17.

47. Ibid., p. 83.

48. Rosenbaum, "A New Heave," p. C13.

49. Sylvia Nasar, "After Tax Changes of 80's, Burden Is No Lighter," *New York Times,* 1 October 1992, p. C1. See also R. C. Longworth, "Job fears Haunt Growing Economy," *Chicago Tribune,* 2 January 1994, pp. A1 and 10.

50. Charles F. Andrain, *Social Policies in Western Industrial Societies* (Berkeley: University of California Press, 1985), p. 194. See also Mishel and Frankel, *State of Working America,* pp. 260–261, for a discussion of three measures of inequality in disposable income in ten democratic countries. The United States is the least equal according to all three measures.

51. "Nation Top-Heavy with Wealth," *Chicago Tribune,* 19 July 1986, p. A1; and U.S. Bureau of the Census, U.S. Department of Commerce, *Statistical Abstract of the United States, 1993* (Washington, D.C.: U.S. Government Printing Office, 1993), p. 462. See also Bureau of the Census, "Household Wealth and Asset Ownership: 1988," *Current Population Reports,* Series P-70, No. 22 (December 1990).

52. Benjamin I. Page, *Who Gets What from Government?* (Berkeley: University of California Press, 1983), p. 213.

53. *New York Times,* 13 May 1983.

54. Peters, *The Politics of Taxation,* p. 168, which reported data for a 1987 survey.

55. *Public Opinion* 8 (February/March 1985), p. 27.

56. "Lotteries Are Now Used in 26 States for Revenue," *New York Times,* national edition, 16 February 1988, p. A8. See also Alan J. Karcher, *Lotteries* (New Brunswick, N.J.: Transaction Books, 1989).

57. R. C. Longworth, "In Europe, A Mighty Money Machine," *Chicago Tribune,* 16 April 1993, pp. 1 and 4, section 3.

Chapter 19 / Domestic Policy / pp. 659–695

1. Isabel Wilkerson, "First Born, Fast Grown: The Manful Life of Nicholas, 10," *New York Times,* 4 April 1993, Sect. 1, p. 1.

2. Karl Zinsmeister, "Growing Up Scared," *Atlantic Monthly,* June 1990, p. 49.

3. U.S. Social Security Administration, *Social Security Bulletin, Annual Statistical Supplement,* 1993, Table 3.A.1, p. 128; *Budget of the United States Government, FY 1995,* Historical Table 3.1, p. 42.

4. "The People, Press & Economics." *A Times Mirror Multi-Nation Study of Attitudes Toward U.S. Economic Issues* (The Gallup Organization, May 1989).

5. Thomas J. Anton, *American Federalism and Public Policy* (Philadelphia: Temple University Press, 1989).

6. Andrew Pollack, "Meeting Lays Bare the Abyss Between AIDS and Its Cure." *New York Times,* 12 August 1994, p. 1.

7. U.S. Centers for Disease Control and Prevention, *Morbidity and Mortality Weekly Report* 42 (19 November 1993), p. 1.

8. Amanda Brown, "AIDS Is Biggest Fear, Health Survey Shows," *Press Association News File,* 23 February 1993 (NEXIS).

9. Rebecca Kolberg, "Americans Worried Less About AIDS, Poll Says," *UPI,* 15 August 1989 (NEXIS).

10. *Budget of the United States Government, FY 1991,* p. 79.

11. Tamar Lewin, "Studies on Teen-Age Sex Cloud Condom Debate," *New York Times,* 8 February 1991, p. A10.

12. *1992 Sourcebook of Criminal Justice Statistics,* Table 2-86, p. 228 (Washington, D.C., 1993).

13. *Washington Post,* 23 August 1989, p. A22.

14. *1992 Sourcebook of Criminal Justice Statistics,* Table 2-90, pp. 230–31.

15. Ibid., Table 2-81, p. 227.

16. W. John Moore, "Rethinking Drugs," *National Journal,* 2 February 1991, pp. 267–271.

17. National Institute on Drug Abuse, *1992 National Household Survey on Drug Abuse: Main Findings,* pp. 19 and 53 (1993).

18. The history of drug abuse in America is based on David Musto, *The American Disease: The Origins of Narcotics Control,* rev. ed. (New York: Oxford University Press, 1987); and David T. Courtwright, *Dark Paradise: Opiate Addiction in America Before 1940* (Cambridge, Mass.: Harvard University Press, 1982.)

19. Elaine Sciolino, "State Department Report Labels Nigeria Major Trafficker of Drugs to U.S.," *New York Times,* 5 April 1994, p. A1.

20. *Chicago Tribune,* 11 February 1990, sec. 1, p. 1.

21. *Budget of the United States, 1995,* p. 208.

22. *1992 Sourcebook of Criminal Justice Statistics,* Table 2-86, p. 228.

23. "Big John," *Time,* 2 March 1987, p. 19.

24. "Poll Shows Support for Treatment, Prevention," *Alcoholism & Drug Abuse Week* 6 (21 March 1994), p. 2.

25. National Institute on Drug Abuse, *1990 National Household Survey on Drug Abuse: Highlights,* pp. 85 and 99. (Washington, 1991).

26. Jann S. Wenner, "Drug War: A New Vietnam?" *New York Times,* 23 June 1990, p. 23.

27. *New York Times,* 27 November 1989, p. 9; *The Gallup Report* (January 1990), pp. 2–9.

28. Linda L. M. Bennett and Stephen Earl Bennett, *Living with Leviathan: Americans Coming to Terms with Big Government* (Lawrence: University Press of Kansas, 1990), pp. 21–24.

29. Shapiro v. Thompson, 396 U.S. 618 (1969).

30. George Gallup, Jr., *The Gallup Poll, Public Opinion 1989* (Wilmington, Del.: Scholarly Resources, 1990), pp. 183–185.

31. I. A. Lewis and William Schneider, "Hard Times: The Public on Poverty," *Public Opinion* 8 (June–July 1985), p. 2.

32. U.S. Bureau of the Census, U.S. Department of Commerce, *Current Population Reports: Money Income and Poverty Status in the United States, 1989,* Series P-60, No. 168, pp. 5–7 (1990); Bureau of the Census, *Poverty in the United States, 1992* Series P-60, No. 185, p. xvii (1993).

33. Bennett and Bennett, *Living with Leviathan,* p. 142.

34. D. Lee Bawden and John L. Palmer, "Social Policy: Challenging the Welfare State," in *The Reagan Record: An Assessment of America's Changing Domestic Priorities,* ed. John L. Palmer and Isabel V. Sawhill (Cambridge, Mass.: Ballinger, 1984), pp. 177–215.

35. Paul C. Light, *Artful Work: The Politics of Social Security Reform* (New York: Random House, 1985), p. 63.

36. *Social Security Bulletin, Annual Statistical Supplement, 1993,* p. 13.

37. Martha Derthick, *Policymaking for Social Security* (Washington, D.C.: Brookings Institution, 1979), pp. 346–347.

38. Julie Kosterlitz, "Who Will Pay?" *National Journal,* 8 March 1985, pp. 570–574.

39. U.S. Bureau of the Census, U.S. Department of Commerce, *Statistical Abstract of the United States, 1988* (Washington, D.C.: U.S. Government Printing Office, 1988), pp. 17, 249.

40. Derthick, *Policymaking,* p. 335.

41. Paul Starr, *The Social Transformation of American Medicine* (New York: Basic Books, 1982), pp. 279–280.

42. Ibid., p. 287.

43. Theodore Marmor, *The Politics of Medicare* (Chicago: Aldine, 1973).

44. *Social Security Bulletin,* p. 14.

45. Ibid.

46. Ibid., Table 2.C.1, p. 87.

47. Lawrence J. Haas, "Big-Ticket Restrictions," *National Journal,* 26 September 1987, p. 2413.

48. Bob Blendon, "The Gridlock Is Us," *New York Times,* 12 June 1994, Sect. 4, p. 3.

49. *Social Security Bulletin,* Table 3.E.8, p. 152.

50. U.S. Bureau of the Census, U.S. Department of Commerce, *Poverty in the United States, 1992* Series P-60, No. 185, p. ix (1993).

51. William Julius Wilson, *The Truly Disadvantaged: The Inner City, the Underclass, and Public Policy* (Chicago: University of Chicago Press, 1987).

52. *Social Security Bulletin,* p. 15.

53. *Work-Related Programs for Welfare Recipients* (Washington, D.C.: Congressional Budget Office, 1987).

54. Mickey Kaus, "Revenge of the Softheads," *New Republic,* 19 June 1989, p. 24.

55. "Pulling Families Out of Welfare Is Proving to Be an Elusive Goal," *New York Times,* 2 April 1990, p. A1.

56. Jeffrey L. Katz, "Clinton Plans Major Shift in the Lives of Poor People," *Congressional Quarterly Weekly Report,* 22 January 1994, p. 121.

57. Jason DeParle, "Welfare as We've Known It," *New York Times,* 19 June 1994, Sect. 4, p. 4.

58. Katz, "Clinton Plans Major Shift," p. 118.

59. *Social Security Bulletin, Annual Statistical Supplement, 1993,* Table 9.H.1, p. 332.

60. Lewis and Schneider, "Hard Times," pp. 3–7.

61. Gallup, *Gallup Poll,* pp. 183–185 (1990).

Chapter 20 / Global Policy / pp. 696–737

1. R. W. Apple, "34 Lands Proclaim a United Europe in Paris Charter," *New York Times,* 22 November 1990, p. 1.

2. Stockholm International Peace Research Institute, *SIPRI Yearbook of World Armaments and Disarmaments, 1992* (New York: Oxford University Press, 1992) pp. 424–56.

3. Stephen John Stedman, "The New Interventionists," in *Foreign Affairs* 72 (February, 1993), p. 7.

4. An ABC News–Washington Post poll taken in February 1993 found 70 percent agreeing with the statement, "Because the United States has limited resources and its own problems at home, it needs to reduce its involvement in world affairs." Only 27 percent agreed with the statement, "Because the United States is the world's strongest and richest country, it has the responsibility to take the lead in world affairs." "Opinion Outlook," *National Journal* 10 (April 1993), p. 894.

5. Alexis de Tocqueville, *Democracy in America* (Oxford: Oxford University Press, 1946), p. 161.

6. "X" [George F. Kennan], "The Sources of Soviet Conduct," *Foreign Affairs* 25 (July 1947), p. 575.

7. Quoted in Arthur M. Schlesinger, Jr., *A Thousand Days* (Boston: Houghton Mifflin, 1965), pp. 704–705.

8. Richard M. Nixon, *U.S. Foreign Policy for the 1970s: A New Strategy for Peace* (Washington, D.C.: U.S. Government Printing Office, 1970), p. 2.

9. Jimmy Carter, "State of the Union," January 23, 1980, *Public*

Papers of the Presidents of the United States (Washington, D.C.: U.S. Government Printing Office, 1981), p. 197.

10. See, for example, Francis Fukayama, *The End of History and the Last Man* (New York: The Free Press, 1992).

11. Daniel Deudney and G. John Ikenberry, "Who Won the Cold War?" *Foreign Policy* 87 (Summer 1992), pp. 128–138.

12. See for example, Paul Kennedy, *Preparing for the Twenty-First Century* (New York: Random House, 1993), especially Chap. 13.

13. Thomas Omestad, "Why Bush Lost," *Foreign Policy* 89 (Winter 1992–1993), pp. 70–81.

14. Quoted in Eric Schmitt, "Somalia Role: Why? U.S. Seeks Clear Rationale for Mission," *New York Times,* 27 August 1993, p. A10.

15. U.S. v. Curtiss-Wright Export Corporation, 299 U.S. 304 (1936).

16. Mary H. Cooper, "Treaty Ratification," *Editorial Research Reports,* 29 January 1988.

17. C. Herman Pritchett, "The President's Constitutional Position," in *Presidency Reappraised,* eds. Rexford Tugwell and Thomas Cronin (New York: Praeger, 1977), p. 23.

18. James Nathan and James Oliver, *Foreign Policy Making* (Boston: Little, Brown, 1983), p. 125.

19. "Duels over Dollars Shuffle," *Congressional Quarterly Weekly Report,* February 1990, p. 606.

20. Duncan Clarke, "Why State Can't Lead," *Foreign Policy* 66 (Spring 1987), pp. 128–142.

21. Harry Crosby (pseudonym), "Too at Home Abroad: Swilling Beer, Licking Boots and Ignoring the Natives with One of Jim Baker's Finest," *Washington Monthly,* September 1991, pp. 16–20.

22. James A. Nathan and James K. Oliver, *Foreign Policy Making and the American Political System,* 2d ed. (Boston: Little, Brown, 1987), p. 44.

23. Quoted in Schlesinger, *A Thousand Days,* p. 406.

24. Quoted in Rodney D. Griffin, "The New C.I.A.," *CQ Researcher,* 11 December 1992, p. 1084.

25. Richard K. Betts, "Analysis, War and Decision Making: Why

Intelligence Failures Are Inevitable," *World Politics* (October 1978), p. 61.

26. Loch K. Johnson, "Now That the Cold War Is Over, Do We Need the CIA?" *The Future of American Foreign Policy,* eds. Charles Kegley and Eugene Wittkopf (New York: St. Martin's Press, 1992), p. 306.

27. Council of State Governments, *State Administrative Officials Classified by Function, 1991–1992* (Lexington, Ky.: Council of State Governments), pp. 160–161.

28. Quoted in Robert Y. Shapiro and Benjamin I. Page, "Foreign Policy and Public Opinion," in *The New Politics of American Foreign Policy,* ed. David Deese (New York: St. Martin's Press, 1993), p. 216.

29. Thomas W. Graham, "Public Opinion and U.S. Foreign Policy Decision Making," in *The New Politics,* pp. 190–191.

30. William Schneider, "Peace and Strength: American Public Opinion on National Security," in *The Public and Atlantic Defense,* eds. Gregory Flynn and Hans Rattinger (Totowa, N.J.: Rowman and Allanheld, 1985). Ole Holsti and James Rosenau identify similar phenomena but use the alternate terminology in "The Structure of Foreign Policy Attitudes Among American Leaders," *Journal of Politics* 52 (February 1990), pp. 94–125, as well as in their earlier book, *American Leadership in World Affairs: Vietnam and the Breakdown of Consensus* (Boston: Allen & Unwin: 1984).

31. Graham, "Public Opinion and U.S. Foreign Policy Decision Making," in *The New Politics,* p. 192.

32. Ibid., p. 194; William Gamson and Andre Modigliani, "Knowledge and Foreign Policy Options: Some Models for Consideration," *Public Opinion Quarterly* 30 (Summer 1966), pp. 187–199; William Gamson and Andre Modigliani, *Untangling the Cold War* (Boston: Little, Brown, 1971).

33. Shapiro and Page, "Foreign Policy and Public Opinion," in *The New Politics,* p. 222.

34. Ibid., pp. 223–229.

35. John E. Rielly, "Public Opinion:

The Pulse of the '90s," *Foreign Policy* 82 (Spring 1991), pp. 79–96.

36. John H. Aldrich, John L. Sullivan, and Eugene Borgida, "Foreign Affairs and Issue Voting: Do Presidential Candidates Waltz Before a Blind Audience?" *American Political Science Review* 83 (March 1989), pp. 123–141.

37. Ibid., p. 136.

38. Graham, "Public Opinion and U.S. Foreign Policy Decision Making," in *The New Politics*, p. 199.

39. Ibid., p. 196.

40. Ibid.

41. George Stuteville, "By Aiding Sikhs, Burton Builds Coffers, 2d Constituency and Political Scorn," *Indianapolis Star*, 14 November 1993, p. 1.

42. John Judis, "Twilight of the Gods," *Wilson Quarterly*, 15 (Autumn 1991), p. 52.

43. Charles Kegley and Eugene Wittkopf, *American Foreign Policy: Pattern and Process*, 4th ed. (New York: St. Martin's Press, 1991), pp. 272–273; Lester Milbrath, "Interest Groups and Foreign Policy," in *Domestic Sources of Foreign Policy*, ed.

James Rosenau (New York: Free Press, 1967), pp. 231–252.

44. Kegley and Wittkopf, *American Foreign Policy*, p. 276.

45. Ibid., p. 310.

46. Donald Snow and Eugene Brown, *Puzzle Palace and Foggy Bottom: U.S. Foreign and Defense Policy-Making in the 1990s* (New York: St. Martin's Press, 1994), p. 170.

47. Ibid., pp. 170–173.

48. Lester Thurow, "When the Lending Stops," *New Perspectives Quarterly* (Fall 1987), p. 14; see also Kevin Phillips, *The Politics of Rich and Poor* (New York: Random House, 1990), Chap. 5.

49. "Competitiveness: Can This War Be Won?," *Time*, 1 April 1991, p. 59.

50. Paul Kennedy, *The Rise and Decline of the Great Powers* (New York: Random House, 1988); also Masahiro Sakamoto, "Pax Americana's Twin Deficits," *New Perspectives Quarterly* (Fall 1987); and Phillips, *The Politics of Rich and Poor*.

51. Daniel S. Papp, *Contemporary International Relations*, 4th ed. (New York: Macmillan, 1994), p. 420.

52. "Hills, in Japan, Stirs a Baby-Bottle Dispute," *New York Times*, 14 October 1989, p. 35.

53. See commentary by A. M. Rosenthal in the *New York Times* 31 March 1989, p. 35; also Kevin Kearns, "Economic Orthodoxies Offered U.S. Students Won't Prepare Them to Work in World Markets," *Chronicle of Higher Education*, 27 March 1991, p. B3.

54. Katie Hafner, "Does Industrial Policy Work? Lessons from Sematech," *New York Times*, 7 November 1993, p. F5.

55. Papp, *Contemporary International Relations*, p. 194.

56. Ibid., pp. 191–192; O.E.C.D., *World Development Report, 1992*, pp. 254–255.

57. Papp, *Contemporary International Relations*, pp. 557–558.

58. See President Clinton's remarks excerpted in "Clinton's Call: Avoid Isolating China on Trade and Rights," *New York Times*, 27 May 1994, p. A4.

59. Douglas Jehl, "No Wish to Jeopardize Billions in Trade and Many Jobs in U.S.," *New York Times*, 27 May 1994, p. A1.

Index to References

Index

Illustration Credits (continued from copyright page)

University Art Gallery, Trumbull Collection; **71:** Granger Collection; **72:** From the Collection of Gilcrease Museum, Tulsa, Oklahoma; **80:** Bettmann; **85:** Tracy W. McGregor Library, Manuscript Division, Special Collections Department, University of Virginia; **91:** Culver.

Chapter 4: **101 (Opener):** Bob Daemmrich/The Image Works; **103:** UPI/ Bettmann; **104** (left): Greg Smith/Sipa Press; **104** (right): William Berry/ Sygma; **109:** Liss/Gamma Liaison; **121:** International Museum of Photography; **123:** George Tames/The New York Times; **125:** Michael Schumann/SABA; **129:** Courtesy of the Mayor's Office, Las Cruces, N.M.; **129:** Katherine Karnow/Woodfin Camp; **129:** Phoebe Bell/Folio; **129:** Steve Leonard/Black Star; **133:** David Falconer/Tony Stone Images; **134:** Jim Schaefer/Sygma.

Chapter 5: **138 (Opener):** Chuck Savage/Stock Market; **140:** Susan May/ SABA; **141:** David Sams/Sipa Press; **145:** Bettmann; **148:** Bob Olson/The Picture Man; **151:** Bob Daemmrich/Stock Boston; **156:** Andrew Holbrooke; **161:** Robert Brenner/Photo Edit; **167:** Bob Riha/Gamma Liaison; **170:** The White House.

Chapter 6: **174 (Opener):** Spencer Grant/Stock Boston; **176:** Les Stone/ Sygma; **179:** Collection of Woody Gilman, Courtesy Life Picture Service; **182:** Culver; **183:** Bettmann; **191:** Jeffrey Markowitz/Sygma; **201:** Tina Gerson/Los Angeles Daily News.

Chapter 7: **212 (Opener):** David Martin/Wide World; **214:** Robb Kendrick; **216:** Division of Rare and Manuscript Collections, Cornell University, Carl A. Kroch Library; **216:** Bachrach Photography; **218:** UPI/Bettmann; **222:** Bob Daemmrich Photography; **225:** Bob Daemmrich/The Image Works; **227:** Denis Farrell/AP/Wide World; **232:** Brown Brothers; **232:** Library of Congress; **245:** AP/Wide World.

Chapter 8: **250 (Opener):** Porter Gifford/Gamma Liaison; **252:** Renato Rotolo/Gamma Liaison; **262:** Library of Congress; **270:** Wide World; **275:** David Stueber/Wide World.

Chapter 9: **285 (Opener):** Larry Downing/Woodfin Camp; **287:** Levy/ Gamma Liaison; **289:** Chromosohm/Sohm/Stock Boston; **301:** Bob Daemmrich; **304:** AP/Wide World; **310:** AP/Wide World.

Chapter 10: **322 (Opener):** Brad Markel/Gamma Liaison; **323:** Tom Meyer/San Francisco Chronicle; **330:** Severy photograph/The Bostonian Society; **331:** Mark Asnin/SABA; **331:** Robb Kendrick; **333:** Denis Paquin/AP/Wide World; **340:** Richard Bloom/© The National Journal; **342:** Michael Newman/Photo Edit; **345:** Terry Ashe/Gamma Liaison; **348:** Charles Moore/Black Star; **351:** Brad Markel/Gamma Liaison.

Chapter 11: **359 (Opener):** Paul Conklin/Photo Edit; **361:** Garry Trudeau/ Universal Press Syndicate; **363:** Kiplinger Washington Collection; **364:** ABC News; **369:** Mark Hall/Reuters/Bettmann; **374:** Brad Markel/Gamma Liaison; **378** (top): Alexandra Avakian/Woodfin Camp; **378** (bottom): Brad Markel/Gamma Liaison; **381:** George Tames; **385:** White House Staff photo; **387:** Paul Conklin; **391:** Terry Ashe/Gamma Liaison.

Chapter 12: **396 (Opener):** Bob Llewellyn; **398** (right): Greg Gibson/ AP/Wide World; **398** (left): Arkansas Daily Gazette/Sipa Press; **400:** Franklin D. Roosevelt Library; **402:** Bettmann; **404:** Larry Downing/ Woodfin Camp; **410:** Ron Edmonds/Wide World; **414:** David Burnett/Contact Press Images; **417:** Martin Simon/SABA; **417:** Dennis Brack/Black Star; **426:** © B. Markel/Liaison; **429:** Luke Frazza/Agence Presse France; **430:** Lyndon Baines Johnson Library.

Chapter 13: **433 (Opener):** Louis Psihoyos/Matrix; **435:** Dennis Brack/Black Star; **437:** Christopher Morris/Black Star; **443:** Dennis Brack/Black Star; **447:** Steve Leonard/Black Star; **449:** J. Scott Applewhite/Wide World; **451:** Bettmann; **452:** Wilfred Bauer/Black Star; **457:** Lisa Quinones/Black Star; **460:** Rick Maiman/Sygma.

Chapter 14: **465 (Opener):** Ron Watts/Black Star; **467:** Karsh, Ottawa/Woodfin Camp; **469:** The National Portrait Gallery, Smithsonian Institution/Art Resource; **476:** Bettmann; **481:** Paul Conklin; **482:** Bettmann; **486–487:** Paul Conklin; **490:** Leighton Mark/UPI; **492:** Val Massenga/© Chicago Tribune Magazine; **497:** Bill Garner; **502:** New York Court of Appeals.

Chapter 15: **508 (Opener):** Paul Conklin/Photo Edit; **510:** Jim Callaway/The Cincinnati Enquirer; **512:** John Berry/Gamma Liaison; **515:** David Rae Morris/Impact Visuals; **525:** G. B. Trudeau; **528:** Schwarz/Gamma Liaison; **540:** Supreme Court Historical Society; **543:** Dennis Brack/Black Star; **547:** Robert Fox/Impact Visuals.

Chapter 16: **552 (Opener):** Fred Phillips/Impact Visuals; **554:** Cynthia Walker/Gamma Liaison; **556:** Danny Lyon/Magnum; **561:** AP/Wide World; **563:** Stanley J. Forman; **566:** Leonard Freed/Magnum; **571:** Brown Brothers; **572:** Michael Springer/Gamma Liaison; **577:** Wide World; **581:** Bob Daemmrich/Tony Stone Images; **585:** Gary Wagner/Sygma.

Chapter 17: **593 (Opener):** Tony Savino/Sipa Press; **595:** Reynolds Enterprise; **601:** Stacy Pick/Stock Boston; **602:** Matthew Ford/Gamma Liaison; **604:** UPI/Bettmann; **605:** Cynthia Johnson/Gamma Liaison; **612:** Jeffrey Lowe/Onyx; **618:** Richard Bloom/SABA.

Chapter 18: **622 (Opener):** Jose L. Pelaez/Stock Market; **624:** Charles Tasnadi/AP/Wide World; **627:** Aventurier/Gamma Liaison; **630:** Brad Markel/Gamma Liaison; **632:** Rick Maiman/Sygma; **637:** Jeffrey Markowitz/Sygma; **640:** Wide World; **642:** Bob Daemmrich Photography; **650:** Crandall/The Image Works; **654:** Reprinted by permission: Tribune Media Service.

Chapter 19: **659 (Opener):** Randy Taylor/Sygma; **661:** Ellen Neipris/Impact Visuals; **666:** The William Helfand Collection; **670:** Adam Scher; **673–674:** Culver Pictures; **681:** Mike Lukovich/Times-Picayune; **684:** Myrleen Ferguson Cate/Photo Edit; **688:** Bernard Boutrit/Woodfin Camp; **691:** Courtesy Maryland State Department of Human Resources; **693:** Center for Disease Control.

Chapter 20: **696 (Opener):** Fabrizio Bensch/Reutes/Bettmann; **698:** Orban/Sygma; **699:** S. Morgan-Spooner/Gamma Liaison; **702:** Photosearch; **704:** FPG; **712:** Lyndon Baines Johnson Library; **716:** Wide World; **720:** Brad Markel/Gamma Liaison; **728:** Jim Borgman/Reprinted with special permission of King Features Syndicate; **732:** Agence-Presse France.

JK 274 .J36 1995
OCLC   31906763
The challenge of democracy

DATE DUE

DEC 0 5 2006	

GAYLORD   PRINTED IN U.S.A.

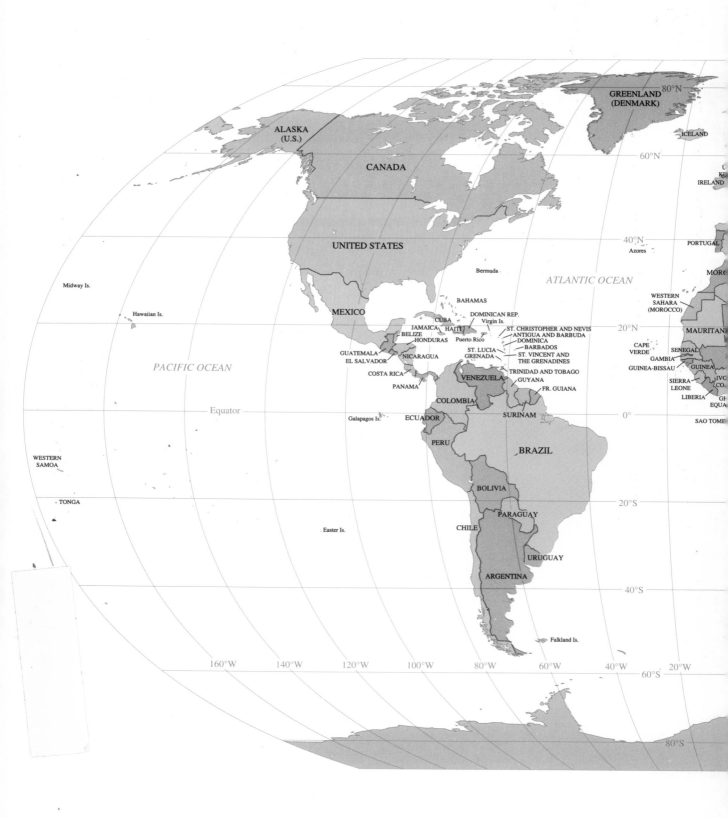